- take your feet off your desk
- it's showtime
- showtime, sportsfans

WEST ACADEMIC PUBLISHING'S LAW SCHOOL ADVISORY BOARD

THE LAW OF MERGERS AND ACQUISITIONS

Fifth Edition

■ ■ ■

Dale A. Oesterle
J. Gilbert Reese Chair
Michael E. Moritz College of Law
The Ohio State University

Jeffrey J. Haas
Professor of Law
New York Law School

AMERICAN CASEBOOK SERIES®

WEST ACADEMIC PUBLISHING

444 Cedar Street, Suite 700
St. Paul, MN 55101
1-877-888-1330

Printed in the United States of America

ISBN: 978-1-68328-979-1

To Pat, Helen, Annie and William

D.A.O.

To my father, Mike, for all his inspiration

J.J.H.

PREFACE

The casebook and the supplementary Teachers' Manual are designed to provide the materials for a three-credit, upper-class law school course on mergers and acquisitions. We have had great success and, well, fun with the course over many years and we offer these materials in the hope that you and your students will enjoy them as well. We recommend that students have available one of the soft cover, statutory supplements for the basic corporations course as they read this material or be able to call up on a computer the federal and state statutes and rules mentioned in the cases and text.

The Teachers' Manual can be acquired in hard copy or found on line at http://lawschool.westlaw.com/TWEN. The online version will feature updates on new events in M & A. A full set of power point slides for class, with diagrams on most of the edited cases in the text, may also be found on-line in our TWEN cite under "course materials." Slides are updated annually.

ACKNOWLEDGMENTS

I am very fortunate to have a supportive and loving family who enable and inspire my work. I am honored to be the husband of Pat and am blessed by and very proud of my children, Helen, Annie and William, and my grandchildren, Harrison and Gracie.

D.A.O.

I am deeply grateful for the confidence that Dale Oesterle has placed in me by adding me as a co-author of his immensely successful casebook on Mergers & Acquisitions. I began using Dale's book when I first started teaching back in the 1990s and have proudly used it ever since. As a former M & A attorney at New York's Cravath, Swaine & Moore, I was extremely impressed with the book's overall organization and, most importantly, the thoughtful insight and analysis Dale provides. Dale's book was and continues to be head-and-shoulders above the rest, and I couldn't have been more delighted to work with Dale in creating this new 5th Edition.

J.J.H.

SUMMARY OF CONTENTS

TABLE OF CONTENTS

TABLE OF CASES

The principal cases are in bold type.

The Law of Mergers and Acquisitions

Fifth Edition

CHAPTER ONE

AN INTRODUCTION TO ACQUISITIONS

■ ■ ■

A. INTRODUCTION

Business entity merger and acquisition transactions (often abbreviated in the book and in modern law practice to *M & A*[1]) are some of the most heavily regulated events in all of American law. Six bodies of legal rules—state contract law, state corporate law, federal securities law, federal and state tax law, federal accounting standards, and federal antitrust law—play lead roles in how parties structure these transactions. Several other areas of the law—labor law, pension plan regulations, environmental law, products liability law, debtor-creditor law, federal bankruptcy law, and law applicable to various regulated industries (banking, utilities, insurance, hospitals, transportation, telecommunications and gaming, for example)—also play minor roles and, depending on the transaction at hand, may even assume lead roles.

A study of the law governing corporate acquisitions, then, is an integration and application of these various systems of rules to the negotiation and structure of a given transaction. Chapter One has three functions: (1) An introduction to legal terminology that hints at the richness of this interwoven texture of the legal doctrines; (2) A discussion of the essential nature of the business side of a deal negotiation; and (3) A brief summary of the overriding policy question of whether mergers and acquisitions are socially valuable. Later chapters focus on relevant areas of legal doctrines, one at a time.

Our approach distinguishes the course from the more common, traditional law school courses that focus on doctrinal areas. Our materials focus on a common business event, a deal, and apply relevant segments of multiple areas of doctrine. The transaction focus of the materials also distinguishes the course from most others in law school that have a litigation focus. We note and study lawsuits over acquisition agreements as they affect acquisition planning, however. Lawyers engaging in an M & A practice appreciate that an acquisition is primarily a controlled process, the process of transferring an operating business from one owner to another.

---

1 Terms of art in the text are identified in italics when they are first used and defined.

B. M & A TERMINOLOGY

1. CUSTOMARY UNDERSTANDING OF BASIC TERMS

A businessperson's definition of a transaction does not often follow the exacting technical terminology of a legal, tax or accounting code. Since businesspeople are your clients, it is necessary to be able to relate to what they understand and what they want to do in a given transaction. A businessperson is likely to have the definitions noted below in mind. This is necessarily an imprecise summary and may evolve in the future.

As you begin your study of M & A, we urge you to have patience with the new vocabulary you will encounter. Learning M & A includes learning a new language, a language that will be unfamiliar to you and not easy to absorb initially. Have patience; unfamiliar terms introduced here appear in context and detail later and will become more familiar. Do not worry about mastering the terms now; we need only get started here.

A businessperson describes a basic deal primarily by identifying (1) who ends up with control of the assets of the constituent firms and (2) the form of the consideration those who gain control (buyers) have to pay others who gave up control (sellers).

Acquisition (or Purchase of the Firm): In an acquisition or purchase of a firm, A, the acquirer, pays for all or substantially all the assets or the controlling stock of another, S. It is a *sale* of S's assets or a sale of S's stock. Consideration is cash or *cash equivalents*, anything of value except voting equity instruments (common stock) in the purchasing firm, S. Debt instruments in S or non-voting preferred stock in S are cash equivalents, for example. The acquiring firm can buy all the assets from the selling firm (an *asset purchase,* often termed an *asset acquisition*) or the controlling ownership equity in the selling firm. If the selling firm is a corporation, in a stock acquisition, the purchaser usually buys more than fifty percent of the voting stock (a *stock purchase,* also termed a *stock acquisition*) in order to gain voting control. In an asset purchase, the selling firm often dissolves after the transaction and passes the transaction proceeds it received on to its shareholders in a liquidating distribution.

In either an asset purchase or a stock purchase, the owners of the selling firm cede control and interest in the selling firm's assets. *After the transaction, the shareholders of the selling firm have no ownership interest in the surviving firm*. Absent special contingent payment provisions, the shareholders of the selling firm no longer have a direct stake in the management of their firm's assets. On the other hand, the shareholders in the acquiring firm retain their relative voting power in the surviving firm through the transaction. In the acquiring firm shareholders' view, their firm has merely changed the form of its assets: cash on its balance sheet has been replaced by S's assets, a factory, for example.

In an asset sale, the acquiring firm may choose not to assume some or even all of the selling firm's liabilities, and the selling firm continues to exist unless dissolved, holding the proceeds it received in the sale. In a stock sale, the acquiring firm has bought the indicia of ownership in the selling firm entity and holds the selling firm entity as a new subsidiary (unless the subsidiary is dissolved into the parent). The liabilities of the selling firm remain with the firm after the control change.

In asset acquisitions, the basic definitional distinction is between the sale of a firm as a business and the sale of some of the firm's property (a *carveout* of a division or subsidiary, for example). The sale of most or all of a firm's operating assets is usually termed an acquisition. In a stock acquisition, businesspeople distinguish between *control transactions* and *non-control transactions* depending on whether the acquiring firm has purchased enough stock to control subsequent elections to the selling firm's board of directors (usually 50.1 percent of the outstanding voting stock).

Merger: In a merger, the owners of one firm pool their interests with those of another firm (known as the *surviving firm*).[2] After the merger, the surviving firm owns the assets and assumes the debts and other liabilities previously owned or owed by the firm that merged out of existence. If the two firms are corporations, the shareholders of the firm that does not survive become shareholders of the surviving firm. The owners of the constituent firms, parties to the transaction, end up as joint owners in the surviving firm after the deal. *The businessperson's distinction between a purchase and a merger then depends primarily on the final position of the shareholders of the selling firm.* In acquisitions, the selling firm's shareholders have no, or very limited, equity in the surviving firm. They *walk* typically with a pocketful of cash.

The relative voting power of a shareholder in either firm in a merger is *diluted* significantly in the surviving firm as a result of the combination, but the economic value of the shares should not fall because the surviving firm now owns the assets of the non-surviving firm. Moreover, in situations where the assets of the non-surviving firm exceed those of the surviving firm, the shareholders of the non-surviving firm may actually receive a controlling stake in the survivor. For example, corporation A and corporation B merge, with corporation B being the survivor. If, immediately prior to the merger, the assets of corporation A exceed those of corporation B, the shareholders of corporation A might end up holding 60 percent of B stock while the shareholders of corporation B hold the remaining 40 percent of B stock.[3]

---

[2] If the two firms pool their interests into a third firm (typically formed for this purpose), the transaction is more properly referred to as a *consolidation* rather than a merger.

[3] This is unimportant if the shareholders of A and B are many and diffuse. It becomes more important when controlling blocks of stock in A or B survive the merger.

If two roughly equal-sized firms merge and the power positions in the survivor are split between the CEOs of the constituent firms, the deal in the investment community is referred to as a *merger of equals*. The CEOs might become co-CEOs (as in the 1998 merger between Travelers Group and Citicorp which resulted in the creation of Citigroup) or shift positions within five years. Experience has shown that these power-sharing arrangements often do not work well in practice and are just public relations ploys to camouflage a sensitive control change.[4]

Merger or Acquisition?: The categories are nuanced. We label as an acquisition transaction, for example, a deal in which either some or all of the shareholders of the selling firm end up with non-ownership interests in the surviving firm (debt instruments such as subordinated debentures). In our example, assume that the shareholders of S, in exchange for their S stock, receive an equivalent value in A bonds. Most businesspeople would say that A has acquired or bought, not merged with, S.

On the other hand, if one of the constituent firms is much larger than the other, common usage would label the transaction an acquisition or purchase of the seller, even if the consideration for the selling firm shareholders is shares in the survivor. Consider, for example, A, a $55 billion corporation, and S, a $5 million corporation. When the firms pool their assets, with the owners of S receiving a few shares in A, the surviving entity, we would more naturally refer to the transaction as a sale of the assets of S to A, rather than a merger of A and S. The S shareholders, as new owners of A shares, would be swallowed up in A's pre-existing shareholder base.

Special Forms of Acquisitions: One often hears the term *takeover* or *tender offer* in acquisition parlance. The term usually describes a stock purchase offer made to shareholders of a publicly traded target firm, in which the acquiring firm buys a controlling block of stock from those shareholders, most often a majority of the outstanding voting stock. The controlling block of stock enables the purchasing firm to elect all the directors to the target's board. With control of the target's board, the acquirer then engages in a *second-step merger*[5] between the acquiring firm (or an acquiring firm subsidiary) and the target to *squeeze out* the remaining target firm shareholders. If, on the announcement of the offer, the acquiring firm does not have the support of the target firm's

---

[4] See, e.g., Alan Brew, *Why Corporate Mergers of Equals Almost Never Work*, FORBES.COM (June 5, 2014) (avail. at https://www.forbes.com/sites/forbesleadershipforum/2014/06/05/why-corporate-mergers-of-equals-almost-never-work/#6bf0daa14176); Rupal Parekh, *A Merger of Equals? No Such Thing*, ADVERTISING AGE (Aug. 4, 2013) (avail. at http://adage.com/article/agency-news/a-merger-equals-thing/243492/); Liz Hoffman, *Co-CEOs Blur Lines in Mergers of Equals*, LAW360.COM (July 30, 2013) (avail. at https://www.law360.com/articles/461158/co-ceos-blur-lines-in-mergers-of-equals).

[5] A second-step merger is also referred to as a *second stage merger*, a *back-end merger* or a *squeeze out merger*.

management, the offer is *hostile* or *unsolicited*. When the purchaser has the support of target management, the offer is *friendly* or *negotiated*.

Leveraged buy-outs, LBOs, (or now more commonly just *buy-outs*) come in several forms. In each, a private group of investors borrows heavily in the *leveraged loan* market to finance the purchase of control of an ongoing business.[6] The surviving entity is heavily *leveraged*, with a debt to equity ratio of over five to one. Some LBOs are carve-outs, a divestiture or split-off, the purchase of the assets of a division or the stock of a wholly-owned subsidiary from a large corporation. In other LBOs, a private group of fewer than 300 participants *takes private* a publicly traded company with over 500 shareholders (a *going-private* transaction).

Various types of single firm *reorganizations* (also called *restructurings*) are accomplished through the formal mechanism of a merger. In one form, a firm shuffles its existing capital structure,[7] changing the nature and mix of its outstanding long-term investment instruments (common and preferred stock, notes, bonds, and debentures). If the firm is eliminating a minority shareholder interest, it is labeled a *squeeze out* (or *freeze out*). Common restructurings include transactions that change the domicile of incorporation (to Delaware from New York, for example) and transactions that change the basic registered form of a business entity (from limited liability company (LLC) to a corporation, for example). Changes in entity form are also called *conversions*. Restructurings also include transactions that merge a parent with a subsidiary in order to create a holding company structure.

2. THE VARYING TYPOLOGIES OF M & A PROFESSIONALS

When tax, accounting, antitrust, state corporate code, and securities law experts use terms such as *merger, asset* or *stock acquisition,* and *reorganization* to describe an acquisition, they are not necessarily

---

[6] The *classic LBO* is an acquisition in which an investment partnership buys the maximum assets using the least amount of its own cash as possible. The partnership borrows against the target's assets and cash flows, putting up one dollar of equity to buy five or six dollars' worth of an ongoing business. The shift in capital structure allows the buyers to more than double the return on their equity if the acquisition proves successful in subsequent years. The financing is layered (with *tranches*). Banks and traditional lenders take senior secured debt; *mezzanine financing* (senior unsecured debt, subordinated or junior debt, and preferred stock) comes from more aggressive lenders demanding short maturities (usually less than seven years); and a thin layer of equity comes from the investment partnership itself. If the partnership includes senior managers of the target firm itself, the LBO is more properly referred to as a *management buy-out* or *MBO*). The classic LBO looks to the target company's improved cash flow to service (*i.e.,* pay down) the new debt over time.

[7] The capital structure of the firm includes all the investment instruments the firm sold to raise capital for its operations. These instruments include all types of stock—common and preferred—and stock rights—options, rights and warrants—and various types of debt—commercial paper, bills, notes, debentures and bonds. A capital side reshuffling is to be distinguished from an operations restructuring, in which a firm changes its organizational structure, adding divisions, for example.

describing the same transaction as would a businessperson. The various regulatory systems that attach consequences to various transaction forms define those basic forms using different criteria, criteria appropriate to the regulatory purpose at issue. Critical to an understanding of regulatory systems that affect large transactions is a careful delineation and comparison of the various classification systems that different experts use. Below is a brief introduction into the different uses of basic terms, such as merger and sale, by experts trained in the details of different regulatory systems. Do not be concerned if you do not understand fully all that follows in this section; we will parse the details of each paragraph below more slowly and more comprehensively in the subsequent chapters of the book.

Tax law distinguishes corporate transactions based on characteristics that are, perhaps, commonly understood by businesspeople. For policy reasons that are not obvious (we will investigate them in later chapters), tax law uses the *merger-sale* distinction as a cornerstone of its system of rules. In tax law, the merger-sale distinction determines whether or not a transaction is a taxable event. Consider the *sale* transaction first. In a stock sale, a selling shareholder recognizes taxable gain or loss; she has changed the form of her investment. A shareholder in a merger, by contrast, is said to continue her investment in the same form, and we do not impose a tax. In an asset sale, the selling firm recognizes taxable gain or loss on the proceeds received for its assets, and if these proceeds are subsequently distributed to the selling firm's shareholders, those shareholders recognize taxable gain or loss as well. On the other hand, if the shareholders in the selling corporation in a stock or asset acquisition receive common voting stock in the acquiring corporation as consideration, there is a consolidation of the shareholder interests in the survivor and the tax code treats the acquisition as a merger, not a sale.

Tax lawyers often categorize transactions by using the sections and subsections of the Internal Revenue Code (IRC). There are, to list common examples, *338 transactions*, referring to § 338 of the IRC and Type A, B, C or D Reorganizations (often shortened to an *A, B, C or D Reorg.*) referring to subsections of IRC § 368(a)(1). For example, an A Reorg is a tax-free statutory merger in which the shareholders of both of the constituent entities to a merger retain a substantial interest in the surviving entity. We will take up accounting and tax issues in Chapter Eight.

State corporate codes are fallen angels. Originally designed around the basic merger/sale distinction noted above, they evolved in the mid-1960s into something quite different. State corporate codes regulate the procedure firms must follow to effect any given transaction. The principal procedural issues include the shareholders' right to vote on a given transaction and the *appraisal rights* (exit rights) of dissenting shareholders. Other important procedural questions include the mechanics of transferring title to assets and debt obligations in the transaction.

At the turn of the century, state corporate codes mandated procedures depending, by and large, on the merger/sale distinction. For example, in a classic merger, the shareholders of both corporations vote and have appraisal rights. In a classic sale, by contrast, the shareholders of the selling firm vote and have appraisal rights. Clever lawyers, however, manipulated the statutory language with ease, structuring sales as statutory mergers and structuring mergers as statutory sales of assets to suit the purposes of their client, usually to avoid select procedural requirements. Rather than attempt to protect the distinction, as Congress has done in the tax code with rules on *step transactions*[8] and the like, the state legislatures, after a brief skirmish, not only abandoned the classic distinction, but amended their codes to legitimize lawyers' planning cleverness.

There is a movement among a handful of state legislatures to synchronize the requirements of the various sections so that it matters less which section applies—to create *equivalency* of rights based on substance. As we shall see, the New York Stock Exchange and our other national stock exchanges have also stepped in with rules designed to have the same effect. The goal of the drafters of the legislation is to make the shareholders' voting rights for a given transaction the same, whatever sections the lawyers use. Most other legislatures have not only refused to join but have reinforced the abandonment of any equivalency notion. Interestingly, as we shall see, even in this climate, the classic merger/sale distinction reappears in different guises in the state courts: the Delaware Supreme Court, for example, uses the distinction as part of its new definition of a fiduciary standard for boards of directors involved in takeover acquisitions. We take up state corporate codes in Chapter Two and fiduciary duty in Chapters Five and Six.

Some of the definitional effects in state corporate codes have been modified by state court case law or even federal case law. By state statute, a surviving firm in a merger assumes all the liabilities of the constituent firms, but an acquiring firm in an asset sale can choose not to assume some or even all of the selling firm's liabilities. Case law on the effect of acquisitions on the tort obligations (and related obligations such as environmental or employment discrimination claims) of the acquired firm, known as *successor liability*, has substantially modified this basic

---

8 The step transaction doctrine (also known as the *substance over form doctrine*) allows the IRS to integrate or combine two or more formally separate transactions into a single, larger transaction for tax purposes. See Commissioner v. Clark, 489 U.S. 726, 738 (1989). In this regard, three tests are employed. The first—the Binding Commitment Test—integrates two transactions if, at the time of the first transaction, there was a binding commitment to engage in the second transaction. See Commissioner v. Gordon, 391 U.S. 83, 96 (1968). The second—the Mutual Interdependence Test—combines two transactions if the legal relationships created by the first transaction would be pointless without the consummation of the second. See American Bantam Car Co. v. Commissioner, 11 T.C. 397, 405 (1948), *aff'd* 177 F.2d 513 (3d Cir. 1949). The third—the End Result Test—combines a series of transactions if each such transaction was effected to achieve the same specific end result. See Penrod v. Commissioner, 88 T.C. 1415, 1429 (1987).

merger/sale distinction. Tort obligations may attach to buying firms in asset sales, for example, even though the buying firms contracted not to assume them. We take up successor liability in Chapter Three.

Other systems of regulation affecting acquisitions do not use the classic merger/sale distinction at all but rely on other basic distinctions. In accounting, a merger/sale distinction, as of 2001, no longer affects the accounting conventions that the surviving firm may use in its financial statements. Under old pooling conventions, in a stock-swap merger the accounts or categories in the financials of the two constituent firms were merely added together to create the financials of the surviving firm.[9] In a sale, the market price paid to the target firm or its shareholders must be reflected in the financials of the purchasing firm. With the phase-out of pooling accounting treatment, purchase accounting, accounting for a sale, will apply to all major acquisitions. We will explain accounting conventions in Chapter Eight, Section A.

The Securities Act of 1933 is concerned mainly with the primary offering of new securities, be they debt or equity securities, to investors through public offerings and unregistered offerings (e.g., private placements). Thus, Securities Act Rule 145 requires that whenever shareholders exchange their old securities for new securities, whether debt or equity, in a transaction, the protections of the 1933 Act apply.[10] This can occur in either a classic merger (stock in one firm is exchanged for stock in the surviving firm) or a classic sale (assets in one firm are exchanged for debt securities in the surviving firm). Moreover, the Securities Exchange Act of 1934 regulates the acquisition of stock from the investing public, known as *tender offers*, regardless of whether the consideration is stock, as in a classic merger, or cash, as in a sale. The Exchange Act also regulates certain events that occur routinely as part of major acquisitions—*proxy solicitations* by publicly held firms, for example—and the timing and content of public disclosures about planned transactions. We take up the mechanics of public offerings, proxy regulation and tender offer regulation in Chapter Two, Section B, and the disclosure requirements in each setting in Chapter Seven, Section A.

The federal antitrust act specific to acquisitions, the Clayton Act, regulates all *business combinations* that pose a threat to competition in relevant product and service markets. The focus is on a combination of the assets of two firms in one entity, regardless of who the shareholders are. Classic mergers and classic sales are both combinations of otherwise

[9] For example, if Firm A had $100,000 of current assets on its balance sheet, while Firm B had $250,000 of current assets on its balance sheet, then under the pooling method the current assets of the combined firms would be $350,000. The current assets of both firms were "pooled" together.

[10] The Securities and Exchange Commission deems the shareholder vote in question to be the equivalent of the shareholders making a *new investment decision*; hence, the need to register the securities in question under the 1933 Act (or rely on a registration exemption).

distinct entities, so both are similarly regulated by the Clayton Act, and antitrust lawyers often refer to either as a merger. The size of the acquisition and the effect of the acquisition on relevant product markets, not whether it is a merger or a sale, are the focus of the legislation. Amendments to the Clayton Act, known as the Hart-Scott-Rodino Antitrust Improvements Act of 1976, affect the timing of public disclosure of acquisition plans. In a similar vein, the law controlling various regulated industries, such as banking or insurance, requires the approval of all large-scale combinations, both classic mergers and sales in the industry, because officials are interested in passing judgment on the capabilities of the new owners. It is unimportant how they came to be new owners. We take up antitrust law in Chapter Nine.

In sum, the legal vocabulary one uses to describe an acquisition varies with the regulatory system in issue. The merger in a "statutory merger" under state corporate law is not the same as a merger in an "A Reorg" under the tax code.

C. WHAT DRIVES M & A ACTIVITY? 5 things

The frequency of acquisitions depends on many factors. During some time periods (the late 1980s for example), M & A activity was robust and plentiful. During other time periods (in the years immediately following the 2008 recession for example), the opposite was true. Significant M & A activity typically depends on one or more of five elements being present in the business environment.

The first element is regulatory change, particularly *deregulation.* (1) Regulatory change, usually accompanied by political change, creates opportunities that did not previously exist. Deregulation took hold in the U.S. beginning in the 1970s. For example, the transportation industry was the first to be addressed, resulting in the deregulation of the railroads (Railroad Revitalization Act of 1976 and the Staggers Rail Act of 1980), airlines (Airline Deregulation Act of 1978), buses (Bus Regulatory Reform Act of 1982) and ocean transportation (Ocean Shipping Act of 1984 and Ocean Shipping Reform Act of 1998). Other industries, including media, telecommunications, financial services, utilities, and health care, have also been deregulated to varying degrees. More recently, in late 2017 the Federal Trade Commission loosened its 30-year-old ban on the cross-ownership of local newspapers and broadcasting stations, a change likely "to touch off a wave of deal making, reordering the local-TV landscape." [11]

The dominant goal of deregulation is to reduce barriers to entry in the newly-deregulated markets, thus facilitating more competitive pricing among industry participants, both existing and newly-created. To help

---

[11] John D. McKinnon & Joe Flint, *FCC Rolls Back Media Ownership Limits*, WALL. S. J., at B4 (Nov. 17, 2017).

offset price competition resulting from deregulation, industry participants often couple together to create larger players in the more competitive market. As a result, industry consolidation through mergers and acquisitions is often stimulated due to regulatory change.

The second element is technological change. This change generates acquisitions as new markets emerge and old ones fade. New innovative competitors acquire and are acquired to access the new markets; obsolete competitors are acquired and reorganized. In particular, technological change often forces existing firms to make *build versus buy* decisions. That is, if a particular firm (likely a larger one) seeks to enter into a particular product market, should it create its own product from scratch or simply acquire an existing firm that already has a competitive product? The firm making that decision will have to weigh the costs associated with developing and testing an entirely new product and then penetrating the market against the cost of acquiring an existing firm that already has a competitive product in place.

The third element is the health of our capital markets. A booming stock market encourages stock swap deals, as high stock prices lead buyers to use their own high priced stock as acquisition consideration, thus preserving valuable cash reserves. A low interest rate environment, by contrast, encourages buyers to borrow to finance acquisitions. Thus, cash is the preferred acquisition currency at that time. A depressed stock market motivates *financial buyers*[12] to purchase firms with high asset values only to turn around and bust those firms up (*i.e.*, sell off assets and business divisions in a piecemeal fashion to the highest bidder).

The fourth element is the existence of dynamic business leaders and their mimics. The human dynamism of the likes of Jack Welch (formerly at GE), Ronald Perelman at Revlon and Carly Fiorina (formerly at Hewlett-Packard) can drive acquisitions. Some call it hubris, others leadership. Regardless, what is the point of being the king or queen unless you rule over a very large kingdom?

The fifth element is a race to size. As one competitor grows through a major acquisition, other competitors soon follow (or attempt to do so).

---

[12] A financial buyer should be distinguished from a *strategic buyer*. A financial buyer is an acquirer, such as a private equity fund, that purchases a controlling stake in a company, if not the entire company. It then implements a strategy designed to make the acquired company leaner and meaner, and hence more profitable. Once the goal is accomplished, the financial buyer sells the acquired company or takes it public, thus pocketing a tidy profit from its investment. Indeed, most financial buyers have a "buy, fix and sell" strategy. A strategic buyer, by contrast, is typically operating in the same industry as the acquired company and seeks to buy that company because it fits strategically with the acquired company's mission. Putting the two companies together creates synergies (value, including cost savings, created by combining two companies that is not available to the separate companies), which is typically the point of strategic purchases. For example, in 2002, Weyerhaeuser Co., which was big in timber and plywood, acquired Willamette Industries, Inc., a leader in white paper products. Putting the two companies together provided Weyerhaeuser with the white paper business it coveted, while also creating approximately $300 million in annual cost savings.

Excessive growth through consolidation, however, generates the need for additional M & A activity of a different variety, to wit, reorganizations, spin-offs, split-offs, and bust-ups. Indeed, a conglomerate often justifies such activity by announcing its intention to refocus on its "core operations"—code words indicating that a previously touted acquisition proved disastrous and now needs to be unwound as soon as possible.

In addition to the foregoing five elements, additional elements may influence M & A activity as well. Consider the following:

CEO Age and Its Relationship to Corporate Takeovers

A study from the Stanford Graduate School of Business and Dartmouth College's Tuck School of Business explored how target firm CEOs' retirement preferences affect the incidence and pricing of corporate takeovers.[13] Interestingly, the study found strong evidence demonstrating that the likelihood of a target firm receiving a successful takeover bid is sharply higher when that firm's CEO is closer to age 65 (*i.e.*, retirement age). The authors found that firms that had CEOs between the ages of 64 and 66 were 5.8 percent more likely to receive a successful takeover bid, versus 4.4 percent for firms with CEOs aged between 59 and 63. This disparity—labeled the *Age-65 Effect* by the authors—corresponds to a 32 percent increase in the odds of a sale.[14]

Importantly, the study found the quality of the deals accepted by firms with older CEOs was still respectable. Takeover premiums and target announcement returns were found to be slightly (insignificantly) higher for retirement age CEOs than younger CEOs. However, combined with the takeover frequency results, the study suggests that retirement CEOs are able to increase deal sales by one-third without sacrificing premiums paid to shareholders. In other words, the quality of deals are relatively the same for younger and older CEOs, but there are simply more deals for older CEOs to close.[15] This increase, however, is not uniform across all types of firms. The Age-65 Effect on takeover frequencies was found to be significantly weaker among stronger-governed firms.[16]

The desire for job security could help explain why younger CEOs are more reluctant to allow their companies to be acquired. As stated by the authors of the study:

---

[13] Dirk Jenter & Katharina Lwellen, *CEO Preferences and Acquisitions*, 1–2 (Rock Ctr. for Corp. Governance at Stanford Univ., Working Paper No. 105, 2014) (avail. at http://papers.ssrn.com/sol3/papers.cfm?abstract_id=1969619).

[14] *Id.* at 3.

[15] *Id.* See also Rachel Feintzeig, *For Corporate Takeovers, 65 Is The Magic Number*, WSJ.COM (Jun. 25, 2014) (avail. at http://blogs.wsj.com/atwork/2014/06/25/for-corporate-takeovers-65-is-the-magic-number/).

[16] *Id.* at 3. Measures of strong governance included: stock ownership by the CEO, blockholders, and directors; board size; board independence; and CEO-chairman duality.

> The target firm's CEO is, arguably, one of the most important actors in the takeover market. The CEO plays a key role in his firm's decisions leading up to a bid (e.g., the decision to seek out a buyer, or to initiate merger talks), and once a bid is made, the CEO leads his firm's response and its negotiations with buyers . . . . *Given this unique role, it is interesting to note that target CEOs' career concerns and retirement preferences are likely to be at odds with shareholders' objectives: target CEOs typically lose their jobs during or shortly after a takeover, and in only a handful of cases does the departing CEO find a new position in a public firm* . . . . This suggests that mergers can represent serious setbacks to target CEOs' careers. Though most CEO compensation contracts recognize these costs—they include golden parachutes or bonuses conditional on mergers—it is unclear to what extent they succeed at eliminating the inherent incentive problem.[17]

Based on the results of the study, potential acquirers and their investment bankers should likely consider the age of the CEO of a potential target firm when making a decision on whether to pursue the acquisition of that company.[18]

D. INTRODUCTION TO M & A NEGOTIATIONS

All acquisitions are complex negotiations, involving a plethora of issues and including conference rooms full of supporting personnel. The parties attempt to discover relevant facts on a long checklist of significant issues, analyze those facts, and generate negotiating positions from an accumulation of trade-offs on all issues of material value. Closing a deal is often as much an administrative challenge as a bargaining challenge. Once the issues are identified and quantified, the number of issues on the table and the imprecision of valuation estimates leave much room for old-fashioned, horse-trading style bargaining.

There is a classic book on the strategy and tactics of negotiating acquisitions by James C. Freund, entitled *Anatomy of a Merger: Strategies and Techniques for Negotiating Corporate Acquisitions* (1975) that we recommend to all lawyers entering the M & A practice.[19] There are also excellent materials on negotiation strategy in general—a favorite is also a classic, David A. Lax and James K. Sebenius, *The Manager as Negotiator: Bargaining for Cooperation and Competitive Gain* (1986). We will not dwell

---

17 *Id.* at 2 (emphasis added) (citations omitted).

18 See Feintzeig, *supra* note 15.

19 His second book, a collection of essays, James C. Freund, *The Acquisition Mating Dance and Other Essays on Negotiating* (1987), is also worth reading. See also Bruce Wasserstein, *Big Deal: The Battle for Control of America's Leading Corporations* (rev. ed. 2000); George P. Barker & George David Smith, *The New Financial Capitalists: Kohlberg Kravis Roberts and the Creation of Corporate Value* (1998).

on negotiation strategy and tactics here. Negotiating points will be mentioned in the issue-specific materials that follow. (In Chapter Four, for example, we examine the multi-issue nature of an acquisition negotiation.) We do, however, need a basic introduction to the acquisition negotiation process and to the identity of the major participants and a basic introduction into deal pricing.

1. A CLASSIC M & A DEAL TIMELINE

The following is a common timeline for a basic acquisition—the cash acquisition of a privately held company.[20] Some differences in timelines for other types of acquisitions are noted.

First, the CEOs (Chief Executive Officers) of the two constituent corporations meet[21] and mutually agree on the potential success of further negotiation and on ballpark financial terms for a deal. The meeting may be at the initiation of either the buyer or the seller[22] or an intermediary.[23] The parties may have established some pre-bargaining confidentiality ground rules in a *confidentially agreement* or a *non-disclosure agreement (NDA)*. Buyers often ask for a *no shop* or *exclusivity agreement* to stop the seller from pursuing other buyers, and sellers often ask for a *standstill agreement*, prohibiting the buyer from purchasing seller stock during the negotiations.

These preliminary negotiations, if fruitful, are often embodied in a *letter of intent* (or *term sheet*), most or all of which is legally non-binding.

---

[20] The sale of most businesses occurs via direct, one-on-one negotiations. A much less used method for selling a business is an auction. The auction can be formal, in which the bidding and time parameters are highly structured, or controlled, in which a limited number of potential bidders are contacted without any specific deadline constraints.

In the context of a *controlled auction*, the seller will identify and contact a list of potential buyers (with a *teaser*, a brief sketch of the seller). Interested buyers will sign a confidentiality agreement and receive an offering memorandum (*book*), which typically is put together by the investment banking firm representing the seller (if any). Potential buyers submit non-binding indications of interest. The seller selects the potential buyers that are the most promising and permits them to conduct a due diligence investigation. The parties selected then submit formal written bids in response to a formal solicitation letter that often is accompanied by a draft acquisition agreement. The seller then selects a leading bidder, and the leading bidder is given a right to exclusive negotiation over the final form of the acquisition agreement.

[21] Anecdotally, a number of these meetings in megadeals occur on the slopes of Vail, Colorado, where the CEOs have gone to relax, escape the eyes of prying parties, and mingle naturally with other business leaders without creating suspicion.

[22] The management of the selling firm may be actively marketing the company. The company will have prepared an offering memorandum, the *book*. The book introduces prospective buyers to the company, its industry, business, and management team. Those who receive the book are usually asked first to sign a confidentiality agreement. Such firms may also have retained a deal intermediary, a business broker, a finder, or an investment bank. Business brokers and investment bankers are agents of the party that engaged them (*buy-side* or *sell-side* advisors) and may not receive compensation from the other side of any deal. Some investment bankers for the seller, however, do, with the seller's assent, offer the buyer financing in the deal. A finder *represents the deal* and may be paid by either or both parties if the deal closes.

[23] Investment bankers, on their own initiative, often research possible deals and present them to identified prospective buyers.

We consider letters of intent and other acquisition documents in Chapter Four. Most CEOs receive advice from their internal financial experts, usually the firm's CFO (Chief Financial Officer), and frequently also from outside investment bankers and accountants with whom they have had a prior long-standing relationship.

The preliminary agreement leads both constituent corporations to formally retain a bevy of experts. The corporations retain, if they have not done so already, lawyers to negotiate and draft the details of the acquisition documents and retain investment bankers and accountants to provide valuation estimates and other financial advice. The lead acquisition planner may come from any of the three professions—law, accounting or investment banking. At the signing of the letter of intent, the seller will typically agree to give the potential buyer exclusive negotiating rights for a period of time while the buyer "does *due diligence*"[24] and drafts and negotiates the details of an acquisition agreement.

In most acquisitions, the buyer conducts a substantial investigation of the seller's business.[25] In stock swap deals the seller will do limited due diligence on the buyer, since the seller is accepting an ownership position in the buyer as payment and thus has a keen interest in the health of the buyer's business. In a due diligence investigation, lawyers and accountants pore over the books and records of the opposing party, checking the accuracy of factual representations and looking for trouble spots. The buyer puts together a due diligence team and a checklist and the information gathered is often formalized in a written report. The due diligence team is assisted, in appropriate cases, by other experts, such as environmental engineers or real estate appraisers, who give assurance on matters of specific importance to the transaction.

After the preliminary discussions, the transaction moves into what experienced lawyers call the mating dance phase. Parties and their advisors negotiate the details of the deal price, the deal structure and the deal documentation. Although lawyers do participate in price and structure negotiations, the part of the M & A transaction thought to belong exclusively to the lawyers is the preparation of the acquisition agreement and related documents. If the buyer needs financing to complete the transaction, it will contact prospective lenders and negotiate financing terms. Lenders will offer firm financing commitments or weaker *highly confident letters*.[26]

---

24 This is a colloquialism for engaging in a due diligence process.

25 The process usually refers to checks on an opposing party but one now hears the term referring to a seller's investigation of its own business during an acquisition, so called sell-side due diligence.

26 A "highly confident" letter is a letter from an investment banking firm stating that it is "highly confident" it can raise the capital necessary for the buyer to acquire the selling firm. The investment banking firm of Drexel Burnham Lambert (of Michael Milken fame) originated the letter in the early 1980s in connection with Carl Icahn's unsuccessful attempt to take over Phillips

Once the CEOs agree on a final price and on a final memorandum of the acquisition agreement, the CEOs present the agreement (an *Agreement of Merger*, for example) to their respective boards of directors. We will study acquisition agreement documents in Chapter Four. The time between the date of the preliminary agreement and the date of board approval varies considerably and may be from two weeks to three months. The directors ask questions, make comments, deliberate and, if all goes well, vote their approval of the acquisition and its associated documentation in a series of board resolutions that will also authorize the CEO to sign the main acquisition agreement for the corporation. The selling firm board often requests an independent investment banker to provide a *fairness opinion*, an opinion that the price offered by the buyer is fair from a financial point of view to the selling firm and its shareholders.

Buyer's counsel prepares a *time and responsibility schedule (T & R List)* that lists the various tasks to be performed by the closing, assigns responsibility for those tasks, and sets times by which the tasks are to be completed.[27] The parties also draft and negotiate a *closing agenda,*[28] a document that lists all the documents due to be delivered at closing. Due diligence investigations continue after board approval and through to the closing to ensure that the seller has satisfied the agreement's conditions before the closing.[29]

If shareholders of one or both of the constituent corporations must vote to ratify the agreement, lawyers prepare shareholder meeting notices and disclosures and the firm calls a special shareholder meeting (or notifies shareholders that the acquisition will be on the agenda at the firm's annual meeting).[30] The time between the board vote and the ratifying shareholder meeting is at least thirty days and often up to three months. If the parties need the approval of a government agency (the Federal Communications Commission for media mergers or the Comptroller of the Currency for bank mergers, for example) or antitrust review from either the Department of Justice or the Federal Trade Commission,[31] the time period is further attenuated. Antitrust review is covered in Chapter Nine. If things go

66. Particularly during the 1980s, highly confident letters enabled corporate raiders to launch takeovers without having the debt portion of their financing in place.

[27] This may also be circulated early in the pre-signing negotiations.

[28] This is sometimes referred to as a *closing checklist* or *closing memorandum*.

[29] *Post-signing* or *Pre-closing due diligence*. In practice this is often more limited and casual than pre-signing due diligence. The buyer often relies on a closing certificate prepared by the seller and does only limited independent investigation that several of the more important conditions (the accuracy of representations and warranties and the absence of any material change in the business, for example) have been satisfied.

[30] In transactions that do not require a shareholder vote, public tender offers, for example, the time period from board approval to the effective transfer of control, through transfers of voting shares, is considerably shorter, sometimes only one month. This is a significant advantage to the buyer anxious to announce and close a deal before any competing bidders appear on the scene. We cover public tender offers in the latter part of Chapter Two.

[31] The parties may need to make a *Hart-Scott-Rodino* (or HSR) filing if required by the Hart-Scott-Rodino Antitrust Improvements Act of 1976.

according to plan, the shareholders of one or both of the constituent corporations approve the acquisition by the requisite majority, usually a majority of all the outstanding voting shares.

If the selling firm is a publicly traded company, the parties must prepare and file their proxy solicitation materials with the Securities and Exchange Commission (SEC). In transactions in which the buyer will issue securities to buyer shareholders, the buyer will have to register the securities under the Securities Act of 1933 or satisfy an exemption to registration. If the transaction is a tender offer the parties must comply with the SEC rules under Section 14(d) of the Securities Exchange Act of 1934. These matters are left to Chapter Two, Section B.

Twenty to thirty days after the shareholder vote, lawyers and CEOs meet to *close* the transaction (a *deferred closing*).[32] If the parties must file materials with the SEC, the closing may be delayed another six months or more. At the closing, once the parties are assured that the conditions in the acquisition agreement are either satisfied or waived, the parties exchange consideration—cash-for-stock, cash-for-assets, or stock-for-stock and so on depending on the deal terms. The closing agenda has been executed, a *closing statement*[33] finalized, and client signatures affixed to the closing documents.

Post-closing, the lawyers make the appropriate filings in addition to getting some well-deserved sleep. In statutory mergers, the parties file the Agreement of Merger (or a short form Certificate of Merger) with an appropriate state official that, among other things, eliminates at least one of the constituent corporations, names the surviving corporation, and establishes the Articles (or Certificate) of Incorporation for the surviving corporation. Deal consideration is delivered to shareholders if necessary,

---

[32] The two-step *deferred closing* transaction detailed in the text is the norm. In some deals, the parties do not sign a binding agreement until the closing. The signing and the closing occur simultaneously (*sign and close* transactions). There are a variety of reasons for this. First, if the parties have signed a letter of intent with a no-shop provision and authorizing the buyer to conduct due diligence, the buyer may resist becoming contractually bound until, satisfied with its investigation, it is ready to close. Second, occasionally the seller is reluctant to sign before closing. The seller may, for example, have announced publicly that the business is for sale and does not want to discourage potential bidders or preclude itself from talking to alternative buyers until the seller is certain the acquisition will close. Third, the negotiations may simply evolve into a simultaneous signing and closing. Due diligence may proceed more rapidly than the negotiations, making a waiting period after signing pointless and needlessly risky. Fourth, there are a few transactions in which the signing and closing are done with limited due diligence and made subject to a *due diligence out*, effectively giving the buyer an option to purchase during a specified period of time at a fixed price.

[33] The closing statement, often part of the closing agenda, sets out the source and application of funds needed to close (sometimes referred to as a *flow of funds memorandum*). In an asset acquisition, for example, the closing statement reflects the purchase price, debits and credits allocated to the parties and the disposition of funds to the seller (and lenders).

often through a paying agent. Finally, the deal is truly done when the participants exchange *deal cubes*[34] and enjoy a closing dinner.[35]

The deferred closing—the time delay between the signing of the *executory* acquisition agreement and its performance (the transfer of consideration for ownership at closing)—has a substantial effect on the structure and nature of an acquisition agreement, as we shall see in Chapter Four. The buyer bears the primary risk of deterioration in the value of the seller's assets, caused either by outside forces or the seller's personnel (theft, shirking or mismanagement), between signing and closing and therefore, as detailed in the next section, must ask for protections or other forms of risk-shifting in the acquisition agreement.

2. RISK ALLOCATION IN DEFERRED CLOSING TRANSACTIONS

Most negotiated acquisitions have substantial time delays between the signing of the acquisition agreement and the closing, the *deferred closing transaction*. Some acquisition techniques, such as cash tender offers, minimize the time delay; others, such as stock swap mergers among equals, may have delays of over eight to ten months. There can be no doubt that deal activity falls as market volatility and uncertainty rises.[36] Whenever there is such a delay, the pricing issues are more complex, as the consequences of changes in the value of one or even both parties during the gap between the time of price setting (signing) and the time of ownership (closing) must be addressed.

Most commonly, the buyer worries that the value of the seller's assets will fall dramatically between signing and closing. In some cases the risk is so substantial that it eliminates any valuation overlap in the bargaining positions and the parties cannot sign to a deal. If the parties can allocate the value deterioration risk to the party most willing to bear it, they can close the deal.

In a *cash deal*, in which the buyer is paying cash for assets or stock,[37] the buyer takes the risk that the value of the selling firm may fall below the deal price by the time of closing. The risk is reflected in the price the buyer is willing to offer, as the buyer will discount the price to account for the risk. Once the deal price is announced, the stock price of the selling

---

[34] Deal cubes contain, in a Lucite block paperweight, a miniaturized pamphlet that records the names of the parties to the deal and the members of the negotiating teams.

[35] Almost always the most memorable and enjoyable part of the deal. Offenses are forgiven and long-term relationships are cemented.

[36] See Robert Dam, Vineet Bhagwat & Jarrad Harford, *The Real Effects of Uncertainty on Merger Activity*, 29 REV. OF FIN. STUDIES 3000 (Issue 11, July 20, 2016).

[37] Payment may be deferred and structured as installment payments or may be by promissory note. When the buyer agrees to installment payments or payments on a note, the parties must negotiate *set-off* rights of the buyer pursing indemnification claims after the closing. Most promissory notes are non-negotiable (cannot be resold by the seller) to protect the buyer's set-off rights.

firm will predominately reflect the deal price, discounted on the chance that the deal will not close. The selling firm value post signing, then, is not independent of the deal price in the trading markets.

A seller, rather than simply refusing the discounted price offered by the buyer, may agree to accept some of the post signing risk of a deterioration in the value of its assets in exchange for a better price from the buyer. The seller may agree, for example, that a decline in the value of the selling firm will trigger negative conditions in the acquisition documents. We discuss these conditions in Chapter Four. The conditions may be triggered by a fall in general industry values or in firm specific values in the target's financials. A serious decline in value may give the buyer the right to walk away from the closing (*a walk right*), forcing the seller to renegotiate the price if it wants to close the deal.[38] It is the acquisition agreement's express conditions then that typically reallocate the risk among the buyer and seller in a typical cash deal.

Some parties also use a *true-up*, a one-time price adjustment mechanism in the acquisition agreement.[39] The purchase price is adjusted based on the state of the balance sheet of the target at the closing date. Usually a set amount (a *target* or *bogey*) is specified for net worth or working capital and payments are made by either buyer or seller for variations from the bogey as reflected in the accounts of the business purchased on the closing date. Note the difference between a true-up and a MAC clause. The MAC clause gives the buyer the right to stop the closing and walk away; the true-up enables the buyer to close the purchase and then claim additional funds from the seller, essentially amounting to a purchase price adjustment.

In *Chicago Bridge & Iron Co. N.V. v. Westinghouse Electric Co. LLC*, 166 A.3d 912 (Del. 2017), the Delaware Supreme Court interpreted a net working capital true-up contained in a purchase agreement narrowly. The purchaser had argued that the seller had represented and warranted that its financial statements were compliant with GAAP when, in fact, they were not. This allegedly led to the seller's post-closing miscalculation of net working capital. Because the purchaser's only option for breaches of representations and warranties was to refuse to close (the "Liability Bar"), the purchaser attempted to fit its complaint under the true-up provision. The Delaware Supreme Court, in reversing the Chancery Court, stated:

> The True Up has an important role to play, but that role is limited and informed by its function in the overall Purchase Agreement. Generally speaking, purchase price adjustments in merger agreements account for changes in a target's business

---

[38] These contract clauses in acquisition agreements are known as *material adverse change clauses (MACs)*.

[39] The amount is usually paid after the closing (and protected by an escrow) but may be paid at closing.

> *between the signing and closing of the merger*. This is especially so when the purchase price is based on the target's value at closing. . . .

Id. at 928 (emphasis added). The Court added:

> [T]he True Up is an important, but *narrow, subordinate, and cabined remedy* available to address any developments affecting [the seller's] working capital that occurred in the period between signing and closing. . . .
>
> By reading the True Up as unlimited in scope and as allowing [the purchaser] to challenge the historical accounting practices used in the represented financials, the Court of Chancery rendered meaningless the Purchase Agreement's Liability Bar.

Id. at 916 (emphasis added).

In *stock deals*, in which the buyer is paying the purchase price with its own stock, the risk allocation of value deterioration must also include the potential decline in the value of the buyer's stock between signing and closing.[40] The delay between signing and closing may be reflected in the deal price terms when the owners of the selling firm take securities in the purchasing firm. In *stock swaps*, a subset of stock deals, shares of one corporation are exchanged for shares of another. To establish a price, the two parties must come to an agreement on the relative value of the two companies. The parties negotiate an exchange ratio for the stock of the constituent corporations based on relative value. After signing the acquisition agreement, the value of one or both of the companies may change dramatically before the closing.

Market-wide trends, such as a substantial decline in the financial markets, industry-specific market trends and company-specific performance may all affect the value of either of the constituent corporations. In stock deals the shareholders of both companies must often ratify the board agreement.[41] This provides an additional check. If the changes occur before any ratifying shareholder meetings, the shareholders of one of the parties may reject the agreement. One can easily point to spectacular failures of large combinations to illustrate the problem.

Moreover, the participants in the securities trading market may judge the exchange ratio itself harshly.[42] More and more frequently, purchasing

---

[40] The risk also exists if the consideration is debt securities in the buyer. The longer the term of the debt and the more subordinated the debt, the greater the risk.

[41] In cash deals, the shareholders of the buyer often do not ratify the board's decision to sign the agreement. We discuss these procedures in Chapter Two.

[42] Sometimes activist hedge funds which own shares in the selling firm will push for changes to the deal terms, seek out a competing third party suitor willing to offer more, or seek to garner shareholder support against the deal in order to thwart it entirely. This is known as *M & A activism*. For example, in 2017 activist hedge fund Jana Partners LLC sought to scuttle EQT Corp.'s proposed $6.7 billion acquisition of Rice Energy, Inc. Jana had previously acquired about 5 percent of EQT's stock and was pushing for EQT to fully separate its pipeline operations from

firms in a stock swap merger are witnessing a fall in their stock price within minutes of the announcement of the transaction. The purchasing firm is the survivor and has agreed to offer newly-issued shares to the shareholders of the selling firm in exchange for all the selling firm's outstanding shares. The fall in stock price is due either to the dilutive effect of the new stock issuance on the surviving firm shareholders or on the financial impact of the transaction in general. The price declines in the purchaser's stock will lower the value received by the selling firm shareholders, and the selling firm may pressure the buyer to offer additional consideration, exacerbating the dilutive effect of the deal on the purchasing firm's shareholders, or may abandon the transaction. The stock price of the target, after a deal is announced, is, of course, now tied to the exchange ratio and the price of the buyer's shares, discounted by the risk that the deal will not close.

Buyers protect themselves against falling value of the seller's assets by inserting conditional convents (e.g., the MAC clauses noted above), similar to those found in cash deals, into acquisition agreements. Sellers, on the other hand, may protect themselves against a decline in the value of the buyer's stock by using a floating exchange rate and walk rights, as well as conditions that are reverse mirrors to those that benefit the buyer for drops in the value of the seller's assets. We cover the covenants and conditions in Chapter Four and the price terms here.

If the firms in a stock swap use a *fixed exchange ratio,* the parties agree on a specified and fixed number of the acquirer's shares that will be exchanged for each share held by the seller's shareholders (e.g., 1.4 to 1 (1.4 buyer shares for each seller share)). The exchange ratio is set when the board votes on the agreement of merger and does not change through the closing. The seller's shareholders bear both general market risk and the specific risk associated with the value of the purchasing firm relative to the value of the selling firm. A decline in value of the purchasing firm relative to the selling firm decreases the value the seller's shareholders receive at the closing. Seller shareholders may refuse to ratify the proposal if the price change precedes their shareholder meeting. The buyer, on the other hand, enjoys the certainty of the fixed exchange ratio, primarily the predictability of the effect of the deal on future earnings per share (either accretive or dilutive[43]). The downside risk for the purchaser is that a sagging exchange value in purchaser stock may encourage third parties to

its exploration and production operations. Because EQT's proposed acquisition of Rice Energy would work against Jana's proposed agenda, Jana pivoted by trying to convince other EQT shareholders to oppose the acquisition. Also in 2017, Warren Buffett's Berkshire Hathaway Inc. made an all-cash $9 billion proposal for the 80 percent stake in Oncor Electric Delivery Company held by Energy Future Holdings Corp. In response, activist hedge fund Elliott Management Corp. successfully found a buyer for the Oncor stake who would pay even more. For more on shareholder activism, see Chapter 11.

[43] A deal that is accretive to earnings means the buyer's earnings per share increases as a result of adding the seller's business to that of the buyer. A deal that is dilutive waters down the buyer's earnings per share.

make competitive offers for the seller. Moreover, a decline in the value of the selling firm could result in the purchaser overpaying for the selling firm when it exchanges its valuable shares for the now less valuable selling firm.

Many sellers ask for downside price protection, that is, adjustments if the buyer's stock falls in value between signing a deal and closing it. Buyers' traditional response is that a fixed exchange ratio reflects the inherent relationship between the companies' fundamental values, and this relationship is not affected by general market volatility. If, so the argument goes, the price decline is due to an industry-wide or market-wide phenomenon, the seller has experienced a comparable price decline in its stock as well, and the economic relationship between the parties is unchanged. Sellers argue in response that the firms may have differing sensitivities to even market-wide price shocks. Some sellers demand, therefore, either a walk-away right (or walk-right), a floating exchange ratio, or a price collar (or a combination of the above).

A seller walk-away right is an express condition in the acquisition agreement that gives the seller the option to walk away from the acquisition closing if the price of the purchasing firm's stock falls below a specified price level between signing and closing. For example, a fixed exchange ratio walk-away would permit the seller to terminate the agreement if, at the time of closing, the purchasing firm's stock has decreased in value by 10 percent from the time of the signing of the agreement, a *single trigger*. Some walk-away clauses have a *double trigger*: the seller may terminate the agreement if the stock value falls a specified percentage or more from the value at the time of the agreement, and if the purchasing firm's stock price falls by a specified percentage relative to a defined peer group of stocks of selected companies.[44]

A *floating exchange ratio* sets the exchange ratio based on an average market price for the purchasing firm's security during a period, usually ten to thirty trading days, prior to the closing (or, less commonly, to the date on which the seller's shareholders will vote to approve the transaction). Thus, the purchasing firm agrees to swap whatever number of its shares will equal a fixed dollar value, calculated using a market average over a set period prior to closing, for a share of the seller. The purchasing firm bears the market risk of a decline in the price of its stock before the closing and, on any decline, will have to issue more shares to each shareholder in the selling firm at the closing.[45] The number of shares that the acquirer

[44] This is popular in the banking industry. In essence, the buyer argues that if the buyer's stock does not fare materially worse than those of its defined peer group, the adjustment mechanism is not appropriate. If the buyer's peers are not the seller's peers, sellers should not accept the argument, however, as the seller's market value may be less sensitive to the conditions causing the injury to the buyer's industry.

[45] There is the opposite problem, an usual one, in which the buyer's stock increases in value and the buyer shares have a greater value at closing than the agreed price for the seller's business. A floating exchange rate gives the buyer *up-side* protection by decreasing the exchange ratio at closing in such a case.

will have to issue to the selling firm's shareholders *floats* with the acquirer's stock price between signing and closing.

There are two problems with the use of a floating exchange ratio. First, the rate must be carefully calculated not to terminate a desirable acquisition solely due to temporary market fluctuations (the Brazilian *real* may be devalued and jolt the market for a short time, for example). The second problem is that a floating exchange ratio exposes the purchasing firm shareholders to the possibility of massive dilution.[46] The potential dilution is limited only by the amount by which the stock price is likely to decline. To manage the dilution risk, the parties use caps and collars.

To protect against extreme dilution, acquisition agreements with floating exchange ratios often put a limit, a dilution *cap*, on the value and thus the number of shares the purchaser is obliged to issue in the exchange.[47] If the exchange ratio hits the cap, the selling firm owners absorb any additional losses in buying firm stock price declines. This can lead to further negotiations over the mechanics of the cap. Selling firms may respond by asking to supplement the cap with a walk-away right if a price decline in the purchasing firm's stock causes the exchange ratio to hit the cap. Purchasing firms, in response, may want the right to waive the cap and avoid the walk-away condition (a *fill or kill option*) and close the deal. Under such an option, the purchaser agrees to issue the full complement of shares required by the floating ratio.

Sellers, playing tit for tat, may also argue for a minimum, or *floor*, in the number of buyer shares paid. If the buyer's share price increases and the floating ratio otherwise would require the buyer to offer fewer shares than the minimum, the seller gets a jump in the value of the exchange. An exchange ratio that has both a cap and floor on the number of shares to be issued in an acquisition is called a *fixed value* or *floating exchange ratio collar*.[48] At the upper and lower limits of the collar, the floating exchange ratio becomes, in essence, a fixed exchange ratio.

Some parties invert the collar: with a *fixed share or floating value collar,* inside a buyer stock price range the parties agree to a fixed exchange ratio, and outside the range agree to a floating ratio. In some fixed

---

46 Dilution refers to the effect on the voting (and economic) power of the outstanding stock caused by substantial new issuances of securities by a firm. Here, the purchasing firm will dilute the outstanding shares held by its existing shareholders by issuing new shares and giving those shares to selling firm shareholders in exchange for their shares in the selling firm.

47 There are variations on the mechanics of the dilution cap. In another form of a dilution cap, the purchaser demands a walk-away right based on a maximum number of shares that the purchaser is willing to issue in the transaction. Selling firms may then negotiate for the right to waive the requirement for additional shares under the floating exchange ratio and hold the purchasing firm to closing the transaction on the shares due at the time the agreement was signed (or on shares due just short of the trigger), a *reverse fill or kill option*.

48 The parties negotiate a range of buyer stock prices, *reference prices*, within which the buyer agrees to issue a constant dollar value of its stock for each share of target stock. The exchange ratio floats for prices inside the range and becomes fixed for prices outside the range at the boundary exchange ratios.

exchange ratio deals, the parties agree to a fixed exchange ratio that is adjusted if the value of the purchasing firm's stock falls by (or increases by) more than a fixed percentage (e.g., plus or minus 10 percent). If the buyer's stock falls by more than 10 percent, for example, the exchange ratio shifts and the purchaser must pay more stock per selling firm share. The adjustment can be automatic or discretionary with the purchaser, a fill or kill option. If automatic, the adjustment is usually capped, with upper limits on the number of shares the purchasing firm will have to deliver, or lower limits on the number of shares the selling firm shareholders will have to accept.

Exchange ratio form and caps and collars are tailored to the circumstances of a particular transaction and the respective concerns and relative bargaining leverage of the parties. Collars are particularly attractive, for example, when stock market prices are very volatile.

NOTE: POST-CLOSING ADJUSTMENTS

In times of heavy economic uncertainty parties may also disagree about firm valuation over extended periods of time *post-closing*. To save a deal, parties shift valuation risk using various types of post-closing adjustments. The common adjustments are true-ups discussed above and *earn outs*, but there are more exotic ones, *contingent value rights* (*CVRs*), for example.

A growing percentage of smaller deals have *earn outs*. If the selling firm is privately held, that is, owned by a small number of shareholders, the parties can agree to a delayed payment schedule, an earn out.[49] An earn out can bridge the gap between a purchaser's conservative valuation of the selling firm (the "base case" view) and the selling firm's higher valuation of itself based on its rosy forecasts (the "optimized case" view). In an earn out, the purchaser pays a minimum purchase price (in cash or purchaser securities) upon which both it and the selling firm can agree. Thereafter, if the selling firm's rosy predictions for the future come true (in whole or in part), the purchaser will make additional purchase price payments (typically a percentage of post-closing profits earned periodically by the newly-purchased operations). Needless to say, the parties often have dramatically divergent views on the value of earn outs. Sellers anticipate receiving large payments in the future, while buyers view sellers' notions as wishful thinking.

In 2017, Diageo PLC, the world's largest spirits maker, agreed to buy upscale tequila brand Casamigos for an upfront payment of $700 million as part of Diago's plan to increase its exposure to the tequila market. If, however, Casamigos hits certain performance targets over the following 10 years, Diageo would pay up to an additional $300 million over that time period. Given that Diageo plans to expand Casamigos internationally, particularly in Europe, the additional payment appears likely to happen. Thus, overall the deal could net actor George Clooney, restauranteur Randy Gerber and real estate tycoon

[49] The technique is largely restricted to privately held companies because of the problems of making multiple post-closing distributions to a large group of public shareholders.

Mike Meldman, the co-founders of Casamigos, $1 billion. We can all sleep soundly now knowing that these three men are *finally* financially secure!

The problem with earn outs is that buyers are tempted to skimp on (maybe even ignore!) the payouts, thus almost daring the former owners to commence (and fund) litigation to recover any amounts owed. This problem is compounded by the buyer's ability to avoid payments through its control of the assets that are generating the payments (*i.e.*, the selling firm's former business). We read a case on such problems in Chapter Four, Section B.2.

If the selling firm is publicly traded and there is a liquid market for the purchaser's securities used in the deal as consideration, the parties can negotiate for *CVRs, contingent value rights*, which are either derivative securities or contractual rights.[50] Sellers taking buyer stock and enjoying significant bargaining leverage in the deal can force a buyer to minimize post-closing risk through CVRs. Thus, as used in this way, CVRs are hedging instruments, providing price protection to selling shareholders who receive stock in the buyer as consideration.[51] Unlike the straight floating exchange ratio, the assurance is tied to post-closing share prices in the buyer. Typically, if the buyer's stock trades below a set price (the target price) for a defined period of time post-closing, the selling shareholders will receive additional compensation (cash, stock or other securities) equal to the difference between the target price and the market price.[52] If the buyer's stock price increases an

---

[50] For excellent articles on CVRs, see Ryan Murr, *Contingent Value Rights: A Middle Ground in M & A Boom*, LA DAILY J. (Sept. 11, 2014); Frank Aquila & Melissa Sawyer, *Contingent Value Rights—Means to an End: Using CVRs to Bridge Valuation Gaps in Public Company M & A Deals*, LexisNexis Emerging Issues Analysis (Sept. 2009).

[51] Merger transactions that utilized CVRs as hedging instruments include Mannkind—Pfizer (2009), Wesfarmers—Coles (2007), ViroLogic—Aclara (2004), Publicis—Saatchi & Saatchi (2000), BNP—Paribas (1999), Viacom—Blockbuster (1994), Viacom—Paramount (1994), and Dow Chemical—Marion Laboratories (1991). In the case of Viacom's successful bid for Paramount, Paramount shareholders had the right to receive in cash or securities (at Viacom's election) the amount by which the trailing sixty-day average trading value of Viacom class B common stock was less than $48 per share (the target price). The initial measurement date was the first anniversary of the closing. The CVR had a floor of $36 per share (most CVRs give the buyer's stock time to recover, if possible, from any decline in trading price associated with the announcement of a deal). Viacom could extend the measurement date forward one or two years and on each extension, the target price and floor price increased. Viacom ended up paying an additional $82 million over the acquisition price to retire the CVRs. See Paramount Communications v. QVC Network, *infra* Chapter Six, Section B.2.

There was some grumbling about the role of market speculators in the payout. Arbitrageurs held very significant positions in both the Viacom/Paramount and Viacom/Blockbuster CVRs—as much as 75 percent of each issue. Because of the CVRs' complexity, the arbitrageurs were able to buy them up at discounts to their intrinsic value. To hedge their bets, the arbitrageurs also bought up the underlying Viacom stock, which, due to the volume of CVRs, helped push up the stock price. Some suggested that the Viacom/Blockbuster transaction was only able to close because arbitrageurs pushed up the Viacom stock price while hedging their positions in the Viacom/Paramount CVRs. In any event, as the maturity of the CVRs approached, the arbitrageurs had to unwind their hedges (*i.e.*, sell the Viacom stock). If that sell-off had resulted in a drop in the stock price, the payout on the CVRs could have been significantly higher than it was. Timely purchases by third-party investors kept the stock price afloat.

[52] Often, there will be a floor price. If the market value of the underlying stock drops below the floor, the holder of the CVR receives only the difference between the target price and the floor.

amount above the CVR price, the CVR pays nothing.[53] Importantly, CVRs represent unsecured obligations of the buyer, and thus holders are subject to the credit risk associated with the buyer.

CVRs can also be used for earn out purposes in the context of a publicly traded selling firm.[54] The selling firm's legacy shareholders would receive cash or securities from the buyer if, on the maturity date,[55] a business line or unit of the selling firm is performing at or above an agreed upon level. This allows the selling firm's shareholders a chance to participate in the future upside of the selling firm's operations without sharing those benefits with the buyer's pre-transaction shareholders. Like earn outs, CVRs used in this way can help bridge valuation gaps that may exist between potential buyers and selling firms, and thus can assist in striking deals in the first instance.

Lastly, CVRs can be linked to the occurrence of value-creating post-closing events relating to the selling firm that are not certain to occur. CVRs used in this context are referred to as *event driven CVRs*. The post-closing events could include the settlement of substantial litigation, the sale of a significant business segment or assets, FDA approval of a new drug, the conclusion of a regulatory investigation, or the culmination of a financial statement restatement. If a specified post-closing event does occur (and, in certain cases, it would have to play out within certain pre-established parameters), the buyer would have to provide the selling firm's legacy shareholders with additional value. Thus, event driven CVRs can help lower the risk of a buyer overpaying for a selling firm. Pharmaceutical and biotech companies utilize event driven CVRs given their reliance on FDA approval for their products.[56]

3. THE DEAL PRICE: VALUATION

In any corporate acquisition, at the center of the negotiation is the question of value, how much is the acquisition target worth as it stands alone and how much will its value increase when combined with the purchaser (what are the *synergistic gains*)? Valuation issues also appear in litigation over acquisitions, in statutory appraisal proceedings or the damage assessment portion of breach of fiduciary duty cases. We will discuss court struggles with valuation issues in statutory appraisal proceedings in Chapter Two, Section A.3.c. We invite those of you who need

---

[53] The CVRs trade in the public securities markets and are only redeemed once, making them useful if there are a large number of selling firm shareholders. CVRs are, in essence, a type of financial future or stock warrant payable by the purchasing firm.

[54] Transactions utilizing CVRs as earn outs include Fresenius SE—App Pharmaceuticals (2008), Onstream Media—Narrowstep (2008), and Minnesota Mining and Manufacturing (*a.k.a.* 3M)—Cardiovascular Devices (1988).

[55] According to NYSE Listing Rule 703.18 ("Contingent Value Rights"), listed CVRs must have a minimum life of at least one year. Maturity dates of between one and three years appear to be the standard in M & A deals.

[56] Deals utilizing event driven CVRs include Sanofi-Aventis—Genzyme (2011), Ligand Pharmaceuticals—Pharmacopeia (2008), Fresenius SE—APP Pharmaceuticals (2008), OSI Pharmaceuticals—Cell Pathways (2003), Antigenics—Aronex Pharmaceuticals (2001), Elan—Liposome (2000), and Ligand Pharmaceuticals—Seragen (1998).

a more in-depth treatment of valuation to take a course in corporate finance in the law or business school.

A few general points on valuation need to be made here. First, and most important, there must be an *overlap* in the valuations of buyer and seller for the deal to close. That is, the buyer must believe that the seller's firm is worth at least as much or more than the seller's managers believe the firm is worth. The buyer, for example, will pay up to $100 million and the seller will take anything over $95 million; the overlap is $5 million. The deal can close at any price between $95 and $100 million. No overlap; no deal.[57] An important part of any negotiation for both parties is creating an accurate valuation of the firm and, if necessary, persuading an opponent to change its valuation to create an overlap.

Second, valuation is a very inexact inquiry, with capable people showing substantial disagreements over values assigned to the same assets. They use several clichés to make the point. Those in the field talk of valuation as an "art not a science,"[58] note that "value is in the eye of the beholder," recommend that buyers respect their "comfort level" feelings on any given valuation, and assert even the best expert opinions can provide only a "range" of values for a firm.[59] Indeed, it is a mark of incompetence when an expert declares a single value. This all means that in practice valuation is a core negotiating point.

Third, in an acquisition there are two separate valuation issues. The first issue is the stand-alone or as-is value of the target company. This is much easier if the target company is publicly traded in a liquid market than if the firm is privately held or otherwise thinly traded; the daily quotes of the secondary trading markets usually provide a good starting point (but only a starting point) to determine a firm's value.[60] The second issue is the extra or added value that the target firm's assets will have

---

[57] Limited bridging mechanisms do exist. One such bridge is an *earn out provision* (discussed in Section D.2 of this Chapter and also in Chapter Four, Section B.2).

[58] Jeffrey J. Haas, CORPORATE FINANCE 69 (1st ed. 2014).

[59] As the Delaware Chancery Court has stated in the context of an appraisal claim:

> [V]aluation decisions are impossible to make with anything approaching complete confidence. Valuing an entity is a difficult intellectual exercise, especially when business and financial experts are able to organize data in support of wildly divergent valuations for the same entity. . . . The value of a corporation is not a point on a line, but a range of reasonable values. . . .

Cede & Co. v. Technicolor, Inc., 2003 WL 23700218, at *2 (Del. Ch.), *aff'd in part, rev'd in part on other grounds,* 884 A.2d 26 (Del. 2005).

[60] Market price is only the starting point because it reflects the value of a single share of common stock—a minority position—in the selling firm in question. Those acquiring entire companies take control of those companies. Having control is valuable, as the acquirer is entitled to directly influence the business strategy of the selling firm going forward. Indeed, an acquirer typically envisions strategies to enhance revenue growth, profitability and capital efficiency at the selling firm. This, in turn, leads the acquirer to pay a control premium for the selling firm—that is, a price per share significantly higher than the per share trading price in the market. See Jeffrey J. Haas, *supra* note 58, at 69–70. Moreover, most selling firms have proprietary, inside information of value that they have not yet disclosed to the trading markets, and thus their per share trading price does not yet reflect that valuable information.

when combined with the assets of the purchasing firm. Is there a strategic fit of the two firms that makes the additive value of their assets larger than the simple sum of their stand-alone values? What is the so-called *synergistic* value? Estimations of synergistic value are a total crapshoot. They make standard expert valuation opinions of privately held companies look downright scientific by comparison.

The juxtaposition of the two valuation issues is most clearly seen if the target's stock is publicly traded. If the stock has a sufficient *float*[61] and the company has made adequate public disclosure, the market price of the stock multiplied by the number of outstanding shares provides that company's *total market capitalization*, which is the starting point for the valuation of the business.[62] But a buyer of the entire publicly traded company will typically pay a sizeable *premium* over the market price of the stock (often averaging around 20 percent). The size of the premium is determined predominately by what the buyer believes it can do with the target company assets that the target company itself is not currently doing.[63]

Valuation is more difficult in those transactions in which the target is privately held and there is no reliable market price for the target stock. The general "rule of thumb" method of valuation, which clients will use as a starting point for more detailed analysis, is often based on *multiples*. The buyer is principally interested in the cash income stream that a given target business will produce over time after the transaction closes. Quick and dirty valuations rely on multiplying some entry on the target's historical financials by an appropriate number (the "multiple"). The method assumes that the historical figures on the target's income statement[64] are, at some level, predictive of future performance.

---

[61] Float refers to the number of outstanding shares of common stock of a publicly traded company that are available for trading in the secondary market. The float of a particular company is equal to (1) the number of outstanding shares of common stock of that company *minus* (2) the sum of (a) the number of shares in the hands of corporate insiders, major shareholders and employees (all of whom trade infrequently, if at all) and (b) the number of shares subject to trading restrictions (*i.e.*, restricted stock). Companies with smaller floats tend to have more volatile stock prices, due to reduced liquidity and wider bid-ask spreads. Corporate actions can directly affect a company's float. For example, stock buy backs reduce the float while reverse stock splits increase the float.

[62] A more comprehensive valuation alternative to total market capitalization is *enterprise value* (or EV for short). EV is calculated as follows: total market capitalization *plus* debt and debt equivalents (preferred stock and minority interests) *less* cash and cash equivalents. Debt and debt equivalents are added to total market capitalization because the buyer of the business in question will have to pay down that business' debts after it acquires the business. Cash and cash equivalents are subtracted from total market capitalization because the buyer is entitled to that cash and cash equivalents after it acquires the business.

[63] See *supra* note 60.

[64] The historical period selected may be the last fiscal year, the last four quarters, the most recent 12 months, or an average of the last three years (or five years). The averaging of earnings over multiple years produces *normalized earnings*. See Jeffrey J. Haas, CORPORATE FINANCE 74 (1st ed. 2014).

Most multiples[65] start with a number on the income statement—net profit figure (*earnings*)—and make customary adjustments. The earnings figure on the income statement used for the valuation may be (1) after taxes (net earnings with tax payments subtracted), (2) before taxes (net earnings before the tax payments have been subtracted),[66] (3) before interest and taxes (*EBIT*), or (4) before interest, taxes, depreciation and amortization (*EBITDA*[67]). Of the four historical earnings calculations, multiples on EBITDA are the most commonly and widely used in informal discussions. EBITDA is a rough approximation of the *net cash flows* of the target.[68] When the multiples are calculated on past numbers rather than expected numbers, they are *trailing* multiples; multiples calculated on expected financial statement numbers (next year's) are *prospective* or *forward* multiples. Most multiples are trailing multiples, and when a simple multiple is reported, it is assumed to be a trailing multiple unless otherwise specified.

As a starting point for analysis and as a comparison of transactions, you will find your clients discussing "the EBITDA multiple" or simply "the multiple." They use the method as a rule of thumb[69] to reduce potentially paralyzing complex calculations for understandable and normal use.[70] EBITDA multiples for deals are routinely reported in the M & A trade press, for example.[71]

The EBITDA multiple used in any given valuation varies widely with the target's industry, the size of the business, the general market and

---

65 One does see multiples of *book value* occasionally for specific businesses, such as banks, and the number comes off the balance sheet (*total equity*).

66 One takes the final figure on the income statement, net earnings, and adds to it the taxes that have been deducted to produce net earnings before taxes.

67 Many pronounce EBITDA as one word ("ebitda"); others pronounce it as three words ("ebit-D-A").

68 To determine past net cash flows, one must add back non-cash expenses that entered into the calculation of net income on the income statement. The principal non-cash expenses are usually depreciation and amortization. These are non-cash charges that represent the diminution in value of assets listed on the balance sheet (depreciation is the term that describes the yearly charge on real and personal property and amortization is the term that describes the charge to intangible property such as patents). EBITDA is not a perfect indicator of cash flows, however, because it leaves out the cash required to fund working capital and equipment replacement. It also excludes cash payments of taxes and interest. We add back taxes paid by the target because the target's tax situation as controlled by the buyer will change, and we add back interest because we are seeking the value of the target to all passive investors (holders of both debt and equity).

Financial experts offer a variety of rationales for using multiples based on net cash flow rather than earnings: net cash flow is less subject to manipulation by management than earnings; net cash flow is generally more stable than earnings; net cash flow is less sensitive to accounting conservatism among companies; and differences in net cash flow are better related to differences in long-run average returns.

69 The rule of thumb can vary industry to industry. The method may use multiples of revenue for insurance agencies and high-tech companies, or multiples of book value for banks and other financial institutions.

70 The calculation of EBITDA is done by averaging the EBITDA figures from at least the last three years.

71 See, e.g., www.thedeal.com (a deal information website listing multiples).

economic conditions and factors intrinsic to the target's operations. The higher the multiple the more aggressive the valuation is, usually based on anticipated high target growth; the lower the multiple the more conservative the valuation, usually based on predictions of flat target growth. Multiples currently collected from data on closed acquisitions show a range of seven to nine on EBITDA for firms in mature, traditional industries.

A ready source of baseline information for appropriate multiples is the publicly available information from publicly traded companies in the same industry with similar characteristics (*comparable companies* or just *comparables*). The multiples of earnings at which comparable companies trade in the stock markets are known; one need only compare the comparable company's stock price to its last published income statement (its *price/earnings ratio* or *P/E ratio* is a multiple using net earnings after tax, for example[72]). Most senior executives know the P/E ratios of the publicly traded firms in their industry and use them as rules of thumb. These comparable P/E multiples, which average, over the last 130 years, around thirteen, understate normal acquisition multiples, however, as they do not reflect a premium for acquiring control of a target's assets and, therefore, must be adjusted upward 20 percent or so.

Business parties to a deal negotiation will know the current multiples for the industry of other recently closed transactions, and these multiples will anchor the negotiation position. The parties seeking a price that represents an aberrant multiple will have the burden of justification.

More sophisticated valuations, prepared by experts when deal discussions are serious, use a *discounted cash flow* (*DCF*) analysis. Experts estimate the future net cash flow of the target and discount the amounts to present value, using a discount rate that reflects the time value of money, the risk of currency inflation, and the risk of volatility in the projections. They will also prepare a more detailed comparables analysis based on various selected financial fundamentals. Finally, they will research comparable transactions to see at what prices comparable companies have been sold in other acquisitions. We will consider these methods in our discussion of appraisal proceedings in Chapter Two, Section A.3. A few experts use *option pricing methods* to value the firm.[73]

---

[72] Because the P/E ratio of a company does not take into consideration the debt on its balance sheet, many professionals prefer the *enterprise ratio* (also known as the *EBITDA ratio*). It is calculated by dividing a company's enterprise value (or EV) (which does take into consideration a company's debt and debt equivalents) by its EBITDA. The ratio indicates the multiple of net cash flow that a given business is worth.

[73] The shareholders hold a synthetic call option on the firm's assets against the firm's creditors, priced at the repayment obligations on the debt. See Black & Scholes, *The Pricing of Options and Corporate Liabilities*, 81 J. POL. ECON. 637 (1973). In other words, the firm is theoretically owned by its creditors, and the shareholders have the option to repurchase the firm from the creditors by paying off the debt owed to those creditors.

The parties use DCF studies to buttress and deepen simple multiple analysis. Keep in mind, however, when the deal closes and managers explain it to others and the press reports it, multiples will be front and center. A headline will be: "A bought S, at 7.2x EBITDA."

E. ARE ACQUISITIONS SOCIALLY BENEFICIAL?

Over the years there have been, and still are, many vocal critics of acquisitions. They make several types of claims. Some go to the core function and purpose of large business entities. Do acquisitions harm customers, non-management employees, the environment, tax collections, local communities, and/or creditors? We discuss these issues in Chapter Three (creditors and the environment), Chapter Eight (tax collections), and Chapter Nine (customers and competitors). The harshest claim, perhaps, is that acquisitions do not benefit the owners (usually the shareholders); that is, shareholders lose value in acquisitions.

One of their more popular claims is that the expectation of joint gains (once labeled synergies[74]) in deals translates into excessive optimism by buyers. Buyers, it seems, can overvalue acquisition gains and, to the delight of target firm shareholders, pay too much for control of the target's assets or, on the other hand, selling firm shareholders can agree to accept too little. Such transactions, some argue, do not add value or may even destroy value. At issue then is whether joint gains exist in sufficient size to explain most acquisitions.

Data does not support the skeptics; empiricists find that the majority of the acquisitions studied in the United States (they necessarily study acquisitions of only publicly traded companies, a subset of about 20 percent of all deals[75]) create and do not destroy value. There are many, many studies; M & A is one of the most widely researched fields in management and finance literature. The primary data on acquisitions comes from *event studies*, studies of the movement of stock prices due to specific events.[76] In

---

[74] The word has fallen out of favor because strategic buyers often used the term to justify megamergers that later turned out to be disasters. See Robert F. Brunner & Arthur Levitt, Jr., DEALS FROM HELL: M & A LESSONS THAT RISE FROM THE ASHES (2005).

[75] Critics note that the sample does not include acquisitions by private companies of public or private companies. It therefore excludes, among others, *financial takeovers* (private buyers of public companies; as opposed to *strategic takeovers* in which one operating company buys another) such as leveraged buy-outs (LBOs) and management buy-outs (MBOs), discussed in Chapter Five. Private equity funds that invested in such takeovers have racked up impressive gains.

[76] Scholars developed the methodology in the 1970s. Event studies assume the semi-strong version of the efficient capital market hypothesis, that is, that all publicly available information is reflected completely and in an unbiased manner in the price of the stock. This means that, since the price of the stock reflects the time and risk discounted present value of all future cash flows that are expected to accrue, no one can earn economic profits on already disclosed publicly available information. Unanticipated events can change the price of the stock and the change should equal the expected changes in the future cash flows of the firm due to the new event. The reverse should also be true: an event has an impact on the financial performance of the firm if it produces an abnormal movement in the price of the stock. Event studies measure stock price to find abnormal returns that correlate with a selected class of events. See generally Sanjai Bhagat

M & A studies, the event is the acquisition announcement. Another form of data comes from *performance studies*, studies in which the authors gather income statement data on the constituent parties before the closing and compare the number with the income statement of the acquisition survivor.[77] Both types of studies have their critics.[78] New methods of analysis continue to appear in the literature.

There is a plethora of studies on the stock price effects of acquisition announcements, and the refinement of the methods used to measure and isolate the effect of the deal on stock price are evolving. Studies that aggregated the wealth effects of both target and bidder firms find that the combined target and bidder returns are positive. See, e.g., Dinara Bayazitova, Matthias Kahl & Rossen Valkanov, *Value Creation for Acquirers: New Methods and Evidence*, Working Paper (July 24, 2011); Sanjai Bhagat, Ming Dong, David Hirshleifer & Robert Noah, *Do Tender Offers Create Value?: New Methods and Evidence,* 76 J. FIN. ECON. 3 (2005). Acquisitions do, on average, create new value.

The event studies have produced other important findings. Perhaps the most significant is the disadvantage of the buying firm in the division of any joint gains created in any given deal. When joint gains exist in acquisitions, studies reveal that buyers give, on average, the lions' share of the added value to the selling firm shareholders. Event studies found that target shareholders do very well; there were uniformly large and significant positive price effects for shareholders of targets. Bidders, on the other hand, do not fare as well.

The findings are not surprising. The selling firm in an acquisition, when publicly traded, usually expects and receives a twenty percent or more *premium* over selling firm share prices. The search for joint gains is necessarily a focus on the buyer's gains. Studies in the 1980s argued that, on average, buyer firm shareholders do not enjoy *any* significant positive wealth effect due to the transactions. Newer studies have reversed the view and found that acquirer shareholder *abnormal returns*[79] are, on average, positive but often small.

An important exception to buyer gains is found in *mega-mergers*, however. In mega-deals—the top one percent by absolute transaction size—buyers do, on average, lose money for their shareholders. This finding

---

& Roberta Romano, *Empirical Studies of Corporate Law*, § 4.3.1 (Aug. 2004), in HANDBOOK FOR LAW AND ECONOMICS (Ed. A. Mitchell Polinsky & Steven Shavell) (collecting studies).

77 See, e.g., Paul Healy, K. Palepu & Richar Ruback, *Does Corporate Performance Improve After Mergers?*, 31 J. FIN. ECON. 21 (1992).

78 Those skeptical of event studies question the presumption of efficient markets or the assumptions used in the studies themselves (the size of the *window* around the announcement data, for example). Critics of performance studies distrust accounting data.

79 Abnormal returns are the difference between a security's expected return and its actual return, triggered by an event.

has led to studies attempting to correlate measures of manager hubris[80] or of higher executive pay[81] with failed mega-deals. The measures of executive hubris can produce a chuckle: we have learned, for example, that a CEO whose picture most often appears in business magazines is more likely to push a bad deal on his/her shareholders.

Another branch of the literature focusing on buyer shareholder gains has found that some forms of deals are consistently better for buying firm shareholders than others. Cash deals are more profitable for buyers than stock swap deals, for example. Scholars continue to struggle to find positive buyer returns in stock swap deals.[82] Transactions in which the acquired company is privately held, for example, show higher success rates.[83] And finally, companies that make acquisitions systematically, through good and bad economic times (the *dedicated* or *serial acquirer*), can also be more successful at generating shareholder value than companies that are occasional acquirers.[84]

QUESTIONS

Should the federal or a state government intervene to impede acquisitions by public companies to protect buying firm shareholders?[85] Or can we expect corporate boards to learn from historical mistakes and the new financial studies?[86]

---

80 Richard Roll, *The Hubris Hypothesis of Corporate Takeover*, 59 J. OF BUS. 197 (1986).

81 J. Harford & K. Li, *Decoupling CEO Wealth and Firm Performance: The Case of Acquiring CEOs*, 62 J. OF FIN. 917 (2007).

82 See Pavel Savor & Qi Lu, *Do Stock Mergers Create Value for Acquirers?*, 64 J. OF FIN. 1061 (2009). In stock swaps the data is confused by a negative signal to the markets by the buying firm that its shares may be over-valued in the trading markets (and thus good currency for consideration in a deal). The bid reveals the firm manager's belief that the buying firm's stock may be over-valued.

83 See, e.g., Kathleen Fuller, Jeffry Netter & Mike Stegemoller, *What do Returns to Acquiring Firms Tell Us? Evidence from Firms that Make Many Acquisitions*, 57 J. OF FIN. 1763, 1768 (2002).

84 Sam Rovit & Catherine Lemire, *Your Best M & A Strategy*, HARV. BUS. REV., Mar. 2003, at 16.

85 See, e.g., James A. Fanto, *Braking Merger Momentum: Reforming Corporate Law Governing Mega-Mergers*, 49 BUFF. L. REV. 249 (2001) (proposing a new standard of court review for board decisions to enter into stock swap mega-mergers; board must bear the burden of establishing that it has reasonable grounds, supported by particularized findings, for believing that the merger will maximize shareholder value and is the best alternative among those currently available to the company, including, among others, the alternative of remaining independent).

86 See Dennis K. Berman, *Dealmakers Got it Right in '03*, WALL. ST. J., Nov. 9, 2004, at C1 ("findings suggest that the M & A world has taken to heart the failures of the previous five years . . . caution rules the boardroom").

CHAPTER TWO

THE BASIC MECHANICS OF THE ACQUISITION PROCESS

■ ■ ■

This Chapter contains a description of the various legal doctrines that mold the basic acquisition forms in American law. State corporate codes provide the core set of rules. Federal securities laws and listing requirements on national securities exchanges amend the rules for publicly traded companies. Federal bankruptcy law trumps state rules for firms in bankruptcy. Chapters Five, Six and Seven supplement the basic rules with managers' duties of care, loyalty, and candor developed primarily through state and federal case law.

A. STATE CORPORATE CODES

1. INTRODUCTION

Corporations are artificial legal entities. Legislatures create and empower them. In the United States, unlike most other countries of the world, individual states recognize corporations at the request of groups of individuals called *incorporators*. All states now use a *registration system*; that is, if the papers filed by incorporators meet minimal, objective administrative standards, a state official must give official recognition to the new corporate entity. Government officials have little or no licensing discretion to deny a request for a *Certificate or Articles of Incorporation*.[1]

The constitution, corporate code, and judicial opinions of the incorporating state control much of the internal governance of a corporation. Since the beginning of the 20th Century, the tiny state of Delaware has been the most popular jurisdiction of incorporation for large, publicly traded multi-state corporations. Over 65 percent of each of our largest five hundred corporations and publicly traded corporations generally are Delaware corporations. Consequently, corporate franchise

---

[1] Delaware statutes refer to the incorporating document as a Certificate of Incorporation. Other states typically call the document Articles of Incorporation. Technically, a Corporate Charter is the document granted by states that recognize corporate entities one at a time by special legislation. A Charter, a Certificate of Incorporation, or Articles of Incorporation, then, is the basic constitutional document of a corporation. Some commentators would also include as part of the corporation's constitutional documents the firm's Bylaws, particularly those adopted at the firm's first meeting of its initial board of directors, known as its organizational meeting. Since we look predominately at the Delaware statutes on acquisitions, the default term for the basic constitutional document of a corporation will be a Certificate of Incorporation.

taxes are the second largest source of tax revenue in Delaware (following personal income tax).[2] Moreover, the Delaware bar profits substantially from legal work generated by Delaware corporations.

Relative to most other states, Delaware's corporate code, entitled the "Delaware General Corporation Law," gives more leeway to corporate managers in their operation of the firm's business.[3] The most important example of Delaware's enhanced managerial freedom is in its provisions on M & A. Indeed, the differences among states' acquisition rules are so significant that one often finds large firms changing their place of incorporation to Delaware on the eve of a major acquisition to take advantage of the Delaware provisions.[4]

Delaware also has a more developed and sophisticated body of precedent on corporate law issues in general and M & A matters in particular. Years of multiple business cases have grown the doctrine and honed the expertise of the trial judges in a limited jurisdiction trial court, the Delaware Chancery Court, and of the appellate justices in the Delaware Supreme Court, that hears appeals from the Chancery Court.[5] This body of case law precedent has proven to be particularly important in acquisitions, which often feature disgruntled shareholders willing to take their grievances to court. In Chapter Six, for example, we will explore how the Delaware Supreme Court defined the responsibilities of the board of directors of the target firm in a hostile tender offer and, thereby, sculptured the contours of our corporate control market.

At the other end of the spectrum on managerial freedom is the California corporate code, which features a heavier regulatory hand. Its acquisition provisions give shareholders of constituent corporations their

---

[2] Since 2018, the *maximum* annual franchise tax payable by most Delaware corporations is $200,000. The maximum rate applies to only 0.2 percent of all Delaware corporations. However, Delaware recently established a new tax category called *Large Corporate Filers*. Franchise tax for a Large Corporate Filer is fixed at $250,000 per year. Large Corporate Filers are defined as Delaware corporations that, as of December 1 of the immediately preceding calendar year: (a) had a class or series of stock listed on a national securities exchange; (b) reported, in financial statements included in their most recent annual report filed with the Securities and Exchange Commission (SEC) or a similar foreign agency, (i) consolidated annual gross revenues or consolidated assets of at least $750 million, and (ii) both consolidated annual gross revenues and consolidated assets of at least $250 million; and (c) would have otherwise been required to pay an annual franchise tax of $200,000.

[3] The state has also developed streamlined procedures for filing corporate documents. A Certificate of Incorporation is processed in two hours, for example.

[4] Other states have mimicked Delaware (Nevada and Maryland) or attempted to draft provisions on acquisitions that are competitive with those of Delaware (Pennsylvania), but the trademark value of a "Delaware corporation" remains strong. A substantial percentage of the country's start-up, high-tech companies, for example, that chooses the corporate form, incorporate in Delaware.

[5] New York and California also have a well-developed body of case law. The success of the Delaware Chancery Court is also due to its swift-moving docket. The Delaware courts decide commercial cases more quickly than do courts in other jurisdictions. The Delaware Chancery Court is well known, for example, for deciding requests for preliminary injunctions and other forms of pre-trial relief very quickly.

strongest set of voting and appraisal rights and, thereby, have the strongest limits on managerial freedom in acquisition planning. Consequently, very few of our large multi-state corporations incorporate in California. California does have, however, one of the highest numbers of annual incorporations of all the states because of the many new small businesses formed in the state. This pattern of large firms incorporating predominately in Delaware and small firms incorporating predominately in their home states (where they have their headquarters), repeats in all other states.[6]

Most states fall somewhere between the Delaware and California models on granting managerial discretion. Nevada, Maryland, Pennsylvania and Virginia have codes that, similar to Delaware's code, give managers more discretion, while New York's code is a bit more restrictive. The legislatures in Pennsylvania and Virginia specifically enacted codes to compete against Delaware for incorporations of large, publicly traded firms. New Jersey and Ohio lean towards a California approach. Several states, most prominently New York and North Carolina, have established special commercial or business law courts to counter the expertise advantage of the Delaware Chancery Court. As of yet, these other states have shown only marginal success in luring large American corporations away from Delaware.

The Committee on Corporate Laws of the Section of Business Law of the American Bar Association exerts a very significant influence on the content of many state corporate codes. The Committee has developed and periodically revises a Model Business Corporation Act (Model Act).[7] Over thirty states use the Model Act as a basis for their domestic corporate codes; another five or so states have adopted selected provisions. The ABA made major revisions to the Model Act in 1999 and 2010 relating to M & A, and in 2016 provided a comprehensive and updated Model Act.[8] Most states adopting the Model Act currently use the 1984 version, a few use the 1969 version (retaining "par value"), and a small number of states have progressed to adopting more recent versions.[9]

---

6 The issue often comes down to cost. For example, a business operating in New York that incorporates in Delaware (but does not operate in Delaware) must (i) pay an annual fee to have a registered agent in Delaware and (ii) pay an annual fee to qualify to do business in New York. Both fees would be avoided if the business simply incorporated in New York and used its New York address for service of process purposes (thus avoiding the need for a registered agent).

7 The Committee produced the original Model Act, modeled on the Illinois Corporate Code, in 1950. The Committee substantially redrafted the Model Act in 1969. After major amendments in 1980, the Committee drafted a substantially revised Model Act in 1984, officially called the Revised Model Business Corporation Act. The Committee reports all proposed and final amendments to the Model Act in *The Business Lawyer*, a journal published by the Section of Business Law of the ABA. The Model Act was most recently updated and amended in a comprehensive manner in 2016.

8 The Committee also made minor changes to the M & A sections in 2003 on conversions.

9 Idaho, Iowa, South Dakota, West Virginia and Wyoming, for example.

This chapter will feature the provisions of the Delaware General Corporation Law and the current version of the Model Act on mergers and acquisitions. Brief mention is made of the California and Ohio provisions, which are unique.

2. THE BASIC PROVISIONS OF STATE CORPORATE CODES RELEVANT TO ACQUISITIONS

The main purposes of the corporate codes are, first, to enable corporations to engage in transactions and, second, to specify the role shareholders play when there are major changes in their firm's capital structure. We tend to overlook the first purpose and fixate on the second, assuming that acquisitions are within the power of modern corporations. It was not always so, however, and some of the peculiarities of state corporate code are explained by their erratic historical evolution.

In the early 1800s, state legislatures chartered corporations one at a time by special act. General corporation codes, although very sketchy, first appeared in the mid-19th century. Since corporations can do only what the legislature expressly enables them to do, many early corporations did not have the power to merge with others or to hold the stock of other corporations (i.e., to own subsidiaries). Most corporations did not have the power to change a narrowly stated purpose of their business. As lawyers sought open-ended powers and purposes for clients in corporate charters, legislatures granted, first in special charters and later in general acts, corporations more general powers that included the power to merge and the power to sell or purchase assets.

The state courts, interpreting the special charters or early general acts, required unanimous shareholder approval for all extraordinary transactions. Courts reasoned that these transactions represented major changes in each shareholder's investment contract with the corporation; therefore, each shareholder had to assent. As corporations grew in size and number, the unanimous vote requirement became excessively restrictive. State legislatures relaxed the shareholder approval requirement for mergers, first to a two-thirds majority of all outstanding shares and later to a simple majority of all outstanding shares. Some states, such as New York, made the change relatively recently.[10]

The Model Act dilutes the vote requirement further and requires only a simple majority of the shareholders attending or represented at a shareholder meeting, provided there is a *quorum*.[11] In exchange for diluting the voting power of shareholders, state legislatures grant

[10] In Ohio, the default rule is a two-third vote of the outstanding shares, which can be reduced in the corporation's Articles to not less than a majority vote of the outstanding shares. Ohio Rev. St. § 1701.78(F).

[11] ABA Model Bus. Corp. Act § 11.04(e) (2016 rev.) (a quorum is a majority of the shares entitled to vote unless a greater number is specified in the Articles).

dissenting shareholders *appraisal rights*, the right to petition the state courts for the "fair" cash value of their shares. Similar to the trend in shareholder voting majority requirements, appraisal rights have eroded substantially over time. We discuss these rights in Section A.3 below.

Enterprising acquisition lawyers, seeking to avoid the voting and appraisal requirements of the codes, turned their attention to those general code sections authorizing corporations to buy and sell property and to hold stock. Could lawyers characterize major acquisitive transactions as asset purchases or as stock purchases rather than statutory mergers?

Early corporate codes did not require shareholder approval by the shareholders of either the selling firm or purchasing firm in asset acquisitions. Indeed, only if the selling firm dissolved was a vote of the selling firm shareholders required. The vote on liquidation once the selling firm had sold its assets was a foregone conclusion, a *fait accompli*, given that the selling firm no longer had any meaningful business operations after the sale. Courts responded by requiring unanimous shareholder approval for asset sales of "all or substantially all" of a corporation's property.[12] Legislatures, to enable a broader use of the technique, amended corporate codes to limit the required ratifying shareholder vote to a majority in asset sales.

In stock purchases, which legislatures authorized once one corporation had the power to hold the stock of another,[13] neither the shareholders of the buying nor selling firm had voting rights. Individual dissenting shareholders of the seller could be troublesome if they refused to tender their shares. The purchasing firm in a simple stock acquisition could not necessarily gain one hundred percent control of the selling firm. Lawyers solved this problem by using a *two-step* acquisition, a stock purchase followed by a *back-end* or *second-step merger* in which the new parent *squeezed out* (forced to exchange their shares for cash) the residual minority shareholders in the new subsidiary. Again, the dissenting shareholders complained to the state courts but the courts, with an occasional hiccup,[14] did not stop the deals.

As we shall see in the materials that follow, the cleverness of lawyers continues unabated. Asset sales structured to achieve the same result of

---

12 Courts categorized the deals as extraordinary transactions, analogous to mergers. In 1915 the Delaware Chancery Court, for example, noted in dicta that the directors of a firm could not sell all or substantially all of the firm's property if a single shareholder objected unless the business is "unprofitable . . . and . . . hopeless" and a majority of the shareholders vote to sell the assets with a view to winding up the business. Butler v. New Keystone Copper Co., 93 A. 380, 383 (Del. Ch. 1915) (the court enforced a charter provision that gave the board the power to sell all the firm's assets on a two-thirds vote of the shareholders). The Delaware legislature enacted the original version of § 271 immediately thereafter. 29 Del. Laws, Ch. 113, § 17 (1917).

13 This was not true until the late 1800s in many states. Pennsylvania did not authorize a corporation to hold the stock of another until the turn of the 20th Century, for example.

14 E.g., Coggins v. New England Patriots Football Club, Inc., 492 N.E.2d 1112 (Mass. 1986) (the court blocked the second step of a two-stage acquisition).

NO SH approval for asset

mergers, reverse asset sales to allocate shareholder voting from the selling firm to the buying firm, and triangular mergers to minimize shareholder voting in the buying firm are all in the M & A lawyers tool kit. Courts confronted with the novel acquisition forms, with minor short-lived exceptions, have refused to reclassify the transactions. Most state legislatures also have permitted, either expressly or by implication, the novel forms by not overruling the state court decisions. California and New Jersey are the two notable exceptions.

The evolution of M & A state law then is a classic case of legal innovation by lawyers, in response to economic developments, as the driving force behind an erosion of the old rules. Most see this as progress; some see it as a conspiracy of the powerful.[15]

The current position of state corporation codes in all states but California is an emphasis on transaction form over transaction substance. That is, the end result of any given transaction has marginal legal significance on whether shareholders vote or have appraisal rights. State codes do not feature a final position analysis that one sees in the merger-sale distinction in tax law or in the combination rules of antitrust law.

The statutory definitions depend more on the *procedure* constituent parties use to effect the transaction than the end position of the parties. If the parties choose to follow the procedure specified under § 251 of the Delaware General Corporation Law, it is a merger. If the parties choose to follow the procedure specified under § 271, it is an asset sale. If either procedure gets the parties to the same result, it is of no legal consequence that the parties have chosen one procedure over another. In other words, the statutes describe procedures to effect mergers and the operative results of a merger, but the statutes do not define a Platonic form of merger.

To learn modern acquisition practice, we will first study the three basic transactional forms in their original forms: the stock swap statutory merger, the cash-for-assets acquisition, and the cash-for-stock acquisition. Second, we will note how, by varying the consideration received in the transactions, the forms can substitute for each other. Third, we will dissect the hybrid forms that lawyers use to plan around statutory mandates. Finally, we will discuss whether the codes, as they have evolved, make sense.

Those states that follow the basic Delaware pattern featured below may have significant deviations from the specific details in the Delaware provisions, and each state's provisions need to be separately consulted relevant to an acquisition.

---

15 E.g., Morton J. Horowitz, THE TRANSFORMATION OF AMERICAN LAW 1870–1960: THE CRISIS OF LEGAL ORTHODOXY, Ch.3 (1992).

a. The Three Basic Forms: The Stock Swap Statutory Merger, the Cash-for-Assets Acquisition, and the Cash-for-Stock Acquisition

The structure of the Delaware General Corporation Law (abbreviated hereinafter as the Del. Gen. Corp. L.) is typical of the structure of most state corporate codes. The authority and procedure for effecting a *statutory merger*[16] is outlined in § 251 and the legal effect of a merger is detailed in §§ 259 to 261. A special *short-form* merger procedure for some parent-subsidiary mergers is contained in § 253. A special *medium-form* merger procedure for negotiated two-step acquisitions that obviates the need for a target shareholder vote is contained in § 251(h). The code covers mergers between domestic and foreign corporations (corporations incorporated in other states) in § 252 and mergers between corporations and entities registered under a separate enabling act in § 254.[17]

The procedure for an asset sale is contained in § 271. The appraisal rights of dissenting shareholders are outlined in § 262 (we will explore these rights in Section A.3 below). Delaware regulates single-firm reorganizations of capital structure in § 242,[18] which specifies the requirements for amending a corporation's charter. The only provision specific to stock acquisitions is § 203, Delaware's anti-takeover statute, which limits hostile tender offers. We will cover this section in detail in Chapter Six, Section C. Although the book summarizes the content of these Delaware sections below, it is wise to get a copy of their full text and refer to the text when relevant.

i. *A Plain Vanilla (or Stock Swap) Statutory Merger*

Diagram 1 illustrates a *stock swap statutory merger*.[19] Two corporations, A Corp. and B Corp., start as separate legal entities with separate owners, their shareholders. In the transaction, B Corp. merges *with and into* A Corp., and thus A Corp. is the *survivor*.[20] There are other structural options: A could merge into B; or A and B could both merge into a new corporation formed for the transaction, C Corp., that survives. A

---

16 The addition of the qualifier *statutory* distinguishes the concept from the meaning of the word "merger" in other contexts (antitrust, for example).

17 Merger of a domestic corporation with an unincorporated association is permitted by § 254; merger of a domestic corporation with a non-stock corporation is enabled by § 257; and merger of a domestic corporation with a limited partnership is authorized in § 263.

Conversion of domestic corporations into other legal entities (limited liability companies, limited partnerships and business trusts) or of other legal entities into corporations is the subject of §§ 265 and 266. We cover conversions in Section A.2.c., *infra*.

18 Section 245 enables a corporation, using § 242 procedures, to "restate" its Certificate of Incorporation in its entirety.

19 The transaction is also known as a *stock-for-stock merger*.

20 The phrase "with and into" is designed to indicate which corporation survives the merger.

merger involving more than two corporations is referred to as a *consolidation*.

In the merger of B into A, B shareholders' stock in B is cancelled and they receive as consideration A Corp. shares (a *stock-for-stock merger* or a *stock swap* merger). A Corp. absorbs the assets and liabilities of B Corp. "as a matter of law." We will investigate further what this means in Chapter Three on successor liability.

Diagram 1

The Plain-Vanilla Statutory Merger: Stock-for-Stock*

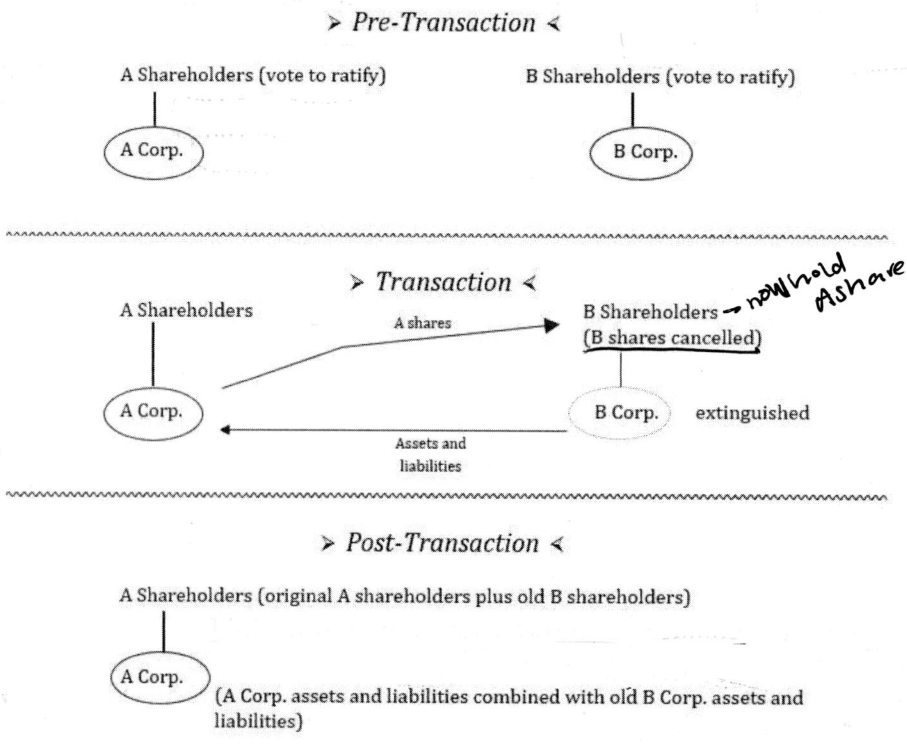

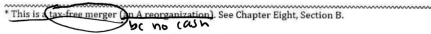

* This is a tax-free merger (an A reorganization). See Chapter Eight, Section B.

After the merger closes, A Corp. survives and B Corp. does not. The shareholders of A Corp. stock hold their stock and the shareholders of old B Corp. stock hold newly-issued A Corp. stock; the ownership interests of A Corp. and B Corp. are *pooled* in the survivor. A Corp. now has added the assets and liabilities of old B Corp. to its own; the assets and liabilities of both constituent corporations are also pooled.

If both A Corp. and B Corp. are Delaware corporations, that is, they had received Certificates of Incorporation from the Delaware Secretary of State, Del. Gen. Corp. L. § 251 controls the acquisition. Section 251(a) authorizes both firms to engage in the transaction and § 251(b) requires that the board of directors of both firms pass a resolution approving an "Agreement of Merger" and a statement "declaring its advisability." The agreement states the terms and conditions of the merger and may amend the Certificate of Incorporation of the survivor.[21]

Both constituent corporations, A Corp. and B Corp., must then submit the agreement to a shareholder vote under § 251(c). A majority of all the *outstanding* shares "entitled to vote" must ratify the agreement.[22] The shareholders of neither constituent corporation can initiate the acquisition vote nor can they amend the agreement; it is an up or down vote. After a successful vote, the parties file the agreement (or a summary of the agreement entitled a "Certificate of Merger") with the Delaware Secretary of State to become effective on a date certain within the next ninety days. On that date, representatives of the constituent corporations meet and "close" the transaction.

The mechanics of who votes in acquisitions deserve special mention. In Delaware the default rule is that shares that do not have general voting rights (non-voting common shares and preferred shares with no voting rights unless there are dividend arrearages) do not vote in major transactions. This seems harsh and a majority of other states do not follow Delaware's example. Yet it is important to note that Delaware firms can and often do provide preferred stock shareholders a separate class vote[23] in acquisitions. In Delaware, the voting power of shareholders granted in the code is a default rule and the parties can change the rule by contract. The parties cannot reduce by contract the voting power of shareholders in the code, however.

The shareholder ratification vote required in the Delaware code is a majority of all outstanding shares entitled to vote, whether or not the shares are actually present or represented at the shareholder meeting by proxy (i.e., without regard to quorum requirements).[24] Since the turnout at shareholder meetings is often less than 75 percent of the outstanding

[21] Thus, a merger is an alternative way in which to amend a corporation's charter.

[22] Outstanding shares are those shares issued by the corporation and in the hands of investors. Any shares repurchased by the corporation itself and not cancelled or retired (*treasury shares*) or held by controlled subsidiaries of the corporation are not considered outstanding for either quorum or voting purposes.

[23] A type of share with a *separate class vote* on a merger means that holders of a majority of the outstanding shares of that type must support the merger for it to proceed. Thus, those shareholders have *veto power* over the transaction.

[24] The Model Act reduces the approval requirement to a majority of those present at the shareholders' meeting if a quorum exists. A quorum is defined as a majority of the "votes entitled to be cast." In theory, under the Model Act, holders of 25–plus percent of the shares could approve a merger. ABA Model Bus. Corp. Act § 11.04(e) (2016 rev.). See also *id.*, § 12.02(e) (shareholder approval of a disposition of all or substantially all of the corporation's assets).

voting shares, a successful vote on a merger can require an affirmative vote of the holders of well over a majority of those shares represented in person or by proxy at the shareholders' meeting (67 percent of the shares present if only 75 percent of the outstanding shares are represented, for example).

There are four major statutory exceptions to the Delaware voting procedures noted above: the 20 Percent Rule, the Short-Form Merger, the Medium-Form Merger, and the Holding Company Exception. Each is explored below.

The 20 Percent Rule. Pursuant to § 251(f), the shareholders of the *surviving firm* in a statutory merger, A Corp. in Diagram 1, do not have a right to vote if: (1) A Corp.'s Certification of Incorporation is unchanged as a result of the merger; (2) the rights, preferences and privileges of their shares survive the merger (their investment contract has not changed); and (3) their shares are not diluted by more than a specified amount, the acquiring company does not issue to the B Corp. shareholders an amount of A shares that exceeds 20 percent of the voting shares of A Corp. outstanding before the transaction.[25] In essence, the exception applies if the original A Corp. shareholders hold at least 83 percent of the A Corp. voting shares (5/6ths) at the conclusion of the transaction.[26] The exception recognizes that when larger firms merge with much smaller firms the transaction is more a purchase of the smaller firm than a merger; thus, the larger firm's shareholders need not ratify the transaction. Some refer to the exception as the *small-scale merger exception*, others call it the *20 percent rule*. See also ABA Model Bus. Corp. Act §§ 6.21(f) & 11.04(h)(4) (2016 rev.) (20 percent trigger).[27]

Short-Form Merger. The second exception to the voting rules involves a statutory merger of a parent corporation and a subsidiary when the parent holds over 90 percent of each class of the subsidiary's voting stock (a *short-form merger*). Section 253 of the Del. Gen. Corp. L. permits the merger of the subsidiary into the parent (an *upstream merger*) solely on a resolution of the parent's board of directors. The shareholders of neither the subsidiary nor the parent have a right to vote on the transaction.[28] If the subsidiary is the surviving corporation (a *downstream merger*), the shareholders of the parent corporation entitled to vote must ratify the

---

[25] The 20 percent figure includes securities or "obligations" convertible into voting shares (convertible debentures, for example) on an "as converted" basis. Options or warrants on voting shares are not to be included. But see ABA Model Bus. Corp. Act § 6.21(f)(2)(i) (2016 rev.) (including "rights exercisable for shares").

[26] In New Jersey, a firm attempting to use the exception cannot issue an amount exceeding 40 percent or more of the pre-existing outstanding shares. N.J. Rev. Stat. § 14A:10–3(4)(c) (2013).

[27] The 20 percent trigger is generally patterned on the listing standards of the national securities exchanges. See ABA Model Bus. Corp. Act § 6.21(f), Off. Cmt. 3 (2016 rev.).

[28] Section 11.04(h) of the ABA Model Bus. Corp. Act gives parent shareholders the right to vote in upstream mergers when the parent's Articles of Incorporation are changed (other than minor changes that a board of directors may make unilaterally under Section 10.05) or when the parent issues stock in the transaction carrying more than 20 percent of the voting power in the parent. ABA Model Bus. Corp. Act, §§ 6.21(f) & 11.04(h) (2016 rev.).

transaction.[29] As we shall see in Chapter Five, short-form mergers have attracted renewed importance in two-step acquisitions due to recent Delaware court precedent.

③ *Medium-Form Merger*. The third exception is the *medium-form merger exception* under Del. Gen. Corp. L. § 251(h). This exception provides a cost-effective and time saving way to accomplish a second-step merger that follows a successful first-step tender offer. Traditionally, the second-step merger in this context was a *long-form* or *single-step merger*, whereby both the mailing of a proxy statement to target shareholders and the holding of an actual shareholder meeting were needed to approve the merger. Doing so is both time consuming and costly—especially in light of the fact that the acquirer will have acquired enough target shares in the successful first-step tender offer to make the merger vote a *fait accompli*.[30]

Prior to the introduction of § 251(h), parties to two-step acquisitions had to avail themselves of *subsequent offering periods*, *top-up options* and *dual-track structures* to help expedite a second-step merger. Subsequent offering periods allow non-tendering target shareholders a second chance to tender their shares into an acquirer's tender offer, thereby enhancing—but certainly not guaranteeing—the acquirer's ability to reach the 90 percent ownership requirement needed to effect a short-form merger under Del. Gen. Corp. L. § 253. A top-up option allows the acquirer to purchase enough additional shares of target company stock which, when added to the shares the acquirer already purchased in a first-step tender offer, allows the acquirer to satisfy the 90 percent ownership requirement under § 253. The acquirer purchases the additional shares directly from the target company itself. Thus, whether the target has enough authorized but unissued shares to satisfy the option is an issue that must be addressed. A dual track structure saves time with respect to a second-step merger, because the first-step tender offer and preparations for the second-step merger occur contemporaneously. How closely the shareholder meeting for the second-step merger can occur to the date on which the first-step tender offer is closed depends on several variables, including whether the Securities and Exchange Commission (SEC) decides to review and comment upon the target company's proxy materials.

Under § 251(h), the need for target company shareholder approval is eliminated if the parties include a provision in their merger agreement

---

29 The ABA has a similar requirement. ABA Model Bus. Corp. Act § 11.04 (2016 rev.).

30 A first-step tender offer typically will contain a *minimum tender condition*. Pursuant to this condition, the acquirer need not close on its tender offer unless the number of shares tendered to it is equal to or higher than the number of shares needed by the acquirer to vote through the second-step merger solely through its own voting power. Thus, the minimum tender condition is normally a majority of all the outstanding shares of the target company's common stock (less the number of target shares already owned, if any, by the acquirer prior to the consummation of the tender offer).

opting into the benefits afforded under that Section.[31] Such a provision allows for the second-step merger to occur immediately following the closing of a successful first-step tender offer without obtaining target shareholder approval. Importantly, use of § 251(h) is explicitly conditioned on the acquirer purchasing that number of shares in the first-step tender offer necessary to satisfy the transactional voting approval requirements under the Delaware Code and in the target corporation's Certificate of Incorporation (if any) *as if § 251(h) were not applicable*. Thus, if the target corporation's charter contains a super majority merger voting provision, or a separate class or series vote, the acquirer's first-step tender offer must satisfy those charter provisions before § 251(h) is available.[32]

Only friendly (i.e., negotiated) deals can benefit from § 251(h), as an agreed upon merger agreement containing an opt-in provision must be approved by the target's board of directors. Moreover, § 251(h) is only available for third party acquisitions. Thus, "going-private" transactions may not use § 251(h).[33] Section 251(h) also requires that the first-step tender offer be for "any and all" shares of the target's stock that, absent § 251(h), would be entitled to vote on the adoption or rejection of the merger agreement; however, the tender offer may be conditioned on the tender of a minimum number or percentage of shares of stock of the target (or any class or series thereof).[34] The tender offer also must be conducted in accordance with the terms provided for in the merger agreement. The consideration offered in the second-step merger must be the same amount and kind as that paid in the first-step tender offer. The merger must be effected as soon as practicable following the consummation of the first-step tender offer, so that non-tendering shareholders will receive the merger consideration quickly—an important policy goal behind § 251(h).

---

[31] Section 251(h) makes clear that parties may use that Section in a non-compulsory manner, thereby not foreclosing their ability to consummate their transaction by other means, such as a top-up option or a § 253 short-form merger.

[32] See Del. Gen. Corp. L. § 251(h)(3). In determining the number of shares that the acquirer must purchase in the first-step tender offer, the Del. Gen. Corp. L. allows the exclusion of so-called *excluded stock*. Excluded stock means (i) treasury stock held by the target corporation, (ii) target stock already owned by the acquirer, (iii) target stock owned by any person that owns, directly or indirectly, all of the outstanding stock of the acquirer, and (iv) target stock owned by any direct or indirect wholly-owned subsidiary of any of the foregoing. See Del. Gen. Corp. L. § 251(h)(6)d. Excluded stock also includes *rollover stock*. Rollover stock consists of shares of stock of the target corporation that are the subject of a written agreement requiring such shares to be transferred, contributed or delivered to the acquirer or any of its affiliates in exchange for stock or other equity interests in the acquirer or an affiliate thereof, so long as such shares are actually transferred, contributed or delivered pursuant to the agreement prior to the time the merger becomes effective. See Del. Gen. Corp. L. § 251(h)(6)g.

[33] Originally, § 251(h) was not available if a party to a merger agreement was an "interested stockholder" as defined in Del. Gen. Corp. L. § 203. This made § 251(h) unavailable in a transaction where shareholders owning 15 percent or more of the target company's voting stock had signed "tender and support" agreements with an acquirer, as it would result in the acquirer being deemed an "interested stockholder" in its own right. A 2014 amendment to § 251(h) removed the "interested stockholder" restriction.

[34] The acquirer may consummate separate offers for separate classes or series of the stock of the target corporation. See Del. Gen. Corp. L. § 251(h)(2).

Section 251(h)'s benefits are only available to acquisition vehicles that are *corporations* and not other types of business entities. Moreover, target corporations need to be either publicly traded or their shares held of record by more than 2,000 shareholders immediately prior to the execution of the merger agreement. In 2016, the Delaware legislature amended § 251(h) to clarify that not all of a target corporation's classes or series of stock need to be listed on an exchange or held of record by more than 2,000 shareholders, so long as *at least one* class or series is. Thus, even if a given target corporation has a series of preferred stock that is not listed or held of record by more than 2,000 shareholders (which is often the case), § 251(h) is still available as long as the target corporation's common stock meets one of these requirements.

Appraisal rights are generally not triggered when an acquirer is using stock of a publicly traded corporation as merger consideration. Nonetheless, appraisal rights are available for all § 251(h) mergers even when that stock is used as merger consideration. Del. Gen. Corp. L. § 262(b)(3). Ordinarily, the Delaware Chancery Court will apply the business judgement standard of review to a merger effected pursuant to § 251(h), so long as target shareholders are disinterested, uncoerced and fully informed when they tender a majority of the corporation's outstanding shares into the first-step tender offer. See *In re Volcano Corp. Shareholders Lit.*, 143 A.3d 727, 738 (Del. Ch. 2016), aff'd, 156 A.3d 697 (Del. 2017).

Since the Delaware legislature added the now widely-used § 251(h) to the Del. Gen. Corp. L. in 2013, other states have begun to follow suit. For example, Maryland, Texas and Virginia have all adopted § 251(h)-like provisions.[35] Moreover, Maryland and Texas, unlike Delaware, allow *non-corporate* acquirers to take advantage of their provisions, thus providing increased structural flexibility. Importantly, the Model Act now provides for a medium-form merger exception to shareholder voting. See ABA Model Bus. Corp. Act § 11.04(j) (2016 rev.).

4) *Holding Company Exception*. The fourth and final voting exception is the *holding company exception* under Del. Gen. Corp. L. § 251(g). No shareholder vote is required when a merger is effected solely to establish a holding company structure. For example, assume A Corp., an operating company, wants to create a holding company structure that would result in A Corp.'s shareholders owning shares in the holding company and A Corp. itself becoming a wholly-owned subsidiary of that holding company. To accomplish this, A Corp. first would drop down[36] a wholly-owned Delaware subsidiary named "Holding Corp." Holding Corp., in turn, would drop down a wholly-owned subsidiary called B Corp. A Corp would then

[35] See Md. Gen Corp. L. § 3–106.1; Tex. Corp. L. §21.459(c); Va. Stock Corp. Act §13.1–718.G.

[36] In a drop down, A Corp. itself acts as an incorporator for a new corporation which becomes a wholly-owned subsidiary of A Corp. The new subsidiary is usually a *shell* corporation, one that has no assets.

merge with and into B Corp. A Corp.'s shareholders would receive shares of Holding Corp. stock as merger consideration. In the end, Holding Corp. owns all the shares of B Corp. B Corp holds all of the assets and liabilities of the former A Corp. by virtue of the merger. Former A Corp. shareholders own all the stock of Holding Corp. In this context, A Corp. shareholders are not entitled to vote on any of these transactions.

The holding company exception has a number of stringent requirements, including the following three. First, Holding Corp. must have a Certificate of Incorporation and Bylaws largely identical to those of the former A Corp. Second, the directors on the Holding Corp. board must be those (and only those) that sat on the board of the former A Corp. Finally, the rights associated with the equity of Holding Corp. must be identical to those associated with the equity of the former A Corp., and thus the rights of the former A Corp. shareholders must not change as a result of the merger.

NOTE: CLASS VOTING

As noted above, Delaware's voting rules do not give voting rights to shares that do not vote in board of director elections (non-voting common and preferred shares, for example) and do not provide for separate class voting. This is very controversial and one of the reasons why Delaware provides more acquisition freedom than most other states.

Class voting enables each class or type of shareholders (or series of shares) to veto an acquisition. A dissident group of preferred shareholders, for example, could veto an acquisition favored by the holders of a majority of the outstanding common shares. The dissident group could be small, just large enough to block the count of a majority vote of the holders of the outstanding preferred shares if holders of a sizable block of preferred shares fail to attend the shareholders meeting (recall that the holders of a mere one-third of the shares could block a successful vote if holders of only three-quarters of the shares attend a meeting).

All but five or six states do not follow Delaware's rules on the absence of separate class voting in mergers. Section 11.04(f) of the Model Act (2016 rev.) provides for class voting on statutory mergers (1) if a class or series of shares is converted into other securities, cash or property, or (2) if the plan of merger contains a provision "that constitutes a proposed amendment to the articles of incorporation of a surviving corporation that requires action by separate voting groups under section 10.04 [relating to amendments to the Articles]." Moreover, if preferred shareholders in the selling firm receive preferred stock in the surviving firm, the preferred shareholders vote as a separate class on the merger, even if the newly-issued preferred stock has similar rights and privileges to their old target shares and regardless of whether the shares vote in director elections. Preferred shareholders of the buying firm vote together with the common shareholders as a single class if there are any amendments to the firm's Certificate of Incorporation but also as a separate class if those amendments affect the rights (whether adversely or not) of the preferred shareholders.[37]

There are other variations. New York, by comparison, gives preferred shareholders two votes; they vote as a separate class and have their votes counted along with the common if the preferred shareholders in the constituent firms end up with preferred shares in the survivor and their rights and privileges under the survivor's constitutional documents are different from those rights in their pre-transaction corporations. N.Y. Bus. Corp. L. §§ 804 & 903. See also Ohio Rev. St. § 1701.78(F) (same).

Class voting is losing favor with the drafters of the Model Act. The Model Act allows a firm to, by amendment to its Articles of Incorporation, eliminate class voting in all cases but those involving reorganizations or recapitalizations or those involving an amendment to the Articles that would otherwise trigger class voting.[38] ABA Model Bus. Corp. Act § 11.04(g) (2016 rev.).

ii. Cash-for-Assets Acquisition

Diagram 2 illustrates a *cash-for-assets acquisition.*[39] In the first step of the transaction, A Corp. pays B Corp. cash consideration for B Corp.'s assets. A Corp. may choose to accept B Corp.'s liabilities, offsetting the dollar amount of the liabilities against the cash price, but A Corp. does not have to do so.[40] There is no change in the constitutional documents of either A or B Corp., nor is there any change in the shares outstanding in either corporation. In the optional but commonplace second step of the transaction, B Corp. dissolves and liquidates, distributing the acquisition consideration previously received from A. Corp. to B's shareholders (after paying off any residual liabilities not assumed by A Corp.). The investment contract held by A Corp. shareholders (the rights and privileges attached to the A Corp. shares) and A Corp.'s constitutional document, its Certificate of Incorporation, is unchanged.

If both A Corp. and B Corp. are Delaware corporations, the transaction is controlled by Del. Gen. Corp. L. §§ 122 and 271. Section 122(4) is a general grant of power to Delaware corporations; the provision empowers A Corp. to buy assets and B Corp. to sell its assets. Another general grant of power, § 122(13), authorizes A Corp. to assume B Corp.'s liabilities (assuming it chooses to do so). Section 271, however, is specific to asset acquisitions and conditions B Corp.'s general authority to sell "all or

37 ABA Model Bus. Corp. Act §§ 10.03(e) & 10.04(b) (2016 rev.).

38 This applies when, for example, the Articles of the surviving firm are amended to change the rights of a preferred class of shareholders.

39 Delaware's original sale of assets provision, enacted in 1917, required the purchasing corporation to pay in "stock or securities." It was not until 1967 that the legislature amended the statute to permit consideration in "money or other property." Lawyers had long before fashioned cash-for-asset acquisitions under the 1917 language by using immediately redeemable notes of the purchaser as consideration.

40 The treatment of B Corp.'s liabilities will be a major subject of negotiation between A Corp. and B Corp.

substantially all" of its assets[41] on a ratifying shareholder vote. Under § 271, B Corp.'s board of directors, whenever it resolves to have the corporation sell "all or substantially all" of B Corp.'s assets, must submit a resolution to its shareholders for a vote. Holders of a majority of the outstanding shares "entitled to vote" must ratify the transaction.[42] B Corp.'s shareholders cannot initiate the transaction nor can they amend the acquisition agreement. A Corp. shareholders are not entitled to vote on the transaction nor can they initiate the transaction. Section 271 covers *split-offs* but not most *spin-offs* or *split-ups*.[43] The Section also does not stop a board from expressly mortgaging or pledging all the firm's assets to secure indebtedness.[44]

The codes of most states other than Delaware contain an important exception to the voting requirement. Over forty-five states permit the disposition of "all or substantially all" of a corporation's assets by the board of directors without shareholder approval if the transaction is in the "regular course of business." E.g., ABA Model Bus. Corp. Act § 12.01(a) (2016 rev.). Most states also except from shareholder voting the redeployment of assets of the parent into a wholly-owned subsidiary. *Id.* § 12.01(c).

---

[41] For purposes of § 271, "the property and assets of the corporation include the property and assets of any subsidiary of the corporation." Del. Gen. Corp. L. § 271(c).

[42] Thus, as is the case with approving a merger under Delaware law, a raw majority vote—without regard to quorum—is required.

[43] A traditional spin-off in which a parent corporation distributes shares of a subsidiary to the parent's shareholders on a pro rata basis is not covered by the section. On the other hand, a split-off in which a parent corporation exchanges shares of a subsidiary to some or all of its shareholders for their shares, a non-pro rata distribution, or an outright sale of the stock of a subsidiary is covered by the section if the subsidiary is large enough. A split-up, or distribution of all of the shares of all parent subsidiaries in complete liquidation, is covered by corporate code sections on dissolutions. See also ABA Model Bus. Corp. Act § 12.01, Off. Cmt. (2016 rev.) (describing treatment of spin-offs, split-offs and split-ups).

[44] See Del. Gen. Corp. L. § 272.

Diagram 2

The Common Asset Acquisition: Cash-for-Assets with the Selling Corporation Dissolving*

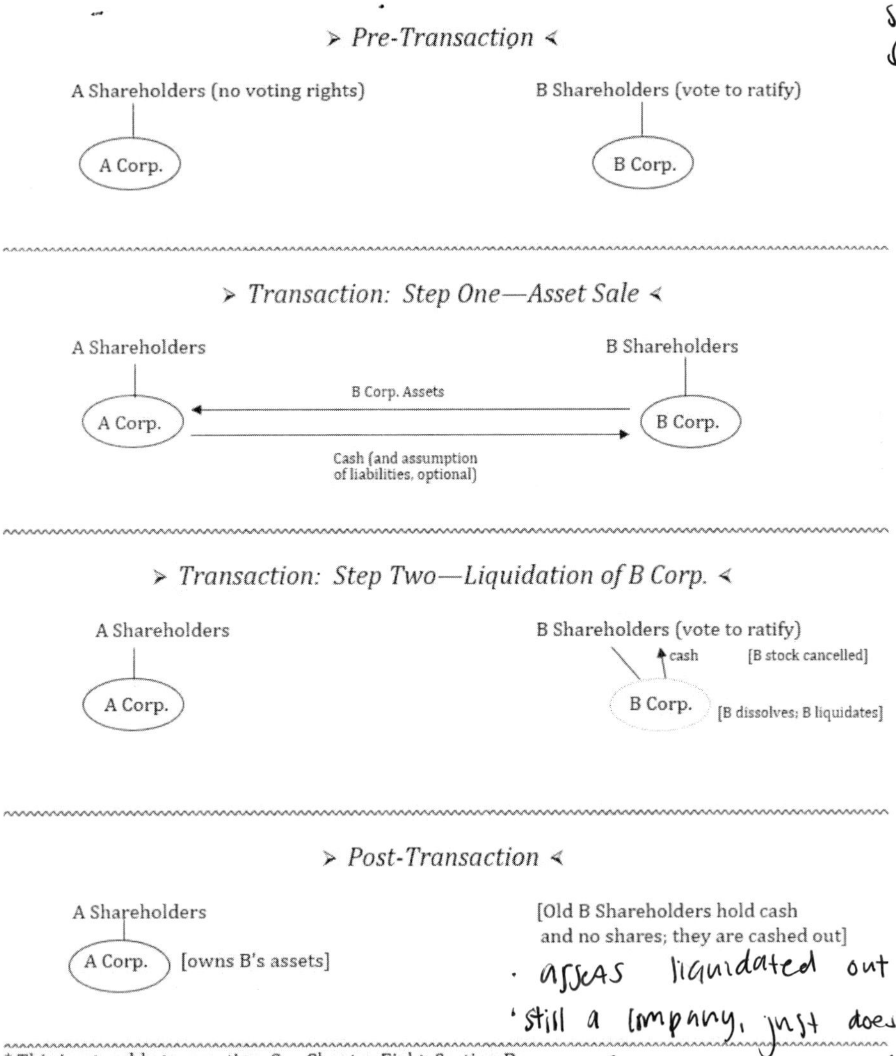

* This is a taxable transaction. See Chapter Eight, Section B.

After an asset acquisition, B Corp. must either reinvest the cash received in operating assets or dissolve and pass the cash in a liquidation distribution back to its shareholders. If B Corp. invests the cash in assets generating passive income—income from the management efforts of others (stock, bonds, or rental property)—the Internal Revenue Code deems B Corp. a personal holding company, which has tax consequences that can be onerous, and the acquisition cannot qualify for tax-free status.[45] In most asset acquisitions then, B Corp. dissolves after the sale of its assets.

The dissolution of the selling corporation is controlled by § 275, which also requires a shareholder vote. The board adopts a resolution on dissolution and submits it to B Corp. shareholders. Holders of a majority of the outstanding shares "entitled to vote" must ratify the resolution.[46] The firm sends a Certificate of Dissolution to the Delaware Secretary of State. On the effective date of the dissolution, the corporation is dissolved and its stock extinguished. The corporation then has three years to wind up, paying its liabilities and passing back to shareholders any residual cash surplus.[47]

After a cash-for-assets transaction, old B Corp. shareholders hold cash consideration (no shares) and A Corp. holds title to B Corp.'s assets (and perhaps is obligated on some or even all of B Corp.'s pre-transaction liabilities). The major differences between Diagram 1 and Diagram 2 are: (a) who votes—A Corp. shareholders do not vote in the asset acquisition; (b) the post-transaction position of the old B shareholders—in the merger the B shareholders hold shares in the survivor and in the asset acquisition the B shareholders are cashed out; and (c) the location of B's pre-transaction liabilities—in an asset acquisition A Corp. may choose not to assume B Corp.'s liabilities, while in a merger A Corp. would assume all those liabilities by operation of law.

Delaware, consistent with its rules on statutory mergers, does not grant the shareholders of the selling firm class voting rights nor grant voting rights to shareholders that do not vote in board elections (non-voting preferred or common shareholders). In what is a surprise to many, most states that require class voting for statutory mergers do not require class voting in asset acquisitions. E.g., ABA Model Bus. Corp. Act § 12.02(e)

---

45 Due to its extensive holdings of securities, under the right circumstances B Corp. also could be deemed an *investment company* (i.e., a mutual fund) and thus have to register as such under the Investment Company Act of 1940, as amended (the "ICA"). 15 U.S.C. § 80a–3(a)(1) (definition of "investment company"). ICA Rule 3a–2, however, provides temporary relief from the ICA's registration requirements to an issuer that, on a *transient basis only*, is deemed to be an investment company because of an unusual business occurrence, such as a sale of significant assets. The transient investment company exemption may be relied upon for a period of up to one year by an issuer that can demonstrate a bona fide intent to be, as soon as is reasonably possible, engaged primarily in a business other than that of investing, reinvesting, owning, holding or trading in securities. An issuer may avail itself of this exemption only once in any three-year period. The one-year period begins on the earlier of (a) the date an issuer owns or proposes to acquire investment securities having a value exceeding 40 per cent of the value of the issuer's total assets (excluding U.S. government securities and cash items) on an unconsolidated basis or (b) the date on which the issuer owns securities and/or cash having a value exceeding 50 per cent of the value of the issuer's total assets on either a consolidated or unconsolidated basis.

46 See *supra* note 42.

47 The Delaware Court of Chancery must approve any winding up period that is more than three years. See Del. Gen. Corp. L. § 278.

(2016 rev.); N.Y. Bus. Corp. L. § 909.[48] The disparity encourages planners to use asset acquisitions. California is the notable exception.[49]

The following case illustrates the difference between a merger, which required class voting, and an asset sale, which did not.

SHIDLER V. ALL AMERICAN LIFE & FINANCIAL CORP.

Supreme Court of Iowa, 1980.
298 N.W.2d 318.

UHLENHOPP, JUSTICE.

* * *

. . . In May, 1973, an attempt was made to merge General United Group, Incorporated (GUG), a domestic corporation (and its subsidiary, United Security Life Company (USL), which need not be separately considered), into All American Delaware Corporation, a foreign corporation, which would be the surviving entity. At that time, GUG had outstanding 105,000 shares of preferred stock, 2,959,650 shares of common stock, and 10,623,150 shares of class B common stock. The preferred and class B common stock had specified conversion rights into common stock. All of the preferred and class B common stock and 67,043 shares of the common stock were owned by another corporation, All American Life & Casualty Company (Casualty), and 2,892,607 shares of the common stock were owned by the public. Casualty also owned all of the stock of All American Delaware, into which GUG was to merge.

* * *

GUG, the domestic corporation, had three classes of stock, preferred, common and class B common. All of Casualty's shares in GUG would be cancelled, and paragraph 4.3(a) of the merger plan stated that each share of the public GUG common stock would, "by virtue of the Merger and without any action on the part of the holder thereof, be converted into and exchanged for $3.25 cash. . . ." Paragraph 4.5 stated that the public common certificates "shall be surrendered by the holder thereof" to the disbursing agent for cash. . . .

Section 496A.70 provides in part that if a class of stock is entitled to vote on a merger, "the plan of merger . . . shall be approved upon receiving

---

[48] In most asset acquisitions, the selling firm dissolves on a vote of its shareholders. The preferred stock, although non-voting, is entitled to its liquidation preference on the distribution. If the acquisition plan requires the preferred shareholders to take stock in the purchasing firm in the liquidation (to stop the dissolving firm from flooding the market with selling firm shares) and the liquidation preference must be paid in cash, the Certificate of Incorporation would have to be amended, changing the terms and conditions of the preferred stock. The preferred shareholders would normally have a class vote on the amendment.

[49] Preferred shareholders in California, asked to accept distributions in a merger or asset sale that are less than their liquidation preferences, have a class vote on the acquisition. Cal. Corp. Code § 1202(b).

the affirmative vote of the holders of at least two-thirds of the outstanding shares of each class of shares entitled to vote as a class thereon and of the total outstanding shares."[Ed.[50]] It then provides:

> Any class of shares of any such corporation shall be entitled to vote as a class if the plan of merger or consolidation, as the case may be, contains any provision, which, if contained in a proposed amendment to articles of incorporation, would entitle such class of shares to vote as a class.

This merger proposal carried by two-thirds of all GUG shares but not by two-thirds of the common stock. Was the common stock entitled to be voted as a class?

Plaintiffs argue that several clauses in section 496A.57 entitled the common to be voted separately. We go no farther than paragraph 3 of that section and specifically to the word "cancellation."[Ed.[51]] Suppose that no merger had been proposed, but an amendment to the articles had been submitted which required that all certificates of GUG common shares be surrendered to a depository for cash, that thereafter the shares of common stock would cease to be stock of the corporation, and that the stock transfer books would be closed. Would not this stock be cancelled in a realistic sense? One day the owner of common stock owns a part of an ongoing enterprise; the next day he does not, he instead has money. His shares are recalled and no further trading is permitted in them; the books are closed. To "cancel" means to "revoke, annul, invalidate." *Webster's Third New International Dictionary* 325 (1969). . . .

* * *

Defendants voice several arguments contrary to this construction of the statutes. One is that this was a "cash out" merger. They say the common stock was not changed or reduced; it was eliminated and money was substituted. But, we find nothing in sections 496A.70 and 496A.57 which differentiates cash out mergers from other varieties. Indeed, the cash out merger is drastic: the stockholder is compelled to give up his stock altogether and separate himself from the ongoing organization; he is ejected. Did not the General Assembly intend that such a class of stock should be entitled to vote separately on its fate?

Defendants further contend that if the General Assembly had intended each class of stock to have separate voting rights on mergers, it could have easily so provided as some states have done. But, the Assembly did not desire to give each class separate voting rights automatically. It desired to

[50] [Ed. The Iowa Corporate Code now requires only a majority vote of the outstanding shares "entitled to be cast." Iowa Code § 490.1104 (2002).]

[51] [Ed. If the selling firm shareholders receive stock in the buyer with identical rights and privileges, do they get a class vote? The issue divides states. E.g., Ohio Rev. Code § 1701.78(F) (no); ABA Model Bus. Corp. Act § 11.04(1)(i) (2016 rev.) (yes).]

give a class separate voting rights if that stock was affected in ways designated in section 496A.57, one of which is cancellation.

Then defendants urge that the merger plan does not use the word "cancel" or "cancellation" regarding this stock, and they say section 496A.57 does not apply unless the merger plan contains a provision "identical" to one of those in the section. We think this argument flies in the face of the *Rath* rationale of realism. The substance, not the precise words, controls. A merger draftsman cannot avoid section 496A.57 by calling an actual cancellation something else.

Defendants also insist that under section 496A.76 the assets of GUG could have been sold, the proceeds could have been distributed, and GUG could have been dissolved without a separate class vote; the holders of common stock would then have no stock, but money instead. Why then, defendants ask, may not substantially the same thing be done by merger?

We may assume *arguendo* that a separate class vote would not be required in such a proceeding, and we lay aside the point that a sale, distribution, and dissolution normally have substantially different consequences than a merger. But, the controlling point is that for reasons it found sufficient, the General Assembly made the requirements of section 496A.70 on merger and of section 496A.76 on sale of assets materially different. We may not make the sections identical by judicial legislation. . . .

* * *

The quoted portion of the articles does however purport to prohibit class voting as between common and class B common. This clause was undoubtedly inserted to give control to Casualty. But, the articles cannot override the statutes. . . .

* * *

Finally, defendants urge plaintiffs' claim that the common was entitled to vote as a class is really academic . . . . Casualty could have converted its other GUG stock to common and thus obtained a two-thirds affirmative vote by the common on the merger. . . .

We lay aside the fact that a conversion of Casualty's other shares to common shares would have involved several other considerations . . . . The significant point is that when the vote on the merger actually occurred in May 1973, Casualty had not in fact converted its other stock or reduced the two-thirds requirement. We deal with the election as it occurred, not as it might have occurred. Many corporations have various classes or series of shares, which have rights of conversion into other shares. Corporate elections under chapter 496A cannot stand or fall on what would have happened if certain hypothetical conversions had previously taken place or if changes in the articles had previously been made; they must stand or fall on what in fact took place. We do not find merit in defendants' final argument.[Ed.[52]]

NOTE: "SUBSTANTIALLY ALL"

The question of what constitutes "substantially all" of the corporate assets under § 271 has produced some surprising results in the Delaware courts. In *Katz v. Bregman*, 431 A.2d 1274 (Del. Ch. 1981), appeal den., 435 A.2d 1044 (Del.1981), the court held that § 271 covered a manufacturing parent's sale of a subsidiary that constituted 51 percent of the parent's total assets, generated about 45 percent of the parent's net sales, and in recent years had been the corporation's only income-producing facility. The Chancery Court had previously reasoned that the crucial question was whether "the sale of assets [is] *quantitatively vital* to the operation of the corporation and is out of the ordinary and substantially affects the existence and purpose of the corporation." *Gimbel v. Signal Companies, Inc.*, 316 A.2d 599, 606 (Del. Ch. 1974), aff'd 316 A.2d 619 (Del. 1974) (emphasis added). See also *Thorpe v. CERBCO*, Inc., 676 A.2d 436 (Del. 1996) (sale of stock of subsidiary that was 68 percent of parent's assets and primary income-generating asset did require a shareholder vote); *Winston v. Mandor*, 710 A.2d 835 (Del. Ch. 1997) (shareholder approval required where corporation sold 60 percent of its net assets but those assets had generated all of its income over a recent six-month period). Subsequent courts refer to the *Gimbel* language as the *"quantitative and qualitative test."* See *Hollinger Inc. v. Hollinger International, Inc.*, 858 A.2d 342, 378 (Del. Ch. 2004).[53]

The Delaware courts answer the question of "quantitative vitality" by examining two sub-issues. First, what percentage of the corporation's *total assets* do the assets being sold represent? Second, what percentage of the corporation's *total income* do the assets being sold generate? If a court determines that the sale in question is of assets that are quantitatively vital, "then [the sale] is beyond the power of the Board of Directors [to effect without stockholder approval]." *Gimbel*, 316 A.2d at 606.

---

[52] [Ed. The Iowa Supreme Court received the case on certification from the United States District Court for the Southern District of Iowa. The plaintiffs had sued in federal court for violations of federal securities law and conversion. The district court dismissed the federal securities claims. The plaintiffs' claims for conversion, based on an illegal taking of their stock in the merger, took over fourteen years to resolve through two trials, two opinions from the District Court and two opinions from the United States Court of Appeals for the Eight Circuit. All because the lawyer for GUG didn't want to engage in an "unnecessary act" of converting the Class B stock to common. In the end, the plaintiffs prevailed collecting $5.40 a share for their stock with interest. The district court set aside, however, the second jury's verdict for $650,000 in punitive damages. See Nelson v. All American Life and Financial Corp., 889 F.2d 141 (8th Cir. 1989) (final published opinion).]

[53] According to the Delaware Chancery Court in *Winston,* 710 A.2d at 843, the sale of assets "transaction must be viewed in terms of its overall effect on the corporation, and there is no necessary qualifying percentage [of assets that need be sold]."

While "out of the ordinary" sales of assets would appear to be a useful metric in deciding whether shareholder approval is necessary, the Delaware Chancery Court, in a partnership-related case entitled *In re Nantucket Island Assoc. Ltd. Partnership Unitholders Litigation*, 810 A.2d 351, 371 (Del. Ch. 2002), has indicated otherwise. According to the Court:

> [T]he only one of the *Gimbel* factors that can be confidently determined is the one that will rarely help decide a case: whether the transaction is "out of the ordinary." That factor is easily satisfied here. But that, of course, would also be true if the partnership sold a quarter of its productive assets. Such a sale would not involve substantially all of a partnership's assets in any common sense way but would also not be an ordinary, run-of-the-mill transaction. Put another way, [the "out of the ordinary"] aspect of the *Gimbel* test will rarely be of much utility in resolving any close case.

Thus, at best, a proposed "out of the ordinary" sale of assets should trigger an analysis to see if *other factors* indicate that shareholder approval is necessary under § 271.[54]

The case of *Hollinger Inc. v. Hollinger Int'l Inc.*, 858 A.2d 342 (Del. Ch. 2004), addressed the thorny issue of whether an asset sale conducted by a wholly-owned, *indirect* subsidiary of a parent company can trigger a vote of the *parent's* shareholders under § 271. The assets being sold were those of the "Telegraph Group" which were held by an indirect, wholly-owned subsidiary of Hollinger International, Inc., a Delaware corporation ("International"). They were being sold to an entity controlled by Frederick and David Barclay. Shareholders of International sought a preliminary injunction preventing International from consummating the sale.

The Telegraph Group assets were held in a sixth-tier U.K. subsidiary of International and not by International itself. Thus, International argued that since International itself was not selling assets, § 271 was inapplicable. However, under § 271(c), "the property and assets of the corporation include the property and assets of any *subsidiary* of the corporation." The Delaware Chancery Court avoided answering the difficult policy question relating to indirect subsidiaries based on its determination that the Telegraph Group did not constitute all or substantially all of International's assets in any event. Nonetheless, and consistent with § 271(c), the Court indicated that if § 271 was not triggered in situations where the assets did constitute all or substantially all of the

---

[54] As the Delaware Chancery Court stated in *Gimbel* itself:

> While it is true that a transaction in the ordinary course of business does not require shareholder approval, the converse is not true. Every transaction out of normal routine does not necessarily require shareholder approval. *The unusual nature of the transaction must strike at the heart of the corporate existence and purpose.*

Gimbel, 316 A.2d at 606 (emphasis added).

H/R

assets of the parent company, then § 271's voting requirement could easily be evaded through the use of a multiple subsidiary structure. *Hollinger*, 858 A.2d at 348.

MBCA

The Model Act abandons the "all or substantially all" phrase entirely; rather, a shareholder vote is triggered whenever a disposition of assets would leave a corporation "without a significant continuing business activity." ABA Model Bus. Corp. Act § 12.02(a) (2016 rev.). The Model Act also contains a safe harbor based on numbers. A significant business activity "conclusively" remains if the continuing business activity represents at least 25 percent of the total assets and 25 percent of either income (before income taxes) or revenues from pre-transaction operations. Although the official comments to the Model Act claim to follow Delaware case law, the standard in the Model Act language appears to be narrower, given the *Katz* case above.

iii. Cash-for-Stock Acquisition

In a *cash-for-stock acquisition*, A Corp. buys B Corp. stock directly from the hands of B Corp. shareholders in exchange for cash. Thus, the transaction is between A Corp. and the shareholders of B Corp.—B Corp. itself is not involved.[55] See Diagram 3 below.

corps can only do what statutes allow

[55] If B Corp. is a publicly traded corporation and A Corp. makes a tender offer for B Corp. shares pursuant to the federal securities laws, B Corp.'s board of directors would have certain duties to perform under those laws. See Section B.2.b.iii, *infra.*

Diagram 3

The Basic Stock Acquisition: Cash-for-Stock*

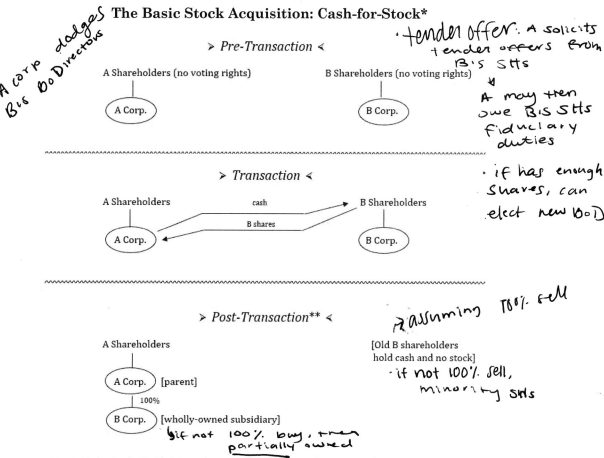

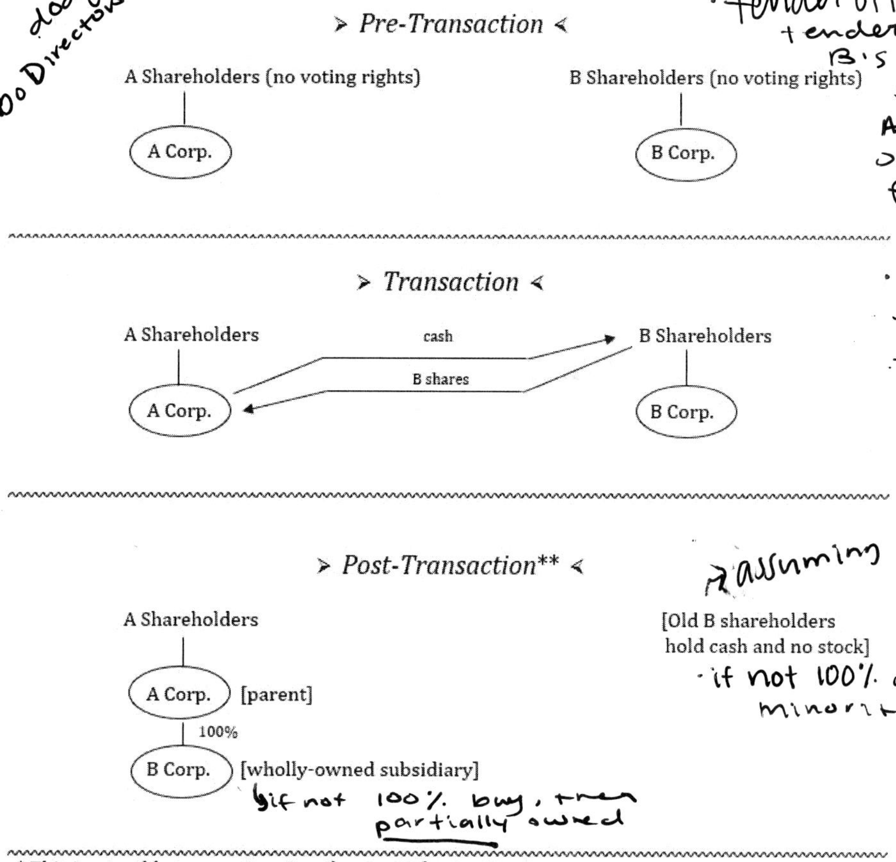

* This is a taxable transaction. See Chapter Eight, Section B.

** This assumes *all* the B shareholders voluntarily took the cash in exchange for their shares.

After the transaction, A Corp. owns the B Corp. stock; A Corp. is the *parent* corporation of a new *subsidiary* corporation, B Corp. The original B Corp. shareholders have tendered and exchanged their shares for cash. There is no change in the certificates of incorporation of either A Corp. or B Corp., nor is there any change in the investment contracts represented by an A Corp. share or a B Corp. share. Only the identity of the owner of the B Corp. shares has changed. If A Corp. cannot convince all the B shareholders to tender their shares for the cash consideration, then a minority block of B Corp. stock remains outstanding. B Corp. would not be a *wholly-owned* subsidiary, but rather a *partially-owned* subsidiary.[56] The remaining original B Corp. shareholders who did not sell become *minority shareholders* of a controlled subsidiary.

---

[56] Both types are together often referred to as controlled subsidiaries.

If both A Corp. and B Corp. are Delaware corporations, the authority for A Corp. to purchase and hold the stock of another corporation is found in §§ 122(4) and (11), part of the laundry list of general corporate powers conferred on Delaware corporations by statute. Section 122(10) also empowers A Corp. to manage the affairs of B Corp. The shareholders of neither A Corp. nor B Corp. have, under any provision of the Del. Gen. Corp. L., a right to vote on the stock acquisition. In theory, B Corp. shareholders do not need the protection of a right to vote because they individually decide whether to accept the consideration offered by A Corp. for their shares. Their *right to refuse the offer* is a substitute for their right to dissent in a vote.[57]

There is a specialized section in the Del. Gen. Corp. L., however, § 203, that applies to stock acquisitions of publicly traded Delaware companies.[58] Within the last twenty years, most states (at last count the number was over forty) have passed *anti-takeover statutes* that restrain stock acquisitions of publicly traded companies. Delaware's § 203 is such a statute. Most anti-takeover statutes give target shareholders voting rights not on the stock acquisition itself but on the *effect* of the acquisition. If the target board disapproves of the stock acquisition, the shareholders may vote on whether (1) the stock acquired by the bidder can be voted going forward or (2) the bidder can, subsequent to a stock acquisition in which some shareholders do not sell into the offer, execute a second-stage, cash-out statutory merger to gain 100 percent of the target stock. Delaware's section, known as a *business combination* or *freeze-out* statute, is of the latter type. Of course, by severely restricting the effect of an acquisition, the legislation in essence regulates the acquisition itself. Indeed, it would perhaps be more honest and understandable simply to condition stock acquisitions on a target shareholder vote or on target management approval. We will discuss state takeover legislation in depth in Chapter Six, Section C.

NOTE: COMPULSORY SHARE EXCHANGES

Section 11.03 in the Model Act provides a procedure for a fourth acquisition form, a *statutory share exchange* (often called a *compulsory share exchange*). In a statutory share exchange, one firm acquires all the outstanding stock in a selling firm through an affirmative vote of the selling firm's shareholders. It contrasts with a typical stock acquisition in which the

---

[57] For an unsuccessful attempt by selling firm shareholders to assert voting rights under a de facto asset sale argument, see Field v. Allyn, 457 A.2d 1089 (Del. Ch. 1983) (two-stage acquisition did not amount to a sale of substantially all of the assets of the corporation).

[58] Publicly traded companies are companies that either (1) have a class of equity securities registered under the Securities Exchange Act of 1934 and listed for trading purposes with one of our national stock exchanges or (2) have (i) a class of equity securities held by more than 2,000 holders of record or 500 non-accredited holders of record and (ii) more than $10 million in assets. A company qualifying under clause (2) above is referred to as a *back-door reporting company*. See Exch. Act § 12(g)(1) & Exch. Act Rule 12g–1.

purchasing firm makes offers to buy shares that each target shareholder may accept or reject. A majority of the shareholders of the acquired firm must approve a statutory share exchange; a majority of the shareholders of the acquiring firm need approve the exchange only if selling firm shareholders receive a substantial number of shares in the acquiring firm as acquisition consideration (usually an amount equal to over 20 percent of the shares outstanding before the acquisition). A dissenting shareholder in the selling corporation may vote no, but if she loses the vote she must nevertheless turn over her shares to the acquiring corporation; the exchange is *compulsory* on an affirmative shareholder vote. Over twenty states have adopted such a provision yet few practitioners use the procedure. The light use of the procedure is due to its poor comparison with a *triangular statutory merger*, an acquisition structure we investigate below in the next subsection.

b. Transaction Planning Alternatives: Change the Consideration Offered

i. Stock-for-Asset Acquisitions

We noted above that the traditional method of pooling the equity interests of two separate corporations is through a stock-for-stock statutory merger. See Diagram 1. Lawyers have long known that an asset acquisition or a stock acquisition can achieve the same end result (serve the same purpose) if the purchasing firm uses as consideration its own common stock rather than cash to buy assets or stock.

For a *stock-for-assets acquisition*, start with Diagram 2. Replace the cash consideration going to B Corp. with A Corp. common stock. Moreover, assume A Corp. not only buys all of B Corp.'s assets but also assumes all of B Corp.'s liabilities. See Diagram 4 below. The result is identical to the post-transaction position in Diagram 1. The shareholders of the constituent firms have pooled their ownership interests in a corporation that itself has the combined assets and liabilities of both firms.

The advantage of a stock-for-assets acquisition or a stock-for-stock acquisition over a stock swap statutory merger is that the shareholders in the purchasing corporation, under the Delaware rules, do not have the right to vote on the transaction nor to claim appraisal rights.[59] Most states currently follow Delaware's lead. A few do not. The states that give shareholders in the purchasing firm voting rights, based on the voting power of the stock issued for use as consideration, are California, New Jersey, and Ohio. See also NYSE Listing Manual Rule 312.03(c) below. As states enact the 1999 amendments to the Model Act, this number will grow.[60] ABA Model Bus. Corp. Act § 6.21(f) (2016 rev.).

---

59 The lack of voting and appraisal rights stems from the fact that no *merger* is involved.

60 Idaho, Iowa, South Dakota, West Virginia and Wyoming have adopted the provision.

Diagram 4

Stock-for-Assets Acquisition*

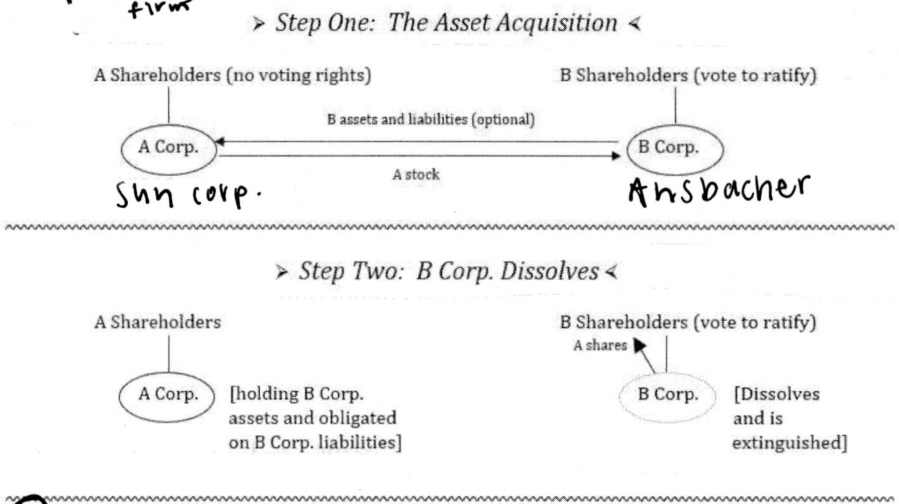

* The tax-free stock acquisition (a C reorganization). See Chapter 8, Section B.

Purchasing firm shareholders who were surprised by the ability of lawyers to circumvent their voting and appraisal rights sought relief in court, asking judges to reclassify stock-for-asset transactions or stock-for-stock acquisitions as de facto *statutory mergers*. With infrequent and largely overruled exceptions, the shareholders lost. The bellwether case is below.

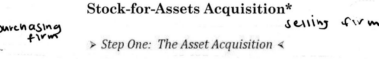

HEILBRUNN V. SUN CHEMICAL CORPORATION

Supreme Court of Delaware, 1959.
150 A.2d 755.

SOUTHERLAND, CHIEF JUSTICE.

This suit is brought by stockholders of Sun Chemical Corporation, a Delaware corporation, against Ansbacher-Siegle Corporation, a New York corporation, and Norman E. Alexander, President of Sun and owner of Ansbacher. Plaintiffs attack the validity of the purchase by Sun of all the assets of Ansbacher. . . .

* * *

Plaintiffs appeal, and contend here, as they did below, that the transaction was by its nature a *de facto* merger.

Although the transaction has been consummated, it is convenient to state many of the facts as they appeared on November 8, 1957, when the proxy statement was sent to the Sun stockholders. They are as follows:

Sun is engaged in the business of manufacturing ink and pigments for ink. It owns a plant at Harrison, New Jersey. It has outstanding 19,000 shares of preferred stock and 1,196,283 shares of common stock. Its balance sheet shows total assets of over $24,000,000. The defendant Alexander is its president, and owns about 2.8 per cent of the common shares.

Ansbacher is engaged in the manufacture of organic pigments. Its products are used in the manufacture of ink, cosmetics, textiles, plastics, and other similar products. Its balance sheet shows total assets of about $1,786,000. The defendant Alexander is its sole beneficial stockholder.

In April of 1956 Alexander, then the owner of about 7,000 shares of Sun, suggested to Sun's then president the possible acquisition of Ansbacher by Sun. Nothing came of the suggestion.

In January 1957, Alexander advised the Sun management that he and five friends and associates owned substantial amounts of Sun shares, and requested representation on the board. Negotiations followed, as a result of which five of the Sun directors resigned, and Alexander and four others named by him were elected to Sun's board. Alexander became president.

In June, 1957, a special committee of Sun's board was appointed to consider whether Sun should own and operate a pigment plant, and if so whether it should rehabilitate its Harrison plant or should acquire or build a new plant. The committee found that Sun's Harrison plant was old, inefficient, and incapable of expansion because of its location. It recommended the acquisition of Ansbacher.

An agreement for the purchase was entered into between Sun and Ansbacher on October 2, 1957. It provides, among other things, as follows:

1. Ansbacher will assign and convey to Sun all of Ansbacher's assets and property of every kind, tangible and intangible; and will grant to Sun the use of its name or any part thereof.

2. Sun will assume all of Ansbacher's liabilities, subject to a covenant that Ansbacher's working capital shall be at least $600,000.

3. Sun will issue to Ansbacher 225,000 shares of its common stock.

4. As soon as possible, after the closing of the transaction, Ansbacher will dissolve and distribute to its shareholders, pro rata, and the shares of the common stock of Sun (subject to an escrow agreement relating to one-fourth of the shares).

5. Ansbacher will use its best efforts to persuade its employees to become employees of Sun.

6. Sun's obligation to consummate the transaction is subject to approval by the holders of a majority of Sun's voting stock, exclusive of shares owned or controlled by Alexander, at a special stockholders' meeting to be thereafter called.

The agreement was approved by the boards of directors of both corporations. A special meeting of Sun's stockholders was called for November 29, 1957. The proxy statement set forth detailed information with respect to the plan of acquisition.

On November 6, 1957, a ruling was obtained from the Commissioner of Internal Revenue that the transaction would constitute a tax-free reorganization under the applicable provisions of the Internal Revenue Code.

Prior to the meeting plaintiffs filed written objections to the transaction, and gave notice of their intention to take legal action.

The approval of the necessary majority of Sun's stockholders was obtained, and the transaction was consummated.

Plaintiffs contend that although the transaction is, in form, a sale of assets of Ansbacher it is in substance and effect a merger, and that it is unlawful because, the merger statute not having been complied with, plaintiffs have been deprived of their right of appraisal and have also suffered financial injury.

The argument that the result of this transaction is substantially the same as the result that would have followed a merger may be readily accepted. As plaintiffs correctly say, the Ansbacher enterprise is continued in altered form as a part of Sun. This is ordinarily a typical characteristic of a merger. . . . Moreover, the plan of reorganization requires the dissolution of Ansbacher and the distribution to its stockholders of the Sun stock received by it for the assets. As a part of the plan, the Ansbacher stockholders are compelled to receive Sun stock. From the viewpoint of Ansbacher, the result is the same as if Ansbacher had formally merged into Sun.

This result is made possible, of course, by the overlapping scope of the merger statute and the statute authorizing the sale of all the corporate assets. This possibility of overlapping was noticed in our opinion in the *Mayflower* case [93 A.2d 107 (Del. 1952)].

There is nothing new about such a result. For many years, drafters of plans of corporate reorganization have increasingly resorted to the use of the sale-of-assets method in preference to the method by merger. Historically, there were reasons for this quite apart from the avoidance of the appraisal right given to stockholders dissenting from a merger. For example, if an interstate merger was not authorized by the statute, a sale of assets could be resorted to. . . .

* * *

The doctrine of *de facto* merger has been recognized in Delaware. It has been invoked in cases of sales of assets for the protection of creditors or stockholders who have suffered an injury because of failure to comply with the statute governing such sales. *Drug, Inc. v. Hunt*, 35 Del. 339, 168 A. 87 (creditor of selling corporation); and *cf. Finch v. Warrior Cement Corp., supra* (stockholder of selling corporation). The contention that it should be applied to cases of the kind here involved depends for its force upon the proposition that the stockholder has been forced against his will to accept a new investment in an enterprise foreign to that of which he was a part, and that his right to an appraisal under the merger statute has been circumvented. . . .

Our Court of Chancery has said that the appraisal right is given to the stockholder in compensation for his former right at common law to prevent a merger. *Chicago Corporation v. Munds*, 20 Del.Ch. 142, 149, 172 A. 452. By the use of the sale-of-assets method of reorganization, it is contended, he has been unjustly deprived of this right.

As before stated, we do not reach this question, because we fail to see how any injury has been inflicted upon the Sun stockholders. Their corporation has simply acquired property and paid for it in shares of stock. The business of Sun will go on as before, with additional assets. The Sun stockholder is not forced to accept stock in another corporation. Nor has the reorganization changed the essential nature of the enterprise of the purchasing corporation, as in *Farris v. Glen Alden Corporation*, 393 Pa. 427, 143 A.2d 25.

Nor is it a case in which the seller can be said to have acquired the purchaser. Sun's net worth is ten times that of Ansbacher. Sun has simply absorbed another company's assets, which are needed, in its own business.

The diminution in the proportional voting strength of the Sun stockholder is not a ground of complaint. Such a consequence necessarily follows any issuance of stock to acquire property.

Plaintiffs made the further point that their proportional interest in the assets has also been diminished. This is, in effect, a charge that the terms of the acquisition are unfair to the Sun minority. Thus, it is said that Ansbacher's net worth is about $1,600,000, and the issuance to Ansbacher of 225,000 shares of Sun stock of the market value of $10.125 a share results in the payment by Sun of a grossly excessive price and in the unjust enrichment of Alexander. It is also said that the report of the committee of Sun's directors admits that the earnings of Ansbacher do not justify the price paid.

These are arguments appropriate to the second cause of action, which the Vice Chancellor refused to dismiss. The legal power to authorize the transaction is one thing. The fairness of its terms and conditions is another. *Allied Chemical & Dye Corporation v. Steel & Tube Co.*, 14 Del.Ch. 64, 122 A. 142. Only the first issue is before us. Plaintiffs are in no way foreclosed from pressing the above contentions when the second cause of action is tried.

* * *

Plaintiffs appear to concede that if the dissolution of Ansbacher and the distribution of Sun stock had not been required by the plan—that is, if Ansbacher had continued as a holding company—the doctrine of *de facto* merger would not apply. This concession exposes the weakness of plaintiffs' case.

How can a Sun stockholder have any concern with what Ansbacher does with the Sun stock after it receives it? Surely the presence or absence of injury to him cannot depend on Ansbacher's decision whether to dissolve and distribute the Sun stock or to continue as a holding company.

Whatever may be the case for giving the right of appraisal to a dissenting stockholder of a selling corporation, as many states have done, there seems little reason, at least in cases like the instant one, to accord it to the stockholders of the purchaser. At all events, no state appears to have done so by statute. . . . And we find no basis in the facts of this case for the granting of such relief in equity on the theory of a *de facto* merger.

* * *

Plaintiffs say that the calling of a stockholders' meeting of Sun is in effect an admission that a merger was involved. On the contrary, the natural inference is that approval of the stockholders was sought because the transaction is one between the corporation and its president. [Ed.[61]]

Some point is sought to be made of the fact that the plan and agreement do not use the words 'purchase' or 'sale'. Nor do they use the word 'merger'. We attach no significance to this omission. One may surmise that the choice of language was influenced by the necessity of devising a tax-free reorganization. But it does not matter what the reason was. The contract was in legal effect one of purchase and sale.

* * *

The judgment of the Court of Chancery is affirmed.

Most all state courts follow *Heilbrunn* and will not reclassify asset sales to be statutory mergers in response to the complaints of shareholders of the purchasing firm who want a right to vote and seek to assert their appraisal rights. Note, however, as discussed above, in a stock-for-assets acquisition like the one in *Heilbrunn,* the California Corporation Code and the Ohio General Corporation Law provide voting and appraisal rights for the pre-existing shareholders in the acquiring firm, unless they will hold

---

[61] [Ed. In transactions between a corporation and another firm owned by one of the corporation's directors, a conflict of interest transaction, a vote of the disinterested shareholders may protect the deal from claims that it is void or voidable. E.g., Del. Gen. Corp. L. § 144 (interested directors). We discuss conflicted deals in Chapter Five, Section C.]

five-sixths or more of the voting power post-acquisition. The Model Act, in § 6.21(f), provides voting but not appraisal rights for shareholders in the acquiring firm.

There have been very few courts that have found for the plaintiff shareholders under a *de facto merger* theory. E.g., *Rath v. Rath Packing Co., supra*; *Farris v. Glen Alden Corp.*, 393 Pa. 427, 143 A.2d 25 (1958); *Applestein v. United Board & Carton Corp.*, 60 N.J.Super. 333, 159 A.2d 146 (Ch.1960), aff'd, 33 N.J. 72, 161 A.2d 474 (1960). The Iowa and Pennsylvania legislatures subsequently repudiated *Rath* and *Farris* in amendments to their states' corporate codes.[62] *Applestein* is the lone example of a successful and unrepudiated application of the de facto merger doctrine to shareholder voting claims in a state Supreme Court case.[63] See N.J. Stat. Ann. § 14A:10–12 (1998 Supp.) (codifying the case). In Chapter Three, we will see that the de facto merger doctrine has considerably more life when target firm *creditors* are the plaintiffs instead of firm shareholders. At the conclusion of the section, we discuss whether the *Heilbrunn* or *Rath* court (or the Delaware or the California legislature) has the better of the argument.

NOTE: REVERSE ASSET SALE

Would the *Heilbrunn* court have held otherwise if the lawyers structured the transaction to be a *reverse asset sale*? In a reverse asset sale, lawyers structure a stock-for-assets acquisition so that the purchasing firm technically sells all of its assets to the selling firm in exchange for a controlling block of stock in the selling firm. That is, the little fish (normally the selling firm) is purposefully allowed to swallow the assets of the bigger fish (normally the purchasing firm). The purchasing firm thereafter dissolves and passes the controlling block of stock in the surviving firm back to the purchasing firm's shareholders.

In Diagram 4 above, assume the A Corp. stock transferred to B Corp. constitutes over 51 percent of the A Corp. stock outstanding after the transfer. Control of A Corp. is transferred to B Corp. and then, on dissolution, to B Corp. shareholders. See the facts of *Rath v. Rath Packing Co.*, 257 Iowa 1277, 136 N.W.2d 410 (1965), for an example of a reverse asset sale.[64] The purpose of a reverse asset sale is to locate shareholder voting or appraisal rights for the

---

[62] The Iowa legislature later rescinded the express rejection of *Rath* on the theory that the new corporation code voting requirements made a *Rath* fact situation impossible. (The Iowa merger statute no longer requires a two-thirds vote of the shareholders.) The Pennsylvania legislature's rejection of *Farris* is found in 15 Pa. Consol. Stat. Ann. § 1904 (2001). See Terry v. Penn Central Corp., 668 F.2d 188, 194 (3d Cir. 1981).

[63] One could construe the *Pratt* case, *infra* Section A.2.b.vi, to also qualify as a de facto merger case that still stands. There has been a smattering of other lower court cases that apply the doctrine. See Kansas City Power & Light Co. v. Western Resources, Inc., 939 F.Supp. 688 (W.D. Mo.1996) (construing Missouri law to reject the doctrine of equal dignity).

[64] The selling firm sought to avoid a two-thirds vote requirement in the state's statutory merger section. An amendment to the firm's Articles of Incorporation, authorizing the issuance of a new controlling block of shares, required only a majority vote. The court voided the transaction.

asset disposition in the buyer, minimizing shareholder vote or appraisal rights due the shareholders of the seller.

These cases may still test courts' tolerance. The *Heilbrunn* court expressly reserved judgment on the issue, citing the *Farris* case. There is also a residual reservation on the issue in *Terry, supra,* 668 F.2d at 194 n.7. After *Hariton,* the next case below, few doubt that the Delaware courts will respect the structure of a reverse asset sale. Other jurisdictions may not; it is an open question.[65]

The *Hariton* case turns on a peculiarity of the Delaware legislation on asset acquisitions; shareholders of the selling firm in asset acquisitions have voting rights, as they do in all states, but do not have appraisal rights. For forty years, transaction planners in a purchase of a Delaware corporation have chosen asset acquisitions over statutory mergers to avoid triggering the appraisal rights of selling shareholders.[66] Shareholders of selling firms in stock-for-asset acquisitions have complained to courts, arguing that they have been deprived of their appraisal rights and that the de facto merger doctrine should apply. In *Hariton,* below, perhaps the best known of all the country's de facto merger cases, the selling firm shareholders' claims failed.

HARITON V. ARCO ELECTRONICS, INC.

Supreme Court of Delaware, 1963.
188 A.2d 123.

SOUTHERLAND, CHIEF JUSTICE.

* * *

A sale of assets is effected under § 271 in consideration of shares of stock of the purchasing corporation. The agreement of sale embodies also a plan to dissolve the selling corporation and distribute the shares so received to the stockholders of the seller, so as to accomplish the same result as would be accomplished by a merger of the seller into the purchaser. Is the sale legal?

The facts are these:

The defendant Arco and Loral Electronics Corporation, a New York corporation, are both engaged, in somewhat different forms, in the electronic equipment business. In the summer of 1961, they negotiated for an amalgamation of the companies. As of October 27, 1961, they entered

---

65 Cf. Union Oil Co. v. U.S., 480 F.2d 807 (Ct.Cl. 1973) (permitted in Ohio).

66 A similar planning choice is available in some other states for cash-for-assets acquisitions but not stock-for-asset acquisitions. The choice causes parties to favor cash-for-assets acquisitions over cash-out mergers. New York, N.Y. Bus. Corp. L. § 910(a)(1)(B), and the ABA Model Bus. Corp. Act § 13.02(a)(3) (2016 rev.), for example, do not give selling shareholders in asset acquisitions appraisal rights if they receive cash in the acquisition within one year of the shareholders' approval of the transaction. The Model Act also conditions the lack of appraisal rights on the absence of a conflict of interest in the transaction.

into a "Reorganization Agreement and Plan." The provisions of this Plan pertinent here are in substance as follows:

1. Arco agrees to sell all its assets to Loral in consideration (inter alia) of the issuance to it of 283,000 shares of Loral.[Ed.[67]]

2. Arco agrees to call a stockholders meeting for the purpose of approving the Plan and the voluntary dissolution.

3. Arco agrees to distribute to its stockholders all the Loral shares received by it as a part of the complete liquidation of Arco.

At the Arco meeting, all the stockholders voting (about 80 percent) approved the Plan. It was thereafter consummated.

Plaintiff, a stockholder who did not vote at the meeting, sued to enjoin the consummation of the Plan on the grounds (1) that it was illegal, and (2) that it was unfair. The second ground was abandoned. . . .

The question before us we have stated above. Plaintiff's argument that the sale is illegal runs as follows:

The several steps taken here accomplish the same result as a merger of Arco into Loral. In a "true" sale of assets, the stockholder of the seller retains the right to elect whether the selling company shall continue as a holding company. Moreover, the stockholder of the selling company is forced to accept an investment in a new enterprise without the right of appraisal granted under the merger statute. Section 271 cannot therefore be legally combined with a dissolution proceeding under § 275 and a consequent distribution of the purchaser's stock. Such a proceeding is a misuse of the power granted under § 271, and a *de facto* merger results.

* * *

We now hold that the reorganization here accomplished through § 271 and a mandatory plan of dissolution and distribution is legal. This is so because the sale-of-assets statute and the merger statute are independent of each other. They are, so to speak, of equal dignity, and the framers of a reorganization plan may resort to either type of corporate mechanics to achieve the desired end. This is not an anomalous result in our corporation law. As the Vice Chancellor pointed out, the elimination of accrued dividends, though forbidden under a charter amendment . . . may be accomplished by a merger. *Federal United Corporation v. Havender*, 24 Del.Ch. 318, 11 A.2d 331.[Ed.[68]]

* * *

Plaintiff concedes, as we read his brief, that if the several steps taken in this case had been taken separately they would have been legal. That is,

[67] [Ed. Loral had 486,500 of Class A common shares outstanding and 362,500 of Class B common shares outstanding. Loral also agreed to assume all of Arco's liabilities.]

[68] [Ed. *Havender* is digested in Section A.2.c of this chapter.]

he concedes that a sale of assets, followed by a separate proceeding to dissolve and distribute, would be legal, even though the same result would follow. This concession exposes the weakness of his contention. To attempt to make any such distinction between sales under § 271 would be to create uncertainty in the law and invite litigation.

We are in accord with the Vice Chancellor's ruling, and the judgment below is affirmed.

NOTE: STOCK AS CONSIDERATION

Consideration in an acquisition can take the form of cash, stock of the buyer, promissory notes, assumption of liabilities or some combination thereof. Numerous factors can affect the form of consideration including, primarily, the buyer's access to cash (usually borrowed) and the seller's willingness to invest in the buyer's business by accepting stock in the buyer. A 2016 survey of acquisition transactions of over $200 million occurring in 2015 involving a strategic buyer and a public company target found that 47 percent were all cash deals, 15 percent were all stock deals and the balance of the deals were combinations of cash and stock.[69]

Recently cash deals have been notably more profitable for the buyer than stock deals. Some claim that the poor returns on stock deals reflect the impact on the trading markets of the negative news on deal announcement that buyer firm managers believe their firm to be overvalued.[70] Buying firms use their own stock as consideration when it is overvalued. Ironically, the best course of action for selling firm shareholders in cash deals is often taking the cash and immediately purchasing buyer firm stock, and in stock deals is often taking the buying firm stock and immediately selling it for cash.

ii. Stock-for-Stock Acquisitions

For a *stock-for-stock acquisition*, start with Diagram 3. Replace the cash consideration going to B Corp. shareholders with A Corp. common stock. See Diagram 5. The result is similar to the post-transaction position in Diagram 1 except that A Corp. holds B Corp.'s assets and liabilities in a wholly-owned subsidiary, a separate legal entity, rather than having combined the B Corp. assets and liabilities with A Corp. assets and liabilities in one legal entity.

The advantage of the parent-subsidiary structure is that, after the transaction, B Corp. creditors of the subsidiary do not have a claim on A Corp. assets held by the parent. This could be of particular importance to

---

[69] See Mergers & Acquisitions Market Trends Subcommittee of the Committee on Negotiated Acquisitions of the American Bar Association's Section of Business Law, *Strategic Buyer/Public Target M & A Deal Points Study* (2016).

[70] See Pavel Savor & Qi Lu, *Do Stock Mergers Create Value for Acquirers?*, 64 J. FIN. 1061 (2009).

A. Corp. if it suspects B Corp. has contingent, unquantified liabilities relating to, for example, environmental problems. By contrast, in a merger B Corp. creditors can execute on A Corp. assets after the transaction. Holders of B Corp. debt receive a boost that translates into a lower B Corp. default risk and, therefore, a windfall increase in the value of the credit they hold.[71]

Diagram 5

Stock-for-Stock Acquisition*

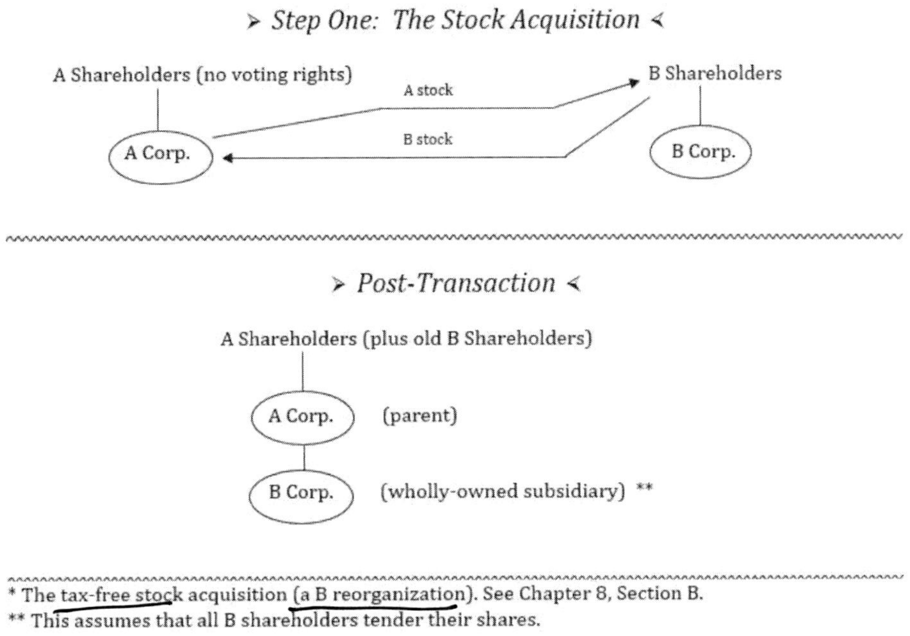

iii. *Cash-Out Mergers*

In a *cash* (or *cash-out) merger transaction*, the shareholders of the selling firm do not end up holding voting common stock in the purchasing firm. Rather, the purchasing firm pays cash for the selling firm's assets or, if cash is not available, pays the selling firm's shareholders in non-voting investments in the purchasing firm (*cash equivalents*)—debentures (debt) or non-voting preferred or common stock (equity). Cash deals are common when (1) cash is cheap (interest rates are low) and acquiring stock is

---

[71] The effect is real. In 2005 investors in MCI bonds were delighted when Verizon Communications, a company with an A2 credit rating from Moody's and an A+ rating from Standard and Poor's, decided to purchase MCI. With Verizon's robust balance sheet buttressing MCI, MCI's creditworthiness increased. As a result, MCI's bonds became less risky, causing the value of the MCI bonds to increase as they rose from junk to investment grade status.

expensive (i.e., the stock price is low due to market conditions),[72] (2) the acquirer does not want to dilute its ownership (i.e., control) structure, or (3) the selling firm shareholders do not want to invest in the buyer.

The traditional cash deals are the cash-for-assets acquisition (Diagram 2), or the cash-for-stock acquisition (Diagram 3). A cash-out is also possible using a statutory merger procedure.[73] For a cash-out statutory merger, start with Diagram 1 and replace the A Corp. shares going to the B Corp. shareholders with cash. See Diagram 6. The end result is identical to the post-transaction position in Diagram 2.

Diagram 6

Cash-Out Merger*

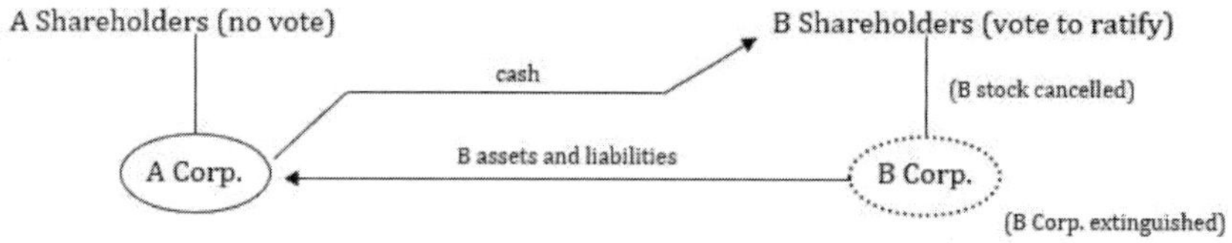

* This is a taxable transaction. See Chapter Eight, Section B.

In cash-out mergers, the A shareholders do not vote if the agreement of merger does not amend the Certificate of Incorporation of A and all A shares outstanding before the deal continue to be outstanding after the deal.

Planners often use cash merger transactions to eliminate minority shareholders, *squeeze-outs* (or *freeze-outs*). In one form of squeeze-out, a corporation drops down (i.e., forms) a new wholly-owned shell subsidiary and merges itself into the subsidiary. See Diagram 9 in Section A.2.c below. All the stock in the corporation is cancelled. The majority shareholders in the original firm receive stock in the surviving firm and the minority shareholders in the original firm receive cash or debt securities; they are squeezed-out.

Another form of squeeze-out eliminates minority shareholders in a subsidiary. The parent corporation can (1) merge the sub into itself (an upstream merger) or (2) merge itself into the sub (a downstream merger) with majority shareholders in the parent retaining shares in the survivor

---

72 When an acquirer's stock price is cheap, more shares have to be issued to cover the acquisition price. The issuance of more shares, however, results in the dilution of the acquirer's existing shareholders.

73 Prior to 1967, Del. Gen. Corp. L. § 251(b) required that the stock of the disappearing constituent corporation in a merger or consolidation be exchanged for "shares or other securities" in the survivor. Prior to 1941, only shares of the survivor were valid consideration. With the 1941 addition of the "other securities" language, clever lawyers used redeemable bonds or notes to get cash into the hands of selling firm shareholders. See, e.g., Coyne v. Park & Tilford Distillers Corp., 154 A.2d 893, 895 (Del. 1959). The 1967 revision authorized the use of cash.

and the minority receiving cash. More commonly, a corporation holding shares in a partially-owned subsidiary (3) drops down a new wholly-owned shell subsidiary and merges the partially-owned sub with and into the wholly-owned sub (see Diagram 8, Stage Two). The firm gives the minority shareholders in the partially-owned subsidiary cash or debt securities (debentures) for their cancelled shares.

The courts have held that merger provisions in corporate codes do authorize such transactions, subject to shareholder claims for fraud or other forms of overreaching. E.g., *Weinberger v. UOP, Inc.*, 457 A.2d 701 (Del. 1983) (a cash-out merger between a parent and its partially-owned subsidiary). Minority shareholders typically do enjoy appraisal rights in such transactions. See Section A.3, *infra*.

In cash merger transactions, preferred shareholders who receive cash for their shares can be surprised by the ease with which firms circumvent liquidation preferences or redemption rights attached to their shares.

RAUCH V. RCA CORP.

United States Court of Appeals, Second Circuit, 1988.
861 F.2d 29.

MAHONEY, CIRCUIT JUDGE.

* * *

This case arises from the acquisition of RCA Corporation ("RCA") by General Electric Company ("GE"). On or about December 11, 1985, RCA, GE, and Gesub, Inc. ("Gesub"), a wholly owned Delaware subsidiary of GE, entered into an agreement of merger. Pursuant to the terms of the agreement, all common and preferred shares of RCA stock (with one exception) were converted to cash, Gesub was then merged into RCA, and the common stock of Gesub was converted into common stock of RCA. Specifically, the merger agreement provided (subject in each case to the exercise of appraisal rights) that each share of RCA common stock would be converted into $66.50, each share of $3.65 cumulative preference stock would be converted into $42.50, and each share of $3.50 cumulative first preferred stock (the stock held by plaintiff and in issue here, hereinafter the "Preferred Stock") would be converted into $40.00. A series of $4.00 cumulative convertible first preferred stock was called for redemption according to its terms prior to the merger.

On February 27, 1986, plaintiff, a holder of 250 shares of Preferred Stock, commenced this diversity class action on behalf of a class consisting of the holders of Preferred Stock. It is undisputed that this action is governed by the law of Delaware, the state of incorporation of both RCA and Gesub. Plaintiff claimed that the merger constituted a "liquidation or dissolution or winding up of RCA and a redemption of the [Preferred Stock]," as a result of which holders of the Preferred Stock were entitled to

$100 per share in accordance with the redemption provisions of RCA's certificate of incorporation, that defendants were in violation of the rights of the holders of Preferred Stock as thus stated; and that defendants thereby wrongfully converted substantial sums of money to their own use. Plaintiff sought damages and injunctive relief.

* * *

According to RCA's Restated Certificate of Incorporation, the owners of the Preferred Stock were entitled to $100 per share, plus accrued dividends, upon the redemption of such stock at the election of the corporation. Plaintiff contends that the merger agreement, which compelled the holders of Preferred Stock to sell their shares to RCA for $40.00, affected a redemption whose nature is not changed by referring to it as a conversion of stock to cash pursuant to a merger. Plaintiff's argument, however, is not in accord with Delaware law.

It is clear that under the Delaware General Corporation Law, a conversion of shares to cash that is carried out in order to accomplish a merger is legally distinct from a redemption of shares by a corporation. Section 251 of the Delaware General Corporation Law allows two corporations to merge into a single corporation by adoption of an agreement that complies with that section. Del. Code Ann. tit. viii, § 251(c) (1983). The merger agreement in issue called for the conversion of the shares of the constituent corporations into cash. The statute specifically authorizes such a transaction. . . . Thus, the RCA-GE merger agreement complied fully with the merger provision in question, and plaintiff does not argue to the contrary.

Redemption, on the other hand, is governed by sections 151(b) and 160(a) of the Delaware General Corporation Law. Section 151(b) provides that a corporation may subject its preferred stock to redemption "by the corporation at its option or at the option of the holders of such stock or upon the happening of a specified event." Del.Code Ann. tit. viii, § 151(b) (1983). In this instance, the Preferred Stock was subject to redemption by RCA *at its election*. . . . Nothing in RCA's certificate of incorporation indicated that the holders of Preferred Stock could initiate a redemption, nor was there provision for any specified event, such as the Gesub-RCA merger, to trigger a redemption.[3]

Plaintiff's contention that the transaction was essentially a redemption rather than a merger must therefore fail. RCA chose to convert

---

[3] Plaintiff points, however, to Del. Code Ann. tit. viii, § 251(e) (1983), which provides that "[i]n the case of a merger, the certificate of incorporation of the surviving corporation shall automatically be amended to the extent, if any, that changes in the amendment are set forth in the agreement of merger." Plaintiff contends that the agreement of merger "purports to alter or impair existing preferential rights." Brief for Plaintiff-Appellant at 14, thus requiring a class vote under other provisions of Delaware law. There are a number of problems with this contention, but the decisive threshold difficulty is that no "existing preferential rights" are altered or impaired in any way, since the holders of Preferred Stock never had any right to initiate a redemption.

its stock to cash to accomplish the desired merger, and in the process chose not to redeem the Preferred Stock. It had every right to do so in accordance with Delaware law. As the district court aptly noted, to accept plaintiff's argument "would render nugatory the conversion provisions within Section 251 of the Delaware Code."

Delaware courts have long held that such a result is unacceptable. Indeed, it is well settled under Delaware law that "action taken under one section [of the Delaware General Corporation Law] is legally independent, and its validity is not dependent upon, nor to be tested by the requirements of other unrelated sections under which the same final result might be attained by different means." *Rothschild Int'l Corp. v. Liggett Group,* 474 A.2d 133, 136 (Del.1984) (quoting *Orzeck v. Englehart,* 41 Del.Ch. 361, 365, 195 A.2d 375, 378 (Del.1963)). The rationale of the doctrine is that the various provisions of the Delaware General Corporation Law are of equal dignity, and a corporation may resort to one section thereof without having to answer for the consequences that would have arisen from invocation of a different section. See *Hariton v. Arco Electronics, Inc.,* 41 Del.Ch. 74, 77, 188 A.2d 123, 125 (Del.1963) ("'the general theory of the Delaware Corporation Law [is] that action taken pursuant to the authority of the various sections of that law constitute acts of independent legal significance and their validity is not dependent on other sections of the Act'") (quoting *Langfelder v. Universal Laboratories, Inc.,* 68 F.Supp. 209, 211 n.5 (D.Del.1946), *aff'd,* 163 F.2d 804 (3d Cir.1947)).

Rothschild Int'l Corp. v. Liggett Group is particularly instructive. In that case, certain preferred shareholders of Liggett were entitled to a $100 per share liquidation preference under Liggett's certificate of incorporation. Liggett, however, undertook a combined tender offer and reverse cash-out merger (similar to the instant transaction) whereby Liggett became a wholly owned subsidiary of Grand Metropolitan Ltd., and the preferred shareholders in question received $70 per share. *Id.,* 474 A.2d at 135–36. A preferred shareholder then brought a class action in which it claimed breach of contract and breach of fiduciary duty, asserting that the transaction was the equivalent of a liquidation of Liggett that entitled preferred shareholders to the $100 per share liquidation preference. The Delaware Supreme Court concluded, however, that "there was no 'liquidation' of Liggett within the well-defined meaning of that term" because "the reverse cash-out merger of Liggett did not accomplish a 'liquidation' of Liggett's assets." *Id* at 136. Accordingly, the Court held that the doctrine of independent legal significance barred plaintiff's claim. *Id.*

In so holding, the Court stated that "[i]t is equally settled under Delaware law that minority stock interests may be eliminated by merger. And, where a merger of corporations is permitted by law, a shareholder's preferential rights are subject to defeasance. Stockholders are charged with knowledge of this possibility at the time they acquire their shares."

Id. at 136–37 (citing *Federal United Corp. v. Havender,* 24 Del.Ch. 318, 332–34, 11 A.2d 331, 338 (Del.1940)). Thus, the defendants were entitled to choose the most effective means to achieve the desired reorganization, "subject only to their duty to deal fairly with the minority interest." *Id.* at 136.

The instant action presents a most analogous situation. Plaintiff claims that the Gesub-RCA merger was, in effect, a redemption. However, there was no redemption within the well-defined meaning of that term under Delaware law, just as there had been no liquidation in *Liggett.* Thus, because the merger here was permitted by law, defendants legitimately chose to structure their transaction in the most effective way to achieve the desired corporate reorganization, and were subject only to a similar duty to deal fairly.

We note in this regard that plaintiff's complaint nowhere alleges that the $40.00 per share conversion rate for the Preferred Stock was unfair. Rather, "[p]laintiff is complaining of a breach of *contractual* rights, entirely divorced from the purported 'fairness' of the transaction." Brief for Plaintiff-Appellant at 23.[4] Moreover, as the district court stated: "Delaware provides specific protection to shareholders who believe that they have received insufficient value for their stock as the result of a merger: they may obtain an appraisal under § 262 of the General Corporation Law." Plaintiff, however, explicitly disavows any appraisal theory or remedy, consistent with her position that fairness is not the issue.

The doctrine of independent legal significance has been upheld by the Delaware courts in related corporate contexts, as well. See, e.g., *Field v. Allyn,* 457 A.2d 1089 (Del.Ch.), *aff'd mem.,* 467 A.2d 1274 (Del.1983) (tender offer followed by cash-out merger does not constitute "sale of assets" to which shareholder meeting provisions of Del. Gen. Corp. Law § 271 are applicable); *Orzeck v. Englehart,* 41 Del.Ch. 361, 195 A.2d 375 (Del.1963) (purchase by corporation with its stock of stock of seven other corporations, as a result of which selling stockholders acquire control of purchasing corporation, does not constitute de facto merger to which statutory appraisal rights apply); *Hariton v. Arco Electronics, Inc.,* 41 Del.Ch. 74, 188 A.2d 123 (Del.1963) (sale of corporate assets for shares of stock of purchasing corporation, followed by distribution of those shares to shareholders of, and dissolution of, selling corporation, does not constitute de facto merger to which statutory appraisal rights apply). Plaintiff's attempt to distinguish these cases on their facts is unavailing. While the details of the transactions may vary from case to case, the principle of the rule is clear and its application here cannot be seriously questioned.

---

[4] In view of this statement, we deem it irrelevant that the merger agreement provides for redemption of a series of $4.00 cumulative convertible first preferred stock, but not for redemption of plaintiff's Preferred Stock. Since the holders of Preferred Stock had no right to initiate a redemption, the only conceivable relevance of the redemption of another class of preferred stock would be to a fairness claim, which plaintiff has forsworn.

* * *

The judgment of the district court dismissing the complaint is affirmed.

The *Rothschild* and *Rauch* cases, among others, put preferred shareholders on notice that corporations can use statutory mergers to avoid liquidation and redemption terms and other protections in their investment contracts. Careful lawyers for preferred shareholders can reinvigorate the protections by drafting a provision in the investment contract (the share certificate) that, for example, stipulates a liquidation preference applies not only in corporate dissolutions but also in cash statutory mergers and other control changes. Such provisions are routine in the convertible, non-cumulative preferred stock taken by venture capitalists in high-tech start-up companies. These provisions are not uniformly included in preferred stock issued by publicly traded firms, however. Why not?

QUESTION

Assuming GE wanted to pay in cash and not GE stock it had three choices: cash-for-assets, cash-for-stock, or a cash-out merger. In *Rauch*, why did GE structure the deal as a reverse triangular cash-out merger? [In a cash-for-assets deal, RCA dissolves and the preferred shareholders get a liquidation distribution. In a cash-for-stock deal, GE will not get 100 percent control of RCA.]

iv. Triangular Acquisitions: The Use of Acquisition Vehicles

In *triangular mergers*, such as the one detailed in the *Rauch* case above and the most common form of triangular acquisition, the purchasing firm *drops down* a wholly-owned shell subsidiary (an *acquisition vehicle*) and the selling firm merges with and into the subsidiary. See Diagram 7 below. Triangular mergers are known as *forward triangular mergers* when the target merges with and into the shell subsidiary (and thus the subsidiary survives) and *reverse triangular mergers* (see *Rauch*, above) when the shell subsidiary merges with and into the target (and thus the target survives).

Technically, the subsidiary is a constituent party to the merger while the parent is not. By statute only the shareholders of a constituent party vote on statutory mergers; thus, the shareholders of the parent do not vote on the merger or have appraisal rights.[74] Since triangular mergers limit the voting rights of purchasing company shareholders and isolate the

---

74 The only shareholder of the subsidiary is the parent itself, and in a triangular merger, the board of directors of the parent vote the stock in favor of the merger through a board resolution. Because the parent initiated the transaction in the first place, the parent vote is a *fait accompli*.

newly-absorbed selling company liabilities in a subsidiary, free from the purchasing company assets, triangular mergers have become a very popular method of acquisition.

Again, the California general corporate code is the exception, giving pre-existing shareholders in the parent voting rights if parent stock is used as consideration, unless those shareholders will hold five-sixths or more of the voting power post-acquisition. Cal. Gen. Corp. L. §§ 1200(e) and 1201(b). See also ABA Model Bus. Corp. Act § 6.21(f) (2016 rev.) (parent shareholder voting rights do not come with appraisal rights, however).

A less popular triangular acquisition is the *triangular asset acquisition*. In a triangular asset acquisition, the purchaser drops down a shell subsidiary and the subsidiary purchases the assets of the target (and the target dissolves). One also sees triangular stock acquisitions in which the purchaser drops down a shell subsidiary and the subsidiary purchases the stock of the target (see *Rothschild*,[75] cited in *Rauch*, above).[76]

[75] In *Rothschild*, Grand Metropolitan used a triangular two-stage stock acquisition. A subsidiary bought stock in a target and then merged with and into the target.

[76] In an odd twist, the shareholders of a parent corporation with a subsidiary used as the purchaser in an asset or stock acquisition do get voting rights in Ohio even though the shareholders of the parent do not have voting rights in a triangular merger. Ohio Rev. St. § 1701.83.

Diagram 7

Forward Triangular Merger*

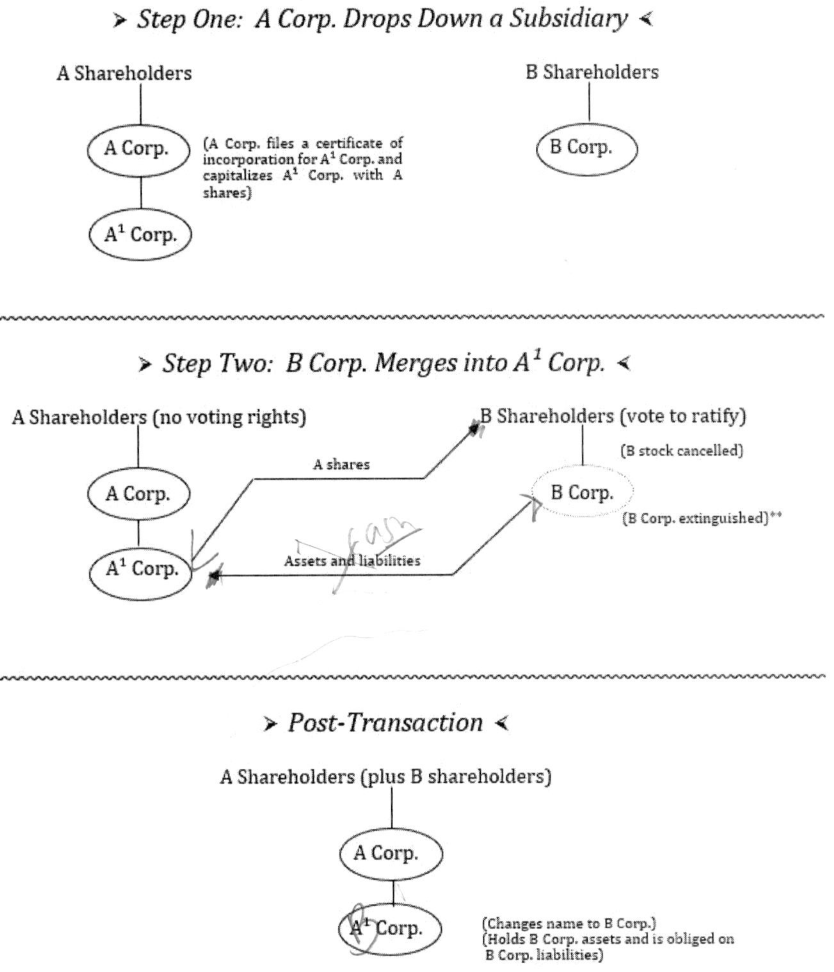

* This is a tax-free forward triangular merger (an A(2)(D) reorganization). See Chapter 8, Section B. If B shareholders receive cash for their shares instead of A Corp. shares, it is a taxable exchange.

** It would be a reverse triangular merger if A[1] Corp. merged into B Corp. with B Corp. surviving. In the exchange, B shareholders all receive A shares (or cash) and A Corp., the shareholder of A[1] Corp., receives the only remaining B Corp. shares, in exchange for its A[1] Corp. shares.

Parent corporation shareholders who seek voting and appraisal rights in a triangular merger under a de facto merger theory have lost when they take the matter to court. E.g., *Terry v. Penn Central*, 668 F.2d 188 (3d Cir. 1981) (parent shareholders in triangular merger do not have voting and appraisal rights). The next case deals with the issue.

EQUITY GROUP HOLDINGS V. DMG, INC.

United States District Court, Southern District of Florida, 1983.
576 F.Supp. 1197.

ARONOVITZ, DISTRICT JUDGE.

* * *

The undisputed facts as stipulated by the parties can be summarized as follows: Defendant, DMG, Inc. ("DMG"), a Florida corporation, is a holding company that has no assets or operations. It is the listed (New York Stock Exchange) parent corporation of a wholly-owned subsidiary, Defendant Diversified Mortgage Investors, Inc. ("DMI"), a Florida corporation. DMG was incorporated in 1980 by DMI for the purpose of carrying out a corporate reorganization. At that time, the shareholders of DMI automatically became shareholders of DMG.

* * *

On October 28, 1983, DMG, Carlsberg and Carlsberg Resources Corporation entered into a Stock Purchase Agreement, pursuant to which DMG agreed to issue two million (2,000,000) shares of DMG voting preferred stock, which had been authorized but unissued, in exchange for forty-four thousand, four hundred, forty-four (44,444) of the one hundred twenty-five thousand (125,000) shares of Carlsberg convertible preferred stock then held by Carlsberg Resources.

Also on October 28, 1983, DMG, DMI, and Carlsberg entered into an Agreement and Plan of Merger (the "Merger Agreement"). Pursuant to the Merger Agreement, Carlsberg will merge into DMI; outstanding shares of Carlsberg will then be converted into DMG common. To accomplish this plan, approximately 12.5 million new shares of Common will be issued to shareholders of Carlsberg. Thereafter, some 64 percent of DMG Common Stock will be owned by Carlsberg shareholders.

* * *

The New York Stock Exchange, wherein DMG is listed, requires that to validate the issuance of the authorized twelve and one-half million shares of DMG common stock that are to be issued to Carlsberg, a majority of DMG shareholders who are represented in person or by proxy at a meeting of shareholders must so vote. See NYSE Company Manual, A–283–284 (January 25, 1978). This election is necessary in order to maintain DMG's listing on the Exchange. Consequently, a shareholders' meeting of DMG has been currently scheduled for December 22, 1983, to vote on a corporate resolution approving the issuance by DMG of the 12.5 million shares of DMG common stock to shareholders of Carlsberg. DMG has also announced that officers and directors of Carlsberg will stand for election to the DMG Board of Directors at the shareholders' meeting scheduled for

December 22, 1983, and that Carlsberg will seek to fill by election four of the seven directorial seats on the DMG Board.

* * *

Plaintiff [a *DMG* shareholder] contends that the two transactions at issue here, *i.e.,* (a) the issuance of two million (2,000,000) voting preferred shares of DMG to Carlsberg, and (b) the merger of DMI and Carlsberg which results in issuance of 12.5 million shares of DMG common to Carlsberg, together constitute a de facto merger of *three* corporations: the present DMG, its subsidiary, DMI and Carlsberg; that the real merger is not only that between DMI and Carlsberg, but between DMG, the parent company, and Carlsberg; that, because Carlsberg is approximately three times the size of DMG, it is really Carlsberg which is surviving and DMG which is ceasing to exist after the merger; and that, if in fact these transactions together do constitute a de facto merger of DMG into Carlsberg, then Florida Corporation Law Section 607.221 requires a full majority of *all outstanding* shares to approve the transaction, rather than a *quorum of shares voted either at the December 22, 1983 meeting or by proxy,* which is all that is required under the rules of the New York Stock Exchange. See NYSE Company Manual A–283, 284 (January 25, 1978).

Plaintiff concedes that the transactions do not fall within the strict statutory wording of Florida Statute Section 607.221, and that therefore this Court would have to declare the transactions a de facto merger in order to find that the statute applies. Plaintiff further argues that if a de facto merger were declared in this case, the appropriate relief would be for the Court to issue a preliminary injunction against holding the shareholder vote at which only a quorum, rather than a full majority, would be required to effectuate the merger. . . .

* * *

On the foregoing basis, the Court finds that the Plaintiff has not met its burden of proof sufficiently to support the issuance of a preliminary injunction. This is not to say that, given more facts and further discovery, the Court could not find that the transaction at issue is a de facto merger requiring a full majority vote of all the outstanding shares of DMG to be approved. . . .

The parties seem to agree that the DMI-Carlsberg Merger, the second of the two transactions at issue here, is a forward triangular merger: a wholly-owned subsidiary is acquiring the assets, liabilities, and stock of the target, a third-party corporation, after which the parent company and its original subsidiary will survive and the target will become part of the subsidiary. The key question before the Court is whether, as Plaintiff alleges, this requires that the Court treat the two transactions—the issuance of two million (2,000,000) shares of DMG voting preferred shares to Carlsberg, and the issuance of 12.5 million shares of common to effectuate a DMI-Carlsberg Merger—as a single transaction. The reason to do so, Plaintiff alleges, is that in reality, Carlsberg will be taking control of DMG, rather than DMG acquiring Carlsberg as part of its subsidiary, DMI. Plaintiff argues that this is so because: (1) Carlsberg is three times the size of DMG; (2) the Carlsberg family will end up controlling a majority of DMG voting shares; (3) the President of Carlsberg will become the President of DMG; and (4) the DMG Board of Directors will be composed of a majority of persons nominated by, and, essentially, voted in by, Carlsberg. These elements, Plaintiff has repeated in its papers as well as orally, constitute a situation in which, in reality, "the minnow is swallowing the whale."

The Court finds that under these facts and circumstances, on the basis of the record before it, Florida law does not necessarily stop or prevent the minnow from swallowing the whale where the business judgment of both the minnow and the whale is that the event will be mutually beneficial to both parties. Without evidence of a breach of fiduciary duty by the Officers/Directors of DMG or DMI or fundamental unfairness, or without allegations or proof of fraud, misrepresentation, *mala fides* or economic harm resulting from such merger, there is not presented to this Court a basis to invoke its equity jurisdiction. . . .

The reason that the minnow may swallow the whale here is simply that nothing appears to prevent this from occurring. Each gets the opportunity to vote on the transaction. Florida law does not define the dilution of voting rights through the issuance of authorized stock as a matter which requires a full shareholder vote and the Florida legislature has specifically abolished preemptive rights. . . . DMG could go forward with the issuance of every one of its authorized but unissued shares, without asking the shareholders for approval. This is not to say that if this were done for fraudulent reasons or illegitimate business purposes, the shareholders would not have numerous causes of action on which to sue, both under state law and under the Federal Securities Laws. The Court is not precluding such actions, or holding that they would not be recognized, in this very case or any other. However, the parties have not presented these issues to the Court in this case . . . .

Similarly, the consideration for both of these transactions is adequate under Florida law, or more than adequate. . . .

Carlsberg is becoming a party to the use of a One Hundred Million ($100,000,000) Dollar tax loss carry-forward with DMG, a substantial consideration regardless of its enhanced position of control of DMG. Similarly, DMG will be less likely to suffer a possible default and non-renewal of a Twenty-three Million ($23,000,000) Dollar loan from Continental Bank due in full December 31, 1983; if default were to occur, it would seriously jeopardize DMG's continued existence. Equity, as well as other shareholders of DMG, will not be harmed *economically* by the Carlsberg-DMG transaction, since the book value of the shares would be roughly equivalent both before and after the DMI-Carlsberg merger. The pre-merger book value would be Two and 77/100 ($2.77) Dollars per share, while the post-merger *pro forma* value would be Two and 70/100 ($2.70) Dollars. . . . In the case at bar, it would be a mistake for the Court to substitute its own judgment for the business judgment of the directors of the corporations involved as to the benefits ultimately to inure to shareholders, absent any evidence of breach of fiduciary duty, or fundamental unfairness, or overreaching. . . .

* * *

. . . The Court does not deny that there is a public interest in corporate democracy at stake here, and that there is merit to Plaintiff's argument that shareholders in a public corporation should be given an opportunity to voice their opinion in a vote on matters of fundamental importance to them. However, it is of importance that the Court is here dealing with shares that were duly authorized by the shareholders of DMG through the 1980 Amendment to DMG's Articles of Incorporation, voted upon by a majority of holders of outstanding stock, which amendments specifically gave the directors the right to issue up to five million (5,000,000) shares of preferred stock *without further shareholder approval.*

The New York Stock Exchange requirement, that a majority of votes cast is required to approve the transaction, also cannot be overlooked. Shareholders are given the right to vote and are free to do so with respect to the DMG issuance of shares to Carlsberg; only the required percentage standard for approval differs between the New York Stock Exchange Rule and the statutory merger standard. The right to vote—or not to do so—is the essence of democracy and is not disregarded in the corporate transactions now before the Court.

Moreover, it cannot be said that corporate suffrage with respect to the shareholders of a parent corporation in a forward triangular merger of its subsidiary with another corporation is a value that the Florida legislature has seen fit to recognize. Florida Statute Section 607.221 guarantees voting rights to the shareholders of the merging subsidiary and the third company, the target or non-surviving corporation; but the section does not contemplate the triangular situation with which the Court is herein faced. The Florida statutes permit the use of the parent's shares as merger consideration. Coupled with the tax advantages and tax-free status of the triangular merger under the Internal Revenue Code, and the convenience of a merger by exchange of stock rather than assets, this is just the type of transaction that the legislature cannot be presumed to have overlooked. In fact, it might be inferred that the legislature intentionally did *not* want to discourage such forms of merger by awarding voting or appraisal rights to the shareholders of the parent. . . .

* * *

ORDERED AND ADJUDGED that Plaintiff's Motion for Preliminary Injunction be and is hereby DENIED.

The Florida statute is in accord with the Del. Gen. Corp. L. and the pre-1999 drafts of the ABA Model Business Corporation Act. The 1999 version of the Model Act gives shareholders of DMG voting rights in the acquisition (but not appraisal rights). In California, the shareholders of DMG would have statutory voting and appraisal rights; that is, a majority of the shareholders of DMG would have to vote to approve the acquisition. Do you prefer the Delaware provision or the California provision?

Shareholders of an acquirer can protect their voting rights in triangular acquisitions with express provisions in a corporation's Certificate of Incorporation.[77] The lack of voting power is a *default rule* and shareholders may opt to change it (an *opt-in* rule). In practice, most shareholders (other than preferred shareholders attempting to protect class voting provisions) do not opt for the protection. Why?

v. Two-Stage Stock Acquisitions

Many stock acquisitions are *two-stage acquisitions*, in which a stock acquisition is followed by a *back-end* or *second-step merger*. In the second stage, the purchasing corporation *drops down* a subsidiary and merges the subsidiary with and into the target, which is now partially-owned by the parent as a result of its successful first stage stock acquisition. See Diagram 8 below. In a drop down, the purchasing corporation itself acts as an incorporator for a new corporation which becomes a wholly-owned subsidiary of the purchasing corporation. The new subsidiary is usually a *shell* corporation, one that has no assets.

The constituent parties to the back-end merger are the wholly-owned, shell subsidiary of the purchasing corporation and the newly-acquired, partially-owned subsidiary that was the target of the stock acquisition. For examples of two-stage stock acquisitions, see *Rothschild*, cited in *Rauch* above, and *Irving Bank* below.

---

[77] They can negotiate for the provisions in the corporate charter when the stock is initially offered or just refuse to buy stock that does not have such protections. See, e.g., Pasternak v. Glazer, 1996 WL 549960 (Del. Ch.), *vacated as moot*, 693 A.2d 319 (Del. 1997) (Certificate of Incorporation gives voting rights to parent shareholders in a triangular merger). In the case, the Delaware Chancery Court stretched language of a Certificate of Incorporation to protect the voting rights of the shareholders of the purchasing corporation; the Delaware Supreme Court vacated the opinion with an opinion that put the holding in doubt. Nevertheless, compare the approach in this case with the Chancery Court's approach to the interpretation of another certificate provision in *Warner Communications* on class voting, mentioned in *Elliott Assoc.* appearing later in the chapter. Class voting gets a much less sympathetic treatment. Note also that courts are using very different conventions when interpreting statutory language in Del. Gen. Corp. L. § 251 (not protecting shareholders' statutory voting rights in triangular acquisitions) than when interpreting the language in a corporate charter.

The purpose of such an acquisition is often speed (as compared to its functional alternative: a single stage cash-out triangular merger); the purchasing firm can gain control of the target faster because it can close the first stage stock acquisition faster than a statutory merger or asset sale. Once the acquirer owns legal control it does not have to worry about competitive bidders. The acquirer can complete the second stage, which takes longer, at its convenience. The second stage, the squeeze-out, is necessary to convert a partially-owned subsidiary into a wholly-owned subsidiary, thus eliminating any remaining minority shareholders in the target (i.e., those that refused to sell their shares during the first stage) in the process.

By virtue of a successful first stage acquisition, the acquirer will own enough shares of the target (more than 50 percent) to vote through the second stage merger through its own voting power. However, § 251(h) of the Del. Gen. Corp. L. provides parties involved in negotiated transactions with a special *medium-form* merger procedure that obviates the need for a target shareholder vote in the first place. For more on the § 251(h) procedure, see *supra* Section A.2.a.i.

Note that a two-stage acquisition can effect a structure identical to the post-transaction structure in Diagram 1 on plain vanilla mergers. Once the two-stage acquisition is complete, one need only merge the wholly-owned subsidiary into the parent with a simple board of directors' resolution (a short-form merger under Del. Gen. Corp. L. § 253). Disgruntled shareholders have, therefore, attacked the transactions as de facto mergers, again without success.

Diagram 8

Two-Stage Acquisition: Stock Acquisition Followed by a Squeeze-Out Statutory Merger

➤ Stage One: Stock Acquisition ◄

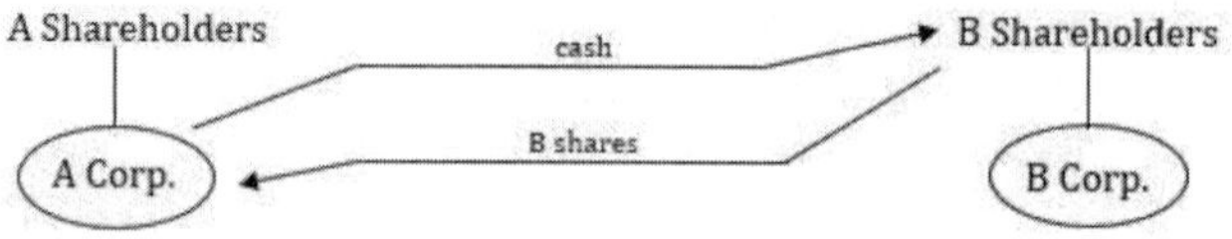

➤ Post-Stage One: A Partially-Owned Subsidiary ◄

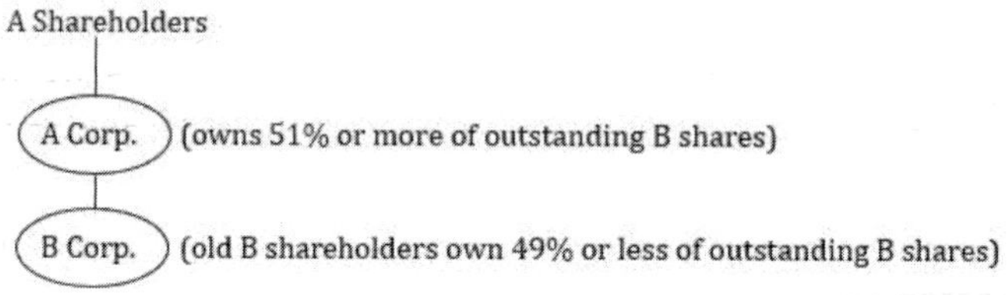

➤ Stage Two: A Squeeze-Out Merger ◄

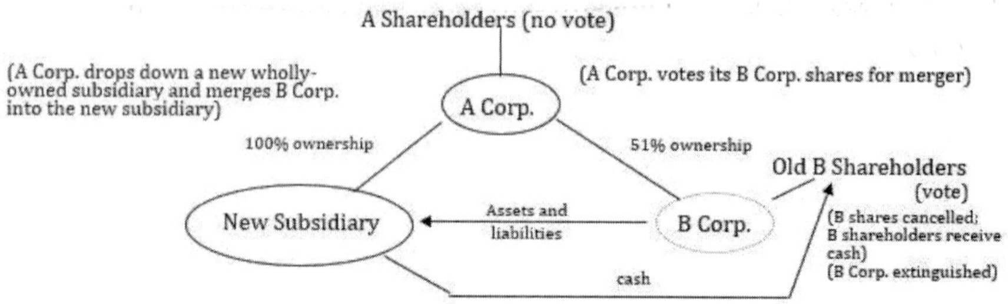

➤ Post-Stage Two ◄

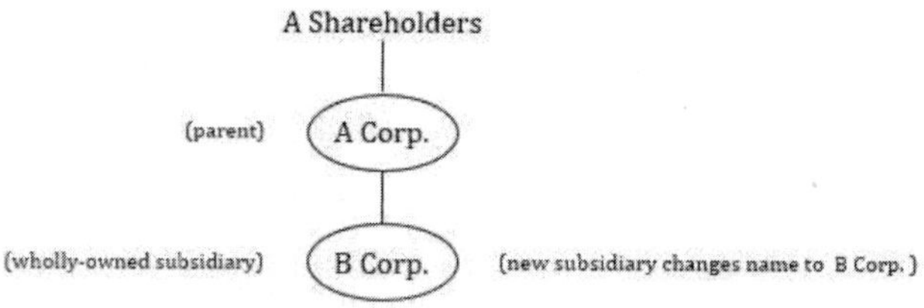

IRVING BANK CORP. V. BANK OF NEW YORK CO., INC.

Supreme Court, New York County, 1988.
530 N.Y.S.2d 757.

HERMAN CAHN, JUSTICE.

Irving Bank Corporation ("IBC") moves for summary judgment, or in the alternative for a preliminary injunction, to prevent Bank of New York ("BNY") from implementing its proposed plan of acquisition of IBC. IBC claims that the plan constitutes a de facto merger, and can only be implemented after approval by two-thirds of BNY's shareholders. BNY seeks dismissal of the complaint on the ground that it fails to state a cause of action. . . . The facts are not in dispute.

* * *

IBC and BNY are both bank holding companies incorporated in the State of New York. In September 1987, BNY announced its intention to acquire IBC. At that time, BNY made an offer to the Board of Directors of IBC to acquire all of the outstanding shares of IBC, which offer was rejected. Over the following months, the proposed acquisition developed into a contested takeover offer, the Board of IBC having not approved the initial offer, nor any subsequent BNY offer. To the contrary, IBC has contested virtually every action taken by BNY in connection with this matter. As a result, several lawsuits are pending before this court involving the two companies and/or their shareholders.

The IBC Board of Directors has stated that it is now in the process of holding an "auction", in relation to this matter. The "auction" is not relevant to the decision of these motions.

. . . BNY's plan of acquisition is basically a two-step process: (1) First, BNY seeks to acquire all or a majority of the outstanding shares of IBC; and (2) thereafter, BNY hopes to consummate a merger between IBC and either BNY or an affiliate of BNY.

The acquisition of IBC's shares would be in exchange for cash and shares of BNY. That is, BNY would pay a certain amount of cash plus between one and two BNY shares for each IBC share acquired.

* * *

IBC brings this action as a shareholder of BNY.[Ed.[78]] It seeks a declaration that BNY's plan of acquisition constitutes a merger, within the meaning of BCL Sec. 903, and thus requires a vote of two-thirds of BNY's shareholders to approve the transaction.[Ed.[79]] It argues, although the form of the plan of acquisition is not one of merger, the substance is that of

[78] [Ed. IBC hopes to delay BNY's acquisition so as to make BNY's cost of carrying the acquisition financing prohibitive.]

[79] [Ed. The New York statute has been amended and now requires only a majority vote of those present or represented by proxy at a shareholders' meeting at which a quorum exists.]

law update

a merger, and the court should apply the "de facto merger doctrine," and treat the acquisition plan as a merger.

BNY disputes the existence of the de facto merger doctrine in New York, and furthermore claims that even where the doctrine is recognized, it would not be applicable in these circumstances.

BNY moves for dismissal on the ground that it has properly complied with the BCL provision that permits its Board to issue common shares for "such consideration, not less than par value thereof, as is fixed from time to time by the board." BCL Sec. 504(c). Therefore, BNY claims any exchange of its shares for IBC shares would be valid. Furthermore, it claims that it already has shareholder authority to issue the shares, since the certificate of incorporation authorizes the issuance of 125,000,000 shares, of which less than 40,000,000 have been issued. Issuance of the proposed 31,000,000 shares in the exchange offer, alleges BNY, has already been, in accordance with statutory requirements, approved by the shareholders of BNY. (BCL Sec. 801).

The shareholders of BNY have not approved any merger of IBC into BNY, or other proposed merger, by two-thirds vote. They did approve a corporate resolution authorizing the planned acquisition (which proposal was submitted to them pursuant to the Rules of the New York Stock Exchange), but by less than a two-thirds vote.

* * *

The de facto merger doctrine has been used by some courts of equity to preserve shareholders' rights where the transaction involved, although not a classic merger, is, in essence, a merger. The courts will look through the form of the transaction to its substance.

. . . The de facto merger doctrine has been applied in this state, but only where it is apparent that the acquired corporation was quickly to be dissolved.

We need not discuss, at this time, extensively the requirements for a de facto merger. It is clear, however, that two factors are necessary: (1) the actual merger must take place soon after the initial transaction, and (2) the seller corporation must quickly cease to exist.

* * *

We note further, that BNY is planning a purchase of the stock, not the assets of IBC. Where the acquirer corporation purchases all the target's assets, leaving the target as a mere shell, the transaction bears a distinct resemblance to a merger. Here, IBC will survive as a corporate entity, with all its assets intact. Although a merger may occur in the future, the instant transaction is not a merger, but the acquisition of a subsidiary. . . .

* * *

---

vi. Partnerships and Long-Term Supply Contracts

The following two cases demonstrate that parties may use either partnership agreements or long-term supply contracts to approximate some of the effects of a stock swap merger. What is lost with either approach? Note that in both Arkansas and New Jersey the courts are unusual in their willingness to apply a de facto merger theory to shareholder claims.

PRATT v. BALLMAN-CUMMINGS FURNITURE CO., 254 Ark. 570, 495 S.W.2d 509 (1973). [In a case dealing with appraisal rights in the wake of the formation of a partnership, the court concluded that the facts as pled established a prima facie case for the application of the de facto merger doctrine. Plaintiffs, minority shareholders of the Ballman-Cummings Furniture Company, sought recovery of the value of their shares pursuant to the Arkansas appraisal statute. Defendants asserted that the transaction was merely the formation of a partnership by two corporations. While the court stopped short of finding that plaintiffs had established grounds for relief, it did state that a prima facie case of de facto merger had been pled and that the trial court thus had incorrectly directed verdict for defendants.

On the pleading, the plaintiff alleged that each constituent corporation, furniture companies, assigned their retail sales operations to the partnership. Each partner agreed to sell all its merchandise to the partnership and the partnership resold the merchandise to the public. The partnership was responsible for billing, merchandising, collection of accounts receivable, and delivery of furniture to customers, thus eliminating the duplication of expenses of the two partner corporations. Moreover, the shipping costs of the two companies working together were substantially lower than if each had shipped its own merchandise. The two corporation partners designated one individual to act as general manager of the partnership and many of the functions of the separate corporations (sales manager, designer, controller, credit collection, and customer relations) were combined under one office in the partnership. One of the corporation partners liquidated in bankruptcy thereafter. The court held that the facts pled were sufficient to state a prima facie case that through the partnership one of the entities had absorbed the identity and assets of the other.]

GOOD v. LACKAWANNA LEATHER CO., 96 N.J.Super. 439, 233 A.2d 201 (Ch.Div.1967). [Plaintiff shareholders sought appraisal rights under a de facto merger theory. The two corporations involved, Good Bros. Leather Co. ("Good Bros.") and Lackawanna Leather Co. ("Lackawanna"), were each part of the leather goods industry: Good Bros. as a leather processing company and Lackawanna as a finisher and seller of leather products. In April 1958, the two corporations proposed a stock swap merger of the two entities, citing as reasons therefore the recent trend among leather finishing companies to develop in-house leather tanning departments rather than rely on outside suppliers. When the plaintiffs perfected their appraisal rights for a block of 20 percent of the shares in each of the two constituent corporations, the boards abandoned the merger. The companies did not have sufficient cash to buy out the minority shares. Following the abandonment of the merger proposal, Good Bros. and Lackawanna developed a symbiotic working relationship. Good Bros. converted approximately 94 percent of its plant and equipment to cash and investment securities. Good Bros. subcontracted its hide processing and sold the hides processed by the subcontractor to Lackawanna, Good Bros.' only customer. Good Bros. also made loans to Lackawanna so that Lackawanna could pay for the processed hides. Finally, Good Bros. built a new leather processing plant and leased the plant to a new corporation, jointly owned by Good Bros. and Lackawanna, which processed hides for Lackawanna. Plaintiffs alleged that, through the use of long-term contractual agreements, the purposes of the merger had been accomplished without satisfying the formal requirements of state law.

Since New Jersey may be the one state that continues to have a robust de facto merger doctrine applicable to shareholder voting rights, see *Applestein v. United Board & Carton Corp.*, 161 A.2d 474 (N.J. 1960), the case is of some importance. But, the court found that in fact there had been no de facto merger, because neither of the constituent corporations had dissolved following the transaction. It held that the development of a close working relationship and the interlocking directorate[80] did not per se constitute a merger. The court noted that the two corporations continued to maintain separate, albeit interlocking, boards of directors, that there had not been an exchange of shares for assets between the two corporations, that Good Bros. had not assumed the liabilities of Lackawanna and that the interest on the loans and the price of the processed hides were at market rates or better. The court was also troubled by the prospect of granting an appraisal remedy when the statute declared that the *consolidated* corporation shall pay to such shareholder the value of his stock. Since there had been no consolidation of enterprises, there was no corporation to be called upon to pay the dissenters the value of their shares.]

c. Single-Firm Reorganizations, Reincorporations and Conversions

Sections 102 and 242 of the Del. Gen. Corp. L. control *amendments to the Certification of Incorporation.* Common amendments include augmenting the corporation's authority to issue shares, often important in

80 Some of the directors on Good Bros.'s board of directors also served on the board of Lackawanna. There were also interlocking officers.

acquisitions in which purchasing firm stock is the consideration, and altering the rights, preferences, and privileges of outstanding shares, particularly preferred shares. The procedure, specified in Del. Gen. Corp. L. § 242(b), requires a board of directors resolution and a ratifying shareholder vote. The holders of shares are entitled to vote as a separate class (even if otherwise specified as non-voting shares) if their shares would be *adversely affected* by the passage of the amendment. A majority vote of the outstanding shares of each class entitled to vote as a separate class is necessary for the passage of the amendment.

Unless the Certificate of Incorporation has express limits, and most do not, many major capital side transactions do not require a shareholder vote. For example, assume a corporation has a conservative debt-equity ratio, and managers decide to issue new subordinated bonds and pass out the proceeds from the bond sale to all the shareholders as an extraordinary dividend, a *dividend recap*. After the one-time extraordinary dividend, shareholders hold shares worth much less than they were before the transaction (offset, of course, by the receipt of a juicy dividend check), and the debt-equity ratio of the firm is much higher. The firm is now highly leveraged. Corporate codes do not require a ratifying shareholder vote on the recapitalization.

Assume, for a second example, that a corporation issues a very large block of preferred stock pursuant to a general grant of authority to its board of directors contained in its Certificate of Incorporation (a *blank check* preferred authorization). The rights and privileges of the stock are not defined in the original Certificate of Incorporation; rather, those rights and privileges will be delineated in a series of board resolutions. Those resolutions will then be folded into a *Certificate of Designation*. When filed with the state, the Certificate of Designation legally becomes part of the Certificate of Incorporation.[81] See Del. Gen. Corp. L. §§ 102(a)(4) and 151(a) (authorizing blank check preferred stock). The stock is a new type of convertible preferred stock (known as poison pill preferred) designed solely to block hostile takeovers. The stock has no dividend or voting rights. The preferred stock converts to common (1 to 1,000) if the board of directors does not approve of the purchase of a large block of common stock by a *hostile* party. The board issues the poison pill preferred stock as a stock dividend to the existing common shareholders. Corporate codes do not require a ratifying vote by common shareholders on the new share issuance.

The separate class voting provisions of Del. Gen. Corp. L. § 242 on statutory recapitalizations and the absence of separate class voting provisions in § 251 on statutory mergers cause lawyers to use statutory

---

81 Thus, while the rights of preferred shareholders are contractual, the "contract" is found within the Certificate of Designation which itself constitutes an *amendment* to the Certificate of Incorporation. The preferred shareholder contract, therefore, is contained within the Certificate of Incorporation.

mergers to avoid separate class voting in recapitalizations.[82] The corporation drops down a wholly-owned subsidiary and merges with and into the subsidiary (a downstream merger), exchanging the stock of the subsidiary for the outstanding stock of the corporation (see Diagram 9) or has the subsidiary merge with and into the parent (an upstream merger). The shareholders of the parent corporation, A Corp., entitled to vote must ratify the transaction by a majority of the outstanding shares. Del. Gen. Corp. L §§ 251 or 253(a).[83]

Similarly, firms incorporated in one state and seeking to *reincorporate* in another, usually Delaware, have long used statutory mergers to accomplish the move. The non-Delaware firm drops down a shell subsidiary incorporated in Delaware, thus becoming a parent corporation. The parent then merges with and into the subsidiary with the subsidiary surviving and changing its name to that of the parent. All the stock in the parent is exchanged for identical shares in the new Delaware corporation and a majority of the outstanding shareholders of the parent entitled to vote must approve. The state of incorporation of the parent controls the voting rights of the shareholders on the reincorporation.

[82] Preferred shareholders in California, asked to accept distributions in a merger or asset sale that are less than liquidation preferences, have a class vote on the acquisition. Cal. Corp. Code § 1202(b).

[83] If the subsidiary stock is distributed "pro rata" to the holders of the stock of the parent, the dissenters do not have appraisal rights. Del. Gen. Corp. L. §§ 253(d) & 262(b)(3) (appraisal rights limited to minority shareholders in the subsidiary). Otherwise, Del. Gen. Corp. L. § 251 applies and the dissenters do have appraisal rights. *Id.*, § 262(b).

Diagram 9

Recapitalizations: A Statutory Merger as an Alternative to a Charter Amendment

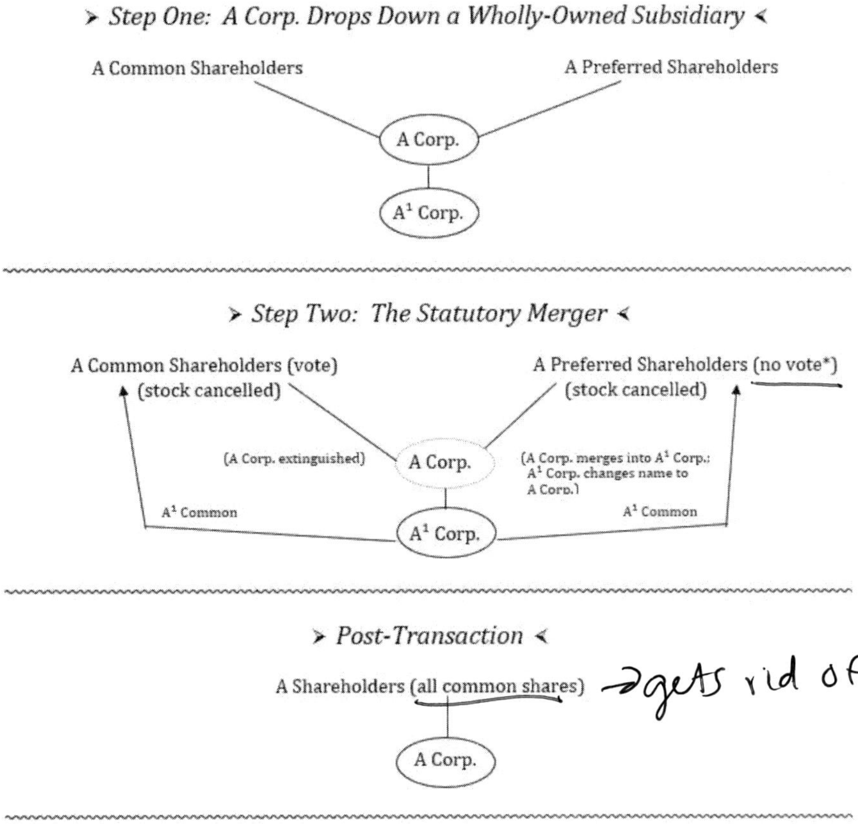

* In Delaware, the preferred shareholders do not vote on the merger unless their voting rights are expressly provided for in the certificate of incorporation. Under the ABA Model Bus. Corp. Act § 11.04(f) (2016 rev.), the preferred shareholders vote as a separate class.

FEDERAL UNITED CORP. V. HAVENDER

Supreme Court of Delaware, 1940.
11 A.2d 331.

Bill in equity to have declared void, as against the complainants, a merger of the defendant, Federal United Corporation, with its wholly-owned subsidiary, Corporation Bond and Share Company, a Delaware corporation, in so far as the merger, in recapitalizing the defendant corporation, undertook to convert complainants' preferred shares into other securities without paying in money dividends accrued thereon.

* * *

On November 30, 1936, by a vote of 91.8 percent of all of the outstanding stock of the defendant corporation, and 100 percent of the stock of its subsidiary, a merger was effected under Section 59 of the General Corporation Law. . . .[Ed.[84]]

* * *

The preferred stock with accumulated dividends was converted into new preferred stock and Class A common stock, so that for each share of the $6 preferred stock there would be given in exchange one share of the new $3 preferred stock of the par value of $50, and six shares of the Class A common stock. . . .

* * *

LAYTON, CHIEF JUSTICE.

* * *

It is for the Legislature not for the court, to declare the public policy of the state; and it is not, therefore, the function of the court to graft an exception on the plain and positive terms of the statute.

* * *

Next to be considered is whether, under the merger and consolidation provisions of the General Corporation Law, and apart from those provisions with respect to a valuation of stock either by agreement or by appraisal, dividends accumulated on the cumulative preference stock of one or more of the constituent companies may be disposed of other than by paying to the dissatisfied shareholder the amount of them in money.

* * *

. . . The substantial elements of the merger and consolidation provisions of the General Corporation Law as they now appear have existed from the time of the inception of the law. It is elementary that these provisions are written into every corporate charter. The shareholder has notice that the corporation whose shares he has acquired may be merged with another corporation if the required majority of the shareholders agree. He is informed that the merger agreement may prescribe the terms and conditions of the merger, the mode of carrying it into effect, and the manner of converting the shares of the constituent corporations into the shares of the resulting corporation. A well understood meaning of the word "convert," is to alter in form, substance, or quality. Substantial rights of shareholders, as is well known, may include rights in respect of voting, options, preferences and dividends. The average intelligent mind must be held to know that dividends may accumulate on preferred stock, and that in the event of a merger of the corporation issuing the stock with another

[84] [Ed. The predecessor to Del. Gen. Corp. L. § 251. For a modern application of *Havender*, see Benchmark Capital Part. IV v. Vague, 2002 WL 1732423 (Del. Ch.), *aff'd* 822 A.2d 396 (Del. 2003).]

corporation, the various rights of shareholders, including the right to dividends on preference stock accrued but unpaid, may, and perhaps must, be the subject of reconcilement and adjustment; in many cases, it would be impracticable to effect a merger if the rights attached to the shares could not be dealt with. . . . Within the time and in the manner provided by the statute, the dissatisfied stockholder, if he so desires, may demand and receive the money value of his shares as that value has been agreed upon or has been determined by an impartial appraisement. Consequently, in a case where a merger of corporations is permitted by the law and is accomplished in accordance with the law, the holder of cumulative preference stock as to which dividends have accumulated may not insist that his right to the dividends is a fixed contractual right in the nature of a debt, in that sense vested and, therefore, secure against attack. Looking to the law, which is a part of the corporate charter, and, therefore, a part of the shareholder's contract, he has not been deceived nor lulled into the belief that the right to such dividends is firm and stable. On the contrary, his contract has informed him that the right is defeasible; and with that knowledge the stock was acquired. . . .

* * *

. . . A holder of preference shares as to which dividends have accumulated through time is not a creditor of the corporation in the ordinary and usual meaning of the word; nor is he the holder of a lien as that word is usually understood. . . .

* * *

There is no invasion of legal or equitable right, nor is there moral wrong, in disposing of dividends on preference stock accumulated through time other than by their payment in money, if the right to such dividends has not the status of a fixed contractual right under the law as it stood when the corporation was formed and the stock was issued, and if the terms of disposal are fair and equitable in the circumstances of the case; and especially is this true where provision is made for payment of the value of the shares to the dissatisfied shareholder. . . .

It is not suggested that the terms of the plan of merger were unfair or inequitable. We conclude, therefore, that the accumulations of dividends on the preference stock of the defendant corporation were lawfully compounded. The complainants were put to their election, either to demand payment in money of the value of their preferred shares as agreed upon, or as ascertained by an appraisement, or to accept the exchange of securities offered by the merger plan. No effort was made to agree upon a valuation of the shares, and no appraisement was sought. Manifestly, under the provisions of the statute, a valuation cannot be demanded now. The complainants must accept the terms of the merger agreement.

* * *

The decree of the court below is reversed, with the direction to enter a decree dismissing the bill of complaint, with costs on the complainants.

Preferred shareholders can contract to protect accumulated and unpaid dividends (*arrearages*) on their cumulative preferred shares from cancellation by a statutory merger if they demand specific language in the investment contracts embodied or incorporated by reference in their share certificates. Why should the default rule be no protection rather than the reverse (requiring an opt-in)? Drafting practice on the question, even by well-known lawyers for high-profile clients, can leave something to be desired. See, e.g., *Warner Comm. v. Chris-Craft Indus.*, 583 A.2d 962 (Del. Ch.), *aff'd without opinion*, 567 A.2d 419 (Del. 1989) (language in the certificate granting a class of preferred shares a super-majority separate class vote if corporate action would "alter or change any rights, preferences or limitations" of the preferred did not apply to the second stage of a two-stage stock acquisition in which the preferred shares in the target were exchanged for preferred shares in the acquiring firm).[85]

The tight construction of the Certificate of Incorporation by the Chancery Court in *Warner* against the preferred shareholders, on boilerplate language, surprised many. After enterprising lawyers representing preferred stock investors wised up and became smarter in their drafting, even the Delaware Supreme Court took notice.

ELLIOTT ASSOC. V. AVATEX CORP.

Supreme Court of Delaware, 1998.
715 A.2d 843.

VEASEY, CHIEF JUSTICE:

* * *

Defendant Avatex Corporation ("Avatex") is a Delaware corporation that has outstanding both common and preferred stock. The latter includes two distinct series of outstanding preferred stock: "First Series Preferred" and "Series A Preferred." Plaintiffs in these consolidated cases are all preferred stockholders of defendant Avatex. The individual defendants are all members of the Avatex board of directors.

Avatex created and incorporated Xetava Corporation ("Xetava")[Ed.[86]] as its wholly-owned subsidiary on April 13, 1998, and the following day

---

[85] See also Sullivan Money Management, Inc. v. FLS Holdings Inc., 1992 WL 345453 (Del. Ch.), *aff'd*, 628 A.2d 84 (Del. 1993) (holding that *Warner* governs and that certificate providing separate class vote to preferred in the event of "change, by amendment to the Certificate . . . or otherwise the terms and provisions of the . . . Preferred Stock so as to affect adversely the rights and preferences of the holders . . . " does not require separate class vote in cash-out merger because the term "or otherwise" did not clearly and expressly apply to mergers).

[86] [Ed. "Xetava" is, of course, "Avatex" spelled backwards.]

announced its intention to merge with and into Xetava. Under the terms of the proposed merger, Xetava is to be the surviving corporation. Once the transaction is consummated, Xetava will immediately change its name to Avatex Corporation. The proposed merger would cause a conversion of the preferred stock of Avatex into common stock of Xetava. The merger will effectively eliminate Avatex' certificate of incorporation, which includes the certificate of designations creating the Avatex preferred stock and setting forth its rights and preferences. The terms of the merger do not call for a class vote of these preferred stockholders. Herein lays the heart of the legal issue presented in this case.

Plaintiffs filed suit in the Court of Chancery to enjoin the proposed merger, arguing, among other things, that the transaction required the consent of two-thirds of the holders of the First Series Preferred stock. . . .

The plaintiffs allege that, because of Avatex' anemic financial state, "all the value of Avatex is [currently] in the preferred stock." By forcing the conversion of the preferred shares into common stock of the surviving corporation, however, the merger would place current preferred stockholders of Avatex on an even footing with its common stockholders. In fact, the Avatex preferred stockholders will receive in exchange for their preferred stock approximately 73% of Xetava common stock, and the common stockholders of Avatex will receive approximately 27% of the common stock of Xetava.

Under the terms of the Avatex certificate of incorporation, First Series stockholders have no right to vote except on:

> (a) any "amendment, alteration or repeal" of the certificate of incorporation "whether by merger, consolidation or otherwise," that
>
> (b) "materially and adversely" affects the rights of the First Series stockholders.[Ed.87]

The text of the terms governing the voting rights of the First Series Preferred Stock is set forth in the certificate of designations . . . .

* * *

[Ed. The Court took great pains to distinguish *Warner Communications Inc. v. Chris-Craft Industries Inc.* The lower court had relied on *Warner* to hold below that the Avatex preferred shares did not have voting rights. A sample of the argument follows.] . . . It is important to keep in mind, however, that the terms of the preferred stock in *Warner* were significantly different from those present here, because in *Warner* the phrase "whether by merger, consolidation or otherwise" was not included.

---

87 [Ed. The Certificate of Designation containing a description of the rights of the preferred shareholders requires, when the preferred have a right to a separate class vote, a super-majority of two-thirds of the outstanding shares.]

The issue here, therefore, is whether the presence of this additional phrase in the Avatex certificate is an outcome-determinative distinction from *Warner.*

* * *

Avatex argued below, and the Court of Chancery appears to have agreed, that *only* a Section 251(b)(3) Amendment to the surviving corporation's charter amounts to an "amendment, alteration or repeal" within the meaning of the provisions defining the voting rights of the preferred stockholders. Accordingly, the argument runs, these provisions would apply *only* in the circumstance (not present here) where Avatex survives the merger and its certificate is amended thereby. Since the proposed merger with Xetava does not contemplate any such amendments to the disappearing Avatex certificate, the argument goes, the transaction can go forward without a First Series class vote.

* * *

The First Series Preferred holders claim to have the right to a class vote only if (a) a transaction effects the "amendment, alteration or repeal" of the rights provided in the certificate, *and* (b) "any right, preference, privilege or voting power of the First Series Preferred" would thereby be materially and adversely affected. For example, plaintiffs make clear that the First Series Preferred would not have a class vote on mergers where they receive the same security in a new entity or are cashed out. The attributes of the First Series Preferred would be intact but for the merger or might be continued if the certificate of the corporation surviving the merger—Xetava—provided for separate classes of stock, guaranteeing to these holders those same attributes. . . .

In our view, the merger does cause the adverse effect because the merger is the corporate act that renders the Avatex certificate that protects the preferred stockholders a "legal nullity," in defendants' words. That elimination certainly fits within the ambit of one or more of the three terms in the certificate: *amendment*, alteration, or *repeal.* The word *repeal* is especially fitting in this context because it contemplates a nullification, which is what defendants concede happens to the Avatex certificate.

[Ed. The Court then discusses its approach to construction of certificates in an attempt to provide guidance to the bar unnerved by *Warner* and its progeny.] Articulation of the rights of preferred stockholders is fundamentally the function of corporate drafters. Construction of the terms of preferred stock is the function of courts. This Court's function is essentially one of contract interpretation against the background of Delaware precedent. These precedential parameters are simply stated: Any rights, preferences, and limitations of preferred stock that distinguish that stock from common stock must be expressly and clearly stated, as provided by statute. Therefore, these rights, preferences, and limitations will not be presumed or implied.[46] The other doctrine states that when there is a hopeless ambiguity attributable to the corporate drafter that could mislead a reasonable investor such ambiguity must be construed in favor of the reasonable expectation of the investor and against the drafter. This latter doctrine is not applicable here because there is no ambiguity.

In our view, the rights of the First Series Preferred are expressly and clearly stated in the Avatex certificate. The drafters of this instrument could not reasonably have intended any consequence other than granting to the First Series Preferred stock the right to consent by a two-thirds class vote to any merger that would result in the elimination of the protections in the Avatex certificate if the rights of the holders of that stock would thereby be adversely affected. The First Series Preferred stock rights granted by the corporate drafters here are the functional equivalent of a provision that would expressly require such consent if a merger were to eliminate any provision of the Avatex certificate resulting in materially adverse consequences to the holders of that security.

* * *

It is important to place what we decide today in proper perspective. The outcome here continues a coherent and rational approach to corporate finance. The contrary result, in our view, would create an anomaly and could risk the erosion of uniformity in the corporation law. The Court of Chancery was mindful of this concern in referring to our general observations in *Kaiser* that the courts should avoid creating enduring uncertainties as to the meaning of boilerplate provisions in financial instruments. To be sure, there are some boilerplate aspects to the preferred stock provisions in the Avatex certificate and those found in other cases. But, one is struck by the disuniformity of some crucial provisions, such as the differences that exist when one compares the provisions in *Warner* and *Sullivan* with those presented here. That lack of uniformity is no doubt a function of (a) the adaptations by different drafters of some standard

[46] Rothschild Int'l Corp. v. Liggett Group Inc., Del. Supr., 474 A.2d 133, 136 (1984). See also Waggoner v. Laster, Del.Supr., 581 A.2d 1127, 1134–35 (1990). In *Waggoner*, the term "strictly construed" was used when describing the judicial approach to determining stock preferences in a case where the holding was that a general reservation clause in a certificate of incorporation was insufficient to expressly reserve authority in the board to establish preferences. We continue to approve that holding, but we do not approve the continued use of the term "strict construction" as appropriately describing the judicial process of analyzing the existence and scope of the contractual statement of preferences in certificates of incorporation or certificates of designations. We believe that the appropriate articulation of that analysis was set forth in our opinion in *Rothschild*: "Preferential rights are contractual in nature and therefore are governed by the express provisions of a company's certificate of incorporation. Stock preferences must also be clearly expressed and will not be presumed." 474 A. 2d at 136. The term "strict construction" (as contrasted to "liberal construction") is often used to describe the approach to statutes in derogation of common law, see *Waggoner*, 581 A. 2d at 1135 n. 9, or to certain contracts (e.g., forfeitures, penalties and restrictive covenants, see 4 WALTER H.E. JAEGER, WILLISTON ON CONTRACTS § 602A (3d ed.1961)). In light of other doctrines, continued use of the term "strict construction" as a substitute for, or gloss on, the Rothschild formulation is problematic. . . .

provisions; (b) negotiations by preferred stock investors seeking certain protections; (c) poor drafting; or (d) some combination of the above. . . .

* * *

NOTE: CONVERSIONS—CHANGES IN ENTITY FORM

The proliferation of small business forms has led to state legislatures amending their business legislation to enable a firm organized under one form to convert to another. Common, for example, is the conversion of a firm organized as a limited liability company (LLC) into a corporation (so as to enable the firm to make an initial public offering (IPO) of its common stock, for example). Again, mergers have been the method of choice. An LLC incorporates a shell Delaware corporation and merges the LLC with and into the corporation. Delaware's corporate code permits mergers between corporations and joint-stock companies, unincorporated associations, trusts, non-stock corporations, limited partnerships, and limited liability companies. See Del. Gen. Corp. L. §§ 254, 256, 257, 263 and 264.

Recently, states have begun to provide a short-form *conversion* procedure in new provisions for their domestic entities. In 1999, Delaware amended its corporate code to provide for conversions of limited liability companies, limited partnerships and business trusts into Delaware corporations and vice versa. Del. Gen. Corp. L. §§ 265–66. When an LLC converts into a corporation, the conversion must be approved in the manner provided for under the LLC act (and in operating agreements executed consistent with the Act). The most important advantage over the old merger procedure is that in the conversion section the corporation's date of existence relates back to the date the LLC commenced its existence. § 265(d). The express effect is that the conversion "shall not be deemed to constitute a dissolution of such other entity," § 265(f),[88] and "shall not be deemed to affect any obligations or liabilities of the other entity incurred prior to its conversion to a corporation . . . or the personal liability of any person incurred prior to such conversion." § 265(e).[89]

d. The Extraterritorial Effect of State Corporate Code Provisions on Shareholder Voting

The protection of local interests has spurred California and New York, among others, to enact legislation that applies to corporations incorporated in other states (*foreign corporations*) that do substantial business within state boundaries. The purpose of such statutes is to subject *tramp* corporations to minimum statutory safeguards applicable to domestic

---

[88] The firm is not, without more, required on the conversion to wind up its affairs, pay its liabilities or distribute its assets. The effect is similar to the "effect of a merger" provision in Del. Gen. Corp. L. § 259. These matters are discussed in detail in Chapter Three.

[89] Foreign non-corporate entities wishing to convert into Delaware corporations must still use the Delaware merger sections, however. Other states include foreign entities in their conversion sections. See, e.g., Colo. Rev. Stat. § 7–90–201(2).

corporations. A tramp corporation is a corporation whose primary contacts are with a foreign jurisdiction and not its state of incorporation. The extraterritorial statutes reduce the benefits for management to incorporate in one state while transacting its principal business in another. Under these provisions, state legislatures apply parts of their corporate codes to foreign corporations, which, of course, must also abide by the corporate codes of the incorporating jurisdiction.

States with added protection for shareholders in acquisitions, New York and California, have sought to apply those protections to tramp corporations doing business locally but incorporated in Delaware and other more lenient jurisdictions. Both states apply some part of their corporate code relating to mergers and acquisitions to qualifying foreign corporations doing business within their states. California subjects foreign corporations with a specified presence in the state[90] to its provisions on shareholder voting and appraisal rights in acquisitions.[91] Cal. Gen. Corp. L. § 2115(b). The section does not apply, however, to publicly traded corporations nor to wholly-owned subsidiaries of foreign corporations not subject to the section. *Id.* § 2115(c). New York's legislation is more limited. A New York statute imposes appraisal rights procedures on all foreign corporations doing business in the State of New York. N.Y. Bus. Corp. L. §§ 623 & 1319(a)(1).

The "internal affairs" doctrine announced in a series of Supreme Court cases on the constitutionality of state anti-takeover statutes would seem to put the California and New York provisions in doubt. See, e.g., *CTS Corp. v. Dynamics Corp. of America,* 481 U.S. 69, 107 S.Ct. 1637, 95 L.Ed.2d 67 (1987) (upholding the Indiana state anti-takeover statute because the statute did not violate the "internal affairs" doctrine). The internal affairs doctrine refers to exclusivity of the incorporating state's control over the structure and organization of domestic corporations. A state attempting to regulate the internal structure of a foreign corporation may violate the Commerce Clause of the United States Constitution if corporations are subject to inconsistent state regulations. However, the only court to reach the issue upheld the California provisions. *Wilson v. Louisiana-Pacific Resources, Inc.*, 138 Cal.App.3d 216, 187 Cal.Rptr. 852 (Cal. App. 1982). Of course, one would expect nothing less of a California court interpreting California corporate law!

The Delaware Courts have, not surprisingly, taken a dim view of the California legislation. Note what is at stake here. If California can impose its own M & A rules on deals that involve Delaware corporations with a

---

[90] Section 2115 applies if a foreign corporation meets certain property, payroll, sales and voting securities tests that indicate significant "contacts" or "presence" in California. See Cal. Gen. Corp. L. § 2115(a).

[91] Sections in the California Code on election and removal of directors and on indemnification of directors also apply to foreign corporations. See Cal. Gen. Corp. L. § 2115(b).

large presence in California, the advantage of incorporating in Delaware is largely lost.

VANTAGEPOINT VENTURE PARTNERS V. EXAMEN, INC.

Supreme Court of Delaware, 2005.
871 A.2d 1108.

HOLLAND, JUSTICE:

* * *

Delaware Action

On March 3, 2005, the plaintiff-appellant, Examen, Inc. ("Examen"), filed a Complaint in the Court of Chancery against VantagePoint Venture Partners, Inc. ("VantagePoint"), a Delaware Limited Partnership and an Examen Series A Preferred shareholder, seeking a judicial declaration that, pursuant to the controlling Delaware law and under the Company's Certificate of Designations of Series A Preferred Stock ("Certificate of Designations"), VantagePoint was not entitled to a class vote of the Series A Preferred Stock on the proposed merger between Examen and a Delaware subsidiary of Reed Elsevier Inc.

California Action

On March 8, 2005, VantagePoint filed an action in the California Superior Court seeking: (1) a declaration that Examen was required to identify whether it was a "quasi-California corporation" under section 2115 of the California Corporations Code;[1] (2) a declaration that Examen was a quasi-California corporation pursuant to California Corporations Code section 2115 and therefore subject to California Corporations Code section 1201(a), and that, as a Series A Preferred shareholder, VantagePoint was entitled to vote its shares as a separate class in connection with the proposed merger; (3) injunctive relief; and (4) damages incurred as the result of alleged violations of California Corporations Code sections 2111(a)(2)(F) and 1201.

---

[1] Section 2115 of the California Corporations Code purportedly applies to corporations that have contacts with the State of California, but are incorporated in other states. See Cal. Corp. Code § 171 (defining "foreign corporation"); and Cal. Corp. Code § 2115(a), (b). Section 2115 of the California Corporations Code provides that, irrespective of the state of incorporation, **foreign corporations' articles of incorporation are deemed amended** to comply with California law and are subject to the laws of California if certain criteria are met. See Cal. Corp. Code § 2115 (emphasis added). To qualify under the statute: (1) the average of the property factor, the payroll factor and the sales factor as defined in the California Revenue and Taxation Code must be more than 50% during its last full income year; and (2) more than one-half of its outstanding voting securities must be held by persons having addresses in California. *Id.* If a corporation qualifies under this provision, California corporate laws apply "to the exclusion of the law of the jurisdiction where [the company] is incorporated." *Id.* Included among the California corporate law provisions that would govern is California Corporations Code section 1201, which states that the principal terms of a reorganization shall be approved by the outstanding shares of each class of each corporation the approval of whose board is required. See Cal. Corp. Code §§ 2115, 1201.

* * *

Facts

Examen was a Delaware corporation engaged in the business of providing web-based legal expense management solutions to a growing list of Fortune 1000 customers throughout the United States. Following consummation of the merger on April 5, 2005, LexisNexis Examen, also a Delaware corporation, became the surviving entity. VantagePoint is a Delaware Limited Partnership organized and existing under the laws of Delaware. VantagePoint, a major venture capital firm that purchased Examen Series A Preferred Stock in a negotiated transaction, owned eighty-three percent of Examen's outstanding Series A Preferred Stock (909,091 shares) and no shares of Common Stock.

On February 17, 2005, Examen and Reed Elsevier executed the Merger Agreement, which was set to expire on April 15, 2005, if the merger had not closed by that date. Under the Delaware General Corporation Law and Examen's Certificate of Incorporation, including the Certificate of Designations for the Series A Preferred Stock, adoption of the Merger Agreement required the affirmative vote of the holders of a majority of the issued and outstanding shares of the Common Stock and Series A Preferred Stock, *voting together as a single class*. Holders of Series A Preferred Stock had the number of votes equal to the number of shares of Common Stock they would have held if their Preferred Stock was converted. Thus, VantagePoint, which owned 909,091 shares of Series A Preferred Stock and no shares of Common Stock, was entitled to vote based on a converted number of 1,392,727 shares of stock.

There were 9,717,415 total outstanding shares of the Company's capital stock (8,626,826 shares of Common Stock and 1,090,589 shares of Series A Preferred Stock), representing 10,297,608 votes on an as-converted basis. An affirmative vote of at least 5,148,805 shares, constituting a majority of the outstanding voting power on an as-converted basis, was required to approve the merger. If the stockholders were to vote by class, VantagePoint would have controlled 83.4 percent of the Series A Preferred Stock, which would have permitted VantagePoint to block the merger. VantagePoint acknowledges, if Delaware law applied, it would not have a class vote.

* * *

Internal Affairs Doctrine

In *CTS Corp. v. Dynamics Corp. of Am.*, the United States Supreme Court stated that it is "an accepted part of the business landscape in this country for States to create corporations, to prescribe their powers, and to define the rights that are acquired by purchasing their shares."[6] In *CTS*, it was also recognized that "[a] State has an interest in promoting stable relationships among parties involved in the corporations it charters, as well as in ensuring that investors in such corporations have an effective voice in corporate affairs."[7] The internal affairs doctrine is a long-standing choice of law principle which recognizes that only one state should have the authority to regulate a corporation's internal affairs—the state of incorporation.

The internal affairs doctrine developed on the premise that, in order to prevent corporations from being subjected to inconsistent legal standards, the authority to regulate a corporation's internal affairs should not rest with multiple jurisdictions. It is now well established that only the law of the state of incorporation governs and determines issues relating to a corporation's internal affairs. By providing certainty and predictability, the internal affairs doctrine protects the justified expectations of the parties with interests in the corporation.

The internal affairs doctrine applies to those matters that pertain to the relationships among or between the corporation and its officers, directors, and shareholders. . . .

The internal affairs doctrine is not, however, only a conflicts of law principle. Pursuant to the Fourteenth Amendment Due Process Clause, directors and officers of corporations "have a significant right . . . to know what law will be applied to their actions"[15] and "stockholders . . . have a right to know by what standards of accountability they may hold those managing the corporation's business and affairs." Under the Commerce Clause, a state "has no interest in regulating the internal affairs of foreign corporations." Therefore, this Court has held that an "application of the internal affairs doctrine is mandated by constitutional principles, except in the 'rarest situations,' " e.g., when "the law of the state of incorporation is inconsistent with a national policy on foreign or interstate commerce."

* * *

Examen is a Delaware corporation. The legal issue in this case—whether a preferred shareholder of a Delaware corporation had the right, under the corporation's Certificate of Designations, to a Series A Preferred Stock class vote on a merger—clearly involves the relationship among a corporation and its shareholders. As the United States Supreme Court held in *CTS*, "no principle of corporation law and practice is more firmly

---

[6] *CTS Corp. v. Dynamics Corp. of Am.*, 481 U.S. 69, 91, 95 L. Ed. 2d 67, 107 S. Ct. 1637 (1987).

[7] *Id.*

[15] *McDermott Inc. v. Lewis*, [531 A.2d 206, 216 (Del.1987)]. [Ed. The quotes in this paragraph are all from this case.]

established than a *State's authority* to regulate domestic corporations, including the authority to *define the voting rights of shareholders*."

In *CTS*, the Supreme Court held that the Commerce Clause "prohibits States from regulating subjects that 'are in their nature national, or admit only of one uniform system, or plan of regulation,' " and acknowledged that the internal affairs of a corporation are subjects that require one uniform system of regulation. In *CTS*, the Supreme Court concluded that "so long as each State regulates voting rights *only in the corporations it has created*, each corporation will be subject to the law of only one State." Accordingly, we hold Delaware's well-established choice of law rules and the federal constitution mandated that Examen's internal affairs, and in particular, VantagePoint's voting rights, be adjudicated exclusively in accordance with the law of its state of incorporation, in this case, the law of Delaware.

* * *

VantagePoint acknowledges that the courts of Delaware, as the forum state, may apply Delaware's own substantive choice of law rules. VantagePoint argues, however, that Delaware's "choice" to apply the law of the state of incorporation to internal affairs issues—notwithstanding California's enactment of section 2115—will result in future forum shopping races to the courthouse. VantagePoint submits that, if the California action in these proceedings had been decided first, the California Superior Court would have enjoined the merger until it was factually determined whether section 2115 is applicable. If the statutory prerequisites were found to be factually satisfied, VantagePoint submits that the California Superior Court would have applied the internal affairs law reflected in section 2115, "to the exclusion" of the law of Delaware—the state where Examen is incorporated.

In support of those assertions, VantagePoint relies primarily upon a 1982 decision by the California Court of Appeals, *Wilson v. Louisiana-Pacific Resources, Inc.*[41] . . .

Wilson was decided before the United States Supreme Court's decision in *CTS* and before this Court's decision in *McDermott*. Ten years after *Wilson*, the California Supreme Court cited with approval this Court's analysis of the internal affairs doctrine in *McDermott*, in particular, our holding that corporate voting rights disputes are governed by the law of the state of incorporation.[45] Two years ago, in *State Farm v. Superior Court*, a different panel of the California Court of Appeals questioned the validity

---

41 *Wilson v. La. Pac. Res., Inc.*, 138 Cal. App. 3d 216, 187 Cal. Rptr. 852 (1982).

45 See *Nedlloyd Lines B.V. v. Superior Court*, 3 Cal. 4th 459, 11 Cal. Rptr. 2d 330, 834 P.2d 1148, 1155 (Cal. 1992), *citing McDermott Inc. v. Lewis*, 531 A.2d 206 (Del. 1987).

of the holding in *Wilson* following the broad acceptance of the internal affairs doctrine over the two decades after *Wilson* was decided.[46] . . .

* * *

3. THE DISSENTING SHAREHOLDERS' APPRAISAL REMEDY

Shareholders of the constituent firms who object to a transaction may have, by state statute, *dissenters' rights* (also *appraisal rights* or *buy out rights*). Shareholders holding appraisal rights may petition a court for the fair value of their shares payable to dissenters in cash by the acquirer. The right is, in essence, a contingent put right on the firm; the strike price is *fair value* as determined by a court and the rights vest on the closing of a transaction. When the appraisal remedy is available, it provides a vital judicial double-check on the fairness of the price that the acquirer paid.

The appraisal remedy in state corporate codes is currently in flux. The remedy's historic origins are no longer salient[92] and it is searching for an elusive, modern justification.[93] State by state disagreements over which shareholders should be entitled to the remedy are common. Moreover, internal to any state code are often idiosyncratic distinctions among deal types. An acquisition planner is well advised to always check the details of the appropriate state provision for any given transaction.

These rights are not trivial. Appraisal proceedings occur frequently enough to be of concern to those planning acquisitions.[94] For example, if a substantial minority block of shareholders demands cash in these proceedings, and the constituent firms in a stock swap acquisition are cash poor, the mere notice by the dissenting shareholders that they might assert their appraisal rights can threaten an acquisition. Many acquisition agreements in stock swap deals expressly condition a closing on the absence of even a small percentage (three percent or more) of target

[46] *State Farm Mut. Auto. Ins. Co. v. Superior Court*, 114 Cal.App.4th 434, 8 Cal.Rptr.3d 56 (2d Dist.2003).

[92] State legislatures granted dissenting shareholders appraisal rights in exchange for loosening the unanimous shareholder vote requirement for statutory mergers. These rights were the quid pro quo for taking away a shareholder's veto power over such transactions. Any shareholder who did not want to go along with the majority of shareholders who approved the transaction could cash out her shares at fair value and move on. See Jeffrey J. Haas, CORPORATE FINANCE 89 (1st ed. 2014).

[93] Some see it as protection for minority shareholders in transactions, others see it as a nuisance given that case law on fiduciary duty provides adequate protections for minority shareholders.

[94] See Wei Jiang, Tao Li, Danquin Mei & Randall Thomas, *Reforming the Delaware Appraisal Statute to Address Appraisal Arbitrage*, 59 J. L. & ECON. (2016) (hereinafter *Reforming Delaware Appraisal*). The authors of this article looked at the 1,566 Delaware corporations involved in transactions in which the appraisal remedy was available during the years 2000–2014. Dissenters in 225 transactions, or approximately 14 percent, sought appraisal rights. The likelihood of an appraisal proceeding was highly correlated to the relative premium offered in the transaction when compared to the pre-transaction market price.

shareholders claiming dissenters' rights. See the facts of *Good v. Lackawanna Leather Co., supra,* in Section A.2.b.vi.

In all types of acquisitions it can be very embarrassing to the parties involved if a state judge awards a dissenting shareholder an amount in cash that is significantly different than the deal consideration. If the award is higher than the deal consideration, it looks like the target's board agreed to sell the target for too low a price, much to the dismay of the target's assenting shareholders. By contrast, if the award is lower than the deal consideration, it looks like the acquiring firm's board overpaid for the target, much to the displeasure of the acquiring firm's shareholders.

There are four central issues in the basic definition of the appraisal remedy: First, what kinds of transactions support the right; second, what are the procedural requirements for perfecting the right; third, how do courts determine "fair value"; and fourth, whether the right is the exclusive remedy for dissenting shareholders. These four central issues are addressed in order in the following four subsections.

a. The Availability of the Appraisal Remedy

Section 262 of the Del. Gen. Corp. L. defines appraisal rights for shareholders of Delaware corporations. It is a hard read with several double-negatives. The *general rule* is that dissenting shareholders in statutory mergers who have a right to vote and minority shareholders in short- and medium-form mergers (who do not have a right to vote) receive appraisal rights.[95] To qualify as a dissenting shareholder, the shareholder must not vote yes on the disputed transaction[96] and must hold the shares from the date of her demand for an appraisal (required before the vote) through the effective date of the acquisition. Del. Gen. Corp. L. § 262(a).

Despite the general rule, mergers involving Delaware corporations do not give rise to the appraisal remedy in four notable instances. The first involves the *market-out exception* under Sections 262(b)(1) and (2) of the Del. Gen. Corp. L. Pursuant to this exception, shareholders whose shares are currently listed on a national securities exchange or, if not listed, are held of record by more than 2,000 shareholders *do not* receive appraisal rights if they are to receive as merger consideration: (a) shares of stock in

95 Delaware, like all states, gives shareholders in short-form mergers appraisal rights even though shareholders of the subsidiary do not vote on the merger. In short-form mergers, a 90 percent or more owned subsidiary can merge with and into its parent (an upstream merger) without a vote of the subsidiary's shareholders. See Del. Gen. Corp. L. § 253. By contrast, only a few states (Maryland, Texas and Virginia) have followed Delaware's lead with respect to medium-form mergers. These mergers are second-step mergers that follow successful friendly first-step tender offers. No vote of the shareholders of the target company (which is now a subsidiary after the first-step tender offer) is needed to approve a second-step merger if, prior to the first-step tender offer, a provision is inserted into the merger agreement between the parties indicating that no such vote would be held (an "opt-in" requirement). In other words, the parties avoid the need to have a shareholder vote if the parties follow the provisions of § 251(h) of the Del. Gen. Corp. L.

96 The shareholder must vote no or abstain, execute a proxy empowering an agent to vote no or abstain, execute a written consent form voting no or abstain, or otherwise not vote at all.

the surviving corporation; (b) shares of stock of another corporation (e.g., a parent company) so long as those shares are listed on a national securities exchange or, if not listed, are held of record by more than 2,000 shareholders; (c) cash in lieu of fractional shares; or (d) any combination of the foregoing.[97]

Importantly, the market-out exception does not apply to shareholders of a public company who receive, among other things, cash (other than for fractional shares) and/or debt securities as merger consideration. Those public shareholders have their appraisal rights restored under § 262(b)(2) of the Del. Gen. Corp. L. This, therefore, is an "exception to the exception."

The market-out exception recognizes that the market is superior to a judge when it comes to fairly valuing the shares of dissenting public shareholders. If those shareholders are to receive stock as merger consideration, the market-out exception encourages them to simply cash out before the merger is consummated by selling their shares in the open market. When dissenting public shareholders are forced to receive cash as merger consideration, by contrast, the market may not provide a fair valuation. Indeed, the trading price of a target company's stock typically trades within a narrow band of the per share cash price being offered by the prospective acquirer. Dissenting public shareholders in that situation should (and do) receive appraisal rights because the market price at which they otherwise could cash out is overly influenced by the cash merger consideration being offered by that acquirer. That consideration may not be fair to the target's shareholders.

The second exception is the *no vote exception* under § 262(b)(1) of the Del. Gen. Corp. L. It states that shareholders of the *surviving corporation* in the merger do not receive appraisal rights if they were not entitled to vote on the merger under § 251(f) of the Del. Gen. Corp. L. Section 251(f) states that shareholders of the surviving corporation are not entitled to vote if (a) the merger agreement does not amend the charter of the surviving corporation, (b) each share of stock after the merger is identical in terms of rights, preferences, privileges, etc. as each share was prior to the merger, and (c) either (1) no shares of the surviving corporation are to be issued as merger consideration in the transaction or (2) the additional shares of the surviving corporation to be issued as merger consideration do not exceed 20 percent of the outstanding shares of the surviving corporation prior to the merger (and thus the dilutive effect to existing surviving corporation shareholders is minimal).

The third exception is the *holding company exception* under § 262(b) of the Del. Gen. Corp. L. Pursuant to it, shareholders of companies engaged in a merger effected solely to create a holding company structure in

[97] Shareholders involved in a § 251(h) medium-form merger are still entitled to appraisal rights even if the merger consideration they receive is publicly traded stock. See Del. Gen. Corp. L. § 262(b)(3).

accordance with § 251(g) of the Del. Gen. Corp. L. do not receive appraisal rights.

Fourth and finally, in 2016 the Delaware legislature modified subsection (g) of § 262 to add a *de minimis exception.* With respect to a constituent corporation to a merger or consolidation with shares listed on a national securities exchange, the Chancery Court *must dismiss* all appraisal proceedings as to all shareholders of shares of that corporation *unless* (1) the total number of shares entitled to appraisal exceeds 1 percent of the outstanding shares of the class or series eligible for appraisal, (2) the value of the consideration provided in the merger or consolidation for such total number of shares exceeds $1 million, or (3) the merger was approved pursuant to the short-form merger provision of Del. Gen. Corp. L. § 253 or 267.[98]

Delaware's appraisal provision is one of the most limited of all such provisions in state corporate codes for several reasons. First, the Delaware provision applies only to mergers; it does not apply in asset sales under § 271,[99] nor to amendments to the Certificate of Incorporation under § 242. Second, as noted above, the Delaware provision has four important exceptions to the general rule that shareholders of the constituent corporations to a merger receive appraisal rights, and thus shareholders do not in those situations. Third, the Delaware provision does not shift attorney or expert witness fees to the corporation if a shareholder prevails absent a court determination of bad faith.

Most jurisdictions do not follow Delaware's lead. For example, most states provide appraisal rights to the shareholders of the selling firm in an asset sale, although some states do not provide appraisal rights in all types of asset sales.[100] Over half the states give appraisal rights to dissenting shareholders on certain amendments to the Articles or Certificate of Incorporation. Some states grant dissenters' rights to shareholders of a corporation in stock acquisitions of a controlling block of its shares.

---

[98] Authors of one study found that about 32 percent of appraisal proceedings in the author's large sample of companies involved stakes below $1 million and constituted less than 1 percent of the company's stock. See *Reforming Delaware Appraisal*, *supra* note 94, at 700. Authors of another study found that the value of the stock holdings of the median appraisal dissenter was $1.8 million and the median percentage ownership was approximately 1 percent of the company in question. See Charles R. Korsmo & Minor Myers, *The Structure of Stockholder Litigation: When Do the Merits Matter?*, 75 OHIO ST. L. J. 829 (2014).

[99] The lack of appraisal rights in asset acquisitions makes Delaware asset acquisitions very attractive to acquisition planners.

[100] The New York Business Corporation Law and 2016 version of the ABA Model Business Corporation Act give appraisal rights to shareholders of corporations selling substantially all their assets for stock in the purchasing corporation except when shareholder approval of an all cash-for-assets transaction is conditioned upon the dissolution of the corporation (and distribution of the cash) within one year from the date of the transaction. N.Y. Bus. Corp. L. § 910 (a)(B); ABA Model Bus. Corp. Act § 13.02(a)(3) (2016 rev.). California provides appraisal rights to selling firm shareholders in stock-for-assets acquisitions but not cash-for-assets acquisitions, regardless of whether the selling firm dissolves. Cal. Gen. Corp. L. § 1300 (omitting reference to § 1001 transactions).

Appraisal rights are controversial and continually evolving.[101] The 1984 version of the ABA Revised Model Business Corporation Act contains a chapter on appraisal rights that is one of the most liberal grants of appraisal rights in the history of state corporate codes. In a complete reversal of approach, the Committee on Corporate Laws recommended in 1999 that states adopt a new chapter that substantially reduces the scope of the chapter that had been in place since 1984. The 2016 version of the Model Act continues to reflect this reduced scope.

The 2016 version of the Model Act competes with Delaware for the title of most conservative state provision. The 2016 version de-links shareholder voting and appraisal rights.[102] Note the contrast with the Delaware provisions. With the 2016 provisions, purchasing firm shareholders in a Model Act state that are entitled to vote on an acquisition because of a 20 percent dilution are not entitled to appraisal rights if the transaction would not alter the terms of the securities they hold.[103] In Delaware such shareholders have appraisal rights. The 2016 Model Act provisions include a market-out exception that is both broader and narrower than the Delaware exemption. The Model Act exemption does apply (that is the Act does not give appraisal rights) to shareholders in publicly traded companies that receive cash for their shares.[104] The Model Act's market-out exception does not apply (appraisal rights do lie) in "conflict-of-interest" transactions or when the consideration is stock in a privately held survivor.[105] The 2016 revision continues to limit appraisal rights in some asset acquisitions; if a selling firm liquidates within a year of a transaction and the shareholders receive cash, selling firm shareholders do not have appraisal rights.[106]

---

[101] The classic attack is in Bayless Manning, *The Shareholders' Appraisal Remedy: An Essay for Frank Coker*, 72 YALE L. J. 223 (1962).

[102] See ABA Model Bus. Corp. Act § 13.02(a)(5) (2016 rev.). Appraisal rights may be augmented, however, by amendments to the Certificate of Incorporation or the Bylaws or by a simple board of directors resolution. See *id.*

[103] The interaction of the 2016 Model Act appraisal rights section with the revisions to its acquisition provisions shows that the ABA agrees substantially with California on voting rights for purchasing corporations in triangular mergers and asset acquisitions. The ABA does not, however, follow California on the grant of appraisal rights in such transactions. Section 6.21(f) of the 2016 Model Act gives voting rights to purchasing shareholders in triangular acquisitions, but Section 13.02 does not seem to give those same shareholders appraisal rights if they dissent (the corporation must be "a party" to the merger).

[104] The Model Act, sensibly, reserves appraisal rights for those shareholders holding illiquid investments or for those shareholders who receive illiquid investments as consideration. The market-out exception in the Model Act is preferable to the Delaware version.

[105] A conflict of interest exists when senior managers or controlling shareholders have interests in both parties in an acquisition. The market exemption is not lost, however, if senior management receives specified financial benefits from employment, consulting, or severance contracts in the transaction.

[106] ABA Model Bus. Corp. Act § 13.02(a)(3) (2016 rev.).

NOTE: CONTRACTUAL MODIFICATION OF APPRAISAL RIGHTS

The Delaware courts have long held that preferred shareholders can contractually waive or modify their rights to appraisal *ex ante*,[107] so long as such waiver or modification is clear.[108] If no such waiver or modification exists, then preferred shareholders have the same appraisal rights as common shareholders in the event of a merger. According to the Delaware Chancery Court:

> As a general rule, preferred stock has the same appraisal rights as common stock, but '[u]nlike common stock, the value of preferred stock is determined solely from the contract rights conferred upon it in the certificate of designation.' Thus, 'when determining the fair value of preferred stock, the court must consider the contract upon which the preferred stock's value was based[.]'

In re Appraisal of Goodcents Holdings, Inc., 2017 WL 2463665, at *3 (Del. Ch.) (quoting *Shiftan v. Morgan Joseph Hldgs., Inc.*, 57 A.3d 928, 942 (Del. Ch. 2012)).

A contractual waiver or modification of appraisal rights for preferred stock is commonplace. *In re Appraisal of Ford Holdings Preferred Stock,* 698 A.2d 973, 977 (Del. Ch. 1997), held that the holders of preferred stock were not entitled to a full-blown appraisal of their shares where the terms of the shares established a predetermined consideration in the event of a merger. As highlighted by Chancellor Allen:

> All of the characteristics of the preferred are open for negotiation; that is the nature of the security. There is no utility in defining as forbidden any term thought advantageous to informed parties, unless that term violates substantive law. Particularly, there is no utility in forbidding the parties creating a preferred stock (the issuer, its advisors and counsel, and the underwriter and its counsel) from establishing a security that has a stated value (or a value established by a stated formula) in the event of stated contingencies.
>
> The general rule applies as with all contracting parties: that which is a valid contract will be enforced either specifically or through a damages action, unless the contract violates positive law or its non-performance is excused. I cannot conclude that a provision that establishes the cash value of a preferred stock in the event of a cash-out merger would violate the public policy reflected in Section 262, given the essentially contractual nature of preferred stock. . . .

The 2016 version of the Model Act has included a contractual waiver for preferred shareholders in its appraisal section, so long as preferred shareholders have the right to vote separately as a group on the transaction in

---

107 See Halpin v. Riverstone Nat'l, Inc., 2015 WL 854724, at *1 (Del. Ch.); In re Appraisal of Metromedia Int'l Group, Inc., 971 A.2d 893, 901–03 (Del. Ch. 2009).

108 Metromedia Int'l Group, Inc., 971 A.2d at 900.

question. If the waiver is added through a charter amendment, the waiver is required to have a one year delayed effective date.[109]

What about common shareholders? Can they contractually waive their right to appraisal? In *Halpin v. Riverstone National, Inc.*, 2015 WL 854724, at *1 (Del. Ch.), the Chancery Court noted that, while the rights of preferred shareholders are largely contractual:

> [T]he relationships between the common stockholders (the residual owners of the corporation), the directors (the fiduciaries managing the corporation on those owners' behalf), and the majority stockholder—if any—having voting control over the corporation (who also stands as a fiduciary to the minority stockholders in certain situations) are in the main governed by the Delaware General Corporation Law and the common law of fiduciary relationships. The question of whether common stockholders can, *ex ante*, waive the right to seek statutory appraisal in the case of a squeeze-out merger of the corporation is therefore more nuanced than is the case with preferred stockholders. That question has not yet been answered by a court of this jurisdiction.

The case itself involved minority common shareholders seeking appraisal of their shares after a June 2014 acquisition of their corporation by a third party. The corporation, however, sought summary judgment based on a stockholders agreement between the corporation and certain minority shareholders, including those seeking appraisal. The agreement provided the corporation with "drag along" rights. In case a change of control transaction was proposed, the corporation could compel the minority to vote in favor of it. Such a favorable vote would render the minority ineligible to seek appraisal. The corporation viewed its "drag along" rights as a forced contractual waiver of appraisal by the minority.

Ruling on other grounds, the Court refused to settle the issue of whether common shareholders, like preferred shareholders, can contractual waive their right to appraisal *ex ante*. Because a majority shareholder existed at the time, the corporation secured that shareholder's written consent to the merger under Del. Gen. Corp. L. § 228 *prior* to asserting its "drag along" rights under the stockholders agreement. The Court noted that the "drag along" provision was entirely prospective:

> [T]he Minority Stockholders agreed to, upon advanced notice, tender or vote in favor of a merger that has been "proposed[d];" the Minority Stockholders did *not* agree to, upon notice after the fact, consent to a merger that has been consummated. The Company bargained for a right it did not exercise, and not the similar right it attempted to exercise. . . . [T]he Company is limited to the benefit of its bargain, which, according to the literal language of the Drag-Along, does not

---

[109] ABA Model Bus. Corp. Act § 13.02(c) (2016 rev.).

> include the power to require Minority Stockholders to consent to a transaction that has already taken place.

Id. at *9.

The Court also refused to entertain the corporation's request for specific performance based on the implied covenant of good faith and fair dealing implicit in the stockholders agreement. According to the Court, the corporation "agreed to drag-along rights that by their unambiguous terms did not apply" retroactively. *Id.* at *10. Thus, the minority shareholders were not "attempting to take advantage of a situation that was unanticipated or unforeseeable at the time of contracting[,]" as both parties were aware that a merger could be carried out by written consent under Del. Gen. Corp. L. § 228. *Id.*

b. The Appraisal Procedure

Under Delaware law, a corporation contemplating a transaction that gives rise to shareholder appraisal rights must notify shareholders of these rights twenty days before the corporation submits the transaction to shareholders for approval. See Del. Gen. Corp. L. § 262(d). Each dissenting shareholder demanding appraisal rights must then notify the corporation of an intent to dissent before the vote on the transaction. If shareholders ratify the transaction, the corporation must notify dissenting shareholders who gave proper notice that appraisal rights are available. This second corporate notification occurs within ten days of the transaction's effective date (not the date of the vote). If the shareholder is unsatisfied with the terms of the merger, she must, within 120 days of the transaction's effective date, file a petition in the Court of Chancery demanding a determination of the fair value of her stock.[110] A trial on the petition can take several years and the dissatisfied shareholder may not receive money for her shares for quite some time, unless the surviving corporation voluntarily chooses to make a payment to the shareholder.[111] From the time of the effective date of the merger until the time the appraisal proceeding is concluded or settled, the dissenting shareholder can neither vote the shares nor receive any distributions on the stock. Del. Gen. Corp. L. § 262(k).[112]

---

110 See Del. Gen. Corp. L. § 262(d). The shareholder can, within 60 days of the effective date, unilaterally withdraw the action and take the terms of the merger. Thereafter, the shareholder can settle the litigation only with the assent of the firm. See *id.*

111 In 2016, the Delaware legislature amended Del. Gen. Corp. L. § 262(h) so as to allow a surviving corporation to pay an amount in cash to dissenting shareholders *prior* to the entry of judgment in an appraisal proceeding. The stated purpose of the amendment was to allow surviving corporations to halt interest from accruing on any amount they prepay, and thus reduce the attractiveness of so-called *interest rate arbitrage*. Indeed, if the surviving corporation makes a prepayment, interest will only accrue on (a) the difference, if any, between the prepayment amount and the fair value of the shares as determined by the Chancery Court and (2) interest already accrued at the time the surviving corporation makes the prepayment, unless accrued interest is also paid at that time.

112 Pursuant to Del. Gen. Corp. L. § 262(h), a shareholder is entitled to interest from the effective date of the merger. In terms of the rate of interest, and whether it should be simple or compound, Section 262(h) states:

The appraisal procedures in the ABA Model Business Corporation Act are significantly different from the procedures in Delaware's corporate code. The Model Act seeks to readjust the balance between the corporation and the dissenting shareholders in favor of shareholders. The principal changes are aimed, first, at eliminating much of the delay in getting funds into the hands of dissenting shareholders; second, at forcing corporations to take more initiative in settling the claims; and third, at shifting more of the expenses of the procedure to the corporation.

As in Delaware, Model Act corporations, in their notice of a shareholder meeting, must inform shareholders of their appraisal rights and dissenting shareholders must give the corporation a written notice before the pivotal shareholder meeting of their intent to demand payment. Model Bus. Corp. Act §§ 1320 & 1321. Once the transaction is effective, however, the Model Act corporation has additional duties.

The Model Act corporation must, within ten days, notify the dissenting shareholders of the maturation of their appraisal rights and send them a specified form. Model Bus. Corp. Act § 1322. If the dissenting shareholder returns the form and his shares within forty days and demands payment, the corporation must pay that shareholder, within thirty days, cash equal to the corporation's estimated fair value for the shares, plus interest. Model Bus. Corp. Act §§ 1322–1324. (In Delaware, a surviving corporation has the right but not the obligation to make such a payment.[113]) If the dissenting shareholder is dissatisfied with the amount, she may, within thirty days of payment, inform the corporation of her estimate of value. Model Bus. Corp. Act § 1326. If the corporation fails to settle the discrepancy, the corporation must commence a proceeding within sixty days of the shareholder's demand to determine the fair value of the shares. If the corporation fails to settle or sue, it must pay the shareholder her demand. Model Bus. Corp. Act § 1330. The effect of the Model Act's procedure is to mandate that a

---

> Unless the Court in its discretion determines otherwise for good cause, interest from the effective date of the merger through the date of payment of the judgment shall be compounded quarterly and shall accrue at 5% over the Federal Reserve discount rate (including any surcharge) as established from time to time during the period between the effective date of the merger and the date of payment of the judgment.

This rate is referred to as the *legal rate of interest* in Delaware.

The 2007 amendment to Del. Gen. Corp. L. § 262(h) resolved a long-running battle over the rate of interest to be awarded, and whether interest would be simple interest or compound interest. Chancellor Chandler, in In re Appraisal of Metromedia Int'l Group, Inc., 971 A.2d 898 (Del. Ch. 2009), noted that the "[t]he question of interest on an appraisal judgment has been mercifully simplified. In 2007, the Delaware General Assembly amended the appraisal statute to provide a simple default rule . . . unless good cause is shown to depart from it." *Id.* at 906. In Merion Capital, L.P. v. 3M Cogent, Inc., 2013 WL 3793896 (Del. Ch.), the Delaware Chancery Court applied the legal rate of interest to the value of the petitioners' shares despite the objections of the respondent. The Court, however, acknowledged that, under Section 262(h), "[a]dopting a different rate [of interest] may be justified where it is necessary to avoid an inequitable result, such as where there has been improper delay or a bad faith assertion of valuation claims." *Id.* at *23.

[113] See Del. Gen. Corp. L. § 262(h); *supra* note 111.

surviving corporation place significant cash in the hands of dissenters soon after the transaction closes.

The most important feature of the Delaware appraisal right is, perhaps, that the dissenting shareholders' attorney and expert fees are not shifted to the corporation unless some equitable exception (such as bad faith) applies.[114] However, one shareholder can seek fees against other shareholders who have also profited from the award.[115] Shareholders in Delaware ought not sue unless they can cover the corporation's offer and the potential expenses of attorneys and experts that can run into six figures. The Model Act gives courts more latitude to shift such expenses to the corporation.[116] ABA Model Bus. Corp. Act § 13.31(a) (2016 rev.).

c. Fair Value

A shareholder perfecting her appraisal rights is entitled to the "fair value" of her shares in cash from the surviving or resulting firm. Del. Gen. Corp. L. § 262(h). There are several intriguing legal questions that set the context of any appraisal valuation. First, does the court start by valuing the entire firm (and give the dissenters a pro rata portion) or calculating the value of just the dissenters' stock (with a discount for those shares' minority status)? Second, what is the relevant date of valuation (just before or after the announcement, at the time of the vote, or at the time of closing)? And third, what is the relationship of the appraisal remedy to actions based on breach of fiduciary duty? Each legal issue is considered in order below. This subsection ends with an example of a court opinion on valuation that answers why the acquisition price agreed to by the parties may not be representative of "fair value."

i. Minority Discounts and the Appraisal Remedy

CAVALIER OIL CORP. V. HARNETT

Supreme Court of Delaware, 1989.
564 A.2d 1137.

WALSH, JUSTICE:

This is an appeal by Cavalier Oil Corporation ("Cavalier") and a cross-appeal by William J. Harnett ("Harnett") from a final judgment of the Court of Chancery determining the fair value of 1,250 shares of stock owned by Harnett in EPIC Mortgage Servicing, Inc. ("EMSI"), a closely-

---

114 See M.G. Bancorporation, Inc. v. Le Beau, 737 A.2d 513, 527 (Del. 1999).

115 See Del. Gen. Corp. L. § 262(j). The court may shift the claimant's "costs of the proceeding" to the firm but these are nominal, including only court filing fees, court reporter copying charges and the like.

116 According to ABA Model Bus. Corp. Act § 13.31(a) (2106 rev.), "The court shall assess the court costs against the corporation, except that the court may assess court costs against all or some of the shareholders demanding appraisal, in amounts which the court finds equitable, to the extent the court finds such shareholders acted arbitrarily, vexatiously, or not in good faith . . . ."

held Delaware corporation. The appraisal action followed a short form merger, pursuant to 8 Del.C. § 253, of EMSI into Cavalier on November 20, 1984.

* * *

Cavalier's final claim of error is directed to the Vice Chancellor's refusal to apply a minority discount in valuing Harnett's EMSI stock. Cavalier contends that Harnett's "de minimus" (1.5 percent) interest in EMSI is one of the "relevant factors" which must be considered under *Weinberger's* expanded valuation standard. In rejecting a minority or marketability discount, the Vice Chancellor concluded that the objective of a section 262 appraisal is "to value the *corporation* itself, as distinguished from a specific fraction of its *shares* as they may exist in the hands of a particular shareholder" [emphasis in original]. We believe this to be a valid distinction.

* * *

The application of a discount to a minority shareholder is contrary to the requirement that the company be viewed as a "going concern." Cavalier's argument, that the only way Harnett would have received value for his 1.5 percent stock interest was to sell his stock, subject to market treatment of its minority status, misperceives the nature of the appraisal remedy. Where there is no objective market data available, the appraisal process is not intended to reconstruct a *pro forma* sale but to assume that the shareholder was willing to maintain his investment position, however slight, had the merger not occurred. Discounting individual share holdings injects into the appraisal process speculation on the various factors that may dictate the marketability of minority shareholdings. More important, to fail to accord to a minority shareholder the full proportionate value of his shares imposes a penalty for lack of control, and unfairly enriches the majority shareholders who may reap a windfall from the appraisal process by cashing out a dissenting shareholder, a clearly undesirable result. . . .

NOTE: PROBLEMS IN APPLICATION—BUILT-IN MINORITY DISCOUNTS AND CONTROL PREMIA

The notion seems simple enough. First, value the firm as an ongoing entity. Next, pro rate the value over the number of shares outstanding. Finally, multiple the per share value so determined by the number of shares held by the dissenters. The concept creates immediate complications, however. Buyers normally pay a premium over market trading price when purchasing an entire firm. The premium represents both a *control premium*, a price paid for legal control of a firm, and a part of a division of any joint gains created specific to the deal (synergy gains, for example). In other words, there is a division between trading prices in liquid markets and acquisition prices. Yet the prices are interconnected because the trading prices reflect the probability and amount of any acquisition price.[117]

If courts use acquisition prices to value a firm, neutral of any gains specific to a deal, then appraisers must adjust trading prices upward to include a control premium. A commonly used figure of firm value, *market capitalization* (or *market cap*), is the stock price of a publicly traded firm times the number of outstanding shares.[118] Is this necessarily too low for a fair value? In other words, the trading markets price non-control shares with a *built in discount* because of their lack of control. Similarly, when appraisers use a comparable publicly held company stock price to value an entire privately held firm (with stock traded in an illiquid market), the comparable firm per share trading price must also be adjusted upwards.[119] Moreover, the adjustment, as noted below, must section off gains specific to a merger. Is this hypothetical inquiry beyond the capacity of courts?

A rule much easier for courts to apply would focus on trading market prices alone (or, for illiquid markets, synthetic trading market prices based on multiples from comparable companies that do have public trading markets). There is some sense to the rule. If minority shareholders sold in the trading markets, would they not exit at a discount? Is not anything over that price a windfall? Did most minority shareholders not buy at prices reflecting a minority discount? Of course, in a merger context, minority shareholders are forced to give up their shares—they are not willing sellers in the secondary market. Should this make a difference?

The control premium issue becomes even more complex when the company being valued is a holding company. A holding company does not produce goods and services itself; rather, its purpose is to own a controlling interest in subsidiary companies that do produce goods and services. Thus, it is a parent corporation which owns, in whole or in part, other corporations.

How should a holding company be valued, and does a control premium play any role? Consider Justice Holland's statements in *M.G. Bancorporation, Inc. v. Le Beau*, 737 A.2d 513, 518, 524–25 (Del. 1999), as he reviews the valuation of MGB, a parent corporation that owned two bank subsidiaries:

> In performing his analysis, [expert witness] Clarke added a control premium to the values of the two subsidiaries to reflect the value of MGB's controlling interest in those subsidiaries. He then added the value of MGB's remaining assets to his valuations of the two subsidiaries. Clarke arrived at an overall fair value of $85 per share for MGB.

---

117 See William J. Carney & Mark Heimendinger, *Appraising the Nonexistent: The Delaware Courts' Struggle with Control Premiums*, 152 U. PA. L. REV. 845 (2003) (probability of a control transaction is already reflected in the market price; where the probability is close to zero, the premium is zero).

118 If one includes in the calculation the assumption that all options and warrants are exercised, the figure is said to be *diluted*; otherwise, it is *undiluted*.

119 See Rapid-American Corp. v. Harris, 603 A.2d 796, 806 (Del.1992) (rejecting valuation because the trial court did not add a control premium to the market price of comparables).

* * *

This Court has held that in valuing a holding company in a statutory appraisal proceeding, pursuant to Section 262, it is appropriate to include a control premium for majority ownership of a subsidiary as an element of the holding company's fair value of the majority-owned subsidiaries.[36] In *Rapid-American*, this Court stated:

> Rapid was a parent company with a 100 percent ownership interest in three valuable subsidiaries. The trial court's decision to exclude the control premium at the corporate level practically discounted Rapid's entire inherent value. The exclusion of a "control premium" artificially and unrealistically treated Rapid as a minority shareholder [of its own subsidiaries]. Contrary to Rapid's argument, Delaware law compels the inclusion of a control premium under the unique facts of this case. Rapid's 100 percent ownership interest in its subsidiaries was clearly a "relevant" valuation factor and the trial court's rejection of the "control premium" implicitly placed a disproportionate emphasis on pure market value.[37]

Based upon the foregoing statements from Rapid-American, the Court of Chancery concluded that [expert witness] Clarke's comparative acquisition approach, which includes a control premium for a majority interest in a subsidiary, was a relevant and reliable methodology to use in a Section 262 statutory appraisal proceeding to determine the fair market value of shares in a holding company.

"The underlying assumption in an appraisal valuation is that the dissenting shareholders would be willing to maintain their investment position had the merger not occurred."[38] Accordingly, the corporation must be valued as a going concern based upon the "operative reality" of the company as of the time of the merger.[39] Therefore, any holding company's ownership of a controlling interest in a subsidiary at the time of the merger is an "operative reality" and an independent element of value that must be taken into account in determining a fair value for the parent company's stock.[40]

The Court of Chancery properly concluded that the rationale of this Court's holding in Rapid-American applied to the MGB appraisal proceeding. Because MGB held a controlling interest in its two subsidiaries, it was necessary to determine the value of those controlling interests in order to ascertain the value of MGB, as a whole, as a going concern on the Merger date. We hold that the Court

---

36 Rapid-American Corp. v. Harris, Del. Supr., 603 A.2d 796, 806 (1992).

37 Rapid-American Corp. v. Harris, 603 A.2d at 806–07 (emphasis added).

38 Cede & Co. v. Technicolor, Inc., Del. Supr., 684 A.2d 289, 298 (1996), *citing* Cavalier Oil Corp. v. Harnett, Del. Supr., 564 A.2d 1137, 1144 (1989). See also Tri-Continental Corp. v. Battye, Del. Supr., 31 Del. Ch. 523, 74 A.2d 71, 72 (1950).

39 Cede & Co. v. Technicolor, Inc., 684 A.2d at 298.

40 Rapid-American Co. v. Harris, 603 A.2d at 806–07.

of Chancery acted in accordance with the statutory parameters of Section 262 by making a per share fair value determination of MGB on the basis of the comparative acquisitions approach applied by Clarke, using the premia that he attributed to MGB's controlling interests in [MGB's two bank subsidiaries].

---

ii. Joint Gains (Synergies) and the Appraisal Remedy

A second issue, in theory distinct from the issue of whether shareholders should suffer a minority discount, is whether minority shareholders should get a portion of the joint gains created specific to the deal. The issue of whether and how to account for the potential gains of an acquisition divides the states. Another way of asking the question is should shareholders receive the value of their shares before the announcement of the merger or after the announcement of the merger when anticipation of the deal closing will be reflected in the share price? As you will see in the *Weinberger* case below, in Delaware the legislature thought it had resolved the matter.

WEINBERGER V. UOP, INC.

Supreme Court of Delaware, 1983.
457 A.2d 701.

MOORE, JUSTICE:

* * *

Fair price obviously requires consideration of all relevant factors involving the value of a company. This has long been the law of Delaware as stated in *Tri-Continental Corp.*, 74 A.2d at 72:

> The basic concept of value under the appraisal statute is that the stockholder is entitled to be paid for that which has been taken from him, viz., his proportionate interest in a going concern. By value of the stockholder's proportionate interest in the corporate enterprise is meant the true or intrinsic value of his stock that has been taken by the merger. In determining what figure represents this true or intrinsic value, the appraiser and the courts must take into consideration all factors and elements which reasonably might enter into the fixing of value. Thus, market value, asset value, dividends, earning prospects, the nature of the enterprise and any other facts which were known or which could be ascertained as of the date of merger and which throw any light on *future prospects* of the merged corporation are not only pertinent to an inquiry as to the value of the dissenting stockholders' interest, but *must be considered* by the agency fixing the value. (Emphasis added.)

This is not only in accord with the realities of present day affairs, but it is thoroughly consonant with the purpose and intent of our statutory law. Under 8 Del.C. § 262(h), the Court of Chancery:

> shall appraise the shares, determining their *fair* value exclusive of any element of value arising from the accomplishment or expectation of the merger, together with a fair rate of interest, if any, to be paid upon the amount determined to be the *fair* value. In determining such *fair* value, the Court shall take into account *all relevant factors*. . . . (Emphasis added.)

It is significant that section 262 now mandates the determination of "fair" value based upon "all relevant factors." Only the speculative elements of value that may arise from the "accomplishment or expectation" of the merger are excluded. We take this to be a very narrow exception to the appraisal process, designed to eliminate use of *pro forma* data and projections of a speculative variety relating to the completion of a merger. But, elements of future value, including the nature of the enterprise, which are known or susceptible of proof as of the date of the merger and not the product of speculation, may be considered. When the trial court deems it appropriate, fair value also includes any damages, resulting from the taking, which the stockholders sustain as a class. If that was not the case, then the obligation to consider "all relevant factors" in the valuation process would be eroded. We are supported in this view not only by *Tri-Continental Corp.,* 74 A.2d at 72, but also by the evolutionary amendments to section 262.

Prior to an amendment in 1976, the earlier relevant provision of section 262 stated:

> (f) The appraiser shall determine the value of the stock of the stockholders. . . . The Court shall by its decree determine the value of the stock of the stockholders entitled to payment therefore. . . .

The first references to "fair" value occurred in a 1976 amendment to section 262(f), which provided:

> (f) . . . the Court shall appraise the shares, determining their fair value exclusively of any element of value arising from the accomplishment or expectation of the merger. . . .

It was not until the 1981 amendment to section 262 that the reference to "fair value" was repeatedly emphasized and the statutory mandate that the Court "take into account all relevant factors" appeared [section 262(h)]. Clearly, there is a legislative intent to fully compensate shareholders for whatever their loss may be, subject only to the narrow limitation that one cannot take speculative effects of the merger into account. . . .

Other states establish an explicit valuation date. N.J. Stat. Ann. 14A:11–3 states that the "fair value" to be awarded dissenting shareholders "shall be determined as of the day prior to the day of the meeting of shareholders at which the proposed action was approved . . . [and] exclude any appreciation or depreciation resulting from the proposed action." In Ohio, a shareholder is entitled to receive the "fair cash value" of her shares as of the day prior to the vote of the shareholders. The "fair cash value" is defined as the "price at which a willing seller who is under no compulsion to sell would be willing to accept and that a willing buyer who is under no compulsion to purchase would be willing to pay[,] . . . any appreciation or depreciation in market value resulting from the proposal submitted to . . . shareholders shall be excluded." Ohio Rev. Code Ann. § 1701.85(C). The valuation date approach is problematic because the share prices on the day before the shareholder vote will reflect the value of the acquisition discounted by the probability that the acquisition will close. Courts must back out the acquisition value in the appraisal, a necessarily hypothetical inquiry. *Armstrong v. Marathon Oil Co.,* 513 N.E.2d 776, 788 (Ohio 1987), cert. den., 498 U.S. 1121, 111 S.Ct. 1076, 112 L.Ed.2d 1181 (1991). California, solving the problem, uses the "day before the first announcement . . . excluding any appreciation or depreciation in consequence of the proposed action." Cal. Gen. Corp. L. § 1300(a). Interestingly, California requires the calculation of "fair *market* value," and not "fair value" or "fair cash value." Does use of the word "market" change anything?

A few states expressly include acquisition value in fair value. New York is the most notable example:

> The court shall . . . fix the value of the shares, which for the purposes of this section, shall be the fair value as of the close of business on the day prior to the shareholders' [approval of the action dissented from]. In fixing the fair value of the shares, the court shall consider the nature of the transaction giving rise to the shareholder's right to receive payment of shares and its effects on the corporation and its shareholders, the concepts and methods then customary in the relevant securities and financial markets for determining fair value of shares of a corporation engaging in a similar transaction under comparable circumstances and all other relevant factors.

N.Y. Bus. Corp. L. § 623(h)(4).

The New York legislature based the statute on the following finding:

> The case law interpretation of fair value has not always reflected the reality of corporate business combinations. These transactions involve the sale of the corporation as a whole, and the corporation's value as an entity may be substantially in excess of the actual or hypothetical market price for shares trading

among investors. Thus, experience has demonstrated that large premiums over market price are commonplace in mergers and in asset acquisitions. In cases where the transaction involves a restructuring of the shareholders' relative interest in the corporation by amendment of the certificate of incorporation, courts may find it appropriate to determine only the fair value of the dissenters' shares, rather than the value of the corporation as a whole, employing traditional valuation concepts.

1982 N.Y. Laws, Ch. 202, § 1.

The Model Act has long used the closing date rather than the date of the shareholder vote as the relevant time. In the 1984 version, "fair value" is determined "immediately before the effectuation of the corporate action to which the dissenter objects, excluding any appreciation or depreciation in anticipation of the corporate action unless exclusion would be inequitable." Rev. Model Bus. Corp. Act § 13.01(3) (1984). The 2016 revision of the section does not include the final "excluding" clause of the 1984 version and invites the court to use "customary and current valuation concepts and techniques generally employed for similar businesses in the context of the transaction requiring appraisal." ABA Model Bus. Corp. Act § 13.01 (2016 rev.) (definition of "fair value").

The Delaware Supreme Court has used the *Weinberger* case analysis to throw a wrench into traditional two-stage acquisitions—stock acquisitions followed by a squeeze-out merger.

CEDE & CO. V. TECHNICOLOR, INC.[120]

Supreme Court of Delaware, 1996.
684 A.2d 289.

HOLLAND, JUSTICE:

. . . The proceeding arises from a cash-out merger of the minority shareholders of Technicolor Incorporated ("Technicolor"), a Delaware corporation. With the approval from a majority of Technicolor's shareholders, MacAndrews & Forbes Group Incorporated ("MAF") merged its wholly-owned subsidiary, Macanfor Corporation ("Macanfor"), into Technicolor. The only defendant-appellee in this appraisal action is Technicolor, the surviving corporation of the merger. The plaintiffs-appellants are Cinerama, Incorporated, the beneficial owner of 201,200

---

[120] [Ed. The litigation began soon after the deal closed in 1983. After multiple opinions by the Delaware Supreme Court that resulted in multiple remands to the Court of Chancery and two trials, the Chancery Court entered final judgment in 2005 on the appraisal. See Cede & Co. v. Technicolor, Inc., 2005 WL 5755422 (Del. Ch.). In the final order, the Delaware Court of Chancery determined that Technicolor owed Cinerama $21.41 a share with pre-judgment interest of 10.32 percent from Jan. 24, 1983 to 1991 and post-judgment interest of simple interest (on the principal) at the statutory rate of 7 percent from Aug. 31, 1991 to payment. The amount rewarded is lower than the merger price and only thirty-eight cents higher than the $21.60 awarded in the first 1991 trial. The opinion in the text is the fourth remand in the litigation.]

shares of Technicolor common stock, and Cede & Company, the record owner of those shares (collectively "Cinerama").

Cinerama contends, inter alia, that the Court of Chancery erred, as a matter of law, in appraising the fair value of its Technicolor shares. According to Cinerama, that legal error was a refusal to include in the valuation calculus "MAF's new business plans and strategies for Technicolor, which the [C]ourt [of Chancery] found were not speculative but had been developed, adopted and implemented" between the date of the merger agreement and the date of the merger. That contention is correct and dispositive of this appeal.

* * *

On October 27, Kamerman [CEO of Technicolor] and Perelman [MAF's controlling shareholder] reached an agreement by telephone. Perelman initially offered $22.50 per share for Technicolor's stock. Kamerman countered with a figure of $23 per share. He also stated that he would recommend its acceptance to the Technicolor Board. Perelman agreed to the $23 per share price.

The Technicolor Board convened on October 29, 1982 to consider MAF's proposal. All nine directors of Technicolor attended the meeting. Kamerman outlined the history of his negotiations with Perelman. Kamerman explained the basic structure of the transaction: a tender offer by MAF at $23 per share for all the outstanding shares of common stock of Technicolor; and a second-step merger with the remaining outstanding shares converted into $23 per share, with Technicolor becoming a wholly owned subsidiary of MAF. Kamerman recommended that MAF's $23 per share offer be accepted in view of the present market value of Technicolor's shares. Kamerman stated that accepting $23 a share was "advisable rather than shooting dice" . . . .

On October 29, 1982, the Technicolor Board agreed to the acquisition proposal by MAF.[Ed.[121]] The Technicolor Board: approved the Agreement and Plan of Merger with MAF; recommended to the stockholders of Technicolor the acceptance of the offer of $23 per share; and recommended the repeal of the supermajority provision in Technicolor's Certificate of Incorporation. Technicolor filed forms 14D–9 and 13D with the Securities and Exchange Commission that reflected those Board actions and recommendations.

In November 1982, MAF commenced an all-cash tender offer of $23 per share to the shareholders of Technicolor. When the tender offer closed on November 30, 1982, MAF had gained control of Technicolor. By December 3, 1982, MAF had acquired 3,754,181 shares, or 82.19 percent,

[121] [Ed. The stock price of Technicolor on October 27, 1982 was $17.375.]

of Technicolor's shares. Thereafter, MAF and Technicolor were consolidated for tax and financial reporting purposes.

The Court of Chancery made a factual finding that, "upon acquiring control" of Technicolor, Perelman and his associates "began to dismember what they saw as a badly conceived mélange of businesses." Perelman testified: "Presumably we made the evaluation of the business of Technicolor before we made the purchase, not after." . . .

Consequently, immediately after becoming Technicolor's controlling shareholder, MAF "started looking for buyers for several of the [Technicolor] divisions." Bear Stearns & Co. was also retained by MAF in December 1982 to assist it in disposing of Technicolor assets. A target date of June 30, 1983 was set for liquidating all of Technicolor's excess assets. As of December 31, 1982, MAF was projecting that $54 million would be realized from asset sales.

In December 1982, the Board of Technicolor notified its stockholders of a special shareholders meeting on January 24, 1983. At the meeting, the Technicolor shareholders voted to repeal the supermajority amendment and in favor of the proposed merger. MAF and Technicolor completed the merger. . . .

The merger was accomplished on January 24, 1983. The parties agree that the appraised value of Technicolor must be fixed as of that date. . . . There is a fundamental disagreement between the litigants, however, concerning the nature of the enterprise to be appraised.

Cinerama argues that the Court of Chancery should have valued Technicolor as it existed on the date of the merger and, in particular, with due regard for the strategies that had been conceived and implemented following the merger agreement by MAF's controlling shareholder, Ronald O. Perelman ("Perelman Plan"). Technicolor argues that the Court of Chancery properly considered Technicolor without regard to the Perelman Plan and only as it existed on or before October 29, 1982, with the then extant strategies that had been conceived and implemented by Technicolor's Chairman, Morton Kamerman ("Kamerman Plan"). According to Cinerama:

> Reduced to its simplest form, the dispute was whether the trial court should value Perelman's Technicolor—a company whose business plans and strategies focused on the processing and duplication of film and videotape and the provision of services to the United States Government and which planned and expected to generate $50 million in cash during 1983 from the sale of unwanted and/or unsuccessful businesses, namely, OHP, CPPD, Gold Key and Audio Visual; or Kamerman's Technicolor—a company whose business plans and strategies assumed diversification away from a concentration on film processing and

videotape duplication for the professional market toward consumer oriented businesses, especially OHP.

The economic experts for both parties used a form of discounted cash flow methodology to value Technicolor. . . .

* * *

[T]he Court of Chancery reasoned that, as a matter of policy, the valuation process in a statutory appraisal proceeding should be the same irrespective of whether a merger is accomplished in one or two steps:

> Delaware law traditionally and today accords to a dissenting shareholder "his proportionate interest in a going concern" and that going concern is the corporation in question, with its asset deployment, business plan, and management unaffected by the plans or strategies of the acquirer. When value is created by substituting new management or by redeploying assets "in connection with the accomplishment or expectation" of a merger, that value is not, in my opinion, a part of the "going concern" in which a dissenting shareholder has a legal (or equitable) right to participate.
>
> If one accepts this principle, the question arises how is it to be applied in a two-step arms'-length acquisition transaction. In such a transaction there will be a period following close [to] the first-step tender offer in which the [majority] acquirer may, as a practical matter, be in a position to influence or change the nature of the corporate business, or to freeze controversial programs until they are reviewed following the second-step merger.

Accordingly, the Court of Chancery concluded that "[f]uture value that would not exist but for the merger . . . even if it is capable of being proven on the date of the merger," is irrelevant in a Delaware statutory appraisal proceeding. (Emphasis added.) Consequently, the Court of Chancery held "that value added to [Technicolor] by the implementation or the expectation of the implementation of Mr. Perelman's new business plan for [Technicolor] is not value to which, in an appraisal action, [Cinerama] is entitled to a pro rata share, but is value that is excluded from consideration by the statutory exclusion for value arising from the merger or its expectation."

* * *

The underlying assumption in an appraisal valuation is that the dissenting shareholders would be willing to maintain their investment position had the merger not occurred. . . . Accordingly, the Court of Chancery's task in an appraisal proceeding is to value what has been taken from the shareholder, i.e., the proportionate interest in the going concern. . . . To that end, this Court has held that the corporation must be valued as an operating entity. . . . We conclude that the Court of Chancery did not adhere to this principle.

* * *

[T]his Court has explained that the dissenter in an appraisal action is entitled to receive a proportionate share of fair value in the going concern on the date of the merger, rather than value that is determined on a liquidated basis. . . . Thus, the company must first be valued as an operating entity. . . .

In a two-step merger, to the extent that value has been added following a change in majority control before cash-out, it is still value attributable to the going concern, *i.e.*, the extant "nature of the enterprise," on the date of the merger. . . . Consequently, value added to the going concern by the "majority acquirer," during the transient period of a two-step merger, accrues to the benefit of all shareholders and must be included in the appraisal process on the date of the merger. . . .

In this case, the question in the appraisal action was the fair value of Technicolor stock on the date of the merger, January 24, 1983, as Technicolor was operating pursuant to the Perelman Plan. . . .

The "accomplishment or expectation" of the merger exception in Section 262 is very narrow, "designed to eliminate use of *pro forma* data and projections of a speculative variety relating to the completion of a merger." *Weinberger v. UOP, Inc.*, 457 A.2d at 713. That narrow exclusion does not encompass known elements of value, including those that exist on the date of the merger because of a majority acquirer's interim action in a two-step cash-out transaction. . . .

QUESTIONS

As a matter of policy, does Chancellor Allen or Justice Holland have the better of the argument? As a matter of acquisition planning, what is the effect of the case on two-stage acquisitions? Can transaction planners use compulsory share exchanges or triangular mergers to avoid allocating a sizable portion of the acquisition synergy to minority shareholders?

The ABA Model Business Corporation Act appears to agree with Justice Holland:

> Clause (i) of the definition of "fair value" in section 13.01 specifies that fair value is to be determined immediately before the effectiveness of the corporate action, which will be after the shareholder vote. Accordingly, section 13.01 permits consideration of changes in the value of the corporation's shares after the shareholder vote but before the effectiveness of the transaction, to the extent such changes are relevant. Similarly, in a two-step transaction

culminating in a merger, fair value is determined immediately before the second step merger, taking into account any interim changes in value.[122]

In the later stages of *Technicolor*, *supra*, a frustrated Chancery Court judge noted the following about the nature of appraisal proceedings:

> Although 8 Del. C. § 262 requires this Court to determine "the fair value" of a share of Technicolor on January 24, 1983, it is one of the conceits of our law that we purport to declare something as elusive as the fair value of an entity on a given date, especially a date more than two decades ago. Experience in the adversarial, battle of the experts' appraisal process under Delaware law teaches one lesson very clearly: valuation decisions are impossible to make with anything approaching complete confidence. Valuing an entity is a difficult intellectual exercise, especially when business and financial experts are able to organize data in support of wildly divergent valuations for the same entity. For a judge who is not an expert in corporate finance, one can do little more than try to detect gross distortions in the experts' opinions. This effort should, therefore, not be understood, as a matter of intellectual honesty, as resulting in the fair value of a corporation on a given date. The value of a corporation is not a point on a line, but a range of reasonable values, and the judge's task is to assign one particular value within this range as the most reasonable value in light of all of the relevant evidence and based on considerations of fairness.[123]

Are concerns about an overmatched judiciary unwarranted? In the case of the Delaware Chancery Court, at least two commentators believe the answer is "yes":

> On the other side of the coin, worries about valuations being performed by "law-trained" judges—sometimes poignantly expressed by the chancellors themselves—are overblown. We are, after all, talking about the Delaware Court of Chancery, not the traffic court of Mandan, North Dakota. The five chancellors are world-leading specialists in corporate law, often with substantial practice experience prior to joining the court. Once on the court, they are tasked with valuation questions on a routine basis. The ability of the unbiased and expert chancellors to perform company valuations strikes us as often more credible than the contingently-

---

122 ABA Model Bus. Corp. Act § 13.01, Off. Cmt. 2B (2016 rev.).

123 Cede & Co. v. Technicolor, Inc., 2003 WL 25579991 (Del. Ch.). See also ABA Model Bus. Corp. Act § 13.01, Off. Cmt. 2B (2016 rev.) (stating, with respect to fair value, that "[c]ustomary valuation concepts and techniques will typically take into account numerous relevant factors, and will normally result in a range of values, not a particular single value.").

compensated investment bankers and corporate officers they are often so anxious to defer to.

Charles Korsmo & Minor Myers, *Reforming Modern Appraisal Litigation*, 41 DEL. J. CORP. L. 279, 324 (2017) (footnote omitted).

---

iii. Is "Deal Value" the Best Evidence of "Fair Value"?

It is often said that something is worth what someone is willing to pay for it. If this is true, then in an appraisal proceeding what weight (if any) should a court give to the merger consideration paid by the buyer for a company in an arm's-length transaction? Consider the case below and the note that follows.

IN RE APPRAISAL OF DELL, INC.

Delaware Court of Chancery, 2016.
2016 WL 3186538, *rev'd in part, aff'd in part, and remanded sub nom. Dell, Inc. v. Magnetar Global Event Driven Master Fund Ltd.*, 177 A.3d 1 (Del. 2017).

MEMORANDUM OPINION

LASTER, VICE CHANCELLOR.

The petitioners owned shares of common stock of Dell Inc. (the "Company"). In 2013, the Company completed a merger that gave rise to appraisal rights (the "Merger"). The petitioners sought appraisal. Based on the evidence presented at trial, the fair value of the Company's common stock at the effective time of the Merger was $17.62 per share.

I. FACTUAL BACKGROUND

* * *

In 1983, at the age of nineteen, Michael Dell started the Company in his freshman dorm room at the University of Texas at Austin. Within two years, the Company achieved annual sales of more than $40 million [from the sale of personal computers ("PCs")]. On June 22, 1988, the Company went public.

* * *

[Ed. Around 2007, Mr. Dell came to believe that the Company needed to evolve to meet three competitive threats. The first came from low-margin PC producers, as the Company sold primarily high-margin, premium-priced PCs. The second was from new products, including Apple Inc.'s iPhone and iPad. Smartphones and tablets both ate into the traditional PC market. The third was cloud-based storage services, such as Amazon Web Services, which adversely affected the Company's server business.

Mr. Dell believed that the Company needed to reduce its reliance on PC sales to end users and increase its sales of software and services to enterprise customers. In 2009, the Company started its transformation, which Mr. Dell planned to achieve through acquisitions. Between 2010 and 2012, the Company spent approximately $14 billion to acquire eleven businesses. Although it would take the Company time to integrate the new businesses and for them to perform in accordance with Mr. Dell's expectations, Mr. Dell and his management team valued the Company post-acquisitions at $22.49 per share (by line of business) and $27.05 per share (by business unit).

Unfortunately, the market did not share Mr. Dell's vision, and continued to value the Company primarily as a seller of PCs. The price of the Company's stock during this period was around $14 per share.

In June 2012, Staley Cates from Southeastern Asset Management ("Southeastern") asked Mr. Dell whether he would consider a management buyout ("MBO"). In August, Egon Durban of Silver Lake Partners ("Silver Lake"), a private equity firm, approached Mr. Dell with the same idea. Mr. Dell decided to consider it. On Friday August 14, 2012, Mr. Dell called Alex Mandl, the Company's lead independent director, and . . . told Mandl that he wanted to pursue an MBO. The Company's stock closed at $12.19 that day.

After Dell's board of directors ("Board") met, Mandl told Mr. Dell that the Board would consider an MBO. Mr. Dell passed on the news to Silver Lake and Kohlberg Kravis Roberts & Co. L.P. ("KKR"). He did not contact Southeastern. The Board formed a special committee (the "Committee") to consider the sale of the company, including a MBO. Mr. Dell threw in with Silver Lake (the "Buyout Group"), agreeing to exchange his Dell stock for equity in a new entity formed to effect the acquisition of Dell.

Upon the advice of its financial advisors, the Committee told Mr. Dell that it would not support a deal below $13.75 per share. Durban of Silver Lake then called Mandl and offered $13.25 a share. Mandl told him that was inadequate. Durban threatened to walk, and Mandl "told him to go ahead." . . . Silver Lake came back at $13.50, but the Committee stood firm.

At this point, Mr. Dell feared the parties had reached an impasse. To resolve the stalemate, Mr. Dell agreed to roll over his Dell shares at a lower valuation than what the public stockholders would receive. With Mr. Dell's commitment, the Buyout Group increased the price it would pay for the public float to $13.65 per share in cash (the "Original Merger Consideration"). The Committee ultimately rejected the Original Merger Consideration as inadequate from a financial point of view.

On July 31, 2013, the Buyout Group made a new offer. Among other things, it agreed to increase the merger consideration to $13.75 per share (the "Final Merger Consideration"). The Committee recommended that the Board approve the revised transaction, which it did.

A special meeting of stockholders took place on September 12, 2013. Under Delaware law, a merger requires the approval of holders of a majority of the outstanding shares, making that the appropriate denominator for consideration. In the Company's case, holders of 57% of the Company's shares voted in favor of the Merger. Because not all stockholders vote, and because a non-vote counts the same as a "no" vote, the percentage always will be higher for the shares that actually voted. In the Company's case, holders of approximately 70% of the shares present at the meeting voted in favor. Both are relatively low margins.]

* * *

A. The Final Merger Consideration As The Best Evidence Of Fair Value

The Company contends that the Final Merger Consideration is the best evidence of the Company's fair value on the closing date. As the proponent of this valuation methodology, the Company bears the burden of establishing its reliability and persuasiveness. In this case, the Final Merger Consideration is certainly a relevant factor, but it is not the best evidence of the Company's fair value.

1. Deal Price As A Subset Of Market Value

The consideration that the buyer agrees to provide in the deal and that the seller agrees to accept is one form of market price data, which Delaware courts have long considered in appraisal proceedings. . . . Traditionally, Delaware decisions focused on stock market prices, rather than the deal price. . . . Chancellor Allen summarized the law as follows:

> It is, of course, axiomatic that if there is an established market for shares of a corporation the market value of such shares must be taken into consideration in an appraisal of their intrinsic value. . . . It is, of course, equally axiomatic that market value, either actual or constructed, is not the sole element to be taken into consideration in the appraisal of stock.

Cede & Co. v. Technicolor, Inc., . . . 1990 WL 161084, at *31 (Del. Ch. Oct. 19, 1990) . . . . Numerous cases support Chancellor Allen's observations that (i) pricing data from a thick and efficient market should be considered and (ii) market price alone is not dispositive.

Recent jurisprudence has emphasized Delaware courts' willingness to consider market price data generated not only by the market for individual shares but also by the market for the company as a whole. If the merger giving rise to appraisal rights "resulted from an arm's-length process between two independent parties, and if no structural impediments existed that might materially distort the 'crucible of objective market reality,'" then "a reviewing court should give substantial evidentiary weight to the merger price as an indicator of fair value." [*Highfields Capital, Inc. v. AXA Fin., Inc.*, 939 A.2d 34, 42 (Del. Ch. 2007).]

Here too, however, the Delaware Supreme Court has eschewed market fundamentalism by making clear that market price data is neither conclusively determinative of no[r] presumptively equivalent to fair value:

* * *

> . . . Requiring the Court of Chancery to defer—conclusively or presumptively—to the merger price, even in the face of a pristine, unchallenged transactional process, would . . . inappropriately shift the responsibility to determine "fair value" from the court to the private parties. . . . Therefore, we reject . . . [the] call to establish a rule requiring the Court of Chancery to defer to the merger price in any appraisal proceeding.

Golden Telecom, Inc. v. Glob. GT LP (Golden Telecom II), 11 A.3d 214, 217–18 (Del. 2010) (footnotes omitted).

Since *Golden Telecom II*, and consistent with the Delaware Supreme Court's teaching in that decision, the Court of Chancery has considered the deal price as one of the "relevant factors" when determining fair value. In at least five decisions, the Court of Chancery has found the deal price to be the most reliable indicator of the company's fair value, particularly when other evidence of fair value was weak.[13]

Depending on the facts of the case, a variety of factors may undermine the potential persuasiveness of the deal price as evidence of fair value. For one, in a public company merger, the need for a stockholder vote, regulatory approvals, and other time-intensive steps may generate a substantial delay between the signing date and the closing date. The deal price provides a data point for the market price of the company as of the date of signing, but as discussed above, the valuation date for an appraisal is the date of

---

[13] *BMC*, . . . 2015 WL 6164771, at *18 (finding merger price to be best indicator of value because of the "uncertainties in the DCF analysis" and because there was an "arm's-length transaction negotiated over multiple rounds of bidding among interested buyers"); *Ramtron*, . . . 2015 WL 4540443, at *20 (finding merger price to be the most reliable evidence of value after deeming management forecasts unreliable and noting that "[a]ny impediments to a higher bid resulted from Ramtron's operative reality, not shortcomings of the Merger process"); *AutoInfo*, . . . 2015 WL 2069417, at *17–18 (deferring to merger price after finding projections unreliable in the context of a "competitive and fair auction"); *Ancestry.com*, . . . 2015 WL 399726, at *23 (finding merger price to be best indicator of value because of weak forecasts and a "robust" sale process); *CKx*, . . . 2013 WL 5878807, at *13 (finding that the merger price was the "most reliable indicator of value" in a case "where no comparable companies, comparable transactions, or reliable cash flow projections exist"). Unlike the current case, none of these decisions involved an MBO. And unlike the current case, reliable projections and persuasive evidence of a significant valuation gap did not exist. In *BMC*, the court found that "the sales process was sufficiently structured to develop fair value of the Company," which is different than the facts of this case. . . . 2015 WL 6164771, at *16. All the cases either involved a more active pre-signing market check or the process was kicked off by an unsolicited third-party bid.

closing. . . . Market pricing indications can change rapidly, whether in the stock market or the deal market.

Another issue is the reality that the M&A market for an entire company has different and less confidence-promoting attributes than the public trading markets:

> Among the other requirements for market efficiency are liquidity and fungibility. Public stock market prices are generally efficient because large numbers of identical shares of stock in a given company trade on a highly liquid market with millions of participants. The deal market, however—dealing as it does with entire companies, rather than individual shares—often lacks both qualities. No two companies are exactly alike, and the market for whole companies is unavoidably chunky, rather than liquid. As such, the deal market is unavoidably less efficient at valuing entire companies (including the value of control) than the stock market is at valuing minority shares.[15]

The limitations on efficient pricing in the market for corporate control "are especially pronounced in the context of MBOs." Iman Anabtawi, *Predatory Management Buyouts*, 49 U.C. Davis L. Rev. 1285, 1320 (2016). . . .

* * *

There is also the recognized problem that an arms' length deal price often includes synergies. This can be true even for a financial buyer, because "the aggregation of shares, which eliminates agency costs in the process, is a value-creating transaction." Lawrence A. Hamermesh & Michael L. Wachter, *Rationalizing Appraisal Standards in Compulsory Buyouts*, 50 B.C. L. Rev. 1021, 1050 (2009). The value of synergies "would not otherwise exist in the enterprise itself" and therefore represent an "'element of value arising from the accomplishment or expectation of the merger or consolidation' that must be excluded" *Id.* at 1029 (quoting 8 *Del. C.* § 262). . . .

These three factors suggest that even with a public company target, deal price will not inevitably equate to fair value. It could be higher or lower. . . . The respondent corporation still may be able to establish that the merger price is the best evidence of fair value—and it often will be—but the corporation must carry its burden on that point. . . .

* * *

3. MBO Status As An Additional Factor

. . . Because of management's additional and conflicting role as buyer, MBOs present different concerns than true arms' length transactions. A

---

15 Charles Korsmo & Minor Myers, *Reforming Modern Appraisal Litigation*, 41 Del. J. Corp. L. (forthcoming 2016) (manuscript at 50), *available at* http://papers.ssrn.com/sol3/papers.cfm?abstract_id=2712088 [hereinafter Modern Appraisal Litigation]. . . .

vast amount of case law . . . and scholarship (both legal . . . and empirical . . .) has addressed MBOs. Although the literature is far from unanimous in its analysis and policy recommendations, . . . the weight of authority suggests that a claim that the bargained-for price in an MBO represents fair value should be evaluated with greater thoroughness and care than, at the other end of the spectrum, a transaction with a strategic buyer in which management will not be retained.

4. The Sale Process In This Case

In this case, the Company's process easily would sail through if reviewed under enhanced scrutiny. The Committee and its advisors did many praiseworthy things, and it would burden an already long opinion to catalog them. In a liability proceeding, this court could not hold that the directors breached their fiduciary duties or that there could be any basis for liability. But that is not the same as proving that the deal price provides the best evidence of the Company's fair value. In this case, a combination of factors undercut the relationship between the Final Merger Consideration and fair value, undermining the persuasiveness of the former as evidence of the latter.

[Ed. The Court first began by addressing whether the *Original* Merger Consideration represented fair value.]

a. The Pre-Signing Phase

The sale process in this case had two phases: (i) a pre-signing phase and (ii) a post-signing go-shop period. The Original Merger Consideration was the product of the pre-signing phase, and the evidence established that it was below fair value. Three factors contributed to this outcome: (i) the use of an LBO pricing model to determine the Original Merger Consideration, which had the effect in this case of undervaluing the Company, (ii) the compelling evidence of a significant valuation gap driven by the market's short-term focus, and (iii) the lack of meaningful pre-signing competition.

i. The LBO Pricing Model

* * *

In this case, the Committee only engaged during the pre-signing phase with financial sponsors. When proposing an MBO, a financial sponsor determines whether and how much to bid by using an LBO model, which solves for the range of prices that a financial sponsor can pay while still achieving particular [internal rates of return, or "IRRs"]. . . . What the sponsor is willing to pay diverges from fair value because of (i) the financial sponsor's need to achieve IRRs of 20% or more to satisfy its own investors and (ii) limits on the amount of leverage that the company can support and the sponsor can use to finance the deal. . . . Although a [discounted cash flow or "DCF"] methodology and an LBO model use similar inputs, they solve for different variables: "[T]he DCF analysis solves for the present value of the firm, while the LBO model solves for the internal rate of return." Donald M. DePamphilis, *Mergers, Acquisitions, and Other Restructuring Activities* 506 (7th ed. 2014). . . .

The factual record in this case demonstrates that the price negotiations during the pre-signing phase were driven by the financial sponsors' willingness to pay based on their LBO pricing models, rather than the fair value of the Company. . . .

* * *

Even if a financial sponsor was willing to accept a lower IRR such that it "could have" paid more for the Company, JPMorgan[, one of the Committee's financial advisors,] concluded that an MBO "would not have been possible for the company" at prices of $19 or more because it would require a level of leverage "that you could not get in the marketplace." . . .

* * *

This was not a case in which the Buyout Group intended to make changes in the Company's business, either organically or through acquisitions. The Buyout Group intended to achieve its returns simply by executing the Company's existing business strategy and meeting its forecasted projections. Mr. Dell identified for the Committee the strategies that he would pursue once the Company was private, and the record establishes that all of them could have been accomplished in a public company setting. [Boston Consulting Group, Inc. ("BCG"), a consultant to the Committee,] recognized and advised the Committee that the *only* benefits Mr. Dell could realize by taking the Company private that were not otherwise available as a public company were accessing offshore cash with less tax leakage (to pay down the acquisition debt) and arbitraging the value of the Company itself by buying low and selling high. . . .

Taken as a whole, the foregoing evidence, along with other evidence in the record, establishes that the Original Merger Consideration was dictated by what a financial sponsor could pay and still generate outsized returns. This fact is a strong indication that the Original Merger Consideration undervalued the Company as a going concern.

ii. The Valuation Gap

A second factor that undermined the persuasiveness of the Original Merger Consideration as evidence of fair value was the widespread and compelling evidence of a valuation gap between the market's perception and the Company's operative reality. The gap was driven by (i) analysts' focus on short-term, quarter-by-quarter results and (ii) the Company's nearly $14 billion investment in its transformation, which had not yet begun to generate the anticipated results. A transaction which eliminates stockholders may take advantage of a trough in a company's performance or excessive investor pessimism about the Company's prospects (a so-called anti-bubble). Indeed, the optimal time to take a company private is after it has made significant long-term investments, but before those investments have started to pay off and market participants have begun to incorporate those benefits into the price of the Company's stock. . . . In *Glassman v. Unocal Exploration Corp.*, 777 A.2d 242 (Del. 2001), the Delaware Supreme Court acknowledged that an appraisal proceeding can and should address the problem of opportunistic timing:

> The determination of fair value must be based on *all* relevant factors, including damages and elements of future value, where appropriate. So, for example, if the merger was timed to take advantage of a depressed market, or a low point in the company's cyclical earnings, or to precede an anticipated positive development, the appraised value may be adjusted to account for those factors.

Id. at 248 . . . .

Proposing an MBO when the stock price is low has the further effect of using the depressed stock price to anchor price negotiations. . . . When a company with a depressed market price starts a sale process, the anchoring effect makes the process intuitively more likely to generate an undervalued bid. . . . Market myopia can accentuate this problem. . . . Investors focused on short-term, quarterly results can excessively discount the value of long-term investments. . . .

The record at trial demonstrated that a significant valuation gap, investor myopia, and anchoring were all present in this case. Mr. Dell identified the opportunity to take the Company private after the stock market failed to reflect the Company's going concern value over a prolonged period. He managed the Company for the long-term and understood that his strategic decisions would drive the stock price down in the short-term. The Company's management team recognized the valuation gap as early as January 2011 . . . . The Committee's advisors reached a similar conclusion. . . .

It bears emphasizing that . . . there is no evidence that Mr. Dell or his management team sought to create the valuation disconnect so that they could take advantage of it. To the contrary, they tried to convince the market that the Company was worth more. Only when the gap persisted despite their efforts, and after both Southeastern and Silver Lake suggested the possibility of an MBO to Mr. Dell, did he eventually decide to pursue the opportunity that the market price was presenting.

* * *

Taken as a whole, the foregoing evidence, along with other evidence in the record, establishes the existence of a significant valuation gap between the market price of the Company's common stock and the intrinsic value of the Company. The anti-bubble both facilitated the MBO and undermined the reliability of the market price as a measure of the Company's value. . . .

iii. Limited Pre-Signing Competition

A third factor that undermined the persuasiveness of the Original Merger Consideration as evidence of fair value was the lack of meaningful price competition during the pre-signing phase. Go-shops in MBO transactions rarely produce topping bids, . . . so the bulk of any price competition occurs before the deal is signed. . . . The price established during the pre-signing phase is therefore critical, and it is the presence or realistic threat of competition during this period that drives up the price. . . .

In this case, the record established that there was minimal competition during the pre-signing phase. The Committee initially engaged with only two financial sponsors, and KKR dropped out after providing its initial expression of interest. . . .

During the pre-signing phase, the Committee did not contact any strategic buyers. . . . Hewlett-Packard Company ("HP") was the obvious choice, [but the] Committee chose not to contact HP. The lack of any outreach to strategic bidders and the assessment that strategic interest was unlikely meant that the financial sponsors did not have to push their prices upward to pre-empt potential interest from that direction.

Without a meaningful source of competition, the Committee lacked the most powerful tool that a seller can use to extract a portion of the bidder's anticipated surplus. The Committee had the ability to say no, and it could demand a higher price, but it could not invoke the threat of an alternative deal. When the Committee made its final demand, Silver Lake stood firm. It was Mr. Dell who bridged the gap by accepting a lower valuation for his rollover shares. . . .

Taken as a whole, there was a lack of meaningful price competition during the pre-signing phase. . . . [B]ecause the offers received in the go-shop period keyed off the Original Merger Consideration, this factor also undermines the reliability of the Final Merger Consideration.

b. The Post-Signing Phase

Although the evidence proved that the Original Merger Consideration was not the best evidence of fair value, the sale process did not stop there. The process entered a second phase, during which Evercore[, a second financial adviser hired by the Committee,] conducted a go-shop. Two higher bids emerged [from private equity firms], one from [The Blackstone Group, L.P. "(Blackstone")] and another from [Carl Icahn and Icahn Enterprises L.P. (together, "Icahn")]. Blackstone eventually withdrew its bid, but Icahn continued to compete. When it appeared that stockholders would vote down the original deal, the Committee and the Buyout Group amended the

Merger Agreement. The amendment provided for the Final Merger Consideration, representing an increase of 23 cents, or 2%, over the Original Merger Consideration.

* * *

. . . The question then becomes whether the increase was sufficient to establish the Final Merger Consideration as fair value. This decision finds that the answer is "no."

As during the pre-signing process, competition from a financial sponsor might have induced the Buyout Group to increase its bid within the confines of the LBO model, but it did not lead to competition at a level indicative of fair value. . . . The 2% bump is consistent with an increase within the confines of the LBO model. Notably, both Blackstone's proposal and the upper range of Icahn's proposal exceeded the Final Merger [Consideration.] . . .

The 2% increase that the Buyout Group offered to secure a favorable vote was all that the go-shop process achieved. Given the evidence that the pre-signing phase did not generate a price that was equivalent to fair value, and in light of the nature of the competition that took place during the go-shop phase, the 2% bump was not sufficient to prove that the Final Merger Consideration was the best evidence of fair value.

* * *

As previously discussed, MBO go-shops rarely generate topping bids. . . . The question for appraisal is whether the Company showed that the structure in fact generated a price that persuasively established the Company's fair value.

* * *

In this case, the structure of the go-shop was relatively open. The length of the go-shop period was forty-five days [which was] "about average" . . . . The steps required to become an "Excluded Party"[Ed.[124]] were also relatively few: A bidder only needed to submit a letter with a general outline of the structure of a transaction sufficient for the Committee to conclude that it "is or could reasonably be expected to result in a Superior Proposal." . . . A party who satisfied that standard would achieve Excluded Party status and could continue to negotiate with the Committee, theoretically until stockholders approved the deal. In this case, an Excluded Party at the end of the forty-five day go-shop period would

124 [Ed. On March 23, 2013, the go-shop period ended. The Committee determined that the Icahn and Blackstone offers were, or could reasonably be expected to lead to, Superior Proposals—i.e., proposals that were financially superior than that offered by the Buyout Group. Anyone who submitted a "Superior Proposal" would qualify as an "Excluded Party." As a result, the Company only would have to pay a $180 million termination fee to the Buyout Group if it entered into a transaction with either Icahn or Blackstone. For non-Superior Proposals and bids produced after the go-shop period, the termination fee increased to $450 million.]

have had another four months before the special meeting, originally scheduled for July 18.

Other structural features of the go-shop were also relatively flexible. The termination fee during the go-shop period for an Excluded Party was $180 million, representing approximately 1% of equity value of the original deal and 40% of the $450 termination fee that otherwise would apply. . . . More importantly, the Merger Agreement [with the Buyout Group] only contemplated a single opportunity for the Buyout Group to match a higher bid, after which the match right in the Merger Agreement expired. The one-time match is more favorable to a topping bidder than an unlimited match right, which is a powerful disincentive. . . .

The main structural problem . . . did not result from the terms of the go-shop in the abstract, but rather stemmed from the size and complexity of the Company. . . . [A] successful topping bid literally would have been unprecedented. The extent of Blackstone's efforts gives a sense of what was required. To get to Excluded Party status, Blackstone had to spend in excess of $25 million and assemble a due diligence team that filled a ballroom, and Blackstone is one of the world's most sophisticated private equity firms. Blackstone also retained Dell's former head of M&A and strategy, Dave Johnson, to lead its acquisition team and had the benefit of his insights.

* * *

A far more significant problem with MBO go-shops is that incumbent management has the best insight into the Company's value, or at least is perceived to have an informational advantage. Competing bidders therefore face threat of the winner's curse . . . . As a third party, the implication is if you bid and you win, you've just learned that you think this company is worth more than management. . . .

* * *

[Another] impediment to competitive bidding was Mr. Dell's value to the Company. . . . [T]he Company's relationship with Mr. Dell was an asset in itself. . . .

To perceive a path to success, a competing bidder had to account for Mr. Dell's value. Mr. Dell was part of the Buyout Group, so the incumbent party to the Merger Agreement had the benefit of that asset. A competing bidder that did not have Mr. Dell as part of its buyout group would be bidding for a company without that asset and would end up with a less valuable [company.]

* * *

[However,] . . . Blackstone and Icahn did not regard Mr. Dell as essential to their bids. Blackstone explored alternative CEO candidates. Icahn described Mr. Dell as a negative factor in an open letter to stockholders . . . . Icahn thought that "[a]ll would be swell at Dell if Michael and the board bid farewell." . . .

As with the other go-shop considerations, Mr. Dell's value to the Company and his association with the Buyout Group were impediments, but not insuperable ones. Exceptional bidders like Blackstone and Icahn could overcome them, but Mr. Dell's unique value and his affiliation with the Buyout Group were negative factors that inhibited the effectiveness of the go-shop process.

d. The Probative Value Of The Sale Process

Taken as a whole, the Company did not establish that the outcome of the sale process offers the most reliable evidence of the Company's value as a going concern. The market data is sufficient to exclude the possibility, advocated by the petitioners' expert, that the Merger undervalued the Company by $23 billion. Had a value disparity of that magnitude existed, then HP or another technology firm would have emerged to acquire the Company on the cheap. What the market data does not exclude is an underpricing of a smaller magnitude, given that all of the participants constructed their bids based on a leveraged financing model and were limited by its constraints.

* * *

QUESTIONS

1. What is the distinction between the "stock market" and the "deal market"?

2. Why was the Court suspicious that the deal price negotiated by the parties did not necessarily reflect the "true" or "intrinsic" value of the company being sold?

3. Why did the Court spend any time discussing whether the *Original* Merger Consideration represented fair value? Shouldn't the Court's sole focus be on the *Final* Merger Consideration?

4. If a buyer utilizing an LBO valuation model demands at least a 20 percent internal rate of return on its investment in connection with a given acquisition, does this necessarily lead to lower offering prices? Is the tail wagging the dog? Or is this a case where the buyer makes its money "going into" a deal?[125]

---

[125] The petitioners in In re Appraisal of PetSmart, Inc., 2017 WL 2303599 (Del. Ch.), argued that an LBO pricing model "will rarely if ever produce fair value because the model is built to allow the [LBO] funds to realize a certain internal rate of return that will always leave some portion of the company's going concern value unrealized." *Id.* at *29. The Delaware Chancery Court, however, rejected this mindset. According to the Court:

> Taken to its logical conclusion, . . . Petitioners' position would suggest that all private equity bidders employing the same model (assuming they strive for the same IRR as

5. What is an "anti-bubble"? Why would it be optimal for management to take a publicly traded company private during an anti-bubble's existence?

6. What is the "winner's curse" and why is it so concerning in the case of an MBO?

When the lower court's decision in *Dell* was appealed, the Delaware Supreme Court reversed in part, affirmed in part and remanded the case back to the Chancery Court:

> The problem with the trial court's opinion is not, as the Company argues, that it failed to take into account the stock price and deal price. The trial court *did consider* this market data. It simply decided to give it no weight. . . . Here, the trial court gave no weight to Dell's stock price because it found its market to be inefficient. But the evidence suggests that the market for Dell's shares was actually efficient and, therefore, likely a possible proxy for fair value. Further, the trial court concluded that several features of management-led buyout ("MBO") transactions render the deal prices resulting from such transactions unreliable. But the trial court's own findings suggest that, even though this was an MBO transaction, these features were largely absent here. Moreover, even if it were not possible to determine the precise amount of that market data's imperfection, . . . the trial court's decision to rely "exclusively" on its own DCF analysis is based on several assumptions that are not grounded in relevant, accepted financial principles.

Dell, Inc. v. Magnetar Global Event Driven Master Fund Ltd., 177 A.3d 1, 5 (Del. 2017).

Despite the *Dell* decision, the Delaware Chancery Court appears increasingly willing to rely on the merger price as a proxy for "fair value," at least when *unaffiliated* mergers are involved. From 2010 through July

---

> Petitioners contend they do) should have bid the same amount for PetSmart. This, of course, did not happen—as shown by the spread between KKR and CD & R's final verbal bid at $78 per share and BC Partners' winning bid at $83 per share. And while it is true that private equity firms construct their bids with desired returns in mind, it does not follow that a private equity firm's final offer at the end of a robust and competitive auction cannot ultimately be the *best* indicator of fair value for the company.

Id. The Court added:

> [T]he LBO model and DCF model both rely upon the same expected cash flows. The LBO model, however, is risk adjusted to account for post-transaction leverage. It follows, then, that the higher rate of return sought by bidders employing an LBO model will be offset by the fact that most of the purchase price is financed with debt which, in turn, creates a higher return on equity. Moreover, companies with a history of lagging performance may be valued more by financial bidders with a plan to turn around the company than strategic bidders who might be less inclined to take on that risk. Stated more simply, there are two sides to the "LBO model" argument.

Id., n. 352; see also DFC Global Corp. v. Muirfield Value Partners, L.P., 2017 WL 3261190, at *22 (Del.) ("That a buyer focuses on hitting its internal rate of return has no rational connection to whether the price it pays as a result of a competitive [sales] process is a fair one.").

2017, the Delaware Chancery Court handed down decisions relating to 12 unaffiliated mergers and 9 affiliated mergers (including *Dell*). The court relied on the merger price exclusively in 7 of the 12 unaffiliated merger cases and partially in an eighth case.[126] The court used a discounted cash flow (DCF) methodology in the other four cases. By contrast, the court used a DCF methodology in *all 9* of the affiliated merger cases (including *Dell*), thus expressing a healthy skepticism of the merger price when a controller or majority shareholder stands on both sides of the transaction. Importantly, almost none of the 9 affiliated merger cases involved a sale process that included a market check with competitive bidding while most of the unaffiliated merger cases did. See Fried Frank, *The Evolving World of Delaware Appraisal* 13–14, M&A/PE Quarterly (Summer 2017).

The Delaware Chancery Court's willingness to defer to the merger price in the case of unaffiliated mergers is illustrated in *In re Appraisal of PetSmart, Inc.*, 2017 WL 2303599 (Del. Ch.). According to the court, the sale process that PetSmart followed in selling itself involved "a robust pre-signing auction among informed, motivated bidders." *Id.* at *40. Indeed, the deal price was "forged in the crucible of objective market reality." *Id.* at *2 (quoting *Van de Walle v. Unimation, Inc.*, 1991 WL 29303, at *17 (Del. Ch.). Given that the PetSmart financial projections available to conduct a DCF valuation "were, at best, fanciful," *id.*, the court relied on the merger price. This was true even though only financial bidders ultimately submitted bids and the most likely strategic bidder (PetSmart's main competitor) was not contacted at all (although the PetSmart board had a reasonable basis for excluding it). It also remained true despite PetSmart's strong post-closing performance that allowed it to distribute an $800 million dividend—a 38 percent return on invested equity—about one year after the closing.[127]

NOTE: IS THERE A LEGAL PRESUMPTION THAT "DEAL VALUE" IS THE BEST EVIDENCE OF "FAIR VALUE"?

DFC Global Corp. v. Muirfield Value Partners, L.P., 2017 WL 3261190 (Del.), involved a challenge to the Delaware Chancery Court's appraisal of shares of DFC Global Corp. resulting from its merger with Lone Star Fund VIII (U.S.), L.P., a private equity acquirer. The Delaware Supreme Court refused to create a legal presumption that deal price is the best evidence of fair value. Its refusal is remarkable given that the Chancery Court had found that:

---

[126] In one of the 8 cases, the court reduced the merger price downward by 0.01 percent to reflect the exclusion of synergies. In the case where the merger price was only partially relied upon, the court gave a one-third weight to each of the merger price, discounted cash flow analysis and comparable analysis.

[127] Cf. In re Appraisal of SWS Group, Inc., 2017 WL 2334852, at *1 (Del. Ch.) (noting that "a public sales process that develops market value is often the best evidence of statutory 'fair value' " and that "the sale of SWS was undertaken in conditions that make the price thus derived unreliable as evidence of fair value").

> i) the transaction resulted from a robust market search that lasted approximately two years in which [41] financial and [three] strategic buyers had an open opportunity to buy without inhibition of deal protections; ii) the company was purchased by a third party in an arm's length sale; and iii) there was no hint of self-interest that compromised the market check.

Id. at *1. The Delaware Supreme Court "decline[d] to engage in that act of creation" because it "has no basis in the statutory text, which gives the Court of Chancery in the first instance the discretion to 'determine the fair value of the shares' by taking into account 'all relevant factors.' " *Id.* (citing Del. Gen. Corp. L. § 262(h)). Noting that the "language [in Del. Gen. Corp. L. § 262(h)] is broad," the Court would continue to apply it *as is* "until the General Assembly wishes to narrow the prism through which the Court of Chancery looks at appraisal value in specific classes of mergers[.]" *Id.*

Despite its refusal to embrace the presumption, the Delaware Supreme Court nonetheless reversed and remanded the case back to the Chancery Court. Because the Chancery Court had determined that the sales process had been robust and conflict-free, the Delaware Supreme Court declined to sustain the Chancery Court's decision to give only a one-third weight to the deal price in determining fair value. In doing so, the Delaware Supreme Court disagreed with the two factors cited by the Chancellor for such reduced reliance. The first factor was that DCF Global was operating "in a trough, with future performance dependent upon the outcome of regulatory decision-making that was largely out of the company's control." *Id.* at *10. The Supreme Court countered this by noting that the market's assessment of future cash flows necessarily considers regulatory as well as other types of risk. The second factor was the alleged unreliability of the deal price when that price is established by a private equity buyer that requires a specific rate of return on its investments. In rejecting this notion, the Delaware Supreme Court noted:

> all disciplined buyers, both strategic and financial, have internal rates of return that they expect in exchange for taking on the large risk of a merger, or for that matter, any sizeable investment of its capital. That a buyer focuses on hitting its internal rate of return has no rational connection to whether the price it pays as a result of a competitive process is a fair one.

Id. at *22.

---

iv. Awarding Interest in Appraisal Proceedings

Should a dissenting shareholder receive interest along with the fair value of her shares once the appraisal proceeding concludes? If so, at what rate? Over what time period? And should it be simple or compound interest? Section 262(h) of the Del. Gen. Corp. L. addresses the issue of interest and states that the Delaware Chancery Court "shall determine the fair value of the shares . . . , *together with interest, if any,* to be paid upon the amount determined to be fair value."[128] Section 262(i) adds that "[T]he Court shall direct the payment of the fair value of the shares, *together with interest, if any,* by the surviving or resulting corporation to the stockholders entitled thereto."[129]

Until 2007, Section 262(i) had an additional sentence: "Interest may be simple or compound, as the Court may direct." Simple interest entails the payment of interest only on the amount of money actually owed (principal). Compound interest, by contrast, entails the payment of interest not only on the amount owed, but on interest itself as it accrues over time. Clearly, a dissenting shareholder would much prefer receiving compound rather than simple interest.

Section 262(i) was amended in 2007 to remove the sentence on compound or simple interest. Moreover, 262(h) was also amended to read "Unless the Court in its discretion determines otherwise for good cause, interest from the effective date of the merger through the date of payment of the judgment shall be *compounded quarterly* and shall accrue at *5% over the Federal Reserve discount rate*[130] (including any surcharge) as established from time to time during the period between the effective date of the merger and the date of payment of the judgment."[131] This rate is referred to as the "legal" or "statutory" rate of interest in Delaware. Consider the following case.

MERION CAPITAL, L.P. v. 3M COGENT, INC.

Delaware Court of Chancery, 2013.
2013 WL 3793896.

MEMORANDUM OPINION

PARSONS, VICE CHANCELLOR.

* * *

---

128 Emphasis added.

129 *Id.*

130 The Board of Governors of the U.S. Federal Reserve System (the "Fed") sets the discount rate. This is the rate of interest a Federal Reserve Bank's lending facility (referred to as its "discount window") charges eligible depository institutions which borrow directly from the Fed. These institutions borrow extremely short-term funds (typically overnight) on a fully secured basis in order to meet their short-term liquidity needs. The Board of Governors can influence the money supply by increasing or decreasing the discount rate. While each Federal Reserve Bank offers three discount window programs—primary credit, secondary credit and seasonal credit—the Fed typically is referring to the primary credit rate when it uses the term "discount rate."

131 Emphasis added.

E. Are Petitioners Entitled to Statutory Interest at the Legal Rate?

[Ed. After setting forth the language of Section 262(h) of the Del. Gen. Corp. L. (which appears in the paragraph preceding this case), the Court stated the following:]

Nevertheless, "[a]dopting a different rate may be justified where it is necessary to avoid an inequitable result, such as where there has been improper delay or a bad faith assertion of valuation claims."[196]

Here, Respondent [3M Cogent, Inc.] argues that this Court should not apply the statutory rate of interest because: (1) awarding prejudgment interest to shareholders who acquired shares after the announcement of the acquisition would be an inequitable result; and (2) [the Shareholder] Petitioners improperly delayed the resolution of this action.

1. Petitioners' post-merger acquisition of shares

3M Cogent emphasizes that Petitioners acquired shares after the Merger was announced. In such circumstances, Respondent contends, it would be inequitable to award interest at the legal rate because Delaware law disfavors the purchase of a lawsuit and statutory interest is not intended to benefit purchasers of after-acquired shares.

In *Salomon Brothers Inc. v. Interstate Bakeries Corp.,*[197] this Court addressed whether one who purchases stock after notice of a transaction is entitled to seek appraisal pursuant to 8 *Del. C.* § 262. The Court stated:

> I find nothing in the purpose or language of § 262 that would defeat [petitioner's] entitlement to an appraisal and I find nothing inequitable about an investor purchasing stock in a company after a merger has been announced with the thought that, if the merger is consummated on the announced terms, the investor may seek appraisal.[198]

In other words, Delaware law does not disfavor the purchase of shares after the announcement of a merger. Indeed, after the trial in *Salomon Brothers,* the Court awarded an 11% rate of interest to the petitioner. As 3M Cogent correctly notes, however, the Court in *Salomon Brothers* did not address whether any reduction or elimination of prejudgment interest might be appropriate.

In support of denying Petitioners an award of statutory interest, Respondent avers that statutory interest was not intended to compensate shareholders who acquired their shares after the merger was announced.

---

[196] *In re Appraisal of Metromedia Int'l Gp., Inc.,* 971 A.2d 893, 907 (Del. Ch. 2009).

[197] 576 A.2d 650 (Del. Ch. 1989), *appeal refused,*571 A.2d 787, 1990 WL 18152 (Del. 1990) (ORDER).

[198] *Id.* at 654.

In *Cede & Co. v. Technicolor, Inc.,*[200] for example, the Delaware Supreme Court stated that "[t]he underlying assumption in an appraisal valuation is that the dissenting shareholders would be willing to maintain their investment position had the merger not occurred."[201] In the same vein, Respondent relies on cases that have recognized that the appraisal right was intended to protect "stockholders—who by reason of the statute lost their common law right to prevent a merger—by providing for the appraisement of their stock and the payment to them of the full value thereof in money."[202]

I am mindful, however, that statutory interest also serves to avoid an undeserved windfall to the respondent in an appraisal action, who "would otherwise have had free use of money rightfully belonging to" the petitioners.[203] Even though a respondent may have been cash-rich, "the [respondent] derived a benefit from having the use of the [petitioners'] funds at no cost."[204]

In sum, the plain language of the appraisal statute calls for the payment of statutory interest unless the Court determines otherwise for good cause shown. Respondent, 3M Cogent, has not shown that it would be inequitable for Petitioners to receive the legal rate of interest for shares acquired after the merger.

2. Petitioners' purported "delay"

Respondent next argues that the Court should refuse to award any interest for the period from April 28, 2011 to February 2, 2012 because Petitioners unreasonably delayed in prosecuting their case. . . .

Petitioners counter that Respondent cannot complain about Petitioners' purported delay because Respondent itself failed to move with alacrity. . . .

For a case of this size and complexity, the trial was completed within a reasonable time period. Even with some excusable delay, the trial was conducted within 20 months of the initial petition. Accordingly, I find that Respondent has not shown any unreasonable or improper delay and, therefore, deny Respondent's request to limit the award of interest on that basis.

---

200 684 A.2d 289 (Del. 1996).

201 *Id.* at 298 (citing *Cavalier Oil Corp. v. Harnett,* 564 A.2d 1137, 1145 (Del. 1989)).

202 *Schenley Indus., Inc. v. Curtis,* 152 A.2d 300, 301 (Del.1959) (citing *Chicago Corp. v. Munds,* 172 A. 452, 455 (Del. Ch.1934)).

203 *Lane v. Cancer Treatment Ctrs. of Am., Inc.,* 2004 WL 1752847, at *36 (Del. Ch. July 30, 2004); *see also Gholl v. Emachines, Inc.,* 2004 WL 2847865, at *18 (Del. Ch. Nov. 24, 2004) ("An award of interest serves two purposes. It compensates the petitioner for the loss of use of its capital during the pendency of the appraisal process and *causes the disgorgement of the benefit respondent has enjoyed during the same period.*" (emphasis added)).

204 *Ryan v. Tad's Enters., Inc.,* 709 A.2d 682, 705 (Del. Ch. 1996), *aff'd,*693 A.2d 1082, 1997 WL 188351 (Del. 1997) (ORDER).

* * *

NOTE: INTEREST RATE ARBITRAGE AND DELAWARE'S RESPONSE

Could an investor "game" the system of appraisal? Assume interest rates paid on money deposits are low when compared to the current statutory rate provided for in Section 262(h) of the Del. Gen. Corp. L. Based on that assumption, would it make financial sense for an investor to purchase stock in a target company after the announcement of a proposed merger involving that company but before the merger vote and then pursue appraisal rights? If you believe your new shares are worth at least the merger consideration being offered by the acquirer, and assuming you can keep a lid on those pesky attorney fees, it may indeed make sense to purchase target company shares post-announcement and pursue those rights. Would a large discrepancy between the current statutory rate and interest rates paid on money deposits create undue pressure on the surviving company to a merger to settle the appraisal proceeding quickly?

Interestingly, the respondent in *Merion Capital, L.P.*, *supra*, argued that the petitioners were indeed gaming the system in that exact way, although its argument was inexplicably buried in a footnote. According to the Delaware Chancery Court:

> In a footnote, Respondent argues that in the current interest rate environment—where the statutory rate of interest is more than seven times the federal discount rate—Petitioners have distorted incentives to seek appraisal. There are risks to both sides in an appraisal proceeding, however, and the applicable interest rate is only one of them. Moreover, "[i]t is beyond the province of courts to question the policy or wisdom of an otherwise valid law. Rather, [I] must take and apply the law as [I] find it, leaving any desirable changes to the General Assembly." *Sheehan v. Oblates of St. Francis de Sales,* 15 A.3d 1247, 1259 (Del. 2011).[132]

Do you find the "we didn't write the law, so go complain to the legislature" argument a convincing *intellectual* argument in this regard?

According to four business school professors, "interest rate arbitrage" is alive and well in Delaware:

> [O]ur study affirms the widely held belief that a significant part of the increase in appraisal petitions has been driven by the lucrative yields provided on the awards in these cases. For every percentage point increase in the yield that arbitrageurs obtain in excess to their alternative risk free investment (e.g., treasury bills with comparable duration), the probability of an appraisal filing increases by about 1.3

---

[132] 2013 WL 3793896, at *25 n. 205.

> percentage points. This implies that the 5% statutory rate above the risk free rate, on its own, has triggered 6.5 percentage points of additional appraisal filings among all eligible M&A deals, or almost 45% of the actual appraisal petitions filed.[133]

Not surprisingly, "there has been a significant uptick in appraisal litigation."[134] Shareholders sought the appraisal remedy 20 times in 2012, 33 times in 2015, and 48 times in 2016.[135] While appraisal actions continue to be brought in only a small number of M & A deals, in 2016 the Delaware legislature decided to take action, amending Del. Gen. Corp. L. § 262(h) in an attempt to tap down interest rate arbitrage. The amendment now allows a surviving corporation to pay an amount in cash to dissenting shareholders *prior* to the entry of judgment in an appraisal proceeding. The stated purpose is to halt interest from accruing on the amount paid, and thus reduce the attractiveness of interest rate arbitrage. Indeed, if the surviving corporation makes a prepayment, interest will only accrue on (a) the difference, if any, between the prepayment and the fair value of the shares as determined by the Chancery Court and (b) interest already accrued at the time the surviving corporation makes the prepayment, unless accrued interest up to that point is also paid at that time.

The amendment does not require that the surviving corporation's prepayment equal or be greater or less than the fair value of the shares to be appraised—i.e., it is not a party admission on valuation. Nor does a prepayment create any inference in that regard. Nevertheless, the amendment is silent on whether dissenters have to return any excess prepayment in the event that the Chancery Court determines that the fair value of the shares appraised is less than the amount prepaid. Thus, surviving corporations making prepayments should be conservative when determining the amount of any prepayment.

---

v. Appraisal Awards and Judicial Review

The Delaware courts have generated some stunning results in appraisal cases. E.g., *In re Emerging Comm.*, 2004 WL 1305745 (Del. Ch.) (in a going-private acquisition shareholders in tender offer/freeze-out merger offered $10.25 a share; court appraisal awarded at $38.05 a share (271.2 percent higher)); *Lane v. Cancer Treatment Centers of America,* 2004 WL 1752847 (Del. Ch.) (in an upstream merger shareholder offered $260 a share; court appraisal awarded $1,345.00 a share (417.3 percent more); *Prescott Group Small Cap v. The Coleman Co.*, 2004 WL 2059515 (Del. Ch.)

---

133 Danqing Mei, Randall Thomas, Tao Li, Wei Jiang, *Reforming the Delaware Law to Address Appraisal Arbitrage*, HARV. L. SCH. FORUM ON CORP. GOV. AND FIN. REG. (May 12, 2016), avail. at https://corpgov.law.harvard.edu/2016/05/12/reforming-the-delaware-law-to-address-appraisal-arbitrage/.

134 Fried Frank, *The Evolving World of Delaware Appraisal*, at 1, M&A/PE Quarterly (Summer 2017).

135 See *id.*

(in a going-private merger shareholders offered $9.31 a share; court appraisal awarded $35.35 a share (279.7 percent more)); *M.G. Bancorporation v. Le Beau*, 737 A.2d 513 (Del. 1999) (minority shareholders in short-form merger offered $41 a share; court appraisal awarded at $85 a share (107.3 percent more)). In comparison to the above, *In re Appraisal of Dell, Inc.*, 2016 WL 3186538 (Del. Ch.), *rev'd in part, aff'd in part, and remanded sub nom. Dell, Inc. v. Magnetar Global Event Driven Master Fund Ltd.*, 177 A.3d 1 (Del. 2017) (in a going-private acquisition shareholders in single step merger offered $13.96 a share; court appraisal awarded $17.62 a share (26.2 percent higher)), seems downright pedestrian.

As seen in the preceding paragraph, appraisal case results can be particularly dramatic in situations involving transactions where a controlling shareholder was merging the target company into itself or another controlled subsidiary. From 2010 through July 2017, the Delaware Chancery Court handed down decisions relating to 9 affiliated mergers (including *Dell*). The appraisal amount awarded in those cases was, on average, 84.1 percent higher than the merger price, with a low of 10.7 percent higher and a high of 258 percent higher. See Fried Frank, *The Evolving World of Delaware Appraisal*, at 14, M&A/PE Quarterly (Summer 2017). Due to the inherent conflict of interest, the courts are looking at affiliated mergers very carefully in appraisal proceedings. One of the deals, *Emerging Communications*, had a price negotiated by a Special Committee of independent directors and accepted by a majority of the minority shareholders twice, first in an open tender offer (majority of the minority tendered) and second in a vote on the second stage merger (majority of the minority voted affirmatively). The lesson is that minority shareholders in controlling shareholder mergers should always, as a strategic matter, dissent.

Despite these dramatic awards, one study found that almost 75 percent of all appraisal proceedings settle before a final determination is made by the court. See Charles R. Korsmo & Minor Myers, *The Structure of Stockholder Litigation: When Do the Merits Matter?*, 75 OHIO ST. L. J. 829, 878–82 (2014).

It is possible, although certainly not likely, that the Delaware Chancery Court could determine that the fair value of the shares held by a dissenter is worth *less* than the deal price. From 2010 through July 2017, the Delaware Chancery Court has handed down three decisions where fair value was, indeed, less than the deal price. See *In re SWS Group*, 2017 WL 2334852 (Del. Ch.) (fair value 7.8 percent lower than merger price); *LongPath Capital, LLC v. Ramtron Int'l Corp.*, 2015 WL 4540443 (Del. Ch.) (fair value determined to be merger price adjusted downward by 0.01 percent to eliminate synergistic value); *Gearrald v. Just Care, Inc.*, 2012

WL 1569818 (Del. Ch.) (fair value 14.4 percent lower than merger price). All three cases involved *unaffiliated* mergers.

The Delaware Supreme Court has underscored that the lower court's valuation will be accorded a high level of deference, so long it properly explains how it reached that valuation.[136] In *M.G. Bancorporation v. Le Beau*, 737 A.2d 513, 526–27 (Del. 1999), the Court noted the following:

> In the absence of legal error, this Court reviews appraisal valuations pursuant to the abuse of discretion standard. The Court of Chancery abuses its discretion when either its factual findings do not have record support or its valuation is not the result of an orderly and logical deductive process.
>
> Appraisal actions are highly complicated matters that the Court of Chancery is uniquely qualified to adjudicate in an equitable manner. Since *Weinberger*, this Court has eschewed choosing any one method of appraisal to the exclusion of all others. Today, we reinforce the substance of this philosophy and support methods that allow the Court of Chancery to perform its statutory role as appraiser, based on a solid foundation of record evidence, independent of the positions of the parties.

---

d. The Exclusivity of the Appraisal Remedy

Another illustration of the uncertain purpose of the appraisal remedy is the courts' struggle with integrating the remedy with claims of breaches of fiduciary duty by managers in acquisitions. Companies ask that the appraisal remedy, if available, be the *exclusive remedy* for shareholders complaining about mergers or other covered transactions. Shareholder plaintiffs would prefer to add appraisal proceedings to their pre-existing arsenal of remedies for attacking transactions—claims for breach of fiduciary duty, securities violations, and fraud. Delaware courts have attempted to carve out an exclusive niche for the appraisal remedy. See *Weinberger, supra* (appraisal remedy exclusive but does not preclude claims "where fraud, misrepresentation, self-dealing, deliberate waste of corporate assets, or gross or palpable overreaching are involved").[137] The remedy in the proceedings based on claims of breach of duty is limited, however, to injunctive relief and *rescissory damages*, damages that put the

---

[136] See DFC Global Corp. v. Muirfield Value Partners, L.P., 2017 WL 3261190, at *31 (Del.) ("[T]he Court of Chancery must exercise its considerable discretion while also explaining, with reference to the economic facts before it and corporate finance principles, why it is according a certain weight to a certain indicator of value.").

[137] The Delaware Supreme Court explained the mechanics of *Weinberger* in two subsequent decisions involving the same litigation, Cede & Co. v. Technicolor, Inc., 542 A.2d 1182 (Del. 1988), and 634 A.2d 345 (Del. 1993) (minority shareholders who discovered evidence of fraud in appraisal proceeding may bring a supplemental equitable proceeding for damages not limited by appraisal award for fair value).

shareholders in the same financial position they would have occupied had the transaction not taken place. See *Andra v. Blount*, 772 A.2d 183 (Del. Ch. 2000) (describing difficulty in applying the *Weinberger* test). The Model Act, purporting to follow Delaware law, limits a dissenting shareholder to its appraisal remedy unless the corporate action "was procured as a result of fraud, a material misrepresentation, or an omission of a material fact necessary to make statements made, in light of the circumstances in which they were made, not misleading[.]" ABA Model Bus. Corp. Act § 13.40(b)(2) (2016 rev.).

Since *Cede & Co. v. Technicolor, Inc.*, 542 A.2d 1182 (Del. 1988) (*Technicolor I*), "the consolidated breach of fiduciary duty action and appraisal proceeding has been a fixture of Delaware law."[138] The breach of fiduciary duty claim seeks an equitable remedy that requires a finding of wrongdoing. The appraisal proceeding seeks a statutory determination of fair value that does not require a finding of wrongdoing. In Technicolor I, the Delaware Supreme Court stated that when presented with such a case, the court should address the breach of fiduciary duty action first, because a finding of liability and the resultant remedy could potentially moot the appraisal proceeding.[139]

The drafters of the Model Act believe that conflicts of interests should affect the basic valuation analysis and, therefore, specifically grant appraisal rights when conflicts exist.[140] If evidence of a conflict of interest or absence thereof affects the basic valuation inquiry, fiduciary duty analysis and valuation analysis become similar.[141] In fiduciary duty cases a court, in the absence of a conflict of interest, defers to the acquisition price under the business judgment rule; in valuation cases a court may use as evidence the actual merger price absent a conflict of interest. The exclusivity issue becomes largely a question of preclusion: Must shareholders file a notice of dissent before the vote to preserve their claims?[142]

---

[138] In re Trados Inc. Shareholder Litigation, 2013 WL 4516775, at *16 (Del. Ch.).

[139] Technicolor I, 542 A.2d at 1188.

[140] See ABA Model Bus. Corp. Act §§ 13.01 (definition of "interested transaction" and "interested person") & 13.02(b)(4) (including Off. Cmt. 2) (interested transactions give rise to appraisal rights) (2016 rev.).

[141] See In re Emerging Comm., 2004 WL 1305745 (Del. Ch.) (the causes were consolidated and one analysis used for both).

[142] Ironically, minority shareholders who do not have appraisal rights (because of a market-out exemption, for example) may have an easier time claiming relief because they do not have to satisfy the requirements in the appraisal statute for perfecting their claims. Cf. Berger v. Pubco Corp., 976 A.2d 132 (Del. 2009) (on quasi-appraisal class actions for minority shareholders that did not file a timely notice to dissent).

QUESTION

In the context of the sale of their company, could directors fully comply with their fiduciary obligations to shareholders and yet fall short of securing fair value for those same shareholders? Consider the following excerpt.

IN RE APPRAISAL OF DELL, INC.

Delaware Court of Chancery, 2016.
2016 WL 3186538, *rev'd in part, aff'd in part, and remanded sub nom. Dell, Inc. v. Magnetar Global Event Driven Master Fund Ltd.*, 177 A.3d 1 (Del. 2017).

MEMORANDUM OPINION

LASTER, VICE CHANCELLOR.

* * *

2. The Appraisal Inquiry Contrasted With The Breach Of Fiduciary Duty Inquiry

[In an appraisal proceeding, an] equally important consideration when evaluating the persuasiveness of the deal price for establishing fair value is the nature of the court's review of the process that led to the transaction. Here, the distinction between a breach of fiduciary duty case and an appraisal proceeding looms large:

> [W]hile the transaction particulars undergirding appraisal are related to and can sometimes overlap with those relevant to the fiduciary duty class action, the emphasis is crucially different. In a fiduciary duty class action, the court is faced with the question of holding individual directors personally liable for having breached their duties to the stockholders. Courts are naturally and properly hesitant to take such a drastic step lest directors become risk-averse, making decisions with an eye toward minimizing the risk of personal liability rather than seeking to maximize expected value for stockholders. An appraisal action asks a substantially more modest question: did the stockholders get fair value for their shares in the merger? If not, the acquirer must make up the difference, but no one is held personally liable.

Modern Appraisal Litigation at [321–22].[Ed.[143]] The two inquiries are different, so a sale process might pass muster for purposes of a breach of fiduciary claim and yet still generate a sub-optimal process for purposes of an appraisal.

The central question in a breach of fiduciary duty case is whether the defendant fiduciaries acted in a manner that should subject them personally to a damages award. To determine whether a breach of duty

---

[143] [Ed. Charles Korsmo & Minor Myers, *Reforming Modern Appraisal Litigation*, 41 Del. J. Corp. L. 279, 321–22 (2017) (footnote omitted) (hereinafter Modern Appraisal Litigation)].

occurred, a court applying Delaware law evaluates the directors' conduct through the lens of a standard of review. "Delaware has three tiers of review for evaluating director decision-making: the business judgment rule, enhanced scrutiny, and entire fairness." *Reis v. Hazelett Strip—Casting Corp.*, 28 A.3d 442, 457 (Del. Ch. 2011). "Enhanced scrutiny is Delaware's intermediate standard of review." *In re Trados Inc. S'holder Litig. (Trados II)*, 73 A.3d 17, 43 (Del. Ch. 2013).

Framed for purposes of an M&A transaction, enhanced scrutiny places the burden on the defendant directors to show that they sought "to secure the transaction offering the best value reasonably available for the stockholders." *Paramount Commc'ns Inc. v. QVC Network Inc.*, 637 A.2d 34, 44 (Del. 1994). In this formulation, "[t]he key verb is 'sought.' Time-bound mortals cannot foresee the future. The test therefore cannot be whether, with hindsight, the directors actually achieved the best price." *In re Del Monte Foods Co. S'holders Litig.*, 25 A.3d 813, 830 (Del. Ch. 2011). "Rather, the duty can only be to try in good faith, in such a setting, to get the best available transaction for the shareholders. Directors are not insurers."[17]

To determine whether directors have satisfied their fiduciary duties in an M&A setting, the enhanced scrutiny standard of review examines (i) the reasonableness of "the decisionmaking process employed by the directors, including the information on which the directors based their decision," and (ii) "the reasonableness of the directors' action in light of the circumstances then existing." *QVC*, 637 A.2d at 44. "Through this examination, the court seeks to assure itself that the board acted reasonably, in the sense of taking a logical and reasoned approach for the purpose of advancing a proper objective, and to thereby smoke out mere pretextual justifications for improperly motivated decisions." *Dollar Thrifty,* 14 A.3d at 598.[Ed.[144]] The reasonableness standard enables a reviewing court "to address inequitable action even when directors may have subjectively believed that they were acting properly." *Del Monte*, 25 A.3d at 830–31. The objective standard does not permit a reviewing court to freely substitute its own judgment for the directors':

> There are many business and financial considerations implicated in investigating and selecting the best value reasonably available. The board of directors is the corporate decisionmaking body best equipped to make these judgments. Accordingly, a court applying enhanced judicial scrutiny should be deciding whether the directors made a reasonable decision, not a perfect decision. If a board selected one of several reasonable alternatives, a court should not second-guess that choice even though it might have

[17] *Citron v. Fairchild Camera & Instrument Corp.*, . . . 1988 WL 53322, at *16 n.17 (Del. Ch. May 19, 1988) (Allen, C.) . . . .

[144] [Ed. In re Dollar Thrifty Shareholder Litig., 14 A.3d 573 (Del. Ch. 2010).]

> decided otherwise or subsequent events may have cast doubt on the board's determination. Thus, courts will not substitute their business judgment for that of the directors, but will determine if the directors' decision was, on balance, within a range of reasonableness.

QVC, 637 A.2d at 45 (emphasis removed). Enhanced scrutiny "is not a license for law-trained courts to second-guess reasonable, but debatable, tactical choices that directors have made in good faith." *In re Toys "R" Us, Inc. S'holder Litig.*, 877 A.2d 975, 1000 (Del. Ch. 2005); *accord Dollar Thrifty*, 14 A.3d at 595–96 ("[A]t bottom *Revlon* is a test of reasonableness; directors are generally free to select the path to value maximization, so long as they choose a reasonable route to get there.").

As these passages show, enhanced scrutiny requires an inquiry into the ends the directors pursued and the means they chose to achieve them. "[T]he reasonableness standard requires the court to consider for itself whether the board is truly well motivated (i.e. is it acting for the proper ends?) before ultimately determining whether its means were themselves a reasonable way of advancing those ends." *Dollar Thrifty*, 14 A.3d at 599. Enhanced scrutiny "mandates that the court look closely at the motivations of the board." *Id.* at 598. What typically generates a finding of breach "is evidence of self-interest, undue favoritism or disdain towards a particular bidder, or a similar non-stockholder-motivated influence that calls into question the integrity of the process." *Del Monte*, 25 A.3d at 831. The test is not whether the outcome was in fact the best transaction reasonably available, and the failure to achieve what actually would have been the best transactional outcome, standing alone, is not a basis for liability. The outcome that the directors achieved will figure into the damages calculation, but only if the matter reaches that phase. The outcome is not part of the liability case.

In an appraisal proceeding, by contrast, the opposite is true. The court does not judge the directors' motives or the reasonableness of their actions, but rather the outcome they achieved. The price is all that matters because the court's inquiry focuses exclusively on the value of the company. How and why the directors achieved fair value or fell short is not part of the case. The sale process is useful to the extent—and only to the extent—that it provides evidence of the company's value on the date the merger closed.

Because the standards differ, it is entirely possible that the decisions made during a sale process could fall within *Revlon*'s range of reasonableness, and yet the process still could generate a price that was not persuasive evidence of fair value in an appraisal. . . . Put differently, even if a transaction passes fiduciary muster, an appraisal proceeding could result in a higher fair value award. . . .

> To be sure, the questions in the two kinds of actions are frequently related. Often, when stockholders do not get fair value for their

> shares, it will be because the board has breached its fiduciary duties. . . . [T]he strongest appraisal claims [should] also present strong fiduciary duty claims, and vice versa. But forcing both types of claims into the same analytical box is a self-evident mistake. Many types of managerial sloth, incompetence, pressure, or collusion that courts have been understandably hesitant to characterize as breaches of fiduciary duty can nonetheless lead to . . . stockholders receiving well below fair value for their shares. In such situations, appraisal constitutes a useful middle course between holding directors personally liable (and potentially granting injunctions) and allowing unfair transactions to escape meaningful scrutiny.

Modern Appraisal Litigation, *supra*, at [322]. "Satisfying one of the various *Revlon*-type tests . . . is not necessarily a market test" sufficient to establish fair value for purposes of appraisal. Charles R. Korsmo & Minor Myers, *Appraisal Arbitrage and the Future of Public Company M&A*, 92 Wash. U.L. Rev. 1551, 1608 (2015).

* * *

e. Modern Application

M.G. BANCORPORATION, INC. V. LE BEAU

Supreme Court of Delaware, 1999.
737 A.2d 513.

HOLLAND, JUSTICE.

* * *

The proceeding arises from a cash-out merger of the minority shareholders of MGB on November 17, 1993 (the "Merger"). MGB was merged into Southwest, which owned over 91 percent of the outstanding shares of MGB's common stock, pursuant to 8 Del. C. § 253. The Petitioners-appellees were the record owners of 18,151 shares of MGB common stock as of the date of the Merger. The Merger consideration was $41 per share.

The Petitioners initiated an appraisal proceeding, in accordance with 8 Del. C. § 262 ("Section 262"), to determine the fair value of MGB's common stock. Following a three-day trial, the Court of Chancery concluded that the fair value of MGB's common stock as of the Merger date was $85 per share. The Respondents were ordered to pay that sum, together with interest, compounded monthly, at the rate of 8 percent from November 17, 1993.

This Court affirms that portion of the judgment by the Court of Chancery that awarded the Petitioners $85 per share. That portion of the judgment that awarded compound interest to the Petitioners, however, is remanded for further consideration.

* * *

The Petitioners are shareholders who owned 18,151 shares of common stock of MGB before the Merger. The Respondents are Southwest and its subsidiary, MGB. Before the Merger, MGB was a Delaware-chartered bank holding company headquartered in Worth, Illinois. MGB had two operating Illinois-chartered bank subsidiaries, Mount Greenwood Bank ("Greenwood") and Worth Bancorp, Inc. ("WBC"). Both banks served customers in the southwestern Chicago metropolitan area. MGB owned 100% of Mount Greenwood and 75.5 percent of WBC.

Before the Merger, Southwest owned 91.68 percent of MGB's common shares. On November 17, 1993, MGB was merged into Southwest in a "short form" merger under 8 Del. C. § 253. Because the Merger was accomplished unilaterally, neither MGB's board of directors nor its minority shareholders were legally required to, or did, vote on the transaction.

Southwest engaged Alex Sheshunoff & Co. Investment Bankers ("Sheshunoff") to determine the "fair market value" of MGB's minority shares for the purpose of setting the Merger price. Sheshunoff determined that the fair market value of MGB's minority shares was $41 per share as of June 30, 1993. Accordingly, MGB's minority shareholders were offered $41 per share in cash as the Merger consideration. The Petitioners rejected that offer, electing instead to pursue their statutory rights, and this appraisal proceeding was commenced.

A stockholders class action based on breach of fiduciary duty was also filed challenging the Merger. On July 5, 1995, the Court of Chancery issued a decision in that companion class action, holding that Sheshunoff had not performed its appraisal in a legally proper manner. The basis for the Court of Chancery's conclusion was that Sheshunoff had determined only the "fair market value" of MGB's minority shares, as opposed to valuing MGB in its entirety as a going concern and determining the fair value of the minority shares as a pro rata percentage of that value.

Petitioners' Valuation

At the December 1996 trial, the Petitioners' expert witness was David Clarke ("Clarke"). He testified that as of the Merger date the fair value of MGB common stock was $58,514,000, or $85 per share. In arriving at that conclusion, Clarke used three distinct methodologies to value MGB's two operating bank subsidiaries: the comparative publicly-traded company approach, yielding a $76.24 to $77.50 per share value; the discounted cash flow ("DCF") method, yielding a $73.96 to $72.23 per share value; and, the comparative acquisitions approach, yielding an $85 per share value.

In performing his analysis, Clarke added a control premium to the values of the two subsidiaries to reflect the value of MGB's controlling interest in those subsidiaries. He then added the value of MGB's remaining assets to his valuations of the two subsidiaries. Clarke arrived at an overall fair value of $85 per share for MGB.

At the trial, the Petitioners also introduced evidence of what MGB's fair value would be if Sheshunoff's prior determination were revised as of the Merger date and if its minority discount were eliminated.

Respondents' Valuation

The Respondents relied upon the expert testimony of Robert Reilly ("Reilly") at trial. He testified that, as of the Merger date, the fair value of MGB common stock was $41.90 per share. Reilly arrived at that conclusion by performing two separate valuations: the discounted cash flow method and a "capital market" analysis. Reilly did not add any control premium to the values of MGB's two subsidiaries, because he determined that a control premium was inappropriate in valuing a holding company such as MGB.

The Respondents did not call anyone from the Sheshunoff firm as an expert witness at trial, even though Sheshunoff's valuation had served as the basis for setting the $41 per share Merger price consideration.

Court of Chancery's Decision

At the conclusion of the trial, the Court of Chancery had before it: three per share values from Clarke; two per share values from Reilly; and a revision by the Petitioners' witness of the Sheshunoff $41 per share computation. The parties' experts' respective valuation conclusions and the revised Sheshunoff valuation were summarized by the Court of Chancery in the following chart:

Valuation in $000s	WBC	75.5% of WBC	Greenwood	Other Assets	Total	Per Share
Petitioners (Clarke)						
Comparative Publicly–Traded Method:	33,059	24,960	20,952	6,814	52,726	76.59
With Control Premium:	43,300	32,692	27,100	6,814	66,606	96.76
DCF Method:	32,075	24,217	20,079	6,814	51,110	74.25
With Control Premium:	44,800	33,824	28,300	6,814	68,938	100.15
Comparative Acquisitions Method:	38,100	28,800	22,900	6,814	58,514	85.00
						85.00 = fair value
Respondents (Reilly)						
Capital Market Method:					28,400	41.26
DCF Method:					29,220	42.45
					Average: 41.90 = fair value	
Sheshunoff (Updated)						
(Without Control Premium)						
Adjusted Book Value						64.13
Adjusted Earnings Value						76.80

The Court of Chancery concluded that $85 per share was the fair value of MGB's stock on the date of the merger.

* * *

The Respondents contend that the Court of Chancery erred by rejecting certain valuation opinions of both parties' experts. The seminal case on this Court's jurisprudence in an appraisal proceeding provides guidance on the admission of expert testimony.[14] Proof of value can be established by any techniques or methods that are generally acceptable in the financial community and otherwise admissible in court, subject only to our interpretation of 8 Del. C. § 262(h).

Reilly's "Capital Market" Approach

The qualifications of the Respondents' expert witness, Reilly, were undisputed at trial. The parties were in sharp disagreement, however, about whether Reilly's "capital market" approach was "generally accepted" within the financial community for valuing banks and bank holding companies. Reilly's capital market analysis used a number of pricing multiples related to the market value of invested capital ("MVIC"). Reilly computed the ratios of MVIC to: earnings before interest and taxes ("EBIT"); earnings before interest, depreciation, and taxes ("EBIDT"); debt

[14] Weinberger v. UOP, Inc., Del. Supr., 457 A.2d 701 (1983).

free net income ("DFNI"); debt free cash flow ("DFCF"); interest incomes; and total book value of invested capital ("TBVIC").[Ed.[145]]

The Petitioners' expert, Clarke, testified that Reilly's capital market approach was not generally accepted in the financial community for valuing banks and bank holding companies. According to Clarke, the financial community focuses upon the ratio of price to book value and price to earnings for purposes of valuing banks and bank holding companies.[Ed.[146]] The Court of Chancery concluded that the Respondents had failed to establish that Reilly's capital market methodology is generally accepted by the financial community for purposes of valuing bank holding companies, as distinguished from other types of enterprises.

The Court of Chancery also determined that Reilly's capital market valuation approach included a built-in minority discount. The Court of Chancery noted that the valuation literature, including a treatise co-authored by Reilly himself, supported that conclusion.[26] The Court of Chancery concluded that because Reilly's capital market method resulted in a minority valuation, even if it had concluded that Reilly's capital market approach was an otherwise acceptable method of valuing a bank holding company, the use of Reilly's capital market approach is improper in a statutory appraisal proceeding.

Delaware Rule of Evidence 702, like its federal counterpart, "establishes a standard of evidentiary reliability."[27] Delaware Rule of Evidence 702 "requires a valid . . . connection to the pertinent inquiry as a precondition to admissibility." When the "factual basis, data, principles, methods, or their application" in an expert's opinion are challenged, the

---

145 [Ed. The Chancery Court noted that, "Reilly's second method for valuing MGB was the "capital market" method, which involved: (1) identifying a portfolio of guideline publicly-traded companies, (2) identifying appropriate pricing multiples for those companies, (3) using the multiples for the guideline companies to calculate the appropriate pricing multiples for MGB and (4) applying the multiples to the corresponding financial indicators for MGB."]

146 [Ed. The Chancery Court noted, "Clarke's comparative publicly-traded company approach involved five steps: (1) identifying an appropriate set of comparable companies, (2) identifying the multiples of earnings and book value at which the comparable companies traded, (3) comparing certain of MGB's financial fundamentals (*e.g.*, return on assets and return on equity) to those of the comparable companies, (4) making certain adjustments to those financial fundamentals, and (5) adding an appropriate control premium. Because the merger date (more specifically, the date before the public announcement of a merger) is normally the time that is relevant, and because the Petitioners made no effort to justify Clarke's use of stock prices going back six weeks before the Merger, the Court cannot accept Clarke's comparative company valuation, despite the validity of the technique itself."]

26 See S.P. Pratt, R.F. Reilly & R.P. Schweis, *Valuing a Business* 194–95, 210 (ed. 1996) (explaining that comparative publicly-traded companies produce a minority discounted valuation); see also C.Z. Mercer, *Valuing Financial Institutions* 198–200 and Chapter Thirteen (1992) (explaining that comparative publicly-traded company valuation technique produces a minority valuation that requires adding a control premium to be accurate).

27 Daubert v. Merrell Dow Pharmaceuticals, Inc., 509 U.S. at 590.

trial judge must decide if the expert's testimony "has a reliable basis in the knowledge and experience of [the relevant] discipline."[29]

Both of those conclusions are fully supported by the record evidence that was before the Court of Chancery and the prior holdings of this Court construing Section 262.[30]

Both parties' experts also gave valuation opinions using the same discounted cash flow methodology. The qualifications of each parties' expert witness were accepted by the Court of Chancery. The propriety of using a discounted cash flow analysis in a statutory appraisal action was also acknowledged. The discounted cash flow methodology has been relied upon frequently by parties and the Court of Chancery in other statutory appraisal proceedings.[Ed.[147]]

Although Reilly and Clarke used the same discounted cash flow methodology, each applied different assumptions. The Court of Chancery determined, for example, that "the difference between Clarke's 12 percent discount rate and Reilly's 18 percent discount rate [was] attributable primarily to their different estimates of MGB's cost of equity capital, and their different assumptions of the company specific risks confronting MGB at the time of the merger." The Court of Chancery disagreed with certain of the other assumptions applied by both of the parties' experts. The Court of Chancery ultimately concluded that it could not rely on the DCF valuation opinion of either party's expert.

The Respondents submit the only significant concern raised by the Court of Chancery with respect to Clarke's DCF analysis involved his use of a 12 percent discount rate, i.e., it incorporated a 1 percent small stock premium based on a 1996 study that may contain post-merger data. The Respondents contend that particular error could have been corrected through a mathematical adjustment, i.e., the addition of a 5.2 percent small stock factor based on a 1992 study (which Clarke had used in several other bank appraisals) results in a 15 percent discount rate. The Respondents have calculated that the substitution of the 15 percent discount rate for Clarke's 12 percent rate produces a fair value for MGB of $57 per share. The Respondents argue the Court of Chancery erred by rejecting their

[29] Kumho Tire Co., LTD v. Carmichael, 119 S. Ct. at 1175, quoting Daubert v. Merrell Dow Pharmaceuticals, Inc., 509 U.S. at 592.

[30] See, e.g., Rapid-American Corp. v. Harris, Del. Supr., 603 A.2d 796 (1992); Weinberger v. UOP, Inc., Del. Supr., 457 A.2d 701 (1983).

[147] [Ed. The Chancery Court noted, "Clarke's DCF valuation analysis involved four steps: (1) projecting the future net cash flows available to MGB's shareholders for ten years after the Merger date, (2) discounting those future cash flows to present value as of the Merger date by using a discount rate based on the weighted average cost of capital ("WACC"), (3) adding a terminal value that represented the present value of all future cash flows generated after the ten year projection period, and (4) applying a control premium to the sum of (2) and (3)." Reilly used a five-year projection.]

adjusted Clarke discounted cash flow valuation of $57 as a reliable indication of fair value.

Having accepted the qualifications of both parties' experts and the propriety of using a discounted cash flow model in this statutory appraisal proceeding, the Court of Chancery was not required to adopt any one expert's methodology or calculations in toto.[33] Similarly, by recognizing the discounted cash flow model as one proper valuation technique, the Court of Chancery was not required to use that methodology to make its own independent valuation calculation by either adapting or blending the factual assumptions of the parties' experts. The ultimate selection of a valuation framework is within the Court of Chancery's discretion.

* * *

Court of chancery
Independently appraised shares

The Respondents contend that the Court of Chancery failed to discharge its statutory obligation to function as an independent appraiser.[Ed.[148]] The record does not support that argument. In its appraisal opinion, the Court of Chancery stated:

> The Court is mindful that $85 per share is more than double the Merger price. The Court is also aware of its role under § 262, which is to determine fair value independently. In discharging that institutional function as an independent appraiser, the Court should, where possible, test the soundness of its valuation conclusion against whatever reliable corroborative evidence the record contains. On that score, the record falls far short of perfection. Limited corroborative evidence is available, however, in the form of Sheshunoff's 1993 fair market valuation, (i) adjusted by Clarke to exclude Sheshunoff's minority discount and (ii) updated by Clarke to reflect value data as of November 17, 1993, the date of the Merger.

In discharging its statutory mandate, the Court of Chancery has the discretion to select one of the parties' valuation models as its general framework or to fashion its own. The Court of Chancery's role as an independent appraiser does not necessitate a judicial determination that is completely separate and apart from the valuations performed by the parties' expert witnesses who testify at trial. It must, however, carefully

[33] Cede & Co. v. Technicolor, Inc., Del. Supr., 684 A.2d 289, 299 (1996).

[148] [Ed. The petitioners' argument is based on the Delaware Supreme Court opinion in Gonsalves v. Straight Arrow Publishers, Inc., 701 A.2d 357 (Del. 1997). The Court invalidated a Chancery Court's decision to use an arbitration style decision-making method designed to restrain the parties from taking extreme positions on value. The Chancery Court told the parties before the argument that it would take one or the other's valuation conclusion based on which was the most reasonable. The Supreme Court held that the Chancery Court failed in its duty to make an "independent appraisal."]

consider whether the evidence supports the valuation conclusions advanced by the parties' respective experts. Thereafter, although not required to do so, it is entirely proper for the Court of Chancery to adopt any one expert's model, methodology, and mathematical calculations in toto if that valuation is supported by credible evidence and withstands a critical judicial analysis on the record.

In this case, the Court of Chancery carefully evaluated the valuation testimony and evidence proffered by the parties' experts. It determined that Reilly's capital market approach is legally impermissible, but even if valid, was improperly applied, thereby requiring the rejection of the values Reilly derived by that method. The Court of Chancery found that both Clarke's and Reilly's DCF analyses were improperly applied, thereby requiring the rejection of the values both experts derived by that approach.

The Court of Chancery concluded that Clarke's comparative acquisition approach was a legally valid method to value MGB and that the credible record evidence supported Clarke's $85 per share determination of MGB's fair value as of the Merger date. In making its independent appraisal valuation, the Court of Chancery could have relied entirely upon Clarke's comparative acquisitions approach. Instead, it critically tested Clarke's comparative acquisition approach by using its own judicial expertise to make corrective adjustments to Sheshunoff's legally improper valuation determination and found corroboration for Clarke's result.

The determination of value in a statutory appraisal proceeding is accorded a high level of deference on appeal. In the absence of legal error, this Court reviews appraisal valuations pursuant to the abuse of discretion standard. The Court of Chancery abuses its discretion when either its factual findings do not have record support or its valuation is not the result of an orderly and logical deductive process.

Appraisal actions are highly complicated matters that the Court of Chancery is uniquely qualified to adjudicate in an equitable manner. Since *Weinberger*, this Court has eschewed choosing any one method of appraisal to the exclusion of all others. Today, we reinforce the substance of this philosophy and support methods that allow the Court of Chancery to perform its statutory role as appraiser, based on a solid foundation of record evidence, independent of the positions of the parties.

* * *

Costs assessment

In their cross-appeal, the Petitioners challenge the Court of Chancery's decision to deny their request for an award of attorneys' and expert witness' fees. Section 262(j) provides that costs may be taxed upon the parties as the court deems equitable under the circumstances. Generally, the Petitioner in an appraisal proceeding "should bear the burden of paying its own expert Witnesses and attorneys," unless some equitable exception applies.[57]

The Petitioners invoked the equitable exception of bad faith conduct on the part of the Respondents. Although some of the cases cited by the Petitioners demonstrate that costs were assessed against the surviving corporation even in the absence of a showing of bad faith, those cases all recognized that the decision to award costs is vested within the Court of Chancery's discretion. The record in this case does not support the contention that the Court of Chancery's decision denying an award of fees to the Petitioners' constituted an abuse of discretion . . . .

NOTE: BATTLE OF THE EXPERTS

The duel of the experts in *Le Beau, supra,* is typical in appraisal cases. Experts hired by each side apply modern financial methods and end-up at vastly different valuations. The differences are often breathtaking; one expert may value a firm three or four hundred percent higher than another. The defense expert always comes in with a price that approximates the deal price and the plaintiff's expert comes in with a staggeringly larger figure. The court must assess the validity of the experts differing assumptions on risk measures, interest rates, comparables and a myriad of other facts. Judges, often not professionally trained in finance, cannot help but feel overmatched and a bit at sea in their analysis.

The battle of the experts should come as no surprise given that each side selects and pays for its own expert witness. Rather than attempting to select the "best expert," each side seeks out the "best *witness*." Does this system provide the courts with the expert assistance which, if the experts were unbiased and objectively chosen, they deserve? The courts' frustration with the system that is in place has been around for decades. Indeed, listen to what Vice Chancellor Hartnett expressed in *Kahn v. U.S. Sugar Corp.*, 1985 WL 4449, at *12, 11 Del. J. Corp. L. 908, 925 (Del. Ch. 1985), as he attempted to value U.S. Sugar Corp.:

> [T]he testimony of the expert witnesses . . . is in hopeless disagreement. Each expert presented impressive credentials. Each expressed an opinion as to value based on dozens of value judgment assumptions. While each assumption was based on some data, almost all of the assumptions were fairly debatable and reasonable men using the same data could conclude that a different percentage multiple, or per acreage figure, etc., should be used.
>
> Quite frankly, there is no rational way that I as the trier of fact could conclude that one expression of value was best. All had flaws, all were based on personal assumptions and opinions and all were

---

[57] Cede & Co. v. Technicolor, Inc., Del. Supr., 684 A.2d 289, 301 (1996); In re Radiology Assoc., Inc., Litig., Del. Ch., 611 A.2d 485, 501 (1991).

expressed by obviously knowledgeable and experienced experts who were retained by one side or the other.

Game theorists have developed decision techniques that courts or legislatures may want to consider. The best known is the *baseball* or *final offer* method in which a judge need only select without adjustment whichever of the two party's valuations is the most reasonable. A variation, *night baseball*, requires the court to accept whichever of the two parties' valuations is closest to that of the judge (or a judicially appointed, neutral expert). The point of these procedures is to reduce the incentive of experts to make extreme valuations. But see *Gonsalves v. Straight Arrow Publishers, Inc.*, 725 A.2d 442 (Del. 1999) (rejecting a final offer procedure used by the Chancery Court; in Delaware the change must come through legislation).

f. Appraisal Arbitrage

Appraisal arbitrage is an investment strategy employed by hedge funds and other shareholder activists. They purchase shares in a target corporation after the record date for a merger involving that company and pursue the appraisal remedy as their investment strategy. The arbitrageurs prefer shares of targets where a large number of "no" votes to the merger are likely. The arbitrageur can earn a return based on (a) any positive difference between the appraised value of their shares (as determined by the court) and the value offered by the acquirer and (b) interest on the appraised value accruing at the statutory rate (5 percent above the Federal Reserve's discount rate) from the date of the merger until the date the judgment is paid.

In 2016, the Delaware legislature attacked appraisal arbitrage by amending Del. Gen. Corp. L. § 262 in two ways. First, as seen *supra*, subsection (h) of § 262 was modified in an attempt to tap down interest rate arbitrage. That subsection now allows a surviving corporation to pay an amount in cash to dissenting shareholders *prior* to the entry of judgment in an appraisal proceeding. The stated purpose is to halt interest from accruing on the prepayment amount, and thus reduce the attractiveness of interest rate arbitrage.

Second, subsection (g) of § 262 was modified by adding a *de minimis exception* to appraisal rights. With respect to a constituent corporation to a merger or consolidation with shares listed on a national securities exchange, the Chancery Court *must dismiss* all appraisal proceedings as to all shareholders of shares of that corporation *unless* (1) the total number of shares entitled to appraisal exceeds 1 percent of the outstanding shares of the class or series eligible for appraisal, (2) the value of the consideration provided in the merger or consolidation for such total number of shares exceeds $1 million, or (3) the merger was approved pursuant to the short-form merger provision of Del. Gen. Corp. L. § 253 or 267.

Another potential challenge to arbitrageurs is the requirement that shares not be voted in favor of the merger (the *Dissenter Requirement*). Del. Gen. Corp. L. § 262(a) (shareholder must neither have "voted in favor of the merger or consolidation nor consented thereto in writing pursuant to [Del. Gen. Corp. L.] § 228"). Given that the majority of all outstanding shares of publicly traded corporations are held in "street name," most investors in reality are only the *beneficial owners* of their shares. Indeed, they hold their shares through banks or brokerage firms which are members of The Depository Trust Company (DTC). DTC was established to facilitate the electronic trading of securities, thus avoiding the hassles associated with using paper stock certificates. Cede & Co., the nominee of DTC, is the actual *record shareholder* for all shares held in street name on the ledgers of publicly traded corporations or their transfer agents.

Importantly, only shareholders of "record" are allowed to pursue appraisal rights (the *Record Holder Requirement*). Del. Gen. Corp. L. § 262(a). Beneficial owners seeking appraisal of their shares, therefore, must request that right through Cede & Co, DTC's nominee. However, DTC primarily holds shares on behalf of its members in fungible bulk, meaning that all of the shares are issued in the name of Cede & Co. without any subdivision into separate accounts of the members' investor customers. Through a "Fast Automated Securities Transfer" account, DTC tracks the number of shares that each member holds using an electronic book entry system. As a result, it is typically very difficult (if not impossible) for an arbitrageur to determine how the shares it has purchased after a record date were voted with respect to the merger.[149]

Three recent Delaware cases[150]—colloquially referred to as the *Appraisal Arbitrage Decisions*[151]—have eschewed imposing a share tracing requirement on shareholders seeking appraisal. In all three cases the Chancery Court deemed it factually impossible for either the petitioners or the surviving corporations to identify how Cede & Co. had voted the shares purchased by the petitioners on behalf of the previous beneficial owners. Therefore, the Chancery Court determined that the petitioners could satisfy the Dissenters Requirement by showing that Cede & Co. had voted at least enough shares *against* the merger to cover the number of shares for which appraisal was sought.[152]

---

[149] Only shareholders of record on the record date are entitled to vote at an upcoming meeting of shareholders. See Del. Gen. Corp. L. § 213(a). Thus, Cede & Co., as record shareholder, is entitled to vote shares held in street name on behalf of beneficial owners. Cede & Co. will vote in accordance with any instructions provided by beneficial owners or their voting service agents (e.g., Institutional Shareholder Services Inc., Broadridge Financial Services, Inc.).

[150] See In re Appraisal of Ancestry.com, Inc., 2015 WL 66825 (Del. Ch. 2015); Merion Capital LP v. BMC Software, Inc., 2015 WL 67586 (Del. Ch. 2015); In re Appraisal of Transkaryotic Therapies, Inc., 2007 WL 1378345 (Del. Ch. 2007).

[151] See In re Appraisal of Dell, Inc., 143 A.3d 20, 36 (Del. Ch. 2016).

[152] *Transkaryotic Therapies*, 2007 WL 1378345, at *4. In *Transkaryotic Therapies*, Cede & Co. had voted some shares in favor of the merger and some against, but the Chancery Court ultimately found that this did not preclude Cede's petition for appraisal with respect to shares not voted in favor of the merger. That is, Cede & Co., having otherwise perfected its appraisal rights with respect to approximately 11 million shares for which appraisal was sought, and having voted

More recently, in *In re Appraisal of Dell Inc.*,[153] the Chancery Court indicated that a different result may follow when it is factually possible to determine how Cede & Co. had voted the shares for which petitioners are seeking appraisal:

> There is language in the Appraisal Arbitrage Decisions which, if applied literally to this case, would preclude the court from considering anything other than Cede's aggregated votes on the Merger. That language suggests that as long as Cede did not vote a quantity of shares in favor of the Merger sufficient to cover the appraisal class, then the Dissenter Requirement is satisfied. The jurists who wrote those passages, however, were deciding cases in which the record did not contain any evidence regarding how Cede voted particular shares and where the parties told the court it was impossible to develop any. In this case, there is evidence about how Cede actually voted particular shares.
>
> Importantly, the Appraisal Arbitrage Decisions did not take the next step and hold that when an investor actually directs that its shares be voted in favor of the merger, and when Cede actually votes shares in accordance with the investor's instructions, then the investor can avoid the implications of the Dissenter Requirement by invoking Cede's aggregate votes on behalf of other investors. Permitting the investor to do so would authorize a non-dissenter to pursue dissenter's rights by "hijack[ing] the ownership rights" of other investors who happened to hold through the same nominee. *Sutter Opportunity Fund 2 LLC v. Cede & Co.*, 838 A.2d 1123, 1129 (Del.Ch.2003). Nothing in the Appraisal Arbitrage Decisions speaks to that factual scenario.
>
> * * *
>
> The evidence [in this case] showing how Cede voted particular blocks of shares provides a basis for distinguishing the Appraisal Arbitrage Decisions. Under those opinions, an appraisal petitioner that held in street name can establish a *prima facie* case that the Dissenter Requirement was met by showing that there were sufficient shares at Cede that were not voted in favor of the merger to cover the appraisal class. This showing satisfies the petitioner's initial burden and enables the case to proceed. If there is no other evidence, then as in the Appraisal Arbitrage Decisions, the *prima facie* showing is dispositive.

approximately 17 million shares against the merger, was able to exercise appraisal rights for the 11 million shares held by the beneficial owner.

[153] 143 A.3d 20 (Del. Ch. 2016).

The analysis, however, need not stop there. Once the appraisal petitioner has made out a *prima facie* case, the burden shifts to the corporation to show that Cede actually voted the shares for which the petitioner seeks appraisal in favor of the merger. The corporation can do this by pointing to documents that are publicly available, such as a Form N-PX.[Ed.[154]] Or the corporation can introduce evidence from Broadridge [Financial Services, Inc.], [International Shareholder Services Inc.], and other providers of voting services, such as internal control numbers and voting authentication records. If the evidence that the corporation adduces is not sufficient to demonstrate that Cede actually voted the shares for which the petitioner seeks appraisal in favor of the merger, then the petitioner can continue to maintain an appraisal action. But if the corporation demonstrates that Cede actually voted the shares for which the petitioner seeks appraisal in favor of the merger, then the Dissenter Requirement is no longer met, and the petitioner cannot obtain seek appraisal for those shares.[155]

4. THE POLICY QUESTIONS

a. California or Delaware?

Delaware law permits parties to a transaction to limit shareholder voting and appraisal rights by changing the form of the transaction while not affecting its essence (the final position of the parties). Form and process count; the substance of the transaction does not. Under Delaware rules, the parties to an acquisition can often place the transaction, without altering its fundamental nature and effect, under two or more provisions of a state corporate code and these alternatives have different requirements for shareholder voting and appraisal rights. Parties are thus free to choose and do choose the provisions with the fewest procedural requirements.

The cases in Section A.2 illustrate that Delaware courts compliment the Delaware legislature and refuse to reclassify transactions based on result or essence. The de facto merger doctrine falls to the equal dignity rule. The Delaware courts will not protect the shareholder voting and appraisal rights in the more liberal of the available sections. In other words, the courts will not nullify the parties' choice by requiring that they meet the requirements of the section that is most protective of shareholders' rights (usually the merger section).

---

[154] [Ed. Form N-PX is required by Section 30 of the Investment Company Act of 1940, as amended. It is filed annually by investment companies (i.e., mutual funds) to report on how they voted shares of stock of publicly traded companies held by them in their investment portfolios. It covers their voting records for the 12-month period ending June 30th, and must be filed with the SEC no later than August 31st.]

[155] *Dell*, 143 A.3d at 52–54.

The effect of the approach is a very lenient climate in Delaware on acquisition planning and form. Planners use the provisions to avoid shareholder voting and appraisal rights whenever practicable.

Most states follow the lead of the Delaware courts in refusing to reclassify transactions. Many states separate from Delaware, however, in their attempt, in the language of their corporate codes, to synchronize the rights of the parties across the various forms. California led the way in this effort in 1977 and, since 1999, the drafters of the Model Act have come on board as well.

The California corporate code is different from Delaware's in two basic respects. First, the California code both attaches shareholder voting rights in a broader array of transactional contexts and, second, attempts to apply the rights equally to parties whose post-transaction position is the same. *Equivalency* of rights based on substance is a fundamental goal of the California provisions. In California, substance does prevail over form. The drafters of the California code attempted to synchronize the code provisions that regulate mergers and acquisitions by their effect on shareholders, not by their technical form; like transactions should be treated alike.

California's corporate code, for example, gives merger-like voting and appraisal rights to shareholders of the buying firm in stock-for-asset sales and in stock-for-stock acquisitions. Cal. Gen. Corp. L. §§ 181(b) & (c) (definition of "reorganization"), 1200(b) & (c) (requiring board approval of acquirer in case of exchange reorganization and sale of assets reorganization, respectively), 1201(a) (shareholder approval), and 1300(a) (grant of appraisal rights).[156] California also gives merger-like voting and appraisal rights to the shareholders of a parent corporation in triangular mergers and in triangular stock-for-asset sales and stock-for-stock acquisitions. *Id.*, §§ 1200(d) (requiring board approval of acquirer in share exchange tender offer), 1201(a) (parent shareholder approval required unless parent shareholders will hold at least five-sixths of voting power post-acquisition), and 1300(a) (grant of appraisal rights).[157]

Two other states, New Jersey and Ohio, have provisions that are similar in some respects to the California provisions. E.g., N.J. Stat. Ann. § 14A:11–12; Ohio Rev. Code Ann. § 1701.83. The statutes of Ohio and New Jersey also make limited attempts at equivalency of rights based on the final position of the parties to an acquisition, and a 1999 revision to the ABA Rev. Model Bus. Corp. Act adopts an equivalency position on voting rights but not on appraisal rights.

---

[156] The purchasing firm must buy "all or substantially all" the assets in an asset acquisition or "control" in a stock acquisition.

[157] California does have some odd exceptions to the equivalency principle. The buying firm shareholders in debt-for-assets acquisitions have voting and appraisal rights if the debt "is not adequately secured and . . . [has] a maturity date in excess of five years." Cal. Gen. Corp. L. § 181(c). The use of similar debt in mergers or debt-for-stock acquisitions does not come with similar voting or appraisal rights.

Which approach is correct, form over substance as in Delaware or substance over form as in California? Since, in most contexts, substance ought to determine rights, not form, the answer seems obvious. When form trumps substance, we normally suspect that someone is getting away with something. Is that suspicion justified here?

Yes and no. Although initially some shareholders were surprised by lawyers' facility at circumventing their voting or appraisal rights, the word is out. The techniques are well known and established and all shareholders have long been on notice to protect their voting rights with contract provisions if they value them sufficiently highly.

More interesting is a second question: Why do our large corporations overwhelmingly prefer the Delaware acquisition rules to the California rules? California's approach on equivalency is surely more elegant and easier to understand and apply. The answer lies in the minimum standards of either jurisdiction. California applies a very robust mandatory requirement on voting and appraisal to all transactions. In Delaware, in the twists and turns of the various sections, planners can find much lower mandatory requirements for any given deal. With equivalency then come stricter mandatory rules. Corporations prefer the voting and appraisal rules that make transactions easier to close. The optimal system would be an equivalency approach of California with the less stringent rules of Delaware. We do not have such a state so Delaware is our best alternative.

This leads, of course, to a follow up question: Are shareholders better or worse off under a system for less stringent voting and appraisal rules? There is the old pro manager explanation; managers favor the flexibility even at the expense of their own shareholders.[158] And the old rebuttal, managers choose rules to maximize the value of the firm to the benefit of their shareholders.[159] But how can shareholders be better off with weak voting and appraisal rights?

The answer lies in the value of transactional flexibility. Shareholders' returns may be higher for a firm that has more transactional flexibility and freedom in modern markets. Couple this understanding with a relaxation of the classic moral principle that shareholders ought to vote and have dissenters' rights in all acquisitions in which there is a *fundamental and*

---

[158] William L. Cary, *Federalism and Corporate Law: Reflections upon Delaware*, 83 YALE L. J. 663 (1974).

[159] See, e.g., Ralph K. Winter, *State Law, Shareholder Protection, and the Theory of the Corporation*, 6 J. LEG. STUD. 251 (1977). This is the "genius of American Corporate law." E.g., Roberta Romano, *The Genius of American Corporate Law* (1993). The strongest evidence of this thesis is event studies that have focused on the effect on stock prices when corporations choose to reincorporate in Delaware. See Roberta Romano, *supra*, at 19–21. When corporations reincorporate in Delaware from other states, we do not see the share price of the corporation drop. Indeed, most studies found a significant positive stock price effect. It is difficult, however, to isolate one factor when studying the cause of share price movements. E.g., Lucian A. Bebchuk, *Federalism and the Corporation: The Desirable Limits on State Competition in Corporate Law*, 105 HARV. L. REV. 1435 (1992) (reincorporation usually accompanied by disclosure of new corporate plan; stock price reaction may be due to investor reaction to new plan).

instantaneous change in their investment,[160] and one has an argument for the Delaware rules.

b. Should Shareholder Voting and Appraisal Rules Be Optional?

At this point one needs to ask whether we could avoid all corporate code classifications of acquisition forms by dropping all the mandatory shareholder voting and appraisal rules. There is much evidence of our retreat from mandatory voting rules in state corporate codes. Are we slowly moving to a system of elective shareholder voting?[161]

Why not generalize the trend and allow shareholders to buy stock in firms that do not have voting rights in acquisitions? Or to put the matter another way, why not permit shareholders to vote generally on whether to vote or *not* vote individually on acquisitions?

State law could simply accept and legitimize all charter or bylaw provisions stipulating acquisition procedures *(open)*, provide standardized terms and procedures that firms could adopt specifically by express shareholder acceptance (*opt in*), or provide terms that firms could replace or modify with other arrangements by express shareholder resolution (*opt out*). Investors would choose rules that (1) minimize agency costs associated with faithless or lazy managers and the opportunistic behavior of other groups of investors (bondholders' interests can be in conflict with the interest of shareholders once the instruments have been sold) and that, at the same time, (2) give appropriate flexibility to their managers to maximize profits.

---

160 First, acquisitions are expected; they are commonplace and routine. Second, modern finance has taught us that what is of primary importance to value are the risk/return characteristics of a stock. A stock's formal rights are but a part of the risk/return calculation. We now well understand, for example, that a change in the contractual attributes of a stock contract is only roughly correlated with substantial changes in the risk attributes of the investment. One can substitute one share for another in an acquisition, triggering voting rights, with little change in the risk/return characteristics of the investment. One can also hold shares through an investment, not changing the form rights of the shares and thus not triggering voting rights, and yet see the risk characteristics of the stock change dramatically (through new leverage, for example). Consider the position of the non-voting, buying firm shareholders in a cash-out merger when the buying firm borrows the purchase price, for example.

161 Under present law, a vote to amend the Articles of Incorporation to authorize the board to issue a block of stock far in excess of all stock outstanding, as occurred in the *Irving Bank* case and the *Equity Group Holdings* case, is in essence a vote not to vote on stock swap mergers that are within the 20 percent rule. Such a charter amendment also authorizes a board to use the new shares as consideration in stock acquisitions, asset acquisitions or triangular mergers (free of even the 20 percent rule). The amendment gives the board the power to make exchange tender offers, as in *Irving Bank,* or execute triangular mergers, as in *Equity Group Holdings.* If a firm also elected to incorporate in Delaware, to avoid the California rules, and not to be listed on the NYSE, such a charter amendment would give a corporation's managers carte blanche to engage in major acquisitions without a shareholder vote. The ABA Model Business Corporation Act does not suggest a total retreat from this. The Model Act contains provisions that provide for shareholder voting in some acquisitions but lower the voting majority required to NYSE standards and drastically reduce shareholder appraisal rights. See, e.g., ABA Model Bus. Corp Act §§ 11.04(e) & 13.02 (2016 rev.).

What procedures provide the best balance in acquisitions and reorganizations? Investors may decide that they do not care to vote on major corporate changes as long as managers' interests are effectively aligned with theirs through compensation packages dependent on stock prices, for example. We could let competition for investment dollars determine the content of the corporate charters that produce the most attractive investment alternatives to participants in the capital markets. The results would vary by type of business or size of firm. At minimum, we would get creative answers to the current line-drawing problems that state codes now so crudely resolve.

One can state the question another way: We empower shareholders with the right to vote on specific transactions, why not empower shareholders with the right to vote on whether they want to vote on transactions (and if so, how)? An argument for opt-out legal rules on shareholder voting and appraisal rights is found in Frank Easterbrook & Daniel Fischel, *The Corporate Contract*, 89 COLUM. L. REV. 1416 (1989).

There is concern that some have against open-ended shareholder choice, *latecomer terms*. Shareholders pay for their shares under a set assumption of voting and appraisal rules and then may be subject to opportunistic or even confiscatory amendments.[162] Mandatory rules stop latecomer terms. But under a robust *nexus-of-contracts theory of corporations*, shareholders investing would worry about latecomer terms and firms, to attract investors and lower their cost of capital, would pre-commit to not adopting any (employing so-called *bonding devices*).[163] We are back to the basic question then. Why can't a firm write its own rules on shareholder voting and appraisal rights that shareholders want and commit to not changing them?

The contract theory of corporations has its critics. Most attack the theory based on the limited information available to investors and, when informed, the limited ability of investors to digest or price the information when they make their investment.[164] A rationale for depriving shareholders of the right to vote in acquisitions may be based on a belief that they will vote against their interest by mistake more often in passing procedural amendments than they will in passing on specific

---

[162] See Easterbrook & Fischel, *supra*, at 1442–44.

[163] Investors, the argument goes, will factor the risk of latecomer terms into the pricing of the beginning terms. If investors can price beginning terms, they ought to be able to price the risk of latecomer terms; that is, the risk of the beginning terms changing over time. If the risk of latecomer terms is high and beginning investors discount the firm's stock to account for the possibility of increased opportunities for opportunistic behavior by managers, incorporators have an incentive to create a charter with provisions that reduce the latecomer term problem. In theory, a firm could pre-commit by requiring super-majority shareholder votes to change procedural rules on acquisitions. Could incorporating in California be a bonding device? Listing on the NYSE?

[164] E.g., Lewis Kornhauser, *The Nexus of Contracts Approach to Corporations: A Comment on Easterbrook and Fischel*, 89 COLUM. L. REV. 1449 (1989).

transactions.[165] Shareholders may be better able to assess the likelihood of opportunistic behavior by their managers in the context of a specific deal than in an open-ended delegation of power to their managers that affects future deals.[166]

Those who disparage the ability of investors to act in their own best interests when they vote on basic procedural rules for acquisitions often overstate their case. No one denies that investors act under conditions of limited information. But, who is better informed: investors or state legislators who draft corporate codes and state judges that struggle to apply them? State legislators and state judges operate under severe conditions of limited information and, at least for state legislators, they may act under conflict-of-interest problems to boot. At issue then is *which* body of individuals, managers seeking funds or state legislators seeking votes, will draft firm operating procedures that best serve the long-term interests of shareholders. Perhaps we should re-evaluate our traditional bias in favor of the legislators.

All this suggests that if firms develop firm-specific pre-commitment devices that are effective and genuine, that is, they engender the confidence of discerning investors, mandatory rules on shareholder voting and appraisal rights may no longer be necessary. We suspect that state legislatures will continue to reduce steadily the scope of mandatory rules in state legislation currently applicable to publicly traded firms and, when politically feasible, eventually eliminate them; all rules in state statutes on shareholder voting in acquisitions for large firms eventually will have opt-out caveats.

Indeed, lawyers could now use the open-ended, contract based Limited Liability Company Codes of some states (Delaware's in particular) to create large, even publicly traded LLCs, with whatever voting rules or appraisal rights clients may wish in major acquisition approval processes. Fitting new LLC forms inside exiting federal securities laws and regulations would be an intriguing experiment.

---

165 This may explain in part why Delaware is able to adopt a provision limiting board liability for due care violations and an anti-takeover statute. Both sections seem to be value decreasing for Delaware firms. See Roberta Romano, *supra* note 159, at 17–19.

166 Votes on specific acquisitions may generate less *rational apathy* than shareholder votes on acquisition procedure. Jeffrey Gordon, *The Mandatory Structure of Corporate Law*, 89 COLUM. L. REV. 1549, 1575–76, 1580 (1989) (explaining rational apathy). The stakes are large, and the decision of whether to exchange one investment for another is similar to the basic investment decision that all shareholders necessarily make in the ordinary course. Shareholder votes on procedural questions may be much harder for shareholders to value (what is the increased risk of opportunistic behavior by managers in the future?) and, even if accurately valued, may represent a much smaller change in share price. Thus, the costs of gathering information for a procedural vote are higher, and the payoff is lower, increasing the incentive for rational apathy. In light of an increased risk of rational apathy generating affirmative votes on procedural questions that hurt shareholder interests, shareholders would seem wise to choose to disable themselves from voting on acquisition procedure, specifically on voting not to vote on individual transactions.

c. The Rational Investor's Choice of Voting and Appraisal Systems

Whether we grant all firms the freedom to cast their own rules based on shareholder choice or we attempt, through state legislatures, to create rules that best approximate what shareholders would otherwise choose, the essential question remains: When will shareholders sensibly request a right to vote or an appraisal right in major acquisitions or reorganizations?

At this point, we ought to revisit our acceptance of the classic assumption that shareholders will want a vote on all "fundamental" changes in the firm to protect their investment. If shareholders are convinced managers will, in a high percentage of deals, act in the best interests of the firm in transactions classified as fundamental, then voting and appraisal rights are unnecessary in these transactions and, perhaps, even dangerous (a class of security holders could block a beneficial transaction to appropriate a larger share of the gains). In sum, rational investors who elect into voting and appraisal systems are balancing the benefits of management flexibility in doing deals against the dangers of managerial mistakes or theft in any given deal.

Assume that we start with the basic proposition that shareholders should want to vote only in transactions when other control mechanisms (post-transaction litigation, for example) are less effective or much more costly than a shareholder vote. The clearest example is a transaction in which managers or controlling shareholders are on both sides of the deal, *conflict of interest transactions*.

Shareholders should want to retain structural protections in conflict of interest transactions. It would be a poor choice, for example, to enable managers to buy their own firm, a *management buy-out*, without shareholder ratification. Voting power to stop such deals is preferable to litigation. This would explain the special stock exchange listing requirements on voting in conflict-of-interest acquisitions, for example. See Section B.1, *infra*. Interestingly, the Delaware courts are imposing majority of minority voting requirements in conflict of interest transactions under doctrines of fiduciary duty. See Chapter Five, Section C.

A special subset of conflict of interest transactions are transactions in which the management team receives substantial *side payments*, specific benefits in a transaction not shared with their shareholders (bribes, and the like).[167] The managers could sell out their shareholders for the personal benefits. Shareholders should want to protect themselves in such transactions by preserving their voting rights.

Finally, special attention is due appraisal rights, a contingent claim on the firm's cash assets. we suspect such rights should always be

---

[167] They are more charitably called golden parachute payments or consulting fees.

negotiated in the stock contract and depend on the specifics of a given investment deal. The only generalizable situation in which appraisal rights would lie would again be in conflict of interest transactions in which minority shareholders could not block the deal by a majority of the minority vote. One would, of course, consider special rules for closely held corporations that would include more appraisal right protections than for publicly traded companies due to the illiquidity of the stock investment.[168] Acquisitions of closely held companies are liquidity events for otherwise often illiquid investments, and as such, deserve more scrutiny. Shareholders in closely held companies would normally ask for more buy out protections.

Again this all suggests that, even under the Delaware provisions, shareholders' voting and appraisal rights are too extensive.

B. PUBLICLY TRADED COMPANIES

1. LISTING REQUIREMENTS OF STOCK EXCHANGES

Our stock markets consist of buyers and sellers of securities trading at mutually agreeable prices. Markets that are deep (have many participants making bids and offers), liquid (have substantial trading volume at any one time), efficient (trading expenses are minimized) and honest (free of manipulation and fraud) are a national asset. A healthy secondary trading market means firms can raise money to capitalize their businesses at lower cost,[169] stock prices act as guideposts to optimal allocations of capital and other investments, and small investors participate in the trading. The markets also provide employment for banks, institutional investors, broker-dealers, accountants, and lawyers—professionals that service the trading markets.

As of March 2018, our stock markets consist of 21 national securities exchanges registered with the Securities and Exchange Commission ("SEC") under Section 6 of the Securities Exchange Act of 1934 (the "Exchange Act" or the "1934 Act"). The two largest *primary listing* exchanges are the New York Stock Exchange, LLC ("NYSE") and The Nasdaq Stock Market LLC ("Nasdaq").[170] A primary listing exchange accepts listing applications from companies who seek to use the exchange

---

168 Most *close corporation codes*, state codes that small companies can elect to have cover their operations, do include buy out rights for shareholders.

169 This is the primary market, a firm selling securities to the public and keeping the net proceeds from the offering. The most important function of the secondary trading market is to support high prices (for a low cost of capital) in the primary markets. If we had no organized secondary market, corporations, in selling shares to the public in the primary market, would promise purchasers that the company would facilitate secondary trading (internally if necessary).

170 Nasdaq is subdivided into three different market tiers: Capital Market (for small capitalization stocks), Global Market (for middle capitalization stocks) and Global Select Market (for large capitalization stocks).

as their home trading location. Companies then may also *dual list* or *cross list* their stock on other exchanges as well.

Each exchange has listing requirements for firms traded on the exchange, and firms agree to those requirements in a listing contract signed with the exchange.[171] Penalties for violating a listing contract include suspension of trading in and de-listing of the firm's securities. An exchange designs listing requirements to attract traders; firms that meet an exchange's listing requirements are, in theory, more attractive to traders than firms that do not. In signing a listing contract, firms promise, among other things, to maintain a minimum float in their securities, to respect conditions on corporate actions that affect outstanding securities, and to be candid and truthful about firm affairs.

Exchanges provide substantial benefits and some problems.[172] On the plus side of the ledger, exchanges have strong incentives to provide rules and enforcement mechanisms that increase investors' returns, and thereby increase investors' demand for listed securities. An exchange has an incentive to create listing rules that are neither too harsh nor too lenient. If the exchange listing requirements are too harsh, firms may view listing as imposing too many costs for the benefit of a listing and choose to list elsewhere. There will be too few securities to trade. If the listing requirements are too lenient, too many firms may engage in acts that defraud or otherwise disadvantage investors and traders will not have confidence in the *bona fides* of the firms listed. In an important sense, the listing requirements are a vital part of the public image and reputation of any exchange. Since the health of trading markets depends on investor confidence, this is no small matter.

The avoidance of the *lemon effect*, so labeled in a famous article by Professor George Akerloff, explains, in part, why our national exchanges have listing requirements.[173] As several of the Asian stock markets know well, spectacular failures of publicly traded companies, which turn out to be notorious swindles, can shock trading market investors and depress the price of all stocks traded in the same market. The smaller and less well known the exchange, the more severe is the adverse reaction to specific scandals. The struggles of exchanges today in emerging market economies should remind us of why the reputation of our own exchanges is so valuable.

The market-wide effect is, in large part, the result of a loss in confidence by traders in the market itself and, perhaps, an inability to

---

[171] An exchange may choose to trade a stock that is listed on another national exchange, the so-called "unlisted trading privilege."

[172] The problems are not covered here. The exchanges generate problems by, for example, attempting to monopolize trading revenues, benefiting the traders in the exchange and not the listed firms.

[173] George Akerloff, *The Market for Lemons: Quality Uncertainty and the Market Mechanism*, 84 Q.J. ECON. 488 (1970).

distinguish accurately the solvency of remaining firms from the collapsed firm. When investors cannot distinguish healthy stocks from unhealthy ones (a.k.a. "lemons"), they view all securities as problematic. As a consequence, investors pay too little for the healthy stocks and too much for the unhealthy ones. This gives healthy firms a strong incentive to find ways to distinguish themselves from their unhealthy cousins and gives unhealthy firms strong incentives to mimic their healthy cousins.

All firms traded in a single market have an incentive to create signaling mechanisms that distinguish them effectively in the eyes of investors from their less solvent or less ethical brethren. The healthy firms use a wide variety of *signaling* devices. They hire outsiders to certify their books, commit managers to shareholder welfare (by compensating them in stock options), and bind managers to pay out cash flow (with high levels of firm debt). If the healthy firms are not largely successful in their efforts, their cost of capital increases relative to the quality of their firm investments and, eventually, the rate of return on their investments falls relative to the lemons' rate of return. If the effect is left unchecked, lemons survive and dominate the market.

One very effective type of signaling device is joining an exclusive club. Firms seek to join a prestigious trading exchange that has a seriously enforced membership policy based on the quality of the firms traded. Each firm has an interest in the health and integrity of all other firms in their exchange. Just as all owners of a McDonald's franchise have an interest in whether other McDonald's franchise owners, wherever located in the country, keep a clean restroom, each firm in an organized identifiable market or exchange has an interest in the *bona fides* of other firms in the market. Firms join the NYSE or the Nasdaq with comprehensive listing requirements designed to, among other things, instill confidence among those in the trading market.

A second solution to the lemon effect is for firms to support a government oversight system that operates to instill, to some reasonable level, minimal confidence in all the national trading markets. We have also created and empowered the SEC to not only supervise and oversee the exchanges but also to create and enforce antifraud or anti-manipulation rules of its own.

An important part of the listing requirements has been their rules on shareholder voting in acquisitions. In several of the cases excerpted earlier in this chapter—*Irving Bank*, *Equity Group Holdings*, and *Pasternak*—listing requirements of the NYSE required shareholder votes in a constituent corporation in an acquisition when state corporate codes did not. The voting requirement has a lower required vote total than most states (a majority of those voting at the meeting rather than a majority of the outstanding shares) and does not require that dissenters have appraisal rights. Below is the text of the requirement from the NYSE.

NEW YORK STOCK EXCHANGE LISTED COMPANY MANUAL[174]

101.00 Introduction

A listing on the New York Stock Exchange is internationally recognized as signifying that a publicly owned corporation has achieved maturity and front-rank status in its industry—in terms of assets, earnings, and shareholder interest and acceptance. Indeed, the Exchange's listing standards are designed to assure that every domestic or non-U.S. company whose shares are admitted to trading in the Exchange market merit that recognition.

* * *

. . . Para. 312.00 Shareholder Approval Policy

Para. 312.01 Shareholders' interest and participation in corporate affairs has greatly increased. Management has responded by providing more extensive and frequent reports on matters of interest to investors. In addition, an increasing number of important corporate decisions are being referred to shareholders for their approval. This is especially true of transactions involving the issuance of additional securities.

Good business practice is frequently the controlling factor in the determination of management to submit a matter to shareholders for approval even though neither the law nor the company's charter makes such approvals necessary. The Exchange encourages this growth in corporate democracy. . . .

Para. 312.02 Companies are urged to discuss questions relating to this subject with their Exchange representative sufficiently in advance of the time for the calling of a shareholders' meeting and the solicitation of proxies where shareholder approval may be involved. All relevant factors will be taken into consideration in applying the policy expressed in this Para. 312.00 and the Exchange will advise whether or not shareholder approval will be required in a particular case.

Para. 312.03 Shareholder approval is a perquisite to listing . . . :

* * *

(c) Shareholder approval is required prior to the issuance of common stock, or of securities convertible into or exercisable for common stock, in any transaction or series of transactions if:

(1) the common stock has, or will have upon issuance, voting power equal to or in excess of 20 percent of the voting power outstanding before the issuance of such stock or of securities convertible into or exercisable for common stock; or (2) the number of shares of common stock to be issued is,

---

[174] The manual is available on line at the NYSE's web site, http://wallstreet.cch.com/LCMTools/PlatformViewer.asp?selectednode=chp%5F1%5F1&manual=%2Flcm%2Fsections%2Flcm%2Dsections%2F (visited April 2018).

or will be equal upon issuance, to or in excess of 20 percent of the number of shares of common stock outstanding before the issuance of the common stock or of securities convertible or exercisable for common stock.

(d) Shareholder approval is required prior to an issuance that will result in a change of control of the issuer.

Para. 312.04 For the Purpose of Para. 312.03:

* * *

(d) Only shares actually issued and outstanding (excluding treasury shares or shares held by a subsidiary) are to be used in making any calculation provided for in Section 312.03(b) and (c). Shares reserved for issuance upon conversion of securities or upon exercise of options or warrants will not be regarded as outstanding.

* * *

(f) "Voting power outstanding" refers to the aggregate number of votes that may be cast by holders of those securities outstanding that entitle the holders thereof to vote generally on all matters submitted to the company's security holders for a vote. . . .

Para. 312.05 Exceptions may be made to the shareholder approval policy of Para. 312.03 upon application to the Exchange when (1) the delay in securing stockholder approval would seriously jeopardize the financial viability of the enterprise and (2) reliance by the company on this exception is expressly approved by the Audit Committee of the Board. . . .

* * *

Para. 312.07 Where shareholder approval is a prerequisite to the listing of any additional or new securities of a listed company, the minimum vote which will constitute shareholder approval for such purposes is defined as approval by a majority of votes cast on a proposal in a proxy bearing on the particular matter.

The Nasdaq has similar rules. See Nasdaq Marketplace Rule 5635. The voting majority required in the NYSE Listed Company Manual is different from the voting majority required by most state corporate codes. The Manual requires only a majority vote of all votes cast on a proposal in a proxy bearing on the particular matter. State corporate codes on acquisitions, if applicable, often require, by contrast, a majority vote of all *outstanding* shares entitled to vote—a much higher standard. E.g., Del. Gen. Corp. L. § 251(a) (mergers). But see ABA Model Bus. Corp. Act § 6.21(f) (2016 rev.) (requiring only a majority vote of those shareholders present or represented at a meeting).

The NYSE also has a special shareholder voting rule for acquisitions in which a senior officer of the acquiring company has a substantial stake in the acquired company, *conflict-of-interest acquisitions*. If a corporation uses over one percent in number of its common stock or its voting stock outstanding before the acquisition as consideration in an acquisition and a director, officer or substantial security holder[175] in the purchasing company has a "substantial direct or indirect" interest in the target, shareholders of the purchasing company must ratify the transaction. NYSE Listed Company Manual § 312.03(b). Nasdaq also requires a vote in conflict-of-interest acquisitions if the consideration offered represents five percent or more of the outstanding shares of the purchaser in either number or voting power. NASD Marketplace Rule 5635(a)(2).

The argument over Delaware's acquisition rules is incomplete unless supplemented by the listing requirements of our national exchanges. Firms assume the NYSE listing requirements when they choose to incorporate in Delaware. Firms may be choosing Delaware's acquisition rules but getting a combination of Delaware and NYSE rules. In other words, the NYSE and our other exchanges act to plug some leaks in the Delaware rules. Interestingly, a combination of Delaware and NYSE rules may replicate California's shareholder voting rules, but the combination does not replicate California's rule on appraisal rights. The NYSE does not augment a shareholder's appraisal rights. Perhaps all that firms are opting out of when they choose to incorporate in Delaware is a robust appraisal regime. In any event, we can speculate: If the NYSE did not have listing requirements on shareholder voting in acquisitions, would firms favor the California approach?

2. FEDERAL SECURITIES LAW

Federal securities law supplements state corporate codes and imposes additional procedural requirements. The additional requirements are substantial in most all acquisitions of publicly traded companies. Also affected are acquisitions of privately held companies if the consideration includes securities. Some of the requirements affect the basic acquisition procedure. The federal rules on (a) soliciting proxies, (b) public tender offers, and (c) the public sale of securities all affect acquisition planning. We consider these rules below, primarily for their effect on acquisitions of a public company. The federal securities laws also penalize acquisition participants for fraudulent or misleading disclosures whether mandated or voluntary; we will take up disclosure issues in Chapter Seven.

The primary effect of the federal rules is to require *public filings with the SEC* by the deal parties when the target is a public company. A company is publicly held if it must register one or more classes of its

[175] A substantial security holder is a shareholder who holds over 5 percent of the issued and outstanding shares of common stock or over 5 percent of the voting power of the firm.

securities under § 12 of the Exchange Act. A company must register a class of securities that is (1) traded on a national stock exchange, or (2) held by over 2,000 shareholders (or 500 shareholders who are not accredited investors as defined in Securities Act Rule 501(a)) at a time when the firm has over $10 million in assets.[176] Exchange Act § 12(a) & (g) and Exchange Act Rule 12g–1. By registering a class of securities with the SEC under the Exchange Act, a company becomes a *reporting company* and must file periodic reports (e.g., an Annual Report on Form 10–K) with the SEC that are also available to the public through, among other sources, the SEC's website (www.sec.gov).

The SEC filings require time and resources to prepare, file and deliver to other parties. Some deals may require filings under multiple sections of the Securities Act and/or the Exchange Act.[177] SEC review of the filings may delay the closing. In the filings, the parties publicly disclose information about the deal and the buyer that they may not disclose publicly in private transactions. Competing bidders may use the information to structure a competing offer. Investors may use the information to challenge the transaction in court.

A primary effect of the required disclosures is to expose parties in acquisitions to high stakes litigation in federal courts for errors in the filed materials. Activist shareholders can use the filings to sue to block the deal, or for damages in failed or disastrous deals; one party can use them to sue the other in hostile deals or failed deals; and the SEC can sue on the filings for a variety of remedies. See Chapter Seven.

a. Shareholder Voting: Proxy Solicitation Regulations

When shareholders vote on acquisitions, state law requires generally that they receive adequate information from company managers on the details of the transaction. State corporate codes do not detail the specific kinds of information that shareholders should have when they vote. See, e.g., Del. Gen. Corp. L. § 251(c).[178] State court case law has developed, under the rubric of a common law on fiduciary duty, on the obligation of a firm to notify its shareholders of all material facts in a transaction.[179] See Chapter Seven, Section C.

Federal securities law stands in stark contrast to state law. If a firm is publicly held, then § 14(a) of the Exchange Act and the twenty "14a" and

---

176 Companies that become reporting companies under the Exchange Act based on their assets and number of shareholders are referred to as *back-door reporting companies*.

177 The SEC has taken strides to consolidate and reconcile the filing requirements of the multiple sections. See, e.g., Regulation M–A.

178 The section only requires that the directors send the shareholders a notice containing a copy of the agreement or a "brief summary . . . as the directors shall deem advisable." A 1998 amendment to § 251(b) requires the directors' resolution approving the merger (which, along with the full agreement, is of record at the shareholder meeting on the merger) to "declar[e] its advisability."

179 See, e.g., Malone v. Brincat, 722 A.2d 5, 10 (Del. 1998).

two "14b" Rules (collectively known as *Regulation 14A*) promulgated by the SEC under the authority of that section apply to the company's *proxy solicitations*. A *proxy* is a delegation of voting power by a shareholder to an agent, the *proxy holder*, who votes the shares at a shareholder meeting; the agency grant is a creation of state law. The SEC rules regulate the solicitation of proxies, requiring that a disclosure document known as a *proxy statement* accompany or precede all solicitations[180] and controlling the content and form of the proxy document itself, the *proxy card*.[181]

Since all large firms routinely solicit proxies from their shareholders in order to do business at shareholder meetings, the rules have substantial bite. Action taken at a shareholder's meeting is not legally binding unless a sufficient number of shares (called a *quorum*) is represented at the meeting either by the shareholders themselves (in person) or by proxy. The diffusion of shareholder holdings in most publicly traded firms requires that the firm solicit proxies to achieve a quorum.[182] In acquisitions, since the required vote is usually a majority of all the outstanding shares (the Delaware requirement), a proxy solicitation is also necessary to gather enough affirmative votes to approve the acquisition.

The disclosure requirements in Regulation 14A for proxy statements are one part of a much larger system of mandatory disclosure requirements that include registration statements for public offerings of securities, periodic reporting requirements for registered companies, and information schedules for public tender offers. The regulations are very detailed on the information that parties must disclose and yet contain open-ended admonitions to add all other material facts as well.[183]

While most of the popular focus on proxy regulations is on shareholder voting for seats on a corporation's board of directors, the rules apply to all matters subject to a shareholder vote. Thus, the regulations promulgated by the SEC specifically cover proxy solicitations for votes required by state corporate codes and exchange listing requirements in acquisitions.

Only one of the parties may have to file proxy materials with the SEC. For example, when the buyer is not publicly traded or the buyer is paying cash and its shareholders do not have the right to vote on the deal, only the seller is required to comply with the solicitation rules.[184] The opposite may

---

[180] See Exch. Act Rule 14a–3.

[181] A proxy card can be analogized to an *absentee ballot* used in political elections.

[182] Moreover, even if management of a registered firm is not soliciting proxies for an upcoming shareholder meeting, the Exchange Act requires the firm to mail an "information statement" to shareholders that contains substantially the same information as a proxy statement contains. Exch. Act § 14(c), Reg. 14C.

[183] See, e.g., Sec. Act Rule 408(a) ("In addition to the information expressly required to be included in a registration statement, there shall be added such further material information, if any, as may be necessary to make the required statements, in the light of the circumstances under which they are made, not misleading.").

[184] Even so, the seller may have to disclose information about the buyer in the seller's proxy statement. In a cash deal, financial and other information about the acquirer in the target's proxy

be true, only the buyer files, if the buyer is publicly traded and the seller is not.[185]

Under Rule 14a–3(a) of Regulation 14A, when an acquisition is the subject of a shareholder vote, a party may not solicit proxies "unless each person solicited is concurrently furnished or has previously been furnished with a written proxy statement containing information specified in Schedule 14A." The proxy statement is the disclosure document sent to shareholders, and it is filed with the SEC under the cover of Schedule 14A.[186] The SEC may or may not comment on the filing depending on the issues on which the shareholders are being asked to vote.[187] When a corporation requests proxies from security holders, it must deliver the mandated proxy statement along with the proxy request, enabling the shareholders, in theory,[188] to make informed voting decisions.[189]

The first five *Items* of Schedule 14A (the numbered items detail what must be in a proxy statement) apply to all proxy statements, regardless of the type of action proposed. They call for the date, time and place of the shareholder meeting (Item 1), information with respect to the revocability of any executed proxy (Item 2), dissenters' appraisal rights, the identity of those soliciting the proxy, the special interest of the solicitors, and others connected with the solicitors (Item 4), and a description of the issuer's outstanding securities and their principal holders (Item 5).

Item 14 of the Schedule is specific to votes on acquisitions by either a buyer or a seller or both. Three other Items also apply to selected acquisitions. Item 12 applies to single-firm exchange reorganizations, and thus covers the modification or exchange of securities. Item 11 applies to

---

statement is required only if that information is *material* to the voting shareholders' evaluation of the transaction. See SEC Schedule 14A, Item 14, Instruction 2(a). For example, disclosure about the acquirer would be required in a cash deal in which target shareholders must vote and the acquisition financing is not assured. See *id.*

185 Providing target financial information is not required in stock swap mergers if the acquirer is using registered securities, the target is a non-reporting company, the acquirer's security holders are not voting on the transaction, and the target is less than 20 percent of the size of the acquirer. See SEC Form S–4, Item 17(b)(7).

186 Schedule 14A is found in Exchange Act Rule 14a–101 ("Information Required in Proxy Statement").

187 Under Exchange Act Rule 14a–6(a), Schedule 14A can be filed in definitive form with the SEC and the proxy statement and proxy card relating thereto can immediately be sent to shareholders, so long as shareholders are being asked to vote on noncontroversial matters such as the election of directors and the appointment or ratification of accountants. When shareholders are being asked to vote on controversial matters, such as a merger, a preliminary Schedule 14A must be filed with the SEC. Such a filing provides the SEC with an opportunity to comment on the filing before proxy materials are disseminated to shareholders.

188 There is little doubt that most shareholders do not read the proxy statement. The few that do are large institutional investors aided by shareholder advisory firms such as Institutional Shareholder Services (ISS for short), a few financial journalists, and plaintiff class action attorneys.

189 In addition, the soliciting firm must mail copies of all literature in final, definitive form, concurrently with their public distribution, to the SEC and to each exchange on which any security of the soliciting firm is listed. Exch. Act Rule 14a–6(b).

shareholder votes on the authorization or issuance of additional securities, often necessary when a buyer uses stock as consideration. Item 19 applies to any amendments to a Charter or Bylaws.

Item 14 of the Schedule requires the disclosure of details about the transaction in issue and about both parties to the transaction. The subsections incorporate by reference other SEC regulations, Regulations S–X, S–K and M–A, and Form S–4.[190] Regulation S–X specifies the accounting conventions that filing parties must use in their required financial documents—balance sheets, income statements and cash flow statements, and amounts to an SEC overlay on generally accepted accounting principles (GAAP). Regulation S–K is more general and contains a variety of informational requirements, including Subpart 1000, Regulation M–A, specific to mergers and acquisitions.

It is worth your time to look up Regulation M–A and skim its contents. You will note a heavy emphasis in the regulations on disclosures about history and performance and very few, narrow requirements for projections and predictions. We will discuss the details of disclosure obligations under federal securities legislation in more detail in Chapter Seven, Section A.

The filing requirement affects the timing of the deal. The soliciting firm must file *preliminary* copies of the proxy statement and the proxy card with the SEC at least ten days before the firm uses the final, *definitive* materials. Exch. Act Rule 14a–6(a). The soliciting firm may mail a preliminary proxy statement to shareholders but usually waits until the proxy statement is final or definitive, because the firm can send the proxy card only with the definitive statement. If the SEC staff decides to comment on the preliminary proxy materials, the soliciting firm must await and resolve the staff comments before mailing the definitive materials. This often takes significantly more than ten days. The firm either changes its materials to satisfy SEC concerns or convinces the SEC staff that the materials as filed are adequate. Once the SEC agrees the firm mails the definitive materials. It is commonplace for the SEC to provide comments (often extensive) on merger and acquisition-related proxy materials.

The preliminary proxy statement is one of the few SEC acquisition filings that a party may file confidentially. Issuers may file preliminary proxy materials confidentially with the SEC pursuant to Exchange Act Rule 14a–(6)(e)(2), provided the transaction is not a "roll-up"[191] or a Rule

---

[190] Regulations S–X and S–K are part of the SEC's integrated disclosure system, whereby disclosure requirements relating to filings under both the Securities Act and the Exchange Act are harmonized. Regulation M–A is technically a subset of Regulation S–K and is designed to provide a laundry list of possible disclosable information in connections with mergers and acquisitions. Form S–4 is the registration statement that issuers file under the Securities Act in connection with registering their securities for use as acquisition consideration.

[191] A roll-up involves the acquisition of a limited life partnership by a publicly traded corporation.

13e–3 "going-private" transaction.[192] Confidential treatment is also contingent on the parties not making any public communication relating to the transaction except those communications specified in Securities Act Rule 135. Rule 135(a)(2)(viii)(D) permits a public disclosure of the names of the parties to a transaction and a brief description of their business, the date, time, and place of the shareholder vote, and a brief description of the transaction and of the basic terms of the transaction. If the parties make public more information than permitted by Rule 135, the SEC will disclose on its website the preliminary filing materials.

There is no general federally-mandated time period between the date the soliciting firm mails the proxy material and the date of the shareholder meeting,[193] but state law requires minimum notice for shareholder meetings. The proxy solicitation usually accompanies any notice of the meeting required by state corporate codes. In Delaware, for example, a corporation must mail notice to its shareholders before any meeting, annual or special, not less than ten days and not more than sixty days before the date of the meeting. Del. Gen. Corp. L. § 222(b). Therefore, publicly traded firms usually solicit proxies by mail during this period. Firms filing definitive proxy materials with their required state notices must have filed their preliminary proxy materials with the SEC well in advance, often thirty days or so, of the proxy solicitation mailing to anticipate potential delays resulting from SEC comments.

The proxy card (the signed grant of agency power to vote) must itself indicate in boldface type on whose behalf the solicitation is made—the firm's board or another interested party. Exch. Act Rule 14a–4(a)(1). The proxies can confer authority to vote only at the next meeting. Exch. Act Rule 14a–4(d)(2) & (3). The proxy must identify clearly and impartially any acquisition or reorganization question submitted to a vote and permit the security holder to choose "between approval or disapproval . . . or abstention." Exch. Act Rule 14a–4(a)(3) & (b)(1).[194] General discretionary proxies—proxies in which a shareholder delegates general voting authority to the proxy holder—are mostly prohibited.[195]

---

192 See Section B.2.b.v, *infra*.

193 An important exception is for proxy statements in acquisitions that incorporate by reference other public filings of publicly traded firms. Note D.3 to SEC Schedule 14A. If an issuer incorporates material by reference in Item 14(e)(1) of the proxy statement, the proxy statement must be delivered twenty days before the date of the vote. See also Exch. Act § 14(h)(1)(J); Exch. Act Rule 14a–6(*l*) (sixty-day minimum period for roll-up transactions unless applicable state law requires a longer period).

194 The requirement of a box for a "no" vote is significant. In board elections, by contrast, the form need only contain boxes for an approval or an abstention vote on any given candidate.

195 A proxy may confer discretionary authority only within specified limitations: matters incident to the conduct of the meeting or unanticipated matters that may come before the meeting; approval of minutes of a prior meeting; shareholder proposals properly omitted from the proxy; or any matter about which the shareholder does not specify a choice, if the form of proxy states in bold type how the proxy holder intends to vote the shares in each such case. Exch. Act Rule 14a–4(c).

NOTE: PRE-COMMENCEMENT DISCLOSURES

In an acquisition that requires the public filing of documents with the SEC, the parties will often publicly announce the transaction before the filings are operational. This is true for tender offers and registration statements discussed in the following two subsections, as well as for proxy statements. The SEC allows such *pre-commencement publications* in defined *safe harbor rules.* Rule 14a–12 in Regulation 14A permits public communications before a firm has provided its shareholders with a written proxy statement. Rules 165 and 135 under the Securities Act apply to public communications before the SEC has declared a registration statement to be effective.[196] Rule 14d–2 under Regulation 14D applies to public communications before a tender offer commences. The safe harbors require pre-commencement communications to contain statements referring shareholders to the full filings and require firms to file the communications with the SEC no later than the date the material is first published, sent or given to shareholders.

The rules have led to multiple and varied questions by participants in acquisitions. SEC interpretations continue to pile up. The requirements apply only to written communications, for example. Does this cover scripts or prepared Q & As in live presentations? (Yes.) Transcripts of live presentations? (Yes.) If an audience of an email is only employees, must the company file on first use? (Yes, if employees are shareholders and the communication is likely to become public.) And so on.

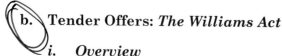

b. Tender Offers: *The Williams Act*

i. Overview

Prior to 1968, bidders used short-lived public offers, known as *Saturday night specials*, to buy control blocks of target stock. The offers lasted for only a few hours, and the bidders took tenders on a first-come, first-served basis as a tactic to create a sense of urgency. Since the bidders offered a substantial premium (the *takeover* or *tender offer premium*) over the market price of the stock, target shareholders rushed to get first in line. Bidders did not reveal their motivation for their offer nor their future plans for the acquired firms.

A Saturday night special-style tender offer generated maximum selling pressure on a dispersed and inadequately informed group of shareholders in publicly traded targets. Shareholders raced to tender their shares, fearful that they would be left out of the offer and lose their chance at the premium price. They had little time to consider the offer, much less gather information relevant to their decision. To stop Saturday night specials, Congress enacted the Williams Act in 1968.[197] The Williams Act

---

196 These two safe harbors are consolidated under Securities Act Rule 425.

197 The Williams Act was named after Senator Harrison ("Pete") Williams, Jr. (1919–2001). He served in the U.S. House of Representatives from 1953 until 1957 and then in the U.S. Senate from 1959 until 1982. In addition to his sponsorship of the Williams Act, he is best known for his

added several sections, most notably §§ 13(d) and (e) and 14(d) and (e), to the Securities Exchange Act of 1934. We will take up § 13(d) in Chapter Seven, Section A.7; §§ 13(e) and 14(d) and (e) on tender offers are the focus of this section. When the Williams Act applies, it has the most significant effect on the form and timing of acquisitions of solvent companies of any federal legislation enacted to date.

The Williams Act regulates tender offers for the registered voting stock of publicly held companies.[198] In a layperson's terms, tender offers are public announcements by an offeror (referred to as a *bidder*) that it will buy stock in a publicly traded company at a set price (a *cash tender offer*) or for a set number of the bidder's securities (an *exchange tender offer*). The value offered is usually well in excess of the current market price of the target shares (the difference referred to as the *takeover* or *tender offer premium*). The offer invites target shareholders to tender their shares to a *depositary* (a bank or trust company) within a set time. If a bidder also places a ceiling on the number of shares it is willing to accept, the offer is a *partial tender offer*. If there is no maximum limit, the offer is an *any-and-all tender offer*. The Williams Act and its accompanying SEC regulations impose various structural requirements on an offer's form and also require bidders to make comprehensive and detailed disclosures upon the announcement of their offers. In addition, the Act prohibits bidders from engaging in open-market purchases in the target firm shares while an offer is alive.

A bidder typically makes its tender offer subject to a number of conditions, regardless of whether that offer is *friendly* (with the target board's approval) or *hostile* (without such approval). Unless these conditions are either satisfied or waived (by the bidder), the bidder need not purchase[199] the shares that target shareholders tender. In a hostile deal, the tender offer will be conditioned on the repeal, redemption or nullification of a target company's takeover defenses (particularly a poison pill). In both hostile and friendly deals, the tender offer is generally conditioned on, among other things: (a) financing to the extent the bidder needs financing, (b) at least a majority of all the outstanding shares of target company stock being tendered into the tender offer (the so-called

---

1981 conviction for taking bribes in the Abscam sting operation. He resigned from the U.S. Senate in 1982 just prior to a scheduled expulsion vote. The Abscam operation is fictionalized in the 2013 Academy Award-nominated feature film *American Hustle*, directed by David O. Russell.

198 While the SEC has extended some of the tender offer rules to cover debt securities in Regulation 14E, it also recognizes that not all tender offers are worthy of regulation. For example, Regulation 14D requires a bidder to file a Schedule TO (which stands for "tender offer") only when it makes a tender offer which, if successful, would result in the bidder beneficially owning *more than five percent* of a class of equity securities of the target company. Exch. Act § 14(d)(1); Exch. Act Rule 14d–1. The requirements in § 14(e) and the rules promulgated thereunder in Regulation 14E apply whether or not the tender offer is subject to Regulation 14D. Section 14(e) is a general antifraud section and authorizes the SEC to pass rules against fraudulent practices in all tender offers. Note, for example, that the minimum twenty-day offering period in Rule 14e–1 thus applies to all tender offers (including tender offers for debt securities), not just tender offers for the stock of publicly traded companies.

199 The act of purchasing tendered shares is referred to as "taking down shares."

minimum tender condition),[200] and the expiration or early termination of the antitrust waiting period under the Hart-Scott-Rodino Antitrust Improvements Act of 1976.[201] If the conditions to a tender offer are not satisfied or waived, the bidder can either (i) terminate the offer or (ii) extend the offer as necessary beyond the initially scheduled period in hopes that the conditions will be satisfied in the near future.

ii. The Structural Framework of a Tender Offer

The Act's sections and the supplementing rules in Regulations 14D and 14E structure the form of the tender offer. Together they require that tender offers have:

(1) a *twenty business day minimum offering period*, Exch. Act Rule 14e–1 (most tender offers are open longer in order to satisfy the tender offer's conditions);

(2) a *ten business day extension* for any material change in the offer;[202]

(3) *shareholder withdrawal rights*[203] coextensive with the offering period, Exch. Act Rule 14d–7(a);

(4) withdrawal rights after sixty days from the initial offer if the offeror has failed to close on the tenders, Exch. Act § 14(d)(5);

---

[200] If the minimum tender condition is satisfied, the bidder will be able to vote through a second-step merger solely through its newly-acquired majority voting power, thus squeezing out remaining target shareholders. If the minimum tender condition is not satisfied, and yet the bidder chooses to waive it and close on its tender offer anyway, the bidder would have to rely on at least some of the remaining target shareholders to vote in favor of the second-step merger to ensure the merger's approval. Because those shareholders did not tender in the first place (presumably because they did not like the deal and the consideration being offered), it is unlikely that many (if any) of those shareholders will vote in favor of a second-step merger that offers them the exact same consideration as the tender offer did. Therefore, most bidders whose tender offers do not satisfy the minimum tender condition will either (a) extend their offers while increasing the price they are offering in order to better entice target shareholders to tender or (b) terminate their tender offers and simply walk away.

[201] The waiting period for all-cash tender offers is 15 days from the date on which the acquiring person files its Hart-Scott-Rodino Notification and Report Form with the Federal Trade Commission and the Premerger Notification Office of the Department of Justice. For all other deals, the waiting period is 30 days from the date on which the latest of the two parties to the transaction has filed its Form. See 15 U.S.C. § 18a(b).

[202] On a price change or an increase or decrease in the number of shares sought by more than two percent, or a change in a dealer's soliciting fee, the tender offer must remain open for at least ten business days after notice of the change. In addition, in exchange tender offers, Exchange Act Rule 14d–4(d)(2) requires that an offer remain open for a minimum period of five to twenty business days after revisions in registration statement material.

[203] A withdrawal right gives a shareholder who has tendered her shares to a depositary agent the right to have her shares returned before the offer closes. This is very useful if a third party offering more money than the original bidder appears on the scene. Indeed, a shareholder can withdraw her shares from the original bidder's tender offer and then tender them into the third party's tender offer.

(5) *pro rata acceptance* for over-subscribed offers,[204] Exch. Act Rule 14d–8;

(6) nondiscrimination among all shareholders holding shares of the type sought, Exch. Act Rule 14d–10(a)(1) (the *all holders* rule); and

(7) the extension of any price increase during the tender offer to all shareholders who have already tendered, Exch. Act Rule 14d–10(a)(2) (the *best price* rule).

Also, from the time of *public announcement* of the tender offer, even if prior to the actual commencement of the tender offer, until the tender offer expires, a bidder may not purchase shares "otherwise than pursuant to such tender offer" (Exch. Act Rule 14e–5), and any short tenders[205] (Exch. Act Rule 10b–4(b)) are prohibited.

Exchange Act Rule 14d–11 permits bidders in tender offers to provide for a period of between three and twenty business days after the expiration of a tender offer, a *subsequent offering period*, during which a shareholder may tender without withdrawal rights. This period is essentially a cleanup period during which target shareholders who failed to tender their shares during a successful tender offer have another chance to tender and receive the tender offer price. By tendering during the subsequent offering period, these shareholders do not have to wait until a second-step merger is completed to get paid for their shares. The period also helps bidders achieve the percentage of target shares necessary to complete a "short-form" merger (typically 90 percent or more), thus avoiding the need for a vote of target shareholders in connection with a second-step merger.[206] Under Exchange Act Rule 14d–7(a)(2), bidders need not offer withdrawal rights to target shareholders who tender their shares during a subsequent offering period; however, Rule 14d–11(e) requires bidders to immediately accept and promptly pay for all securities as they are tendered during the subsequent offering period.

The most obvious benefit of the tender offer rules that catches the eye is the twenty-day minimum offering period. It can be a mirage. Bidders can always extend their offers voluntarily for additional periods of time (typically one or more additional 20 business day periods). Voluntary extensions are common in both friendly and hostile tender offers, as it is highly unlikely (if not impossible) for all of the conditions to a tender offer (especially a hostile one) to be met within a single 20 business day time

---

204 Assume, for example, an acquirer wants only fifty-one shares out of 100 outstanding, there are four shareholders each holding twenty-five share blocks, and three of the four shareholders tender all their shares. The acquirer must accept 51/75s of each of the three blocks (17 shares) to acquire the desired fifty-one shares. In other words, the bidder returns to each of the three tendering shareholders 49/75s of their stock (8 shares) and pays a tender offer premium on 17 shares.

205 Speculators may not borrow stock and tender the borrowed stock into a tender offer.

206 See Del. Gen. Corp. L. § 253.

frame. Moreover, the SEC may delay the offer by requesting changes in the offering materials. In exchange tender offers, as noted in the next section, the buyer must file a registration statement on Form S–4 under the Securities Act.

The tender offer rules leave in place the timing advantages of cash tender offers. The buyer can acquire control of the target company and thus take over its board quickly. In negotiated transactions, this shortens a process that could take over a year to around one month. The short time period reduces the risk of competing bidders, changing market conditions, and material adverse changes in the operations of the target company. Some acquisition planners also point to the reduced role of proxy advisory services such as Institutional Shareholder Services (ISS) in tender offers as another advantage over mergers. A planner also avoids the risk in mergers that shareholders will sell their shares after the record date, not grant a proxy with the sale, and fail to vote in favor of the merger proposal. As noted below, the timing advantages of an exchange tender offer over a merger, while still significant, are less pronounced.

NOTE: THE BEST PRICE RULE AND SEVERANCE PAYMENTS

The SEC adopted amendments to its tender offer best price rules to resolve the uncertainty generated by conflicting federal circuit court decisions on the treatment of compensatory, severance and other employee benefit arrangements granted to a target's directors, employees, and other shareholders. Some courts had held that the compensation had to be included in the directors' and employees' calculation of the value paid on their shares pursuant to the tender offer and, if included, resulted in such shareholders receiving more than others in violation of the best price rule. The SEC clarified that the best price rule applies only to consideration paid for securities tendered in a tender offer and does not include compensation arrangements subject to two conditions. First, the compensation paid to the employee-shareholder is for past services performed, future services to be performed or future services to be refrained from performing (e.g., a non-compete). Second, the compensation must not be calculated based on the number of shares tendered or to be tendered by the employee-shareholder. The independent directors of the target, or, if the bidder is a party, the bidder must approve the arrangements. Exch. Act Rule 14d–10(d). Until the clarification, deal planners had shied away from using tender offers in negotiated deals to protect severance payments to the employee-shareholders. With the Commission clarification, two-step transactions have made a comeback in negotiated transactions.

NOTE: MARKET MANIPULATION AND MINI-TENDER OFFERS

Exchange Act Rule 14e–8 is designed to prevent prospective bidders from manipulating the market for the target company's stock. The Rule makes it illegal for any person to announce a plan to make a tender offer that has not yet commenced if that person (a) does not have a bona fide intent to launch the offer within a reasonable time period and complete it, (b) intends for the announcement to manipulate the market price of the stock of the bidder or target company, or (c) lacks a reasonable belief[207] that it will have the means to purchase the securities it is seeking to buy. This Rule is important because news that a particular company is about to be put "in play" (i.e., made the target of a tender offer) typically drives up that company's stock price. Public announcements of a potential tender offer trigger the obligation to file all written communications with the SEC. Exch. Act Rule 14d–2(b).

The SEC has also indicated that the antifraud provisions of Regulation 14E apply to so-called *mini-tender offers*. Mini-tender offers are tender offers for less than 5 percent of a company's registered voting securities that typically offer a price *less* than the current market price of the stock in question. The filing, disclosure, and procedural requirements of Exchange Act Section 14(d) and Regulation 14D do not apply. Are buyers able to design mini-tender offers as first-come, first-served offers and omit withdrawal rights and pro-rationing? The SEC takes the position that the antifraud provisions of Exchange Act Section 14(e) and the substantive and procedural requirements of Regulation 14E do apply to such offers.[208]

How could mini-tender offers possibly succeed when the offering price is *below* the trading price of the stock in question? Apparently, there were enough ignorant investors in the world who accepted these tender offers to make them worth the bidders' time and expense to launch them. Many who tendered were simply unaware what the current market price of their stock was, or upon receiving a legal disclosure document in the mail simply assumed they were required to tender.[209] Others wrongly assumed that all tender offers include a premium price.

---

[207] See Hartmarx Corp. v. Abboud, 326 F.3d 862, 868–69 (7th Cir. 2003) (discussing "reasonable belief" requirement). The SEC's adopting release readily acknowledged that Exchange Act Rule 14e–8's "reasonable belief" requirement was a slippery one and would probably be a locus of future litigation. In an attempt to provide some guidance on what constitutes a "reasonable belief," the SEC noted that "[a]lthough not required, a commitment letter or other evidence of financing ability (e.g., funds on hand or an existing credit facility) would in most cases be adequate to satisfy the rule's requirement that the bidder have a reasonable belief that it can purchase the securities sought." *Final Rule: Regulation of Takeovers and Security Holder Communications*, SEC Rel. 34–42055, 1999 WL 969596, at *17 (Oct. 22, 1999). The SEC stated that "[o]f course, if a target or other party decided to litigate under [Exchange Act Rule 14e–8], the plaintiff would have the burden of showing that the bidder either did not have an intent to commence and complete the offer or did not reasonably believe it had the ability to purchase the securities." *Id.*

[208] See *Commission Guidance on Mini-Tender Offers and Limited Partnership Tender Offers*, SEC Rel. 34–43069, 2000 WL 1190808, at *3 (July 24, 2000).

[209] The SEC has indicated that some bidders do not adequately disseminate the tender offer disclosure to security holders:

> Often, bidders . . . will deliver the offering documents to The Depository Trust Company ("DTC"). These bidders rely on DTC to forward a notice of the offer electronically to DTC's participant broker-dealers and banks. In some cases, the participants then send information to their customers for whom the participants hold securities in street name. Generally, bidders make no effort to send offering documents to security holders who hold their securities in their own name, rather than through brokers or banks in street name.
>
> The information sent by the broker-dealer or bank participants to customers often is limited to notice of the tender offer, the expiration date, and, in some cases, the price. The

The SEC interprets the general antifraud language of Exchange Act Section 14(e) to prohibit mini-tender offers for less than the market price unless full and prominent disclosure of this fact is made to target shareholders. Moreover, mini-tender offers at or above the market price, without withdrawal rights, and where the offeror intends to close the offer only if the market price rises above the offer price (a free call option) are also prohibited.[210]

Regulation 14E requires a mini tender offer to be open for twenty business days, ten business days following a change in price, and that the bidder promptly pay for or return securities when the tender offer expires. The SEC also interprets Section 14(e) to require bidders to disclose and disseminate material information to target shareholders. The SEC recommends disclosures on, among other things, offer price, price changes, ability to finance the offer, identity of the bidder, plans or proposals of the offeror, and conditions and terms on the offer. As mentioned above, the SEC's list of recommended disclosures is also a prominent statement on whether the offer price is below the market price.

iii. Bidder and Target Disclosure

In addition to the form requirements, the tender offer regulations add a heavy layer of multiple disclosure obligations on bidders and target companies.

a) Bidder Disclosure

In a normal cash tender offer, the bidder typically posts a summary announcement of a tender offer (known as the summary ad) in the Wall Street Journal.[211] While a summary ad invites target shareholders to

---

> participants do not always request copies of the offering documents from DTC. Even if the participants do obtain the offering documents, they may decide not to send them to their customers. Therefore, security holders may make investment decisions without receiving material information about the tender offer.

Id. at *5.

[210] In these situations, a bidder would continue extending its offer until such time as the market price of the stock rose above the offer price. Because shareholders who tendered had no withdrawal rights, the extensions could continue indefinitely. Once the stock price did rise above the offer price, the bidder would sell the tendered shares at the market price and use the proceeds to pay for the tendered shares at the lower offer price, thus pocketing the difference. Typically, the bidder would not pay tendering shareholders for 30 days or more. The bidder in this situation never bears any risk. However, tendering shareholders are harmed because their funds are withheld for a significant amount of time in violation of the prompt payment requirements of Exchange Act Rule 14e–1(c). In addition, the SEC believes this payment practice violates Exchange Act Rule 14e–8 if the bidder lacked a reasonable belief that it will have the means to purchase the securities it is seeking to buy when it launched the mini-tender offer. Moreover, if the bidder intended never to purchase the shares unless the market price rose above the offer price, and did not disclose this intent, the SEC believes that this would be a "fraudulent, deceptive or manipulative practice" within the meaning of Section 14(e). See *id.* at *6.

[211] A formal tender offer commences at 12:01 a.m. on the date when the bidder (1) publishes a *long-form notice* of the tender offer in a newspaper, (2) publishes a *summary advertisement* of the tender offer in a newspaper, or (3) provides to shareholders definitive copies of the tender offer materials. See Exch. Act Rule 14d–2(a). The required content of a long-form, a summary form, and a tender offer solicitation are all specified in the SEC rules. In almost all cases, a bidder commences a formal tender offer by the use of a summary advertisement of the type often seen in the financial

request formal offering materials from the bidder's information agent, a bidder actively seeks (and is also legally required) to send those materials to those shareholders.[212] In this regard, under Exchange Act Rule 14d–5(a)(3) the target company can choose either to (a) send the bidder's offering materials to the target's shareholders (at the bidder's cost and expense) within three business days of delivery of the bidder's offering materials or (b) provide a list of target shareholders to the bidder so that the bidder can send its materials out directly. In most instances, the target will provide a list of target shareholders because the bidder, which typically already owns some shares of the target's stock before it commences its tender offer, normally demands a list of target shareholders pursuant to its legal right to do so under state corporate law.[213]

On the day its tender offer is announced, the bidder files a Schedule TO[214] with the SEC, delivers a copy of the schedule to the target and to all national exchanges on which the target's stock is traded, and mails (or has the target mail) to the shareholders of the target the main disclosure exhibit to its Schedule TO, namely the Offer to Purchase or OP. It also sends them the means to tender, a Letter of Transmittal or LT.

The Schedule TO disclosures required of the bidder depend on the type of deal. Item 10 of Schedule TO requires the bidder to include its own financial statements if material to the investor's decision of whether to sell, hold, or tender the relevant securities. The bidder's financial statements are not material in an all-cash tender offer if the offer is not subject to a financing condition and either (a) the bidder is a reporting company that has filed its periodic reports with the SEC electronically or (b) the offer is for all outstanding securities of a subject class. Schedule TO, Instruction 2 to Item 10. If the offeror is not a reporting company, the financial statements need not be audited if they are not available or obtainable

pages of the *Wall Street Journal*. Summary ads usually form a vertical rectangle flowing from the top to the bottom of one-third of one page of a newspaper. A summary ad describes the basic terms of the offer and invites target shareholders to request formal offering materials from the bidder's "information agent." Summary ads are typically published in Section C ("Money & Investing") of the *Wall Street Journal*, although they appear in the *New York Times* and *Los Angeles Times* occasionally. These ads *cannot* include a transmittal letter enabling shareholders to tender their securities pursuant to Exchange Act Rule 14d–6(d)(3).

[212] See Exch. Act Rule 14d–4(a)(2)(ii).

[213] See, e.g., Del. Gen. Corp. L. § 220(b)(1). Demanding a list of shareholders under state law is particularly important in the context of a *hostile* tender offer. If, under Rule 14d–5(a)(3), the bidder were to allow the target company to decide whether to mail out the bidder's materials or provide the bidder with a list of shareholders, the target could decide to mail out the bidder's materials. However, once the bidder delivered its expensive and voluminous materials to the target, those materials might "accidentally" wind up in the dumpster behind the target's headquarters!

[214] Exch. Act Rule 14d–100. Schedule TO applies to tender offers by independent parties, issuer *self-tender offers* (a corporation tenders for its own shares), and going-private transactions (a tender offer than reduces the number of shareholders to under 300 or causes the delisting of its shares from a national stock exchange or Nasdaq (see Exch. Act Rule 13e–1(a)(3)(ii)), although the requirements of Schedule TO differ somewhat for the different types of transactions. Schedule TO can also be used to amend a previously filed Schedule 13D pursuant to Exchange Act Rule 13d–2. See Cover Page of Schedule TO and General Instruction B to Schedule TO.

"without unreasonable cost or expense." *Id.*, Instruction 7 to Item 10. If the offeror is a natural person, she must disclose her net worth. *Id.*, Instruction 4 to Item 10. If a bidder makes a cash tender offer and anticipates a follow-up second-step merger using securities as consideration, the bidder must include post-merger *pro forma* financial information in the tender offer statement. *Id.*, Instruction 5 to Item 10. This requirement, however, is limited to "negotiated" deals in which the size of the target exceeds 20 percent of the value of the acquirer.

The vast majority of the information included in a Schedule TO is incorporated by reference into the Schedule from the Schedule's two main exhibits—the Offer to Purchase and the Letter of Transmittal. The Offer to Purchase, usually well over thirty pages, sets forth the terms of the offer—the number of shares to be purchased, the offer price and the length of time the offer will be open. Additional required disclosure includes details on withdrawal rights, conditions to the offer, tax considerations, past contacts and negotiations between the parties, the source and amount of funds to be used to purchase shares, the purpose of the acquisition and the bidder's plans for the target company post-acquisition. The Letter of Transmittal is the document that shareholders must complete to tender their shares into the tender offer.

If the SEC staff reviews the filed Schedule TO and returns comments to the bidder, the bidder and the SEC negotiate the comments while the tender offer is open. If unsatisfied by the bidder's responses, the SEC may ask the bidder to send additional information to the target shareholders and may ask the bidder to extend the tender offer period so that shareholders can consider the new material.

Shareholders respond to the offer by tendering their shares to a named intermediary, usually a commercial bank or trust company, referred to as a *depositary*. The tendering shareholders attach the Letter of Transmittal to their shares; the paying agent accumulates the shares and pays all shareholders when the offer expires and the bidder takes down shares for payment. If a shareholder wishes to withdraw shares, she must submit a *letter of withdrawal* accompanied by a *signature guarantee,* verifying that the signature of the shareholder is authentic. Shareholders often wait until the last minute before tendering their shares in the hope that better offers from other bidders will materialize (a bidding war). As the expiration date approaches, brokers, acting on behalf of shareholders, may submit a *notice of guaranteed delivery*, guaranteeing that the broker will deliver shares within five business days; the paying agent will include the shares so guaranteed in the closing.

b) Target Disclosure

The target firm, within ten business days of the commencement of the tender offer, must send a notice to its shareholders (1) recommending the offer, (2) rejecting the offer, (3) expressing no opinion on the offer and remaining neutral, or (4) stating that it is unable to take a position on the offer. Exch. Act Rule 14e–2. Before the expiration of the ten-day period, the target can issue a *stop-look-and-listen request* to its shareholders, asking that they refrain from tendering their shares until the managers of the target can make and distribute their Rule 14e–2 decision.

Whenever the target recommends that its security holders accept or reject an outstanding offer to tender, the firm must file a *Schedule 14D–9* with the SEC and deliver a copy to its shareholders,[215] the bidder, and any national stock exchanges on which the stock is traded. If the tender offer has been negotiated ahead of time with target management (the normal case), the target issues its affirmative recommendation that its shareholders accept the offer and tender their shares. If, however, the tender offer in question is hostile, the recommendation of target's management is typically the polar opposite. Typically, management will recommend that shareholders not tender their shares because the consideration being offered by the bidder is "inadequate from a financial point of view." That is a fancy way of saying the bidder is not offering enough money for the target's shares. Delaware case law refers to an inadequate financial offer as *substantive coercion* and thus a legal justification for the board of directors of a Delaware corporation to adopt takeover defenses.[216]

If the target buys back some of its own stock after receiving notice of an unwanted tender offer by an independent party, it must file a Rule 13e–1 Statement with the SEC, and if the issuer stock repurchase is in the form of a competing tender offer, the issuer must file and disseminate its own full blown Schedule TO instead. Within a Rule 13e–1 Statement, a target must disclose, among other things, the purpose of its stock purchases, its plans for the repurchased securities (e.g., retire them, hold them in treasury, resell them at a later date), and the source and amount of funds used to make the purchases. Rule 13e–1(a). Without such disclosure, a rise in the target's stock price (caused by the target's own purchases) could lead the market into thinking an additional third party is interested in the target and that a bidding war might ensue.

If the issuer buys enough shares to reduce the number of shareholders to less than 300 or cause the delisting of its shares from a national stock

go private

[215] Targets may communicate with their shareholders in anticipation of a tender offer not yet launched without filing a full Schedule 14D–9, if all written communications so used are filed with the SEC on the date of first use. Exch. Act Rule 14d–9(a). The target's obligation to file a full Schedule 14D–9 arises on the day the target first makes a solicitation or recommendation with respect to a commenced (and not merely announced) tender offer or within ten days of the commencement of the offer, whichever comes first. Exch. Act Rule 14(d)–9(b) & (g).

[216] See, e.g., Unitrin, Inc. v. Amer. Gen. Corp., 651 A.2d 1361, 1383–85 (Del. 1995).

exchange or Nasdaq (i.e., it *goes private*),[217] it must file a *Schedule 13E–3*.[218] More on going-private transactions appears in Section B.2.b.v below.

If the bidder and target have negotiated to allow the bidder to select, other than by shareholder vote, a majority of the directors of the target after a successful tender offer, then the target must file a disclosure statement at least ten days before the date on which the designees take office. Exch. Act Rule 14f–1. The statement includes information about the new directors and their compensation.

iv. What Is a Tender Offer?

The Williams Act does not define the term tender offer, and the drafters appear to have purposely avoided placing any useful definitional guidance in the Act's legislative history.[219] At first glance, this seems truly odd, given that the main purpose of the Williams Act is to regulate tender offers. However, Congress left the boundaries of the Williams Act's coverage open-ended and undefined lest enterprising Wall Street folks and their lawyers do end runs around a static definition. The Act does not explicitly require that all large-scale stock acquisitions take the form of a regulated tender offer. Thus, the Act leaves some room for large-scale stock acquisitions through open-market trades or privately negotiated deals. Apparently, Congress expected the SEC and the courts to define the boundaries of the term tender offer and thus the scope of the Act.

tender offer happens:

The only SEC rule relevant to the definition of a tender offer is Exchange Act Rule 14d–2, which defines when a classic tender offer commences. Under Rule 14d–2(b), a tender offer commences when the bidder first publishes or gives security holders the means to tender securities in the offer (i.e., sends a letter of transmittal) or publishes a statement regarding how the transmittal form may be obtained. Everything short of mailing a transmittal form or otherwise instructing shareholders on how to tender their shares does not commence a tender offer. However, all written communications concerning an anticipated tender offer must be filed with the SEC on the date of first use under cover of Schedule TO.[220] In addition, the very first such communication must be

---

[217] See Exch. Act Rule 13e–3(a)(3)(ii).

[218] Exch. Act Rule 13e–100. If the going-private transaction is accomplished by means of a tender offer, the issuer may file a combined Schedule TO and Schedule 13E–3 under cover of Schedule TO. However, the issuer must provide all information called for by both schedules (taking into consideration redundancies).

[219] According to the Second Circuit:

> The term "tender offer," although left somewhat flexible by Congress' decision not to define it, nevertheless remains a word of art. Section 14(d)(1) was never intended to apply to *every* acquisition of more than 5% of a public company's stock. If that were the case there would be no need for § 13(d)(1), which requires a person, *after* acquiring more than 5%, to furnish the issuer, stock exchange and the SEC with certain pertinent information.

Hanson Trust PLC v. SCM Corp., 774 F.2d 47, 59 (2d Cir. 1985) (emphasis added).

[220] Pre-commencement communications can also be filed with the SEC on Form 8–K. See Cover of Form 8–K. The Form is discussed in Chapter Seven.

delivered to the target and any competing bidders on its date of first use. Exch. Act Rule 14d–2(b). Furthermore, each written communication must contain a prominent legend advising target shareholders to read the tender offer statement when it becomes available.[221]

While the SEC has been reluctant to write any rules on the definitional boundaries of a tender offer,[222] the good news is that most parties engaging in tender offers comply with the mandates of the Williams Act. Trouble arises, however, when someone conducts an *unconventional tender offer*. The SEC periodically stresses its position that, under the Williams Act, the term tender offer goes beyond the conventional tender offer to include acquisition programs that present the type of abuses that Congress intended to eliminate. This position leaves us to speculate on what constitutes an unconventional tender offer.[223]

In defining an unconventional tender offer, the SEC's help is limited to an eight-part "flexible factors" test, set forth in *amicus* briefs condemning particular acquisitions. See, e.g., *Hoover Industries, v. Fuqua Inc.*, 1979 WL 1244, at *4 (N.D. Ohio 1979) (listing all eight factors); *Wellman v. Dickinson*, 475 F.Supp. 783, 823–24 (S.D.N.Y. 1979) (listing only the first seven factors as the eighth factor was inapplicable to the case), aff'd on other grounds, 682 F.2d 355 (2d Cir. 1982), cert. den., 460 U.S. 1069, 103 S.Ct. 1522, 75 L.Ed.2d 946 (1983); *SEC v. Carter Hawley Hale Stores, Inc.,* 760 F.2d 945, 950–52 (9th Cir. 1985) (listing all eight factors).

The factors listed by the SEC that identify a tender offer are:

(1) Whether there is an active and widespread solicitation of public shareholders for shares of an issuer;

(2) Whether the solicitation is made for a substantial percentage of the issuer's stock;

---

[221] The legend must also advise shareholders that they can obtain tender offer materials for free on the SEC's website and explain which materials are available for free from the offeror.

[222] There was a fleeting moment of hope in 1979. In that year, a federal district court admonished the agency for failing to provide proper guidance for investors and rejected the agency's flexible-factor approach. The SEC grudgingly responded with two attempts to define tender offer, one in a proposed rule and the other in a proposed legislative amendment. See *Acquisitions of Substantial Amounts of Securities and Related Activities Undertaken During and Following a Tender Offer for Those Securities*, SEC Rel. 34–24976, 1987 WL 847508 (Oct. 1, 1987) (hereinafter *Acquisitions of Substantial Amounts of Securities*). Predictably, the definitions in these proposals were overly broad and drew harsh criticism. Some critics were so desperate for clarification, however, that they were willing to accept these overly-inclusive definitions in order to achieve some predictability. In any event, the SEC has not acted on either proposal. Some use language of the proposed rule as guidance, but the eight-factor test, incorporated in case law, has more legal authority.

[223] One example of an unconventional tender offer is the *street sweep*. This is the practice of a bidder purchasing large blocks of stock up and down the streets of New York's financial district—figuratively sweeping up shares on Wall Street.

8 flex. factors

street sweep

(3) Whether the offer to purchase is made at a premium over the prevailing market price;

(4) Whether the terms of the offer are firm rather than negotiable;

(5) Whether the offer is contingent on the tender of a fixed minimum number of shares, and perhaps, subject to the ceiling of a fixed maximum number to be purchased;

(6) Whether the offer is open for only a limited period of time;

(7) Whether the offerees are subjected to pressure to sell their stock; and

(8) Whether public announcements of a purchasing program concerning the target company precede or accompany a rapid accumulation of large amounts of target company securities.

The SEC's eight-part test leaves much to the imagination. The SEC describes each factor in the test only vaguely, and some of the factors appear to overlap. The SEC also routinely attaches a catchall equivocation to the test: "The Commission repeatedly has cautioned that not all eight factors are entitled to equal weight and that neither all, nor even a majority, of the eight factors need be present."[224] The SEC has not indicated which of these factors are determinative or which can be missing in a determination. (Thanks SEC!) However, it has added that the eight "factors really serve one ultimate purpose—to identify whether a purchase program places pressure on shareholders to respond hastily before having a chance to consider material information."[225]

Judicial interpretations of the SEC's eight-factor test fall all over the map.[226] The common thread throughout these opinions, if one can be found, is the notion that stock acquisitions do not violate the Williams Act unless, prior to an acquisition, a purchaser publicizes its intention to use a street sweep to gain control of a target. Publicity can take the form of general press releases, public announcements aimed at all shareholders, or communications to a large number of individual shareholders. Courts view such publicity, when followed by large-scale private and open-market purchases at premium prices, as too close to traditional tender offers.

The SEC distinguishes privately negotiated purchase programs and open-market purchase programs from unconventional tender offers. In

---

224 *Acquisitions of Substantial Amounts of Securities*, *supra* note 222, at *7.

225 *Id.*

226 One district court interpreted the test to include in its definition of tender offer "all methods of takeover by a large-scale stock purchase program." See Wellman v. Dickinson, 475 F.Supp. 783, 825 (S.D.N.Y. 1979). One court has explicitly rejected the test as too vague. Brascan Ltd. v. Edper Equities Ltd., 477 F.Supp. 773, 791 (S.D.N.Y. 1979). Finally, other courts have viewed the test as a shapeless authority, finding in it whatever they want to find. E.g., SEC v. Carter Hawley Hale Stores, Inc., 587 F.Supp. 1248, 1252–57 (C.D.Cal. 1984), *aff'd*, 760 F.2d 945 (9th Cir. 1985).

privately negotiated purchase programs, the SEC focuses on the number of direct solicitations and, to a lesser extent, the sophistication of those solicited as critical variables. Apparently, if the acquirer solicits enough shareholders, the SEC considers a stock acquisition to be a tender offer, even when general publicity of the sweep is absent. The general market notification (which creates the pressure to sell) results from the large number of individual contacts, rather than a simple press release. The SEC's approach finds support in some judicial opinions. On its face, though, this approach seems inconsistent in that it allows an acquirer to purchase from sellers, regardless of sophistication and number, in the open markets with no public comment and the enticement of a steadily rising price, but prohibits the same acquirer from directly contacting shareholders with an unadorned offer to purchase at a price slightly in excess of market.

Not all courts have bought into the SEC's flexible factors test. Consider the Second Circuit's approach in the following case.

HANSON TRUST PLC v. SCM CORPORATION

United States Court of Appeals, Second Circuit, 1985.
774 F.2d 47.

Before MANSFIELD, PIERCE and PRATT, CIRCUIT JUDGES.

Opinion

MANSFIELD, CIRCUIT JUDGE:

Hanson Trust PLC, HSCM Industries, Inc., and Hanson Holdings Netherlands B.V. (hereinafter sometimes referred to collectively as "Hanson") appeal from an order of the Southern District of New York, 617 F.Supp. 832 (1985), Shirley Wohl Kram, Judge, granting SCM Corporation's motion for a preliminary injunction restraining them, their officers, agents, employees and any persons acting in concert with them, from acquiring any shares of SCM and from exercising any voting rights with respect to 3.1 million SCM shares acquired by them on September 11, 1985. The injunction was granted on the ground that Hanson's September 11 acquisition of the SCM stock through five private and one open market purchases amounted to a "tender offer" for more than 5% of SCM's outstanding shares, which violated §§ 14(d)(1) and (6) of the Williams Act, and rules promulgated by the Securities and Exchange Commission (SEC) thereunder. *See* 17 C.F.R. §§ 240.14(e)(1) and 240.14d–7. We reverse.

The setting is the familiar one of a fast-moving bidding contest for control of a large public corporation: first, a cash tender offer of $60 per share by Hanson, an outsider, addressed to SCM stockholders; next, a counterproposal by an "insider" group consisting of certain SCM managers and their "White Knight," Merrill Lynch Capital Markets (Merrill), for a "leveraged buyout" at a higher price ($70 per share); then an increase by Hanson of its cash offer to $72 per share, followed by a revised SCM-Merrill leveraged buyout offer of $74 per share with a "crown jewel" irrevocable lock-up option to Merrill designed to discourage Hanson from seeking control by providing that if any other party (in this case Hanson) should acquire more than one-third of SCM's outstanding shares (66⅔% being needed under N.Y.Bus.L. § 903(a)(2) to effectuate a merger[Ed.[227]]) Merrill would have the right to buy SCM's two most profitable businesses (consumer foods and pigments) at prices characterized by some as "bargain basement." The final act in this scenario was the decision of Hanson, having been deterred by the SCM-Merrill option (colloquially described in the market as a "poison pill"), to terminate its cash tender offer and then to make private purchases, amounting to 25% of SCM's outstanding shares, leading SCM to seek and obtain the preliminary injunction from which this appeal is taken. A more detailed history of relevant events follows.

SCM is a New York corporation with its principal place of business in New York City. Its shares, of which at all relevant times at least 9.9 million were outstanding and 2.3 million were subject to issuance upon conversion of other outstanding securities, are traded on the New York Stock Exchange (NYSE) and Pacific Stock Exchange. Hanson Trust PLC is an English company with its principal place of business in London. HSCM, a Delaware corporation, and Hanson Holdings Netherlands B.V., a Netherlands limited liability company, are indirect wholly-owned subsidiaries of Hanson Trust PLC.

On August 21, 1985, Hanson publicly announced its intention to make a cash tender offer of $60 per share for any and all outstanding SCM shares. Five days later it filed the tender offer documents required by § 14(d)(1) of the Williams Act and regulations issued thereunder. The offer provided that it would remain open until September 23, unless extended, that no shares would be accepted until September 10, and that

> "Whether or not the Purchasers [Hanson] purchase Shares pursuant to the Offer, the Purchasers may thereafter determine, subject to the availability of Shares at favorable prices and the availability of financing, to purchase additional Shares in the open market, in privately negotiated transactions, through another tender offer or otherwise. Any such purchases of additional Shares might be on terms which are the same as, or more or less favorable than, those of this Offer. The Purchasers also reserve the right to dispose of any or all Shares acquired by them." *Offer to Purchase For Cash Any and All Outstanding Shares of Common Stock of SCM Corporation* (Aug. 26, 1985) at 21.

---

[227] [Ed. New York has since reduced the necessary vote to a majority vote.]

On August 30, 1985, SCM, having recommended to SCM's stockholders that they not accept Hanson's tender offer, announced a preliminary agreement with Merrill under which a new entity, formed by SCM and Merrill, would acquire all SCM shares at $70 per share in a leveraged buyout sponsored by Merrill. Under the agreement, which was executed on September 3, the new entity would make a $70 per share cash tender offer for approximately 85% of SCM's shares. If more than two-thirds of SCM's shares were acquired under the offer the remaining SCM shares would be acquired in exchange for debentures in a new corporation to be formed as a result of the merger. On the same date, September 3, Hanson increased its tender offer from $60 to $72 cash per share. However, it expressly reserved the right to terminate its offer if SCM granted to anyone any option to purchase SCM assets on terms that Hanson believed to constitute a "lock-up" device. *Supplement Dated September 5, 1985, to Offer to Purchase,* at 4.

The next development in the escalating bidding contest for control of SCM occurred on September 10, 1985, when SCM entered into a new leveraged buyout agreement with its "White Knight," Merrill. The agreement provided for a two-step acquisition of SCM stock by Merrill at $74 per share. The first proposed step was to be the acquisition of approximately 82% of SCM's outstanding stock for cash. Following a merger (which required acquisition of at least 66⅔%), debentures would be issued for the remaining SCM shares. If any investor or group other than Merrill acquired more than one-third of SCM's outstanding shares, Merrill would have the option to buy SCM's two most profitable businesses, pigments and consumer foods, for $350 and $80 million respectively, prices which Hanson believed to be below their market value.

Hanson, faced with what it considered to be a "poison pill," concluded that even if it increased its cash tender offer to $74 per share it would end up with control of a substantially depleted and damaged company. Accordingly, it announced on the Dow Jones Broad Tape at 12:38 P.M. on September 11 that it was terminating its cash tender offer. A few minutes later, Hanson issued a press release, carried on the Broad Tape, to the effect that "all SCM shares tendered will be promptly returned to the tendering shareholders."

At some time in the late forenoon or early afternoon of September 11 Hanson decided to make cash purchases of a substantial percentage of SCM stock in the open market or through privately negotiated transactions. Under British law Hanson could not acquire more than 49% of SCM's shares in this fashion without obtaining certain clearances, but acquisition of such a large percentage was not necessary to stymie the SCM-Merrill merger proposal. If Hanson could acquire slightly less than one-third of SCM's outstanding shares it would be able to block the $74 per share SCM-Merrill offer of a leveraged buyout. This might induce the latter to work out an agreement with Hanson, something Hanson had unsuccessfully sought on several occasions since its first cash tender offer.

Within a period of two hours on the afternoon of September 11 Hanson made five privately-negotiated cash purchases of SCM stock and one open-market purchase, acquiring 3.1 million shares or 25% of SCM's outstanding stock. The price of SCM stock on the NYSE on September 11 ranged from a high of $73.50 per share to a low of $72.50 per share. Hanson's initial private purchase, 387,700 shares from Mutual Shares, was not solicited by Hanson but by a Mutual Shares official, Michael Price, who, in a conversation with Robert Pirie of Rothschild, Inc., Hanson's financial advisor, on the morning of September 11 (before Hanson had decided to make any private cash purchases), had stated that he was interested in selling [Mutual's] SCM stock to Hanson. Once Hanson's decision to buy privately had been made, Pirie took Price up on his offer. The parties negotiated a sale at $73.50 per share after Pirie refused Price's asking prices, first of $75 per share and, later, of $74.50 per share. This transaction, but not the identity of the parties, was automatically reported pursuant to NYSE rules on the NYSE ticker at 3:11 P.M. and reported on the Dow Jones Broad Tape at 3:29 P.M.

Pirie then telephoned Ivan Boesky,[Ed.[228]] an arbitrageur who had a few weeks earlier disclosed in a Schedule 13D statement filed with the SEC that he owned approximately 12.7% of SCM's outstanding shares. Pirie negotiated a Hanson purchase of these shares at $73.50 per share after rejecting Boesky's initial demand of $74 per share. At the same time Rothschild purchased for Hanson's account 600,000 SCM shares in the open market at $73.50 per share. An attempt by Pirie next to negotiate the cash purchase of another large block of SCM stock (some 780,000 shares) from Slifka & Company fell through because of the latter's inability to make delivery of the shares on September 12.

Following the NYSE ticker and Broad Tape reports of the first two large anonymous transactions in SCM stock, some professional investors surmised that the buyer might be Hanson. Rothschild then received telephone calls from (1) Mr. Mulhearn of Jamie & Co. offering to sell between 200,000 and 350,000 shares at $73.50 per share, (2) David Gottesman, an arbitrageur at Oppenheimer & Co. offering 89,000 shares at $73.50, and (3) Boyd Jeffries of Jeffries & Co., offering approximately 700,000 to 800,000 shares at $74.00. Pirie purchased the three blocks for

[228] [Ed. In the late 1980s, Boesky pled guilty to insider trading charges unrelated to the SCM deal. He agreed to cooperate with the SEC by informing against junk bond king Michael Milken in return for a more lenient prison sentence. Author James B. Stewart wrote about Boesky's criminal activities in his book *Den of Thieves*. The famous Gordon Gekko character (played by Michael Douglas and earning him the 1987 Academy Award for Best Actor) of Oliver Stone's 1987 feature film *Wall Street* is widely believed to be based, at least in part, on Boesky. Like the Gekko character, Boesky also delivered a speech on the positive aspects of "greed" when he spoke at the 1986 commencement ceremony of the School of Business of the University of California, Berkeley.]

Hanson at $73.50 per share. The last of Hanson's cash purchases was completed by 4:35 P.M. on September 11, 1985.

In the early evening of September 11 SCM successfully applied to Judge Kram in the present lawsuit for a restraining order barring Hanson from acquiring more SCM stock for 24 hours. On September 12 and 13 the TRO was extended by consent pending the district court's decision on SCM's application for a preliminary injunction. Judge Kram held an evidentiary hearing on September 12–13, at which various witnesses testified, including Sir Gordon White, Hanson's United States Chairman .... Sir Gordon White testified that on September 11, 1985, after learning of the $74 per share SCM-Merrill leveraged buyout tender offer with its "crown jewel" irrevocable "lock-up" option to Merrill, he instructed Pirie to terminate Hanson's $72 per share tender offer, and that only thereafter did he discuss the possibility of Hanson making market purchases of SCM stock. ...

SCM argued before Judge Kram (and argues here) that Hanson's cash purchases immediately following its termination of its $72 per share tender offer amounted to a *de facto* continuation of Hanson's tender offer, designed to avoid the strictures of § 14(d) of the Williams Act, and that unless a preliminary injunction issued SCM and its shareholders would be irreparably injured because Hanson would acquire enough shares to defeat the SCM-Merrill offer. Judge Kram found that the relevant underlying facts (which we have outlined) were not in dispute, ... and concluded that "[w]ithout deciding what test should ultimately be applied to determine whether Hanson's conduct constitutes a 'tender offer' within the meaning of the Williams Act ... SCM has demonstrated a likelihood of success on the merits of its contention that Hanson has engaged in a tender offer which violates Section 14(d) of the Williams Act." ... The district court, characterizing Hanson's stock purchases as "a deliberate attempt to do an 'end run' around the requirements of the Williams Act," ... made no finding on the question of whether Hanson had decided to make the purchases of SCM before or after it dropped its tender offer but concluded that even if the decision had been made after it terminated its offer preliminary injunctive relief should issue. From this decision Hanson appeals.

DISCUSSION

A preliminary injunction will be overturned only when the district court abuses its discretion. ...

Since, as the district court correctly noted, the material relevant facts in the present case are not in dispute, this appeal turns on whether the district court erred as a matter of law in holding that when Hanson terminated its offer and immediately thereafter made private purchases of a substantial share of the target company's outstanding stock, the purchases became a "tender offer" within the meaning of § 14(d) of the

Williams Act. Absent any express definition of "tender offer" in the Act, the answer requires a brief review of the background and purposes of § 14(d).

* * *

The typical tender offer, as described in the Congressional debates, hearings and reports on the Williams Act, consisted of a general, publicized bid by an individual or group to buy shares of a publicly-owned company, the shares of which were traded on a national securities exchange, at a price substantially above the current market. . . . The offer was usually accompanied by newspaper and other publicity, a time limit for tender of shares in response to it, and a provision fixing a quantity limit on the total number of shares of the target company that would be purchased.

Prior to the Williams Act a tender offeror had no obligation to disclose any information to shareholders when making a bid. The Report of the Senate Committee on Banking and Currency aptly described the situation: "by using a cash tender offer the person seeking control can operate in almost complete secrecy. At present, the law does not even require that he disclose his identity, the source of his funds, who his associates are, or what he intends to do if he gains control of the corporation." . . .

* * *

The purpose of the Williams Act was, accordingly, to protect the shareholders from that dilemma by insuring "that public shareholders who are confronted by a cash tender offer for their stock will not be required to respond without adequate information." *Piper v. Chris-Craft Industries,* 430 U.S. 1, 35, (1977); *Rondeau v. Mosinee Paper Corp.,* 422 U.S. 49, 58, (1975).

Congress took "extreme care," . . . however, when protecting shareholders, to avoid "tipping the balance of regulation either in favor of management or in favor of the person making the takeover bid." . . . Indeed, the initial draft of the bill, proposed in 1965, had been designed to prevent "proud old companies [from being] reduced to corporate shells after white-collar pirates have seized control[.]" . . . In the end, Congress considered it crucial that the act be neutral and place " 'investors on an equal footing with the takeover bidder' . . . without favoring either the tender offeror or existing management." *Piper, supra,* 430 U.S. at 30 . . . .

Congress finally settled upon a statute requiring a tender offer solicitor seeking beneficial ownership of more than 5% of the outstanding shares of any class of any equity security registered on a national securities exchange first to file with the SEC a statement containing certain information specified in § 13(d)(1) of the Act, as amplified by SEC rules and regulations. Congress' failure to define "tender offer" was deliberate. Aware of "the almost infinite variety in the terms of most tender offers" and concerned that a rigid definition would be evaded, Congress left to the court and the SEC the flexibility to define the term. . . .

Although § 14(d)(1) clearly applies to "classic" tender offers of the type described above . . . , courts soon recognized that in the case of privately negotiated transactions or solicitations for private purchases of stock many of the conditions leading to the enactment of § 14(d) for the most part do not exist. The number and percentage of stockholders are usually far less than those involved in public offers. The solicitation involves less publicity than a public tender offer or none. The solicitees, who are frequently directors, officers or substantial stockholders of the target, are more apt to be sophisticated, inquiring or knowledgeable concerning the target's business, the solicitor's objectives, and the impact of the solicitation on the target's business prospects. In short, the solicitee in the private transaction is less likely to be pressured, confused, or ill-informed regarding the businesses and decisions at stake than solicitees who are the subjects of a public tender offer.

These differences between public and private securities transactions have led most courts to rule that private transactions or open market purchases do not qualify as a "tender offer" requiring the purchaser to meet the pre-filing strictures of § 14(d). *Kennecott Copper Corp. v. Curtiss-Wright Corp.,* 449 F.Supp. 951, 961 (S.D.N.Y.), *aff'd in relevant part,* 584 F.2d 1195, 1206–07 (2d Cir.1978); *Stromfeld v. Great Atlantic & Pac. Tea Co., Inc.,* 496 F.Supp. 1084, 1088–89 (S.D.N.Y.), *aff'd mem.,* 646 F.2d 563 (2d Cir.1980); *SEC v. Carter-Hawley Hale Stores, Inc.,* 760 F.2d 945, 950–53 (9th Cir. 1985); *Brascan Ltd. v. Edper Equities, Ltd.,* 477 F.Supp. 773, 791–92 (S.D.N.Y.1979); *Astronics Corp. v. Protective Closures Co.,* 561 F.Supp. 329, 334 (W.D.N.Y.1983); *LTV Corp. v. Grumman Corp.,* 526 F.Supp. 106, 109 (E.D.N.Y.1981); *Energy Ventures, Inc. v. Appalachian Co.,* 587 F.Supp. 734, 739–41 (D.Del.1984); *Ludlow v. Tyco Laboratories, Inc.,* 529 F.Supp. 62, 67 (D.Mass.1981); *Chromalloy American Corp. v. Sun Chemical Corp.,* 474 F.Supp. 1341, 1346–47 (E.D.Mo.), *aff'd,* 611 F.2d 240 (8th Cir.1979). The borderline between public solicitations and privately negotiated stock purchases is not bright and it is frequently difficult to determine whether transactions falling close to the line or in a type of "no man's land" are "tender offers" or private deals. This has led some to advocate a broader interpretation of the term "tender offer" than that followed by us in *Kennecott Copper Corp. v. Curtiss-Wright Corp., supra,* 584 F.2d at 1207, and to adopt the eight-factor "test" of what is a tender offer, which was recommended by the SEC and applied by the district court in *Wellman v. Dickinson,* 475 F.Supp. 783, 823–24 (S.D.N.Y.1979), *aff'd on other grounds,* 682 F.2d 355 (2d Cir.1982), *cert. denied,* 460 U.S. 1069, 103 S.Ct. 1522, 75 L.Ed.2d 946 (1983), and by the Ninth Circuit in *SEC v. Carter Hawley Hale Stores, Inc., supra.* The eight factors are:

"(1) active and widespread solicitation of public shareholders for the shares of an issuer;

8 factor test

(2) solicitation made for a substantial percentage of the issuer's stock;

(3) offer to purchase made at a premium over the prevailing market price;

(4) terms of the offer are firm rather than negotiable;

(5) offer contingent on the tender of a fixed number of shares, often subject to a fixed maximum number to be purchased;

(6) offer open only for a limited period of time;

(7) offeree subjected to pressure to sell his stock; [and]

* * *

[(8)] public announcements of a purchasing program concerning the target company precede or accompany rapid accumulation of large amounts of the target company's securities." (475 F.Supp. at 823–24).

Although many of the above-listed factors are relevant for purposes of determining whether a given solicitation amounts to a tender offer, the elevation of such a list to a mandatory "litmus test" appears to be both unwise and unnecessary. As even the advocates of the proposed test recognize, in any given case a solicitation may constitute a tender offer even though some of the eight factors are absent or, when many factors are present, the solicitation may nevertheless not amount to a tender offer because the missing factors outweigh those present. *Id.*, at 824; *Carter, supra*, at 950.

We prefer to be guided by the principle followed by the Supreme Court in deciding what transactions fall within the private offering exemption provided by § [4(a)2] of the Securities Act of 1933, and by ourselves in *Kennecott Copper* in determining whether the Williams Act applies to private transactions. That principle is simply to look to the statutory purpose. In *S.E.C. v. Ralston Purina Co.*, 346 U.S. 119, (1953), the Court stated, "the applicability of § [4(a)(2)] should turn on whether the particular class of persons affected need the protection of the Act. An offering to those who are shown to be able to fend for themselves is a transaction 'not involving any public offering.' " *Id.*, at 125. Similarly, since the purpose of § 14(d) is to protect the ill-informed solicitee, the question of whether a solicitation constitutes a "tender offer" within the meaning of § 14(d) turns on whether, viewing the transaction in the light of the totality of circumstances, there appears to be a likelihood that unless the pre-acquisition filing strictures of that statute are followed there will be a substantial risk that solicitees will lack information needed to make a carefully considered appraisal of the proposal put before them.

Applying this standard, we are persuaded on the undisputed facts that Hanson's September 11 negotiation of five private purchases and one open market purchase of SCM shares, totalling 25% of SCM's outstanding stock, did not under the circumstances constitute a "tender offer" within the meaning of the Williams Act. Putting aside for the moment the events preceding the purchases, there can be little doubt that the privately negotiated purchases would not, standing alone, qualify as a tender offer, for the following reasons:

(1) In a market of 22,800 SCM shareholders the number of SCM sellers here involved, six in all, was miniscule compared with the numbers involved in public solicitations of the type against which the Act was directed.

(2) At least five of the sellers were highly sophisticated professionals, knowledgeable in the market place and well aware of the essential facts needed to exercise their professional skills and to appraise Hanson's offer, including its financial condition as well as that of SCM, the likelihood that the purchases might block the SCM-Merrill bid, and the risk that if Hanson acquired more than 33 1/3% of SCM's stock the SCM-Merrill lockup of the "crown jewel" might be triggered. Indeed, by September 11 they had all had access to (1) Hanson's 27-page detailed disclosure of facts, filed on August 26, 1985, in accordance with § 14(d)(1) with respect to its $60 tender offer, (2) Hanson's 4-page amendment of that offer, dated September 5, 1985, increasing the price to $72 per share, and (3) press releases regarding the basic terms of the SCM-Merrill proposed leveraged buyout at $74 per share and of the SCM-Merrill asset option agreement under which SCM granted to Merrill the irrevocable right under certain conditions to buy SCM's consumer food business for $80 million and its pigment business for $350 million.

(3) The sellers were not "pressured" to sell their shares by any conduct that the Williams Act was designed to alleviate, but by the forces of the market place. Indeed, in the case of Mutual Shares there was no initial solicitation by Hanson; the offer to sell was initiated by Mr. Price of Mutual Shares. Although each of the Hanson purchases was made for $73.50 per share, in most instances this price was the result of private negotiations after the sellers sought higher prices and in one case price protection, demands which were refused. The $73.50 price was not fixed in advance by Hanson. Moreover, the sellers remained free to accept the $74 per share tender offer made by the SCM-Merrill group.

(4) There was no active or widespread advance publicity or public solicitation, which is one of the earmarks of a conventional tender offer. Arbitrageurs might conclude from ticker tape reports of two large anonymous transactions that Hanson must be the buyer. However, liability for solicitation may not be predicated upon

disclosures mandated by Stock Exchange Rules. See *S.E.C. v. Carter-Hawley Hale Stores, Inc., supra,* 760 F.2d at 950.

(5) The price received by the six sellers, $73.50 per share, unlike that appearing in most tender offers, can scarcely be dignified with the label "premium." The stock market price on September 11 ranged from $72.50 to $73.50 per share. Although risk arbitrageurs sitting on large holdings might reap sizeable profits from sales to Hanson at $73.50, depending on their own purchase costs, they stood to gain even more if the SCM-Merrill offer of $74 should succeed, as it apparently would if they tendered their shares to it. Indeed, the $73.50 price, being at most $1 over market or 1.4% higher than the market price, did not meet the SEC's proposed definition of a premium, which is $2.00 per share or 5% above market price, whichever is greater. SEC Exchange Act Release No. 16,385 (11/29/79) [1979–80] Fed.Sec.L.Rep. ¶ 82,374.

(6) Unlike most tender offers, the purchases were not made contingent upon Hanson's acquiring a fixed minimum number or percentage of SCM's outstanding shares. Once an agreement with each individual seller was reached, Hanson was obligated to buy, regardless what total percentage of stock it might acquire. Indeed, it does not appear that Hanson had fixed in its mind a firm limit on the amount of SCM shares it was willing to buy.

(7) Unlike most tender offers, there was no general time limit within which Hanson would make purchases of SCM stock. Concededly, cash transactions are normally immediate but, assuming an inability on the part of a seller and Hanson to agree at once on a price, nothing prevented a resumption of negotiations by each of the parties except the arbitrageurs' speculation that once Hanson acquired 33 ⅓% or an amount just short of that figure it would stop buying.

In short, the totality of circumstances that existed on September 11 did not evidence any likelihood that unless Hanson was required to comply with § 14(d)(1)'s pre-acquisition filing and waiting-period requirements there would be a substantial risk of ill-considered sales of SCM stock by ill-informed shareholders.

There remains the question whether Hanson's private purchases take on a different hue, requiring them to be treated as a "*de facto*" continuation of its earlier tender offer, when considered in the context of Hanson's earlier acknowledged tender offer, the competing offer of SCM-Merrill and Hanson's termination of its tender offer. After reviewing all of the undisputed facts we conclude that the district court erred in so holding.

In the first place, we find no record support for the contention by SCM that Hanson's September 11 termination of its outstanding tender offer was false, fraudulent or ineffective. Hanson's termination notice was clear, unequivocal and straightforward. Directions were given, and presumably are being followed, to return all of the tendered shares to the SCM shareholders who tendered them. Hanson also filed with the SEC a statement pursuant to § 14(d)(1) of the Williams Act terminating its tender offer. As a result, at the time when Hanson made its September 11 private purchases of SCM stock it owned no SCM stock other than those shares revealed in its § 14(d) pre-acquisition report filed with the SEC on August 26, 1985.

The reason for Hanson's termination of its tender offer is not disputed: in view of SCM's grant of what Hanson conceived to be a "poison pill" lock-up option to Merrill, Hanson, if it acquired control of SCM, would have a company denuded as the result of its sale of its consumer food and pigment businesses to Merrill at what Hanson believed to be bargain prices. Thus, Hanson's termination of its tender offer was final; there was no tender offer to be "continued." Hanson was unlikely to "shoot itself in the foot" by triggering what it believed to be a "poison pill," and it could not acquire more than 49% of SCM's shares without violating the rules of the London Stock Exchange.

Nor does the record support SCM's contention that Hanson had decided, before terminating its tender offer, to engage in cash purchases. Judge Kram referred only to evidence that "Hanson had *considered* open market purchases before it announced that the tender offer was dropped" (emphasis added) but made no finding to that effect. Absent evidence or a finding that Hanson had decided to seek control of SCM through purchases of its stock, no duty of disclosure existed under the federal securities laws.

Second, Hanson had expressly reserved the right in its August 26, 1985, pre-acquisition tender offer filing papers, whether or not tendered shares were purchased, "*thereafter* . . . to purchase additional Shares in the open market, in privately negotiated transactions, through another tender offer or otherwise." (Emphasis added). . . . Thus, Hanson's privately negotiated purchases could hardly have taken the market by surprise. Indeed, professional arbitrageurs and market experts rapidly concluded that it was Hanson which was making the post-termination purchases.

Last, Hanson's prior disclosures of essential facts about itself and SCM in the pre-acquisition papers it filed on August 26, 1985, with the SEC pursuant to § 14(d)(1), are wholly inconsistent with the district court's characterization of Hanson's later private purchases as "a deliberate attempt to do an 'end run' around the requirements of the Williams Act." On the contrary, the record shows that Hanson had already filed with the SEC and made public substantially the same information as SCM contends that Hanson should have filed before making cash purchases. The term "tender offer," although left somewhat flexible by Congress' decision not to define it, nevertheless is a word of art. Section 14(d)(1) was never intended to apply to *every* acquisition of more than 5% of a public company's stock. If that were the case there would be no need for § 13(d)(1), which requires a person, *after* acquiring more than 5%, to furnish the issuer, stock exchange and SEC with certain pertinent information. Yet the expansive definition of "tender offer" advocated by SCM, and to some extent by the SEC as amicus, would go far toward rendering § 13(d)(1) a dead letter. In the present case, we were advised by Hanson's counsel upon argument on September 23 that on that date it was filing with the SEC the information required by § 13(d)(1) of the Williams Act with respect to its private purchases of SCM stock. In our view, that is all that is required by the Act in the present circumstances.

* * *

In the present case we conclude that since the district court erred in ruling as a matter of law that SCM had demonstrated a likelihood of success on the merits, based on the theory that Hanson's post-tender offer private purchases of SCM constituted a *de facto* tender offer, it was an abuse of discretion to issue a preliminary injunction. Indeed, we do not believe that Hanson's transactions raise serious questions going to the merits that would provide a fair ground for litigation. In view of this holding it becomes unnecessary to rule upon the district court's determination that the balance of hardships tip in favor of SCM and that absent preliminary relief it would suffer irreparable injury. However, our decision is not to be construed as an affirmance of the district court's resolution of these issues.

* * *

The order of the district court is reversed, the preliminary injunction against Hanson is vacated, and the case is remanded for further proceedings in accordance with this opinion. The mandate shall issue forthwith.

QUESTIONS

1. The Court states that "[i]f Hanson could acquire slightly less than one-third of SCM's outstanding shares it would be able to block the $74 per share SCM-Merrill offer of a leveraged buyout." Is the Court correct in its assessment? If so, what was Hanson's strategy in this regard?

2. After reading that the initial draft of the Williams Act labeled corporate raiders *white-collar pirates*, is it easier to sympathize with those who criticize the Williams Act for being too pro-target management? See Note, Critics of the Williams Act, *infra* Section B.2.b.v.

3. According to the Court, "the solicitee in the private transaction is less likely to be pressured, confused or ill-informed regarding the businesses and

decisions at stake than solicitees who are the subjects of a public tender offer." Why?

4. Are you persuaded by the Court's comparison of a private placement under Securities Act § 4(a)(2) (as interpreted by the U.S. Supreme Court in the famous *Ralston Purina* decision) to the situation a tender offer presents? Private placements involve *offers to sell* securities, while tender offers involve *offers to buy* securities. Should they be treated similarly?

5. Is the Court's "totality of the circumstances" test any better than the SEC's flexible factors test? When the Court provides its seven reasons as to why Hanson's privately negotiated purchases do not, standing alone, qualify as a tender offer, which of the reasons reflect Securities Act private placement factors and which reflect the SEC's eight factors? Is the Court simply covering its "you know what" by referencing the SEC's eight factors?

6. Why would SCM's expansive definition of "tender offer" potentially render § 13(d)(1) of the Exchange Act a "dead letter" according to the Court?

7. Hanson's purchases all occurred on September 11, 1985, and its counsel informed the Court that it was filing a Schedule 13D on Hanson's behalf on September 23, 1985. The Court then noted "that is all that is required by the [Williams] Act in the present circumstances." But was Hanson *late* with its filing? See Exchange Act § 13(d)(1) & Rule 13d–1(a) (filing must occur within 10 days after the acquisition).

v. Issuer Tender Offers and Going-Private Transactions

An offer by a corporation to purchase its own outstanding securities is a form of recapitalization known as an *issuer tender offer*. An offer by someone other than the issuer is a *third-party tender offer*.[229] Thus far in our discussion of § 14(d) of the Exchange Act and the SEC rules thereunder, we have been assuming a third-party tender offer. Issuer tender offers for the issuer's own equity securities—assuming the issuer is a reporting company—must comply with Exchange Act Rule 13e–4. All issuer tender offers, like all third-party tender offers, must comply with § 14(e) of the Exchange Act and Regulation 14E. Rule 13e–4 imposes on issuer tender offers disclosure, form and timing requirements identical to those imposed on third-party tender offers noted above.

The SEC has also passed a series of rules and a schedule under a general grant of authority under § 13(e) of the Exchange Act, an open-ended antifraud provision on issuer stock repurchases, aimed at regulating *going-private transactions*. Exch. Act Rules 13e–3 to 13e–100.[230] In a going-private transaction, a publicly traded company, that is, a company that reports under § 12 of the Exchange Act, buys back enough of its shares to transform itself into a company whose stock is no longer registered. A

[229] The first party is the target issuer, the second is the target shareholder, and the third is the independent bidder.

[230] Exchange Act Rule 13e–100 is also known as Schedule 13E–3.

publicly traded company becomes a privately held company if, as a result of purchasing enough of its own shares, it reduces the number of its shareholders to fewer than 300 or causes the delisting of its shares from a national stock exchange or Nasdaq.[231] The consideration offered in the transaction to selling shareholders is usually cash or debt securities in the issuer, or a combination of the two. The stock repurchase can come in many forms, an issuer cash tender offer, a cash merger or a cash-for-assets acquisition.

Going-private transactions involve a tremendous conflict of interest. When current management offers to buy out public shareholders and establishes the price at which to do so, the interests of management and shareholders diverge. Indeed, if the managers (who owe fiduciary duties to the shareholders) negotiate a good deal for themselves, that deal naturally comes at the expense of the shareholders. Accordingly, the SEC promulgated Rule 13e–3 and Schedule 13E–3 to address going-private transactions and the conflict of interest they pose.

Because of this inherent conflict of interest, two major differences exist between Schedule 13E–3 for going-private issuer repurchases and Schedule TO for issuer and third-party tender offers. First, Item Eight of Schedule 13E–3 incorporates by reference Item 1014 of Regulation M–A. Item 1014 requires a statement on the "fairness" of a going-private transaction with supporting rationale. By requiring a statement on fairness, the issuer becomes liable on the assertion under the general antifraud provisions of the securities acts if the statement is misleading. All material factors behind the statement must be itemized and disclosed.

Second, Item 9 of Schedule 13E–3 incorporates Item 1015 of Regulation M–A. Item 1015 requires the disclosure of all reports or appraisals from outside parties "materially relating" to the fairness of the offer. In a Schedule 13E–3, the issuer, as a fiduciary to the selling shareholders, must disclose all its valuation information while outside bidders are more secretive. Thus, the issuer must disclose *all valuation reports and opinions* it has received. It simply cannot cherry pick the best valuation report or opinion (in this case, the one giving the lowest possible valuation) of several it may have received.

If the going-private transaction is accomplished by means of a tender offer, the issuer may file a combined Schedule TO and Schedule 13E–3 under cover of Schedule TO. However, the issuer must provide all information called for by both schedules (taking into consideration redundancies).

Rule 13e–3 provides an important exemption from a Schedule 13E–3 filing for second-step cleanup transactions occurring within one year after the termination of a tender offer by a third party buyer. However, the

---

231 See Exch. Act Rule 13e–3(a)(3)(ii).

exemption is subject to a number of conditions. These include the second-step consideration being at least equal to the highest consideration offered in the tender offer and the third party buyer having disclosed in its tender offer its intention to engage in a going-private transaction. See Rule 13e–3(g)(1). The rule has significant problems in application, however.

NOTE: CRITICS OF THE WILLIAMS ACT

Supporters of the Williams Act focus on one or both of two goals.[232] The Act's first goal is to enable target shareholders to evaluate a tender offer's merits more effectively. The Act thus requires disclosures by bidders and relaxes deadline pressure. The provisions mandating a minimum offering period, withdrawal periods, and pro rata acceptance for oversubscribed offers all act to delay any tender offer's closing date in order to ensure that target shareholders have time to consider and act on the offer's merits. The Act gives the target shareholders adequate information about the bid and the time to digest the information. Absent the Act, bidders can make a raw offer, without information on itself or its plans, at premium prices and stampede shareholders into tendering by announcing that the offer will be open for a short time and that the buyer will accept less than all the shares on a first-come, first-served basis.

The Act's second goal, which is independent of and not necessary to the first, is to protect shareholder equality in control changes. Bidders must include all shareholders in an offer, must accept oversubscribed offers pro rata, may not purchase in the markets while an offer is pending, must give any price increases to all those who tendered before the increases, and must legally commence their tender offer on the date when they first provide shareholders with the means to tender. Moreover, the Act prevents those who tender from avoiding the pro rata limitations through short tenders or hedged tenders. These provisions prohibit price discrimination among shareholders once a tender offer has begun, arguably to protect small shareholders who otherwise could not command the premiums that large shareholders could command.

Critics of the Williams Act believe the Act limits the number of tender offers that would otherwise replace inefficient managers. Without the threat of tender offers, managers have more room to shirk their responsibilities. The Act reduces the return on tender offers in three ways. First, a bidder must disclose all material facts about the target, including its plans for the target if it obtains control. Other bidders and the target itself can use the information revealed without compensation. Competing bidders can free-ride on the initial bidder's search costs, to defeat the bid. Targets can mimic a bidder's plans to take value out of winning a bid. Second, the Act's waiting period enhances the possibility of competitive bids or defensive maneuvers by target managers. Third, the SEC rules prohibit price discrimination among target shareholders, raising the costs of a control acquisition to the price demanded by the last

---

[232] The classic justification for the Williams Act is contained in Chief Justice Burger's opinion in Rondeau v. Mosinee Paper Corp., 422 U.S. 49, 95 S.Ct. 2069, 45 L.Ed.2d 12 (1975), *infra* Chapter Seven, Section A.7.b.

shareholder (the *hold-out shareholder*) whose shares are needed to complete the control block.

As a consequence, critics argue, the Act raises the cost of successful takeovers and shelters managerial inefficiency. If the Williams Act were repealed, the argument continues, "lightning fast" bids ("Saturday night specials") could be launched, competitive bidders and target managers would not have time to react, and it would become possible to consummate a tender offer at a lower price. Managers would be more concerned about their job performance, lest they encourage a tender offer from depressed stock prices caused by their subpar efforts, and shareholders would receive the benefit of higher stock prices across the board from consistently better performing managers.

There is evidence that the Williams Act does reduce the number of tender offers made in any given year. In the years immediately following the passage of the Williams Act in 1968, takeover premiums increased from 32 percent to 53 percent, and the frequency of takeovers declined. See Jarrell & Bradley, *The Economic Effects of Federal and State Regulation of Cash Tender Offers*, 23 J.L. & ECON. 371, 373, 388, 405 (1980). After the Act, the number of takeovers did not exceed pre-Act levels for eleven years.

There are also questions about some of the specific SEC rules. The statutory language of the Williams Act itself does not require that all tender offers go to all shareholders, nor does the Act prohibit a bidder from privately buying shares during a tender offer. The SEC added those obligations by rule. Absent SEC rules, a bidder could comply with the Act even if it purchased stock outside the tender offer before, during, and after the tender offer and at prices differing from the tender offer price. The Act's literal language also allows a bidder to discriminate among shareholders by targeting the tender offer to subgroups of shareholders (those with large blocks of shares, for example).

There is a respectable argument that an equal sharing rule may hurt target shareholders. The rule does stop some deals at the margin. Some bidders will not be able to pay enough to obtain a majority of the shares under an equal price rule but would be able to close the deal if allowed to discriminate among shareholders on price. The argument is that target shareholders should prefer a rule that allowed unequal division of control acquisition gains if such a rule maximizes the total gains produced in all acquisitions regardless of how the gains are distributed in any one transaction. Through diversification, shareholders could eliminate much of the risk of adverse discrimination in any one transaction and enjoy a proportionate share of the larger aggregate gains that such a rule would produce, a share that would exceed their share of the gains under an equal-division rule. Moreover, the shareholders would benefit from the increased pressure on target firm managers to keep stock prices up.

c. Stock Deals: Regulation of Public Offerings

The Securities Act of 1933 protects the purchasers of *securities*, broadly defined to include both debt and equity investment securities, in *public offerings*. In the classic public offering, a firm sells securities to the public as a means of raising capital to fund its business. The very first public offering of securities by a firm is referred to as its *initial public offering* or *IPO*. If a firm offers securities to the public, defined roughly as over thirty-five or so people, the firm must register the securities for sale with the SEC under the Securities Act. The registration statement includes, in large part, a *preliminary prospectus*, which the firm must ultimately deliver in final form to the buying investors by the time of the final delivery of the security sold. The prospectus is a disclosure document containing information about the issuing firm and the security sold.

The SEC has decided to apply the Securities Act to all acquisitions in which target shareholders receive securities in the bidder as all or part of their acquisition consideration if the number of shareholders is large.[233] This decision seems a bit odd with respect to mergers and assets sales, as the Securities Act only applies to "sales" of securities and "offers to sell" securities.[234] Target shareholders in a merger or asset sale technically are not "selling" their shares. Rather, they are simply *voting* on whether to approve a merger or an asset sale. This is particularly true in a stock-for-assets acquisition, because the recipient of the stock consideration is (at least initially) the target company itself, and not the target shareholders.

As seen in Securities Act Rule 145(a), however, the SEC has taken the position that a sale of securities has in fact occurred in the context of a stock swap statutory merger and a stock-for-assets acquisition. Accordingly, the acquirer must register the shares it is issuing with the SEC under the Securities Act. The SEC's position is that target shareholders are being asked to vote on whether to accept a new or different security for their existing securities. In substance, therefore, the shareholders are making a *new investment decision*. The SEC believes this triggers Securities Act disclosure requirements.

The Securities Act requirements change significantly the timetable for all noncash acquisitions of publicly traded companies. The public offering registration rules add buyer information disclosure requirements in negotiated mergers and asset acquisitions that may not be required by the proxy solicitation rules and the Williams Act's tender offer rules. The combination filing requirements of the various disclosure systems adds substantial complexity to such deals.

---

[233] If the number of target shareholders is small, the offering may qualify for a registration exemption under the Securities Act. The exemption to registration most commonly relied on for acquisitions is the private placement exemption found in Section 4(a)(2) of the Securities Act and safe harbor Rule 506 of Regulation D promulgated by the SEC thereunder. Buyers using Regulation D must file a Form D within fifteen days of the closing. The text in this subsection of the book focuses on the full registration required for acquisitions of publicly traded companies and not on the use of an exemption.

[234] Sec. Act § 5(a).

For negotiated statutory mergers, compulsory stock exchanges, and asset sales, the buyer registers the securities it is using as acquisition consideration on a *Form S–4 registration statement*. The Form S–4 also acts as the seller's proxy statement, and the combined disclosure document contained therein is referred to as a *proxy statement/prospectus*. See Exch. Act Rule 14a–101, Schedule 14A, Item 14, Instruction 1. The Form S–4 may also serve as a proxy statement for the purchaser if the purchaser's shareholders also vote, in which case the combined disclosure document contained therein is referred to as a *joint proxy statement/prospectus*.[235]

If a purchaser uses a Form S–4 and incorporates by reference other public disclosure documents it has filed with the SEC under the Exchange Act, it must send the form at least twenty days in advance of the date of the shareholders' meeting. If the purchaser does not want to assume liability for the seller's representations in its proxy statement, or the purchaser wants to narrow the twenty-day notice requirement, then it can register the transaction on a basic Form S–1 instead of a Form S–4; however, Form S–1 does not permit liberal incorporation by reference of other Exchange Act periodic reports, as does Form S–4, and thus is more expensive to prepare and distribute.

A registration statement, according to the Securities Act, automatically becomes effective twenty days after filing unless the SEC declares it effective sooner (a concept known as *acceleration*) or takes action to toll the running of the period. In practice, the SEC demands that all registrants waive the twenty-day period. See Sec. Act Rule 473 (providing for a paragraph on the cover of a registration statement that is a continuing amendment) and Sec. Act Rule 461 (used by the SEC to condition acceleration on the issuer's filing a delaying amendment). The delaying amendment gives the SEC time to screen the registration statements and decide which ones to review thoroughly.[236] The SEC staff will not disclose its criteria for selection.

If the SEC does not review an issuer's registration statement, the issuer receives notice five days after filing and may ask that the registration statement become effective any time, on forty-eight hours' notice. If the SEC does review an issuer's registration statement, the SEC, on the overwhelming majority of reviewed registration statements,

---

[235] The only substantive differences between the disclosure documents sent to the purchaser's shareholders and the target's shareholders relate to the Cover Letter from the CEO/Chair of the Board, the Notice of Meeting and the proxy card, as each will be customized for the purchaser's shareholders or the target's shareholders, as the case may be.

[236] In reviewing registration statements, the SEC does not approve or pass on the merits of the securities being offered. The sole task of the SEC is to ensure that the registration statement is, on its face, accurate and complete. The SEC is free to decide, after declaring a statement effective, that the statement was in fact misleading or false. The Securities Act and case law on the Act provide for substantial civil and criminal liabilities against the issuer and its managers and others involved with the registration statement if there are material misstatements or omissions in the statement. See Sec. Act §§ 11 & 17.

requests additional information. In garden-variety stock offerings that do not involve tender offers, this *letter of comment* appears, on average, for filings by repeat registrants thirty days after filing. Once an issuer has satisfied the concerns in the letter—and this may take several weeks to several months after the SEC sends its letter of comment—the SEC will declare the registration statement *effective*. The review and comment process is a significant factor in the timing of the transaction because the buyer cannot offer its securities for sale or mail the proxy statement/prospectus until the registration statement is effective.[237]

The purchaser may mail a preliminary prospectus to target shareholders but ordinarily will not because the purchasing firm cannot include a proxy card in the mailing.[238] In practice, the parties to a negotiated stock swap merger publicly announce their transaction immediately after reaching a definitive agreement. This announcement usually takes the form of a written joint press release followed by a joint press conference and then presentations to analysts by senior officials of both parties. In the usual case, under Securities Act Rules 165 and 425, the acquirer will be required to file with the SEC the text of the initial joint press release, any scripts prepared for the initial press conference if the script is distributed, transcripts of any financial presentations distributed to securities analysts, and texts and transcripts of any subsequent new or amended public written communications until the closing of the merger. The target makes similar filings pursuant to Exchange Act Rule 14a–12(b) under cover of Schedule 14A.

If an acquisition takes the form of an exchange tender offer, a bidder makes a public offer to exchange target stock for stock or debt in the buyer (or the buyer's parent), the Securities Act rules supplement the Williams Act rules.[239] The addition of the Securities Act rules affects the form and timing of the tender offer.

---

[237] In theory, a party can attempt to minimize SEC review by issuing securities previously registered and placed up on an *acquisition shelf*. To do so, a buyer files an initial Form S–4 registration statement—which is subject to full SEC review—to register securities to be offered in connection with future acquisitions under Securities Act Rule 415(a)(1)(viii). See also Form S–4, Instruction H. After the SEC has declared an acquisition shelf effective, the buyer can use the shares in future acquisitions, taking them down off the registration shelf as needed. However, in all acquisitions of publicly traded companies, the buyer must file a post-effective amendment to its Form S–4 to add information about each transaction. The amendment itself is subject to SEC review, and it is almost certain that the SEC will do so. The need to file a post-effective amendment, and the SEC's ability to review that amendment, largely defeats the timing advantage of using an acquisition shelf. Also diminishing the usefulness of an acquisition shelf is the requirement that the issuer may only register securities in an amount which, at the time the Form S–4 becomes effective, the issuer reasonably expects to be offered and sold within two years from the initial effective date of the registration. Sec. Act Rule 415(a)(2). Acquisition shelves are seldom used in practice as a result.

[238] Securities Act Rule 460, requiring delivery of a preliminary prospectus for acceleration of the effective date, has an exception for Rule 145 transactions (acquisitions).

[239] A third level of filings is required if the exchange tender offer involves ratifying votes by either the bidder or target shareholders or if the tender offer requires that the right to vote the

Prior to 2000, a bidder could not commence an exchange tender offer (i.e., send tender offer materials to target shareholders) until the SEC declared its Securities Act registration statement effective. This effectively prevented a bidder from using an exchange tender offer in a bidding contest for a target. It also meant that a bidder was effectively prevented from launching a *hostile* exchange tender offer because of the time delays generally associated with Securities Act registration. Indeed, because a Securities Act registration statement is a public document, a bidder had no way to surprise or sneak up on the target company. Thus, prior to 2000 virtually all bidding contests and hostile takeovers involved all-cash tender offers to which the Securities Act did not apply.

In order to level the playing field between cash tender offers and exchange tender offers, the SEC now allows a bidder (or an issuer itself) to commence its exchange tender offer upon the filing of, and *prior* to the effectiveness of, its Securities Act registration statement.[240] However, Securities Act Rule 162(a) requires a bidder to file with the SEC a Securities Act registration statement that includes a preliminary prospectus containing all information, including pricing information, necessary for a target shareholder to make an informed investment decision. In its adopting release, the SEC promised expedited review of exchange tender offer filings to further reduce the regulatory disparity between the treatment of cash tender offers and exchange tender offers.[241]

To commence an exchange tender offer before effectiveness of a registration statement, a bidder files a combination registration statement and tender offer statement with the SEC and distributes the statement to target shareholders. Sec. Act Rule 162(a). Target shareholders may tender their securities prior to effectiveness of the registration statement but the bidder cannot accept the tenders until the SEC declares the registration statement to be effective. *Id.*[242]

The application of the Securities Act public offering rules to exchange tender offers casts doubt on *stock lock-ups*, a common exchange tender offer planning device. In a stock lock up, the bidder asks, prior to the

stock passes on tender. Such tender offers involve proxy solicitations and come under proxy solicitation requirements.

[240] See Exch. Act Rules 14d–4(b) (for third party exchange tender offers) and 13e–4(e)(2) (for issuer exchange tender offers). These Rules apply to exchange tender offers in which the consideration consists either solely or partially of securities registered under the Securities Act. Early commencement is at the option of the bidder or issuer. Exchange offers can commence as early as the filing of a registration statement, or on a later date selected by the bidder or issuer up to the date of effectiveness of its Securities Act registration statement.

[241] See *Regulation of Takeovers and Security Holder Communications*, SEC Rel. 33–7760, 1999 WL 969596, at *21 (Oct. 22, 1999).

[242] A bidder engaged in an exchange tender offer enjoys relaxed "gun jumping" restrictions under the Securities Act. Unlike most other issuers of securities, a bidder can freely communicate with target shareholders about an anticipated exchange tender offer both before and after it files its Form S–4 registration statement with the SEC. If, however, it communicates in writing, a bidder must file all those materials with the SEC under Securities Act Rules 165, 424 and 425.

commencement of the exchange offer, controlling target company shareholders to commit to tender their shares into the offer. The SEC staff has indicated that it will not construe the offers to violate the Securities Act if the agreements only include officers, directors, founders, and five percent shareholders of the target holding less than one hundred percent of the stock.

In exchange tender offers, the SEC supplements the requirements of Exchange Act Rule 14e–5, prohibiting the bidder from purchasing target shares outside the tender offer, with Regulation M. Regulation M prohibits the bidder and the target (if friendly) from purchasing bidder securities that are used in an exchange tender offer as long as the offer remains open. Reg. M, Rules 101 & 102.[243]

NOTE: GOING PUBLIC WITH A REVERSE MERGER

In a *reverse merger* a privately held company *goes public* by merging into an existing public shell company (i.e., a public company with no real assets or liabilities). In the stock-for-stock merger, the public shell company survives and a controlling block of stock in the shell (typically 85 percent) is given to the owners of the privately held company, which merges out of existence. All the assets and liabilities of the privately held company are subsumed within the public shell by virtue of the merger. The Certificate of Merger changes the name of the public shell to that of the private company. The publicly held survivor then aggressively broadens its trading market to make its securities more liquid. The company courts new market makers, prepares audited financials for public reports, and eventually applies for a listing on the NASD bulletin board or the Nasdaq.

Several well-known firms have successfully used the procedure. The firms get the benefit of a liquid market for its shares; the shares increase in value and the market provides a valuation benchmark for the firm. However, recent accounting scandals in a number of Chinese reverse merger companies have tarnished the procedure's reputation.

The advantage of the procedure is the minimal time it takes to get registered in the public capital markets. The merger into a shell takes much less time than a traditional merger because there is only minimal due diligence.

The SEC's disdain for companies "going public" through a reverse merger is palpable. The SEC believes the procedure allows "not-ready-for-prime-time" companies to go public at a time when they can't attract a legitimate underwriter to conduct an underwritten IPO. A reverse merger does not raise new capital. Moreover, no registration statement is filed that has been vetted by underwriters who are subject to potential liability for a materially false and misleading registration statement under Securities Act § 11(a).

---

[243] Regulation M also applies to stock swap mergers and stock-for-assets acquisitions, if the acquirer is using registered securities as consideration.

If the surviving public firm wants to raise capital in the future for its operations, it must conduct a registered public offering or satisfy one of the offering exemptions (a private placement of public equity, a *PIPE*, for example). If the founders of the privately held company want to sell their newly-acquired stock in the public company (to get cash), they must do a secondary registered offering or satisfy the resale requirements of Securities Act Rule 144 for affiliates (e.g., controlling officials can dribble out their shares to the market under the one percent rule).

NOTE: SPECIAL PURPOSE ACQUISITION COMPANIES (SPACS)

A growing number of mid-sized companies are agreeing to mergers with *special purpose acquisition companies (SPACs)*, formally known as *blank check companies*.[244] A SPAC is a shell company that has no operations but that has raised funds by going public through a registered *initial public offering* (*IPO*).[245] The Form S–1 registration statement lists the organizer's intention of merging with or acquiring another company with the proceeds of the IPO.[246] Most of the proceeds from the IPO are held in a trust[247] and released only when the acquisition is completed. The managers of a SPAC must complete an acquisition in 18 to 24 months that uses at least 80 percent of the SPAC funds or return the funds to its shareholders. The completion of the acquisition is known as *de-SPACing*.

SPAC founders are generally experienced investment fund managers, private equity investors, investment bankers, business executives or even

---

[244] Technically, a SPAC is generally exempt from Securities Act Rule 419 regulating blank check companies. This is because its securities do not qualify as *penny stocks* as its shareholders' equity exceeds $5 million and the minimum bid price of its common stock exceeds $4 per share. See Sec. Act Rule 419(a)(2) & Exch. Act Rule 3a51–1. Nevertheless, most SPACs follow the "spirit" of Rule 419 with some notable differences. Thus, like blank check companies, 95 percent or more of the net proceeds raised by a SPAC will be deposited into a trust account, the fair value of the first business target of the SPAC will equal at least 80 percent of the funds held in the trust account, and the securities issued by the SPAC will begin trading in the secondary market on the date of the SPAC's initial public offering. With respect to trading, the SPAC must file Form 8–Ks under the Exchange Act containing updated financial information prior to the initial business combination.

[245] Prospective investors in a typical SPAC offering are offered *units* at a price at or around $10 per unit. Each unit consists of one share of the SPAC's common stock and one to two warrants exercisable for one share of such common stock. The components of the units become separately tradable a set number of days after the offering. Warrants are not exercisable until the business combination occurs and are redeemable by the SPAC for nominal value if SPAC common stock trades above a predetermined market price. Underwriters for SPAC deals include Cantor Fitzgerald & Co., Citigroup, Deutsche Bank and EarlyBirdCapital, Inc., one of the very first securities firms underwriting SPAC offerings.

[246] During 2017, a new use for a SPAC was proposed by venture capital firm Social Capital. It went public with a SPAC, Social Capital Hedosophia Holdings Corp., on September 13, 2017, raising $600 million in the process. The SPAC planned to use the proceeds to acquire a minority stake in one of the more than 150 private U.S. technology companies valued at $1 billion or more. By doing so, the SPAC would offer public investors a chance to indirectly trade interests in that private company by directly trading interests in the SPAC. As a result, there would be no need for that private company to conduct an initial public offering, thus allowing it to avoid the hassles of being a publicly traded company. See Maureen Farrell, *Tech Firms Offered Alternative to IPOs*, WALL ST. J., Aug. 24, 2017, at B1.

[247] This is necessary to prevent the SPAC from being considered an "investment company" (i.e., a mutual fund) under the Investment Company Act of 1940.

former politicians.[248] SPACs typically leverage their IPO funds to buy bigger companies. Prior to completing the IPO, a SPAC may not take any steps to identify an acquisition target. Any acquisition by a SPAC requires the approval by a majority of the shares held by the SPAC's public shareholders.[249] Holders of the shares who vote against the deal may also choose to have their shares redeemed. In practice this gives any 20 percent block of the shareholders the right to wind up the SPAC. After the acquisition, the surviving company is public and must file periodic reports under the Exchange Act. While historically SPAC securities traded on the OTC-Bulletin Board, since 2008 both the Nasdaq and the NYSE permit the listing of SPAC securities.[250]

The heyday of SPACS occurred in 2007 during which 66 SPACs raised over $12 billion. Things came to a crashing halt, however, when the Great Recession hit, with only one SPAC IPO raising a meager $36 million occurring in all of 2009. Momentum picked up again beginning in 2013 as SPACs raised over $1.4 billion. In 2016, SPACs raised over $3.7 billion in U.S. markets, a year which included the largest SPAC offering since 2008 (CF Corp.'s $600 million IPO). In 2017, TPG Pace Energy Holdings raised $600 million and became the first SPAC to list its securities on the main NYSE market (NYSE) as opposed to the NYSE's small cap equity market (NYSE MKT). Through August 2017, 22 SPACs have raised $6.9 billion during 2017.

How successful have SPACs been at de-SPACing? Between 2003 and 2015, 235 SPACs completed IPOs. Of those, 127 successfully completed acquisitions (de-SPACing), 5 had announced acquisition targets and 27 were still searching for acquisition targets. However, 76 SPACs were unable to de-SPAC and were forced into liquidation.[251]

NOTE: SECURITIES ACT § 3(a)(9) EXCHANGES

The Securities Act contains a special exemption from registration for securities distributed in voluntary exchanges and recapitalizations. The exemption is contained in § 3(a)(9) for "any security exchanged by the issuer with its existing security holders exclusively where no commission or other remuneration is paid or given directly or indirectly for soliciting such exchange."

Exchange transactions may occur in a wide variety of circumstances—for example, an exchange of new debt securities for existing debt securities or an exchange of common stock for preferred stock. The § 3(a)(9) exemption is quite

---

248 Notable officers of SPACs include former Apple executive Steve Wozniak, former CEO of Apollo Investment Corp. Michael Gross, and former undersecretary for Homeland Security Asa Hutchinson.

249 Since 2011 both the NYSE and the Nasdaq allow a SPAC to conduct a tender offer that complies with Exchange Act Rule 13e–4 and Regulation 14E for shareholders' shares in lieu of a shareholder vote, unless a vote is otherwise required by law. See NYSE Listed Company Manual § 102.06, at ¶ c; Nasdaq IM–5101–2(e).

250 See NYSE Listed Company Manual § 102.06; Nasdaq IM–5101–2.

251 Cynthia M. Krus & Harry S. Pangas, *A Primer on Special Purpose Acquisition Companies*, at 2 (Mar. 2016) (avail. at http://www.publiclytradedprivateequity.com/portalresource/SPACsOverview.pdf).

narrow. The issuer of both securities in the exchange must be the exact same entity (and not a subsidiary), no part of the offering may be made to anyone other than existing security holders, the existing security holders must not be required to part with anything of value except their existing securities (and thus new capital may not be raised in an exchange offer),[252] and the issuer cannot pay anyone for soliciting proxies.

C. BUYING DISTRESSED COMPANIES

Why would a purchaser want to acquire a financially troubled company? Some financially troubled companies support a positive operating cash flow, that is, their revenues exceed their operating costs and expenses, but the companies have over-leveraged capital structures—too much debt. The positive operating returns are smaller than the payments due on the firm's capital debts. Purchasers of financially troubled companies are willing to buy the operations of such companies but not assume their debts.

Classic stock acquisitions and statutory mergers will not work unless troubled companies restructure first;[253] the stock acquired is worthless and the debts absorbed in a merger exceed the value of the assets acquired. The company can restructure by agreement outside of bankruptcy or restructure under the supervision of a federal bankruptcy judge, a non-consensual restructuring.[254] In a *workout*, a consensual out-of-bankruptcy court agreement, a financially distressed company and its significant creditors adjust the company's obligations. If the workout fails,[255]

---

[252] There are two limited exceptions to Section 3(a)(9)'s prohibition on additional consideration. First, pursuant to Securities Act Rule 150, an issuer can make payments to its security holders "in connection with an exchange of securities for outstanding securities, when such payments are part of the terms of the offer of the exchange." Based on no-action relief granted by the SEC Staff, these payments may include cash or a cash equivalent and may even be paid by an affiliate of the issuer. See The News Corporation Limited, SEC No-Action Letter, 1992 WL 108015 (May 15, 1992); International Controls Corp., SEC No-Action Letter, 1990 WL 286830 (Aug. 6, 1990); and Carolina Wholesale Florists, Inc., SEC No-Action Letter, 1976 WL 12584 (Aug. 17, 1976). Second, Securities Act Rule 149 allows a security holder to make a cash payment to the issuer that may be necessary "to effect an equitable adjustment, in respect of dividends or interest paid or payable on the securities involved in the exchange, as between such security holder and other security holders of the same class accepting the offer of exchange." Thus, an equitable adjustment would be permitted when, due to the timing of interest payments and sales between security holders, one security holder receives the benefit of an interest payment due to another security holder. The issuer would be within its rights to require the unjustly enriched security holder to reimburse the issuer for the extra interest payment under these circumstances.

[253] Restructuring usually entails a relaxation or cancellation of outstanding interest and principal repayment obligations. Some creditors will take cash in exchange for their distressed debt. Others may accept substantial equity positions in the restructured firm.

[254] In a Chapter 11 bankruptcy reorganization, a debtor does not need the consent of all the affected parties. Individual creditors who dissent can lose to a favorable majority vote of their class and entire classes of dissenting creditors can be ignored under a "cramdown" provision. See Bankruptcy Code § 1129.

[255] Workouts are thus a negotiated alternative to bankruptcy and all interested parties will agree to a workout only if they believe that an out-of-court restructuring is more favorable for them than the likely outcome of a bankruptcy case. There are many reasons why workouts fail. Creditors may distrust the firm's managers or lack confidence in the business plan and supporting

management (in a voluntary filing) or firm creditors (in an involuntary filing) seek relief under Chapter 11 of the federal Bankruptcy Code. Chapter 11 provides a court-supervised reorganization procedure to restructure a troubled firm's debt.[256]

Asset acquisitions do not, in theory, require that a financially troubled company restructure before the acquisition. Of course, a purchaser acquires a firm's operating assets, assumes only those debts necessary to run the company (trade creditor obligations and salary contracts are examples) and does not assume the crushing obligations of the firm's passive creditors. An asset acquisition also can be part of a workout. After the acquisition, the selling firm dissolves and liquidates, paying creditors by priority.

The problem with such asset acquisitions, as we shall see in Chapter Three, is that creditors, frustrated with less than complete payment in the dissolution, will attempt to follow the assets and sue the buyer under a de facto merger theory. Buyers who want to cut off such exposure either have to get releases from all seller creditors on the sale or rely on formal bankruptcy proceedings to cut off their claims. The asset acquisition becomes part of a Chapter 11 reorganization proceeding or, less often, a Chapter 7 liquidation proceeding.

Bankruptcy offers several advantages. First, the bankruptcy rules preempt the state corporate code rules on acquisition procedure. Second, a bankruptcy court can order that a sale of assets be "free and clear" of almost all claims and interests (a concept known as *burnishing* the assets),[257] with certain tort claims being the exception. Third, a buyer can avoid non-assignability clauses on valuable leases, some licenses, franchises and other contracts.[258] Fourth, a buyer can avoid the application of federal securities law to securities offered in the deal.[259]

There are two fundamental methods of acquiring assets of a debtor firm in a Chapter 11 case. The trustee (or debtor-in-possession (*DIP*))[260] may sell the assets under § 363(b)(1) of the Bankruptcy Code or the sale may be part of an approved *plan of reorganization* under § 1129.[261] A § 363

---

projections of management. Creditors may want to attack payments or transfers to other claimants as preferences or fraudulent conveyances. Or the sheer number of creditors whose participation is necessary for a successful restructuring and the complexity of the issues on priority of payment that need to be resolved may make it impossible to negotiate final agreement.

256 A merger with the debtor, once its debts have been restructured, can be part of a Chapter 11 plan of reorganization. Bankruptcy Code § 1123(a)(5).

257 Bankruptcy Code §§ 363(f) & 1141(c).

258 Bankruptcy Code § 365.

259 Bankruptcy Code §§ 1125 & 1145(a)(1).

260 A debtor-in-possession is the old management of the company, and in the case of a corporate debtor, the old board of directors.

261 See also §§ 1123(a)(5) and (b)(4) of the Bankruptcy Code.

sale is usually for cash,[262] thus providing the debtor with an immediate infusion of needed cash. In a plan of reorganization, the plan not only provides for the sale of the business but also provides for a distribution of the proceeds received on the sale. The plan can include the distribution of *reorganization securities*, equity or subordinated debt securities issued by the reorganized entity to the predecessor firm's creditors.

In a § 363 sale, any "out of the ordinary course of business" transaction must comply with notice and hearing requirements. The federal rules of bankruptcy procedure require at least twenty days' notice by mail of a proposed sale, unless the court, for good cause, reduces the period and accepts another method. Notice goes to all interested parties, providing them with an opportunity to examine the price and terms of the proposed sale. Those claimants that object may request a hearing on the transaction, but a bankruptcy court may approve the sale over the objections of creditors and equity holders.[263] The notice requirement also provides competing bidders, if any, with an opportunity to come forward with a better offer. Trustees (or debtors-in-possession) have a fiduciary and statutory duty to obtain the highest and best offer for the firm. Although both public auctions and private sales are possible under the federal rules, public auctions appear to be the preferred means of obtaining the highest or best price.

A plan of reorganization that includes a sale of the firm must specify a proposed treatment of all the debtor firm's outstanding claims and interests.[264] The holders of each class of claims (debt holders) and interests (equity holders) vote on the plan. A class of claims accepts the plan only if the holders of at least two-thirds of the amount of the claims in the class that vote approve and more than one-half of the number of the claims in the class that vote approve. A class of interests accepts a plan only if the holders of at least two-thirds of the amount of the interests in the class that vote approve. A judge may confirm a Chapter 11 plan despite a non-accepting class vote in a *cramdown*, if the plan pays the dissenting class in full before distributing any property to a junior class.[265] In the case of an

[262] A secured creditor can *credit bid* for the assets. This means that a secured creditor may buy the assets not with cash but instead by agreeing to reduce the amount of debt the debtor owes to it. See Bankruptcy Code § 363(k); In re Chrysler, 576 F.3d 108, 116 (2d Cir. 2009), *vacated as moot sub nom.* Ind. State Police Pension Trust v. Chrysler LLC, 130 S.Ct. 1015 (2009).

[263] The bankruptcy court's order approving the sale is a final order and appealable as of right. The right to appeal can delay the closing of the sale and affect the purchase price. Accordingly, § 363(m) of the Bankruptcy Code provides special protection to good faith purchasers. A sale to a good faith purchaser cannot be reversed or modified on appeal unless prior to closing the appellant obtained a stay pending appeal. In effect, the section moots the appeal once the closing of the transaction has occurred. In re Chateaugay Corp., 988 F.2d 322, 325 (2d Cir.1993).

[264] The plan must provide to each creditor at least the value that creditor would receive in a liquidation under Chapter 7 of the Bankruptcy Code. § 1129(a)(7)(ii). The requirement is known as *the best interests test* and is the floor of consideration that must be paid under a Chapter 11 plan. Additionally, no class of claims may receive more than its claim amount. § 1129(b).

[265] This is known as the *absolute priority rule*. The absolute priority rule provides that a Chapter 11 plan of reorganization is fair and equitable as to the holders of *senior* claims or interests that are not repaid in full, so long as the holders of *junior* claims or interests do not receive or retain property under the plan on account of such junior claim or interest. § 1129(b). In other

insolvent debtor, it is relatively simple to confirm a plan over the dissent of common shareholders because typically there are no classes junior to that class.

A sale of the firm under a plan of reorganization is more time-consuming, expensive and difficult than a § 363 sale, but the plan approval process is designed to be more protective of the community of claimants in a Chapter 11 case. Section 363 sales can swallow the safeguards in the plan process (a *sub rosa* plan of reorganization). Federal courts have long held, therefore, that a § 363 sale requires that the debtor demonstrate special circumstances requiring swift action.

For example, the Court in *In re the Lionel Corp.*, 722 F.2d 1063 (2d Cir. 1983), held that a bankruptcy judge must be presented at a Section 363(b) asset sale hearing with a *good business reason* to grant an application for a Section 363 sale. Otherwise, the grant is an abuse of discretion. *Id.* at 1071. *Lionel* also sets forth some of the factors a bankruptcy judge should consider when deciding whether to approve a sale under Section 363. These include, among others:

- The amount of time that has elapsed since the bankruptcy filing;
- The likelihood that a Chapter 11 plan of reorganization will be proposed and confirmed in the near future;
- The effect of the proposed asset sale on future plans of reorganization;
- The proceeds to be obtained from the disposition of assets vis-á-vis any appraisals of the property; and
- "Most importantly perhaps," whether the asset(s) is increasing in value or decreasing in value. See *id.*

Section 363 sales have become quite common. E.g., Douglas G. Baird & Robert K. Rasmussen, *The End of Bankruptcy,* 55 STAN. L. REV. 751, 751–52 (2002) (reorganizations have been replaced by Section 363 sales). The federal government used Section 363 in the Great Recession bailouts of both Chrysler and General Motors. *In re Chrysler, infra; In re Motors Liq. Co.*, 430 B.R. 65 (S.D.N.Y. 2010) (General Motors' § 363 sale was not a sub rosa plan of reorganization).

A typical Section 363 sale takes the form of a *controlled auction.* The debtor in possession (*DIP*) reaches an asset purchase agreement with an initial bidder, a *stalking horse.* The agreement is subject to higher and better bids. The stalking horse is rewarded with a break-up fee of between one and five percent of the sale price, expense reimbursements, minimum

---

words, if a plan allows those lower down the repayment food chain to receive something of value when senior claimants or interest holders are not being made whole, then those senior claimants or interest holders should not be forced to accept that plan.

increments for overbids, qualification requirements for competing bidders, and deadlines for competing bids and a final auction. The DIP submits the agreement and bidding procedures to the Bankruptcy Judge for approval. Competing bidders have less time than the stalking horse for due diligence and a limited ability to renegotiate the asset purchase agreement signed by the stalking horse. The winning bidder is expected to sign an agreement with limited conditions and post-closing remedies. The entire process may be completed in less than three months.

IN RE CHRYSLER

United States Court of Appeals Second Circuit, 2009.
576 F.3d 108, *vacated as moot*, 558 U.S. 1087 (2009).

DENNIS JACOBS, CHIEF JUDGE:

* * *

In a nutshell, Chrysler LLC and its related companies (hereinafter "Chrysler" or "debtor" or "Old Chrysler") filed a pre-packaged bankruptcy petition under Chapter 11 on April 30, 2009. The filing followed months in which Chrysler experienced deepening losses, received billions in bailout funds from the Federal Government, searched for a merger partner, unsuccessfully sought additional government bailout funds for a stand-alone restructuring, and ultimately settled on an asset-sale transaction pursuant to 11 U.S.C. § 363 (the "Sale"), which was approved by the Sale Order. The key elements of the Sale were set forth in a Master Transaction Agreement dated as of April 30, 2009: substantially all of Chrysler's operating assets (including manufacturing plants, brand names, certain dealer and supplier relationships, and much else) would be transferred to New Chrysler in exchange for New Chrysler's assumption of certain liabilities and $2 billion in cash. Fiat S.p.A agreed to provide New Chrysler with certain fuel-efficient vehicle platforms, access to its worldwide distribution system, and new management that is experienced in turning around a failing auto company. Financing for the sale transaction—$6 billion in senior secured financing, and debtor-in-possession financing for 60 days in the amount of $4.96 billion—would come from the United States Treasury and from Export Development Canada. The agreement describing the United States Treasury's commitment does not specify the source of the funds, but it is undisputed that prior funding came from the Troubled Asset Relief Program ("TARP"), 12 U.S.C. § 5211(a)(1), and that the parties expected the Sale to be financed through the use of TARP funds. Ownership of New Chrysler was to be distributed by membership interests, 55% of which go to an employee benefit entity created by the United Auto Workers union, 8% to the United States Treasury and 2% to Export Development Canada. Fiat, for its contributions, would immediately own 20% of the equity with rights to acquire more (up to 51%), contingent on payment in full of the debts owed to the United States Treasury and Export Development Canada.

* * *

The Indiana Pensioners characterize the Sale as an impermissible, *sub rosa* plan of reorganization. . . . As the Indiana Pensioners characterize it, the Sale transaction "is a 'Sale' in name only; upon consummation, new Chrysler will be old Chrysler in essentially every respect. It will be called 'Chrysler.' . . . Its employees, including most management, will be retained. . . . It will manufacture and sell Chrysler and Dodge cars and minivans, Jeeps and Dodge Trucks. The real substance of the transaction is the underlying reorganization it implements." . . .

Section 363(b) of the Bankruptcy Code authorizes a Chapter 11 debtor-in-possession to use, sell, or lease estate property outside the ordinary course of business, requiring in most circumstances only that a movant provide notice and a hearing. 11 U.S.C. § 363(b). We have identified an "apparent conflict" between the expedient of a § 363(b) sale and the otherwise applicable features and safeguards of Chapter 11. *Comm. of Equity Sec. Holders v. Lionel Corp. (In re Lionel Corp.),* 722 F.2d 1063, 1071 (2d Cir.1983); *cf. Braniff,* 700 F.2d at 940.

* * *

In the twenty-five years since *Lionel*, § 363(b) asset sales have become common practice in large-scale corporate bankruptcies. . . . A law review article recounts the phenomenon:

> Corporate reorganizations have all but disappeared. . . . TWA filed only to consummate the sale of its planes and landing gates to American Airlines. Enron's principal assets, including its trading operation and its most valuable pipelines, were sold within a few months of its bankruptcy petition. Within weeks of filing for Chapter 11, Budget sold most of its assets to the parent company of Avis. Similarly, Polaroid entered Chapter 11 and sold most of its assets to the private equity group at BankOne. Even when a large firm uses Chapter 11 as something other than a convenient auction block, its principal lenders are usually already in control and Chapter 11 merely puts in place a preexisting deal.

Douglas G. Baird & Robert K. Rasmussen, *The End of Bankruptcy,* 55 Stan. L. Rev. 751, 751–52 (2002) (internal footnotes omitted). In the current economic crisis of 2008–09, § 363(b) sales have become even more useful and customary.[6] The "side door" of § 363(b) may well "replace the main

---

[6] For instance, Lehman Brothers sold substantially all its assets to Barclays Capital within five days of filing for bankruptcy. Lehman Brothers filed for bankruptcy in the early morning hours of September 15, 2008. On September 20, 2008, the bankruptcy court approved the sale to Barclays of Lehman's investment banking and capital markets operations, as well as supporting infrastructure including the Lehman headquarters in midtown Manhattan for $1.7

route of Chapter 11 reorganization plans." Jason Brege, Note, *An Efficiency Model of Section 363(b) Sales,* 92 Va. L. Rev. 1639, 1640 (2006).

Resort to § 363(b) has been driven by efficiency, from the perspectives of sellers and buyers alike. The speed of the process can maximize asset value by sale of the debtor's business as a going concern. Moreover, the assets are typically burnished (or "cleansed") because (with certain limited exceptions) they are sold free and clear of liens, claims and liabilities. See infra (discussing § 363(f) and tort issues). A § 363 sale can often yield the highest price for the assets because the buyer can select the liabilities it will assume and purchase a business with cash flow (or the near prospect of it). Often, a secured creditor can "credit bid," or take an ownership interest in the company by bidding a reduction in the debt the company owes. See 11 U.S.C. § 363(k) (allowing a secured creditor to credit bid at a § 363(b) sale).

This tendency has its critics. . . . The objections are not to the quantity or percentage of assets being sold: it has long been understood (by the drafters of the Code, and the Supreme Court) that § 363(b) sales may encompass all or substantially all of a debtor's assets. Rather, the thrust of criticism remains what it was in *Lionel:* fear that one class of creditors may strong-arm the debtor-in-possession, and bypass the requirements of Chapter 11 to cash out quickly at the expense of other stakeholders, in a proceeding that amounts to a reorganization in all but name, achieved by stealth and momentum. . . .

As § 363(b) sales proliferate, the competing concerns identified in *Lionel* have become harder to manage. Debtors need flexibility and speed to preserve going concern value; yet one or more classes of creditors should not be able to nullify Chapter 11's requirements. A balance is not easy to achieve, and is not aided by rigid rules and prescriptions. *Lionel*'s multi-factor analysis remains the proper, most comprehensive framework for judging the validity of § 363(b) transactions.

* * *

The Indiana Pensioners argue that the Sale is a *sub rosa* plan chiefly because it gives value to unsecured creditors (*i.e.,* in the form of the ownership interest in New Chrysler provided to the union benefit funds) without paying off secured debt in full, and without complying with the procedural requirements of Chapter 11. However, Bankruptcy Judge Gonzalez demonstrated proper solicitude for the priority between creditors and deemed it essential that the Sale in no way upset that priority. The lien holders' security interests would attach to all proceeds of the Sale: "Not one penny of value of the Debtors' assets is going to anyone other than the First-Lien Lenders." . . . As Bankruptcy Judge Gonzalez found, all the

billion. See *Bay Harbour Mgmt., L.C. v. Lehman Bros. Holdings Inc. (In re Lehman Bros. Holdings Inc.),* No. 08-cv-8869(DLC), 2009 WL 667301, at *8 (2009) (affirming the § 363(b) sale order).

equity stakes in New Chrysler were entirely attributable to *new* value-including governmental loans, new technology, and new management—which were not assets of the debtor's estate. . . .

The Indiana Pensioners' arguments boil down to the complaint that the Sale does not pass the discretionary, multifarious *Lionel* test. The bankruptcy court's findings constitute an adequate rebuttal. Applying the *Lionel* factors, Bankruptcy Judge Gonzalez found good business reasons for the Sale. The linchpin of his analysis was that the only possible alternative to the Sale was an immediate liquidation that would yield far less for the estate—and for the objectors. The court found that, notwithstanding Chrysler's prolonged and well-publicized efforts to find a strategic partner or buyer, no other proposals were forthcoming. In the months leading up to Chrysler's bankruptcy filing, and during the bankruptcy process itself, Chrysler executives circled the globe in search of a deal. But the Fiat transaction was the *only* offer available. . . .

The Sale would yield $2 billion. According to expert testimony—not refuted by the objectors—an immediate liquidation of Chrysler as of May 20, 2009 would yield in the range of nothing to $800 million. . . . Crucially, Fiat had conditioned its commitment on the Sale being completed by June 15, 2009. While this deadline was tight and seemingly arbitrary, there was little leverage to force an extension. To preserve resources, Chrysler factories had been shuttered, and the business was hemorrhaging cash. According to the bankruptcy court, Chrysler was losing going concern value of nearly $100 million each day. . . .

On this record, and in light of the arguments made by the parties, the bankruptcy court's approval of the Sale was no abuse of discretion. With its revenues sinking, its factories dark, and its massive debts growing, Chrysler fit the paradigm of the melting ice cube. Going concern value was being reduced each passing day that it produced no cars, yet was obliged to pay rents, overhead, and salaries. Consistent with an underlying purpose of the Bankruptcy Code—maximizing the value of the bankrupt estate—it was no abuse of discretion to determine that the Sale prevented further, unnecessary losses. . . .

The Indiana Pensioners exaggerate the extent to which New Chrysler will emerge from the Sale as the twin of Old Chrysler. New Chrysler may manufacture the same lines of cars but it will also make newer, smaller vehicles using Fiat technology that will become available as a result of the Sale—moreover, at the time of the proceedings, Old Chrysler was manufacturing no cars at all. New Chrysler will be run by a new Chief Executive Officer, who has experience in turning around failing auto companies. It may retain many of the same employees, but they will be working under new union contracts that contain a six-year no-strike provision. New Chrysler will still sell cars in some of its old dealerships in the United States, but it will also have new access to Fiat dealerships in the European market. Such transformative use of old and new assets is precisely what one would expect from the § 363(b) sale of a going concern. . . .

* * *

NOTE: GOVERNMENT BROKERED DEALS

The Great Recession of 2008 led the federal government to broker several large acquisitions. In all cases, the government gave buyers financial incentives to purchase troubled companies. Chrysler and General Motors were pre-packaged bankruptcy acquisitions in which the government provided significant financing. Other brokered acquisitions included Bank of America's purchase of Countrywide, the nation's largest mortgage lender, and, two months later, of Merrill Lynch, a 94-year old brokerage house. Both targets were facing severe solvency problems and both deals were stock swaps. The acquisitions created the nation's largest retail bank. With the acquisitions, Bank of America assumed the substantial mortgage-related liabilities of both financial institutions. The deals proved to be a disaster, requiring Bank of America to take huge write-offs for the value of the toxic assets held by both of the targets, and eventually cost the Bank of America CEO, Kenneth D. Lewis, his job.

Similarly, the government pressured JPMorgan to purchase Bear Stearns, a failing investment bank, and later Washington Mutual, a failed commercial bank. Unlike the Bank of America deal, JPMorgan did very, very well in the deal at the expense of the government and Bear Stearns shareholders.

With each brokered buy-out there were upset investors in either the buyer or the seller arguing that the government had deprived them of value in its rush to keep the troubled institutions afloat. With the government in the picture amid cries of a crisis, the parties often avoided traditional shareholder ratification requirements as well as other legal procedural protections. In other words, exigency trumped law. See Steven M. Davidoff & David Zaring, *Regulation by Deal: The Government's Response to the Financial Crisis*, 61 ADMIN. L. REV. 463 (2009).

CHAPTER THREE

SUCCESSORSHIP TO ASSETS AND LIABILITIES

■ ■ ■

A. ACQUISITION NEGOTIATION AS A MULTI-ISSUE BARGAIN

1. INTRODUCTION TO MULTI-ISSUE BARGAINING THEORY

As noted in Chapter One, the parties' valuations must create an overlap (*joint gains* in the parlance of negotiation theorists) for the deal to close. The overlap may just reflect a disagreement in the current valuation of the seller or, more commonly, the overlap may reflect the buyer's view that the seller's assets will have a higher value once under the control of the buyer.[1] Parties that start bargaining only to find that there is no overlap often can create an overlap by allocating specific assets and liabilities to the party that values them the most favorably, persuading the opposite party to revalue (you are using the wrong multiple), or by allocating specific risks to the party willing to bear them at the least cost.

Once an overlap is found to exist, the bargaining is not over; the allocation of the gains from the overlap remains. The division of the joint gains is also significant to any analysis of negotiation tactics and strategy in acquisitions. Both parties to an acquisition are trying to create the joint gains, a cooperative endeavor, and at the same time, split the mutual gains thus generated, a competitive endeavor. Most negotiation theorists focus on the creative side of negotiations and understate or disparage the competitive side. This is a mistake. Professors Lax and Sebenius recognize the inherent interrelationship between the two endeavors in their identification of the fundamental tension in bargaining; the tension between *claiming* and *creating* value in negotiations. See David A. Lax & James K. Sebenius, THE MANAGER AS NEGOTIATOR 29–30, 33–35 (1986).

Consider an example of a buyer willing to pay up to $100 million and a seller willing to sell for over $95 million, creating an overlap of $5 in bargaining positions. Does the buyer pay $100, losing all the joint gains, or

---

[1] Synergy due to integration of firm assets is a form of this claim. Strategic buyers often search for synergy. Another form of the claim is that the buyer can better manage the seller's assets to *unlock value*. Financial buyers, hedge funds and private equity funds, seek to unlock value.

$95, capturing all the joint gains? Lax & Sebenius caution us that the tactics used in the identification of the overlap in prices necessary to the deal can also determine which of the two parties can claim the largest portion of the joint gains. This point can get lost in the prescriptions of some negotiation theorists.[2]

The part of the negotiation that deserves special mention in these materials and that is covered in more depth later in the book (Chapter Four) is the *lawyer to lawyer* negotiation over the preparation of the acquisition agreement once the business principals have agreed to the basics of a deal. The business people negotiate the basic terms of the transaction and hand the deal over to their lawyers to prepare an agreement. The business people may view the agreement as a "fill-in-the-blanks of a form" style endeavor and can be surprised (and unhappy) when their lawyers ask them to take positions on conflicted drafting issues. The lawyers, anxious to protect their client's interest, may be over-zealous, lack an appreciation of the fragile nature of the deal, and thereby endanger its closing. The lawyer-to-lawyer negotiation under these circumstances is much discussed in books, conferences and professional conversation.

In a sophisticated acquisition negotiation, the buyer and the seller do not negotiate solely over a single price for the firm. They often negotiate by item to maximize the joint gains achieved by the parties in the acquisition. The seller and the buyer may disagree on the value of some of the seller's significant rights and obligations. The seller, for example, may value select income-producing assets more highly than the buyer, or the seller may calculate the cost of select obligations to be less than the cost estimated by the buyer. If so, the seller ought not to transfer these assets and obligations in the acquisition. Rather, the seller should dispose of them before or after the acquisition or retain them, as it sees fit. In other words, the parties can maximize the value of the deal by allocating the rights and obligations to the party that places the highest value on those producing income and places the least cost on those requiring expenditures or obligations.

A simple example illustrates the point. A seller with an ongoing business that produces gears for all types of machinery has the prospect of paying significant product liability claims. The firm has already paid to settle three product liability lawsuits and anticipates several more. The value of the business to the seller without the claims is $575,000. The value of the business to the buyer without the claims is $600,000, creating an overlap of $25,000.[3] Assume, however, that the seller, more confident of the quality of the gears it has produced, values the product liability claims (in discounted present value terms) at a negative $50,000, putting the total present value of the firm to the seller at $525,000. The buyer, on the other

---

[2] E.g., Roger Fischer & William L. Ury, GETTING TO YES (1981) (focusing on creating the overlap).

[3] Both parties are better off with any deal priced in the overlap.

hand, believes that gears produced during the seller's ownership of the firm will generate liability that will cost, in present dollars, $100,000, putting the total present value of the firm to the buyer at $500,000. There is no overlap in valuations and no room for a deal if the buyer must absorb the contingent liabilities.

On the other hand, if the seller agrees to retain responsibility for all product liability claims based on gears produced when the seller owned the firm, the deal can close at a price between $600,000 and $575,000. In essence, the buyer agrees to pay the seller for assuming the contingent claims because the seller places a lower cost on them than does the buyer. From a position of no valuation overlap, the parties have created a joint gain of $25,000[4] that they now split in negotiations over the purchase price. If we do not allow the parties to allocate the contingent claims in an acquisition, then we destroy the deal at the cost of denying the buyer—the party that values most highly the seller's gear-producing assets, perhaps because it can produce gears at a lower marginal cost—the ability to produce gears using the assets.

Our example applies not only to obligations that are liabilities but also to rights or assets that have positive value. In our basic example, substitute a valuable patent for the contingent liabilities and assume the same basic valuation of the gear business; the buyer values the business at $600,000 without the patent and the seller values the business at $575,000 without the patent. The buyer believes the firm with the patent is worth $650,000 because it values the patent held by the seller, in present dollars, at $50,000. The seller believes the firm with the patent is worth $750,000 because it values the patent at $175,000. If the seller retains the patent, the deal works; otherwise it does not. If the buyer must have permission from the patent owner to produce a line of gears, the parties can agree to grant buyer a non-exclusive license with royalties paid per gear produced so that the seller retains, in essence, the full economic fruits of the patent.

The tension between "creating" and "claiming" value is pronounced in multi-issue bargaining. The parties must subdivide the issues, reveal relative strength of utility on the various issues so defined, and make tradeoffs, issue by issue, that maximize their joint gains. See Lax & Sebenius, *supra*, at 91, 115.

A party in a multi-issue bargain can pursue claiming tactics to maximize its share of whatever joint gains are created. For example, a party can overstate interest in some issues (to overstate the value of a concession) and understate interest in others (to prevent from being squeezed). In an extreme case, a party can feign a completely new interest

4 The joint gain is calculated by comparing the combined position of the buyer and the seller before the acquisition and their combined position after the acquisition. If, for example, the seller is a poor negotiator and sells the firm, without liabilities, for $575,000, the seller is no better or worse off and the buyer has bought a firm it values at $600,000 for $575,000, for a net gain to the buyer of $25,000.

that it hopes to "concede" for something of real value. The lure of claiming tactics is individual gain. However, claiming tactics put at risk the creation of joint value (a sub-optimal deal for both sides or no deal at all)—and ethics.

In our example of a negotiation over the sale of a gear-manufacturing business in which the parties disagreed over the value of future product liability claims and over the value of a patent, we have a classic example of the fundamental tension in multi-issue bargaining between claiming and creating value. If the seller wanted to be a pure "value claimer," it would start negotiations with an exaggerated value on the patent, grossly undervalue the size of potential product liability claims, and exaggerate the value of the firm neutral of the liability and the patent. What is the danger of this approach?[5] On the other hand, if the seller wanted to be a pure "value creator," it would disclose, accurately and fully, its belief about the value of the patent, about the size of the potential product liability claims, and about the value of the firm neutral of both the liability and the patent. What is the danger of this approach?[6] How should a seller decide whether to disclose or hold back material information?[7]

QUESTION

Which type of acquisition makes multi-issue bargaining the easiest?

2. EXTERNALITIES AND OTHER FORMS OF OPPORTUNISTIC BEHAVIOR IN ACQUISITIONS

The darker side of acquisitions (and recapitalizations as well) consists of the parties' creation of joint gains by evading preexisting obligations to third parties who are not represented in the bargaining. If the parties are successful in using an acquisition to avoid or overburden obligations owed to third parties, they can split the gains created by the evasion or additional burden.

Consider our example of the gear firm with significant potential product liability claims. The reason for the disparate evaluation of the claims between buyer and seller may be that the two parties have different predictions about the number and success of future claims, given the quality of the seller's production runs. On the other hand, the buyer and the seller may agree on their predictions on the number and likely success of future claims—that is, both value them at a minus $100,000 if someone has to pay them—but the seller may believe that it can use an asset acquisition to avoid at least half the claims. The seller attempts to sells its

---

[5] Deadlock and the loss of any part of the $25,000 joint gains.

[6] Your opponent does not reciprocate with equal candor. A deal is struck but you lose any part of the $25,000 joint gains. Your opponent offers you $575,001 for the company (without the patent and you keep the liability) and will not budge. You take the deal for a $1 gain.

[7] Of course, this question separates the suckers from the pros.

business, retains the liabilities, and dissolves, distributing the sale proceeds to its shareholders before putative plaintiffs can sue the firm to collect for their injuries.

Since the product liability claimants are not represented in the acquisition (indeed many future claimants may not know at the time of the acquisition that they will have claims and thus are interested parties in the deal), the claimants cannot protect themselves from the consequences of the deal. If the seller is correct that it can avoid half the product liability claims in the aftermath of an acquisition, then the seller and the buyer have created a joint gain of $50,000 through the acquisition, which they can divide, at the expense of the contingent claimants. Economists label these costs to product liability claimants, among others, *externalities*, *third-party effects*, or social costs not borne by the contracting parties.[8] An important function of our legal system is to protect potential victims of externalities in deals.

All contingent claimants, including those with environmental or employment discrimination claims, are potential acquisition victims. Another common victim of acquisitions is the United States government. If the parties to an acquisition are motivated solely by tax savings, that is, the parties pay significantly less total tax after the acquisition than before, then they have created joint gains that the parties can divide at the expense of the United States Treasury. It matters little which of the two parties to an acquisition actually realizes the tax gains, because the parties can allocate the value of the gains among themselves in the purchase price. We will discuss the efforts of Congress and the Internal Revenue Service to combat tax-motivated acquisitions in Chapter Eight, Section B.

In designing legal protections for contingent claimants, we could begin with a rule that refuses to allow the seller to retain the liabilities in any acquisition. In other words, the courts could simply attach the liabilities to the buyer, regardless of the parties' efforts to contract otherwise. This stops acquisitions designed largely to avoid future liabilities, but it also stops legitimate acquisitions in which the seller and the buyer, both intending to pay all valid claims, simply disagree on their assessment of the present value of the future claims. Unless judges can argue successfully that such a rule blocks far fewer legitimate acquisitions than harmful acquisitions, or that an alternative rule that distinguishes the harmful from the beneficial acquisitions is not workable, our courts must design rules that

[8] The identification of externalities is not an exact science. For example, one could argue that, theoretically, the retail purchasers of the gears, when they decided how much they were willing to pay for the gears, ought to have "priced" or "internalized" the possibility that their product liability claims, if any, could be cut off by an acquisition of the producer. In other words, absent a contract warranty that the seller will not attempt to defeat the product liability claims through an acquisition, the purchaser of gears ought to pay fractionally less for the gears. This assumes more knowledge and sophistication on the part of gear customers than is normally the case, however, and the argument does not cover those injured by defective gears that were not gear customers (innocent bystanders, for example).

catch the harmful acquisitions and permit legitimate deals. As you read the cases on contingent liabilities in the chapter, you can assess the success of our courts in this endeavor.

Another class of potential claimants are parties who have long term contractual relationships with the seller, the value of which may be adversely affected by an acquisition. This class includes creditors—long-term bondholders to suppliers, licensors of intellectual property rights, real estate or personalty lessors, and employees (white collar or blue collar, unionized or non-unionized). Members of this class can claim damage in any specific acquisition: the creditors can see the value of their debt decrease as the default risk of the debt increases; licensors or lessors may find their grants of permission overburdened or their potential income from royalties or rent diminished; and employees may find themselves out of work or working for less. With the occurrence of any of these events in an acquisition, the injured parties usually ask for legal redress.

Their argument has bite. In each case, the aggrieved party has incurred substantial costs (or foregone significant nonrecurring opportunities) in reliance on a continuing relationship with the firm, and these costs may have put the party at a strategic disadvantage. If the firm refuses (or threatens to refuse, to gain a bargaining advantage) to honor its promises, the aggrieved party loses the value of its sunk costs. Consider, for example, the position of a middle manager who has spent several years learning how to manage a small part of the seller's business. If she is fired, she will lose the value of her skills that are tailored to the specific people and assets that she manages. Other employers will not pay her for the true value of these skills. An employer, realizing her predicament, is tempted to offer her a reduced salary, well below the increases the employer implicitly promised to pay her when she was hired and to expropriate some of the value of her asset-specific skills. Yet she resists, relying on her claim for contract damages in court. Can the employer sell the business to a third party, who can threaten to terminate her free of any contract claims and thus extract a reduced salary agreement? This kind of behavior is often labeled as *opportunistic* by economists.

Bondholders have made a similar claim. A firm asks for and receives cash from investors in exchange for the firm's promise to repay the principal in the future and to pay a fixed interest for the privilege of using the money. Is there an implicit promise that the firm will maintain its capital structure in more or less the same basic pattern? Once the firm collects the cash from the bondholders, does it breach the implicit promise by adding so much additional debt that the risk of default on the original bonds is substantially increased? Even if so, can the firm sell to a third party, which materially increases the firm's leverage, without consideration for the selling firm's implicit promise?

In theory, parties who contract with a firm need not be helpless victims of acquisitions. They can protect themselves in a variety of ways in their initial contracts against any potential acquisition. At the time of contracting, they can negotiate for specific promises or warranties against opportunistic behavior. Or they can simply demand additional compensation for absorbing the risk of opportunistic behavior (that is, they can discount the value of the firm's return promise to pay); they *price the risk*. Our middle manager could, for example, at the time of her hiring have demanded in writing a schedule of raises and a generous severance payment for any loss of her position without cause, or a higher initial salary (with a signing bonus, perhaps) if the firm was unwilling to satisfy her demand for a detailed written contract. In other words, contractual claimants such as the middle manager are not victims of externalities; they can, theoretically, price or internalize the costs of a firm's prospective avoidance of their claims.

If theory matches reality, the role of legal rules in protecting contract claimants is very limited. The judges ought to be empowered only to interpret contract language or to provide gap fillers or default terms if the contract language is silent or ambiguous. Does the middle manager's contract with the seller contain any implicit protections against loss of employment due to control changes? If both parties have perfect information, the courts' choice of default terms as favoring one party or the other does not matter, as long as the courts are predictable over time. We presume the parties have accepted whatever default rule is in force by their choice not to explicitly contract to avoid it and they have priced it in their deal. In our example, it ought not to matter if courts favor the firm by assuming that the middle managers have no protection against control changes if the contract is silent.

In theory, then, applicable legal rules are relevant in contract cases only to facilitate and order the judge's function of finding and carrying out the intent of the parties to the original bargain. The best example of a system of legal rules that seems, with minor exceptions, to take its basic character from this view is the system of rules covering the status of creditors (particularly long-term creditors) and real estate lessors in acquisitions. When reading the materials, ask yourself whether the rules for patent licensors also fit in this category.

On the other hand, theory does not always match fact. Some classes of parties may have bargaining disadvantages stemming from the asymmetric distribution of information, lack of bargaining capacity, poor perspicacity about the future, or flagging market power. Economists refer to these cases as market failures; in such cases, we cannot rely on unregulated private autonomy to order the parties' affairs in socially useful ways. When such cases exist, lawmakers must first identify the systemic disadvantages and then design appropriate legal protections. These choices are politically charged, with interest groups claiming special needs. Strong views, couched in morality and political theory but tinged with self-interest, are the order of the day. The examples in the following materials of bargaining situations that our society currently includes in this category of market failures are contained in Section C of this Chapter, dealing with collective bargaining agreements and with employee pension and welfare benefit plans.

Note that the legislative and judicial processes may themselves be the vehicles for opportunistic behavior. Some groups who do not deserve or need protection may use these processes to extract value from their contractual counterparts that was not part of their original bargains. Our middle manager gets a windfall at the expense of the seller if she explicitly gives up a control change clause in favor of a larger initial salary and is later able to convince a court that she deserves damages for the loss of her job due to an acquisition. She also may be able to convince a state legislature to pass a statute protecting her position in acquisitions. Finally, there is the very pragmatic argument advanced by some that acquisitions are one of the time-honored methods of avoiding otherwise overly burdensome governmental regulation. If a firm has negotiated collective bargaining agreements that prove to be too generous in light of economic conditions, it is easier to sell the assets of the firm to another party, which takes the firm free of the contracts, than to negotiate wage concessions.

QUESTION

Which type of acquisition provides the easiest vehicle for opportunistic behavior?

B. TRANSFER OR VESTING OF ASSETS IN ACQUISITIONS

1. STATUTORY MERGERS: ASSETS *VEST* IN SURVIVOR

All state codes have specific statutes on the effect of a statutory merger on the preexisting rights and obligations of the constituent parties. Delaware's provisions are §§ 259 and 261 in the Delaware General Corporation Law. As a general matter, the statutes contain language directing that all rights and obligations of the constituent parties pass to the surviving entity in a statutory merger *"as a matter of law."* Assets and debts "shall be vested in the corporation surviving . . . ." Do the merger statutes override contracts that are implicitly or expressly *non-assignable* or *non-transferable*? In other words, if one firm holds non-assignable contracts with a third party, can a second firm merge with the first and claim rights under the contracts? Does your answer depend on which firm survives in the merger? The following case is a landmark decision on the intersection of federal law on patents and state law on the effect of mergers.

PPG INDUSTRIES, INC. V. GUARDIAN INDUSTRIES CORP.

United States Court of Appeals, Sixth Circuit, 1979.
597 F.2d 1090, *cert. denied,* 444 U.S. 930.

LIVELY, CIRCUIT JUDGE.

The question in this case is whether the surviving or resultant corporation in a statutory merger acquires patent license rights of the constituent corporations. . . .

Prior to 1964 both PPG and Permaglass, Inc., were engaged in fabrication of glass products which required that sheets of glass be shaped for particular uses. Independently of each other, the two fabricators developed similar processes that involved "floating glass on a bed of gas, while it was being heated and bent." This process is known in the industry as "gas hearth technology" and "air float technology"; the two terms are interchangeable. After a period of negotiations, PPG and Permaglass entered into an agreement on January 1, 1964 whereby each granted rights to the other under "gas hearth system" patents already issued and in the process of prosecution. . . .

Eleven patents are involved in this suit. Nine of them originated with Permaglass and were licensed to PPG as exclusive licensee under Section 3.2, subject to the non-exclusive, non-transferable reservation to Permaglass set forth in Section 3.3. Two of the patents originated with PPG. Section 4.1 granted a non-exclusive, non-transferable license to Permaglass with respect to the two PPG patents. . . .

As of December 1969, Permaglass was merged into Guardian pursuant to applicable statutes of Ohio and Delaware. Guardian was engaged primarily in the business of fabricating and distributing windshields for automobiles and trucks. It had decided to construct a facility to manufacture raw glass and the capacity of that facility would be greater than its own requirements. Permaglass had no glass manufacturing capability and it was contemplated that its operations would utilize a large part of the excess output of the proposed Guardian facility.

The "Agreement of Merger" between Permaglass and Guardian did not refer specifically to the 1964 agreement between PPG and Permaglass. However, among Permaglass' representations in the agreement was the following:

> (g) Permaglass is the owner, assignee, or licensee of such patents, trademarks, trade names, and copyrights as are listed and described in Exhibit "C" attached hereto. None of such patents, trademarks, trade names, or copyrights is in litigation

and Permaglass has not received any notice of conflict with the asserted rights of third parties relative to the use thereof.

Listed on Exhibit "C" to the merger agreement are the nine patents originally developed by Permaglass and licensed to PPG under the 1964 agreement that are involved in this infringement action.

Shortly after the merger was consummated PPG filed the present action, claiming infringement by Guardian in the use of apparatus and processes described and claimed in eleven patents, which were identified by number and origin. The eleven patents were covered by the terms of the 1964 agreement. PPG asserted that it became the exclusive licensee of the nine patents which originated with Permaglass under the 1964 agreement and that the rights reserved by Permaglass were personal to it and non-transferable and non-assignable. PPG also claimed that Guardian had no rights with respect to the two patents, which had originated with PPG because the license under these patents was personal to Permaglass and non-transferable and non-assignable except with the permission of PPG. . . .

One of the defenses pled by Guardian in its answer was that it was a licensee of the patents in suit. It described the merger with Permaglass and claimed it "had succeeded to all rights, powers, ownerships, etc., of Permaglass, and, as Permaglass' successor, defendant is legally entitled to operate in place of Permaglass under the January 1, 1964 agreement between Permaglass and plaintiff, free of any claim of infringement of the patents. . . ."

Questions with respect to the assignability of a patent license are controlled by federal law. It has long been held by federal courts that agreements granting patent licenses are personal and not assignable unless expressly made so. . . . This has been the rule at least since 1852 when the Supreme Court decided *Troy Iron & Nail v. Corning*, 55 U.S. (14 How.) 193, 14 L.Ed. 383 (1852). . . . The district court recognized this rule in the present case, but concluded that where patent licenses are claimed to pass by operation of law to the resultant or surviving corporation in a statutory merger there has been no assignment or transfer. . . .

Guardian relies on two classes of cases where rights of a constituent corporation have been held to pass by merger to the resultant corporation even though such rights are not otherwise assignable or transferable. It points out that the courts have consistently held that "shop rights" do pass in a statutory merger. . . . A shop right is an implied license which accrues to an employer in cases where an employee has perfected a patentable device while working for the employer. Though the employee is the owner of the patent, he is estopped from claiming infringement by the employer. This estoppel arises from the fact that the patent work has been done on the employer's time and that the employer has furnished materials for the experiments and financial backing to the employee.

The rule that prevents an employee-inventor from claiming infringement against a successor to the entire business and good will of his employer is but one feature of the broad doctrine of estoppel that underlies the shop right cases. No element of estoppel exists in the present case. The license rights of Permaglass did not arise by implication. They were bargained for at arm's-length and the agreement that defines the rights of the parties provides that Permaglass received non-transferable, non-assignable personal licenses. We do not believe that the express prohibition against assignment and transfer in a written instrument may be held ineffective by analogy to a rule based on estoppel in situations where there is no written contract and the rights of the parties have arisen by implication because of their past relationship.

The other group of cases, which the district court and Guardian found to be analogous, holds that the resultant corporation in a merger succeeds to the rights of the constituent corporations under real estate leases. . . . The most obvious difficulty in drawing an analogy between the lease cases and those concerning patent licenses is that a lease is an interest in real property. As such, it is subject to the deep-rooted policy against restraints on alienation. Applying this policy, courts have construed provisions against assignability in leases strictly and have concluded that they do not prevent the passage of interests by operation of law. . . . There is no similar policy that is offended by the decision of a patent owner to make a license under his patent personal to the licensee, and non-assignable and non-transferable. In fact, the law treats a license as if it contained these restrictions in the absence of express provisions to the contrary . . .

The quoted language from Sections 3, 4 and 9 of the 1964 agreement evinces an intent that only Permaglass was to enjoy the privileges of licensee. If the parties had intended an exception in the event of a merger, it would have been a simple matter to have so provided in the agreement . . . We conclude that if the parties had intended an exception in case of a merger to the provisions against assignment and transfer they would have included it in the agreement . . .

The district court also held that the patent licenses in the present case were not transferred because they passed by operation of law from Permaglass to Guardian. This conclusion is based on the theory of continuity that underlies a true merger. However, the theory of continuity relates to the fact that there is no dissolution of the constituent corporations and, even though they cease to exist, their essential corporate attributes are vested by operation of law in the surviving or resultant corporation. . . . It does not mean that there is no transfer of particular assets from a constituent corporation to the surviving or resultant one.

The Ohio merger statute provides that following a merger all property of a constituent corporation shall be "deemed to be *transferred* to and vested in the surviving or new corporation without further act or deed. . . ."

(emphasis added). Ohio Revised Code, [former] § 1701.81(A)(4). This indicates that the transfer is by operation of law, not that there is no transfer of assets in a merger situation. The Delaware statute, which was also involved in the Permaglass-Guardian merger, provides that the property of the constituent corporations "shall be vested in the corporation surviving or resulting from such merger or consolidation,. . . ." 8 Del.C. § 259(a). The Third Circuit has construed the "shall be vested" language of the Delaware statute as follows: "In short, the underlying property of the constituent corporations is *transferred* to the resultant corporation upon the carrying out of the consolidation or merger. . . ." *Koppers Coal & Transportation Co. v. United States,* 107 F.2d 706, 708 (3d Cir.1939) (emphasis added).

In his opinion in *Koppers,* Judge Biggs disposed of arguments very similar to those of Guardian in the present case, based on the theory of continuity. Terming such arguments "metaphysical" he found them completely at odds with the language of the Delaware statute. *Id.* Finally, on this point, the parties themselves provided in the merger agreement that all property of Permaglass "shall be deemed transferred to and shall vest in Guardian without further act or deed. . . ." A transfer is no less a transfer because it takes place by operation of law rather than by a particular act of the parties. The merger was effected by the parties and the transfer was a result of their act of merging.

Thus, Sections 3, 4 and 9 of the 1964 agreement between PPG and Permaglass show an intent that the licenses held by Permaglass in the eleven patents in suit not be transferable. While this conclusion disposes of the license defense as to all eleven patents, it should be noted that Guardian's claim to licenses under the two patents, which originated with PPG is also defeated by Section 11.2 of the 1964 agreement. This section addresses a different concern from that addressed in Sections 3, 4, and 5. The restrictions on transferability and assignability in those sections prevent the patent licenses from becoming the property of third parties. The termination clause, however, provides that Permaglass' license with respect to the two PPG patents will terminate if the ownership of a majority of the voting stock of Permaglass passes from the 1964 stockholders to designated classes of persons, even though the licenses themselves might never have changed hands.

Apparently, PPG was willing for Permaglass to continue as licensee under the nine patents even though ownership of its stock might change. These patents originated with Permaglass and so long as Permaglass continued to use the licenses for its own benefit a mere change in ownership of Permaglass stock would not nullify the licenses. Only a transfer or assignment would cause a termination. However, the agreement provides for termination with respect to the two original PPG patents in the event of an indirect takeover of Permaglass by a change in the ownership of a majority of its stock. The fact that PPG sought and obtained a stricter provision with respect to the two patents which it originally owned in no way indicates an intention to permit transfer of licenses under the other nine in case of a merger. None of the eleven licenses was transferable; but two of them, those involving PPG's own development in the field of gas hearth technology, were not to continue even for the benefit of the licensee if it came under the control of a manufacturer of automobiles or a competitor of PPG in the glass industry "other than the present owners" of Permaglass. A consistency among the provisions of the agreement is discernible when the different origins of the various patents are considered. . . .

QUESTIONS

1. Would the result in *PPG Industries* be different if Guardian had merged into Permaglass? See, e.g., *Meso Scale Diagnostics LL v. Roach Diagnostics GMBH,* 2011 WL 1348438 (Del. Ch. 2011) (question open). If Guardian had bought all the Permaglass stock? (Note the effects of § 11.2 in the 1964 agreement.) See *Institut Pasteur v. Cambridge Biotech Corp.*, 104 F.3d 489 (1st Cir. 1997) (stock sale not an assignment of patent license held by firm). Why is the form of the transaction critical?

2. Assume Permaglass is lessee on a real estate lease that is *expressly* "non-assignable." After the merger, can Guardian Industries claim to be the lessee under the old lease? E.g., *Dodier Realty & Investment v. St. Louis National Baseball Club*, 238 S.W.2d 321 (Mo. 1951) (yes).[9] How is it that a patent license that has no clause on assignment does not transfer in a merger and an expressly non-assignable real estate lease does transfer? What is inherently different about the two contracts that justifies this disparate treatment? Can the holding be explained by the nature of the return payments—royalties in licenses and rent in leases?[10] Or does the holding depend exclusively on the federal nature of the right? See *Cincom Systems v Novelis Corp.*, 2007 WL 128999 (S.D. Ohio 2007) (copyright license did not vest in survivor in merger).

---

[9] See also Imperial Enterprises v. Fireman Fund Insurance, 535 F.2d 287 (5th Cir. 1976) (same result with an insurance policy).

[10] State law on the assignment of personal licenses often involves a balancing test. E.g., Trubowith v. Riverbank Canning, 182 P.2d 182 (Cal. 1947) ("validity depends on whether it affects the interests of the parties protected."). If applied to the *PPG* facts, for example, the court would not assume a merger was a transfer but would investigate whether the merger led to a substantial change in the economic relationship between the licensee and licensor (i.e., added a substantial burden to the license). If so, the license would not transfer; if not, it would. Changes in form of the licensee business, for example, such as a recapitalization or reincorporation would not void the license. So the *PPG* case represents a major difference in doctrine. There is some indication that state legislatures intend to overrule even the balance test limitation in the effect of merger statute language.

NOTE: FEDERAL PRE-EMPTION AND STATE "EFFECT OF MERGER" STATUTES

State courts and state legislatures that have focused on the issue, joined by several academics, do not like the *PPG* decision. See *TXO Production Co. v. M.D.Mark., Inc.*, 999 S.W.2d 137 (Tex. Civ. App. 1999) (discussing *PPG*). Why? The state of Texas has attempted to nullify the decision by changing its law on the effect of mergers. Until 1987, the Texas statute stated that assets of the constituent corporation were "deemed to be transferred to and vested in" the survivor. The language was similar to the language in the 1984 version of the Rev. Model Act § 11.07(a)(3) (" . . . is vested in the survivor without reversion or impairment . . . "). In 1987, the Texas legislature amended the language to state that the assets of constituent corporations are "deemed to be, and without any transfer or assignment having occurred, vested in" the surviving corporation. Tex. Bus. Corp. Act. Art. 5.06A (Vernon 1999). Comments of the drafters indicated that they intended to nullify the *PPG* case. *TXO Production Co.*, 999 S.W. 2d at 141 n3. See also Colo. Rev. Stat. § 7–111–106(1)(b)0 (" . . . a merger does not constitute a conveyance, transfer, or assignment . . . ") Did they succeed? The Ohio statute in place at the time *PPG* was decided was based on the 1969 version of the Model Act (" . . . deemed to be transferred to and vested in the surviving or new corporation . . . "). Ohio has since modified its statute (assets " . . . are vested in the surviving or new entity without further act . . . ") Ohio Gen. Corp. L. § 1701.82 (a)(3). Does the new language change the holding of *PPG*? See *Cincom Sys., Inc. v. Novelis Corp*, 581 F.3d 431 (6th Cir. 2009) (no).

The *PPG* decision holds that the nature of a patent license is a question of federal law (a license is personal) but that a contract that assigns a patent license is a matter of state law. Assume a patent license is expressly non-assignable or non-transferable, could a state court hold that the contract clause implies that the parties intended the patent license vest in a survivor in a merger (because they implicitly recognized and accepted the effect of the merger statute language)?

2. STOCK ACQUISITIONS: NO VESTING OR TRANSFER

BRANMAR THEATRE CO. V. BRANMAR, INC.

Court of Chancery of Delaware, 1970.
264 A.2d 526.

SHORT, VICE CHANCELLOR.

. . . Plaintiff was incorporated under the laws of Delaware on June 7, 1967. The owners of its outstanding capital stock were the Robert Rappaport family of Cleveland, Ohio. On June 9, 1967, plaintiff and defendant entered into a lease agreement for a motion picture theatre in the Branmar Shopping Center, New Castle County, Delaware. The lease, sixteen pages in length, recites that the lessor is to erect a theatre building in the shopping center. It provides for the payment of rent by the lessee to the lessor of $27,500 per year plus a percentage of gross admissions receipts, plus five percent of any amounts paid to the lessee by refreshment concessionaires. The percentage of admissions figure is regulated by the type of attractions in the theatre, the minimum being five per cent and the maximum ten. The lease provides for a twenty-year term with an option in the lessee to renew for an additional ten years. The lessee is to provide the lessor with a loan of $60,000, payable in installments, to be used for construction. The lessee is to provide, at its cost, whatever fixtures and equipment are necessary to operate the theatre. Paragraph 12 of the lease, the focal point of this lawsuit, provides:

> "Lessee shall not sublet, assign, transfer, or in any manner dispose of the said premises or any part thereof, for all or any part of the term hereby granted, without the prior written consent of the Lessor, such consent shall not be unreasonably withheld."

Joseph Luria, the principal for Branmar Shopping Center testified at trial that he negotiated the lease agreement with Isador Rappaport; that he made inquiries about Rappaport's ability to manage a theatre and satisfied himself that Rappaport had the competence and the important industry connections to successfully operate the theatre. It appears that Rappaport and his son operate a successful theatre in Cleveland, Ohio and have owned and operated theatres elsewhere.

Following execution of the lease, the Rappaports were approached by Muriel Schwartz and Reba Schwartz, operators of ten theatres in the Delaware and neighboring Maryland area, with an offer to manage the theatre for the Rappaports who had no other business interests in the Wilmington area. This offer was not accepted but the Schwartzes subsequently agreed with the Rappaports to purchase the lease from plaintiff and have it assigned to them. An assignment was executed by plaintiff to the Schwartzes. Defendant rejected the assignment under the power reserved in Paragraph Twelve of the lease. On May 29, 1969, the Schwartzes purchased the outstanding shares of plaintiff from the Rappaports. Upon receipt of notice of the sale defendant advised plaintiff that it considered the sale of the shares to the Schwartzes to be a breach of Paragraph Twelve of the lease and the lease to be null and void.

Defendant argues that the sale of stock was in legal effect an assignment of the lease by the Rappaports to the Schwartzes, was in breach of Paragraph Twelve of the lease, and that it was, therefore, justified in terminating plaintiff's leasehold interest. That in the absence of fraud, and none is charged here, transfer of stock of a corporate lessee is ordinarily not a violation of a clause prohibiting assignment is clear from the authorities. . . . Defendant contends, however, that this is not the ordinary case. Here, it says, due to the nature of the motion picture business, the performance required was by the Rappaports personally. But, while defendant's negotiations were with a member of the Rappaport family when the lease was executed it chose to let the theatre to a corporation whose stock might foreseeably be transferred by the then stockholders. In the preparation of the lease, a document of sixteen pages, defendant was careful to spell out in detail the rights and duties of the parties. It did not, however, see fit to provide for forfeiture in the event the stockholders sold their shares. Had this been the intent it would have been a simple matter to have so provided. . . .

Defendant contends that the evidence clearly shows that the Schwartzes do not have the connections in the industry to obtain first quality motion pictures which is of prime importance to a landlord under "a percentage rental agreement." If these were the facts defendant's theory that the lease called for personal performance by the Rappaports might have some merit. . . .

If the question of ability to perform to defendant's best advantage is material at all, it is as between the Schwartzes and the Rappaports and there is simply no competent evidence in the record to answer this question. Moreover, defendant's characterization of the lease as "a percentage rental agreement" is not justified. The rental terms are not based solely on percentages but on a substantial stipulated annual rent plus percentages. What difference in dollars the percentages would amount to depending upon the identity of the theatre's management does not appear.

Conditions and restrictions in a deed or lease, which upon a breach work a forfeiture of estate, are not favored by the law. . . . This rule rests on the principle that the party having the power to stipulate in his own favor should not neglect to make his exactions clear and further 'that every man's grant is to be taken most strongly against himself. . . .' The disfavor in which forfeitures are viewed gives a special reason for invoking this general rule of construction against the person whose granting language is appealed to as the source of a claimed forfeiture. . . .

Defendant suggests that since "the Rappaports" could not assign the lease without its consent they should not be permitted to accomplish the same result by transfer of their stock. But, the rule that precludes a person from doing indirectly what he cannot do directly has no application to the present case. The attempted assignment was not by the Rappaports but by plaintiff corporation, the sale of stock by its stockholders. Since defendant has failed to show circumstances to justify ignoring the corporation's separate existence, reliance upon the cited rule is misplaced. . . .

NOTE: CONTROL CHANGE CLAUSES

The lawyers for PPG could have better protected the patent licenses and reservations against assignment or transfer with a *control change clause*, a clause aimed at prohibiting transfers under any and all of the various forms of acquisitions. Such a clause would also have been useful to Branmar's lawyers when they drafted the real estate lease. Note how the clause that follows stops assignment or transfer in a reverse merger (Guardian merging into Permaglass with Guardian shareholders receiving a controlling block of Permaglass stock) and in a stock acquisition:

> *Assignment.* Licensee may not assign this Agreement without Licensor's prior written consent. For purposes of this Section, a Change in Control shall be deemed an assignment. "Change in Control," as used herein, shall mean (1) a sale of all or substantially all of Licensee's assets, (2) a merger or consolidation in which the Licensee is not the surviving corporation, (3) a reverse merger in which the Licensee is the surviving corporation but the shares of common stock of Licensee outstanding immediately preceding the merger are converted by virtue of the merger into other property, whether in the form of securities, cash or otherwise, or (4) an acquisition by any person or entity of securities of the Licensee representing at least fifty percent (50 percent) of the combined voting power entitled to vote in the election of directors.

NOTE: PURCHASING HIGH-TECH COMPANIES

The goal of a company purchasing a high-tech company is often the acquisition of coveted rights to intellectual property in the form of licenses that the target either holds (*license-in* agreements) or grants (*license-out* agreements). In many privately held technology companies, license agreements may constitute the majority or even all of the assets of significant value. Under a license-in, the target has obtained the right to use intellectual property from a third-party licensor that either owns the property or has received the right to further license it from yet another business (a right to *sublicense*). Under a license-out, the target itself has licensed for value intellectual property that it owns or has the right to sublicense.

Before lawyers drafting technology licenses became attuned to the possibility of sophisticated transaction planning, anti-transfer clauses in licenses were brief. A common type of assignment provision in license agreements was one that prohibits assignment by either party without consent of the other. It forces a party that wants to transfer a license agreement in an asset acquisition to renegotiate the license agreement with the other party. One also sees in older technology licenses clauses that prohibit an assignment "by operation of law." These clauses stop transfers of the licenses in forward direct or triangular mergers (the law in reverse mergers is still uncertain). *PPG Industries* made the clauses unnecessary in patent licenses as it requires renegotiation with third-party patent licensors in forward direct or triangular mergers, mergers in which the target does not survive. The older anti-assignment provisions (and *PPG Industries*) do not, however, stop transfers of control of a license in a stock acquisition. As a consequence, stock acquisitions of high-tech companies with intellectual property became the preferred acquisition technique. Modern license drafting practice has caught up, however, using control change clauses that plan for all the different transaction possibilities.

The liquidity of technology licenses in acquisitions has led lawyers to draft specific license terms in anticipation of stock acquisitions.

Clauses on Competitors: Parties to a license agreement do not want to end up in an undesirable or unintended relationship with a competitor. If a competitor buys a licensee, the licensor may find itself licensing technology to a competitor. If a competitor buys a licensor, the licensee may be paying royalties to a competitor and a sublicense would inadvertently assist a competitor in expanding market share. The parties to the license find it useful, therefore, to identify likely competitors and, for those firms on the list, require consent for all transfers or a right to terminate prior to the transfer.

Clauses on the Scope of the License: Licenses often contain scope restrictions. The agreements specify the intellectual property that the licensee has a right to use, the permitted uses and who may or may not be entitled to use the intellectual property. For example, the use of the intellectual property may be limited to a specific division, subsidiary, or business of the licensee. These limitations can limit the value of the license in the hands of purchasers. In the example noted, the purchaser cannot, without renegotiation, use the purchased intellectual property anywhere in the acquirer's operations.

Clauses on Licensee Fees and Royalties: The license fee and royalty structure negotiated by the target and a third party may not reflect the value of the newly-acquired intellectual property in the hands of the buyer. If the licensee pricing scale is based on units manufactured under the license and the buyer produces dramatically more or less units than the target, then the pricing agreement in the original license over or under prices the property. To correct such problems, parties in licenses covenant for changes in financial terms contingent on acquisitions.

Clauses on Exclusivity: Licenses often include exclusivity provisions that grant the licensee exclusive territorial rights in an area or the exclusive right to use the technology on specific product lines. The licensor usually reserves the right to terminate the license or convert the license to a non-exclusive license if the licensee fails to meet certain royalty milestones. Acquisition of the licensee may dramatically change the appropriateness of the milestones. Again, license agreements may require renegotiation of such clauses contingent on acquisitions.

While most of the clauses noted protect licensors from surprises due to the acquisition of licensees, there are nasty surprises for the purchasers of licensors as well. For example, acquisitions of targets that have granted open-end licenses, in which the license grants the licensee use of "all intellectual property owned by the licensor" can grant a licensee everything originally owned by the target and everything owned by the purchaser if the purchaser does not maintain the target as a subsidiary after the acquisition.

3. ASSET ACQUISTIONS: TRANSFERS AND TRADEOFFS

The purchaser of a privately held company, focusing on limiting exposure to the liabilities of the seller, often will prefer an asset acquisition. In an asset acquisition, the purchaser has an opportunity to determine, within limits, which liabilities of the seller it will contractually assume. There are some recognized exceptions to the buyer's ability to avoid seller's liabilities (we explore these in Section C on successor liability below), but none of the exceptions prevent a buyer from attempting to minimize exposure with protections in an asset acquisition agreement. Unlike a stock acquisition or merger, in which a creditor's claims stay with the survivor,[11] a creditor in an asset sale can proceed directly against even a dissolved seller or the seller's shareholders for a period of time (typically three years).[12] A buyer concerned about long-term exposure to seller liabilities can require the seller to maintain insurance coverage or to escrow funds for post-closing liabilities.

In exchange for control over exposure to the seller's liabilities, the buyer incurs significant transactional disadvantages. First, asset transactions are typically more complicated and more time-consuming than stock purchases and statutory mergers. The acquisition contract must describe all assets purchased with specificity. At closing lawyers must document the transfer of the assets to the buyer and asset-specific filings or recordings may be necessary to effect the transfer. This will require separate assignment documents for real property deeds, leases, patents, trademarks and other intellectual property, motor vehicle registrations and any other evidences of transfer that a general bill of sale and assignment cannot cover. These transfers may involve assets in a number of states, each with different forms and requirements for filing and recording.

Second, among the assets included are valuable contract rights, leases, joint venture or strategic alliances, government contracts and insurance policies. These contract rights often are assignable only with the consent of other parties. This gives hold-up power to those parties, who might extract additional concessions for their assent. Third, government licenses, permits or other authorizations granted to the seller may require applications to government agencies to approve the transfer or re-issue the permits. The administrative delays or hearings necessary to securing the

---

[11] The shareholders of the selling firm are only liable on the claims indirectly, if at all, if a buyer seeks indemnification for post-closing claims through the indemnification provisions in an acquisition agreement.

[12] This can also include the seller's directors if the board has the seller distribute the proceeds of the sale in liquidation to its shareholders without making adequate provision for the firm's outstanding liabilities.

approvals can be substantial and risky (if, for example, the seller has a "grandfathered right" that is personal to the seller).

Glitches in the acquisition paper work can cause post-closing problems.

CHEMETALL GMBH v. ZR ENERGY, INC.

United States Court of Appeals, Seventh Circuit, 2003.
320 F.3d 714.

WILLIAMS, CIRCUIT JUDGE.

After Chemetall GMBH acquired the assets of Morton International, Joseph T. Fraval left Morton and formed a competing company, Zr Energy, Inc. Chemetall sued Fraval for breach of his agreement with Morton to not use or disclose its confidential information. A jury found in favor of Chemetall. Fraval appeals the district court's denial of his motion to dismiss Chemetall's breach of contract claim, which the court treated as a motion for summary judgment . . . . [W]e conclude that the motion was properly denied . . . .

* * *

Fraval was employed by Morton International (and its predecessors), where for 20 years he was involved in the production and marketing of zirconium powder, a chemical used in various pyrotechnic applications, including automobile air bags. Fraval signed an Employee Trade Secret Agreement with Morton in which he promised not to reveal confidential information regarding "improvements, inventions, or know-how relating to" Morton's business. The agreement was to be effective during and after his employment and was to "inure to the benefit of [Morton's] successors and assigns."

Morton later sold its zirconium powder business to Chemetall. The Asset Purchase Agreement between Chemetall and Morton required Morton to keep secret the assets and information acquired by Chemetall and to have its employees undertake equivalent secrecy obligations. Three years after the sale, Fraval left Morton and, with Arnold Berkovitz, formed Zr Energy to produce and market zirconium powder.

Chemetall's amended complaint alleged that Fraval breached his confidentiality agreement with Morton, now enforceable by Chemetall by reason of its acquisition of Morton's zirconium powder business . . . .

* * *

Turning to the merits of the breach of contract claim, the parties agree that Illinois law applies. . . .

Fraval's agreement with Morton was explicitly intended to "inure to the benefit of [Morton's] successors and assigns." "An assignment of a right is a manifestation of the assignor's intention to transfer a particular right by which the assignor's right to performance is terminated in whole or in part, and the assignee acquires the right." . . .

Fraval relies on two provisions of the Morton/Chemetall Asset Purchase Agreement that identify assets excluded from the sale. First, Fraval points to Paragraph 9.13, which, he argues, excludes his Employee Trade Secret Agreement from the sale to Chemetall:

> No employee of Seller shall become an employee of Purchaser as a result of this transaction and Purchaser shall not assume any liability or obligation with respect to any employee of Seller, including, but not limited to, any employment or consulting agreement entered into by Seller.

We do not read this provision as negating an assignment to Chemetall of the right to enforce Fraval's confidentiality obligation. As applied to the Trade Secret Agreement, Paragraph 9.13 means that Chemetall declined to assume Morton's obligations (that Chemetall declined to become his employer, for example), but it says nothing about whether Chemetall acquired Morton's rights—rights that are, according to the Trade Secret Agreement, assignable by Morton.

Second, Paragraph 2(i) of the Asset Purchase Agreement generally excludes any assets not listed in the Agreement, and according to Fraval, his Trade Secret Agreement was not contained on the list of included assets. Confidential information relating to the acquired assets was, however, expressly included in the sale to Chemetall, and the obligations of Morton and its employees with respect to that information was also referenced in the Purchase Agreement:

> 18(a) After the Closing, Seller shall keep secret and retain in strictest confidence, and shall not use for the benefit of itself or others any of the subject Assets or information pertaining thereto and shall not disclose such information to anyone outside of the Purchaser. . . .
>
> (b) All of Seller's employees who have been active in the Business, at any time before the Closing Date, shall be bound to a secrecy undertaking in accordance with paragraph 18(a).

These terms do not conclusively establish the parties' intent with respect to Fraval's pre-existing confidentiality agreement; nevertheless, we think the terms are consistent with an intent to preserve those obligations for the benefit of Chemetall. We therefore agree with the district court that these terms do not foreclose an intent to assign Fraval's confidentiality agreement to Chemetall. Thus, the district court was correct to deny

Fraval's pretrial motion and allow evidence on the question of the parties' intent.[13]

Most publicly traded companies will have placed debt securities in the public markets. The contract rights of the debt holders are contained in a *trust indenture,* a formal document whose *covenants* provide rights and protections to the debt holders. The trust indenture sets out the rights of debt holders with respect to security over the assets of the company, defines any restrictions on the company's operations and financing activities, assigns the relative ranking of the indebtedness, and grants the rights and remedies that are available to the debt holders if the trust indenture covenants are violated. In particular, covenants typically: (a) restrain the issuance of new debt, (b) restrict the amount of prior-ranking indebtedness that may be issued, (c) govern asset acquisitions, asset dispositions, sale/leasebacks, and mergers and consolidations, (d) restrict junior debt redemption, (e) restrict borrowings by subsidiaries, and (f) restrict the payment of dividends to shareholders. Covenants protect the security of the debt holders under the trust indenture. Enforcement of the trust indenture, and its covenants, usually requires approval by a certain percentage of the debt holders. The so-called *boiler plate* covenants are common in most trust indentures. The boiler plate covenants on acquisitions: (1) prohibit acquisitions that weaken the asset security behind the outstanding debt and (2) require the survivor on acceptable acquisitions to assume the debt (*successor obligor clauses*). On default of any of the covenants, the holders of fifty percent of the debt may demand *acceleration* for all debt holders, the immediate payment of the outstanding principal and interest on the debt. Satisfying the covenants, therefore, is central to any acquisition of a publicly traded company.

In most cases on successor obligor clauses, the bondholders sue to stop asset sales in which a buyer does not agree to accept liability on the bonds, arguing, for example, that piece-by-piece asset sales violate the clause. See, e.g., *Liberty Media Corp. v Bank of N.Y. Mellon Trust Co., N.A.*, 2011 WL 1632333 (Del. Ch.). In the following case, the bondholders sued to stop a buyer from assuming the liability under the clause. Why?

---

13 Chemetall introduced evidence at trial that both Morton and Chemetall intended that the confidentiality agreement be assigned, and as noted above, Fraval is not challenging on appeal the sufficiency of that evidence.

SHARON STEEL CORP V. CHASE MANHATTAN BANK

United States Court of Appeals, Second Circuit, 1982.
691 F.2d 1039, *cert. denied*, 460 U.S. 1012 (1983).

WINTER, CIRCUIT JUDGE.

Between 1965 and 1977, UV issued debt instruments pursuant to five separate indentures, the salient terms of which we briefly summarize. In 1965, UV issued approximately $23 million of 5 3/8 percent subordinated debentures due in 1995, under an indenture naming The Chase Manhattan Bank, N.A. ("Chase") as the trustee ("First Chase Indenture")[Ed.[14]]. . . . In 1968, the City of Port Huron, Michigan, issued approximately $22 million in Industrial Development Revenue Bonds, bearing 6 ¼ percent interest and due in 1993, under an indenture also naming Chase as the trustee ("Second Chase Indenture"). Similarly, in 1968, the County of Itawamba, Mississippi, issued approximately $13 million in Industrial Development Revenue Bonds due in 1993, under an indenture naming Union Planters National Bank of Memphis as the trustee ("Union Planters Indenture"). In 1977, UV issued $75 million of 8 7/8 percent debentures due in 1997 under an indenture naming Manufacturers Hanover Trust Company ("Manufacturers") as the trustee ("Manufacturers Indenture"). At the same time, UV issued $25 million of 9 ¼ percent senior subordinated notes due in 1987 pursuant to an indenture under which United States Trust Company of New York ("U.S. Trust") is the trustee ("U.S. Trust Indenture"). . . .

The debentures, notes, and guaranties are general obligations of UV. Each instrument contains clauses permitting redemption by UV prior to the maturity date, in exchange for payment of a fixed redemption price (which includes principal, accrued interest and a redemption premium) and clauses allowing acceleration as a non-exclusive remedy in case of a default. The First Chase Indenture,[4] the Port Huron Lease Guaranty, the

---

14 [Ed. The rights of bondholders are stipulated in a private contract called an Indenture, which includes, among other things, various promises (covenants). Bond indenture forms are now highly standardized. The indentures provide for the appointment of an indenture trustee, usually a large commercial bank, to oversee and enforce the terms of the indenture. The bonds in the case bore rates of interest at lower than prevailing market rates, that is, the market rates of interest had raised after the bonds had been sold. This meant that the current market value of the bonds, the amount the bonds would fetch if resold on the open market, was less than the bonds' face amount (par, the amount payable on maturity). UV therefore did not want to pay off the bonds face value with the cash proceeds of its asset sales, it wanted to sell the bonds to someone else who would do what UV would do if it had not liquidated, that is, hold the bonds to maturity. UV and the purchaser, Sharon, could split the value of the benefit on not paying off the bonds.]

4 Section 13.01 of the First Chase Indenture reads as follows:

> Nothing in this Indenture or any of the Debentures contained shall prevent any merger or consolidation of any other corporation or corporations into or with the Company, or any merger or consolidation of the Company (either singly or with one or more corporations), into or with any other corporation, or any sale, lease, transfer or other disposition of all or substantially all of its property to any corporation lawfully entitled to acquire the same or prevent successive similar consolidations, mergers, sales, leases, transfers or other dispositions to which the Company or its successors or assigns or any subsequent successors or assigns shall be a party; provided, however, and the Company

Union Planters Lease Guaranty, the Manufacturers Indenture and the U.S. Trust Indenture each contains a "successor obligor" provision allowing UV to assign its debt to a corporate successor which purchases "all or substantially all" of UV's assets. If the debt is not assigned to such a purchaser, UV must pay off the debt. While the successor obligor clauses vary in language, the parties agree that the differences are not relevant to the outcome of this case.

The Liquidation of UV

During 1977 and 1978, UV operated three separate lines of business. One line, electrical equipment and components, was carried on by Federal Pacific Electric Company ("Federal"). In 1978, Federal generated 60 percent of UV's operating revenue and 81 percent of its operating profits. It constituted 44 percent of the book value of UV's assets and 53 percent of operating assets. UV also owned and operated oil and gas properties, producing 2 percent of its operating revenue and 6 percent of operating profits. These were 5 percent of book value assets and 6 percent of operating assets. UV also was involved in copper and brass fabrication, through Mueller Brass, and metals mining, which together produced 13 percent of profits, 38 percent of revenue and constituted 34 percent of book value assets and 41 percent of operating assets. In addition to these operating assets, UV had cash or other liquid assets amounting to 17 percent of book value assets.

On January 19, 1979, the UV Board announced its intention to liquidate UV, subject to shareholder approval. . . . On March 26, 1979, UV's shareholders approved the sale of Federal and the liquidation plan. The following day, UV filed its Statement of Intent to Dissolve with the Secretary of State of Maine, its state of incorporation. On March 29, the sale of Federal to the Reliance Electric subsidiary for $345 million in cash was consummated . . . On July 23, 1979, UV announced that it had entered into an agreement for the sale of most of its oil and gas properties to Tenneco Oil Company for $135 million cash. The deal was consummated as of October 2, 1979 and resulted in a net gain of $105 million to UV.

covenants and agrees, that any such consolidation or merger of the Company or any such sale, lease, transfer or other disposition of all or substantially all of its property, shall be upon the condition that the due and punctual payment of the principal of, interest and premium, if any, on, all of the Debentures, according to their tenor, and the due and punctual performance and observance of all the terms, covenants and conditions of this Indenture to be kept or performed by the Company shall, by an indenture supplemental hereto, executed and delivered to the Trustee, be assumed by any corporation formed by or resulting from any such consolidation or merger, or to which all or substantially all of the property of the Company shall have been sold, leased, transferred or otherwise disposed of (such corporation being herein called the "successor corporation"), just as fully and effectively as if the successor corporation had been the original party of the first part hereto, and such supplemental indenture shall be construed as and shall constitute a novation thereby releasing the Company (unless its identity be merged into or consolidated with that of the successor corporation) from all liability upon, under or with respect to any of the covenants or agreements of this Indenture but not, however, from its liability upon the Debentures.

The Sale to Sharon Steel

In November 1979, Sharon proposed to buy UV's remaining assets. UV and Sharon entered into an "Agreement for Purchase of Assets" and an "Instrument of Assumption of Liabilities" on November 26, 1979. Under the purchase agreement, Sharon purchased all of the assets owned by UV on November 26 (*i.e.,* Mueller Brass, UV's mining properties and $322 million in cash or the equivalent) for $518 million ($411 million of Sharon subordinated debentures due in 2000—then valued at 86 percent or $353,460,000—plus $107 million in cash). Under the assumption agreement, Sharon assumed all of UV's liabilities, including the public debt issued under the indentures. UV thereupon announced that it had no further obligations under the indentures or lease guaranties, based upon the successor obligor clauses.

On December 6, 1979, in an attempt to formalize its position as successor obligor, Sharon delivered to the Indenture Trustees supplemental indentures executed by UV and Sharon. The Indenture Trustees refused to sign. Similarly, Sharon delivered an assumption of the lease guaranties to both Chase and Union Planters but those Indenture Trustees also refused to sign.

The Successor Obligor Clauses

Successor obligor clauses are "boilerplate" or contractual provisions, which are standard in a certain genre of contracts. Successor obligor clauses are found in virtually all indentures. Such boilerplate must be distinguished from contractual provisions, which are peculiar to a particular indenture and must be given a consistent, uniform interpretation. Boilerplate provisions are thus not the consequence of the relationship of particular borrowers and lenders and do not depend upon particularized intentions of the parties to an indenture. There are no adjudicative facts relating to the parties to the litigation for a jury to find and the meaning of boilerplate provisions is, therefore, a matter of law rather than fact.

Moreover, uniformity in interpretation is important to the efficiency of capital markets. . . . Whereas participants in the capital market can adjust their affairs according to a uniform interpretation, whether it is correct or not as an initial proposition, the creation of enduring uncertainties as to the meaning of boilerplate provisions would decrease the value of all debenture issues and greatly impair the efficient working of capital markets. Such uncertainties would vastly increase the risks and, therefore, the costs of borrowing with no offsetting benefits either in the capital market or in the administration of justice. Just such uncertainties would be created if interpretation of boilerplate provisions were submitted to juries sitting in every judicial district in the nation.

Sharon's argument is a masterpiece of simplicity: on November 26, 1979, it bought everything UV owned; therefore, the transaction was a "sale" of "all" UV's "assets." In Sharon's view, the contention of the Indenture Trustees and Debentureholders that proceeds from earlier sales in a predetermined plan of piecemeal liquidation may not be counted in determining whether a later sale involves "all assets" must be rejected because it imports a meaning not evident in the language.

Sharon's literalist approach simply proves too much. If proceeds from earlier piecemeal sales are "assets," then UV continued to own "all" its "assets" even after the Sharon transaction since the proceeds of that transaction, including the $107 million cash for cash "sale," went into the UV treasury. If the language is to be given the "literal" meaning attributed to it by Sharon, UV's "assets" were not "sold" on November 26 and the ensuing liquidation requires the redemption of the debentures by UV. Sharon's literal approach is thus self-defeating.

Sharon argues that the sole purpose of successor obligor clauses is to leave the borrower free to merge, liquidate or to sell its assets in order to enter a wholly new business free of public debt and that they are not intended to offer any protection to lenders. On their face, however, they seem designed to protect lenders as well by assuring a degree of continuity of assets. Thus, a borrower that sells all its assets does not have an option to continue holding the debt. It must either assign the debt or pay it off.

Sharon seeks to rebut such inferences by arguing that a number of transactions, which seriously dilute the assets of a company, are perfectly permissible under such clauses. For example, UV might merge with or sell its assets to a company that has a miniscule equity base and is debt heavy. They argue from these examples that the successor obligor clause was not intended to protect borrowers from the kind of transaction in which UV and Sharon engaged.

We disagree. In fact, a substantial degree of protection against diluting transactions exists for the lender. Lenders can rely, for example, on the self-interest of equityholders for protection against mergers that result in a firm with a substantially greater danger of insolvency. So far as the sale of assets to such a firm is concerned, that can occur but substantial protection still exists since the more debt heavy the purchaser, the less likely it is that the seller's equityholders would accept anything but cash for the assets. A sale to a truly crippled firm is thus unlikely given the self-interest of the equityholders. After a sale, moreover, the lenders would continue to have the protection of the original assets. In both mergers and sales, complete protection against an increase in the borrower's risk is not available in the absence of more specific restrictions, but the self-interest of equityholders imposes a real and substantial limit to that increase in risk. The failure of successor obligor clauses to provide even more protection hardly permits an inference that they are designed solely for the benefit of borrowers.

Sharon poses hypotheticals closer to home in the hope of demonstrating that successor obligor clauses protect only borrowers: *e.g.*, a transaction involving a sale of Federal and the oil and gas properties in the regular course of UV's business followed by an $18 per share distribution to shareholders after which the assets are sold to Sharon and Sharon assumes the indenture obligations. To the extent that a decision to sell off some properties is not part of an overall scheme to liquidate and is made in the regular course of business it is considerably different from a plan of piecemeal liquidation, whether or not followed by independent and subsequent decisions to sell off the rest. A sale in the absence of a plan to liquidate is undertaken because the directors expect the sale to strengthen the corporation as a going concern. A plan of liquidation, however, may be undertaken solely because of the financial needs and opportunities or the tax status of the major shareholders. In the latter case, relatively quick sales may be at low prices or may break up profitable asset combinations, drastically increasing the lender's risks if the last sale assigns the public debt. In this case, for example, tax considerations compelled completion of the liquidation within 12 months. The fact that piecemeal sales in the regular course of business are permitted thus does not demonstrate that successor obligor clauses apply to piecemeal liquidations, allowing the buyer last in time to assume the entire public debt.

We hold, therefore, that protection for borrowers as well as for lenders may be fairly inferred from the nature of successor obligor clauses. The former are enabled to sell entire businesses and liquidate, to consolidate or merge with another corporation, or to liquidate their operating assets and enter a new field free of the public debt. Lenders, on the other hand, are assured a degree of continuity of assets.

Where contractual language seems designed to protect the interests of both parties and where conflicting interpretations are argued, the contract should be construed to sacrifice the principal interests of each party as little as possible. An interpretation which sacrifices a major interest of one of the parties while furthering only a marginal interest of the other should be rejected in favor of an interpretation which sacrifices marginal interests of both parties in order to protect their major concerns.

Of the contending positions, we believe that the Indenture Trustees and Debentureholders best accommodate the principal interests of corporate borrowers and their lenders. Even if the UV/Sharon transaction is held not to be covered by the successor obligor clauses, borrowers are free to merge, consolidate, or dispose of the operating assets of the business. Accepting Sharon's position, however, would severely impair the interests of lenders. Sharon's view would allow a borrowing corporation to engage in a piecemeal sale of assets, with concurrent liquidating dividends to that point at which the asset restrictions of an indenture prohibited further distribution. A sale of "all or substantially all" of the remaining assets could then be consummated, a new debtor substituted, and the liquidation of the borrower completed. The assignment of the public debt might thus be accomplished, even though the last sale might be nothing more than a cash for cash transaction in which the buyer purchases the public indebtedness. The UV/Sharon transaction is not so extreme, but the sale price paid by Sharon did include a cash for cash exchange of $107 million. Twenty-three percent of the sale price was, in fact, an exchange of dollars for dollars. Such a transaction diminishes the protection for lenders in order to facilitate deals with little functional significance other than substituting a new debtor in order to profit on a debenture's low interest rate. We hold, therefore, that boilerplate successor obligor clauses do not permit assignment of the public debt to another party in the course of a liquidation unless "all or substantially all" of the assets of the company at the time the plan of liquidation is determined upon are transferred to a single purchaser.

C. SUCCESSOR LIABILITY

1. ASSET ACQUISITIONS AND STATE LAW ON SUCCESSOR LIABILITY

Successor liability is the name given a group of legal doctrines that allocate liabilities in an acquisition. In acquisitions, the parties allocate liabilities in the acquisition contract using acquisition structure and supplementing specific agreements. The surprises come when courts do not respect the allocation. Most cases on successor liability, therefore, are cases in which a court attaches a creditor's claim to a purchaser that had thought it had left the liability with the seller.

In state corporate law, successor liability issues depend on the form of the transaction. State corporate law codes provide that when two firms merge, the surviving firm (or the new firm in the case of a consolidation) succeeds to the liabilities of the disappearing firm (or firms) automatically, as a matter of law. In a stock acquisition, the selling firm does not change form and retains all prior liabilities. In contrast, when the successor firm acquires some or all of the assets of the predecessor firm, the general rule is that the successor does not assume any liabilities, except as negotiated. Judges use several doctrines to disregard the parties' allocation in selected cases.

In asset acquisitions, the problem cases occur when a purchaser elects not to assume some of the major liabilities of the seller in the acquisition. If the seller does not pay the liabilities in full with the proceeds of the acquisition, the aggrieved creditors may attempt to follow the assets to the new owner and sue the buyer. The most sympathetic claimants are those *long-tail* (or *contingent* or *unvested*) claimants whose injuries do not occur until after the acquisition has closed and the seller has dissolved.

Products liability claimants are a high profile subgroup of long-tail claimants. The states fall into two camps on successor liability in products liability cases. The larger camp, represented by Illinois, follows a traditional rule of four exceptions, the most important of which is for *de facto mergers*. The smaller camp, represented by California, Michigan, and New Jersey, takes a more aggressive stance in favor of the long-tail creditors. The first case, *Cargo Partner*, details the basic de facto merger doctrine, the second case, *Ruiz*, deals with successor liability on products liability claims and conflicts of law problems.

CARGO PARTNER AG V. ALBATRANS, INC.

United States Court of Appeals, Second Circuit, 2003.
352 F.3d 41.

SACK, CIRCUIT JUDGE.

. . . Cargo Partner brought this diversity action against the defendant-appellee Chase, Leavitt (Customhouse Brokers) Inc. ("Chase-Leavitt") seeking to recover on a trade debt owed by Chase-Leavitt to Cargo Partner. Cargo Partner also brought suit against Albatrans, alleging that by purchasing all of Chase-Leavitt's assets, Albatrans became liable for Chase-Leavitt's debts, including its debt to Cargo Partner. . . .

* * *

It is undisputed that New York law applies to this case. Under New York law, there are at least three ways in which a corporation can acquire the business of another: The purchaser can buy the seller's capital stock, it can buy the seller's assets, or it can merge with the seller to form a single corporation. In the first case, the purchaser does not become liable for the seller's debts unless the stringent requirements for piercing the corporate veil are met. . . . Likewise, the purchaser of a corporation's assets does not, as a result of the purchase, ordinarily become liable for the seller's debts. . . . The amount paid for the assets would ordinarily be available to satisfy those debts, at least in part. So long as the buyer pays a bona fide, arm's-length price for the assets, there is no unfairness to creditors in thus limiting recovery to the proceeds of the sale—cash or other consideration roughly equal to the value of the purchased assets would take the place of the purchased assets as a resource for satisfying the seller's debts. Moreover, as the magistrate judge observed, allowing creditors to collect against the purchasers of insolvent debtors' assets would "give the creditors a windfall by increasing the funds available compared to what would have been available if no sale had taken place."[Ed.[15]] . . . Only in

[15] [Ed. The magistrate also noted that the imposition of expanded successor liability to trade creditors would make it more difficult for an insolvent business to be sold as a going concern,

the third case, when two corporations merge to become a single entity, is the successor corporation automatically liable for the debts of both predecessors; it *is* both predecessors.

New York recognizes four common-law exceptions to the rule that an asset purchaser is not liable for the seller's debts, applying to: (1) a buyer who formally assumes a seller's debts; (2) transactions undertaken to defraud creditors; (3) a buyer who de facto merged with a seller; and (4) a buyer that is a mere continuation of a seller. See *Schumacher,* 59 N.Y.2d at 245, 451 N.E.2d at 198, 464 N.Y.S.2d at 440 (1983). . . .[3]

A de facto merger occurs when a transaction, although not in form a merger, is in substance "a consolidation or merger of seller and purchaser." . . . Applying New York law, we have observed that:

> [T]o find that a de facto merger has occurred there must be [1] a continuity of the selling corporation, evidenced by the same management, personnel, assets and physical location; [2] a continuity of stockholders, accomplished by paying for the acquired corporation with shares of stock; [3] a dissolution of the selling corporation[;] and [4] the assumption of liabilities by the purchaser.
>
> *Arnold Graphics Indus.,* 775 F.2d at 42 . . . .[4]

* * *

We have no need to . . . determine whether all four factors must be present for there to be a de facto merger. Whichever test applies, we are confident that the doctrine of de facto merger in New York does not make a corporation that purchases assets liable for the seller's contract debts absent continuity of ownership.

The purpose of the doctrine of de facto merger is to "avoid [the] patent injustice which might befall a party simply because a merger has been called something else." . . . While each of the four factors in Fitzgerald (and their similar counterparts in Arnold) distinguish mergers from asset sales, continuity of ownership is the essence of a merger. . . . It is, by contrast, the nature of an asset sale that the seller's ownership interest in the entity is given up in exchange for consideration; the parties do not become owners together of what formerly belonged to each. Continuity of ownership might not alone establish a de facto merger, but as the magistrate judge correctly

increasing the likelihood of a piecemeal sale of assets at a lower price and thus reducing the amount available to creditors. Cargo Partner AG v. Albatrans, 207 F. Supp. 86, 112 (S.D.N.Y. 2002).]

[3] Some courts have observed that the mere-continuation and de-facto-merger doctrines are so similar that they may be considered a single exception.

[4] For example, a transaction in which a corporation acquires the assets of another corporation by (1) purchasing the assets of the seller with its stock; (2) assuming the liabilities of the seller; and (3) continuing the operations of the seller through itself but dissolving the seller would likely be treated as a de facto merger.

observed, it "is the 'substance'" of a merger. . . . Because there is no continuity of ownership here, the asset purchase was not "a merger . . . called something else."

* * *

It is true that a number of states, beginning with Michigan in *Turner v. Bituminous Casualty Co.*, 397 Mich. 406, 429–30, 244 N.W.2d 873, 883 (1976), and California in *Ray v. Alad Corp.*, 19 Cal.3d 22, 30–34, 560 P.2d 3, 8–11, 136 Cal.Rptr. 574, 579–82 (1977), have relaxed the requirement of continuity of ownership in products-liability cases. . . . But see . . . *Flaugher v. Cone Automatic Mach. Co.*, 30 Ohio St. 3d 60, 507 N.E.2d 331, 335–37 (1987). As far as we know it has never been applied, in this state or elsewhere, outside of the products-liability context.[Ed.[16]] This apparently reflects its use, specific to that area of law, to maintain strict liability for products despite the transfer of the assets that were used to produce them. . . .

* * *

. . . For the foregoing reasons, the decision and order of the district court dismissing the plaintiff's complaint with respect to Cargo Partner's assertion of the de facto merger doctrine is affirmed.

QUESTION

Are the parties more likely to treat trade creditors unfairly in stock-for-assets acquisitions than in cash-for-assets acquisitions?

RUIZ V. BLENTECH CORPORATION

United States Court of Appeals, Seventh Circuit, 1996.
89 F.3d 320.

CUDAHY, CIRCUIT JUDGE.

Felipe Ruiz's case turns on a rather mystifying choice-of-law problem. Ruiz, a citizen of Illinois, suffered an injury in his home state from an allegedly defective product manufactured in California by a California corporation. The manufacturer has dissolved, but another California corporation has followed in its footsteps by purchasing its principal assets and continuing its business. Ruiz seeks to make the successor corporation answer for his tort claims against the manufacturer. Illinois and California have different rules for determining when one corporation is responsible, as a successor, for the tort liabilities of its predecessors. The district court

---

[16] [Ed. See also Bielagus v. EMRE of New Hampshire Corp, 826 A,2d 559 (N.H. 2003) (refusing to apply continuity of enterprise or substantial continuation test to a commercial contract).]

concluded that Illinois' rules, which are less favorable to Ruiz, should apply. . . . We affirm.

Felipe Ruiz operated a screw conveyor in a food processing plant in Schiller Park, Illinois. On June 16, 1992, he somehow became entangled in the conveyor's machinery and sustained several grievous injuries, the most severe of which left him paralyzed. He soon filed a lawsuit in an Illinois state court, bringing claims of strict products liability and negligence, among others. The case was removed to the district court on the basis of diversity jurisdiction.

. . . Another defendant was Custom Stainless Equipment, the California corporation that had manufactured the conveyor in 1983 and had dissolved in 1986. The last defendant was an entity that Ruiz identified as the successor to Custom Stainless' liabilities in tort. When Custom Stainless dissolved, it sold all of its assets for cash to Blentech, another California corporation. Blentech continued to manufacture Custom Stainless' product lines under its own name, using the same product designs, the same factory, the same management, and the same employees. Ruiz contended in the district court that California law defined the relationship between Custom Stainless and Blentech and, therefore, between Blentech and himself. According to Ruiz's interpretation of that law, Blentech's assimilation of Custom Stainless included an assumption of strict liability for any defective products that Custom Stainless had manufactured.

. . . The fifth defendant, Blentech, resisted Ruiz's claim by arguing that it did not belong in the case at all. Blentech maintained that its purchase of Custom Stainless' assets had not involved a conveyance of Custom Stainless' tort liabilities, and it made this argument the basis for a motion for summary judgment. . . .

With respect to Ruiz's claim against Blentech, the choice-of-law analysis had crucial importance. Only two states have significant contacts with the issues raised. California was the place of the legal relationship between Custom Stainless and Blentech; and Illinois was the place of Ruiz's residence and his injury. The decisive issue in the case was whether Blentech had succeeded to Custom Stainless' liabilities by virtue of its purchase of Custom Stainless' assets and its business. Illinois and California shared a basic rule about corporate successor liability, but California provided an exception to that rule that was not available in Illinois.

Illinois mandates that, as a general rule of corporate law, a corporation that purchases the principal assets of another corporation does not assume the seller's liabilities arising from tort claims or from any other kind of claims. . . . Illinois does recognize four exceptions to this rule. The purchasing corporation assumes the seller's liabilities when: (1) it expressly agrees to assume them[Ed.[17]]; (2) the asset sale amounts to a de facto merger; (3) the purchaser is a mere continuation of the seller; (4) the sale is for the fraudulent purpose of escaping liability for the seller's obligations. . . . California's corporate law establishes the same general rule and the same four exceptions. *Ray v. Alad Corp.*, 19 Cal.3d 22, 136 Cal.Rptr. 574, 578, 560 P.2d 3, 7 (1977).

California departs from the Illinois rules, however, by adopting a fifth exception. That exception provides that a corporation that purchases a manufacturing business and continues to produce the seller's line of products assumes strict liability in tort for defects in units of the same product line previously manufactured and distributed by the seller. *Ray*, 136 Cal.Rptr. at 582, 560 P.2d at 11. This "products line" exception applies in cases involving tort claims where: (1) the plaintiff lacks an adequate remedy against the seller/manufacturer; (2) the purchaser knows about product risks associated with the line of products that it continues; and (3) the seller transfers goodwill associated with the product line.

The difference between Illinois' and California's rules is decisive here because Ruiz's case against Blentech depends entirely upon whether the "products line" exception applies. . . . Blentech did not acquire Custom Stainless' obligations to Ruiz under one of the four standard exceptions to the general rule of successor liability. Blentech has not agreed to assume that obligation. It did expressly agree to assume all of Custom Stainless' tort liabilities arising before the date of the asset sale in 1986, but it emphatically disclaimed all liabilities arising after that date, and Ruiz was not injured until 1992. Neither did Blentech and Custom Stainless combine their corporate identities, either through a de facto merger or through some other means. In either Illinois or California, a court will conclude that an asset sale merges two corporations or makes the buyer the continuation of the seller only if it finds an identity of ownership between the two. In effect, the de facto merger and continuation exceptions are identical; each exception depends upon an identity of ownership between the seller and purchaser. . . . When Custom Stainless sold its assets to Blentech, Custom Stainless' owners received cash, not stock, and they have not participated in the ownership of Blentech in any way. Finally, Ruiz makes no allegation that the asset sale between Blentech and Custom Stainless was an occasion

17 [Ed. The assumption, as all students of contract law know, can be *express* or *implied*. A determination of whether the purchaser expressly assumes an obligation of the seller focuses typically on provisions in the asset purchase agreement, usually the definition of the term "assumed liabilities" and the indemnity clause. Recently, courts have struggled with whether a general assumption of liability or indemnification clause includes an assumption of huge unforeseen claims. Compare Mobay Corp. v. Allied-Signal, Inc., 761 F.Supp. 345 (D. N.J. 1991) (purchaser did not, with a general indemnification clause, assume unforeseen Superfund or CERCLA claims), with Kessinger v. Grafco, Inc., 875 F.2d 153 (7th Cir. 1989) (purchaser, with a general assumption clause, did assume unforeseen products liability claims). A buyer's implied assumption of a seller's obligation is determined by the buyer's conduct indicating an intent to assume. If the buyer's conduct or oral representations are communicated to the claimant and relied on by the claimant, the equitable doctrine of estoppel may apply (the purchaser may be estopped from denying the assumption).]

for fraud; moreover, nothing in the record even remotely supports such an allegation. Thus, Blentech can be liable to Ruiz only if the "products line" exception applies. . . .

. . . The district court should have conducted one analysis for issues of successor liability and a separate analysis for issues of tort liability. As a matter of corporate law, the issue of successor liability pertains to different significant contacts than does the tort law issue of liability for Ruiz's injury. California clearly has the most significant contacts with a sale of corporate assets by one California corporation to another. Here both corporations have their principal places of business in California. Consequently, California corporate law should determine what liabilities, if any, were conveyed when Custom Stainless sold its business to Blentech. It is equally clear that Illinois has the most significant relationship to an alleged tort befalling one of its citizens within its borders. . . .

Part of the uncertainty over the nature of the "products line" exception comes from the fact that the exception has a variety of sources each of which articulates a different rationale for the exception and each of which places it within a different realm of substantive law. The way in which the exception is characterized may depend upon the source from which it comes. Michigan law has apparently established the "products line" exception as a means of making it easier to prove that the predecessor and successor corporations have effected a de facto merger, although the reasoning behind this conclusion is not entirely clear. *See Turner v. Bituminous Casualty Co.,* 397 Mich. 406, 244 N.W.2d 873, 879–80 (1976).[Ed.[18]] Therefore, in Michigan, the exception seems to be an instrument of corporate law that defines what must pass through an asset sale. In New Jersey, on the other hand, the Supreme Court has held that the exception has nothing to do with determining whether a de facto merger occurred. Instead, the court there held that the exception is an instrument for preserving the system of strict liability for products liability claims by imposing duties on manufacturers. *See Ramirez v. Amsted Indus., Inc.*, 86 N.J. 332, 431 A.2d 811, 819–20 (1981).

For our purposes, California's understanding of the nature of the "products line" exception is what matters. . . . At least with respect to this argument, Ruiz does not ask us to generate an abstract version of the exception out of the air and make it a part of Illinois law. In any event, this would be a futile effort because Illinois courts have so emphatically rejected this request when other claimants have made it. . . . California courts have quite clearly established that the exception is a matter of products liability

[18] [Ed. The Michigan test is often termed the continuity-of-enterprise doctrine and is understood to represent an expansion of the traditional de facto merger exception. While the de facto merger exception requires that the assets be sold for stock because such a transaction is the functional equivalent of a statutory merger, the continuity-of-enterprise exception dispenses with that requirement on the grounds that sales for stock and sales for cash should receive equal treatment.]

law, not corporate law. The California Supreme Court derived the exception from its line of cases prescribing strict liability in tort for injuries resulting from defective products. . . . Moreover, California has limited the application of the exception to cases in which it preserves a plaintiff's ability to collect on a valid strict liability claim. . . . In this way, California has established the "products line" exception as a means of advancing the cost-shifting purposes behind its regime of strict liability for injuries caused by defective products. Unlike Michigan, California has not employed the exception generally as a means to limit efforts by corporations to erase corporate identity in the course of asset sales. Instead, California uses the exception to insure that manufacturers generally will bear the costs of defective products.

As we have noted, Ruiz could maintain his case against Blentech only if the "products line" exception applied. Because the exception is a matter of California tort law, not California corporate law, it does not apply to this case. The judgment of the district court is, therefore, AFFIRMED.

DOMINE v. FULTON IRON WORKS, 76 Ill. App. 3d 253, 395 N.E.2d 19 (App. Ct. Ill. 1979):[19] . . . [W]e do not believe that the holding of the California Supreme Court in *Ray* is in conformity with the law of strict liability in this state.[Ed.[20]] . . . The corporate successor to the manufacturer of an allegedly defective product, who takes succession after the product has left the manufacturer's control, is clearly outside of the original producing and marketing chain. Such a corporate successor cannot fairly be said to have participated in placing the product into the stream of commerce. . . . In *Liberty Mutual Insurance Co. v. Williams Machine & Tool Co.* (1975), 62 Ill.2d 77, 82, 338 N.E.2d 857, 860, the court made it clear that: "The major purpose of strict liability is to place the loss caused by defective products on those who create the risk and reap the profit by placing a defective product in the stream of commerce."

The other policy considerations underlying imposition of strict liability are: (1) that the public interest in human life and health requires protection of law, and (2) that the manufacturer solicits and invites use of the product, thereby representing to the public that it is safe and suitable for use. The corporate successor to the manufacturer of a defective product cannot be said to have created the risk, and, except in a very remote way, does not reap the profit derived from sale of the product. Moreover, the successor

---

19 A later Illinois Court of Appeals case, Nguyen v. Johnson Mach. & Press Corp., 104 Ill. App.3d 1141, 433 N.E.2d 1101, 1111 (1982), added that, in rebuttal to the risk-spreading rationale of the New Jersey Supreme Court that followed *Ray*, the court doubted whether all successor companies, particularly small entrepreneurs, could spread the costs of injuries caused by manufactured products. The Illinois court noted that many small companies were unable to obtain insurance policies covering liability for injuries caused by a predecessor's products.

20 [Ed. Illinois courts pioneered strict liability in Suvada v. White Motor Co., 32 Ill.2d 612, 210 N.E.2d 182 (1965).]

corporation has neither invited use of the product nor represented to the public that the product is safe and suitable for use. Finally, we do not believe that the public interest in human life and health would be served by adoption of *Ray*.

NOTE: A DUTY TO WARN?

Some courts have held that a successor corporation that acquires the assets of another may have a duty to warn the predecessor's customers of product risks. The successor must have actual or constructive notice of the product's risks, know of the location of the owner, and have a relationship with the owner. A successor that continues service contracts entered into by a predecessor is at risk under the doctrine. E.g., *Schumacher v. Richards Shear Co.,* 59 N.Y. 239, 464 N.Y.S.2d 437, 451 N.E.2d 195,199 (1983).

2. SUCCESSOR LIABILITY AND FEDERAL STATUTES

a. Labor Law: A New Doctrine

GOLDEN STATE BOTTLING CO. V. NLRB

Supreme Court of the United States, 1973.
414 U.S. 168, 94 S.Ct. 414, 38 L.Ed.2d 388.

MR. JUSTICE BRENNAN delivered the opinion for a unanimous Court.

The principal question for decision in this case is whether the bona fide purchaser of a business, who acquires and continues the business with knowledge that his predecessor has committed an unfair labor practice in the discharge of an employee, may be ordered by the National Labor Relations Board to reinstate the employee with backpay.

Petitioners are Golden State Bottling Co., Inc. (Golden State), and All American Beverages, Inc. (All American). All American bought Golden State's soft drink bottling and distribution business after the National Labor Relations Board had ordered Golden State, "its officers, agents, successors, and assigns" to reinstate with back pay a driver-salesman, Kenneth L. Baker, whose discharge by Golden State was found by the Board to have been an unfair labor practice. In a subsequent backpay specification proceeding to which both Golden State and All American were parties, the Board found that All American continued after the acquisition to carry on the business without interruption or substantial changes in method of operation, employee complement, or supervisory personnel. In that circumstance, although All American was a bona fide purchaser of the business, unconnected with Golden State, the Board found that All American, having acquired the business with knowledge of the outstanding

Board order, was a "successor" for purposes of the National Labor Relations Act and liable for the reinstatement of Baker with backpay . . . .[2] We affirm.

* * *[5]

. . . [T]he board's order against All American strikes an equitable balance.[6] When a new employer, such as All American, has acquired substantial assets of its predecessor and continued, without interruption or substantial change, the predecessor's business operations, those employees who have been retained will understandably view their job situations as essentially unaltered. Under these circumstances, the employees may well perceive the successor's failure to remedy the predecessor employer's unfair labor practices arising out of an unlawful discharge as a continuation of the predecessor's labor policies. To the extent

2 [Ed. The NLRB position is summarized in the following footnote in the opinion:]

"To further the public interest involved in effectuating the policies of the Act and achieve the 'objectives of national labor policy, reflected in established principles of federal law,' we are persuaded that one who acquires and operates a business of an employer found guilty of unfair labor practices in basically unchanged form under circumstances which charge him with notice of unfair labor practice charges against his predecessor should be held responsible for remedying his predecessor's unlawful conduct.

In imposing this responsibility upon a bona fide purchaser, we are not unmindful of the fact that he was not a party to the unfair labor practices and continues to operate the business without any connection with his predecessor. However, in balancing the equities involved there are other significant factors, which must be taken into account. Thus, 'it is the employing industry that is sought to be regulated and brought within the corrective and remedial provisions of the Act in the interest of industrial peace.' When a new employer is substituted in the employing industry there has been no real change in the employing industry insofar as the victims of past unfair labor practices are concerned, or the need for remedying those unfair labor practices. Appropriate steps must still be taken if the effects of the unfair labor practices are to be erased and all employees reassured of their statutory rights. And, it is the successor who has taken over control of the business who is generally in the best position to remedy such unfair labor practices most effectively. The imposition of this responsibility upon even the bona fide purchaser does not work an unfair hardship upon him. When he substituted himself in place of the perpetrator of the unfair labor practices, he became the beneficiary of the unremedied unfair labor practices. Also, his potential liability for remedying the unfair labor practices is a matter which can be reflected in the price he pays for the business, or he may secure an indemnity clause in the sales contract which will indemnify him for liability arising from the seller's unfair labor practices."

5 We recognize that, unlike the situation in Wiley where state law provided some support for holding the successor by consolidation liable, . . . the general rule of corporate liability is that, when a corporation sells all of its assets to another, the latter is not responsible for the seller's debts or liabilities, except where (1) the purchaser expressly or impliedly agrees to assume the obligations; (2) the purchaser is merely a continuation of the selling corporation; or (3) the transaction is entered into to escape liability. The perimeters of the labor-law doctrine of successorship, however, have not been so narrowly confined. . . . Successorship has been found 'where the new employer purchases a part or all of the assets of the predecessor employer; (and) where the entire business is purchased by the new employer . . . . The refusal to adopt a mode of analysis requiring the Board to distinguish among mergers, consolidations, and purchases of assets is attributable to the fact that, so long as there is a continuity in the 'employing industry,' the public policies underlying the doctrine will be served by its broad application. . . .

6 A purchasing company cannot be obligated to carry out under s 10(c) every outstanding and unsatisfied order of the Board. For example, because the purchaser is not obligated by the Act to hire any of the predecessor's employees, . . . the purchaser, if it does not hire any or a majority of those employees, will not be bound by an outstanding order to bargain issued by the Board against the predecessor or by any order tied to the continuance of the bargaining agent in the unit involved. . . .

that the employees' legitimate expectation is that the unfair labor practices will be remedied, a successor's failure to do so may result in labor unrest as the employees engage in collective activity to force remedial action. Similarly, if the employees identify the new employer's labor policies with those of the predecessor but do not take collective action, the successor may benefit from the unfair labor practices due to a continuing deterrent effect on union activities. Moreover, the Board's experience may reasonably lead it to believe that employers intent on suppressing union activity may select for discharge those employees most actively engaged in union affairs, so that a failure to reinstate may result in a leadership vacuum in the bargaining unit. . . .

Avoidance of labor strife, prevention of a deterrent effect on the exercise of rights guaranteed employees by s 7 of the Act, . . . protection for the victimized employee—all-important policies subserved by the National Labor Relations Act . . . —are achieved at a relatively minimal cost to the bona fide successor. Since the successor must have notice before liability can be imposed, "his potential liability for remedying the unfair labor practices is a matter which can be reflected in the price he pays for the business, or he may secure an indemnity clause in the sales contract which will indemnify him for liability arising from the seller's unfair labor practices." . . . If the reinstated employee does not effectively perform, he may, of course, be discharged for cause. . . .

* * *

We agree with the Court of Appeals and add only the observation that its conclusion is buttressed by the consideration that an order requiring reinstatement and backpay is aimed at "restoring the economic status quo that would have obtained but for the company's wrongful refusal to reinstate . . . ." . . .[10]

Affirmed.

The federal circuit courts have used the *notice test* of *Golden State Bottling*, a test substantially broader than the common law successor liability test noted above, in finding successor liability in a variety of cases based on claims under federal statutes regulating employment. The courts have used the notice test in employment discrimination cases, see, e.g., *Rojas v. TK Commun., Inc.*, 87 F.3d 745 (5th Cir. 1996) (Title VII); *EEOC v. Vucitech*, 842 F.2d 936 (7th Cir. 1988) (same) and in cases on liability for pension obligations (delinquent pension contributions, termination liability and multi-employer withdrawal liability). E.g., *Chicago Truck*

---

[10] It is apparent that had Golden State already reinstated Baker with back pay before the sale of its business, and thereby fully complied with the Board's order, All American would have had no more obligation to employ him in the continuing business than it had to employ any of Golden State's other employees. . . .

Drivers, Helpers and Warehouse Workers Union Pension Fund v. Tasemkin, 59 F.3d 48 (7th Cir. 1995); *Stotter Div. of Graduate Plastic Co. v. District 65, United Auto Workers*, 991 F.2d 997 (2d Cir. 1993); *Brend v. Sames Corp.*, 2002 WL 1488877 (N.D. Ill.). See also *Steinbach v. Hubbard*, 15 F.3d 843 (9th Cir. 1994) (a claim for minimum wage under the Fair Labor Standards Act).

When dealing with collective bargaining agreements, however, the Supreme Court went off on another tangent altogether. Under state law a collective bargaining agreement, as a contractual obligation of the seller, would pass to the survivor in mergers, would remain with the seller (now owned by the buyer) in stock acquisitions,[21] and would pass to the buyer in asset acquisitions only if expressly assumed (or, if not, as a matter of equity under the de facto merger doctrine).[22] Consider how far we are from this basic set of rules in the following case on *successor employers*.

FALL RIVER DYEING & FINISHING CORP. V. NLRB

Supreme Court of the United States, 1987.
482 U.S. 27, 107 S.Ct. 2225, 96 L.Ed. 2d 22.

JUSTICE BLACKMUN delivered the opinion of the Court.

. . . For over 30 years before 1982, Sterlingwale operated a textile dyeing and finishing plant in Fall River, Mass. In the late 1970s the textile-dyeing business, including Sterlingwale's, began to suffer from adverse economic conditions and foreign competition. After 1979, business at Sterlingwale took a serious turn for the worse because of the loss of its export market, . . . and the company reduced the number of its employees. . . . Finally, in February 1982, Sterlingwale laid off all its production employees, primarily because it no longer had the capital to continue the converting business. . . . It retained a skeleton crew of workers and supervisors to ship out the goods remaining on order and to maintain the corporation's building and machinery. . . . In the months following the layoff, Leonard Ansin, Sterlingwale's president, liquidated the inventory of the corporation and, at the same time, looked for a business partner with whom he could "resurrect the business. . . . Ansin felt that he owed it to the community and to the employees to keep Sterlingwale in operation. . . .

For almost as long as Sterlingwale had been in existence, its production and maintenance employees had been represented by the United Textile Workers of America, AFL-CIO, Local 292 (Union). . . .

---

21 See U.S. Can Co. v. NLRB, 984 F.2d 864 (7th Cir. 1993) (Easterbrook, J., "perplexed" as to why the NLRB did not apply state law on a stock acquisitions to hold a target bound on a collective bargaining agreement).

22 The contract could contain protections against acquisitions, as do indentures or patent licenses that provide rights against sellers that negotiate acquisitions that do not satisfy specific covenants.

In late summer 1982, however, Sterlingwale finally went out of business. It made an assignment for the benefit of its creditors, . . . primarily Ansin's mother, who was an officer of the corporation and holder of a first mortgage on most of Sterlingwale's real property, . . . and the Massachusetts Capital Resource Corporation (MCRC), which held a security interest on Sterlingwale's machinery and equipment. . . . Ansin also hired a professional liquidator to dispose of the company's remaining assets, mostly its inventory, at auction. . . .

During this same period, a former Sterlingwale employee and officer, Herbert Chace, and Arthur Friedman, president of one of Sterlingwale's major customers, Marcamy Sales Corporation (Marcamy), formed petitioner Fall River Dyeing & Finishing Corp. . . . Chace and Friedman formed petitioner with the intention of engaging strictly in the commission-dyeing business and taking advantage of the availability of Sterlingwale's assets and work force. . . . Accordingly, Friedman had Marcamy acquire from MCRC and Ansin's mother Sterlingwale's plant, real property, and equipment . . . , and convey them to petitioner.[1] . . . Petitioner also obtained some of Sterlingwale's remaining inventory at the liquidator's auction. . . . Chace became petitioner's vice president in charge of operations and Friedman became its president. . . .

In September 1982, petitioner began operating out of Sterlingwale's former facilities and began hiring employees. . . . It advertised for workers and supervisors in a local newspaper, . . . and Chace personally got in touch with several prospective supervisors. . . . Petitioner hired 12 supervisors, of whom 8 had been supervisors with Sterlingwale and 3 had been production employees there. . . . In its hiring decisions for production employees, petitioner took into consideration recommendations from these supervisors and a prospective employee's former employment with Sterlingwale. . . . Petitioner's initial hiring goal was to attain one full shift of workers, which meant from 55 to 60 employees. . . .

By letter dated October 19, 1982, the Union requested petitioner to recognize it as the bargaining agent for petitioner's employees and to begin collective bargaining. . . . Petitioner refused the request, stating that, in its view, the request had "no legal basis." . . . At that time, 18 of petitioner's 21 employees were former employees of Sterlingwale. . . . By November of that year, petitioner had employees in a complete range of jobs, had its production process in operation, and was handling customer orders . . . , by mid-January 1983, it had attained its initial goal of one shift of workers. . . . Of the 55 workers in this initial shift, a number that represented over half the workers petitioner would eventually hire, 36 were former Sterlingwale employees. . . . Petitioner continued to expand its work force, and by mid-April 1983, it had reached two full shifts. For the first time, ex-Sterlingwale

1 Petitioner did not acquire one of the three buildings formerly used by Sterlingwale, App. 200–201, and closed one that it did acquire, *id.*, at 195.

employees were in the minority but just barely so (52 or 53 out of 107 employees). . . .

Although petitioner engaged exclusively in commission dyeing, the employees experienced the same conditions they had when they were working for Sterlingwale. The production process was unchanged and the employees worked on the same machines, in the same building, with the same job classifications, under virtually the same supervisors. . . . Over half the volume of petitioner's business came from former Sterlingwale customers, and, in particular, Marcamy. . . .

. . . Essentially for the reasons given by the Court of Appeals . . . however, we find that the Board's determination that there was "substantial continuity" between Sterlingwale and petitioner and that petitioner was Sterlingwale's successor is supported by substantial evidence in the record. Petitioner acquired most of Sterlingwale's real property, its machinery and equipment, and much of its inventory and materials.[10] It introduced no new product line. Of particular significance is the fact that, from the perspective of the employees, their jobs did not change. Although petitioner abandoned converting dyeing in exclusive favor of commission dyeing, this change did not alter the essential nature of the employees' jobs because both types of dyeing involved the same production process. The job classifications of petitioner were the same as those of Sterlingwale; petitioner's employees worked on the same machines under the direction of supervisors most of whom were former supervisors of Sterlingwale. The record, in fact, is clear that petitioner acquired Sterlingwale's assets with the express purpose of taking advantage of its predecessor's work force.

We do not find determinative of the successorship question the fact that there was a 7-month hiatus between Sterlingwale's demise and petitioner's start-up. Petitioner argues that this hiatus, coupled with the fact that its employees were hired through newspaper advertisements—not through Sterlingwale employment records, which were not transferred to it—resolves in its favor the "substantial continuity" question. . . .[11] We thus must consider if and when petitioner's duty to bargain arose.

---

[10] Petitioner makes much of the fact that it purchased the assets of Sterlingwale on the "open market." . . . Petitioner, however, overlooks the fact that it was formed with the express purpose of acquiring Sterlingwale's assets, a purpose it accomplished by having its parent company acquire some of Sterlingwale's major assets and then transferring them to petitioner. So long as there are other indicia of "substantial continuity," the way in which a successor obtains the predecessor's assets is generally not determinative of the "substantial continuity" question. . . .

[11] Similarly, in light of the general continuity between Sterlingwale and petitioner from the perspective of the employees, we do not find determinative the differences between the two enterprises cited by petitioner. Petitioner's change in marketing and sales . . . appears to have had no effect on the employer-employee relationship. That petitioner did not assume Sterlingwale's liabilities or trade name, *id.*, at 16, also is not sufficient to outweigh the other factors. . . . Moreover, the mere reduction in petitioner's size, in comparison to that of Sterlingwale . . . , does not change the nature of the company so as to defeat the employees' expectations in continued representation by their Union. . . .

In *Burns,* the Court determined that the successor had an obligation to bargain with the union because a majority of its employees had been employed by Wackenhut. . . . The "triggering" fact for the bargaining obligation was this composition of the successor's work force. . . . In other situations, as in the present case, there is a start-up period by the new employer while it gradually builds its operations and hires employees. In these situations, the Board, with the approval of the Courts of Appeals, has adopted the "substantial and representative complement" rule for fixing the moment when the determination as to the composition of the successor's work force is to be made. If, at this particular moment, a majority of the successor's employees had been employed by its predecessor, then the successor has an obligation to bargain with the union that represented these employees. . . . Accordingly, as found by the Board and approved by the Court of Appeals, mid-January was the period when petitioner reached its "substantial and representative complement." Because at that time the majority of petitioner's employees were former Sterlingwale employees, petitioner had an obligation to bargain with the Union then. . . .

JUSTICE POWELL, with whom THE CHIEF JUSTICE and JUSTICE O'CONNOR join, dissenting.

In this case, the undisputed evidence shows that petitioner is a completely separate entity from Sterlingwale. There was a clear break between the time Sterlingwale ceased normal business operations in February 1982 and when petitioner came into existence at the end of August. In addition, it is apparent that there was no direct contractual or other business relationship between petitioner and Sterlingwale. . . . Although petitioner bought some of Sterlingwale's inventory, it did so by outbidding several other buyers on the open market. Also, the purchases at the public sale involved only tangible assets. Petitioner did not buy Sterlingwale's trade name or goodwill, nor did it assume any of its liabilities. And, while over half of petitioner's business (measured in dollars) came from former Sterlingwale customers, apparently this was due to the new company's skill in marketing its services. There was no sale or transfer of customer lists, and given the 9-month interval between the time that Sterlingwale ended production and petitioner commenced its operations in November, the natural conclusion is that the new business attracted customers through its own efforts. No other explanation was offered. . . . Any one of these facts standing alone may be insufficient to defeat a finding of successorship, but together they persuasively demonstrate that the Board's finding of "substantial continuity" was incorrect. . . .

Even if the evidence of genuine continuity were substantial, I could not agree with the Court's decision. As we have noted in the past, if the presumption of majority support for a union is to survive a change in ownership, it must be shown that there is both a continuity of conditions *and* a continuity of work force. . . . This means that unless a majority of the new company's workers had been employed by the former company, there is no justification for assuming that the new employees wish to be represented by the former union, or by any union at all. . . . Indeed, the rule hardly could be otherwise. It would be contrary to the basic principles of the NLRA simply to presume in these cases that a majority of workers supports a union when more than half of them have never been members, and when there has been no election. . . .

In my view, the Board's decision to measure the composition of petitioner's work force in mid-January is unsupportable. . . . In fact, less than three months after the duty to bargain allegedly arose, petitioner had nearly doubled the size of its mid-January work force by hiring the remaining 50-odd workers it needed to reach full production. This expansion was not unexpected; instead, it closely tracked petitioner's original forecast for growth during its first few months in business. Thus, there was no reasonable basis for selecting mid-January as the time that petitioner should have known that it should commence bargaining.

QUESTION

Why are control change clauses, requiring consent on control changes, not more common in collective bargaining agreements? Should courts supply them if labor unions do not bargain for them? Can labor unions waive the successor employer doctrine in exchange for higher wages?

NOTE: SUCCESSORSHIP OF A DUTY TO ARBITRATE OR A DUTY TO BARGAIN

There is a distinction between rights deriving from a collective bargaining agreement and rights deriving from the National Labor Relations Act (NLRA), as were in issue in *Fall River Dyeing & Finishing* and *Golden State Bottling*. A collective bargaining agreement is fundamentally a contract between workers and an employer. Parties litigate claims deriving from the NLRA as *unfair labor practice* claims; the National Labor Relations Board adjudicates those claims, subject to appellate review. An important unfair labor practice claim against a successor employer, as was in issue in *Fall River Dying & Finishing*, is the refusal to bargain with a recognized labor union.

Imposing a duty to bargain on a successor employer is not as severe as imposing a duty to arbitrate on a successor employer and the Supreme Court has done the former while refusing to do the latter on a given set of facts. *NLRB v. Burns Intern. Sec. Serv. Inc.*, 406 U.S. 272, 281–82, 287–88 (1972):

> It does not follow, however, from Burns' duty to bargain that it was bound to observe the substantive terms of the collective-

> bargaining contract the union had negotiated with Wackenhut and to which Burns had in no way agreed. . . .
>
> * * *
>
> We also agree with the Court of Appeals that holding either the union or the new employer bound to the substantive terms of an old collective-bargaining contract may result in serious inequities. A potential employer may be willing to take over a moribund business only if he can make changes in corporate structure, composition of the labor force, work location, task assignment, and nature of supervision. Saddling such an employer with the terms and conditions of employment contained in the old collective-bargaining contract may make these changes impossible and may discourage and inhibit the transfer of capital. On the other hand, a union may have made concessions to a small or failing employer that it would be unwilling to make to a large or economically successful firm. . . .

Imposing a duty to bargain on a successor is significant for various reasons. It recognizes a bargaining relationship between an employer and a union and an agency relationship between a union and a group of employees. Without it, a union has to engage in an organizing drive, which is typically very costly and has an uncertain outcome. When the duty to bargain applies, the employer must bargain with the union over mandatory topics, risking an economic strike if a contract is not signed. Under §§ 8(a)(5) and 8(b)(3), it is an unfair labor practice for an employer or a union "to refuse to bargain collectively."

Section 8(d) defines collective bargaining as "the performance of the mutual obligation of the employer and the representative of the employees to meet at reasonable times and confer in good faith with respect to wages, hours, and other terms and conditions of employment." While the parties have an obligation to meet and confer in good faith, that obligation "does not compel either party to agree to a proposal or require the making of a concession." Moreover, the new employer may be unable to institute changes unilaterally in mandatory topics without first bargaining to impasse. Finally, the duty to bargain forces the parties to disclose information in certain defined contexts. For example, when an employer claims that it is financially unable to meet the union's demands, it must corroborate such claims on request.

Once a business and a union sign a collective bargaining agreement, parties are expected to abide by the terms of the agreement. If either side believes the other is not following the terms of the agreement, that party may seek relief before the NLRB. Most collective bargaining agreements have arbitration clauses creating a duty to arbitrate grievances before the claims can reach the NLRB. When a successor employer refuses to pay wages stipulated under a collective bargaining agreement signed by a predecessor employer (and not expired at the time of the acquisition) and refuses to arbitrate the union's resulting grievance, the Supreme Court has held that the successor employer has breached its duty to arbitrate. See *John Wiley & Sons, Inc. v. Livingston*, 376 U.S. 543, 550–51 (1964):

> While the principles of law governing ordinary contracts would not bind to a contract an unconsenting successor to a contracting party, a collective bargaining agreement is not an ordinary contract. . . . Central to the peculiar status and function of a collective bargaining agreement is the fact, dictated both by circumstance . . . , and by the requirements of the National Labor Relations Act, that it is not in any real sense the simple product of a consensual relationship. Therefore, although the duty to arbitrate, as we have said . . . , must be founded on a contract, the impressive policy considerations favoring arbitration are not wholly overborne by the fact that Wiley did not sign the contract being construed. . . . We thus find Wiley's obligation to arbitrate this dispute in the Interscience contract construed in the context of a national labor policy.
>
> We do not hold that in every case in which the ownership or corporate structure of an enterprise is changed the duty to arbitrate survives. As indicated above, there may be cases in which the lack of any substantial continuity of identity in the business enterprise before and after a change would make a duty to arbitrate something imposed from without, not reasonably to be found in the particular bargaining agreement and the acts of the parties involved. . . .

Subsequent courts have struggled with a now divided successor employer standard. There seems to be one class of successor employers that has a duty to bargain but not a duty to arbitrate and another than must arbitrate terms. The delineation of the two classes is not well defined. See *Local 348-S, UFCW, AFL-CIO v. Meridian Mgt. Corp.*, 583 F.3d 65 (2d Cir. 2010) (2–1 for a broad rather than a narrow application of a duty to arbitrate to successor employers). Moreover, once a successor employer has a duty to arbitrate, what does an arbitrator do? Logically one would suspect that the entire collective bargaining contract applies to the new employer, but some courts have suggested that the arbitrator has the power to rewrite the terms of the contract for the new employer. *Id.* (J. Livingston in dissent referred to the standard as a "freewheeling balancing test").[23]

Courts have made it clear that an asset purchaser cannot avoid a duty to bargain, or in an appropriate case a duty to arbitrate, by discriminating against employees of the seller because of their union status. For example, a new employer may not discover from the old employer the union

---

[23] The Livingston dissent attempts to apply state law on corporate form to the duty to arbitrate test, a very sensible endeavor. The Supreme Court should reconsider the broad language of the *Wiley* decision that divorced the successor employer test from state law on acquisition form. The irony is that the acquisition in *Wiley* was a statutory merger and the Court did not need to create a successor employer test to hold the survivor bound by a collective bargaining agreement of a constituent party to the merger; state law provided for it.

sympathies of its employees and refuse to hire those identified as sympathetic. The cases suggest that, if a new employer maintains the old operations intact, hiring new, inexperienced, nonunion employees in preference to experienced union employees, judges will presume anti-union animus. By contrast, if a purchaser substantially changes operations so that experience in the old operation would be of little value in the new operation, no such inference lies.

In *Burns*, the defendant, held to be a successor employer, did not buy the assets of their predecessor; there was no acquisition. See also *Canteen Corp. v NLRB*, 103 F.3d 1355 (7th Cir. 1997). The employer provided services previously provided by its predecessor. This is the ultimate extension of the successor liability concept. Liability not only attaches to assets or a business sold for value but also to a job site.

The challenge for the drafters of a doctrine of successor employer is to preserve an employer's option of selling assets to a new business, particularly if the old business is marginally solvent, while blocking acquisitions designed primarily to break collective bargaining agreements on existing, successful businesses. Labor economists label the wage reduction motivation opportunistic behavior. Firms use acquisitions to secure a larger share of the joint surplus generated by the interaction of a wealth-producing employee group and the firm's capital assets. See, e.g., Edward B. Rock & Michael L. Wachter, *Labor Law Successorship: A Corporate Law Approach*, 92 MICH. L. REV. 203 (1993). Does *Fall River Dyeing & Finishing* establish the right rule?

b. Environmental Liabilities

NEW YORK V. NATIONAL SERVICES INDUS., INC.

United States Court of Appeals, Second Circuit, 2006.
460 F.3d 201.

SOTOMAYOR, CIRCUIT JUDGE.

This appeal presents a question of successor liability under the Comprehensive Environmental Response Compensation and Liability Act of 1980 ("CERCLA"), 42 U.S.C. §§ 9601–9675 (2000). Specifically, the question before us is whether federal common law for purposes of determining corporate successor liability under CERCLA incorporates state law—in this case, New York law—or displaces state law in favor of a uniform national rule derived from traditional common-law principles. We must then determine whether, under the applicable governing law, defendant-counterclaimant-appellee National Service Industries, Inc. ("NSI") is liable as the legal successor to Serv-All Uniform Rental Corp. ("Serv-All"). For the reasons that follow, we find that we need not decide whether federal common law under CERCLA would displace state law because the claim of plaintiff-counter-defendant-appellant the State of

New York ("the State") would fail under either New York or traditional common law. That is, we hold that New York follows the traditional common-law rules of successor liability, which would govern if state law did not provide the rule of decision, and which require some evidence of continuity of ownership to find the existence of a de facto merger, and thus, successor liability. For that reason, we also hold that the State's common-law unjust enrichment and restitution claims fail. . . .

I. Facts

From 1962 to 1988, Serv-All operated a uniform rental business that served customers on Long Island. It delivered its clients clean uniforms, and picked up and cleaned the soiled ones. Until the mid-1980s, Serv-All cleaned the uniforms itself using a dry-cleaning process. In 1978, it arranged to have several dozen drums of perchloroethelyne, a hazardous substance used in dry cleaning, disposed of at the Blydenburgh Landfill in Islip, New York. In soil, perchloroethelyne decomposes into several chemicals, including vinyl chloride. Both perchloroethelyne and vinyl chloride are considered hazardous substances under CERCLA. *See* 42 U.S.C. § 9602; 40 C.F.R. § 302.4 (2005). Since 1983, the Blydenburgh Landfill has been listed in the New York Registry of Hazardous Waste Sites and in 1987 was added to the National Priority List of contaminated sites. Because Serv-All arranged for the disposal of the perchloroethelyne, the parties do not dispute that Serv-All was a potentially responsible party under CERCLA. *See* 42 U.S.C. § 9607(a)(3).

In October 1988, Serv-All sold almost all of its assets, including its customer list, current contracts, trucks, good will, and the right to use its name to Initial Service Investments ("Initial") for approximately $2.2 million. Ralph Colantuni and William Lepido, Serv-All's owners, also signed a covenant not to compete with Initial in the area for seven years. Initial operated the uniform rental business in large measure as Serv-All had done before the sale. It used the Serv-All name and trucks, and employed some of Serv-All's management and support personnel and all but one of Serv-All's former drivers. Initial did not continue Serv-All's practice of dry-cleaning uniforms, however, but instead laundered them in water at one of its facilities.

After the transaction, Serv-All changed its name to C-L Dissolution Corporation and adopted a liquidation plan. On January 27, 1989, C-L Dissolution Corporation formally dissolved. In 1992, NSI bought all shares of Initial's stock. On August 31, 1995, Initial merged into NSI.

Meanwhile, the State conducted a clean-up of the Blydenburgh Landfill, for which it incurred response costs that, as of 2002, exceeded $12 million with interest. . . .

* * *

II. Choice of Law

The first question before us is what law provides the rule of decision governing corporate successor liability under CERCLA. We conclude, like the district court did, that we need not decide this question because the outcome would be the same whether we apply state law or a national rule derived from traditional common-law principles. To reach this conclusion, however, we review the analysis by which CERCLA choice-of-law questions should be resolved.

CERCLA does not specifically provide that a successor corporation may be held liable for response costs. Nevertheless, we have held that CERCLA encompasses successor liability. Thus, strictly speaking, federal law (i.e., federal common law) governs successor liability under CERCLA. *See United States v. Kimbell Foods, Inc.,* 440 U.S. 715, 727, 99 S.Ct. 1448, 59 L.Ed.2d 711 (1979). In giving content to that law, however, we must decide whether to "adopt state law or . . . fashion a nationwide federal rule." *Id.* at 728, 99 S.Ct. 1448. . . .

* * *

B.

Generally, "[i]n the absence of congressional guidance on the issue of what law to apply, we look to the three-part test enunciated by the Supreme Court in *United States v. Kimbell Foods, Inc.*" *VKK Corp. v. Nat'l Football League,* 244 F.3d 114, 122 (2d Cir.2001). Under *Kimbell Foods,* courts determining whether federal common law should displace state law must consider: (1) whether the federal program, by its very nature, requires uniformity; (2) whether application of state law would frustrate specific objectives of the federal program; and (3) whether application of a uniform federal rule would disrupt existing commercial relationships based on state law. 440 U.S. at 728–29, 99 S.Ct. 1448. . . .

The choice-of-law question is a complicated one that has led our sister circuits to reach different answers. [Ed. The First, Sixth, Ninth, and Eleventh Circuits look to state law and the Third and Fourth Circuits favor the application of a uniform federal common law rule.]

. . . [T]he *Kimbell Foods* factors appear to favor the absorption (non-displacement) of state law. . . . Although CERCLA is a federal statute for which there is presumably an interest in uniform application, where there is no conflict between federal policy and the application of state law, "a mere federal interest in uniformity is insufficient to justify displacing state law in favor of a federal common law rule." *Betkoski II,* 112 F.3d at 91 (citing *O'Melveny & Myers,* 512 U.S. at 87–88, 114 S.Ct. 2048); *VKK Corp.,* 244 F.3d at 121–22; *see also Kamen v. Kemper Fin. Servs.,* 500 U.S. 90, 98, 111 S.Ct. 1711, 114 L.Ed.2d 152 (1991) ("The presumption that state law should be incorporated into federal common law is particularly strong in areas in which private parties have entered legal relationships in the expectation that their rights would be governed by state-law standards. . . . Corporate law is one such area.").

Here, NSI points to no conflict between the application of state law and the federal interests at issue in CERCLA, and we fail to see one. . . . New York law embraces successor liability and the tests it uses to define successor liability are not unduly restrictive. In fact, according to the State, New York's standards for finding successor liability under the de facto merger exception are *more* expansive than traditional common-law principles. Nevertheless, because the State's claim fails under either New York law or traditional common-law principles, we need not, and thus do not, decide whether CERCLA requires the displacement of state law in this instance.

II. The Law of Successor Liability

Under both New York law and traditional common law, a corporation that purchases the assets of another corporation is generally not liable for the seller's liabilities. . . . Hence, as noted above, a buyer of a corporation's assets will be liable as its successor if: "(1) it expressly or impliedly assumed the predecessor's tort liability, (2) there was a consolidation or merger of seller and purchaser, (3) the purchasing corporation was a mere continuation of the selling corporation, or (4) the transaction is entered into fraudulently to escape such obligations." *Schumacher,* 59 N.Y.2d at 245, 464 N.Y.S.2d 437, 451 N.E.2d 195; *accord N. Shore Gas Co.,* 152 F.3d at 651 (traditional common-law principles).

A.

The exception for the "consolidation or merger of seller and purchaser" is at issue here. The State claims that Serv-All's sale of its assets to Initial (now NSI) was, in fact, a de facto merger of Serv-All into Initial. As noted, "[a] de facto merger occurs when a transaction, although not in form a merger, is in substance 'a consolidation or merger of seller and purchaser.' " *Cargo Partner AG v. Albatrans, Inc.,* 352 F.3d 41, 45 (2d Cir.2003) (quoting *Schumacher,* 59 N.Y.2d at 245, 464 N.Y.S.2d 437, 451 N.E.2d 195). At common law, the hallmarks of a de facto merger include: (1) continuity of ownership; (2) cessation of ordinary business and dissolution of the acquired corporation as soon as possible; (3) assumption by the purchaser of the liabilities ordinarily necessary for the uninterrupted continuation of the business of the acquired corporation; and (4) continuity of management, personnel, physical location, assets, and general business operation. *See generally N. Shore Gas Co.,* 152 F.3d at 652 & n. 6; . . . .

NSI does not dispute, for purposes of this appeal, that the transaction between Initial (now NSI) and Serv-All satisfies the last three elements of the test: Initial assumed Serv-All's customer contracts, kept the Serv-All name, uniforms, vehicles, and many of its employees, and the former Serv-All company ceased to exist soon after the sale. Both parties also agree that there is no continuity of ownership between Initial, the purchasing corporation, and Serv-All, the selling corporation, because the transaction was for cash and there is no evidence that the previous owners of Serv-All have continued to profit from the company in any way. Moreover, the State does not dispute that if traditional common law were to supply the rule of decision, the four-part de facto merger test would apply. . . . Nor does it challenge the district court's conclusion that under the four-part test there has been no de facto merger because there is no evidence of continuity of ownership between NSI and Serv-All. . . . Instead, the State asserts that New York law is broader than traditional common law and is unsettled with respect to whether a de facto merger requires continuity of ownership. . . .

* * *

. . . Accordingly, because we find that New York would not depart from the traditional common law to find a de facto merger in the absence of any evidence of continuity of ownership, we are not presented with an "exceptional" circumstance that would require certification of this question to the New York Court of Appeals. . . .

NOTE: SUCCESSOR LIABILITY UNDER CERCLA—MERE CONTINUATION OR SUBSTANTIAL CONTINUITY?

Some circuits, applying a federal common law would apply the *substantial continuity* (or *continuity of enterprise*) rule from the labor law cases.[24] Others, like the Second Circuit have held that the substantial continuity test is not a sufficiently established part of the common law and that the doctrinal origin of the test, the *mere continuation* test, is more appropriate. Moreover, those circuit courts applying state law from Michigan or New Jersey would use the substantial continuity test. The substantial continuity test relaxes the continuity of ownership requirement of the mere continuation test. The substantial continuity test focuses on the continuity of the business rather than on ownership: Are the same employees doing the same jobs under the same supervisors, working conditions, and production processes and producing the same products for the same customers?

Which test is preferable on pure policy grounds?

Judge Leval, concurring in an earlier opinion in the *National Services Industries* case,[25] criticizes the fairness of applying the substantial continuity test to CERCLA claims.

---

[24] For an example see North Shore Gas Co. v. Salomon, Inc., 152 F.3d 642 (7th Cir. 1998) (applying a "hybrid" test).

[25] New York v. National Services Indus., Inc., 352 F.3d 682, 693–94 (2d Cir. 2003) (Leval, J., concurring).

If a seller's CERCLA liability could be imposed on a purchaser of assets merely because it continued substantially unchanged from the operations of the seller, the rule would result in disastrously unfair consequences, which furthermore would be harmful to the economy as a whole. In many circumstances, a purchaser of assets, buying with the intention of continuing the business being sold, would have no knowledge, and no reasonable way of learning, that the assets were burdened with liability. Businesses that engage in illegal dumping of toxic wastes often do so in secret, arranging for furtive nocturnal dumping by unlicensed carriers. Such a seller will have no records of its illegal dumping and will certainly not volunteer the information to the purchaser of its assets. In addition, in many instances, the dumping that gives rise to liability was done long in the past, at a time when such activities were unregulated and no records were maintained. Even assuming good faith among all participants in the purchase and sale, there may be no reasonable way for the purchaser to learn about the seller's history of disposal of toxic wastes because none of the present employees of the seller were employed when the disposal occurred and the seller has no records of the disposal.

Thus, a good faith buyer of assets, who does all reasonable due diligence, and has no reason to suspect liability, may learn too late that assets purchased at full going-business value came with a hidden liability that might vastly exceed their value. Business assets purchased in good faith for $1 million might easily bring liabilities of $5 million or $10 million in cleanup costs.

A rule of successor liability that threatened good-faith buyers with huge, unpredictable liability would also impose serious systemic costs on the economy. Such a rule would depress the price purchasers would be willing to pay for assets, as buyers would risk acquiring massive hidden liability. At the very least, buyers would need to purchase expensive liability insurance, which would reduce the market value of assets offered for sale. Asset purchasers might also favor piecemeal purchases at breakup value, in preference to purchasing at going-business value to continue the operation, resulting in both depression of the market value of the assets and the destruction of the jobs of those previously employed in the seller's operation. Nor is the unfairness that would result from the imposition of such capricious, arbitrary liabilities on innocent good faith purchasers nullified by the theoretical availability of insurance. This is so for at least three reasons. First, as noted, insurance would impose premium costs on all purchasers, thus diminishing the value of the assets being sold. Second, insurance policies have limits on the amount of coverage. Cleanup costs can be so extraordinarily high as to exceed the available coverage. Third, an arbitrary and unfair imposition of a substantial liability on a blameless party is no less unfair or arbitrary (although less drastic) when its impact is dispersed by the insurance mechanism among numerous blameless parties.

Those who favor the substantial test for CERCLA liabilities on the other side, see *North Shore Gas*, want the private assets that produced the pollution available to pay for the pollution cleanup. Using an acquisition to separate the assets from the liability appears inherently unfair regardless of the bona fides of the purchaser. Moreover, if the purchaser knows the substantial continuity rule, she knows the risks of any asset purchase and can take steps to protect herself. She is on notice. She, as noted in the next subsection, can buy new insurance, do an investigation of the seller's business, demand indemnification backed by an escrow of the acquisition funds and so on. She has only herself to blame if she is surprised.

Judge Leval would impose successor CERCLA liability on an asset purchaser only if the purchaser is a participant in a fraudulent attempt to avoid the liability. The owners in a single-firm reorganization qualify under the mere continuation exception. If the same owners and the same business buy their former business they are liable as successor. If an independent purchaser buys the assets they are not. Judge Leval does not discuss fairness for independent purchasers who have actual notice of the CERCLA liabilities.[26]

An economist would argue that fairness is not the issue. The key to environmental regulation is forcing those who pollute to internalize fully all costs of contamination. If regulation is successful, all business decisions must fully factor in the cost of the environmental risk of any activity. Continuing the theory, if regulation successfully does internalize contamination costs, a clear social benefit also exists for allowing firms to allocate freely potential environmental liabilities in acquisitions. In a typical acquisition, the firm that can absorb the risk at the lowest cost, whether the selling firm or the buying firm, will retain or acquire the liabilities. The other party to the negotiation will pay to avoid the liabilities. Several possible explanations, excluding avoidance behavior, exist as to why one firm may be able to bear the risk at a lower cost. For instance, one firm may be better able to diversify the risk of incurring large cleanup costs or may be better able to handle cleanup situations when they occur.

In practice, however, the benefits of free transferability may be outweighed by the enforcement costs. CERCLA's absolute prohibition of contracts releasing liability reflects the belief that if firms are allowed to transfer environmental liabilities, the firms will find a way to avoid the liabilities at the expense of the government. A second best solution (second best because it does not allow for efficient allocations of environmental liability in acquisitions) is a rule that irrevocably ties environmental liability to the

---

26 Are they liable based on the notice? Or must they have specific notice that the liabilities will not be satisfied after the acquisition (even if the purchase proceeds are applied)? Or specific notice that the purchase proceeds will not be used towards the liabilities at all (they will be diverted)? If one adopts some form of a notice test exception to a fairness test, will only actual notice do or will constructive notice (the purchase should have known) also suffice? If only actual notice causes purchaser liability then all purchasers will be, to the extent possible, purposefully ignorant.

operating assets of a business. In theory, if purchasers of a business must pay for any environmental damage caused by the sellers' prior operation of the business, then purchasers will pay less for the business on transfer and the seller will have internalized the environmental costs of any of its pre-transaction activity. See generally Merritt B. Fox, *Corporate Successors under Strict Liability: A General Economic Theory and the Case of CERCLA,* 26 WAKE FOREST L. REV. 183 (1991).

Because of enormous information disparities between purchaser and seller on the extent of the seller's environmental liability exposure, a second best rule, represented by the substantial continuity doctrine, may only be practical if the successor had fair notice of the liability so that it had the opportunity to discount the price it paid for the assets in the acquisition.[27] The substantial continuity test applies only when the particular circumstances of a transaction suggest that the corporate actors knew or *should have known* about environmental liability.

This is similar to the statutory innocent landowner defense[28] for owners of contaminated land. The purchaser in an asset acquisition would have to establish that it did not know, or had no reason to know, about the environmental liability at the time of the transaction. The defense would impose an affirmative duty on prospective landowners to conduct an appropriate inquiry into the history and past uses of the land to be acquired, consistent with commercial or customary practice. Factors that courts would examine include any specialized knowledge or experience of the purchaser, the sophistication of the contracting parties, the relationship of the purchase price to the property in an uncontaminated state, commonly known or reasonably ascertainable information, and the ability to detect such contamination by an appropriate inspection. A court would scrutinize the quality of the due diligence performed by the asset purchaser and determine if the purchaser should have known about the pre-transaction liability and could have allocated the liability prior to the sale. Are judges up to the task? Judges have applied the innocent landowner defense for purchasers of contaminated land very parsimoniously.

---

27 A rule of absolute successor liability will cause purchasers to so heavily discount the value of the selling firm that firm level acquisitions will decline relative to other types of asset sales—bust-up auctions, for example.

28 CERCLA § 101(35), 42 U.S.C. § 9601(35). The innocent landowner defense has a tortured statutory base. An innocent landowner is excluded from the definition of "contractual relationship" with a prior owner, someone who is within the definition of person. An innocent landowner is a purchaser of a contaminated site who did not know, or had no reason to know, that hazardous substances were present at the property. *Id.* § 101(35)(A)(1), 42 U.S.C. § 9601(35)(A)(i). To establish that a purchaser had no reason to know, it must be established by a preponderance of the evidence that the purchaser undertook an "appropriate inquiry" into the past ownership and uses of the property using "good commercial or customary practices." *Id.* § 101(35)(B), 42 U.S.C. § 9601(35)(B).

c. How Can a Purchaser in an Asset Acquisition Minimize Its Involuntary Exposure to Seller's Liabilities?

Wary purchasers use a combination of strategies to minimize nasty surprises—unpriced, unwittingly absorbed liabilities from asset acquisitions. First, purchasers conduct a thorough due diligence investigation of the seller's business, liabilities, and insurance before the closing. Second, purchasers insist on several specialized provisions in the acquisition agreement. The purchaser agrees to assume only specifically identified liabilities and secures a comprehensive and thorough set of specific warranties from the seller warranting that there are no other outstanding problems that could lead to additional liabilities. There are, among others, specific warranties on litigation, labor disputes, products liability, and environmental claims. The warranties are backed by an indemnification clause from the seller and, if possible, from the seller's shareholders. The seller secures the indemnification obligation by funding an escrow account or by providing a bond or some other form of purchaser insurance (we will cover acquisition agreements in Chapter Four). Third, the purchaser uses a triangular acquisition to place the new assets in a wholly-owned subsidiary. Fourth, to the extent possible in light of business imperatives, the purchaser minimizes the appearance of business continuity, avoiding factors that might lead a court to impose successor liability. The purchaser, for example, requires the seller to maintain its separate corporate existence and its own liability insurance for a specific time following the sale (this is not practical in a tax-free reorganization).[29] Fifth, in transactions where the assets or divisions are based in different states, or where the seller and buyer are based in different states, the purchase agreement can contain a choice-of-law provision that applies the law of a state other than California, Michigan, New Jersey, or Alabama.

3. PURCHASING ASSETS FROM A BANKRUPT COMPANY

Can a purchaser cut off all claims of successor liability by buying the assets of a company in bankruptcy? During an ongoing bankruptcy proceeding, a buyer can purchase assets: (1) from a secured lender that has foreclosed (see *Chicago Truck Drivers* below), (2) from a bankruptcy trustee or debtor-in-possession in a § 363(b) sale (see *Ninth Avenue Remedial Group* below), or (3) pursuant to a plan of reorganization in a Chapter 11 proceeding. Bankruptcy Code § 1123. The general rule is that Chapter 11 *cleanses* the assets sold of the seller's liabilities. The purchaser buys the assets *free and clear* of claims, liens, and other encumbrances. See, e.g., Bankruptcy Code § 363(f). There are some important exceptions, however.

---

[29] The purchaser can, to the extent commercially reasonable, also minimize the number of successor managers or employees it retains, relocate the operating facilities, change the name or details of the product, and so on.

If a purchaser has taken title to a contaminated site in bankruptcy, CERCLA liability follows the asset, even if the contamination occurred prior to the bankruptcy proceeding. See *In re Chateaugay Corp.*, 944 F.2d 997 (2d Cir. 1991) (EPA cleanup orders survive bankruptcy). An asset purchaser is liable under CERCLA as a current owner for all contamination at the site regardless of when it occurred (unless it can use the very narrow "innocent purchaser" defense).

CERCLA is silent on two related questions—successors liability when the environmental claim arises out of the disposal of hazardous substances off-site by a predecessor prior to its bankruptcy proceeding and successor liability when the claim arises out of the operation by a predecessor of a contaminated site owned by another party. A purchaser in an asset acquisition may not know about the off-site disposal (it was performed by an operating unit of the seller that either no longer exists or was not acquired by the asset purchaser, for example) nor about the predecessor's operation of a contaminated site.

NINTH AVENUE REMEDIAL GROUP V. ALLIS-CHALMERS CORP.

United States District Court, N.D. Indiana, 1996.
195 B.R. 716.

LOZANO, DISTRICT JUDGE.

. . . This case concerns the Ninth Avenue Dump Superfund site in Gary, Indiana. The site, which operated as a chemical and industrial waste disposal facility during the 1970's, has been contaminated by releases or threatened releases of the hazardous substances dumped there. Plaintiff, Ninth Avenue Remedial Group, has conducted and is conducting cleanup activities at the Ninth Avenue site under the approval of the Environmental Protection Agency ("EPA"). . . . The Group and its members now sue several Defendants under the Comprehensive Environmental Response Compensation and Liability Act of 1980 as amended ("CERCLA"), 42 U.S.C. §§ 9607 and 9613, for contributions to the cleanup costs which amount to over $20 million. . . .

According to Clark, Apex Oil Company ("Apex") purchased Clark Oil & Refining Corporation ("Old Clark") in 1981. In December of 1987, Apex and its subsidiaries, including Old Clark, sought protection from creditors under Chapter 11 of the Bankruptcy Code. After a period of negotiations, the Horsham Corporation, through its subsidiary, AOC Acquisition Corporation, agreed to purchase certain assets of Apex and its subsidiaries, including many of Old Clark's facilities. AOC Acquisition later changed its name to Clark Refining & Marketing, Inc., now a Defendant in this action.

The asset purchase agreement between Apex and AOC/Clark provided that Clark would not assume any liability for claims arising from the operation of Old Clark's facilities prior to the sale. . . .

In November 1988 the bankruptcy court approved the agreement for the sale of assets to AOC/Clark "free and clear of all liens, claims, taxes, encumbrances, obligations, contractual commitments, and interests," pursuant to 7 U.S.C. § 363(f). In addition, the order provided that "the rights of creditors and other parties in interest asserting a lien or other interest against the Purchased Assets shall attach to the Purchase Price; . . . liens and interests against the Purchased Assets shall be of no further force and effect." *Id.* Two years later, in August 1990, the bankruptcy court entered an order confirming the Chapter 11 reorganization plan for Apex and its subsidiaries. The order discharged the debtors of any claims arising prior to the confirmation order. . . .

. . . Applying the traditional successorship doctrine to the case at hand, the only successorship exception that appears relevant from the motions and responses before the Court is the third exception for mere continuity of business enterprise. In other words, Clark would be liable for claims against Old Clark if Clark is merely a continuity of Old Clark's business. Under the traditional application of the mere continuity exception, a corporate successor is the continuation of the predecessor if only one corporation remains after the transfer of assets and there is identity of stockholders and directors between the two corporations. . . . Some courts have adopted a similar but broader test for business continuity, called the "substantial continuity" or "continuity of enterprise" test, to determine successor liability under CERCLA. . . . The courts that have applied the substantial continuity test have concluded that environmental cleanup is one of those situations in which public policy dictates that the traditional notions of successor liability should be broadened. . . .[Ed.[30]]

The substantial continuity test does consider identity of stock, stockholders, and corporate officers, but those factors are not determinative. . . . Under the substantial continuity test, the court considers, in addition, a series of factors to determine whether one corporation is the successor of another: (1) retention of the same employees; (2) retention of the same supervisory personnel; (3) retention of the same production facilities in the same location; (4) production of the same product; (5) retention of the same name; (6) continuity of assets; (7) continuity of general business operations; and (8) whether the successor holds itself out as a continuation of the previous enterprise. . . . The court should also consider whether "the transfer to the new corporation was part of an effort to continue the business of the former corporation yet avoid its existing or potential state or federal environmental liability. . . ."

---

[30] [Ed. This is not without controversy. See New York v. National Service Indus., *supra*, holding that the test violates the Supreme Court opinion in *Bestfoods*.]

. . . The Seventh Circuit has used the substantial continuity exception when determining successor liability under federal common law in cases involving employment discrimination and union pension funds. . . . Applying the substantial continuity successor liability exception as the Seventh Circuit did in *Tasemkin* and *G-K-G,* this Court will find a successor liable for CERCLA claims under the broader substantial continuity exception if the successor knew or had notice of the potential CERCLA liability[2] and there was substantial continuity in the operation of the business before and after the sale. . . .

Clark's foremost argument in its motions to dismiss and/or for summary judgment is that when it purchased Old Clark's assets during the bankruptcy proceedings, the bankruptcy court approved the sale of the assets free and clear of all liens and claims including Plaintiffs' claims. If Clark is correct, the sale would preclude liability regardless of the successorship doctrine.

The fact that the asset sale in this case took place in the context of bankruptcy is not determinative of the question of liability. The *Tasemkin* case, 59 F.3d 48, discussed liability as applied to a successor that acquired the assets in a bankruptcy foreclosure. The bankruptcy debtor owed money to a union pension fund. The union sued the company that had obtained the assets of the debtor during the bankruptcy proceedings. The Seventh Circuit held that the fact that the new owner acquired the company in a bankruptcy foreclosure was irrelevant to the question of liability as applied to successors. *Id.* at 51.

Clark, however, argues that the sale of assets specifically approved by the bankruptcy court was "free and clear" of all potential liabilities: Pursuant to 11 U.S.C. § 363(f), the transfer and conveyances of the purchased assets to [Clark] shall be free and clear of all liens, claims, taxes, encumbrances, obligations, contractual commitments and interests. . . . Section 363(f) of Title 11 of the U.S. Code gives a bankruptcy trustee the power to sell the assets of the debtor "free and clear of any interests in such property."

The courts have not defined "free and clear of any interest in such property" under 11 U.S.C. section 363(f) clearly. . . . In dicta, the Seventh Circuit stated that section 363(f) refers only to liens. *Zerand-Bernal, Inc. v. Cox,* 23 F.3d 159, 163 (7th Cir.1994). . . . In *Zerand,* a product made by the debtor prior to the section 363 sale injured the plaintiff, several years after the sale. The plaintiff sued the buyer under product liability. The order approving the sale included a provision making the sale " 'free and clear of

[2] *Tasemkin* and *G-K-G* both require that the successor have notice of the claim. Neither of the cases imposes a duty on the asset purchaser to inquire about possible claims before the purchase. . . . Because the motions and the responses did not raise this issue, the Court does not decide whether a successor must inquire about potential CERCLA liabilities during the purchase if it wants to claim later that successor liability does not apply because it had no notice of the claim.

any liens, claims or encumbrances of any sort or nature' " and confirming the terms of the sale agreement. *Id.* at 161. The appellate court stated that even though the assets had been sold free and clear of liens and encumbrances, the victim in that case was not trying to enforce the lien and the sale order did not preclude his claims. *Id.* at 163.

Defendant urges the Court to look at the plain meaning of the word "interest." Defendant argues that "interest" includes a broad category of interests such as liens, claims, rights, etc. . . .

Other cases in other circuits support a broad interpretation of section 363(f). Those courts have used section 363(f) to preclude claims against successors who purchased assets in a bankruptcy sale even when the claims were not based on in rem interests.[Ed.[31]]

Two main arguments underlay the decisions in the cases cited above: first, that fear of successor liability will discourage potential buyers in sales conducted pursuant to bankruptcy; second, that the successorship doctrine frustrates the orderly scheme of the bankruptcy laws by allowing some unsecured creditors to recover without regard to the priority order of the bankruptcy proceedings. *Tasemkin*, 59 F.3d at 50–51. Defendant proposes these arguments in its briefs to support its motions.

The Seventh Circuit, however, has criticized these arguments. *See Tasemkin*, 59 F.3d at 50 (citing *Forde*, 437 F.Supp. 631). The appellate court found the first argument unconvincing because asset purchasers generally face the risk of successor liability whether or not the sellers are bankrupt. The court found no reason to give special protection to the purchasers of the assets of a bankruptcy debtor. The appellate court also rejected the second argument because it found that the priority order established during the bankruptcy proceeding becomes irrelevant once the bankruptcy proceedings are completed. *Id.* . . .

---

[31] [Ed. The cases cited were several district court or bankruptcy court cases. The list now includes In re Chrysler, 576 F.3d 108 (2d Cir. 2010); In re Trans World Airlines, 322 F.3d 283 (3d Cir. 2003); In re Leckie Smokeless Coal Co., 99 F.3d 573 (4th Cir. 1996). According to the Second Circuit in *Chrysler*:

> To allow the claimants to assert successor liability claims against [the purchaser] while limiting other creditors' recourse to the proceeds of the asset sale would be inconsistent with the Bankruptcy Code's priority scheme. Appellants ignore this overarching principle and assume that tort claimants faced a choice between the Sale and an alternative arrangement that would have assured funding for their claims. But had appellants successfully blocked the Sale, they would have been unsecured creditors fighting for a share of extremely limited liquidation proceeds. Given the billions of dollars of outstanding secured claims against Old Chrysler, appellants would have fared no better had they prevailed.
>
> The possibility of transferring assets free and clear of existing tort liability was a critical inducement to the Sale. As in *TWA*, a sale of the assets of [Old Chrysler] at the expense of preserving successor liability claims was necessary in order to preserve some [55],000 jobs, . . . and to provide funding for employee-related liabilities, including retirement benefits [for more than 106,000 retirees].

576 F.3d at 126 (citations omitted).]

In *Zerand*, the Seventh Circuit also criticized the idea that buyers in bankruptcy proceedings should be protected from successor liability. 23 F.3d at 163. The court dismissed the notion that bankruptcy courts have the power to enjoin all future lawsuits against buyers at bankruptcy sales in order to maximize the sale price. To do so, the appellate court concluded, would encourage bankruptcy filings to allow debtors to sell free of all liabilities, an advantage that asset sellers do not have outside the bankruptcy laws.

In deciding whether the sale to Clark precludes successor liability for Plaintiffs' CERCLA claims, the Court does not have to decide what type of interests are covered by the section 363(f) language, because the Court can decide on other grounds. As explained *infra*, the cases suggest that if the CERCLA claim could have been a claim in bankruptcy against Old Clark, the bankruptcy court had the equitable power to discharge the claim against the asset purchaser independently of section 363(f). If the claim arose after the consummation of the bankruptcy proceedings, the bankruptcy court did not have the power to discharge that claim. . . .

In conclusion, it appears that while the bankruptcy courts might have the power to sell assets free and clear of any interest that could be brought against the bankruptcy estate during bankruptcy,[9] either through section 363(f) or through the powers of the bankruptcy court under other sections of the Code, a sale free and clear does not include future claims that did not arise until after the bankruptcy proceedings concluded. . . . Applying that interpretation to this case, the Court finds that the asset sale approved by the bankruptcy court precludes suits against Clark for any claim that could have been brought against Old Clark during the bankruptcy. However, if the CERCLA claim did not arise until after the bankruptcy proceedings concluded, the bankruptcy court could not have discharged a claim which did not even exist at the time. . . .

To decide whether Plaintiffs' claim was discharged by the bankruptcy court, it becomes important to determine whether Plaintiffs had a CERCLA claim against Old Clark which they should have brought against it during the bankruptcy proceedings. . . .

Applying the law as stated by the appellate court, the bankruptcy proceedings that led to the sale and purchase of the Clark assets discharged the CERCLA claims asserted by Plaintiffs if the claimants (1) had actual or constructive knowledge that a release or threatened release of

---

9 In *Zerand*, the Seventh Circuit stated in dicta that bankruptcy discharges protect only the debtor and not the successor. 23 F.3d at 163. This is the most extreme interpretation possible of the effect of a bankruptcy discharge. This Court hesitates to adopt this conclusion when it does not have to do so. Even if the bankruptcy discharge did not apply to Clark, successor liability will not apply if Plaintiffs could have brought a claim against the predecessor in the bankruptcy proceedings. This is because successor liability is limited when the plaintiff could have obtained a remedy from the predecessor. *But see Tasemkin*, 59 F.3d at 51 (stating that the prior availability of relief from the predecessor is a factor of significant weight, but it is not dispositive to the question of successor liability).

hazardous substances had occurred, and (2) could tie Old Clark, the bankruptcy debtor, to the release prior to the confirmation of the bankruptcy reorganization. . . . [T] he Court cannot determine whether the bankruptcy proceedings discharged the CERCLA claim for the disposal of waste generated by Old Clark at the Ninth Avenue site.

QUESTIONS

After the case, who will buy an old refinery? Is the claimant knowledge qualifier helpful? In *New York v. National Service Industries*, *supra*, the Second Circuit rejected the substantial continuity test for CERCLA cases. How would this case be decided in the Second Circuit?

CHICAGO TRUCK DRIVERS, HELPERS AND WAREHOUSE WORKERS UNION PENSION FUND v. TASEMKIN, 59 F.3d 48 (7th Cir. 1995): [Tasemkin Furniture Company went into Chapter 7 bankruptcy liquidation proceedings. One of the unsatisfied unsecured claimants was the firm's pension fund, owed some $300,000. The secured lender foreclosed on the collateral and sold the assets to a second company, Tasemkin Inc. The second firm operated the same business from fewer locations, employed largely the same staff and relied primarily on the same suppliers. The owner of the second firm was the daughter-in-law of the owner of the failed firm, the president was the son. The foreclosure was not a § 363(f) asset sale conducted by a bankruptcy trustee. The bankruptcy proceeding closed in 1992 and two years later the pension fund sued Tasemkin under a theory of successor liability. The Seventh Circuit reversed the district court's order granting a motion to dismiss.] . . . [T]he case stands for the proposition that it is desirable, perhaps even necessary, to shield purchasers of failing businesses from liability incurred by predecessors. Such protection is viewed as a means of encouraging market growth and the fluidity of corporate capital. Fear of successor liability, this argument runs, would "chill" sales in bankruptcy and as a result harm employees of the failed concern who might have retained jobs with the successor business. . . . This argument pertains equally well, however, to a company nearing the brink of bankruptcy. The potential for chilling does not vary as a function of a company's precise degree of distress, and there is no reason to accord the purchasers of formally bankrupt entities some special measure of insulation from liability that is unavailable to ailing but not yet defunct entities. (Of course, it is neither certain nor clear that the chilling effect need give us pause: purchasers can demand a lower price to account for pending liabilities of which they are aware, and under federal successorship principles will not be held responsible for liabilities of which they had no notice.) . . . In so holding we do not suggest that a creditor's prior opportunity to satisfy the claim against the predecessor is irrelevant. . . . Instead of being dispositive . . . the availability of relief from the predecessor is a factor to be considered along with other factors. . . . Here, those facts include the apparent nature of the acquisition . . . , which clearly had the effect, intended or no, of frustrating unsecured creditors while resurrecting virtually the identical enterprise. . . .

QUESTIONS

Are the employees of Tasemkin better or worse off with the ruling? What if the family is the only willing bidder on the furniture company operations?

D. LAWS STOPPING ASSET STRIPPING

If only a portion of a firm's assets are being transferred, if a firm is being liquidated after a business failure, or if the seller values some significant assets or liabilities more highly than the buyer does, the parties typically will choose to structure the transaction as a sale of assets, rather than as a merger,[32] and identify specifically which assets and liabilities are transferred. So long as the buyer pays fair market value for the assets it buys and the seller applies the consideration received in the acquisition to the residual debts of the business, creditors of the seller are *better off* by a rule that permits the parties to allocate assets and liabilities to the highest valuing party. If, on the other hand, the seller in the acquisition uses the transaction as a vehicle to avoid applying the money received to the debts of the business and instead distributes the consideration received to its shareholders, then creditors are worse off. The seller is *asset stripping* the business.

Opportunistic sellers have used three strategies to hurt the creditors. All three involve an asset sale. Following an asset sale those who control the seller, now a non-operating company holding passive assets (cash or stock in the purchaser) and still on the hook for all long-tail liabilities, attempt to distribute the assets to themselves and other shareholders ahead of the creditors. There are three methods of distribution. First, they *liquidate and dissolve* the seller, passing the sale proceeds out as liquidation proceeds. The *dissolution* provisions of state corporate codes apply to the distributions. Second, they cause the seller to declare either a one-time, *extraordinary dividend* or share redemption using the sale proceeds as the dividend or the repurchase payment. The *legal capital statutes* in state corporate codes and state statutes on *fraudulent conveyances* apply to stop the distributions. And third, the mafia version,

[32] This is not always true. For example, in a case in which the purchaser wants only some of the seller's assets, the parties could restructure the target before an acquisition, with a spin-off, for example, and use a statutory merger to acquire the desired assets after the restructuring.

they cause the seller to enter into a variety of sweetheart deals with shareholders, milking the assets over time.[33] State common law on breach of *fiduciary duty*, state statutes on *conflict-of-interest*, and state statutes on *fraudulent conveyances* apply to this alternative. In both the second and third alternatives, after the shareholders milk the seller of all its assets, the selling firm becomes an empty shell company, the shareholders stop the payment of the state franchise fees, and the state dissolves the shell as a matter of law for non-payment.

The success of the three alternatives depends in part on the deficiencies in the countervailing law and in serendipity. If the claimants sit on their rights, they lose them. For claimants that suspect they have claims against a seller pursuing one of these alternatives, they are put to an election—claim or pass. The doctrine of successor liability in asset sales that holds the purchaser liable for the debts of the seller is a doctrine that reflects our dissatisfaction with (and ignorance of, perhaps) these other legal protections.

1. DISSOLUTION PROTECTION

All state corporation codes provide for the dissolution of corporations. Under the traditional approach, state codes permit corporations to dissolve and liquidate by a board resolution ratified by a shareholder vote. In a *voluntarily dissolution*, the corporation winds up its affairs, and *liquidates*, paying off its creditors and distributing any surplus to shareholders.

In liquidation, the corporation notifies individually all known creditors and publishes a general notice in a widely circulated newspaper. Most traditional corporate law statutes bar claims of creditors who come forward after the statutorily mandated notice and claims period. As to known creditors, this system is satisfactory. If the selling firm receives fair value for the assets, existing creditors of the seller are no worse off and, when the seller dissolves, have an opportunity to present their claims for payment ahead of any distributions to shareholders.[34]

The statutory structure provides an opportunity for asset buyers and sellers to share the gains of jointly externalizing risk onto unknown future tort and environmental creditors—the long-tail or contingent claimants. These claims are based on injuries that occur, mature or are discovered after dissolution. The future victims cannot negotiate during the winding-

---

[33] Controlling shareholders can distribute corporate assets as excessive salary payments through sales of the assets for less than fair market value, through loans to shareholders at less than market interest rates, through guarantees of shareholder debt on which the shareholder defaults, through loans from shareholders to the firm in which the firm defaults on the underlying debt and assets pledged as security are forfeited to the shareholders, and so on. See Bayless Manning & Jim Hanks, A CONCISE TEXTBOOK ON LEGAL CAPITAL 13–16 (3d ed. 1990).

[34] Under the 1999 version of the ABA Model Business Corporation Act, a dissolved corporation must notify all known claimants in writing, who then have 120 days to present their claims. If the claim is rejected, the claimant must sue on the claim within ninety days of the rejection. ABA Model Bus. Corp. Act § 14.06 (1999).

up period with the dissolving firm to price the risk of future liabilities, and sellers will liquidate not having internalized the full costs of their business decisions on potential tort victims or environmental claimants. Limited protection is available for long-tail claimants under traditional statutes. If a long-tail claim matures shortly after the liquidation distributions to the selling firm shareholders, the claimants have the statutory *wind-up* period, usually three to five years,[35] to sue the firm or the shareholders individually (if the firm has already distributed all of its assets).[36] Each shareholder is liable only to the extent of the shareholder's personal distribution in liquidation from the firm (or a pro rata share of the claim if less).[37] Long-tail claimants in this group can recover only by chasing a diffuse group of shareholders.

Long-tail claimants whose claims mature after the statutory cut off period are generally out of luck. Some attempt to sue based on improper notice. The targets of such a suit are the firm's directors and all shareholders receiving a corporation distribution on liquidation. The failure of the dissolution procedure to resolve all claims unsettles the managers and shareholders of dissolving firms. Delaware has taken the lead with an innovative approach to provide more post-dissolution certainty.

The default procedure in the Delaware general corporate law requires that a dissolving corporation make provision to pay all contingent, conditional, or unmatured contractual claims known to the corporation. Del. Gen. Corp. L. § 281(b)(i). Section 281(b)(ii) also requires that a dissolving corporation formulate a plan of distribution to make such provision for claims "that have not been made known, or that have not

---

35 That is, the claimants get the benefit of the statute of limitations on their type of claim, capped by the statutory period on claims after dissolution (3 to 5 years).

36 The traditional rule is best illustrated by § 105 of the 1979 Model Bus. Corp. Act. The provision authorized suits against a dissolved corporation for two years after dissolution. Some state courts held that the provision barred claims that arose after the two-year period, other courts held the statute did not provide a statute of limitations but only affected a claimant's ability to sue a firm as opposed to its shareholders. See *Note, Corporate Life after Death: CERCLA Preemption of State Corporate Dissolution Law,* 88 MICH. L. REV. 131, 149–55 (1989) (discussing the 1979 Model Act).

In recognition of the problems with the traditional provisions, the 1984 version of the Model Business Corporation Act extended the claim period to five years from the traditional two-year period on the assumption that most of the long-tail claims would arise during that period. ABA Model Bus. Corp. L. § 14.07(c). At the same time, the 1984 revision clarified that the section had the effect of a statute of limitation on long-term claims and not just a statement on the capacity of a dissolved firm to be sued. ABA Model Bus. Corp. L. § 14.07(d) (1984). Technically, the statutory period for asserting the claims begins on the date the dissolving corporation publishes, in a general circulation paper, a notice of its intent to liquidate. *Id.* If not barred, claims may be enforced against the dissolved corporation to the extent of undistributed assets and against shareholders to the extent of the shareholders' pro rata share of the obligation or the value of the assets distributed in liquidation, whichever is less. *Id.* The 2000 version reduces the period of presenting claims after publication of notice from five years back to three years.

37 If a firm distributes its assets before the expiration of the period, it must make "reasonable" provision for claims that could be brought in the period. See ABA Model Bus. Corp. Act § 14.09(a) (2000).

arisen, but that, based on facts known to the corporation . . . , are likely to arise or to become known to the corporation . . . within ten years of the date of dissolution." If the amount provided is insufficient, claimants may pursue shareholders for amounts received in the liquidating distribution or their pro rata share of the claim, whichever is less, subject to the statute of limitations on the claim. Del. Gen. Corp. L. § 282(a).[38] Directors of a dissolved corporation are personally liable if such a plan of distribution was not formulated properly or the amounts set aside were not "reasonable" at the time the plan was made. *Id.* § 281(c).

For shareholders and directors in dissolving corporations who want to cut off liability on long-tail claims, an optional safe harbor procedure is available in § 281(a).[39] A dissolving corporation may petition the Court of Chancery to determine the amount and form of security that is "reasonably likely to be sufficient to provide compensation for claims that have not been made known to the corporation or that have not risen but that, based on facts known to the corporation or successor entity, are likely to arise or to become known to the corporation or successor entity within 5 years after the date of dissolution or such longer period of time as the Court of Chancery may determine not to exceed 10 years after the date of dissolution." Del. Gen. Corp. L. § 280(c)(3). The court may appoint a guardian ad litem to represent the long-tail claimants. *Id.* On compliance with the court decree, shareholders are not liable for any claims begun after the three-year winding-up period established by § 278, Del. Gen. Corp. L. § 282(b), and directors are not personally liable to any claimants. Del. Gen. Corp. L. § 281(c).

The difficulty of fashioning an adequate security arrangement under § 280(c)(3) is the subject of the following case.

IN RE REGO COMPANY

Court of Chancery of Delaware, 1992.
623 A.2d 92.

ALLEN, CHANCELLOR.

. . . I conclude that, as presently constituted, the security aspects of the Company's plan of final distribution are not sufficient to meet the statutory requirements. . . .

---

[38] Here Delaware differs from the current version of the Model Act. The Act has a three year bar on these claims. See ABA Model Bus. Corp. Act § 14.07(c)(3) (2016 rev.). In Delaware the three year bar applies only to the safe harbor procedure in Section 280(a). Del. Corp. L. § 282(b).

[39] The 2000 amendments to the Model Business Corporation Act also add a new section, § 14.08, that, similar in effect to the Delaware provision noted in the text, creates a court proceeding that gives directors and shareholders a safe harbor in providing for contingent claims that are not barred by publication. The firm provides security for claims that "are reasonably estimated to arise" within three years of the effective date of dissolution. The three-year period is considerably shorter than the potential ten-year period provided for in the Delaware statute.

. . . [T]he question of a dissolving corporation's duty, if any, to potential future claimants is problematic in at least two ways. First, the problem of compensation to persons injured by defective products or by undiscovered and actionable environmental injury, caused by dissolved corporations, is of obvious social concern. If, in the context of a corporate dissolution, the corporation law does not treat these possible contingencies responsibly, it can be expected that other legal doctrines, such as successor liability doctrines, will be stretched and shaped to address them. A default in corporation law may mean that the market for the sale of corporate assets as part of a dissolution will be chilled by the prospect of buyers being forced involuntarily to assume unknown future liabilities. This is a practical problem that the law governing the creation and dissolution of corporate entities might well address. Secondly, the few adjudicated cases that hold that the trust fund doctrine[Ed.[40]] is inapplicable to claims arising after the expiration of the wind-up period, may seem to corporate directors to give insufficient comfort to permit them safely to make a final distribution, if they have reason to know that future claims are quite likely to arise.

. . . The new Delaware procedure codified at Sections 280–282 of the Delaware Corporate Law addresses both of these concerns. It structures a mechanism (alternative mechanisms actually) which under certain circumstances, for the first time recognizes rights in unknown future corporate claimants and provides a level of assurance to such persons that, as part of the corporate dissolution process, reasonable provision will be made for their future claims. Equally important, the new procedure offers to directors and shareholders (and perhaps transferees) assurance that, if the Court of Chancery approves security provisions for corporate claimants, then they will be protected from potential future claims arising from the decision to distribute the corporation's assets on dissolution. . . .

RegO elected to follow the new elective provisions of Sections 280 and 281(a). . . . RegO engaged in the business of manufacturing and marketing valves and other components for systems using liquified petroleum, anhydrous ammonia and other compressed gases. . . . Due to its explosive nature, systems transporting or using L.P. gas are involved from time to time in accidents resulting in property damage and/or personal injury. Victims of these incidents, of course, often bring suit against all parties associated with the LP system involved in the accident. As a result, RegO, as a component parts manufacturer, has often been required to appear as a defendant in such product liability actions. . . .

RegO proposes a plan for the payment and the security of its known and future unknown creditors including the establishment of a Claimants Trust and the transfer to the trust of all of RegO's assets. . . .

[40] [Ed. Under the trust fund doctrine, the shareholders hold their distributions in liquidation in trust for unpaid, unbarred claimants.]

The central issue presented by this proceeding arises under Section 280(c). It is whether the Claimants Trust provides security that will be sufficient for the claims of present claimants, and will be reasonably likely to be sufficient for claims that have not been made known or that have not yet arisen, but that based on facts known to RegO are likely to arise or become known, prior to the expiration of applicable statutes of limitation.

In addressing this question, one must first ask the factual question whether the assets held by RegO are likely to offer security that will be adequate to reasonably assure the payment of all foreseeable future claims. As noted above, I conclude that they are not. . . .

Next one must ask whether that fact disables RegO from proceeding to wind-up its affairs pursuant to Sections 280 and 281(a). I conclude that in the situation in which a dissolved corporation is dedicating all of its assets to the security arrangement offered under Section 280(c), that the inadequacy of those assets to offer full security ought not to deprive the directors of the corporation from proceeding under Section 280 and Section 281(a). . . . That is, sufficiency of the security agreement may be achieved in spite of the inability to assure or secure future compensation in full to all foreseeable future claimants. Where the dissolved corporate assets are in total inadequate to secure full compensation to all foreseeable future claimants, the sufficiency of the security arrangement will inescapably involve questions of the fairness of the proposed security among various claimants or classes of claimants. . . .

Thus, the more difficult questions presented by the Claimants Trust are whether its terms, especially the preference that it accords to present claimants over unknown or future claimants, is appropriate. . . . I conclude that, in light of the legislative intent reflected in Section 281(b), and less vividly but no less recognizably in Section 281(a), this preference is not justified in this factual context. . . .

One of the potential creditors of RegO, Emerson, objected to an extraordinary dividend of $38 million that RegO paid on the eve of dissolution. Emerson had attacked the dividend in another proceeding. Its attack was based on state insolvency statutes and on state fraudulent conveyance acts.

2. INSOLVENCY STATUTES

Limitations on dividends and redemptions are found in the *legal capital statutes* of all corporate codes. The statutes are in a state of evolution; some states have the old statutes (legal capital statutes), with *par value* shares, and some states have retained the solvency provisions of the old statutes (*insolvency statutes*) and rejected any par value calculations. Section 6.40 of the ABA Model Business Corporation Act (2016 rev.), a modern statute, provides as follows:

> (a) A board of directors may authorize and the corporation may make distributions to its shareholders subject to restrictions by the articles of incorporation and the limitation in subsection (c). . . .
>
> (c) No distribution may be made if, after giving it effect:
>
> (1) the corporation would not be able to pay its debts as they become due in the usual course of business [Ed. the *equity insolvency test*]; or
>
> (2) the corporation's total assets would be less than the sum of its total liabilities plus . . . the amount that would be needed, if the corporation were to be dissolved at the time of the distribution, to satisfy the preferential rights upon dissolution of shareholders whose preferential rights are superior to those receiving the distribution. [Ed. the *balance sheet test*]

Any director that votes for or assents to a distribution made in violation of § 6.40 is personally liable to the corporation for the amount of the illegal distribution; however, the party asserting liability must establish that, when taking the action in question, the director did not comply with the standard of conduct set forth in § 8.30 of the Model Act. ABA Model Bus. Corp. Act § 8.32 (2016 rev.). Any proceeding against a director must be brought within two years of the illegal distribution. *Id.* A director found liable can assert contribution rights against other directors who violated their duties. She can also seek recoupment from any shareholder who received the illegal distribution knowing it was illegal when made. *Id.*

3. FRAUDULENT CONVEYANCE PROTECTION

Fraudulent conveyance laws protect a creditor's right to *execute* on assets of debtors[41] in the event of defaults. If a debtor has transferred property to frustrate collection efforts by creditors, creditors may sue under state law to set aside any improper transfers and obtain a lien on the transferred property. Trustees in bankruptcy (or debtors in possession) are empowered under federal law to recover for the benefit of creditors the value of any property improperly removed from the bankrupt debtor's estate. Fraudulent conveyance provisions are found in § 548 of the Federal Bankruptcy Code, 11 U.S.C.A. § 548, and in state acts, which are typically modeled on either the Uniform Fraudulent Conveyance Act (1918) (UFCA)

---

41 Force the judicially supervised sale of the property and claim the sale proceeds.

or the newer Uniform Fraudulent Transfer Act (1984) (UFTA).[42] A trustee in bankruptcy is also empowered to invoke state fraudulent conveyance law to invalidate pre-bankruptcy transfers. 11 U.S.C.A. § 544(b). The statutes have a long heritage, deriving from Statute of 13 Elizabeth, passed by the English Parliament in 1571.

The UFTA and insolvency statutes in state corporate codes overlap in effect, but the UFTA is broader in scope. The insolvency statutes apply only to corporate distributions to shareholders, dividends or share repurchases. The UFTA § 5(a) applies to any transfer of property by any debtor to anybody and for any purpose whenever there is actual intent to defraud creditors or whenever the transferor receives value which is less than "reasonably equivalent value." The difference between the value received and reasonably equivalent value is treated as a gratuitous transfer that creditors or their representative can recover under UFTA § 7. Moreover, UFTA § 8 does not recognize the innocent receipt of a gratuitous fraudulent transfer as a defense.

The UFTA, like the UFCA before it, catches transfers that show an "actual intent to hinder, delay or defraud creditors" (the *actual intent* test). UFTA § 4(a)(1). More important, perhaps, is the *constructive intent* test in UFTA §§ 4(a)(2) and 5. A transfer is deemed fraudulent when the seller does not receive "reasonably equivalent value in exchange" and the seller's remaining assets are "unreasonably small in relation to the business" remaining, UFTA § 4(a)(2)(I); the seller knew or should have known that it would "incur debts beyond [its] ability to pay as they became due," UFTA § 4(a)(2)(ii); or "the debtor was insolvent at that time or the debtor became insolvent as a result of the transfer," UFTA § 5. Creditors whose claims attached "before or after the transfer was made" can use the first two theories of relief; creditors whose claims predate the transfer can also use the third theory.

Federal courts have struggled with whether the UFTA and its predecessor, the UFCA, provide relief for creditors in bankrupt companies that have recently undergone leveraged buy-outs (LBOs) or other leveraged recapitalizations.

---

[42] Forty-three states and the District of Columbia have adopted the UFTA. The remaining states continue to apply its predecessor, the UFCA or the common law.

Diagram 10

A Leveraged Buy-Out

➤ ***Step One*** ➤

(An LBO fund creates an acquisition shell company. The company borrows substantial amounts of cash from institutional investors.)

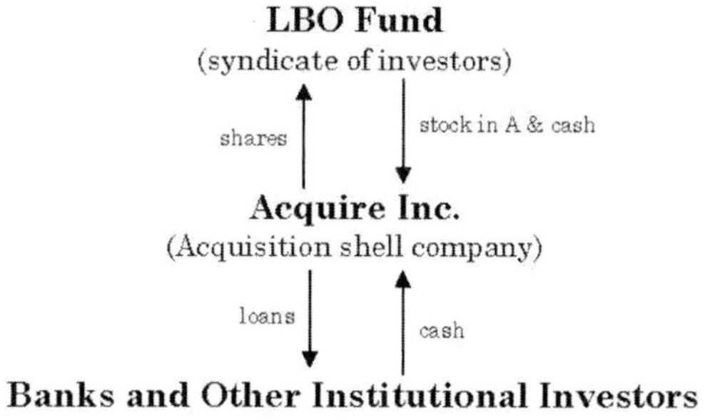

➤ ***Step Two*** ➤

(Acquire Inc. purchases a controlling block of stock in the target, A Inc.)

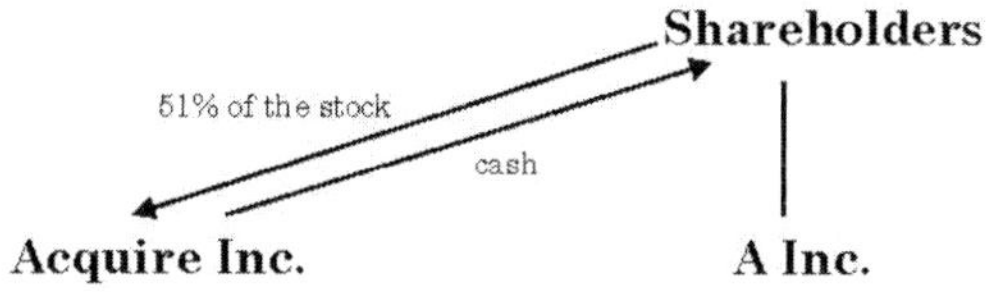

➤ ***Step Three*** ➤

(Acquire Inc. merges into A Inc.)

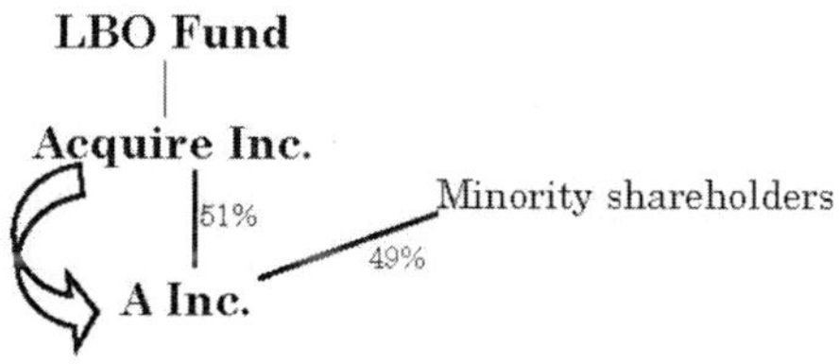

Acquire Inc.'s shareholders (less than 300) receive all the outstanding common stock in A Inc. A Inc.'s minority shareholders exchange their voting stock for debt securities or non-voting preferred stock in A Inc. Acquire Inc.'s massive debts attach by "operation of law" to A Inc.

➤ ***Step Four*** ≺

(A Inc. manipulates its assets and capital structure to generate cash to pay off the acquisition financing.)

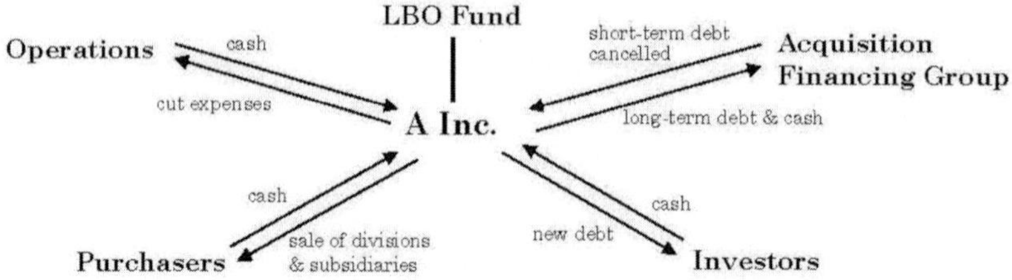

BOYER V. CROWN STOCK DISTR., INC.

United States Court of Appeals, Sixth Circuit, 2009.
587 F.3d 787.

POSNER, CIRCUIT JUDGE.

These appeals arise from the Chapter 7 bankruptcy of Crown Unlimited Machine, Inc. The trustee in bankruptcy filed an adversary action charging the defendants—a defunct corporation and its shareholders, members of a family named Stroup—with having made a fraudulent conveyance in violation of Ind. Code § 32–18–2–14(2) (section 4(a)(2) of the Uniform Fraudulent Transfer Act), a statute enforceable in a bankruptcy proceeding. See 11 U.S.C. § 544(b). After an evidentiary hearing, the bankruptcy judge awarded the trustee $3,295,000 plus prejudgment interest. The district judge affirmed and the defendants have appealed. The trustee has cross-appealed, seeking an additional $590,328.

Crown was a designer and manufacturer of machinery for cutting and bending tubes. Most of the machinery it made was custom-designed to the buyer's specifications, and only two other companies manufactured custom-designed machinery of that type. In January 1999 the defendants agreed to sell all of Crown's assets to Kevin E. Smith, the president of a company in a similar line of business. The price was $6 million. Crown agreed to employ Smith until the closing, so that he could assure himself of the value of the business before committing to buying it.

He decided to go through with the deal. At the closing, on January 5, 2000, Crown received from a new corporation, formed by Smith, $3.1 million in cash and a $2.9 million promissory note. The new corporation (also named Crown Unlimited Machine, Inc., the name being among the assets sold to the new Crown) had borrowed the $3.1 million from a bank. Although the loan was secured by all of Crown's assets, the annual interest rate (a floating rate) initially exceeded 9 percent. The rate suggests—since inflation expectations were low at the time—that the bank considered the risk of default nontrivial.

The promissory note was payable on April 1, 2006, with interest at an annual rate of 8 percent. Although that translates into an interest expense of $232,000 a year, the agreement of sale specified that the new corporation would be required to pay only $100,000 a year on the note, with the first payment due in April 2001, unless new Crown's sales exceeded a specified high threshold. The note, like the bank loan, was secured by all of Crown's assets, but the promisee's (old Crown's) security interest was subordinated to the bank's. Although the interest rate on the note was lower than the interest rate on the bank loan, even though the note was not as well secured, there was, as we'll see, little chance that the note would ever be paid; and after the first two $100,000 interest payments, it wasn't.

Smith's personal assets were meager. He contributed only $500 of his own money toward the purchase.

Just prior to the closing, old Crown transferred $590,328 from its corporate bank account to a separate bank account so that it could be distributed to Crown's shareholders as a dividend. This was done pursuant to an understanding of the parties that, depending on the company's performance between the initial agreement and the closing, the Stroups would be permitted to keep some of Crown's cash that would otherwise have been transferred to the new corporation as part of the sale; the sale, since it was of all of Crown's assets, included whatever money was in the corporation's bank account.

After the closing, old Crown (renamed Crown Stock Distribution, Inc.) distributed the entire $3.1 million in cash that it had received to its shareholders, and ceased to be an operating company.

New Crown was a flop. It declared bankruptcy in July 2003, and its assets were sold pursuant to 11 U.S.C. § 363 (which authorizes a sale, if approved by the bankruptcy judge, of assets of the debtor) for $3.7 million. The buyer was a new company of which Smith is now the president. Most of the money realized in the sale was required for paying off the bank; very little was left over to pay the claims of new Crown's unsecured creditors, who were owed some $1.6 or $1.7 million and on whose behalf the trustee in bankruptcy brought the adversary action. . . .

* * *

We begin our analysis with the trustee's argument for recharacterizing the transaction. In a conventional LBO, an investor buys the stock of a corporation from the stockholders with the proceeds of a loan secured by the corporation's own assets. . . . It follows that if all the assets are still fully secured when the corporation declares bankruptcy, the unsecured creditors cannot satisfy any part of their claims from a sale of the assets. If the trustee loses this suit, the unsecured creditors will have recovered only $150,000—less than 10 cents on the dollar.

Should the acquired company be doomed to go broke after and because of the LBO—if the burden of debt created by the transaction was so heavy that the corporation had no reasonable prospect of surviving—the payment to the shareholders by the buyer of the corporation is deemed a fraudulent conveyance because in exchange for the money the shareholders received they provided no value to the corporation but merely increased its debt and by doing so pushed it over the brink. . . . A corporate transfer is "fraudulent" within the meaning of the Uniform Fraudulent Transfer Act, even if there is no fraudulent intent, if the corporation didn't receive "reasonably equivalent value" in return for the transfer and as a result was left with insufficient assets to have a reasonable chance of surviving indefinitely. . . .

Some courts have been reluctant to apply the Act as written to leveraged buyouts. See *Kupetz v. Wolf,* 845 F.2d 842, 847–50 (9th Cir.1988); *United States v. Tabor Court Realty Corp., supra,* 803 F.2d at 1297; *Wieboldt Stores, Inc. v. Schottenstein,* 94 B.R. 488, 503 (N.D.Ill.1988). They sympathize with minority shareholders who have no power to prevent such a deal. They may also agree with the scholars who have argued that many LBOs are welfare-enhancing transactions because by making the managers owners (managers are often the buyers in an LBO) and thus fusing ownership with control, an LBO increases the managers' incentive to operate the corporation with a view to maximizing its value rather than their salaries and perks. These scholars also argue that devices that facilitate transfers of corporate control increase the mobility of capital. . . .

The reluctance of the courts in the decisions we cited is not easy to square with the language of the Uniform Fraudulent Transfer Act. And anyway the "equities," as we shall see, do not favor lenient treatment in this case. Moreover, although before the LBO Smith was briefly a member of Crown's management, the LBO did not close a gap between managers and shareholders. LBOs, though by burdening the acquired corporation with additional debt they increase the risk of bankruptcy (because debt is a fixed cost, and therefore unlike a variable cost does not shrink when the debtor's output shrinks), can indeed have redeeming economic value when the corporation is publicly held and the managers have a low equity stake prior to the transaction. In a publicly held corporation there is a separation of ownership from control, and the managers may use their control to manage the company in a way that will increase their personal wealth rather than maximize the profits of the corporation; the conflict of interest is eliminated by making the managers the owners. But this rationale for an LBO is missing from this case because both old and new Crown were closely held corporations. And while the economic literature also argues that the increased risk of bankruptcy that an LBO creates concentrates the minds of the managers (just as, according to Samuel Johnson, the prospect of being hanged concentrates the mind of the condemned person), this is hard to take seriously in the present case; for the owner-manager had only a $500 stake in the company.

But the critical difference between the LBO in this case and a bona fide LBO is that this LBO was *highly* likely to plunge the company into bankruptcy. There was scant probability that the transaction would increase the firm's value; on the contrary, it left the firm with so few assets that it would have had to be extremely lucky to survive.

The transaction differed, however, in two formal respects from a conventional overleveraged LBO: the buyer bought the assets of the corporation, rather than stock in the corporation; and despite a load of debt and a dearth of cash, the corporation limped along for three-and-a-half years before collapsing into the arms of the bankruptcy court. . . .

* * *

. . . But to assess the significance of this point one must distinguish between insolvency and the acknowledgment of insolvency and between insolvency and a lack of adequate capital. A firm might be insolvent in the bankruptcy sense of negative net worth—its liabilities exceeded its assets, . . . yet it might continue operating as long as it was able to raise enough money to pay its debts as they became due, or even longer if its creditors were forbearing.

By encumbering all the company's assets, the sale reduced its ability to borrow on favorable terms, as it could offer no collateral to lenders. And by surrendering most of old Crown's cash (the cash that was paid as a dividend) and obligating itself to pay $100,000 a year to the defendants and $495,000 a year to service the $3.1 million bank loan, without receiving anything in return except Smith's $500, new Crown was forced to engage in continual borrowing during its remaining life, and on unfavorable terms. Seven months before it declared bankruptcy it had run up $8.3 million in debt and its assets were worth less than half that amount.

New Crown thus had made payments and incurred obligations without receiving "reasonably equivalent value" in return. Even if it was not actually insolvent *ab initio,* as a result of the lack of equivalence it began life with "unreasonably small" assets given the nature of its business. That was what the bankruptcy judge meant when he said that new Crown survived as long as it did only on "life support." That was a finding of fact to which we defer.

The difference between insolvency and "unreasonably small" assets in the LBO context is the difference between being bankrupt on the day the LBO is consummated and having at that moment such meager assets that bankruptcy is a consequence both likely and foreseeable. . . . Focusing on the second question avoids haggling over whether at the moment of the transfer the corporation became "technically" insolvent, a question that only accountants could relish having to answer. . . .

But one has to be careful with a term like "unreasonably small." It is fuzzy, and in danger of being interpreted under the influence of hindsight bias. One is tempted to suppose that because a firm failed it must have been inadequately capitalized. The temptation must be resisted. . . . But new Crown started life almost with no assets at all, for all its physical assets were encumbered twice over, and the dividend plus new Crown's interest obligations drained the company of virtually all its cash. It was naked to any financial storms that might assail it. So the statutory condition for a fraudulent conveyance was satisfied—or so at least the bankruptcy judge could and did find without committing a clear error.

The fact that mistakes by the buyer hastened the company's demise is not a defense. Whether a transfer was fraudulent when made depends on conditions that existed when it was made, not on what happened later to affect the timing of the company's collapse. . . . Not that the length of the interval between the LBO and the collapse is irrelevant to determining the effect of the transfer. It is pertinent evidence. The longer the interval, the less likely that the collapse was fated at the formation of the new company . . . . An inadequately capitalized company may be able to stagger along for quite some time, concealing its parlous state or persuading creditors to avoid forcing it into a bankruptcy proceeding in which perhaps only the lawyers will do well.

* * *

As for the "dividend," it was an integral part of the LBO, although the trustee stumbled by failing to present evidence concerning old Crown's dividend policy. . . . We know as well that the dividend represented 50 percent of Crown's 1999 profits, which was unreasonably high given the cash needs of the business. Crown's owners drained it of cash—all unbeknownst to the corporation's present and future unsecured creditors. These indications that the dividend was part of the fraudulent transfer rather than a normal distribution of previously earned profits—that it wasn't an ordinary dividend but rather the withdrawal of an asset vital to the acquiring firm—were sufficient to place a burden on the defendants of producing evidence that it was a bona fide dividend, a burden they failed to carry.

* * *

. . . The trustee is entitled to the judgment awarded by the bankruptcy judge, plus the $590,328 dividend. After the claims of all creditors have been satisfied and the costs of administering the bankruptcy paid, any money remaining in the hands of the trustee must be returned to the defendants. . . .

The fraudulent conveyance attack on failed LBOs has succeeded in a limited number of cases. In *Lippi v. City Bank*, 955 F.2d 599 (9th Cir. 1992), and *United States v. Tabor Court Realty Corp.*, 803 F.2d 1288 (3d Cir. 1986), lenders to the purchasers in an LBO had their security interests set aside as fraudulent conveyances and in *Lippi* and *Wieboldt Stores v. Schottenstein*, 94 B.R. 488 (N.D.Ill. 1988), departing shareholders in the target had their stock sales set aside as fraudulent conveyances (they were constructive redemptions). Those most injured by LBO collapses are existing creditors of the target whose claims may be effectively subordinated to the claims of the LBO lender (which are secured by the assets of the target firm).[43] Contractual creditors can protect themselves from LBOs by requiring loan covenants restricting their debtor firms from engaging in LBO deals. Creditors generally choose higher interest rates to omit the covenants. So-called non-adjusting creditors (involuntary creditors such as tort claimants)[44] cannot protect themselves because they cannot bargain for interest rates to offset the risk and are, therefore, at the most risk in such deals.

Most fraudulent conveyance claims against LBO structures fail, however. See, e.g., *In re PNP Holdings Corp.*, 1998 WL 133560 (9th Cir.) (jury question). Plaintiffs often flounder on their heavy burden of proving that the target firm was insolvent at the time of the LBO. Parties to the LBO, the new equity owners and the new lenders (defendants in a fraudulent conveyance statute claim), do not invest unless they are convinced the firm can survive. Their return on their investment depends on the success of the re-leveraged firm. Moreover, the departing directors, to protect themselves from claims based on breach of fiduciary duty, often hire expert consultants that provide *solvency opinions,* opinions that the firm, immediately after the LBO, will be solvent. E.g., *Moody v. Security Pacific Business Credit, Inc.*, 971 F.2d 1056 (3d Cir. 1992) (new management skills and new access to credit not "reasonably equivalent value" as a matter of law, but firm solvent at time of LBO); cf. *SPC Plastics Corp. v. Griffith*, 224 B.R. 27 (6th Cir. 1998) (summary judgment for debtor affirmed on grounds that new management skills and new access to credit could not be equivalent value; summary judgment for debtor on insolvency reversed).

---

[43] LBO transactions can affect the value of existing claims even if the target remains solvent. The transaction increases the target firm's debt to equity ratio (leverage) and this lowers the value of outstanding debt. For example, an LBO prompts rating agencies to reduce the target's bond ratings. See, e.g., Metro. Life Ins. Co. v. RJR Nabisco, 716 F.Supp.1504 (S.D.N.Y. 1989) (see Chapter Six, Section C.2).

[44] Some argue that voluntary creditors that extend credit on fixed terms, like some trade creditors whose claims are so small that it is impractical to monitor, should also be included in this category. E.g., Lucian Arye Bebchuk & Jesse M. Fried, *The Uneasy Case for the Priority of Secured Claims in Bankruptcy,* 105 YALE. L.J. 857, 869–70 (1996).

4. BULK SALES ACTS

States enacted bulk sales legislation in the early 1900s to remedy a type of fraud on creditors perpetuated by unscrupulous trading merchants. A merchant would finance the purchase of his inventory (*stock in trade*),[45] then sell his entire inventory (*in bulk*) to a single purchaser and abscond with the proceeds, leaving the creditors that had financed his purchase of inventory unpaid. The creditors had a right to sue the merchant on the unpaid debts, but that right often was of little practical value. Even if the merchant-debtor was found and served successfully with process, those creditors who succeeded in obtaining a judgment often were unable to satisfy it because the defrauding seller had spent or hidden the sale proceeds. Nor did the creditors ordinarily have recourse to the merchandise sold. The transfer of the inventory to an innocent buyer, a good faith purchaser, effectively immunized the goods from the reach of the seller's creditors. The buyer asserted the *bona fide purchaser* for value defense.

State legislatures thought that the law of fraudulent conveyances was inadequate. When the buyer in bulk was in league with the seller or paid less than full value for the inventory, fraudulent conveyance law enabled the defrauded creditors to void the sale and apply the transferred inventory toward the satisfaction of their claims against the seller. But fraudulent conveyance law provided no remedy when purchasers bought for adequate value and in good faith—without reason to know of the seller's intention to pocket the proceeds and disappear.

State legislatures responded with *bulk sales laws*. The Uniform Commissioners on State Laws simplified and codified the state laws in a *Bulk Transfer Act* added as Article 6 of the Uniform Commercial Code in the early 1950s. All fifty states adopted a version of the Article. By 1987, the Commissioners had a radical change of heart and recommended that states repeal entirely the Bulk Transfer Act or replace it with a much tamer *Bulk Sales Act*. Over forty states (including Delaware) have repealed their Bulk Transfer Act and close to ten states (including California) have adopted the Revised Article 6 Bulk Sales Act. The effect of the laws is that whenever the parties have structured an asset sale of a business, the transaction planners must review all applicable transfer acts or bulk sales laws to determine what requirements are applicable.

Common to all bulk sales laws is the imposition of a duty on the buyer whenever it purchases the stock in trade of a seller, a sale "in bulk," to notify the seller's creditors of the impending sale. The laws applied only when the seller sold an inventory (stock) and when the purchaser did not agree to assume the seller's inventory financing debts in full.[46] Original

---

[45] Borrow money secured by the inventory.

[46] If the purchaser does assume the seller's debts, the purchaser must be solvent after the assumption and must give written notice of the assumption within thirty days of the sale. UCC § 6–103(3)(j) (1987).

Article 6—the Bulk Transfer Act—requires that a purchaser send notice ten days before whichever occurs first: the purchaser closes, the purchaser takes possession of the goods, or the purchaser pays for the goods. In those jurisdictions that have adopted optional § 6–106 in their Bulk Transfer Act, the purchaser also must assure that the new consideration for the transfer is applied to pay debts of the transferor.

The buyer's failure to comply with these and any other statutory duties generally affords the seller's creditors a remedy analogous to the remedy for fraudulent conveyances: the creditors acquire the right to set aside the sale and can reach the transferred inventory in the hands of the buyer. Like its predecessors, the Bulk Transfer Act is remarkable in that it obligates buyers in bulk to incur costs to protect the interests of the seller's creditors, with whom they usually have no relationship. Even more striking is that the Bulk Transfer Act affords creditors a remedy against a good faith purchaser for full value without notice of any wrongdoing on the part of the seller.

Compliance with the provisions of the Bulk Transfer Act can be burdensome, particularly when the transferor has a large number of creditors. When the transferor is actively engaged in business at a number of locations, assembling a current list of creditors may not be possible. Mailing a notice to each creditor may prove costly. When the goods that are the subject of the transfer are located in several jurisdictions, the transferor may be obligated to comply with Article 6 as enacted in each jurisdiction. The widespread enactment of non-uniform amendments makes compliance with Article 6 in multiple-state transactions problematic. Moreover, the Bulk Transfer Act requires compliance even when there is no reason to believe that the transferor is conducting a fraudulent transfer, e.g., when the transferor is scaling down the business but remaining available to creditors.

The benefits that compliance affords to creditors are insubstantial and do not justify the burdens and risks that the Article imposes upon good faith purchasers of business assets. The Bulk Transfer Act requires that notice be sent only ten days before the transferee takes possession of the goods or pays for them, whichever happens first. Given the delay between sending the notice and its receipt, creditors have scant opportunity to avail themselves of a judicial or nonjudicial remedy before the transfer has been consummated. In some cases, the Bulk Transfer Act has the unintended effect of injuring, rather than aiding, creditors by discouraging the sale of the debtor's business. Those purchasers who recognize the burdens and risks that Article 6 imposes upon them sometimes agree to purchase in bulk only at a reduced price. Others refuse to purchase in bulk at all, leaving the creditors to realize only the liquidation value, rather than the going concern value, of the business goods.

The National Conference of Commissioners on Uniform State Laws revised Article 6 in 1987 to reduce the burdens and risks imposed upon good-faith buyers of business assets while increasing the protection afforded to creditors. There are numerous changes. Among the most important, the new Article applies only when the buyer has notice, or after reasonable inquiry would have notice, that the seller will not continue to operate the same or a similar kind of business after the sale. UCC § 6–102(1)(c). When the seller is indebted to a large number of persons (over 200), the buyer need neither obtain a list of those persons nor send individual notices to each person but instead may give notice by filing with a state official. UCC §§ 6–105(2) & 6–104(2). The notice period has also increased from ten days to forty-five days. UCC § 6–105(5). A buyer who makes a good faith effort to comply with the requirements of this Article or to exclude the sale from the application of this Article, or who acts on the good faith belief that this Article does not apply to the sale, is not liable for noncompliance. UCC § 6–107(3). A buyer's noncompliance does not render the sale ineffective or otherwise affect the buyer's title to the goods; rather, the liability of a non-complying buyer is for damages caused by the noncompliance. UCC §§ 6–107(1) & 6–107(8). Finally, the bulk sales law of the jurisdiction of the seller's chief executive office or place of business controls. UCC § 6–103(1) & (2).

To avoid the time, effort and potential disruption of complying with bulk sales acts, parties to asset acquisitions may agree to waive compliance based upon the seller's agreement to indemnify the purchaser against seller creditor claims. If the purchaser does not trust the indemnification protection and there is otherwise insufficient security (no escrow), then wise purchasers comply with the act.

5. SUBSIDIARIES AND LIMITED LIABILITY PROTECTIONS

Owners of insolvent firms with healthy operating business burdened by overwhelming tort or environmental liabilities have looked to schemes involving subsidiaries to unlock the value in the operating assets. The owners attempted to sell or otherwise isolate the healthy operations free from the liabilities. All the schemes involved attempts to invoke the limited liability of parent firms for the debts of their subsidiaries. The most notorious of the schemes is in the following case.

SCHMOLL V. ACANDS, INC.

United States District Court, District of Oregon, 1988.
703 F.Supp. 868, *affirmed,* 977 F.2d 499 (9th Cir. 1992).

PANNER, CHIEF JUDGE.

Plaintiff Raymond Schmoll brings this products liability action against Raymark Industries Inc. and Raytech Corporation (Raytech). The issue is whether Raytech is liable as a successor for Raymark Industries' production, sale and distribution of products containing asbestos. I find that Raytech is a successor in liability to Raymark Industries. . . .

Raymark Industries manufactured and distributed energy absorption and transmission products, including asbestos and asbestos-containing products. Since the early 1970's, Raymark Industries has been named in an ever-increasing number of asbestos related personal injury lawsuits. By June 26, 1988, Raymark Industries had been named as a defendant in more than 68,000 cases. Approximately 1,000 new cases are filed each month. Raymark Industries has suffered severe financial declines as a result of the asbestos litigation. In 1981, Raymark Corporation had a net worth of $112.4 million. By 1985, the reported net worth of the company had dropped to $3.6 million. . . .

The corporate restructuring involved a complex series of transactions that transformed Raybestos-Manhattan into Raymark Industries and Raytech. The steps of this restructuring are diagrammed and described below.

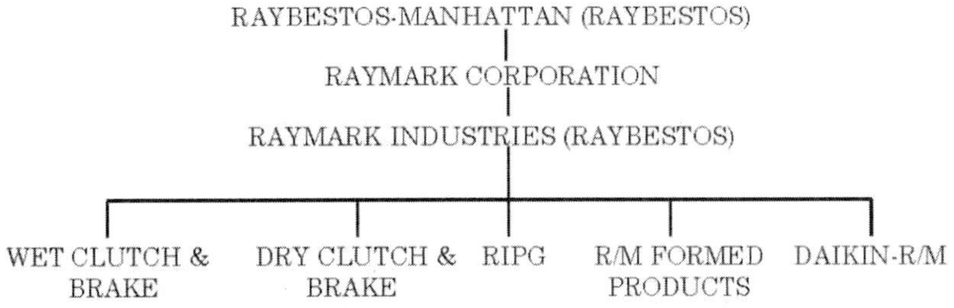

STEP 1: Raybestos-Manhattan (Raybestos), originally organized as a New Jersey corporation in 1929, was reorganized as a Connecticut corporation in 1976. In 1982, Raybestos-Manhattan changed its name to Raymark Industries and created Raymark Corporation as a holding company for Raymark Industries. Raymark Corporation's only asset was the stock of Raymark Industries. In 1985, Raymark Industries' assets included two operating divisions, Wet Clutch & Brake (WC & B) and Dry Clutch & Brake (DC & B); the stock of a German subsidiary, Raybestos Industrie—Produkte G.m.b.H. (RIPG); the stock of a shell corporation, R/M Formed Products; and a 50 percent interest in a foreign joint venture, Daiken—R/M.

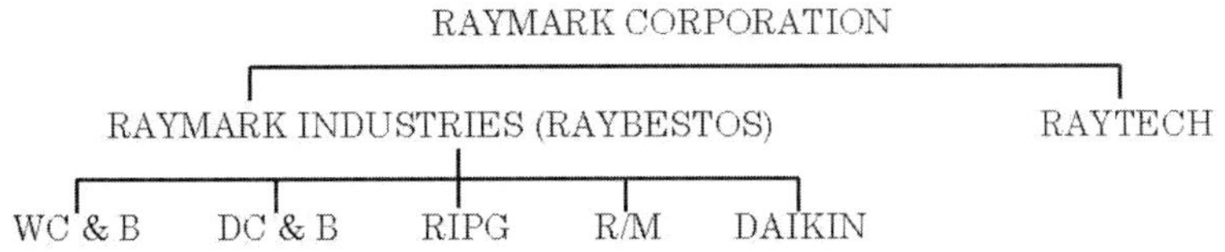

STEP 2: In June 1986, Raymark Corporation created Raytech as a wholly owned subsidiary.

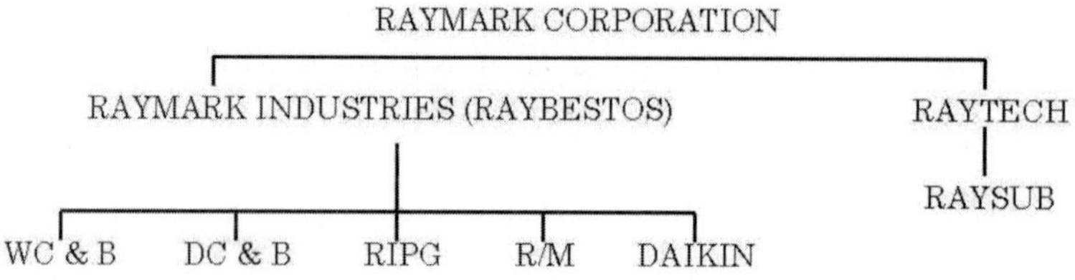

STEP 3: Raytech then created Raysub as a wholly-owned subsidiary. Raytech and Raysub were created solely to carry out the merger described in the next step.

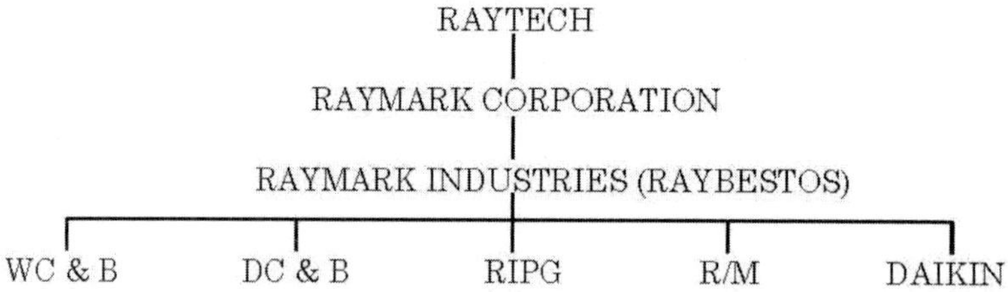

STEP 4: In October 1986, Raymark Corporation merged into Raysub, with Raymark Corporation surviving as a wholly-owned subsidiary of Raytech. In this merger, each outstanding share of Raymark common stock was converted into one share of Raytech stock. Raytech, designated the "holding company," was entirely owned by the former shareholders of Raymark Corporation. As a result of this merger, Raytech, the parent of Raysub, became the parent of Raymark Corporation. Raytech then owned 100 percent of the stock of Raymark Corporation, which owned 100 percent of the stock of Raymark Industries.

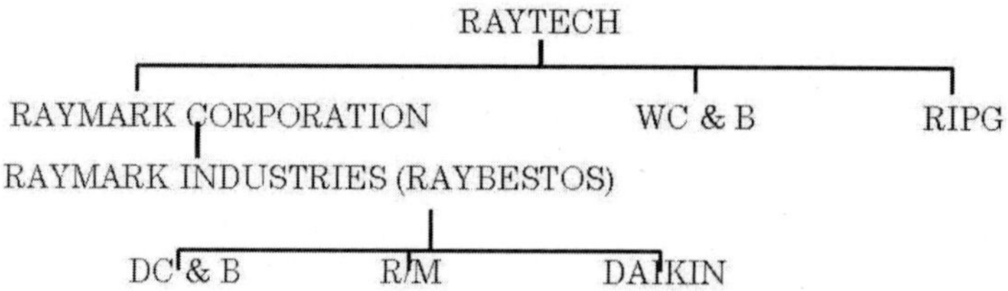

STEP 5: In 1987, Raytech purchased Raymark Industries' two most profitable assets, the Wet Clutch and Brake Division and RIPG stock. Raytech purchased the Wet Clutch and Brake Division for $76.9 million. Payment consisted of approximately $15 million in cash, $10 million worth of Raytech stock at closing with another $6 million in stock to be transferred later,[47] and $46 million in unsecured notes. The Wet Clutch and Brake Division, the largest of Raymark Industries' business operations, had significant profit potential. Furthermore, the asbestos claims against Raymark Industries did not arise from the Wet Clutch and Brake Division.

Raytech also purchased the RIPG stock owned by Raymark Industries for $8.2 million. RIPG does not manufacture or sell its asbestos products in the United States and has never been named in asbestos-related litigation. Terms of the sale included a cash payment of $3.9 million, with the balance financed by an unsecured note.

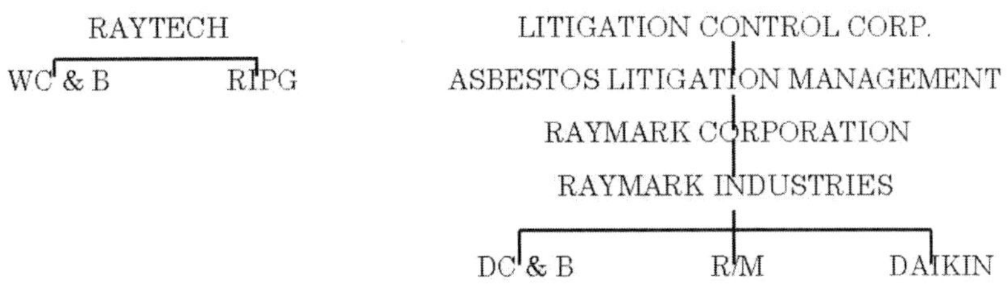

STEP 6: In 1988, Raytech sold Raymark Corporation, and thus Raymark Industries, to Asbestos Litigation Management (ALM) for $1 million. ALM paid $50,000 in cash and a $950,000 unsecured promissory note for all Raymark Corporation's assets and liabilities.

ALM is a wholly owned subsidiary of Litigation Control Corporation (LCC), whose business includes claims processing, document control and retention, and other services to companies involved in complex litigation. ALM serves only companies defending asbestos litigation. ALM now owns the stock of Raymark Corporation, whose only asset is Raymark Industries' stock.

As a result of this involved corporate restructuring, Raytech now owns WC & B and RIPG, the two historically lucrative businesses of Raymark Industries, without the drain of asbestos-related litigation. By selling the

[47] Though stock transferred to Raymark had an apparent market value of $10 million, it is unlikely that Raymark could have sold those shares for anything approaching that value. Any attempt by Raymark to market large blocks of these shares would have had a devastating effect on the price of Raytech shares. Dr. Albert Fitzpatrick, plaintiff's business expert, stated that Raymark probably would have had to accept a 90 percent discount in order to sell these shares as a block.

stock of Raymark Corporation, Raytech was able to dispose of a subsidiary whose asbestos-related expenses had decreased its earnings by $8.6 million during the first quarter of 1988.

. . . Raymark Industries had valuable assets, RIPG and Wet Clutch & Brake. It conveyed these assets to Raytech, which was owned by Raymark Industries' former shareholders. This transaction left Raymark Industries with staggering asbestos liabilities, unprofitable operations, unsecured notes, and stock which could not be sold in large blocks without a deep discount.

Present and future asbestos tort claimants, as Raymark Industries' potential creditors, were likewise left with little in the transaction. The money Raytech paid for Raymark Industries' profit-generating assets will not adequately compensate present and future claimants. If Raytech escapes liability for Raymark Industries' torts, these creditors will no longer have access to Raymark Industries' valuable assets or to the potential stream of profits generated by these assets.

In the present case, the context of the corporate restructuring and the participants' statements show that the elaborate transfer of assets was designed to escape liability. Raymark Industries has experienced severe financial problems because of asbestos litigation. By April 1, 1988, nearly 34,000 asbestos related personal injury cases were pending against Raymark Industries. These claims exceed $33 billion. Trying cases to verdict has cost an average of $59,000. Raymark Industries has been assessed more than $75,000,000 in punitive damages from asbestos litigation. Raymark Industries has already exhausted approximately 71 percent of its almost $400 million in insurance coverage.

In response to Raymark Corporation's financial difficulties, Craig Smith and other officers and directors, with the advice of counsel, developed the sophisticated corporate restructuring scheme. The New York law firm of Debevoise & Plimpton advised Raytech's board of directors that:

> It should be possible under existing case law for Raytech to acquire assets or businesses of Raymark without thereby subjecting Raytech or such acquired assets or businesses to liability for the asbestos-related claims against Raymark under the doctrines of successor liability, piercing the corporate veil or fraudulent conveyance. . . .

Raymark Corporation's 1985 annual report stated that the company's long-term strategy was:

> to protect and enhance shareholder investment, to maximize the amounts available for deserving asbestos-injured claimants[48] and

[48] Raymark Industries' 1988 Settlement Guidelines provides a maximum payment of $452. In a recent case involving clear asbestos liability and death from mesothelioma, Raymark Industries offered nothing. The jury returned a verdict of $1.7 million in compensatory damages

> to limit exposure for asbestos claims only to businesses currently threatened, thus enabling our other businesses and any new business opportunities to grow, unshadowed by the cloud of asbestos liability.

Another purpose of the corporate restructuring was:

> to gain access to new sources of capital and borrowed funds which could be used to finance the acquisition and operation of new businesses in a corporate restructure that should not subject Raytech or such acquired businesses to the asbestos related liabilities of Raymark. . . .

I find that, although the corporate restructuring meets the technical formalities of corporate form, it was designed with the improper purpose of escaping asbestos-related liabilities.[49] Raymark Corporation changed from the parent of Raymark Industries to the subsidiary of Raytech to the subsidiary of ALM. Raytech purchased Raymark Corporation's two valuable assets and then sold the remainder to ALM for $1 million. It is inconceivable that in an arm's-length corporate transaction, a buyer would have purchased an entity so lacking in assets and laden with liabilities.

There is no just reason to respect the integrity of these transactions. Raymark Industries made substantial profits from the production of asbestos-containing products. Raymark Industries should not be allowed to avoid liability by transferring its profitable assets leaving no more than a corporate shell unable to satisfy its asbestos-related obligations.

This case presents serious equitable considerations. At least 21 million American workers have been directly exposed to significant amounts of asbestos at the work place since 1940 and millions more have been indirectly exposed. . . . Tens of thousands of people become ill or die from asbestos-related diseases every year. . . . Asbestos-related lawsuits are filed in corresponding numbers.[50]

It is ironic that, while Raymark Industries prides itself for not following Johns-Manville Corporation's (Manville) lead by filing bankruptcy, Raymark is in effect attempting a bankruptcy-like reorganization without affording creditors the protections of formal bankruptcy. In December 1986, the United States Bankruptcy Court for the Southern District of New York confirmed a Plan of Reorganization of Manville. The Plan created a personal injury trust of $3 billion to cover all

---

against Raymark Industries. Sawyer v. Raymark Industries, Inc., No. 87–542 (D.Haw. Dec.6, 1988).

49 Plaintiff notes that if he were attempting to set aside the transactions, rather than hold Raytech responsible for Raymark Industries' torts, the court could hold as a matter of law that the transactions constituted fraudulent conveyances under the Uniform Fraudulent Transfer Act, Or.Rev.Stat. § 95.200–310.

50 Through April 1, 1988, Raymark Industries has been named in 68,057 separate actions involving 84,724 individual plaintiffs. In 1988, 1,209 cases have been filed per month. Raymark Industries projects additional filings through 1997 of approximately 61,200 cases . . .

of Manville's present and future, known and unknown asbestos injury liabilities. . . .

The success or failure of Raymark Corporation's attempts to escape asbestos liability will provide direction to other companies seeking to avoid such responsibility. Upholding the integrity of such transactions would unjustly elevate form over substance.[Ed.[51]]

CELOTEX CORP. v. HILLSBOROUGH HOLDINGS CORP., 176 B.R. 223 (M.D. Fla. 1994): [In late 1987 Kohlberg, Kravis, Roberts and Company, through Hillsborough Holdings Corporation (HHC), arranged a $2.4 billion leveraged buy-out of Jim Walter Corporation on the assumption that the asbestos product claims against a Jim Walter subsidiary, Celotex Corporation, that had once made asbestos products could be confined to the subsidiary.] Prior to 1987, the old Jim Walter Corporation ("JWC") acted as a holding company, owning all the stock in various subsidiaries, including Celotex. In 1987, JWC was the subject of a multi-step leveraged buy-out (the "LBO"), in which JWC was acquired by and merged into a newly formed corporation called Hillsborough Acquisition Corporation ("HAC"). HAC then transferred all of JWC's assets, except Celotex, to two newly-created holding companies, HHC and Walter Industries. HAC next changed its name to Jim Walter Corporation. HHC [Ed. Should this be HAC?] sold this "new" Jim Walter Corporation, along with its subsidiary Celotex, to a third party, the Jasper Corporation. [Celotex and its subsidiaries faced massive potential tort liabilities arising out of asbestos claims in an aggregate amount far exceeding their net worth. The other two new holding companies held all old Jim Walter's other subsidiaries, which were profitable and financially sound. After the sale of new Jim Walter Corporation, HHC sought to sell the remaining old Jim Walter assets, which it believed were free of the Celotex liabilities. A suit against HHC and Walter Industries brought by eighty thousand asbestos victims so unsettled bond investors and potential asset buyers that Hillsborough was forced to seek bankruptcy court protection. The plaintiffs sought to have the corporate veil between old Jim Walter and its subsidiary, Celotex, removed, leaving the company and its successors, HHC and Walter Industries, liable for any judgments against Celotex. The federal district court affirmed the bankruptcy judge's refusal to pierce the veil in 1994 and the parties settled while the case was on appeal. HHC agreed to put $375 million into Celotex, which was in its own Chapter 11 proceeding, and Celotex agreed to seek an injunction in its plan of reorganization that

---

[51] [Ed. After the case, Raytech Corporation filed a Chapter 11 petition. See Raytech Corp. v. White, 54 F.3d 187 (3d Cir. 1995), *cert. denied*, 516 U.S. 914 (1995) (9th Circuit case collaterally estops Raytech from relitigating successor liability).]

prohibited the asbestos claimants from seeking any further relief from HHC or its affiliates.]

The first claim for asbestos related injuries was filed in 1966. Since that time hundreds of thousands of claims have been filed; with an average of nearly 300,000 claims per year filed for the last three years. Defendants have spent an estimated $54 billion on asbestos litigation. Liability for asbestos is no longer centered on asbestos manufacturers or auto parts. Affected companies include insulation makers, a can maker, an industrial gas producer, a tile maker, railroads, electronics producers, a boilermaker, and a media giant. The recent trend in the litigation seems to be toward suing peripheral companies, firms that used asbestos in refineries, power plants, plumbing supply, and distributors. So when savvy dealmakers look at potential acquisitions they include in their checklist potential asbestos liability.

The *Schmoll* case demonstrates the difficulty of even the most elaborate strategies designed to separate profitable assets from asbestos claims. If a transaction does not have an underlying business rationale beyond escaping asbestos liability, courts seem to find a way to apply some form of liability shifting doctrine be it successor liability or disregarding a parent-sub separation. Purchases of assets for cash by independent third parties (if the seller retains the proceeds of the sale and applies them fully to the asbestos claims), seemingly the safest transaction, may run afoul of the fraudulent conveyance statutes. See *W.R. Grace &Co. v. Sealed Air Corp.*, 281 B.R. 852 (Bankr. Ct. D. Del. 2002).[52] The author has found only one case in which an asset acquisition for cash in the face of asbestos liabilities was not set aside for one reason or another. *Lippe v. Bairnco*, 99 Fed. App'x 274 (2d Cir. 2004) (plaintiff's experts evidence on fair value excluded as inherently incredible).

NOTE: SECTION 524(g) PROCEEDINGS FOR ASBESTOS CLAIMS

The safest way to buy asbestos-tainted assets is through a Chapter 11 bankruptcy proceeding. Many of the current deals to buy asbestos-linked assets are done under the protection of the bankruptcy court. Purchasers often resort to a specialized proceeding under § 542(g) of the Bankruptcy Code, part of a plan of reorganization process. In a § 524(g) proceeding, the bankruptcy court appoints a representative for future claimants, who assists in creating a settlement that resolves and discharges future claims. Upon completion of the

---

52 There are two issues: First, whether the transaction was for "fair value" and, second, whether the debtor corporation was insolvent at the time of the deal. The second question may turn on the details of a state's statute. The Uniform Fraudulent Conveyances Act (UFCA) refers to "probable liability" or "existing debts" in determining solvency. The Uniform Fraudulent Transfers Act (UFTA) does not, taking a pure balance sheet approach (corporation insolvent when "the sum of the debtor's debts is greater than all of the debtor's assets").

proceeding, a federal district court issues a permanent injunction against future claims. The injunction sanitizes the seller's balance sheet.

The disadvantage of the § 542(g) process is that is can be a slow and expensive proceeding, and some faltering companies might not survive long enough to complete the acquisition. The advantages of doing a deal outside of bankruptcy, speed and less publicity, translate into a lower likelihood of competition from other purchasers.

Deals for solvent but heavily liability-burdened firms that parties do outside of bankruptcy are usually triangular asset acquisitions. The purchaser quantifies the risk of the asbestos claims, reduces the sale price accordingly, and purchases the assets of the seller through a wholly owned subsidiary, isolating the new subsidiary from the parent's operations. The seller may retain primary liability on the liabilities, but the purchase recognizes the risk of exposure on the liabilities under a de facto merger theory should the seller default. Purchasers therefore routinely seek *indemnification* from the seller on the outstanding liabilities if the buyer must pay them, but the seller guarantee is only as good as the financial resources backing it. If the indemnification is based on the seller's insurance the buyer must do due diligence on the target's insurance. If indemnification is insufficient, as it often is, the buyer may be able to purchase its own specialized insurance to plug gaps in their risk profile.

The strategy of isolating the liabilities in a subsidiary also has some risk as well, as creditors may ask a court to *disregard the entity (pierce the corporate veil).*

UNITED STATES V. BESTFOODS

Supreme Court of the United States, 1998.
524 U.S. 51, 118 S.Ct. 1876, 141 L.Ed.2d 43.

JUSTICE SOUTER delivered the opinion of the Court.

The United States brought this action for the costs of cleaning up industrial waste generated by a chemical plant. The issue before us, under the Comprehensive Environmental Response, Compensation, and Liability Act of 1980 (CERCLA), 94 Stat. 2767, as amended, 42 U.S.C. § 9601 et seq., is whether a parent corporation that actively participated in, and exercised control over, the operations of a subsidiary may, without more, be held liable as an operator of a polluting facility owned or operated by the subsidiary. We answer no, unless the corporate veil may be pierced. But a corporate parent that actively participated in, and exercised control over, the operations of the facility itself may be held directly liable in its own right as an operator of the facility.

* * *

In 1957, Ott Chemical Co. (Ott I) began manufacturing chemicals at a plant near Muskegon, Michigan, and its intentional and unintentional dumping of hazardous substances significantly polluted the soil and ground water at the site. In 1965, respondent CPC International Inc. incorporated a wholly owned subsidiary to buy Ott I's assets in exchange for CPC stock. The new company, also dubbed Ott Chemical Co. (Ott II), continued chemical manufacturing at the site, and continued to pollute its surroundings. CPC kept the managers of Ott I, including its founder, president, and principal shareholder, Arnold Ott, on board as officers of Ott II. Arnold Ott and several other Ott II officers and directors were also given positions at CPC, and they performed duties for both corporations.

In 1972, CPC sold Ott II to Story Chemical Company, which operated the Muskegon plant until its bankruptcy in 1977. Shortly thereafter, when respondent Michigan Department of Natural Resources (MDNR) examined the site for environmental damage, it found the land littered with thousands of leaking and even exploding drums of waste, and the soil and water saturated with noxious chemicals. MDNR sought a buyer for the property who would be willing to contribute toward its cleanup, and after extensive negotiations, respondent Aerojet-General Corp. arranged for transfer of the site from the Story bankruptcy trustee in 1977. Aerojet created a wholly owned California subsidiary, Cordova Chemical Company (Cordova/California), to purchase the property, and Cordova/California in turn created a wholly owned Michigan subsidiary, Cordova Chemical Company of Michigan (Cordova/Michigan), which manufactured chemicals at the site until 1986.[5]

By 1981, the federal Environmental Protection Agency had undertaken to see the site cleaned up, and its long-term remedial plan called for expenditures well into the tens of millions of dollars. To recover some of that money, the United States filed this action under § 107 in 1989, naming five defendants as responsible parties: CPC, Aerojet, Cordova/California, Cordova/Michigan, and Arnold Ott. (By that time, Ott I and Ott II were defunct.) . . .

* * *

---

[5] Cordova/California and MDNR entered into a contract under which Cordova/California agreed to undertake certain cleanup actions, and MDNR agreed to share in the funding of those actions and to indemnify Cordova/California for various expenses. The Michigan Court of Appeals has held that this agreement requires MDNR to indemnify Aerojet and its Cordova subsidiaries for any CERCLA liability that they may incur in connection with their activities at the Muskegon facility. See Cordova Chemical Co. v. Dept. of Natural Resources, 212 Mich.App. 144, 536 N.W.2d 860 (1995), appeal denied, 453 Mich. 901, 554 N.W.2d 319 (1996). [Ed. The EPA will, in very limited circumstances, agree not to sue prospective purchasers of contaminated property in exchange for promises to remediate. 60 Fed. Reg. 34,792 (July 3, 1995). The so-called "brown-fields" initiative is very controversial. Several bills introduced in Congress have sought more aggressive brown-field redevelopment. See William Buzbee, *Brownfields, Environmental Federalism, and Institutional Determinism*, 21 WM. & MARY ENVT'L L. & POL'Y REV. 1 (1997).]

It is a general principle of corporate law deeply "ingrained in our economic and legal systems" that a parent corporation (so-called because of control through ownership of another corporation's stock) is not liable for the acts of its subsidiaries. . . .

But there is an equally fundamental principle of corporate law, applicable to the parent-subsidiary relationship as well as generally, that the corporate veil may be pierced and the shareholder held liable for the corporation's conduct when, inter alia, the corporate form would otherwise be misused to accomplish certain wrongful purposes, most notably fraud, on the shareholder's behalf. . . .[10]

If the act rested liability entirely on ownership of a polluting facility, this opinion might end here, but CERCLA liability may turn on operation as well as ownership, and nothing in the statute's terms bars a parent corporation from direct liability for its own actions in operating a facility owned by its subsidiary. . . .

Under the plain language of the statute, any person who operates a polluting facility is directly liable for the costs of cleaning up the pollution. See 42 U.S.C. § 9607(a)(2). This is so regardless of whether that person is the facility's owner, the owner's parent corporation or business partner, or even a saboteur who sneaks into the facility at night to discharge its poisons out of malice. If any such act of operating a corporate subsidiary's facility is done on behalf of a parent corporation, the existence of the parent-subsidiary relationship under state corporate law is simply irrelevant to the issue of direct liability. . . .

This much is easy to say; the difficulty comes in defining actions sufficient to constitute direct parental "operation." . . . To sharpen the definition for purposes of CERCLA's concern with environmental contamination, an operator must manage, direct, or conduct operations specifically related to pollution, that is, operations having to do with the leakage or disposal of hazardous waste, or decisions about compliance with environmental regulations.

* * *

The well-taken objection to the actual control test, however, is its fusion of direct and indirect liability; the test is administered by asking a question about the relationship between the two corporations (an issue going to indirect liability) instead of a question about the parent's interaction with the subsidiary's facility (the source of any direct liability). If, however, direct liability for the parent's operation of the facility is to be kept distinct from derivative liability for the subsidiary's own operation,

[10] Some courts and commentators have suggested that this indirect, veil-piercing approach can subject a parent corporation to liability only as an owner, and not as an operator . . . We think it is otherwise, however. If a subsidiary that operates, but does not own, a facility is so pervasively controlled by its parent for a sufficiently improper purpose to warrant veil piercing, the parent may be held derivatively liable for the subsidiary's acts as an operator.

the focus of the enquiry must necessarily be different under the two tests. "The question is not whether the parent operates the subsidiary, but rather whether it operates the facility, and that operation is evidenced by participation in the activities of the facility, not the subsidiary. Control of the subsidiary, if extensive enough, gives rise to indirect liability under piercing doctrine, not direct liability under the statutory language." Oswald 269; . . . .

In addition to (and perhaps as a reflection of) the erroneous focus on the relationship between CPC and Ott II, even those findings of the District Court that might be taken to speak to the extent of CPC's activity at the facility itself are flawed, for the District Court wrongly assumed that the actions of the joint officers and directors are necessarily attributable to CPC. . . .

. . . The Government would have to show that, despite the general presumption to the contrary, the officers and directors were acting in their capacities as CPC officers and directors, and not as Ott II officers and directors, when they committed those acts.[13] . . .

* * *

In our enquiry into the meaning Congress presumably had in mind when it used the verb "to operate," we recognized that the statute obviously meant something more than mere mechanical activation of pumps and valves, and must be read to contemplate "operation" as including the exercise of direction over the facility's activities. . . .

Identifying such an occurrence calls for line drawing yet again, since the acts of direct operation that give rise to parental liability must necessarily be distinguished from the interference that stems from the normal relationship between parent and subsidiary. Again, norms of corporate behavior (undisturbed by any CERCLA provision) are crucial reference points. Just as we may look to such norms in identifying the limits of the presumption that a dual officeholder acts in his ostensible capacity, so here we may refer to them in distinguishing a parental officer's oversight of a subsidiary from such an officer's control over the operation of the subsidiary's facility. "[A]ctivities that involve the facility but which are consistent with the parent's investor status, such as monitoring of the subsidiary's performance, supervision of the subsidiary's finance and capital budget decisions, and articulation of general policies and procedures, should not give rise to direct liability." Oswald 282. The critical question is whether, in degree and detail, actions directed to the facility by

---

[13] We do not attempt to recite the ways in which the Government could show that dual officers or directors were in fact acting on behalf of the parent. Here, it is prudent to say only that the presumption that an act is taken on behalf of the corporation for whom the officer claims to act is strongest when the act is perfectly consistent with the norms of corporate behavior, but wanes as the distance from those accepted norms approaches the point of action by a dual officer plainly contrary to the interests of the subsidiary yet nonetheless advantageous to the parent.

an agent of the parent alone are eccentric under accepted norms of parental oversight of a subsidiary's facility.

* * *

6. THE DEBTOR'S RESIDUAL STRATEGY: BLEED AND DEFAULT

Our legal system uses a grab bag of approaches aimed at minimizing defaults on cleanup debts. At the core of all of these approaches is a flypaper strategy designed to stick any and all parties in the vicinity with liability in the hope that one of them will be solvent at the time of execution. First, CERCLA restricts a selling firm's ability to transfer completely its liability to a second firm. A buying firm may agree to pay all the selling firm's liabilities, but the selling firm remains liable if the buying firm defaults. Second, our legal system attaches environmental liabilities to assets, so that anyone buying the assets must often assume the liabilities. In CERCLA, for example, the statute attaches liability to the original and subsequent landowners of contaminated land, subject to a very narrow "innocent landowners" defense that excludes most contract purchasers. Courts applying CERCLA have also attached liability to non-contaminated assets under the various doctrines of the common law of successor liability. A selling firm can agree to indemnify a buying firm for any cleanup costs attributable to the selling firm's business before the acquisition, but a buying firm runs the risk of the selling firm's insolvency or dissolution.

Thus, in an acquisition, our legal system collects on environmental obligations by following both the assets in the hands of the buyers as well as the proceeds of the sale in the hands of the sellers. In any acquisition, the system, in theory, doubles the security behind any environmental claims once the business is sold. The disadvantage of this approach is that it imposes not only significant restraints on acquisitions, but also restraints on the alienation and use of otherwise productive property.

In theory, the law holds buyers responsible for cleanup obligations of the seller. The seller, forced to absorb a reduction in prices any buyer will pay for a firm that has outstanding cleanup obligations, fully internalizes the costs of any acts that have generated these environmental obligations. Accordingly, the theory goes, the seller will consider the cleanup costs in its balancing of the costs and benefits of any act that leads to such costs. In practice, however, the theory breaks down on two fronts. First, since cleanup costs at present cannot be accurately estimated by buyers, buyers often cannot price them in an acquisition. Buyers walk, looking for other assets that do not have any environmental risk, rather than absorb the price risk.[53] Sellers, not able to absorb severe discounts that necessarily

---

[53] Buyers could also agree to participate in a piecemeal sale of the seller. Buyers of a small piece of the business (except the contaminated land itself) cannot be said to buy the business itself and are free from successor liabilities. The seller loses the goodwill value of the business (its

take account of the variability of the cleanup costs, find it more profitable to soldier along, pulling money out of the firm whenever they can, draining its assets, and eventually refusing to pay taxes or other government fees until the government executes on the land and takes ownership.[54] This is the ultimate dodge. Avoid liability as long as one can, drain all cash out of the operation (in salaries and dividends), avoid any new capital contributions, and ultimately escheat the land to the government, creating a *brown field*.[55] The effect is the reverse doughnut blight around inner cities of abandoned manufacturing facilities.[56]

Second, even if the costs are estimable, they are difficult to price in a deal because the statutes do not allow either party to escape them completely after the transaction; one party must always guarantee the cleanup obligations of the other. The statutes cause the seller to remain secondarily liable after any acquisition, subject to the risk of the buyer's insolvency or dissolution, which the seller must price in the acquisition. The situation also works in reverse: if the buyer seeks contractual indemnification from the seller for cleanup costs, the buyer is subject to the risk of the seller's insolvency or dissolution. Thus, the parties must price not only the cleanup costs but also the risk of secondary liability on those costs in any given acquisition. The combination of the variability of cleanup costs and the variability of secondary guarantees makes many deals impossible.

---

reputational value). However, the seller must find a way to distribute the sale proceeds to owners without subjecting the distributions to attack. This is the dissolution and fraudulent conveyance problem noted above.

54 Several statutory exemptions from the definition of "owner" exist. One such exclusion applies to state or local governments that acquired title to a contaminated facility involuntarily through bankruptcy, tax delinquency, abandonment, eminent domain, etc. CERCLA § 101(20)(D). It is possible, therefore, to buy land from a government unit and not be in a "contractual relationship" with a prior statutory "owner" under the innocent purchaser defense. Moreover, even if the defense does not apply, states (and the federal government) will often provide special protections from liability to those who purchase contaminated land from the state (or federal government). See note 5 in *Bestfoods, supra* (state of Michigan indemnification agreement), citing Cordova Chemical Co. v. Dept. of Natural Resources, 212 Mich.App. 144, 536 N.W.2d 860 (1995), appeal denied, 453 Mich. 901, 554 N.W.2d 319 (1996).

55 With the federal government bogged down in Superfund litigation, the states have begun to design their own brown-field redevelopment programs in cooperation with the EPA. Forty-seven states now have voluntary clean-up programs and more than twenty offer financial incentives to firms that undertake brown-field redevelopment. Pennsylvania, for example, offers statutory relief from liability, a streamlined review process and straightforward clean-up standards. Some state regulators have become more tolerant of "risk-based clean-up," a pseudonym for sprucing up land only to a level consistent with its proposed future use. Property zoned for industrial use does not have to meet the same standards as that for residential use.

Moreover, the technology for cleaning up industrial contamination has improved steadily. With the new technology came a willingness of insurance companies to cover risks associated with transferring environmentally impaired properties. The insurance has generated a new industry, private companies specialized in buying and redeveloping brown-field sites. When there is money to be made in cleaning up brown-fields, there is a way out.

56 The new factories locate on virgin land in rural locations.

CHAPTER FOUR

ACQUISITION DOCUMENTS

■ ■ ■

Most acquisitions follow a predictable trail in the production of documents. There may be substantial variety in the documents themselves, of course, reflecting the terms of a given deal. In this chapter, we investigate the basic acquisition documents. In the preliminary negotiations, one often sees a letter of intent, a confidentiality agreement and (if one of the parties is publicly traded) a public announcement. Lawyers undertaking a legal audit, also known as a *legal due diligence investigation*, will use an acquisition review checklist to prepare for both signing the acquisition agreement and the subsequent closing. The acquisition agreement follows, with sections on price, representations and warranties, covenants, conditions and indemnification. Supporting documents include the disclosure letter or schedule and, if key managers of the seller are staying on to run the business, one or more employment agreements. Closing documents include the supplement to the disclosure letter or schedule and opinions of counsel and may include a non-negotiable promissory note and an escrow agreement.

For those who wish for forms that are more complete or further discussion of the details of the documents, there are excellent materials authored by the Committee on Mergers and Acquisitions of the Section of Business Law of the American Bar Association. American Bar Association, Committee on Mergers and Acquisitions, Section on Business Law, *Model Stock Purchase Agreement with Commentary* (2d ed. 2010); *Model Asset Purchase Agreement with Commentary* (2001); and *Model Merger Agreement for the Acquisition of a Public Company* (2011). The American Bar Association, Section on Business Law, *Manual on Acquisition Review* (1995), is a due diligence checklist with commentary. Also important is the American Bar Association, *Guidelines for the Preparation of Closing Opinions* (2002) and the *Statement of the Role of Customary Practice in the Preparation and Understanding of Third-Party Legal Opinions* (Aug. 2008), articulating a national consensus on the role, content and interpretation of legal opinions delivered at closing to parties to the transaction. The following sections use provisions from the ABA forms as well as some privately created.

Students interested in documents used in recent acquisitions can find samples in the filings of publicly traded firms that are available without charge on the SEC's web site (www.sec.gov). There are also several online services that charge for collecting such documents. See LexisNexis

Transactional Advisor, Securities Practice Center and LexisNexis Securities Mosiac.

A. PRELIMINARY DOCUMENTS

1. CONFIDENTIALITY AGREEMENTS

The *confidentiality agreement* (or *nondisclosure agreement* or *NDA*) is usually the first document the parties sign in an acquisition negotiation. It is usually in the form of a letter. A seller ought not to give a prospective purchaser sensitive business information until the purchaser has signed a confidentiality agreement.[1] A confidentiality agreement defines confidential information very broadly[2] and obligates the buyer to keep information received in strict confidence. Most agreements also include a provision on the secrecy of the deal negotiations as well. A buyer may also request a seller to sign a confidentiality agreement if the buyer is offering stock or notes in the acquisition, and thus a "mutual" NDA is executed. The buyer in such deals will usually disclose information to the seller necessary to value the consideration. A disclosure may include, for example, information on future business plans or financial capacity.

It is typical for certain information to be carved out from a confidentiality agreement. One frequently sees exceptions for generally available public information, information already in the hands of the purchaser at the time of signing or "independently developed" information. For example, the following is a standard carve out provision:

> Recipient shall have no obligation under this Agreement to maintain in confidence any information that: (a) is in the public domain at the time of disclosure, (b) though originally

---

[1] Sometimes parties consolidate the Agreement into the letter of intent, but the better practice is to keep the two documents separated. The seller intends the confidentiality agreement to be an enforceable contract and parts of the letter of intent are not enforceable. Combining the two documents can confuse their intended legal status. Moreover, if confidential information is transferred and the letter of intent is never executed, that information is not protected.

[2] Consider the following provision:

> For purposes of this Agreement, "**Confidential Information**" means all information and material which is proprietary to Discloser, whether or not marked as "confidential" or "proprietary," and which is disclosed to or obtained by Recipient, which relates to Discloser's past, present or future research, marketing, technology, development or business activities. Without limiting the generality of the foregoing, the defined term Confidential Information covers all information or materials prepared by or for Discloser and includes, without limitation, all of the following: financial documentation, processes, procedures, "know-how," new product or new technology information, manufacturing, development or marketing techniques, marketing plans and materials, development or marketing timetables, strategies and development plans, including trade names, trademarks, customer, supplier or personal names and other information related to customers, suppliers or personnel, pricing policies, financial information, trade secrets, research, source code, prototypes, and other information of a similar nature, whether or not reduced to writing or other tangible form, and any other nonpublic business information. Confidential Information also includes all information received from others that Discloser is obligated to treat as confidential.

> Confidential Information, subsequently enters the public domain other than by breach of Recipient's obligations hereunder or by breach of another entity's obligation of confidentiality, (c) is shown by documentary evidence to have been known by Recipient prior to its receipt from Discloser or (d) is independently developed by Recipient without access to or utilization of any Confidential Information. Recipient shall be entitled to disclose Confidential Information to the extent required pursuant to a court order or as otherwise required by law, provided that Recipient gives Discloser reasonable prior notice of any such proposed disclosure and complies with any applicable protective order or equivalent.

Most confidentiality agreements also require the recipient of the confidential information to use that information solely for a defined purpose. In the M & A context, the purpose to determine whether to pursue a deal between the parties. The agreement also limits the identity of those at the recipient who can see the information. For example:

> Recipient may use the Confidential Information only to further the Purpose and only in accordance with the terms of this Agreement. Recipient may disclose Confidential Information only to consultants, counsel or full-time employees of Recipient who have: (a) a demonstrable need to know such Confidential Information and (b) been informed of Recipient's obligations hereunder. A breach of such promise shall be considered a material breach hereunder. Recipient hereby agrees to indemnify and hold harmless Discloser against any loss of any kind arising out of the use or disclosure of Confidential Information by any person, including full-time employees, to which Recipient has disclosed Confidential Information. Recipient agrees to segregate all tangible Confidential Information from other information or materials to prevent commingling.

Most agreements also control all interviews of the seller's employees by a potential buyer and require a return or destruction of all confidential information on the termination of negotiations. Some agreements, particularly those in acquisitions of high tech companies, prohibit the buyer from hiring selling company employees for a period of years.[3] Most agreements contain caveats that the agreement does not obligate either party to consummate a deal or commit to any terms of a deal. Additionally,

---

3 Consider the following provision:

> For a period of one year following the date of this Agreement, the Recipient will not induce, solicit, aid or encourage any employee or contractor of Discloser to leave such employ, or employ in connection with any Competitive Activity (as defined below), any employee or contractor of Discloser within one year after such individual has left the employ of Discloser. For purposes of this Agreement, "**Competitive Activity**" means directly or indirectly performing any services for, or owning any interest in, any corporation, partnership, proprietorship, business or other entity (other than the Discloser) which engages in the business of Discloser.

the agreement does not obligate either party to negotiate further in good faith or otherwise. There is also a disclaimer of any representations or warranties on the accuracy or completeness of any information provided.[4] The reasons for the disclaimers are evident from the discussion in the following section. Anti-assignment provisions are also typical.[5]

Finally, confidentiality agreements typically require the recipient to consent to equitable relief. Take the following provision:

> Recipient acknowledges that monetary damages alone may not be a sufficient remedy for unauthorized disclosure and use of Confidential Information and that Discloser shall be entitled, without waiving any other rights or remedies, to such injunctive or equitable relief as may be deemed proper by a court of competent jurisdiction. If either party employs attorneys to enforce any rights arising out of or relating to this Agreement, the prevailing party shall be entitled to recover reasonable attorney's fees.

Although confidentiality agreements as a part of merger negotiations are ubiquitous, in the past one rarely saw lawsuits based on breaches of the agreements. The exception to this is litigation over a relatively modern practice, the use of *standstill* provisions in the sale of public companies. A standstill provision prevents a potential buyer from disrupting the negotiations by acquiring shares of the seller in the open market or by soliciting proxies. Thus, a standstill provision prohibits a potential buyer from gaining leverage over the seller through those activities. The duration of the standstill period may range from six months to two years.

If a seller is running a controlled auction for the company, the standstill provisions force all bidding parties to operate within the boundaries of the bidding process established by the seller—that is, to play nice. The agreements stop, for example, a bidder from submitting a low offer only to submit a topping bid after the seller announces and accepts the winning bid among competitors in the auction. The standstill pressures all bidders to put their best offer forward in the formal auction.[6]

---

4 The disclaimer is not preclusive. AES Corp. v. Dow Chem. Co., 325 F.3d 174, *cert. denied*, 540 U.S. 1068, 124 S.Ct. 805, 157 L.Ed.2d 732 (2003) (remanded; provision is evidence of non-reliance).

5 Consider the following provision:

> Recipient shall not assign any rights or delegate any obligations under this Agreement or otherwise transfer or assign this Agreement (voluntarily or by operation of law) without the prior written consent of Discloser. Any assignment or delegation without written consent shall be null and void and of no force or effect.

6 See Ventas, Inc. v. Health Care Prop. Investors, Inc., 635 F. Supp. 2d 612 (W.D. Ky. 2009) In *Ventas*, a potential buyer submitted a topping bid for a target company after the completion of an auction for a target company, much to the dismay of the winning bidder. The winning bidder brought a suit against the topping bidder for tortious interference with the purchase agreement entered into by the target and the winning bidder after completion of the auction. To prove such a claim, the court held that the winning bidder must show: (1) the existence of a contract; (2) the topping bidder's knowledge of the contract; (3) that the topping bidder

If the acquisition closes, some of the purchaser's obligations under a confidentiality agreement are no longer binding (information relating to assets and liabilities transferred to the buyer) and some are (information relating to assets and liabilities retained by the seller). Thus, either the confidentiality agreement itself or the basic acquisition agreement needs to deal with the extent to which parties modify confidentiality obligations on closing. Typical practice is for the parties to agree that a confidentiality agreement is superseded by provisions in the basic agreement. The buyer often insists on a termination date (*sunset*) for the confidentially obligation if the acquisition does not close.

If the parties do not sign a confidentiality agreement, the seller still has some protections under state law. State law protects trade secrets.[7] Forty-seven states, the District of Columbia, the U.S. Virgin Islands and Puerto Rico have adopted a version of the Uniform Trade Secrets Act (1979 with 1985 Amendments) (UTSA). Section 1(4) defines information as a trade secret if it "(a) derives economic value, actual or potential, from not being generally known to, and not being readily ascertainable by proper means by, other persons who can obtain economic value from its disclosure or use, and (b) is the subject of efforts that are reasonable under the circumstances to maintain its secrecy."[8] Several states have criminal statutes as well specifically addressed to the misappropriation of trade secrets. At issue is the definition of reasonable efforts to maintain secrecy. The execution of the confidentiality agreement itself is such an effort; the failure to execute such an agreement could be evidence of the opposite.

2. LETTERS OF INTENT

A buyer and a seller often enter into a *letter of intent*[9] at the conclusion of a successful first phase of negotiations. The letter, usually prepared by counsel for the purchaser, indicates the nature of the contemplated transaction and summarizes its basic terms, including price, terms of payment and the principal conditions to the closing. Conditions may include, for example, approval by government agencies and consent by third parties, raising of financing by the buyer, and achievement of stated net earnings by the target. The buyer and seller anticipate that a definitive

intended to cause the target to breach the contract; (4) that the topping bidder's conduct caused the target's breach; (5) that this breach resulted in damages to the winning bidder; and (6) that the topping bidder had no privilege or justification to excuse its conduct. *Id.* at 618–19.

7 The federal Economic Espionage Act of 1996 also protects against theft of trade secrets, so long as the theft was committed by someone with the knowledge or intent that the theft will benefit a foreign power.

8 Prior to the development of the UTSA, improper use or disclosure of a trade secret was traditionally a common law tort. U.S. courts widely adopted §§ 757 and 758 of the Restatement of Torts (1939), which set forth the basic principles of trade secret law prior to the UTSA. Part of the impetus behind the development of the UTSA was the omission of § 757 from the Restatement of Torts, 2d (1978).

9 Other terms for an interim letter are an *agreement in principle, memorandum of understanding,* or *term sheet.*

written acquisition agreement will follow and ultimately supplant the letter of intent.

The parties to most letters of intent do not view the letter as a legally binding obligation of the parties to actually do a deal; instead, it is a moral obligation to close the deal on the stipulated terms. However, at the option of the parties, letters of intent can be binding contracts with open-ended terms. The strongest form of such a contract is an agreement on essential terms with other terms implicitly agreed to as whatever is reasonable based on custom and practice. E.g., *Itek Corp. v. Chicago Aerial Ind., Inc.*, 248 A.2d 625 (Del. 1968). The weakest form of such a contract is an agreement to bargain in good faith towards a deal based on the terms in the letter of intent. E.g., *Teachers Ins. & Annuity Assoc. v. Tribune Co.*, 670 F.Supp. 491 (S.D.N.Y. 1987).[10] Courts are left to determine whether letters of intent are binding contracts when the parties do not include explicit language on their legal effect. The cases are fact-specific as judges and juries seek to discern the parties' objective intent; there is much room in such trials for effective courtroom advocacy after the fact. See, e.g., *R.G. Group, Inc. v. Horn & Hardart Co.,* 751 F.2d 69 (2d Cir. 1984).

Good lawyers drafting the letters include explicit language on the binding nature of the deal terms.[11] Nevertheless, evidence of subsequent communications can overcome even such explicit language. Courts have found oral statements such as "looks like we have a deal" or even a simple handshake to indicate intent to be bound. E.g., *American Cyanamid Co. v. Elizabeth Arden Sales Corp.*, 331 F.Supp. 597 (S.D.N.Y. 1971).

Even letters of intent that are not legally binding on the basic terms of a deal may, however, have a miscellany of subparts that the parties agree are legally binding—a "no-shop" clause, due diligence inspection rights, an allocation of fees and expenses, or a confidentiality provision, for example. Confidentiality provisions normally should be in a separate agreement, negotiated before the signing of a letter of intent. Letters thus have subsections of non-binding obligations and binding obligations. Examples of some types of legally binding provisions follow.

Clients like letters of intent; their lawyers often do not. Both the buyer and seller in an acquisition prefer a preliminary commitment from the other before they incur the substantial costs of negotiating a definitive agreement and performing or allowing to be performed a due diligence review of the selling company. Both parties can see if there are "deal-breaking" terms and conditions. The letter also helps the buyer in lining up financing and establishes a clear trigger for compliance with regulatory

[10] Resourceful plaintiffs' lawyers also use promissory estoppel and restitutionary theories (quantum meruit) to ask for relief in a failed acquisition. E.g., W.R. Grace & Co. v. Taco Tico Acq., 454 S.E.2d 789 (Ga. App. 1995) (denying relief on both theories).

[11] Language that a letter of intent is "subject to a formal written agreement" may not be enough. E.g., Computer Systems of America, Inc. v. IBM Corp., 795 F.2d 1086 (1st Cir. 1986) ("subject to" language is merely a condition subsequent to a valid contract).

filings (under the Hart-Scott-Rodino Act, see Chapter Nine, Section C) and for public announcements. Their lawyers worry that courts will use the agreement to give a disgruntled party relief if an anticipated deal does not close.[12] Negotiations of a letter can sometimes become mired in detail that is best reserved for negotiations over a comprehensive, definitive agreement.

Letters of intent also affect subsequent bargaining leverage. Sellers push buyers into settling key terms in some detail before buyers have access to the seller's records and information. Once those terms are agreed upon, the party asking for changes in the terms of a signed letter of intent, usually the buyer, has the burden of justification: "I thought we had a deal" is the seller's response to any request for a modification of the terms. A buyer asking for a downward purchase price adjustment after conducting due diligence will likely be met by seller indignation and threats to scuttle the deal. Once the parties sign a letter of intent, however, the buyer does have a generic bargaining advantage as the letters create an expectation of an acquisition on the part of keenly interested third parties—investors, lenders, customers and vendors—that may pressure seller managers to close a deal and accede to buyers' additional demands.

In exchange for an early memorialization of the deal terms, buyers usually ask for an *exclusive dealing* commitment (an *exclusivity provision*) that prevents the seller from soliciting or considering offers from other interested buyers. Exclusivity provisions are often the primary goal of buyers entering into letters of intent. Some lawyers believe that exclusivity provisions, coupled with fees for breach,[13] make the effect of letters of intent more favorable on balance to buyers than sellers. Buyers also want to preserve maximum flexibility to change the terms once they learn more about the selling company, and sellers, on the other hand, want a clear understanding on the price and other key parts of the acquisition agreement, including understandings on employment agreements for key seller executives who will be staying on post-closing.[14]

Cases on letters of intent usually find courts careful to follow the express written language of the letters on what is binding and what is not. There are some notable exceptions, however. The exceptions make for

---

[12] For a must read classic case see AIH Acq. Corp. v. Alaska Indus. Hardware, Inc., 306 F.Supp.2d 455 (S.D.N.Y. 2004), *vacated and remanded to a new judge*, 2004 WL 1496864 (2d Cir. 2004).

[13] Buyers want, at minimum, reimbursement for reasonable costs and expenses incurred in the course of pursuing the acquisition. Parties may agree upon a specific liquidated damages amount in lieu of expense reimbursement, a *break up fee*. Aggressive buyers require large break-up fees or *topping fees*. A break up fee is an amount paid in addition to expense reimbursement. A topping fee is an amount equal to a percentage of the difference between a higher third party offer and the buyer's offer.

[14] Sellers' insistence on detail can sometimes bog down the Letter of Intent negotiation to the point where the parties should simply enter into negotiations on the main acquisition agreement itself.

hilarious reading and it pains us to choose only one to present here.[15] The exceptions follow a pattern: two parties negotiate happily past the letter of intent stage and the buyer, usually prompted by a higher bid from someone else, cancels the deal. The aggrieved buyer sues on contract and manages to get to a jury. The plaintiff's trial lawyers scour emails, press releases and oral conversations looking for casual positive affirmations of a deal. Did they shake hands on a deal or raise a glass to toast a deal? Did someone say, without contradiction, "we have a deal"?

The jury, oblivious to the arcane and stylized customs and understandings of this country's small, tightly knit band of acquisition attorneys, finds a binding contract, relying on what passes as normal, oral deal talk to overcome contrary written language in the formal documents. The jury's approach is straightforward: when principals shake hands on a deal or otherwise toast or celebrate a deal, they have a contract. The court then finds room for the jury verdict in the conflicted evidence, an endeavor that often includes a tortured, twisted interpretation of the written language.

Whenever such a case appears in the advance sheets, as it does every five to seven years or so, the country's acquisition lawyers, who drafted the documents or some like them, are amazed and left sputtering in surprise and anger. A jury and then a court once again have refused to respect the lawyers' common understandings of their normal practice. The small band of acquisition lawyers then grudgingly redrafts boilerplate language in an effort to stave off the next "travesty of justice."

Consider justice, Texas style:

TEXACO, INC. V. PENNZOIL CO.

Court of Appeals of Texas, First Dist., 1987.
729 S.W.2d 768, *writ of error refused* 748 S.W.2d 631 (Tex. 1988),
cert. denied, 485 U.S. 994, 108 S.Ct. 1305, 99 L.Ed.2d 686 (1988).

WARREN, JUSTICE.

This is an appeal from a judgment awarding Pennzoil damages for Texaco's tortious interference with a contract between Pennzoil and the "Getty entities" (Getty Oil Company, the Sarah C. Getty Trust, and the J. Paul Getty Museum).

The jury found, among other things, that:

(1) At the end of a board meeting on January 3, 1984, the Getty entities intended to bind themselves to an agreement providing for the purchase of Getty Oil stock, whereby the Sarah C. Getty Trust would own

[15] See, e.g., Turner Broadcasting Sys. Inc. v. McDavid, 303 Ga.App. 593, 693 S.E.2d 873 (Ct.App. 2010) (the expiration of a letter of intent under a termination clause nullified the effect of language in the letter that the terms in the letter did not create a binding contract; later oral representation that "we have a deal" created an oral agreement).

4/7ths of the stock and Pennzoil the remaining 3/7ths; and providing for a division of Getty Oil's assets, according to their respective ownership if the Trust and Pennzoil were unable to agree on a restructuring of Getty Oil by December 31, 1984;

(2) Texaco knowingly interfered with the agreement between Pennzoil and the Getty entities;

(3) As a result of Texaco's interference, Pennzoil suffered damages of $7.53 billion:

(4) Texaco's actions were intentional, willful, and in wanton disregard of Pennzoil's rights; and,

(5) Pennzoil was entitled to punitive damages of $3 billion.[Ed.[16]]

* * *

Though many facts are disputed, the parties' main conflicts are over the inferences to be drawn from, and the legal significance of, these facts. There is evidence that for several months in late 1983, Pennzoil had followed with interest the well-publicized dissension between the board of directors of Getty Oil Company and Gordon Getty, who was a director of Getty Oil and also the owner, as trustee, of approximately 40.2 percent of the outstanding shares of Getty Oil. On December 28, 1983, Pennzoil announced an unsolicited, public tender offer for 16 million shares of Getty Oil at $100 each.

Soon afterwards, Pennzoil contacted both Gordon Getty and a representative of the J. Paul Getty Museum, which held approximately 11.8 percent of the shares of Getty Oil, to discuss the tender offer and the possible purchase of Getty Oil. In the first two days of January 1984, a "Memorandum of Agreement" was drafted to reflect the terms that had been reached in conversations between representatives of Pennzoil, Gordon Getty, and the Museum.

Under the plan set out in the Memorandum of Agreement, Pennzoil and the Trust (with Gordon Getty as trustee) were to become partners on a 3/7ths to 4/7ths basis respectively, in owning and operating Getty Oil. Gordon Getty was to become chairman of the board, and Hugh Liedtke, the chief executive officer of Pennzoil, was to become chief executive officer of the new company.

The Memorandum of Agreement further provided that the Museum was to receive $110 per share for its 11.8 percent ownership, and that all other outstanding public shares were to be cashed in by the company at $110 per share. Pennzoil was given an option to buy an additional 8 million shares to achieve the desired ownership ratio. The plan also provided that

[16] [Ed. The $10.53 billion verdict, which began almost immediately to collect interest at the staggering rate of $3 million a day, pushed Texaco, the country's fifth-largest corporation, into bankruptcy. The parties later settled for $3 billion.]

Pennzoil and the Trust were to try in good faith to agree upon a plan to restructure Getty Oil within a year, but if they could not reach an agreement, the assets of Getty Oil were to be divided between them, 3/7ths to Pennzoil and 4/7ths to the Trust.

The Memorandum of Agreement stated that it was subject to approval of the board of Getty Oil, and it was to expire by its own terms if not approved at the board meeting that was to begin on January 2. Pennzoil's CEO, Liedtke, and Gordon Getty, for the Trust, signed the Memorandum of Agreement before the Getty Oil board meeting on January 2, and Harold Williams, the president of the Museum, signed it shortly after the board meeting began. Thus, before it was submitted to the Getty Oil board, the Memorandum of Agreement had been executed by parties who together controlled a majority of the outstanding shares of Getty Oil.

The Memorandum of Agreement was then presented to the Getty Oil board, which had previously held discussions on how the company should respond to Pennzoil's public tender offer. A self-tender by the company to shareholders at $110 per share had been proposed to defeat Pennzoil's tender offer at $100 per share, but no consensus was reached.

The board voted to reject recommending Pennzoil's tender offer to Getty's shareholders, then later also rejected the Memorandum of Agreement price of $110 per share as too low. . . . [Ed.: The Board never signed the Memorandum of Agreement or any subsequent draft of the Memorandum.]

* * *

The Museum's lawyer told the board that, based on his discussions with Pennzoil, he believed that if the board went back "firm" with an offer of $110 plus a $5 stub, Pennzoil would accept it. After a recess, the Museum's president (also a director of Getty Oil) moved that the Getty board should accept Pennzoil's proposal provided that the stub be raised to $5, and the board voted fifteen to one to approve this counter-proposal to Pennzoil. The board then voted themselves and Getty's officers and advisors indemnity for any liability arising from the events of the past few months. Additionally, the board authorized its executive compensation committee to give "golden parachutes" (generous termination benefits) to the top executives whose positions "were likely to be affected" by the change in management. There was evidence that during another brief recess of the board meeting, the counter-offer of $110 plus a $5 stub was presented to and accepted by Pennzoil. After Pennzoil's acceptance was conveyed to the Getty board, the meeting was adjourned, and most board members left town for their respective homes.

That evening, the lawyers and public relations staff of Getty Oil and the Museum drafted a press release describing the transaction between Pennzoil and the Getty entities. The press release, announcing an agreement in principle on the terms of the Memorandum of Agreement but with a price of $110 plus a $5 stub, was issued on Getty Oil letterhead the next morning, January 4, and later that day, Pennzoil issued an identical press release.

. . . Meanwhile, also on January 4, Pennzoil's lawyers were working on a draft of a formal "transaction agreement" that described the transaction in more detail than the outline of terms contained in the Memorandum of Agreement and press release.

On January 5, the Wall Street Journal reported on an agreement reached between Pennzoil and the Getty entities, describing essentially the terms contained in the Memorandum of Agreement. The Pennzoil board met to ratify the actions of its officers in negotiating an agreement with the Getty entities, and Pennzoil's attorneys periodically attempted to contact the other parties' advisors and attorneys to continue work on the transaction agreement.

The board of Texaco also met on January 5, authorizing its officers to make an offer for 100% of Getty Oil and to take any necessary action in connection therewith. . . .

* * *

At noon on January 6, Getty Oil held a telephone board meeting to discuss the Texaco offer. The board voted to withdraw its previous counter-proposal to Pennzoil and unanimously voted to accept Texaco's offer. Texaco immediately issued a press release announcing that Getty Oil and Texaco would merge.

. . . The merger agreement between Texaco and Getty Oil was signed on January 6; the stock purchase agreement with the Museum was signed on January 6; and the stock exchange agreement with the Trust was signed on January 8, 1984.

* * *

[Ed.: Texaco made numerous objections to the jury instructions; it lost on all of them. Only the Court ruling on Texaco's objection to the jury instruction on a contract between Pennzoil and Getty Oil follows.]

Texaco contends that under controlling principles of New York law, there was insufficient evidence to support the jury's finding that at the end of the Getty Oil board meeting on January 3, the Getty entities intended to bind themselves to an agreement with Pennzoil.

Pennzoil responds that the question of the parties' intent is a fact question, and the jury was free to accept or reject Texaco's after-the-fact testimony of subjective intent. Pennzoil contends that the evidence showed that the parties intended to be bound to the terms in the Memorandum of Agreement plus price terms of $110 plus a $5 stub, even though the parties may have contemplated a later, more formal document to memorialize the agreement already reached. Pennzoil also argues that the binding effect of the Memorandum of Agreement was conditioned only upon approval of the board, not also upon execution of the agreement by a Getty signator.

Under New York law, if parties do not intend to be bound to an agreement until it is reduced to writing and signed by both parties, then there is no contract until that event occurs. . . . If there is no understanding that a signed writing is necessary before the parties will be bound, and the parties have agreed upon all substantial terms, then an informal agreement can be binding, even though the parties contemplate evidencing their agreement in a formal document later. . . .

If the parties do intend to contract orally, the mere intention to commit the agreement to writing does not prevent contract formation before execution of that writing . . . and even a failure to reduce their promises to writing is immaterial to whether they are bound. . . .

* * *

It is the parties' expressed intent that controls which rule of contract formation applies. To determine intent, a court must examine the words and deeds of the parties, because these constitute the objective signs of such intent. . . . Only the outward expressions of intent are considered—secret or subjective intent is immaterial to the question of whether the parties were bound. . . .

* * *

. . . Texaco contends that the evidence of expressed intent not to be bound establishes conclusively that there was no contract at the time of Texaco's alleged inducement of breach. Texaco argues that this expressed intent is contained in (1) the press releases issued by the Getty entities and Pennzoil, which stated that "the transaction is subject to execution of a definitive merger agreement"; (2) the phrasing of drafts of the transaction agreement, which Texaco alleges "carefully stated that the parties' obligations would become binding only 'after the execution and delivery of this Agreement' "; and (3) the deliberate reference by the press releases to the parties' understanding as an "agreement in principle."

* * *

Any intent of the parties not to be bound before signing a formal document is not so clearly expressed in the press release to establish, as a matter of law, that there was no contract at that time. The press release does refer to an agreement "in principle" and states that the "transaction" is subject to execution of a definitive merger agreement. But the release as a whole is worded in indicative terms, not in subjunctive or hypothetical ones. The press release describes what shareholders *will* receive, what Pennzoil *will* contribute, that Pennzoil *will* be granted an option, etc.

The description of the transaction as subject to a definitive merger agreement also includes the need for stockholder approval and the completion of various governmental filing and waiting requirements. There was evidence that this was a paragraph of routine details, that the referred to merger agreement was a standard formal document required in such a transaction under Delaware law, and that the parties considered these technical requirements of little consequence.

* * *

Texaco also contends that explicit language of reservation in drafts of Pennzoil's transaction agreement indicates the parties' expressed intent not to be bound without a signed writing. Texaco asserts that "Pennzoil's lawyers carefully stated that the parties' obligations would become binding only 'after the execution and delivery of this Agreement.' "

That assertion is not accurate. In fact, "after the execution and delivery of this Agreement" was merely used as an introductory phrase before each party's obligations were described, *e.g.*, after the execution and delivery of this Agreement, Pennzoil shall terminate the tender offer; . . . Pennzoil and the Company shall terminate all legal proceedings; . . . the Company shall purchase all shares held by the Museum; etc. Other clauses in the transaction agreement did not contain that phrase, *e.g.*, the Company *hereby* grants to Pennzoil the option to purchase up to 8 million shares of treasury stock; *on or prior to the effective date*, Pennzoil and the Trustee shall form the merging company; etc.

A reasonable conclusion from reading the entire drafts is that the phrase "after the execution and delivery of this Agreement" was used chiefly to indicate the timing of various acts that were to occur, and not to impose an express precondition to the formation of a contract. . . . Again, the language upon which Texaco relies does not so clearly express an intent not to be bound to resolve that issue or to remove the question from the ambit of the trier of fact.

Next, Texaco states that the use of the term "agreement in principle" in the press release was a conscious and deliberate choice of words to convey that there was not yet any binding agreement. Texaco refers to defense testimony that lawyers for Getty Oil and the Museum changed the initial wording of the press release from "agreement" to "agreement in principle" because they understood and intended that phrase to mean that there was no binding contract with Pennzoil.

* * *

Pennzoil and Texaco presented conflicting evidence at trial on the common business usage and understanding of the term "agreement in principle." Texaco's witnesses testified that the term is used to convey an invitation to bid or that there is no binding contract. Pennzoil's witnesses testified that when business people use "agreement in principle," it means that the parties have reached a meeting of the minds with only details left to be resolved. There was testimony by Sidney Petersen, Getty Oil's chief executive officer, that an "agreement in principle" requires the parties to proceed to try to implement the details of the agreement in good faith, and that that was the case with the agreement in principle with Pennzoil.

The jury was the sole judge of the credibility of the witnesses and was entitled to accept or reject any testimony it wished, as well as to decide what weight to give the testimony. . . . There was sufficient evidence at trial on the common business usage of the expression "agreement in principle" and on its meaning in this case for the jury reasonably to decide that its use in the press release did not necessarily establish that the parties did not intend to be bound before signing a formal document.

* * *

The next factor showing intent to be bound is whether there was agreement on all essential terms of the alleged agreement. Texaco contends that numerous items of "obvious importance" were still being negotiated at the time Pennzoil claims a contract had been formed. [Ed.: The Court discusses each of Texaco's arguments on the lack of agreement on essential terms. The Court found that the jury had evidence to conclude (1) that the parties did agree explicitly on some terms that they borrowed from the Memorandum of Agreement, (2) that some terms on which there was no explicit agreement could be implied by custom and practice, and (3) that finally other terms were not essential.]

* * *

There was sufficient evidence for the jury to conclude that the parties had reached agreement on all essential terms of the transaction with only the mechanics and details left to be supplied by the parties' attorneys. Although there may have been many specific items relating to the transaction agreement draft that had yet to be put in final form, there is sufficient evidence to support a conclusion by the jury that the parties did not consider any of Texaco's asserted "open items" significant obstacles precluding an intent to be bound.

The fourth factor that Texaco discusses as showing that the parties did not intend to be bound before executing a formal contract is the magnitude and complexity of the transaction. There is little question that the transaction by which Getty Oil was to be taken private by the Trust and Pennzoil involved an extremely large amount of money. It is unlikely that parties to such a transaction would not have expected a detailed written document, specifically setting out the parties' obligations and the exact mechanics of the transaction, whether it was to be executed before the parties intended to be bound or only to memorialize an agreement already reached.

We agree with Texaco that this factor tends to support its position that the transaction was such that a signed contract would ordinarily be expected before the parties would consider themselves bound. However, we cannot say, as a matter of law, that this factor alone is determinative of the question of the parties' intent.

The trial of this case lasted many weeks, with witnesses for both sides testifying extensively about the events of those first days of January 1984. Eyewitnesses and expert witnesses interpreted and explained various aspects of the negotiations and the alleged agreement, and the jury was repeatedly made aware of the value of Getty Oil's assets and how much money would be involved in the company's sale. There was testimony on how the sale of the company could be structured and on the considerations involved in buying and restructuring, or later liquidating, the company. But there was also testimony that there were companies that in the past had bound themselves to short two-page acquisition agreements involving a lot of money, and Getty's involvement banker testified that the Texaco transaction included "one page back-of-the-envelope kinds of agreements" that were formalized. The Memorandum of Agreement containing the essential terms of the Pennzoil/Getty agreement was only four pages long.

Although the magnitude of the transaction here was such that normally a signed writing would be expected, there was sufficient evidence to support an inference by the jury that that expectation was satisfied here initially by the Memorandum of Agreement, signed by a majority of shareholders of Getty Oil and approved by the board with a higher price, and by the transaction agreement in progress that had been intended to memorialize the agreement previously reached.

The record as a whole demonstrates that there was legally and factually sufficient evidence to support the jury's finding in Special Issue No. 1 that the Trust, the Museum, and the Company intended to bind themselves to an agreement with Pennzoil at the end of the Getty Oil board meeting on January 3, 1984. Point of Error 46 is overruled.

* * *

3. INVESTMENT BANKER ENGAGEMENT LETTERS

Parties to an acquisition are more frequently engaging financial advisors to assist them in finding acquisition partners, negotiating the terms of transactions, and performing research and due diligence on an opposing party. The advisor is an investment banker who may also run any auction and issue a fairness opinion justifying a deal's terms to shareholders. Before commencing work, the investment banker will require the execution of an *engagement letter*.

The letter outlines the services provided by the investment banker, indicating whether those services are exclusive or not, and specifies compensation.[17] Compensation for the investment banker is structured typically as a *success fee*, a fee contingent on the completion of an acquisition, in addition to reimbursement of costs and expenses.[18] Some bankers also insist on a separate nonrefundable monthly retainer fee, usually credited against the success fee if earned. The letter also may specify a separate fee for delivering a fairness opinion.[19]

The success fee is typically a percentage of the total transaction value.[20] "Fees based on percentages often decrease according to the size of the transaction, [and the percentages typically become] progressively smaller as the overall amount of the transaction fee increases."[21] A success fee gives the investment banker a strong incentive to close a deal and, if representing a seller, to maximize the price received by the selling firm.

The most heavily negotiated term in the letter is the definition of *covered transactions*, a description of the transactions that, if completed, will trigger the payment of a fee. Many companies seek to carve-out certain potential acquisition partners on the basis that they already have a relationship with those partners. Thus, why pay an investment banker to make an introduction to those partners? Investment bankers counter that their services go well beyond mere introductions, as noted above. Most letters also contain a *tail period*, a time period after the termination of the engagement (six months to two years) in which a transaction with any other party will still trigger the payment of the fee.[22]

---

[17] The initial draft of the engagement letter is typically produced by counsel to the investment banker. Recipients of the initial draft should proceed with caution: "investment bankers often propose broad, and perhaps over-reaching, engagement letters initially". Louis R. Dienes & Alison M. Pear, *An Annotated Form of Investment Banker Engagement Letter*, CAL. BUS. L. PRACTITIONER (Vol. 25, No. 4) (Fall 2010), at 112 (hereinafter *Engagement Letter*). The investment banker's major objectives in the engagement letter "will include: (1) defining the type of transaction for which it is being engaged broadly, so that the client's liability for payment of the banker's fee is triggered easily; (2) defining the exclusivity of its services as broadly as possible; (3) limiting the circumstances that allow the client to avoid paying its fee; and (4) limiting indemnification liability." *Id.* at 109.

[18] It is typical to place a cap on expenses or require prior approval from the company for any expense in excess of a predetermined amount.

[19] If the transaction in question is a going-private transaction (whereby an existing publicly traded company is being turned back into a privately held company), Item 1015(b)(5) of SEC Regulation M–A requires the company in question to state whether it or an affiliate determined the amount of consideration to be paid to the investment banking firm or whether the investment banking firm recommended the amount of consideration to be paid.

[20] What qualifies as "transaction value" must be adequately agreed to by the parties and set forth in the engagement letter. If consideration other than cash is involved, how is that non-cash consideration valued? For example, if the seller receives an earn out payable in subsequent years or warrants to purchase stock in the acquirer that have a multiple-year exercise period, what value is placed on that consideration today?

[21] *Engagement Letter*, *supra* note 17, at 111.

[22] Often tails are limited to transactions with only those potential acquisition partners to whom the investment banker made an introduction during the term of the engagement. Other times, the tail covers a transaction with any third party under the theory that the investment banker created "buzz" about the company in question that ultimately led to a deal (albeit after the engagement ended). In most cases, tails will not apply if the company terminated the engagement letter for "good reason or cause" (as defined in the letter).

An engagement letter typically sets forth several additional provisions. For example, it likely will contain a list of circumstances that allow a party to escape paying the success fee. Inevitably, it also will contain an indemnification provision. In this regard, companies must indemnify the investment banker in the event it is dragged into litigation relating to the transaction covered by the engagement letter. Often indemnification obligations are set forth in an annex or schedule attached to the engagement letter. Indemnification obligations survive any termination of the engagement.

B. THE ACQUISITION AGREEMENT AND SUPPORTING DOCUMENTS

1. THE BASIC AGREEMENT

Most acquisition agreements follow much the same structure. Section 1 is a glossary of defined terms. Section 2 contains the details of the basic exchange—the stock or assets to be acquired, the consideration to be paid and the timetable for the closing. We considered some of the pricing considerations in Chapter One, Section D.2. The next sections, usually Sections 3 and 4, contain the *representations and warranties* of the seller and purchaser, respectively. Following the reps and warranties are two sections on *covenants*, usually Section 5 on pre-closing covenants for the seller and Section 6 on pre-closing covenants for the purchaser. Section 7 contains post-closing covenants. The next two sections, often Sections 8 (for the purchaser) and 9 (for the seller), contain *conditions precedent* to the obligations of both parties to execute the exchange at the closing. The next section usually outlines the circumstances in which each party may terminate the deal (Section 10 on *termination*). The section on termination is often followed by a section on *indemnification*[23] (Section 11), specifying remedies for each party's breach of the agreement. A final section (Section 12) contains miscellaneous provisions. Each type of provision is discussed below.

Key agreement provisions will vary based on the structure of the transaction. The major difference between a stock purchase acquisition of a privately held company and an asset acquisition is in Section 2 on the basic exchange. In an asset acquisition, Section 2 and its accompanying Schedules must identify the assets that the purchaser is buying. In addition, the purchaser's agreement on which liabilities it will assume (if any) are specified with care. In many asset acquisitions, the purchaser agrees to assume those liabilities ordinary and necessary to the daily operations of the business purchased but does not assume extraordinary or

[23] Many acquisition agreements have a separate section on post-closing covenants of the seller. The covenants deal with employees and employee benefits, payment of selected liabilities, assistance in post-closing legal proceedings, customer and business relations, and a covenant not to compete.

contingent liabilities. Exhibits to an asset purchase agreement include assignment and assumption documents.

A stock acquisition is memorialized in a stock purchase agreement signed by the selling shareholders and the buyer. An acquisition agreement of a publicly traded company is much shorter; the document has very limited seller representations and warranties (based primarily on seller's current SEC filings) and no post-closing indemnification rights against seller's public shareholders.

a. Defined Terms

The lawyers for the buyer and seller typically spend an inordinate amount of time (and clients' money) negotiating over *defined terms.* A particular word or phrase that is used throughout the acquisition agreement will be defined up front in Section 1. Thereafter, whenever the word or phrase is used throughout the agreement, it will appear in a capitalized form. For example, once the seller's headquarters is defined, the word "headquarters" will appear as "Headquarters" throughout the agreement, the initial capitalization indicating that it is a defined term.

Why is such an effort spent defining terms? Consider the alternative. Ambiguous terms in an agreement are "interpreted" by the court based on what the court believes is the intent of the parties. Why leave it to a court when the parties themselves can simply define what they mean up front? Hence, defined terms. Moreover, crafty lawyers can shift risk from the buyer to the seller (or vice versa) by carefully defining a term in a way that favors their client.

It is not unusual for an acquisition agreement to contain page after page of defined terms—perhaps including 50 to 150 specific defined terms. Some defined terms are mundane ("Business Day"), while others are more specific to the deal at hand ("Chase Bank Facility"). Many defined terms include in their definition one or more *other* defined terms. What follows are but a few examples of defined terms culled from an asset acquisition agreement. Do the definitions favor the seller, buyer or neither party?

> "**Law**" means any statute, law, ordinance, regulation, rule, code, order, constitution, treaty, common law, judgment, decree, other requirement or rule of law of any Governmental Authority.[24]

---

[24] We're willing to bet you *thought* you knew what the word "Law" meant! Notice the inclusion of another defined term—Governmental Authority. That is defined as:

> "**Governmental Authority**" means any federal, state, local or foreign government or political subdivision thereof, or any agency or instrumentality of such government or political subdivision, or any self-regulated organization or other non-governmental regulatory authority or quasi-governmental authority (to the extent that the rules, regulations or orders of such organization or authority have the force of Law), or any arbitrator, court or tribunal of competent jurisdiction.

"**Intellectual Property**" means all intellectual property and industrial property rights and assets, and all rights, interests and protections that are associated with, similar to, or required for the exercise of, any of the foregoing, however arising, pursuant to the Laws of any jurisdiction throughout the world, whether registered or unregistered, including any and all: (a) trademarks, service marks, trade names, brand names, logos, trade dress, design rights and other similar designations of source, sponsorship, association or origin, together with the goodwill connected with the use of and symbolized by, and all registrations, applications and renewals for, any of the foregoing; (b) internet domain names, whether or not trademarks, registered in any top-level domain by any authorized private registrar or Governmental Authority, web addresses, web pages, websites and related content, accounts with Twitter, Facebook and other social media companies and the content found thereon and related thereto, and URLs; (c) works of authorship, expressions, designs and design registrations, whether or not copyrightable, including copyrights, author, performer, moral and neighboring rights, and all registrations, applications for registration and renewals of such copyrights; (d) inventions, discoveries, trade secrets, business and technical information and know-how, databases, data collections and other confidential and proprietary information and all rights therein; (e) patents (including all reissues, divisionals, provisionals, continuations and continuations-in-part, re-examinations, renewals, substitutions and extensions thereof), patent applications, and other patent rights and any other Governmental Authority-issued indicia of invention ownership (including inventor's certificates, petty patents and patent utility models); (f) software and firmware, including data files, source code, object code, application programming interfaces, architecture, files, records, schematics, computerized databases and other related specifications and documentation; (g) royalties, fees, income, payments and other proceeds now or hereafter due or payable with respect to any and all of the foregoing; and (h) all rights to any Actions of any nature available to or being pursued by Seller to the extent related to the foregoing, whether accruing before, on or after the date hereof, including all rights to and claims for damages, restitution and injunctive relief for infringement, dilution, misappropriation, violation, misuse, breach or default, with the right but no obligation to sue for such legal and equitable relief, and to collect, or otherwise recover, any such damages.

"**Material Adverse Effect**" means any event, occurrence, fact, condition or change that is, or could reasonably be expected to become, individually or in the aggregate, materially adverse to

(a) the business, results of operations, condition (financial or otherwise), prospects or assets of the Business, (b) the value of the Purchased Assets, or (c) the ability of Seller to consummate the transactions contemplated hereby on a timely basis.

"**Transaction Documents**" means this [Asset Purchase] Agreement, the Bill of Sale, the Assignment and Assumption Agreement, the Intellectual Property Assignments, the Non-Competition, Non-Solicitation and Transition Services Agreements, and the other agreements, instruments and documents required to be delivered at the Closing.

---

b. The Basic Exchange

The basic exchange between the parties, typically contained in Section 2 of the acquisition agreement, will depend on whether the transaction is an asset acquisition, a stock acquisition or a merger. Compare the representative sample language from each type of agreement in the subsections that follow. How are they similar? How are they different? Which are easy and elegant, and which are messy and involved? Notice the extensive use of defined terms in all three agreements.

i. Asset Purchase Agreement

Article II

Purchase and Sale

2.1 Purchase and Sale of Assets. Subject to the terms and conditions set forth herein, at the Closing, Seller shall sell, assign, transfer, convey and deliver to Buyer, and Buyer shall purchase from Seller, free and clear of any Encumbrances, all of Seller's right, title and interest in, to and under each of the following assets, properties and rights of every kind and nature, whether real, personal or mixed, tangible or intangible (including goodwill), wherever located and whether now existing or hereafter acquired (other than the Excluded Assets), which relate to, or are used or held for use in connection with, the Business (collectively, the "Purchased Assets"):

(a) all information relating to past, present and prospective customers of the Business ("**Customers**"), including Customer lists, purchasing histories, maintenance records, Customer complaints and inquiry files and renewal amounts and dates;

(b) all Transferred Intellectual Property Assets, including the Seller Name and the domain names and URLs set forth on Section 2.1(b) of the Disclosure Schedules (collectively, the "**Seller Website**") and the "Seller" trademark Reg. No. 3,282,367;

(c) all of the furniture, fixtures, equipment, office equipment, supplies, computers, telephones, other tangible personal property, inventory, packaging, supplies, parts and other inventories set forth on Section 2.1(c) of the Disclosure Schedules (the "**Tangible Personal Property**");

(d) all books and records, including, but not limited to, books of account, ledgers and general, financial and accounting records, machinery and equipment maintenance files, price lists, distribution lists, supplier lists, production data, quality control records and procedures, research and development files, records and data (including all correspondence with any Governmental Authority), sales material and records (including pricing history, total sales, terms and conditions of sale, sales and pricing policies and practices), strategic plans, internal financial statements, marketing and promotional surveys, material and research and files relating to the Transferred Intellectual Property Assets and the Transferred Intellectual Property Licenses ("**Books and Records**"); *provided, however*, that after the Closing, Buyer will promptly provide Seller with access to and copies of any original documents comprising the Books and Records which Seller reasonably requests;

(e) all Customer contracts, including all master service agreements, dedicated team agreements, maintenance agreements, and work-in-progress Contracts with Customers of the Business, and those vendor relationships, reseller Contracts, strategic vendor alliances, Transferred Intellectual Property Licenses and other Contracts used in connection with the Business which are set forth on Section 2.1(e) of the Disclosure Schedules (the "**Assigned Contracts**");

(f) all prepaid expenses, credits, advance payments, claims, security, refunds, rights of recovery, rights of set-off, rights of recoupment, deposits, charges, sums and fees (including any such item relating to the payment of Taxes);

(g) all of Seller's rights under warranties, indemnities and all similar rights against third parties and all agreements with third parties not to compete with the Business or solicit any of the employees, clients, Customers or suppliers of the Business, including the right to enforce Contracts with Business Employees who have agreed not to compete with the Business or solicit any of the employees, clients, Customers or suppliers of the Business;

(h) all rights to any [Legal] Actions of any nature available to or being pursued by Seller to the extent related to the Business, the Purchased Assets or the Assumed Liabilities, whether arising by way of counterclaim or otherwise;

(i) all telephones numbers of the Business; and

(j) all goodwill and the going concern value of the Business.

2.2 Excluded Assets. Notwithstanding the foregoing, the Purchased Assets shall not include the following assets (collectively, the "**Excluded Assets**"):

(a) cash and cash equivalents;

(b) bank accounts of Seller;

(c) all accounts or notes receivable held by Seller, and any security, claim, remedy or other right related to any of the foregoing, in each case relating exclusively to products sold and services provided by Seller prior to the Closing Date;

(d) all the Contracts of Seller other than the Assigned Contracts (the "**Excluded Contracts**");

(e) any leases for real property and all security deposits associated therewith;

(f) the vehicle set forth on Section 2.2(f) of the Disclosure Schedules;

(g) all insurance benefits, including rights and proceeds, arising from or relating to the Business for all periods prior to the Closing Date;

(h) the corporate seals, organizational documents, minute books, stock books, Tax Returns, books of account or other records of Seller that are not Books and Records;

(i) all the rights to any of Seller's claims for any federal, state, local, or foreign tax refunds;

(j) all Seller Benefit Plans and assets attributable thereto;

(k) all assets and Liabilities of Seller relating exclusively to businesses of Seller other than the Business (including Seller's product business); and

(*l*) the rights which accrue or will accrue to Seller under the Transaction Documents.

2.3 Assumed Liabilities. Subject to the terms and conditions set forth herein, Buyer shall assume and agree to pay, perform and discharge when due only the following Liabilities of Seller (collectively, the "**Assumed Liabilities**"), and no other Liabilities:

(a) Liabilities under Assigned Contracts that are set forth on Section 2.3(a) of the Disclosure Schedules and for which performance is required from and after the Closing and for which the applicable Customer has not prepaid for such services, but only to the extent that (i) such Liabilities are required to be performed on or after the Closing and (ii) such Liabilities were incurred in the ordinary course of business and do not relate to any failure to perform, improper performance, or other breach, default or violation by Seller on or prior to the Closing Date; and

(b) payments to subcontractors of Seller with respect to services to be performed for the benefit of a Customer, but only to the extent that payments will be owing to Buyer from such Customer in respect of such services.

2.4 Excluded Liabilities. Buyer shall not assume and shall not be responsible to pay, perform or discharge any Liabilities of Seller or any of its Affiliates of any kind or nature whatsoever other than the Assumed Liabilities (the "**Excluded Liabilities**"). Seller shall, and shall cause each of its Affiliates to, pay and satisfy in due course all Excluded Liabilities which they are obligated to pay and satisfy. Without limiting the generality of the foregoing, the Excluded Liabilities shall include, but not be limited to, the following:

(a) any Liabilities of Seller arising out of or incurred in connection with the negotiation, preparation, investigation and performance of this Agreement, the other Transaction Documents and the transactions contemplated hereby and thereby, including fees and expenses of counsel, accountants, consultants, advisers and others;

(b) any Liability for (i) Taxes of Seller (or any stockholder or Affiliate of Seller) or relating to the Business, the Purchased Assets or the Assumed Liabilities for any Pre-Closing Tax Period; (ii) Taxes that arise out of the consummation of the transactions contemplated hereby or that are the responsibility of Seller pursuant to Section 6.10 [of this Agreement]; or (iii) other Taxes of Seller (or any stockholder or Affiliate of Seller) of any kind or description (including any Liability for Taxes of Seller (or any stockholder or Affiliate of Seller) that becomes a Liability of Buyer under any common law doctrine of de facto merger or transferee or successor liability or otherwise by operation of contract or Law);

(c) any Liabilities relating to or arising out of the Excluded Assets;

(d) any Liabilities in respect of any pending or threatened [Legal] Action arising out of, relating to or otherwise in respect of the operation of the Business or the Purchased Assets to the extent such Action relates to such operation on or prior to the Closing Date, including any Liability arising as a result of any proceeding relating to any alleged action or omission prior to the Closing Date by or on behalf of Seller related to the performance of any

Contract, for any accident or injury, infringement of Intellectual Property or violations of Law;

(e) any Liabilities of Seller arising under or in connection with any Seller Benefit Plan;

(f) any Liabilities with respect to Business Employees who are terminated on or prior to the Closing Date;

(g) any Liabilities of Seller for any present or former employees, officers, directors, retirees, independent contractors or consultants of Seller, including any Liabilities associated with any claims for wages or other benefits, bonuses, accrued vacation, workers' compensation, severance, retention, termination or other payments;

(h) any trade accounts payable of Seller;

(i) any Liabilities relating to utilities associated with any leases for real property (including data lines, phone, electric, water service, cleaning and other building services);

(j) any Liabilities of the Business relating or arising from unfulfilled commitments, quotations, purchase orders, Customer orders or work orders, except for Liabilities that are Assumed Liabilities pursuant to Section 2.3;

(k) any Liabilities to indemnify, reimburse or advance amounts to any present or former officer, director, employee or agent of Seller (including with respect to any breach of fiduciary obligations by same);

(*l*) any Liabilities under the Assigned Contracts that are not Assumed Liabilities;

(m) any Liabilities under the Excluded Contracts or any other Contracts (i) which are not validly and effectively assigned to Buyer pursuant to this Agreement; (ii) which do not conform to the representations and warranties with respect thereto contained in this Agreement; or (iii) to the extent such Liabilities arise out of or relate to a breach by Seller of such Contracts prior to Closing;

(n) any Liabilities associated with debt, loans or credit facilities of Seller and/or the Business owing to financial institutions; and

(*o*) any Liabilities arising out of, in respect of or in connection with the failure by Seller or any of its Affiliates to comply with any Law or Governmental Order.

2.5 Consideration. In consideration for the purchase and sale of the Purchased Assets, at the Closing Buyer shall (a) wire immediately available funds in the amount of U.S.$156,000.000.00 to a Seller bank account designated in writing by the Seller prior to the Closing, and (b) assume the Assumed Liabilities.

---

ii. Stock Purchase Agreement

Article II

Purchase and Sale of Shares

2.1 Purchase and Sale. Subject to the terms and conditions of this Agreement, at the Closing (as defined in Section 3 of this Agreement), the Shareholders shall sell, convey, transfer, and assign, upon the terms and conditions hereinafter set forth, to Buyer, free and clear of all liens, pledges, claims, and encumbrances of every kind, nature and description, and Buyer shall purchase and accept from the Shareholders the Shares, which comprise all of the outstanding capital stock of the Company.

2.2 Purchase Price. Buyer shall purchase the Shares for aggregate consideration (the "**Purchase Price**") as follows:

(a) At the Closing, the Buyer shall pay to the Shareholders the sum of nine hundred eighty five thousand dollars ($985,000.00) by wire transfer of immediately available funds to such bank account of the Shareholders as the Shareholders shall designate in writing prior to the Closing.

(b) On October 1, 2017, the Buyer shall issue to the Shareholders two hundred thousand (200,000) shares of the Buyer's common stock (the "**Common Stock**"), which shall be restricted stock. Such stock shall be subject to vesting as provided in Exhibit A attached hereto.[25]

(c) On September 30, 2017, the Buyer shall deliver to Comerica, Inc. (the "**Escrow Agent**") the sum of five hundred thousand dollars ($500,000.00) (the "**Escrow Amount**"). The Escrow Amount shall be held by the Escrow Agent and distributed to the Shareholders pursuant to the terms and conditions of the Escrow Agreement attached hereto as Exhibit B, to be entered into by the Buyer, the Shareholders and the Escrow Agent at or prior to the Closing, and shall be subject to set off, in accordance with Section 13.5 hereof, in the event that the Company or the Shareholders breach the representations and warranties contained in Section 5 of this Agreement.[26]

---

25 Thus, in this deal the selling shareholders are receiving both cash and stock in the buyer. However, the stock vests with the selling shareholders over a period of years.

26 It is not unusual for the buyer to place a portion of the cash purchase price (here, a total of $500,000) in escrow. That money is available to satisfy any claims the buyer has against the selling shareholders for any breach of their representations and warranties running in favor of the

(d) After Closing, the Shareholders shall be entitled to receive up to five percent (5%) of all gross customer receipts less credit card and transaction expenses, discounts, returns, and bad debt expenses ("**Net Revenue**") from products or services that present listing information procured from permitted, active data feeds from all Multiple Listing Service ("**MLS**") partners ("**MLS Relationships**") listed or described on the MLS Scorecard provided in Exhibit C attached hereto ("**Revenue Sharing Payments**").[27] Such Revenue Sharing Payments shall be payable quarterly for ten (10) consecutive fiscal quarters following the Closing Date, beginning with the quarter ended December 31, 2017. Each quarterly Revenue Sharing Payment shall be calculated as provided in Exhibit C hereto, and shall be subject to set off, in accordance with Section 13.5 hereof, in the event that the Company or the Shareholders breach the representations and warranties contained in Section 5 of this Agreement. For purposes of this paragraph, "**permitted**" shall mean (i) allowed pursuant to the terms of a written contract or (ii) allowed pursuant to usage where no written contract is required, and "**active**" shall mean capable of being accessed, regardless of whether such data feed was actually accessed.

---

iii. Merger Agreement

Article II

The Merger

2.01. The Merger. (a) At the Effective Time, Merger Subsidiary[28] shall be merged (the "**Merger**") with and into the Target Company in accordance with the requirements of the General Corporation Law of the State of Delaware (the "**Delaware Law**"), whereupon the separate existence of Merger Subsidiary shall cease, and the Target Company shall

---

buyer. If, after a period of time (typically one year), any monies remain in escrow, the escrow agent will pay that out to the selling shareholders.

27 This is an odd deal in that the selling shareholders are entitled to share in certain revenues generated by the buyer's business over the next two and a half years. Of course, the buyer can offset those revenues against any claims the buyer has relating to breaches by the selling shareholders of their representations and warranties running in favor of the buyer. The provision has the flavor of an earn out provision sometimes found in acquisition agreements. See Note, Post-Closing Adjustments, in Chapter One, Section D.2.

28 This is the wholly owned subsidiary formed by the acquirer to effect a triangular merger. Because the target company is the surviving company in the merger, the merger is referred to as a *reverse triangular merger*. Had Merger Subsidiary survived the merger (i.e., the Target Company had merged with and into Merger Subsidiary), the merger would be called a *forward triangular merger*.

be the surviving corporation in the Merger (the "**Surviving Corporation**").

(b) As soon as practicable after satisfaction or, to the extent permitted hereunder, waiver of all conditions to the Merger, the Target Company and Merger Subsidiary will file a certificate of merger with the Secretary of State of the State of Delaware and make all other filings or recordings required by Delaware Law in connection with the Merger. The Merger shall become effective at such time as the certificate of merger is duly filed with the Secretary of State of the State of Delaware or at such later time as is specified in the certificate of merger (the "**Effective Time**").

(c) From and after the Effective Time, the Surviving Corporation shall possess all the rights, privileges, powers and franchises and be subject to all of the restrictions, disabilities and duties of the Target Company and Merger Subsidiary, all as provided under Delaware Law.

(d) The closing of the Merger (the "**Closing**") shall take place (i) at the law offices of Smith & Wollensky LLP, 797 Third Avenue, New York, NY, as soon as practicable, but in any event within three business days after the day on which the last to be fulfilled or waived of the conditions set forth in Article 8 (other than those conditions that by their nature are to be fulfilled at the Closing, but subject to the fulfillment or waiver of such conditions) shall be fulfilled or waived in accordance with this Agreement or (ii) at such other place and time or on such other date as the Target Company and Acquirer may agree in writing (the "**Closing Date**").

2.02. Conversion of Shares. (a) At the Effective Time by virtue of the Merger and without any action on the part of the shareholder thereof:

(i) each share of Target Company common stock (the "**Shares**") held by the Target Company itself as treasury stock or owned by Acquirer or any subsidiary of Acquirer immediately prior to the Effective Time (together with the associated Target Company Right (as defined in Section 3.05), if any)[29] shall be canceled, and no payment shall be made with respect thereto;

(ii) each share of common stock of Merger Subsidiary outstanding immediately prior to the Effective Time shall be converted into and become one share of common stock of the Surviving Corporation with the same rights, powers and privileges as the shares so converted and shall constitute the only outstanding shares of capital stock of the Surviving Corporation[30]; and

---

[29] A Target Company Right is the poison pill right deemed attached to each outstanding share of Target Company common stock. At the time of this deal, the Target Company had a poison pill takeover defense in place.

[30] Thus, by virtue of the merger, all shares of Merger Subsidiary stock (which are solely owned by the Acquirer) are converted into one share of Surviving Corporation stock. That Surviving Corporation share will be the only share left outstanding as a result of the merger, and

(iii) each Share (together with the associated Target Company Right) outstanding immediately prior to the Effective Time shall, except as otherwise provided in Section 2.02(a)(i), be converted into the right to receive 1.32015 (the "Exchange Ratio") shares of fully paid and nonassessable common stock, without par value, of Acquirer ("Acquirer Common Stock").[31]

(b) All Acquirer Common Stock issued as provided in this Section 2.02 shall be of the same class and shall have the same terms as the currently outstanding Acquirer Common Stock. Acquirer shall, following the Closing, except as provided in Section 2.03(c), pay all stamp duties and stamp duty reserve tax, if any, imposed in connection with the issuance or creation of the Acquirer Common Stock in connection with the Merger.

(c) From and after the Effective Time, all Shares (together with the associated Target Company Rights) converted in accordance with Section 2.02(a)(iii) shall no longer be outstanding and shall automatically be canceled and retired and shall cease to exist, and each holder of a certificate representing any such Shares shall cease to have any rights with respect thereto, except the right to receive the Merger Consideration (as defined below) and any dividends payable pursuant to Section 2.03(f). From and after the Effective Time, all certificates representing the common stock of Merger Subsidiary shall be deemed for all purposes to represent the number of shares of common stock of the Surviving Corporation into which they were converted in accordance with Section 2.02(a)(ii).

(d) The Acquirer Common Stock to be received as consideration pursuant to the Merger by each holder of Shares (together with cash in lieu of fractional shares of Acquirer Common Stock as specified below) is referred to herein as the "**Merger Consideration**".

(e) For purposes of this Agreement, the word "**Subsidiary**" when used with respect to any Person means any other Person, whether incorporated or unincorporated, of which (i) more than fifty percent of the securities or other ownership interests or (ii) securities or other interests having by their terms ordinary voting power to elect more than fifty percent of the board of directors or others performing similar functions with respect to such corporation or other organization, is directly owned or controlled by such Person or by any one or more of its Subsidiaries. For purposes of this Agreement, "**Person**" means an individual, a corporation, a limited liability company, a partnership, an association, a trust or any other entity

---

thus the Acquirer will be the only shareholder left which owns shares in the Surviving Corporation. Through this process the Target Company (a.k.a. the Surviving Corporation) in a reverse triangular merger ends up as a wholly owned subsidiary of the Acquirer at the conclusion of the transaction.

[31] This is a stock-for-stock merger, whereby Target Company shareholders are receiving 1.32015 shares of Acquirer stock in exchange for each share of the Target Company stock they hold.

or organization, including a government or political subdivision or any agency or instrumentality thereof.

2.03. Surrender and Payment. (a) Prior to the Effective Time, Acquirer shall appoint an agent reasonably acceptable to the Target Company (the "**Exchange Agent**") for the purpose of exchanging certificates representing Shares (the "**Certificates**") for the Merger Consideration. Acquirer will make available to the Exchange Agent, as needed, the Merger Consideration to be paid in respect of the Shares. Promptly after the Effective Time, Acquirer will send, or will cause the Exchange Agent to send, to each holder of record at the Effective Time of Shares a letter of transmittal for use in such exchange (which shall specify that the delivery shall be effected, and risk of loss and title shall pass, only upon proper delivery of the Certificates to the Exchange Agent) in such form as the Target Company and Acquirer may reasonably agree, for use in effecting delivery of Shares to the Exchange Agent.

(b) Each holder of Shares that have been converted into a right to receive the Merger Consideration, upon surrender to the Exchange Agent of a Certificate, together with a properly completed letter of transmittal, will be entitled to receive the Merger Consideration in respect of the Shares represented by such Certificate. Until so surrendered, each such Certificate shall, after the Effective Time, represent for all purposes only the right to receive such Merger Consideration.

(c) After the Effective Time, there shall be no further registration of transfers of Shares. If, after the Effective Time, Certificates are presented to the Surviving Corporation, they shall be canceled and exchanged for the consideration provided for, and in accordance with the procedures set forth, in this Article II.

(d) Any portion of the Merger Consideration made available to the Exchange Agent pursuant to Section 2.03(a) that remains unclaimed by the holders of Shares one year after the Effective Time shall be returned to Acquirer, upon demand, and any such holder who has not exchanged his Shares for the Merger Consideration in accordance with this Section prior to that time shall thereafter look only to Acquirer for payment of the Merger Consideration in respect of his Shares. Notwithstanding the foregoing, Acquirer shall not be liable to any holder of Shares for any amount paid to a public official pursuant to applicable abandoned property laws. Any amounts remaining unclaimed by holders of Shares three years after the Effective Time (or such earlier date immediately prior to such time as such amounts would otherwise escheat to or become property of any governmental entity) shall, to the extent permitted by applicable law, become the property of Acquirer free and clear of any claims or interest of any Person previously entitled thereto.

(f) No dividends or other distributions with respect to Acquirer Common Stock issued in the Merger shall be paid to the holder of any unsurrendered Certificates until such Certificates are surrendered as provided in this Section. Subject to the effect of applicable laws, following such surrender, there shall be paid, without interest, to the record holder of the Acquirer Common Stock issued in exchange therefor (i) at the time of such surrender, all dividends and other distributions payable in respect of such Acquirer Common Stock with a record date after the Effective Time and a payment date on or prior to the date of such surrender and not previously paid and (ii) at the appropriate payment date, the dividends or other distributions payable with respect to such Acquirer Common Stock with a record date after the Effective Time but with a payment date subsequent to such surrender. For purposes of dividends or other distributions in respect of Acquirer Common Stock, all Acquirer Common Stock to be issued pursuant to the Merger (but not options therefor issued pursuant to Section 2.04 unless actually exercised at the Effective Time) shall be entitled to dividends pursuant to the immediately preceding sentence as if issued and outstanding as of the Effective Time.

2.04. Stock Options. (a) At the Effective Time, each outstanding option to purchase Shares (a "**Target Company Stock Option**") granted under the Target Company's plans identified in Schedule 2.04 as being the only compensation or benefit plans or agreements pursuant to which Shares may be issued (collectively, the "**Target Company Stock Option Plans**"), whether vested or not vested, shall be deemed assumed by Acquirer and shall thereafter be deemed to constitute an option to acquire, on the same terms and conditions as were applicable under such Target Company Stock Option prior to the Effective Time (in accordance with the past practice of the Target Company with respect to interpretation and application of such terms and conditions), the number (rounded down to the nearest whole number) of shares of Acquirer Common Stock determined by multiplying (x) the number of Shares subject to such Target Company Stock Option immediately prior to the Effective Time by (y) the Exchange Ratio, at a price per share of Acquirer Common Stock (rounded up to the nearest whole cent) equal to (A) the exercise price per Share otherwise purchasable pursuant to such Target Company Stock Option divided by (B) the Exchange Ratio. In addition, prior to the Effective Time, the Target Company will make any amendments to the terms of such stock option or compensation plans or arrangements that are necessary to give effect to the transactions contemplated by this Section. The Target Company represents that no consents are necessary to give effect to the transactions contemplated by this Section.

(b) Acquirer shall take all corporate action necessary to reserve for issuance a sufficient number of shares of Acquirer Common Stock for delivery pursuant to the terms set forth in this Section 2.04.

(c) At the Effective Time, each award or account (including restricted stock, stock equivalents and stock units, but excluding Target Company

Stock Options) outstanding as of the date hereof ("**Target Company Award**") that has been established, made or granted under any employee incentive or benefit plans, programs or arrangements and non-employee director plans maintained by the Target Company on or prior to the date hereof which provide for grants of equity-based awards or equity-based accounts shall be amended or converted into a similar instrument of Acquirer, in each case with such adjustments to the terms and conditions of such Target Company Awards as are appropriate to preserve the value inherent in such Target Company Awards with no detrimental effects on the holders thereof. The other terms and conditions of each Target Company Award, and the plans or agreements under which they were issued, shall continue to apply in accordance with their terms and conditions, including any provisions for acceleration (as such terms and conditions have been interpreted and applied by the Target Company in accordance with its past practice). The Target Company represents that (i) there are no Target Company Awards or Target Company Stock Options other than those reflected in Section 3.05 and (ii) all employee incentive or benefit plans, programs or arrangements and non-employee director plans under which any Target Company Award has been established, made or granted and all Target Company Stock Option Plans are disclosed in Schedule 2.04.

(d) At the Effective Time, Acquirer shall file with the Securities and Exchange Commission (the "**SEC**") a registration statement on an appropriate form or a post-effective amendment to a previously filed registration statement under the Securities Act of 1933, as amended (the "**1933 Act**"), with respect to the Acquirer Common Stock subject to options and other equity-based awards issued pursuant to this Section 2.04, and shall use its reasonable best efforts to maintain the current status of the prospectus contained therein, as well as comply with any applicable state securities or "blue sky" laws, for so long as such options or other equity-based awards remain outstanding.

2.05. Adjustments. If at any time during the period between the date of this Agreement and the Effective Time, any change in the outstanding shares of capital stock of Acquirer or the Target Company (except as permitted under this Agreement) shall occur, including, without limitation, by reason of any reclassification, recapitalization, stock split or combination, exchange or readjustment of shares, or any stock dividend thereon with a record date during such period, the Merger Consideration shall be appropriately adjusted.

2.06. Fractional Shares. (a) No fractional shares of Acquirer Common Stock shall be issued in the Merger, but in lieu thereof each holder of Shares otherwise entitled to a fractional share of Acquirer Common Stock will be entitled to receive, from the Exchange Agent in accordance with the provisions of this Section 2.06, a cash payment in lieu of such fractional shares of Acquirer Common Stock . . . .

* * *

(c) As soon as practicable after the determination of the amount of cash, if any, to be paid to holders of Shares in lieu of any fractional shares of Acquirer Common Stock, the Exchange Agent shall make available such amounts to such holders of Shares without interest.

* * *

2.09. Shares Held by Target Company Affiliates. Anything to the contrary herein notwithstanding, any shares of Acquirer Common Stock (or certificates therefor) issued to affiliates of the Target Company pursuant to Section 2.03 shall be subject to the restrictions described in [Securities Act Rules 144 and 145], and such shares (or certificates therefor) shall bear a legend describing such restrictions.

---

c. Representations and Warranties

Representations (reps) are statements of past or existing facts about the seller or buyer made by the seller or buyer and running in favor of the other party. The seller's common reps cover not only matters routine to all businesses (a good standing representation, for example) but also cover, among other things, environmental claims, employee benefits, intellectual property and products liability claims, each of which could result in significant liabilities of the buyer after closing. For example, the seller might represent to the buyer that "over the last 12 months, there has been no unionizing activity at the seller's plant."

The buyer's reps deal mainly with a buyer's ability and authority to enter into the acquisition in the first place and to consummate the closing, particularly as it relates to financing. For example, the buyer might represent to the seller that "it has the funding necessary to pay the purchase price of the assets being sold pursuant to this agreement."

Intentional misrepresentations (a.k.a. "lies" or "fraud") are actionable in tort, and under the right circumstances a plaintiff could even sue for punitive damages. However, the key word is "intentional." What if there had been unionizing activity at the seller's plant, but the seller's management was unaware of it? Technically, the seller's representation to the contrary would not be actionable due to a lack of intent.

To take the intent element off of the table, buyers require sellers (and vice versa) to warrant or guarantee that their representations are, indeed, true. Thus, by making a representation also a *warranty* (hence, "reps and warranties"), the seller *guarantees* that there has been no unionizing activity at the seller's plant. The seller's intent is irrelevant. Breaches of warranty are, of course, actionable in contract. Absent highly exceptional circumstances, buyers bringing a breach of contract action cannot sue for punitive damages.

The seller's reps and warranties are detailed descriptions about the business being sold and are much more plentiful in number than those of the buyer. This is because the buyer uses the seller's reps and warranties for three important purposes. First, the seller's reps and warranties help the buyer learn about the seller's business and reveal existing or potential problems or liabilities. For example, if the seller cannot represent and warrant that "over the last 12 months, there has been no unionizing activity at the seller's plant," the logical inference drawn by the buyer is that there *has* been such activity. This realization could turn off the buyer to the point it ceases pursuing a deal. Alternatively, it could lead the buyer to restart negotiations on purchase price under the theory that a unionized seller workforce will create a less profitable business in the future.

Second, the seller's reps and warranties help the buyer conduct its due diligence. In addition to their informational content noted above, many reps and warranties contain *laundry lists*. For example, if the seller represents and warrants that "all of the seller's employee benefit plans are listed in Section 3.13 of the Disclosure Letter," the buyer can then ask to review the laundry list of plans for due diligence purposes. Any problems or holes discovered by the buyer will be raised at the negotiating table.

Lastly, the buyer will use the seller's reps and warranties as a potential trigger to walk away from the deal after the main acquisition agreement has been signed but before the closing. Indeed, one of the conditions to the buyer's obligation to close will be that "the seller's representations and warranties remain true and correct in all material respects as if made on and as of the date of the closing."[32] In the event they are not, the buyer can choose to walk away from the deal (as a condition to closing will not have been met), or use the threat of walking away to demand a downward purchase price adjustment or other concessions from the seller.

Here are a few of seller's representations and warranties taken from a recent asset purchase agreement:

> **Section 4.01 Organization and Qualification of Seller.** Seller is a corporation duly organized, validly existing and in good standing under the Laws of the State of Delaware and has all necessary corporate power and authority to own, operate or lease

[32] This condition to closing is known as the "bring down" of reps and warranties. Reps and warranties relate to past and existing states of affair and are made as of the date of the acquisition agreement (i.e., the date of signing). Buyers require sellers to reaffirm the accuracy of sellers' reps and warranties "as of the date of the closing" as if those reps and warranties were made as of that later date, thus "bringing down" those reps and warranties to the closing date.

the properties and assets now owned, operated or leased by it and to carry on the Business as currently conducted.

Section 4.02 Authority of Seller. Seller has all necessary corporate power and authority to enter into this Agreement and the other Transaction Documents to which Seller is a party, to carry out its obligations hereunder and thereunder and to consummate the transactions contemplated hereby and thereby. The execution and delivery by Seller of this Agreement and any other Transaction Document to which Seller is a party, the performance by Seller of its obligations hereunder and thereunder and the consummation by Seller of the transactions contemplated hereby and thereby have been duly authorized by all requisite corporate action on the part of Seller. This Agreement has been duly executed and delivered by Seller, and (assuming due authorization, execution and delivery by Buyer) this Agreement constitutes a legal, valid and binding obligation of Seller enforceable against Seller in accordance with its terms, except as such enforceability may be limited by bankruptcy, insolvency, reorganization, fraudulent conveyance or transfer or similar Laws affecting the enforcement of creditors' rights generally or general principles of equity (whether considered in a proceeding at law or in equity). When each other Transaction Document to which Seller is or will be a party has been duly executed and delivered by Seller (assuming due authorization, execution and delivery by each other party thereto), such Transaction Document will constitute a legal and binding obligation of Seller enforceable against it in accordance with its terms, except as such enforceability may be limited by bankruptcy, insolvency, reorganization, fraudulent conveyance or transfer or similar Laws affecting the enforcement of creditors' rights generally or general principles of equity (whether considered in a proceeding at law or in equity).

* * *

Section 4.05 Undisclosed Liabilities. Seller has no Liabilities with respect to the Business, except (a) those which are adequately reflected or reserved against in the Balance Sheet as of the Balance Sheet Date, and (b) those which have been incurred in the ordinary course of business consistent with past practice since the Balance Sheet Date and which are not, individually or in the aggregate, material in amount.

* * *

Section 4.11 Legal Proceedings. Except as set forth on Section 4.11 of the Disclosure Schedules, there are no Actions pending or, to Seller's Knowledge, threatened against or by Seller (a) relating to or affecting the Business, the Purchased Assets or the Assumed Liabilities; or (b) that challenge or seek to prevent, enjoin or otherwise delay the transactions contemplated by this Agreement. No event has occurred or circumstances exist that may give rise to, or serve as a basis for, any such Action. There are no outstanding Governmental Orders and no unsatisfied judgments, penalties or awards against, relating to or affecting the Business.

* * *

Section 4.13 Employment Matters.

(a) Business Employees. Section 4.13(a) of the Disclosure Schedules contains a list[33] of all Business Employees and sets forth for each such individual the following: (i) name; (ii) title or position (including whether full or part time); (iii) hire date; (iv) current annual base compensation rate; and (v) commission, bonus or other incentive-based compensation. Seller is not a party to or bound by any collective bargaining or other agreement with a labor organization representing any of the Business Employees.

(b) No Complaints or Notices. To the Knowledge of Seller, there are no pending or threatened notices or complaints from or on behalf of any of the Business Employees as to any conduct or situation which, if established, could reasonably be expected to constitute a violation of federal, state or local law by Seller.

(c) No Stoppage. During the past three (3) years, Seller has not experienced any organized slowdown, work interruption, strike or work stoppage by the Business Employees.

(d) Benefit Plans. The Seller Benefit Plans have been operated and administered in compliance in all material respects with the provisions of applicable Law, including ERISA and the [Tax] Code. No Seller Benefit Plan is subject to the minimum funding standards of Section 302 of ERISA or Section 412 of the [Tax] Code, and no Seller Benefit Plan is subject to Title IV of ERISA.

One of the more important representations and warranties relates to a seller's financial statements. A seller is typically required to provide the buyer with the seller's audited financial statements for the past several fiscal years and unaudited financial statements as of the end of an interim period subsequent to the conclusion of the most recent fiscal year. Buyers are often surprised when told that the seller's auditors are not normally

[33] This is a nice example of a laundry list used by the buyer for due diligence purposes.

liable to the buyer for inaccurate financials.[34] Buyers can attempt to make auditors liable by asking for a reliance letter from them, but accounting firms are increasingly unwilling to give them. The buyer's primary protection then is a rep and warranty from the seller regarding the quality of those statements. The rep and warranty is also supplemented by another rep and warranty relating to the accuracy of the seller's financial books and records.

A frequent subject of dispute is the appropriate degree of assurance by the seller on the quality of the financial statements. The buyer wants a seller representation that the statements are *complete and correct*, while the seller objects that the standard is in excess of the fair presentation principles of GAAP (Generally Accepted Accounting Principles) used by accountants to prepare them.[35] Moreover, buyers often attempt to obtain assurances about specific line items in the financials that go well beyond fair presentation in accordance with GAAP.[36] For example, buyers may ask for a seller rep and warranty that no undisclosed liabilities exist, which goes beyond what is required by GAAP for a balance sheet.[37]

The purchaser of a publicly traded company has the comfort of having access to substantial public information about the seller (all subject to the powerful antifraud provisions of the federal securities laws) and hence does not need a comprehensive set of representations and warranties.[38] Moreover, the reps and warranties of a publicly traded seller typically do not survive beyond the closing, because clawing money back from the former public shareholders of the seller is obviously difficult if not impossible. Thus, a publicly traded seller's reps and warranties mainly facilitate buyer due diligence, while also providing the buyer with a walk right because their accuracy as of the closing date is a condition to closing.

---

[34] E.g., Credit Alliance Corp. v. Arthur Anderson & Co., 65 N.Y.2d 536, 546–47 (1992).

[35] Fights over seller financial statement representations become even more acute when the seller is a privately held company that does not have its financial statements audited in the first place.

[36] Judges can misunderstand this. E.g., Delta Holdings, Inc. v. National Distillers & Chemical Corp., 945 F.2d 1226 (2d Cir. 1991), *cert. denied*, 503 U.S. 985, 112 S.Ct. 1671, 118 L.Ed.2d 390 (1992) (in essence, specific representation on some items means other items covered by a general representation are not as significant).

[37] A Buyer-Favorable Representation: Seller has no liability except for liabilities reflected or reserved against in the Balance Sheet or the Interim Balance Sheet and current liabilities incurred in the Seller's ordinary course of business since the date of the Interim Balance Sheet.

A Seller-Favorable Representation: Seller has no liability of the nature required to be disclosed in a balance sheet prepared in accordance with GAAP except for those set forth in a Schedule attached to this agreement.

[38] The seller will commonly represent that it has made all required filings of periodic reports with the SEC and that the filings comply with the federal securities acts in all material respects. Occasionally the buyer also asks the seller to separately represent that the financial statements in the annual and quarterly reports have been prepared in accordance with GAAP, "fairly present the financial condition" of the seller, and are "correct and complete in all material respects."

NOTE: REPRESENTATIONS INSURANCE

The motivations of both sides on drafting representations and warranties in an acquisition are at odds. The buyers want comfort that the company being purchased is what it is represented to be and does not contain hidden blemishes. Sellers want maximum liquidity and finality; they want to take their money and run. A new type of insurance policy, *Representations and Warranties Insurance* (RWI), can bridge the gap between otherwise incompatible positions. Under RWI, if the maker of an insured representation or warranty breaches it, the insurer is obligated to pay for the loss resulting from the breach. Ideally, insurers step in only after an arms-length negotiation is mature. This is not "bad deal" insurance; the insurance is not a safeguard for lack of care in structuring a deal or for a poor job of due diligence investigation by the buyer. Moreover, RWI does not address all types of representations and warranties; the insurance is not a means for obtaining insurance for otherwise uninsurable risks, such as asset valuations or breaches that an insured already knows exist.

NOTE: LET THE RISK SHIFTING BEGIN—WEASELING OUT OF REPS AND WARRANTIES BY THE SELLER

Everyone knows that assets sold "*as is*" garner low prices. For example, if you buy a used car "as is," you're going to get a great price, but there's a reason for that. You and not the seller bear the risk of something going wrong with that car in the future. Hence, you better do your due diligence on that car (e.g., have a mechanic inspect it) prior to the purchase.

By contrast, assets sold with a warranty garner the higher prices that a seller is seeking. However, if there are problems with the assets during the warranty period, the seller and not the buyer is on the hook for fixing the problem. The money the seller spends fixing problems covered by the warranty essentially amounts to an after-the-fact purchase price reduction.

In an acquisition deal, buyers rarely buy businesses "as is." Buyers require sellers to make an elaborate series of reps and warranties running in favor of buyers. Since the reps are also warranties, sellers are guaranteeing that their representations are true. A breach of a rep and warranty costs sellers money, as sellers must compensate buyers for the difference between what was promised and what was delivered.

Because sellers hate giving money back to buyers, they seek to water down their reps and warranties through *knowledge qualifiers, materiality qualifiers* and *exceptions lists*. All three mechanisms shift the risk of future problems back onto buyers. Therefore, buyers must be very careful where and when they allow those mechanisms to be inserted into agreements.

Knowledge Qualifications. Sellers will seek to insert a *knowledge qualifier* into as many reps and warranties as possible. That is, a seller will want to insert "to the best of its knowledge" or "to its knowledge" in front of a given representation. Doing so reintroduces the element of *intent* back into the rep and warranty—something the warranty aspect was designed to eliminate.

For example, take the following environmental issue. The buyer purchases the seller's manufacturing business. Post-closing, the buyer discovers that waste from the seller's factory has been leaching into the underground aquafer and contaminating a nearby creek. Understandably, the buyer is furious at the thought of spending $2 million on remediation efforts and demands that the seller pay the tab. The acquisition agreement contains one of the following two environmental reps and warranties. Which would you prefer if you were the buyer or seller?

> "The Seller represents and warrants that its business has been operated in compliance with all Environmental Laws."

> "The Seller represents and warrants that, ***to Seller's knowledge***, its business has been operated in compliance with all Environmental Laws."

The first rep and warranty is a *blanket guarantee* that the seller's business has been operated in accordance with all Environmental Laws (as defined). The seller's knowledge is irrelevant, and thus the seller's intent is irrelevant. The seller has breached its rep and warranty and will have to pay for the remediation. The second rep and warranty, by contrast, is not a blanket guarantee. The seller will only have breached the rep and warranty if the seller's management *knew* about the contamination problem and thus lied to the buyer. In this case, the buyer *will have no recourse* against the seller if it purchases the seller's business only to learn post-closing about the contamination. The seller has *shifted the risk* of the unknown contamination onto the buyer by use of a knowledge qualifier.

The issue in the debate over the inclusion of knowledge qualifiers is straightforward: *Which party should bear the economic risk of unknown facts?* In seeking to insert a knowledge qualifier into a particular rep and warranty, sellers will claim that they can only affirm what they know. Buyers will resist, stating that the seller's knowledge is irrelevant to the accuracy of the basic statement and that even if the representation is false and the seller does not know that it is false, the seller should bear the risk of the inaccuracy of the statement. As a fall back position, buyers will insist on a constructive knowledge qualification, a *reasonable* or under *due inquiry* standard, in addition to an actual knowledge qualifier; the representation imputes to a party knowledge that the party would have had if it had made a reasonable inquiry: "to Seller's knowledge *after due inquiry* . . . ."

Materiality Qualifications. Sellers will also seek to water down their reps and warranties by inserting a *materiality qualifier* into many of their reps and warranties. A rep that there have been no adverse changes in the business between signing and closing, for example, usually contains an express materiality qualifier (e.g., "except for those changes which do not materially and adversely affect the business"). Take our environmental example from above. If the buyer refuses to allow a knowledge qualifier, the seller may still attempt to insert a materiality qualifier. Compare the following two environmental reps and warranties. Which would you prefer if you were the buyer or seller?

> "The Seller represents and warrants that its business has complied with all Environmental Laws."

> "The Seller represents and warrants that its business has complied **in all material respects** with all Environmental Laws."

The first rep and warranty is a *blanket guarantee* that the seller's business has been operated in accordance with all Environmental Laws (as defined). The second rep and warranty, by contrast, is a blanket guarantee only with respect to *material* environmental law violations. Thus, costs associated with nonmaterial environmental law violations (fines, etc.) are borne by the buyer. The seller has *shifted the risk* of nonmaterial environmental violations onto the buyer by use of a materiality qualifier.

Of course, sellers would love to include both knowledge and materiality qualifiers:

> "The Seller represents and warrants that, ***to Seller's knowledge***, its business has complied **in all material respects** with all Environmental Laws."

What risks does the buyer shoulder now if it accepts this version of the rep and warranty?

Some of the seller's reps and warranties are so fundamental that even technical inaccuracies may be important to the buyer. A good standing representation or a representation on outstanding stock in a stock purchase agreement must be accurate; no breach is trivial to a buyer. Why?

Buyers often prefer to put materiality qualifications in the remedy sections rather than in the individual reps and warranties themselves. Thus, although all reps and warranties must be completely true, only material breaches give a right to damages and only a material failure of a condition gives a walk right. Buyers often seek to protect themselves against technically true but misleading disclosures by the seller by including a *10b–5 representation*. This is a representation similar in form to Rule 10b–5 under the Exchange Act that puts the burden on the seller to provide the proper context for each disclosure.[39]

Exceptions Lists. The most blatant risk shifting in seller reps and warranties occurs through the use of exceptions lists. Take the following example:

> "***Except as set forth on Section 4.11 of the Disclosure Schedules***, there are no Actions pending or, to Seller's knowledge, threatened against or by Seller (a) relating to or affecting the Business, the Purchased Assets or the Assumed Liabilities; or (b) that challenge or

[39] Damages for breach of such a representation do not require proof of reliance or scienter under the indemnification provisions, however.

seek to prevent, enjoin or otherwise delay the transactions contemplated by this Agreement."

Everything the seller lists on the exceptions list (Section 4.11 of the Disclosure Schedules in the example above) *will not* violate the seller's rep and warranty. Thus, everything on that list is the *buyer's problem* going forward.

Given the risk shifting aspect of an exceptions list, buyers must carefully scrutinize everything the seller puts on the list prior to executing the acquisition agreement. Such scrutiny often leads to disagreement over whether a given item should be included on the list in the first place. If it is taken off the list, it's the seller's problem. If it stays, it's the buyer's problem. Often arguments over what stays on the list lead to purchase price renegotiations, with the buyer arguing "If you want to keep it on the list and for me to accept that risk, I deserve a purchase price reduction."

d. Covenants and Conditions

Breach of a *covenant*, a promise, will result in liability by the breaching party if the transaction does not close. The covenants in an acquisition agreement are of two types: affirmative covenants ("thou shall"), in which the parties commit to perform specified acts in the future, and negative covenants ("thou shall not"), in which the parties commit *not* to perform specified acts in the future. The seller must make most of the promises because it controls the business between signing and closing (the *pre-closing* period), and thus its actions or inaction directly impact the business. However, some covenants will apply to the *post-closing* period.

Pre-closing covenants reflect issues that arise from a *delayed* or *staggered* closing. The buyer attempts to preserve the quality of the business and facilitate the closing. The seller promises, among other things, to give the purchaser access to its records, to take organizational steps to consummate the acquisition (obtaining governmental consents and favorable shareholder votes), to run the company between the signing of the agreement and the closing so as not to diminish the company's value (i.e., operate solely in the "ordinary course"), and to use best efforts to satisfy the conditions for closing specified in subsequent sections. A sample "operation of the business" covenant follows:

> **5.01. Conduct of the Target Company.** From the date of this Agreement until the Closing Date, the Target Company and its Subsidiaries shall conduct their business in the ordinary course consistent with past practice and shall use their reasonable best efforts to preserve intact their business organizations and relationships with third parties. Without limiting the generality of the foregoing, except with the prior written consent of Acquirer or as contemplated by this Agreement, and, in the case of clauses (g), (i), (j) and (l) below, except in the ordinary course of business

not representing a new strategic direction of the Target Company, from the date of this Agreement until the Closing Date:

(a) the Target Company will not, and will not permit any of its Subsidiaries to, adopt or propose any change in its certificate of incorporation or by-laws;

(b) the Target Company will not, and will not permit any of its Subsidiaries to, adopt a plan or agreement of complete or partial liquidation, dissolution, merger, consolidation, restructuring, recapitalization or other material reorganization of the Target Company or any of its Subsidiaries (other than a merger or consolidation between its wholly-owned Subsidiaries);

(c) the Target Company will not, and will not permit any of its Subsidiaries to, issue, sell, transfer, pledge, dispose of or encumber any shares of, or securities convertible into or exchangeable for, or options, warrants, calls, commitments or rights of any kind to acquire, any shares of capital stock of any class or series of the Target Company or its Subsidiaries other than (i) issuances pursuant to the exercise of convertible securities outstanding on the date hereof or issuances pursuant to stock based awards or options that are outstanding on the date hereof and are reflected in Section 3.05 or are granted in accordance with clause (ii) below and (ii) additional options or stock-based awards to acquire Shares granted under the terms of any Target Company Stock Option Plan as in effect on the date hereof in the ordinary course consistent with past practice;

(d) the Target Company will not, and will not permit any of its Subsidiaries to, (i) split, combine, subdivide or reclassify its outstanding shares of capital stock, or (ii) declare, set aside or pay any dividend or other distribution payable in cash, stock or property with respect to its capital stock other than (x) regular quarterly cash dividends payable by the Target Company or such Subsidiary consistent with past practice (including periodic dividend increases consistent with past practice), but which for the sake of clarity shall not include any special dividend or (y) dividends paid by any Subsidiary of the Target Company to the Target Company or any wholly-owned Subsidiary of the Target Company;

(e) the Target Company will not, and will not permit any of its Subsidiaries to, redeem, purchase or otherwise acquire directly or indirectly any of the Target Company's capital stock, except for repurchases, redemptions or acquisitions (x) required by the terms of its capital stock or any securities outstanding on the date hereof, (y) required by or in connection with the respective terms, as of the date hereof, of any Target Company Stock Option Plan or any dividend reinvestment plan as in effect on the date hereof in the ordinary course of the operations of such plan consistent with past practice or (z) effected in the ordinary course consistent with past practice;

(f) the Target Company will not amend the terms (including the terms relating to accelerating the vesting or lapse of repurchase rights or obligations) of any outstanding options to purchase Shares;

(g) the Target Company will not, and will not permit any of its Subsidiaries to, make or commit to make any capital expenditure;

(h) the Target Company will not, and will not permit any of its Subsidiaries to, increase the compensation or benefits of any director, officer or employee, except for normal increases in the ordinary course of business consistent with past practice or as required under applicable law or any existing agreement or commitment;

(i) the Target Company will not, and will not permit any of its Subsidiaries to, acquire a material amount of assets (as measured with respect to the consolidated assets of the Target Company and its Subsidiaries taken as a whole) of any other Person;

(j) the Target Company will not, and will not permit any of its Subsidiaries to, sell, lease, license or otherwise dispose of any material assets or property except pursuant to existing contracts or commitments;

(k) except for any such change which is not significant or which is required by reason of a concurrent change in GAAP, the Target Company will not, and will not permit any of its Subsidiaries to, change any method of accounting or accounting practice (other than any change for tax purposes) used by it;

(l) the Target Company will not, and will not permit any of its Subsidiaries to, enter into any material joint venture, partnership or other similar arrangement;

(m) the Target Company will not, and will not permit any of its Subsidiaries to, take any action that would make any representation or warranty of the Target Company hereunder inaccurate in any material respect at, or as of any time prior to, the Closing Date; and

(n) the Target Company will not, and will not permit any of its Subsidiaries to, agree or commit to do any of the foregoing.

One class of controversial pre-closing covenants concerns *deal protection,* efforts to discourage competing bidders. The target board is limited by its fiduciary duty to its shareholders in agreeing to such provisions. See Chapter Five. A *no-shop* covenant prohibits a seller from actively soliciting other bidders and a *no-talk* clause prohibits the disclosure of non-public information to competing bidders that appear on their own. Bidders often call deal protection measures *stalking horse protections.* Acquisitions are risky; a prospective purchaser can expend time, effort, and significant sums of money on due diligence and professional services rendered in connection with a pending transaction and not successfully close. Moreover, a losing initial bidder (the *jilted suitor* or *buyer*) may have aided the seller by establishing a floor price that the seller uses to negotiate for a higher offer (the initial bidder is a stalking horse). The initial bidder also aids the winning bidder by providing a credible assurance of the selling firm's intrinsic value. Thus, prospective bidders may be reluctant to make an initial offer for the seller for fear that the bidder's time and effort will be wasted when another bidder appears. Deal protection covenants, if used properly, encourage a balky bidder to bid. Legal deal protection covenants include those designed to return a jilted suitor back to the *status quo ante* if it loses out on a deal.

The opposite of a no-shop clause is a *go-shop* clause, enabling the directors of the seller to actively solicit competing offers for a limited time period (typically twenty to fifty days) after signing. The clauses are common in conflict of interest transactions, when managers are buying the company they manage for other shareholders (a *management buy-out*). Indeed, go-shops aid directors of the seller in satisfying their fiduciary duties to their shareholders in the context of those transactions. See *In re Appraisal of Dell, Inc.*, 2016 WL 3186538 (Del. Ch.), *rev'd in part, aff'd in part, and remanded sub nom. Dell, Inc. v. Magnetar Global Event Driven Master Fund Ltd.*, 177 A.3d 1 (Del. 2017), *supra* Chapter 2, Section A.3.c.iii.

Post-closing transitional covenants obligate the parties to work together after the closing on the smooth transfer of all the assets and liabilities to the buyer. There are often several covenants relating to employee retention and benefits, for example. Post-closing protective covenants, non-competition and non-solicitation of employee clauses and confidentiality agreements all stop actions by the seller that may diminish the value of the business transferred.

If one party does not satisfy a *condition*, the other (unless it waives the condition) may refuse to close (walk). An unsatisfied closing condition is often referred to as a *walk right* or an *out.* There is a fundamental difference between closing conditions, on the one hand, and representations and warranties and covenants, on the other. A breach of a rep and warranty or a covenant (a promise) gives remedies under the indemnification section; the failure of a condition, unless waived by the party to whom the condition runs, justifies a refusal to perform its obligations (i.e., close). Most all representations and warranties and covenants also are included in conditions, subject in most cases to a materiality qualification.[40] Conditions besides those covering reps and warranties and covenants also exist. Thus, if a seller breaches one of those conditions, the buyer can walk but cannot close and then sue for damages. Only if the breach fails to satisfy another covenant, such as the *best efforts clause*,[41] is a seller liable in damages. For example, the failure of the seller to deliver an estoppel certificate[42] gives the purchaser the election to walk at the closing but, since delivery is not a covenant of the seller, not the right to sue for damages unless the seller has violated its best efforts obligation.

The conditions precedent to the obligations of the purchaser and seller specify what must be true for the parties to be bound at the closing to execute the basic exchange (cash-for-stock; cash-for-assets; and so on). These provisions therefore detail what each party can expect from the other at the closing. One of the important conditions is a *bring down clause* in which the seller reaffirms all of its representations and warranties as accurate as of the closing date.[43] Thus, each rep and warranty operates (often subject to a materiality condition) as a closing condition. Other conditions include the performance of each of the pre-closing covenants, the acquisition of all necessary governmental consents, the executions of opinions of counsel, and the presentation of the required supplementary documents (an escrow agreement, an employment agreement, a release and an estoppel certificate, for example). In the acquisition of a publicly traded company, the conditions may include *comfort letters* from the SEC on the accounting effect of the transaction and *fairness opinions* from independent investment bankers on the reasonableness of the price. A buyer seeking a very broad walk right will ask for a *due diligence out*, making the buyer's obligation to purchase subject to the buyer's

---

[40] Since the closing condition and many of the individual reps and warranties each have materiality qualifiers, the closing condition often has a *double materiality scrape*. This is a clause that, for the purpose of calculating the materiality qualifier in the closing condition, all materiality qualifiers in the reps and warranties are disregarded. Without this, breaches of reps and warranties, immaterial in their individual instances but material when viewed collectively, would not result in the failure of the condition and thus wouldn't allow the buyer to walk.

[41] The seller will usually covenant to use its best efforts to satisfy all the conditions. A seller will also covenant to provide such documents and to take such actions as a buyer may reasonable request.

[42] In a stock acquisition, each selling shareholder must deliver a release and estoppel certificate releasing the buyer from all claims but those based on a breach of the acquisition agreement.

[43] The negotiation of a materiality qualifier on this closing condition is significant. Buyers want the bring down clause to specify that the representations are *true and correct* at the time of closing. Sellers ask for *true and correct in all material respects* language.

satisfactory completion of a due diligence investigation on the seller's operations.[44]

Sellers will negotiate for a materiality qualification on many of the conditions. Sellers want purchasers' walk rights contingent on only non-trivial failures of conditions; that is, the purchaser can refuse to close only if there are material inaccuracies in the reps and warranties, for example. In public company acquisitions there is often included an overarching *material adverse change clause (MAC)* that gives the buyer a walk right if the business of the target significantly declines in value between the signing and the closing. Many MAC clauses contain *carve-outs*, exclusions of specified events or circumstances. A common carve out is for global, national or regional political conditions; another is for industry wide changes or developments. The leading cases on MAC clauses, one of which, *Hexion Specialty Chemicals, Inc.*, is in Section D.2 below, are skeptical of buyers' arguments under the provisions, holding that the clauses do not act as an escape hatch for buyers that have changed their minds after signing the agreement *(buyer's remorse).*

Financing conditions provide a buyer with a walk right if the buyer fails to secure financing for the acquisition payment. The condition is accompanied by a buyer representation that the buyer has received *commitment letters*[45] or *highly confident letters*[46] from lenders (and, in private equity fund acquisitions, an *equity financing commitment letter* from the sponsor fund) and a covenant that the buyer will use *commercially reasonable efforts* (or *reasonable best efforts*) to obtain financing on the terms specified in the letters. In triangular mergers, mergers between a seller and a shell acquisition subsidiary of the sponsoring buyer, a best efforts clause of the shell is little comfort if the buyer walks without financing. Monetary claims against the empty shell are worthless and specific performance is impossible (the shell has no funds and the target, as a third party, has questionable standing to enforce the commitment letters).

---

[44] Sellers will resist as this language grants a buyer very close to an open option on the purchase.

[45] A lender commits to debt financing for a substantial part of the acquisition price. The commitment papers describe the type of financing and the structure and terms of the proposed financing. The documents also contain conditions for the financing. Most letters contain their own MAC clause. All letters will condition financing on evidence that the buyer can satisfy one or more financial metrics. The typical funding metric is a *pro forma leverage ratio* (the ratio of funded debt, including all acquisition debt, to EBITDA). Many fee letters that accompany the commitment letter (but are not shown to the seller) provide that a buyer must pay a committing lender a portion of the termination fee received from the seller.

[46] An investment bank indicates its belief that the buyer will be able to secure financing. The highly confident letters were popular in the 80s and 90s. Now sellers demand fully executed commitment papers on financial commitments for the full amount of the debt financing required for the acquisition.

NOTE: ACQUISITION FINANCING

Financing type and structure is limited only by the imagination. Common in acquisition financing are senior secured credit facilities, mezzanine or subordinated debt, high yield bonds, debentures and notes and bridge facilities. A *senior secured credit facility*, a loan provided by a lender (or group of lenders, a *loan syndicate*), is similar in form to a traditional commercial loan from a commercial bank. The buyer's obligation to repay is secured by all the buyer's current and future assets. Additional debt funding at higher interest rates is available from lenders that specialize in *mezzanine* or *subordinated* debt financing. The obligation to repay is subordinated to the right of payment on other indebtedness of the buyer. The obligations are not secured by a security interest in the assets of the buyer. *High yield bonds* (a.k.a. *junk bonds*), *debentures* and *notes* are term loans with extended maturities that are sold to a broad group of investors. The Securities Act of 1933 treats the bonds, debentures and notes as an offering of securities; most are issued in private placements to a *placement agent* (typically an investment banking firm) that immediately flips them (resells them) to qualified institutional buyers (*QIBs*)[47] under Securities Act Rule 144A.[48] A buyer will use *bridge financing*, borrowing funds short term (under a year) to bridge the time between the closing and the completion of permanent financing (a high yield debt offering, for example).

e. Termination and Indemnification Clauses

After a failed closing, a party may want to force a closing and either or both parties may want to sue for damages. After a closing, a buyer may sue for breach when a transaction closes and the buyer discovers major problems in the business. General principles of contract law excuse performance, closing, if the other party commits a material breach of a contract. Contract law also provides for recovery of damages for breach and a variety of equitable remedies as well—rescission, specific performance, injunctive relief and reformation. Plaintiffs asserting an alleged breach of a representation and warranty may also make claims based on modern evolutions of the old action of common law fraud.[49] These claims are more

---

[47] See Securities Act Rule 144A(a)(1) (definition of "qualified institutional buyer").

[48] Some issuers register their securities offerings with the SEC at the outset and sell the securities through underwriters to the public. Other issuers offer their securities through private placements to qualified institutional buyers, typically with the use of Securities Act Rule 144A. Still other issuers seek the best of both worlds. They will issue their securities through private placements while committing to register mirror image securities with the SEC within a specified time period. Once the SEC grants effectiveness to their offerings, those issuers then exchange the registered mirror image securities for those they previously privately placed (a so-called *A/B Exchange*). Investors receiving the registered mirror image securities can then freely sell them in the secondary market, as issuers will have listed those securities for trading on a stock exchange as part of the registration process.

[49] Federal securities law, state statutes on negligent misrepresentation, deceptive trade practice statutes, and state blue sky laws all have grown out of the state action of common law fraud.

difficult to prove and win than contract claims,[50] but often appear as alternative counts in a complaint.[51]

Against this extensive backdrop of judicial remedies, the parties negotiate *termination* and *indemnification* clauses attempting to recast the scope and form of relief otherwise available. Sellers attempt to limit the remedies and buyers attempt to expand on the remedies. The clauses are often the most hotly negotiated clauses in the agreement and depend heavily on the relative bargaining positions of the parties.

The termination clause confirms that a party's decision not to close does not relieve either party of any liability for breach. The parties may include a *fiduciary out*,[52] allowing the seller to terminate an agreement in light of a higher bid, or a *drop-dead date*, a future date at which either party may refuse to close without penalty. Parties who do not want to rely on general legal and equitable rights and remedies provide for *termination fees* for a jilted buyer[53] and *reverse termination fees* for a jilted seller (also known as *break-up fees*).[54] A party may pay the fee without triggering a breach. The fees are usually combined with an express limitation on claims for relief outside the fee.

Most indemnification sections, providing for damages if one party breaches, provide sellers with a *basket* amount, a minimum amount that a buyer's damages must exceed before the seller owes anything. This deductible recognizes that a seller's reps and warranties on an ongoing business are unlikely to be perfectly accurate and that the parties do not

---

50 A plaintiff must prove additional elements (e.g., intent) over those required by contract claims to prevail.

51 As discussed earlier, a seller's breach of a representation gives rise to a claim in tort, and punitive damages may even be available. However, the seller's misrepresentation must be intentional, and intent is often difficult to establish. To take intent off the table, a buyer will insist that a seller's representations also be made warranties (guarantees). Breach of a warranty gives rise to a claim in contract. Intent is irrelevant in that context.

52 The Delaware Supreme Court's poorly considered decision in Omnicare, Inc. v. NCS Healthcare, Inc., 818 A.2d 914 (Del. 2003), has caused a lively debate over whether Delaware law requires fiduciary out clauses in acquisition agreements that require a vote of the selling firm shareholders. See Orman v. Cullman, 2004 WL 2348395, at *7 (Del. Ch.) (no, if minority shareholders have a separate, effective approval right).

53 Termination fees are often triggered by the seller's exercise of a fiduciary out right to terminate the acquisition due to a target board accepting a higher offer or a shareholder vote against the transaction. The fee may also be triggered by a change in the recommendation to shareholders by the target board or by a no vote by target shareholders. The size of the fee attracts the attention of the Delaware courts when it is so large that it acts to deter rival bids. See, e.g., In re Lear Corp. Shareholder Litig., 926 A.2d 94 (Del. Ch. 2007). Most fees are two to four percent of the equity value of the target, with maximum fees hitting 6.3 percent. See Phelps Dodge Corp. v. Cyprus Amax Mineral Co., 1999 WL 1054255 (Del. Ch.) (questioning a 6.3 percent fee in dicta).

54 Reverse termination fees are paid by the buyer when a transaction does not close due to the failure of a closing condition (the failure to obtain financing, for example). The relationship of reverse termination fees to specific performance clauses has been the subject of some very sloppy drafting. See United Rentals, Inc. v. RAM Holdings, 937 A.2d 810 (Del. Ch. 2007).

want disputes over insignificant amounts.[55] Parties typically negotiate extensively over the workings of the indemnification provisions, including basket and cap amounts.

The buyers intend the indemnification section to specify and add to otherwise available remedies and to provide that the remedies *survive* the closing.[56] Clauses may offer protection not dependent on a breach; they may simply reallocate risk.[57] A seller negotiates for an exclusive declaration of remedies in the indemnification clause and an *as is* sale, no survival of the remedies after the closing. A survival clause enables a purchaser that has not discovered a major problem with the seller's business to sue the seller for a false representation after closing.[58] The purchaser's remedies must survive the closing and a court must hold that the purchaser was not at fault somehow for not finding the defect in its acquisition review of the seller's business (that the purchaser did not somehow assume the risk).

NOTE: BOUNDARIES TO PROVISIONS ON LIMITING REMEDIES

A seller often attempts to limit a buyer's remedies through contract provisions in which the buyer: (a) disclaims all express or implied representations other than those expressly set out in the agreement (a *non-reliance clause*), (b) agrees that indemnification under the terms of the agreement is the buyer's exclusive remedy, and/or (c) agrees that the sale is *as is, where is*. At issue is the effectiveness of the language. The issue is cleanest, perhaps, on claims of some version of fraud that require an aggrieved party to prove reliance (often by *clear and convincing* evidence). Will a non-reliance provision in a contract serve to defeat the claim?

There is a split in the federal courts over whether the non-reliance clauses defeat claims based on the federal securities laws.[59] See *AES Corp. v. Dow Chemical Co.*, 325 F.3d 174 (3d Cir. 2003) (non-reliance clause is evidence of non-reliance but not conclusive); but see *Harsco Corp. v. Segui*, 91 F.3d 337 (2d

---

[55] If reps and warranties already have materiality qualifiers included within them, then a basket provision often includes a *double materiality scrape*. That is a clause which, for the purpose of calculating basket amounts, disregards the materiality qualification in the reps and warranties.

[56] In the acquisition of a publicly traded company, the consideration will be disbursed to a dispersed group of seller shareholders either on or immediately after the acquisition. Post-closing relief from those shareholders often is not practicable so the acquisition agreement usually does not give the purchaser general indemnification rights against the selling company shareholders. The only indemnification section is one that protects the officers and directors of the selling company from liability from claims arising from the transaction.

[57] Indemnification from liabilities unknown at the time of signing or closing is such an example.

[58] In asset acquisitions, the seller dissolves soon after the transaction and indemnification clauses must apply to the target shareholders.

[59] The Supreme Court decision in Landreth Timber Co. v. Landreth, 471 U.S. 681, 105 S.Ct. 2297, 85 L.Ed.2d 692 (1985), made all stock acquisitions, even if privately negotiated and even if the seller was a privately held corporation, subject to the general antifraud proscriptions in Exchange Act Rule 10b–5. Rule 10b–5 claims immediately became an attractive alternative to breach of contract claims for frustrated buyers.

Cir. 1996). Similarly, there is also a split in state courts over whether the clauses defeat claims based on common law fraud. See *ABRY V.L.P. v. F & W Acq, LLC*, 891 A.2d 1032 (Del. Ch. 2006) (non-reliance clauses do not shield affirmative misrepresentations but the burden of proof to overcome the language is very high); but see *Consolidated Edison, Inc. v. Northeast Utilities*, 249 F. Supp.2d 387 (S.D.N.Y. 2003) (summary judgment granted based on non-reliance clause; clause must be *specific* to false representation, however), *rev'd on other grounds*, 426 F.3d 524 (2d Cir. 2005).

Most clauses on survival, such as § 11.1 in the American Bar Association's Model Stock Purchase Agreement, purport to give the purchaser who does discover a false representation in the acquisition review a right to *close-and-sue* (some refer to the practice as *sandbagging*).[60] That is, the purchaser with knowledge of a false representation can close without revealing its discovery to the seller, and then sue the seller for a rebate on the purchase price after the closing. Some courts may refuse to respect the language of a clause that permits the strategy of sandbagging using the common law doctrine of reliance, a required element of damage relief. Compare *Hendricks v. Callahan,* 972 F.2d 190, 195–96 (8th Cir. 1992) (not enforceable), with *CBS v. Ziff Davis Publishing Co.*, 553 N.E.2d 997 (N.Y. 1990) (enforceable).[61] Once a very sharp practice against naïve sellers,[62] knowledgeable sellers have fashioned protections. They can insist on anti-sandbagging clauses, that a purchaser reveal its discoveries before or at the closing and renegotiate the price to reflect the discovery, waive the problem or walk away from the deal.[63] Now that the issue is out in the open, some buyers now insist on *pro-sandbagging* provisions!

f. Boilerplate

The final section of miscellaneous provisions contains those boilerplate provisions that your first-year course in contracts taught you were necessary. Many of the boilerplate provisions address the resolution of

---

[60] There is the related issue of substitute performance. At common law a breaching party may condition substitute performance, closing recognizing a breach, on a waiver of contract claim. An opposing party may not, relying on contract language, accept the performance and sue under the original contract. See U.S. v. Lamont, 155 U.S. 303, 15 S.Ct. 97, 39 L.Ed. 160 (1894). At issue is whether a buyer can avoid the effect of the doctrine by express contract language.

[61] The ABA drafters disagree with *Hendricks*. The case, they say, deprives buyers of the benefit of their bargain. Representations and warranties are risk allocation devices, not just assurances regarding the accuracy of facts.

[62] Such a rule encourages purchasers to be silent at the closing, purposefully misleading the seller on the purchaser's due diligence findings, rather than negotiate the conflict. It encourages litigation as the purchaser's incentive to settle is significantly reduced post-closing. The purchaser, with the deal no longer at risk, has an inexpensive lottery ticket for litigation.

[63] Savvy sellers may also ask the purchasers to execute at closing a release on known but undisclosed defects. Purchasers who refuse to sign the release show their hand, prompting a renegotiation of the price.

disputes. There are provisions on governing law, consent to jurisdiction of certain courts, waiver of jury trial, and arbitration. Some clauses aid courts in interpreting the basic contract: There are provisions on integration (remember the *parol evidence rule*?), waiver, severability, section headings, form of notices, time is of the essence, choice of governing law, and so on. There are also a few provisions that add material terms to the deal, the provision on successors and assigns, the payment of expenses, and on who may make public announcements about the transaction.

g. Negotiations Over the Documents

The custom in acquisition practice is for the purchaser's lawyers to prepare the first draft of the acquisition agreement and present the draft to the seller's lawyers, who negotiate for changes, additions and deletions. The sellers return a marked-up draft (a *redline*) as a prelude to the negotiation.[64] The purchaser's lawyers rely on forms to prepare their initial draft. Common errors by a purchaser's lawyer include using a mark-up of the last acquisition in which the firm participated. First, the mark-up may not reflect the nuances of the current acquisition. Second, the mark-up, one in a long series, may not reflect current legal developments. Third, the mark-up is the negotiated final deal, not a purchaser's first draft (opening salvo). A purchaser's first draft should provide negotiating room for concessions. The room for concessions is more than a bargaining tactic to gain an advantage if a seller does not ask for changes, it is a disclosure/discovery device. When a seller asks for concessions to a representation and warranty declaring, for example, no environmental risks, the seller must justify the change and reveal information about the company in the process ("We may have a problem in a sink hole on the back forty.").

On the other hand, when a purchaser uses an extreme first draft, it risks declaring to the seller that the purchaser (or the purchaser's attorney) is unreasonable and overzealous. This could awaken a suspicion in the seller that the purchaser is opportunistic or neurotic (or both) and not someone with whom the seller wants to be in a cooperative deal. It could kill some deals and, at a minimum, put the seller's attorneys on notice that it will be a nit-picky negotiation, driving up everyone's lawyer fees and exasperating one or both parties. In this vein, we caution that the black letter of the American Bar Association's Model Stock Purchase Agreement is, in most legal communities outside of New York, a relatively aggressive purchaser's first draft. It is an excellent educational tool but a buyer's lawyers ought to temper its language for use as a first draft in most acquisitions.

---

[64] Whenever a lawyer marks up a draft, she should redline or otherwise indicate the changes. It is inappropriate to mark up a draft and return it without indicating where the changes are in the hopes that one can slip some important changes by a busy attorney on the other side.

The drafters of a well-crafted agreement generally aim to minimize judicial involvement in the interpretation of the agreement's express language (as opposed to, for example, the necessary involvement of a judge in factual disagreements). Use of defined terms helps immensely in this regard. Courts will respect the plain meaning of an agreement's language unless the written contract's terms are ambiguous. There are limits to what attorneys can accomplish with even the most thorough and detailed of documents. The most obvious limit is the capacity of general jurisdiction judges to understand and appropriately enforce stock acquisition documents when confronted with subsequent disputes. The now-routine complexity of acquisition documents augments the risk that judges may not interpret them in accordance with the understandings of the parties who signed them. If the risk of judicial error becomes substantial, parties may want to investigate alternative dispute resolution mechanisms that guarantee a sophisticated decision maker who understands these transactions.

There is a serious question about whether acquisition forms currently in wide use have evolved into a monster of interwoven and overlapping provisions. First, the drafters of a typical acquisition agreement address the same issues in multiple sections. For example, in the ABA Model Stock Purchase Agreement, the accuracy of representations and warranties in sections 3 and 4 serve as the basis for closing conditions in sections 8 and 9, which in turn provide a right to terminate in section 10, and as a basis for covenants in section 6 and for indemnification under section 11 and other common law remedies under section 12. Whew!

Second, acquisition agreements invariably contain numerous representations that overlap with other representations both specific and general. A single factual event, therefore, could constitute a breach. In the ABA Model Stock Purchase Agreement an error in the value of inventory stated in the seller's financials, for example, is a violation of the representations in 3.4 (Financial Statements), 3.5 (Books and Records), 3.6 (Real and Personal Property), 3.9 (Inventories), 3.14 (Compliance with Legal Requirements), and 3.29 (Disclosure).[65] To reiterate the first point above, the error would also breach covenants 6.2 and conditions 8.1, 8.2, and 8.3, and constitute a termination event in 10.1, an indemnification event in 11.2 and be the basis for contract remedies in 12.11. Whew (again)!

In several notable cases, courts have struggled with the complexity of the language of acquisition agreements. The Delaware Chancery Court, in *United Rentals,* excerpted in the next section, found a conflict in the remedy section on the exclusivity of a termination fee.[66] The Delaware Superior

---

65 We may have missed one or two.

66 See also Matria Healthcare Inc. v. Coral SR LLC, 2007 WL 763303 (Del. Ch.) (conflict between post-closing adjustment and indemnification provisions).

Court, in *DCV Holdings*,[67] struggled with the multiple representations breached by a charge of price fixing against the seller's executives. Some of the representations had different knowledge qualifiers and others did not. The judge held that one representation, with a knowledge qualifier, superseded the others that did not have the qualifier, rather than apply each representation separately and independently. Drafters now include more language to deal with each case and the basic form document grows anew.[68]

Another limit to contract detail is the parties' inability to reduce important terms of an agreement to well-defined written obligations because of intricate or uncertain future contingencies. Drafting definitive contractual language may be impractical because of the parties' inability to identify uncertain future conditions or because of their inability to characterize complex adaptations when the contingencies can be identified in advance. In these situations, the parties may create *relational* contracts and rely on broad provisions requiring, for example, good faith and fair dealing (which are implied in all contracts even if not expressly included), best efforts, or material performance. Open-ended contract terms rely essentially on the parties' stake in their business reputation and on their underlying sense of business values and ethics. When these restraints fail, such terms give substantial discretion to the sensibilities of enforcing courts.

A last, ubiquitous limit on contracting is a group of common law doctrines that cannot be nullified by explicit contract terms. The basic principle of contract law is a respect for and facilitation of parties ordering their private affairs. Thus, many contract rules of law apply only in the absence of an expression of intention by the parties and the parties may change them if they see fit. This basic principle has exceptions, however. A small but powerful body of elite doctrines, embodying notions of essential fairness that have a long pedigree, empowers judges to overlook the express language of even the most detailed contracts to reach results that add to and may even contradict a contract's stipulated terms.[69] The doctrines have

---

[67] DCV Holdings, Inc. v. Conagra, Inc., 2005 WL 698133 (Del.), *aff'd*, 889 A.2d 954 (Del. 2005).

[68] Whether and how complexity benefits clients (as opposed to their lawyers) are serious questions. Is the transaction bar creating a need for their services? The authors wonder why, in private stock acquisitions, for example, the core acquisition agreements (exclusive of special deal terms) contain much more than, other than authorization formalities, a (1) representation of clean and complete financials with (2) closing adjustments at closing for changes in operations within an acceptable range, (3) a covenant to preserve the value in the business to the closing, and (4) a right to walk for unacceptably large changes in the operations or value of the business. The common law provides a full set of remedies for breach or fraud. Anything else may be just gilding the lily as a way of extracting fees in an otherwise high dollar exchange. The authors cannot recall of an acquisition that would not have been covered adequately by these provisions.

[69] The doctrines of fraud and misrepresentation trump all contract language. The doctrines of mistake, material breach, waiver, substituted performance, accord and satisfaction and remedies are part of basic contract law and each doctrine has a core essence in application that the parties cannot alter or waive by contract language.

always been a part of contract analysis, although there is some recent concern about their expanding breadth. Parties will attempt to avoid them with clever language, but courts resist the limitations.[70]

Litigators and their clients, burdened with litigation over the meaning of acquisition documents, have been heard to voice a skeptical, pragmatic view of how judges ultimately decide cases using these wild-card doctrines. There is apparently a "pervasive perception" that acquisition agreements are so "labyrinthine that neither the parties nor the lawyers who drafted them understand them" and that since "the reason for courts to show deference to contracts disappears . . . [i]t appears acceptable for judges and juries to do what they think is fair under the circumstances of the case before them." John S. Lowe, *Developments in Nonregulatory Oil and Gas Law: Are We Moving Toward a Kinder and Gentler Law of Contracts?*, Proc. 42nd Ann. Inst. on Oil and Gas Law and Taxation (1991). The effect, they argue, is a spiral of deepening frustration: "Resolution of disputes on equitable principles tends to spur drafters to ever more detailed contractual expositions of their intent in an attempt to recapture the predictive function of the contract, which in turn is likely to result in long and complicated provisions that fuel the predilection of the courts to ignore the literal words." *Id.*

The spiral description seems apt in light of the number of recent cases in which judges have struggled with the explicit language of acquisition agreements. In any event, the spiral can be avoided both by judges who have patience with crafted detail in high-risk, high-stake deals and by lawyers who do not burden stock acquisition agreements with needless and numbing verbiage.[71] The bedrock of common law that empowers parties to order their private affairs through legally enforceable contracts has safety valves, however, that parties and their lawyers should not ignore.

When lawyers disagree over language in drafts of an acquisition agreement, they have two options: negotiate a compromise or, if they cannot, return to their clients and present them with the controversy. The client can decide to compromise or deadlock. Lawyers, who do not want to budge and yet are hesitant to tell clients of an impasse[72] (clients often see these matters as technical issues and can lose patience with their lawyers),

---

70 See. e.g., Abry Partners V, L.P. v. F & W Acq., LLC, 891 A.2d 1032 (Del. Ch. 2006) (liability limiting provisions invalid to the extent they purported to shield affirmative misrepresentations).

71 Consider the cautionary words of Bayless Manning, former Dean of the Stanford Law School and a partner in Paul, Weiss, Rifkind, Wharton & Garrison in New York City:

> We lawyers have an all too familiar propensity to believe that the solution to any problem is more drafting. As a group, we continue to believe that particularity conquers ambiguity. That belief is ill-founded. . . . We would do well to adopt as our drafting model the Constitution of the United States rather than the Internal Revenue Code.

Bayless Manning, *Principles of Corporate Governance: One Viewer's Perspective on the ALI Project*, 48 BUS. LAW. 1319, 1331 (1993).

72 To ask if clients want to hold out or concede the question.

will resort to arguments over custom in M & A practice. The lawyer who is asking for something novel, outside normal practice, has the burden of persuasion. So lawyers (1) debate custom and practice *on the street*,[73] (2) then debate over who is deviating from custom and practice (asking for special treatment),[74] and (3) finally debate over whether the bargaining power of a client whose lawyer is asking for special language is strong enough to demand and get it (whether the demand is "reasonable").[75] If one client is anxious to close the deal and the other client is reluctant, skip to step (3). So important is the practice that lawyers have developed resources that collect data on the frequency of the use of acquisition clauses.[76] The data supports an argument for who is closer to the practice on the street.

UNITED RENTALS, INC. V. RAM HOLDINGS, INC.

Delaware Court of Chancery, 2007.
937 A.2d 810.

CHANDLER, CHANCELLOR.

* * *

First, the language of the Merger Agreement presents a direct conflict between two provisions on remedies, rendering the Agreement ambiguous and defeating plaintiff's motion for summary judgment. Second, the extrinsic evidence of the negotiation process, though ultimately not conclusive, is too muddled to find that plaintiff's interpretation of the Agreement represents the common understanding of the parties. Third, under the forthright negotiator principle, the subjective understanding of one party to a contract may bind the other party when the other party knows or has reason to know of that understanding. Because the evidence in this case shows that defendants understood this Agreement to preclude the remedy of specific performance and that plaintiff knew or should have known of this understanding, I conclude that plaintiff has failed to meet its burden and find in favor of defendants.

* * *

1. *The Merger Agreement*

The Merger Agreement contains two key provisions at issue in this case. Section 9.10, entitled "Specific Performance," provides:

---

[73] E.g., "that provision you're asking for isn't 'market'."

[74] This is usually collapsed into the debate over number 1.

[75] Here a deal lawyer's reputation in the legal community comes into play, for every lawyer knows that she may be on the less powerful end of a document negotiation tomorrow.

[76] The Mergers and Acquisitions Committee of the Section of Business Law of the ABA conducts annual *deal point studies*. These studies cover public/public acquisitions, private/private acquisitions and international transactions. The studies are available at http://apps.americanbar.org/dch/committee.cfm?com=CL560003 (visited Sept. 2017). See also *SRS Acquiom M & A Deal Terms Study* (2017) (avail. at www.srsacquiom.com/resources/2017-srs-acquiom-ma-deal-terms-study/).

> The parties agree that irreparable damage would occur in the event that any of the provisions of this Agreement were not performed in accordance with their specific terms or were otherwise breached. Accordingly, (a) [RAM Holdings] and [RAM Acquisition] shall be entitled to seek an injunction or injunctions to prevent breaches of this Agreement by the Company and to enforce specifically the terms and provisions of this Agreement, in addition to any other remedy to which such party is entitled at law or in equity and (b) the Company shall be entitled to seek an injunction or injunctions to prevent breaches of this Agreement by [RAM Holdings] or [RAM Acquisition] or to enforce specifically the terms and provisions of this Agreement and the Guarantee to prevent breaches of or enforce compliance with those covenants of [RAM Holdings] or [RAM Acquisition] that require [RAM Holdings] or [RAM Acquisition] to (i) use its reasonable best efforts to obtain the Financing and satisfy the conditions to closing set forth in Section 7.1 and Section 7.3, including the covenants set forth in Section 6.8 and Section 6.10 and (ii) consummate the transactions contemplated by this Agreement, if in the case of this clause (ii), the Financing (or Alternative Financing obtained in accordance with Section 6.10(b)) is available to be drawn down by [RAM Holdings] pursuant to the terms of the applicable agreements but is not so drawn down solely as a result of [RAM Holdings] or [RAM Acquisition] refusing to do so in breach of this Agreement. *The provisions of this Section 9.10 shall be subject in all respects to Section 8.2(e) hereof, which Section shall govern the rights and obligations of the parties hereto (and of [Cerberus Partners], the Parent Related Parties, and the Company Related Parties) under the circumstances provided therein.*

Section 8.2(e), referred to in the specific performance provision in section 9.10, is part of Article VIII, entitled "Termination, Amendment and Waiver." Article VIII provides specific limited circumstances in which either RAM or URI can terminate the Merger Agreement and receive a $100 million termination fee. The relevant portion of section 8.2(e) of the Merger Agreement provides:

> Notwithstanding anything to the contrary in this Agreement, including with respect to Sections 7.4 and 9.10, (i) the Company's right to terminate this Agreement in compliance with the provisions of Sections 8.1(d)(i) and (ii) and its right to receive the Parent Termination Fee pursuant to Section 8.2(c) or the guarantee thereof pursuant to the Guarantee, and (ii) [RAM Holdings]'s right to terminate this Agreement pursuant to Section 8.1(e)(i) and (ii) and its right to receive the Company Termination Fee pursuant to Section 8.2(b) shall, in each case, be the sole and exclusive remedy, including on account of punitive damages, of (in

the case of clause (i)) the Company and its subsidiaries against [RAM Holdings], [RAM Acquisition], [Cerberus Partners] or any of their respective affiliates, stockholders, general partners, limited partners, members, managers, directors, officers, employees or agents (collectively "*Parent Related Parties*") and (in the case of clause (ii)) [RAM Holdings] and [RAM Acquisition] against the Company or its subsidiaries, affiliates, stockholders, directors, officers, employees or agents (collectively "*Company Related Parties*"), for any and all loss or damage suffered as a result thereof, and upon any termination specified in clause (i) or (ii) of this Section 8.2(e) and payment of the Parent Termination Fee or Company Termination Fee, as the case may be, none of [RAM Holdings], [RAM Acquisition], [Cerberus Partners] or any of their respective Parent Related Parties or the Company or any of the Company Related Parties shall have any further liability or obligation of any kind or nature relating to or arising out of this Agreement or the transactions contemplated by this Agreement as a result of such termination.

. . .

In no event, whether or not this Agreement has been terminated pursuant to any provision hereof, shall [RAM Holdings], [RAM Acquisition], [Cerberus Partners] or the Parent Related Parties, either individually or in the aggregate, be subject to any liability in excess of the Parent Termination Fee for any or all losses or damages relating to or arising out of this Agreement or the transactions contemplated by this Agreement, including breaches by [RAM Holdings] or [RAM Acquisition] of any representations, warranties, covenants or agreements contained in this Agreement, and *in no event shall the Company seek equitable relief or seek to recover any money damages in excess of such amount from [RAM Holdings], [RAM Acquisition], [Cerberus Partners] or any Parent Related Party or any of their respective Representatives.*

The parties dispute the effect of section 8.2(e) on section 9.10.

* * *

URI argues that the plain and unambiguous language of the merger agreement allows for specific performance as a remedy for the Ram Entities' breach. . . .

* * *

Reading the Agreement as a whole and with the aid of the fundamental canons of contract construction, I conclude that URI's interpretation is reasonable. . . .

* * *

Though defendants fail to demonstrate that plaintiff's interpretation of the Merger Agreement is unreasonable as a matter of law, defendants do succeed in offering a reasonable alternative interpretation. . . . The relationship between sections 9.10 and 8.2(e), as set forth in section 9.10 is, defendants contend, clear: section 9.10 is "subject to" section 8.2(e). Section 8.2(e) then provides that "in no event shall [URI] seek equitable relief or seek to recover any money damages in excess of such amount [*i.e.*, the $100 million termination fee] from [RAM or Cerberus]." RAM argues that section 8.2(e) operates to prohibit URI from seeking any form of equitable relief (including specific performance) under all circumstances, relegating URI's relief to only the $100 million termination fee. . . .

* * *

Therefore, I must consider extrinsic evidence to ascertain the meaning of the Merger Agreement.

* * *

The Court heard testimony from seven witnesses over a two-day trial in order to resolve the factual issue of what was the common understanding of the parties with respect to remedies in the Merger Agreement. The Merger Agreement, of course, is a contract, and the Court's goal when interpreting a contract "is to ascertain the shared intention of the parties." Thus, URI, which seeks to specifically enforce the Merger Agreement, bore the burden of persuasion in demonstrating that the common understanding of the parties was that this contract allowed for the remedy of specific performance and that URI is entitled to such a remedy. URI has failed to meet its burden.

* * *

The Court must emphasize here that the introduction of extrinsic, parol evidence does not alter or deviate from Delaware's adherence to the objective theory of contracts. . . . [T]he private, subjective feelings of the negotiators are irrelevant and unhelpful to the Court's consideration of a contract's meaning, because the meaning of a properly formed contract must be shared or common. That is not to say, however, that a party's subjective understanding is never instructive. On the contrary, in cases where an examination of the extrinsic evidence does not lead to an obvious, objectively reasonable conclusion, the Court may apply the forthright negotiator principle. Under this principle, the Court considers the evidence of what one party *subjectively* "believed the obligation to be, coupled with evidence that the other party knew or should have known of such belief." . . .

The evidence presented at trial conveyed a deeply flawed negotiation in which both sides failed to clearly and consistently communicate their client's positions. First, I find that the extrinsic evidence is not clear enough to conclude that there is a single, shared understanding with respect to the availability of specific performance under the Merger Agreement. Second, I employ the forthright negotiator principle to make two additional findings. With respect to URI, I find that even if the Company believed the Agreement preserved a right to specific performance, its attorney . . . categorically failed to communicate that understanding to the defendants during the latter part of the negotiations. Finally, with respect to RAM, although it could have easily avoided this entire dispute by striking section 9.10(b) from the Agreement, I find that its attorney did communicate to URI his understanding that the Agreement precluded any specific performance rights. Consequently, I conclude that URI has failed to meet its burden and determine that the Merger Agreement does not allow a specific performance remedy.

* * *

After the Delaware Chancery Court decision, United Rentals announced it would not appeal and Apollo paid the $100 million reverse termination fee and walked. Deal lawyers, uncomfortable with the forthright negotiator analysis, started putting disclaimers of the rule in agreements. Will they work? Moreover, all deal attorneys began to choreograph deal negotiations to put written *understanding statements* of express deal language before their opponents. Attorneys began to negotiate understanding statements as well as the deal language itself. Faced with an understanding statement, an opponent had to challenge the statement; remaining silent became too risky.

QUESTION

Why do good lawyers present to their clients for signing an agreement with conflicting provisions on critical sections?

2. SUPPLEMENTAL DOCUMENTS

Exhibits and additional agreements on specific matters often supplement the basic acquisition document. The following list identifies some of those documents.

The Disclosure Letter (or Schedules):[77] As noted in the language of the "good standing" representation above, many of the representations refer to

---

[77] If the securities of the buyer or seller are, or will be, publicly traded, a party may have to file an acquisition agreement with the SEC. See Reg. S–K, Item 601(b)(2). Information filed with the SEC is publicly available. The SEC may refuse a request for confidential treatment. See Sec. Act Rule 406 and Exch. Act Rule 24b–2. Item 601(b)(2) does not require the filing of disclosure letters or schedules unless they are *material.* The temptation to hide sensitive information in schedules is obvious. The SEC has argued that the practice may make a representation in the disclosed acquisition agreement misleading, even if there is an open-ended reference to an

a *disclosure letter* that supplements the acquisition agreement. The letter has sections for lists of items that correspond with specified representations. Sometimes a list contains a full itemization. For example, a part of the disclosure letter will contain a list of all real property, leaseholders of other interests owned by the seller, and a corresponding representation will affirm that the list in the disclosure letter is "complete and accurate" and that "seller owns, with good and marketable title, all property it purports to own" and so on. Other parts of the disclosure letter may contain exceptions to a blanket statement in the representations. For example, a representation will state that there are no contracts with relatives of board members other than those listed in the letter and the letter will list a contract between the firm and a mother-in-law.[78] Some parties append *schedules* to an acquisition agreement, one schedule per representation section, rather than use a disclosure letter, but the effect is the same. Parties negotiate the content of the letters or schedules because the documents serve, in effect, to limit, modify, complete or expand the representations of sellers.

The Employment or Non-Competition Agreement: If the purchaser wants the services of one or more of the employees of the seller, the purchaser may demand an employment agreement that binds the employee to stay with the business after the acquisition. The employment agreement will often contain a non-competition clause, discouraging a retained individual from leaving the purchaser's employment within one to three years after the acquisition. If, on the other hand, the purchaser is not planning to employ seller personnel with access to sensitive business information, the purchaser may demand a non-competition agreement to stop employees of the seller from competing with the business once the purchaser takes over. This can be accomplished by a restrictive covenant in the acquisition agreement (only if the employee is a signatory) or by means of a separate agreement.

Courts do not like non-competes and will enforce them only if they are reasonable in geographic scope and duration and are necessary to protect clear business interests in trade secrets and goodwill. E.g., *Wilson v. Electro Marine Systems, Inc.*, 915 F.2d 1110, 1115 (7th Cir. 1990) (New York and Illinois law).

---

undisclosed schedule or letter. See, e.g., Glazer Capital Mgmt. v. Magistri, 549 F.3d 736 (9th Cir. 2008); *SEC Section 21(a) Report concerning The Titan Corp.*, SEC Rel. No. 34–51283, 2005 WL 1074830 (Mar. 1, 2005).

[78] Information that constitutes an exception to a representation may relate to embarrassing acts or omissions of the seller. In extreme cases, the act or omission may give rise to potential criminal or civil penalties or give a road map to plaintiff's attorneys. In such cases, seller's counsel argues for confidentiality of the letter, even to the point of asserting that the letter is not technically part of the acquisition agreement and does not have to be filed with government agencies such as the Securities and Exchange Commission. This is dangerous, implicating the purchaser as well if the refusal to disclose is itself yet another violation.

Earn out Agreement: Earn out agreements provide contingent pricing mechanisms, usually to bridge the negotiating impasse between a seller's and a buyer's projections of the future revenues or value of the company. They are most likely to be used when the seller is a private company, but not always. The seller, by nature, believes the company has excellent prospects, while the buyer is more skeptical. An earn out is also attractive if a purchaser has financing problems and cannot fund the full purchase price. The seller partially finances the acquisition.

In earn outs, the buyer pays the seller part of the purchase price as a percentage of future revenues or earnings, usually EBITDA (earnings before interest, tax, depreciation and amortization). Earn outs are distinguished from post-closing adjustments that modify the purchase price to account for changes in the financials of the seller during the period between the date of the signing and the closing.

Earn outs can create substantial post-closing disputes between purchasers and sellers. A buyer will naturally want to change aspects of the purchased business in order to integrate the acquired operations into its pre-existing business. Moreover, there may be a synergistic effect from the combination. Allocating revenue and accounting for operations to calculate the earn out payment often puts the parties at odds. It is more common to provide for special dispute resolution procedures in the agreements, usually the appointment of neutral accountants as arbitrators.

O'TOOL V. GENMAR HOLDINGS, INC.

United States Court of Appeals, Tenth Circuit, 2004.
387 F.3d 1188.

BRISCOE, CIRCUIT JUDGE.

Defendants Genmar Holdings, Inc., Genmar Industries, Inc., and Genmar Manufacturing of Kansas, Inc., appeal a jury verdict in favor of plaintiffs Horizon Holdings, LLC (f/k/a Horizon Marine LC) and Geoffrey Pepper on plaintiffs' claim for breach of contract.

. . . In early 1997, Pepper, his wife, and a group of investors purchased an industrial building in Junction City, Kansas, and formed their own recreational boat manufacturing company, Horizon Marine LC (Horizon). . . .

Pepper's initial goal was to manufacture and sell aluminum jon boats (a/k/a utility boats) he had designed. He hoped to subsequently expand Horizon's product line to include pontoon and deck boats. Horizon began producing jon boats in October 1997. By early 1998, Horizon had not earned a profit and, in Pepper's words, was "still struggling." . . .

In August 1998, defendants Genmar Holdings, Inc., and Genmar Industries, Inc., (collectively "Genmar") approached Pepper about purchasing Horizon. Genmar, the world's largest recreational boat manufacturer, manufactures approximately eighteen different brands of boats in approximately twelve manufacturing plants throughout the United States. . . .

Negotiations culminated in the sale of Horizon to Genmar in December 1998. Under the terms of the parties' written purchase agreement, Genmar created a new subsidiary, defendant Genmar Manufacturing of Kansas, LLC (GMK), that assumed all of the assets and liabilities of Horizon. GMK also offered written employment agreements to Pepper, who assumed the presidency of GMK, and to Pepper's daughter and son-in-law, both of whom assumed managerial positions with GMK similar to the ones they held with Horizon.

The purchase price paid by Genmar for Horizon was comprised of two components: (1) cash consideration of $2.3 million dollars; and (2) "earn-out consideration." The purchase agreement detailed how the "earn-out consideration" was to be calculated:

> For a period of five (5) years from and after the Closing, Purchaser agrees to remit to Seller as additional consideration and part of the aggregate Purchase Price hereunder an amount equal to a percentage of all annual gross revenues ("Annual Gross Revenues"), subject to achieving certain gross profit percentages [13 percent or more in the first year of GMK's operation, and 14 percent or more thereafter], from the sale of (i) Seller's Horizon (or any direct successor) brand boats, trailers, pre-rigging, parts and accessories (collectively the "Seller Products") and (ii) the manufacture of Purchaser's boats (Genmar Holdings' brands) in Seller's Junction City, Kansas plant facility after the Closing Date, in each case of (i) and (ii) above based upon the annual published dealer list price to a maximum of $5,200,000 (the "Earn-Out Consideration").

Id. at 3–4. At closing, Genmar made an advance payment of $200,000 of earn-out consideration to Horizon, which amount was to be deducted from earn-out consideration payments due to Horizon after the second quarter of 1999.

Pepper's understanding of the earn-out provision was that production of Horizon boats and accessories would afford GMK the most potential for achieving gross revenues and in turn maximize the earn-out consideration. This was because, in addition to receiving a dealer list price for each Horizon boat sold to a dealer, GMK would receive gross revenues for engines, trailers, and other accessories that were sold with the Horizon boats. Pepper was confident he could achieve the maximum earn-out consideration because, in part, Genmar executives had assured him that Horizon boats would "be the champion of th[e] [GMK] facility." . . .

Pepper's expectations and assumptions for GMK's operations were challenged almost immediately after the deal was closed. In early 1999, Pepper was informed by Genmar of a possible trademark conflict with the Horizon brand name and the Horizon brand of boats was renamed "Nova" (one of two trademark names already registered by Genmar). Further, and more problematically for Pepper, it became evident in early 1999 that two of Genmar's own brands of boats, Ranger and Crestliner, would become the priority of the GMK facility. Specifically, Genmar instructed Pepper that, in the event of production conflicts, GMK should give priority to production of Crestliner boats. Genmar also instructed Pepper to focus all of GMK's engineering efforts on developing fifteen new Ranger boat designs.

Genmar's focus on the Crestliner and Ranger brands created dual problems for Pepper and GMK. First, the design of new Ranger models was expensive for GMK (who was expected by Genmar to bear all design and production costs) since the dimensions and materials for the Ranger models were completely different than the existing Nova designs. Second, the Ranger models were significantly harder to build than the relatively simple designs of the Nova and Crestliner boats. That fact, combined with GMK's inexperienced workforce, resulted in longer production times and higher costs for the Ranger boats.

Genmar's focus on the Crestliner and Ranger brands also created a dilemma for Pepper. As noted, the parties' written purchase agreement provided that the earn-out consideration to be paid to Horizon/Pepper by Genmar would be based on GMK's gross revenues meeting or exceeding a certain level. However, because GMK was inefficient at building the new Ranger models, and because it received only a set reimbursement for each Ranger boat (equal to its estimated cost of production), it actually lost money on each Ranger boat produced. With respect to the Crestliner boats, GMK also received only a set reimbursement (again equal to its estimated cost of production), and received no revenues from engines, trailers, or accessories sold with the Crestliner boats.

* * *

By November 1999, GMK's gross revenues and production were far under budget. Specifically, GMK's gross revenues fell $360,000 short of budget, or $222,000 actual gross revenues versus $582,000 budgeted gross revenues. At the same time, GMK's backlog of orders for Nova boats grew by more than 300,000 units to a total of 616,000 units. The results for December 1999 were similar. GMK's gross revenues fell $209,000 short of budget, or $372,000 versus $581,000. GMK's controller and vice-president of finance attributed these problems to Genmar's continued focus on Crestliner and Ranger boats at the expense of Nova boats.

On December 21, 1999, Pepper was called to a meeting at Genmar's corporate offices in Minneapolis, Minnesota. During the meeting, Oppegaard criticized Pepper's performance as president of GMK and effectively demoted him, offering him an undefined engineering position with Genmar. Oppegaard further instructed GMK to cease production of Nova pontoon and deck boats, and to increase its emphasis on production of Ranger boats.

* * *

On April 5, 2000, Genmar terminated Pepper, his daughter, and his son-in-law from their respective positions at GMK. Under the terms of his employment contract with Genmar, Pepper was prohibited from working in the recreational boat manufacturing industry for a period of two years. Following plaintiffs' terminations, Genmar began converting, or "flipping," GMK's existing Nova dealers to other Genmar brands. . . . Effective July 2001, GMK, at Genmar's direction, completely stopped manufacturing the Nova brand of boats.

Genmar closed the GMK facility in May 2002 and consolidated manufacturing of its aluminum boats into another facility. According to Genmar's estimates, it lost approximately $15 million dollars on the GMK transaction, and GMK never showed a profit. Genmar acknowledged, however, that during the years of GMK's operation, the Ranger and Crestliner subsidiaries were profitable, as was Genmar as a whole. Genmar further acknowledged these profits were attributable, in part, to production of boats at the GMK facility. Genmar also acknowledged its Crestliner manufacturing plant, which prior to the Horizon acquisition produced Ranger aluminum boats, performed better from a financial standpoint after the Ranger production was shifted to the GMK facility. Finally, Genmar acknowledged that it continues to manufacture and sell boats based on designs created by Pepper.

* * *

. . . Plaintiffs' surviving claims were tried to a jury in November 2002. The jury found in favor of Pepper and Horizon on their claim for breach of the purchase agreement and awarded them $2.5 million in damages. The jury also found in favor of Cassandra and John O'Tool on their claims for breach of employment contracts. . . .

* * *

Judgment as a matter of law—breach of contract claim

Defendants contend the district court erred in denying their motion for judgment as a matter of law on the breach of contract claim asserted by plaintiffs Horizon and Pepper. . . .

* * *

"Under Delaware law, an implied covenant of good faith and fair dealing inheres in every contract." *Chamison v. Healthtrust, Inc.*, 735 A.2d 912, 920 (Del. Ch. 1999). "As such, a party to a contract has made an implied covenant to interpret and to act reasonably upon contractual language that is on its face reasonable." *Id.* "This implied covenant is a judicial convention designed to protect the spirit of an agreement when, without violating an express term of the agreement, one side uses oppressive or underhanded tactics to deny the other side the fruits of the parties' bargain." *Id.* "It requires the [finder of fact] to extrapolate the spirit of the agreement from its express terms and based on that 'spirit,' determine the terms that the parties would have bargained for to govern the dispute had they foreseen the circumstances under which their dispute arose." *Id.* at 920–21. The "extrapolated term" is then "implie[d] . . . into the express agreement as an implied covenant," and its breach is treated "as a breach of the contract." "The implied covenant cannot contravene the parties' express agreement and cannot be used to forge a new agreement beyond the scope of the written contract." *Id.*

The overarching theme of the breach of implied covenant theory asserted by Pepper and Horizon is "that Genmar's entire course of conduct frustrated and impaired [their] realization of the Earn-Out" provided in the parties' agreement. In particular, Pepper and Horizon point to the following actions taken by Genmar following its acquisition of Horizon: (1) changing the brand name of the boats from Horizon to Nova; (2) immediately shifting GMK's production priority from Horizon/Nova boats to Ranger and Crestliner boats; (3) requiring GMK, rather than Ranger or another subsidiary, to bear the costs of designing and producing the new line of Ranger boats; (4) failing to give Pepper operational control over GMK; (5) reimbursing GMK only at "standard cost" for the manufacture of Ranger and Crestliner boats, thereby impairing realization of the earn-out triggers; (6) discontinuing the Horizon/Nova brand of boats; (7) "flipping" Horizon/Nova dealers to other Genmar brands; and (8) shutting down the GMK facility.

Defendants contend all of these actions were expressly contemplated under the terms of the parties' agreement and thus could not form the basis for a violation of the implied covenant of good faith and fair dealing. . . . [W]e disagree.

* * *

Defendants also argue that plaintiffs' "implied covenant claim . . . fails because there is no evidence the parties would have agreed to the obligations the District Court imposed by implication." . . . For example, defendants contend there is no "basis to find that the parties 'would have agreed' that Pepper would have complete discretion to refuse to manufacture Ranger and Crestliner boats." . . . "Nor," defendants argue, "is there any basis to find that the parties 'would have agreed' to maintain the Horizon name." . . .

Defendants' arguments, in our view, ignore the spirit of the parties' agreement. As noted, the agreement expressly stated the purchase price paid by defendants to Pepper/Horizon would be comprised of two components: (1) cash consideration upon closing; and (2) earn-out consideration, based upon GMK meeting or exceeding certain gross revenue goals, for five years following closing. The obvious spirit of this latter component was that Pepper, as president of GMK, would be given a fair opportunity to operate the company in such a fashion as to maximize the earn-out consideration available under the agreement (approximately $5.2 million dollars over five years).

* * *

Lastly, defendants contend there was no evidence that Genmar acted with the intent to harm plaintiffs, i.e., "to injure plaintiff's contractual rights."[Ed.[79]] . . . Instead, defendants contend, "the decisions [plaintiffs] claim[ ] breached an implied duty constitute nothing other than Genmar's reasonable (although ultimately unsuccessful) business efforts to make the Junction City facility profitable for the first time in its operating life."

In denying defendants' post-trial motion, the district court rejected an identical argument. In particular, the court noted that "copious evidence was presented at trial demonstrating that defendants acted with . . . 'dishonest purpose' or 'furtive design.' " . . . For example, the district court noted that "ample evidence" was presented "that defendants had ulterior motives for acquiring Horizon . . . , including the desire to remove a potentially significant competitor from the market and the desire to obtain a facility in the 'southern' market dedicated primarily to the production of Ranger boats." . . . Reduced to its essence, the district court concluded

> the evidence was sufficient to support the conclusion that defendants believed (but were ultimately incorrect) that they could still turn a profit of Ranger and Crestliner boats at Genmar Kansas while simultaneously preventing Mr. Pepper from realizing any earn-out by stifling the production of Horizon boats and reimbursing Genmar Kansas only at standard cost for the production of other boats.

. . . After carefully reviewing the trial transcript, we conclude the district court's summary of the evidence is accurate and sufficient to rebut defendants' assertion that there was no evidence they intended to harm plaintiffs. The district court properly denied defendants' motion for JMOL.

* * *

RICHMOND v. PETERS, 1999 WL 96736 (6th Cir.) (unpublished opinion): . . . In 1989, Frederick Richmond agreed to sell UForma Shelby Business Forms, Inc., a business forms printing business, to Samuel

---

[79] [Ed. But see Sonoran Scanners, Inc. v. Perkinelmer, Inc., 585 F.3d 535 (1st Cir. 2009) (asset purchase agreement contained an implied term that buyer would use reasonable efforts to "develop and promote" technology purchased; the implied term did not, like an implied duty of good faith and fair dealing, require a finding of intent to harm or bad faith)].

Peters. At that time, the business was operating at a considerable loss. Richmond and Peters entered into a stock purchase agreement that set the purchase price at $3.6 million, to be paid in annual installments. The amount of each annual installment was to equal one-half the amount by which the aggregate profits of UForma Shelby and Miami Systems, Inc. (a similar entity owned by Peters) exceeded the 1988 and 1989 average annual profits of Miami Systems alone. The shares of UForma stock were placed in escrow until the purchase price was paid in full. The agreement recognized that this formula might result in no payment being made during some years. It also provided that Peters was to operate UForma Shelby according to "sound business practices" similar to those employed in operating Miami Systems and included an integration clause that provided that the agreement set forth the entire understanding between the parties.

As determined by the formula set forth in the stock purchase agreement, Peters paid Richmond $496,057 for the year 1990 and $147,368 for the year 1991. The combined earnings of UForma Shelby and Miami Systems as reported in their audited financial statements were insufficient to trigger a payment under the formula for the years 1992 through 1995. . . .

Richmond's complaint against Peters for breach of contract and breach of fiduciary duty alleged that further payments were due and that Peters had not operated UForma Shelby and Miami Systems in accordance with sound business practices. He also alleged that Peters breached fiduciary duties of loyalty and good faith. . . .

Peters moved for judgment as a matter of law after Richmond rested his case. The court granted the motion, determining that Ohio law imposed no fiduciary duty on Richmond and declining to imply any duties the parties had not included in the agreement. . . .

Peters and Richmond are both established businessmen who were represented by counsel in the course of this transaction. They negotiated at arm's-length and knowingly entered into an agreement that does not expressly impose a fiduciary relationship. Although the agreement requires Peters to run the business according to "sound business practices," and annual payments were variable and determined by the profits of the venture, we conclude that these facts alone do not alone establish a fiduciary relationship between the parties. On this record, there is no evidence of "mutual knowledge of confidentiality or the undue exercise of power or influence," *Anchor*, 94 F.3d at 1024, to turn their ordinary business relationship into a fiduciary relationship. Without evidence of either of these factors, we cannot infer a fiduciary duty from this agreement. . . .

QUESTIONS

What is the difference between a claim based on a breach of fiduciary duty and one based on a breach of a duty of good faith and fair dealing? In acquisitions agreements with earn outs, how much flexibility does the new owner have in managing the acquired assets?

3. ACQUISITION REVIEW DOCUMENTS

The purchaser's attorneys use an acquisition review checklist to do a thorough legal audit of the seller's business. Many lawyers refer to the audit as *legal due diligence*, a reference from the due diligence investigation conducted by an underwriter's counsel in a public offering of securities.[80] The audit precedes the signing of a definitive acquisition agreement to help the purchaser accurately price the seller's business and continues after the signing in preparation for the closing to give the purchaser, at the time of closing, a high level of confidence in the accuracy and completeness of the seller's representations and warranties in the acquisition agreement.

The acquisition review begins with an *engagement letter* from the purchaser to its lawyers, specific to the transaction. The lawyers then send a *document request* to the lawyers for the seller asking for copies of documents needed to answer questions on the checklist. The purchaser's lawyers then prepare a *work program*, with deadlines, and prepare answers to the questions on a comprehensive checklist.

The checklist typically mirrors a seller's common representations and warranties in acquisition agreements. The following questions, for example, are for a **single** representation, the "Organization and Qualification of Seller" representation in most acquisition agreements, a sample of which was in Section B.1.c. *supra.* A legal audit checks the representation for the purchaser.

A. Documents Customarily Reviewed

To conduct the acquisition review, obtain, and review the documents listed below.

___1. Certified copies of the Company's Certificate or Articles of Incorporation and all amendments thereto to date, as well as any proposed amendments.

---

[80] An underwriter can avoid liability for a materially false and misleading Securities Act registration statement relating to securities it is underwriting if it pleads and proves the *due diligence defense.* To succeed, the underwriter must demonstrate that it "had, after reasonable investigation, reasonable ground to believe and did believe" that the registration statement was accurate and free of material omissions. Sec. Act § 11(b)(3). The availability of the due diligence defense is designed to encourage underwriters to be *gatekeepers of informational veracity*, thus helping to protect public investors from fraudulent issuer disclosure contained in registration statements.

___2. Certified copies of the Company's Bylaws, as amended to date.

___3. Minute books of the Company, including minutes of the meetings of the board of directors, any committees (whether of the board or otherwise), and shareholders, for the last five years to date.

___4. List of all jurisdictions in which the Company is currently qualified to do business as a foreign corporation.

___5. List of locations of all plants, offices, or other facilities of the Company.

___6. Certificates of Authority or Qualification issued by each jurisdiction in which the Company is authorized to do business as a foreign corporation.

___7. Certificates of Existence (where available) or Good Standing (long form) or Tax Certificates issued by the appropriate governmental authority in the state of the Company's incorporation and in each state in which the Company is qualified to transact business as a foreign corporation.

___8. All documents with respect to any partnership or joint venture affiliations of the Company, including partnership or joint venture agreements and all other documents necessary and appropriate under applicable state law to determine the due organization, qualification, or good standing of each such partnership or joint venture with which the Company is affiliated.

B. Procedures to Be Followed

The following checklist outlines the basic inquiries to be addressed, issues to be resolved, and procedures to be followed in an acquisition review of the Company's organization and good standing.

1. <u>Due Incorporation and Due Organization</u>

___a. Confirm that the Certificate or Articles of Incorporation and all amendments thereto were properly executed and filed by examining these documents in conjunction with applicable state law.

___b. Review minute books to confirm that:

___(1) the initial election of directors was procedurally correct under applicable law.

___(2) the board of directors held an organizational meeting in a timely manner after incorporation documents were filed.

___(3) bylaws of the Company were properly adopted.

___(4) necessary officers were elected.

___(5) stock was properly authorized and issued.

___(6) the minimum consideration for starting business, pursuant to state law, was received.

___c. Compare the review of minute books with the review of provisions of the Certificate or Articles of Incorporation and Bylaws (e.g., as to the number of directors authorized to be elected) to confirm that all organizational actions taken by the Company were taken in accordance with these documents, as well as with applicable law.

2. Valid Existence and Good Standing

___a. Confirm that the Company has not ceased to exist as a corporation through merger, forfeiture of its charter, nonpayment of taxes, etc., by examining the minute books, all filings made with state agencies, and Good Standing or Tax Certificates issued by appropriate state authorities.

3. Bylaws

Review the Bylaws with particular attention to the following items:

___a. The quorum, notice, and other procedural requirements for meetings of both shareholders and directors.

___b. The number and qualification of directors, provisions regarding removal of directors, and filling vacancies on the board.

___c. Any classification or staggering with respect to the election of directors.

___d. Officers required to be elected.

___e. Provisions concerning the indemnification of directors and officers.

___f. Provisions addressing how to amend the Bylaws.

___g. Provisions requiring the signature of certain officers on stock certificates and other corporate documents.

___h. Special voting provisions, including provisions permitting director or shareholder action without a meeting, including telephone meetings.

4. Minutes

Review the minutes of the meetings of the Company's directors, any committee, whether created by the board of directors or otherwise, and shareholders, with particular attention to the following items:

___a. All material contracts and transactions were identified, including employment contracts, pension plans, leases, loans, acquisitions, and other transactions, and any pending or threatened litigation.

___b. Shareholders' and directors' meetings have been held at least annually.

___c. At each meeting of directors or shareholders at which any corporate action was taken, a quorum of either group was present as provided in the Bylaws.

___d. Directors who voted with respect to corporate action were, at every such meeting, properly elected by the shareholders.

___e. Directors properly authorized all issuances of shares of the Company and valued any noncash consideration paid for issued shares.

___f. Any director or shareholder vote taken in connection with material corporate transactions, including mergers, consolidations, etc., of the Company, was duly recorded.

5. Qualification as a Foreign Corporation

___a. Determine all jurisdictions in which the Company is currently qualified to do business as a foreign corporation, and obtain Certificates of Authority or Certificates of Good Standing (e.g., relating to payment of taxes) for each of these jurisdictions.

___b. Inquire about the location of all offices, plants, or other facilities of the Company, as well as all jurisdictions in which the Company has significant contacts in any connection.

___c. Determine necessity for qualification in other jurisdictions.

___d. If the Company may be changing its name in connection with the transaction, confirm that the new name can be used in all relevant states of incorporation or qualification by conducting a name search with the appropriate state governmental authority.

6. Company's Subsidiaries, Predecessors, and Affiliates

___a. With respect to subsidiaries and affiliates of the Company, perform all routine organizational and good standing inquiries as outlined above. The scope of such an investigation in the context of predecessor entities will depend on how long ago the acquisition occurred and the importance of the predecessor to the Company's current holdings.

___b. Confirm that, except as disclosed in the Company's books and acquisition documents, no outstanding shares of any subsidiary of the Company are held by any individual or entity other than the Company.

___c. Determine whether any subsidiary or affiliate has voted the Company's shares, particularly if such action is prohibited by law.

___d. Review the organizational documents of any entities previously acquired by the Company, and determine whether they were properly acquired (e.g., the previously acquired entity's stock was valid and properly authorized at the time of acquisition).

___e. Review predecessor entities with respect to material contracts and other obligations or liabilities the Company may have assumed.

___f. Determine whether the Company or any of its subsidiaries have or operate under any partnership or joint venture agreements and, if so, obtain and review such agreements to ensure that such entities are properly and currently organized. Further investigation of any affiliates concerning material contracts, for example, will depend on counsel's assessment of the importance of such affiliates to the Company.

4. CONTINGENT TERMS IN, AMENDMENTS TO AND ABANDONMENT OF ACQUISITION AGREEMENTS

State corporate codes provide expressly for the amendment or abandonment of an acquisition agreement after either board approval or shareholder approval. We must take care to distinguish abandonment from amendment, however, although in practice the concepts are often related. Whenever shareholders vote to ratify a board resolution, any substantial changes to the terms and conditions after the vote have the potential to affect the integrity of the ratifying vote unless a revote is required. State codes attempt to give deal flexibility to the boards of the negotiating parties while at the same time respecting the integrity of the shareholder vote. You can ask yourself whether the balance in the legislation is sensible.

The state codes make it clear that, after a shareholder vote, a board of one of the parties may still abandon a deal (refuse to close) subject to the contract rights of the other side. If a board bases its decision to abandon a deal on the failure of a material deal condition, then the other side cannot complain. The state codes (1) enable a corporation to put such conditions in the deal terms and thus have them submitted to the ratifying shareholders and (2) enable boards to abandon deals after a ratifying shareholder vote. If a board decision to abandon a deal is, however, a breach of an acquisition agreement, then, although the board has the power to abandon, the other side can seek damages and in rare cases specific performance in contract. These cases are the subject of Section D below.

Amendments, on the other hand, are modifications of the terms and conditions of a deal, agreed to by both sides. The state corporate codes enable boards to agree to amendments only in limited circumstances. Otherwise, the integrity of the shareholder vote on terms and conditions is threatened, as the board may obtain shareholder ratification on one set of terms and then change the deal. Amendments that exceed those terms that a code permits require a new shareholder ratifying vote. In practice, abandonment and amendments are often linked. One party threatens abandonment, based on the failure of a closing condition, further negotiations ensue, and the parties negotiate an amendment.

So, the package of rights on deal modifications has three parts. First, state codes provide that an acquisition agreement, once signed, may contain terms that vary with future events. The ABA Model Bus. Corp. Act § 11.02(f) (2016 rev.), for example, expressly permits parties to a merger to adopt terms "dependent on facts ascertainable outside the plan" of merger, provided that those facts are objectively ascertainable.[81]

The provision restates traditional contract law that allows for parties to condition agreements on subsequent events and not run afoul of the doctrine of illusory promises, which states that a party who has the power of unilateral termination is not bound as there is no "mutuality of obligation" supporting a contract. See, e.g., 1A Corbin on Contracts § 166 (1963). In traditional contract doctrine, if a condition relates to an event that is outside the unfettered discretion of one of the parties, the promise to perform is not illusory and the contract valid. Thus, for example, traditional contract doctrine would support a purchase price adjustment mechanism based on stock market conditions. ABA Model Bus. Corp. Act § 1.20(k)(2)(ii) (2016 rev.), however, unlike the corresponding provision in Del. Gen. Corp. L. § 251(b), specifically includes "a determination or action by . . . the corporation or any other party to a plan or filed document." The language explicitly protects a condition based on a favorable shareholder vote and protects conditions based on a favorable due diligence investigation. To the extent the language attempts to protect contract language that gives a unilateral right to a party to terminate without consequence before closing, it may be contrary to the illusory promise doctrine.[82]

Second, most corporate codes provide that an acquisition agreement may provide expressly that a board of directors retains the power to *abandon* unilaterally a merger before the merger's effective date (usually the closing date) even after any ratifying shareholder vote. E.g., Del. Gen. Corp. L. § 251(d) (mergers and consolidations), § 271(b) (asset sales). Thus,

---

81 ABA Model Bus. Corp. Act § 1.20(k) (2016 rev.) elaborates as follows:

Whenever a provision of this Act permits any of the terms of a plan or a filed document to be dependent on facts objectively ascertainable outside the plan or filed document, the following provisions apply:

(1) The manner in which the facts will operate upon the terms of the plan or filed document must be set forth in the plan or filed document.

(2) The facts may include:

(i) any of the following that is available in a nationally recognized news or information medium either in print or electronically: statistical or market indices, market prices of any security or group of securities, interest rates, currency exchange rates, or similar economic or financial data;

(ii) a determination or action by any person or body, including the corporation or any other party to a plan or filed document; or

(iii) the terms of, or actions taken under, an agreement to which the corporation is a party, or any other agreement or document.

82 The drafters have apparently confused the doctrine with an "objectively ascertainable" standard. If a party retains complete control over its performance, it has not entered into a contract, even if its decision to perform or not perform is "objectively ascertainable."

a board has the *power* to act on unsatisfied conditions in the acquisition agreement (exercise an out or walk right) or just refuse to close and breach the contract subject to the other side's contract rights. The Model Act has an opt-out provision (parties may abandon agreements in accordance with any procedures set forth in the plan of merger or, if no such procedures exist, in the manner determined by the board of directors) in contrast to the opt-in provision in the Delaware code. ABA Model Bus. Corp. Act § 11.08 (2016 rev.) (the official comment adding that "[t]he power to abandon a transaction does not affect any contract rights that other parties may have"). Good practice in a Delaware corporation then is to always include the power in an acquisition agreement.

Rather than abandon a deal, some boards prefer to let their shareholders vote a deal down when circumstances surrounding the deal sour. In 1998 the Delaware legislature amended Del. Gen. Corp. L. § 251 governing mergers to require that the board of directors declare the "advisability" of a merger agreement before submitting it to the shareholders. The section was also amended to provide that a merger agreement might require that it be submitted to the shareholders even if the board, subsequent to its initial approval thereof, determines that the agreement is no longer advisable and recommends that the shareholders reject it. The Model Act requires the following:

> In submitting the plan of merger . . . to the shareholders for approval, the board of directors shall recommend that the shareholders approve the plan . . . unless (i) the board of directors makes a determination that because of conflicts of interest or other special circumstances it should not make such a recommendation or (ii) [the board of directors determines it no longer recommends the matter]. If either (i) or (ii) applies, the board shall inform the shareholders of the basis for its so proceeding.

ABA Model Bus. Corp. Act §§ 8.26 & 11.04(b) (2016 rev.).

Finally, the board has the power to enter into *amendments,* often based on a threat to abandon based on the failure of deal conditions. Amendments are *mutual* agreements of the parties to change the terms of an otherwise legally binding contract. A plan of merger may contain a provision that allows for parties to an agreement to amend the plan freely after the initial joint board resolutions accepting the agreement and before any shareholder vote in ratification as long as nothing has been filed with the secretary of state. Once shareholders ratify an agreement, however, the parties' ability to amend the agreement is very limited. After shareholder ratification, a plan of merger may not be amended to change the consideration paid under the plan, to change the articles of incorporation of the survivor or to otherwise materially change the terms and conditions of the plan to adversely affect a ratifying group of shareholders. E.g., Del.

Gen. Corp. L. § 251(d); ABA Model Bus. Corp. Act § 11.02(g) (2016 rev.). Parties must resubmit to shareholders for new ratification any deal modifications that exceed these limits. Interestingly, neither the Delaware code nor the Model Act makes any provision for post-shareholder ratification amendments to asset sale agreements.[83]

C. CLOSING DOCUMENTS

At the closing, the parties deliver or execute additional documents that satisfy conditions in the basic agreement.

The Supplement to the Disclosure Letter (or Schedules): The seller has an obligation to update the information in the representations between the signing and the closing due to a covenant promising prompt notification and a *bring down* clause in the conditions precedent to the buyer's obligation to close. Any updated information is usually included in a *supplement to the disclosure letter* (or *schedules)* and brought to the closing (or transmitted in advance of the closing to the purchaser). A seller's failure to update the disclosure letter breaches both a covenant—giving a right to damages—and a condition—giving the buyer a walk right.

Alternatively, a material change detailed in the supplement to the disclosure letter may itself constitute a breach of the representations as of the time of the signing date (particularly if there is no knowledge qualification). This breach gives an indemnification right and a walk right. A seller is therefore in a bind if it discovers facts that it should include in a supplement to the disclosure letter. Moreover, because of the delay between signing and closing and the complexity of most businesses, such updates are inevitable and routine to most deals. The bind, if not addressed in the language of the acquisition agreement, means sellers are signing an agreement that they will, in most cases, inevitably breach.

Most sellers negotiate for language that permits a disclosure in the supplement to cure any breach of the representations at signing. Since the supplement itself will negate any breach of the representations at closing, a carefully updated supplement will protect a seller from any claims of breach. Sellers, therefore, will take extra care to make full and timely disclosures. Purchasers are uncomfortable with such language because they have negotiated the price at signing without the benefit of the new information and, once a seller delivers a supplement to the disclosure letter containing new information, purchasers want the freedom to renegotiate the price or, short of a successful renegotiation, the freedom to walk. Therefore, purchasers insist on some form of protection from severe (the

---

[83] One could read this either to allow all such amendments without limitation or to prohibit all such amendments without a new ratifying vote.

supplement is no cure at all)[84] to modest (the purchaser can walk but has no indemnification rights on representations or covenants relevant to the updated material).[85] The modest solution encourages the parties to renegotiate the price at closing[86] rather than terminate the deal and sue.

Closing Opinions by Lawyers: Custom and practice in acquisitions have developed a call for legal opinions to be delivered at the closing to parties to the transaction. They are known as *third-party legal opinions* because the opinion giver makes them to parties other than her own client (usually the opposite party in the acquisition). The opinion recipient's counsel and the opinion giver usually negotiate the content of the opinion. The opinion giver is in an awkward position. A third party demands her assurances on matters specific to the acquisition and her client demands that she provide them to facilitate the closing. Yet, the broader the assurances in an opinion, the more personal risk the opinion maker assumes on post-closing claims made by third parties angry over disadvantageous deals. In essence, the opinion maker becomes a party to the transaction (albeit for limited purposes) while trying to service a client.

The Section of Business Law of the American Bar Association, recognizing the quandary of transaction lawyers asked to write closing opinions, produced a *Third Party Legal Opinion Report* (1991). In the Report, the Section attempted to establish a national consensus on what was reasonable practice in closing opinions. In essence, the Report attempted to establish a ceiling on what opposing counsel could reasonably demand from other lawyers in closing opinions. The Report did two things: first, it drafted a *Legal Opinion Accord*, a code to which parties could agree to be bound in acquisition agreements. The Accord standardizes lawyers' assurances, with an extensive definitional gloss. Second, the Report included *Guidelines for the Negotiation and Preparation of Third-Party Legal Opinions*. The Guidelines, later supplemented by *Legal Opinion Principles* and redrafted in 2002,[87] provide guidance for those lawyers who do not adopt (or whose opposite parties refuse to accept) the Legal Opinion Accord.[88] Since most lawyers do not use the Accord, the Guidelines have

---

84 See, e.g., *ABA Model Stock Purchase Agreement*, Section 11.2(a). If so, why ever do a supplement? The agreement also requires, as a covenant, a promise to disclose relevant new information.

85 An intermediate position would be a provision giving the purchaser a walk right with full indemnification if it walks but, if a purchaser elects to close, it waives any claim.

86 Both sides will lose on termination under such conditions. The purchaser loses its sunk costs on investigation and negotiation fees and any profits from the deal, and the seller loses its costs and profits as well. The joint losses will most likely create an overlap for renegotiation of the price. If, on the other hand, the purchaser can recover its costs and lost profits from the seller in litigation (including attorney fees), then the incentive for the purchaser to renegotiate is seriously reduced (equal to the uncompensated expenses of litigation plus the present value of the risks of judicial errors favoring the seller).

87 Committee on Legal Opinions, ABA Section of Business Law, *Guidelines for the Preparation of Closing Opinions,* 57 BUS. LAW. 875 (2002).

88 The current version of both the Guidelines and the Principles are contained in 57 BUS. LAW. 875 (2002).

become the more dominant document of the two.[89] The most recent development is an attempt to discourage lawyers from requiring legal opinions in deals based on a cost-benefit analysis of the practice.[90] The effort has paid dividends with deal point studies finding a substantial and continuing decline in the number of deals requiring closing opinions.[91]

For a flavor of what the Guidelines do, some sections are set out below.

GUIDELINES FOR THE PREPARATION OF CLOSING OPINIONS

Committee on Legal Opinions, Section of Business Law of the American Bar Association.
57 BUS. LAW. 875 (2002).

* * *

1.2 COVERAGE

The opinions included in a closing opinion should be limited to reasonably specific and determinable matters that involve the exercise of professional judgment by the opinion giver. The benefit of an opinion to the recipient should warrant the time and expense required to prepare it. . . .

* * *

1.4 PROFESSIONAL COMPETENCE

Opinion givers should not be asked for opinions that are beyond the professional competence of lawyers. To the extent a matter such as financial statement analysis, economic forecasting, or valuation is relevant to an opinion, an opinion giver may properly rely on a factual certificate or assumption. . . .

* * *

3.1 GOLDEN RULE

An opinion giver should not be asked to render an opinion that counsel for the opinion recipient would not render if it were the opinion giver and possessed the requisite expertise. Similarly, an opinion giver should not refuse to render an opinion that lawyers experienced in the matters under consideration would commonly render in comparable situations, assuming that the requested opinion is otherwise consistent with these Guidelines and the opinion giver has the requisite expertise and in its professional judgment is able to render the opinion. Opinion givers and counsel for

89 See also *Statement on the Role of Customary Practice in the Preparation and understanding of Third Party Legal Opinions*, 63 BUS. LAW. 1277 (2008) (approved by multiple bar and legal groups).

90 See ABA Guidelines, Section 1.2 (2002).

91 Nontax legal opinions are now rare in acquisitions of public companies. A 2009 ABA Study found legal opinions were required in only 58 percent of the private deals studied.

opinion recipients should be guided by a sense of professionalism and not treat opinions simply as if they were terms in a business negotiation. . . .

Classic examples of assurances in closing opinions now include the valid creation and existence of a client[92] and the validity of a client's actions taken in connection with the approval and closing of the acquisition.[93] One party's delivery of a required legal opinion is a condition to the other party's obligation to close. This has the effect of making the underlying matters on which a lawyer opines conditions to the closing as well. Legal opinions are limited to verifiable matters of legal compliance. Lawyers will refuse to give legal opinions that require their judgment on the materiality of a violation of a representation and will not give opinions on matters that they cannot know or reasonably investigate (compliance with all applicable laws, for example) or on legal matters that are uncertain (application of the antitrust laws, for example).

Lawsuits over closing opinions are very infrequent, but they do appear occasionally.[94]

DEAN FOODS COMPANY V. PAPPATHANASI

Massachusetts Superior Court, 2004.
2004 WL 3019442.

VANGESTEL, J.

* * *

There were negotiations in the late fall of 1997 and winter of 1998 between Scangas Bros. Holding, Inc. ("SBHI") and Garelick Farms Inc. ("Garclick") concerning the sale of the stock of SBHI to Garelick. SBHI was a holding company that held all of the capital stock of West Lynn Creamery. . . .

* * *

---

92 The following language is an illustration:

Each Acquired Company is a corporation duly organized, validly existing and in good standing under the laws of its jurisdiction of incorporation as set forth in the Disclosure Letter, with full corporate power and authority to own its properties and to engage in its business as presently conducted or contemplated, and is duly qualified and in good standing as a foreign corporation under the laws of each other jurisdiction in which it is authorized to do business as set forth in the Disclosure Letter. One or more of the Acquired Companies, free and clear of all adverse claims, own all of the outstanding capital stock of each of the Subsidiaries of record [and beneficially]. All of the outstanding shares of capital stock of each Acquired Company have been duly authorized and validly issued and are fully paid and nonassessable and were not issued in violation of the preemptive rights of any Person.

93 Other examples include certification of record ownership of capital stock and of the condition of a company's official records.

94 See also Marcus v. Frome, 329 F.Supp.2d 464 (S.D.N.Y. 2004).

. . . Ultimately, on June 30, 1998, Suiza Foods Corporation ("Suiza"), through its wholly-owned subsidiary Garelick Farms, Inc., purchased all outstanding stock in SBHI, the parent company of West Lynn Creamery. Rubin and Rudman represented SBHI, West Lynn Creamery and the selling shareholders in connection with the sale. In the Stock Purchase Agreement, the West Lynn Creamery sellers made the following representations to Suiza:

> *Absence of Litigation.* Except as set forth in *Schedule 2.10* of the Company Disclosure Schedule, there is no claim, action, suit, litigation, proceeding, arbitration or investigation of any kind, at law or in equity (including actions or proceedings seeking injunctive relief), pending or, to the Company's knowledge, threatened against the Company or any of its subsidiaries, and neither the Company or any of its subsidiaries is subject to any continuing order of, consent decree, settlement agreement or other similar written agreement with, or continuing investigation by, any Governmental Entity, or any judgment, order, writ, injunction, decree or award of any Governmental Entity or arbitrator, including, without limitation, cease-and-desist or other orders.

The Stock Purchase Agreement also required the West Lynn Creamery sellers to deliver an opinion of counsel to Garelick/Suiza. Thus, on June 30, 1998, Rubin and Rudman issued an Opinion Letter to Garelick. Paragraph 9 of the Opinion Letter—the particular paragraph of greatest significance to this case—stated:

> 9. To our knowledge, except as set forth in *Schedule 2.10* of the Company Disclosure Schedule, there is no claim, action, suit, litigation, proceeding, arbitration or, [sic] investigation of any kind, at law or in equity (including actions or proceedings seeking injunctive relief), pending or threatened against the Company or any of its subsidiaries and neither the Company nor any of its subsidiaries is subject to any continuing order of, consent decree, settlement agreement or other similar written agreement with, or continuing investigation by, any Governmental Entity, or any judgment, order, writ, injunction, decree or award of any Governmental Entity or arbitrator, including, without limitation, cease-and-desist or other orders.

The Opinion Letter also stated that, for the purposes of the foregoing opinion, Rubin and Rudman "have relied upon the representations of factual matters contained in the Purchase Agreement and have made no independent investigation of such factual matters; however, nothing has come to our attention which causes us to doubt the accuracy thereof." The Opinion Letter stated that "[i]n rendering our opinions we have examined such materials as we have deemed relevant to those opinions. . . ."

There also is a separate paragraph in the Opinion Letter that reads as follows:

> With respect to matters stated to be "to our knowledge," we call your attention to the fact that we have not made any independent review or investigation of agreements (other than those expressly referred to herein), instruments, orders, writs, judgments, rules, regulations or decrees by which our clients or any of their properties may be bound, nor have we made any investigations as to the existence of actions, suits, investigations or proceedings, if any, pending or threatened against our clients, except to the extent that any of the above is disclosed in any exhibit or schedule to the Purchase Agreement. However, nothing has come to our attention which causes us to doubt the accuracy of such exhibits or schedules.

The Opinion Letter closes with the following:

> This opinion letter is rendered solely to you and for your benefit in connection with the transaction described herein and may not be relied upon in any manner or for any other purpose by, or circulated or delivered to, [sic] other person or entity, except your successors and assigns, without our prior written consent.

* * *

. . . In June 1998, Rubin and Rudman had a written policy concerning the issuance and preparation of opinion letters. The policy stated in part (with emphasis in the original):

> 3. *Approval of Opinions.* Our Firm's policy is that certain partners must approve opinion letters covered by this policy.
>
> The person who proposes to issue the opinion letter must bring the draft opinion to a partner authorized to approve opinion letters in the particular area, *with the completed back-up file or binder.* It is the responsibility of the reviewing partner (the "countersigning partner") to review the opinion letter, satisfy himself or herself as to its propriety and also the existence and completeness of the contents of the opinion file or binder. If there is no such back-up, the opinion cannot be approved or issued.
>
> If the countersigning partner reviews the opinion and back-up and finds it in order, he or she should approve it. This may be signified by both signing the opinion letter itself or, if two signatures on a letter seems odd or out of place, the countersigning partner may merely sign the copy of the opinion in our back-up file. Only partners may sign opinion letters. Obviously, if the countersigning partner does not agree with the substance of the opinion, the Practice Area Leader, the Managing

Partner, the Assistant Managing Partner or the Firm Chairman ought to be consulted immediately to resolve the disagreement.

The countersigning partner should keep a copy of the opinion he has approved for his or her own file.

As of June 30, 1998, Jason A. Sokolov ("Mr. Sokolov"), a partner at Rubin and Rudman, was asked by Mr. Barton [who was the seller's deal lawyer and also a partner] to countersign the Opinion Letter. In actuality, however, the Opinion Letter was not signed by any individual lawyer. Rather, it was signed:

Very truly yours,

/s/ Rubin and Rudman LLP

Rubin and Rudman LLP

* * *

On March 26, 2001, West Lynn Creamery entered into an agreement to plead guilty to a Criminal Information charging it with a conspiracy to defraud the United States by impeding, impairing, obstructing and defeating the lawful government functions of the Internal Revenue Service, in violation of 18 U.S.C. § 371. . . . The plea agreement . . . resulted in West Lynn Creamery paying a fine of $7,200,000 and a special assessment of $400.

* * *

Attorneys' fees in the amount of $2,021,400.75 and costs of $149,953.86, aggregating $2,171,354.50, are said to have been incurred by the WLC group in responding to and resolving the criminal charges against West Lynn Creamery. . . .

RULINGS OF LAW

The plaintiffs' three claims against the defendants are: negligent misrepresentation, common law negligence, and violations of G.L. c. 93A. The claims for negligent misrepresentation and for common law negligence, in the context of this case, are essentially overlapping. Thus, the Court will focus primarily on the negligent misrepresentation claim.

> "In order to recover for negligent misrepresentation[,] a plaintiff must prove that the defendant (1) in the course of his business, (2) supplie[d] false information for the guidance of others (3) in their business transactions, (4) causing and resulting in pecuniary loss to those others (5) by their justifiable reliance upon the information, and (6) with failure to exercise reasonable care or competence in obtaining or communicating the

information." *Nota Constr. Corp. v. Keyes Assocs., Inc.*, 45 Mass.App.Ct. 15, 19–20, 694 N.E.2d 401 (1998)[Ed.[95]] . . . .

* * *

The specific context in which this case must be examined is the rendering of an opinion or report by a law firm to an entity that is not its client. The particular kind of opinion involved here is often referred to as a "no litigation" opinion. . . .

* * *

As noted above, the purpose of the "no litigation" opinion is to do nothing more than provide comfort to the opinion recipient, the plaintiffs here, that the opinion preparers, Mr. Barton, with some help from Messrs. Altman, Speleotis and Sokolov, all acting for Rubin and Rudman, did not know the list of pending or threatened litigation and investigations "set forth in *Section 2.10* of the Company Disclosure Schedule" to be incomplete or unreliable. Further, that comfort was reinforced by Rubin and Rudman's statement that "nothing has come to [its] attention which causes [it] to doubt the accuracy thereof."

* * *

This Court concludes and rules that the information that Mr. Altman provided to Mr. Barton at the June 16, 1998, meeting regarding the status of the Gavriel grand jury subpoena [Ed.: Altman, a partner at Rubin and Rudman had handled the subpoena for West Lynn Creamery] and the rebate investigation as it related to West Lynn Creamery, had Altman known that the information was for the purpose of an opinion stating that Rubin and Rudman knew of no threatened governmental investigation of West Lynn Creamery, would have fallen below the standard of a reasonably competent white-collar criminal defense lawyer. [At the meeting, Altman told Barton he thought the investigation had "gone away."]

It does not excuse the situation for Mr. Altman to say he did not understand corporate transactions or for Mr. Barton to say he relied solely on Mr. Altman's expertise regarding the handling of the grand jury subpoena and its significance for purposes of the opinion being rendered. A see-no-evil, hear-no-evil, speak-no-evil approach cannot be what the TriBar Report is teaching the opinion-writing bar.[9] Both sides' experts were in agreement on this point.

---

[95] [Ed. Note: Negligent misrepresentation is a fraud claim with a reduced state of mind requirement; the law replaces scienter with negligence. The doctrine pares down the class of potentially liable defendants, however, to those with a pecuniary duty to provide accurate information or those in a *special relationship* to the plaintiff. See Corp. Prop. Assoc. 14 Inc. v. CHR Holding Corp., 2008 WL 963048 (Del. Ch.).]

[9] This Court particularly does not accept Rubin and Rudman's expert's view—apparently strongly held, and certainly strongly stated—that trial lawyers are unable to comprehend the elegant nuances of corporate opinion letters or that matters relating to grand jury subpoenas are too "arcane" for corporate lawyers to be expected to divine.

* * *

Mr. Altman, however, was not the opinion preparer. Indeed, he testified that he did not even know that what he was being asked about at the June 16, 1998, meeting was to be considered for inclusion in a Rubin and Rudman opinion letter. He claims not to have known about the opinion letter until the commencement of this lawsuit. This surprised the Court, but it accepts the testimony as given. This testimony suggests not so much a failure on Mr. Altman's part, but rather a significant breakdown in the careful process established at Rubin and Rudman regarding opinion letters. Mr. Barton did not carry his investigation far enough; and Mr. Sokolov seems to have overlooked the firm's policy on opinion letters.

There is a dramatic difference in asking a lawyer in Mr. Altman's position whether he thinks a grand jury investigation has gone away, and asking him whether his law firm can decline to reveal the grand jury investigation in an opinion letter that confirms the absence of pending or threatened investigations, while being embroidered with the nothing-has-come-to-our-attention-which-causes-us-to-doubt-the-accuracy-thereof language.

It cannot be consistent with the customary practice relating to opinion letters, so elaborately expressed in the TriBar Report, to permit the opinion preparer to avoid his obligations to the opinion recipient by the simple artifice of blindly adopting the report of a fellow attorney's handling of a criminal grand jury subpoena for the client in question when that fellow attorney does not even know that he is providing grist for an opinion letter mill.[10]

* * *

The Rubin and Rudman defendants did not conduct the inquiry that they were required to make by customary practice. The confirmation they gave, grounded as it was as on errors of fact, created for the recipients the comfort that an ongoing investigation did not exist *and* that nothing had come to the attention of Rubin and Rudman that cast doubt about the accuracy of that report.

* * *

The plaintiffs were definitely "one of a limited group of persons for whose benefit and guidance Rubin and Rudman intended to supply . . . information."

* * *

[10] All that either Mr. Altman or Mr. Barton had to do was place a telephone call to Mr. Merberg [Ed. Gavriel's criminal defense lawyer.]. If either of them had done so, they would have learned that the rebate investigation had not gone away. Rather, Gavriel, on March 25, 1998, had entered a plea agreement that included a provision that he would cooperate fully with law enforcement and government attorneys in an ongoing investigation.

The last sentence of the Rubin and Rudman Opinion Letter contains Rubin and Rudman's intent: "This opinion letter is rendered solely to you and for your benefit in connection with the transaction described herein and may not be relied upon in any manner or for any other purpose by, or circulated or delivered to, [sic] other person or entity, except your successors and assigns, without our prior written consent."

Further, the Opinion Letter was a condition of the closing; it was present at the closing; and the closing was accomplished.[11] See *Prudential Ins. Co., supra,* 80 N.Y.2d at 384–385, 590 N.Y.S.2d at 834–835, 605 N.E.2d 318.

* * *

The Court finds the amount of the fine and special assessment—$7,200,400—to be an appropriate amount for assessment as an element of damages as a direct consequence of the Opinion Letter's misleading failure to warn of the grand jury subpoena/rebate investigation. . . .

* * *

The Court also agrees that those reasonable attorneys' fees and expenses that were incurred after the June 30, 1998 closing, and were responsive to the matter as it became known on September 10, 1998, are the only other element of damages. . . .

* * *

. . . [A]lthough the Court finds the entity Rubin and Rudman LLP liable pursuant to Count VI for negligent misrepresentation and Count VIII for common law negligence, it does not find any of the three individual Rubin and Rudman defendants separately liable therefor. The misrepresentations and the negligence was the collective act or failure to act of the entity. No individual act or failure to act of any of the individual owners, standing alone, was directed at the plaintiffs or caused the plaintiffs harm. As to Messrs. Altman, Barton or Speleotis, none individually made any representations to any of the plaintiffs, nor did any of them individually commit any negligent acts toward any of the plaintiffs. It was the firm itself that had the duty and acted collectively with regard to the WLC group.

* * *

The Release: In an acquisition, the principal shareholders (and perhaps other agents, employees and officers of the seller) deliver a Release

---

[11] The Court does not accept the implication in the closing argument for the Rubin and Rudman defendants that the Opinion Letter was just an extraneous, perhaps redundant, piece of paper lying unnoticed and uncared for in a rack of documents at the closing, or that its existence as a requirement of closing was somehow—no evidence showed how—waived by the plaintiffs.

at the closing. The Release usually covers all claims which the releasing parties had, or arising from any matter that existed, as of the closing date against the purchaser and the selling company.[96] Without such a Release, for example, if a purchaser asserts claims against individual shareholders of the seller, the individuals might assert that the claims relate to actions taken by them as officers and directors of the seller and present a claim for indemnification against the successor of the seller, the purchaser. The Release affects a clean break from the prior owners.

The Non-negotiable Promissory Note: If the purchaser delivers a promissory note to the sellers at the closing as part of the exchange, the note will contain standard terms, the interest rate, the amortization schedule, the manner of payment, events of default and remedies. The sellers want the promissory note to be negotiable (i.e., transferrable), and the buyers want the opposite.[97] If the note is non-negotiable, the seller cannot pass it on to a holder in due course (free from purchaser claims under the acquisition agreement). UCC § 3–302.

Moreover, a non-negotiable note is subject to the purchaser's set-off rights for any claims the purchaser may have for breach of the acquisition agreement.[98] As such, the note secures, in a fashion, the obligations of the agreement. Other issues to be resolved include the interest rate, the manner of payment, whether the note can be prepaid without penalty, whether the note is secured, the availability of a guarantor, and the priority of the purchaser's obligation relative to the purchaser's other debts. Potential collateral could include the stock or assets received by the purchaser in the acquisition. In a stock acquisition, if the assets of the acquired company secure the note, the transaction generates fraudulent transfer (conveyance) risks.[99]

Documents on Performance Guarantees—an Escrow Agreement: The Escrow Agreement provides for an escrow of funds available to the purchaser to satisfy claims the purchaser may have or develop under the acquisition agreement for matters such as the seller's breach of a representation. An escrow agreement may provide funds for indemnification claims, for purchase price adjustment claims (true-ups) or both. Sellers often ask that access to the escrowed funds be the purchaser's exclusive post-closing remedy. Most escrow agreements provide for an institutional escrow agent that dispenses the funds under the terms

---

96 In a stock acquisition (or a reverse merger) the selling company is a released party; in an asset acquisition the selling company is a releasing party.

97 To be negotiable, the note must contain language of being "payable to order or to bearer." UCC § 3–104(1). Moreover, the note cannot be conditional ("on the terms and conditions of the acquisition agreement," for example). UCC § 3–104(1)(b).

98 See D'Oench, Duhme & Co. v. FDIC, 315 U.S. 447, 62 S.Ct. 676, 86 L.Ed. 956 (1942) (set-off rights not effective against holders in due course).

99 With the lien the firm has made a transfer without receiving equivalent value (the shareholders, not the firm, receive the note) and, if the entity is or becomes insolvent in the transfer, the transfer may be voided by creditors of the firm.

specified.[100] If the purchaser makes no claims against the funds, they revert to the seller after a specified period of time.

Bills of Sale and Assignment and Assumption Agreements: In asset acquisitions, the seller delivers to the buyer bills of sale and assignment and assumption agreements that transfer assets and liabilities. The seller often collapses the agreements into one document. Some practitioners separate the bill of sale and the assignment and assumption agreement. The bill of sale transfers assets and contractual rights; the assignment and assumption agreement transfers all contractual obligations and rights. The seller signs the bill of sale unilaterally; the assignment and assumption agreement is a two-party agreement. There are usually general agreements referring to assets and contract rights specified in the purchase agreement and, in some cases, specific agreements on leases, copyrights, patents, service marks and trademarks.

D. LITIGATION AMONG PARTIES TO ACQUISITION CONTRACTS

1. BUYER PURCHASES A *PIG IN A POKE*

MEDCOM HOLDING CO. V. BAXTER TRAVENOL LABS., INC.

United States Court of Appeals, Seventh Circuit, 1997.
106 F.3d 1388.

ESCHBACH, CIRCUIT JUDGE:

* * *

In 1986, Baxter sold to MHC all of the outstanding capital stock of Medcom for $3.77 million[Ed.[101]] pursuant to a Stock Purchase Agreement (the "SPA"). In the SPA, Baxter made several representations and warranties as of the date of the SPA and as of the date of closing. The representations and warranties include the following: that no material fact was undisclosed that was necessary to prevent previous statements from being misleading; that all representations, statements, and information provided to MHC (including the schedules and financial statements contained in the SPA) were true in all material respects; and that Baxter would pay the amount of any overstatement in the September 30, 1986 balance sheet, which it represented had been prepared in accordance with generally accepted accounting principles ("GAAP").

Subsequent to MHC's purchase of Medcom, MHC discovered various facts that it claims were part of a scheme by Baxter to defraud MHC. In

---

[100] A party may propose that its counsel act as an escrow agent. There is some conflict among state bar opinions on the practice. Professional liability insurers actively discourage it.

[101] [Ed. Baxter had purchased Medcom only four years earlier for $50 million. Medcom, owned by Baxter, racked up four years of heavy losses.]

particular, MHC alleged that Baxter falsely represented and warranted that Medcom had a balance sheet with $10 million in assets at book value when Baxter knew that Medcom had a pertinent asset value of only $1 million. Among other evidence of this alleged scheme to defraud, MHC pointed to evidence that Baxter had written down Medcom's assets to a total of $1 million in precisely the same manner as the two earlier write-downs, but this time the write-down was reflected only on the Medcom accounting records held at Baxter's corporate offices. It was not reflected on Medcom's September 30, 1986 balance sheet given to MHC. MHC also pointed to evidence that Medcom's Chairman and CEO, Robert Funari, had prepared an analysis of the realizable value of Medcom's assets that was several million dollars less than the value represented to MHC and that A.D. Little, a valuation firm, had conducted a preliminary appraisal that indicated that Medcom's assets were worth only $2.5 million.

Baxter presented testimony that Medcom's balance sheet was accurate, fairly presented, and in accordance with GAAP. Baxter also presented evidence that A.D. Little's valuation was a preliminary, unissued draft and did not include substantial fixed assets that were included in the sale to MHC. Baxter also produced testimony that Funari's personal valuation was based on market value, whereas the balance sheet concerned book value.

MHC alleged that Baxter had falsely represented the status of Medcom's marketable domestic training programs. The June 1986 offering memorandum for the stock, the "Blue Book," stated that Medcom had a "current library" of over 1600 audiovisual training programs that it marketed in the United States for nurse, physician and consumer health education. The Blue Book also stated that the Famous Teachings in Modern Medicine ("FTMM") and the Video Journal of Medicine Series for Physician Education "currently contain over 500 active programs. . . ." MHC alleged that two-thirds of the programs were neither "current" nor "active" and could not be sold for current medical instruction. Baxter argued that the Blue Book simply contained an accounting of the number of programs, not a representation as to the contents or marketability of the programs. Baxter also countered MHC's claim with evidence that the vast bulk of programs in Medcom's library were "ethically saleable" in 1986.

MHC alleged that Baxter falsely represented in the Blue Book the existence of a pending $3 million sale of programs to the Daharan Medical Center in Saudi Arabia. Baxter did not disclose that it had information that this sale would not take place and that the sale of any additional programs in Saudi Arabia was unlikely. MHC further alleged that Baxter failed to disclose that millions of dollars worth of previous sales were the results of bribes, not the quality of the product. Baxter introduced evidence that prospective buyers were told, "that they should put no value on the Saudi Arabian business when looking at Medcom." . . .

MHC also alleged that Baxter did not disclose that the Saudi programs had been the subject of a lawsuit brought by Medcom's founder, Richard Fuisz, (the "Fuisz litigation") against Baxter and Medcom, alleging improper payments to Saudi officials and their family members. Nor did Baxter disclose that the settlement of the suit subjected the purchaser of Medcom to potential liability. Baxter produced evidence that the Fuisz litigation was settled before Baxter sold Medcom to MHC, Baxter was responsible for payment of the settlement, and Baxter was bound by the confidentiality provisions of the settlement agreement. Therefore, Baxter was not obligated to disclose the litigation.

MHC alleged that Baxter misrepresented in the June 1986 Blue Book the existence of a newsletter joint venture with the UCLA teaching hospital despite the fact that Baxter already had cancelled this venture by letter in April 1986. Baxter claimed that Medcom had simply given notice to UCLA that Medcom would terminate its contract with UCLA effective October 31, 1986. Baxter claimed that notice was given once Baxter decided to sell Medcom so that any future buyer would not be contractually obligated to keep publishing the unprofitable newsletter. . . .

* * *

Based on these and other similar claims, MHC alleged that Baxter had schemed to defraud MHC and was liable for damages on a number of theories. Baxter disputed all the claims and argued both that it was not liable and that it had caused MHC no damages.

* * *

The first trial, *Medcom I*, took place over the course of six weeks in 1990. Of the five counts in MHC's original complaint, only three of the counts were tried: Count I alleged violations of Section 10–b of the Securities Exchange Act of 1934, 15 U.S.C. § 78j(b) and Rule 10b–5, 17 C.F.R. § 240.10b–5 (collectively "Rule 10b–5"); Count IV alleged fraud under Illinois common law; and Count V alleged breach of contract. The *Medcom I* jury found Baxter liable on all three counts and awarded to MHC compensatory damages in the amount of $5,725,000 and punitive damages in the amount of $10,000,000. The jury also specifically found that Baxter breached the SPA as it related to EPI.

On the special verdict form, the jury made specific findings on actual damages. The jury awarded $3,500,000 on MHC's claims relating to Medcom's domestic programs and $2,225,000 on MHC's claims relating to Medcom's September 30, 1986 balance sheet. The jury awarded zero damages on MHC's claims regarding the UCLA Newsletter, the FTMM physician programs, and Medcom's Saudi Arabian operations. The *Medcom I* jury further broke down these awards to $1 million on Count I, $3 million on Count IV and $1,725,000 on Count V. . . .

* * *

On a common law fraud claim, Illinois law permits Medcom to be placed in the same financial position it would have been in had the misrepresentation been true.... To prove damages for the domestic programs library, MHC had to establish the amount of lost profits from the obsolete programs that Baxter had represented as "current" programs....

* * *

MHC also sought damages based on the $10.6 million balance sheet. MHC relied upon the warranty in the SPA providing that Baxter would pay MHC the amount of any overstatement in the balance sheet. Thus, the district court found that the award must be justified by reference to the breach of contract claim.

MHC produced one witness, Michael Reagan of the accounting firm of Deloitte, Haskins & Sells, to testify to the amount of overstatement. Reagan testified that a 40 percent reduction of the balance sheet was appropriate, resulting in approximately $4.1 million in damages. The jury returned a verdict in the amount of $2,225,000.

Reagan analyzed the balance sheet overstatement line-item by line-item. For each item that he concluded that Baxter had overstated in the balance sheet, he testified as to why he reached this conclusion and by how much Baxter had overstated the value of the asset. Reagan was cross-examined on each balance sheet line-item. He also testified extensively on both direct and cross examination regarding his workpapers, which were provided to the jury as exhibits. In addition, Baxter called an accounting expert, who rebutted each of Reagan's opinions line-item by line-item. Baxter's expert also suggested that Reagan's entire analysis should be rejected and that there were flaws that should lead to partial rejection of some line-items....

* * *

MHC also seeks reinstatement of the *Medcom I* jury's award of $10 million in punitive damages....

* * *

... As we have noted, Illinois courts "take rather a dim view of punitive damages, and insist that the plaintiff seeking them demonstrate not only simple fraud, but gross fraud, breach of trust, or other extraordinary or exceptional circumstances clearly showing malice and willfulness." ...

* * *

... In light of the dim view Illinois courts take of punitive damages, we agree that punitive damages were not warranted. We affirm the district court's order denying punitive damages.

* * *

In *Medcom I*, the jury found that Baxter's failure to transfer EPI [Ed. EPI was a wholly-owned subsidiary of Medcom.] to MHC on September 30, 1986, breached the SPA. The district court granted specific performance to plaintiff MHC, required Baxter to transfer and deliver all of its stock in EPI to MHC, and ordered Baxter to account for the benefits Baxter received from possession of EPI since September 30, 1986. . . .

The district court awarded approximately $1.1 million to MHC. . . .

* * *

The evidence at *Medcom I* was sufficient to support the jury's verdicts on liability and on compensatory damages. The district court erred in failing to enter judgment on these verdicts. . . .

We affirm the district court's denial of punitive damages. We also affirm the district court's award of $1,117,645 pursuant to the EPI accounting. . . .

* * *

PROUTY v. GORES TECHNOLOGY GROUP, 18 Cal.Rptr.3d 178 (App. 2004): [Employees of the target company can enforce against the acquirer provisions of an acquisition agreement in which purchaser promised not to terminate employees during the sixty days following the closing and to provide specified severance benefits to employees terminated within ninety days of the closing.]

Regarding third party beneficiaries, section 10.5 of the stock sale agreement stated the agreement is "not intended to confer upon any Person other than the parties hereto, the Company [VeriFone], [and other entities not relevant here] any rights or remedies hereunder." . . .

* * *

GTG argues the express language of section 10.5 of the agreement and section 8(b) of the amendment preclude plaintiffs from being third party beneficiaries. Plaintiffs argue that despite sections 10.5 and 8(b), GTG and Hewlett-Packard adopted section 6 of the amendment with the express intent to benefit plaintiffs, thus making them third party beneficiaries who could enforce the agreement. . . .

* * *

Applying the law of third party beneficiaries to the language of the contract discloses GTG and Hewlett-Packard expressly intended to grant plaintiffs the promises contained in section 6 of the amendment. Indeed, section 6 is a classic third party provision. It is patently intended to preclude early termination of the affected employees and to provide those terminated soon after the closing with severance benefits similar to what they would have received had they been terminated when employed by Hewlett-Packard. The provision expressly benefits them, and only them.

* * *

GTG disagrees with our conclusion, asserting section 10.5 precludes plaintiffs from becoming third party beneficiaries. . . .

* * *

Section 6 of the amendment does conflict with section 10.5 of the stock purchase agreement. . . . [W]hen a general and particular provision are inconsistent, the particular and specific provision is paramount to the general provision. . . . Section 6 of the amendment thus is an exception to section 10.5 of the original contract and section 8(b) of the amendment, and the plaintiffs can enforce it.". . .

* * *

2. THE BUYER REFUSES TO CLOSE

NOTE: THE BOOM AND BUST OF PRIVATE EQUITY IN THE NAUGHT DECADE

A *private equity* buyout fund raises money from passive investors to fund the equity portion of heavily-leveraged *going-private deals*. The fund creates a wholly owned shell subsidiary, funds the subsidiary with some cash, raises additional proceeds from multiple credit facilities, takes the cash and buys all the stock of a publicly traded company (in a two-step stock acquisition/clean up statutory merger). Since the number of shareholders in a target, now a portfolio company of the fund, is reduced to under 300, the target firm goes private, and is no longer subject to the public company reporting obligations of Section 12 of the Securities Exchange Act of 1934.

Private equity deals dominated the boom from 2002 to 2007 before the bust in 2008. The 2007 acquisition of Chrysler LLC by Cerberus Capital Management and the $44 billion acquisition of Texas Utility TXU Inc. were two of the many highlights of the era. Private equity deals use very sophisticated capital structures—the intricately layered senior, subordinated, unsecured and preferred stock financing. When the credit market collapsed in 2008, private equity deals dried up for a time. Those deals that had been negotiated before the collapse and not set for closing until after the collapse saw private equity funds scrambling to terminate deals. Litigation over the busted deals invariably focused on acquisition contract language. One of the more notable of the busted deal cases follows. It involved Apollo Management, one of the high profile private equity funds of the era.

HEXION SPECIALTY CHEMICALS, INC. V. HUNTSMAN CORP.

Delaware Court of Chancery, 2008.
965 A.2d 715.

LAMB, VICE CHANCELLOR.

* * *

The plaintiffs and counterclaim defendants in this action are Hexion Specialty Chemicals, Inc., Apollo Global Management, LLC, and various entities through which Apollo Global Management conducts its business (Apollo Global Management and its related entities are collectively referred to as "Apollo"). Hexion, a New Jersey corporation, is the world's largest producer of binder, adhesive, and ink resins for industrial applications. Apollo Global Management, a Delaware limited liability company, is an asset manager focusing on private equity transactions. Through its ownership in Hexion's holding company, Apollo owns approximately 92% of Hexion.

The defendant and counterclaim plaintiff in this action is Huntsman Corporation, a Delaware corporation. Huntsman, a global manufacturer and marketer of chemical products, operates five primary lines of business: Polyurethanes, Advanced Materials, Textile Effects, Performance Products and Pigments.

* * *

On July 12, 2007, Hexion and Huntsman signed a merger agreement whereby Hexion agreed to pay $28 per share in cash for 100% of Huntsman's stock.[1] The total transaction value of the deal was approximately $10.6 billion, including assumed debt. The plaintiffs filed suit in this court on June 18, 2008 seeking declaratory judgment on three claims: (1) Hexion is not obligated to close if the combined company would be insolvent and its liability to Huntsman for failing to close is limited to no more than $325 million; (2) Huntsman has suffered a Company Material Adverse Effect ("MAE"); and (3) Apollo has no liability to Huntsman in connection with the merger agreement. On July 2, 2008, Huntsman filed its answer and counterclaims requesting declaratory judgment that: (1) Hexion knowingly and intentionally breached the merger agreement; (2) Huntsman has not suffered an MAE; and (3) Hexion has no right to terminate the merger agreement. Also, Huntsman's counterclaims seek an order that Hexion specifically perform its obligations under various sections of the merger agreement, or, alternatively, and in the event Hexion fails to perform, the award of full contract damages. . . .

* * *

In May 2007, Huntsman, through its financial advisor Merrill Lynch & Co., Inc., began to solicit bids for the company. Apollo (through Hexion)

---

1 Apollo is not a party to the merger agreement.

and Basell, the world's largest polypropylene maker, emerged among the potential buyers. Huntsman signed confidentiality agreements and began to negotiate merger agreements with both Hexion and Basell. On June 25, 2007, Huntsman rejected Hexion's offer of $26 per share and executed a merger agreement with Basell for $25.25 per share. The same day, but after the agreement was signed, Hexion raised its bid to $27 per share. Basell refused to raise its bid, stating that its deal remained superior because it was more certain to close.[4] On June 29, 2007, Huntsman re-entered negotiations with Hexion after Hexion further increased its bid to $27.25 per share. On July 12, 2007, Huntsman terminated its deal with Basell and signed an all cash deal at $28 per share with Hexion.

* * *

One day before the signing of the merger agreement, Hexion signed a commitment letter with affiliates of Credit Suisse and Deutsche Bank (the "lending banks") to secure financing for the deal. In section 3.2(e) of the merger agreement, Hexion represented that the "aggregate proceeds contemplated to be provided by the Commitment Letter will be sufficient . . . to pay the aggregate Merger Consideration." The commitment letter required a "customary and reasonably satisfactory" solvency certificate from the Chief Financial Officer of Hexion, the Chief Financial Officer of Huntsman, or a reputable valuation firm as a condition precedent to the lending banks obligation to provide financing.

* * *

Due to the existence of a signed agreement with Basell and Apollo's admittedly intense desire for the deal, Huntsman had significant negotiating leverage. As a result, the merger agreement is more than usually favorable to Huntsman. For example, it contains no financing contingency and requires Hexion to use its "reasonable best efforts" to consummate the financing. In addition, the agreement expressly provides for uncapped damages in the case of a "knowing and intentional breach of any covenant" by Hexion and for liquidated damages of $325 million in cases of other enumerated breaches. The narrowly tailored MAE clause is one of the few ways the merger agreement allows Hexion to walk away from the deal without paying Huntsman at least $325 million in liquidated damages.

* * *

Initially, Hexion and Apollo were extremely excited about the deal with Huntsman. . . . While Huntsman's Pigments business had been slowing since shortly after signing, Hexion and Apollo's view of the deal did

[4] A transaction between Huntsman and Hexion would take longer to close because it required a more detailed antitrust review than a deal between Huntsman and Basell. Also, the proposed transaction with Hexion would be more highly levered than the proposed transaction with Basell.

not seem to change dramatically until after receipt of Huntsman's disappointing first quarter numbers on April 22, 2008. Following receipt of these numbers, Apollo revised its deal model and concluded that the transaction would produce returns much lower than expected. . . .

* * *

Hexion argues that its obligation to close is excused as a result of a Company Material Adverse Effect in the business of Huntsman. For the reasons detailed below, Hexion's argument fails. . . .

* * *

Section 6.2(e) of the merger agreement states that Hexion's obligation to close is conditioned on the absence of "any event, change, effect or development that has had or is reasonably expected to have, individually or in the aggregate," an MAE. MAE is defined in section 3.1(a)(ii) as:

> any occurrence, condition, change, event or effect that is materially adverse to the financial condition, business, or results of operations of the Company and its Subsidiaries, taken as a whole; *provided, however,* that in no event shall any of the following constitute a Company Material Adverse Effect: (A) any occurrence, condition, change, event or effect resulting from or relating to changes in general economic or financial market conditions, except in the event, and only to the extent, that such occurrence, condition, change, event or effect has had a disproportionate effect on the Company and its Subsidiaries, taken as a whole, as compared to other Persons engaged in the chemical industry; (B) any occurrence, condition, change, event or effect that affects the chemical industry generally (including changes in commodity prices, general market prices and regulatory changes affecting the chemical industry generally) except in the event, and only to the extent, that such occurrence, condition, change, event or effect has had a disproportionate effect on the Company and its Subsidiaries, taken as a whole, as compared to other Persons engaged in the chemical industry. . . .

The parties disagree as to the proper reading of this definition. Hexion argues that the relevant standard to apply in judging whether an MAE has occurred is to compare Huntsman's performance since the signing of the merger agreement and its expected future performance to the rest of the chemical industry. Huntsman, for its part, argues that in determining whether an MAE has occurred the court need reach the issue of comparing Huntsman to its peers if and only if it has first determined that there has been an "occurrence, condition, change, event or effect that is materially adverse to the financial condition, business, or results of operations of the Company and its Subsidiaries, taken as a whole. . . ." Huntsman here has the better argument. The plain meaning of the carve-outs found in the proviso is to prevent certain occurrences which would *otherwise* be MAE's being found to be so. If a catastrophe were to befall the chemical industry and cause a material adverse effect in Huntsman's business, the carve-outs would prevent this from qualifying as an MAE under the Agreement. But the converse is not true—Huntsman's performance being disproportionately worse than the chemical industry in general does not, in itself, constitute an MAE. Thus, unless the court concludes that the company has suffered an MAE as defined in the language coming before the proviso, the court need not consider the application of the chemical industry carve-outs.

* * *

. . . [B]ecause, as discussed below, Huntsman has not suffered an MAE, the court need not reach the question of whether Huntsman's performance has been disproportionately worse than the chemical industry taken as a whole.

* * *

For the purpose of determining whether an MAE has occurred, changes in corporate fortune must be examined in the context in which the parties were transacting. In the absence of evidence to the contrary, a corporate acquirer may be assumed to be purchasing the target as part of a long-term strategy. The important consideration therefore is whether there has been an adverse change in the target's business that is consequential to the company's long-term earnings power over a commercially reasonable period, which one would expect to be measured in years rather than months. A buyer faces a heavy burden when it attempts to invoke a material adverse effect clause in order to avoid its obligation to close. Many commentators have noted that Delaware courts have never found a material adverse effect to have occurred in the context of a merger agreement. This is not a coincidence. The ubiquitous material adverse effect clause should be seen as providing a "backstop protecting the acquirer from the occurrence of unknown events that substantially threaten the overall earnings potential of the target in a durationally-significant manner. A short-term hiccup in earnings should not suffice; rather [an adverse change] should be material when viewed from the longer-term perspective of a reasonable acquirer." This, of course, is not to say that evidence of a significant decline in earnings by the target corporation during the period after signing but prior to the time appointed for closing is irrelevant. Rather, it means that for such a decline to constitute a material adverse effect, poor earnings results must be expected to persist significantly into the future.

* * *

Hexion focuses its argument that Huntsman has suffered an MAE along several lines: (1) disappointing results in Huntsman's earnings performance over the period from July 2007 through the present; (2) Huntsman's increase in net debt since signing, contrary to the expectations of the parties; and (3) underperformance in Huntsman's Textile Effects and Pigments lines of business.

* * *

. . . Huntsman's expert Zmijewski testified at trial, the terms "financial condition, business, or results of operations" are terms of art, to be understood with reference to their meaning in Regulation S–K and Item 7, the "Management's Discussion and Analysis of Financial Condition and Results of Operations" section of the financial statements public companies are required to file with the SEC. In this section, a company is required to disclose its financial result for the period being reported, along with its pro forma financial results for the same time period for each of the previous two years. Zmijewski testified at trial that these results are analyzed by comparing the results in each period with the results in the same period for the prior year (i.e., year-end 2007 results to year-end 2006 results, first-quarter 2005 results to first-quarter 2004 results, and so forth). The proper benchmark then for analyzing these changes with respect to an MAE, according to Zmijewski (and the analysis the court adopts here), is to examine each year and quarter and compare it to the prior year's equivalent period. Through this lens, it becomes clear that no MAE has occurred. Huntsman's 2007 EBITDA was only 3% below its 2006 EBITDA, and, according to Huntsman management forecasts, 2008 EBITDA will only be 7% below 2007 EBITDA. Even using Hexion's much lower estimate of Huntsman's 2008 EBITDA, Huntsman's 2008 EBITDA would still be only 11% below its 2007 EBITDA. . . .

* * *

These results do not add up to an MAE, particularly in the face of the macroeconomic challenges Huntsman has faced since the middle of 2007 as a result of rapidly increased crude oil and natural gas prices and unfavorable foreign exchange rate changes. Ultimately, the burden is on Hexion to demonstrate the existence of an MAE in order to negate its obligation to close, and that is a burden it cannot meet here.

* * *

Hexion urges that Huntsman's results of operations cannot be viewed in isolation, but should be examined in conjunction with Huntsman's increase in net debt. As of the end of June 2007, Huntsman forecast that its net debt at the end of 2008 would be $2.953 billion. At the time, its net debt stood at $4.116 billion. It expected that this reduction in debt would be financed by the divestiture of three of its divisions (which was accomplished by the end of 2007) and by its operating cash flows. Things did not go according to plan. Driven largely by dramatic increases in the prices of inputs and growth in accounts receivables, working capital expanded during this time by $265 million, while foreign exchange effects on the outstanding debt balances resulted in a dollar-denominated increase in the notional value of Huntsman's debt of an additional $178 million. All told, rather than shrinking by a billion dollars, Huntsman's net debt since signing has expanded by over a quarter of a billion dollars.

. . . This argument initially appears attractive, but examination of Apollo's initial deal-model negates any persuasive power it might have initially held. In all four of the cases which Apollo modeled, Huntsman's net debt at closing is assumed to be $4.1 billion. All of Hexion's assumptions about the value of the deal were predicated on Huntsman's net debt levels on that order—the projected decrease in Huntsman's net debt of a billion dollars was simply an added attraction. Hexion cannot now claim that a 5% increase in net debt from its expectations in valuing the deal, even combined with the reduced earnings, should excuse it from its obligation to perform on the merger agreement.

* * *

Both in its pretrial brief and at trial, Hexion focused most of its attention on two Huntsman divisions which have been particularly troubled since the signing of the merger agreement—Pigments and Textile Effects. . . .

First, as already discussed, under the terms of the merger agreement, an MAE is to be determined based on an examination of Huntsman taken as a whole. A close examination of two divisions anticipated to generate at most a fourth of Huntsman's EBITDA is therefore only tangentially related to the issue. Although the results in each of these two divisions, if standing alone, might be materially impaired, as already illustrated above, Huntsman as a whole is not materially impaired by their results. If it is unconvincing to say Huntsman's business as a whole has been materially changed for the worse, it is even more unconvincing to claim that 75% of Huntsman's business is fine, but that troubles in the other 25% materially changes the business as a whole.

Additionally, there is reason to believe that much of Huntsman's troubles in each of these divisions are short-term in nature. . . .

* * *

III.

Both parties seek declaratory judgment on the subject of knowing and intentional breach. Hexion seeks a declaratory judgment that no "knowing and intentional breach" of the merger agreement has occurred, and therefore its liability for any breach of the merger agreement is capped at $325 million. Huntsman seeks the obverse—a declaratory judgment that Hexion has engaged in a "knowing and intentional breach" of the merger agreement, and therefore it is entitled to full contract damages, not capped or liquidated by the $325 million figure in section 7.3(d) of the merger agreement. For the reasons detailed below, the court concludes that Hexion has engaged in a knowing and intentional breach, and that the liquidated damages clause of section 7.3(d) is therefore inapplicable.

* * *

. . . Thus a "knowing and intentional" breach is a deliberate one—a breach that is a direct consequence of a deliberate act undertaken by the breaching party, rather than one which results indirectly, or as a result of the breaching party's negligence or unforeseeable misadventure. In other words, a "knowing and intentional" breach, as used in the merger agreement, is the taking of a deliberate act, which act constitutes in and of itself a breach of the merger agreement, even if breaching was not the conscious object of the act. It is with this definition in mind that Hexion's actions will be judged.

* * *

Section 5.12(a) of the merger agreement contains Hexion's covenant to use its reasonable best efforts to consummate the financing:

> (a) [Hexion] shall use its reasonable best efforts to take, or cause to be taken, all actions and to do, or cause to be done, all things necessary, proper or advisable to arrange and consummate the Financing on the terms and conditions described in the Commitment Letter, including (i) using reasonable best efforts to (x) satisfy on a timely basis all terms, covenants and conditions set forth in the Commitment Letter; (y) enter into definitive agreements with respect thereto on the terms and conditions contemplated by the Commitment Letter; and (z) consummate the Financing at or prior to Closing; and (ii) seeking to enforce its rights under the Commitment Letter. Parent will furnish correct and complete copies of all such definitive agreements to the Company promptly upon their execution.

Put more simply, to the extent that an act was both commercially reasonable and advisable to enhance the likelihood of consummation of the financing, the onus was on Hexion to take that act. To the extent that Hexion deliberately chose not to act, but instead pursued another path designed to *avoid* the consummation of the financing, Hexion knowingly and intentionally breached this covenant.

* * *

IV.

Hexion strenuously argues, and urges the court to declare, that on a pro forma basis (assuming the merger closes on the financing terms contemplated in the commitment letter), the combined entity will be insolvent. . . .

* * *

The court thus finds itself asked to referee a battle of the experts in which there is no clear answer and no possibility of splitting the difference. For the reasons briefly discussed below, the court determines not to reach the issue of solvency at this time because that issue will not arise unless and until a solvency letter or opinion is delivered to the lending banks and those banks then either fund or refuse to fund the transaction.

. . . Huntsman is correct that the solvency of the combined entity is not a condition precedent to Hexion's obligations under the merger agreement. In fact, looking only at terms of the merger agreement, Hexion's avowed inability to deliver a suitable solvency opinion does not negate its obligation to close: rather, the receipt of such an opinion is merely a condition precedent to Huntsman's duty to close, protects Huntsman (and its shareholders), and is, therefore, waivable by Huntsman. To put it differently, Hexion's fear that it has agreed to pay too high a price for Huntsman does not provide a basis for it to get out of the transaction.

* * *

. . . For the reasons discussed elsewhere in this opinion, the court is issuing a judgment and order that will require Hexion to specifically perform its covenants and obligations under the merger agreement (other than its obligation to close). Thus, if the other conditions to closing are met, Hexion will be obligated to call upon the lending banks to perform on their funding obligations. In that circumstance, the banks will then have to choose whether to fund on the basis of the solvency letter delivered by Huntsman or, instead, reject that letter as unsatisfactory and refuse to fund. If the lending banks refuse to fund, they will, of course, be opening themselves to the potential for litigation, including a claim for damages for breach of contract. In such litigation, the prospective insolvency of the combined entity would likely be an important issue.

If the banks agree to fund, Hexion will then have to determine whether it considers it in its best interests to close the transaction, or instead refuse to close, subjecting itself to the possibility of an additional finding of knowing and intentional breach of contract and uncapped contract damages. If Hexion chooses to close, the issue will be moot. If it does not, the posture of the matter, and the decision presented to the court, will be far more concrete and capable of judicial resolution than the issue now framed by the parties.

For the foregoing reasons, the court will not now resolve the question of whether the combined entity would be solvent or not. That issue may arise in the future in the course of this litigation or some related action, but it is not now properly framed by the terms of the merger agreement and the status of the transaction. Thus, the issue is not ripe for a judicial determination.

V.

Huntsman asks the court to enter a judgment ordering Hexion and its merger subsidiary, Nimbus, to specifically perform their covenants and obligations under the merger agreement. For the reasons explained below, the court finds that, under the agreement, Huntsman cannot force Hexion to consummate the merger, but that Huntsman is entitled to a judgment ordering Hexion to specifically perform its other covenants and obligations.

The court first examines whether the merger agreement, somewhat unusually, contains a provision prohibiting the issuance of an order specifically directing Hexion to comply with its duty to close the transaction. Section 8.11 provides that generally a non-breaching party may seek and obtain specific performance of any covenant or obligation set forth in the agreement. However, that section goes on to state, in virtually impenetrable language, as follows: "In circumstances where [Hexion is] obligated to consummate the Merger and the Merger has not been consummated on or prior to the earlier of the last day of the Marketing Period or the Termination Date (other than as a result of [Huntsman's] refusal to close in violation of this Agreement) the parties acknowledge that [Huntsman] shall *not* be entitled to enforce specifically the obligations of [Hexion] to consummate the Merger."

* * *

In view of these provisions, and considering all the circumstances, the court concludes that it is appropriate to require Hexion to specifically perform its obligations under the merger agreement, other than the obligation to close. . . . When it is known whether the financing contemplated by the commitment letter is available or not, Hexion and its shareholders will thus be placed in the position to make an informed judgment about whether to close the transaction (in light of, among other things, the findings and conclusions in this opinion) and, if so, how to finance the combined operations. As the parties recognize, both Hexion and Huntsman are solvent, profitable businesses. The issues in this case relate principally to the cost of the merger and whether the financing structure Apollo and Hexion arranged in July 2007 is adequate to close the deal and fund the operations of the combined enterprise. The order the court is today issuing will afford the parties the opportunity to resolve those issues in an orderly and sensible fashion.

* * *

Before the decision came down, Huntsman had countersued Apollo (and its founders) and the two banks financing the acquisition, Credit Suisse and Deutsche Bank, in Texas state court. It claimed tortious interference of two contracts, the deal with Hexion and the lost deal with

Basel. After the Delaware decision, Hexion was in a very awkward position. It had to attempt to close or pay substantial damages that would bankrupt the company. Not surprisingly, the financing banks refused to fund the deal, relying on Hexion's own arguments of the insolvency of the resulting company. Hexion sued the financing banks on their commitment letters and all parties entered into negotiations to solve the mess. The Delaware court had given Huntsman a substantial strategic advantage but it had developed liquidity problems and was finding it difficult to fund the litigation. In December of 2008, Apollo and Hexion paid Huntsman $750 million in cash and bought $250 million in Huntsman convertible notes. In June of the next year, the financing banks paid Huntsman $632 million in cash and agreed to provide a low rate $1.1 billion loan. See Steven M. Davidoff, GODS AT WAR 94–95 (2009).

QUESTION

Are MACs "dead"? Expect traditional MACs to be supplemented or replaced by more specific closing conditions tied to earnings targets, sales level, or lack of customer defections and other quantifiable terms that may excuse performance unequivocally.

CONSOLIDATED EDISON, INC. V. NORTHEAST UTILITIES

United States Court of Appeals, Second Circuit, 2005.
426 F.3d 524.

JACOBS, CIRCUIT JUDGE.

* * *

This case arises from the failed multi-billion dollar merger between CEI [Consolidated Edison, Inc.] and NU [Northeast Utilities]. Among the terms and conditions of the underlying merger agreement ("Agreement"), CEI agreed to purchase all of NU's outstanding shares for $3.6 billion—$1.2 billion over the prevailing market price. . . .

On March 5, 2001, shortly before the scheduled closing, CEI declared that NU had suffered a material adverse change that "dramatically lowered" NU's valuation, and declined to proceed with the merger unless NU would agree to a lower share price. NU rejected the share-price reduction, treated CEI's demand as an anticipatory repudiation and breach of the Agreement, and declared that the merger was "effectively terminate[d]."

CEI brought suit against NU for (*inter alia*) breach of contract, fraudulent inducement, and negligent misrepresentation, while NU counterclaimed for breach of contract, alleging that CEI's proposed share-price reduction was attributable to buyer's remorse in a sinking stock market rather than any change in NU's condition. On cross-motions for partial summary judgment, the district court dismissed CEI's claims of fraudulent inducement and negligent misrepresentation, but allowed the dueling breach-of-contract claims to proceed. The substance of those contract claims has little bearing on this appeal; at issue here is whether the $1.2 billion shareholder premium can be claimed as damages arising from CEI's alleged breach of the Agreement.

* * *

The first question presented is whether any NU shareholders (as of any date) enjoy the right, as third-party beneficiaries, to sue CEI for the $1.2 billion premium that CEI would have paid but for its allegedly wrongful failure to complete the merger.

New York law governs the Agreement. *See* Agreement, art. VIII, § 8.07. [A 308.] Under New York law, a contractual promise can be enforced by a non-party who is an intended third-party beneficiary of that promise. . . . The question, therefore, is whether CEI and NU intended to confer on NU's shareholders a right to enforce CEI's promise to complete the merger (and thus a claim against CEI for the $1.2 billion premium). The answer is no. Undoubtedly, the merger agreement confers on NU's shareholders certain rights as third-party beneficiaries, so that after the "NU Effective Time," *i.e.*, the moment at which the merger was to be complete, the shareholders could have enforced CEI's contractual obligation to pay them the $1.2 billion premium. However, as the NU Effective Time never arrived, CEI's duty to pay the premium did not arise.

* * *

The Agreement treats third-party rights at article VIII, section 8.06. That provision states that there are none, with two exceptions:

> *This Agreement* . . . (i) *constitutes the entire agreement,* and supersedes all prior agreements and understandings, both written and oral, among the parties with respect to the subject matter of this Agreement . . . and (ii) *except for the provisions of Article II and Article 5.08,* [is] *not intended to confer upon any person other than the parties any rights or remedies.*

Agreement, art. VIII, § 8.06 (emphasis added).

One exception to that foreclosure of third-party rights—article V, section 5.08—concerns the personal liability of CEI and NU's trustees, directors, and officers during and after the merger, and has no bearing on this case. The other—Article II—describes what occurs upon the arrival of the NU Effective Time, and is important. In particular, section 2.01(b) states that at the "NU Effective Time" each outstanding NU share "shall be converted into the right to receive" cash or stock in the post-merger company. *Id.*, art. II, § 2.01(b)(ii), (ii)(A)–(B). That consideration would include the shareholder premium at issue here. Reading article VIII's general foreclosure of third-party beneficiary rights together with the exception in article II, section 2.01, we see that the only third-party right conferred on NU's shareholders is a right, arising *upon completion of the merger,* to receive payment for their shares. Since it is undisputed that the NU Effective Time never arrived, that right never arose.

* * *

The intent of CEI and NU to limit the third-party right (in the way set out above) is further manifested in the overall context and scheme of the Agreement. The express third-party right of NU shareholders to compel payment of the consideration due to them post-merger implements a contract right that NU could not enforce on their behalf: At and after the NU Effective Time, NU would no longer exist as an independent entity, but CEI would not yet have established the fund from which NU's shareholders would be paid. *See* Agreement, art. II, § 2.04. NU argues that even without the grant of such a third-party right, the shareholders may have been able to compel payment for their shares through claims of conversion, quasi-contract, implied contract, or accounting. That may be, but the most direct, simple, and potent remedy would be an action at law in contract; and that is exactly what the Agreement provides.

If we were to find a third-party right for shareholders to seek damages for breach of the duty to merge before the NU Effective time, that right would overwhelm the careful arrangements that the Agreement makes for that contingency, and would unduly limit the signatories' own freedom of action to accept or hazard the contractual consequences of non-performance.

Article VII, section 7.01 explains the circumstances under which the Agreement may be "terminated" by either party prior to the merger's completion. Section 7.01(e) provides that NU may terminate:

> *if CEI shall have breached or failed to perform in any material respect any of its* representations, warranties, covenants or other *agreements* contained in this Agreement, which breach or failure to perform (A) would give rise to the failure of a condition set forth in Section 6.03(a) *or* (b), *and* (B) is incapable of being cured by CEI or *is not cured by CEI within a reasonable period of time following receipt of written notice from NU of such breach or failure to perform.*

(emphasis added). If, as NU alleges, CEI unjustifiably refused to complete the merger, CEI breached article VI, section 6.03(b)—which requires that CEI perform "in all material respects all obligations [ ] to be performed by it under this Agreement at or prior to the Closing Date"—and that breach was not cured within a reasonable time (ever, in fact) after NU's notice of breach. Thus, section 7.01(e) covers termination in the event of just such a breach as is alleged by NU.

The effect of a section 7.01(e) termination is set out in section 7.02. The first part of section 7.02 states:

> *In the event of termination* of this Agreement *by* either *NU* or CEI as provided in Section 7.01, *this Agreement shall forthwith become null and void* and have no effect, *without any liability or obligation on the part of CEI* or NU, *other than* the provisions of *Section 3.01(q), Section 3.02(o),* the penultimate sentence of *Section 5.04(a), Section 5.09,* this *Section 7.02* and *Article VIII,* which provisions shall survive such termination . . .

(emphasis added). Termination therefore would result in no "liability or obligation on the part of CEI" except for what is required by the provisions enumerated in section 7.02.

None of those provisions, however, provides support for the shareholders' right to sue CEI under these circumstances. Sections 3.01(q) and 3.02(*o*) ("Brokers"), and section 5.04 ("Access to Information; Confidentiality; Advice of Changes") have no bearing on this appeal. Section 5.09 ("Fees and Expenses") specifies fees and expenses owed by one party to the other. In particular, [i] CEI and NU agreed to share the costs of various regulatory filings and taxes associated with the merger, *id.* § 5.09(a); [ii] NU agreed to pay CEI a $110 million "Termination Fee" if, under certain circumstances, the Agreement were terminated and NU thereafter entered into an acquisition agreement with a third party, *id.* § 5.09(b); [iii] NU promised to pay a $20 million "expense reimbursement fee" to CEI if the Agreement were terminated under certain circumstances, *id.* § 5.09(c), and CEI made a similar promise, *id.* § 5.09(d); and [iv] NU agreed to cover CEI's costs and expenses if it were to prevail in any suit against NU to procure payment of the Termination Fee or expense reimbursement fee, *id.* § 5.09(e). None of these provisions contemplate the NU shareholders' right to sue CEI for the lost $1.2 billion premium; and any such right would overwhelm the specified and limited remedies available to each party in the event of breach and termination of the Agreement.

* * *

That leaves the second part of section 7.02, which states that where "termination results from the willful and material breach by a party of any of its representations, warranties, covenants or agreements set forth in the Agreement":

> *such termination shall not relieve any party of any liability or damages resulting from its willful and material breach of this Agreement* (including any such case in which a Termination Fee or any expense reimbursement fee is payable pursuant to Section 5.09), *to the extent any such liability or damage suffered by the*

party entitled to such payment exceeds the amount of such payment . . .

(emphasis added). This wording—which sets out the consequences of a "willful and material breach"—is at the heart of the matter, but this part of section 7.02 applies only to "liability or damage suffered by *the party,*" not by *non-parties,* and therefore, not by NU's shareholders.

In sum, article VII—which governs breach and termination of the Agreement—provides no support for the shareholders' right to sue CEI for failure to complete the merger. To the contrary, that article reflects the parties' intent [i] to limit the damages resulting from a breach of the Agreement to those owed to each other; and even then, [ii] to liquidate and limit those damages, except in the case of a willful and material breach. By setting out and limiting the consequences of breach, the Agreement affords each party a critical power to abandon the merger if it is willing to suffer the stipulated consequences, a power that would be illusory if such abandonment could trigger a potential billion-dollar liability to the shareholders.

* * *

NOTE: TERRORISM AND MAC CLAUSES

The issue of terrorism has made its way into the acquisition documents of deals. Most often, language on terrorism is surfacing in the "material adverse change," or MAC, clauses in the acquisition contract. The new language allows companies to pull out of deals in the event of "acts of terrorism" or, more infrequently, expressly prevents the other side from using acts of terrorism to walk away from a deal. Even before the events of September 11th, lawyers had been haggling over the details of MACs and *force majeure* or *acts of God* clauses.[102] The clauses have become increasingly more elaborate as parties have fine-tuned allocations of risk in light of calamities. MACs were once confined to abrupt changes in the financial condition of a party, as opposed to the industry or economy in which it operates. Courts have construed the traditional *force majeure* clause to cover only war or conflicts between sovereigns, as opposed to acts of terror.

[102] *Force majeure* clauses represent the parties' contractual agreement on acts of impracticability that will warrant the suspension of performance, either temporarily or permanently, by one or both parties.

3. SELLER REFUSES TO CLOSE

NACCO INDUSTRIES, INC. v. APPLICA INCORPORATED

Court of Chancery of Delaware 2009.
997 A.2d 1.

LASTER, VICE CHANCELLOR.

* * *

Defendant Harbert Management Corporation is an investment manager that oversees a hedge fund complex. The Complaint names as defendants the Harbert-affiliated entities that were involved in the Applica transaction. . . .

Defendant Applica is a Florida corporation headquartered in Miramar, Florida. Applica markets, distributes, and sells small household appliances. Applica is now a portfolio company of Harbinger. Prior to being taken private by Harbinger, Applica's common stock traded on the New York Stock Exchange.

Plaintiff NACCO is a Delaware corporation with its principal place of business in Mayfield Heights, Ohio. NACCO is a holding company whose shares trade on the New York Stock Exchange. NACCO owns plaintiff HB-PS Holding Company, Inc. ("Hamilton Beach"), a Delaware corporation with its principal place of business in Glen Allen, Virginia. Hamilton Beach is a designer, marketer, and distributor of small electric household appliances and commercial products for restaurants, hotels, and bars.

* * *

In early 2005, NACCO approached Applica about a strategic transaction with Hamilton Beach. The parties signed a non-disclosure agreement, exchanged confidential information, and began discussions. Applica broke off talks, inviting NACCO to re-approach in early 2006.

Applica proved more receptive in 2006. In January, Applica's board authorized merger discussions with NACCO. On February 16, Applica and NACCO updated their non-disclosure agreement, and NACCO agreed to a standstill provision that limited its ability to act unilaterally to acquire Applica. When NACCO found itself in a bidding contest for Applica some seven months later, the consequences of agreeing to the standstill would prove critical, because NACCO ended up competing against Harbinger, which was not similarly restricted and had used its freedom and the cover of allegedly false Schedule 13 disclosures to accumulate a large block of Applica stock.

On February 28, 2006, Applica announced publicly that it was exploring strategic alternatives. In March, Applica began making outgoing calls to potential strategic partners.

On May 2, 2006, Applica's board of directors decided to pursue NACCO's merger proposal. During the week of May 24, Applica conducted due diligence on Hamilton Beach's operations. On June 6, NACCO sent Applica a draft merger agreement. On July 23, the parties executed a merger agreement (the "Hamilton Beach Merger Agreement"). In the contemplated transaction, NACCO would spin off Hamilton Beach, which would acquire Applica in a stock-for-stock merger. Following the transaction, NACCO's stockholders would own 75% and Applica's stockholders 25% of the resulting entity. In advance of the spin-off, Hamilton Beach would pay a $110 million cash dividend to NACCO. The parties announced the Hamilton Beach Merger Agreement on July 24.

* * *

On September 14, 2006, Harbinger announced a bid to acquire all of the Applica shares it did not yet own at $6.00 per share. Although Harbinger had been on the scene for some time, this announcement heralded a change in Harbinger's public role.

Harbinger began purchasing Applica stock on February 24, 2006 . . . .

* * *

On August 17, 2006, Harbinger filed another Schedule 13D disclosing that its position now amounted to 39.24% of Applica's outstanding stock. . . .

In all of its August 2006 Schedule 13D filings, Harbinger continued to state that it was holding its shares for investment purposes and not with any plan or intention to influence or control Applica. . . .

On September 14, 2006, Harbinger topped the Hamilton Beach Merger by offering to acquire all of the outstanding shares of Applica that Harbinger did not already own for $6.00 per share. In conjunction with its bid, Harbinger filed a Schedule 13D/A amending the disclosure in its prior Schedule 13 forms. The amended disclosure stated that rather than acquiring its shares for "investment purposes," Harbinger "acquired [its] Shares of [Applica] in order to acquire control of [Applica]." . . .

* * *

On October 10, 2006, Applica notified NACCO that it was terminating the Hamilton Beach Merger Agreement and would enter into a merger agreement with Harbinger. Under the Hamilton Beach Merger Agreement, Applica was permitted to terminate the agreement to accept a "Superior Proposal."

* * *

. . . Applica paid NACCO the $4 million termination fee and $2 million in expense reimbursement that the Hamilton Beach Merger Agreement called for in the event the agreement was validly terminated to accept a topping bid. Applica then entered into a merger agreement with Harbinger (the "Harbinger Merger Agreement").

* * *

Between December 15, 2006, and January 17, 2007, NACCO and Harbinger bid against each other for Applica. On December 15, NACCO launched a tender offer for Applica at $6.50 per share. Harbinger matched. On December 21, NACCO raised its bid to $7.00. Harbinger matched. Incremental bidding continued, with NACCO ultimately offering $8.05 per share on January 16, 2007.

On January 17, 2007, Harbinger raised its bid to $8.25 per share. In consideration for the increased bid, Applica nearly doubled Harbinger's termination fee—from $4 million to $7 million—and increased Harbinger's expense reimbursement from $2 million to $3.3 million.

NACCO points out that throughout the bidding, Harbinger had the benefit of owning a nearly 40% block that it had acquired for much lower prices at a time when NACCO was limited by a standstill agreement. Harbinger thus effectively was bidding for 60% of Applica, while NACCO was bidding for the whole thing. Put differently, every time NACCO put a dollar on the table, Harbinger could match with 60 cents. NACCO claims Harbinger only enjoyed this advantage because of its fraudulent Section 13 disclosures.

On January 24, 2007, Applica's stockholders approved the Harbinger Merger Agreement. NACCO terminated its offer.

* * *

Shortly after Applica's stockholders approved the Harbinger merger, Applica and Salton entered into a merger agreement. Harbinger was the driving force behind the deal. On December 28, 2007, the Salton-Applica transaction closed. [Ed. Salton was owned by Harbinger.] Harbinger owned 92% of the combined company.

* * *

II. LEGAL ANALYSIS

A. Count I States A Claim For Breach Of Contract.

The Hamilton Beach Merger Agreement became effective as of July 23, 2006. From that point on, Applica was bound by Section 6.12 of the agreement, entitled "No Solicitation." Count I of the Complaint asserts that Applica breached Section 6.12.

I find it helpful to break Section 6.12 into subparts. Under Sections 6.12(a) and (b), Applica had the obligation to stop all discussions about any competing transaction. Framed in customary language, these sections stated:

(a) [Applica] will immediately cease, terminate and discontinue any discussions or negotiations with any Person conducted before the date of this Agreement with respect to any [Applica] Competing Transaction. . . .

(b) Prior to the Effective Time, [Applica] will not, and will cause its Affiliates and representatives not to, directly or indirectly solicit, initiate or encourage any inquiries or proposals from, discuss or negotiate with, or provide any non-public information to, any Person (other than [NACCO], [Hamilton Beach] and their respective representatives) relating to any merger, consolidation, share exchange, business combination or other transaction or series of transactions involving [Applica] that is conditioned on the termination of this Agreement or could reasonably be expected to preclude or materially delay the completion of the Merger (an "*[Applica] Competing Transaction*").

I will refer to these subsections as the "No-Shop Clause."

Section 6.12(d) created an exception to the No-Shop Clause. In similarly customary language, Section 6.12(d) permitted Applica "to engage in any discussions or negotiations with, or provide any information to, any Person" if Applica "received an unsolicited bona fide written offer regarding an [Applica] Competing Transaction from a third party (which has not been withdrawn) and its board of directors has determined in good faith that there is a reasonable likelihood that such [Applica] Competing Transaction would constitute [an Applica] Superior Proposal." Section 6.12(e) defined "Applica Superior Proposal" as, in substance, an Applica Competing Transaction "which the board of directors of [Applica] concludes, after consultation with its financial advisors and following the receipt of the advice of its outside counsel, would, if consummated, result in a transaction that is more favorable to the [Applica] Shareholders than the Transactions." I will refer to this aspect of Section 6.12(d) as the "Superior Proposal Clause."

In addition to the No-Shop and Superior Proposal Clauses, Sections 6.12(c) and (d) required Applica to keep NACCO informed of any inquiry or proposal relating to an Applica Competing Transaction. Section 6.12(c) provided:

> [Applica] will promptly (and in any event within 24 hours) notify [NACCO] of its or any of its officers', directors' or representatives' receipt of any inquiry or proposal relating to, an [Applica] Competing Transaction, including the identity of the Person submitting such inquiry or proposal and the terms thereof.

In language following the Superior Proposal Clause, Section 6.12(d) provided that "[Applica] will use its commercially reasonable efforts to keep [NACCO] informed promptly of the status and terms of any such proposal or offer and the status and terms of any such discussions or negotiations and will promptly provide [NACCO] with any such written proposal or offer." I will refer to these aspects of Section 6.12 as the "Prompt Notice Clause."

* * *

In asserting its breach of contract claim, NACCO first focuses on the period of time from July 23, 2006, when the Hamilton Beach Merger Agreement became effective, until September 14, when Applica advised NACCO that it had received Harbinger's $6.00 per share proposal. I find that the Complaint contains allegations sufficient to support a claim for breach of the Hamilton Beach Merger Agreement during this period under the plaintiff-friendly Rule 12(b)(6) standard.

* * *

The No-Shop Clause and Prompt Notice Provision thus covered the outgoing communication by Applica management and the incoming call from Salton. They also covered the discussions regarding Harbinger's dissatisfaction with the Hamilton Beach Merger Agreement and its request for a waiver of the vote-stripping effect of the Florida Act, which related to a "transaction or series of transactions that . . . could reasonably be expected to preclude or materially delay the completion of the Merger."

* * *

As a second basis for its breach of contract claim, NACCO focuses on the time period starting on September 14, 2006, when Applica advised NACCO that it had received Harbinger's $6.00 per share proposal. On that date, Applica exercised its right under the Superior Proposal Clause to enter into discussions with Harbinger. NACCO alleges that from that point on, NACCO breached its obligations under the Prompt Notice Clause to "use its commercially reasonable efforts to keep [NACCO] informed promptly of the status and terms of [Harbinger's proposal] and the status and terms of any such discussions or negotiations."

* * *

These allegations readily support a claim that Applica did not act in a commercially reasonable fashion by effectively going radio silent between September 14 and October 10, 2006. . . .

* * *

Defendants argue aggressively that despite having pled breaches of the Hamilton Beach Merger Agreement, NACCO has not sufficiently pled damages and thus its contract claims should be dismissed. The crux of the "no damages" argument is that NACCO subsequently engaged in a bidding war for Applica and lost. Having been defeated in the marketplace, the defendants claim that NACCO should not have a remedy in court.

* * *

I am comfortable inferring at the pleading stage that if NACCO succeeds in establishing a breach of the Hamilton Beach Merger Agreement, it will be able to establish harm sufficient to invoke this Court's remedial powers. NACCO is entitled to make its case that it should receive its full expectancy damages for breach of the Hamilton Beach Merger Agreement. If it cannot obtain expectancy damages, then NACCO is entitled to prove an alternative damages measure, such as its reliance interest.

In terms of any reliance-based recovery, NACCO will have to contend with its receipt of a bargained-for $4 million termination fee and $2 million in expense reimbursement. But as is customary in merger agreements, Applica's right to terminate the Hamilton Beach Merger Agreement under Section 8.1(h) and pay the fees without further liability depended on Applica complying with its obligations under Section 6.12, including the No-Shop and Prompt Notice Clauses. And Section 8.2 of the Hamilton Beach Merger Agreement excludes from the limitation on liability any termination resulting "from the willful and material breach by a party of any of its representations, warranties or covenants in this Agreement." It is far from clear at this stage that NACCO is bound contractually or factually to the termination fee and expense reimbursement as a measure of recovery.

* * *

C. Count IV States A Claim For Fraud.

. . . I conclude that I have jurisdiction to consider NACCO's fraud claim and that a claim has been adequately pled.

* * *

The fraud claim turns exclusively on statements that Harbinger made in its Section 13 filings between March 8 and August 17, 2006. . . .

* * *

NACCO claims that Harbinger falsely stated it was acquiring shares for investment purposes when in fact it was purchasing shares to control or influence Applica, at a time when it had plans for a merger involving Applica, and at a time when it had plans to defeat NACCO's acquisition of Applica. . . .

* * *

Based on the allegations of the Complaint, NACCO has pled sufficiently that Harbinger's statements regarding its investment intent in its Schedule 13G and 13D filings were false or misleading. In reaching this conclusion, I recognize that my federal colleague considered a similar issue in the context of NACCO's applications for a temporary restraining order, preliminary injunction, and expedited discovery, and wrote that "the Court does not perceive any falsity in Harbinger's filing when they are properly viewed alongside unfolding events." *NACCO Indus., Inc. v. Applica Inc.*, 2006 WL 3762090, at *7 (N.D. Ohio Dec. 20, 2006). That ruling was made in a different procedural posture and on a different record. The district court was asked on a highly expedited basis to consider applications for equitable relief. The district judge did so solely on a paper record consisting of NACCO's complaint, which did not contain references to e-mails and other documents from the Delaware action because the defendants stood on their confidentiality designations.

The district court's determination, made in the context of weighing the likelihood of success for purposes of an injunction application, was necessarily tentative and preliminary. It would not have been binding on the district court in a further proceeding, and it is not binding on me. I, by contrast, am tasked with judging the sufficiency of the Complaint under Rules 9(b) and 12(b)(6). Those rules mandate different standards than were applied by the district court, and I must grant all reasonable inferences to the plaintiff. Given the differences in procedural posture, it is understandable that the district court and I could reach different conclusions. For purposes of the motion to dismiss, I believe that NACCO has sufficiently alleged facts supporting a reasonable inference that Harbinger's statements were false or materially incomplete.

* * *

I am frankly troubled by the reliance inquiry. Even based on the unusual and extreme facts pled in the Complaint, I view it as a close call.

* * *

Prior to the execution of the Hamilton Beach Merger Agreement, if NACCO understood that Harbinger was interested in control or influence and accumulating a large stake for that purpose, NACCO could have sought to have Applica take action in response, and NACCO's and Applica's interests would have been aligned. NACCO could have asked Applica to modify NACCO's standstill agreement so that NACCO could buy shares, and Applica might have agreed to let NACCO take some balancing position. This Court has recognized that the board of directors of a target corporation must comply with its fiduciary duties when enforcing standstill provisions.... The Applica board could well have concluded that permitting NACCO to take a limited balancing position would assist the board in retaining control of its process and obtaining the best transaction reasonably available.

More likely, NACCO could have suggested that Applica cap Harbinger with a rights plan. This is an action that Applica logically would have taken in response to the threat of a creeping takeover.... NACCO also might have suggested that Applica sue Harbinger for Section 13 violations, and to protect its process, Applica might have done so.

After the execution of the Hamilton Beach Merger Agreement, if NACCO had learned the truth about Harbinger's plans, NACCO had the same ability to ask Applica to release NACCO from its standstill or adopt a rights plan. And at that point, NACCO also had rights under the Hamilton Beach Merger Agreement, which required Applica in Section 6.4 to use "reasonable best efforts to cause all of the conditions" to closing to be met.

In addition, had Harbinger's disclosures been candid, NACCO could have moved earlier to enforce the Hamilton Beach Merger Agreement. If NACCO had been able to move earlier, this Court might have been able to accommodate the expedited trial that NACCO originally requested. Because of the factual disputes in this case, this Court only could have issued a mandatory injunction or other affirmative and compulsory relief, such as an order of specific performance, after trial. . . . As events turned out, NACCO did not seek relief until November 13, 2006, and this Court was unable to schedule a timely expedited trial. I do not fault NACCO for deciding not to continue the expedited proceeding it filed in Delaware once it became clear that mandatory relief was effectively unavailable. With truthful disclosures from Harbinger, NACCO might well have filed suit sooner.

In reaching these conclusions, I recognize that the Applica board had some interest in facilitating a topping bid, and that passively allowing Harbinger to establish a position served that goal. We will never know with certainty what would have happened along the alternative timeline I am forced to contemplate. But for present purposes, I conclude that NACCO has alleged a reasonable theory as to why Harbinger sought to mislead NACCO through its Schedule 13 filings and how NACCO reasonably relied to its detriment on Harbinger's disclosures.

This is not to say that NACCO could rely naïvely on what Harbinger said. At some point, NACCO was obligated to protect itself. But this is a difficult line to draw. After Applica announced publicly that it was exploring strategic alternatives, arbitrageurs and hedge funds would naturally move into the stock. Harbinger's initial Schedule 13 filings were thus relatively routine. Nor did Harbinger's continued buying give rise to immediate concerns. Sophisticated investors could readily be expected to continue to accumulate shares after the announcement of the Hamilton Beach Merger Agreement. This transaction contemplated a stock-for-stock merger to create a new entity that would benefit from the synergistic effects of the combination. Investors like Harbinger could recognize the potential value of this transaction and seek to get in on the ground floor, potentially via significant stakes.

In candor, I have sympathy for the proposition that at some point it became unreasonably naïve for NACCO to trust that a hedge fund engaging in conduct resembling a creeping takeover wanted only to receive its ratable share of the benefits of the existing deal. But the line when NACCO's reliance became unreasonable is difficult to draw and is not something I will address on a motion to dismiss. I also resist the idea of insulating wrongdoers and penalizing victims because a fraud arguably became sufficiently apparent that the victim should have known better. I likewise resist the idea that some market players could insulate themselves at the pleadings stage from claims based on false disclosures by arguing that others should know how close to the line they like to play and that their disclosures really should never be believed.

* * *

E. Count III States A Claim For Tortious Interference With Contract.

* * *

. . . As traditionally framed, a claim for tortious interference with contract requires "(1) a contract, (2) about which defendant knew and (3) an intentional act that is a significant factor in causing the breach of such contract (4) without justification (5) which causes injury." *Irwin & Leighton, Inc. v. W.M. Anderson Co.*, 532 A.2d 983, 992 (Del. Ch. 1987) (Allen, C.). There can be no meaningful dispute about the existence of the Hamilton Beach Merger Agreement or Harbinger's knowledge of it. Based on my analysis of Count I, NACCO has pled a claim for breach of contract and has alleged injury flowing from the breach. The issues are therefore elements (3) and (4).

This Court has held that a plaintiff pled a claim for tortious interference with a covenant not to compete when the defendants set out to form a competing business and intentionally solicited the assistance and involvement of an individual whom they knew was bound by the covenant. . . .

I . . . believe that the detailed allegations of fraudulent statements that I discussed in analyzing Count IV provide a sufficient basis for a claim of tortious interference. . . .

* * *

For purposes of the tortious interference analysis, I also take into account Harbinger's success in acquiring a nearly 40% stock position, facilitated at least in part through its false disclosures. . . . Harbinger similarly obtained an unfair advantage over NACCO by accumulating a large stock position based on false disclosures. Because of Harbinger's actions, NACCO did not receive the full benefit of the contractual protections that NACCO bargained for, including the superior proposal mechanism for filtering Applica's access to topping bids. NACCO instead faced a competing bidder with a significant leg up thanks to its improper activities.

* * *

QUESTION

Private equity funds were furious with the holding in this case. Why?

E. MERGERS IN REGULATED INDUSTRIES

One of the most important conditions in any acquisition agreement is a requirement that the parties have secured all necessary government approvals. This is essential in deals that involve *regulated industries*. An array of federal and state agencies govern mergers in specified businesses such as broadcast communications, health care, insurance, commercial banking, public utilities, and national transportation. The number of deals subject to government regulatory oversight is a significant proportion of all acquisitions. In each case, an agency is responsible both for ongoing oversight and for approval of any corporate combinations.

The potential overlap of these regulatory frameworks and the general antitrust law (detailed in Chapter Nine) raises two questions. First, there is the question of which agency or agencies have the authority to review a merger. Second, there is the question of what standard applies to the review of a merger in each particular industry. Usually, Congress does not exempt industry participants from the antitrust laws. There are important exceptions. Rail mergers, as noted in the *Conrail* case in Chapter Six, Section C.2, are subject to the exclusive supervision of the Surface Transportation Board (formerly the Interstate Commerce Commission). While the agencies use standards that generally follow the antitrust provisions, agencies often have more flexibility to consider factors other than competitive effects in markets in analyzing a proposed transaction. In any event, a deal in a regulated industry must always await regulatory approval before it can close.

The approval usually adds time, uncertainty and complexity to the basic deal. Deal participants make an application for approval and respond to information requests. Public authorities make a recommendation, take testimony from all interested parties, issue a final decision and, often, must defend the decision in a judicial appeal.

A good example of these proceedings includes Oregon Electric Utility Co.'s application to purchase Portland General Electric Co. (PGE), a $2.36 billion subsidiary of the bankrupt Enron Corporation. Oregon Electric submitted its application to the Oregon Public Utility Commission (OPUC) and, in July 2004, the staff recommended against that sale to the commissioners. In September of 2004, however, the staff reversed itself and recommended the sale if PGE agreed to thirty-eight specified conditions. The key condition was a $75 million rate credit spread over five years, a one percent rate reduction. State law requires that OPUC find a "net benefit" to the ratepayers in any utility acquisition. Citizen groups demanded a larger concession in the public hearings. On March 10, 2005, OPUC denied Oregon Electric's application. Ultimately, in April 2006, PGE cancelled Enron's stock ownership and issued new shares to its creditors as part of its bankruptcy plan of reorganization. Since then, it has been an independent publicly owned corporation whose shares trade on the NYSE under the ticker symbol "POR."

The facts of *Allegheny* detail a merger in a regulated industry, utilities.

ALLEGHENY ENERGY, INC. V. DQE, INC.

United States Court of Appeals, Third Circuit, 1999.
171 F.3d 153.

POLLAK, J.

This is a diversity case in which an interlocutory appeal has been taken from the denial of a preliminary injunction. The appeal presents a question of Pennsylvania law. The question is whether, on the particular facts of this case, the loss by one publicly traded corporation of a contractual opportunity to acquire another publicly traded corporation through a corporate merger constitutes irreparable harm. In concluding that the plaintiff—the would-be acquiring corporation—was not entitled to a preliminary injunction compelling specific performance of the merger agreement, the district court ruled that if the plaintiff prevailed on the merits it would have an adequate remedy at law in the form of an action for damages. Plaintiff's contention that the loss of the numerous expected benefits of the merger was not quantifiable as damages, and hence constituted irreparable injury, was rejected by the district court. On this appeal, plaintiff renews that contention. We conclude that, in the context of this case, plaintiff's contention is soundly based. Accordingly, we will vacate the judgment of the district court and remand for further proceedings.

* * *

Allegheny Energy, Inc. ("Allegheny") and DQE, Inc. ("DQE")—both of which are utility companies whose shares are traded on the New York Stock Exchange—entered into a merger agreement on April 7, 1997. The agreement envisioned a combined company in which DQE would be a wholly-owned subsidiary of Allegheny. Allegheny is a utility holding company that provides electricity generation, transmission and distribution, chiefly in Pennsylvania, Maryland and West Virginia; its principal operating subsidiary is West Penn, a franchised electric service provider in western Pennsylvania. DQE is also a utility holding company; its principal operating subsidiary is Duquesne, a franchised provider in western Pennsylvania.

* * *

Section 6.1 of the merger agreement has provided rules for the period between the signing of the agreement and consummation of the merger—a consummation contingent both on the stockholder approvals referred to above and on approvals by the relevant regulatory boards.[3] Among the interim rules is a prohibition on any action "that would prevent the Merger from qualifying for 'pooling of interests' accounting treatment." . . .[4]

Other agreement provisions allow either party to abort the agreement prior to consummation under certain conditions. . . .[5]

On August 1, 1997 (about four months after the merger agreement was signed), pursuant to the Pennsylvania restructuring legislation, Duquesne and West Penn—the parties' major operating subsidiaries—each filed restructuring plans with the PUC, and the two filed joint applications for PUC and Federal Energy Regulatory Commission ("FERC") approval of the merger. Almost eight months later, on March 25, 1998, PUC administrative law judges issued recommendations in the Duquesne and

---

[3] Section 6.1 states that each company must operate "in the ordinary and usual course" of business and "use its best efforts" to "preserve its business organization intact and maintain its existing relations and goodwill." Moreover, it generally prohibits either party from unilaterally repurchasing stock, encumbering assets, changing stock-based compensation plans, or changing any compensation and benefit plan. . . .

[4] Under certain circumstances, stock-for-stock mergers may be structured to take advantage of an accounting method—pooling of interests accounting treatment—that provides financial advantages to the newly combined company by permitting the absorbed corporation's assets to be recorded at book value. . . . Valuing the absorbed corporation's assets at book value permits two savings: the combined company avoids recording the absorbed corporation's goodwill and avoids recording the (often higher) fair market value of the absorbed corporation's assets. . . . The combined company is thus freed from the requirement of amortizing the greater costs against its earnings over the ensuing years. . . . A combined corporation emerging from a merger accounted for under the pooling of interests method therefore would report higher annual earnings than the same corporation emerging from a merger accounted for under the traditional purchase method. . . .

In order to qualify for pooling of interests accounting treatment, a merger must meet several conditions. Those requirements fall into three groups: (1) characteristics of the combining companies; (2) manner of the combination; and (3) absence of pre and post-combination transactions. Accounting Principles Board Opinion No. 16, "Business Combinations" (1970). *See also* generally AICPA Accounting Interpretations of APB Opinion No. 16. The third group of requirements is at issue in this case. The APB Opinion and Interpretations identify a number of actions that can frustrate pooling of interests accounting treatment if taken after the signing of a merger agreement and before consummation of the merger. Many of those actions can be taken unilaterally, and several—such as a new stock award plan for officers and directors—can occur without prior public announcement.

[5] Section 8.1 permits termination by mutual written consent of both boards of directors. Section 8.3 permits Allegheny to terminate the agreement under certain circumstances, including a material breach by DQE that cannot be cured within thirty days. Section 8.4 permits DQE to terminate the agreement under certain circumstances, including a material breach by Allegheny that cannot be cured within thirty days. . . .

West Penn restructuring cases. On May 29, 1998, the PUC modified the administrative law judges' recommendations in the two cases. West Penn was disallowed approximately $1 billion of the $1.6 billion in allegedly stranded costs that it had requested. . . .

In a July 23, 1998 Order, the PUC held that the merged company would have to prove that it had mitigated its market power at a market power hearing to be held in the year 2000. Should the merged company fail at that time to establish that it had mitigated its market power, the PUC would order it to divest itself of 2500 megawatts of generation by July 1, 2000. . . .

The FERC—which like the PUC has jurisdiction over market power issues—also found certain elements of the parties' joint proposal related to market power to be inadequate. On September 16, 1998, the FERC ordered the companies either to divest DQE's Cheswick plant prior to the merger or to submit to a hearing on market power mitigation. . . .

DQE was concerned with what it viewed as the "material adverse effects" of the PUC Order in the West Penn case, the PUC market power order, and the FERC market power order. On October 5, 1998, DQE informed Allegheny that, pursuant to Section 8.2(a) of the merger agreement, it was terminating the agreement. Allegheny immediately filed a complaint in the United States District Court for the Western District of Pennsylvania, seeking specific performance of the merger agreement, and—fearing that DQE would take action to scuttle pooling of interests accounting treatment—filed an accompanying motion seeking both a temporary restraining order and a preliminary injunction "enjoining DQE from taking any action that it is precluded from taking without Allegheny's consent under Section 6.1 of the Merger Agreement" until Allegheny's claim for specific performance was decided. . . .

* * *

Allegheny argues that it is entitled to specific performance—not just money damages—because of "the inherent uniqueness of a company sought to be acquired, and the irreparable harm suffered by the party acquiring the company by the loss of the opportunity to own or control that business." . . . DQE disagrees, arguing that corporate combinations are regularly valued.

Pennsylvania law conforms to the general rules regarding the availability of specific performance. "Specific performance should only be granted . . . where no adequate remedy at law exists." *Clark v. Pennsylvania State Police*, 496 Pa. 310, 436 A.2d 1383, 1385 (Pa. 1981) (citing *Roth v. Hartl*, 365 Pa. 428, 75 A.2d 583 (Pa. 1970)). . . .

These general rules are unremarkable. . . .

* * *

We think it clear that the agreed-upon Allegheny-DQE merger constitutes a unique, non-replicable business opportunity for Allegheny. The Joint Proxy Statement filed with the SEC and mailed to both corporations' shareholders describes several respects in which the integration of DQE and Allegheny could be expected to produce particular benefits: the contiguity of Allegheny's and DQE's service territories; DQE's particular expertise—"better than its peer companies"—in "developing unregulated businesses;" the complementarity of Allegheny's "winter-peaking, low cost, efficient operations, and suburban and rural customer base" with DQE's "summer-peaking operations and urban customer base;" the "strategic fit" of DQE's "regulated and unregulated energy products and services" and Allegheny's "core businesses;" "the combined company's ability to take advantage of future strategic opportunities and to reduce its exposure to changes in economic conditions in any segment of its business;" and the expectation that the "combined company [would] . . . have the critical mass necessary to compete in a deregulated utility environment." In the measured prose of the Joint Proxy Statement, "the synergies estimated by the managements of [Allegheny] and DQE appear to be achievable." DQE has not undertaken to identify any available merger partner, other than itself, whose acquisition by Allegheny would yield even one, let alone all, of these very considerable business opportunities. Accordingly, if DQE has breached the merger agreement, Allegheny is entitled to specific performance.

* * *

Subsequent History of the *Allegheny* Case

The case was set for trial and both the District Court and the Third Circuit, on appeal, held that DQE was entitled to terminate the merger agreement. *Allegheny Energy, Inc. v. DQE, Inc.*, 2000 WL 767578 (3d Cir.) (unpublished). DQE terminated the agreement arguing that the financial fallout of Federal Energy Regulatory Commission and Pennsylvania Commission orders involving Allegheny's main subsidiary, West Penn, would be substantial.

West Penn, making up 45 percent of Allegheny's operations, was required to restructure its operations on unfavorable terms. The merger agreement contained a "no material adverse effect" condition that applied to both parties. The condition defined "material adverse effect" to include only effects "taken as a whole" on the parent and subsidiaries and to include regulatory authority orders only if the "effect on one party exceeds such effect on the other party." The Third Circuit struggled with the clause, finding the language "ambiguous . . . the product of negotiation and compromise." The Third Circuit, although noting the existence of facts that supported Allegheny's interpretation that the clause excluded the effects of the specific orders in question, in the end simply deferred to the trial court's findings.

NOTE: REGULATORY EXTORTION?

As noted earlier, mergers in regulated industries are subject to merit regulation by state or federal officials. These approvals can take time and are often the result of attenuated negotiations.

For example, in 2004 the merger of two insurance companies, Anthem Inc. and Wellpoint Health Networks, Inc., required the approval of ten states' insurance commissioners. The $16.4 billion deal sought to create the country's largest managed health care organization. The California Insurance Commissioner, John Garamendi, had authority over a small part of the proposed merger. Wellpoint operated a subsidiary, Blue Cross Life and Health Insurance, in California. His opposition effectively blocked the merger, even though California's Department of Managed Health Care had approved the deal. Once he opposed the merger, insurance commissioners in other states, who had already approved the deal, withdrew their approvals.

Garamendi reversed his position when Anthem agreed to contributions of over $265 million over 20 years to low-income health programs in California. Included in the amount was, for example, $15 million in scholarships for low-income students entering the nursing field, channeled through California's community college network. The scholarship pays not only for tuition but also for childcare and transportation. Another $15 million goes to outreach and enrollment for the state's Health Families and Medi-Cal programs to cover more children. One-hundred million dollars was dedicated to low-income health care projects over 20 years.

The $265 million figure would rise, dollar-for-dollar, if the total amount of golden parachutes paid to departing Wellpoint executives exceeded that amount.

Garamendi also extracted numerous conditions on the operations of the subsidiary including financial constraints on affiliated transactions, dividend payments and rate changes and components. There were several other agreements as well. Among other things, Anthem agreed not to cherry pick clients; agreed to work with Garamendi's staff to develop a new program for indemnity insurance programs and preferred provider organizations to increase coverage for prevention and early detection in specific services; and agreed to boost the percentage of premiums it spends for medical care.

A Wall Street Journal editorial on Garamendi's approval of the merger called it "political extortion." *Garamendi's Tollgate*, WALL ST. J., Nov. 29, 2004, at A14 ("feudal highwayman"). Mr. Garamendi responded with the following letter to the editor:

> "As insurance commissioner of California, it is my duty to protect the rights of insurance consumers in this state. As you assert in your Nov. 29 editorial "Garamendi's Tollgate," I indeed held out for a

better deal for California consumers when Anthem Inc. proposed a $16.4 billion merger with Wellpoint Health Networks. And I got it. The original proposal from Anthem saddled policyholders with a $4 billion bill to pay for the cash cost of the merger, executive compensation and transaction costs. Anthem quantified the annual benefits of the merger at $250 million, so in 16 years policyholders would get their money back with no interest. Certainly the journal would sneer at that return on investment. Adding to the consumer insult were the extraordinary golden parachutes for Wellpoint executives that ranged in value from $200 million to $600 million. Consider that California has more than a million uninsured children; $250 million would purchase health insurance for 200,000 children. California law and most state laws require that I judge the merits of a merger on six criteria. Two of them provide that I may disapprove the transaction if I find that the buyer's plans to change the structure of the entity are not "fair and reasonable to policyholders." It was clear to me that this deal was prejudicial to the interest of the policyholders that I am required by law to protect. There is no law requiring me to protect the greedy excess of corporate executives. Anthem eventually saw the merits of my objection to the merger and agreed to limit premiums so that no part of blue cross life and health company's premium dollar will be used to pay for the cash cost of the merger. Anthem agreed to invest $200 million of its assets in health projects in underserved communities in California, contribute $35 million to fund and support health clinics in those same communities, contribute $15 to the community college system for the training of 2,500 nurses, and another $15 million to enroll children in the healthy families programs. You can characterize my action any way you want, but let me be clear: I will not tolerate corporate greed at the expense of the people I am elected to protect. I vowed to create the best consumer protection agency in the nation and I aim to do just that."

John Garamendi, *"I Take My Job as Consumer Protector Seriously,"* Letter to the Editor, WALL ST. J., Dec. 14, 2005, at A15.

CHAPTER FIVE

FIDUCIARY DUTY IN NEGOTIATED ACQUISITIONS

■ ■ ■

A. INTRODUCTION

As you will note in the cases below, the Delaware Supreme Court uses three basic tests for judging the actions of a selling firm's board in a negotiated acquisition: the basic *business judgment rule* applied in *Smith v. Van* Gorkom, *infra*; the *enhanced scrutiny test* or *Unocal* test (a threshold test for the business judgment rule), applied to deals in which a seller blocks a tender offer or negotiates with one bidder to the exclusion of another (as in *Revlon v. MacAndrews*,[1] *infra*); and the *entire fairness test*, applied to deals in which the directors do not satisfy the requirements of the business judgment rule (e.g., when they are operating under conflicts of interest). E.g., *Mills Acquisition Co. v. Macmillan, Inc.*, *infra*. The enhanced scrutiny test applies to all takeover defenses and is the subject of Chapter Six on hostile bids; the test applies to negotiated acquisitions only when a seller blocks one bidder to protect a negotiated deal with another. Although *deal protection* is an important part of many negotiated deals, we will delay considering the issue, for purposes of educational clarity and economy, until Chapter Six, Section B.2.

In both this Chapter and the next, look for the basic definition of each test and for the facts that are crucial to the court's choice of a test in any given case. Other states have historically followed the lead of the Delaware courts. The increasing complexity of the Delaware jurisprudence, however, is leading some states to chart their own course.

A board of directors owes a fiduciary duty to the corporation. The duty has several components of which the most important are a duty of loyalty, a duty of care, and a duty of candor. The duty of care is a duty not to be lazy, a duty not to shirk one's responsibility for basic skill and competence. The duty of loyalty is a duty not to put one's personal welfare ahead of the

---

[1] The Delaware Supreme Court has stated that the *Unocal* test and the *Revlon* test are applications of the same test. See Paramount Communications v. QVC Network (Chapter Six, Section B.2). The enhanced scrutiny test from *Unocal* applies when a board blocks a takeover or when a board favors one bidder over another. If a board runs a *fair sale* (often a *fair auction*), that is, the board gives all bidders an equal opportunity to buy the firm, the unadorned business judgment rule applies. The *Revlon* case analysis, relevant to whether the firm has given all bidders an equal opportunity, has become, therefore, a part of negotiated acquisition doctrine.

firm's, a duty not to serve "two masters". A duty of candor is a duty to convey to shareholders accurate information on firm matters.

A firm may sue its own board for breaches of the duties. Since managers do not usually sue managers (unless the management team has changed), the shareholders of the firm may sue, in the firm's stead (in *derivative actions*), on the duties. When shareholders allege an injury to themselves as shareholders and not to the firm, they can sue *directly*. See *Tooley v. Donaldson, Lufkin, and Jenrette, Inc.*, 845 A.2d 1031, 1033 (Del. 2004). Since acquisitions usually involve payouts to shareholders, most shareholder claims for breaches of the duties in acquisitions are direct actions. See, e.g., *Parnes v. Bally Entertainment Corp.*, 722 A.2d 1243 (Del. 1999).

B. THE DUTY OF CARE

When plaintiff shareholders may bring claims of a breach of a duty of care, the board attempts to invoke the protections of the *business judgment rule*. If successful the board elevates the standard of culpability to gross negligence; when not successful, under Delaware jurisprudence, the base, fall back standard of culpability is the *entire fairness test*. The application of the entire fairness test in this context in Delaware is a doctrinal hiccup; under traditional doctrine the duty of care, absent the business judgment rule, would be based on ordinary negligence (a duty to use the care others similarly situated would ordinarily and customarily use). Other states that have reached the issue often do use negligence as the base standard.

1. THE TARGET BOARD'S DECISION TO SELL THE COMPANY

SMITH V. VAN GORKOM

Supreme Court of Delaware, 1985.
488 A.2d 858.

HORSEY, JUSTICE.

This appeal from the Court of Chancery involves a class action brought by shareholders of the defendant Trans Union Corporation ("Trans Union" or "the Company"), originally seeking rescission of a cash-out merger of Trans Union into the defendant New T Company ("New T"), a wholly-owned subsidiary of the defendant, Marmon Group, Inc. ("Marmon"). Alternate relief in the form of damages is sought against the defendant members of the Board of Directors of Trans Union, New T, and Jay A. Pritzker and Robert A. Pritzker, owners of Marmon. . . .

Under Delaware law, the business judgment rule is the offspring of the fundamental principle, codified in 8 Del.C. § 141(a), that the business and affairs of a Delaware corporation are managed by or under its board of directors. . . . In carrying out their managerial roles, directors are charged with an unyielding fiduciary duty to the corporation and its shareholders. . . . The business judgment rule exists to protect and promote the full and free exercise of the managerial power granted to Delaware directors. . . . The rule itself "is a presumption that in making a business decision, the directors of a corporation acted on an informed basis, in good faith and in the honest belief that the action taken was in the best interests of the company. . . ." Thus, the party attacking a board decision as uninformed must rebut the presumption that its business judgment was an informed one.

The determination of whether a business judgment is an informed one turns on whether the directors have informed themselves "prior to making a business decision, of all material information reasonably available to them."

Under the business judgment rule there is no protection for directors who have made "an unintelligent or unadvised judgment. . . ." A director's duty to inform himself in preparation for a decision derives from the fiduciary capacity in which he serves the corporation and its stockholders. . . . We think the concept of gross negligence is also the proper standard for determining whether a business judgment reached by a board of directors was an informed one.

In the specific context of a proposed merger of domestic corporations, a director has a duty under 8 Del.C. 251(b), along with his fellow directors, to act in an informed and deliberate manner in determining whether to approve an agreement of merger before submitting the proposal to the stockholders. Certainly in the merger context, a director may not abdicate that duty by leaving to the shareholders alone the decision to approve or disapprove the agreement. . . .

On the record before us, we must conclude that the Board of Directors did not reach an informed business judgment on September 20, 1980 in voting to "sell" the Company for $55 per share pursuant to the Pritzker cash-out merger proposal. [Ed.: Jay A. Pritzker was a well-known takeover specialist.] Our reasons, in summary, are as follows:

The directors (1) did not adequately inform themselves as to Van Gorkom's role in forcing the "sale" of the Company and in establishing the per share purchase price; (2) were uninformed as to the intrinsic value of the Company; and (3) given these circumstances, at a minimum, were grossly negligent in approving the "sale" of the Company upon two hours' consideration, without prior notice, and without the exigency of a crisis or emergency.

As has been noted, the Board based its September 20 decision to approve the cash-out merger primarily on Van Gorkom's [Ed. the Chief Executive Officer and Chairman of the Board of Trans Union] representations. . . . Without any documents before them concerning the proposed transaction, the members of the Board were required to rely entirely upon Van Gorkom's 20-minute oral presentation of the proposal. No written summary of the terms of the merger was presented; the directors were given no documentation to support the adequacy of $55 price per share for sale of the Company; and the Board had before it nothing more than Van Gorkom's statement of his understanding of the substance of an agreement which he admittedly had never read, nor which any member of the Board had ever seen.

Under 8 Del.C. § 141(e), "directors are fully protected in relying in good faith on reports made by officers. . . ." The term "report" has been liberally construed to include reports of informal personal investigations by corporate officers. . . . However, there is no evidence that any "report," as defined under § 141(e), concerning the Pritzker proposal, was presented to the Board on September 20.[16] Van Gorkom's oral presentation of his understanding of the terms of the proposed Merger Agreement, which he had not seen, and Romans' brief oral statement of his preliminary study regarding the feasibility of a leveraged buy-out of Trans Union do not qualify as § 141(e) "reports" for these reasons: the former lacked substance because Van Gorkom was basically uninformed as to the essential provisions of the very document about which he was talking. Romans' statement was irrelevant to the issues before the Board since it did not purport to be a valuation study. At a minimum for a report to enjoy the status conferred by § 141(e), it must be pertinent to the subject matter upon which a board is called to act, and otherwise be entitled to good faith, not blind, reliance. . . .

The defendants rely on the following factors to sustain the Trial Court's finding that the Board's decision was an informed one: (1) the magnitude of the premium or spread between the $55 Pritzker offering price and Trans Union's current market price of $38 per share [Ed. Court's note[2] moved here]; (2) the amendment of the Agreement as submitted on September 20 to permit the Board to accept any better offer during the "market test" period; (3) the collective experience and expertise of the Board's "inside" and "outside" directors; and (4) their reliance on Brennan's legal advice that the directors might be sued if they rejected the Pritzker proposal. We discuss each of these grounds seriatim:

---

[16] In support of the defendants' argument that their judgment as to the adequacy of $55 per share was an informed one, the directors rely on the BCG study and the Five Year Forecast. However, no one even referred to either of these studies at the September 20 meeting; and it is conceded that these materials do not represent valuation studies. Hence, these documents do not constitute evidence as to whether the directors reached an informed judgment on September 20 that $55 per share was a fair value for sale of the Company.

[2] [Ed. The common stock of Trans Union was traded on the New York Stock Exchange. Over the five year period from1975 through 1979, Trans Union's stock had traded within a range of a high of $39 1/2 and a low of $24 1/4. Its high and low range for 1980 through September 19 (the last trading day before announcement of the merger) was $38 1/4–$29 1/2.]

> A substantial premium may provide one reason to recommend a merger, but in the absence of other sound valuation information, the fact of a premium alone does not provide an adequate basis upon which to assess the fairness of an offering price. Here, the judgment reached as to the adequacy of the premium was based on a comparison between the historically depressed Trans Union market price and the amount of the Pritzker offer. Using market price as a basis for concluding that the premium adequately reflected the true value of the Company was a clearly faulty, indeed fallacious, premise, as the defendants' own evidence demonstrates.

The record is clear that before September 20, Van Gorkom and other members of Trans Union's Board knew that the market had consistently undervalued the worth of Trans Union's stock, despite steady increases in the Company's operating income in the seven years preceding the merger. . . . Van Gorkom testified that he did not believe the market price accurately reflected Trans Union's true worth; and several of the directors testified that, as a general rule, most chief executives think that the market undervalues their companies' stock. Yet, on September 20, Trans Union's Board apparently believed that the market stock price accurately reflected the value of the Company for the purpose of determining the adequacy of the premium for its sale.

In the Proxy Statement, however, the directors reversed their position. There, they stated that, although the earnings prospects for Trans Union were "excellent," they found no basis for believing that this would be reflected in future stock prices. With regard to past trading, the Board stated that the prices at which the Company's common stock had traded in recent years did not reflect the "inherent" value of the Company. But having referred to the "inherent" value of Trans Union, the directors ascribed no number to it. Moreover, nowhere did they disclose that they had no basis on which to fix "inherent" worth beyond an impressionistic reaction to the premium over market and an unsubstantiated belief that the value of the assets was "significantly greater" than book value. By their own admission they could not rely on the stock price as an accurate measure of value. Yet, also by their own admission, the Board members assumed that Trans Union's market price was adequate to serve as a basis upon which to assess the adequacy of the premium for purposes of the September 20 meeting.

The parties do not dispute that a publicly-traded stock price is solely a measure of the value of a minority position and, thus, market price represents only the value of a single share. Nevertheless, on September 20, the Board assessed the adequacy of the premium over market, offered by Pritzker, solely by comparing it with Trans Union's current and historical stock price. . . .

Indeed, as of September 20, the Board had no other information on which to base a determination of the intrinsic value of Trans Union as a going concern. As of September 20, the Board had made no evaluation of the Company designed to value the entire enterprise, nor had the Board ever previously considered selling the Company or consenting to a buy-out merger. Thus, the adequacy of a premium is indeterminate unless it is assessed in terms of other competent and sound valuation information that reflects the value of the particular business.

Despite the foregoing facts and circumstances, there was no call by the Board, either on September 20 or thereafter, for any valuation study or documentation of the $55 price per share as a measure of the fair value of the Company in a cash-out context. It is undisputed that the major asset of Trans Union was its cash flow. Yet, at no time did the Board call for a valuation study taking into account that highly significant element of the Company's assets.

We do not imply that an outside valuation study is essential to support an informed business judgment; nor do we state that fairness opinions by independent investment bankers are required as a matter of law. Often insiders familiar with the business of a going concern are in a better position than are outsiders to gather relevant information; and under appropriate circumstances, such directors may be fully protected in relying in good faith upon the valuation reports of their management. *See* 8 Del.C. § 141(e). . . .

Here, the record establishes that the Board did not request its Chief Financial Officer, Romans, to make any valuation study or review of the proposal to determine the adequacy of $55 per share for sale of the Company. On the record before us: The Board rested on Romans' elicited response that the $55 figure was within a "fair price range" within the context of a leveraged buy-out. No director sought any further information from Romans. No director asked him why he put $55 at the bottom of his range. No director asked Romans for any details as to his study, the reason why it had been undertaken or its depth. No director asked to see the study, and no director asked Romans whether Trans Union's finance department could do a fairness study within the remaining 36-hour period available under the Pritzker offer.

Had the Board, or any member, made an inquiry of Romans, he presumably would have responded as he testified: that his calculations were rough and preliminary; and, that the study was not designed to determine the fair value of the Company but rather to assess the feasibility of a leveraged buy-out financed by the Company's projected cash flow, making certain assumptions as to the purchaser's borrowing needs. Romans would have presumably also informed the Board of his view, and the widespread view of Senior Management, that the timing of the offer was wrong and the offer inadequate.

The record also establishes that the Board accepted without scrutiny Van Gorkom's representation as to the fairness of the $55 price per share for sale of the Company—a subject that the Board had never previously considered. The Board thereby failed to discover that Van Gorkom had suggested the $55 price to Pritzker and, most crucially, that Van Gorkom had arrived at the $55 figure based on calculations designed solely to determine the feasibility of a leveraged buy-out.[19] No questions were raised either as to the tax implications of a cash-out merger or how the price for the one million share option granted Pritzker was calculated.

We do not say that the Board of Directors was not entitled to give some credence to Van Gorkom's representation that $55 was an adequate or fair price. Under § 141(e), the directors were entitled to rely upon their chairman's opinion of value and adequacy, provided that such opinion was reached on a sound basis. Here, the issue is whether the directors informed themselves as to all information that was reasonably available to them. Had they done so, they would have learned of the source and derivation of the $55 price and could not reasonably have relied thereupon in good faith.

None of the directors, Management or outside, were investment bankers or financial analysts. Yet the Board did not consider recessing the meeting until a later hour that day (or requesting an extension of Pritzker's Sunday evening deadline) to give it time to elicit more information as to the sufficiency of the offer, either from inside Management (in particular Romans) or from Trans Union's own investment banker, Salomon Brothers, whose Chicago specialist in merger and acquisitions was known to the Board and familiar with Trans Union's affairs.

Thus, the record compels the conclusion that on September 20 the Board lacked valuation information adequate to reach an informed business judgment as to the fairness of $55 per share for sale of the Company.[20]

This brings us to the post-September 20 "market test" upon which the defendants ultimately rely to confirm the reasonableness of their September 20 decision to accept the Pritzker proposal. In this connection, the directors present a two-part argument: (a) that by making a "market test" of Pritzker's $55 per share offer a condition of their September 20 decision to accept his offer, they cannot be found to have acted impulsively

---

19 As of September 20, the directors did not know: that Van Gorkom had arrived at the $55 figure alone and subjectively, as the figure to be used by Controller Peterson in creating a feasible structure for a leveraged buy-out by a prospective purchaser; that Van Gorkom had not sought advice, information, or assistance from either inside or outside Trans Union directors as to the value of the Company as an entity or the fair price per share for 100% of its stock; that Van Gorkom had not consulted with the Company's investment bankers or other financial analysts; that Van Gorkom had not consulted with or confided in any officer or director of the Company except Chelberg; and that Van Gorkom had deliberately chosen to ignore the advice and opinion of the members of his Senior Management group regarding the adequacy of the $55 price.

20 For a far more careful and reasoned approach taken by another board of directors faced with the pressures of a hostile tender offer, *see* Pogostin v. Rice, *supra* at 623–627.

or in an uninformed manner on September 20; and (b) that the adequacy of the $17 premium for sale of the Company was conclusively established over the following 90 to 120 days by the most reliable evidence available—the marketplace. Thus, the defendants impliedly contend that the "market test" eliminated the need for the Board to perform any other form of fairness test either on September 20, or thereafter.

Again, the facts of record do not support the defendants' argument. There is no evidence: (a) that the Merger Agreement was effectively amended to give the Board freedom to put Trans Union up for auction sale to the highest bidder; or (b) that a public auction was in fact permitted to occur. The minutes of the Board meeting make no reference to any of this. Indeed, the record compels the conclusion that the directors had no rational basis for expecting that a market test was attainable, given the terms of the Agreement as executed during the evening of September 20. . . .

> The Merger Agreement, specifically identified as that originally presented to the Board on September 20, has never been produced by the defendants, notwithstanding the plaintiffs' several demands for production before as well as during trial. No acceptable explanation of this failure to produce documents has been given to either the Trial Court or this Court. . . .

Van Gorkom states that the Agreement as submitted incorporated the ingredients for a market test by authorizing Trans Union to receive competing offers over the next 90-day period. However, he concedes that the Agreement barred Trans Union from actively soliciting such offers and from furnishing to interested parties any information about the Company other than that already in the public domain. Whether the original Agreement of September 20 went so far as to authorize Trans Union to receive competitive proposals is arguable. . . .

The defendants attempt to downplay the significance of the prohibition against Trans Union's actively soliciting competing offers by arguing that the directors "understood that the entire financial community would know that Trans Union was for sale upon the announcement of the Pritzker offer, and anyone desiring to make a better offer was free to do so." Yet, the press release issued on September 22, with the authorization of the Board, stated that Trans Union had entered into "definitive agreements" with the Pritzkers; and the press release did not even disclose Trans Union's limited right to receive and accept higher offers. Accompanying this press release was a further public announcement that Pritzker had been granted an option to purchase at any time one million shares of Trans Union's capital stock at 75 cents above the then-current price per share.

Thus, notwithstanding what several of the outside directors later claimed to have "thought" occurred at the meeting, the record compels the conclusion that Trans Union's Board had no rational basis to conclude on September 20 or in the days immediately following, that the Board's acceptance of Pritzker's offer was conditioned on (1) a "market test" of the offer; and (2) the Board's right to withdraw from the Pritzker Agreement and accept any higher offer received before the shareholder meeting.

The directors' unfounded reliance on both the premium and the market test as the basis for accepting the Pritzker proposal undermines the defendants' remaining contention that the Board's collective experience and sophistication was a sufficient basis for finding that it reached its September 20 decision with informed, reasonable deliberation. . . .[21]

Part of the defense is based on a claim that the directors relied on legal advice rendered at the September 20 meeting by James Brennan, Esquire, who was present at Van Gorkom's request. . . .

Several defendants testified that Brennan advised them that Delaware law did not require a fairness opinion or an outside valuation of the Company before the Board could act on the Pritzker proposal. If given, the advice was correct. However, that did not end the matter. Unless the directors had before them adequate information regarding the intrinsic value of the Company, upon which a proper exercise of business judgment could be made, mere advice of this type is meaningless; and, given this record of the defendants' failures, it constitutes no defense here.[22]

A second claim is that counsel advised the Board it would be subject to lawsuits if it rejected the $55 per share offer. It is, of course, a fact of corporate life that today when faced with difficult or sensitive issues, directors often are subject to suit, irrespective of the decisions they make. However, counsel's mere acknowledgement of this circumstance cannot be rationally translated into a justification for a board permitting itself to be stampeded into a patently unadvised act. While suit might result from the rejection of a merger or tender offer, Delaware law makes clear that a board acting within the ambit of the business judgment rule faces no ultimate liability. . . . Thus, we cannot conclude that the mere threat of litigation, acknowledged by counsel, constitutes either legal advice or any valid basis upon which to pursue an uninformed course.

---

[21] Trans Union's five "inside" directors had backgrounds in law and accounting, 116 years of collective employment by the Company and 68 years of combined experience on its Board. Trans Union's five "outside" directors included four chief executives of major corporations and an economist who was a former dean of a major school of business and chancellor of a university. The "outside" directors had 78 years of combined experience as chief executive officers of major corporations and 50 years of cumulative experience as directors of Trans Union. Thus, defendants argue that the Board was eminently qualified to reach an informed judgment on the proposed "sale" of Trans Union notwithstanding their lack of any advance notice of the proposal, the shortness of their deliberation, and their determination not to consult with their investment banker or to obtain a fairness opinion.

[22] Nonetheless, we are satisfied that in an appropriate factual context a proper exercise of business judgment may include, as one of its aspects, reasonable reliance upon the advice of counsel. This is wholly outside the statutory protections of 8 Del.C. § 141(e) involving reliance upon reports of officers, certain experts and books and records of the company.

[Ed.: The court also held that the board did not "cure" its breach of its duty of care with its later efforts to consider whether there were other potential bidders at the October 6 and January 26 meetings.]

The defendants ultimately rely on the stockholder vote of February 10 for exoneration. The defendants contend that the stockholders' "overwhelming" vote approving the Pritzker Merger Agreement had the legal effect of curing any failure of the Board to reach an informed business judgment in its approval of the merger[Ed.[3]] . . . [W]e find that Trans Union's stockholders were not fully informed of all facts material to their vote on the Pritzker Merger . . . . We list the material deficiencies in the proxy materials:

(1) The fact that the Board had no reasonably adequate information indicative of the intrinsic value of the Company, other than a concededly depressed market price, was without question material to the shareholders voting on the merger. . . .

Accordingly, the Board's lack of valuation information should have been disclosed. Instead, the directors cloaked the absence of such information in both the Proxy Statement and the Supplemental Proxy Statement. Through artful drafting, noticeably absent at the September 20 meeting, both documents create the impression that the Board knew the intrinsic worth of the Company. . . . [Ed. The list continues with judicial demands that the board explicitly disclose that it was ignorant and had failed to investigate before the court would say that it had fully informed the shareholders, a demand, of course, that is impossible for a board to meet.]

MCNEILLY, JUSTICE, dissenting:

. . . Directors of this caliber are not ordinarily taken in by a "fast shuffle." I submit they were not taken into this multi-million dollar corporate transaction without being fully informed and aware of the state of the art as it pertained to the entire corporate panorama of Trans Union. . . . These men knew Trans Union like the back of their hands and were more than well qualified to make on the spot informed business judgments concerning the affairs of Trans Union including a 100% sale of the corporation. Lest we forget, the corporate world of then and now operates on what is so aptly referred to as "the fast track". These men were at the time an integral part of that world, all professional business men, not intellectual figureheads. . . .

---

[3] [Ed. In Gantler v. Steven, 965 A.2d 695 (Del. 2009), the Court overruled the statement in *Van Gorkom* that a fully informed vote of shareholders would defeat a shareholder claim. The Court held that such a vote would reinstate a business judgment rule standard for a board decision.]

NOTE: THE EFFECT OF VAN GORKOM ON STOCK PRICES, FAIRNESS OPINIONS, D & O INSURANCE, AND SHIELD STATUTES

Researchers have found that, in spite of all the attention the case has received in the business community, it had no effect on the market value of Delaware corporations. Michael Bradley & Cindy A. Schipani, *The Relevance of the Duty of Care Standard in Corporate Governance*, 75 IOWA L. REV. 1 (1989) (hereinafter *Relevance*). The finding is consistent with the view that the decision had no real impact on the way Delaware corporations were managed or the way the stock of these firms was priced by the market. Perhaps investors believed that later courts would construe the decision narrowly, applying it only to takeovers, and that liability under the decision's reasoning could be easily avoided by obtaining a fairness opinion from an investment banker and otherwise creating a proper paper trail for any acquisition decision. The *Van Gorkom* case did create more work for independent investment bankers. There was a surge in the demand for one-page *fairness opinions* to target boards in takeovers at $500,000 a pop and up. Target boards' use of fairness opinions seems to have returned to pre-1986 levels, but the portion of revenues that the financial industry earns for deal advisory services (usually paid on a contingency basis and relative to the size of the deal) has sky-rocketed. See Helen M. Bowers, *Fairness Opinions and the Business Judgment Rule: An Empirical Investigation of Target Firms' Use of Fairness Opinions*, 96 NW. U. L. REV. 567 (2002). The case also created more work for lawyers, who craft board procedures and draft merger agreements to minimize the risk of liability under the decision. What procedures do they recommend?[4]

Interestingly, however, directors' and officers' liability insurance (D & O insurance) rates increased more than twelve-fold in the year the decision was rendered. See *Relevance*, at 73. Moreover, the common stock of firms that write D & O insurance rose significantly in price. This increase in equity led the authors of the study to suggest that "insurers were able to increase their premiums beyond the actuarially fair level. . . . Increase in liability premiums was not due to an expected increase in liability claims. Rather, the increase in premiums was due to the inelasticity of demand for corporate liability insurance and the hyperbole surrounding the Trans Union decision." *Id.* at 75.

Since *Van Gorkom,* selling firms have not had any trouble purchasing fairness opinions to support whatever view of the price the board holds ("is fair" or "is not fair"). The running joke in the M&A community is that "there is nothing fair about fairness opinions." The press has focused on the more sensational examples of valuation discrepancies in the opinions.[5] For example,

---

[4] At issue is whether the procedures increase the probability of good decisions. Compare Fred S. McChesney, *A Bird in the Hand and Liability in the Bush: Why Van Gorkom Still Rankles, Probably*, 96 NW. U.L. REV. 631 (2002) (no), with Lynn A. Stout, *In Praise of Procedure: An Economic and Behavioral Defense of* Smith v. Van Gorkom *and the Business Judgment Rule*, 90 NW. U.L. REV. 675 (2002) (yes).

[5] Gretchen Morgenson, *Just How Fair are Fairness Opinions?*, INT'L HERALD TRIB., May 31, 2005, at 13. See also Gretchen Morgenson, *Mirror, Mirror, Who is the Unfairest?*, N.Y. TIMES, May 29, 2005, Sec. 3, at 1.

for acquisitions in 2004 in which both the acquirers and targets sought fairness opinions, the target's advisers typically valued the merger consideration received by their clients, relative to the offer price, at 34 percent higher than their counterparts for the acquirers. Defenders of fairness opinion practice argue that the opinions are misperceived: A fairness opinion is not intended to determine whether the financial terms of a transaction are the best possible terms available. An opinion is intended to opine on whether the financial terms of a transaction are within a *range of fairness*.

The most poignant criticism of fairness opinions is that conflicts of interest color the valuation: An opinion provider, usually an investment bank, often provides a range of other lucrative services to the hiring company (some in the deal itself—it is the deal underwriting, market-maker, lender or asset manager—and others not deal related) and the opinion providers often are paid a substantial bonus if the deal closes ("success fees"). The Financial Industry Regulatory Authority (FINRA), the self-regulatory organization that regulates National Association of Securities Dealers (NASD) member broker-dealers, responded to the criticism with Rule 5150.[6] The Rule requires a full disclosure of the success fee arrangement and of any other work done for a client, but does not otherwise change prevailing practice.

The lasting effect of the *Van Gorkom* case on corporate law came in the immediate legislative enactment of *shield statutes*. Delaware's is in § 102(b)(7) in the Delaware General Corporation Law:

> (b) . . . [T]his certificate of incorporation may also contain . . . the following: . . .
>
> (7) A provision eliminating or limiting the personal liability of a director to the corporation or its shareholders for monetary damages for breach of fiduciary duty as a director, provided that such provision shall not eliminate or limit the liability of a director; (i) For any breach of the director's duty of loyalty to the corporation or its stockholders; (ii) for acts or omissions not in good faith or which involve intentional misconduct or a knowing violation of law; (iii) under section 174 of this title [Unlawful Distributions]; or (iv) for any transaction from which the director derived an improper personal benefit. . . .

Over forty states have adopted a version of the Delaware shield statutes). At their first annual shareholder meeting held after the adoption of § 102(b)(7), over 300 firms passed charter amendments (known as *raincoat* provisions) waiving director liability to the full extent allowed under the provision. The Model Act has a cleaner version of the Delaware section in § 2.02(b)(4) (subsection (ii) of the Delaware provision, with its good faith language which has caused problems in application, is omitted as duplicative of section (iv)). ABA Model Bus. Corp. Act § 2.02(b)(4) (2016 rev.). Some states have much

[6] Originally NASD Rule 2290 (eff. Dec. 8, 2007). Investment banks that provide fairness opinions are typically registered broker-dealers and NASD members. The Rule requires member firms of the NASD to comply with specified disclosure and procedural requirements in rendering fairness opinions.

stronger shield statutes. See, e.g., Ohio Gen. Corp. L § 1701.59(D) (an opt out rather than an opt in provision). These shield provisions substantially weakened all shareholders suits against boards for damages based on claims of breaches of the duty of care.

Researchers studying the effect of § 102(b)(7) found that the passage of the law correlated with a significant decrease in the equity value of firms incorporated in Delaware relative to those incorporated elsewhere. See *Relevance*, at 74. The results startled the authors of the study: The cumulative abnormal return to Delaware firms over the months surrounding the effective date of the section was a negative 2.96 percent, the largest drop found in any recent research on various other takeover defenses. Moreover, the researchers found that most of the 559 firms that elected to adopt the protections of the Delaware statute experienced a second significant decrease in the market value of their common stock when they first announced their intention to pass amendments to their articles to make use of the section. The authors concluded that "available evidence seems to be mounting that legal rules are important constraints on the behavior of corporate managers." *Id.* at 70.

NOTE: THE DELAWARE DOCTRINAL QUAGMIRE—OF THRESHOLDS AND FALL-BACK TESTS

The primary advantage of the business judgment rule is that the defendants, if they are successful in asserting the defense, can win the case on summary motions without going through a full trial. The summary motions may be motions to dismiss on the pleadings, summary judgment motions that include deposition testimony, or motions for preliminary injunctions that require the court to declare whether there is a "substantial likelihood" of success on the merits at trial. If the board loses the summary motions then a full trial becomes inevitable. The parties usually settle after a decision on summary motions; the plaintiff settles for nuisance value with a loss on the motions and the defendant settles for big bucks to avoid the embarrassments of trial if the reverse is true.

Van Gorkom was an odd decision in many ways.[7] Doctrinally it established a precedent for expanding the *thresholds* of the business judgment rule. The language of the case itself was odd in that the new threshold for information was a gross negligence test, identical in effect to the business judgment rule itself, for which the new test was a threshold. More significantly, the court took a classic business decision, a decision to act or gather more information, when unaffected by conflict of interest, outside the business judgment rule. Why do judges know more than boards about when to act and when to do further research? This threshold approach reappeared in hostile takeover cases later.

---

[7] There is a sound argument for the proposition that the board took what it knew to be a good deal for its shareholders, based on a comparison of the sales premium to the average sales premiums of other comparable company sales. The Chancery Court, on remand, was going to struggle granting damages for shareholder injury. The Court's abuse on common notions of finance to rely on notions of an *intrinsic value* apart from a market price in a liquid and deep public market also raised eyebrows.

Here is the sequence. In *Unocal* in 1985, the court established a new threshold for target defenses to hostile tender offers, the *enhanced scrutiny* test.[8] In *Revlon* in 1986 the new threshold applied to efforts to block one bidder (the *raider*) and sell to another (the *white knight*). The target has to run a fair form of auction, the threshold, before the business judgment rule applies. Inevitably, the *Revlon* threshold came to apply whenever a company agrees to sell itself in any form of negotiated acquisition. See Chapter Six, Section B.2. Did the company treat all hopeful friendly suitors fairly in the sales process? Moreover, the *Unocal* threshold came to apply in any case of a negotiated deal with a single suitor if the deal included deal protections covenants, as most now do. As such, the *Unocal* and *Revlon* thresholds now eclipse the business judgment rule with respect to negotiated deals that do not involve conflicts of interest. When applying the *Revlon* threshold in multiple suitor cases, the Delaware courts now struggle to get back to a synthetic business judgment rule analysis ("we do not tell boards how to structure sales . . . " and so on.)[9] Added to that is the now difficult line drawing exercise of exactly when the *Revlon* threshold applies. The deal protection cases and auction cases appear below in Chapter Six.

A second new threshold analysis appeared with the *Disney* case[10] on executive compensation. The good faith language in Del. Gen. Corp. L. § 102(b)(7) and traditional case law has long been a condition of applying a business judgment rule analysis. Most had assumed it was an alternative statement of a requirement that there were no conflicts of interest. The *Disney* court held that the good faith language was an independent test based on a deliberate disregard of one's duties as a board member. This new understanding of old language created a new threshold for applying the business judgment rule in acquisitions. Although the Delaware court, in response perhaps to heavy criticism, has defined the new doctrine very narrowly; so narrowly that it now has a questionable independent sphere of effect—the new threshold will occupy acquisition lawyers. As seen in the *Lyondell* case below, the *Revlon* and *Disney* threshold tests now apply to any analysis of a common negotiated acquisition between independent, sophisticated parties.

The failure to meet a threshold meant the plaintiffs had defeated the business judgment rule defense. What test applied? Many before 1993 had assumed that a failure to claim the advantages of the business judgment rule in a duty of care case meant that the board of directors would be tried under an unadorned *negligence* standard. Delaware does not specify a basic duty of care test in its corporation code, e.g., Del. Gen. Corp. L. § 141(a), but many states do. The Model Act, for example, states that "members of the board of directors . . . when becoming informed . . . or devoting attention to their

---

[8] This test has bifurcated into a multiple layered test as we shall see in the next Chapter.

[9] One now reads, for example, that the *Revlon* analysis has two "key features": determining the adequacy of the decisionmaking process employed by the directors; and determining the reasonableness of the directors' actions under the circumstances then existing. See, e.g., In re Dollar Thrifty Shareholder Litig., 14 A.3d 573, 596 (Del. Ch. 2010).

[10] In re Disney Derv. Litig., 906 A.2d 97 (Del. 2006)

oversight duties, shall discharge their duties with the care that a person in a like position would reasonably believe appropriate under similar circumstances." ABA Model Bus. Corp. Act § 8.30(b) (2016 rev.). See also Ohio § 1701.59(B) ("director shall perform the director's duties . . . in good faith, in a manner in or not opposed to the best interests of the corporation, and with the care that an ordinarily prudent person in a like position would use under similar circumstances"). This is a version of a classic negligence test. The Delaware Supreme Court in one of the many bad opinions in the horrific *Technicolor* litigation, rejected the negligence test in favor of an *entire fairness test* as the basic standard if a board is not protected by the business judgment rule. *Cede & Co v. Technicolor, Inc.,* 634 A.2d 345, 361 (Del. 1993). Other states may not follow this analysis.

What is the difference between an entire fairness test and a true negligence test? Consider the *Technicolor* case itself. On remand, the Chancellor, after one of the longest trials in Delaware court history, held that the price was entirely fair. The Delaware Supreme Court affirmed, and gave a road map for Delaware law on the application of the test in duty of care cases. *Cinerama, Inc. v. Technicolor*, 663 A.2d 1156 (Del. 1995). The entire fairness test has two parts, a *fair dealing* analysis and a *fair price* analysis, and then a "disciplined balancing" of the two tests. Under the fair dealing analysis, the court investigates the timing of the transaction, the initiation of the transaction, the negotiation of the transaction, the structure of the transaction, the disclosure to directors, the approval of directors, the disclosure to shareholders, and the approval of the shareholders. In the fair price analysis, the court assesses whether the price was the "highest price reasonably available." Keep in mind that all this effort to affirm a deal came in a strategic deal in which there was no conflict of interest; it was a deal between two sophisticated, independent parties, with top flight lawyers and investment bankers as advisors. A negligence based decision would have included substantial deference to custom and practice.

2. THE PURCHASING BOARD'S DECISION TO ACQUIRE A COMPANY

ASH V. MCCALL

Delaware Court of Chancery, 2000.
2000 WL 1370341.

CHANDLER, CHANCELLOR.

Shareholder plaintiffs Arlene Ash, Noel Saito, Kimberly Madajczyk and Sydney H. Dalman assert derivative claims on behalf of McKesson HBOC, Inc. ("McKesson HBOC" or the "Company"), a Delaware corporation, which was formed through the merger of McKesson Corporation ("McKesson") and HBOC & Co. ("HBOC") on January 12, 1999. Approximately 3 1/2 months after McKesson's acquisition of HBOC became effective, McKesson HBOC issued the first of what appears to be three downward revisions of revenues, earnings, net income, and other financial information, for financial years 1996–1998. The complaint generally asserts claims related to these revisions. Pending before me is defendants' motion to dismiss. . . . After the merger, six directors from each pre-merger company comprised the combined Company's board of directors. . . .

The due care claim alleges that the directors of McKesson and the directors of HBOC breached their duty of care by failing to inform themselves of all reasonably available material information before deciding to enter into, and recommend, the merger. Put another way, plaintiffs contend that the directors breached their duty of care by failing to detect HBOC's accounting irregularities during the course of due diligence investigations performed in connection with the merger.

red flags

Here lies the heart of the lawsuit against former McKesson directors and, to a lesser extent, former HBOC directors.[21] Plaintiffs contend that the directors missed several "red flags" that should have alerted them to the accounting problems, in the course of full-scale due diligence, before they approved the merger. Plaintiffs then allege that the directors failed to identify the accounting defects, with some degree of mental culpability ranging from actual knowledge to gross recklessness, reckless disregard, just plain recklessness and, finally, gross negligence.

The notion that McKesson directors had actual knowledge of HBOC's earnings overstatements and nonetheless proceeded with the merger finds no support in the amended complaint. Moreover, it is simply illogical to presume that McKesson directors would knowingly cause McKesson to acquire a company with significant, undisclosed earnings misstatements. Nothing in the pleadings remotely suggests a reason why McKesson would purposefully buy such a company; nor do the pleadings offer anything by way of explanation—not a single fact or theory that could possibly support such a conclusion.

Taking all the facts in the complaint as true, and reading every conceivable inference in plaintiffs' favor, inexorably leads to the conclusion that plaintiffs' claims sound in negligence, at most. The McKesson board determined that it was in McKesson's strategic interests to enter the healthcare information technology business. It then acted on that objective

---

[21] I characterize this claim as primarily directed against the McKesson directors because the merger represented something of a windfall to the HBOC shareholders to the extent that the losses borne by HBOC shareholders in connection with the accounting irregularities were serendipitously halved (or thereabout) by virtue of the merger. In other words, because HBOC shareholders received properly valued McKesson stock for their own improperly or, rather, overvalued HBOC stock, and held only a 60 percent interest in the combined company, as opposed to all of it when the irregularities were disclosed and the stock price plummeted, HBOC shareholders bore only 60 percent of whatever losses accrued from the accounting irregularities, as opposed to 100%. Former McKesson shareholders, undoubtedly to their chagrin, bore the remaining 40 percent of the losses. Put more simply, by reducing their ownership interest in the company containing the earnings overstatements from 100% to 60% through the merger, HBOC shareholders reduced their exposure to the overstatements by the same amount.

by pursuing a business combination with HBOC—one of the leading companies in the field. It hired expert accounting and financial advisors to perform due diligence on HBOC—DeLoitte & Touche and Bear Stearns, respectively. After DeLoitte and Bear Stearns completed their due diligence reviews, with the participation of McKesson management, they waived "green flags" to the McKesson board, in effect saying, "This merger is financially and strategically sound." The McKesson directors approved the merger.

Defendants characterize the "red flags" that plaintiffs make so much of as "dated," "obscure," and "inconsequential" relative to the prominent "green flags" given to the directors by the accounting and financial experts who conducted due diligence reviews in advance of the merger. When plaintiffs' "red flags" are juxtaposed with the clean bill of health given by DeLoitte and Bear Stearns after due diligence reviews, the complaint permits one conclusion: that the McKesson directors' reliance on the views expressed by their advisors was in good faith. What would plaintiffs have the McKesson board do in the course of making an acquisition other than hire a national accounting firm and investment bank to examine the books and records of the target company? Nothing in the pleadings otherwise casts doubt on the good faith of the McKesson directors.[23]

Undaunted by the facts alleged in their own complaint, plaintiffs contend that "there is no authority for defendants' argument that the directors here are entitled to abdicate their duties to their experts." It is, in reality, plaintiffs' argument that is without basis in fact or law. Directors of Delaware corporations quite properly delegate responsibility to qualified experts in a host of circumstances. One circumstance is surely due diligence review of a target company's books and records. To delegate this assignment is not an "abdication" of duty.

The complaint here, fairly read, alleges that the McKesson directors were advised by their experts (DeLoitte and Bear Stearns) and that they relied on their expertise in conducting due diligence ancillary to the proposed merger. So the question becomes whether such directors are to be "fully protected" on the basis that they relied in good faith on qualified experts under 8 Del. C. § 141(e). The McKesson board is entitled to the presumption that it exercised proper business judgment, including proper reliance on experts. Plaintiffs have not rebutted the presumption with particularized facts creating reason to believe that the McKesson board's conduct was grossly negligent. That is, plaintiffs have not alleged particularized facts (in contrast with conclusions) that, if proved, would show that (1) the directors in fact did not rely on the expert, or (2) that their reliance was not in good faith, or (3) that they did not reasonably believe

[23] If these facts demonstrate anything, it is merely that DeLoitte, Bear Stearns, and McKesson management performed shoddy due diligence. Plaintiffs have not brought claims against any of these parties.

that the experts' advice was within the experts' professional competence, or (4) that the directors were at fault for not selecting experts with reasonable care, or (5) that the issue (here, alleged accounting deficiencies in HBOC's financial records) was so obvious that the board's failure to detect it was grossly negligent regardless of the experts' advice, or (6) that the board's decision was so unconscionable as to constitute waste or fraud. This complaint is devoid of particularized allegations along these lines and is, therefore, incapable of surviving a motion to dismiss.

> In determining whether the complaint creates any doubt that the McKesson directors used due care in approving the merger, the Court considers whether the directors: (i) informed themselves of available critical information before approving the transaction; (ii) considered expert opinion; (iii) provided all Board members with adequate and timely notice of the [transaction] before the full Board meeting and of its purpose; or (iv) inquired adequately into the reasons for or terms of [the transaction]. . . .

Plaintiffs have not alleged facts creating a reasonable doubt that the McKesson directors did not act in accordance with any of these guidelines. Plaintiffs' allegations that directors were less than fully informed of reasonably available material information or that they considered the merger in any other procedurally unsound manner relies entirely on the wisdom of hindsight. The complaint fails to create a reasonable doubt that the informational component of the McKesson directors' decision-making process, measured by the concept of gross negligence, included consideration of all material information reasonably available.

Defendants have also directed the Court's attention to exculpatory charter provisions, enacted under 8 Del. C. § 102(b)(7), in McKesson's and the combined McKesson HBOC's articles of incorporation. Although the exculpatory provisions serve as adequate independent grounds for dismissing the due care claim, I principally rely on plaintiffs' failure to allege particularized facts, creating a reasonable doubt that the merger, at the time it was entered into, was other than a valid exercise of business judgment. . . .

[A]lthough it is not pleaded in the existing complaint, certain allegations made in the amended complaint and during oral argument on the motion suggest that the current shareholders of the combined McKesson HBOC may be able to assert a claim for breach of fiduciary duty directly against the directors of the combined company as a result of the directors' decision not to pursue a potential claim against the former directors of HBOC for the (alleged) fraud in connection with HBOC's accounting practices. If the directors of the combined company decided not to pursue this potential claim in a manner that is grossly negligent or self-interested, such decision may itself give rise to a potential claim for breach of the fiduciary duties of care or loyalty. That claim would be separate and distinct from a claim based on the failure of HBOC's directors to oversee or monitor properly the accounting practices at HBOC before the merger. . . .

. . . Although one may speculate as to the reasons behind McKesson's disinclination to take legal action against HBOC and its officers and directors, such speculation is completely idle absent nonconclusory allegations of fact.[58]

NOTE: THE "SHOP 'TIL YOU DROP" '90S—THE ATTACK ON BUYER'S BOARDS

During the '90s, Enron's Jeffrey Skilling, WorldCom's Bernard J. Ebbers and Tyco International's L. Dennis Kozlowski were the vanguard of a new breed of growth-driven CEOs. This generation of CEOs used aggressive acquisition programs to post impressive growth rates. Mergers were not a compliment to their basic core business; mergers *were* their basic core business. The growth rates fueled high stock prices, which gave them the currency to make the acquisitions.

The companies with an aggressive acquisition strategy included Cisco Systems, AT&T, GE, JDS, Uniphase and Ariba. These high tech companies used their stratospheric stock prices to buy the revenues of other companies. Many of the aggressive deal-makers also took on huge debt loads, convinced that rapid growth rates produced by the acquisitions would cover the debts.

The "dot.com crash" in 2000 embarrassed many of the celebrated deal-makers of the '90s. Their companies had to take record-setting write-downs to account for the falling value of acquired companies.[11] Scandal stalked the group as several of the companies were found to have used accounting gimmicks to hide debt and inflate earnings so as to prop up their stock prices. Ebbers lost his job. He was found guilty of nine counts of securities fraud and filing false statements with securities regulators and is currently serving prison time. Kozlowski left Tyco, was found guilty of misappropriating $400 million, and sentenced to a minimum of 8 years. Skilling was sentenced to 24 months and fined $45 million.

Investors punished the companies in the stock market. The losers in this game were often the shareholders of stable acquired companies who received

---

58 . . . The notion of a paralyzed board is belied somewhat by the aggressive steps to disclose the problem and to remove certain senior managers. On the other hand, the current board's failure or refusal to pursue potential claims against HBOC's former directors and managers, or against those firms that performed the due diligence, supports the notion of an incapacitated board. But I need not address this issue now, given that plaintiffs will be afforded an opportunity to plead more particular facts about what the HBOC directors knew concerning the accounting improprieties, and when they knew it, in the context of either a direct attack on the current board's failure to pursue the claim or in a double derivative action, as mentioned earlier. Such facts, together with additional facts regarding the board's composition, would assist a court in determining whether the board is structurally unable to make an independent and disinterested judgment regarding the potential claim against HBOC.

11 AOL Time Warner holds the current record for goodwill write-offs at $54 billion.

an inflated currency (frequently pumped by dubious accounting and promotional techniques) for their shares. Many selling firm shareholders held the shares received in the acquiring company and rode them down. The classic example is Qwest's acquisition of US West. Qwest went public in 1997 at around $5 a share, the stock rose to over $60 a share, the company used the stock to buy US West, a baby Bell, in a stock swap in 2000, and the stock dropped back to $6 a share by early 2002. US West shareholders lost billions in stock value. Many of those shareholders bought US West stock as a fairly secure investment (they put the stock in pension and college fund plans) and did not bail out on the acquisition. Only those Qwest founders and backers who got in before the IPO, when Qwest was private, made money. The founders sold on the way down. Joe Nacchio, the CEO of Qwest, netted over $100 million in personal gains from Qwest stock and salary in 2001, when his stock dropped two-thirds of its value.

In a few cases, the acquiring shareholders lost more than the selling company shareholders on stock deals. Lucent, Cisco and GE, for example, used their overpriced stock to purchase the overpriced stock of other high tech companies. The shareholders of both the acquiring and acquired companies were exchanging inflated stock for inflated stock. At issue was whose stock is the more inflated. An exchange of an 80 percent inflated stock of the acquirer for a 95 percent inflated stock of the acquired benefits the shareholders of the acquired companies.

The '90s were unique in another respect as well. Founders of high tech companies made personal fortunes on companies that never turned a profit. Many of the founders, such as Gary Winnick at Global Crossing, sold their founder's stock (and, perhaps, stock obtained from exercising compensatory options) on the way down, netting millions. Winnick made over $730 million on a $20 million investment, while his company, which went public in 1997 and filed for bankruptcy in 2002, never made a profit.

The sorry performance of deals in the 90's[12] leads some to call for a strengthening of legal standards applied to the managers of purchasers in an effort to discourage acquisitions. Courts could, for example, no longer give boards of directors of purchasers the benefit of the business judgment rule when evaluating acquisitions; an ordinary negligence standard could be the litmus test. Others argue that shareholders of acquiring corporations should have veto power with enhanced voting rights.[13]

[12] See David Henry, *Mergers: Why Most Big Deals Don't Pay Off*, BUS. WEEK, Oct. 14, 2002, at 60 (61 percent of buyers destroyed their own shareholders wealth in 302 mergers studied between July 1995 and Aug. 2001; average return for all buyers was 4.3 percent below their industry peers and 9.2 percent below the S&P 500). See also Sara B. Moeller, Frederik P. Schlingemann, & Rene M. Stulz, *Firm Size and the Gains from Acquisitions*, 73 J. FIN. ECON. 201 (2004) (finding dramatic losses to bidder share prices on acquisition announcements after 1997).

[13] E.g., Lawrence A Hamermesh, *Premiums in Stock-for-Stock Mergers and Some Consequences in the Law of Director Fiduciary Duties*, 152 U. PA. L. REV. 881 (2003) (when purchasing firm shareholders vote, control premium paid in the acquisition is reduced on average by 19 percent).

The calls for reform now seem premature in light of the natural market correction evident in evidence after the 2001 debacle. Managers became more reluctant to propose acquisitions to their boards and boards became more reluctant to approve them.[14] Often criticized for virtually rubber stamping deal proposals during the M & A waves of the past two decades, company directors now give nothing a free pass.[15] Cursory review has been replaced by intense grilling of managers and advisers. Everything from price to strategy to post-deal execution must be justified. And the board won't hesitate to flex its power if all the pieces don't fit together. Directors want to know whether the due diligence has been properly performed, whether the buyer understands the transaction, whether the target is a strategic fit, and whether there is a sound post deal implementation plan. In other words, the market does, at some level, self-correct.[16]

Moreover, any government reform retarding buy-side acquisition decisions has costs. A change in the business judgment rule for acquisitions will stop some deals shareholders would prefer their managers make. New stiffer rules for acquisitions would also create line drawing problems as courts grapple with, for example, the definition of a purchase acquisition (is a stock purchase of 40 percent of the outstanding voting shares enough?). A change in the voting rules would add cost, time, and complexity to deals. At issue is whether firms should set their own voting processes or depend on state legislatures for optimal rules.

Alleging violations of a duty of care is not the only way to attack a negotiated merger with an unrelated party. Dissenting shareholders can also contest their manager's efforts to persuade shareholders to support the deal. Consider the contested Hewlett-Packard vote below:

---

14 E.g., David Henry, *Have Dealmakers Wised Up?*, BUS. WEEK, Feb. 21, 2005 at 36 ("acquirers appear to have learned important lessons from the failures of the past").

15 See, e.g., Martin Sikora, *Dealmakers Battle the Perfect Storm,* MERGERS & ACQUISITIONS, vol. 38, No. 2, Feb. 2003 (describing harsh board reviews of deals).

16 Data on bidder returns in acquisition can be very fuzzy. One has to compare a hypothetical company that does not do a deal to a company that does a deal. The company may show negative returns on a deal but may also have had more negative returns it if had not done a deal (it was in a declining industry, for example). See generally Robert Brunner, *Applied Mergers & Acquisitions*, Ch.3 (2004). But see Leonce Bargerona, Frederik Schlingemanna & Rene Stulz, *Why do Private Acquirers Pay So Little Compared to Public Acquirers?*, 89 J. FIN. ECON. 375 (2008) (managers of large publicly traded companies overbid for targets). Studies do find that the largest value loss suffered by bidders in acquisitions is correlated with entrenched managers in the bidder. R. Christopher Small, *The Sources of Value Destruction in Acquisitions by Entrenched Managers,* 106 J. FIN. ECON. 247 (2012).

HEWLETT V. HEWLETT-PACKARD CO.

Delaware Court of Chancery, 2002.
2002 WL 549137 (unpublished opinion).

CHANDLER, CHANCELLOR.

. . . HP and Compaq are each publicly traded Delaware corporations and global providers of computers and computer-related products and services. Hewlett and van Bronkhorst are co-trustees of The William R. Hewlett Revocable Trust (the "Trust"), which owns 72,802,148 shares representing approximately 3.75 percent of HP's outstanding stock. The Hewlett Parties beneficially own 75,748,594 shares of HP representing approximately 3.90 percent of HP's outstanding stock.[2]

On September 4, 2001, HP and Compaq entered into an agreement by which the two companies would be combined. Under the terms of this proposed merger, Compaq stockholders would be issued 0.6325 of a share of HP common stock for each share of Compaq stock they owned, representing in the aggregate approximately 35.7 percent of the combined company. HP stockholders would continue to hold the same number of shares they owned before the merger but, because of the new HP shares issued to former Compaq shareholders, the equity ownership percentage of the existing HP stockholders would be considerably diluted. Consummation of the proposed merger required a majority vote of HP stockholders voting at a meeting where a majority of the outstanding HP shares were present and properly approved the issuance of HP stock to Compaq stockholders.

Immediately following the announcement of the proposed merger, HP's stock price dropped 18.7 percent from $23.21 to $18.87 (representing an aggregate loss of approximately $8.5 billion in stockholder value). By early November 2001, the price of HP's shares had dropped 27.2 percent. This continued decline in share price contrasts with a 9.9 percent gain in share value realized by an index of comparable companies.

On November 6, 2001, in reaction to this decline in value that Hewlett believed confirmed his concerns over the proposed merger, Hewlett publicly announced that he, the Trust, the William and Flora Hewlett Foundation, and his two sisters would all vote against the proposed merger. That same day, David Woodley Packard, son of HP's other founder, announced that he would also vote against the transaction. Later the Packard Foundation also announced its shares would be voted against the proposed merger. The Hewlett Parties, the William and Flora Hewlett Foundation, Hewlett's two sisters, David Packard, and the Packard Foundation collectively represent approximately 18 percent of HP's voting shares. By a definitive proxy

[2] Hewlett has also been a director of HP for approximately 15 years and is the son of the late William R. Hewlett, one of HP's founders.

statement dated February 5, 2002, the Hewlett Parties solicited proxies in opposition to the proposed merger.

On March 19, 2002, HP held a stockholders meeting to vote on the proposed transaction. After the meeting, HP publicly claimed that the proposed merger was approved by a slim margin. The independent inspector responsible for certifying the vote, however, has not informed either party of any preliminary results of the voting.

The Vote-Buying Claim

The Hewlett Parties' allegation with regard to proxies cast in favor of the proposed merger by Deutsche Bank is essentially, although not captioned as such in the complaint, a vote-buying claim. Deutsche Bank holds at least 25 million shares of HP. The plaintiffs allege that Deutsche Bank's last-minute switch from voting 17 million of its shares against the merger to voting those shares for the merger was the result of a combination of inducement and coercion, orchestrated by HP's management, which caused Deutsche Bank to vote in favor of the proposed merger for reasons other than those based upon the merits of the transaction.[4]

* * *

The appropriate standard for evaluating vote-buying claims is articulated in *Schreiber v. Carney* [447 A.2d 19 (Del. Ch. 1982)]. *Schreiber* indicates that vote-buying is illegal per se if "the object or purpose is to defraud or in some way disenfranchise the other stockholders." *Schreiber* also notes, absent these deleterious purposes, that "because vote-buying is so easily susceptible of abuse it must be viewed as a voidable transaction subject to a test for intrinsic fairness." At first blush this proposition seems difficult to reconcile with the General Assembly's explicit validation of shareholder voting agreements in § 218(c). Significantly, however, it was the management of the defendant corporation that was buying votes in favor of a corporate reorganization in *Schreiber*. Shareholders are free to do whatever they want with their votes, including selling them to the highest bidder. Management, on the other hand, may not use corporate assets to buy votes in a hotly contested proxy contest about an extraordinary transaction that would significantly transform the corporation, unless it can be demonstrated, as it was in *Schreiber*, that management's vote-buying activity does not have a deleterious effect on the corporate franchise.[10]

[4] Presumably, if only 17 million of Deutsche Bank's 25 million shares were switched from voting against to voting for the merger, Deutsche Bank still voted 8 million (or approximately 1/3) of its shares against the merger.

[10] Significantly, the vote-buying at issue in *Schreiber* was ratified in an independent and fully informed vote of the disinterested shareholders. Such ratification carries substantial weight when the Court is determining whether a vote-buying arrangement has a deleterious effect on the shareholder franchise, even if the vote-buying transaction is subject to a test of intrinsic fairness.

. . . Initially, I believe the facts as alleged in the complaint support a reasonable inference that the switch of Deutsche Bank's vote of 17 million shares to favor the merger was the result of the enticement or coercion of Deutsche Bank by HP management. The Hewlett Parties allege that just four days before the stockholders meeting Deutsche Bank was named as a co-arranger of a multi-billion dollar credit facility. That same day (March 15), Deutsche Bank had submitted all of its proxies and voted 25 million shares against the merger. On Monday, March 18, it is alleged that Deutsche Bank expressed fear over losing future business as a result of HP's negative reaction to Deutsche Bank's vote against the HP management-sponsored merger. Finally, the complaint alleges that, on March 19, the date of the special stockholder meeting, HP delayed the meeting while HP management was involved in a purportedly coercive telephone conference and then closed the polls immediately after Deutsche Bank switched 17 million of its votes as a result of the understanding arrived at during that call. As stated above, however, a vote-buying agreement is not illegal per se, even when company management is buying votes. The more difficult question is whether or not the facts alleged support a reasonable inference that the agreement had a materially adverse effect on the franchise of the other HP shareholders.

The Hewlett Parties' primary argument as to why the alleged vote-buying agreement between HP and Deutsche Bank is illegal is that HP management used corporate funds (in essence, funds in which all of HP shareholders have a common interest as owners of HP) to purchase votes in favor of a transaction favored by management that management was required to put to a shareholder vote. Furthermore, HP management failed to use any devices, such as a ratifying vote of independent shareholders, which would protect the integrity of the vote on the proposed merger.

The allegations of the Hewlett Parties, if true, are particularly troubling. The extraordinary transaction at issue in this case is one of the limited types of transactions a corporate board cannot unilaterally cause its corporation to consummate. Because the transaction would have a fundamental impact on the ownership interests of a company's shareholders, the board must present the proposal to the shareholders for approval. If the allegations of the Hewlett Parties are true, the implication is that HP management was concerned that the proposed merger, which they supported, would not be supported by a majority of HP's shareholders. Despite the fact that it was for the shareholders to make the ultimate determination of whether to approve the proposed merger, HP management purportedly used the shareholders' own money (in the form of corporate funds) to buy votes in opposition to HP shareholders who did not favor the merger. These actions, if they in fact were taken impermissibly, tipped the balance in favor of HP management's view of how the vote should turn out and made it proportionally more difficult for shareholders opposing the merger to defeat the transaction. In my opinion, that is an improper use of corporate assets by a board to interfere with the shareholder franchise. Whether the shareholders disagreed with, did not believe, or even did not understand the information presented to them by HP management about the proposed merger, it was the right of the shareholders to cast their votes on the proposed merger without impermissible interference from HP management.

... Accepting the allegations of the complaint as true in this case, however, I conclude that the plaintiffs have stated a cognizable vote-buying claim.

The Disclosure Claim

The Hewlett Parties' second claim is that in soliciting proxies in favor of the proposed merger, HP management knowingly made numerous materially false and misleading public statements with regard to the integration of HP and Compaq. Those statements purportedly convinced Institutional Shareholder Services ("ISS") to recommend to its subscribers that they vote in favor of the proposed merger.[15] That recommendation caused at least one of HP's largest shareholders, Barclays Global Investors ("Barclays"), to vote for the proposed merger.[16] Because of the extremely narrow margin of victory claimed by HP management, the vote by Barclays of more than 60 million shares (representing 3.1 percent of HP's voting shares) in favor of the proposed merger was likely outcome determinative.

To support this claim, the Hewlett Parties allege that in the months leading up to the stockholder vote, HP management repeatedly said, at investor and analyst conferences, to the media, and elsewhere, that HP's efforts to integrate its business with that of Compaq were progressing at least as well as planned. HP management gave assurances that HP was going to achieve at least $2.5 billion in cost savings in the first two years after the merger while losing no more than 5 percent of revenue, and having to layoff only 15,000 employees. . . .

In contrast to the public statements made by HP management, plaintiffs allege that at the time those statements were made, management knew that the integration plan was not on track, that projected cost savings and revenue losses were not what investors expected, and that the reality of the integration meant that HP was going to have to have higher revenues, to cut other costs, or to layoff 24,000, not 15,000, HP employees. . . .

---

15 ISS is a subscription service that "helps institutional investors research the financial implications of proxy proposals and cast votes that will protect and enhance shareholder returns." The ISS recommendation to vote for the proposed merger was subscribed to by institutional stockholders holding as much as 23% of HP shares. Compl. ¶ 7(b).

16 Before ISS had issued its recommendation to vote for the proposed merger, Barclays had stated that it would unconditionally vote its shares in accordance with the ISS recommendation.

Legal Standard for a Disclosure Claim

In a proceeding under § 225(b), the Court is permitted to "hear and determine the result of any vote of stockholders . . . upon matters other than the election of directors." Part of that power includes the power to determine the validity of votes cast. To the extent that HP management procured proxies by disclosing material information that it knew to be false, therefore, the plaintiffs' disclosure claim is cognizable in a proceeding under § 225(b). To be actionable in this context, false or misleading statements must be material to those receiving the statements, which means that there must be a "substantial likelihood that the disclosure of the [the additional information] would have been viewed by the reasonable investor as having significantly altered the 'total mix' of information made available" to the shareholders.

I must at this stage of the litigation, it would be impossible for me to hold, as a matter of law, that the Hewlett Parties failed to state a cognizable disclosure claim in this § 225 action. . . .[24]

NOTE: SUBSEQUENT HISTORY IN THE HEWLETT-PACKARD CASE

After a trail on the merits, the Chancery Court found for the defendants:

> Based on all of the testimony and exhibits and for the reasons set forth above, I conclude that plaintiffs have failed to prove that HP disseminated materially false information about its integration efforts or about the financial data provided to its shareholders. In addition, I conclude that plaintiffs have failed to prove that HP management improperly enticed or coerced Deutsche Bank into voting in favor of the merger. Accordingly, I will enter judgment in favor of HP and dismiss the plaintiffs' complaint.

Hewlett v. Hewlett-Packard Co., 2002 WL 818091, at *16 (Del. Ch.).

The matter was far from closed, however. Walter Hewlett's lawsuit was a catalyst for the SEC and for the federal district attorney for the Southern District of New York to launch investigations into the conduct of Hewlett-Packard and Deutsche Bank during the proxy battle. These investigations

---

[24] I reiterate that the plaintiffs in this case have done more than just allege in conclusory form that they thought the defendant was lying. Such a bare-bones allegation would not be sufficient to invoke § 225 after a party lost a proxy contest. The plaintiffs here have specifically identified reports to management by the integration team that can be verified and that would, accepting the alleged facts as true, prove the bad faith of HP management. The credibility of these allegations, made primarily upon information and belief, is bolstered by the fact that one of the plaintiffs, Walter Hewlett, is a director of the defendant corporation and as such has access to confidential company documents. Finally, the alleged misstatements pertain to integration, an issue that was particularly important to ISS, an institution that was effectively able to dictate the vote of a block of shares that we now know was likely outcome determinative. It is in light of all of these factors that I conclude that the plaintiffs may proceed with this challenge under § 225.

found that HP agreed to pay $2 million to the investment banking division of Deutsche Bank, contingent on the approval and completion of the merger.[17] During the investigation, an anonymous employee leaked a voicemail message from Carly Fiorina, Chairman and CEO of HP, to Robert Wayman, CPO of HP, in which she said, "We may have to do something extraordinary for (Deutsche Bank) to bring 'em over the line here."[18] As a result of the investigation, the investment advisory unit of Deutsche Bank agreed to pay a $750,000 settlement for failing to disclose a conflict of interest as required when it voted its clients' proxies.

CEO Fiorina dropped Walter Hewlett off the list of management nominees for the board in 2003. HP struggled, losing market share to competitors IBM and Dell, and Fiorina herself was eased out two and one-half years after the acquisition. She left with a $21 million goodbye package. HP stock jumped seven percent on the news of her exit. In 2016, Ms. Fiorina ran to become the Republican nominee for president, losing out to Donald Trump.

NOTE: THIRD PARTY VOTE BUYING

When a potential acquirer makes a bid for a target, the bid is at a substantial premium over market price and the acquirer's shares often drop two to five percent on the announcement. Bidder shareholders are not thrilled and target shareholders are ecstatic. Target shareholders, therefore, have an interest in whether the bidder shareholders will approve the acquisitions. Some dabbling by the target shareholders in bidder shares is enviable. They may buy a few bidder shares to prop up the price, but this is expensive. In a new tactic, a target shareholder buys bidder shareholder votes without buying the shares, a much cheaper method of influencing the bidder vote. Should the move be prohibited?[19]

In the takeover of King Pharmaceuticals by Mylan Laboratories, a hedge fund, Perry Corporation, owned seven million shares of King. Perry had bought the shares on the announcement of the deal, acting as an arbitrageur and betting that the deal would close; the market price at purchase was $12 and the deal price was $16.50. To encourage the deal to close, Perry negotiated a very sophisticated swap trade with two investment houses so that it controlled the ownership and voting rights of ten percent of Mylan shares but with limited or no exposure to fluctuations in the Mylan share price. Perry bought the shares and the investment banks, on Perry's behalf, sold the same number of shares short, removing the risk of price declines for both sides. Perry bought voting power with the economic consequences of share ownership. Gossip on Wall Street is that target shareholders used the same tactic in the 2002 proxy fight over the $24 billion merger of Hewlett-Packard and Compaq.

---

17 Bloomberg News, *Deutsche Bank Settles Proxy-Votes Case*, N.Y. TIMES, Aug. 20, 2002, at C3.

18 Markoff, John, *U.S. Agencies Looking into Hewlett Vote,* N.Y. TIMES, Apr. 16, 2002, at C1.

19 Note that the target itself is prohibited from purchasing shares in the bidder during an exchange tender offer by Regulation M.

The Courts have yet to rule definitively on whether to respect agreements that *uncouple* voting rights from the economic consequences on the underlying stock.[20]

C. DUTY OF LOYALTY: CONFLICT OF INTEREST TRANSACTIONS

Many transactions are between entities in which some of the same parties have ownership stakes or other interests on both sides of the deal. The cases present the danger that minority shareholders of the target will be cheated if their conflicted managers breach a duty of loyalty to the firm and sell the firm too cheaply in a sweetheart deal to themselves. The first subsection details the general principles. The next two subsections deal with parent-subsidiary combinations. In the second subsection, the parent, controlling a subsidiary, merges with the subsidiary; in the third subsection, the parent purchases the outstanding stock of the subsidiary it does not already own (and then cleans up with a short-form merger if necessary). In the fourth subsection, the target firm (or its insiders) repurchases shares on the eve of an acquisition. In the fifth subsection, a single firm recapitalizes.

1. GENERAL PRINCIPLES: WHEN ARE DIRECTORS DISINTERESTED AND INDEPENDENT?

When a firm's senior managers have a stake in the purchaser in a leveraged buy-out (a form of *financial acquisition*), the takeover is called a management buy-out (MBO). Managers of the target may also have an interest in the acquiring firm in *strategic acquisitions* (between two operating companies). If a majority of the directors are conflicted or if there is a controlling or dominating shareholder, the deal, without more, must meet a strict *entire or intrinsic fairness* test. The test requires both fair dealing (a fair process) and a fair price. See *Weinberger v. UOP, Inc.*, in the next subsection.[21] If the board violates a duty of candor, however, it is a per se violation of the entire fairness test. E.g., *Sealy Mattress Co. v. Sealy, Inc.*, 532 A.2d 1324, 1335 (Del. 1987).

To mitigate the sting of an entire fairness review, the seller firm may use *cleansing* processes to take conflicted individuals out of the approval process. The selling firm could decide to be represented in the negotiations by a *special negotiating committee* (*SC*) of *disinterested, independent* directors, who employ independent counsel and investment advisors.[22]

[20] See, e.g., Crown EMAK Partners, LLC v. Kurz, 992 A.2d 377 (Del. 2010) (finding no uncoupling on the facts of the case).

[21] The test also applies to mergers of LLCs into corporations. See Solar Cells v. True North Partners, LLC, 2002 WL 749163 (Del. Ch.).

[22] For an example of a special committee decision to sell to a management group that the courts respected, see Barkan v. Amsted Industries, Inc., 567 A.2d 1279 (Del. 1989). For an example of a court-approved special committee auction in which one of the bidders was a management

Firms may also require a ratification vote by a majority of the shareholders that are not interested or conflicted; a *majority of the minority*.

ORMAN V. CULLMAN

Court of Chancery of Delaware, 2002.
794 A.2d 5.

CHANDLER, CHANCELLOR.

General Cigar, a Delaware Corporation with its principal executive offices located in New York, New York, is a leading manufacturer and marketer of premium cigars. The Company has exclusive trademark rights to many well-known brands of cigars, including seven of the top ten brands that were previously manufactured in Cuba.

The Company went public in an initial public offering ("IPO") of 6.9 million shares of Class A stock at $18.00 per share on February 28, 1997. As of March 30, 2000, the Company had approximately 13.6 million shares of Class A and 13.4 million shares of Class B common stock outstanding. Class A stock was publicly traded and Class B stock was not publicly traded. Class A stock had one vote per share and Class B had ten votes per share. Even though Class B shares had ten times—the voting power of Class A shares, the Company's Certificate of Incorporation required equal consideration in exchange for Class A and Class B shares in the event of a sale or merger. At the time of the proposed merger, the Cullman Group owned approximately 162 shares of Class A and 9.9 million shares of Class B. Although this aggregated to approximately 37 percent of the Company's total outstanding stock, the Cullman Group had voting control over the Company because the 9.9 million Class B shares it owned represented approximately 74 percent of that class, which enjoyed a 10:1 voting advantage over Class A shares. The Cullman Group's equity interest, therefore, gave it approximately 67 percent of the voting power in the corporation.

. . . In the early fall of 1999, Swedish Match approached certain members of the Cullman Group (the "Cullmans") about purchasing the interest in General Cigar owned by its Public Shareholders. This was seen to be a logical business combination because General Cigar had a strong presence in the United States premium cigar market and Swedish Match had strength in the international cigar and smokeless tobacco markets through its established network of international contacts and resources. At a November 4, 1999 General Cigar board meeting, the Cullmans informed the Board of Swedish Match's interest. The Board then authorized the Cullmans to pursue discussions with Swedish Match assisted by defendant

group, see In re RJR Nabisco, 1989 WL 7036 (Del. Ch.) (Allen, Chancellor). The special committee procedure comes from Del. Gen Corp. L. § 144(a)(1) (Interested Directors), which the courts apply by analogy.

director Solomon's financial advising firm, Peter J. Solomon & Company ("PJSC").

Negotiations between the Cullmans and Swedish Match continued during November and December 1999. By the end of December 1999 the structure for a proposed transaction had been determined. That structure included: 1) a sale by the Cullman Group of approximately one-third of its equity interest in the Company to Swedish Match at $15.00 per share; 2) immediately following the Cullman Group's private sale, a merger in which all shares in the Company held by the Unaffiliated Shareholders would be purchased for $15.00 per share; 3) Cullman Sr. and Cullman Jr. maintaining their respective positions as Chairman and President/Chief Executive Officer of the surviving company and having the power to appoint a majority of the board; 4) three years after the merger, the Cullman Group having the power to put its remaining equity interest to the Company and the Company having the power to call such interest; and 5) an agreement by the Cullman Group that should the proposed transaction with Swedish Match not close, it would vote against any other business combination for a period of one year following the termination of the proposed transaction.

Once the negotiations reached agreement on the above points, the Board created a special committee (the "Special Committee"), consisting of outside defendant directors Lufkin, Israel, and Vincent, to determine the advisability of entering into the proposed transaction. The Special Committee retained independent legal and financial advisors—Wachtell, Lipton, Rosen & Katz and Deutsche Bank Securities, Inc., respectively—to assist them in this endeavor. In early January 2000 the Special Committee received copies of the proposed agreements previously reached between the Cullmans and Swedish Match. After a review of these proposals by the Special Committee and its legal and financial advisors, the Special Committee directly negotiated with Swedish Match over the terms of the agreement. The substantive changes in the terms of the transaction resulting from negotiations by the Special Committee appear to be that the amount of consideration to be received by the Unaffiliated Shareholders for each of their Class A shares increased from $15.00 to $15.25 and the length of time the Cullman Group would not vote in favor of another business combination if the challenged merger failed to close increased from twelve to eighteen months. On January 19, 2000 the Special Committee unanimously recommended approval of the transaction as modified as a result of their negotiations. That same day, the General Cigar Board unanimously approved the transaction.

The relevant terms of the final transaction recommended to the Company's shareholders, and subject to approval of the Unaffiliated Shareholders, included an initial private sale by the Cullman Group of 3.5 million shares of its Class B stock, representing about one-third of its

General Cigar equity interest, to Swedish Match for $15.00 per share. The Cullman Group was to retain its remaining equity interest, which would then consist of approximately 162 Class A shares and 6.4 million Class B shares. Following the merger, that remaining interest would aggregate to approximately 36 percent of the total outstanding equity interest in the Company.[24] Immediately following this private sale, a merger would take place in which all publicly owned Class A and Class B shares (those not owned by the Cullman Group) would be purchased for $15.25 per share.

In addition to the Cullman Group's continuing equity position and voting control in the surviving company, several provisions of the proposed transaction assured ongoing participation of the Cullman Group in the day-to-day operations of that company. Cullman Sr. would retain his position as Chairman of the Board of the surviving company and Cullman Jr. would continue to serve as President and CEO of the surviving company. The Cullman Group would have the power to appoint a majority of the board of the surviving company after the merger.

Additionally, beginning three years from the date of the merger, the Cullman Group would have the option to put some or all of its remaining equity interest to the surviving company and the surviving company would have a reciprocal right to call some or all of the company's stock retained by the Cullman Group. The Cullman Group also agreed to vote against any proposed merger transaction for eighteen months should the transaction with Swedish Match not be consummated.

Finally, the transaction was structured in such a way that the Cullman Group could not dictate its approval. Despite the fact that the Cullman Group possessed voting control over the Company both before and after the proposed transaction, approval of the merger required that a majority of the Unaffiliated Shareholders of Class A stock, voting separately as a class, vote in favor of the transaction.[27]

Fiduciary Duty Claims

". . . A cardinal precept of the General Corporation Law of the State of Delaware is that directors, rather than shareholders, manage the business and affairs of the corporation."[30] The business judgment rule is a recognition of that statutory precept. The rule "is a presumption that in making a business decision the directors of a corporation acted on an informed basis, in good faith and in the honest belief that the action taken was in the best interests of the company." Therefore, the judgment of a

24 Because of the disproportionate 10:1 voting strength of the Class B shares compared to the Class A shares, the Cullman Group continued to have voting control over the surviving company and, therefore, the merger did not constitute a sale or transfer of control.

27 In order to assure the Unaffiliated Shareholders had the unobstructed right to determine whether or not the merger would close, the Cullman Group "agreed to vote any Class A shares held by them pro rata in accordance with the vote of the Unaffiliated Shareholders."

30 Aronson v. Lewis, Del. Supr., 473 A.2d 805, 811 (1984) (citing 8 Del. C. § 141(a)).

properly functioning board will not be second-guessed and "[a]bsent an abuse of discretion, that judgment will be respected by the courts." Because a board is presumed to have acted properly, "[t]he burden is on the party challenging the decision to establish facts rebutting the presumption."

One way for a plaintiff to overcome this burden, for example, is to allege facts demonstrating a squeeze out merger or a merger between two corporations under the control of a controlling shareholder. If facts of that nature are sufficiently alleged, the business judgment presumption is rebutted and entire fairness is the standard of review. "A controlling or dominating shareholder standing on both sides of a transaction . . . bears the burden of proving its entire fairness."[34] Although procedural safeguards may be put in place that shift the burden to the plaintiff to prove the unfairness of the merger (i.e., the negotiation and approval of the transaction by a special committee of independent and disinterested directors or the requirement of approval by a majority of the company's minority shareholders), "[e]ntire fairness remains the proper focus of judicial analysis in examining an interested merger, irrespective of whether the burden of proof remains upon or is shifted away from the controlling or dominating shareholder." Regardless of whether the burden of proof is shifted to the plaintiff, however, "[t]he initial burden" under entire fairness is borne by the controlling party "who stands on both sides of the transaction."[36]

Here, however, although the Cullman Group was the controlling shareholder of the target company both before and after the merger, the

---

[34] Kahn v. Lynch Communication Sys., Inc., Del. Supr., 638 A.2d 1110, 1115 (1994).

[36] Usually, the entire fairness standard only applies at the outset ("ab initio") in certain special circumstances, viz, a squeeze out merger or a merger between two companies under the control of a controlling shareholder. See, e.g., Kahn v. Lynch, *supra*. Entire fairness review is not automatically triggered when a non-controlling shareholder appears on both sides of a challenged transaction. Moreover . . . , the business judgment standard may apply even when some (but less than a majority) of the directors lack independence and/or are interested in the transaction . . . This distinction is of vital importance due to the effects, as a practical matter, of a determination that entire fairness is the appropriate standard from the outset ("ab initio").

As our Supreme Court has recognized, a determination that entire fairness is the appropriate standard of review "is often of critical importance." *Lynch*, 638 A.2d at 1116. That conclusion normally will preclude dismissal of a complaint on a Rule 12(b)(6) motion to dismiss. Once the business judgment rule presumption is rebutted, the burden of proof shifts to the defendant, who must either establish the entire fairness of the transaction or show that the burden of disproving its entire fairness must be shifted to the plaintiff. A determination of whether the defendant has met that burden will normally be impossible by examining only the documents the Court is free to consider on a motion to dismiss—the complaint and any documents it incorporates by reference. Besides foreclosing dismissal under Rule 12(b)(6), the requirement of an entire fairness review may also preclude the entry of a final judgment even after discovery on a motion for summary judgment, but only if there remains at that point unresolved questions of material fact on either of the two prongs of the entire fairness test. The more difficult of these two prongs to establish on a paper record, however, is the "fair price" prong. *See* Weinberger v. UOP, Inc., 457 A.2d 701, 711 (1983) (explaining that an entire fairness review is not bifurcated and considers both fair dealing and fair price and that fair price "relates to [all relevant] economic and financial considerations of the proposed [transaction]"). Although not inevitable in every case, in those cases in which entire fairness is the initial standard, the likely end result is that a determination of that issue will require a full trial.

Cullman Group did not stand on both sides of the challenged merger. Instead it was approached by, and began initial negotiations with, an unaffiliated third party, Swedish Match. A Special Committee of independent directors then completed those negotiations. Therefore, the burden remains on Orman to allege other facts sufficient to overcome the business judgment presumption. Specifically, Orman must allege facts that raise a reasonable doubt as to whether the Board breached either its duty of care or its duty of loyalty to the corporation. In his complaint, Orman alleges that the Board breached its duty of loyalty.

As a general matter, the business judgment rule presumption that a board acted loyally can be rebutted by alleging facts which, if accepted as true, establish that the board was either interested in the outcome of the transaction or lacked the independence to consider objectively whether the transaction was in the best interest of its company and all of its shareholders. To establish that a board was interested or lacked independence, a plaintiff must allege facts as to the interest and lack of independence of the individual members of that board. To rebut successfully business judgment presumptions in this manner, thereby leading to the application of the entire fairness standard, a plaintiff must normally plead facts demonstrating "that a majority of the director defendants have a financial interest in the transaction or were dominated or controlled by a materially interested director." I recognize situations can exist when the material interest of a number of directors less than a majority may rebut the business judgment presumption and lead to an entire fairness review. That is when an " 'interested director fail[ed] to disclose his interest in the transaction to the board and a reasonable board member would have regarded the existence of the material interest as a significant fact in the evaluation of the proposed transaction.' " Nevertheless, in this case the interest that may be attributed to the Cullman Group or other Board members was disclosed to the Board and, therefore, Orman still must establish that a majority of the Board was interested and/or lacked independence.

If a plaintiff alleging a duty of loyalty breach is unable to plead facts demonstrating that a majority of a board that approved the transaction in dispute was interested and/or lacked independence, the entire fairness standard of review is not applied and the Court respects the business judgment of the board. Whether a particular director is disinterested or independent is a recurring theme in Delaware's corporate jurisprudence. We reach conclusions as to the sufficiency of allegations regarding interest and independence only after considering all the facts alleged on a case-by-case basis.

The *Aronson* Court set forth the meaning of "interest" and "independence" in this context. It defined interest as "mean[ing] that directors can neither appear on both sides of a transaction nor expect to derive any personal financial benefit from it in the sense of self-dealing, as opposed to a benefit which devolves upon the corporation or all stockholders generally." This definition was further refined in *Rales v. Blasband* when our Supreme Court recognized that "[d]irectoral interest also exists where a corporate decision will have a materially detrimental impact on a director, but not on the corporation and the stockholders." It should be noted, however, that in the absence of self-dealing, it is not enough to establish the interest of a director by alleging that he received any benefit not equally shared by the stockholders. Such benefit must be alleged to be material to that director. Materiality means that the alleged benefit was significant enough "in the context of the director's economic circumstances, as to have made it improbable that the director could perform her fiduciary duties to the . . . shareholders without being influenced by her overriding personal interest."

On the separate question of independence, the *Aronson* Court stated that "[i]ndependence means that a director's decision is based on the corporate merits of the subject before the board rather than extraneous considerations or influences." Such extraneous considerations or influences may exist when the challenged director is controlled by another. To raise a question concerning the independence of a particular board member, a plaintiff asserting the "control of one or more directors must allege particularized facts manifesting 'a direction of corporate conduct in such a way as to comport with the wishes or interests of the corporation (or persons) doing the controlling.' The shorthand shibboleth of 'dominated and controlled directors' is insufficient." This lack of independence can be shown when a plaintiff pleads facts that establish "that the directors are 'beholden' to [the controlling person] or so under their influence that their discretion would be sterilized."

Subjective test

In determining the sufficiency of factual allegations made by a plaintiff as to either a director's interest or lack of independence, the Delaware Supreme Court has rejected an objective "reasonable director" test and instead requires the application of a subjective "actual person" standard to determine whether a particular director's interest is material and debilitating or that he lacks independence because he is controlled by another.

General Cigar had an eleven-member board. In order to rebut the presumptions of the business judgment rule, Orman must allege facts that would support a finding of interest or lack of independence for a majority, or at least six, of the Board members. Orman asserts, and defendants appear to concede, that the four members of the Cullman Group were interested because they received benefits from the transaction that were not shared with the rest of the shareholders.[49] Orman, therefore, would

[49] "Four of the Company's eleven directors have a conflict of interest in recommending adoption of the Merger Agreement because, as members of the [Cullman Group], they will continue to have an equity interest in the Surviving Corporation. As a result, they will receive the benefits

have to plead facts making it reasonable to question the interest or independence of two of the remaining seven Board members to avoid dismissal based on the business judgment rule presumption. With varying levels of confidence, Orman's complaint alleges that each of the seven remaining Board members—Israel, Vincent, Lufkin, Barnet, Sherren, Bernbach, and Solomon—were interested and/or lacked independence.[50]

---

of future earnings, growth and increased value of General Cigar, and be subject to the risks of such ownership, while [the cashed-out Unaffiliated Shareholders] will no longer receive any such benefit or be subject to such risks."

50 . . . Although interest and independence are two separate and distinct issues, these two attributes are sometimes confused by parties. . . .

As described above, a disabling "interest," as defined by Delaware common law, exists in two instances. The first is when (1) a director personally receives a benefit (or suffers a detriment), (2) as a result of, or from, the challenged transaction, (3) which is not generally shared with (or suffered by) the other shareholders of his corporation, and (4) that benefit (or detriment) is of such subjective material significance to that particular director that it is reasonable to question whether that director objectively considered the advisability of the challenged transaction to the corporation and its shareholders. The second instance is when a director stands on both sides of the challenged transaction. See 8 Del.C. § 144. This latter situation frequently involves the first three elements listed above. As for the fourth element, whenever a director stands on both sides of the challenged transaction he is deemed interested and allegations of materiality have not been required.

"Independence" does not involve a question of whether the challenged director derives a benefit from the transaction that is not generally shared with the other shareholders. Rather, it involves an inquiry into whether the director's decision resulted from that director being controlled by another. A director can be controlled by another if in fact he is dominated by that other party, whether through close personal or familial relationship or through force of will. A director can also be controlled by another if the challenged director is beholden to the allegedly controlling entity. A director may be considered beholden to (and thus controlled by) another when the allegedly controlling entity has the unilateral power (whether direct or indirect through control over other decision makers), to decide whether the challenged director continues to receive a benefit, financial or otherwise, upon which the challenged director is so dependent or is of such subjective material importance to him that the threatened loss of that benefit might create a reason to question whether the controlled director is able to consider the corporate merits of the challenged transaction objectively.

Confusion over whether specific facts raise a question of interest or independence arises from the reality that similar factual circumstances may implicate both interest and independence, one but not the other, or neither. By way of example, consider the following: Director A is both a director and officer of company X. Company X is to be merged into company Z. Director A's vote in favor of recommending shareholder approval of the merger is challenged by a plaintiff shareholder.

Scenario One. Assume that one of the terms of the merger agreement is that director A was to be an officer in surviving company Z, and that maintaining his position as a corporate officer in the surviving company was material to director A. That fact might, when considered in light of all of the facts alleged, lead the Court to conclude that director A had a disabling interest.

Scenario Two. Assume that director C is both a director and the majority shareholder of company X. Director C had the power plausibly to threaten director A's position as officer of corporation X should director A vote against the merger. Assume further that director A's position as a corporate officer is material to director A. Those circumstances, when considered in light of all of the facts alleged, might lead the Court to question director A's independence from director C, because it could reasonably be assumed that director A was controlled by director C, since director A was beholden to director C for his position as officer of the corporation. Confusion over whether to label this disability as a disqualifying "interest" or as a "lack of independence" may stem from the fact that, colloquially, director A was "interested" in keeping his job as a corporate officer. Scenario Two, however, raises only a question as to director A's independence since there is nothing that suggests that director A would receive something from the transaction that might implicate a disabling interest.

If a plaintiff's allegations combined all facts described in both Scenario One and Scenario Two, it might be reasonable to question both director A's interest and independence. Conversely, if all

Directors Israel and Vincent

Perhaps the weakest allegations of interest and/or lack of independence are aimed at directors Israel and Vincent, who were both members of the Special Committee that investigated the advisability of the merger and negotiated with Swedish Match. The complaint states that these two defendants "had longstanding business relations with members of the Cullman Group which impeded and impaired their ability to function independently and outside the influence of the Cullman Group." The only fact pled in support of this assertion is the mere recitation that Israel and Vincent had served as directors of General Cigar since 1989 and 1992, respectively.

. . . The naked assertion of a previous business relationship is not enough to overcome the presumption of a director's independence. . . . [A]llegations concerning longstanding business relations fail as a matter of law to place in issue the independence of directors Israel and Vincent.[56]

Director Lufkin

Orman asserts that director Lufkin, who was the third member of the Special Committee, lacked independence and was also interested in the merger transaction. . . . Defendant Lufkin had been a Board member of General Cigar or its predecessor since 1976." . . . Lufkin's supposedly disabling interest results from the fact that he was "a founder of Donaldson, Lufkin & Jenrette ("DLJ") [and that] DLJ, or a successor or affiliate thereof, was one of two lead underwriters in the Company's IPO and obtained a substantial fee as a result thereof." This bare statement of fact does not suggest, or even lead to a reasonable inference of, a disabling interest on the part of Lufkin as that statement does not show that he " 'will receive a personal financial benefit from [the] transaction that is not equally shared by the stockholders.' "

---

the facts in both scenarios were alleged except for the materiality of Director A's position as a corporate officer (perhaps because director A is a billionaire and his officer's position pays $20,000 per year and is not even of prestige value to him) then neither director A's interest nor his independence would be reasonably questioned. The key issue is not simply whether a particular director receives a benefit from a challenged transaction not shared with the other shareholders, or solely whether another person or entity has the ability to take some benefit away from a particular director, but whether the possibility of gaining some benefit or the fear of losing a benefit is likely to be of such importance to that director that it is reasonable for the Court to question whether valid business judgment or selfish considerations animated that director's vote on the challenged transaction.

56 I note that Israel and Vincent, as well as each of the other Board members, were also shareholders of General Cigar. As a general matter, that is a fact that weighs in support of the presumption that a director objectively considered the merits of the proposed corporate transaction in determining how to cast his vote on that transaction. A director who is also a shareholder of his corporation is more likely to have interests that are aligned with the other shareholders of that corporation as it is in his best interest, as a shareholder, to negotiate a transaction that will result in the largest return for all shareholders. . . .

Director Barnet

The only fact alleged in support of Orman's allegation of director Barnet's interest is that he "has an interest in the transaction since he will become a director of the surviving company." No case has been cited to me, and I have found none, in which a director was found to have a financial interest solely because he will be a director in the surviving corporation. To the contrary, our case law has held that such an interest is not a disqualifying interest.[61] Even if I were to infer that Orman was alleging that the fees Barnet was to receive as a director with the surviving company created a disabling interest, without more, that assertion would also fail. . . .

Director Bernbach

Orman alleges that director Bernbach was both interested in the merger and lacked the independence to make an impartial decision regarding that transaction because he has "a written agreement with the Company to provide consulting services [and that] [i]n 1998 . . . Bernbach was paid $75,000 for such services . . . and additional funds since that date."

. . . At this stage of the litigation, the facts supporting this allegation are sufficient to raise a reasonable inference that director Bernbach was controlled by the Cullman Group because he was beholden to the controlling shareholders for future renewals of his consulting contract. . . . Even though there is no bright-line dollar amount at which consulting fees received by a director become material, at the motion to dismiss stage and on the facts before me, I think it is reasonable to infer that $75,000 would be material to director Bernbach and that he is beholden to the Cullman Group for continued receipt of such fees.

Director Solomon

Orman alleges that "Defendant Solomon has an interest in the transaction since his company, PJSC, stands to reap fees of $3.3 million if the transaction is effectuated." The reasonable inference that can be drawn from this contention is that if the merger is consummated PJSC will receive $3.3 million. If the merger is not consummated PJSC will not receive $3.3 million . . . Because director Solomon's principal occupation is that of "Chairman of Peter J. Solomon Company Limited and Peter J. Solomon Securities Company Limited," it is reasonable to assume that director Solomon would personally benefit from the $3.3 million his company would receive if the challenged transaction closed. I think it would be naive to say, as a matter of law, that $3.3 million is immaterial. In my opinion, therefore, it is reasonable to infer that director Solomon suffered a disabling interest

61 *See* Krim v. ProNet, Inc., Del.Ch., 744 A.2d 523, 528 n. 16 (1999) ("[T]he fact that several directors would retain board membership in the merged entity does not, standing alone, create a conflict of interest.").

when considering how to cast his vote in connection with the challenged merger when the Board's decision on that matter could determine whether or not his firm would receive $3.3 million.

Directors Bernbach and Solomon, at this stage, cannot be considered independent and disinterested. Orman has thus pled facts that make it reasonable to question the independence and/or disinterest of a majority of the General Cigar Board—the four Cullman Group directors, plus Bernbach and Solomon, or six out of the eleven directors. Accordingly, I cannot say, as a matter of law, that the General Cigar Board's actions are protected by the business judgment rule presumption. Defendants' motion to dismiss the fiduciary duty claims—based as it is on a conclusion that the challenged transaction was approved by a disinterested and independent board—must be denied.

Reaching this decision with regard to the loyalty of the Board that approved the merger, however, does not rebut the business judgment presumption at this stage of the litigation. It merely means that the business judgment presumption may not be used as the basis to dismiss Orman's fiduciary duty claims for failure to state a cognizable claim. Further discovery is necessary to determine whether the facts—as they truly existed at the time of the challenged transaction, rather than those accepted as necessarily true as alleged—are sufficient to rebut the business judgment rule presumption and to trigger an entire fairness review. Thus it is unnecessary for me presently to consider Orman's allegations concerning the purported unfairness of the price and process of the merger. Such allegations will become relevant only if the business judgment presumption is finally determined to have been successfully rebutted. . . .

In addition, because I conclude that it is impossible to say, as a matter of law, that information concerning the fair market value of the Company's headquarters building is immaterial, I cannot currently accept defendants' contention that a fully informed vote of a majority of the Company's Unaffiliated Shareholders ratified any possible breaches of fiduciary duties in connection with the Board's consideration of the challenged merger. If it were later determined that this omission was not material, however, shareholder ratification might become an important issue.[Ed.[23]]

Finally, the pleadings (and reasonable inferences drawn therefrom) are insufficient for me to make a determination with respect to the possible cleansing effect resulting from the actions of General Cigar's Special

---

[23] [Ed. The plaintiffs later dropped the incomplete disclosure claim based on the market value of the headquarters, and the Delaware Court of Chancery later granted summary judgment against the defendants based on the shareholder vote. The court held that a fully informed "majority of the minority" stockholder vote ratified the transaction. 2004 WL 2348395 (Del. Ch.). The Court held that a voting lock-up provision in the Cullman's stock sale agreement did not *coerce* the shareholder vote. The lock-up required the Cullman group to vote their shares of Class B common stock for the merger and against any alternative transaction for a period of eighteen months after any termination of the agreement.]

Committee. The complaint provides no bases upon which I can draw conclusions confidently as to whether or not the Special Committee's negotiations with Swedish Match were indeed arms-length and indicative of a properly functioning and properly motivated committee.[Ed.[24]]

NOTE: SARBANES-OXLEY AND LISTING REQUIREMENTS ON THE DEFINITION OF INDEPENDENT

Federal securities legislation, the Sarbanes-Oxley Act of 2002 (SOX),[25] and exchange listing standards[26] have refined definitions of "independent" directors. SOX applies to all publicly traded corporations and the listing requirements on any exchange apply to those corporations listed on the exchange. Under SOX a corporation must have an audit committee comprised solely of independent directors. Independent directors are non-executive directors that have not accepted "any consulting, advisory, or other compensatory fee from the issuer." SOX § 301; Exch. Act Rule 10A–3(b)(1)(ii)(A) (implementing required language from SOX). The NYSE listing requirements go further and require that all listed companies have a majority of independent directors and have compensation, nomination and audit committees made up of only independent directors.[27] An independent director can have "no material relationship" with a listed company. There is a three-year cooling off period for many of the most common kinds of connections that undermine independence. If the corporation has a controlling shareholder, the requirements for a majority of independent directors on the board and for independent director-only compensation and nominating committees do not apply. Only the audit committee independent director-only rules apply. The controlling shareholder exemption is limited, however, because all conflict-of-interest transactions in listed companies must be approved by a firm's audit committee. Do these definitions of "independent" apply in evaluating the independence of board members in duty of loyalty cases in state courts? Should they?

Once a court finds a director to be independent and disinterested, the director is largely immune from shareholder derivative actions for monetary damages involving acquisition decisions.

---

[24] [Ed. The Court had found the three members of the SC to be disinterested and independent. Also the deal, as the Court noted, was not of the type in which the entire fairness test applies *ab initio*. Why did a business judgment rule presumption not attach to the committee on the pleadings?]

[25] Sarbanes-Oxley Act of 2002 § 301, 15 U.S.C. § 78j–1(m)(3)(B) (audit committees).

[26] *Order Approving Proposed Rule Changes and Amendments No. 1 Thereto*, SEC Rel. 34–48745, 2003 WL 22509738 (Nov. 4, 2003) (approving the NYSE and NASD proposals on board structure).

[27] See NYSE Listing Co. Manual Rules 3.03A1–6. The Nasdaq has a similar rule. See Nasdaq Marketplace Rule 5605.

QUESTIONS

Steve Friedman and Rebecca Dew grew up on the same block in Jacksonville, Florida. Steve and Rebecca became good friends while attending the same schools. They both even attended Florida State University together, although their relationship was always platonic. Over the years, Steve and Rebecca have remained good friends and even find the time to play golf together at least once a month. While Steve became an executive for an advertising agency, Rebecca rose through the corporate ranks and eventually became the CEO of Riverside Aerospace Inc. ("RAI"), a publicly traded Delaware corporation. When an opening on the RAI board became available, Rebecca decided to ask her friend Steve to fill the open seat. Steve gratefully accepted. Steve's advertising agency doesn't do any work for RAI, and thus Steve's only affiliation with RAI is as a director of the company.

Does Steve Friedman qualify as an "independent director" under: (a) Delaware law? (b) NYSE listing requirements? or (c) SOX? How likely is it that Steve will vote against any proposal that Rebecca champions?

IN RE CORNERSTONE THERAPEUTICS, INC. STOCKHOLDER LITIG., 115 A.3d 1173 (Del. 2015): [The plaintiff sought monetary damages against a director protected by an exculpatory charter provision. The Delaware Supreme Court reversed a Chancery Court decision and held that plaintiffs' must plead either duty of loyalty or bad faith claims specifically against the director regardless of the underlying standard of review for the board's conduct (whether under *Revlon*, *Unocal*, the business judgment rule or the entire fairness test) and regardless of whether the transaction is an interested or conflicted transaction.] . . . In this decision, we hold that even if a plaintiff has pled facts that, if true, would require the transaction to be subject to the entire fairness standard of review, and the interested parties to face a claim for breach of their duty of loyalty, the independent directors do not automatically have to remain defendants. When the independent directors are protected by an exculpatory charter provision and the plaintiffs are unable to plead a non-exculpated claim against them, those directors are entitled to have the claims against them dismissed, in keeping with this Court's opinion in *Malpiede v. Townson* [780 A.2d 1075 (Del. 2001)] . . . .

Our common law of corporations has rightly emphasized the need for independent directors to be willing to say no to interested transactions proposed by controlling stockholders. For that reason, our law has long inquired into the practical negotiating power given to independent directors in conflicted transactions. Although it is wise for our law to focus on whether the independent directors can say no, it does not follow that it is prudent to create an invariable rule that any independent director who says yes to an interested transaction subject to entire fairness review must remain as a defendant until the end of the litigation, regardless of the absence of any evidence suggesting that the director acted for an improper motive. For more than a generation, our law has recognized that the negotiating efforts of independent directors can help to secure transactions with controlling stockholders that are favorable to the minority. Indeed, respected scholars have found evidence that interested transactions subject to special committee approval are often priced on terms that are attractive to minority stockholders. We decline to adopt an approach that would create incentives for independent directors to avoid serving as special committee members, or to reject transactions solely because their role in negotiating on behalf of the stockholders would cause them to remain as defendants until the end of any litigation challenging the transaction. . . .

NOTE: EXECUTIVES AS LOOSE CANNONS IN ACQUISITION NEGOTIATIONS

Dow Chemical Co. fired and then sued one of its executive vice presidents, Romeo Kreinberg, alleging that he had breached his fiduciary duty to the company by discussing a possible buy-out of the company without informing the company's board of directors of the discussions. A federal district court held that the claim survived a motion to dismiss in *Dow Chemical Co. v. Reinhard*, 2007 WL 2780545 (E.D. Mich. 2007). Does a CEO have the power to initiate buy-out negotiations without informing the board? The issue made headlines when Merrill Lynch CEO Stanley O'Neal, later fired, approached Wachovia Bank with a merger proposal without informing his board of his intentions. Most employment documents (and hiring board resolutions) do not contain a relevant explicit authorization. Does a CEO have the inherent power to initiate buy-out discussions without board express authorization? Initiating merger discussions does not itself seem to require board authorization. When a CEO attempts to sign a confidentiality agreement on behalf of his company, however, he may not be authorized to do so without an express resolution of the board—it is a close question. The board must, however, sign any deal negotiated by the CEO. Of this, there can be no doubt. And when the CEO leaves his board out of the loop in the negotiations, this decision to sign may be viewed by courts as a fait accompli rather than an independent business decision, well-informed and deliberated. This is the rub. The court may not respect the board's decision to sign. A CEO negotiating a deal without prior board notification is questionable practice.

IN RE SS&C TECHNOLOGIES, INC., SHAREHOLDERS LITIGATION, 911 A.2d 816 (Del. Ch. 2006): [Court refused to approve a settlement of a shareholder class action] . . . Stone, SS&C's CEO, instigated this transaction through the use of corporate resources but without prior authorization from the board of directors. He did so in order to identify a transaction in which he could both realize a substantial cash payout for some of his shares and use his remaining shares and options to fund a sizeable investment in the resulting entity. When Stone identified Carlyle as his chosen partner and negotiated a price at which he was willing to sell a portion of his shares, Carlyle sent a letter to the board of directors making a proposal to acquire the rest of the shares at that price, indicating Stone's agreement to its terms. In response, the board of directors formed a special committee that retained expert legal and financial advisors. But, after a brief effort to identify another buyer, that committee reached agreement with Carlyle at a price only slightly higher than Carlyle negotiated with Stone.

These facts, on their face, raise a series of questions about both Stone's conduct and that of the board of directors. For instance, did Stone misuse the information and resources of the corporation when, acting in his official capacity but without board authorization, he hired an investment banker to help him identify a private equity partner to suit his needs? Another question is whether, given Stone's precommitment to a deal with Carlyle, the board of directors was ever in a position to objectively consider whether or not a sale of the enterprise should take place. Similarly, did Stone's general agreement to do a deal with Carlyle make it more difficult for the special committee to attract competing bids, especially from buyers not interested in having Stone own a significant equity interest in the surviving enterprise? And, did Stone's negotiation of a price range with Carlyle unfairly impede the special committee in securing the best terms reasonably available? These are only some of the important legal issues that result from the way Stone and the board of directors formulated the private equity buy-out of SS&C Technologies.

None of these issues is adequately addressed by the plaintiffs' counsel in connection with the proposed settlement. Indeed, the plaintiffs' submissions, both written and oral, fail to come to grips with the fact that Stone had an array of conflicting interests that made him an unreliable negotiator or that the special committee was placed in a difficult position by Stone's preemptive activities. Most surprisingly, at the hearing, the plaintiffs' counsel told the court that Stone took no cash out of the deal and instead rolled all of his stock and options into equity in the new deal. Suffice it to say that a manager who has the opportunity to both take $72.6 million in cash from the transaction and roll a portion of his equity into a large equity position in the surviving entity has a different set of motivations than one who does not.

2. SQUEEZE-OUT MERGERS: ACQUISITIONS OF A MINORITY INTEREST IN A CONTROLLED SUBSIDIARY

WEINBERGER V. UOP, INC.

Supreme Court of Delaware, 1983.
457 A.2d 701.

MOORE, JUSTICE.

This post-trial appeal was reheard en banc from a decision of the Court of Chancery. It was brought by the class action plaintiff below, a former shareholder of UOP, Inc., who challenged the elimination of UOP's minority shareholders by a cash-out merger between UOP and its majority owner, The Signal Companies, Inc. . . .

In ruling for the defendants, the Chancellor re-stated his earlier conclusion that the plaintiff in a suit challenging a cash-out merger must allege specific acts of fraud, misrepresentation, or other items of misconduct to demonstrate the unfairness of the merger terms to the minority.[Ed.[28]] We approve this rule and affirm it.

> The Chancellor also held that even though the ultimate burden of proof is on the majority shareholder to show by a preponderance of the evidence that the transaction is fair, it is first the burden of the plaintiff attacking the merger to demonstrate some basis for invoking the fairness obligation. We agree with that principle. However, where corporate action has been approved by an informed vote of a majority of the minority shareholders, we conclude that the burden entirely shifts to the plaintiff to show that the transaction was unfair to the minority. . . . But in all this, the burden clearly remains on those relying on the vote to show that they completely disclosed all material facts relevant to the transaction.

Here, the record does not support a conclusion that the minority stockholder vote was an informed one. Material information, necessary to

[28] [Ed. The court here is dividing those monetary claims that a shareholder must make in an appraisal proceeding, see Chapter 2, Section A.3, and those monetary claims that a shareholder can bring in a general action. The doctrine, sometimes referred to as the *exclusivity of the appraisal remedy*, directs that claims based solely on an inadequate stock price in the squeeze-out should be brought only in an appraisal proceeding. In an appraisal proceeding, the shareholder asks only for the fair value of her stock. Claims brought in a general action may ask the court to enjoin a merger or grant rescissory damages. The boundaries are difficult to draw in practice, however. See, e.g., Rabkin v. Philip A. Hunt Chemical Corp., 498 A.2d 1099 (Del 1985) (claims of unfair dealing based on timing of squeeze-out merger appropriate in general action); Cede & Co. v. Technicolor, Inc., 542 A.2d 1182 (Del 1988) (after-discovered fraud claim appropriate in general action); Cavalier Oil Corp. v. Harnett, 564 A.2d 1137 (Del 1989) (corporate opportunity claim that relates directly to value of stock appropriate in appraisal proceeding); Gonsalves v. Straight Arrow Publ. Inc., 701 A.2d 357 (Del. 1997) (claims of excessive CEO compensation not appropriate in appraisal proceeding).]

acquaint those shareholders with the bargaining positions of *Signal* and *UOP*, was withheld under circumstances amounting to a breach of fiduciary duty. We therefore conclude that this merger does not meet the test of fairness, at least as we address that concept, and no burden thus shifted to the plaintiff by reason of the minority shareholder vote. Accordingly, we reverse and remand for further proceedings consistent herewith. . . .

A primary issue mandating reversal is the preparation by two UOP directors, Arledge and Chitiea, of their feasibility study for the exclusive use and benefit of Signal. [Ed.: Arledge and Chitiea were also directors and officers of Signal. Arledge was Vice President and Director of Planning of Signal; Chitiea was Senior Vice President and Chief Financial Officer of Signal.] This document was of obvious significance to both Signal and UOP. Using UOP data, it described the advantages to Signal of ousting the minority at a price range of $21–$24 per share. . . .

[I]t is clear from the record that neither Arledge nor Chitiea shared this report with their fellow directors of UOP. . . . This conduct hardly meets the fiduciary standards applicable to such a transaction. . . . None of UOP's outside directors who testified stated that they had seen this document. . . .

The Arledge-Chitiea report speaks for itself in supporting the Chancellor's finding that a price of up to $24 was a "good investment" for Signal. It shows that a return on the investment at $21 would be 15.7 percent versus 15.5 percent at $24 per share. This was a difference of only two-tenths of one percent, while it meant over $17,000,000 to the minority. Under such circumstances, paying UOP's minority shareholders $24 would have had relatively little long-term effect on Signal, and the Chancellor's findings concerning the benefit to Signal, even at a price of $24, were obviously correct. . . .

Certainly, this was a matter of material significance to UOP and its shareholders. Since the study was prepared by two UOP directors, using UOP information for the exclusive benefit of Signal, and nothing whatever was done to disclose it to the outside UOP directors or the minority shareholders, a question of breach of fiduciary duty arises. This problem occurs because there were common Signal-UOP directors participating, at least to some extent, in the UOP board's decision-making processes without full disclosure of the conflicts they faced.[7] . . .

[7] Although perfection is not possible, or expected, the result here could have been entirely different if UOP had appointed an independent negotiating committee of its outside directors to deal with Signal at arm's length. . . . Since fairness in this context can be equated to conduct by a theoretical, wholly independent, board of directors acting upon the matter before them, it is unfortunate that this course apparently was neither considered nor pursued. . . . Particularly in a parent-subsidiary context, a showing that the action taken was as though each of the contending parties had in fact exerted its bargaining power against the other at arm's length is strong evidence that the transaction meets the test of fairness. . . .

Given the absence of any attempt to structure this transaction on an arm's length basis, Signal cannot escape the effects of the conflicts it faced, particularly when its designees on UOP's board did not totally abstain from participation in the matter. There is no "safe harbor" for such divided loyalties in Delaware. When directors of a Delaware corporation are on both sides of a transaction, they are required to demonstrate their utmost good faith and the most scrupulous inherent fairness of the bargain. . . . The requirement of fairness is unflinching in its demand that where one stands on both sides of a transaction, he has the burden of establishing its entire fairness, sufficient to pass the test of careful scrutiny by the courts. . . .

There is no dilution of this obligation where one holds dual or multiple directorships, as in a parent-subsidiary context. . . . Thus, individuals who act in a dual capacity as directors of two corporations, one of whom is parent and the other subsidiary, owe the same duty of good management to both corporations, and in the absence of an independent negotiating structure (see note 7, *supra*), or the directors' total abstention from any participation in the matter, this duty is to be exercised in light of what is best for both companies. . . . The record demonstrates that Signal has not met this obligation.

The concept of fairness has two basic aspects: fair dealing and fair price. The former embraces questions of when the transaction was timed, how it was initiated, structured, negotiated, disclosed to the directors, and how the approvals of the directors and the stockholders were obtained. The latter aspect of fairness relates to the economic and financial considerations of the proposed merger, including all relevant factors: assets, market value, earnings, future prospects, and any other elements that affect the intrinsic or inherent value of a company's stock. . . . However, the test for fairness is not a bifurcated one as between fair dealing and price. All aspects of the issue must be examined as a whole since the question is one of entire fairness. However, in a non-fraudulent transaction we recognize that price may be the preponderant consideration outweighing other features of the merger.[Ed.[29]] Here, we address the two basic aspects of fairness separately because we find reversible error as to both. . . .

ROSENBLATT v. GETTY OIL CO., 493 A.2d 929 (Del. 1985): In this class action brought on behalf of the minority stockholders of Skelly Oil Company (Skelly) we review a Court of Chancery decision holding that the

[29] [Ed. On the troublesome issue of how to value the minority shares once the court decided that there was no arm's-length negotiation between the boards of the parent and the subsidiary, the court noted that the Chancery Court on remand could include a "nonspeculative" amount representing value generated by the merger plan itself. "[E]lements of future value, including the nature of the enterprise, which are known or susceptible of proof may be considered."]

1977 stock-for-stock merger of Skelly and Mission Corporation (Mission) into Getty Oil Company (Getty) was entirely fair to the plaintiffs. . . . Immediately before this merger Getty directly owned 7.42 percent of Skelly's outstanding shares and 89.73 percent of Mission, which in turn held 72.6 percent of Skelly's stock. . . .

Beginning with the burden of proof, we agree with the trial court that the plaintiffs' allegations were sufficient to challenge the fairness of the merger ratio. . . . Clearly, Getty, as majority shareholder of Skelly, stood on both sides of this transaction and bore the initial burden of establishing its entire fairness. . . . However, approval of a merger, as here, by an informed vote of a majority of the minority shareholders, while not a legal prerequisite, shifts the burden of proving the unfairness of the merger entirely to the plaintiffs. . . . Getty, nonetheless, retained the burden of showing complete disclosure of all material facts relevant to that vote. . . .[Ed.[30]]

On the basis of this record we are satisfied that Getty dealt fairly with Skelly throughout the transaction. . . . Plaintiffs seek to compare this action to *Weinberger* by claiming that a memorandum, dated October 14, 1976, prepared by Robert J. Menzie, a Getty financial officer, was never disclosed to Skelly. In particular, plaintiffs liken this document, projecting a $52,165,000 after-tax decrease in Getty's 1976 earnings, in comparison to its 1975 earnings, to the Arledge and Chitiea report in *Weinberger*. . . .

[T]he Arledge-Chitiea report, used secretly by and exclusively for Signal, was prepared by two Signal directors, who were also UOP directors, using UOP information obtained solely in their capacities as UOP directors. *Weinberger*, 457 A.2d at 705. Here, the decreased earnings projection was prepared by a member of Getty's management for Getty's use as part of its annual reporting function. . . .

[30] [Ed. In the later opinion of Kahn v. Lynch Communication Systems, 638 A.2d 1110 (Del. 1993), the Delaware Supreme Court clarified that in a squeeze-out case the test is always one of entire fairness. Approval of the transaction by an independent committee of directors or by an informed majority of minority shareholders shifts the burden of proof on the issue of fairness from the controlling or dominating shareholder to the challenging shareholder/plaintiff but does not change the test; it remains an entire fairness inquiry. In the *Kahn* case, the court held that the independent negotiating committee did not engage in arm's-length bargaining, and the burden of proof did not shift to the plaintiff when the committee surrendered to an ultimatum, the threat of a hostile tender offer at a lower price, accompanying the controlling shareholder's final offer. On remand, the chancery court found that the transaction satisfied both the fair-dealing and fair-price parts of an entire fairness review. The Supreme Court affirmed, noting that the minority vote on the freeze-out merger was not coerced because the controlling shareholder and the minority shareholders all received the same price and there was full disclosure. In other words, the shareholder vote cured the defective Special Committee negotiations. Kahn v. Lynch Communication Systems, Inc., 669 A.2d 79 (1995). In a subsequent case, Kahn v. Tremont Corp., 694 A.2d 422 (Del. 1997), the court also held that a Special Committee's failure to act in an independent or informed matter left the burden of proof on the defendants. For another case in which the defendant directors carried their burden of proving entire fairness, see Cinerama, Inc. v. Technicolor, Inc., 663 A.2d 1156 (Del. 1995).]

While it has been suggested that *Weinberger* stands for the proposition that a majority shareholder must under all circumstances disclose its top bid to the minority, that clearly is a misconception of what we said there. The sole basis for our conclusions in *Weinberger* regarding the non-disclosure of the Arledge-Chitiea report was because Signal appointed directors on UOP's board, who thus stood on both sides of the transaction, violated their undiminished duty of loyalty to UOP. It had nothing to do with Signal's duty, as the majority stockholder, to the other shareholders of UOP.

As to the approval of the merger proposal by the Getty and Skelly boards, the record shows that their action was taken on an informed basis. . . . After careful scrutiny of the methods employed by the parties, the process of information gathering, the negotiations, and all relevant economic and financial factors, we conclude that the Chancellor's findings regarding fairness of the price paid the Skelly minority shareholders were entirely correct. . . .

GLASSMAN v. UNOCAL EXPLORATION, 777 A.2d 242 (Del. 2001) (Berger, Justice): [The exclusive remedy for minority shareholders in short-form merger transactions, 8 Del. C. § 253, is an appraisal remedy. The entire fairness test first articulated in *Weinberger v. UOP, Inc.* is not applicable once the parent owns over 90 percent of the sub. A subsequent Delaware Chancery Court case held, however, that the controlling shareholder does owe a fiduciary duty of disclosure to the minority shareholders, so the minority shareholders may make a fully informed decision on whether to exercise their appraisal rights].[31]

NOTE: CLEANSING PROCESSES EFFECT ON THE STANDARD OF REVIEW

Kahn v. Lynch Communication Systems, 638 A.2d 1110 (Del. 1993), discussed in an editor's note in *Rosenblatt,* above, resolved a split in two Delaware Court of Chancery decisions on the issue of whether, in a merger between a controlling shareholder and a firm (an interested merger), an informed majority of the minority shareholder vote or a vote by a special committee of disinterested directors could change the standard of judicial review from entire fairness to the business judgment rule. The court held that when the defendants prove a successful ratification, the standard of review does not change, but the burden of proof does. When the defendant successfully uses a cleansing process, the plaintiff must prove that the transaction was unfair. A majority of the minority favorable vote on the transaction, if fully informed and if the minority shareholders are paid that same price per share as is received by the controlling shareholder, may carry the burden of proving

---

[31] E.g., Erickson v. Centennial Beauregard Cellular, LLC, 2003 WL 1878583 (Del. Ch. 2003) (motion to dismiss denied in short-form merger).

entire fairness, however. *Kahn v. Lynch Communication Systems,* 669 A.2d 79, 86 (Del. 1995) (affirming result after remand).

Many states, following the Model Business Corporation Act, do not agree with *Kahn*. Their courts hold that a valid cleansing process shifts the standard of review to the business judgment rule in controlling shareholder cases. ABA Model Bus. Corp. Act Ch. 8, Subch. F (2016 rev.). The Model Act's drafters believed that, as a practical matter, a judicial analysis of a special committee's effectiveness or of the disclosures to inform minority shareholders would involve a close examination of the transaction's fairness. Once a court concludes that a special committee operated as an effective proxy for arm's-length, non-coerced bargaining or that an informed, non-coerced majority of the minority shareholders approved the deal, any additional layer of entire fairness evaluation seems repetitious. Cf. *Auerback v. Bennett,* 393 N.E. 2d 994 (N.Y. 1979) (summary judgment granted; business judgment rule applies to special litigation committee if independent and disinterested).

Delaware's Chancery Court has, at times, questioned the *Lynch* rule[32] and has refused to follow the rule in selected sub-classes of duty of loyalty cases involving cleansing processes. In cases *not* involving a conflicted controlling shareholder, the Chancery Court has held that the process in issue re-instates a business judgment rule analysis. See, e.g., *In re PNB Holding Co. Shareholders Litig.*, 2006 WL 2403999, at *14 n. 69 (Del Ch.); *Cooke v. Oolie,* 2000 WL 710199 (Del. Ch.) (business judgment rule applies if no controlling shareholders, directors conflicted, and disinterested director approval);[33] *In re Wheelabrator Tech. Shareholder Litg.*, 663 A.2d 1194 (Del. Ch. 1995) (business judgment rule applies if informed vote of a majority of the minority). Cf. *Lewis v. Vogelstein,* 699 A.2d 327 (Del. Ch. 1997) (shareholder ratification must be unanimous in cases of *waste*, "an exchange to which no reasonable person not acting under compulsion and in good faith could agree").

The Delaware Supreme Court itself has two lines of cases that apply the business judgment rule to a transaction when there is a vote of a "fully informed, uncoerced majority of the disinterested shareholders." In *Corwin v KKR Financial Holdings LLC,* 125 A. 3d 304 (Del. 2015), the court applied the business judgment rule when there was no controlling shareholder and a majority of the minority vote. In *Kahn II,* the case that follows, the court applied the rule with a controlling shareholder if a company used *both* a special committee and a majority of the minority vote. What remains open is whether a properly functioning special committee operating without a majority of the minority vote receives the protections of the business judgment rule.

The Delaware court's refusal to reinstate the business judgment rule for a properly functioning special committee's determinations without minority

---

[32] See, e.g., In re Pure Resources, Inc., Shareholders Litig., 808 A.2d 421, 444 n.43 (Del. Ch. 2002).

[33] A case in which there was a conflict of interest in a majority of the directors, a functioning SC, and no controlling or dominating shareholder would be similar to a case in which only a minority of the board was conflicted and the non-conflicted directors all supported the deal and there was no controlling or dominating shareholder.

shareholder ratification rests, perhaps, on the court's uneasiness with the independence of disinterested directors elected by a controlling shareholder and with the power of majority shareholders to intimidate minority shareholders with an implicit threat of retribution if the transaction failed. See *Kahn v. Lynch Comm. Sys.*, 638 A.2d 1110, 1116–17 (Del. 1993). In this regard, William T. Allen[34] has stated:

> . . . But I must confess a painful awareness of the ways in which the device may be subverted and rendered less than useful. . . .
>
> * * *
>
> Consider the outside director who is asked to serve on a special committee to preside over a sale of the company. While he may receive some modest special remuneration for this service, he and his fellow committee members are likely to be the only persons intensely involved in the process who do not entertain the fervent hope of either making a killing or earning a princely fee. Couple that with the pressure that the seriousness and urgency of the assignment generate; the unpleasantness that may be required if the job is done right; and, the fact that no matter what the director does he will probably be sued for it, and you have, I think, a fairly unappetizing assignment.
>
> Combine these factors with those . . . that create feelings of solidarity with management directors, particularly the corporation's CEO, and it becomes, I would think, quite easy to understand how some special committees appear as no more than, in T.S. Eliot's phrase, "an easy tool, deferential, glad to be of use."

William T. Allen, *Independent Directors in MBO Transactions: Are They Fact or Fantasy?*, 45 BUS. LAW. 2055, 2056, 2060–61 (1990). But see *In re CNX Gas Corp. Shareholders Litig.*, 2010 WL 2291842, at *13 (Del. Ch.) (Lasker, V.C.): "Post-*Lynch* experience shows that special committees can negotiate effectively with controllers and that both special committees and minority stockholders can reject squeeze-out proposals."

QUESTIONS

What is the practical effect of the Delaware Court refusing to apply the business judgment rule to a ratifying decision of an independent board or a ratifying vote of disinterested shareholders? How easy is it for defendants in a conflict-of-interest deal to win a summary judgment motion in Delaware courts based on a ratification process designed to cleanse the conflict?[35] In Delaware is judicial certification now just a normal part of the procedure in conflict-of-interest deals? A recent study found that minority shareholders in squeeze-out

---

[34] For many years a respected Chancellor of the Delaware Chancery Court.

[35] See, e.g., Krasner v. Moffett, 826 A.2d 277 (Del. 2003) (merger recommended by special committee could not be dismissed without factual inquiry).

deals routinely claim more than their pro rata share of firm value in the deals.[36] Have the courts been too protective?

KAHN V. M & F WORLDWIDE CORP.

Supreme Court of Delaware, 2014.
88 A.3d 635.

minority SHS in MFW

HOLLAND, JUSTICE:

[MacAndrews & Forbes Holdings, Inc. ("M & F" or "MacAndrews & Forbes"), a holding company entirely owned by Ronald Perelman, owned 43% of the common stock of M & F Worldwide Corp. ("MFW"). In 2011, M & F sought to acquire the remaining common stock of MFW that it did not already own through a single step merger (the "Merger"). From the outset, M & F's merger proposal was made contingent upon two stockholder-protective procedural conditions. First, M & F required the Merger to be negotiated and approved by a special committee of independent MFW directors (the "Special Committee"). Second, M & F required that the Merger be approved by a majority of stockholders unaffiliated with M & F (*i.e.*, a "majority of the minority"). The Merger closed in December 2011, after it was approved by a vote of 65.4% of MFW's minority stockholders.

Plaintiff minority stockholders (the "Appellants") sought post-closing relief against M & F, Ronald Perelman and the other twelve MFW directors (including the four members of the Special Committee) (the "Defendants") for breach of fiduciary duty. After the Appellants were provided with extensive discovery, the Defendants then moved for summary judgment, which the Court of Chancery granted.[Ed.[37]]

The Court of Chancery found that the case presented a "novel question of law," specifically, "what standard of review should apply to a going private merger conditioned upfront by the controlling stockholder on approval by both a properly empowered, independent committee and an informed, uncoerced majority-of-the-minority vote." The Court of Chancery held that business judgment review, rather than entire fairness, should be applied to a very limited category of controller mergers. That category consisted of mergers where the controller voluntarily relinquishes its control—such that the negotiation and approval process replicate those that characterize a third-party merger. Finding that this had, in fact, occurred in this case and that the Appellants had failed to raise any genuine issue of material fact indicating the contrary, the Court of Chancery then reviewed the Merger under the business judgment standard and granted summary judgment for the Defendants.]

---

[36] Thomas Bates, Michal Lemmon & James Lunch, *Shareholder Wealth Effects and Bid Negotiation in Freeze Out Deals, Are Minority Shareholders Left Out in the Cold?*, 81 J. FIN. ECON. 681 (2006) (no).

[37] [Ed. In re MFW Shareholders Litigation, 67 A.3d 396 (Del. Ch. 2013).]

* * *

ANALYSIS

What Should Be the Review Standard?

Where a transaction involving self-dealing by a controlling stockholder is challenged, the applicable standard of judicial review is "entire fairness," with the defendants having the burden of persuasion. In other words, the defendants bear the ultimate burden of proving that the transaction with the controlling stockholder was entirely fair to the minority stockholders. In *Kahn v. Lynch Communication Systems, Inc.* . . . ,[6] however, this Court held that in "entire fairness" cases, the defendants may shift the burden of persuasion to the plaintiff if either (1) they show that the transaction was approved by a well-functioning committee of independent directors; **or** (2) they show that the transaction was approved by an informed vote of a majority of the minority stockholders.

This appeal presents a question of first impression: what should be the standard of review for a merger between a controlling stockholder and its subsidiary, where the merger is conditioned *ab initio* upon the approval of **both** an independent, adequately-empowered Special Committee that fulfills its duty of care, and the uncoerced, informed vote of a majority of the minority stockholders. The question has never been put directly to this Court.

. . . . The Appellants submit . . . that statements in *Lynch* and its progeny could be (and were) read to suggest that even if both procedural protections were used, the standard of review would remain entire fairness. However, in *Lynch* and the other cases that Appellants cited, . . . the controller did not give up its voting power by agreeing to a non-waivable majority-of-the-minority condition. That is the vital distinction between those cases and this one. . . .

* * *

Business Judgment Review Standard Adopted

We hold that business judgment is the standard of review that should govern mergers between a controlling stockholder and its corporate subsidiary, where the merger is conditioned *ab initio* upon both the approval of an independent, adequately-empowered Special Committee that fulfills its duty of care; and the uncoerced, informed vote of a majority of the minority stockholders. We so conclude for several reasons.

First, entire fairness is the highest standard of review in corporate law. It is applied in the controller merger context as a substitute for the dual statutory protections of disinterested board and stockholder approval, because both protections are potentially undermined by the influence of the

---

[6] . . . 638 A.2d 1110 (Del.1994).

controller. However, as this case establishes, that undermining influence does not exist in every controlled merger setting, regardless of the circumstances. The simultaneous deployment of the procedural protections employed here create a countervailing, offsetting influence of equal—if not greater—force. That is, where the controller irrevocably and publicly disables itself from using its control to dictate the outcome of the negotiations and the shareholder vote, the controlled merger then acquires the shareholder-protective characteristics of third-party, arm's-length mergers, which are reviewed under the business judgment standard.

Second, the dual procedural protection merger structure optimally protects the minority stockholders in controller buyouts. As the Court of Chancery explained:

> [W]hen these two protections are established up-front, a potent tool to extract good value for the minority is established. From inception, the controlling stockholder knows that it cannot bypass the special committee's ability to say no. And, the controlling stockholder knows it cannot dangle a majority-of-the-minority vote before the special committee late in the process as a deal-closer rather than having to make a price move.

Third, and as the Court of Chancery reasoned, applying the business judgment standard to the dual protection merger structure:

> . . . is consistent with the central tradition of Delaware law, which defers to the informed decisions of impartial directors, especially when those decisions have been approved by the disinterested stockholders on full information and without coercion. Not only that, the adoption of this rule will be of benefit to minority stockholders because it will provide a strong incentive for controlling stockholders to accord minority investors the transactional structure that respected scholars believe will provide them the best protection, a structure where stockholders get the benefits of independent, empowered negotiating agents to **bargain for the best price and say no** if the agents believe the deal is not advisable for any proper reason, plus the critical ability to determine for themselves whether to accept any deal that their negotiating agents recommend to them. A transactional structure with both these protections is fundamentally different from one with only one protection.[11]

Fourth, the underlying purposes of the dual protection merger structure utilized here and the entire fairness standard of review both converge and are fulfilled at the same critical point: **price.** Following *Weinberger v. UOP, Inc.*, this Court has consistently held that, although entire fairness review comprises the dual components of fair dealing and fair price, in a non-fraudulent transaction "price may be the preponderant

---

[11] Emphasis added.

consideration outweighing other features of the merger."[12] The dual protection merger structure requires two price-related pretrial determinations: first, that a fair price was achieved by an empowered, independent committee that acted with care; and, second, that a fullyinformed, uncoerced majority of the minority stockholders voted in favor of the price that was recommended by the independent committee.

The New Standard Summarized

To summarize our holding, in controller buyouts, the business judgment standard of review will be applied *if and only if:* (i) the controller conditions the procession of the transaction on the approval of both a Special Committee and a majority of the minority stockholders; (ii) the Special Committee is independent; (iii) the Special Committee is empowered to freely select its own advisors and to say no definitively; (iv) the Special Committee meets its duty of care in negotiating a fair price; (v) the vote of the minority is informed; and (vi) there is no coercion of the minority.[14]

If a plaintiff that can plead a reasonably conceivable set of facts showing that any or all of those enumerated conditions did not exist, that complaint would state a claim for relief that would entitle the plaintiff to proceed and conduct discovery. If, after discovery, triable issues of fact remain about whether either or both of the dual procedural protections were established, or if established were effective, the case will proceed to a trial in which the court will conduct an entire fairness review.

This approach is consistent with *Weinberger, Lynch* and their progeny. A controller that employs and/or establishes only one of these dual procedural protections would continue to receive burden-shifting within the entire fairness standard of review framework. Stated differently, unless *both* procedural protections for the minority stockholders are established *prior to trial,* the ultimate judicial scrutiny of controller buyouts will continue to be the entire fairness standard of review.

Having articulated the circumstances that will enable a controlled merger to be reviewed under the business judgment standard, we next address whether those circumstances have been established as a matter of undisputed fact and law in this case.

---

12 Weinberger v. UOP, Inc., 457 A.2d 701, 711 (Del.1983).

14 The Verified Consolidated Class Action Complaint would have survived a motion to dismiss under this new standard.... [The Appellants' multiple] ... allegations about the sufficiency of the price call into question the adequacy of the Special Committee's negotiations, thereby necessitating discovery on all of the new prerequisites to the application of the business judgment rule.

Dual Protection Inquiry

* * *

We begin by reviewing the record relating to the independence, mandate, and process of the Special Committee. In *Kahn v. Tremont Corp.*, this Court held that "[t]o obtain the benefit of burden shifting, the controlling stockholder must do more than establish a perfunctory special committee of outside directors."[38]

Rather, the special committee must "function in a manner which indicates that the controlling stockholder did not dictate the terms of the transaction and that the committee exercised real bargaining power 'at an arms-length.' "[39] As we have previously noted, deciding whether an independent committee was effective in negotiating a price is a process so fact-intensive and inextricably intertwined with the merits of an entire fairness review (fair dealing and fair price) that a pretrial determination of burden shifting is often impossible. Here, however, the Defendants have successfully established a record of independent committee effectiveness and process that warranted a grant of summary judgment entitling them to a burden shift prior to trial.

We next analyze the efficacy of the majority-of-the-minority vote, and we conclude that it was fully informed and not coerced. That is, the Defendants also established a pretrial majority-of-the-minority vote record that constitutes an independent and alternative basis for shifting the burden of persuasion to the Plaintiffs.

The Special Committee Was Independent

The Appellants do not challenge the independence of the Special Committee's Chairman, Meister. They claim, however, that the three other Special Committee members—Webb, Dinh, and Byorum—were beholden to Perelman because of their prior business and/or social dealings with Perelman or Perelman-related entities.

* * *

To evaluate the parties' competing positions on the issue of director independence, the Court of Chancery applied well-established Delaware legal principles.[26] To show that a director is not independent, a plaintiff must demonstrate that the director is "beholden" to the controlling party "or so under [the controller's] influence that [the director's] discretion

---

[38] Kahn v. Tremont Corp., 694 A.2d 422, 429 (Del.1997) (citation omitted). . . .

[39] [*Id.*] at 429 (citation omitted).

[26] The record does not support the Appellants' contention that that the Court of Chancery "relied heavily" on New York Stock Exchange ("NYSE") rules in assessing the independence of the Special Committee, and that the application of such rules "goes against longstanding Delaware precedent." The Court of Chancery explicitly acknowledged that directors' compliance with NYSE independence standards "does not mean that they are necessarily independent under [Delaware] law in particular circumstances." The record reflects that the Court of Chancery discussed NYSE standards on director independence for illustrative purposes. . . .

would be sterilized."[27] Bare allegations that directors are friendly with, travel in the same social circles as, or have past business relationships with the proponent of a transaction or the person they are investigating are not enough to rebut the presumption of independence.

A plaintiff seeking to show that a director was not independent must satisfy a materiality standard. The court must conclude that the director in question had ties to the person whose proposal or actions he or she is evaluating that are sufficiently substantial that he or she could not objectively discharge his or her fiduciary duties. Consistent with that predicate materiality requirement, the existence of some financial ties between the interested party and the director, without more, is not disqualifying. The inquiry must be whether, applying a subjective standard, those ties were *material,* in the sense that the alleged ties could have affected the impartiality of the individual director.

* * *

[The Delaware Supreme Court then carefully reviewed the findings of the Court of Chancery with respect to the independence of Webb, Dinh, and Byorum.] The record supports the Court of Chancery's holding that none of the Appellants' claims relating to Webb, Dinh or Byorum raised a triable issue of material fact concerning their individual independence or the Special Committee's collective independence.

The Special Committee Was Empowered

It is undisputed that the Special Committee was empowered to hire its own legal and financial advisors, and it retained Willkie Farr & Gallagher LLP as its legal advisor. After interviewing four potential financial advisors, the Special Committee engaged Evercore Partners ("Evercore"). The qualifications and independence of Evercore and Willkie Farr & Gallagher LLP are not contested.

Among the powers given the Special Committee in the board resolution was the authority to "report to the Board its recommendations and conclusions with respect to the [Merger], including a determination and recommendation as to whether the Proposal is fair and in the best interests of the stockholders. . . ." The Court of Chancery also found that it was "undisputed that the [S]pecial [C]ommittee was empowered not simply to 'evaluate' the offer, like some special committees with weak mandates, but to negotiate with [M & F] over the terms of its offer to buy out the noncontrolling stockholders. This negotiating power was accompanied by the clear authority to say no definitively to [M & F]" and to "make that decision stick." MacAndrews & Forbes promised that it would not proceed with any going private proposal that did not have the support of the Special Committee. Therefore, the Court of Chancery concluded, "the MFW

---

[27] *Rales v. Blasband,* 634 A.2d 927, 936 (Del.1993) (citing *Aronson v. Lewis,* 473 A.2d 805, 815 (Del.1984)).

committee did not have to fear that if it bargained too hard, MacAndrews & Forbes could bypass the committee and make a tender offer directly to the minority stockholders."

The Court of Chancery acknowledged that even though the Special Committee had the authority to negotiate and "say no," it did not have the authority, as a practical matter, to sell MFW to other buyers. MacAndrews & Forbes stated in its announcement that it was not interested in selling its 43% stake. Moreover, under Delaware law, MacAndrews & Forbes had no duty to sell its block, which was large enough, again as a practical matter, to preclude any other buyer from succeeding unless MacAndrews & Forbes decided to become a seller. Absent such a decision, it was unlikely that any potentially interested party would incur the costs and risks of exploring a purchase of MFW.

Nevertheless, the Court of Chancery found, "this did not mean that the MFW Special Committee did not have the leeway to get advice from its financial advisor about the strategic options available to MFW, including the potential interest that other buyers might have *if MacAndrews & Forbes was willing to sell*."[36] The undisputed record shows that the Special Committee, with the help of its financial advisor, did consider whether there were other buyers who might be interested in purchasing MFW, and whether there were other strategic options, such as asset divestitures, that might generate more value for minority stockholders than a sale of their stock to MacAndrews & Forbes.

The Special Committee Exercised Due Care

The Special Committee insisted from the outset that MacAndrews (including any "dual" employees who worked for both MFW and MacAndrews) be screened off from the Special Committee's process, to ensure that the process replicated arm's-length negotiations with a third party. In order to carefully evaluate M & F's offer, the Special Committee held a total of eight meetings during the summer of 2011.

* * *

In scrutinizing the Special Committee's execution of its broad mandate, the Court of Chancery determined there was no "evidence indicating that the independent members of the special committee did not meet their duty of care. . . ." To the contrary, the Court of Chancery found, the Special Committee "met frequently and was presented with a rich body of financial information relevant to whether and at what *price* a going private transaction was advisable." The Court of Chancery ruled that "the plaintiffs d[id] not make any attempt to show that the MFW Special Committee failed to meet its duty of care. . . ." Based on the undisputed record, the Court of Chancery held that, "there is no triable issue of fact regarding whether the [S]pecial [C]ommittee fulfilled its duty of care." In

[36] Emphasis added.

the context of a controlling stockholder merger, a pretrial determination that the *price* was negotiated by an empowered independent committee that acted with care would shift the burden of persuasion to the plaintiffs under the entire fairness standard of review.

Majority of Minority Stockholder Vote

We now consider the second procedural protection invoked by M & F—the majority-of-the-minority stockholder vote. Consistent with the second condition imposed by M & F at the outset, the Merger was then put before MFW's stockholders for a vote. On November 18, 2011, the stockholders were provided with a proxy statement, which contained the history of the Special Committee's work and recommended that they vote in favor of the transaction at a price of $25 per share.

The proxy statement disclosed, among other things, that the Special Committee had countered M & F's initial $24 per share offer at $30 per share, but only was able to achieve a final offer of $25 per share. The proxy statement disclosed that the MFW business divisions had discussed with Evercore whether the initial projections Evercore received reflected management's latest thinking. It also disclosed that the updated projections were lower. The proxy statement also included the five separate price ranges for the value of MFW's stock that Evercore had generated with its different valuation analyses.

Knowing the proxy statement's disclosures of the background of the Special Committee's work, of Evercore's valuation ranges, and of the analyses supporting Evercore's *fairness opinion,* MFW's stockholders—representing more than 65% of the minority shares—approved the Merger. In the controlling stockholder merger context, it is settled Delaware law that an uncoerced, informed majority-of-the-minority vote, without any other procedural protection, is itself sufficient to shift the burden of persuasion to the plaintiff under the entire fairness standard of review. The Court of Chancery found that "the plaintiffs themselves do not dispute that the majority-of-the-minority vote was fully informed and uncoerced, because they fail to allege any failure of disclosure or any act of coercion."

Both Procedural Protections Established

Based on a highly extensive record, the Court of Chancery concluded that the procedural protections upon which the Merger was conditioned-approval by an independent and empowered Special Committee and by a uncoerced informed majority of MFW's minority stockholders-had *both* been undisputedly established *prior to trial.* We agree and conclude the Defendants' motion for summary judgment was properly granted on all of those issues.

Business Judgment Review Properly Applied

We have determined that the business judgment rule standard of review applies to this controlling stockholder buyout. Under that standard, the claims against the Defendants must be dismissed unless no rational person could have believed that the merger was favorable to MFW's minority stockholders. In this case, it cannot be credibly argued (let alone concluded) that no rational person would find the Merger favorable to MFW's minority stockholders.

Conclusion

For the above-stated reasons, the judgment of the Court of Chancery is affirmed.

NOTE: COMPENSATION OF SPECIAL NEGOTIATING COMMITTEES

Is a sense of duty enough? Courts could encourage firms to realign the incentives of directors on special committees by tailoring their compensation to their performance in acquisition negotiations. Paying outside directors solely in stock or stock options rather than cash would have the effect of aligning them financially with the firm's shareholders in takeovers if they hold their stock during the period of their directorship. Since the amount of stock held by individual directors may not be large and the potential gains on their shares in a takeover not significant (particularly if a director is new), a firm could offer cash bonuses tied directly to stock price increases resulting from the acts of the special committee in response to an MBO. Such compensation packages would have the added advantage of signaling to the markets and to the special committee directors themselves that the firm has a serious commitment to having an independent board negotiate to maximize shareholder wealth in all MBOs.[40] Novel methods of compensation would eliminate much of the tacit conflict of interest pressures (Should I be loyal to the CEO that appointed me?) that result when special committees respond to an MBO. Unfortunately, the creation of specially compensated and empowered directorships has never received serious consideration. Courts could act as a stimulus to novel compensation methods by declaring that special committees so compensated are the only ones that courts will judge under the unadorned, traditional business judgment rule.

---

[40] One could also generalize the system to all takeovers, particularly those in which the management team is threatened with the loss of their jobs. See Dale A. Oesterle, *Target Managers as Negotiators*, 71 CORNELL L. REV. 53, 70–71 (1985). The special director, of course, may lose his job upon completion of a tender offer, but he realizes no gain by defeating a tender offer unless the post-tender offer stock price exceeds the weighted average of the tender offer price and the anticipated second-stage merger price. Moreover, the special director's reputation as a negotiating agent, which could earn him opportunities to act in a similar capacity for other companies, depends on his success in negotiating the best price.

3. TENDER OFFERS FOR MINORITY SHARES BY CONTROLLING SHAREHOLDERS—THE *COERCION* TEST

In 2001 a Delaware Vice Chancellor in the *Siliconix* litigation[41] noted that a combination of two previous Delaware Supreme Court cases made it possible to accomplish a buy-out of a minority interest without satisfying the entire fairness test required in *Kahn*. Instead of using a triangular statutory merger, the buyer acquires the minority shares through a two-step transaction, a tender offer and a short-form merger. The tender offer, under a 1996 opinion,[42] required only that there be no deception or coercion and the short-form merger statute, under a 2001 opinion,[43] limited shareholders' remedies to their statutory appraisal rights. Private equity funds immediately started doing *Siliconix deals* to take advantage of the disparity in judicial review. Control premiums paid in two-step deals were lower that the premiums paid in one step mergers and the two-step deals closed with more frequency and faster.

Later Chancery Court opinions noted the inconsistency and suggested that the Supreme Court (1) lighten the *Kahn* standard and (2) tighten the tender offer test. Waiting for Supreme Court action the Chancery Court itself tightened the *coercion* test under the tender offer standard.[44] A tender offer is not coercive if the offer: (1) is conditioned on tenders by a majority of the minority shareholders, (2) promises a follow up, short-form merger, and (3) is unaccompanied by any retributive threats. The coercion test has now been supplanted (or supplemented?) by a *unitary test*.[45]

IN RE CNX GAS CORPORATION SHAREHOLDERS LITIGATION

Court of Chancery of Delaware, 2010.
4 A.3d 397.

LASTER, VICE CHANCELLOR.

Representatives of a putative class of minority stockholders have challenged a controlling stockholder freeze-out structured as a first-step tender offer to be followed by a second-step short-form merger. The plaintiffs have sued the controlling stockholder, its controlled subsidiary, and the four members of the subsidiary board. Three of the subsidiary directors are also directors of the controller. The fourth is an independent outsider and the sole member of the special committee formed to respond to the controller's tender offer. The plaintiffs have moved for a preliminary injunction against the transaction.

---

41 In re Siliconix, Inc. Shareholders Litig., 2001 WL 716787 (Del. Ch. 2001).

42 Solomon v. Pathe Comm., 672 A.2d 35 (Del. 1996).

43 Glassman v. Unocal Exploration, 777 A.2d 242 (Del. 2001).

44 In re Pure Resources, Inc., Shareholders Litig., 808 A.2d 421 (Del. Ch. 2002).

45 In re Cox Communications Inc. Shareholder Litig., 879 A.2d 604 (Del. Ch. 2005).

. . . On April 28, 2010, CONSOL commenced a tender offer to acquire the outstanding public shares of CNX Gas at a price of $38.25 per share in cash (the "Tender Offer"). The price represents a premium of 45.83% over the closing price of CNX Gas's common stock on the day before CONSOL announced the Dominion Transaction and its intent to acquire the shares of CNX Gas that it did not already own ($26.23). The Tender Offer price represents a 24.19% premium over the closing price of CNX Gas's common stock on the day before CONSOL announced the T. Rowe Price agreement ($30.80).

CONSOL has committed to effect a short-form merger promptly after the successful consummation of the Tender Offer. In the merger, remaining stockholders will receive the same consideration of $38.25 per share in cash. Consummation of the Tender Offer is subject to a non-waivable condition that a majority of the outstanding minority shares be tendered, excluding shares owned by directors or officers of CONSOL or CNX Gas. The T. Rowe Price shares are included in the majority-of-the-minority calculation. With the T. Rowe Price shares locked up, CONSOL only needs to obtain an additional 3,006,316 shares, or approximately 12% of the outstanding stock, to satisfy the condition.

At a special meeting held on April 15, the CNX Gas board unanimously approved the formation of a special committee. . . . The scope of the authority that the CNX Gas board provided to the Special Committee was limited. The Special Committee was authorized only to review and evaluate the Tender Offer, to prepare a Schedule 14D–9, and to engage legal and financial advisors for those purposes. The resolution did *not* authorize the Special Committee to negotiate the terms of the Tender Offer or to consider alternatives.

After the April 15 board meeting, the Special Committee retained Skadden, Arps, Slate, Meagher & Flom LLP ("Skadden") as its legal advisor and Lazard, Ltd. ("Lazard") as its financial advisor. . . . Even though the Special Committee was technically not authorized to negotiate, Pipski decided to seek a price increase. . . . Five days later, on May 10, the day before the Schedule 14D–9 was due, the CNX Gas board retroactively granted the Special Committee authority to negotiate. On the next day, May 11, Pipski and his advisors held a call with CONSOL senior executives and their advisors. CONSOL declined to increase the price.

Later on May 11, the Special Committee issued the Schedule 14D–9. The Special Committee stated in the Schedule 14D–9 that it "determined not to express an opinion on the offer and to remain neutral with respect to the offer." The Special Committee cited its "concerns about the process by which CONSOL determined the offer price" and its "view that CONSOL was unwilling to negotiate the offer price." The Schedule 14D–9 noted that a member of CONSOL management previously suggested that CNX Gas stock was worth more than $38.25. The Schedule 14D–9 also reported that the CNX Gas board refused to expand the size of the Special Committee or grant it the full power of the board in connection with the offer.

* * *

The Tender Offer is scheduled to close tomorrow. . . .

* * *

Cox Communications rendered the *Lynch* and *Siliconix* standards coherent by explaining that the business judgment rule should apply to any freeze-out transaction that is structured to mirror *both* elements of an arms' length merger, *viz.* approval by disinterested directors *and* approval by disinterested stockholders. . . .

* * *

Under the *Cox Communications* framework, if a freeze-out merger is both (i) negotiated and approved by a special committee of independent directors and (ii) conditioned on an affirmative vote of a majority of the minority stockholders, then the business judgment standard of review presumptively applies[Ed.[46]]. . . . If the transaction does not incorporate both protective devices, or if a plaintiff can plead particularized facts sufficient to raise a litigable question about the effectiveness of one of the devices, then the transaction is subject to entire fairness review. *Id.* The viability of a challenge to a controlling stockholder merger in which both protective devices are used thus can be assessed prior to trial, either on the pleadings or via motion for summary judgment. . . .

Likewise under the *Cox Communications* framework, if a first-step tender offer is both (i) negotiated and recommended by a special committee of independent directors and (ii) conditioned on the affirmative tender of a majority of the minority shares, then the business judgment standard of review presumptively applies to the freeze-out transaction. . . . As with a merger, if both requirements are not met, then the transaction is reviewed for entire fairness. . . .

Post-*Lynch* experience shows that special committees can negotiate effectively with controllers and that both special committees and minority stockholders can reject squeeze-out proposals. The 2008 exchange offer in this case was withdrawn when minority stockholders responded negatively. I am currently presiding over a challenge to a controlling transaction in which the majority-of-the-minority tender condition failed twice. . . . Last fall the directors of iBasis adopted a rights plan in response to a tender offer by its controlling stockholder, Royal KPN. The iBasis directors filed two lawsuits against Royal KPN, took one of the lawsuits through trial, and ultimately extracted a price increase from $2.25 to $3 per share. In 2005, minority stockholders at Cablevision Systems

[46] [Ed. The Vice Chancellor seems to be assuming a modification of the Delaware Supreme Court holding in *Lynch*.]

Corporation rejected a going private transaction proposed by the Dolan family, which controlled 74% of the company's voting power, despite its 51% premium over market. In 2003, the outside directors of Next Level Communications, Inc. resisted a *Siliconix* tender offer and filed suit against the controlling stockholder to enjoin the transaction. . . . In *Siliconix* itself, the exchange offer that was the subject of the decision ultimately failed to satisfy its majority-of-the-minority condition. These examples augur in favor of a unified standard under which independent directors and unaffiliated stockholders are given the tools to negotiate with controllers, backstopped by meaningful judicial review for fairness when those tools are withheld.

* * *

The Tender Offer does not pass muster under the unified standard. First and most obviously, the Special Committee did not recommend in favor of the transaction. That fact alone is sufficient to end the analysis and impose an obligation on CONSOL to pay a fair price.

Second, the Special Committee was not provided with authority comparable to what a board would possess in a third-party transaction. Initially, the Special Committee was authorized only to review and evaluate the Tender Offer, to prepare a Schedule 14D–9, and to engage legal and financial advisors for those purposes. The Special Committee was not authorized to negotiate or to consider other alternatives. . . .

The CNX Gas board majority grounded its decision on CONSOL's unwillingness to sell its CNX Gas shares. Given CONSOL's position as a controlling stockholder and the additional rights CONSOL possessed under its various agreements with CNX Gas, any effort to explore strategic alternatives likely would have been an exercise in futility. But that was a decision for Pipski and his advisors to make. Armed with an appropriate delegation of authority, Pipski and the creative minds at Skadden and Lazard might have devised ways to increase the Special Committee's leverage. They might have filed litigation against CONSOL. Or they might have considered some form of rights plan.

* * *

These principles apply directly here. A controller making a tender offer does not have an inalienable right to usurp or restrict the authority of the subsidiary board of directors. A subsidiary board, acting directly or through a special committee, can deploy a rights plan legitimately against a controller's tender offer, just as against a third-party tender offer, to provide the subsidiary with time to respond, negotiate, and develop alternatives. The fact that the subsidiary's alternatives may be limited as a practical matter does not require that the controller be given a veto over the board decision-making process. Prolonged and inequitable use of the rights plan by the subsidiary remains subject to traditional review under

Unocal Corp. v. Mesa Petroleum Co., 493 A.2d 946 (Del.1985). Unlike dispersed stockholders, a controller typically also will have the ability to use its voting power to remove and replace incumbent directors and, if it wishes, force through its chosen transaction via merger.

Because a board in a third-party transaction would have the power to respond effectively to a tender offer, including by deploying a rights plan, a subsidiary board should have the same power if the freeze-out is to receive business judgment review. This does not mean that a special committee must use that power. The shadow of pill adoption alone may be sufficient to prompt a controller to give a special committee more time to negotiate or to evaluate how to proceed. What matters is that the special committee fulfills its contextualized duty to obtain the best transaction reasonably available for the minority stockholders. Here, the Special Committee was deprived of authority that a board would have in a third-party transaction. Under *Cox Communications,* this fact provides a separate and independent basis to review a controlling stockholder freeze-out for entire fairness.

* * *

The absence of Special Committee approval imposes an obligation on the defendants to show that the Tender Offer price is fair. . . .

* * *

. . . A plaintiff seeking to enjoin a tender offer must show that a post-trial award of money damages would not be a sufficient remedy. . . . If the defendants fail to establish that the tender price is fair, an award of money damages can be fashioned. No question has been raised, much less evidence presented, to cast doubt on CONSOL's solvency or ability to satisfy a damages award. The plaintiffs therefore have not shown any threat of irreparable harm. Given the availability of monetary relief, the balance of the equities favors the denial of the motion for preliminary injunction. . . .

QUESTION

How frequently can a deal satisfy the majority-of-minority tender condition?[47]

[47] For example, if the controlling shareholder owns forty percent of the stock, it needs another fifty percent (83 percent of the outstanding minority shares; fifty percent of sixty percent) to get to ninety percent voting control in order to execute the short-form merger under Del. Gen. Corp. Law § 253. If the controlling shareholder owns eighty-five percent of the stock, it needs only another five percent of the shares outstanding (33 percent of the minority shares; 5 percent of 15 percent) to get to ninety percent. The majority-of-minority tender condition is redundant for the forty percent shareholders and a real burden for the eighty-five percent shareholder.

NOTE: EMPIRICAL EVIDENCE

Two studies have found that minority shareholders in a freeze-out tender offer receive lower cumulative abnormal returns on average that do the minority shareholders in a pure freeze-out merger. Fernan Restrepo, *Judicial Review and Gains of Minority Shareholders in Freeze-Out Transactions*, 3 HARV. BUS. L. REV., Issue 2 (Aug. 1, 2013) (summarizing studies).

NOTE: DUTY OF THE SPECIAL COMMITTEE TO EXERCISE HOLD UP POWER IN SQUEEZE-OUTS

The *Siliconix* line of cases is odd in juxtaposition with the *Unocal* line of cases discussed in the next Chapter. *Unocal* empowers boards of directors facing hostile takeovers to be active in blocking hostile bidders. Courts must decide whether a decision to adopt a *poison pill* (or *rights*) plan is a breach of fiduciary duty. In *Siliconix* deals, the target board's representative, the special committee, may breach its fiduciary duty by *not* adopting, or threatening to adopt, a poison pill plan so as to maximize its negotiating power with a controlling shareholder. A poison pill plan is the only method of blocking a deal outside of litigation when a majority of the shares are held by a controlling shareholder.[48] If a board does not use a poison pill plan (or the threat of one) must it, in the alternative, sue (or threaten to sue) to block the deal? Moreover, under *Siliconix*, a board's filings under federal securities rules on tender offers become the subject of a fiduciary duty inquiry. How must, as a matter of state law, a target board satisfy its disclosure obligations under Exchange Act Rules 14e–2 and 14d–9 (see Chapter Two, Section B.2.b.iii)? Similar issues can occur in squeeze-out triangular mergers.

4. MINORITY STOCK REPURCHASES IN ANTICIPATION OF AN ACQUISITION[49]

LAWTON V. NYMAN

United States Court of Appeals, First Circuit, 2003.
327 F.3d 30.

LYNCH, CIRCUIT JUDGE.

* * *

Nyman Manufacturing Company was a closely held, fourth-generation family-owned company in Rhode Island that manufactured paper and plastic dinnerware. Robert Nyman, the President and CEO of the company,

---

[48] Cf. Malpiede v. Townson, 780 A.2d 1025 (Del. 2001) (allegation that board was grossly negligent in failing to adopt poison pill plan that might have allowed the board to negotiate for a higher bid; dismissed on a § 102(b)(7) exculpatory charter provision defense).

[49] See also Alessi v. Beracha, 849 A.2d 939 (Del. Ch. 2004) (claim that directors breached a fiduciary duty of disclosure by failing to disclose merger negotiations at a time when the corporation was repurchasing its common stock survives a motion to dismiss).

and his brother Kenneth, the Vice-President of Manufacturing, had worked in the business their entire adult lives.

There were two classes of company stock: Class A shares, which were non-voting, and Class B shares, which were voting stock. The company's articles of incorporation authorized 13,500 shares of Class A stock and 1,500 shares of Class B stock. Traditionally, one or two family members owned all of the Class B stock, while the Class A shares were dispersed throughout the family. No dividends were ever paid on either class of stock. Robert and Kenneth Nyman had each inherited 375 shares of the Class B voting stock from their uncle; this was the entirety of the issued Class B stock. Because they were the controlling shareholders, we refer to them as the majority shareholders of the company. In the beginning of 1995, there were 8,385 shares of Class A stock outstanding. Judith Lawton, the sister of Robert and Kenneth, owned Class A stock, as did her husband and eight children. The Lawtons together owned 952 Class A shares. . . .

The company teetered on the verge of bankruptcy in the late 1980s. In 1991, the company's performance again began to suffer. In 1994, after three consecutive years of losses, the company hired Keith Johnson, a specialist in turning around and then selling companies, as a consultant. Johnson was made the Chief Financial Officer and Treasurer in August 1994, and his liability stems from his position as an officer. He was promised an equity share of the company if he could revive the company's flagging profits.

By the spring of 1995, it appeared that the fortunes of the ailing company were being reversed. Earlier, in the fiscal year ending March 25, 1995, the company reported a profit of nearly $1.6 million, in vivid contrast with its past losses. . . .

* * *

The company's fiscal year ended on March 29, 1996. The unaudited financials showed a profit of $3.5 million and a quadrupling of shareholder equity. . . .

* * *

On May 8, 1996, the company, over Johnson's signature, sent letters to all Class A shareholders except Robert and Kenneth, their spouses, and the Walfred Nyman Trust, offering to redeem their shares for $200 per share. . . .

Several statements in the letter were not accurate. The record shows that the impetus to redeem the shares came from the company, not that the company made the offer in response to several inquiries from other minority shareholders concerning their desire to sell their stock. The record also shows that there was no bank-imposed deadline of May 22, as the letter implied. One lender had imposed no deadlines and the other had imposed a deadline of July 29. . . .

The next day, on May 9, 1996, Johnson reported to Heller Financial, Inc. that Nyman's fiscal year-end profit was estimated to be $3.533 million, and he included a copy of Nyman's unaudited FY 1996 financial statement. The unaudited financials were not disclosed to plaintiffs, nor was the decision to retain a consultant, nor was the fact that the defendants were in May engaged in discussions to acquire other companies. The letter also implied that the $200 a share price was based on "favorable economic factors and current estimates of operating results," but did not disclose what was meant by this. The stock price of $200 a share was based on neither current market value nor book value. Defendants did not seek to have an appraisal done.

* * *

Most of the Lawtons met on the evening of May 10 and, after ruminating over the weekend, all of the Lawtons who held stock in Nyman Manufacturing Co. agreed to sell their shares. . . . Because this stock was redeemed by the company, the redemption increased defendants' share of the Class A stock.

* * *

The officers also purchased all Class A and B shares in the company treasury on June 25. For these they signed promissory notes totaling $973,000 that called for interest payments to be made commencing on June 30, 1997. . . .

By June 1996, the book value of the shares was $527.50. The district court accepted the valuation of defendants' expert, William Piccerelli, that in May and June 1996, the fair market value of the company's stock was approximately $303 a share.

Johnson at some point discovered that the Van Leer Corporation . . . had funds available to acquire other companies. . . . The sale closed on September 29, 1997.

Van Leer purchased all of Nyman Manufacturing's stock for $28,164,735.00. After deducting closing costs of $980,383.00, and an escrow amount of $1,423,331.00, set aside to satisfy a potential liability of the company, the net amount paid to shareholders was $25,761,021.00. Some $1,667.38 was paid for each of the 13,500 Class A shares and options, and $2,167.59 was paid for each of the 1,500 Class B shares, 1.3 times the price of the Class A shares. . . .

* * *

This case involves the narrow question of the duties owed by officers and directors, including those who are majority controlling shareholders in a closely held corporation, to minority shareholders when the defendants offer to buy, or have the corporation redeem, the shares of minority shareholders. What precise duties are owed in this situation is also a question on which there is no direct precedent in Rhode Island law. . . .

* * *

Rhode Island law would, we think, similarly recognize a heightened duty of disclosure in a close corporation setting by officers who are majority shareholders with undisclosed information, who are purchasing minority shares or causing the corporation to do so. It would also, we think, impose an objective rather than a subjective standard of materiality. . . .

Materiality depends on all the circumstances. . . . Here there were only two possible types of buyers for plaintiffs' shares—the defendants (either directly or by causing redemption of the shares) or an outside buyer looking to acquire the company. Here the defendants did not disclose their decision to work toward selling the company, their decision to hire a consultant, or their acquisition talks in May with other companies. Each is pertinent to the question of whether there was an outside buyer for the shares.

The mere causing of a closely held corporation to offer an inadequate price by majority shareholders to minority shareholders is not itself sufficient to establish a breach. It may be evidence, though, as to breach of other duties. And if a majority shareholder violates his duties of disclosure and the minority shareholder sells at an inadequate price, the minority shareholder can seek damages based on the difference between the offered price and the fair value of the stock. *See Sugarman v. Sugarman,* 797 F.2d 3, 8 (1st Cir. 1986) (applying Massachusetts law in freeze-out scenario).

If the finding of breach of fiduciary duty turned purely on the definiteness of the plan to sell, this would be a difficult liability issue. However, the case does not turn on that isolated proposition, but instead on an interrelated series of non-disclosures and misrepresentations. There is ample evidence to support the district court's finding of breach of fiduciary duty.

* * *

The evidence supports the plaintiffs' theory that these defendants engaged in a concerted, accelerating effort to buy up the minority shareholders' stock, thus increasing the defendants' ownership of the company, in anticipation of a sale of the company. We understand the district court to have concluded that the non-disclosure of the possibility of a sale was material, even at this early stage, because it motivated the defendants' actions and was information which would aid and be important to the plaintiffs in evaluating the offer made.

* * *

Of course, with the May 1996 redemption offer the plaintiffs knew that defendants (and their families) were attempting to get sole ownership of the company. This might have led a reasonable investor to ask why and to seek further information. Still, this is not enough to render immaterial as a matter of law the undisclosed and misrepresented information. In all events, the district court's fact finding that there was a violation is supportable.

Thus, the evidence reasonably can be interpreted to show a scheme by defendants to obtain total ownership of the company for less than fair value through a variety of devices, anticipating a future sale. The devices fall into two general categories: first, the failure to disclose that management had decided to try to sell the company and, second, the withholding of other material information as to the redemption and misrepresentation of other information. For example, while defendants on May 9 thought it was material to Nyman's lenders that they have the company's unaudited financials, the defendants failed to disclose that information to the plaintiffs. To effectuate this scheme, defendants pressured plaintiffs to sell by imposing false deadlines, telling Judith Lawton this was a "once in a lifetime opportunity," failing to disclose financial information which would call into question the adequacy of the price offered, and timing the offer so that plaintiffs would not have the audited financial results while defendants simultaneously disclosed financial results to lenders. . . .

We find no clear error in the conclusion that this totality of information would be germane and material to a selling minority shareholder and we uphold the liability finding. . . .

* * *

[Remanded for a recalculation of damages.[Ed.[50]]]

NEMEC v. SHRADER, 991 A.2d 1120 (Del. 2010) (Steele, C.J.[51]): [The company redeemed the stock of two retired executives before selling its government business division. The Court dismissed claims that the board breached the Company's Stock Plan's implied covenant of good faith and fair dealing, and its fiduciary duty.] "The Chancellor found no cognizable claim for a breach of the implied covenant because the Stock Plan explicitly authorized the redemption's price and timing, and Booz Allen, Nemec, and Wittkemper received exactly what they bargained for under the Stock Plan. The Chancellor wrote "[c]ontractually negotiated put and call rights are intended by both parties to be exercised at the time that is most advantageous to the party invoking the option."

---

50 [Ed. See also Neubauer v. Goldfarb, 133 Cal. Rptr. 2d 218 (Cal. Ct. App. 2003) (waiver of directors' duty of disclosure in a buy-sell agreement with a minority shareholder is void as against public policy).]

51 Two of the five Justices dissented.

. . . Our colleagues' thoughtful dissent suggests that we neglect to note that the challenged conduct (redeeming the retired stockholders shares) must *"further a legitimate interest of the party relying on the contract"* [emphasis supplied by the dissent]. The Company's directors, at the time of the decision to redeem owed fiduciary duties to the corporation and its stockholders. The redemption would not affect the Company directly. However, a failure to redeem the now retired stockholders' shares consistent with the Company's right under the stock plan would directly reduce the working stockholders' distribution by $60 million. If the Company's directors had not exercised the Company's absolute contractual right to redeem the retired stockholders shares, the working stockholders had a potential claim against the directors for favoring the retired stockholders to the detriment of the working stockholders.

The Company's redemption of the retired stockholders' shares now produces the retirees' accusation that the Company breached the covenant of fair dealing and good faith implied in the stock plan. The directors did nothing unfair and breached no fiduciary duty by causing the Company to exercise its absolute contractual right to redeem the retired stockholders' shares at a time that was most advantageous to the Company's working stockholders. The fact that some directors were in the group of working stockholders who received a *pro rata* share of the $60 million did not make it an interested transaction because those director stockholders received the same *pro rata* benefit as all other stockholders similarly situated. The directors made a rational business judgment to exercise the Company's contractual right for the $60 million benefit to all working stockholders rather than to take no action and be accused of favoritism to the retired stockholders.

. . . Crafting, what is, in effect, a post contracting equitable amendment that shifts economic benefits from working to retired partners would vitiate the limited reach of the concept of the implied duty of good faith and fair dealing. Delaware's implied duty of good faith and fair dealing is not an equitable remedy for rebalancing economic interests after events that could have been anticipated, but were not, that later adversely affected one party to a contract. Rather the covenant is a limited and extraordinary legal remedy. As the Chancellor noted in his opinion, the doctrine " 'requires a party in a contractual relationship to refrain from arbitrary or unreasonable conduct which has the effect of preventing the other party to the contract from receiving the fruits of the bargain.' " These plaintiff-appellants got the benefit of their actual bargain, and now urge us to expand the doctrine of the implied duty of good faith and fair dealing. A party does not act in bad faith by relying on contract provisions for which that party bargained where doing so simply limits advantages to another party. We cannot reform a contract because enforcement of the contract as written would raise "moral questions." The policy underpinning the implied duty of good faith and fair dealing does not extend to post contractual rebalancing of the economic benefits flowing to the contracting parties."

5. RECAPITALIZATIONS

LEVCO ALTERNATIVE FUND V. READER'S DIGEST ASSOC.

Supreme Court of Delaware, 2002.
2002 WL 1859064 (unpublished).

Before WALSH, BERGER, and STEELE, JUSTICES.

(1) This is an expedited appeal from the Court of Chancery following denial of an application for a preliminary injunction. The appellants-plaintiffs below are Class A non-voting shareholders of Reader's Digest Association, Inc. ("RDA"), a Delaware corporation, who seek to prevent the implementation of a recapitalization of RDA scheduled for shareholder vote on August 14, 2002. . . .

(2) The recapitalization plan at issue calls for RDA to: (i) purchase all the shares of its Class B voting stock at a premium ratio of 1.24 to 1 with the newly issued common stock at one vote per share; (ii) recapitalize each share of the Class A non-voting stock into one share of the new voting common stock; (iii) create a staggered Board of Directors; and (iv) eliminate the ability of shareholders to act by written consent.

(3) The key to the recapitalization proposal is the agreement by RDA to purchase 3,636,363 shares of Class B Voting Stock owned by the DeWitt Wallace-Reader's Digest Fund and the Lila Wallace Reader's Digest Fund (the "Funds") at $27.50 per share for an aggregate purchase price of approximately $100 million. The Funds currently control 50 percent of the Class B voting stock. Following the recapitalization, the funds will hold 14 percent of the new voting stock.

(4) The appellants sought a preliminary injunction in the Court of Chancery asserting that the purported recapitalization was ultra vires to the extent it contravened RDA's charter-based requirement to treat all classes of shareholders identically. Appellants alleged that the recapitalization resulted in financial detriment to the Class A shareholders. Appellants also argued that the Special Committee established to evaluate the fairness of the transaction breached its fiduciary duty to consider the separate interests of the Class A shareholders. RDA and its directors do not dispute that the directors owe a fiduciary duty to the Class A shareholders but contend that they discharged that duty through the intensive negotiations between the Funds and the Special Committee, composed of three outside directors.

(5) Appellants contend that the recapitalization violates Article IV(*l*) of the Reader's Digest certificate of incorporation, which provides that Class A and Class B stock "shall participate share and share alike in all

dividends and distributions of assets upon liquidation or otherwise and shall be identical in all other respects. . . ." As appellants read the certificate, on all matters except voting rights, Class A and Class B stock must be treated identically.

(6) The Court of Chancery held that the recapitalization does not violate Article IV. We review that decision of law de novo, and conclude that the trial court correctly interpreted the disputed provision. . . . First, the recapitalization is not a dividend or a distribution of assets, as those terms are commonly understood. Second, the "identical in all other respects" language, read in context, refers to the other stock rights and preferences identified in the first eleven subsections of Article IV—conversion rights, redemption preferences, etc. It does not mandate identical treatment of Class A and Class B stock in a recapitalization.

(7) Appellants next assert that the directors, including the Special Committee, were subject to the control of the Funds and were thus required to demonstrate the entire fairness of the transaction. Appellants further contend that the directors breached their duty of care. . . .

(8) Although the Court of Chancery did not elaborate on the burden of proof, we think it significant here that the initial burden of establishing entire fairness rests upon the party who stands on both sides of the transaction. *Kahn v. Lynch Comm. Sys., Inc.*, 638 A.2d 1110, 1117 (Del. 1994). That burden may shift, of course, if an independent committee of directors has approved the transaction. *Emerald Partners v. Berlin*, 726 A. 2d 1215, 1221 (Del.1999). While we agree with the Court of Chancery that the independent committee who negotiated the recapitalization believed it was operating in the interests of the corporation as an entity, we conclude that the committee's functioning, to the extent it was required to balance the conflicting interests of two distinct classes of shareholders, was flawed both from the standpoint of process and price.

(9) With respect to the unfair dealing claim, the Special Committee never sought, nor did its financial advisor, Goldman Sachs, ever tender, an opinion as to whether the transaction was fair to the Class A shareholders. Goldman Sachs directed its fairness opinion to the interests of RDA as a corporate entity. Given the obvious conflicting interests of the shareholder classes, the conceded absence of an evaluation of the fairness of the recapitalization on the Class A shareholders is significant. While the Class A shareholders received voting rights, their equity interests decreased by at least $100 million without either their consent or an objective evaluation of the exchange. In short, while the Special Committee believed, perhaps in good faith, that the transaction was in the best interests of the corporation, arguably, it never focused on the specific impact upon the Class A shareholders of RDA's payment of $100 million to the Class B shareholders.

(10) With respect to the premium paid to the Class B shareholders, given RDA's tenuous financial condition, having recently committed to a large acquisition, incurring additional debt in order to pay $100 million to the Class B shareholders is a matter of concern. The net result of the transaction was to significantly reduce the post-capitalization equity of the corporation. To the extent that the directors did not secure sufficient information concerning the effect of the recapitalization premium on the Class A shareholders, a serious question is raised concerning the discharge of their duty of care . . .

(11) We are not required, nor was the Court of Chancery, to determine the final merits of appellants' claims but, in our view, they stand a reasonable probability of success. . . . [Reversed.]

D. LEGAL DUTIES OF CONTROLLING SHAREHOLDERS IN NEGOTIATED ACQUISITIONS

The general rule is that a shareholder selling a block of stock, even a controlling block of stock, does not have to include other shareholders in the sale. The other shareholders or the firm itself cannot contest the controlling shareholder's decision to sell its own stock (a *free trade* rule). The other shareholders do not have *tag along rights* (or a right of an *equal opportunity to participate*) in the sale. The first subsection describes the general free trade rule and the subsequent subsections contain exceptions or modifications to the general rule.

1. NO OBLIGATION TO SHARE PROCEEDS FROM THE SALE OF A CONTROLLING BLOCK OF STOCK

ZETLIN V. HANSON HOLDINGS, INC.[52]

Court of Appeals of New York, 1979.
48 N.Y.2d 684, 421 N.Y.S.2d 877, 397 N.E.2d 387.

MEMORANDUM: . . . Plaintiff Zetlin owned approximately 2 percent of the outstanding shares of Gable Industries, Inc., with defendants Hanson Holdings, Inc., and Sylvestri together with members of the Sylvestri family, owning 44.4 percent of Gable's shares. The defendants sold their interests to Flintkote Co. for a premium price of $15 per share, at a time when Gable was selling on the open market for $7.38 per share. It is undisputed that the 44.4 percent acquired by Flintkote represented effective control of Gable.

---

[52] See also Harris v. Carter, 582 A.2d 222, 234 (Del. Ch. 1990) ("shareholder has a right to sell his or her stock and in the ordinary case owes no duty in that connection to other shareholders acting in good faith").

Recognizing that those who invest the capital necessary to acquire a dominant position in the ownership of a corporation have the right of controlling that corporation, it has long been settled law that, absent looting of corporate assets, conversion of a corporate opportunity, fraud or other acts of bad faith, a controlling stockholder is free to sell, and a purchaser is free to buy, that controlling interest at a premium price. . . .

Certainly, minority shareholders are entitled to protection against such abuse by controlling shareholders. They are not entitled, however, to inhibit the legitimate interests of the other stockholders. It is for this reason that control shares usually command a premium price. The premium is the added amount an investor is willing to pay for the privilege of directly influencing the corporation's affairs.

In this action plaintiff Zetlin contends that minority stockholders are entitled to an opportunity to share equally in any premium paid for a controlling interest in the corporation. This rule would profoundly affect the manner in which controlling stock interests are now transferred. It would require, essentially, that a controlling interest be transferred only by means of an offer to all stockholders, i.e., a tender offer. This would be contrary to existing law and if so radical a change is to be effected it would best be done by the Legislature. . . .

NOTE: THE EMPIRICAL EVIDENCE ON THE EFFECT OF BLOCK TRADES ON MINORITY SHAREHOLDERS

Is a tag along rule in the best interest of target shareholders? Note that any firm can voluntarily adopt some form of a tag along rule in its constitutional documents and its investment contracts. Or, put another way, the no tag along rule is a default rule. Would shareholders price stock in a corporation with a tag along rule higher?

A study of large-block trades between 1978 and 1982 found that when block sellers receive premiums, stock prices of shares held by non-participating shareholders typically increase, but not to the price per share received by the blockholder. Michael J. Barclay & Clifford G. Holderness, *The Law and Large-Block Trades*, 35 J. L. & ECON. 265 (1992). The authors concluded that blockholders use their voting power to improve firm management (creating the stock price increases) and to consume corporate benefits (salary) to the exclusion of minority shareholders (hence their willingness to pay premiums). Non-participating shareholders, therefore, participate ratably in any post-transaction value increases. They also found that although state law does not require that minority shareholders necessarily receive the same price per share in a follow-up merger or stock acquisition as was paid for a negotiated block, most block purchasers pay minority shareholders at least as much per share as they report having paid the block seller. The authors conclude that the primary effect of allowing block sellers to receive control premiums is to transfer the blocks to those who are more effective monitors and managers, to the benefit of both minority shareholders and the block-trading parties. They conclude that laws effecting a reduction in the frequency of block trades would reduce the wealth of minority shareholders.

Do the data and conclusions of the authors depend on existing protections in sale of control cases (the looting, sale of office and corporate opportunity doctrines)? Or do the data support a more complete deregulation of block sales? See Einer Elhauge, *The Triggering Function of Sale of Control Doctrine*, 59 U. CHI. L. REV. 1465 (1992) (looting, sale of office and corporate opportunity doctrines are valuable "triggers," identifying classes of cases in which block transfers may injure minority shareholders rather than benefit them).

NOTE: THE WILLIAMS ACT AS AN EXCEPTION TO THE FREE TRADE RULE

The most notable exception to the no tag along rule is in the Williams Act. A public tender offer must give an equal opportunity of participation to all shareholders, large and small alike. Exch. Act Rule 14d–10.[53] Privately negotiated purchases of large blocks of stock are still permitted, however, as long as they are not unconventional tender offers and do not occur alongside pending tender offers. Should the SEC require, as has been proposed, that all large-scale acquisitions of publicly held firms be in the form of public tender offers regulated under the Williams Act?

2. THE DUTY NOT TO SELL TO A "LOOTER"

INSURANSHARES CORP. OF DEL. V. NORTHERN FISCAL CORP.

District Court, E.D. Pennsylvania, 1940.
35 F.Supp. 22.

KIRKPATRICK, DISTRICT JUDGE.

This is a suit brought by a corporation against its former officers, directors, certain of its former stockholders, and others, to recover damages incurred by the corporation as a result of the sale of its control to a group who proceeded to rob it of most of its assets. The plaintiff is an investment trust, specializing in shares of small life insurance companies. . . .

Certain of the defendants were, prior to December 21, 1937, the owners of 75,933 of the corporation's total outstanding 284,032 shares. These defendants will be referred to collectively as the management group [a syndicate of Philadelphia banks and affiliates]. . . . The board of directors of the corporation was composed entirely of this management group or their nominees. . . . On December 21, 1937, the management group transferred the control of the corporation to the Boston group, none

---

[53] See Chapter Two, Section B.2.b.ii.

of whom had ever had any interest of any kind in it. With the control, as that term is here used, went plenary power under the by-laws to sell, exchange or transfer all of the securities in the corporation's portfolio, as well as access to and physical possession of them. In this case, acquisition of control was the indispensable first step of a scheme . . . , the purpose of which was to strip the corporation of its valuable assets, leaving its mere shell to the remaining stockholders. The project was carried out with thoroughness and dispatch, but its subsequent steps and its disastrous results to the corporation are not in dispute and need not be detailed here.

The actual transfer was made in accordance with a program to which the Philadelphia group assented and the steps of which they followed. Immediate and complete passing of control was ensured by the successive resignation of the old directors, each resignation being followed by the election of a new member of the board, on the nomination of the Boston group. At the same time, the management group sold and delivered their stock to the Boston group.

. . . Those who control a corporation, either through majority stock ownership, ownership of large blocks of stock less than a majority, officeholding, management contracts, or otherwise, owe some duty to the corporation in respect of the transfer of the control to outsiders. The law has long ago reached the point where it is recognized that such persons may not be wholly oblivious of the interests of everyone but themselves, even in the act of parting with control, and that, under certain circumstances, they may be held liable for whatever injury to the corporation made possible by the transfer. Without attempting any general definition, and stating the duty in minimum terms as applicable to the facts of this case, it may be said that the owners of control are under a duty not to transfer it to outsiders if the circumstances surrounding the proposed transfer are such as to awaken suspicion and put a prudent man on his guard—unless a reasonably adequate investigation discloses such facts as would convince a reasonable person that no fraud is intended or likely to result. Thus, whatever the extent of the primary duty may be, circumstances may be sufficient to call into being the duty of active vigilance and inquiry. If, after such investigation, the sellers are deceived by false representations, there might not be liability, but if the circumstances put the seller on notice and if no adequate investigation is made and harm follows, then liability also follows.

From a careful reading of the voluminous evidence in this case, I have become convinced that facts and circumstances leading up to this sale, . . . were sufficient to indicate to any reasonable man in his position that the Boston group were acquiring the control of the corporation by improper means and for an improper purpose.

I have just referred to acquisition by improper means. What happened was that the buyers had arranged with Paine, Webber & Co. that the latter would advance the price of the purchase (some $310,000) on an unsecured loan, and that, immediately after they had obtained control, the portfolio, or as much of it as was necessary, would be pledged with Paine, Webber & Co. as collateral, sold by them from time to time, the proceeds applied to liquidating the note, and the balance turned over. Comment as to the legality and ethics of this procedure is unnecessary, but the point is that if Hepburn had good reason to suspect that the purchase was to be financed in toto with the corporation's assets, it would be fair warning of the fraudulent nature of the whole thing. So, in considering whether the circumstances of this sale called for a real investigation, one matter of importance is what was known or to be inferred as to the manner in which the purchase was to be financed.

On turning to the record, one learns, with some surprise, that this same corporation had been systematically looted some five years before by a different group who bought control, using exactly the same means of financing the deal, and who stole the assets of the corporation in much the same general way. This episode was known in all of its details to Hepburn. In fact, the banks had become stockholders, unwillingly, as a result of the wreckage caused by it. In June, 1937, the persons responsible for the loss had settled their liability from some $650,000, of which perhaps half had come into the treasury of the corporation. This, of course, is not proof that a new group would do the same thing, but it certainly was a vivid reminder of the special dangers to which these small and helpless investment trusts were constantly exposed. . . .

Hepburn [head of the management group] had fair notice that, whatever the plans of the purchasers might be, one part of their program was to have a large part of the corporation's assets converted into cash and available in that form the minute they took over control. It appears that the corporation had invested some $400,000 of its assets (including the cash received from the settlement of the suit against its earlier looters) in certificates of New England Fund—another investment trust of a somewhat different type. The terms of this trust provided that holders of these certificates could obtain either the cash value of the purchase or the underlying securities which they represented upon five days notice to the New England Fund. A special meeting of the board of directors of Insuranshares was called for December 16, five days before the date fixed for closing. The directors were advised that the purchasers wanted a resolution passed apparently authorizing Solomont without any restrictions to get the money from the New England Fund on December 21—the day to which the closing had been postponed (the five days' notice had already been given by Blair on the morning of the 16th). They balked at this, but finally did pass a resolution directing the New England Fund to transfer the certificates to Solomont upon his being elected and qualified as treasurer of Insuranshares. As a matter of fact, immediately after the consummation of the deal, Solomont flew to Boston with the certificates and succeeded in turning them into cash.

Fourthly, the inflated price paid by the Boston group for the banks' shares has already been considered as evidence that they were primarily interested in buying control, but I do not think it can be disregarded as being also some indication that they had an improper purpose in view. Why were the purchasers willing to pay so much for control? I should think this question might well have occurred to one who was selling it. No doubt if this corporation had been an industrial, mining, or commercial enterprise, whose physical assets and business might have potentialities which a purchaser might believe he could develop if given control, the price would not mean very much. It was, however, merely an investment company, and the ultimate assets—what was really being sold—were nothing but the ready equivalent of cash in marketable securities.

Fifthly, Hepburn and the banks were specifically warned at least twice of the danger of carrying out the deal with parties about whom they knew so little. Simmons, the corporation's lawyer, discussed the matter at length at a conference at which Hepburn was present, and embodied his thought in a memorandum, which Hepburn may or may not have received and brought to Hardt's attention. He 'pointed out the possible consequences to you individually should Insuranshares suffer a loss through the operations of a group of men to whom you made possible the acquisition of the stock of the company.' . . .

. . . There was simply too much of the sort of thing described for this transaction to pass as a perfectly normal stock sale. I think that the circumstances were such as to indicate to any reasonable person to whom Hepburn's knowledge of what was going on could be imputed, that there was more than a possibility of fraud and consequent injury to the corporation in the sale. That being so, there plainly was a duty upon the sellers to make a genuine effort to obtain and verify such information as they reasonably could get about the means by which the purchase was to be financed and the character, aims and responsibility of the purchasers, or, in the absence of adequate information, to refrain from making the sale.

. . . Specifically, the banks, with all their credit facilities made absolutely no investigation of the financial standing and resources of the purchasers and at no time received any information to indicate to them that the purchasers had any money whatever. They knew that money to pay for the stock would be somehow forthcoming through Paine, Webber. In spite of their knowledge of the methods in which at least two previous fraudulent purchases of investment trusts had been financed by brokerage houses with the trusts' portfolios, they made no effort to find out what was to be behind Paine, Webber's certified check. As to the first of these points there can be no question that any sort of investigation would have revealed that the purchasers were not remotely able to finance a $300,000 deal from their own resources. As to the second, the performance of Paine, Webber & Co. throughout was so naive as to make it quite likely that, if any inquiry had been made, the whole method of financing would have been cheerfully disclosed. At any rate, it is not necessary to speculate as to what would have been the result if the duty of reasonable investigation had been performed. If, after inquiry, facts had been refused or misrepresented, a different question would be presented. The fact is that no genuine investigation was made.

I realize that it is expecting a great deal of businessmen, or anyone else, for that matter, to say that they should make searching inquiries which might result in disclosing facts which would upset an advantageous and apparently perfectly legal piece of business. And, by the same token, it takes no stretch of the imagination to conclude that Hepburn was not making any great effort to inform himself about the means which these three Boston lawyers were going to adopt to enable them to buy an investment trust for $300,000.

. . . [Defendants] take the position that in the present case, the banks at least owed absolutely no duty of any kind to the plaintiff corporation or its remaining stockholders. The point at which they draw the line is that the duty does not come into existence as to mere stockholders 'except when those stockholders do not content themselves with the ordinary functions of stockholders, but take upon themselves the powers and prerogatives of directors.' As a corollary to this proposition, the defendants contend that in cases where a duty does exist it is only in respect of direct dealings with the corporate property, and can never attach to dealings in its stock.

The fundamental difficulty with the defendants' position is that it fails to recognize that this case involves more than a question of liability—even that of majority stockholders, which these defendants were not—in respect of the sale of corporate stock. What is involved here, as has been pointed out, is a sale of control by a minority, but controlling, interest. The duties and liabilities in such case may be more than I have assumed them to be for the purposes of this case, but they are certainly not less. I have stated them as narrowly as possible, and I think that as so stated they are well grounded in the law.

HARRIS v. CARTER, 582 A.2d 222 (Del. Ch. 1990) (Allen, Chancellor): [Citing *Insuranshares Corp. of Del.*, above, as a "leading case."] . . . I conclude that while a person who transfers corporate control to another is surely not a surety for his buyer, when the circumstances would alert a reasonably prudent person to a risk that his buyer is dishonest or in some material respect not truthful, a duty devolves upon the seller to make such inquiry as a reasonably prudent person would make, and generally to exercise care so that others who will be affected by his actions should not be injured by wrongful conduct.

The cases that have announced this principle have laid some stress on the fact that they involved not merely a sale of stock, but a sale of control over the corporation. . . . That circumstance is pleaded here as well. . . . I assume without deciding that a duty of care of a controlling shareholder that may in special circumstances arise in connection with a sale of corporate control is breached only by grossly negligent conduct. . . .

3. THE FIDUCIARY DUTY OF THE BOARD TO PROTECT MINORITY SHAREHOLDERS

Delaware courts hold that whenever the board of directors must participate in some way in the sale of the controlling block, the board has a duty to protect the interests of the minority shareholders. The cases are controversial because the Delaware courts, using the squeeze out cases (Sections C.2 and 3 above) as a guide, invoke the entire fairness test to judge the actions of the board.

Consider the effect: The free trade rule prohibits the board from interfering with a straight sale of a controlling block. There is no fiduciary analysis of the board passivity. Once the controlling shareholder asks the board to participate in some way in the sale, the Court jumps over a business judgment rule analysis directly to an entire fairness analysis on the board's decision. First, the defendants cannot win the case on summary motions; trial becomes inevitable. The best the defendant can do under the *Kahn v. Lynch* case is shift the burden of proof on entire fairness by relying on a disinterested, independent Special Committee.[54] Second, the board is required to exercise some form of *holdup power* to negotiate terms for its decision. The board cannot negotiate for a better deal with other buyers because the controlling shareholder could block any alternate deal but it could holdup the controlling shareholder's sale to extract a higher price. This does protect minority shareholders but it also smacks of raw opportunism, the extortion of cash to remove an artificial roadblock to the deal.[55] And third, lawyers wonder whether the obligation of a firm to exercise some form of holdup power in sales of controlling blocks of stock could swallow the general rule.

Two of these cases follow.[56] Note the circumstances that frame the issue in each case:

---

54 There is no shareholder vote or tender of shares so a majority of the minority condition cannot apply.

55 At some level, of course, a board's use of hold up power to hurt majority shareholders in favor of minority shareholders is also a breach of fiduciary duty.

56 See also Black v. Hollinger Int'l, Inc., 872 A.2d 559 (Del. 2005) (partially owned subsidiary adopted poison pill plan to stop sale of controlling parent; plan valid to stop controlling shareholder of parent from taking a corporate opportunity of the sub).

McMULLIN v. BERAN, 765 A.2d 910 (Del. 2000): [A corporate parent (Arco), owning 80 percent of a subsidiary, Chemical, negotiated a two-step acquisition by a third party, Lyondell. The plaintiff, a minority shareholder of Chemical, argued that Arco sold the subsidiary too cheaply because Arco was, at the time, desperate for cash. She argued that a higher price for Chemical shares could have been obtained if the deal was for stock instead of cash or if the sale had happened at another time. The Court of Chancery granted a motion to dismiss and the Delaware Supreme Court reversed, holding that in transactions of this type the directors of the controlled corporation had a duty to secure the best value reasonably available for all subsidiary shareholders.] "This case relates to a complete sale of Chemical. The chemical board owed fiduciary duties of care, loyalty and good faith to all chemical shareholders in recommending a sale of the entire corporation. . . . [W]hen a board is presented with the majority shareholder's proposal to sell the entire corporation to a third party, the ultimate focus on value maximization is the same as if the board itself had decided to sell the corporation to a third party. When the entire sale to a third-party is proposed, negotiated and timed by a majority shareholder, however, the board cannot realistically seek any alternative because the majority shareholder has the right to vote its shares in favor of the third-party transaction it proposed for the board's consideration. Nevertheless, in such situations, the directors are obliged to make an informed and deliberate judgment, in good faith, about whether the sale to a third party that is being proposed by the majority shareholder will result in a maximization of value for the minority shareholders."

Note the irony here. The controlling shareholder has voluntarily negotiated a sale in which the minority shareholders tag along at the same price. The controlling shareholder could have sold its block without them and left the back-end, squeeze-out merger to the purchaser. For its trouble, the controlling shareholder has been sued and must prove at trial that the price offered the minority shareholders, the same price the controlling shareholder is content to accept for its own shares, is fair. The Court has held, in essence, that whenever a controlling shareholder agrees to a minority shareholder tag along, the shareholder must justify the price under an entire fairness test at trial. At trial a judge will speculate on whether the controlling shareholder sold its shares too dearly.

IN RE DIGEX, INC. SHAREHOLDER LITIGATION, 789 A.2d 1176 (Del. Ch. 2000) (Chandler, C.): [In September of 2000, WorldCom and Intermedia Communications announced a triangular merger agreement. Intermedia's most valuable asset was a 52-percent equity interest, 94-percent voting interest in Digex, a Delaware corporation. WorldCom, intent on engaging in restructuring transactions involving Digex after the acquisition, conditioned the deal on a decision of the Digex board to waive the protections of Del Corp. L. § 203, the Delaware anti-takeover statute. The acquisition would have triggered the section's protections and WorldCom would have been blocked from engaging in post-closing transactions with Digex for three years. The Digex board complied. The court held that the entire fairness test applied to the decision and granted a motion for a preliminary injunction against the closing.] "The trade put before the Digex board was simple: waive § 203 and give up the protections granted by the terms of the statute in exchange for a stronger corporate parent who had much to offer . . . and the end of the burdensome relationship with Intermedia. Was this the best deal available? . . . [I]t is impossible to say. Perhaps Digex could have extracted something more from WorldCom, perhaps not. . . . [T]he waiver really did present Digex with bargaining leverage against Intermedia and WorldCom. This leverage simply was not used—could not be used—because of the decision of the interested directors."

[The Court also noted that the board's failure to use the holdup power of Section 203 did not mean that the board should have auctioned the subsidiary to other buyers. The Court noted in dicta that the board of the subsidiary has no *Revlon* duties, no duty to auction the subsidiary, when a controlling parent corporation sells itself.] "In this case . . . no "change of control is proposed. . . . [The subsidiary's] minority existed before the proposed merger and it will not change under the proposed transaction. What will change is ownership of [the subsidiary's] majority shareholder. . . . Finally it is important to recognize that any effort [of the sub board] to sell [the sub] in a *Revlon*-style auction would appear to be futile. . . . Where, as here, a majority shareholder can block proposed transactions involving a sale of control, the courts will not require a board of directors to engage in a futile exercise, even though the board continues to owe requisite fiduciary duties to its shareholders. . . ."

This is not a small subset of transactions. All companies incorporated in Delaware are subject to Del. Gen. Corp. L. § 203, with its *upstream trigger*, and most have not waived it. Add to those companies the number of companies that have poison pill plans in place, also with *upstream triggers*, that is, they are triggered by the sale of companies that hold blocks of stock as well as the sale of the blocks themselves, and one has a substantial number of our larger companies that must waive either § 203 and/or a poison pill to enable controlling shareholders to sell their blocks of stock or, for that matter, to sell themselves (or have their controlling shareholders sell blocks of stock in them).

QUESTIONS

At issue is what a board is obliged to do when a shareholder sells its controlling block of stock. Should the Digex board have demanded a cash payment for a § 203 waiver? Some form of special protection for minority shareholders in subsequent transactions with WorldCom? Is the duty of the board to negotiate limited to cases in which a controlling shareholder requests an affirmative act of the board (i.e., a § 203 waiver request)? Or do the directors have an obligation to use affirmatively whatever leverage is available (for example, to refuse to cooperate with a due diligence investigation) or an obligation to create negotiating leverage (adopting a poison pill plan with a trigger that fires on changes of ownership in firms that own controlling blocks of stock)?[57]

4. THE DUTY NOT TO SELL AN OFFICE

ESSEX UNIVERSAL CORP. V. YATES[58]

United States Court of Appeals, Second Circuit, 1962.
305 F.2d 572.

LUMBARD, CHIEF JUDGE.

. . . The defendant Herbert J. Yates, a resident of California, was president and chairman of the board of directors of Republic Pictures Corporation, a New York corporation which at the time relevant to this suit had 2,004,190 shares of common stock outstanding. Republic's stock was listed and traded on the New York Stock Exchange. In August 1957, Essex Universal Corporation, a Delaware corporation owning stock in various diversified businesses, learned of the possibility of purchasing from Yates an interest in Republic. Negotiations proceeded rapidly, and on August 28 Yates and Joseph Harris, the president of Essex, signed a contract in which Essex agreed to buy, and Yates agreed "to sell or cause to be sold" at least 500,000 and not more than 600,000 shares of Republic stock. The price was set at eight dollars a share, roughly two dollars above the then market price on the Exchange. Three dollars per share was to be paid at the closing on September 18, 1957 and the remainder in twenty-four equal monthly payments beginning January 31, 1958. The shares were to be transferred on the closing date, but Yates was to retain the certificates, endorsed in blank by Essex, as security for full payment. In addition to other provisions not relevant to the present motion, the contract contained the following paragraph:

---

[57] See Black v. Hollinger Int'l, Inc., 872 A.2d 559 (Del. 2005) (Chancery Court had held that it did not rule on whether a firm had a duty to adopt a poison pill to stop the sale of a controlling parent, only on whether the pill once adopted was valid).

[58] [Ed. Applied in Cooke v. Oolie, 2000 WL 710199, at *19 n. 58 (Del. Ch.).]

"6. Resignations.

Upon and as a condition to the closing of this transaction if requested by Buyer at least ten (10) days prior to the date of the closing:

(a) Seller will deliver to Buyer the resignations of the majority of the directors of Republic.

(b) Seller will cause a special meeting of the board of directors of Republic to be held, legally convened pursuant to law and the by-laws of Republic, and simultaneously with the acceptance of the directors' resignations set forth in paragraph 6(a) immediately preceding will cause nominees of Buyer to be elected directors of Republic in place of the resigned directors."

Before the date of the closing, as provided in the contract, Yates notified Essex that he would deliver 566,223 shares, or 28.3 per cent of the Republic stock then outstanding, and Essex formally requested Yates to arrange for the replacement of a majority of Republic's directors with Essex nominees pursuant to paragraph 6 of the contract. This was to be accomplished by having eight of the fourteen directors resign seriatim, each in turn being replaced by an Essex nominee elected by the others; such a procedure was in form permissible under the charter and by-laws of Republic, which empowered the board to choose the successor of any of its members who might resign. . . .

[Ed.: Yates refused to close the deal and Essex sued. Yates filed a motion for summary judgment.]

It is established beyond question under New York law that it is illegal to sell corporate office or management control by itself (that is, accompanied by no stock or insufficient stock to carry voting control). . . . The same rule apparently applies in all jurisdictions where the question has arisen. . . . The rationale of the rule is undisputable: persons enjoying management control hold it on behalf of the corporation's stockholders, and therefore may not regard it as their own personal property to dispose of as they wish.[3] Any other rule would violate the most fundamental principle of corporate democracy, that management must represent and be chosen by, or at least with the consent of, those who own the corporation.

Essex was, however, contracting with Yates for the purchase of a very substantial percentage of Republic stock. If, by virtue of the voting power carried by this stock, it could have elected a majority of the board of directors, then the contract was not a simple agreement for the sale of office to one having no ownership interest in the corporation, and the question of its legality would require further analysis. Such stock voting control would incontestably belong to the owner of a majority of the voting stock, and it

[3] The cases have made no distinction between contracts by directors or officers to resign and contracts by persons who in actuality control the actions of officers or directors to procure their resignations, and of course none should exist.

is commonly known that equivalent power usually accrues to the owner of 28.3 percent of the stock. For the purpose of this analysis, I shall assume that Essex was contracting to acquire a majority of the Republic stock, deferring consideration of the situation where, as here, only 28.3 percent is to be acquired.

Republic's board of directors at the time of the aborted closing had fourteen members divided into three classes, each class being "as nearly as may be" of the same size. Directors were elected for terms of three years, one class being elected at each annual shareholder meeting on the first Tuesday in April. Thus, absent the immediate replacement of directors provided for in this contract, Essex as the hypothetical new majority shareholder of the corporation could not have obtained managing control in the form of a majority of the board in the normal course of events until April 1959, some eighteen months after the sale of the stock. The first question before us then is whether an agreement to accelerate the transfer of management control, in a manner legal in form under the corporation's charter and by-laws, violates the public policy of New York.

There is no question of the right of a controlling shareholder under New York law normally to derive a premium from the sale of a controlling block of stock. In other words, there was no impropriety *per se* in the fact that Yates was to receive more per share than the generally prevailing market price for Republic stock. . . .

The next question is whether it is legal to give and receive payment for the immediate transfer of management control to one who has achieved majority share control but would not otherwise be able to convert that share control into operating control for some time. I think that it is. . . .

The easy and immediate transfer of corporate control to new interests is ordinarily beneficial to the economy and it seems inevitable that such transactions would be discouraged if the purchaser of a majority stock interest were required to wait some period before his purchase of control could become effective. Conversely it would greatly hamper the efforts of any existing majority group to dispose of its interest if it could not assure the purchaser of immediate control over corporation operations. I can see no reason why a purchaser of majority control should not ordinarily be permitted to make his control effective from the moment of the transfer of stock.

Thus if Essex had been contracting to purchase a majority of the stock of Republic, it would have been entirely proper for the contract to contain the provision for immediate replacement of directors. Although in the case at bar only 28.3 percent of the stock was involved, it is commonly known that a person or group owning so large a percentage of the voting stock of a corporation which, like Republic, has at least the 1,500 shareholders normally requisite to listing on the New York Stock Exchange, is almost certain to have share control as a practical matter. If Essex was contracting to acquire what in reality would be equivalent to ownership of a majority of stock, i.e., if it would as a practical certainty have been guaranteed of the stock voting power to choose a majority of the directors of Republic in due course, there is no reason why the contract should not similarly be legal. Whether Essex was thus to acquire the equivalent of majority stock control would, if the issue is properly raised by the defendants, be a factual issue to be determined by the district court on remand. . . .

FRIENDLY, CIRCUIT JUDGE (concurring).

[D]evelopments over the past decades seem to me to show that such a clause violates basic principles of corporate democracy. To be sure, stockholders who have allowed a set of directors to be placed in office, whether by their vote or their failure to vote, must recognize that death, incapacity or other hazard may prevent a director from serving a full term, and that they will have no voice as to his immediate successor. But the stockholders are entitled to expect that, in that event, the remaining directors will fill the vacancy in the exercise of their fiduciary responsibility. A mass seriatim resignation directed by a selling stockholder, and the filling of vacancies by his henchmen at the dictation of a purchaser and without any consideration of the character of the latter's nominees, are beyond what the stockholders contemplated or should have been expected to contemplate. This seems to me a wrong to the corporation and the other stockholders which the law ought not countenance, whether the selling stockholder has received a premium or not. . . . To hold the seller for delinquencies of the new directors only if he knew the purchaser was an intending looter is not a sufficient sanction. The difficulties of proof are formidable even if receipt of too high a premium creates a presumption of such knowledge, and, all too often, the doors are locked only after the horses have been stolen. Stronger medicines are needed—refusal to enforce a contract with such a clause, even though this confers an unwarranted benefit on a defaulter, and continuing responsibility of the former directors for negligence of the new ones until an election has been held. Such prophylactics are not contraindicated, as Judge Lumbard suggests, by the conceded desirability of preventing the dead hand of a former "controlling" group from continuing to dominate the board after a sale, or of protecting a would-be purchaser from finding himself without a majority of the board after he has spent his money. A special meeting of stockholders to replace a board may always be called, and there could be no objection to making the closing of a purchase contingent on the results of such an election. I perceive some of the difficulties of mechanics such a procedure presents, but I have enough confidence in the ingenuity of the corporate bar to believe these would be surmounted.

Hence, I am inclined to think that if I were sitting on the New York Court of Appeals, I would hold a provision like Paragraph 6 violative of public policy save when it was entirely plain that a new election would be a mere formality—i.e., when the seller owned more than 50 percent of the stock.

. . . When an issue does arise, the "practical certainty" test is difficult to apply. The existence of such certainty will depend not merely on the proportion of the stock held by the seller but on many other factors—whether the other stock is widely or closely held, how much of it is in "street names," what success the corporation has experienced, how far its dividend policies have satisfied its stockholders, the identity of the purchasers, the presence or absence of cumulative voting, and many others. Often, unless the seller has nearly 50 percent of the stock, whether he has "working control" can be determined only by an election; groups who thought they had such control have experienced unpleasant surprises in recent years. . . .

5. THE DUTY NOT TO USURP CORPORATE OPPORTUNITIES

THORPE V. CERBCO, INC.

Supreme Court of Delaware, 1996.
676 A.2d 436.

WALSH, JUSTICE.

In this appeal from the Court of Chancery we address the duties owed to a corporation by controlling shareholders who are also directors. The shareholder-plaintiff in this derivative suit, Merle Thorpe ("Thorpe") alleged that the controlling shareholders of CERBCO, Inc. had usurped an opportunity which belonged to the corporation. That opportunity was the potential sale of control of one of CERBCO's subsidiaries. . . .

CERBCO is a holding company with voting control of three subsidiaries. At the relevant time, 1990, only one of these subsidiaries, Insituform East, Inc. ("East"), was profitable. The continued profitability of East was in doubt, however, because its regional license to conduct its primary business was about to expire. This license to exploit a process used in the in-place repair of pipes was obtained from Insituform of North America, Inc. ("INA").

CERBCO's capital structure consisted of two classes of stock. Class A was entitled to one vote per share, and Class B was entitled to 10 votes per share. In addition, the Class B shares were empowered to elect 75 percent of the board of directors. The Erikson brothers constituted CERBCO's controlling group of shareholders, owning 247,564 or 78 percent of the outstanding Class B shares, and 111,000 or 7.6 percent of the outstanding shares of Class A. Thus, while the Eriksons owned 24.6 percent of CERBCO's total equity, they exercised effective voting control with approximately 56 percent of the total votes. The Eriksons also constituted two of the four members of CERBCO's board of directors.

East's capital structure and that of the other two subsidiaries is similar to that of CERBCO. East's certificate of incorporation provides for each of the 318,000 Class B shares to have ten votes, while the 4.3 million Class A shares have one vote each. In addition, the Class B shares elect 75 percent of the board of directors. CERBCO owned 1.1 million shares of Class A (26 percent of the outstanding Class A shares) and 93 percent of the Class B shares.

In the fall of 1989, INA explored the possibility of acquiring one of its sublicensees.... In January 1990, Krugman met with the Eriksons to discuss the possibility of INA's acquiring East. At this first meeting Krugman was unaware of CERBCO's capital structure, which conferred control on the Eriksons, and presumably approached the Eriksons in their representative capacities as officers and directors. Although the factual record is disputed as to what occurred at this meeting, the Chancellor found that the Eriksons made a counterproposal to Krugman after he expressed interest in purchasing East from CERBCO. This counterproposal involved the Eriksons' selling their controlling interest in CERBCO to INA. It is unclear whether or not the Eriksons explicitly stated that they would block an attempt by INA to buy East from CERBCO. Nevertheless, the Chancellor found that Krugman was led to believe that the Eriksons would permit only the transaction involving their sale of CERBCO stock to INA....

The Eriksons did not inform CERBCO's outside directors, George Davies and Robert Long, that INA had approached the Eriksons with the intention of buying East from CERBCO, but did inform them of INA's interest in buying the Eriksons' stock. Upon learning this, Davies suggested to Robert Erikson that CERBCO sell East to INA, but Robert Erikson rejected this idea.

At the February 22, 1990 CERBCO board meeting, Davies asked whether INA had ever been interested in buying East. The Eriksons denied that INA had ever made such an offer, and had INA done so, the Eriksons indicated that they would likely vote their shares to reject it. According to draft minutes of the February 22, 1990 meeting, Rogers & Wells, who regularly served as counsel to CERBCO, advised the members of the Board that, as part of a proposed letter of intent that was being negotiated between the parties, INA would be given access to CERBCO's books and records for its due diligence review prior to the execution of a final agreement. The outside directors agreed.

In addition to securing the cooperation of CERBCO officials in making CERBCO's records available in INA's due diligence examination, the Eriksons also sought board approval of their use of Rogers & Wells as their personal counsel in their negotiations with INA. Rogers & Wells gave

CERBCO its written statement that, in its opinion, there was no conflict of interest between the Eriksons and CERBCO because the proposed transaction was a private deal by the Eriksons that did not implicate CERBCO's interests. The board thereafter consented to the representation.

On March 12, 1990, the Eriksons and INA signed a letter of intent ("LOI") for the sale of the Eriksons' controlling interest in CERBCO for $6 million. The letter of intent required the Eriksons to give INA access to CERBCO's books and records, subject to INA's agreement to keep the information confidential, and required INA to indemnify the Eriksons for any costs associated with litigation arising from the consummation of the proposed transaction. It also restricted the Eriksons' activities with respect to other potential buyers:

> The Sellers (or either of them) shall not for a period from the date hereof to the first to occur of (a) April 23, 1990, (b) the Closing or (c) the date of abandonment by INA of negotiations regarding the Stock Purchase Agreement, elicit, enter into, entertain or pursue any discussions or negotiations with any other person or entity with respect to the sale of any of the Shares or any other transaction the effect of which if completed, would frustrate the purposes of this letter.

The LOI required that the parties not disclose its terms unless such disclosure was required by law. The outside directors reviewed the letter at a March 1990 INA sublicensees convention in Hawaii.

On May 11, 1990, Thorpe lodged a demand with the CERBCO board that the proposed transaction be rejected or that the Eriksons provide an accounting for the control premium associated with the sale of their Class B shares. In July, the two outside directors formed a special committee, which terminated representation by Rogers & Wells and hired Morgan, Lewis & Bacchius to represent CERBCO.

While negotiations between the Eriksons and INA continued, the LOI expired and on May 30 INA paid the Eriksons $75,000 to extend the terms through August 1, 1990.

At the September 14, 1990 CERBCO board meeting, the board considered an alternative transaction involving the issuance of authorized CERBCO Class B stock to INA so that it could have a measure of control over East. The Eriksons objected to this proposal, which would destroy not only the Eriksons' control value, but that of the other CERBCO shareholders.

On September 18, 1990, the letter of intent between the Eriksons and INA expired without consummation of the sale. Evidently, the Eriksons and INA were unable to agree on such issues as indemnification for liabilities that might arise out of an SEC suit pending at the time, and the payment of litigation costs related to the transaction which the Eriksons had already incurred.

Thorpe filed suit on August 24, 1990, contending that the Eriksons had diverted from CERBCO the opportunity to sell East to INA so that the Eriksons could instead sell their control over CERBCO. . . .

The fundamental proposition that directors may not compete with the corporation mandates the finding that the Eriksons breached the duty of loyalty. *Guth v. Loft*, Inc., Del.Supr., 5 A.2d 503, 510 (1939). . . . When INA's president, Krugman, approached the Eriksons, he did so to inquire about INA's purchase of CERBCO's shares in East, not the purchase of the Eriksons' shares in CERBCO. Since the Eriksons were approached in their capacities as directors, their loyalty should have been to the corporation. The Chancellor correctly found that the Eriksons had breached that duty of loyalty through self-interest in subsequent actions. The Eriksons should have informed the CERBCO board of INA's interest in gaining control of East since INA originally wanted to deal with CERBCO. . . .[7]

Once INA had expressed an interest in acquiring East, CERBCO should have been able to negotiate with INA unhindered by the dominating hand of the Eriksons. . . . The Eriksons were entitled to profit from their control premium and to that end compete with CERBCO but only after informing CERBCO of the opportunity. Thereafter, they should have removed themselves from the negotiations and allowed the disinterested directors to act on behalf of CERBCO. . . .

In applying the corporate opportunity doctrine, *Guth v. Loft* requires the Court to examine several elements:

> [I]f there is presented to a corporate officer or director a business opportunity which the corporation is financially able to undertake, is, from its nature, in the line of the corporation's business and is of practical advantage to it, is one in which the corporation has an interest or a reasonable expectancy, and, by embracing the opportunity, the self-interest of the officer or director will be brought into conflict with that of his corporation, the law will not permit him to seize the opportunity for himself.

5 A.2d at 511.

In this case, it is clear that the opportunity was one in which the corporation had an interest. Despite this fact, CERBCO would never be able to undertake the opportunity to sell its East shares. Every economically viable CERBCO sale of stock could have been blocked by the

---

[7] Because of CERBCO's clear interest in the opportunity in this case, disclosure to the board of directors was required. . . . Disclosure to and informed approval by the board may insulate a director from liability where the corporate opportunity doctrine otherwise applies. . . . A director who opts not to inform the board of the opportunity acts at his peril, unless he is ultimately able to demonstrate post hoc that the corporation was not deprived of an opportunity in which it had an interest in or capability of engaging. . . .

Eriksons under § 271. Since the corporation was not able to take advantage of the opportunity, the transaction was not one which, considering all of the relevant facts, fairly belonged to the corporation. *See Fliegler v. Lawrence,* Del.Supr., 361 A.2d 218, 220 (1976) (finding no liability since corporation was not financially or legally able to take advantage of opportunity).

Generally, the corporate opportunity doctrine is applied in circumstances where the director and the corporation compete against each other to buy something, whether it be a patent, license, or an entire business. This case differs in that both the Eriksons and CERBCO wanted to sell stock, and the objects of the dispute, their respective blocks of stock to be sold, were not perfectly fungible. In order for the Eriksons and CERBCO to compete against one another, their stock must have been rough substitutes in the eyes of INA. If INA considered none of the CERBCO transactions to be an acceptable substitute to the INA-Erikson transaction, then the opportunity was never really available to CERBCO. Thus, those transactions which were not economically rational alternatives need not be considered by a court evaluating a corporate opportunity scenario.

The Chancellor thoroughly examined the evidence presented by the parties to determine that only one transaction presented a serious alternative to an Erikson-INA deal. This one viable alternative involved the sale of all of CERBCO's East stock for a price of $12.8 million. . . .

After dispensing with unrealistic alternatives, we are left to consider a CERBCO sale of all its East stock to INA. Whether or not the Eriksons had a right to block an alternative transaction turns on whether this transaction would constitute all or substantially all of CERBCO's assets and require shareholder approval under § 271. We are satisfied that the Court of Chancery correctly applied the law to the facts of this case in making the determination that, in 1990, CERBCO's investment in East constituted substantially all of CERBCO's assets. . . .

In the opinion below, the Chancellor determined that the sale of East would constitute a radical transformation of CERBCO. In addition, CERBCO's East stock accounted for 68 percent of CERBCO's assets in 1990 and this stock was its primary income generating asset. We therefore affirm the decision that East stock constituted "substantially all" of CERBCO's assets as consistent with Delaware law.

Because the alternative transaction would have been covered by § 271, the Eriksons had the statutory right as shareholders to veto this transaction. Given their power, the Eriksons would obviously never allow CERBCO to enter a transaction against their economic interests. Damages cannot be awarded on the basis of a transaction that has a zero probability of occurring due to the lawful exercise of statutory rights. . . .

While the failure of CERBCO to sell East to INA is certainly related to the Eriksons' faithlessness, that failure did not proximately result from the breach. Instead the Eriksons' § 271 rights are ultimately responsible for the nonconsummation of the transaction. Even if the Eriksons had behaved faithfully to their duties to CERBCO, they still could have rightfully vetoed a sale of substantially all of CERBCO's assets under § 271. Thus, the § 271 rights, not the breach, were the proximate cause of the nonconsummation of the transaction. Accordingly, transactional damages are inappropriate. . . .

Even though the corporation may not have been able to effectuate the transaction because of the Eriksons' rights under § 271, some recovery is warranted because of the breach of fiduciary duty. . . . Once disloyalty has been established, the standards evolved in *Oberly v. Kirby* and *Tri-Star* require that a fiduciary not profit personally from his conduct, and that the beneficiary not be harmed by such conduct. While there are no transactional damages in this case, we find the Eriksons liable for damages incidental to their breach of duty. Specifically the Eriksons are liable to CERBCO for the amount of $75,000 received from INA in connection with the letter of intent. . . . In addition, the Eriksons must reimburse CERBCO for any expenses, including legal and due diligence costs, that the corporation incurred to accommodate the Eriksons' pursuit of their own interests prior to the deal being abandoned by the Eriksons and INA.

CHAPTER SIX

A TARGET BOARD'S DECISION TO BLOCK A STOCK ACQUISITION

■ ■ ■

A. INTRODUCTION TO TAKEOVER DEFENSES

1. A CLASSIFICATION OF THE DEFENSES

As noted in Chapter Two, an acquirer in a stock acquisition need not deal directly with the selling firm's board of directors; the opposite party to the deal is the selling firm's shareholders. In the past, boards have been dismayed to find that control of their firms has passed to a new owner without their consent or participation. Boards concerned about reducing their vulnerability to unwanted takeovers fashioned a growing number of defenses to insert themselves back into the decision to sell. Later, state legislatures memorialized some of these devices in state anti-takeover statutes.

Bidders and target shareholders, frustrated by the defenses, contest them in court. There are two separate legal issues. First, are the defenses void *ab initio* as outside the power of the board of directors to adopt? And, second, if the defenses are prima facie valid, have the directors abused their discretion (breached their fiduciary duty to their shareholders) in deploying or refusing to defuse a defense on the facts of a particular case? The courts, after dabbling with the first question,[1] have now largely left the field to the defending corporations, with one important exception, and look hard at only the second question. When a state has adopted an anti-takeover statute the first issue is, of course, moot, but the second issue remains.

There are three different kinds of takeover defenses relevant to our study of board power. The categories are defined by the role of shareholders in the creation of each defense: first, takeover defenses that require specific shareholder ratification (e.g., *shark repellent* certificate amendments); second, takeover defenses put in place by the board using very general grants of authority contained in a firm's certificate or articles of incorporation (e.g., a firm uses a charter provision authorizing the

[1] For example, several federal district court judges found poison pill plans, in effect, an unauthorized delegation of power to a firm's board of directors. E.g., Minstar Acquiring Corp. v. AMF, Inc., 621 F.Supp. 1252 (S.D.N.Y.); Ascaro, Inc. v. Court, 611 F.Supp. 468 (D.N.J. 1985). We believe the judges were correct, but the Delaware Supreme Court put flight to their position in *Revlon, infra*.

issuance of *blank check* preferred stock to promulgate a *poison pill* plan); and third, takeover defenses based on the board's general powers as granted in a state corporate code (e.g., a board uses a code provision authorizing a board to contract for the sale of firm assets to erect a *crown jewel* defense). In the first category, shareholders must vote to approve the specific defense in question. In the second category, shareholders, unless the general grant is in a firm's original charter, must vote to amend a firm's charter to give the board the general power. And in the third category, shareholders do not necessarily vote at all, unless they vote to amend a charter to remove the board's power to effectuate the defense.

The shareholders are not powerless, however, with respect to defenses promulgated without specific ratification (categories two and three). They can, using the shareholder resolution procedure provided under Exchange Act Rule 14a–8 (Shareholder Proposals), vote to recommend that a board withdraw specific defenses that it has chosen to put in place. Moreover, a board deciding to use a takeover defense in categories two or three could choose to ask for a positive shareholder ratification, although unnecessary, to protect them from shareholder derivative litigation. In suits by shareholders, the courts have held that certain defenses that fall in each of the three categories are beyond the power of the board or are an abuse of the board's power. Moreover, our national exchanges prohibit some takeover defenses that would otherwise fall in the first category.

The following is a general introduction to some of the popular defenses that fall in each of the three categories. This list is intended to be neither exhaustive nor thoroughly explanatory; we leave this to the rich facts of the cases we will study in this chapter. As you read each case in the chapter, note the details of each defense employed and consider the usefulness of each defense.

Shark Repellant Amendments to Certificates or Articles of Incorporation: Certificate amendments that require a specific shareholder vote are called *shark repellent* amendments. Drafters of early shark repellent amendments designed them to retard the ability of someone with newly-acquired voting power from taking control of the firm's board of directors. The amendments provided for a staggered or classified board of directors (only a minority, usually one-third, of the board seats are the subject of an election in any one year), for eliminating shareholder voting through the written consent procedure (a method of voting that does not require a formal shareholders' meeting), for limiting the right of shareholders to call a special meeting of shareholders, for prohibiting the removal of a sitting director unless for cause, for limiting the creation of new seats on the board of directors, and for giving the remaining members of the board the sole authority to appoint new directors if a director resigns, becomes incapacitated or dies midterm.

Shark repellent certificate amendments proved, at first, to be only marginally effective. Once an acquirer purchased a controlling block of stock, existing board members owed the new owner fiduciary duties. Most board members who could not respond to the new owner's requests simply resigned rather than continue in an uncomfortable lame duck capacity, at constant risk of being the object of a suit brought by the new controlling shareholder. Moreover, courts prohibit the existing board from finding ways of diluting the ownership of a new controlling owner once the new owner has the controlling block of stock. *Condec Corp. v. Lukenheimer Co.*, 230 A.2d 769 (Del. Ch. 1967) (the court enjoined the issuance of a large block of new shares to a friendly party after an unwanted buyer had otherwise obtained control).

show stoppers

Lawyers, therefore, designed a second round of certificate amendments with much more punch—indeed, state anti-takeover legislation often mimics these second-generation charter amendments. The more powerful amendments contain provisions for a supermajority vote for all business combinations between a controlling shareholder and the firm if the controlling shareholder acquired control without the specific approval of a pre-existing board of directors or if the controlling shareholder does not meet fair price criteria.[2] Some certificate amendments give non-tendering shareholders the right to put their stock to the firm for a specified period of time at a generous price after a successful stock acquisition. Others reduce the voting rights of one who has made a successful stock acquisition unless the acquisition meets specified fair price requirements or unless the voting rights are approved by non-selling shareholders.

The most extreme form of this sophisticated class of certificate amendments is amendments that change the voting rights of outstanding common stock. In *time-phased* or *tenure* voting plans, a firm gives multiple votes per share to all outstanding common shareholders, but the multiple votes disappear on the transfer of the underlying stock and reappear when a shareholder holds the stock for three or four years. See *Williams v. Geier*, 671 A.2d 1368 (Del. 1996). In *capped voting* plans, a firm limits the voting power of shares based on the number of shares owned. Shareholders who purchase shares in excess of the triggering amount do not receive voting rights on the excess shares. Finally, a recapitalization can simply create two classes of voting stock (*two-tier voting stock*). One class, sold exclusively

---

[2] This type of shark repellent amendment, which was the foundation for second-generation state anti-takeover statutes, often combines fair price and supermajority provisions. Both provisions require that an acquirer of a set percentage of the target's stock cannot engage in a second-stage merger or asset sale transactions with the target unless a supermajority, often over 85 percent, of the outstanding target shareholders approve. The fair price version exempts transactions from the supermajority vote if the price offered shareholders in the transaction meets certain criteria, usually indexed to the highest price paid by the acquirer for its initial block of target stock. Moreover, most of the provisions also contain a clause that prohibits firms from repealing them unless by supermajority vote. Most of the more sophisticated provisions have come to contain a "board-out" clause, empowering a target board to waive the provision for a specific acquirer before it has made a triggering acquisition.

to insiders, has concentrated voting power and diluted economic rights to equity (rights to corporate distributions, dividends, redemptions and liquidation payments). The other class has limited voting power and full economic rights.

Poison Pill Plans: The major disadvantages of certificate amendments adopted by shareholder vote are: first, they take time to put in place; second, they are not flexible; and third, the firm must justify them in comprehensive disclosure documents required by the federal proxy solicitation regulations. In response, clever corporate lawyers designed new defenses that could be implemented without a simultaneous shareholder vote—firms could employ them in less time and did not have to justify them in proxy statements. The most popular of these defenses is a *poison pill plan*, a dividend distribution of stock, stock rights, or other securities (notes, for example) that have special redemption or conversion options. Since stock rights are now the preferred form of delivery, poison pill plans are now often referred to as *stock rights plans*. An unapproved stock acquisition of a specified percentage of a firm's stock (a *trigger*) activates (*vests*) the options in these instruments. The options, once vested and exercised, *severely dilute* the value of the target shares held by the bidder. Ouch!

Poison pill plans are designed so that no bidder can afford to trigger them with an unapproved stock acquisition.[3] Boards retain the right to waive the effects of a plan, usually through a right to redeem the outstanding securities for a nominal fee. Thus, buyers must negotiate with the board before acquiring a triggering block of stock, seeking the board's approval of the acquisition and the board's agreement that it will redeem the outstanding conversion rights. In other words, poison pill plans force bidders to negotiate with the target board in stock acquisitions, acquisitions that the bidder could otherwise consummate without the board's approval.

[3] But see William J. Carney & Leonard A. Silverston, *The Illusory Protections of the Poison Pill*, 79 NOTRE DAME L. REV. 179 (2003) (buyers can "swallow the pill," paying an affordable premium). The authors do not take into account the risk of the target immediately replacing a triggered pill with a second (*reloaded*) poison pill, see *Selectica, infra*, locking in the bidder's diluted stock position.

Poison pill plans, which began as distributions of convertible preferred stock, have evolved into distributions of stock rights[4] and convertible debt.[5] Current forms of poison pill plans have evolved into very stylized complex edifices of language and structure, the mechanics of which have yet to be tested in the courts.[6] Some firms, concerned about the legality of any one plan in a given jurisdiction and hedging their bets, will put in place two or even three plans—each based on a different underlying security. A board, to be able to create one of the popular poison pill plans, must have the authority to issue rights, debt or preferred stock with rights and privileges set by board resolution at the time of issuance.

---

4 The two principal types of share rights plans, the most popular type of poison pill plan, are a *call plan*, under which the holder has a contingent right to buy securities of the target or the acquirer at a deep discount from their market value, and a *put* or *back-end plan*, under which the holder has a contingent right to require the issuer or the acquiring company to purchase the holder's securities, at a generous premium. There are two types of call plans, the older "flip-over/flip-in" plans and the newer automatic "flip-in" plans. Call plans are much more common than are put plans. Keep in mind that drafters of such plans intend that the rights issued will never vest; the details of the plans are a deterrent to hostile bidders, like the doomsday bomb in the movie "Doctor Strangelove." (In the movie, the United States triggered the bomb by mistake.)

To implement a call plan, a company issues to its shareholders one contingent share right for each share of common stock outstanding. The issuance is in the nature of a dividend authorized by the directors and need not be approved by the shareholders. The typical call right entitles the holder (once the right becomes exercisable due to a triggering stock acquisition) to buy stock at half price in certain situations. In the case of a merger between the rights issuer and an acquirer, the rights holders can buy, at half price, the stock of the company surviving the merger (whether the survivor is the issuer or the acquirer), a flip-over. If an acquirer of the issuer's shares does not pursue a back-end merger but engages in certain kinds of self-dealing transactions with its new subsidiary, the rights holders can purchase shares of the target at half price, a flip-in. The call right thus allows the issuer's shareholders to block a squeeze-out second-stage merger or other methods of self-dealing.

The right is initially "stapled" to the common stock; that is, it trades together with the common stock. The rights vest ten days after a third party acquires a specified percentage (often 15 percent or more) of the company's stock (a "triggering event") without the target board's approval. Once vested, the company issues separate rights certificates, and the rights become exercisable and transferable separately from the common stock. The unvested rights have a stated term of ten years and target directors may redeem them at a nominal price (for example, ten cents) at any time before they vest. This means that the plans have built-in "sunset" provisions and must be periodically re-issued. The redemption feature allows the board to remove the plan to negotiate an acquisition of the company.

The vested rights permit holders to buy a share of the common stock of the issuer or acquirer (depending on the circumstances) at a price that is typically a multiple of the market price (usually three) of the common stock on the date of issuance of the right. This option is seriously out-of-the-money (the exercise price is much higher than the value of the underlying asset) and holders will not exercise it. The right is a sham. The core of the plan is the supplemental option described below to buy stock having a market value of twice the exercise price of the right, an in-the-money option.

In the older plans, if a merger occurs after the rights have become exercisable, the holder of each right is entitled to purchase that number of the surviving company's shares whose market value is triple or twice the exercise price of the right. This feature is sometimes referred to as a "flip-over" provision because the target shareholder's right "flips over" into a right to buy stock in the surviving company, even if that company is not the same as the original issuer of the right. The flip-over is protected by a flip-in. If a third party acquires 15 percent or more of the target's stock and does not execute a back-end merger of the target into the acquirer, but attempts to engage in certain self-dealing transactions that are, in essence, substitutes for the back-end merger, the holder of each right (other than the purchaser who triggered the rights, whose rights become null and void) can claim the issuer's shares with a market value of triple or twice the exercise price of the right. Self-dealing transactions typically are defined to include any transaction in which the 15-percent holder or one of its affiliates merges into the target, transfers assets to the

A charter provision on preferred stock that empowers the board to issue novel kinds of preferred stock is called a *"blank check" preferred* provision. Most states require an express declaration in a firm's certificate of incorporation that its board can issue preferred stock with rights and privileges set at the time of issuance. E.g., Del. Gen. Corp. L. §§ 102(a)(4) & 151(a). This means that at some point the shareholders must have voted to authorize the blank check provision.[7] On the other hand, most state

---

target in exchange for target stock, buys any target assets whose aggregate fair market value exceeds a specified amount, receives any compensation from the target other than for full-time employment, or receives disproportionate benefits as a result of any loan, advance, financial assistance, or tax advantage provided by the target. This feature is sometimes referred to as a "flip-in," because the right can be "flipped" into a position in the stock of the target company. See generally Richards, Layton & Finger, *Model Poison Pill* (2000).

The later, more powerful call plans omit the "flip-over" feature entirely and eliminate the contingent part of the "flip-in" provisions. The flip-in rights become exercisable to buy stock of the issuer at a fraction of market value whenever the acquirer buys more than a threshold amount of the issuer's stock, even if the acquirer does not engage in any coercive or self-dealing transactions. The acquirer who triggers the options for other shareholders does not have such an option. The other shareholders, exercising their new options, *substantially dilute* the value the acquirer's stock. In extreme forms, the acquirer simply loses much of the value of the triggering stock purchase (at minimum, the value of 15 percent of the voting stock).

The genius of the call plan is that it does not require a shareholder vote, has neutral tax consequences, does not affect earnings reports, and is not a public offering under the Securities Act of 1933. Shareholders do not vote because the distribution is a form of stock dividend declared by the board. Neither the distribution of the rights, nor the subsequent "unstapling" of the rights from the common stock and the distribution of rights certificates, constitutes a taxable event for the company or its shareholders; rather, the rights are treated for tax purposes as capital assets in the hands of most shareholders. Each right probably would have a basis of zero, and its holding period would relate back to the holding period of the common stock from which the right was separated. The rights are out of the money when issued, so they do not dilute earnings per share. Moreover, because the redemption date is neither fixed nor determinable, accounting guidelines would not require recognition of the redemption amount as a long-term obligation of the issuer. The rights issuer need not register with the SEC the common stock issuable upon exercise of the rights because the rights will not be exercised—and the stock will not be issued—until some future triggering event has occurred.

Under a put plan, as under a call plan, a company's board issues rights to shareholders as a dividend, without shareholder approval. A put right typically enables its holder (other than a holder of more than a specified percentage of the company's stock, that is, the plan is discriminatory among shareholders) to "put" to the issuer a share of common stock for a specified amount of cash, debt securities, preferred stock, or a combination of the above, in the event that a third party acquires more than a specified percentage of the company's stock and does not offer to buy the rest of the stock at a specified price (which is usually equal to the value of the cash or securities receivable if the rights are exercised). The price can be a fixed amount, which gives shareholders (other than a 15-percent holder) the right to exchange a share for a specific value in notes or cash if a third party acquired 15 percent of the issuer's stock and does not offer to buy all outstanding shares at the specified price. Alternatively, the price can be set by a formula to equal the highest price per share paid by a bidder in acquiring the issuer's stock.

A put plan raises legal questions not raised by a call plan, including the need to comply with restrictions under loan agreements and state corporation statutes concerning the redemption of stock. A put plan also might raise fraudulent conveyance issues, on the theory that the company has given rights holders the right to put shares to the company for excessive consideration.

[5] See the facts of *Revlon, infra.*

[6] The authors knows of only two that have been triggered. Insiders triggered one by mistake; a bidder triggered a *NOL plan* (with a low threshold five percent trigger) to contest the plan's validity in court. See *Selectica, infra.*

[7] In the proxy materials that accompanied proxy solicitations for such amendments, detailed disclosures of the specifics of any one plan or any one takeover defense were not necessary. Only a general comment that the amendments empowered the board to adopt a defense in the

corporate codes provide that boards have a default power (absent a contrary provision in the certificate) to issue stock rights and to place debt with the terms set by the board at the time of issuance. Del. Gen. Corp. L. §§ 122(13) & 157. So stock rights and convertible debt plans may not require even a general form of shareholder authorization.[8]

The ease of adopting a poison pill plan avoids the necessity of pre-bid planning; a target can adopt an effective poison pill plan after a hostile bidder makes an unwanted offer. This has led one author to conclude that all firms operate as if they have a pill in place (a *shadow pill*), even if they formally do not. John Coates IV, *Takeover Defenses in the Shadow of the Pill: A Critique of the Scientific Evidence*, 79 TEX. L. REV. 271 (2000).

Some of the new variations on shareholder rights plans are intended to confine their scope. One is the so-called *chewable pill*, a plan constructed so that it will not stand in the way of a well-priced offer, an offer that a publicly traded target ought not refuse. The chewable pill simply dissolves when a respectable offer is on the table. There are two versions. The first version specifies a condition for the pill's evaporation—a fully financed all-cash offer at a generous premium over the target's trading price. More recently, proponents have asked for an alternative that scraps the specific price condition in favor of evaporation on a favorable vote of the shareholders.[9] A second is a *TIDE* provision (three year independent director evaluation), a sunset provision that requires a firm's independent directors to reconsider the plan every three years. A third is a provision in the plan (or in the corporation's charter) that requires a shareholder ratification vote. Most of the ratification rules have a fiduciary-out, however, permitting boards to adopt a plan without a vote if the directors determine it is in the best interests of the corporation.

Another poison pill variation is the *morning after pill*. The pill is a shareholder rights plan that is ready to go at a moment's notice once a hostile threat materializes. The directors can approve the plan immediately upon the materialization of the threat because the plan has *previously been prepared* and is simply awaiting their approval. Directors,

---

future usually sufficed. Since most publicly traded firms have long since adopted blank check preferred provisions in their certificates of incorporation authorizing the board generally to create the plans, or they rely on stock rights or convertible debt for their plans, poison pills may more appropriately now belong in the next category of defenses, those that can be put in place without shareholder action.

[8] However, if a call plan allows shareholders to exchange one kind of stock for another in the issuer or to otherwise buy stock, the firm must have sufficient authorization in its charter to issue the new stock.

[9] Opponents of the condition-specific plan say the condition will telegraph the terms of an offer that a target will accept before the target even contemplates a deal. Moreover, the target board may not be able to shop the company for a better price once the condition is satisfied. Opponents of the updated version say that taking away a board's discretion disables a board from acting as a sales agent in the shareholders' interest—checking the highly competitive acquisition market for better offers or checking whether a bid squares with recent purchase prices for peer companies. The latter complaint seems strained, however, as the board, even though stripped of the power to decide, can always recommend to their shareholders what action to take.

however, do not approve the plan in advance to avoid alienating those shareholders who dislike poison pills (that is, almost all of them).

The most effective method of neutralizing poison pill plans is an election to replace incumbent directors with directors that will redeem the rights (and waive the provisions of state anti-takeover statutes). This refocused everyone's attention on shareholder voting mechanics (who may call special shareholder meetings, shareholder voting by written consent, board classification) and resurrected the importance of the first generation shark repellant charter amendments. Staggered or classified boards in combination with poison pills have proven to be potent deterrents to combination hostile tender offer/proxy contests. See Section B.3. below. A staggered board prevents a hostile bidder from soliciting proxies to elect a slate of candidates that will proceed with the acquisition. The combination of a poison pill and a staggered board has proven to be very effective against the last remaining method of closing a hostile takeover.

"Two-Tier" Voting Stock: A less popular and more controversial member of this category of defenses that require general but not specific shareholder authorization is stock exchange offers or stock dividends that put in place a two-tier voting stock system. In the exchange tender offer, a firm offers stock with diluted voting power and concentrated claims on equity for its outstanding common stock. The insiders do not tender, the outsiders do, and the insiders end up with concentrated voting power. A board must have authorization in its certificate, or must amend the corporation's certificate to grant the board authorization, to issue the non-voting or diluted voting common stock. The existing shareholders must vote to ratify the charter amendment. Again, many publicly traded firms have amended their certificates to give their boards this authority and even though unused, the provisions are available should the need arise. In stock distributions, a firm issues super voting stock as a stock dividend on its common stock with a transfer restriction that converts the super voting stock to lower voting common stock if the new stock is sold. Insiders hold and outsiders trade. In its more extreme form, the firm simply issues the new super voting stock and sells the new stock only to insiders; however, the firm must get fair value for the stock. The insiders must pay cash or get the stock over time in a compensation grant program. If the stock has no economic rights (no rights to dividend or liquidation distributions), the firm can argue that it has a discounted value. The existing shareholders must vote to ratify the charter amendment.

Many technology and media firms, such as Google (now Alphabet, Inc.), put two-tier voting stock plans in their charter at the time of their Initial Public Offering (IPO); the founders hold and do not sell super voting stock and the regular voting stock is sold to the public. In the March 2017 Snap, Inc. IPO, the company offered only non-voting Class A shares to the public. The Snap IPO led to The Council of Institutional Investors and other powerful trade organizations to lobby global index providers to revise their policies to bar non-voting shares from their indices. The critics argued that the passive investors in index funds would be forced to invest in non-voting shares and that the shares erode public company governance. S&P Dow Jones and FTSE Russell, two powerful index providers, moved quickly to comply. The matter is still open, however.[10]

Lock-ups and Other Asset-Based Strategies: The third category of defenses—those that do not require any shareholder vote, even at the most general level of authorization—is the most wide-ranging. Boards of directors use their inherent power over firm assets to make the firm unattractive to unwanted bidders. These defenses are often less attractive than a poison pill plan, because the defenses in the third category usually require that the board expend assets or make major changes in the capital structure of the firm.[11] The board sells or gives contingent rights to the key firm asset to a third party (the *crown jewel* or *asset lock-up* defense), buys the target stock held by an unwanted bidder directly from that bidder (*greenmail*), gives top managers handsome severance payments contingent on control changes (*golden parachutes*), or issues stock or contingent stock rights (a *stock lock-up*) to a friendly party (a *white squire*) subject to reselling restrictions (a *standstill agreement*). The firm makes acquisitions of its own to create antitrust problems for the bidder (the *Clayton* defense), to create national defense concerns if the bidder is foreign (the *Pentagon play*), or to acquire control of the bidder in a reverse acquisition (the *Pac-Man* defense).

A common modern defense in this category is a radical restructuring (the *dividend recap*). The target adds leverage by selling debt and passing the cash proceeds of the placement back to its own shareholders in a huge one-time stock dividend. By leveraging, a firm exhausts its debt capacity and its cash reserves so that a bidder cannot use the firm's own assets to finance an acquisition, the strategy of choice of leveraged buyout firms.

NOTE: THE ANTIDOTE TO TAKEOVER DEFENSES—SHAREHOLDER RESOLUTIONS

Rule 14a–8, promulgated under § 14 of the Securities Exchange Act of 1934, grants a security holder owning at least one percent or $1,000 in market

---

[10] The prospectus for the Snap, Inc. IPO was fascinating for another reason besides the fact that non-voting shares of Class A common stock were being offered to the public. Nowhere to be found in the prospectus was a discussion on whether *appraisal rights* would be afforded to holders of the Class A non-voting shares in the case of a merger involving Snap. When Professor Haas contacted Snap's legal counsel, Cooley LLP in Palo Alto, California, and asked whether appraisal rights would be available to public shareholders in accordance with § 262 of the Del. Gen. Corp. L., no answer was volunteered. Frankly, it boggles the mind that the issue was not addressed in the Snap prospectus. If counsel believes that shareholders are not entitled to appraisal rights, their determination should have been prominently disclosed in the "Risk Factors" section of the prospectus.

[11] Important exceptions are the contingent contracts such as lock-ups or golden parachutes.

value of voting securities the right to present proposals for inclusion in the corporation's proxy solicitation materials for upcoming shareholder meetings. The security holder must have held the securities for at least one year (ownership through an employee stock ownership plan counts), and the proposals must be timely. The proponent may not only ask for a shareholder vote on a specific proposition but also draft a 500-word supporting statement that the firm must include in the corporation's proxy statement. The rule gives even small shareholders an opportunity to initiate a referendum on various aspects of corporate policy and operation.[12]

A shareholder can use Rule 14a–8 to have shareholders vote on the appropriateness of a takeover defense adopted by their managers without a ratifying vote (e.g., a poison pill plan). The evidence on the success of shareholder resolutions on acquisition defenses shows a marked trend in favor of dissident shareholders. Anti-poison pill and broad declassification proposals have been among the most popular resolutions and attracted the highest vote totals in recent years. Compare this with shareholder support for resolutions on social and environmental issues, which historically receive an average of less than ten percent of the shareholder vote.

Most Rule 14a–8 resolutions are *recommendations* to the board (precatory), and some boards ignore the results.[13] In response, shareholder activists are asking firms to include binding bylaw amendments in the firm's proxy materials. Firms argue that the proposals are an illegal constraint on the management power of boards of directors. A recent Delaware court decision supports their view.[14] The SEC has taken the position that firms can omit such proposals as "improper under state law."[15] Even if a bylaw is considered validly adopted by shareholder resolution, boards in some states have the power to amend the bylaws and could promptly repeal them.[16] Frustrated shareholders have turned to a new tactic: director qualification bylaws. The bylaw disqualifies directors from re-nomination if they fail to support a shareholder approved Rule 14a–8 proposal.

The role of shareholder advisory groups, such as the Council of Institutional Investors (CII), the Investor Responsibility Research Center (IRRC), and Institutional Shareholder Services (ISS), has shifted power

---

[12] Without the rule (or if a shareholder proposal does not come under the rule), a shareholder has to bear the expense of preparing and mailing his own proxy and proxy statement, complying with all the proxy solicitation rules contained in Securities and Exchange Commission Regulation 14A. For all but the largest shareholders this is prohibitively expensive. The shareholder may also present a proposal from the floor at the shareholder meeting, see Exchange Act Rule 14a–4. Unless the shareholder has successfully solicited proxies in advance, management's voting power is usually sufficient to reject the proposal, however. Thus, Rule 14a–8 is an essential and often exclusive mechanism for shareholder activism.

[13] Boards justify their action by pointing to Del. Gen. Corp. L. § 141(a): "The business and affairs of every corporation organized under this chapter shall be managed by or under the direction of a board of directors . . ."—*not* the shareholders.

[14] CA, Inc. v. AFSCME Employees Pension Plan, 953 A.2d 227 (Del. 2008) (bylaws that divest boards of discretion over the business affairs of the company are void).

[15] Mattel, Inc., SEC No-Action Letter, 2002 WL 833515 (Mar. 25, 2002).

[16] See Centaur Partner IV v. National Intergroup Inc., 582 A.2d 923 (Del 1990) (applying Del. Gen. Corp. L. § 109(a); bylaw provision that prohibits repeal by directors is void).

significantly to shareholders. The advisory groups sell their advice to institutional shareholders, who rely on their advice when voting their shares (partly to defend themselves against attacks by their investors on their voting records). Most of the groups do not like takeover defenses, particularly supermajority provisions, classified boards and poison pill plans. The groups attack the defenses on multiple fronts. First, the groups track shareholder proposals and recommend positive votes against the defenses. ISS is the country's leading proxy advisor and its recommendations to institutional investors on any shareholder vote are very influential.[17] Second, the groups make recommendations on votes for individual directors and an important part of their recommendations turns on a director's voting record on takeover defenses and on responses to shareholder resolutions on takeover defenses. Shareholders, supported by the advisory groups, run *Vote No* (more accurately *Withhold Vote*[18]) campaigns against directors, for example, that do not follow approved shareholder proposals. ISS, for example, recommends that shareholders withhold their vote for directors who have voted to adopt or renew a poison pill plan without shareholder approval.[19] And third,[20] the groups publish *corporate governance ratings* for each company and the ratings decline if a firm has takeover defenses in place. ISS has indicated, for example, that responsiveness to shareholder proposals will affect its governance rating. These ratings can affect stock price.

The effect of shareholder resolutions and advisory group activity on director elections has been dramatic. Resolutions pressing companies to drop staggered board terms and hold annual elections for all directors attracted an average favorable vote of 74 percent of the voting shareholders in 2011.[21] Less than thirty percent of companies in the S&P 500 index now have classified boards (compared with 50 percent in 2005).[22] Less than 14 percent of the companies in the S&P 500 have poison pill plans in place (compared with 51 percent in 2004). Shareholder resolutions attacking supermajority provisions attracted an average favorable vote over 60 percent of the shareholders in 2011 and seventy five percent of the shareholders in 2010. The overall effect is that just 35 percent of our larger companies now have supermajority voting requirements for acquisitions. Less favorable but still impressive gains have

---

17 An ISS recommendation can make a fifteen to twenty percent difference in the outcome of a given vote on shareholder proposals.

18 Shareholders cannot vote *no* on management nominees; they can only vote yes or abstain. A "vote no" campaign is, therefore, a request that shareholders check the abstain box.

19 See ISS, 2011 U.S. Proxy Voting Guidelines Summary (Dec. 16, 2010)

20 One could also argue that the "say on pay" vote mandated by the Dodd-Frank Act will also eventually pressure directors to act on shareholder proposal recommendations. See Exch. Act § 14A & Exch. Act Rule 14a–21. ISS currently has had less success on influencing those votes than it does on influencing votes on shareholder resolutions and director elections.

21 See ISS, 2011 U.S. Postseason (Sept. 29, 2011) (containing the data for the paragraph). These tendencies continue to date. See ISS 2016 Board Practices Study (June 1, 2016) (over 80 percent of S&P 500 companies do not have staggered boards).

22 Interestingly, the smaller the company the more likely it is to have takeover defenses in place. The percentage of companies in the Russell 200 that have classified boards in place and those that have poison pill plans in place is 15 percent and 19 percent, respectively. Do the institutional investors that take the advice of ISS pay less attention to these companies?

followed shareholder resolutions lowering the threshold of calling special meetings and seeking the right to act by written consent.

NOTE: THE ANTIDOTE TO THE ANTIDOTE? NEW STATE STATUTES

The successful attack on classified boards has led firms to lobby state legislatures for new statutes that (1) make classified boards mandatory (or opt out rather than opt in provisions) and (2) empower boards to adopt poison pill plans with *delayed hand* provisions. See Section C, *infra*. The later type statute overrules the *Quickturn Design* case that follows. So far three states, Iowa, Indiana, and Oklahoma, have passed pro-classified board provisions and another four, Georgia, Maryland, Virginia, and Pennsylvania, have passed delayed hand provisions. ISS will, no doubt, reflect these devices in its new corporate governance ratings. Shareholders in notable Oklahoma and Indiana companies will now press their companies to reincorporate in Delaware.

2. DEFENSES VOID "AB INITIO"

QUICKTURN DESIGN SYSTEMS, INC. V. SHAPIRO

Delaware Supreme Court, 1998.
721 A.2d 1281.

HOLLAND, JUSTICE.

* * *

At the time Mentor commenced its bid, Quickturn had in place a Rights Plan that contained a so-called "dead hand" provision. That provision had a limited "continuing director" feature that became operative only if an insurgent that owned more than 15 percent of Quickturn's common stock successfully waged a proxy contest to replace a majority of the board. In that event, only the "continuing directors" (those directors in office at the time the poison pill was adopted) could redeem the rights.

During the same August 21, 1998 meeting at which it amended the special meeting by-law, the Quickturn board also amended the Rights Plan to eliminate its "continuing director" feature, and to substitute a "no hand" or "delayed redemption provision" into its Rights Plan. The Delayed Redemption Provision provides that, if a majority of the directors are replaced by stockholder action, the newly elected board cannot redeem the rights for six months if the purpose or effect of the redemption would be to facilitate a transaction with an "Interested Person."[21]

---

[21] The "no hand" or Delayed Redemption Provision is found in a new Section 23(b) of the Rights Plan, which states:

> (b) Notwithstanding the provisions of Section 23(a), in the event that a majority of the Board of Directors of the Company is elected by stockholder action at an annual or special meeting of stockholders, then until the 180th day following the effectiveness of such election (including any postponement or adjournment thereof), the Rights shall not be

It is undisputed that the DRP would prevent Mentor's slate, if elected as the new board majority, from redeeming the Rights Plan for six months following their election, because a redemption would be "reasonably likely to have the purpose or effect of facilitating a Transaction" with Mentor, a party that "directly or indirectly proposed, nominated or financially supported" the election of the new board. Consequently, by adopting the DRP, the Quickturn board built into the process a six month delay period in addition to the 90 to 100 day delay mandated by the By-Law Amendment.

* * *

In this appeal, Mentor argues that the judgment of the Court of Chancery should be affirmed because the Delayed Redemption Provision is invalid as a matter of Delaware law. According to Mentor, the Delayed Redemption Provision, like the "dead hand" feature in the Rights Plan that was held to be invalid in Toll Brothers,[29] will impermissibly deprive any newly elected board of both its statutory authority to manage the corporation under 8 Del.C. § 141(a) and its concomitant fiduciary duty pursuant to that statutory mandate. We agree.

* * *

One of the most basic tenets of Delaware corporate law is that the board of directors has the ultimate responsibility for managing the business and affairs of a corporation. Section 141(a) requires that any limitation on the board's authority be set out in the certificate of incorporation. The Quickturn certificate of incorporation contains no provision purporting to limit the authority of the board in any way. The Delayed Redemption Provision, however, would prevent a newly elected board of directors from *completely* discharging its fundamental management duties to the corporation and its stockholders for six months. While the Delayed Redemption Provision limits the board of directors' authority in only one respect, the suspension of the Rights Plan, it nonetheless restricts the board's power in an area of fundamental importance to the shareholders—negotiating a possible sale of the corporation. Therefore, we hold that the Delayed Redemption Provision is invalid under § 141(a), which confers upon any newly elected board of directors *full* power to manage and direct the business and affairs of a Delaware corporation.

* * *

---

redeemed if such redemption is reasonably likely to have the purpose or effect of facilitating a Transaction with an Interested Person.

Substantially similar provisions were added to Sections 24 ("Exchange") and 27 ("Supplements and Amendments") of the Rights Plan.

[29] Carmody v. Toll Brothers, Inc., Del.Ch., C.A. No. 15983, Jacobs, V.C., 1998 WL 418896 (July 24, 1998) ("*Toll Brothers*"). See Bank of New York Co., Inc. v. Irving Bank Corp., N.Y. Sup. Ct., 139 Misc.2d 665, 528 N.Y.S.2d 482 (1988). . . .

The Delayed Redemption Provision would prevent a new Quickturn board of directors from managing the corporation by redeeming the Rights Plan to facilitate a transaction that would serve the stockholders' best interests, even under circumstances where the board would be required to do so because of its fiduciary duty to the Quickturn stockholders. . . .

NOTE: STOCK EXCHANGE RESTRICTIONS ON VOTING RIGHTS PLANS

A failsafe strategy for target boards to stop unwanted stock acquisitions is to limit the voting power of the outstanding common stock not held by the firm's insiders. A purchaser cannot take control of the board without purchasing the insiders' shares. As noted above, there were several ways to limit the voting power of outstanding stock and several ways to affect the limitation. The more problematic approach is to vary the voting rights of shareholders holding a single class of voting common stock. The firm could, for example, cap the voting power of any one shareholder, regardless of the number of shares held (a *voting cap plan*), or could restrict the voting power of shares for several years after any transfer (a *time-phased plan*). But, capping voting power disadvantages existing control groups. And time-phased plans basing voting power on the length of time the shares have been held also generate unexpected problems.[23]

---

[23] Gamco Investors, Inc. v. Century Telephone Enterprises, C.A. 91–1027 (W.D. La., Aug. 14, 1991), 7 M&A CORP. GOV. L. REP. 315: [In 1987, Century, a public corporation incorporated under the laws of Louisiana, instituted a time-phased voting plan for its stock which provided ten votes per share for shareholders who had beneficially held their shares either (1) as of March 31, 1987, or (2) for a period of forty-eight consecutive months beginning with the effective date of the proposal. The super voting rights were lost upon sale of the shares, but a new beneficial owner of former ten vote shares could acquire ten for one rights himself by holding the shares for forty-eight months. The purpose of instituting the ten for one voting rights was to encourage long term investment into the company. . . .

Over time, Century's directors discovered several problems with the time-phased voting plan which they had not foreseen. First, the percentage of Century stock held by institutional investors had grown from 30 percent in 1987 to 56 percent in 1990. Century was particularly concerned that institutional investors, such as the plaintiff, might acquire sufficient voting power in the corporation to seize control of Century without paying a premium. This was particularly troubling in light of the plaintiff's highly publicized comments that Century was a likely takeover target.

Second, Century was unable to use the "pooling of assets" method of accounting in making acquisitions in exchange for Century stock. . . . Third, Century came to realize that determination of ten-vote status could be difficult because of problems in interpreting the various criteria set out in the time-phase voting provisions and that such difficulties could lead to problems between Century and its shareholders.

Changing all shares back to one vote shares was considered, but was quickly rejected because of the difficulty of persuading ten vote shareholders to give up their ten votes per share and because the disenfranchisement of the ten votes per share would violate the New York Stock Exchange rules and would subject Century to delisting. . . .

Century decided that the best solution to the above-stated problems would be to amend the Articles of Incorporation to freeze the time-phased voting plan as it then stood. . . . Under Louisiana law, no separate vote was required by the one vote shares because they did not constitute a separate class of stock. . . .]

The technique most favored by target managers is the creation of two classes of stock. One class would have the predominant equity interest in the firm—holders would receive full dividends and have full rights on liquidation—but would also have limited or no voting rights. The second class would have very limited equitable rights—holders would receive little or no portion of any dividend or liquidation distributions—but would also have super-voting rights. A firm's insider control group would hold some of the first class, for their returns, and all of the second class, for control.

There are three methods of implementing a two-tier voting stock plan in an ongoing company. First, a firm can amend its certificate of incorporation to limit the rights of outstanding shares and authorize the issuance of the new super-voting shares, which are sold or distributed exclusively to insiders. Second, the firm can amend its certificate of incorporation to authorize the issuance of non-voting or limited-voting shares, if the articles did not do so already, and then distribute the new non-voting shares or limited-voting shares through a self-tender offer, exchanging the new shares for the outstanding voting shares. Insiders would not participate in the exchange and would retain the voting shares. Third, a firm can amend its certificate of incorporation to authorize the issuance of super-voting shares with transfer restrictions and distribute the new shares as a stock dividend.

Shareholders, when asked to approve voting power recapitalization proposals, seem too pliant in light of economic studies finding that such recapitalizations have significant negative effects on stock price.[24] Shareholders seem overly susceptible to *sweeteners*, a cash payment contingent on their exchange of voting for non-voting stock, to subtle retributive threats (the risk of what happens to a company if a controlling shareholder is peeved) and to heavy effective lobbying by managers (using corporate funds). Academics explain the success of the votes on *rational apathy*, the shareholders' incentive not to inform themselves adequately to vote with perspicuity because the cost of gathering the information is higher than any gain in stock value that may occur from an educated vote.[25] Moreover, we wonder whether even intelligent voters can assess the cost of permanent disenfranchisement; the loss of the ability to embarrass managers, a club rarely used but always behind the door, may have subtle but significant value in ensuring day-to-day management accountability.

Our stock exchanges have been sensitive to investor concerns on the issue. The New York Stock Exchange has had a long-standing policy that favors companies with one vote per share of common stock. In its current form the policy accepts pre-existing dual class voting stock structures but expressly discourages listed companies from engaging in new voting recapitalization changes. The rule stops our largest companies from implementing voting

---

[24] See *Voting Rights Listing Standards; Disenfranchisement Rule*, SEC Rel. Nos. 34-25891, 1988 WL 1000037 (July 7, 1988), and 34-25891A, 1988 WL 1000039 (July 13, 1988) (both discussing SEC Office of Economic Analysis studies).

[25] See *Voting Rights Listing Standards; Disenfranchisement Rule*, SEC Rel. No. 34-25891, 1988 WL 1000037 (July 7, 1988) (Comments of Professor Weiss).

recapitalizations as pure takeover defenses. NYSE Listed Company Manual § 313.00(A):

> Voting rights of existing shareholders of publicly traded common stock . . . cannot be disparately reduced or restricted through any corporate action or issuance. Examples of such corporate action or issuance include, but are not limited to, the adoption of time phased voting rights plans, the adoption of capped voting rights plans, the issuance of super voting stock, or the issuance of stock with voting rights less than the per share voting rights of the existing common stock through an exchange offer.[Ed.[26]]

The Nasdaq has a similar rule. See Nasdaq Marketplace Rule 5640 and IM-5640.

3. EMPIRICAL DATA ON THE USE AND EFFECT OF THE TAKEOVER DEFENSES

Researchers since the mid-1980s have studied the effect of takeover defenses on the stock price of adopting corporations. The early studies found that on the adoption of the more severe anti-takeover defenses, the stock price of a corporation dropped significantly.[27] Newer, more

---

[26] [Ed. The policy permits the listing of voting common stock when a company has outstanding non-voting common stock and vice versa. § 313(B). The policy does not apply to companies with existing dual class capital structures. § 313, Supp. Material, 10.]

[27] See Gregg A. Jarrell & Annett B. Poulsen, *Shark Repellents and Stock Prices: The Effects of Antitakeover Amendments Since 1980*, 19 J. FIN. ECON. 127 (1987) (fair price amendments have been found to have no significant effects, while classified board and supermajority clauses have been found in some studies to have significant negative impacts on target shareholder wealth); Sanjai Bhagat & Richard H. Jefferies, *Voting Power in the Proxy Process: The Case of Anti-takeover Charter Amendments*, 30 J. FIN ECON. 193 (1991) (same); Gregg A. Jarrell & Annett B. Poulsen, *Dual-Class Recapitalizations as Antitakeover Mechanisms,* 20 J. FIN. ECON. 130 (1988) (dual-class voting stock recapitalizations are associated with significant negative stock price effects); Michael Ryngaert, *Effects of Poison Pills on Shareholder Wealth,* 20 J. FIN. ECON. 377 (1988) (adoption of the more restrictive of the poison pill plans correlates with stock price declines; court decisions validating a poison pill also correlate with price declines, while price increases follow court decisions to invalidate a pill.); Choi, Kamma & Weintrop, *The Delaware Courts, Poison Pills, and Shareholder Wealth*, 2 J. L., ECON. & ORG. 375 (1989) (the overall wealth effect for 133 Delaware corporations was $1.97 billion); Larry Y. Dann & Harry DeAngelo, *Corporate Financial Policy and Corporate Control: A Study of Defensive Adjustments in Asset and Ownership Structure*, 20 J. FIN. ECON. 87 (1988) (severe corporate restructuring of assets through acquisition programs or divestiture or of stock structure through stock issuances or repurchases, undertaken without a shareholder vote, correlated with significant negative stock price effects); David J. Dennis, *Defensive Changes in Corporate Payout Policy, Share Repurchases and Special Dividends*, 45 J. FIN. ECON. 1433 (1990) (announcement of defensive share repurchases is associated with an average negative impact on the share price of the target firm while special, large-scale dividend payments generally increase the wealth of target firm shareholders); W.H. Mikkelson & R.S. Ruback, *Target Repurchases and Common Stock Returns*, 22 RAND J. OF ECON. 544 (1991) (greenmail payments correlate with negative abnormal returns if not followed by a successful bid). The newer studies on point are, Vincente Cunat, Mireia Gine, & Maria Guadaulup, *Price and Probability: Decomposing the Takeover Effect of Anti-Takeover Provisions,* SSRN 2713906 (Aug. 2016) (found large and significant effects of removing anti-takeover provisions) and Joathan Karpoff, *Do Takeover Defenses Deter Takeover?*, 30 REV. OF FIN. STUDIES 2359 (July 2017) (14 defenses empirically related to likelihood of takeover).

There is a sizable dissent to the content in the preceding paragraph of this footnote. See John C. Coates IV, *Takeover Defenses in the Shadow of the Pill: A Critique of the Scientific Evidence*, 79 TEX. L. REV. 271 (2000). Professor Coates argues that such studies on poison pill plans do not

sophisticated studies, based on broader measures of restrictions on shareholders' rights confirm the basic finding.[28] Classified boards continue to attract significant negative attention.[29]

Most studies that addressed the question have found that firms with defenses in place sold for higher premiums in takeovers than firms did without defenses.[30] Once a bidder appears, takeover defenses enable target firm shareholders to claim more value if the acquisition is successful. In other words, the defenses give target-firm managers the ability to negotiate for a higher acquisition price. Other studies claim that poison pills have a neutral impact on offer premiums.[31] There is no doubt that M & A advisors believe that takeover defenses lead to higher takeover premiums.

---

support claims that they decrease firm value on adoption. He argues that since poison pill plans can be adopted quickly by target boards, a board's announcement that it has adopted a plan does not distinguish the firm significantly from those who have not but could have. Shark repellant amendments, on the other hand, he notes, which take time to adopt and, in some cases, time to repeal and, therefore, cannot be adopted quickly so as to respond to a pending bid, do distinguish target firms that have the amendments from those who do not. Professor Coates rejects the common view that the actual adoption of a pill adds crucial information (affecting a firm's value), that is, the firm is signaling that its management will use its power to block bids and/or negotiate to extract additional value from bidders. Consistent with his analysis, one seeking to measure the wealth effects of poison pills could attempt to find and focus on a legal event, a case, that validated poison pills. The Moran v. Household Finance case, decided in 1985, is the obvious candidate; those that have focused on the case find negative firm wealth effects associated with the decision. Martijn Cremers & Allen Ferrell, *Thirty Years of Shareholder Rights and Firm Valuation*, 69 J. FIN. 1167 (2014).

28 See generally Alma Cohen & Charles Wang, *How Do Staggered Boards Affect Shareholder Value?*, 108 J. FIN. ECON. 627 (2013) (negative effects); Martijn Cremers & Allen Ferrell, *supra* note 27 (discussing results of studies that find negative wealth effects from firms than score poorly on the IRRC G-index, an index of twenty four variables that measure restrictions on shareholder rights and the number of anti-takeover measures); Martijn Creamers & Vinay Nair, *Governance Mechanisms and Equity Prices*, 60 J. FIN. 2859 (2005); Paul Gompers, Joy Ishii, & Andrew Metrick, *Corporate Goverance and Equity Prices,* Q.J. OF ECON. 118 (2003). See also Lucian Bebchuk, Alma Cohen, & Allen Ferrell, *What Matters in Corporate Governance?*, 22 REV. OF FIN. STUDIES 783 (Feb. 2009) (focusing on an *entrenchment index* of six variables, classified boards, limits on shareholder amendments to bylaws, poison pills, golden parachutes, and supermajority requirements for mergers and for charter amendments, and finding significant reductions in firm value correlated with an increase in the index). There is substantial controversy over these findings. See Yakov Amihud, Markus Schmid, & Steven Davidoff Solomon, *Do Staggered Boards Affect Firm Value?*, SSRN 2948141 (June 29, 2017) (no effect).

29 Olubumni Faleye, *Classified Boards, Firm Value, and Managerial Entrenchment*, 83 J. FIN. ECON. 501 (Feb. 2007); Lucian B. Bebchuk & Alma Cohen, *The Cost of Entrenched Boards*, 78 J. FIN. ECON. 409 (Nov. 2005) (classified boards correlate with lower shareholder value). But see Esteban Afonso & M. Wintoki, *Explaining the Staggered Board Discount*, SSRN 1927471 (Oct. 5, 2011) (weak, deeply discounted firms use classified boards).

30 See, e.g., Randall Heron & Erik Lie, *On the Use of Poison Pills and Defensive Payouts by Takeover Targets,* 79 J. BUS. 1783 (July 2006). See also Thomas Bates & Michael Lemmon, *Breaking Up is Hard to Do? An Analysis of Termination Fee Provisions and Merger Outcomes*, 69 J. FIN. ECON. 469 (2003) (termination fees produce higher completion rates and greater takeover premiums). There is contrary opinion. See, e.g., Vincente Cunat, Mireia Gine & Maria Guadaulup, *Price and Probability: Decomposing the Takeover Effect of Anti-Takeover Provisions,* SSRN 2713906 (Aug. 2016).

31 While acknowledging that firms that have adopted pills before a bid receive higher premiums than firms that have not, Professor Coates argues that the correlation does not prove causation. Coates, *supra* note 27, at 311–313. If bidders can adopt pills post-bid, he argues, then pre-bid pills have no causal connection to premiums. Professor Coates, with two co-authors, has also found that staggered boards of directors, backed by poison pill plans, do not provide higher

How do we reconcile the first phenomenon—defenses correlate with a decrease in, or have no effect on the value of a firm—with the second—defenses increase the acquisition price to the benefit of target shareholders? Stock declines on the adoption of takeover defenses reflect the new disincentive that the defenses create for search efforts by all potential bidders. When firms can use takeover defenses to increase acquisition prices, the defenses reduce returns on search and bidding costs for bidders. Takeover defenses also increase the probability that target managers will be able to defeat a pending offer or entice a second bidder to create an auction. Higher takeover prices and the increased possibility of failure increase the potential cost of any potential takeover, discourage first bidders at the margin, and thereby deny some target shareholders a significant potential increase in the value of their shares by discouraging initial bidders from putting their firms *in play*. In essence, there are fewer takeovers,[32] but the ones that happen close at higher prices. The stock prices' effect on the adoption of defenses tell us that the lost value to potential takeover targets in fewer takeovers exceeds or is equal to the increased value in takeover prices.[33]

NOTE: HIGH-TECH COMPANY IPOs AND ANTI-TAKEOVER DEFENSES

From the Netscape IPO in 1995 through the tech wreck in March of 2000, a slew of high tech companies made initial public offerings (IPOs) of their common stock, transposing themselves from privately held to publicly traded companies. The companies often had a history of negative earnings and did not anticipate profits for several years. They did own gobs of potentially valuable intellectual property, however. Profits would come from maturing operations or the sale of the company and its intellectual property to mature companies

---

premiums in hostile deals that are eventually completed. Lucian Arye Bebchuk, John C. Coates IV & Guhan Subramanian, *The Powerful Anti-Takeover Force of Staggered Boards: Theory, Evidence, and Policy*, 54 STAN. L. REV. 887 (2002). They also could not find evidence of higher premiums in friendly deals. Lucian Arye Bebchuk, John C. Coates IV & Guhan Subramanian, *The Powerful Antitakeover Force of Staggered Boards: Further Findings and a Reply to Symposium Participants,* 55 STAN. L. REV. 885 (2002). The data is controversial. See, e.g., Marcel Kahan & Edward Rock, *Corporate Constitutionalism: Anti-Takeover Charter Provisions as Precommitment,* 152 U. PA. L. REV. 473, 504 (2003) (data do not warrant conclusion). See also Thomas Bates, David Becher & Michael Lemmon, *Board Classification and Managerial Entrenchment: Evidence from the Market for Corporate Control*, 87 J. FIN. ECON. 656 (Mar. 2008) (classified boards do not reduce target shareholder returns and do not reduce the size of takeover premiums received but do show a larger portion of the transaction surplus allocated to target shareholders and are associated with small negative firm wealth effects).

[32] See John Pound, *The Effect of Antitakeover Amendments on Takeover Activity: Some Direct Evidence*, 30 J. L. & ECON. 353 (1987). There is a difference between the frequency of takeovers in general and the frequency with which takeovers close once a target is identified. One would expect, consistent with the theory, larger differences in the first number than the second. See Heron & Lie, *supra* note 30 (poison pills do not reduce the frequency of takeovers once targets are identified).

[33] But see Thomas Bates, David Becher & Michael Lemmon, *supra* note 31. They find that the existence of a classified board does reduce slightly the likelihood of a target receiving a takeover bid but argue that the economic consequence is small.

(such as Cisco, Lucent, or Tyco). Most such companies incorporated in Delaware or restated their certificate of incorporation in Delaware for the IPO and had the opportunity to opt out of § 203, the Delaware anti-takeover statute, on incorporation or reincorporation. Most high tech firms did not do so, in spite of the firms' interest in maximizing their salability or liquidity.[34] Many of the certificates also contained shark repellant amendments. Moreover, the prospectuses for the IPOs (the final written selling document required by the SEC), in the "Risk Factors" section, often explained the firms' failure to opt out of § 203 and their choice of shark repellant amendments with some surprising language. Here is an example:

> Our certificate of incorporation and bylaws contain provisions which could delay or prevent a change in control even if the change in control would be beneficial to our stockholders.

Michael J. Halloran, Lee F. Benton, Robert V. Gunderson, Jr., Jorge del Calvo & Benjamin M. Vandegrift, VENTURE CAPITAL & PUBLIC OFFERING NEGOTIATION (3d ed. 2002) at 28–28 (sample prospectus). What is going on here?[35]

B. FIDUCIARY DUTY AND A BOARD'S DECISION TO BLOCK TAKEOVERS

1. INTRODUCTION TO THE ENHANCED SCRUTINY TEST (THE *UNOCAL* TEST)

Introduction to Hostile Tender Offers: The archetypical hostile tender offer consisted of a cash tender offer for fifty-one percent of the outstanding voting shares, closed in the minimum twenty days allowed by the Williams

[34] The seminal article is Robert Daines & Michael Kausnes, *Do IPO Charters Maximize Firm Value? Anti-Takeover Protection in IPOs*, 17 J. L. ECON. & ORG. 83 (2001).

[35] For a positive explanation see William C. Johnson, Jonathan M. Karpoff, & Sangho Yi, *Why Do IPO Firms Have Takeover Defenses?* (Sept 6, 2011) (commits firm to operating strategy to the benefit of dependent customers, suppliers or strategic partners). For a negative explanation see, e.g., Laura Field & Jonathan M. Karpoff [Ed. yes same fellow], *Takeover Defense of IPO Firms*, 57 J. FIN. 1857 (2002) (explained by agency conflict between managers and non-managerial shareholders at the IPO stage). The authors found that takeover defenses in IPO firms are negatively related to subsequent acquisition likelihood and unrelated to takeover premiums for those firms that are acquired. The defenses are positively related to managers' compensation and negatively related to managerial ownership at the time of the IPO and to measures of how closely the managers are monitored by non-managerial shareholders at the IPO. The authors conclude that IPO managers, when they can, appear to shift the cost of takeover protection onto non-managerial shareholders. See also John C. Coats IV, *Explaining Variation in Takeover Defenses: Blame the Lawyers*, 89 CAL. L. REV. 1301 (2001); Lucian A. Bebchuk, *Why Firms Adopt Antitakeover Arrangements,* 152 U. PA. L. REV. 713 (2003) (various explanations; none support a value increasing role for takeover protections, however). Professor Oesterle believes in a "giddy with glee/I'm a prodigy" theory; the private investors have hit big and stand to make millions, they will not jeopardize collecting their winnings in the IPO by arguing with the founders over what are, at the time to the investors, trifles. (It could also be a "don't rock the boat" theory.) The founders, worried about control over their "baby" once the company has gone public and the subject of sycophantic adulation by all their giddy investors, ask for management entrenchment protections and get them. (I'm a prodigy, why should I not continue to control the company?"). See also Lucian Bebchuk & Kobi Kastiel, *The Untenable Case for Perpetual Dual-class Stock,* 103 VA. L. REV. 585 (2017).

Act, followed by a squeeze-out merger of the remaining minority shareholders using *junk bonds*, subordinated debentures of the acquirer.[36] The offer created stampede pressure on target shareholders by offering a premium over market price in the tender offer and a lower value in junk bonds in the squeeze-out. The Delaware Supreme Court came to call the price differential, *structural coercion*. The blended price of the total offer, fifty-one percent times the tender offer price and forty-nine percent times the back-end merger price,[37] could be lower than target shareholders would be willing to accept under less rushed conditions. In cases of substantial price differentials, it was possible that the blended price was lower than the market price of the target company.

30-60%

The straw man coercive tender offer then was a cash tender offer, squeeze-out merger combination with a substantial price differential at a blended price that was only a small premium over the pre-deal market price of the target. In practice this deal, the fear of which drove the early case law, was as rare as hen's teeth. In most all hostile deals, the cash tender offer was for a substantial premium over market price (thirty to sixty percent) and the back-end value of the junk bonds was equal to the tender offer price.[38] Target shareholders who believed that the firm could nick the bidder for a higher premium (and a bigger slice of the elusive joint gains or synergy in the deal), even though their board tells them not to tender, felt pressured to tender anyway because they could not trust their fellow shareholders to hold out.[39] The Delaware Supreme Court came to label this *opportunity loss* or *substantive coercion* (depending on whether the target board was looking at alternative sales or firm value when it recommended that target shareholders hold out).[40] There was little or no structural coercion, except perhaps for the time value of money lost waiting on the back-end price. Structural coercion may have been rare but opportunity loss or substantive coercion is easy to assert and hard to disprove. Target shareholders pondering a bid always wonder whether they

---

[36] Junk bonds are unsecured debt obligations of the acquirer subordinated to all other acquirer debt. They bear a high risk and, therefore, a high rate of interest. In some cases, the "junk" was non-voting preferred stock. The junk could be sold into the markets for cash once target shareholders received it in the back-end merger. The value of the bonds promised, if there is no active trading market in the instruments created, is hard to determine, however, and it tested investment bankers valuation skills.

[37] This assumes that all target shareholders would tender all their shares and, under the pro rata takeup rules of the Williams Act, would get the blended price. If 100 percent of the target shareholders tender, for example, 51 percent of each block of shares is included in the tender offer and 49 percent is included in the back-end merger. If 80 percent of the outstanding shareholders tender, the bidder would take up 51/80ths of each block tendered in the first stage and 49/80ths of each block in the second stage.

[38] The back-end price had to survive the target shareholder's requests for appraisal. Most acquirers were out of cash by the back-end and could not risk a substantial number of target shareholder's perfecting and pursuing their appraisal rights. Why? See Chapter 2, Section A.3.

[39] This is a version of a *collective action problem*. The shareholders, acting individually, would agree to accept an offer that they would, acting collectively (through a vote, for example), reject.

[40] The terminology and the distinction is troublesome.

can get a higher price and wonder whether other shareholders will listen to a board's cry that they should refuse. In any event, the potential horror of *coercive*[41] hostile tender offers rushed the courts into supporting target board efforts to block unwelcome tender offers.

The first major case on unwelcome tender offers is not included in robust form in the text. *Unocal Corporation v. Mesa Petroleum Co*, 493 A.2d 946 (Del. 1985). The legal test, the *Unocal* standard, gets its name from the case. The case is not in the text because the defense that the court sanctioned was a defensive, coercive, self-tender offer that excluded the bidder. The target tendered for its own shares at a premium price, excluded the bidder's shares, and shareholders recognized that those that did not tender would be left with lower value "stub stock." The SEC passed a rule against the practice, including self-tender offers in the *all-holders rule*, which prohibits discriminatory tender offers. See Exch. Act Rule 14d–10(a)(1). It goes without saying that the irony of naming a test after a case in which the tactic sanctioned by a state court is now illegal as a matter of federal law is palpable. Moreover, the court sanctioned, as a defense, a structurally coercive offer, one of the very few ever made in any context. It reminds one of the Williams Act, named after a Senator who later ended up in jail for taking bribes.

The more important case was the second, *Moran v. Household International, Inc.*, 500 A.2d 1346 (Del 1985), in which the Delaware Supreme Court validated an early form of a poison pill plan. The decision is seen by M & A practitioners and corporate law scholars as the central legal event that opened the way for target companies to unilaterally deploy takeover defenses. The decision represented a major shift in power from shareholders to corporate boards in corporate control contests. Significantly, the holding was not expected; it was a surprise[42] and, therefore, an identifiable shock to stock prices. Before the decision, less than five firms in one-thousand had a poison pill plan in place. Within three years of the decision, 600 firms in one-thousand had adopted one. Studies of the effect of the case on stock prices show a stunning negative effect in the markets.[43]

The modern formulation of the *Unocal* test, with its addendum from *Unitrin*[44] in 1995, is well described in the following case:

---

[41] The label *coercive* necessarily drives any analysis.

[42] The SEC wrote an amicus brief in the case arguing that the poison pill plan was illegal. Professor Oesterle was a young academic at the time and can remember the astonishment of his colleagues in corporate law on the holding. See Martin Lipton & Paul K. Rowe, *Pills, Polls and Professors: A Reply to Professor Gilson*, 27 DEL. J. CORP. L. 1 (2002) (*Household* "changed everything").

[43] See, e.g., Martijn Cremers & Allen Ferrell, *Thirty Years of Shareholder Rights and Firm Valuation*, 69 J. FIN. 1167 (2014) (the negative association of the G-index—a measure of limits on shareholder rights—with firm value began with the date of the case).

[44] Unitrin, Inc. v. American General Corp., 651 A.2d 1361 (Del. 1995).

AIR PRODUCTS AND CHEMICALS, INC. V. AIRGAS, INC.

Court of Chancery of Delaware, 2011.
16 A.3d 48.

CHANDLER, CHANCELLOR.

* * *

Plaintiff Air Products is a Delaware corporation headquartered in Allentown, Pennsylvania that serves technology, energy, industrial and healthcare customers globally. . . . The Shareholder Plaintiffs are Airgas stockholders. . . . Airgas is a Delaware corporation headquartered in Radnor, Pennsylvania. . . .

. . . Before its September 15, 2010 annual meeting, Airgas was led by a nine-member staggered board of directors, divided into three equal classes with one class (three directors) up for election each year. Other than McCausland [the CEO], the rest of the board members are independent outside directors. . . . At the 2010 annual meeting, three Airgas directors (McCausland, Brown, and Ill) lost their seats on the board when three Air Products nominees were elected. On September 23, 2010, Airgas expanded the size of its board to ten members and reappointed McCausland to fill the new seat. Thus, Airgas is now led by a ten-member staggered board of directors, nine of whom are independent.

As of the record date for the 2010 annual meeting, Airgas had 83,629,731 shares outstanding. From October 2009 (when Air Products privately approached Airgas about a potential deal) until today, Airgas's stock price has ranged from a low of $41.64 to a high of $71.28. For historical perspective, before then it had been trading in the $40s and $50s (with a brief stint in the $60s) through most of 2007–2008, until the financial crisis hit in late 2008. The stock price dropped as low as $27 per share in March of 2009, but quickly recovered and jumped back into the mid-$40s. In the board's unanimous view, the company is worth at least $78 in a sale transaction at this time ($60-ish unaffected stock price plus a 30% premium), and left alone, most of the Airgas directors "would say the stock will be worth north of $70 by next year." In the professional opinion of one of Airgas's independent financial advisors, the fair value of Airgas as of January 26, 2011 is "in the mid to high seventies, and well into the mid eighties." McCausland currently owns approximately 9.5% of Airgas common stock. The other directors collectively own less than 2% of the outstanding Airgas stock. Together, the ten current Airgas directors own approximately 11% of Airgas's outstanding stock. . . .

As a result of Airgas's classified board structure, it would take two annual meetings to obtain control of the board. In addition to its staggered board, Airgas has three main takeover defenses: (1) a shareholder rights plan ("poison pill") with a 15% triggering threshold, (2) Airgas has not opted out of Delaware General Corporation Law ("DGCL") § 203, which prohibits business combinations with any interested stockholder for a period of three years following the time that such stockholder became an interested stockholder, unless certain conditions are met, and (3) Airgas's Certificate of Incorporation includes a supermajority merger approval provision for certain business combinations. Namely, any merger with an "Interested Stockholder" (defined as a stockholder who beneficially owns 20% or more of the voting power of Airgas's outstanding voting stock) requires the approval of 67% or more of the voting power of the then-outstanding stock entitled to vote, unless approved by a majority of the disinterested directors or certain fair price and procedure requirements are met.

Together, these are Airgas's takeover defenses that Air Products and the Shareholder Plaintiffs challenge and seek to have removed or deemed inapplicable to Air Products' hostile tender offer. . . .

A. The Unocal *Standard*

Because of the "omnipresent specter" of entrenchment in takeover situations, it is well-settled that when a poison pill is being maintained as a defensive measure and a board is faced with a request to redeem the rights, the *Unocal* standard of enhanced judicial scrutiny applies. Under that legal framework, to justify its defensive measures, the target board must show (1) that it had "reasonable grounds for believing a danger to corporate policy and effectiveness existed" (i.e., the board must articulate a legally cognizable threat) and (2) that any board action taken in response to that threat is "reasonable in relation to the threat posed."

The first hurdle under *Unocal* is essentially a process-based review: "Directors satisfy the first part of the *Unocal* test by demonstrating good faith and reasonable investigation." Proof of good faith and reasonable investigation is "materially enhanced, as here, by the approval of a board comprised of a majority of outside independent directors."

But the inquiry does not end there; process alone is not sufficient to satisfy the first part of *Unocal* review—"under *Unocal* and *Unitrin* the defendants have the burden of showing the reasonableness of their investigation, the reasonableness of their process and *also of the result that they reached*." That is, the "process" has to lead to the finding of a threat. Put differently, no matter how exemplary the board's process, or how independent the board, or how reasonable its investigation, to meet their burden under the first prong of *Unocal* defendants must actually articulate some legitimate threat to corporate policy and effectiveness.

Once the board has reasonably perceived a legitimate threat, *Unocal* prong 2 engages the Court in a substantive review of the board's defensive actions: Is the board's action taken in response to that threat proportional to the threat posed? In other words, "[b]ecause of the omnipresent specter that directors could use a rights plan improperly, even when acting subjectively in good faith, *Unocal* and its progeny require that this Court also review the use of a rights plan objectively." This proportionality review asks first whether the board's actions were "draconian, by being either preclusive or coercive." [Ed. This is the *Untirin* addendum.] If the board's response was not draconian, the Court must then determine whether it fell "within a range of reasonable responses to the threat" posed.

. . . In *Moran v. Household International, Inc.,* written shortly after the *Unocal* decision in 1985, the Delaware Supreme Court first upheld the legality of the poison pill as a valid takeover defense. Specifically, in *Moran,* the Household board of directors "react[ed] to what it perceived to be the threat in the market place of coercive two-tier tender offers" by adopting a stockholder rights plan that would allow the corporation to protect stockholders by issuing securities as a way to ward off a hostile bidder presenting a structurally coercive offer. The *Moran* Court held that the *adoption* of such a rights plan was within the board's statutory authority and thus was not *per se* illegal under Delaware law. But the Supreme Court cabined the use of the rights plan as follows:

> [T]he Rights Plan is not absolute. When the Household Board of Directors is faced with a tender offer and a request to redeem rights, they will not be able to arbitrarily reject the offer. They will be held to the same fiduciary standards any other board of directors would be held to in deciding to adopt a defensive mechanism, the same standard they were held to in originally approving the Rights Plan.

Hostile B says show threat, if wanna stop it, redeem rights plan by BoD

The Court went on to say that "[t]he Board does not now have unfettered discretion in refusing to redeem the Rights. The Board has no more discretion in refusing to redeem the Rights than it does in enacting any defensive mechanism." Accordingly, while the Household board's adoption of the rights plan was deemed to be made in good faith, and the plan was found to be reasonable in relation to the threat posed by the "coercive acquisition techniques" that were prevalent at the time, the pill at that point was adopted merely as a preventive mechanism to ward off future advances. The "ultimate response to an actual takeover," though, would have to be judged by the directors' actions taken at that time, and the board's "use of the Plan [would] be evaluated when and if the issue [arose]."

Notably, the pill in *Moran* was considered reasonable in part because the Court found that there were many methods by which potential acquirors could get around the pill. One way around the pill was the "proxy out"—bidders could solicit consents to remove the board and redeem the rights. In fact, the Court did "not view the Rights Plan as much of an impediment on the tender offer process" at all. After all, the board in *Moran* was not classified, and so the entire board was up for reelection annually—meaning that all of the directors could be replaced in one fell swoop and the acquiror could presumably remove any impediments to its tender offer fairly easily after that. . . .

A. Has the Airgas Board Established That It Reasonably Perceived the Existence of a Legally Cognizable Threat?

1. *Process*

Under the first prong of *Unocal,* defendants bear the burden of showing that the Airgas board, "after a reasonable investigation . . . determined in good faith, that the [Air Products offer] presented a threat . . . that warranted a defensive response." . . .

In examining defendants' actions under this first prong of *Unocal,* "the presence of a majority of outside independent directors coupled with a showing of reliance on advice by legal and financial advisors, 'constitute[s] a prima facie showing of good faith and reasonable investigation.'" Here, it is undeniable that the Airgas board meets this test.

First, it is currently comprised of a majority of outside independent directors—including the three recently-elected insurgent directors who were nominated to the board by Air Products. Air Products does not dispute the independence of the Air Products Nominees, and the evidence at trial showed that the rest of the Airgas board, other than McCausland, are outside, independent directors who are not dominated by McCausland.

Second, the Airgas board relied on not one, not two, but three outside independent financial advisors in reaching its conclusion that Air Products' offer is "clearly inadequate." . . . In addition, the Airgas board has relied on the advice of legal counsel, and the three Air Products Nominees have retained their own additional independent legal counsel (Skadden, Arps). In short, the Airgas board's process easily passes the smell test.

2. *What is the "Threat?"*

Although the Airgas board meets the threshold of showing good faith and reasonable investigation, the first part of *Unocal* review requires more than that; it requires the board to show that its good faith and reasonable investigation ultimately gave the board "grounds for concluding that a threat to the corporate enterprise existed." In the supplemental evidentiary hearing, Airgas (and its lawyers) attempted to identify numerous threats posed by Air Products' $70 offer: It is coercive. It is opportunistically timed. It presents the stockholders with a "prisoner's dilemma." It undervalues Airgas—it is a "clearly inadequate" price. The merger arbitrageurs who have bought into Airgas need to be "protected from themselves." The arbs are a "threat" to the minority. The list goes on.

The reality is that the Airgas board discussed essentially none of these alleged "threats" in its board meetings, or in its deliberations on whether to accept or reject Air Products' $70 offer, or in its consideration of whether to keep the pill in place.

. . . [T]he only threat that the board discussed—the threat that has been the central issue since the beginning of this case—is the inadequate price of Air Products' offer. Thus, inadequate price, coupled with the fact that a majority of Airgas's stock is held by merger arbitrageurs who might be willing to tender into such an inadequate offer, is the only real "threat" alleged.

In the end, it really is "All About Value." Airgas's directors and Airgas's financial advisors concede that the Airgas stockholder base is sophisticated and well-informed, and that they have all the information necessary to decide whether to tender into Air Products' offer.

a. Structural Coercion

Air Products' offer is not structurally coercive. A structurally coercive offer involves "the risk that disparate treatment of non-tendering shareholders might distort shareholders' tender decisions." It is for all shares of Airgas, with consideration to be paid in all cash.[3] The offer is backed by secured financing. There is regulatory approval. The front end will get the same consideration as the back end, in the same currency, as quickly as practicable. Air Products is committed to promptly paying $70 in cash for each and every share of Airgas and has no interest in owning less than 100% of Airgas. Air Products would seek to acquire any non-tendering shares "[a]s quick[ly] as the law would allow." It is willing to commit to a subsequent offering period. In light of that, any stockholders who believe that the $70 offer is inadequate simply *would not tender* into the offer—they would risk nothing by not tendering because if a majority of Airgas shares did tender, any non-tendering shares could tender into the subsequent offering period and receive the exact same consideration ($70 per share in cash) as the front

b. Opportunity Loss

Opportunity loss is the threat that a "hostile offer might deprive target stockholders of the opportunity to select a superior alternative offered by target management or . . . offered by another bidder." . . . Air Products' offer poses no threat of opportunity loss. The Airgas board has had, at this point, over sixteen months to consider Air Products' offer and to explore "strategic alternatives going forward as a company." After all that time, there is no alternative offer currently on the table, and counsel for defendants represented during the October trial that "we're not asserting that we need more time to explore a specific alternative." The "superior alternative" Airgas is pursuing is simply to "continue[ ] on its current course and execute[ ] its strategic [five year, long term] plan."

c. Substantive Coercion

Inadequate price and the concept of substantive coercion are inextricably related. The Delaware Supreme Court has defined substantive coercion, as discussed in Section II.*C*, as "the risk that [Airgas's] stockholders might accept [Air Products'] inadequate Offer because of 'ignorance or mistaken belief' regarding the Board's assessment of the long-term value of [Airgas's] stock." In other words, if management advises stockholders, in good faith, that it believes Air Products' hostile offer is inadequate because in its view the future earnings potential of the company is greater than the price offered, Airgas's stockholders might nevertheless reject the board's advice and tender.

In the article that gave rise to the concept of "substantive coercion," Professors Gilson and Kraakman argued that, in order for substantive coercion to exist, two elements are necessary: (1) management must actually expect the value of the company to be greater than the offer—and be correct that the offer is in fact inadequate, and (2) the stockholders must reject management's advice or "*believe* that management will not deliver on its promise." Both elements must be present because "[w]ithout the first element, shareholders who accept a structurally non-coercive offer have not made a mistake. Without the second element, shareholders will believe management and reject underpriced offers."

Defendants' argument involves a slightly different take on this threat, based on the particular composition of Airgas's stockholders (namely, its large "short-term" base). In essence, Airgas's argument is that "the substantial ownership of Airgas stock by these short-term, deal-driven investors poses a threat to the company and its shareholders"—the threat that, because it is likely that the arbs would support the $70 offer, "shareholders will be coerced into tendering into an inadequate offer." The threat of "arbs" is a new facet of substantive coercion, different from the substantive coercion claim recognized in *Paramount*. There, the hostile tender offer was purposely timed to confuse the stockholders. . . . In contrast, here, defendants' claim is not about "confusion" or "mistakenly tendering" (or even "disbelieving" management)—Air Products' offer has been on the table for over a year, Airgas's stockholders have been barraged with information, and there is no alternative offer to choose that might cause stockholders to be confused about the terms of Air Products' offer. Rather, Airgas's claim is that it needs to maintain its defensive measures to prevent control from being surrendered for an unfair or inadequate price. The argument is premised on the fact that a large percentage (almost half) of Airgas's stockholders are merger arbitrageurs—many of whom bought into the stock when Air Products first announced its interest in acquiring Airgas, at a time when the stock was trading much lower than it is today—who would be willing to tender into an inadequate offer because they stand to make a significant return on their investment even if the offer grossly undervalues Airgas in a sale. "They don't care a thing about the fundamental value of Airgas." In short, the risk is that a majority of Airgas's stockholders will tender into Air Products' offer despite its inadequate price tag, leaving the minority "coerced" into taking $70 as well. The defendants do not appear to have come to grips with the fact that the arbs bought their shares from long-term stockholders who viewed the increased market price generated by Air Products' offer as a good time to sell.

The threat that merger arbs will tender into an inadequately priced offer is only a legitimate threat if the offer is indeed inadequate. The only way to protect stockholders [from a threat of substantive coercion] is for courts to ensure that the threat is real and that the board asserting the threat is not imagining or exaggerating it." . . . [M]anagement presented a single scenario in its revised five-year plan—no double dip recession; reasonably optimistic macroeconomic growth assumptions. Everyone at trial agreed that "reasonable minds can differ as to the view of future value." But nothing in the record supported a claim that Airgas fudged any of its numbers, nor was there evidence that the board did not act at all times in good faith and in reasonable reliance on its outside advisors. The Air Products Nominees found the assumptions to be "reasonable." They do not see "any indication of a double-dip recession."

The next question is, if a majority of stockholders *want* to tender into an inadequately priced offer, is that substantive coercion? Is that a threat that justifies continued maintenance of the poison pill? Put differently, is there evidence in the record that Airgas stockholders are so "focused on the short-term" that they would "take a smaller harvest in the swelter of August over a larger one in Indian Summer"? . . . [T]here is at least some evidence in the record suggesting that this risk may be real. Moreover, both Airgas's expert as well as *Air Products' own expert* testified that a large number—if not all—of the arbitrageurs who bought into Airgas's stock at prices significantly below the $70 offer price would be happy to tender their shares at that price regardless of the potential long-term value of the company. Based on the testimony of both expert witnesses, I find sufficient evidence that a majority of stockholders might be willing to tender their shares regardless of whether the price is adequate or not—thereby ceding control of Airgas to Air Products. . . .

yes, a threat

Ultimately, it all seems to come down to the Supreme Court's holdings in *Paramount* and *Unitrin.* In *Unitrin,* the Court held: "[T]he directors of a Delaware corporation have the prerogative to determine that the market undervalues its stock and to protect its stockholders from offers that do not reflect the long-term value of the corporation under its present management plan." When a company is not in *Revlon* mode, a board of directors "is not under any *per se* duty to maximize shareholder value in the short term, even in the context of a takeover." The Supreme Court has unequivocally "endorse[d the] conclusion that it is not a breach of faith for directors to determine that the present stock market price of shares is not representative of true value or that there may indeed be several market values for any corporation's stock." As noted above, based on all of the facts presented to me, I find that the Airgas board acted in good faith and relied on the advice of its financial and legal advisors in coming to the conclusion that Air Products' offer is inadequate. And as the Supreme Court has held, a board that in good faith believes that a hostile offer is inadequate may "properly employ[ ] a poison pill as a proportionate defensive response to protect its stockholders from a 'low ball' bid."

B. *Is the Continued Maintenance of Airgas's Defensive Measures Proportionate to the "Threat" Posed by Air Products' Offer?*

Turning now to the second part of the *Unocal* test, I must determine whether the Airgas board's defensive measures are a proportionate response to the threat posed by Air Products' offer. Where the defensive measures "are inextricably related, the principles of *Unocal* require that [they] be scrutinized collectively as a unitary response to the perceived threat." Defendants bear the burden of showing that their defenses are not preclusive or coercive, and if neither, that they fall within a "range of reasonableness."

1. *Preclusive or Coercive*

A defensive measure is coercive if it is "aimed at 'cramming down' on its shareholders a management-sponsored alternative." Airgas's defensive measures are certainly not coercive in this respect, as Airgas is specifically *not* trying to cram down a management sponsored alternative, but rather, simply wants to maintain the status quo and manage the company for the long term.

A response is preclusive if it "makes a bidder's ability to wage a successful proxy contest and gain control [of the target's board] . . . 'realistically unattainable.' " Air Products and Shareholder Plaintiffs argue that Airgas's defensive measures are preclusive because they render the possibility of an effective proxy contest realistically unattainable. . . . [N]o bidder to my knowledge has ever successfully stuck around for two years and waged two successful proxy contests to gain control of a classified board in order to remove a pill. So does that make the combination of a staggered board and a poison pill preclusive?

This precise question was asked and answered four months ago in *Versata Enterprises, Inc. v. Selectica, Inc.* . . . The Delaware Supreme Court rejected this argument, stating that. . . . *[W]e hold that the combination of a classified board and a Rights Plan do not constitute a preclusive defense*.". . . . The Court concluded: "The fact that a combination of defensive measures makes it more difficult for an acquirer to obtain control of a board does not make such measures realistically unattainable, i.e., preclusive. . . . I am thus bound by this clear precedent to proceed on the assumption that Airgas's defensive measures are not preclusive if they delay Air Products from obtaining control of the Airgas board (even if that delay is significant) so long as obtaining control at some point in the future

~~is realistically attainable~~. I now examine whether the ability to obtain control of Airgas's board in the future is realistically attainable.

- Air Products has already run one successful slate of insurgents. Their three independent nominees were elected to the Airgas board in September. Airgas's next annual meeting will be held sometime around September 2011. Accordingly, if Airgas's defensive measures remain in place, Air Products has two options if it wants to continue to pursue Airgas at this time: (1) It can call a special meeting and remove the entire board with a supermajority vote of the outstanding shares, or (2) It can wait until Airgas's 2011 annual meeting to nominate a slate of directors. . . .

Whether it is realistic to believe that Air Products can, at some point in the future, achieve a 67% vote necessary to remove the entire Airgas board at a special meeting is (in my opinion) impossible to predict given the host of variables in this setting, but the sheer lack of historical examples where an insurgent has ever achieved such a percentage in a contested control election must mean something. Commentators who have studied actual hostile takeovers for Delaware companies have, at least in part, essentially corroborated this common sense notion that such a victory is not realistically attainable. Nonetheless, while the special meeting may not be a realistically attainable mechanism for circumventing the Airgas defenses, that assessment does not end the analysis under existing precedent.

Even if Air Products is unable to achieve the 67% supermajority vote of the outstanding shares necessary to remove the board in a special meeting, it would only need a simple majority of the voting stockholders to obtain control of the board at next year's annual meeting. Air Products has stated its unwillingness to wait around for another eight months until Airgas's 2011 annual meeting. There are legitimately articulated reasons for this—Air Products' stockholders, after all, have been carrying the burden of a depressed stock price since the announcement of the offer. But that is a business determination by the Air Products board. The reality is that obtaining a simple majority of the voting stock is significantly less burdensome than obtaining a supermajority vote of the outstanding shares, and considering the current composition of Airgas's stockholders (and the fact that, as a result of that shareholder composition, a majority of the voting shares today would likely tender into Air Products' $70 offer), if Air Products and those stockholders choose to stick around, an Air Products victory at the next annual meeting is very realistically attainable. . . .

2. *Range of Reasonableness*

"If a defensive measure is neither coercive nor preclusive, the *Unocal* proportionality test requires the focus of enhanced judicial scrutiny to shift to the range of reasonableness." The reasonableness of a board's response is evaluated in the context of the specific threat identified—the "specific nature of the threat [ ] 'sets the parameters for the range of permissible defensive tactics' at any given time." Here, the record demonstrates that Airgas's board, composed of a majority of outside, independent directors, acting in good faith and with numerous outside advisors concluded that Air Products' offer clearly undervalues Airgas in a sale transaction. The board believes in good faith that the offer price is inadequate by no small margin. Thus, the board is responding to a legitimately articulated threat.

This conclusion is bolstered by the fact that the three Air Products Nominees on the Airgas board have now wholeheartedly joined in the board's determination—what is more, they believe it is their fiduciary duty to keep Airgas's defenses in place. And Air Products' *own directors* have testified that (1) they have no reason to believe that the Airgas directors have breached their fiduciary duties (2) even though plenty of information has been made available to the stockholders, they "agree that Airgas management is in the best position to understand the intrinsic value of the company," and (3) if the shoe were on the other foot, they would act in the same way as Airgas's directors have.

Air Products chose to replace a minority of the Airgas board with three *independent directors* who promised to take a "fresh look." Air Products ran its nominees expressly premised on that independent slate. It could have put up three nominees premised on the slogan of "shareholder choice." It could have run a slate of nominees who would promise to remove the pill if elected. It could have gotten three directors elected who were resolved to fight back against the rest of the Airgas board.

[T]the maintenance of the board's defensive measures must fall within a range of reasonableness here. The board is not "cramming down" a management-sponsored alternative—or *any* company-changing alternative. Instead, the board is simply maintaining the status quo, running the company for the long-term, and consistently showing improved financial results each passing quarter. The board's actions do not *forever* preclude Air Products, or any bidder, from acquiring Airgas or from getting around Airgas's defensive measures if the price is right. In the meantime, the board is preventing a change of control from occurring at an inadequate price. This course of action has been clearly recognized under Delaware law: "directors, when acting deliberately, in an informed way, and in the good faith pursuit of corporate interests, may follow a course designed to achieve long-term value even at the cost of immediate value maximization."

Shareholder plaintiffs argue in their Post-Supplemental Hearing brief that Delaware law adequately protects any non-tendering shareholders in the event a majority of Airgas shareholders did tender into Air Products' offer . . . [W]hen Air Products would then seek to effect a long-form merger on the back end—as it has stated is its intention—any deal would be subject to entire fairness and claims for appraisal rights. . . . [O]n the back end, control will have already been conveyed to Air Products. The enormous value of synergies will not be factored into any appraisal. Additionally, much of the projected value in Airgas's five year plan is based on the expected returns from substantial investments that Airgas has already made—e.g., substantial capital investments, the SAP implementation. There is no guarantee (in fact it is unlikely) a fair value appraisal today would account for that projected value—value which Airgas's newest outside financial advisor describes as "orders of magnitude greater than what's been assumed and which would give substantially higher values." . . .

There is no question that poison pills act as potent anti-takeover drugs with the potential to be abused. Counsel for plaintiffs (both Air Products and Shareholder Plaintiffs) make compelling policy arguments in favor of redeeming the pill in this case—to do otherwise, they say, would essentially make all companies with staggered boards and poison pills "takeover proof." The argument is an excellent sound bite, but it is ultimately not the holding of this fact-specific case, although it does bring us one step closer to that result.

As this case demonstrates, in order to have any effectiveness, pills do not—and cannot—have a set expiration date. To be clear, though, this case does not endorse "just say never." What it does endorse is Delaware's long-understood respect for reasonably exercised managerial discretion, so long as boards are found to be acting in good faith and in accordance with their fiduciary duties (after rigorous judicial fact-finding and enhanced scrutiny of their defensive actions). The Airgas board serves as a quintessential example.

Directors of a corporation still owe fiduciary duties to *all stockholders*—this undoubtedly includes short-term as well as long-term holders. At the same time, a board cannot be forced into *Revlon* mode any time a hostile bidder makes a tender offer that is at a premium to market value. The mechanisms in place to get around the poison pill—even a poison pill in combination with a staggered board, which no doubt makes the process prohibitively more difficult—have been in place since 1985, when the Delaware Supreme Court first decided to uphold the pill as a legal defense to an unwanted bid. That is the current state of Delaware law until the Supreme Court changes it. . . .

QUESTIONS

On reading the decision, Air Products, as it had promised, dropped its bid and walked away. Are the Airgas shareholders better off for it? If the three Air Products nominees to the Airgas board had not "turned" and supported the Airgas defense, would the case have come out differently? What role did Delaware's promotion of itself as a home for large corporations play in the decision?

PARAMOUNT COMMUNICATIONS, INC. v. TIME, INC., 571 A.2d 1140 (Del. 1989): . . . On March 3, 1989, Time's board, with all but one director in attendance, met and unanimously approved the stock-for-stock merger with Warner. . . . The common stock of Warner would then be converted into common stock of Time at the agreed upon ratio. . . . Time sent out extensive proxy statements to the stockholders regarding the approval vote on the merger. . . . On June 7, 1989, these wishful assumptions were shattered by Paramount's surprising announcement of its all-cash offer to purchase all outstanding shares of Time for $175 per share. The following day, June 8, the trading price of Time's stock rose from $126 to $170 per share. . . . Time's board decided to recast its consolidation with Warner into an outright cash and securities acquisition of Warner by Time; and Time so informed Warner. Time accordingly restructured its proposal to acquire Warner as follows: Time would make an immediate all-cash offer for 51 percent of Warner's outstanding stock at $70 per share. The remaining 49 percent would be purchased at some later date for a mixture of cash and securities worth $70 per share. To provide the funds required for its outright acquisition of Warner, Time would assume 7–10 billion dollars worth of debt, thus eliminating one of the principal transaction-related benefits of the original merger agreement. . . . [Ed.: Time refused to negotiate with Paramount and erected a variety of takeover defenses that applied only to Paramount—a stock lock-up, a poison pill plan, and a no-shop clause. The court held that the Time board had not put the company up for sale and therefore that the duty enunciated in *Revlon* to hold a fair auction and sell to the highest bidder was not applicable to the Warner acquisition. Furthermore, it held that Time's board in refusing to even negotiate with Paramount met the requirements of the basic *Unocal* test.]

. . . The board's prevailing belief was that Paramount's bid posed a threat to Time's control of its own destiny and the retention of the "Time Culture" [generally, the editorial style of Time Magazine; the editors and writers believed that the takeover would threaten the magazine's independence and integrity]. . . .

[T]he Time board reasonably determined that inadequate value was not the only legally cognizable threat that Paramount's all-cash, all-shares offer could present. Time's board concluded that Paramount's eleventh hour offer posed other threats. One concern was that Time shareholders might elect to tender into Paramount's cash offer in ignorance or a mistaken belief of the strategic benefit which a business combination with Warner might produce. Moreover, Time viewed the conditions attached to Paramount's offer as introducing a degree of uncertainty that skewed a comparative analysis. Further, the timing of Paramount's offer to follow issuance of Time's proxy notice was viewed as arguably designed to upset, if not confuse, the Time stockholders' vote. Given this record evidence, we cannot conclude that the Time board's decision of June 6 that Paramount's offer posed a threat to corporate policy and effectiveness was lacking in good faith or dominated by motives of either entrenchment or self-interest. . . .

. . . [T]he Chancellor found that Time's responsive action to Paramount's tender offer was not aimed at "cramming down" on its shareholders a management-sponsored alternative, but rather had as its goal the carrying forward of a pre-existing transaction in an altered form. Thus, the response was reasonably related to the threat. The Chancellor noted that the revised agreement and its accompanying safety devices did not preclude Paramount from making an offer for the combined Time-Warner company or from changing the conditions of its offer so as not to make the offer dependent upon the nullification of the Time-Warner agreement. Thus, the response was proportionate. . . .

After the *Paramount Communications v. Time* case, the Delaware courts had to decide which *threats* justified a board's use of blocking devices. Two of those cases follow.

VERSATA ENTERPRISES v. SELECTICA, INC., 5 A.3d 586 (Del. 2010): [Selectica, after it went public, never had a profitable year. The company amassed $160 million in net operating losses (NOLs). The NOLs had substantial value because the company could use the NOLs to offset future taxable income. The company loses, however, a substantial portion of the NOLs when it goes through an *ownership change*, defined in Section 382 of the Internal Revenue Code. The definition of ownership change includes a change in the stock ownership of the company by more than 50 percent over a rolling three year period. Only five percent shareholders are included in the calculation, however. To protect its NOLs Selectica adopted a poison pill plan with a trigger of an unapproved stock purchase of 4.99 percent. A rejected hostile bidder, Versata, purchased enough shares in the open market to trigger the pill. Selectica diluted Versata's equity interest by half under the authority of the pill. All shareholders other than Versata received an additional share of Selectica stock. Selectica then put a new poison pill plan in place with a 4.99 percent trigger, *a reloaded poison pill*. The Court held that the Selectica board's decisions met the *Unocal* test.] "As we held in *Moran*, the adoption of a Rights Plan is not absolute. In other cases, we have upheld the adoption of a Rights Plans in specific defensive circumstances while simultaneously holding that it may be inappropriate for a Rights Plan to remain in place when those specific circumstances change dramatically. The fact that the NOL Poison Pill was reasonable under the specific facts and circumstances of this case, should not be construed as generally approving the reasonableness of a 4.99% trigger in the Rights Plan of a corporation with or without NOLs.

To reiterate *Moran,* "the ultimate response to an actual takeover bid must be judged by the Directors' actions at that time." If and when the Selectica Board "is faced with a tender offer and a request to redeem the [Reloaded NOL Poison Pill], they will not be able to arbitrarily reject the offer. They will be held to the same fiduciary standards any other board of directors would be held to in deciding to adopt a defensive mechanism." The Selectica Board has no more discretion in refusing to redeem the Rights Plan "than it does in enacting any defensive mechanism. Therefore, the Selectica Board's future use of the Reloaded NOL Poison Pill must be evaluated if and when that issue arises."

YUCAIPA AMERICAN ALLIANCE FUND II, L.P. v. RIGGIO, 1 A.3d 310 (Del. Ch. 2010) (Strine, V.C.): [A hedge fund manager, Burkle, acquired eighteen percent of the stock in a struggling, publicly traded book seller, Barnes & Noble. The founder of B&N, Riggio, owned thirty percent of its shares. The B&N board adopted a poison pill plan with a twenty percent trigger to stop Burkle and excepted Riggio's control block. Burkle sued to enjoin the pill. The Court refused on the grounds that the B&N board was reasonably concerned about the effects on shareholders of a *creeping tender offer*.] "On this record, I have no reason to conclude that Yucaipa would consciously propose options that would injure others for its own profits. But that is hardly the measure of whether a board such as Barnes & Noble's might put in place a rights plan to address the threat that Yucaipa might pose. Despite its protestations, Yucaipa's prior investing history is replete with the sorts of investments that often lead to transactions in which public stockholders are treated differently. Although Yucaipa seems to have mostly entered on friendly terms, the terms it extracted have often given it control rights not available more generally to stockholders and its influence has resulted in important managerial changes. To this point, it is reasonable to infer that the leveraged buyout options that Burkle pondered with investment banks regarding Barnes & Noble would have involved Yucaipa remaining as an equity investor and the other stockholders being cashed out. Indeed, it appears that Yucaipa prefers private company investments and would enjoy the chance to be an investor in a private Barnes & Noble.

No doubt our law provides substantial protections for other investors in the event that a large stockholder with board representation proposes a going private transaction or engages in other forms of unfair value extraction, but that does not mean that the Barnes & Noble board was not entitled to take reasonable, non-preclusive action to ensure that an activist investor like Yucaipa did not amass, either singularly or in concert with another large stockholder, an effective control bloc that would allow it to make proposals under conditions in which it wielded great leverage to seek advantage for itself at the expense of other investors. Precisely by cabining Yucaipa at a substantial, but not overwhelming, level of voting influence, the board preserved for itself greater authority to protect the company's public stockholders. . . .

. . . [T]he board was concerned that Yucaipa could, along with Aletheia as an admiring and devoted fellow traveler [Ed. A second hedge fund], essentially form a control bloc without paying a control premium. Wielding effective voting control, Yucaipa and Aletheia could then propose options, such as a leveraged buyout in which they remained as controlling stockholders, that might be less attractive to the company's other stockholders than would either the status quo or the sale of the company in an open shopping process. Contrary to Yucaipa's view, I do not believe that this concern is at all unreasonable. . . .

Although Yucaipa dismisses the notion, it is possible that, absent the Rights Plan, Barnes & Noble could find itself in a situation where the Riggios increased their voting power substantially in response to Yucaipa and Aletheia open market purchases, resulting in a situation when the remaining public stockholders (such as holders of index funds that might not sell into the market if Barnes & Noble remained, as it now is, a public company) were relegated to a minority. In such a scenario, either Yucaipa or Aletheia might actually be the ones who sell out, or the company could end up with three large bloc holders having acquired their stock for less than might have been paid to the more dispersed Barnes & Noble investors had the company been sold in a process run by the board. I do not pretend to have the capacity to tease out what results such an open market free-for-all would have for Barnes & Noble's smaller investors, but I do believe it was reasonable for the board to fear that the outcome would be less desirable than if a rights plan cabined the situation." [Under pressure from shareholders, B&N put itself up for sale. Only one bidder, John Malone, expressed interest. He backed out and purchased from the company a small block of preferred shares convertible into a 17 percent interest in the common.]

NOTE: EMPIRICAL EVIDENCE ON BLOCKED TAKEOVERS

Shareholders in target firms that are the subject of hostile takeovers receive average premiums of approximately 50 percent over the pre-takeover market value of their stock.[45] Firms that resist takeovers show abnormal returns of about 20 percent on their stock for two years (reflecting the market's optimism that a takeover will yet happen) and then returns drift between a negative 5 to 10 percent for the subsequent three years.[46] It is little wonder

---

[45] In negotiated takeovers, the premiums average closer to twenty-five percent. As we shall see in Section B.3, *infra*, true hostile takeovers are now very rare.

[46] Michael Bradley, Anand Desai & E. Han Kim, *The Rationale Behind Interfirm Tender Offers: Information or Synergy?*, 11 J. FIN. ECON. 183 (1988); See also Lucian Arye Bebchuk, John C. Coates IV & Guhan Subramanian, *The Powerful Antitakeover Force of Staggered Boards,* NBER Working Paper 8974 2002 (firms that remain independent made shareholders worse off); Dalida

then that the Delaware Supreme Court opinion in *Unocal*, legitimizing takeover defenses, correlated with a negative wealth change for all Delaware corporations.[47]

Time's rejection of Paramount's bid, for example, proved to be disastrous for Time shareholders. Time turned down a $200 a share offer from Paramount (it was rumored that Paramount would have paid up to $220 a share) and two years later the stock was trading at below $100 a share and three years later the stock traded at $120 a share. The company acquired Warner and did not turn a profit for the next six or so years (after paying interest and preferred dividends). Warner's managers were, however, richly paid up front. Steve Ross, the CEO of Warner and the main architect of the acquisition, pocketed personally $190 million and his fellow managers another $700 million. As if that were not enough, as the new CEO of Time-Warner, Ross was paid another $70 million or so in salary for 1990. AOL then bought Time-Warner for AOL stock, yet another disastrous deal for the already beleaguered Time shareholders, now AOL shareholders. See Kara Swisher & Lisa Dickey, THERE MUST BE A PONY HERE SOMEWHERE: THE AOL TIME WARNER DEBACLE AND THE QUEST FOR A DIGITAL FUTURE (2003).

One clear result of the takeover defenses is to give target managers a bigger slice of the acquisition premium so they will waive the defenses. Consider the following case on "CICs":

IN RE MONY GROUP INC. SHAREHOLDER LITIGATION, 853 A.2d 661 (Del. Ch. 2004): [Shareholders sought a preliminary injunction against a shareholder vote on a cash-for-stock merger between two companies in the insurance industry. Managers of the target had Change in Control Agreements (golden parachutes or CICs) in place as part of their compensation packages. The original deal had the managers receiving $205 million of the deal proceeds just to pay off the parachutes, a whopping 15 percent of the total deal price. On shareholder complaints, a chagrined board negotiated the covenants down to $79 million, about 6 percent of the total transaction value. The court found that golden parachutes averaged, as a percentage of deal price in the financial services industry, about 3.4 percent. The amended payoff to the target managers in the case was, therefore, still well above the 75th percentile for such transaction. The court held that the board had not breached its fiduciary duty in negotiating the contracts but that it had breached a duty of candor in the proxy materials for the deal]: "The history of AXA's bidding shows that there is essentially a 1:1 ratio between the value of the CICs and the amount per share an acquiror offers. The Cook Analysis, then, shows that as a

---

Kadyrzhanova & Matthew Rhodes-Kropf, *Concentrating on Governance*, 65 J. FIN. 5 (2011) (positive wealth effects from defenses that delay bidders; negative wealth effects from defenses that stop bidders).

[47] See Kamma, Sreenivas, Weintrop & Weir, *Investors' Perceptions of the Delaware Supreme Court Decision in Unocal v. Mesa*, 20 J. FIN. ECON. 419 (1988).

percentage of deal value, the money that will be paid to beneficiaries of the CICs is above the amount paid in CICs in more than 75 percent of comparable transactions. The court is persuaded that, in the circumstances presented, the Proxy Statement needs to include disclosure of information available to the Board about the size of the CICs as compared to comparable transactions. The materiality of such disclosure is heightened by the Board's rejection of the Original Offer for reasons relating, at least in part, to the outsized CICs. Given that history, the stockholders are entitled to know that the CICs remain unusually large, when faced with the decision whether to vote to approve the $31 per share merger price, vote "no," or demand appraisal. Putting it differently, the record supports the conclusion that there is a substantial likelihood that disclosure of the information described in footnote 44 " 'would [be] viewed by the reasonable investor as having significantly altered the "total mix" of information made available.' "[48]

A very clever article by Professors Kahan and Rock[49] breaks academic commentators into three groups: the Hamiltonians, who favor target board veto power in takeovers;[50] the Jacksonians, who favor target shareholder choice in response to any given takeover bid;[51] and the Madisonians, who believe shareholders may rationally endow a board with some power in deciding how to sell the company.[52] Professor Oesterle is grouped with the Madisonians, see the excerpt below.

Professors Kahan and Rock do not join any one group[53] but support a system of pure constitutional choice. Firms should decide for themselves, they argue, which constitutional structure they would prefer; in other

[48] Following the issuance of the opinion, the parties modified the merger agreement. One of the modifications was for managers with parachutes to forego certain restricted stock options valuing $7.4 million, with the resultant savings being used to fund a special dividend of $.10 per share that would be payable to shareholders of record immediately prior to closing.

[49] Marcel Kahan & Edward Rock, *Corporate Constitutionalism: Antitakeover Charter Provisions as Pre-Commitment*, 152 U. PA. L. REV. 473 (2003).

[50] E.g., Richard Kihlstrom & Michael Wachter, *Corporate Policy and the Coherence of Delaware Takeover Law,* 152 U. PA. L. REV. 723 (2003). Boards possess nonpublic information about company value, cannot disclose the information accurately to shareholders, and can be trusted to act in their shareholders' interest (most of the time).

[51] E.g., Frank H. Easterbrook & Daniel R. Fischel, *The Proper Role of a Target's Management in Responding to a Tender Offer,* 94 HARV. L. REV. 1161 (1981) (arguing for board passivity). Managers, to retain the private benefits of control, often resist takeovers even when in the best interests of shareholders. Boards should be limited to providing information to shareholders and (to some) to soliciting other bidders to stimulate an auction.

[52] The board is a useful bargaining agent and can implement a value-maximizing selling strategy. E.g., Dale A. Oesterle, *Target Managers as Negotiating Agents for Target Shareholders in Tender Offers: A Reply to the Passivity Thesis,* 71 CORNELL L. REV. 53 (1985); Dale A. Oesterle, *The Negotiation Model of Tender Offer Defenses and the Delaware Supreme Court*, 72 CORNELL L. REV. 117 (1986).

[53] They may believe themselves to be extreme Madisonians because they believe the constitutional choice will be a shareholder choice.

words, firms should be able to choose any one of the three constitutional models. Indeed, they argue, this is largely what we have in place now.

The question is very similar to (and perhaps just a subset of) the one presented in Chapter 2, Section A.4, on the best rules for how shareholders should vote in negotiated acquisitions. In that Section, we asked whether shareholders should be free to set up any voting system they preferred rather than have to work within the boundaries of the mandatory rules of state corporate law. The troubling persistence of value-reducing anti-takeover defenses,[54] particularly the classified boards/poison pill plan combinations, and the ubiquity of value-reducing state anti-takeover legislation (Section C, *infra*), the protections of which firms do not waive, suggest that a pure shareholder choice model may not be working optimally. The success of shareholder resolutions supported by institutional shareholders that defang some popular takeover defenses is promising, however. Continued impatience with state law on takeover defenses has led some to argue for a more interventionist federal law.[55]

In 2003, the Delaware Supreme Court injected a *Unocal* threshold analysis into all *deal protection covenants* used in negotiated acquisitions. *Omnicare, Inc. v. NCS Healthcare, Inc.*, 818 A.2d 914 (Del. 2003). The case had two vigorous dissenters, a very rare practice in Delaware Supreme Court decisions on business matters.[56] All board decisions to sign major contracts limit future board discretion;[57] yet the Court held that in acquisitions with delayed closings a board cannot bind itself to close through deal protection covenants. The opinion was all the more questionable because of its odd facts; the central deal protection device in the case hinged on a side deal between the buyer and controlling shareholders who agreed to vote for the deal. Subsequent courts have struggled to protect controlling shareholder stock deals[58] and to apply the language of the case to traditional deal protection covenants in acquisition agreements, no-shop and no-talk clauses (discussed in Chapter Four). Courts in other jurisdictions have rejected the reasoning[59] and the Chancery Court has been openly critical of the decision, citing the dissent.[60] It is only a matter of time before the opinion will be substantially revisited and limited, perhaps, to *agree to recommend* (to shareholders) clauses and the like.

---

54 See the data discussed in Section A.3 above.

55 See e.g., Lucian Arye Bebchuk & Allen Ferrell, *A New Approach to Takeover Law and Regulatory Competition*, 87 VA. L. REV. 101 (2001) (arguing for an optional body of substantive federal takeover law).

56 The dissenters argued for a traditional business judgment rule analysis.

57 See, e.g., Jewel Cos. Inc. v. Pay Less Drug Stores Northwest, 741 F.2d 1555 (9th Cir. 1984).

58 See Orman v. Cullman, 2004 WL 2348395 (Del. Ch.).

59 E.g., Monty v. Leis, 123 Cal. 641 (Cal. App. 2011)

60 E.g., In re Toys "R" Us, Inc. Shareholder Litig., 877 A.2d 975, 1016 (Del. Ch. 2007) (an "aberrational departure").

OMNICARE, INC. v. NCS HEALTHCARE, INC.

Supreme Court of Delaware, 2003.
818 A.2d 914.

HOLLAND, JUSTICE.

NCS Healthcare, Inc. ("NCS"), a Delaware corporation, was the object of competing acquisition bids, one by Genesis Health Ventures, Inc. ("Genesis"), a Pennsylvania corporation, and the other by Omnicare, Inc. ("Omnicare"), a Delaware corporation. . . .

The board of directors of NCS, an insolvent publicly traded Delaware corporation, agreed to the terms of a merger with Genesis. Pursuant to that agreement, all of the NCS creditors would be paid in full and the corporation's stockholders would exchange their shares for the shares of Genesis, a publicly traded Pennsylvania corporation. Several months after approving the merger agreement, but before the stockholder vote was scheduled, the NCS board of directors withdrew its prior recommendation in favor of the Genesis merger.

In fact, the NCS board recommended that the stockholders reject the Genesis transaction after deciding that a competing proposal from Omnicare was a superior transaction. The competing Omnicare bid offered the NCS stockholders an amount of cash equal to more than twice the then current market value of the shares to be received in the Genesis merger. The transaction offered by Omnicare also treated the NCS corporation's other stakeholders on equal terms with the Genesis agreement.

The merger agreement between Genesis and NCS contained a provision authorized by Section 251(c) of Delaware's corporation law. It required that the Genesis agreement be placed before the corporation's stockholders for a vote, even if the NCS board of directors no longer recommended it. At the insistence of Genesis, the NCS board also agreed to omit any effective fiduciary clause from the merger agreement. In connection with the Genesis merger agreement, two stockholders of NCS, who held a majority of the voting power, agreed unconditionally to vote all of their shares in favor of the Genesis merger. Thus, the combined terms of the voting agreements and merger agreement guaranteed, ab initio, that the transaction proposed by Genesis would obtain NCS stockholder's approval. . . .

The dispositive issues in this appeal involve the defensive devices that protected the Genesis merger agreement. The Delaware corporation statute provides that the board's management decision to enter into and recommend a merger transaction can become final only when ownership action is taken by a vote of the stockholders. Thus, the Delaware corporation law expressly provides for a balance of power between boards and stockholders which makes merger transactions a shared enterprise and ownership decision. Consequently, a board of directors' decision to adopt defensive devices to protect a merger agreement may implicate the stockholders' right to effectively vote contrary to the initial recommendation of the board in favor of the transaction.

It is well established that conflicts of interest arise when a board of directors acts to prevent stockholders from effectively exercising their right to vote contrary to the will of the board. The "omnipresent specter" of such conflict may be present whenever a board adopts defensive devices to protect a merger agreement. The stockholders' ability to effectively reject a merger agreement is likely to bear an inversely proportionate relationship to the structural and economic devices that the board has approved to protect the transaction. . . .

There are inherent conflicts between a board's interest in protecting a merger transaction it has approved, the stockholders' statutory right to make the final decision to either approve or not approve a merger, and the board's continuing responsibility to effectively exercise its fiduciary duties at all times after the merger agreement is executed. These competing considerations require a threshold determination that board-approved defensive devices protecting a merger transaction are within the limitations of its statutory authority and consistent with the directors' fiduciary duties . . . [D]efensive devices adopted by the board to protect the original merger transaction must withstand enhanced judicial scrutiny under the *Unocal* standard of review, even when that merger transaction does not result in a change of control.

. . . A board's decision to protect its decision to enter a merger agreement with defensive devices against uninvited competing transactions that may emerge is analogous to a board's decision to protect against dangers to corporate policy and effectiveness when it adopts defensive measures in a hostile takeover contest. In applying *Unocal*'s enhanced judicial scrutiny in assessing a challenge to defensive actions taken by a target corporation's board of directors in a takeover context, this Court held that the board "does not have unbridled discretion to defeat perceived threats by any draconian means available. Similarly, just as a board's statutory power with regard to a merger decision is not absolute, a board does not have unbridled discretion to defeat any perceived threat to a merger by protecting it with any draconian means available. . . .

. . . In this case, the Court of Chancery did . . . find as a fact . . . that NCS's public stockholders (who owned 80 percent of NCS and overwhelmingly supported Omnicare's offer) will be forced to accept the Genesis merger because of the structural defenses approved by the NCS board. Consequently, the record reflects that any stockholder vote would have been robbed of its effectiveness by the impermissible coercion that predetermined the outcome of the merger without regard to the merits of the Genesis transaction at the time the vote was scheduled to be taken. Deal protection devices that result in such coercion cannot withstand

Unocal's enhanced judicial scrutiny standard of review because they are not within the range of reasonableness.

Although the minority stockholders were not forced to vote for the Genesis merger, they were required to accept it because it was a fait accompli. The record reflects that the defensive devices employed by the NCS board are preclusive and coercive in the sense that they accomplished a fait accompli . . . Those tripartite defensive measures—the Section 251(c) provision, the voting agreements, and the absence of an effective fiduciary out clause—made it "mathematically impossible" and "realistically unattainable" for the Omnicare transaction or any other proposal to succeed, no matter how superior the proposal. . . .

Under the circumstances presented in this case, where a cohesive group of stockholders with majority voting power was irrevocably committed to the merger transaction, "[e]ffective representation of the financial interests of the minority shareholders imposed upon the [NCS board] an affirmative responsibility to protect those minority shareholders' interests." The NCS board could not abdicate its fiduciary duties to the minority by leaving it to the stockholders alone to approve or disapprove the merger agreement because two stockholders had already combined to establish a majority of the voting power that made the outcome of the stockholder vote a foregone conclusion. . . .

. . . The directors of a Delaware corporation have a continuing obligation to discharge their fiduciary responsibilities, as future circumstances develop, after a merger agreement is announced. Genesis anticipated the likelihood of a superior offer after its merger agreement was announced and demanded defensive measures from the NCS board that completely protected its transaction. Instead of agreeing to the absolute defense of the Genesis merger from a superior offer, however, the NCS board was required to negotiate a fiduciary out clause to protect the NCS stockholders if the Genesis transaction became an inferior offer. By acceding to Genesis' ultimatum for complete protection in futuro, the NCS board disabled itself from exercising its own fiduciary obligations at a time when the board's own judgment is most important, i.e. receipt of a subsequent superior offer.

Any board has authority to give the proponent of a recommended merger agreement reasonable structural and economic defenses, incentives, and fair compensation if the transaction is not completed. To the extent that defensive measures are economic and reasonable, they may become an increased cost to the proponent of any subsequent transaction. Just as defensive measures cannot be draconian, however, they cannot limit or circumscribe the directors' fiduciary duties. . . .

The NCS board was required to contract for an effective fiduciary out clause to exercise its continuing fiduciary responsibilities to the minority stockholders. The issues in this appeal do not involve the general validity of either stockholder voting agreements or the authority of directors to insert a Section 251(c) provision in a merger agreement. In this case, the NCS board combined those two otherwise valid actions and caused them to operate in concert as an absolute lock up, in the absence of an effective fiduciary out clause in the Genesis merger agreement.

VEASEY, CHIEF JUSTICE, with whom STEELE, JUSTICE, joins dissenting.[Ed.[61]]

. . . The essential fact that must always be remembered is that this agreement and the voting commitments of Outcalt and Shaw concluded a lengthy search and intense negotiation process in the context of insolvency and creditor pressure where no other viable bid had emerged. . . .It is now known, of course, after the case is over, that the stockholders of NCS will receive substantially more by tendering their shares into the topping bid of Omnicare than they would have received in the Genesis merger, as a result of the post-agreement Omnicare bid and the injunctive relief ordered by the Majority of this Court. Our jurisprudence cannot, however, be seen as turning on such ex post felicitous results. Rather, the NCS board's good faith decision must be subject to a real-time review of the board action before the NCS-Genesis merger agreement was entered into. . . .

Going into negotiations with Genesis, the NCS directors knew that, up until that time, NCS had found only one potential bidder, Omnicare. Omnicare had refused to buy NCS except at a fire sale price through an asset sale in bankruptcy. Omnicare's best proposal at that stage would not have paid off all creditors and would have provided nothing for stockholders. . . . Negotiations with Genesis led to an offer paying creditors off and conferring on NCS stockholders $24 million—an amount infinitely superior to the prior Omnicare proposals.

But there was, understandably, a sine qua non. In exchange for offering the NCS stockholders a return on their equity and creditor payment, Genesis demanded certainty that the merger would close. If the NCS board would not have acceded to the Section 251(c) provision, if Outcalt and Shaw had not agreed to the voting agreements and if NCS had insisted on a fiduciary out, there would have been no Genesis deal! Thus, the only value-enhancing transaction available would have disappeared. . . .

A lock-up permits a target board and a bidder to "exchange certainties." Certainty itself has value. The acquirer may pay a higher price for the target if the acquirer is assured consummation of the transaction. The target company also benefits from the certainty of completing a

[61] [Ed. Dissenting opinions are rare in the Delaware Supreme Court; rarer still are 3 to 2 opinions. Before *Omnicare*, the last such split was in Smith v. Van Gorkom, *supra*, over twenty years earlier. For a well known case that supports the dissenters, see Jewel Cos. Inc. v. Pay Less Drug Stores Northwest, Inc., 741 F.2d 1555 (9th Cir.) (best efforts and no-other-deal clauses upheld in case for tortious interference with contract).]

transaction with a bidder because losing an acquirer creates the perception that a target is damaged goods, thus reducing its value. . . .

Situations will arise where business realities demand a lock-up so that wealth enhancing transactions may go forward. Accordingly, any bright-line rule prohibiting lockups could, in circumstances such as these, chill otherwise permissible conduct. . . .

[W]e believe that the better rule in this situation is that the business judgment rule should apply . . . .

We respectfully disagree with the Majority's conclusion that the NCS board breached its fiduciary duties to the Class A stockholders by failing to negotiate a "fiduciary out" in the Genesis merger agreement. What is the practical import of a "fiduciary out?" It is a contractual provision, articulated in a manner to be negotiated that would permit the board of the corporation being acquired to exit without breaching the merger agreement in the event of a superior offer.

In this case, Genesis made it abundantly clear early on that it was willing to negotiate a deal with NCS but only on the condition that it would not be a "stalking horse." Thus, it wanted to be certain that a third party could not use its deal with NCS as a floor against which to begin a bidding war. As a result of this negotiating position, a "fiduciary out" was not acceptable to Genesis. . . .

By deterring bidders from engaging in negotiations like those present here and requiring that there must always be a fiduciary out, the universe of potential bidders who could reasonably be expected to benefit stockholders could shrink or disappear. Nevertheless, if the holding is confined to these unique facts, negotiators may be able to navigate around this new hazard.

STEELE, JUSTICE, dissenting.

. . . The contract terms that NCS' board agreed to included no insidious, camouflaged side deals for the directors or the majority stockholders nor transparent provisions for entrenchment or control premiums. At the time the NCS board and the majority stockholders agreed to a voting lockup, the terms were the best reasonably available for all the stockholders, balanced against a genuine risk of no deal at all. The cost benefit analysis entered into by an independent committee of the board, approved by the full board and independently agreed to by the majority stockholders cannot be second guessed by courts with no business expertise that would qualify them to substitute their judgment for that of a careful, selfless board or for majority stockholders who had the most significant economic stake in the outcome.

We should not encourage proscriptive rules that invalidate or render unenforceable precommitment strategies negotiated between two parties to a contract who will presumably, in the absence of conflicted interest, bargain intensely over every meaningful provision of a contract after a careful cost benefit analysis. Where could this plain common sense approach be more wisely invoked than where a board, free of conflict, fully informed, supported by the equally conflict-free holders of the largest economic interest in the transaction, reaches the conclusion that a voting lockup strategy is the best course to obtain the most benefit for all stockholders?

. . . The majority's proscriptive rule limits the scope of a board's cost benefit analysis by taking the bargaining chip of foregoing a fiduciary-out "off the table" in all circumstances. . . . Lockup provisions attempt to assure parties that have lost business opportunities and incurred substantial costs that their deal will close. I am concerned that the majority decision will remove the certainty that adds value to any rational business plan. . . .

QUESTIONS

What happened to the fall back argument that if the threshold tests of *Unocal* were not met the defendants could prevail on an entire fairness test? Since no-shop or no-talk clauses are not *preclusive*, they do not appear, on their own, to require fiduciary-out conditions to be enforceable. Is there any way practitioners can still use voting lock-ups by controlling shareholders in deals?[62]

BRAZEN V. BELL ATLANTIC CORP.

Supreme Court of Delaware, 1997.
695 A.2d 43.

VEASEY, CHIEF JUSTICE.

In this appeal, the issues facing the Court surround the question of whether a two-tiered $550 million termination fee in a merger agreement is a valid liquidated damages provision or whether the termination fee was an invalid penalty and tended improperly to coerce stockholders into voting for the merger. . . .

In 1995, defendant below—appellee, Bell Atlantic Corporation, and NYNEX Corporation entered into merger negotiations. In January 1996, NYNEX circulated an initial draft merger agreement that included a termination fee provision. Both parties to the agreement determined that the merger should be a stock-for-stock transaction and be treated as a

---

[62] See Orman v. Cullman, 2004 WL 2348395 (Del. Ch.) (yes; use majority of minority shareholder vote conditions). What if the supplementing "force-the-vote" provision has a fiduciary-out?

merger of equals. Thus, to the extent possible, the provisions of the merger agreement, including the termination fee, were to be reciprocal.

Representatives of Bell Atlantic and NYNEX agreed that a two-tiered $550 million termination fee was reasonable for compensating either party for damages incurred if the merger did not take place because of certain enumerated events. The termination fee was divided into two parts. First, either party would be required to pay $200 million if there were both a competing acquisition offer for that party and either (a) a failure to obtain stockholder approval, or (b) a termination of the agreement. Second, if a competing transaction were consummated within eighteen months of termination of the merger agreement, the consummating party would be required to pay an additional $350 million to its disappointed merger partner. . . .

The express language in section 9.2(e) of the agreement unambiguously states that the termination fee provisions "constitute liquidated damages and not a penalty." The Court of Chancery correctly found that liquidated damages, by definition, are damages paid in the event of a breach of a contract. While a breach of the merger agreement is not the only event that would trigger payment of the termination fee, the express language of section 9.2(c) states that a party's breach of section 7.2 (which provides that the parties are required to take all action necessary to convene a stockholders' meeting and use all commercially reasonable efforts to secure proxies to be voted in favor of the merger), coupled with other events, may trigger a party's obligation to pay the termination fee.

Thus, we find no compelling justification for treating the termination fee in this agreement as anything but a liquidated damages provision, in light of the express intent of the parties to have it so treated.

In *Lee Builders v. Wells*, [103 A.2d 918, 919 (1954),] a case involving a liquidated damages provision equal to 5 percent of the purchase price in a contract for the sale of land, the Court of Chancery articulated the following two-prong test for analyzing the validity of the amount of liquidated damages: "Where the damages are uncertain and the amount agreed upon is reasonable, such an agreement will not be disturbed." . . . We find . . . that the termination fee safely passes both prongs of the *Lee Builders* test.

To be a valid liquidated damages provision under the first prong of the test, the damages that would result from a breach of the merger agreement must be uncertain or incapable of accurate calculation. Plaintiff does not attack the fee on this ground. Given the volatility and uncertainty in the telecommunications industry due to enactment of the Telecommunications Act of 1996 and the fast pace of technological change, one is led ineluctably to the conclusion that advance calculation of actual damages in this case approaches near impossibility.

Plaintiff contends, however, that the $550 million fee violates the second prong of the *Lee Builders* test, i.e., that it is not a reasonable forecast of actual damages, but rather a penalty intended to punish the stockholders of Bell Atlantic for not approving the merger. Plaintiff's attack is without force. Two factors are relevant to a determination of whether the amount fixed as liquidated damages is reasonable. The first factor is the anticipated loss by either party should the merger not occur. The second factor is the difficulty of calculating that loss: the greater the difficulty, the easier it is to show that the amount fixed was reasonable. In fact, where the level of uncertainty surrounding a given transaction is high, "[e]xperience has shown that . . . the award of a court or jury is no more likely to be exact compensation than is the advance estimate of the parties themselves." Thus, to fail the second prong of *Lee Builders*, the amount at issue must be unconscionable or not rationally related to any measure of damages a party might conceivably sustain.

Here, in the face of significant uncertainty, Bell Atlantic and NYNEX negotiated a fee amount and a fee structure that take into account the following: (a) the lost opportunity costs associated with a contract to deal exclusively with each other; (b) the expenses incurred during the course of negotiating the transaction; (c) the likelihood of a higher bid emerging for the acquisition of either party; and (d) the size of termination fees in other merger transactions. The parties then settled on the $550 million fee as reasonable given these factors. Moreover, the $550 million fee represents 2 percent of Bell Atlantic's market capitalization of $28 billion. This percentage falls well within the range of termination fees upheld as reasonable by the courts of this State. We hold that it is within a range of reasonableness and is not a penalty.

This is not strictly a business judgment rule case. If it were, the Court would not be applying a reasonableness test. The business judgment rule is a presumption that directors are acting independently, in good faith and with due care in making a business decision. It applies when that decision is questioned and the analysis is primarily a process inquiry. Courts give deference to directors' decisions reached by a proper process, and do not apply an objective reasonableness test in such a case to examine the wisdom of the decision itself.

Since we are applying the liquidated damages rubric, and not the business judgment rule, it is appropriate to apply a reasonableness test, which in some respects is analogous to some of the heightened scrutiny processes employed by our courts in certain other contexts. Even then, courts will not substitute their business judgment for that of the directors, but will examine the decision to assure that it is, "on balance, within a range of reasonableness." Is the liquidated damages provision here within the range of reasonableness? We believe that it is, given the undisputed record showing the size of the transaction, the analysis of the parties concerning lost opportunity costs, other expenses and the arms-length negotiations.

Plaintiff further argues that the termination fee provision was coercive. Plaintiff contends that (a) the stockholders never had an option to consider the merger agreement without the fee, and (b) regardless of what the stockholders thought of the merits of the transaction, the stockholders knew that if they voted against the transaction, they might well be imposing a $550 million penalty on their company. Plaintiff contends that the termination fee was so enormous that it "influenced" the vote. Finally, plaintiff argues that the fee provision was meant to be coercive because the drafters deliberately crafted the termination fees to make them applicable when Bell Atlantic's stockholders decline to approve the transaction as opposed to a termination resulting from causes other than the non-approval of the Bell Atlantic stockholders. We find plaintiff's arguments unpersuasive.

First, the Court of Chancery properly found that the termination fee was not egregiously large. Second, the mere fact that the stockholders knew that voting to disapprove the merger may result in activation of the termination fee does not by itself constitute stockholder coercion. Third, we find no authority to support plaintiff's proposition that a fee is coercive because it can be triggered upon stockholder disapproval of the merger agreement, but not upon the occurrence of other events resulting in termination of the agreement.

In *Williams v. Geier*, [671 A.2d 1368, 1382–83 (1996),] this Court enunciated the test for stockholder coercion. Wrongful coercion that nullifies a stockholder vote may exist "where the board or some other party takes actions which have the effect of causing the stockholders to vote in favor of the proposed transaction for some reason other than the merits of that transaction." But we also stated in *Williams v. Geier* that "[i]n the final analysis . . . the determination of whether a particular stockholder vote has been robbed of its effectiveness by impermissible coercion depends on the facts of the case."

In this case, the proxy materials sent to stockholders described very clearly the terms of the termination fee. Since the termination fee was a valid, enforceable part of the merger agreement, disclosure of the fee provision to stockholders was proper and necessary. Plaintiff has not produced any evidence to show that the stockholders were forced into voting for the merger for reasons other than the merits of the transaction. To the contrary, it appears that the reciprocal termination fee provisions, drafted to protect both Bell Atlantic and NYNEX in the event the merger was not consummated, were an integral part of the merits of the transaction. Thus, we agree with the finding of the Court of Chancery that, although the termination fee provision may have influenced the stockholder vote, there were "no structurally or situationally coercive factors" that made an otherwise valid fee provision impermissibly coercive in this setting. . . .

QUESTIONS

Is *Bell* consistent with *Omnicare*? If an acquisition agreement stipulates that payment of a termination fee is payable solely on the exercise of an option of a party to walk (is not based on a breach of contract), is a liquidated damage analysis based on reasonableness appropriate?

2. BLOCKING ONE BIDDER TO FAVOR ANOTHER: THE *REVLON* ZONE

REVLON, INC. V. MACANDREWS & FORBES HOLDINGS, INC.

Supreme Court of Delaware, 1986.
506 A.2d 173.

MOORE, JUSTICE.

. . . The prelude to this controversy began in June 1985, when Ronald O. Perelman, chairman of the board and chief executive officer of Pantry Pride, met with his counterpart at Revlon, Michel C. Bergerac, to discuss a friendly acquisition of Revlon by Pantry Pride. Perelman suggested a price in the range of $40–50 per share, but the meeting ended with Bergerac dismissing those figures as considerably below Revlon's intrinsic value. All subsequent Pantry Pride overtures were rebuffed, perhaps in part based on Mr. Bergerac's strong personal antipathy to Mr. Perelman. . . .

On August 19, the Revlon board met specially to consider the impending threat of a hostile bid by Pantry Pride.[3] At the meeting, Lazard Freres, Revlon's investment banker, advised the directors that $45 per share was a grossly inadequate price for the company. Felix Rohatyn and William Loomis of Lazard Freres explained to the board that Pantry Pride's financial strategy for acquiring Revlon would be through "junk bond" financing followed by a break-up of Revlon and the disposition of its assets. With proper timing, according to the experts, such transactions could produce a return to Pantry Pride of $60 to $70 per share, while a sale of the company as a whole would be in the "mid 50" dollar range. Martin Lipton, special counsel for Revlon, recommended two defensive measures: first, that the company repurchase up to 5 million of its nearly 30 million outstanding shares; and second, that it adopt a Note Purchase Rights Plan.

---

[3] There were 14 directors on the Revlon board. Six of them held senior management positions with the company, and two others held significant blocks of its stock. Four of the remaining six directors were associated at some point with entities that had various business relationships with Revlon. On the basis of this limited record, however, we cannot conclude that this board is entitled to certain presumptions that generally attach to the decisions of a board whose majority consists of truly outside independent directors. . . .

Under this plan, each Revlon shareholder would receive as a dividend one Note Purchase Right (the Rights) for each share of common stock, with the Rights entitling the holder to exchange one common share for a $65 principal Revlon note at 12 percent interest with a one-year maturity. The Rights would become effective whenever anyone acquired beneficial ownership of 20 percent or more of Revlon's shares, unless the purchaser acquired all the company's stock for cash at $65 or more per share. In addition, the Rights would not be available to the acquiror, and prior to the 20 percent triggering event the Revlon board could redeem the rights for 10 cents each. Both proposals were unanimously adopted.

Pantry Pride made its first hostile move on August 23 with a cash tender offer for any and all shares of Revlon at $47.50 per common share and $26.67 per preferred share, subject to (1) Pantry Pride's obtaining financing for the purchase, and (2) the Rights being redeemed, rescinded or voided.

The Revlon board met again on August 26. The directors advised the stockholders to reject the offer. Further defensive measures also were planned. On August 29, Revlon commenced its own offer for up to 10 million shares, exchanging for each share of common stock tendered one Senior Subordinated Note (the Notes) of $47.50 principal at 11.75 percent interest, due in 1995, and one-tenth of a share of $9.00 Cumulative Convertible Exchangeable Preferred Stock valued at $100 per share. Lazard Freres opined that the notes would trade at their face value on a fully distributed basis.[4] Revlon stockholders tendered 87 percent of the outstanding shares (approximately 33 million), and the company accepted the full 10 million shares on a pro rata basis. The new Notes contained covenants which limited Revlon's ability to incur additional debt, sell assets, or pay dividends unless otherwise approved by the "independent" (non-management) members of the board.

At this point, both the Rights and the Note covenants stymied Pantry Pride's attempted takeover. The next move came on September 16, when Pantry Pride announced a new tender offer at $42 per share, conditioned upon receiving at least 90 percent of the outstanding stock. Pantry Pride also indicated that it would consider buying less than 90 percent, and at an increased price, if Revlon removed the impeding Rights. While this offer was lower on its face than the earlier $47.50 proposal, Revlon's investment banker, Lazard Freres, described the two bids as essentially equal in view of the completed exchange offer.

The Revlon board held a regularly scheduled meeting on September 24. The directors rejected the latest Pantry Pride offer and authorized

4 Like bonds, the Notes actually were issued in denominations of $1,000 and integral multiples thereof. A separate certificate was issued in a total principal amount equal to the remaining sum to which a stockholder was entitled. Likewise, in the esoteric parlance of bond dealers, a Note trading at par ($1,000) would be quoted on the market at $100.

management to negotiate with other parties interested in acquiring Revlon. Pantry Pride remained determined in its efforts and continued to make cash bids for the company, offering $50 per share on September 27, and raising its bid to $53 on October 1, and then to $56.25 on October 7.

In the meantime, Revlon's negotiations with Forstmann and the investment group Adler & Shaykin had produced results. The Revlon directors met on October 3 to consider Pantry Pride's $53 bid and to examine possible alternatives to the offer. Both Forstmann and Adler & Shaykin made certain proposals to the board. As a result, the directors unanimously agreed to a leveraged buyout by Forstmann. The terms of this accord were as follows: each stockholder would get $56 cash per share; management would purchase stock in the new company by the exercise of their Revlon "golden parachutes";[5] Forstmann would assume Revlon's $475 million debt incurred by the issuance of the Notes; and Revlon would redeem the Rights and waive the Notes covenants for Forstmann or in connection with any other offer superior to Forstmann's. The board did not actually remove the covenants at the October 3 meeting, because Forstmann then lacked a firm commitment on its financing, but accepted the Forstmann capital structure, and indicated that the outside directors would waive the covenants in due course. Part of Forstmann's plan was to sell Revlon's Norcliff Thayer and Reheis divisions to American Home Products for $335 million. Before the merger, Revlon was to sell its cosmetics and fragrance division to Adler & Shaykin for $905 million. These transactions would facilitate the purchase by Forstmann or any other acquiror of Revlon.

When the merger, and thus the waiver of the Notes covenants, was announced, the market value of these securities began to fall. The Notes, which originally traded near par, around 100, dropped to 87.50 by October 8. One director later reported (at the October 12 meeting) a "deluge" of telephone calls from irate noteholders, and on October 10 the Wall Street Journal reported threats of litigation by these creditors.

Pantry Pride countered with a new proposal on October 7, raising its $53 offer to $56.25, subject to nullification of the Rights, a waiver of the Notes covenants, and the election of three Pantry Pride directors to the Revlon board. On October 9, representatives of Pantry Pride, Forstmann and Revlon conferred in an attempt to negotiate the fate of Revlon, but could not reach agreement. At this meeting Pantry Pride announced that it would engage in fractional bidding and top any Forstmann offer by a slightly higher one. It is also significant that Forstmann, to Pantry Pride's exclusion, had been made privy to certain Revlon financial data. Thus, the parties were not negotiating on equal terms.

---

[5] In the takeover context "golden parachutes" generally are understood to be termination agreements providing substantial bonuses and other benefits for managers and certain directors upon a change in control of a company.

Again privately armed with Revlon data, Forstmann met on October 11 with Revlon's special counsel and investment banker. On October 12, Forstmann made a new $57.25 per share offer, based on several conditions.[6] The principal demand was a lock-up option to purchase Revlon's Vision Care and National Health Laboratories divisions for $525 million, some $100–$175 million below the value ascribed to them by Lazard Freres, if another acquiror got 40 percent of Revlon's shares. Revlon also was required to accept a no-shop provision. The Rights and Notes covenants had to be removed as in the October 3 agreement. There would be a $25 million cancellation fee to be placed in escrow, and released to Forstmann if the new agreement terminated or if another acquiror got more than 19.9 percent of Revlon's stock. Finally, there would be no participation by Revlon management in the merger. In return, Forstmann agreed to support the par value of the Notes, which had faltered in the market, by an exchange of new notes. Forstmann also demanded immediate acceptance of its offer, or it would be withdrawn. The board unanimously approved Forstmann's proposal because: (1) it was for a higher price than the Pantry Pride bid, (2) it protected the noteholders, and (3) Forstmann's financing was firmly in place.[7] The board further agreed to redeem the rights and waive the covenants on the preferred stock in response to any offer above $57 cash per share. The covenants were waived, contingent upon receipt of an investment banking opinion that the Notes would trade near par value once the offer was consummated. . . .

We turn first to Pantry Pride's probability of success on the merits. The ultimate responsibility for managing the business and affairs of a corporation falls on its board of directors. 8 Del.C § 141(a). In discharging this function the directors owe fiduciary duties of care and loyalty to the corporation and its shareholders. . . . These principles apply with equal force when a board approves a corporate merger pursuant to 8 Del.C. § 251(b) . . . and of course they are the bedrock of our law regarding corporate takeover issues. . . . While the business judgment rule may be applicable to the actions of corporate directors responding to takeover threats, the principles upon which it is founded—care, loyalty and independence—must first be satisfied. . . .

If the business judgment rule applies, there is a "presumption that in making a business decision the directors of a corporation acted on an

[6] Forstmann's $57.25 offer ostensibly is worth $1 more than Pantry Pride's $56.25 bid. However, the Pantry Pride offer was immediate, while the Forstmann proposal must be discounted for the time value of money because of the delay in approving the merger and consummating the transaction. The exact difference between the two bids was an unsettled point of contention even at oral argument.

[7] Actually, at this time about $400 million of Forstmann's funding was still subject to two investment banks using their "best efforts" to organize a syndicate to provide the balance. Pantry Pride's entire financing was not firmly committed at this point either, although Pantry Pride represented in an October 11 letter to Lazard Freres that its investment banker, Drexel Burnham Lambert, was highly confident of its ability to raise the balance of $350 million. Drexel Burnham had a firm commitment for this sum by October 18.

informed basis, in good faith and in the honest belief that the action taken was in the best interests of the company." *Aronson v. Lewis,* 473 A.2d at 812. However, when a board implements anti-takeover measures there arises "the omnipresent specter that a board may be acting primarily in its own interests, rather than those of the corporation and its shareholders. . . ." *Unocal Corp. v. Mesa Petroleum Co.*, 493 A.2d at 954. This potential for conflict places upon the directors the burden of proving that they had reasonable grounds for believing there was a danger to corporate policy and effectiveness, a burden satisfied by a showing of good faith and reasonable investigation. *Id.* at 955. In addition, the directors must analyze the nature of the takeover and its effect on the corporation in order to ensure balance—that the responsive action taken is reasonable in relation to the threat posed. *Id.*

The first relevant defensive measure adopted by the Revlon board was the Rights Plan, which would be considered a "poison pill" in the current language of corporate takeovers—a plan by which shareholders receive the right to be bought out by the corporation at a substantial premium on the occurrence of a stated triggering event. *See generally Moran v. Household International, Inc.,* Del. Supr., 500 A.2d 1346 (1985). By 8 Del. C. §§ 141 and 122(13),[11] the board clearly had the power to adopt the measure. *See Moran v. Household International, Inc.*, 500 A.2d at 1351. Thus, the focus becomes one of reasonableness and purpose.

The Revlon board approved the Rights Plan in the face of an impending hostile takeover bid by Pantry Pride at $45 per share, a price which Revlon reasonably concluded was grossly inadequate. Lazard Freres had so advised the directors, and had also informed them that Pantry Pride was a small, highly leveraged company bent on a "bust-up" takeover by using "junk bond" financing to buy Revlon cheaply, sell the acquired assets to pay the debts incurred, and retain the profit for itself.[63] In adopting the Plan, the board protected the shareholders from a hostile takeover at a price below the company's intrinsic value, while retaining sufficient flexibility to address any proposal deemed to be in the stockholders' best interests.

To that extent the board acted in good faith and upon reasonable investigation. Under the circumstances it cannot be said that the Rights Plan as employed was unreasonable, considering the threat posed. Indeed, the Plan was a factor in causing Pantry Pride to raise its bids from a low of

[11] The relevant provision of Section 122 is:

"Every corporation created under this chapter shall have power to:

(13) Make contracts, including contracts of guaranty and suretyship, incur liabilities, borrow money at such rates of interest as the corporation may determine, issue its notes, bonds and other obligations, and secure any of its obligations by mortgage, pledge or other encumbrance of all or any of its property, franchises and income, ..." 8 Del.C. § 122(13). . . .

[63] As we noted in *Moran,* a "bust-up" takeover generally refers to a situation in which one seeks to finance an acquisition by selling off pieces of the acquired company presumably at a substantial profit. *See Moran,* 500 A.2d at 1349, n. 4.

$42 to an eventual high of $58. At the time of its adoption the Rights Plan afforded a measure of protection consistent with the directors' fiduciary duty in facing a takeover threat perceived as detrimental to corporate interests. *Unocal,* 493 A.2d at 954–55. Far from being a "show-stopper," as the plaintiffs had contended in *Moran*, the measure spurred the bidding to new heights, a proper result of its implementation. *See Moran*, 500 A.2d at 1354, 1356–67.

Although we consider adoption of the Plan to have been valid under the circumstances, its continued usefulness was rendered moot by the directors' actions on October 3 and October 12. At the October 3 meeting the board redeemed the rights conditioned upon consummation of a merger with Forstmann, but further acknowledged that they would also be redeemed to facilitate any more favorable offer. On October 12, the board unanimously passed a resolution redeeming the Rights in connection with any cash proposal of $57.25 or more per share. Because all the pertinent offers eventually equaled or surpassed that amount, the Rights clearly were no longer any impediment in the contest for Revlon. This mooted any question of their propriety under *Moran* or *Unocal.*

The second defensive measure adopted by Revlon to thwart a Pantry Pride takeover was the company's own exchange offer for 10 million of its shares. The directors' general broad powers to manage the business and affairs of the corporation are augmented by the specific authority conferred under 8 Del. C. § 160(a), permitting the company to deal in its own stock. . . . However, when exercising that power in an effort to forestall a hostile takeover, the board's actions are strictly held to the fiduciary standards outlined in *Unocal.* These standards require the directors to determine the best interests of the corporation and its stockholders, and impose an enhanced duty to abjure any action that is motivated by considerations other than a good faith concern for such interests. . . .

The Revlon directors concluded that Pantry Pride's $47.50 offer was grossly inadequate. In that regard the board acted in good faith, and on an informed basis, with reasonable grounds to believe that there existed a harmful threat to the corporate enterprise. The adoption of a defensive measure, reasonable in relation to the threat posed, was proper and fully accorded with the powers, duties, and responsibilities conferred upon directors under our law. . . .

However, when Pantry Pride increased its offer to $50 per share, and then to $53, it became apparent to all that the break-up of the company was inevitable. The Revlon board's authorization permitting management to negotiate a merger or buyout with a third party was a recognition that the company was for sale. The duty of the board had thus changed from the preservation of Revlon as a corporate entity to the maximization of the company's value at a sale for the stockholders' benefit. This significantly altered the board's responsibilities under the *Unocal* standards. It no longer faced threats to corporate policy and effectiveness, or to the stockholders' interests, from a grossly inadequate bid. The whole question of defensive measures became moot. The directors' role changed from defenders of the corporate bastion to auctioneers charged with getting the best price for the stockholders at a sale of the company.

This brings us to the lock-up with Forstmann and its emphasis on shoring up the sagging market value of the Notes in the face of threatened litigation by their holders. Such a focus was inconsistent with the changed concept of the directors' responsibilities at this stage of the developments. The impending waiver of the Notes covenants had caused the value of the Notes to fall, and the board was aware of the noteholders' ire as well as their subsequent threats of suit. The directors thus made support of the Notes an integral part of the company's dealings with Forstmann, even though their primary responsibility at this stage was to the equity owners.

The original threat posed by Pantry Pride—the break-up of the company—had become a reality which even the directors embraced. Selective dealing to fend off a hostile but determined bidder was no longer a proper objective. Instead, obtaining the highest price for the benefit of the stockholders should have been the central theme guiding director action. Thus, the Revlon board could not make the requisite showing of good faith by preferring the noteholders and ignoring its duty of loyalty to the shareholders. The rights of the former already were fixed by contract. . . . The noteholders required no further protection, and when the Revlon board entered into an auction-ending lock-up agreement with Forstmann on the basis of impermissible considerations at the expense of the shareholders, the directors breached their primary duty of loyalty.

The Revlon board argued that it acted in good faith in protecting the noteholders because Unocal permits consideration of other corporate constituencies. Although such considerations may be permissible, there are fundamental limitations upon that prerogative. A board may have regard for various constituencies in discharging its responsibilities, provided there are rationally related benefits accruing to the stockholders. *Unocal,* 493 A.2d at 955. However, such concern for non-stockholder interests is inappropriate when an auction among active bidders is in progress, and the object no longer is to protect or maintain the corporate enterprise but to sell it to the highest bidder.

Revlon also contended that . . . it had contractual and good faith obligations to consider the noteholders. However, any such duties are limited to the principle that one may not interfere with contractual relationships by improper actions. Here, the rights of the noteholders were fixed by agreement, and there is nothing of substance to suggest that any of those terms were violated. The Notes covenants specifically contemplated a waiver to permit sale of the company at a fair price. The Notes were accepted by the holders on that basis, including the risk of an unreason-able

adverse market effect stemming from a waiver. Thus, nothing remained for Revlon to legitimately protect, and no rationally related benefit thereby accrued to the stockholders. Under such circumstances we must conclude that the merger agreement with Forstmann was unreasonable in relation to the threat posed.

A lock-up is not per se illegal under Delaware law. . . . Such options can entice other bidders to enter a contest for control of the corporation, creating an auction for the company and maximizing shareholder profit. Current economic conditions in the takeover market are such that a "white knight" like Forstmann might only enter the bidding for the target company if it receives some form of compensation to cover the risks and costs involved. . . . However, while those lock-ups which draw bidders into the battle benefit shareholders, similar measures which end an active auction and foreclose further bidding operate to the shareholders' detriment. . . .

. . . Forstmann had already been drawn into the contest on a preferred basis, so the result of the lock-up was not to foster bidding, but to destroy it. The board's stated reasons for approving the transactions were: (1) better financing, (2) noteholder protection, and (3) higher price. As the Court of Chancery found, and we agree, any distinctions between the rival bidders' methods of financing the proposal were nominal at best, and such a consideration has little or no significance in a cash offer for any and all shares. The principal object, contrary to the board's duty of care, appears to have been protection of the noteholders over the shareholders' interests.

While Forstmann's $57.25 offer was objectively higher than Pantry Pride's $56.25 bid, the margin of superiority is less when the Forstmann price is adjusted for the time value of money. In reality, the Revlon board ended the auction in return for very little actual improvement in the final bid. The principal benefit went to the directors, who avoided personal liability to a class of creditors to whom the board owed no further duty under the circumstances. Thus, when a board ends an intense bidding contest on an insubstantial basis, and where a significant by-product of that action is to protect the directors against a perceived threat of personal liability for consequences stemming from the adoption of previous defensive measures, the action cannot withstand the enhanced scrutiny which *Unocal* requires of director conduct. *See Unocal*, 493 A.2d at 954–55.

In addition to the lock-up option, the Court of Chancery enjoined the no-shop provision as part of the attempt to foreclose further bidding by Pantry Pride. . . . The no-shop provision, like the lock-up option, while not per se illegal, is impermissible under the *Unocal* standards when a board's primary duty becomes that of an auctioneer responsible for selling the company to the highest bidder. The agreement to negotiate only with Forstmann ended rather than intensified the board's involvement in the bidding contest.

It is ironic that the parties even considered a no-shop agreement when Revlon had dealt preferentially, and almost exclusively, with Forstmann throughout the contest. After the directors authorized management to negotiate with other parties, Forstmann was given every negotiating advantage that Pantry Pride had been denied: cooperation from management, access to financial data, and the exclusive opportunity to present merger proposals directly to the board of directors. Favoritism for a white knight to the total exclusion of a hostile bidder might be justifiable when the latter's offer adversely affects shareholder interests, but when bidders make relatively similar offers, or dissolution of the company becomes inevitable, the directors cannot fulfill their enhanced *Unocal* duties by playing favorites with the contending factions. Market forces must be allowed to operate freely to bring the target's shareholders the best price available for their equity.[16] Thus, as the trial court ruled, the shareholders' interests necessitated that the board remain free to negotiate in the fulfillment of that duty.

The court below similarly enjoined the payment of the cancellation fee, pending a resolution of the merits, because the fee was part of the overall plan to thwart Pantry Pride's efforts. We find no abuse of discretion in that ruling. . . .

PARAMOUNT COMMUNICATIONS, INC. V. QVC NETWORK, INC.

Supreme Court of Delaware, 1994.
637 A.2d 34.

VEASEY, CHIEF JUSTICE.

In this appeal we review an order of the Court of Chancery dated November 24, 1993 (the "November 24 Order"), preliminarily enjoining certain defensive measures designed to facilitate a so-called strategic alliance between Viacom Inc.("Viacom") and Paramount Communications Inc. ("Paramount") approved by the board of directors of Paramount (the "Paramount Board" or the "Paramount directors") and to thwart an unsolicited, more valuable, tender offer by QVC Network Inc. ("QVC"). In affirming, we hold that the sale of control in this case, which is at the heart of the proposed strategic alliance, implicates enhanced judicial scrutiny of the conduct of the Paramount Board under *Unocal Corp. v. Mesa Petroleum Co.*, Del. Supr. 493 A.2d 946 (1985), and *Revlon, Inc. v. MacAndrews & Forbes Holdings, Inc.*, Del. Supr., 506 A.2d 173 (1986). We further hold that the conduct of the Paramount Board was not reasonable as to process or result. . . .

---

16 By this we do not embrace the "passivity" thesis rejected in *Unocal*. *See* 493 A.2d at 954–55, nn. 8–10. The directors' role remains an active one, changed only in the respect that they are charged with the duty of selling the company at the highest price attainable for the stockholders' benefit.

On September 12, 1993, the Paramount Board met again and unanimously approved the Original Merger Agreement whereby Paramount would merge with and into Viacom. The terms of the merger provided that each share of Paramount common stock would be converted into 0.10 shares of Viacom Class A voting stock, 0.90 shares of Viacom Class B nonvoting stock, and $9.10 in cash. In addition, the Paramount Board agreed to amend its "poison pill" Rights Agreement to exempt the proposed merger with Viacom. The Original Merger Agreement also contained several provisions designed to make it more difficult for a potential competing bid to succeed. We focus, as did the Court of Chancery, on three of these defensive provisions: a "no-shop" provision (the "No-Shop Provision"), the Termination Fee, and the Stock Option Agreement.

First, under the No-Shop Provision, the Paramount Board agreed that Paramount would not solicit, encourage, discuss, negotiate, or endorse any competing transaction unless: (a) a third party "makes an unsolicited written, bona fide proposal, which is not subject to any material contingencies relating to financing"; and (b) the Paramount Board determines that discussions or negotiations with the third party are necessary for the Paramount Board to comply with its fiduciary duties.

Second, under the Termination Fee provision, Viacom would receive a $100 million termination fee if: (a) Paramount terminated the Original Merger Agreement because of a competing transaction; (b) Paramount's stockholders did not approve the merger; or (c) the Paramount Board recommended a competing transaction.

The third and most significant deterrent device was the Stock Option Agreement, which granted to Viacom an option to purchase approximately 19.9 percent (23,699,000 shares) of Paramount's outstanding common stock at $69.14 per share if any of the triggering events for the Termination Fee occurred. In addition to the customary terms that are normally associated with a stock option, the Stock Option Agreement contained two provisions that were both unusual and highly beneficial to Viacom: (a) Viacom was permitted to pay for the shares with a senior subordinated note of questionable marketability instead of cash, thereby avoiding the need to raise the $1.6 billion purchase price (the "Note Feature"); and (b) Viacom could elect to require Paramount to pay Viacom in cash a sum equal to the difference between the purchase price and the market price of Paramount's stock (the "Put Feature"). Because the Stock Option Agreement was not "capped" to limit its maximum dollar value, it had the potential to reach (and in this case did reach) unreasonable levels. . . .

On October 21, 1993, QVC filed this action and publicly announced an $80 cash tender offer for 51 percent of Paramount's outstanding shares (the "QVC tender offer"). Each remaining share of Paramount common stock would be converted into 1.42857 shares of QVC common stock in a second-step merger. The tender offer was conditioned on, among other things, the invalidation of the Stock Option Agreement, which was worth over $200 million by that point.[5] QVC contends that it had to commence a tender offer because of the slow pace of the merger discussions and the need to begin seeking clearance under federal antitrust laws. . . .

[Ed.: Viacom raised its price to $85 per share and QVC responded with a tender offer at $90 per share.] At its meeting on November 15, 1993, the Paramount Board determined that the new QVC offer was not in the best interests of the stockholders. The purported basis for this conclusion was that QVC's bid was excessively conditional. . . .

The General Corporation Law of the State of Delaware (the "General Corporation Law") and the decisions of this Court have repeatedly recognized the fundamental principle that the management of the business and affairs of a Delaware corporation is entrusted to its directors, who are the duly elected and authorized representatives of the stockholders. 8 Del. C. § 141(a). . . . Under normal circumstances, neither the courts nor the stockholders should interfere with the managerial decisions of the directors. The business judgment rule embodies the deference to which such decisions are entitled. . . .

Nevertheless, there are rare situations which mandate that a court take a more direct and active role in overseeing the decisions made and actions taken by directors. In these situations, a court subjects the directors' conduct to enhanced scrutiny to ensure that it is reasonable. The decisions of this Court have clearly established the circumstances where such enhanced scrutiny will be applied. *E.g., Unocal*, 493 A.2d 946; *Moran v. Household Int'l, Inc.*, Del. Supr., 500 A.2d 1346 (1985); *Revlon*, 506 A.2d 173 . . . The case at bar implicates two such circumstances: (1) the approval of a transaction resulting in a sale of control, and (2) the adoption of defensive measures in response to a threat to corporate control. . . .

When a majority of a corporation's voting shares are acquired by a single person or entity, or by a cohesive group acting together, there is a significant diminution in the voting power of those who thereby become minority stockholders. . . . In the absence of devices protecting the minority stockholders, stockholder votes are likely to become mere formalities where there is a majority stockholder. . . . Absent effective protective provisions, minority stockholders must rely for protection solely on the fiduciary duties owed to them by the directors and the majority stockholder, since the minority stockholders have lost the power to influence corporate direction through the ballot. The acquisition of majority status and the consequent privilege of exerting the powers of majority ownership come at a price. That price is usually a control premium which recognizes not only the value of a

[5] By November 15, 1993, the value of the Stock Option Agreement had increased to nearly $500 million based on the $90 QVC bid. *See* Court of Chancery Opinion, 635 A.2d 1245, 1271.

control block of shares, but also compensates the minority stockholders for their resulting loss of voting power.

In the case before us, the public stockholders (in the aggregate) currently own a majority of Paramount's voting stock. Control of the corporation is not vested in a single person, entity, or group, but vested in the fluid aggregation of unaffiliated stockholders. In the event the Paramount-Viacom transaction is consummated, the public stockholders will receive cash and a minority equity voting position in the surviving corporation. Following such consummation, there will be a controlling stockholder who will have the voting power to: (a) elect directors; (b) cause a break-up of the corporation: (c) merge it with another company; (d) cash-out the public stockholders; (e) amend the certificate of incorporation; (f) sell all or substantially all of the corporate assets; or (g) otherwise alter materially the nature of the corporation and the public stockholders' interests. Irrespective of the present Paramount Board's vision of a long-term strategic alliance with Viacom, the proposed sale of control would provide the new controlling stockholder with the power to alter that vision.

Because of the intended sale of control, the Paramount-Viacom transaction has economic consequences of considerable significance to the Paramount stockholders. Once control has shifted, the current Paramount stockholders will have no leverage in the future to demand another control premium. As a result, the Paramount stockholders are entitled to receive, and should receive, a control premium and/or protective devices of significant value. There being no such protective provisions in the Viacom-Paramount transaction, the Paramount directors had an obligation to take the maximum advantage of the current opportunity to realize for the stockholders the best value reasonably available. . . .

The consequences of a sale of control impose special obligations on the directors of a corporation.[13] In particular, they have the obligation of acting reasonably to seek the transaction offering the best value reasonably available to the stockholders. . . . In pursuing this objective, the directors must be especially diligent. . . . In particular, this Court has stressed the importance of the board being adequately informed in negotiating a sale of control. . . . Moreover, the role of outside, independent directors becomes particularly important because of the magnitude of a sale of control transaction and the possibility, in certain cases, that management may not necessarily be impartial. . . .

---

[13] We express no opinion on any scenario except the actual facts before the Court, and our precise holding herein. Unsolicited tender offers in other contexts may be governed by different precedent. For example, where a potential sale of control by a corporation is not the consequence of a board's action, this Court has recognized the prerogative of a board of directors to resist a third party's unsolicited acquisition proposal or offer. *See* . . . *Time-Warner*, 571 A.2d at 1152. The decision of a board to resist such an acquisition, like all decisions of a properly-functioning board, must be informed, *Unocal*, 493 A.2d at 954–55, and the circumstances of each particular case will determine the steps that a board must take to inform itself, and what other action, if any, is required as a matter of fiduciary duty.

Barkan teaches some of the methods by which a board can fulfill its obligation to seek the best value reasonably available to the stockholders. 567 A.2d at 1286–87. These methods are designed to determine the existence and viability of possible alternatives. They include conducting an auction, canvassing the market, etc. Delaware law recognizes that there is "no single blueprint" that directors must follow. *Id.* at 1286–87. . . .

In determining which alternative provides the best value for the stockholders, a board of directors is not limited to considering only the amount of cash involved, and is not required to ignore totally its view of the future value of a strategic alliance. . . . Instead, the directors should analyze the entire situation and evaluate in a disciplined manner the consideration being offered. Where stock or other non-cash consideration is involved, the board should try to quantify its value, if feasible, to achieve an objective comparison of the alternatives.[14] In addition, the board may assess a variety of practical considerations relating to each alternative including:

> [an offer's] fairness and feasibility; the proposed or actual financing for the offer, and the consequences of that financing; questions of illegality, . . . the risk of non-consum[m]ation; . . . the bidder's identity, prior background and other business venture experiences; and the bidder's business plans for the corporation and their effects on stockholder interests.

Macmillan, 559 A.2d at 1282 n.29. These considerations are important because the selection of one alternative may permanently foreclose other opportunities. While the assessment of these factors may be complex, the board's goal is straightforward: Having informed themselves of all material information reasonably available, the directors must decide which alternative is most likely to offer the best value reasonably available to the stockholders. . . .

Board action in the circumstances presented here is subject to enhanced scrutiny. Such scrutiny is mandated by: (a) the threatened diminution of the current stockholders' voting power; (b) the fact that an asset belonging to public stockholders (a control premium) is being sold and may never be available again; and (c) the traditional concern of Delaware courts for actions which impair or impede stockholder voting rights. . . .

The key features of an enhanced scrutiny test are: (a) a judicial determination regarding the adequacy of the decisionmaking process employed by the directors, including the information on which the directors based their decision; and (b) a judicial examination of the reasonableness

---

[14] When assessing the value of non-cash consideration, a board should focus on its value as of the date it will be received by the stockholders. Normally, such value will be determined with the assistance of experts using generally accepted methods of valuation. *See* In re RJR Nabisco, Inc. Shareholders Litig., Del. Ch., C.A. No. 10389, Allen, C. (Jan. 31, 1989), reprinted at 14 DEL. J. CORP. L. 1132, 1161.

of the directors' action in light of the circumstances then existing. The directors have the burden of proving that they were adequately informed and acted reasonably.

Although an enhanced scrutiny test involves a review of the reasonableness of the substantive merits of a board's actions, a court should not ignore the complexity of the directors' task in a sale of control. There are many business and financial considerations implicated in investigating and selecting the best value reasonably available. The board of directors is the corporate decisionmaking body best equipped to make these judgments. Accordingly, a court applying enhanced judicial scrutiny should be deciding whether the directors made a *reasonable* decision, not a *perfect* decision. If a board selected one of several reasonable alternatives, a court should not second-guess that choice even though it might have decided otherwise or subsequent events may have cast doubt on the board's determination. Thus, courts will not substitute their business judgment for that of the directors, but will determine if the directors' decision was, on balance, within a range of reasonableness. . . .

We now turn to duties of the Paramount Board under the facts of this case and our conclusions as to the breaches of those duties which warrant injunctive relief. . . . We conclude that the Paramount directors' process was not reasonable, and the result achieved for the stockholders was not reasonable under the circumstances.

When entering into the Original Merger Agreement, and thereafter, the Paramount Board clearly gave insufficient attention to the potential consequences of the defensive measures demanded by Viacom. . . . [T]he Paramount Board made no effort to eliminate or modify these counterproductive devices, and instead continued to cling to its vision of a strategic alliance with Viacom. . . . When the Paramount directors met on November 15 to consider QVC's increased tender offer, they remained prisoners of their own misconceptions and missed opportunities to eliminate the restrictions they had imposed on themselves. Yet, it was not "too late" to reconsider negotiating with QVC. . . .

Viacom argues that it had certain "vested" contract rights with respect to the No-Shop Provision and the Stock Option Agreement. In effect, Viacom's argument is that the Paramount directors could enter into an agreement in violation of their fiduciary duties and then render Paramount, and ultimately its stockholders, liable for failing to carry out an agreement in violation of those duties. Viacom's protestations about vested rights are without merit. This Court has found that those defensive measures were improperly designed to deter potential bidders, and that such measures do not meet the reasonableness test to which they must be subjected. They are consequently invalid and unenforceable under the facts of this case.

The No-Shop Provision could not validly define or limit the fiduciary duties of the Paramount directors. To the extent that a contract, or a provision thereof, purports to require a board to act or not act in such a fashion as to limit the exercise of fiduciary duties, it is invalid and unenforceable. . . .

WILLIAM T. ALLEN, JACK B. JACOBS & LEO E. STRINE, JR., *FUNCTION OVER FORM: A REASSESSMENT OF STANDARDS OF REVIEW IN DELAWARE CORPORATION LAW,* 56 BUS. LAW. 1287 (2001): . . . From a technical corporation law perspective, however, those results [of the Delaware Supreme Court takeover cases] were often rationalized in a manner that gave inadequate guidance to lawyers whose task was to plan, and render advice to clients about, transactions based upon these post-1985 judicial opinions. Indeed, the multi-billion dollar transaction between two major corporations reviewed in *Paramount Communications, Inc. v. QVC Network, Inc.* was based explicitly on one such opinion.[64]

ARNOLD v. SOCIETY FOR SAVINGS BANCORP, INC., 650 A.2d 1270 (Del. 1994): "The directors of a corporation "have the obligation of acting reasonably to seek the transaction offering the best value reasonably available to the stockholders," in at least the following three scenarios: (1) "when a corporation initiates an active bidding process seeking to sell itself or to effect a business reorganization involving a clear break-up of the company,"; (2) "where, in response to a bidder's offer, a target abandons its long-term strategy and seeks an alternative transaction involving the break-up of the company"; or (3) when approval of a transaction results in a "sale or change of control." In the latter situation, there is no "sale or change in control" when " '[c]ontrol of both [companies] remain[s] in a large, fluid, changeable and changing market.' "

When a target corporation is in what lawyers now refer to as the *Revlon zone*, the Delaware courts will analyze the board of directors'

[64] In *QVC*, the Viacom-Paramount merger agreement was justified under the rationale of the Delaware supreme court as stated in its last decision bearing on the subject, Paramount Communications, Inc. v. Time Inc. (Time-Warner), 571 A.2d 1140 (Del. 1990). In *Time-Warner*, the court affirmed the ruling of the Chancellor that the *Time-Warner* combination did not invoke duties under Revlon, Inc. v. MacAndrews & Forbes Holdings, Inc., 506 A.2d 173 (Del. 1986), but explicitly premised its affirmance on a different rationale than the court of chancery had used. *Time-Warner*, 571 A.2d at 1150. Under the Chancery approach in *Time-Warner*, the later Viacom-Paramount merger would clearly have invoked *Revlon*. Under the supreme court's *Time-Warner* opinion, it was far less clear that the Viacom-Paramount merger implicated *Revlon*. In *QVC*, the Delaware supreme court embraced the Chancery approach in Time-Warner, holding that the Viacom-Paramount merger triggered *Revlon* scrutiny, but disclaiming any responsibility for causing confusion among the transactional planners. *QVC*, 637 A.2d at 46–48 (embracing rationale used by Chancery Court in *Time-Warner* case and indicating that this should not have been surprising).

conduct using an enhanced level of scrutiny that focuses on whether the directors acted reasonably in obtaining the best value for target shareholders. Outside the *Revlon* zone, the Delaware courts will evaluate the activities of the board of directors of the target defending against unwanted bidders using the less rigorous *Unocal* proportionality test. Experience with the two tests has shown that defendants can win against a *Unocal* based claim on summary motions but rarely will win on summary motions against a *Revlon* based claim. Consider the effect of the dichotomy on acquisition structure. If one publicly traded company acquires another in a stock-for-stock deal, the business judgment rule applies to the decision to merge and the *Unocal* test applies to deal protection provisions (defenses used to deter an unwanted second bidder). If, on the other hand, the acquiring company pays in cash (or debt instruments), the *Revlon* duties apply to the sale process and decision. If the transaction is structured to give target shareholders a choice of stock or cash, *Revlon* duties apply. See, e.g., *In re Lukens Inc. Shareholders Litigation*, 757 A.2d 720, 732 n.25 (Del. Ch. 1999) (62 percent of the consideration was cash and 38 percent was stock in the acquirer).

Revlon is no longer constrained by its factual context and has evolved into a much larger role in all acquisitions. Revlon's situation was a classic *raider* (Pantry Pride), *white knight* (Forstmann) contest. The board did not want to sell to a raider and sought out a white knight to sell to instead. The Court quite reasonably held that in a sale to a white knight, the raider could not be left out of the bidding. The logic of the case, that in sales and changes of control a board must seek the best price for its shareholders, came to apply to all cases in which a target company sells itself, regardless of whether there was a disfavored bidder on the scene.[65] The *Revlon* entire fairness analysis now supplanted a business judgment rule analysis to all board decisions to sell the firm. The Court has struggled to get the genie back in the bottle.

LYONDELL CHEMICAL CO. V. RYAN

Delaware Supreme Court, 2009.
970 A.2d 235.

BERGER, JUSTICE.

. . . The class action complaint [by Lyondell shareholders] challenging this $13 billion cash merger [between Lyondell and Basel] alleges that the Lyondell directors breached their "fiduciary duties of care, loyalty and candor . . . and . . . put their personal interests ahead of the interests of the Lyondell shareholders." Specifically, the complaint alleges that: 1) the merger price was grossly insufficient; 2) the directors were motivated to approve the merger for their own self-interests; 3) the process by which the

[65] How does one judge whether a bidder is "disfavored"?

merger was negotiated was flawed; 4) the directors agreed to unreasonable deal protection provisions; and 5) the preliminary proxy statement omitted numerous material facts. The trial court rejected all claims except those directed at the process by which the directors sold the company and the deal protection provisions in the merger agreement.

The remaining claims are but two aspects of a single claim, under *Revlon v. MacAndrews & Forbes Holdings, Inc.*, that the directors failed to obtain the best available price in selling the company. As the trial court correctly noted, *Revlon* did not create any new fiduciary duties. It simply held that the "board must perform its fiduciary duties in the service of a specific objective: maximizing the sale price of the enterprise." The trial court reviewed the record, and found that Ryan might be able to prevail at trial on a claim that the Lyondell directors breached their duty of care. But Lyondell's charter includes an exculpatory provision, pursuant to 8 Del. C. § 102(b)(7), protecting the directors from personal liability for breaches of the duty of care. Thus, this case turns on whether any arguable shortcomings on the part of the Lyondell directors also implicate their duty of loyalty, a breach of which is not exculpated. Because the trial court determined that the board was independent and was not motivated by self-interest or ill will, the sole issue is whether the directors are entitled to summary judgment on the claim that they breached their duty of loyalty by failing to act in good faith.

This Court examined "good faith" in two recent decisions. In *In re Walt Disney Co. Deriv. Litig.*, the Court discussed the range of conduct that might be characterized as bad faith, and concluded that bad faith encompasses not only an intent to harm but also intentional dereliction of duty . . . . The *Stone* Court . . . clarified any possible ambiguity about the directors' mental state, holding that "imposition of liability requires a showing that the directors knew that they were not discharging their fiduciary obligations."

. . . [T]he trial court reviewed the existing record under a mistaken view of the applicable law. Three factors contributed to that mistake. First, the trial court imposed *Revlon* duties on the Lyondell directors before they either had decided to sell, or before the sale had become inevitable. Second, the court read *Revlon* and its progeny as creating a set of requirements that must be satisfied during the sale process. Third, the trial court equated an arguably imperfect attempt to carry out Revlon duties with a knowing disregard of one's duties that constitutes bad faith.

. . . The Court of Chancery identified several undisputed facts that would support the entry of judgment in favor of the Lyondell directors: the directors were "active, sophisticated, and generally aware of the value of the Company and the conditions of the markets in which the Company operated." They had reason to believe that no other bidders would emerge, given the price Basell had offered and the limited universe of companies that might be interested in acquiring Lyondell's unique assets. Smith negotiated the price up from $40 to $48 per share—a price that Deutsche Bank opined was fair. Finally, no other acquiror expressed interest during the four months between the merger announcement and the stockholder vote.

Other facts, however, led the trial court to "question the adequacy of the Board's knowledge and efforts. . . ." After the Schedule 13D was filed in May, the directors apparently took no action to prepare for a possible acquisition proposal. The merger was negotiated and finalized in less than one week, during which time the directors met for a total of only seven hours to consider the matter. The directors did not seriously press Blavatnik for a better price, nor did they conduct even a limited market check. Moreover, although the deal protections were not unusual or preclusive, the trial court was troubled by "the Board's decision to grant considerable protection to a deal that may not have been adequately vetted under *Revlon*."

The trial court found the directors' failure to act during the two months after the filing of the Basell Schedule 13D critical to its analysis of their good faith. . . .

The problem with the trial court's analysis is that *Revlon* duties do not arise simply because a company is "in play." The duty to seek the best available price applies only when a company embarks on a transaction—on its own initiative or in response to an unsolicited offer—that will result in a change of control. Basell's Schedule 13D did put the Lyondell directors, and the market in general, on notice that Basell was interested in acquiring Lyondell. The directors responded by promptly holding a special meeting to consider whether Lyondell should take any action. The directors decided that they would neither put the company up for sale nor institute defensive measures to fend off a possible hostile offer. Instead, they decided to take a "wait and see" approach. That decision was an entirely appropriate exercise of the directors' business judgment. The time for action under *Revlon* did not begin until July 10, 2007, when the directors began negotiating the sale of Lyondell.

The Court of Chancery focused on the directors' two months of inaction, when it should have focused on the one week during which they considered Basell's offer. During that one week, the directors met several times; their CEO tried to negotiate better terms; they evaluated Lyondell's value, the price offered and the likelihood of obtaining a better price; and then the directors approved the merger. The trial court acknowledged that the directors' conduct during those seven days might not demonstrate anything more than lack of due care. But the court remained skeptical about the directors' good faith—at least on the present record. That lingering concern was based on the trial court's synthesis of the *Revlon* line of cases, which led it to the erroneous conclusion that directors must follow one of several courses of action to satisfy their *Revlon* duties.

There is only one *Revlon* duty—to "[get] the best price for the stockholders at a sale of the company." No court can tell directors exactly how to accomplish that goal, because they will be facing a unique combination of circumstances, many of which will be outside their control. . . .

The Lyondell directors did not conduct an auction or a market check, and they did not satisfy the trial court that they had the "impeccable" market knowledge that the court believed was necessary to excuse their failure to pursue one of the first two alternatives. As a result, the Court of Chancery was unable to conclude that the directors had met their burden under *Revlon*. In evaluating the totality of the circumstances, even on this limited record, we would be inclined to hold otherwise. But we would not question the trial court's decision to seek additional evidence if the issue were whether the directors had exercised due care. Where, as here, the issue is whether the directors failed to act in good faith, the analysis is very different, and the existing record mandates the entry of judgment in favor of the directors.

As discussed above, bad faith will be found if a "fiduciary intentionally fails to act in the face of a known duty to act, demonstrating a conscious disregard for his duties." . . . [T]there are no legally prescribed steps that directors must follow to satisfy their *Revlon* duties. Thus, the directors' failure to take any specific steps during the sale process could not have demonstrated a conscious disregard of their duties. More importantly, there is a vast difference between an inadequate or flawed effort to carry out fiduciary duties and a conscious disregard for those duties. . . .

[I]f the directors failed to do all that they should have under the circumstances, they breached their duty of care. Only if they knowingly and completely failed to undertake their responsibilities would they breach their duty of loyalty. The trial court approached the record from the wrong perspective. Instead of questioning whether disinterested, independent directors did everything that they (arguably) should have done to obtain the best sale price, the inquiry should have been whether those directors utterly failed to attempt to obtain the best sale price.

Viewing the record in this manner leads to only one possible conclusion. The Lyondell directors met several times to consider Basell's premium offer. They were generally aware of the value of their company and they knew the chemical company market. The directors solicited and followed the advice of their financial and legal advisors. They attempted to negotiate a higher offer even though all the evidence indicates that Basell had offered a "blowout" price. Finally, they approved the merger agreement, because "it was simply too good not to pass along [to the stockholders] for their consideration." We assume, as we must on summary judgment, that the Lyondell directors did absolutely nothing to prepare for Basell's offer, and that they did not even consider conducting a market check before agreeing to the merger. Even so, this record clearly establishes that the Lyondell directors did not breach their duty of loyalty by failing to act in good faith. . . .

[T]he decision of the Court of Chancery is reversed and this matter is remanded for entry of judgment in favor of the Lyondell directors. . . .

QUESTION

If the Delaware Chancery Court, with all its expertise of and focus on Delaware precedent, cannot figure out these rules, how can the rest of us? For a follow-up slap down of the Chancery Court by the Delaware Supreme Court, see *C&J Energy Services, Inc. v City of Miami*, 107 A.3d 1049 (Del. 2014) (*Revlon* requires an "effective" but not "active" market check and there is "no specific route that a board must follow").

The high water mark of judicial intervention in a board's decision on how to sell the company may be the following case.

IN RE NETSMART TECHNOLOGIES, INC. SHAREHOLDERS LITIGATION, 924 A.2d 171 (2007) (STRINE, V. C.): "This case literally involves a microcosm of a current dynamic in the mergers and acquisitions market. Netsmart Technologies, Inc. has entered into a "Merger Agreement" with two private equity firms, . . . Insight and Bessemer. If the $115 million "Insight Merger" (or "Merger") is consummated, Netsmart's stockholders will receive $16.50 per share and the buyers will take the micro-cap company, whose shares are currently listed on the NASDAQ, private.

In October 2005, Netsmart completed a multi-year course of acquisitions by purchasing its largest direct competitor. . . . After that acquisition was announced, private equity buyers made overtures to Netsmart management. These overtures were favorably received and management soon recommended, in May 2006, that the Netsmart board consider a sale to a private equity firm. Relying on the failure of sporadic, isolated contacts with strategic buyers stretched out over the course of more than a half-decade to yield interest from a strategic buyer, management, with help from its long-standing financial advisor, William Blair & Co., L.L.C., steered the board away from any active search for a strategic buyer. Instead, they encouraged the board to focus on a rapid auction process involving a discrete set of possible private equity buyers. . . . The Merger Agreement prohibits the Netsmart board from shopping the company but does permit the board to consider a superior proposal. A topping bidder would only have to suffer the consequence of paying Insight a 3% termination fee. No topping bidder has emerged to date and a stockholder vote is scheduled to be held next month, on April 5, 2007.

A group of shareholder plaintiffs now seeks a preliminary injunction against the consummation of this Merger. . . .

Having decided to sell the company for cash, the Netsmart board assumed the fiduciary duty to undertake reasonable efforts to secure the highest price realistically achievable given the market for the company. This duty—often called a *Revlon* duty for the case with which it is most commonly associated—does not, of course, require every board to follow a judicially prescribed checklist of sales activities. Rather, the duty requires the board to act reasonably, by undertaking a logically sound process to get the best deal that is realistically attainable. . . .

What is important and different about the *Revlon* standard is the intensity of judicial review that is applied to the directors' conduct. Unlike the bare rationality standard applicable to garden-variety decisions subject to the business judgment rule, the *Revlon* standard contemplates a judicial examination of the reasonableness of the board's decision-making process. Although linguistically not obvious, this reasonableness review is more searching than rationality review, and there is less tolerance for slack by the directors. Although the directors have a choice of means, they do not comply with their *Revlon* duties unless they undertake reasonable steps to get the best deal.

. . . The plaintiffs' second argument has much more force. That argument is that the Special Committee and Netsmart board did not have a reliable basis to conclude that the Insight deal was the best one because they failed to take any reasonable steps to explore whether strategic buyers might be interested in Netsmart. . . .

I believe on this score that the plaintiffs are, if this preliminary record is indicative of the ultimate record in the case, likely to be successful on this point. . . . [T]he board's consideration of whether to seek out strategic buyers was cursory and poorly documented at best.

What was never done by Conway, William Blair, or the board was a serious sifting of the strategic market to develop a core list of larger healthcare IT players for whom an acquisition of Netsmart might make sense. Perhaps such an effort would have yielded no names. But it might have. . . .

. . . Moreover, the ultimate results obtained by pursuing the directors' strategy of excluding strategic buyers were less than exciting . . . . As plaintiffs point out, the implied transaction multiples that the Insight Merger ultimately entailed were all (except one) below both [their expert's] median and mean for comparable transactions[.]

Similarly, the implied transaction value of $115 million of a $16.50 share price fell below even the lower range of [their expert's] DCF value of Netsmart, which was $142 million to $202 million or roughly $20 to $29 per share. . . .

Of course, one must confront the defendants' argument that they used a technique accepted in prior cases. The Special Committee used a limited, active auction among a discrete set of private equity buyers to get an attractive "bird in hand." But they gave Netsmart stockholders the chance for fatter fowl by including a fiduciary out and a modest break-up fee in the Merger Agreement. By that means, the board enabled a post-signing, implicit market check. Having announced the Insight Merger in November 2006 without any bigger birds emerging thereafter, the board argues that the results buttress their initial conclusion, which is that strategic buyers simply are not interested in Netsmart. . . .

Precisely because of the various problems Netsmart's management identified as making it difficult for it to attract market attention as a micro-cap public company, an inert, implicit post-signing market check does not, on this record, suffice as a reliable way to survey interest by strategic players. Rather, to test the market for strategic buyers in a reliable fashion, one would expect a material effort at salesmanship to occur. To conclude that sales efforts are always unnecessary or meaningless would be almost un-American, given the sales-oriented nature of our culture. In the case of a niche company like Netsmart, the potential utility of a sophisticated and targeted sales effort seems especially high. . . .

In the absence of such an outreach, Netsmart stockholders are only left with the possibility that a strategic buyer will: (i) notice that Netsmart is being sold, and, assuming that happens, (ii) invest the resources to make a hostile (because Netsmart can't solicit) topping bid to acquire a company worth less than a quarter of a billion dollars. In going down that road, the strategic buyer could not avoid the high potential costs, both monetary (e.g., for expedited work by legal and financial advisors) and strategic (e.g., having its interest become a public story and dealing with the consequences of not prevailing) of that route, simply because the sought-after-prey was more a side dish than a main course. It seems doubtful that a strategic buyer would put much energy behind trying a deal jump in circumstances where the cost-benefit calculus going in seems so unfavorable. Analogizing this situation to the active deal jumping market at the turn of the century, involving deal jumps by large strategic players of deals involving their direct competitors in consolidating industries is a long stretch.

Similarly, the current market trend in which private equity buyers seem to be outbidding strategic buyers is equally unsatisfying as an excuse for the lack of *any* attempt at canvassing the strategic market. Given Netsmart's size, the synergies available to strategic players might well have given them flexibility to outbid even cash-flush private equity investors. Simply because many deals in the large-cap arena seem to be going the private equity buyers' way these days does not mean that a board can lightly forsake any exploration of interest by strategic bidders.

In this regard, a final note is in order. Rightly or wrongly, strategic buyers might sense that CEOs are more interested in doing private equity deals that leave them as CEOs than strategic deals that may, and in this case, certainly, would not. That is especially so when the private equity deals give management, as Scalia aptly put it, a "second bite at the apple" through option pools. With this impression, a strategic buyer seeking to top Insight might consider this factor in deciding whether to bother with an overture.

Here, while there is no basis to perceive that Conway or his managerial subordinates tilted the competition among the private equity bidders, there is a basis to perceive that management favored the private equity route over the strategic route. Members of management desired to continue as executives and they desired more equity. A larger strategic buyer would likely have had less interest in retaining all of them and would not have presented them with the potential for the same kind of second bite. The private equity route was therefore a clearly attractive one for management, all things considered."

[Ed.: The Court allowed the company to hold a shareholder vote on the merger once the firm had made additional requested disclosures to its shareholders.]

QUESTIONS

Would *Netsmart* be decided the same after *Lyondell*, *supra*? Would the result have changed if the price had been higher? Or do we have a new procedural requirement for all private equity purchases of small companies?

Would the result have been different if a straight business judgment analysis had applied? What is the "omnipresent specter" of a conflict of interest in this case?

IN RE DEL MONTE FOODS COMPANY SHAREHOLDERS LITIGATION, 25 A.3d 813 (Del. Ch. 2011) [Lasker, V.C.]: On November 24, 2010, Del Monte Foods Company ("Del Monte" or the "Company") entered into an agreement and plan of merger with Blue Acquisition Group, Inc. and its wholly owned acquisition subsidiary, Blue Merger Sub Inc. Blue Acquisition Group is owned by three private equity firms: Kohlberg, Kravis, Roberts & Co. ("KKR"), Centerview Partners ("Centerview"), and Vestar Capital Partners ("Vestar"). . . . The Merger Agreement contemplates a $5.3 billion leveraged buyout of Del Monte (the

"Merger"). If approved by stockholders, each share of Del Monte common stock will be converted into the right to receive $19 in cash. The consideration represents a premium of approximately 40% over the average closing price of Del Monte's common stock for the three-month period ended on November 8, 2010. The $19 price is higher than Del Monte's common stock has ever traded.

The stockholders of Del Monte are scheduled to vote on the Merger. . . . The plaintiffs seek a preliminary injunction postponing the vote. They originally asserted that the individual defendants, who comprise the Del Monte board of directors (the "Board"), breached their fiduciary duties . . . by failing to act reasonably to pursue the best transaction reasonably available . . . .

This case is difficult because the Board predominantly made decisions that ordinarily would be regarded as falling within the range of reasonableness for purposes of enhanced scrutiny. Until discovery disturbed the patina of normalcy surrounding the transaction, there were only two Board decisions that invited serious challenge: first, allowing KKR to team up with Vestar, the high bidder in a previous solicitation of interest, and second, authorizing Barclays Capital, the financial advisor to Del Monte, to provide buy-side financing to KKR.

Discovery revealed a deeper problem. Barclays secretly and selfishly manipulated the sale process to engineer a transaction that would permit Barclays to obtain lucrative buy-side financing fees. On multiple occasions, Barclays protected its own interests by withholding information from the Board that could have led Del Monte to retain a different bank, pursue a different alternative, or deny Barclays a buy-side role. Barclays did not disclose the behind-the-scenes efforts of its Del Monte coverage officer to put Del Monte into play. Barclays did not disclose its explicit goal, harbored from the outset, of providing buy-side financing to the acquirer. Barclays did not disclose that in September 2010, without Del Monte's authorization or approval, Barclays steered Vestar into a club bid with KKR, the potential bidder with whom Barclays had the strongest relationship, in violation of confidentiality agreements that prohibited Vestar and KKR from discussing a joint bid without written permission from Del Monte.

Late in the process, at a time when Barclays was ostensibly negotiating the deal price with KKR, Barclays asked KKR for a third of the buy-side financing. Once KKR agreed, Barclays sought and obtained Del Monte's permission. Having Barclays as a co-lead bank was not necessary to secure sufficient financing for the Merger, nor did it generate a higher price for the Company. It simply gave Barclays the additional fees it wanted from the outset. In fact, Barclays can expect to earn slightly more from providing buy-side financing to KKR than it will from serving as Del Monte's sell-side advisor. Barclays' gain cost Del Monte an additional $3 million because Barclays told Del Monte that it now had to obtain a last-minute fairness opinion from a second bank.

On the preliminary record presented in connection with the injunction application, the plaintiffs have established a reasonable probability of success on the merits of a claim for breach of fiduciary duty against the individual defendants, aided and abetted by KKR. By failing to provide the serious oversight that would have checked Barclays' misconduct, the directors breached their fiduciary duties . . . .

To hold that the Del Monte directors breached their fiduciary duties for purposes of granting injunctive relief does not suggest, much less pre-ordain, that the directors face a meaningful threat of monetary liability. On this preliminary record, it appears that the Board sought in good faith to fulfill its fiduciary duties, but failed because it was misled by Barclays. Unless further discovery reveals different facts, the one-two punch of exculpation under Section 102(b)(7) and full protection under Section 141(e) makes the chances of a judgment for money damages vanishingly small. The same cannot be said for the self-interested aiders and abetters. But while the directors may face little threat of liability, they cannot escape the ramifications of Barclays' misconduct. For purposes of equitable relief, the Board is responsible.

To remedy (at least partially) the taint from Barclays' activities, the plaintiffs ask that the vote on the Merger be enjoined for a meaningful period (30 to 45 days) and that the parties to the Merger Agreement be enjoined from enforcing the deal protections during that time. The defendants are enjoined preliminarily from proceeding with the vote on the Merger for a period of 20 days. Pending the vote on the Merger, the parties to the Merger Agreement are enjoined from enforcing the no-solicitation and match-right provisions in Section 6.5(b), (c) and (h), and the termination fee provisions relating to topping bids and changes of recommendation in Section 8.5(b). The injunction is conditioned on the plaintiffs posting a bond in the amount of $1.2 million.[Ed.[66]]

NOTE: THE BEGINNINGS OF A DELAWARE SUPREME COURT PULL BACK?

It is noteworthy that the author of the previous opinion wrote a book chapter in 2016 entitled *Changing Attitudes: The Stark Results of Thirty Years of Evolution in Delaware M&A Litigation*, SSRN 2982603 (June 2017). In that chapter, the author indicated that the Delaware Supreme Court was deregulating its jurisprudence on "third-party" acquisitions. Current doctrine

---

[66] [Ed. After extensive shopping of the company in the twenty day hiatus, no other bidders made offers. The shareholders voted overwhelmingly for the deal. The Court later awarded interim attorney fees to the plaintiffs of $2.75 million.]

is more favorable towards selling boards in single-bidder negotiations in three areas: (1) the legitimacy of deal protection measures in single-bidder offers; (2) a respect for third-party contract rights; and (3) a deference to the outcome of shareholder voting. He notes that the doctrinal movement is the result of the rise of sophisticated institutional investors who often influence M & A outcomes and a skepticism with the value of M & A litigation to investors. He cites the *C&J Energy* case, cited in the Question after the *Lyondell* case above, as one of his leading examples.

NOTE: THE DISPARAGING OF FINANCIAL BUYERS—A MEDIA PASTIME

Financial buyers accomplish single firm major reorganizations from outside, rather than inside. Financial buyers purchase companies (usually taking them private in the process) and reorganize and recapitalize the companies purchased. Financial buyers spot corporations that they believe should make major operational changes or otherwise be reorganized or recapitalized to maximize shareholder value, and whose managers have been slow to make appropriate changes. They do not often purchase targets to combine target assets with the assets of an otherwise ongoing operating company, as do *strategic buyers.*

In the '80s the financial buyers were known as *LBO funds* and the acquisitions were often hostile. In the first decade of this century, the buyers, now known as *private equity funds,* negotiated transactions with the support of managers. In both decades financial buyers have had very bad press. Most of it related to their enormous gains, brushing alterations of established companies, use of extreme leverage, focus on shareholder profit, and arrogance.[67] Those who are happy, the shareholders of the purchased companies who collect a healthy control premium and the investors in the buy-out fund who enjoy heady returns, are quiet.

Sometimes financial buyers make mistakes and their portfolio companies end up in bankruptcy,[68] but many times they have been on the cutting edge of industry changes.[69] The financial takeovers of the '80s were a correction of the

---

[67] See Evan Thomas & Daniel Gross, *Taxing the Superrich*, NEWSWEEK, Jan. 10, 2008; Daniel Gross, *Borrowers are out in the Cold*, NEWSWEEK, Mar. 3, 2008.

[68] The bankruptcy of several LBOs at the end of the '80s accelerated the political backlash that gave us state anti-takeover legislation and judicial approval of poison pill plans. Over 60 percent of all new restaurants end up losing money, yet we do not pass statutes against restaurants. Just as in any business venture, some acquisitions succeed and some fail. The market rewards the successes and penalizes the failures.

[69] Examples of financial takeovers in the '80s, followed by major operational changes, include takeovers of retail clothing companies that operated downtown department stores, which were more valuable as office buildings; takeovers of airlines which were paying employees too much after the industry had been deregulated; and takeovers of oil and gas companies which were wasting resources on marginally productive oil and gas exploration. Examples of financial takeovers in the '80s that led to reorganizations include takeovers of dinosaur conglomerates, which needed to both sell under-performing divisions and refocus on their specialty divisions. Examples of financial takeovers in the '80s that led to recapitalizations include takeovers that releveraged target firms to obtain the tax advantages of debt and to realign the incentives of managers.

conglomerate mergers of the '70s.[70] Financial buyers in the naught decade were governance experts, replacing stodgy boards of directors with streamlined, efficient management teams.[71]

3. BLOCKING PROXY CONTESTS: THE BLASIUS TEST

The decision of state courts and state legislatures to respect target boards' blocking power in tender offers aimed at target shareholders has led insurgents to fall back on a weapon of the '60s: the proxy fight. An insurgent makes a tender offer (often called a *bear hug*) at an attractive price conditional on the support of the target board. If the target board resists, the bidder conditions its tender offer on winning a proxy fight for control of the target board.[72] Once an insurgent wins control of the board, it has the board redeem outstanding poison pill plans and waive any applicable state anti-takeover laws. After board action, the bidder closes its tender offer.

The proxy fight, by itself expensive and hard to win because shareholders often see it as a personality dispute with everyone eventually tarred by the revelations, is focused by the tender offer: "Vote for the insurgents and receive X dollars." Shareholders can understand and vote on an offer of a premium sales price for their stock. A combination tender offer/proxy fight is much more expensive and takes much more time than a mid-'80s-style hostile tender offer.

The expense and time delay of a combination tender offer/proxy fight limits the number of buyers that use the strategy. In most combination proxy contests/hostile tender offers that do occur, target managers get a sense of the likely outcome of the shareholder vote before it is held and succumb to the hostile bidder (a negotiated acquisition) or find another suitor (a white knight). In a few cases over the years, the shareholder vote has been held and a bidder's nominees have replaced insiders on a target board.

Target boards, intent on defending against combination tender offer/proxy fights, rely on a staggered election of directors, which is then

---

70 Financial takeovers in the '80s were often followed by strategic acquisitions as the financial buyer spun off companies to strategic buyers, or resold the residual firm once changes were in place, again often to strategic buyers or back to the public. In a sense, many financial buyers were intermediaries—dealers of companies they bought. As such, financial takeovers added liquidity to the acquisition market.

71 See Dale Oesterle, *Are Leveraged Buyouts a Form of Governance Arbitrage?*, 3 BROOKLYN J. OF CORP. FIN. & COMM. LAW 53 (2008).

72 We continue to see sporadic proxy fights as the main weapon in a contest for control. In the '90s, Kirk Kerkorian used the threat of a proxy fight to change Chrysler's dividend and repurchase policies, and Carl Icahn mounted an unsuccessful proxy fight to force RJR Nabisco to split up its tobacco and food businesses. For more on activist shareholders, see Chapter 11.

coupled with a poison pill plan.[73] Hostile bidders cannot gain control of a board for two years. There remain a small group of bidders that run a proxy contest anyway, particularly if one of the board members up for re-election is an incumbent CEO. See *Air Products, supra* Section B.1. Success at the ballot box did not mean that the bidder has gained control of the target. Moreover, the new board members can be "turned"; although nominated by a bidder, the new board members have a fiduciary responsibility to the target and all of its shareholders, and thus must evaluate the hostile bid from the target shareholders' perspective.

NOTE: THE NEW DEFINITION OF HOSTILE

The acquisition boom in the '90s and then the 2000s looked very different from the boom of the '80s. Are economics and softening regulations the explanation? Not entirely. The hostility in our courts and in our state legislatures towards hostile, leveraged buyouts had chased most raiders (financial buyers) from the scene by the early '90s. A hostile deal in the '80s was one that threatened to *close* hostile, without target management support. Now a hostile deal is one that is unsupported by target management when first announced but *needs target management support to close*. It starts hostile but must close *friendly*. There has been a shift in terminology. Under the new parlance, a hostile takeover is one that is initially announced without the support of the target board and is successful when the bidder puts enough pressure on the target board to get the target board to negotiate and ultimately capitulate.

The Delaware courts, while tolerant of takeover defenses to tender offers, are much less tolerant of takeover defenses that preclude proxy contests. See, e.g., *Unitrin, supra* (dicta); *Stroud v. Grace*, 606 A.2d 75, 92 n.3 (Del. 1992) (requiring a *compelling justification* for tactics that disenfranchise shareholders).

BLASIUS INDUSTRIES, INC. V. ATLAS CORP.[74]

Court of Chancery of Delaware, 1988.
564 A.2d 651.

ALLEN, CHANCELLOR.

. . . Blasius is a new stockholder of Atlas. It began to accumulate Atlas shares for the first time in July, 1987. On October 29, it filed a Schedule 13D with the Securities Exchange Commission disclosing that, with affiliates, it then owed 9.1 percent of Atlas' common stock. It stated in that

---

[73] How does a company create a staggered board in a hurry? Through a defensive restructuring. See, e.g., Hilton Hotels Corp. v. ITT Corp, 978 F.Supp.1342 (D. Nev. 1997) (restructure invalid).

[74] The Delaware Supreme Court has adopted the "basic tenets" of *Blasius*. See Stroud v. Grace, 606 A.2d 75, 92 (Del. 1992).

filing that it intended to encourage management of Atlas to consider a restructuring of the Company or other transaction to enhance shareholder values. It also disclosed that Blasius was exploring the feasibility of obtaining control of Atlas, including instituting a tender offer or seeking "appropriate" representation on the Atlas board of directors. . . .

On December 30, 1987, Blasius caused Cede & Co. (the registered owner of its Atlas stock) to deliver to Atlas a signed written consent (1) adopting a precatory resolution recommending that the board develop and implement a restructuring proposal, (2) amending the Atlas bylaws to, among other things, expand the size of the board from seven to fifteen members—the maximum number under Atlas' charter, and (3) electing eight named persons to fill the new directorships. Blasius also filed suit that day in this court seeking a declaration that certain bylaws adopted by the board on September 1, 1987 acted as an unlawful restraint on the shareholders' right, created by Section 228 of our corporation statute, to act through consent without undergoing a meeting.

The reaction was immediate. . . . [T]he board voted to amend the bylaws to increase the size of the board from seven to nine and appointed John M. Devaney and Harry J. Winters, Jr. to fill those newly created positions. Atlas' Certificate of Incorporation creates staggered terms for directors; the terms to which Messrs. Devaney and Winters were appointed would expire in 1988 and 1990, respectively.

In increasing the size of Atlas' board by two and filling the newly created positions, the members of the board realized that they were thereby precluding the holders of a majority of the Company's shares from placing a majority of new directors on the board through Blasius' consent solicitation, should they want to do so. Indeed the evidence establishes that that was the principal motivation in so acting.

. . . The board then voted to reject the Blasius proposal. . . .

One of the principal thrusts of plaintiffs' argument is that, in acting to appoint two additional persons of their own selection, including an officer of the Company, to the board, defendants were motivated not by any view that Atlas' interest (or those of its shareholders) required that action, but rather they were motivated improperly, by selfish concern to maintain their collective control over the Company. That is, plaintiffs say that the evidence shows there was no policy dispute or issue that really motivated this action, but that asserted policy differences were pretexts for entrenchment for selfish reasons. If this were found to be factually true, one would not need to inquire further. The action taken would constitute a breach of duty. *Schnell v. Chris Craft Industries*, Del. Supr., 285 A.2d 437 (1971); *Giuricich v. Emtrol Corp.*, Del. Supr., 449 A.2d 232 (1982). . . .

On balance, I cannot conclude that the board was acting out of a self-interested motive in any important respect on December 31. I conclude rather that the board saw the "threat" of the Blasius recapitalization proposal as posing vital policy differences between itself and Blasius. It acted, I conclude, in a good faith effort to protect its incumbency, not selfishly, but in order to thwart implementation of the recapitalization that it feared, reasonably, would cause great injury to the Company.

The real question the case presents, to my mind, is whether, in these circumstances, the board, even if it is acting with subjective good faith (which will typically, if not always, be a contestable or debatable judicial conclusion), may validly act for the principal purpose of preventing the shareholders from electing a majority of new directors. The question thus posed is not one of intentional wrong (or even negligence), but one of authority as between the fiduciary and the beneficiary (not simply legal authority, i.e., as between the fiduciary and the world at large).

It is established in our law that a board may take certain steps—such as the purchase by the corporation of its own stock—that have the effect of defeating a threatened change in corporate control, when those steps are taken advisedly, in good faith pursuit of a corporate interest, and are reasonable in relation to a threat to legitimate corporate interests posed by the proposed change in control. *See Unocal Corp. v. Mesa Petroleum Co.*, Del. Supr., 493 A.2d 946 (1985) . . . . Does this rule—that the reasonable exercise of good faith and due care generally validates, in equity, the exercise of legal authority even if the act has an entrenchment effect—apply to action designed for the primary purpose of interfering with the effectiveness of a stockholder vote? Our authorities, as well as sound principles, suggest that the central importance of the franchise to the scheme of corporate governance, requires that, in this setting, that rule not be applied and that closer scrutiny be accorded to such transaction.

The shareholder franchise is the ideological underpinning upon which the legitimacy of directorial power rests. Generally, shareholders have only two protections against perceived inadequate business performance. They may sell their stock (which, if done in sufficient numbers, may so affect security prices as to create an incentive for altered managerial performance), or they may vote to replace incumbent board members.

It has, for a long time, been conventional to dismiss the stockholder vote as a vestige or ritual of little practical importance. It may be that we are now witnessing the emergence of new institutional voices and arrangements that will make the stockholder vote a less predictable affair than it has been. Be that as it may, however, whether the vote is seen functionally as an unimportant formalism, or as an important tool of discipline, it is clear that it is critical to the theory that legitimates the exercise of power by some (directors and officers) over vast aggregations of property that they do not own. Thus, when viewed from a broad, institutional perspective, it can be seen that matters involving the integrity of the shareholder voting process involve consideration not present in any other context in which director's exercise delegated power.

. . . The distinctive nature of the shareholder franchise context also appears when the matter is viewed from a less generalized, doctrinal point of view. From this point of view, as well, it appears that the ordinary considerations to which the business judgment rule originally responded are simply not present in the shareholder voting context. That is, a decision by the board to act for the primary purpose of preventing the effectiveness of a shareholder vote inevitably involves the question who, as between the principal and the agent, has authority with respect to a matter of internal corporate governance. That, of course, is true in a very specific way in this case which deals with the question who should constitute the board of directors of the corporation, but it will be true in every instance in which an incumbent board seeks to thwart a shareholder majority. A board's decision to act to prevent the shareholders from creating a majority of new board positions and filling them does not involve the exercise of the corporation's power over its property, or with respect to its rights or obligations; rather, it involves allocation, between shareholders as a class and the board, of effective power with respect to governance of the corporation. . . . Action designed principally to interfere with the effectiveness of a vote inevitably involves a conflict between the board and a shareholder majority. Judicial review of such action involves a determination of the legal and equitable obligations of an agent towards his principal. This is not, in my opinion, a question that a court may leave to the agent finally to decide so long as he does so honestly and competently; that is, it may not be left to the agent's business judgment.

. . . In two recent cases dealing with shareholder votes, this court struck down board acts done for the primary purpose of impeding the exercise of stockholder voting power. In doing so, a per se rule was not applied. Rather, it was said that, in such a case, the board bears the heavy burden of demonstrating a compelling justification for such action. . . .

The board was . . . presented with a consent solicitation by a 9 percent shareholder. Moreover, here it had time (and understood that it had time) to inform the shareholders of its views on the merits of the proposal subject to stockholder vote. The only justification that can, in such a situation, be offered for the action taken is that the board knows better than do the shareholders what is in the corporation's best interest. While that premise is no doubt true for any number of matters, it is irrelevant (except insofar as the shareholders wish to be guided by the board's recommendation) when the question is who should comprise the board of directors. The theory of our corporation law confers power upon directors as the agents of the shareholders; it does not create Platonic masters. It may be that the Blasius restructuring proposal was or is unrealistic and would lead to injury to the corporation and its shareholders if pursued. Having heard the evidence, I am inclined to think it was not a sound proposal. The board certainly viewed it that way, and that view, held in good faith, entitled the board to take certain steps to evade the risk it perceived. It could, for example, expend corporate funds to inform shareholders and seek to bring them to a similar point of view. . . . But there is a vast difference between expending corporate funds to inform the electorate and exercising power for the primary purpose of foreclosing effective shareholder action. A majority of the shareholders, who were not dominated in any respect, could view the matter differently than did the board. If they do, or did, they are entitled to employ the mechanisms provided by the corporation law and the Atlas certificate of incorporation to advance that view. They are also entitled, in my opinion, to restrain their agents, the board, from acting for the principal purpose of thwarting that action.

I therefore conclude that, even finding the action taken was taken in good faith, it constituted an unintended violation of the duty of loyalty that the board owed to the shareholders. . . .

MM COMPANIES, INC. v. LIQUID AUDIO, INC., 813 A.2d 1118 (Del. 2003): [A shareholder of a publicly traded Delaware corporation seeks to buy the company. Its offer is rejected and it announces that it will nominate candidates for the two board seats up for election at the next annual meeting. The company has a board of five members, staggered into three classes, one of which was elected in any given year. The shareholder also announces that it will seek an amendment to the company's bylaws to increase the size of the board from five to nine members and attempt to fill the new four positions with its candidates (obtaining six of the nine seats). The bylaw amendment requires a two-thirds vote of the shareholders. When it becomes apparent that the shareholder's nominees will be elected, the company announces an amendment to its bylaws to increase the size of the board to seven members and the incumbent board appoints two individuals to fill the new positions. At the shareholders' meeting, the dissident shareholder's two nominees were elected but its proposal to expand the board by four seats fails. The Supreme Court, reversing the Chancery Court,[75] invalidated the company's bylaw amendment adding two seats to the board.] "The *Unocal* standard of review applies because the Liquid Audio board's action was a 'defensive measure taken in response to some threat to corporate policy and effectiveness which touches upon issues of control.' The compelling justification standard of *Blasius* also had to be applied *within* an application of the *Unocal* standard to that specific

---

[75] The Chancery Court had held that the board's actions did not make it harder for the shareholder to obtain control. Under both the initial and expanded size of the board, the shareholder would need the support of two-thirds of the shareholders to prevail; support by only a plurality of the shares would leave the shareholder with only minority representation in either case (two of five or two of seven).

defensive measure because the primary purpose of the Board's action was to interfere with or impede the effective exercise of the shareholder franchise in a contested election for directors. . . .

As this case illustrates, such defensive actions by a board need not actually prevent the shareholders from attaining any success in seating one or more nominees in a contested election for directors and the election contest need not involve a challenge for outright control of the board of directors. . . .

One of the most venerable precepts of Delaware's common law corporate jurisprudence is the principle that 'inequitable action does not become permissible simply because it is legally possible.'[76] At issue in this case is not the validity generally of either a bylaw that permits a board of directors to expand the size of its membership or a board's power to appoint successor members to fill board vacancies. In this case, however, the incumbent Board timed its utilization of these otherwise valid powers to expand the size and composition of the Liquid Audio board for the primary purpose of impeding and interfering with the efforts of the stockholders' power to effectively exercise their voting rights in a contested election for directors."

QUESTION

Blasius and *Liquid Audio* are examples of what some have called an "ineffective staggered board," a classified board that can be circumvented by a clever bidder because the shark repellant amendments were incomplete.[77] What should courts do when target mangers take last second steps to shore up their mistake?

MORAN v. HOUSEHOLD INTERNATIONAL, INC., 490 A.2d 1059 (Del. Ch. 1985): [Poison pill plan triggered by a twenty percent stock acquisition or by the "formation of a group of persons holding 20% [of the target stock] to act together for the purpose of conducting a proxy contest." The Court held the trigger reasonable under a *Unocal* analysis, noting that under the plan a 19.9 percent shareholder could solicit and gather proxies on its own and not trigger the plan. The mere receipt of a proxy did not create a "group" between the proxy solicitor and the proxy grantor under

---

76 Schnell v. Chris-Craft, Indus., Inc., 285 A.2d 437, 439 (Del. 1971).

77 Most of the errors come in charter amendments that leave too much room in the bylaws to change the composition of the board. Common errors include a classified board specified in the bylaws and not the firm's charter, a failure to control in the charter special elections and consent solicitations on the removal and re-appointment of directors, and a failure to control in the charter the size of the board.

the terms of the plan. The plan definition of group required an agreement to jointly fund and run a proxy contest.][78]

CHESAPEAKE CORP v. SHORE, 771 A.2d 293 (Del. Ch. 2000) (Strine, V.C.): [The target combined a share repurchase program with a supermajority voting requirement for ratifying mergers. The Court held the supermajority bylaw invalid under both *Blasius* and *Unocal* tests. The Vice Chancellor suggested that the two test be merged.] "In reality, invocation of the *Blasius* standard of review usually signals that the court will invalidate the board action under examination. Failure to invoke *Blasius,* conversely, typically indicates that the board action survived (or will survive) review under *Unocal*. . . . Given this interrelationship and the continued vitality of *Schnell v. Chris-Craft,* one might reasonably question to what extent the *Blasius* 'compelling justification' standard of review is necessary as a lens independent of or to be used within the *Unocal* frame. If *Unocal* is applied by the court with a gimlet eye out for inequitably motivated electoral manipulations or for subjectively well-intentioned board action that has preclusive or coercive effects, the need for an additional standard of review is substantially lessened. Stated differently, it may be optimal simply for Delaware courts to infuse our *Unocal* analyses with the spirit animating *Blasius* and not hesitate to use our remedial powers where an inequitable distortion of corporate democracy has occurred. This is especially the case when a typical predicate to the invocation of *Blasius* is the court's consideration of *Unocal* factors, such as the board's purpose and whether the board's actions have preclusive or coercive effects on the electorate."

NOTE: HEDGE FUNDS STEP UP AS SHAREHOLDER ACTIVISTS

Since the turn of the century, hedge funds, recognizing that takeovers and proxy contests were too expensive and too risky given the defenses available to target boards, have used another strategy—the so-called activist shareholder approach. Hedge funds are lightly regulated, actively managed investment pools available only to high-net worth individuals and institutions. Some hedge funds (activists) discovered that they could earn substantial returns by buying small stakes in underperforming companies and pressuring the managers to alter course.

An activist fund purchases a stake in a target small enough to avoid triggering any poison pill plan or state anti-takeover statute (usually less than ten percent). Other hedge funds join but do not explicitly coordinate, forming a wolf pack that does not satisfy any "group" definition under a pill or a statute. A fund will use, for example, an aggressive Schedule 13D filing to notify other funds and investors of its intentions. The leading fund then demands that the

---

[78] See also Yuciapa American Allinace Fund II, L.P. v. Riggio, 1 A.3d 310 (Del. Ch. 2010) (refusing to apply the *Blasius* test to a poison pill).

board give it a board seat, drop its poison pill, sell the company, execute a spin-off, announce a special cash stock dividend or stock buyback, or halt a pending merger. If the managers refuse, the fund threatens a hostile proxy contest for whatever board seats are up for election. The threat seems to work even against staggered boards if a notable insider, the CEO or CFO, is up for election on the board. The parallel investing by other hedge funds, support from sympathetic traditional institutional investors, and endorsements by proxy advisory firms make the lead fund's chance of winning an election to a seat or seats probable. The tactic is different from the full blown proxy contest for control of the board because the leading fund is content to threaten a proxy contest for a minority position (i.e., is pushing a so-called "short slate").

The strategy has become so dominate and so often affects acquisitions and acquisition strategies that we have added a short Chapter 11 to the casebook on the phenomenon.

4. PLAINTIFFS' LAWYERS FEES: A COST IN ALL NEGOTIATED DEALS?

The *Kahn* entire fairness test and the *Unocal* or *Revlon* enhanced scrutiny test attract plaintiffs' attorneys like moths to light. A lawsuit comes on the heels of most every major negotiated deal announcement that involves a controlling shareholder (*Kahn*), deal protection provisions (*Unocal*), or a change of control (*Revlon*). Payments to plaintiffs' attorneys are now considered part of the cost of a deal.

IN RE COX COMMUNICATIONS SHAREHOLDER LITIGATION, 879 A.2d 604 (Del.Ch. 2005): [The Court considers what are appropriate attorney's fees for the plaintiffs' attorneys in the settlement of a class action attack on a controlling shareholder transaction. In the decision, the Court described common litigation practice in a *Kahn* based attack.] "For both the proponents of mergers with controlling stockholders (i.e., controllers and the directors involved in the transactions, all of whom become defendants in lawsuits attacking those transactions) and the plaintiffs' lawyers who file suits, this incentive effect of *Lynch* manifested itself in a unique approach to 'litigation.' Instead of suing once a controller actually signs up a merger agreement with a special committee of independent directors, plaintiffs sue as soon as there is a public announcement of the controller's intention to propose a merger. . . . After the suits are filed, the special committee gets down to its work. The litigation meanwhile remains dormant for the obvious reason that there is no agreed-upon transaction to challenge, by way of injunction or otherwise.

After the special committee completes its analysis of value and is ready to negotiate price and conditions, the activity heats up and the special committee begins bargaining—the so-called 'first track.' At some point in the negotiation process, the defendants—usually through the controller—open up a 'second track' of negotiations with the plaintiffs' counsel.

Increasingly, in this second track, the plaintiffs engage a financial advisor of their own, whose work is shared with the defendants in an effort to show that the controller's original offer was unfair and that a higher price should be paid in order to avoid a lawsuit. This second track proceeds in partial isolation from the first track in the sense that the plaintiffs' counsel is not made privy to all of the back and forth of the first track.

Indeed, the artistry of defense counsel is to bring the first and second tracks to the same destination at the same time. At some point towards the very end of the first track, the controller frames the negotiation with the special committee in a manner so that it can assure itself that the special committee is likely to accept a particular price subject to the negotiation of an acceptable merger agreement and the delivery of a final fairness opinion from the special committee's financial advisor. When that price is known but before there is a definitive deal, defense counsel (who by now has a sense of the plaintiffs' bargaining position) makes its 'final and best offer' to plaintiffs' counsel. The plaintiffs' counsel then accepts via an MOU that is subject to confirmatory discovery.

As the objectors point out and this court has often noted in settlement hearings regarding these kind of cases in the past, the ritualistic nature of a process almost invariably resulting in the simultaneous bliss of three parties—the plaintiffs' lawyers, the special committee, and the controlling stockholders—is a jurisprudential triumph of an odd form of tantra. I say invariably because the record contains a shocking omission—the inability of the plaintiffs, despite their production of expert affidavits, to point to one instance in the precise context of a case of this kind (i.e., cases started by attacks on negotiable going-private proposals) of the plaintiffs' lawyers refusing to settle once a special committee has agreed on price with a controller.

That bears repeating. In no instance has there been a situation when the controller's lawyer told the plaintiffs' lawyer this is my best and final offer and received the answer, 'sign up your deal with the special committee, and we'll meet you in the Chancellor's office for the scheduling conference on our motion to expedite.' Rather, in every instance, the plaintiffs' lawyers have concluded that the price obtained by the special committee was sufficiently attractive, that the acceptance of a settlement at that price was warranted.

The objectors use this admittedly material fact to buttress another argument they make about *Lynch*. That argument, which is again something members of this court have grasped for some time, rests in the ease for the plaintiffs' lawyers of achieving 'success' in this ritual. When a controlling stockholder announces a 'proposal' to negotiate a going private merger, the controller is, like any bidder, very unlikely to present his full reserve price as its opening bid. Moreover, given the nature of *Lynch* and its progeny, and their emphasis on the effectiveness of the special committee as a bargaining agent, the controller knows, and special committee members will demand, that real price negotiations proceed after the opening bid, and that those negotiations will almost certainly result in any consummated deal occurring at a higher price.

For plaintiffs' lawyers, the incentives are obvious. By suing on the proposal, the plaintiffs' lawyers can claim that they are responsible, in part, for price increases in a deal context in which price increases are overwhelmingly likely to occur. Added to this incentive is the fact that the plaintiffs' lawyers know that the *Lynch* standard gives them the ability, on bare satisfaction of notice pleading standards and Rule 11, to defeat a motion to dismiss addressed to any complaint challenging an actual merger agreement with a special committee, even one conditioned on Minority Approval. Because of this ability, the plaintiffs' claims always have settlement value because of the costs of discovery and time to the defendants. Add to this another important ingredient, which is that once a special committee has negotiated a material price increase with the aid of well-regarded financial and legal advisors, the plaintiffs' lawyers can contend with a straight-face that it was better to help get the price up to where it ended than to risk that the controller would abandon the deal. Abandonment of the deal, the plaintiffs' lawyers will say with accuracy, will result in the company's stock price falling back to its pre-proposal level, which is always materially lower as it does not reflect the anticipation of a premium-generating going private transaction. Having vigorously aided the special committee to get into the range of fairness and having no reason to suspect that the special committee was disloyal to its mission, the plaintiffs' lawyers can say, in plausible good faith, that it was better for the class to take this improved bid, which is now well within the range of fairness, rather than to risk abandonment of the transaction. Moreover, for those stockholders who wish to challenge the price, appraisal still remains an option.

In seeking fees in these cases, the plaintiffs' lawyers have been pragmatic. Recognizing that they, at best, can claim 'shared credit' with the special committee, the plaintiffs' lawyers have tempered their fee requests and have asked for a relatively small percentage of the 'benefit'—i.e., the difference between the price of the controller's opening bid and the final merger price agreed to by the special committee. But, at the same time, the rewards that they reap are substantial, especially when measured on an hourly basis and against the relative lack of risk that this kind of litigation entails. With the incentive that *Lynch* provides to defense counsel to settle the case and put the threat of continued litigation behind them, the plaintiffs' bar knows that the defendants will be willing to concede that the price increase was due in some material way to their desire to settle the litigation. Furthermore, the plaintiffs know that this court had been modest in awarding fees in this context, so that defendants do not fear that a settlement would result in demands for huge fees that would either draw objectors or cause the controller (if it agrees to pay the fee, as is almost always the case) to bear too much additional pain. All in all, this is a story that the objectors regard as indicative of a broken element of our system of representative litigation."

QUESTION

The process puts a premium on the perspicacity of a judge to look through the entreaties of a unified set of parties who support a settlement. How do shareholders fair in all this?

C. STATE ANTI-TAKEOVER STATUTES

NOTE: THE GO-GO '80S—THE DECADE OF GREED?

The '80s was an extraordinary decade in acquisition practice. The size of the deals was unprecedented; the language colorful; and new larger-than-life personalities occupied the press. There were $20-billion deals, $100-million professional fees, bust-ups and greenmail, bear hugs, good-bye kisses, poison pills, lock-ups, extraordinary gains in wealth by some, extraordinary losses by others, and public battles between raiders goaded on by arbs and defenders who sought help from white knights. Movie producers,[79] novelists,[80] and politicians[81] were attracted to the spectacle and most condemned it. It was the decade of greed and opportunism. Gordon Geckos (the oily-haired Michael Douglas)[82] were behind the takeovers, and Andrew Jorgensons (the homespun Gregory Peck)[83] were defending companies like the venerable New England Wire & Cable.

An increasing mountain of studies by financial economists who have put the period under a microscope suggests that the public condemnation of the '80s was, at minimum, too harsh, and perhaps simply wrong. Hostile takeovers have now lost their stigma and are a routine option of our blue chip companies

---

[79] See *Wall Street* (Twentieth Century Fox 1987), *Other People's Money* (Warner Bros. 1991), and *Barbarians at the Gate* (Home Box Office 1992).

[80] See Stephen W. Frey, *The Takeover* (1995). Facts were better than fiction and non-fiction writers were busy as well. See, e.g., George Anders, *Merchant of Debt: KKR and the Mortgaging of American Business* (1992); Bryan Burrough & John Helyar, *Barbarians at the Gate: The Fall of RJR Nabisco* (1990); Michael Lewis, *Liar's Poker: Rising Through the Wreckage on Wall Street* (1989); Dan G. Stone, *April Fools: An Insider's Account of the Rise and Collapse of Drexel Burnham* (1990).

[81] Then-Arkansas Governor William Jefferson Clinton made attacks on raiders a core part of his stump speech in the 1992 presidential campaign. See, e.g., Chris Black, *Gov. Clinton of Arkansas Joins the Presidential Race*, BOSTON GLOBE, Oct. 4, 1991, at 1.

[82] Gecko, played by Michael Douglas (who won an Oscar for the role) in the movie *Wall Street,* was a corporate raider who was outwitted by Bud Fox (played by Charlie Sheen) in an attempted takeover of Blue Star Airline. *Wall Street, supra* note 79.

[83] Larry "the Liquidator" (played by Danny DeVito) in the movie *Other People's Money,* successfully took over Jorgenson's company. *Other People's Money, supra* note 79.

(e.g., IBM, AT&T, and Johnson & Johnson) and old-line investment banks.[84] But the anti-takeover fervor in the '80s had real consequences. Our legacy from the hyperbole is laws—enacted or declared during the tumult, and surviving like the flotsam from a storm—which affect modern acquisition practice. State legislatures were active participants, enacting by the early '90s a plethora of legislation designed to stop takeovers that did not have target board clearance.

1. ANTI-TAKEOVER STATUTES THAT STRIP PURCHASED SHARES OF RIGHTS OR POWERS

BNS, INC. V. KOPPERS COMPANY, INC.

United States District Court, D. Delaware, 1988.
683 F.Supp. 458.

SCHWARTZ, CHIEF JUDGE.

. . . Constitutional Challenges

1. Background: State Takeover Statutes

Following the United States Supreme Court's decision in *Edgar v. MITE Corp.*, 457 U.S. 624, 102 S. Ct. 2629, 73 L. Ed. 2d 269 (1982), which invalidated the Illinois Business Takeover Act on commerce clause grounds, and in effect struck down virtually every other state takeover statute, many states enacted "second generation" takeover legislation. . . . In the portion of the *MITE* opinion constituting the opinion of the Court, Justice White found the Illinois statute indirectly burdened interstate commerce, and held that the burden imposed outweighed any legitimate state interests promoted by the statute. *MITE*, 457 U.S. at 643–46. . . .

State legislatures addressed the problem of regulating tender offers in the wake of *MITE* by reconstructing their statutes into four forms more closely resembling traditional state corporation laws: control share acquisitions statutes,[7] fair price provision statutes,[8] right of redemption statutes,[9] and business combination statutes. . . .[10] By reconstructing their

[84] Goldman Sachs Group, a Wall Street giant that for years prided itself on not advising hostile takeovers ("We defend against raiders"), now is a leading advisor on hostile deals.

[7] *See* Ind. Code Ann. § 23–1–42 (Burns Supp.1986); Minn. Stat. Ann. § 302A.671 (West 1985 & Supp.1987); Mo. Ann. Stat. § 351.407 (Vernon Supp.1987); Ohio Rev. Code Ann. §§ 1701.831 (Anderson 1985). [Ed. A bidder not approved by the board cannot vote the newly-acquired shares without a favorable vote of the remaining shareholders.]

[8] *See, e.g.*, Md. Corps. & Ass'ns Code Ann. §§ 3–601 to –603 (1985 & Supp.1986). [Ed. A bidder not approved by the board cannot merge its firm into the target unless the remaining target shareholders are paid a "fair price" (the price paid any other shareholder for a period of time prior to the merger) or a majority of them approve.]

[9] *See, e.g.*, Pa. Stat. Ann. tit. 15 §§ 1408(B), 1409(C), 1910 (Purdon Supp.1986); Me. Rev. Stat. Ann. tit. 13–A, § 910 (Supp.1986); Utah Code Ann. § 16–10–76.5 (Supp.1986). [Ed. A redemption statute, also known as an appraisal statute, gives shareholders a put right for "fair value" contingent on a triggering stock acquisition.]

[10] Ind. Code Ann. § 23–1–43 (Burns Supp.1986); Ky. Rev. Stat. Ann. § 271A.397(3) (Baldwin Supp. 1986); Mo. Ann. Stat. § 351.459 (Vernon Supp. 1987); N.Y. Bus. Corp. Law

takeover statutes in the form of traditional corporate governance regulation, states hoped to avoid the commerce clause infirmities of the Illinois legislation invalidated in *MITE*. . . . Several of the second generation statutes, such as those of Indiana and Maryland, combine two or more types of post-MITE state takeover regulation. Because the Supreme Court's affirmation of Indiana's second generation statute in *CTS Corp. v. Dynamics Corp.*, [481 U.S. 69 (1987),] . . . rests on certain features of that law in relation to the Williams Act, a brief description of Indiana's control share acquisition statute clarifies analysis of the constitutionality of the Delaware statute.

Indiana's control share acquisition statute operates quite differently from the Delaware approach. The Indiana statute strips acquired blocks of shares of voting rights, allowing for reinstatement of voting rights following shareholder approval. The acquiror's voting rights resume if a majority of the disinterested—i.e., non-acquiror, non-management—shares vote to restore the acquiror's voting rights at the next annual meeting or at a special shareholders meeting held within fifty days of the acquiror's request (and paid for by the acquiror). *See* Ind. Code Ann. § 23–1–42–3, –7, –10(b). A separate part of Indiana's takeover statute aims at post-transaction business combinations, resembling the fourth type of state response to *MITE*. *See* Ind. Code Ann. § 23–1–43.

The most important statutory reaction to *MITE* for current purposes is the business combination statute. First enacted by New York, and most recently by Delaware, this type of statute prohibits certain business combinations between an "interested shareholder" and the target corporation for an extended period of time—five years in the case of New York's statute, and three years in Delaware's § 203.[12] Business combination statutes typically contain exceptions allowing for friendly offerors to consummate post-takeover transactions. Common examples include board approval, or board approval plus a vote of a supermajority of the stockholders. Business combination restrictions shield shareholders from the coerciveness of front-end loaded, two-tier offers by preventing the offeror from effecting the second step of the offer unless the target's board of directors and, in some instances, the target's shareholders, approve the transaction.

2. *The Delaware Statute*

Delaware's statute, which may qualify as a "third generation" statute, having been passed after *CTS*, is modeled after the kind of second

§ 912(a)(5) (McKinney 1986). [Ed. A business combination statute prohibits all back-end mergers for a period of years after a triggering stock acquisition not approved by the target board.]

[12] *See* Del.Code Ann. 8, § 203(a); N.Y. Bus. Corp. Law § 912 (McKinney 1986).

generation statute pioneered in New York.[15] Section 203 encompasses a variety of transactions between a stockholder and the corporation of whose outstanding voting stock the stockholder owns at least 15 percent. The full statute is reproduced in the appendix to this opinion, but, put simply, it prevents "business combinations," broadly defined, between an "interested stockholder"[17] and the target corporation[18] for a three-year period, unless one of the exceptions to the statute applies.

Subsection (a) of § 203 sets forth three ways an interested stockholder otherwise subject to the section may escape its moratorium on business combinations. Subsection (b) lists circumstances in which the section will not apply at all. Subsection (a) allows a tender offeror to consummate a second step merger or other business combination where: (1) the board approves the combination prior to the date the offeror becomes an interested stockholder; (2) the transaction which transforms the stockholder into an interested stockholder results in the interested stockholder owning at least 85 percent of the outstanding voting stock, excluding for the purposes of calculating that percentage shares owned by officers who are also directors and certain employee stock plans; (3) the board of directors approves the business combination after the person becomes an interested stockholder and the proposed combination is authorized by 66 2/3 of the outstanding voting stock not owned by the interested stockholder.

Subsection (b) lists six circumstances in which § 203 will not apply. Subsection (b)(1) permits newly-organized corporations to exempt themselves from the statute. Subsection (b)(2) gives the board of directors of a Delaware corporation until May 3, 1988, to amend the corporation's bylaws to "opt-out" of the coverage of the statute. Because the terms of the directors on Koppers's board are staggered, BNS cannot avail itself of this provision of the statute.

The third subparagraph, (b)(3), gives stockholders the power to amend the corporation's bylaws or certificate of incorporation in order to place the corporation outside the statute. Such an amendment will not be effective for twelve months, however. Further, a successful offeror is forbidden from

---

15 Delaware's law is less restrictive in that the moratorium on combinations lasts only three years rather **than** five, and in some of its provisions for avoiding restrictions on business combinations. *See* N.Y. Bus. Corp. Law § 912 (McKinney 1986).

17 The statute defines an interested stockholder as: "any person (other than the corporation and any direct or indirect majority-owned subsidiary of the corporation) that (i) is the owner of 15 percent or more of the outstanding voting stock of the corporation. . . . For the purpose of determining whether a person is an interested stockholder, the voting stock of the corporation deemed to be outstanding shall include stock deemed to be owned by the person through application of paragraph (8) of this subsection but shall not include any other unissued stock of such corporation which may be issuable pursuant to any agreement, arrangement or understanding, or upon exercise of conversion rights, warrants or options, or otherwise."

18 The law reaches beyond hostile takeovers, covering almost every situation in which an investor's equity proportion rises above 15 percent without prior board approval.

using a stockholder amendment opt-out. Only persons who become interested stockholders after the amendment may take advantage of it.

Subsection (b)(4) exempts certain small companies not listed on a national exchange, quoted through a national securities association, or with fewer than 2,000 stockholders. The fifth subsection provides that persons who become interested stockholders inadvertently, e.g., through gift or inheritance, are not bound by § 203.

The sixth subsection of 203(b) releases a bidder from combination restrictions when management—or a third party approved by management—proposes a merger, sale of substantial assets, or tender or exchange offer for more than 50 percent of the outstanding voting stock. In that event, the bidder may devise a competing proposal within twenty days of the announcement of the management-endorsed proposal. This exception allows stockholders an opportunity to consider competing bids.

3. Preemption . . .

Congress added the Williams Act . . . to the system of federal securities regulation to fill a gap in the disclosure scheme set up by the 1933 and 1934 securities laws. . . . In the familiar words of the bill's sponsor, Senator Williams:

> Every effort has been made to avoid tipping the balance of regulatory burden in favor of management or in favor of the offeror. The purpose of this bill is to require full and fair disclosure for the benefit of stockholders while at the same time providing the offeror and management equal opportunity to fairly present their case.

113 Cong. Rec. 854–55 (1967) (statement of Sen. Williams). The Securities Act of 1933 and the Exchange Act of 1934 provided for disclosure to investors in every area of securities transfers but that to which the Williams Act addresses itself: tender offers and the stock acquisitions which typically precede them. Hence, prior to 1968, shareholders were privy to information about issuers, the financial condition of issuers, plans for the funds raised from the issue, information relevant to securities bought or sold in the secondary markets, and a variety of other facts . . . but were not provided with similar information regarding the tender offeror.

Between the 1930's and the 1960's, cash tender offers grew in popularity as a mode of corporate acquisition. . . . Responding to the increasing number of corporate transactions beyond the scope of the regulatory framework, Congress constructed a statute imposing several disclosure requirements on tender offerors and their targets. The rationale for requiring disclosure was (and is) shareholder protection. Shareholders were at a disadvantage compared to a potential acquiror in terms of information relevant to making a decision on the merits of the offer. In mandating disclosure, Congress deliberately contemplated requirements that would have a neutral effect on the balance of power between target management and the acquiror. . . .

This "careful balance," *CTS*, 107 S.Ct. at 1645, is not an end in itself. It is rather Congress's judgment regarding the means for achieving shareholder protection. *See CTS*, 107 S.Ct. at 1645–46. . . . Consequently, as the *CTS* Court points out, incidental effects on the relative positions of offerors and target managements caused by legislation intended to promote shareholder welfare do not contravene the purposes of the Williams Act.

> Of course, by regulating tender offers, the Act makes them more expensive and thus deters them somewhat, but this type of reasonable regulation does not alter the balance between management and offeror in any significant way. The principal result of the Act is to grant shareholders the power to deliberate collectively about the merits of tender offers. . . .

In examining the application of the preemption doctrine to the Delaware act, the threshold inquiry is the reach of the state legislation. If the state law does not intrude upon the federally regulated field, the state law is not endangered by the supremacy clause and further preemption analysis is unnecessary. Delaware argues here that because literal compliance with both the Williams Act and § 203 is possible, and because § 203 does not affect the tender offer process itself, the preemption analysis ends. This argument rests on a too narrow view of the scope of the Williams Act. As the *CTS* Court recognized, statutes which regulate the ability of a successful offeror to control the target, whether through voting rights restrictions or otherwise, plainly implicate Williams Act policies. *See CTS*, 107 S.Ct. at 1645–46.

The purpose of the Delaware legislation, as presented in the synopsis to the act and in certain testimony during the hearings, is to protect shareholders from the coercive aspects of some tender offers. Given this plain statement of legislative purpose, the argument that the act does not affect Williams Act goals seems disingenuous. Admittedly, the Williams Act confines its provisions to disclosure requirements and procedural guidelines for the actual tender offer, and does not address the rights of a successful offeror once the tender is completed. The point of requiring disclosure, however, is to give stockholders sufficient, balanced information upon which to choose whether to tender their shares. The Delaware Act operates to restrict the choice of stockholders, albeit for the shareholders' own welfare. The legislature has determined that restricting stockholder choice merely corrects for the coerciveness inherent in many tender offers by eliminating the possibility of second-step freezeouts at a lower price.[23]

---

[23] A freezeout occurs when a controlling shareholder forces minority shareholders to surrender their shares in exchange for cash or debt securities. Without fair price or other protection, a corporation's shareholders could be pressured into surrendering their shares in the

This Court need not disturb that legislative judgment, but the fact remains that the law restricts shareholder choice in the hostile tender offer context. Preventing states from unduly interfering with the tender offer itself but allowing them to deprive the tender offeror of perhaps the most important fruit of gaining control, i.e., a business combination, would permit a de facto frustration of the goals of the Williams Act.

Having passed through the threshold inquiry concerning the statutes' overlap, preemption scrutiny of the Delaware Act must begin with the proposition that the power of the states to regulate tender offers does not extend to complete eradication of hostile offers. Delaware contests this proposition. Delaware's argument assumes that *any* advantage given to management in the name of shareholder protection, however significant, is in keeping with the Williams Act. This contention stretches *CTS*'s reasoning too far. A statute that favors management to an extreme degree in effect will foreclose hostile tender offers entirely. . . .

From the premise that the state cannot eliminate hostile tender offers comes the hoary question to what extent a state may limit them. CTS contemplates some degree of limitation, but does not set forth a pellucid test. Therefore, this Court must infer from *Piper v. Chris-Craft . . . , Edgar v. MITE . . . ,* and *CTS Corp. v. Dynamics Corp . . .* what degree of restriction of tender offers is constitutional. . . . The fair import of the cases . . . is that even statutes with substantial deterrent effects on tender offers do not circumvent Williams Act goals, so long as hostile offers which are beneficial to target shareholders have a meaningful opportunity for success. Applying the analysis of *CTS* to § 203 and assessing the effects of § 203's exceptions shows that the statute and the Williams Act can co-exist. . . .

The statute offers protection to independent shareholders by preventing certain dealings between a successful offeror and the target corporation. In so doing, the statute eliminates most unsanctioned (by the target's board with or without the shareholders) freezeouts, or post-tender offer mergers between the offeror and the company whereby remaining shareholders are forced to sell their stock for cash or securities. Preventing unapproved mergers also effectively eliminates many leveraged buyouts, in which the assets of the target company provide resources for servicing the debt incurred by the bidder in taking control. . . .

. . . This Court is unable, though, to divine the full extent of the advantage bestowed on incumbent management by the law, and on this record cannot find that the advantage outweighs the benefits conferred on shareholders.

---

first stage of a tender offer, for fear that a second stage freezeout at a lower price will follow. This coercive aspect of "front-loaded" two-step, or two-tier offers, provides a significant amount of the current momentum toward and justification for state legislation regulating takeovers. . . .

Finally, the Delaware statute does not interpose the state government's views of fairness between willing buyers and sellers. Instead, § 203 permits incumbent management and a minority of the stockholders to impose their views of fairness on willing but sometimes overreaching buyers and willing but sometimes coerced sellers. Legislative judgment that management may be trusted to act in the best interests of shareholders is subject to criticism. . . . Nevertheless, entrusting management to protect shareholders is the norm in current corporate law. Moreover, the heightened judicial scrutiny of management imposed by Delaware law in the takeover context, *see Unocal Corp. v. Mesa Petroleum*, 493 A.2d 946 (Del. 1985), no doubt also will apply to the decisions of boards with respect to proposed business combinations. Therefore, notwithstanding the pro-management tilt of the Delaware statute, Delaware's § 203 more probably than not is within the sphere of constitutional state regulation of tender offers.

Section 203 alters the balance between target management and the offeror, perhaps significantly. Yet the section will be constitutional notwithstanding its pro-management slant, so long as it does not prevent an appreciable number of hostile bidders from navigating the statutory exceptions.

Leaving aside for the moment the exceptions specified in subsection (b), there are three major "outs" or escapes of subsection (a). The first, board approval, however, will necessarily be absent in the hostile takeover context, leaving the bidder with just two escape routes. These two outs work in favor of target management, and accordingly to the detriment of the offeror. But on this record, the statute appears to offer hostile bidders the necessary degree of opportunity to effect a business combination.

The second escape route relieves the offeror from the statute's strictures if eighty-five percent of the stockholders (excluding shares held by officer-directors and certain employee stock ownership plans ("ESOPs")),[26] tender their shares. This escape may place a heavy burden on the offeror hoping to consummate the transaction despite the opposition of management, but the evidence is conflicting.

According to Commissioner Grundfest, an investigation by the SEC revealed "no example in the history of hostile takeovers . . . where a hostile bidder obtained 90 percent of a target's shares if management was hostile through to the end." Hearings at 24. Apparently in response to this concern, the recommended bill lowered the percentage exemption from 90 percent to 85 percent, and excluded some management and ESOP shares from the calculation. Whether this relaxation will permit a sufficient number of hostile-to-the-end offers remains to be seen. Commissioner Grundfest suggested a threshold figure of 75 percent, "or some other realistic

[26] The statute excludes ESOPs which do not allow participating employees to determine confidentially whether the ESOP shares will be tendered in a tender or exchange offer.

figure. . . ." Grundfest recommended that the 75 percent figure exclude all shares held by management. . . . In another letter . . . , Grundfest likened a 65 percent threshold to a political "victory by a landslide. . . ."

In the other corner on the 85 percent question, Martin Lipton commented that "[i]t will be a rare situation where a tender offer will not attract 85 percent of the target's non-management stock. . . ." Similarly, Raymond Groth, of First Boston, stated that "the vast majority of tender offers which are not abandoned have resulted in the acquisition of more than 85 percent of the shares of the target. . . ."

This Court, however, is not prepared to rule on the appropriate percentage of post-tender ownership required to insulate minority stockholders from coercive two-tier bids in the absence of facts refuting the state's determination, as contrasted to unsubstantiated intuitive opinion. Such facts are not present here;[27] accordingly, subsection (a)(2) must be viewed as giving hostile offerors an opportunity to consummate their offers and receive full control despite management opposition.

The third escape, board approval *and* approval of two-thirds of the nontendering stockholders (again excluding the offeror, but including management), subsection (a)(3), also possibly places a substantial burden on would-be acquirors. The vote requires the offeror to woo and win two-thirds of the very group—including management—that refused initially to tender. This supermajority vote contrasts with that in place in Indiana, where tendering and nontendering shareholders—excluding management—vote on the rights of the acquiror by a simple majority. Standing alone, this exception might well be illusory.

In sum, the effects of the three exceptions contained in subsection (a) are not easily predictable. The legislature's judgment is that those escapes, together with the exceptions specified in subsection (b), allow offers beneficial to shareholders to proceed, and thus save the statute from constitutional infirmity.

Notwithstanding § 203's possible injurious effects, because it benefits stockholders, and because the legislature presumably has balanced the countervailing effects and found the degree of stockholder protection to

[27] The Court notes the irony of the defendant Koppers's position here compared to its position before the federal court in Los Angeles, where Koppers has intervened in a proceeding between BNS and the federal government concerning antitrust implications of the proposed takeover. The California litigation has provoked Koppers to argue that BNS will be unable to take control of Koppers, in part because of the well documented "five percent" of shareholders that do not respond to any tender offer, regardless of price. This phenomenon of 5 percent of shareholders not responding, along with Koppers management and directors' holdings of 3.4 percent, effectively prevents BNS, according to Koppers, from purchasing 90 percent of the outstanding shares of Koppers. . . . In this litigation, however, a tender offer resulting in 85 percent ownership, in order to avoid the statute, is lauded by Koppers as a perfectly reasonable requirement. . . . Given the management's ownership of 3.4 percent and the fact that 5 percent of shareholders make no response to a tender offer, the reality is BNS must receive 92 percent of the remaining outstanding shares to navigate the second escape route.

offset potential harm to stockholders, the Court concludes that the statute will be in all likelihood constitutional and not preempted. If the method Delaware has chosen to protect stockholders in fact on balance harms them, then at that time reconsideration of the statute's congruence with the Williams Act will be warranted.

Subsection (b)'s provisions, with the exception of subsection (b)(6), which allows competitive bidding in certain circumstances, do not materially alter the effect of the statute. Subsection (b)(1), which permits newly-organized companies to exempt themselves from the statute, of course does not apply to all of the companies now in existence. Subsection (b)(2) (allowing the board of a company to opt-out of the statute) will expire in early May of this year, and will be primarily applicable to non-staggered boards. Subsection (b)(3) by its own terms is ineffective for a year, and may not be used by a successful offeror. Subsection (b)(4) merely excludes certain small companies from the statute. Subsection (b)(5) provides that stockholders whose ownership rises above the fifteen percent threshold inadvertently are not subject to the statute, and therefore does not cover hostile tender offers.

4. Commerce Clause Defects

The second constitutional defect of the statute, *BNS* asserts, is that it places an undue burden on interstate commerce. This argument is unpersuasive. The three-step commerce clause inquiry set forth in *CTS* reveals that the statute harmonizes well with commerce clause dictates in the state takeover regulation context.

The *CTS* Court analyzed the Indiana statute's compliance with the commerce clause by using a three-part test: (1) are the effects of the statute discriminatory?; (2) does the statute create an impermissible risk of inconsistent regulation?; and (3) does the statute promote stable corporate relationships and protect shareholders? The answers to these questions demonstrate that the plaintiff's commerce clause arguments miss the mark.

The effects of Delaware's regulation of corporations it charters in the area of business combinations are not discriminatory. States may regulate their own corporate citizens. "No principle of corporate law is more firmly established than a State's authority to regulate domestic corporations. . . ." *CTS*, 107 S.Ct. at 1649. Section 203 does not discriminate between offerors which are Delaware corporations and offerors which are not incorporated here.

The second part of the CTS commerce clause test, pertaining to the risk of inconsistent regulation, also may be answered negatively. The *MITE* Court strongly criticized the Illinois statute because of its extraterritorial effects. *See Edgar v. MITE Corp.*, 457 U.S. 624, 642, 102 S.Ct. 2629, 2640, 73 L.Ed.2d 269 (1982) (plurality opinion of White, J.).

Conversely, the *CTS* Court identified an advantage of Indiana's statute as being that it applied only to Indiana corporations with a significant number of Indiana resident shareholders. The fact that a vast majority of Delaware's corporations do not have their main office in Delaware or many resident shareholders does not prevent Delaware from regulating tender offers affecting these corporations and does not inevitably create a risk of inconsistent regulation.

Thirdly, the Delaware statute both promotes stable corporate relationships and protects shareholders. In so doing, the statute reflects valid state concerns.[31] Indications that the stated purpose of the statute may not wholly conform with the legislature's true motives, however strong, must be ignored where the statute does accomplish the stated purpose. The Constitution does not require state corporate law to be pure of concern for the state's financial well-being, so long as the statute does not circumvent the policies of the commerce clause. . . .

RP ACQUISITION CORPORATION v. STALEY CONTINENTAL, INC., 686 F.Supp. 476 (D. Del. 1988) (Roth, J.): [Another plaintiff gathered additional facts in a subsequent case to contest Judge Schwartz's tentative finding in *BNS* of a "meaningful opportunity of success."]

". . . First of all, § 203 helps protect independent shareholders. By making post-acquisition mergers more difficult, § 203 discourages potential makers of two tier coercive offers from launching such bids. It also discourages potential makers of 'any and all' offers calculated to achieve a 51 percent tender and to be followed by a freeze-out. In addition, making these mergers more difficult hampers leveraged buyouts, whereby the target corporation is saddled with the debt the acquiror has incurred in taking control.

Of course, at the same time that § 203 achieves shareholder protection, it also exercises substantial deterrent effects on tender offers. § 203 can deprive an acquiror of what it may consider an essential element of control

---

[31] The legislative history of the Delaware Act reflects a mixed bag of motives. Prominent among these was the legislative perception that takeover tactics employed by individuals such as T. Boone Pickens and Carl Icahn were harmful to stockholders and target corporations. No less prominent, however, was the worry that failure to enact a anti-takeover law would jeopardize the $170 million in franchise taxes and fees, currently representing 17 percent of gross state revenues, which Delaware receives each year from corporations appreciative of the state's corporate law policies. The testimony before the joint judiciary committees of the Delaware legislature is replete with references to revenues, but these references take us less far than the plaintiff wishes to go. The statute's furtherance of Delaware's pecuniary interests does not automatically render it unconstitutional. Along with the concerns voiced for protecting state revenues, other witnesses expressed concerns for shareholder welfare, and the legislators vigorously questioned both opponents and proponents of the bill. While the legislative history of section 203 is not free of protectionist sentiment, neither is it devoid of concern for the group putatively benefited—the stockholders of Delaware corporations. It is manifestly not this Court's place to reject the legislature's offered justification for section 203 absent clear proof that this justification is only a pretense. Such proof is missing.

of the target corporation, the ability to effect a business combination. For example, the acquiror may no longer be able to realize quickly the possible synergy resulting from the merger and integration of the target corporation into itself. Highly leveraged offerors may find their borrowed funds harder to obtain since lenders may hesitate to loan funds knowing that they will have to wait three years for repayment, increasing carrying costs and risk. The making of tender offers may thus be generally dampened. The deterrence of § 203 inhibits not only coercive offers but also any-or-all bids such as RP's.

The crucial inquiry, then, is whether hostile offers still have a meaningful opportunity for success despite the operation of § 203. The defendants maintain the exceptions to § 203 do preserve such an opportunity for success. Plaintiff asserts these exceptions are illusory.

The 85 percent exception is illusory, according to the plaintiff, because (1) hostile offers have historically failed to achieve that percentage of ownership and (2) typically, at least 16 percent of the stock is in the hands of shareholders who are blindly pro-management and/or shareholders who are entirely non-responsive to any corporate communication (the 'dead shares'). . . . [T]he S.E.C. concludes at most 50 percent (13 out of 26) of the hostile tender offers reached 85 percent share holdings. These percentages undercut plaintiff's own argument and indicate hostile offers will have a 'meaningful opportunity for success' under the 85 percent exception.

More importantly, we find this historical record not persuasive for present purposes. . . . [L]evels of ownership which offerors achieved in the past are not an accurate prognosticator of the levels of ownership offerors will reach when faced with § 203. Before passage of the Delaware law, offerors had no specific incentive to reach 85 percent ownership. Now, they may extend the duration of the offer to reach 85 percent ownership. Alternatively, they may offer more consideration to reach 85 percent in which case shareholders would benefit, receiving greater consideration for the control premium they are collectively surrendering. On the other hand, management may try to place 15 percent of the outstanding stock in steadfastly loyal (but not excluded) hands, eliminating the possibility of a successful hostile tender offer. But until an accurate, rather than hypothetical, record can be assembled, whether the 85 percent exception 'will permit a sufficient number of hostile-to-the-end offers,' as Chief Judge Schwartz commented in *BNS*, is an issue 'which remains to be seen.' . . .

. . . While truly dead shares apparently do exist, we find plaintiff's statistics probably overestimate their existence. It is a distinct possibility that, should offerors increase their bids in an effort to reach 85 percent ownership, dead shares will be wondrously resuscitated. . . . S.E.C. Commissioner Joseph A. Grundfest . . . calculated dead shares to be 'a minimum of 3 percent and more commonly about 5 percent of the shares . . . .' In short, we find that, despite the existence of dead shares, hostile tender offers retain a meaningful opportunity for success under the 85 percent exception. . . ."

Professor Subramanian and his co-authors, studying a wide sample of deals after 1988 affected by § 203, found that in practice the 85 percent standard leaves no meaningful opportunity for success; it is illusory. Guhan Subramanian, Steven Herscovici & Brian Barbetta, *Is Delaware's Antitakeover Statute Unconstitutional? Evidence From 1988–2008*, 65 BUS. LAWYER 685 (2010). Is the statute unconstitutional? Consider the following case.

WLR FOODS, INC. v. TYSON FOODS, INC., 65 F.3d 1172 (4th Cir. 1995): "Tyson further asserts that the Williams Act preempts the Virginia statutes because the Virginia statutory scheme does not provide a bidder with a 'meaningful opportunity for success' in effecting a hostile takeover. The 'meaningful opportunity for success test' has been used by several district courts to assess whether state statutes are preempted by the Williams Act. *See, e.g., BNS, Inc. v. Koppers Co., Inc.*, 683 F.Supp. 458, 469 (D. Del. 1988). . . . We . . . reject the meaningful opportunity for success test. As we stated above, the purpose of the Williams Act is to protect independent investors from bidders and management by ensuring that the investors have access to information. The statute does not, however, have as an independent purpose the creation of an environment for bidders that is conducive to takeovers. Tyson attempts to use the 'meaningful opportunity for success' test to shift the focus of the Williams Act from protection of investors to protection of bidders. However, the Williams Act is simply not designed to protect a company in Tyson's position; 'the Williams Act does not create a right to profit from the business of making tender offers.' *Amanda*, 877 F.2d at 504–05.

The four Virginia statutes may work to give target management an advantage in the tender offer context. The preemption question we address here, however, is whether Virginia's decision to allow management access to a set of defensive mechanisms in the takeover situation frustrates the Williams Act's goal of investor protection. We hold that it does not. . . ."

NOTE: THE PROLIFERATION OF ANTI-TAKEOVER STATUTES

The *Koppers* case provides a detailed description of Delaware's business combination (or *freeze-out*) statute and a brief account in the footnotes of several other popular types of state anti-takeover statutes. The Court describes Indiana's *control share acquisition statute* and Maryland's *fair price statute*. Also common are *poison pill validation statutes*[85] and *assumption of labor*

---

[85] See Michal Barzuza, *The State of State Antitakeover Law*, 95 VA. L. REV. 1973 (2009).

contract statutes.[86] Pennsylvania's *disgorgement statute* described in the case is rare, however.[87] There are many variations among the state statutes and most states that have one type of statute also have others. Pennsylvania, for example, has a control share act, a business combination statute, a poison pill validation statute, a severance pay statute, a redemption statute and a disgorgement statute. The total count of states with some form of anti-takeover legislation is around thirty-five.[88]

State legislatures passed many of the state statutes in extreme haste at the request of an individual or local firm worried about a takeover threat. For example, when rumors circulated about a takeover of Boeing Corporation, the governor of Washington signed a bill, which had been drafted by *Boeing counsel*, that the Washington legislature had approved in an emergency session. Arizona state officials, at the request of Greyhound Corporation, introduced, adopted, and signed into law the Arizona Control Share Act in three days. It took Illinois only two days and Minnesota only one to pass their statutes. The governor of Massachusetts signed the Massachusetts statute in the offices of Gillette, a takeover target at the time. Whose interests were state officials representing in promulgating the legislation?

Most scholars who have studied the effect of the passage of state anti-takeover statutes on shareholder wealth have found the passage of the acts correlates with stock price declines for domestic corporations.[89] The degree of the shareholder wealth loss is, not surprisingly, correlated with the severity of the anti-takeover statute. Constituency statutes, business combination

---

[86] The new owner must assume the labor agreements of the purchased company.

[87] Also rare are *severance statutes* (providing for severance payments to workers on unapproved acquisitions), *anti-greenmail statutes* (disabling a target board from buying the toe-hold stake of a potential bidder at a premium price without shareholder approval), *control share cash out statutes* (giving a board call rights on a bidder's stock), and *golden parachute restrictions* (disabling a board from paying severance checks to executives after a takeover).

[88] See www.SharkRepellent.net. The exact number depends on which statutes one counts as anti-takeover statutes. Does a statute mandating a classified board structure count? In any event, two-thirds of our largest corporations are incorporated in five states, all of which have anti-takeover laws (Delaware, New York, Ohio, Pennsylvania and Massachusetts). Delaware has two state takeover laws: a three-year freeze-out statute and a succession of labor contract provision. The other four states have some of the most extensive and innovative defensive takeover regulations in the country.

[89] See Roberta Romano, THE GENIUS OF AMERICAN CORPORATE LAW, 62–66 (1993) (collecting studies). See also Robert M Daines, *Do Classified Boards Affect Firm Value? Takeover Defenses After the Pill* (2004, working paper) (discussing a 1990 Massachusetts law that imposed staggered boards on all Massachusetts public companies, even if the charters did not so provide; stock price of Massachusetts companies declined). A new study takes issue with these findings. See Emiliano M. Catan & Marcel Kahan, *The Law and Finance of Anti-Takeover Statutes*, 68 STAN L. REV. 629 (2016) (they find significant errors in three of the older studies). The authors main argument focuses on the dramatic variation in the context of the adoption of individual state statutes and the failure of the studies to take these major contextual differences into account. Their conclusion that their study calls into doubt "most empirical knowledge about the real economic effects of takeover threats" seems broad. The jumble of private side and statutory defenses rushed to the front in the '80s takeover battle will make clean data on the effect of individual soldiers obscure to say the least. There is less doubt, however, on the total impact of the defenses on the major players, the buyers and the targets. Tactics changed dramatically as both sides felt the bite of the evolving defenses; the participants believed in their effectiveness. See also Ronald J Gilson & Alan Schwartz, *Defensive Tactics and Optimal Search: A Simulation Approach*, SSRN 2805529 (posted July 7, 2016).

statutes, control share acquisition statutes and poison pill validation statutes yield negative abnormal returns, on average, for affected companies. Fair price statutes, on the other hand, have neutral effects.[90] The three states that have gained notoriety for the extreme nature of their anti-takeover statutes—Massachusetts, Ohio, and Pennsylvania—show the most substantial reductions in firm value. Pennsylvania and Ohio have adopted statutes that enable the disgorgement of all the short-term profits made by a hostile bidder.[91]

The Delaware statute, like most state anti-takeover statutes (excepting the appraisal statute in Pennsylvania), does not present a substantial additional deterrent to hostile takeovers; it adds yet another defensive weapon to an already potent arsenal of defenses—poison pill plans and second generation shark repellant amendments. Before the adoption of the statute, the Delaware courts had been faced with supervising the decisions of target boards in creating and holding onto poison pill plans; the statute does not materially change their responsibility. The Delaware courts must now also decide, under their increasingly intricate edifice of fiduciary duty case law, legal challenges to both a board's decision not to waive a firm-specific poison pill plan and its decision not to waive the statutory three-year cooling-off period. See, e.g., *Airgas, supra* Section B.1.; *Digex, supra* Chapter Five, Section D.3. The statutes have thus become another part of a basic fiduciary duty analysis of the target board's actions in response to a takeover.

2. STATUTES PROTECTING AND ENHANCING THE DISCRETION OF TARGET BOARDS

The 1985 and 1986 cases on takeover defenses produced by the Delaware Supreme Court (e.g., *Unocal, Moran,* and *Revlon*, among others) that put the Delaware courts in the middle of evaluating the use of common takeover defenses led to other states adopting statutes that accept or modify a Delaware style analysis. The statutes include statutes that validated poison pill plans, statutes that applied liability shield statutes to takeover defenses, and statutes that recast directors' duties of loyalty and care in the takeover setting (*BJR* and *constituency statutes*).

Most poison pill validation statutes codify the *Moran* and *Revlon* cases, empowering boards to adopt poison pill plans even if they discriminate against shares held by a bidder. Some of the statutes that validate poison pill plans exceed the boundaries of the Delaware cases, however. Three states—Georgia, Maryland, and Virginia—for example, authorize a board to limit a future board's discretion in redeeming a pill (*delayed hand* or *dead hand* statutes). Massachusetts' statute applies a business judgment rule standard, not an enhanced standard of review, to board decisions on the adoption and use of a poison pill.

---

[90] Romano, *supra* note 89.

[91] See Alma Cohen Bebchuk & Allen Ferrell, *Does the Evidence Favor State Competition in Corporate Law?*, 90 CAL. L. REV. 1175, 1801 (2002).

Similarly, several states do not follow Delaware's limited application of liability shield statutes to takeovers. Liability shield statutes protect directors from damage suits. See Chapter Five, Section B.1. Delaware's liability shield statute, Section 102(b)(7), does not seem to apply in *Unocal* or *Revlon* enhanced scrutiny cases.[92] Six states—Maryland, Indiana, North Carolina, Ohio, Pennsylvania and Virginia—apply liability shield statutes to directors' actions in takeover cases either expressly or indirectly by declaring that a basic business judgment analysis (BJR statute), not an enhanced scrutiny analysis, applies in evaluating a target board's decisions. Those statutes that apply the business judgment rule expressly reject *Unocal* and *Revlon*.

Ohio Gen. Corp. Law § 1701.59

(D)(1) A director shall not be found to have violated the director's duties [of care] under division (B) of this section unless it is proved by clear and convincing evidence that the director has not acted in good faith, in a manner the director reasonably believes to be in or not opposed to the best interests of the corporation, or with the care that an ordinarily prudent person in a like position would use under similar circumstances, in any action brought against a director, including actions involving or affecting any of the following:

> (a) A change or potential change in control of the corporation, including a determination to resist a change or potential change in control . . . .
>
> (b) A termination or potential termination of the director's service to the corporation as a director; . . .

(E) A director shall be liable in damages . . . only if it is proved by clear and convincing evidence . . . that the director's action or failure to act involved an act or omission undertaken with deliberate intent to cause injury to the corporation or undertaken with reckless disregard for the best interests of the corporation. . . .

---

[92] In footnote 34 of *Mills Acquisition,* the Delaware Supreme Court noted, "We made it abundantly clear that *both* duties [duty of care and loyalty] were involved in *Revlon*, and that both had been breached." Mills Acq. Corp. v. Macmillan, Inc., 559 A.2d 1261, 1284 n. 34 (Del. 1989). This means that § 102(b)(7) ought not apply to situations that call for enhanced scrutiny. But good pleading is required. See Arnold v. Society For Savings Bancorp, Inc., 650 A.2d 1270 (Del. 1994): [The plaintiff sought a preliminary injunction against a statutory merger. The court held that a certificate provision based on § 102(b)(7) justified summary judgment for the defendants both on a claim based on a breach of disclosure obligations in the proxy statements and on a claim of breach of fiduciary duty due to the use of a no-shop and a lock-up provision in the acquisition agreement. The later holding, in response to the plaintiff's argument that an analysis of takeover defenses necessarily involves the duty of loyalty, demonstrates that the Delaware courts will parse the particulars of the allegation in acquisition cases.] ". . . As to plaintiff's third claim, though the granting of no-shop and lock-up rights can under certain circumstances implicate the duty of loyalty, without any additional, supportive factual basis for his claim, sufficient at least to create a genuine issue of material fact, plaintiff's reliance on *Mills* and *Unocal* is unpersuasive. . . ." For a similar result, see Malpiede v. Townson, 780 A.2d 1075 (Del. 2001).

QUESTION

Does *Unocal's* enhanced scrutiny test apply in Ohio state courts?

Constituency statutes allow directors of target boards to consider constituencies other than shareholders in responding to takeover offers. Thirty-five states have such statutes. The statutes, in essence, necessarily modify a *Unocal* analysis and reject a pure *Revlon* analysis. Courts applying constituency statutes often declare that their state does not follow the two Delaware cases.[93] Significantly, Delaware has as yet refused to adopt any version of the constituency statutes and the drafters of the Revised Model Business Corporation Act have refused to put such a provision in their Model Act.

Constituency statutes in several states—e.g., Connecticut, Iowa, Louisiana, Missouri, Oregon, and Tennessee—apply only to change-of-control contests, but in the rest of the states, the statutes apply to all board decisions. The constituency statutes are permissive. They permit directors to *consider* the interests of constituencies other than shareholders, typically employees, creditors, suppliers, customers, and communities, among other *stakeholders*, and a few allow for consideration of the "national and state economies." Some statutes contain simply a laundry list of groups, including shareholders, whose interests a board *may* consider. Two statutes, those of Indiana and Pennsylvania, direct that a board ought not to consider the interests of any one group (an oblique reference to shareholders) as dominant.

The New York statute is typical of most of the state statutes. N.Y. Bus. Corp. L. § 717:

> (b) In taking action, including, without limitation, action which may involve or relate to a change or potential change in the control of the corporation, a director shall be entitled to consider, without limitation, (1) both the long-term and the short-term interests of the corporation and its shareholders and (2) the effects that the corporation's actions may have in the short-term or in the long-term upon any of the following:
>
> (i) the prospects for potential growth, development, productivity and profitability of the corporation; (ii) the corporation's current

---

[93] See, e.g., Dynamics Corp. of America v. WHX Corp., 967 F.Supp. 59, 64 (D. Conn. 1997) (applying New York law); Seidman v. Central Bancorp., 2003 WL 2158509 (Mass. Super. Ct.); Steiner v. Losyniak, No. 601661/97, slip op. (N.Y. App. Div. June11, 1997). See also Invacare Crop. v. Healthdyne Techs., 968 F.Supp. 1578 (N.D. Ga. 1997) (constituency statute pre-empts *Blasius* analysis).

> employees; (iii) the corporation's retired employees and other beneficiaries receiving or entitled to receive retirement, welfare or similar benefits from or pursuant to any plan sponsored, or agreement entered into, by the corporation; (iv) the corporation's customers and creditors; and (v) the ability of the corporation to provide, as a going concern, goods, services, employment opportunities and employment benefits and otherwise to contribute of the communities in which it does business.
>
> Nothing in this paragraph shall create any duties owed by any director to any person or entity to consider or afford any particular weight to any of the foregoing or to abrogate any duty of the directors, either statutory or recognized by common law or court decisions.

The constituency statutes operate to protect directors' acts from judicial review in suits by shareholders. How? Is fiduciary duty to everyone in essence fiduciary duty to no one?

NORFOLK SOUTHERN v. CONRAIL, C.A. Nos. 96-7167, 96-7350 (E.D. Pa., Nov. 19, 1996) (unpublished oral opinion), *affirmed* Nos. 97-1006, 97-1009 (3d Cir., Mar. 7, 1997): In October 1996, CSX Corp. offered to buy Conrail in a two-step stock acquisition for over $8 billion and Conrail agreed. Norfolk Southern, worried about its competitive position vis-à-vis a merged CSX and Conrail, made its hostile tender offer after CSX had announced its deal. Norfolk Southern offered approximately *$1 billion* more for Conrail than CSX had agreed to pay.

The CSX acquisition had an odd structure for a friendly, negotiated deal. The Conrail board first agreed to allow CSX to buy 19.9 percent of the Conrail stock and then consented to a front-end loaded, two-tiered tender offer. CSX offered to pay $110 in cash per share to those Conrail shareholders who had tendered their stock into a partial tender offer (for only 20 percent of the shares) and then would freeze out the remaining shareholders at a low price, exchanging CSX convertible preferred stock worth less than $100 for their shares. The Conrail board also agreed to a "lock-out" clause preventing itself from shopping for any other merger partner for one year or retracting its poison pill for a 270-day period if the CSX merger fell apart. Conrail later augmented the lock-out in exchange for a sweetened deal from CSX, extending the lock-out to two years.

In four rounds of legal hearings before a federal district court judge in Philadelphia, Conrail and CSX prevailed in their argument that the Pennsylvania anti-takeover statutes empowered the Conrail board to refuse to deal with Norfolk Southern. Conrail's lawyers called a Conrail director to the stand who recounted with pride his role on the Unocal Corporation board of directors that defeated a hostile bid made by one of the best-known '80s takeover artists, T. Boone Pickens. The Conrail CEO, LeVan, pontificated about a long-term "strategic vision" that his shareholders, many of whom were now arbitrageurs, were incapable of appreciating. In the background, LeVan negotiated with favored bidder CSX for an enlarged paycheck (an additional $2.3 million a year) and a promise that he would be the CEO in two years. LeVan's response to disgruntled shareholders who saw $1 billion of their money left on the table? "If you don't like the [Pennsylvania] law, don't buy the stock."[94]

Federal District Court Judge Van Artsdalen described as "myopic" Delaware case law that focuses on target shareholders' interests and applauded the Pennsylvania constituency statute[95] that permitted Conrail's board to look at the railway's "role in the national economy."[96]

> It seems clear that the Pennsylvania statutes to which I have referred were enacted with the decisions of the Delaware State Courts and particularly *Unocal Corporation v. Mesa Petroleum Corporation*, and *Revlon, Incorporated v. MacAndrews and Forbes Holdings, Incorporated*, that they had that clearly in mind and in order to exclude those and similar decisions that seem to mandate or suggest that the primary or perhaps only consideration in a situation where there is an attempted takeover of a rival competition or a takeover or a merger between corporations is what is the best financial deal for the stockholders in the short term. And most of the evidence that has been presented in this case is based on the contention that somehow the offer that has been made by NS is a superior offer financially.
>
> Although those decisions [*Unocal* and *Revlon*] may be fine for the shareholders whose only interest is that of a short-term financial investment to maximize their profits, it completely ignores the economic utility and value of corporations as a form of business enterprise that produces goods and services for the public and the national economy, in this case railroad services.

Knowledgeable industry analysts bemoaned the judge's lack of business sophistication, noting that the Conrail CEO's "strategic vision"

---

94 See Holman W. Jenkins, Jr., *Once Again, Railroad Shareholders Take It in the Caboose*, WALL ST. J., Nov. 19, 1996, at A23.

95 The Pennsylvania constituency statute, passed at the close of the '80s, frees a target from any obligation to sell itself to the highest bidder. The law allows a target to take into consideration not only its shareholders' interests but also the interests of employees and communities affected by the target's business. 15 Pa. Cons. Stat. Ann. § 1715. The statute was part of a multipart package of anti-takeover provisions passed in 1990. A study on the impact of the statute found that they, when passed, cost shareholders in Pennsylvania companies an immediate $4 billion in share value. See Samuel H. Szewczyk & George P. Tsetsekos, *State Intervention in the Market for Corporate Control: the Case of Pennsylvania Senate Bill 1310*, 31 J. FIN. ECON. 3 (1992).

96 The court also noted that under the Pennsylvania constituency statute, in a change of control situation, the decision of a majority of disinterested directors is presumed to satisfy their fiduciary duties unless it is proven by "clear and convincing evidence" that the disinterested directors did not act in good faith after reasonable investigation.

was nothing more than an attempt to maintain an unnecessary railroad monopoly in the northeast at the expense of the railroad's customers.[97]

Conrail's victories in federal court were trumped by its defeat in a Conrail shareholder meeting, however. The Pennsylvania statutes also require a shareholder vote for any stock acquisitions over 20 percent.[98] When Conrail put the 20 percent tender offer to a vote of its shareholders, it lost, even though with CSX's 19.9 percent stake and the 13 percent stake held by Conrail employees expected to vote with CSX, CSX needed only a few more votes to attain a majority. It did not get them. Apparently, the Conrail shareholders were in disagreement with Federal District Court Judge Van Artsdalen over the best interests of their company.

After the shareholder vote, the three parties were in deadlock with Norfolk Southern, threatening an old-fashioned proxy fight for control of the Conrail board. CSX had spent $2 billion on Conrail stock and $16 million on acquisition expenses and Norfolk Southern had spent $1 billion on Conrail stock and $75 million on expenses; Moody's Investors Service downgraded the ratings of the long-term debt of both companies, citing the costs and uncertainties connected with the merger battle.

Sense finally prevailed among the suitors when the federal agency regulating railroads, the Surface Transportation Board, balked at approving the CSX/Conrail merger.[99] Norfolk Southern and CSX agreed on a plan to split Conrail between them. CSX would buy Conrail for $10.5 billion and sell routes to Norfolk Southern. On the news of the agreement, the stock of both CSX and Conrail closed up. The effect was to reverse the disastrous Penn Central merger of 1968, which combined the Pennsylvania and New York Central railroads. LeVan's plans to keep the company intact failed, but he walked away with a compensation and stock-options package worth millions.

SARAH S. NICKERSON, THE SALE OF CONRAIL: PENNSYLVANIA'S ANTI-TAKEOVER STATUTES VERSUS SHAREHOLDER INTERESTS

72 TUL. L. REV. 1369, 1406–09 (1998).

Who Won?

Clearly, Conrail's shareholders won, as the $115 per share price they will receive represents more than a 60 percent premium on the price of

---

97 See Holman W. Jenkins, Jr., *supra* note 94.

98 15 Pa. Cons. Stat. Ann. §§ 2561–2568.

99 The Surface Transportation Board governs rail mergers. The STB decides whether a combination is "consistent with the public interest," using a multifactor test. The statutory test includes, among other things, consideration of the effect of the merger on public transportation, on rail carrier employees, on competition among rail carriers, and on rail prices. Why did the STB balk at the CSX-Conrail deal when the federal district court judge approved it using similar criteria? The STB wanted two balanced east-west rail lines, not one dominant line in the east.

Conrail's stock just prior to the takeover battle. Conrail's customers will obtain competitive rail lines into New York, which will likely lead to lower rates and may ultimately benefit the public if the prices of goods are reduced to reflect decreases in transportation costs. But Conrail's customers will only benefit if service into New York remains strong, which in turn will hinge on both companies' ability to make major infrastructure investments as Conrail's facilities are in need of expansion and modernization. It is unclear whether CSX or Norfolk is paying more for Conrail than either can afford or than the routes are actually worth. Almost immediately, analysts began speculating as to whether the total purchase price of $10.2 billion, the highest in the history of railroad acquisitions, was too high. . . .

Conrail's employees and management and the city of Philadelphia are the biggest losers. Estimates indicate that Norfolk and CSX will lay off approximately 2,000 workers, and it seems likely that most of these will be Conrail employees. There is now no hope that CSX will move its headquarters from Richmond, Virginia, to Conrail's hometown, Philadelphia. Without Conrail, Philadelphia stands to lose not only tax revenue but also significant charitable contributions which the railroad made to local community organizations. With respect to Conrail's management, their vision of the company's best interest was thwarted, and they were, as one analyst described it, "left on the sidelines" to watch as Conrail was broken apart. However, the deal was not a total failure for LeVan. Industry sources estimated that his personal severance package would amount to more than $22 million. Given his financial settlement and the high price CSX and Norfolk were forced to pay, even Snow, CSX's chairman and LeVan's biggest ally, speculated in the aftermath of the deal whether LeVan, despite his courting of CSX and professed interest in preserving the company, was really just maneuvering to maximize shareholder value.

Conrail's shareholders will receive a huge return on their investment arguably at the expense of other stakeholders, including Conrail's employees and perhaps the city of Philadelphia. Stakeholder literature suggests that "a substantial part of the takeover premium [in this case 60 percent over the price of Conrail's stock just prior to the takeover battle] consists of a *wealth transfer* from stakeholders to shareholders." This conclusion derives from the concept that a corporation is "a nexus or web of explicit and implicit contracts establishing rights and obligations among various" parties including employees, creditors, shareholders, management, and the local community.[Ed.[100]] Each party enters into an

[100] [Ed. The implicit contract argument is often attributed to economists Andrei Schleifer and Lawrence Summers. It is explained in *Do Poison Pills Make You Strong?*, ECONOMIST, June 29, 1991 at 59:

> The debate hinges on the economics of contracts. Most of the people who have a stake in any particular investment project want contracts with known risks and secure returns: employees want a fixed wage, bank lenders want regular payments of

explicit or implicit contract with the corporation when it provides something of value to the corporation in the expectation of receiving a

---

interest, landowners want rent, and so on. But if every stakeholder needed a fixed return, agreed in advance, few projects would ever get started. That is where the concept of the "share contract" comes in. After all the fixed-risk contracts have been settled out of the firm's income, shareholders keep the rest. They accept the risks not covered in the various fixed-return contracts—the "residual risk."

To make such a contract appeal to investors, shareholders are granted certain rights—crucially, the right to hire and fire managers, and to sell the shares to an investor who values the firm more highly than they do. Without these rights, the argument runs, the residual risk of shareholding would be unacceptable and fewer projects would be undertaken. Shareholders are special. Their rights can be infringed only at great economic cost.

The new theory claims that shareholders are not the only ones to face residual risks. A paper by Andrei Shleifer, now at Harvard University, and Lawrence Summers, now chief economist at the World Bank [Ed. once chief economic advisor to President Obama], first brought the idea to economists' attention, spawning a new literature. Shleifer and Summers argued that although non-shareholders seem to have contracts without residual risk, they have entered into unwritten contracts that do expose them to it. These implicit contracts are based on trust—between employers and managers, managers and shareholders, suppliers and buyers.

Why have such contracts? Predicting the distant future is hard; writing a contract to cover all possibilities is nice for lawyers, but a nuisance for everybody else. Yet without long-term commitments, shareholders will lose. For instance, shareholders should want workers to learn about their jobs, and to become more skillful at doing them. But this learning is risky: much that the workers learn will be firm-specific, with little value to any other employer. Workers will be more willing to take this risk if they trust managers to carry on employing them.

Managers who make such implicit contracts, reckon Shleifer and Summers, have every reason to honor them. Building a reputation for trustworthy management is valuable. So even if it might pay the company to break some implicit contracts, it will choose not to because this would hurt its ability to enter into such contracts in future. But suppose new managers feel no obligation to honor merely implicit contracts agreed to by their predecessors. By breaking these contracts, they can reduce the firm's costs. Hostile takeovers can reward shareholders, in effect, by mugging other stakeholders. One costly side-effect may be that it becomes harder to enter into trust-based contracts throughout the economy.

If correct, this theory supports the view that hostile takeovers promote short-termism, that merger policy should take account of all the firm's stakeholders, and that poison pills may not always be nasty. When ICI improved its redundancy terms and protected its pension fund, it might be argued, it was not reducing the value of the company. It was merely formalizing earlier trust-based agreements.

The economics of this new approach makes sense in principle. The question is how great the costs of undermining implicit contracts are in practice. Might they be big enough to outweigh the benefits of a vigorous market for corporate control?

But implicit contracts are not necessarily efficient. Many look economically absurd. Consider a corporate headquarters full of senior employees living a life of leisure. To a would-be predator, this looks like fat. But, say Shleifer and Summers, it might be the implicit reward for workers at the end of a long, hard-working career. If so, it seems likely to be a highly inefficient deal. An implicit commitment to maintain a certain size of payroll also looks like a bad contract. The spread of portable pensions and shorter and more flexible employment contracts seems to make better economic sense. Where stakeholders do bear residual risk, they can be given an equity stake, or formal profit-sharing—better that than vague promises of "you can trust us."

A further criticism is that breaking implicit contracts may not be as attractive to new management as the new theory suggests. Managers know that a reputation for trust is hard to get and easy to lose.

Shleifer and Summers were surely right to point to the existence of implicit corporate contracts. But the case for taming the market for corporate control is still far from proven.

return on its investment. Where a stakeholder's contract is implicit, the investment is unprotected and thus vulnerable to being expropriated by the shareholders, because the contract is "judicially unenforceable."

Employees, for instance, make an investment in their employer when they obtain company-specific knowledge and skills. An implicit contract arises as a result of this investment, in which the employee agrees to be paid less in relation to the value of his product in the early stages of his career in exchange for a promise by his employer of job security and payment in the later stages of his career at a rate greater than the value of his productivity. In this way the employee accepts a deferment of compensation. Where this implicit contract is breached and employment is involuntarily terminated as a result of a hostile takeover, the shareholders arguably expropriate value that belonged to the employees by robbing the employees of their deferred compensation.

Similarly, communities make an investment in a company and enter an implicit contract when they provide "specialized infrastructure, tax breaks and other benefits." The community gives value to the corporation up front with the expectation that it will benefit over the long term from having the company in the community. If the company relocates as the result of a hostile takeover before the community has benefited or even recouped its costs, then the community is arguably robbed of the value of its investment by the shareholders.

Thus, under this stakeholder analysis of implicit contracts, the premium Conrail's shareholders will receive is suspect and leads to several questions. Is the equity provided by shareholders of greater value than the labor supplied by employees or the infrastructure or tax breaks supplied by the local community? Is it fair to reward the shareholder at the expense of the other stakeholders when the shareholder, because he is able to diversify his investments, arguably assumes less risk than the stakeholders whose investments are by their nature non-diversifiable . . . ?

QUESTIONS

Ms. Nickerson worries about wealth transfers from employees and citizens of Philadelphia to shareholders in the acquisition. Can Conrail shareholders claim that before the acquisition a poor management team, running a nearly insolvent railroad, was, over time, affecting a wealth transfer from shareholders to managers, employees, and citizens? How do we decide who has the superior claim for an inappropriate "wealth transfer"?

Acquisitions are often alternatives to bankruptcy reorganizations. In bankruptcy, how would the employees of Conrail have fared?

Do we need the Conrail board or a federal district court judge to fret about the country's economic welfare and the health of its eastern railroads when there already is a government agency in place, the Surface Transportation Board, expressly empowered to oversee railway acquisitions to protect the public interest?

The contested leveraged buyout of RJR Nabisco described in the following case was the largest leveraged buyout in the '80s and featured some of Wall Street's best-known lawyers and investment bankers. A bestseller was written about the contest, Bryan Burrough & John Helyar, BARBARIANS AT THE GATE: THE FALL OF RJR NABISCO (1990), which was later made into a rather bad HBO movie. All serious students of mergers, acquisitions, and reorganizations should read the book.

METROPOLITAN LIFE INS. CO. v. RJR NABISCO, INC.

United States District Court, Southern District of New York, 1989.
716 F.Supp. 1504.

WALKER, DISTRICT JUDGE:

The corporate parties to this action are among the country's most sophisticated financial institutions, as familiar with the Wall Street investment community and the securities market as American consumers are with the Oreo cookies and Winston cigarettes made by defendant RJR Nabisco, Inc. (sometimes "the company" or "RJR Nabisco"). The present action traces its origins to October 20, 1988, when F. Ross Johnson, then the Chief Executive Officer of RJR Nabisco, proposed a $17 billion leveraged buy-out ("LBO") of the company's shareholders, at $75 per share.[1] Within a few days, a bidding war developed among the investment group led by Johnson and the investment firm of Kohlberg Kravis Roberts & Co. ("KKR"), and others. On December 1, 1988, a special committee of RJR Nabisco directors, established by the company specifically to consider the competing proposals, recommended that the company accept the KKR proposal, a $24 billion LBO that called for the purchase of the company's outstanding stock at roughly $109 per share. . . .

Plaintiffs now allege, in short, that RJR Nabisco's actions have drastically impaired the value of bonds previously issued to plaintiffs by, in effect, misappropriating the value of those bonds to help finance the LBO and to distribute an enormous windfall to the company's shareholders. As

---

1 A leveraged buy-out occurs when a group of investors, usually including members of a company's management team, buy the company under financial arrangements that include little equity and significant new debt. The necessary debt financing typically includes mortgages or high risk/high yield bonds, popularly known as "junk bonds." Additionally, a portion of this debt is generally secured by the company's assets. Some of the acquired company's assets are usually sold after the transaction is completed in order to reduce the debt incurred in the acquisition.

a result, plaintiffs argue, they have unfairly suffered a multimillion dollar loss in the value of their bonds. . . .[4]

The bonds implicated by this suit are governed by long, detailed indentures, which in turn are governed by New York contract law.[10] No one disputes that the holders of public bond issues, like plaintiffs here, often enter the market after the indentures have been negotiated and memorialized. Thus, those indentures are often not the product of face-to-face negotiations between the ultimate holders and the issuing company. What remains equally true, however, is that underwriters ordinarily negotiate the terms of the indentures with the issuers. Since the underwriters must then sell or place the bonds, they necessarily negotiate in part with the interests of the buyers in mind. Moreover, these indentures were not secret agreements foisted upon unwitting participants in the bond market. No successive holder is required to accept or to continue to hold the bonds, governed by their accompanying indentures; indeed, plaintiffs readily admit that they could have sold their bonds right up until the announcement of the LBO. . . .

The indentures at issue clearly address the eventuality of a merger. They impose certain related restrictions not at issue in this suit, but no restriction that would prevent the recent RJR Nabisco merger transaction. . . . The indentures also explicitly set forth provisions for the adoption of new covenants, if such a course is deemed appropriate. . . .

In effect, plaintiffs contend that express covenants were not necessary because an *implied* covenant would prevent what defendants have now done. . . . Thus, in cases like *Van Gemert v. Boeing Co.,* 520 F.2d 1373 (2d Cir.), *cert. denied,* 423 U.S. 947, 96 S.Ct. 364, 46 L.Ed.2d 282 (1975) ("Van Gemert I"*),* and *Pittsburgh Terminal Corp. v. Baltimore & Ohio Ry. Co.,* 680 F.2d 933 (3d Cir.), *cert. denied,* 459 U.S. 1056, 103 S.Ct. 475, 74 L.Ed.2d 621 (1982)—both relied upon by plaintiffs—the courts used the implied covenant of good faith and fair dealing to ensure that the bondholders received the benefit of their bargain as determined from the face of the contracts at issue. In *Van Gemert I,* the plaintiff bondholders alleged inadequate notice to them of defendant's intention to redeem the debentures in question and hence an inability to exercise their conversion rights before the applicable deadline. The contract itself provided that notice would be given in the first place. *See, e.g., id* at 1375 ("A number of provisions in the debenture, the Indenture Agreement, the prospectus, the registration statement . . . and the Listing Agreement . . . dealt with the

---

[4] Agencies like Standard & Poor's and Moody's generally rate bonds in two broad categories: investment grade and speculative grade. Standard & Poor's rates investment grade bonds from "AAA" to "BBB." Moody's rates those bonds from "AAA" to "Baa3." Speculative grade bonds are rated either "BB" and lower, or "Bal" and lower by Standard & Poor's and Moody's, respectively. *See, e.g., Standard and Poor's Debt Rating Criteria* at 10–11. No one disputes that, subsequent to the announcement of the LBO, the RJR Nabisco bonds lost their "A" ratings.

[10] Both sides agree that New York law controls this Court's interpretation of the indentures, which contain explicit designations to that effect. . . .

possible redemption of the debentures . . . and the notice debenture-holders were to receive . . . "). Faced with those provisions, defendants in that case unsurprisingly admitted that the indentures specifically required the company to provide the bondholders with notice. *See id.* at 1379. While defendant there issued a press release that mentioned the possible redemption of outstanding convertible debentures, that limited release did not "mention even the tentative dates for redemption and expiration of the conversion rights of debenture holders." *Id.* at 1375. Moreover, defendant did not issue any general publicity or news release. Through an implied covenant, then, the court fleshed out the full extent of the more skeletal right that appeared in the contract itself, and thus protected plaintiff's bargained-for right of conversion.[21] As the court observed,

> What one buys when purchasing a convertible debenture in addition to the debt obligation of the company . . . is principally the expectation that the stock will increase sufficiently in value that the conversion right will make the debenture worth more than the debt. . . . *Any loss* occurring to him from failure to convert, as here, *is not from a risk inherent in his investment but rather from unsatisfactory notification procedures.*

Id. at 1385 (emphasis added, citations omitted). . . . Similarly, the court in *Pittsburgh Terminal* applied an implied covenant to the indentures at issue because defendants there "took steps to prevent the Bondholders from receiving information which they needed *in order to receive the fruits of their conversion option should they choose to exercise it." Pittsburgh Terminal*, 680 F.2d at 941 (emphasis added).

The appropriate analysis, then, is first to examine the indentures to determine "the fruits of the agreement" between the parties, and then to decide whether those "fruits" have been spoiled—which is to say, whether plaintiffs' contractual rights have been violated by defendants. . . .

A review of the parties' submissions and the indentures themselves satisfies the Court that the substantive "fruits" guaranteed by those contracts and relevant to the present motions include the periodic and regular payment of interest and the eventual repayment of principal. *See, e.g.*, Bradley Aff. Exh. L, § 3.1 ("The Issuer covenants . . . that it will duly and punctually pay . . . the principal of, and interest on, each of the Securities . . . at the respective times and in the manner provided in such Securities . . . "). According to a typical indenture, a default shall occur if the company either (1) fails to pay principal when due; (2) fails to make a timely sinking fund payment; (3) fails to pay within 30 days of the due date thereof any interest on the date; or (4) fails duly to observe or perform any of the express covenants or agreements set forth in the agreement. . . .

---

[21] Since newspaper notice, for instance, was promised in the indenture, the court used an implied covenant to ensure that meaningful, reasonable newspaper notice was provided. *See id* at 1383.

Plaintiffs' Amended Complaint nowhere alleges that RJR Nabisco has breached these contractual obligations; interest payments continue and there is no reason to believe that the principal will not be paid when due.

[T]his Court holds that the "fruits" of these indentures do not include an implied restrictive covenant that would prevent the incurrence of new debt to facilitate the recent LBO. To hold otherwise would permit these plaintiffs to straightjacket the company in order to guarantee their investment. These plaintiffs do not invoke an implied covenant of good faith to protect a legitimate, mutually contemplated benefit of the indentures; rather, they seek to have this Court create an additional benefit for which they did not bargain.

Although the indentures generally permit mergers and the incurrence of new debt, there admittedly is not an explicit indenture provision to the contrary of what plaintiffs now claim the implied covenant requires. That absence, however, does *not* mean that the Court should imply into those very same indentures a covenant of good faith so broad that it imposes a new, substantive term of enormous scope. This is so particularly where, as here, that very term—a limitation on the incurrence of additional debt—has in other past contexts been expressly bargained for; particularly where the indentures grant the company broad discretion in the management of its affairs, as plaintiffs admit . . . , particularly where the indentures explicitly set forth specific provisions for the adoption of new covenants and restrictions . . . , and *especially* where there has been no breach of the parties' bargained-for contractual rights on which the implied covenant necessarily is based. While the Court stands ready to employ an implied covenant of good faith to ensure that such bargained-for rights are performed and upheld, it will not, however, permit an implied covenant to shoehorn into an indenture additional terms plaintiffs now wish had been included. . . .

Plaintiffs argue in the most general terms that the fundamental basis of all these indentures was that an LBO along the lines of the recent RJR Nabisco transaction would never be undertaken, that indeed *no* action would be taken, intentionally or not, that would significantly deplete the company's assets. Accepting plaintiffs' theory, their fundamental bargain with defendants dictated that nothing would be done to jeopardize the extremely high probability that the company would remain able to make interest payments and repay principal over the 20 to 30 year indenture term—and perhaps by logical extension even included the right to ask a court "to make sure that plaintiffs had made a good investment. . . ." But as Judge Knapp aptly concluded in Gardner, "Defendants . . . were under a duty to carry out the terms of the contract, but not to make sure that plaintiffs had made a good investment. The former they have done; the latter we have no jurisdiction over. . . ." Plaintiffs' submissions and MetLife's previous undisputed internal memoranda remind the Court that a "fundamental basis" or a "fruit of an agreement" is often in the eye of the beholder, whose vision may well change along with the market, and who may, with hindsight, imagine a different bargain than the one he actually and initially accepted with open eyes.

The sort of unbounded and one-sided elasticity urged by plaintiffs would interfere with and destabilize the market. And this Court, like the parties to these contracts, cannot ignore or disavow the marketplace in which the contract is performed. Nor can it ignore the expectations of that market—expectations, for instance, that the terms of an indenture will be upheld, and that a court will not, *sua sponte,* add new substantive terms to that indenture as it sees fit. The Court has no reason to believe that the market, in evaluating bonds such as those at issue here, did not discount for the possibility that any company, even one the size of RJR Nabisco, might engage in an LBO heavily financed by debt. That the bonds did not lose any of their value until the October 20, 1988 announcement of a possible RJR Nabisco LBO only suggests that the market had theretofore evaluated the risks of such a transaction as slight.

> The Court recognizes that the market is not a static entity, but instead involves what plaintiffs call "evolving understanding[s]. . . ." Just as the growing prevalence of LBO's has helped change certain ground rules and expectations in the field of mergers and acquisitions, so too it has obviously affected the bond market, a fact no one disputes. . . .

To respond to changed market forces, new indenture provisions can be negotiated, such as provisions that were in fact once included in the 8.9 percent and 10.25 percent debentures implicated by this action. New provisions could include special debt restrictions or change-of-control covenants. There is no guarantee, of course, that companies like RJR Nabisco would accept such new covenants; parties retain the freedom to enter into contracts as they choose. But presumably, multi-billion dollar investors like plaintiffs have some say in the terms of the investments they make and continue to hold. And, presumably, companies like RJR Nabisco need the infusions of capital such investors are capable of providing.

Whatever else may be true about this case, it certainly does not present an example of the classic sort of form contract or contract of adhesion often frowned upon by courts. In those cases, what motivates a court is the strikingly inequitable nature of the parties' respective bargaining positions. . . . Plaintiffs here entered this "liquid trading market," with their eyes open and were free to leave at any time. Instead they remained there notwithstanding its well understood risks. . . .

In the final analysis, plaintiffs offer no objective or reasonable standard for a court to use in its effort to define the sort of actions their "implied covenant" would permit a corporation to take, and those it would not.[28] Plaintiffs say only that investors like themselves rely upon the "skill" and "good faith" of a company's board and management . . . and that their covenant would prevent the company from "destroy[ing] . . . the legitimate expectations of its long-term bondholders. . . ." As is clear from the preceding discussion, however, plaintiffs have failed to convince the Court that by upholding the explicit, bargained-for terms of the indenture, RJR Nabisco has either exhibited bad faith or destroyed plaintiffs' *legitimate,* protected expectations.

[C]ourts are properly reluctant to imply into an integrated agreement terms that have been and remain subject to specific, explicit provisions, where the parties are sophisticated investors, well versed in the market's assumptions, and do not stand in a fiduciary relationship with one another.

It is also not to say that defendants were free willfully or knowingly to misrepresent or omit material facts to sell their bonds. Relief on claims based on such allegations would of course be available to plaintiffs, if appropriate—but those claims properly sound in fraud, and come with requisite elements. Plaintiffs also remain free to assert their claims based on the fraudulent conveyance laws, which similarly require specific proof.[30] Those burdens cannot be avoided by resorting to an overbroad, superficially appealing, but legally insufficient, implied covenant of good faith and fair dealing. . . .

[P]laintiffs advance a claim that remains based, their assertions to the contrary notwithstanding, on an alleged breach of a fiduciary duty. . . . *Simons v. Cogan*, 549 A.2d 300, 303 (Del.1988), the recent Delaware Supreme Court ruling . . . held, *inter alia,* that a corporate bond "represents a contractual entitlement to the repayment of a debt and does not represent an equitable interest in the issuing corporation necessary for the imposition of a trust relationship with concomitant fiduciary duties." Before such a fiduciary duty arises, "an existing property right or equitable interest supporting such a duty must exist." *Id.* at 304. A bondholder, that court concluded, "acquires no equitable interest, and remains a creditor of the corporation whose interests are protected by the contractual terms of the indenture." *Id.* . . .

[T]his Court finds Simons persuasive, and believes that a New York court would agree with that conclusion. . . .

. . . Before a court recognizes the duty of a "punctilio of an honor the most sensitive," it must be certain that the complainant is entitled to more than the "morals of the market place," and the protections offered by

---

[28] Under plaintiffs' theory, bondholders might ask a court to prohibit a company like RJR Nabisco not only from engaging in an LBO, but also from entering a new line of business—with the attendant costs of building new physical plants and hiring new workers—or from acquiring new businesses such as RJR Nabisco did when it acquired Del Monte.

[30] As noted elsewhere, plaintiffs can also allege violations of express terms of the indentures.

actions based on fraud, state statutes or the panoply of available federal securities laws. This Court has concluded that the plaintiffs presently before it—sophisticated investors who are unsecured creditors—are not entitled to such additional protections. . . .[Ed.[101]]

QUESTION

Do the constituency statutes[102] discussed above change the result in the *RJR Nabisco* case?

The trust indentures at issue in *RJR Nabisco* are controlled by the Trust Indenture Act of 1939 that applies to debt securities in principal amount of $5 million or more. The Act sets minimum criteria for bond trustees and requires a unanimous vote of the bondholders to alter principal or interest payment obligations. The Act does not contain requirements that protect bondholders in acquisitions. However, many trust indentures do contain such provisions. Covenants in an indenture may limit stock repurchases, prohibit a merger or sale of substantially all the assets unless the surviving company agrees to be bound by the indentures, and contain anti-dilution clauses to protect convertible debt.[103] As the bondholders in *RJR Nabisco* discovered, none of the traditional clauses gave much protection in modern LBOs.

---

[101] [Ed.: A few counts survived the motion for summary judgment, counts based on state law for common law fraud and fraudulent conveyance. In January of 1991, the case settled and the settlement restored to the plaintiffs much of the value of the RJR bonds that had been lost subsequent to the LBO in 1989. George Anders, *RJR and Insurer Settle Suit on Rights of Bondholders*, WALL ST. J., Jan. 25, 1991, at C13. The plaintiffs were paid in cash, new debt securities, common stock and a reduced term on some existing debt. RJR also agreed to pay the plaintiff's legal fees of $15 million.]

[102] Wyoming passed a unique provision, the Wyoming Management Stability Act in response to the holding. Wy. Stat. § 17–18–101–403. Under the Act, Wyoming corporations may put a list in place of "bondholder protections" by filing a document, which is approved in the same manner as a bylaw amendment (which boards can do by simple resolution in Wyoming), with the secretary of state. The list includes a requirement of bondholder consent to all acquisitions and control changes. A filing corporation may set voting requirements at fifty to ninety percent of the value of the bonds at maturity.

[103] The position of the bondholders in the RJR Nabisco LBO parallels the situation of the holders of convertible debt in MGM in 1973. Convertible debentures are vulnerable to devaluation in acquisitions. The debenture holders in the dissolving corporation may find their convertibility vanish when the equity securities disappear or may find that the equity securities in the survivor are worth much less because of its additional leverage. In 1974 the Delaware Chancery Court held, in Harff v. Kerkorian, 324 A.2d 215 (Del.Ch. 1974), that the MGM board did not owe a fiduciary duty to convertible debenture holders when the corporation issued an extraordinary cash dividend and impaired the value of their conversion right. Since that case, trust indentures with new issues of convertible debentures routinely include anti-dilution provisions that apply in acquisitions. Such covenants may provide, for example, formulae to adjust the conversion ratio and to flip-over the conversion right into stock of the survivor.

After leveraged buy-outs and leveraged recaps became popular, issuers of debt securities were forced to increase yields to place new issues. Some, however, found that they could lower yields by offering *poison put* (or *event risk*) covenants in the trust indenture agreements that spell out the rights of the debt holders. The covenants enable investors to sell the bonds back to the issuer on the occurrence of a triggering event, defined to include changes of control, leveraged recapitalizations, and, in most cases, a severe credit downgrade (to triple B minus or lower). A second strategy is to increase the coupon rate on bonds with the occurrence of a specified triggering event that results in a credit downgrade (some also decrease the coupon rate on a credit upgrade).

A 1991 study reports that in sample companies that underwent major capital restructurings between 1983 and 1988, only 10 percent of investment grade bonds had been downgraded to speculative grade by August, 1989. The authors of the study also report a corresponding rise in covenants protecting bondholders from event risks. Forty percent of investment grade industrial bonds issued in 1989 and 1990 contained these special covenants and cost between 25 to 45 basis points in yield. Leland Crabbe, *Event Risk: An Analysis of Losses to Bondholders and "Super Poison Put" Bond Covenants,* 66 J. FIN. 689 (1991). When LBOs waned in the early '90s so did the covenants; by late 1991 event risk covenants covered less than one percent of new investment grade issues. Marcel Kahan & Michael Klausner, *Antitakeover Provisions in Bonds: Bondholder Protection or Management Entrenchment?*, 40 UCLA L. REV. 31 (1993). Professors Kahan and Klauser also found that managers often used event risk covenants to further their own control interests in the firm at the expense of shareholder value while giving only marginal protection to bond values. The covenants exempted *management* buyouts that could depress bond values and cover even unleveraged hostile takeovers that did not threaten bond values.

MCMAHAN & COMPANY V. WHEREHOUSE ENTERTAINMENT, INC.

United States Court of Appeals, Second Circuit, 1990.
900 F.2d 576.

PRATT, CIRCUIT JUDGE:

. . . Defendant Wherehouse Entertainment, Inc. offered 6 1/4 percent convertible subordinated debentures whose key selling feature was a right of holders to tender the debentures to Wherehouse in the case of certain triggering events which might endanger the value of the debentures. The tender right was to arise if:

(a) A person or group . . . shall attain the beneficial ownership . . . of an equity interest representing at least 80 percent of the voting power . . . unless such attainment has been approved by a majority of the Independent Directors;

(b) The Company . . . consolidates or merges . . . unless approved by a majority of the Independent Directors;

(c) The Company . . . incurs . . . any Debt . . . excluding . . . Debt which is authorized or ratified by a majority of the Independent Directors, immediately after the incurrence of which the ratio of the Company's Consolidated Total Debt to its Consolidated Capitalization exceeds .65 to 1.0.

Indenture § 5.02, 11–12 (June 15, 1986). . . .

The offering materials defined an "Independent Director" as "a director of the Company" who was not a recent employee but who was a member of the board of directors on the date of the offering or who was subsequently elected to the board by the then-Independent Directors. . . . The reason offered for this unusual right to tender was that it would be a protection against certain forms of take-over attempts, including leveraged buy-outs. . . .

Plaintiffs are financial institutions that purchased 34 percent of the convertible debentures. Eighteen months after the purchase, Wherehouse entered into a merger agreement with defendants WEI Holdings, Inc. and its subsidiary WEI Acquisition Corp. The practical effect of the merger, accomplished through a leveraged buy-out, left Wherehouse with a debt approaching 90 percent of its capitalization and left plaintiffs' debentures valued at only approximately 50 percent of par. Plaintiffs attempted to exercise their right to tender, but the company refused to redeem the debentures on the ground that the "board of directors" had approved the merger. . . .

We hold that the district court erred in granting summary judgment to the defendants; because plaintiffs have raised a triable issue as to whether the written and oral representations about the right to tender these debentures were materially misleading to a reasonable investor in violation of § 11 and § 12 of the 1933 Securities Act and also of § 10(b) of the 1934 Securities Exchange Act. . . .

. . . Plaintiffs claim that these offering materials misstated the right to tender and omitted important information about it in violation of § 11. They argue that a reasonable investor would have believed that the right to tender was valuable because it was presented as a right to be exercised at the holder's option and as a protection against takeovers that might affect the security of the debentures. In truth, however, the right to tender was illusory, they argue, because it was designed to be exercised only at the option of management and therefore was intended to protect the interest of shareholders, not of debentureholders.

Plaintiffs are correct that the offering materials can reasonably be read to present the option to tender as a valuable right. The language used was invariably language of entitlement. . . . Further, a jury could reasonably view the presentation of the right to tender as a special feature to protect investors, for the offering materials stressed the purported value of the right in any takeover transaction which would threaten the value of the debentures. . . .

Finally, the right was restricted only in that it was subject to action by "the Independent Directors. . . ." A jury could reasonably find that this repeated use of the word "unless" encouraged the inference that exercise of the right would be the norm and that waiver would be the exception.

Although the offering materials explain that the Independent Directors would be chosen from the company's board of directors, the term "Independent Director" implies a special status, some distinction from an "ordinary" director. The term suggests that these directors would be "independent" of management and the normal obligations of board members to act in the interests of shareholders. Thus the restriction could reasonably be understood to mean that in the case of a triggering event, the right to tender would arise *unless* the Independent Directors find the event to be in the interests of the debentureholders. . . .

By thus representing that in a takeover context the Independent Directors would be considering the interests of debentureholders, the defendants implied that the Independent Directors had a duty to protect the debentureholders' interests. Defendants, however, have shown nothing in their corporate charter or by-laws that would have permitted, much less required, these Independent Directors to favor debentureholders over shareholders. Moreover, at the time of the approval of this merger, the Independent Directors constituted all but one of the "ordinary" directors on the board. As ordinary directors, they had a fiduciary duty to protect the interest of shareholders in any takeover situation, regardless of debentureholders' interests or rights. It is inevitable, then, that the so-called Independent Directors had no independence; they would never protect the interest of debentureholders except by coincidence because, as ordinary directors, they were required by law to protect the interests of the shareholders. From this perspective, there is merit in plaintiffs' contentions that the right to tender was illusory and that the representations of it in the offering materials were misleading. . . .

AIR LINE PILOTS ASS'N INT'L v. UAL CORP., 897 F.2d 1394 (7th Cir. 1990): [The board violated their fiduciary duty to their shareholders by including an anti-takeover device in the corporation's contract with one of its labor unions.] "There is abundant evidence that these provisions were adopted not to resolve a conflict between United and the machinists and thus head off a possible strike, as United and the machinists contend in this litigation, but to prevent the pilots from taking over the company. . . . So these are anti-takeover devices, and of a unique lethality because unlike the usual 'poison pills' the company could not rescind them. . . . Delaware law requires that defensive measures, and a fortiori defensive measures as irrevocable as these, be adopted with due concern for the interests of shareholders. The challenged covenants were adopted in haste and with due regard for nothing except their probable efficacy in defeating the pilots' takeover attempt. They violate Delaware law."

NOTE: DATA ON STAKEHOLDER WELFARE IN ACQUISITIONS

The flip side of any finding that, on average, bidding firms have successfully squeezed additional cash flow out of targets' operations is that the bidding firms did it by injuring—expropriating the wealth from—third parties. The obvious candidates for abuse are the federal government (the target pays less taxes), bondholders (the target adds leverage and lowers the value of old debt), employees (the target releases employees and otherwise lowers wages and benefits), and customers (the combination of target/bidder has enough market share to charge monopolistic prices). The data gathered demonstrates, however, that, on average, bidder gains from disadvantaging any one of the groups explain only a small portion of the premiums paid to target shareholders.[104] This is not to say, however, that in any given case a bidder did not take value from these constituencies in an acquisition.

Financial economists also found evidence that bidders do not buy firms to expropriate wealth from bondholders, blue-collar employees, customers and other non-shareholder constituencies. Studies of companies that had just been purchased in leveraged acquisitions found there were substantial reductions in the number of white-collar employees.[105] The effect of leveraged acquisitions on wage reductions (including pension reductions) of union employees was negative but not as pronounced.[106] Indeed one study found, in the aggregate, no statistically significant wage changes in leveraged buyouts.[107] Another found no statistically significant wage changes from hostile takeovers over those present in friendly takeovers.[108] There were, of course, notable exceptions, such as Carl Icahn's acquisition of TWA.

---

[104] See Abbie Smith, *Corporate Ownership Structure and Performance: The Case of Management Buyouts: Evidence from 1985–89*, 27 FIN. MGMT. 143 (1990); Sanjai Bhagat, Andrei Shleifer & Robert Vishny, *Hostile Takeovers in the 1980s: The Return to Corporate Specialization*, BROOKINGS PAPERS ON ECONOMIC ACTIVITY 1 (1990).

[105] See Frank R. Lichtenberg & Donald Siegel, *The Effects of Leveraged Buyouts on Productivity and Related Aspects of Firm Behavior*, 27 J. FIN. ECON. 165 (1990).

[106] Brian Becker, *Union Rents as a Source of Takeover Gains Among Target Shareholders*, 49 INDUS. & LAB. REL. REV. 3 (1995).

[107] See Lichtenberg & Siegel, *supra* note 105.

[108] See Joshua Rosett, *Do Union Wealth Concessions Explain Takeover Premiums? The Evidence on Contract Wages,* 27 J. FIN. ECON. 263 (1990). See also Smith, *supra* note 104;

A study of the effect of management buyouts on a firm's outstanding non-convertible bonds found that the bondholders lost about 3 percent of the market value of the bonds.[109] However, bonds with strong covenant protection actually *gained* value.[110] Finally, leveraged acquisitions that created significant consolidations of market power (disadvantaging customers) were the exception, not the rule.[111]

D. THE PERFORMANCE OF THE DELAWARE COURTS

Given the focus of the nation's M & A attorneys on every new Delaware M & A case, it is astonishing to note the number of other states that do not follow Delaware case law on acquisitions. Either by statute or by case law alone, a majority of the other states have rejected important parts or even all of Delaware's fiduciary duty analysis in takeovers.[112] A majority of the states have constituency statutes that implicitly opt out of *Revlon* (and perhaps *Unocal* as well). A number of the states (at least ten[113]) have rejected explicitly by statute or by case law the analysis in either *Unocal, Revlon*, or *Blasius*. Very few courts in other states (seven[114]) have held that their state will follow the basic Delaware analysis. Add to the mix states that have rejected *Weinberger*[115] (or *Kahn*) on negotiated acquisitions and you have widespread rejection of basic Delaware doctrine in acquisitions.

It is easy to claim, as many have that have noticed the phenomenon,[116] that the other states which have rejected Delaware's analysis have done so to protect managers at the expense of their shareholders (and everyone else for that matter). Support for their claim comes predominately from the observation that the other states offer more protection to manager's discretion in acquisitions than does Delaware case law and the history of the state's anti-takeover statutes. The state legislatures wrote most of the anti-takeover statutes at the behest of local, publicly traded corporations

---

Jagadeesh Gokhale, Erica L. Groshen & David Neumark, *Do Hostile Takeovers Reduce Extramarginal Wage Payments?*, 77 REV. ECON. & STAT. 470 (1995).

[109] See Douglas O. Cook, John C. Easterwood & John D. Martin, *Bondholder Wealth Effects of Management Buyouts*, 21 FIN. MGMT. 102 (1992).

[110] See Paul Asquith & Thierry A. Wizman, *Event Risk, Covenants, and Bondholder Returns in Leveraged Buyouts,* 27 J. FIN. ECON. 27 (1990).

[111] See Andrei Shleifer & Robert W. Vishny, *The Takeover Wave of the 1980s*, 249 SCIENCE 745 (Aug. 17, 1990); Judith A. Chevalier, *Do LBO Supermarkets Charge More? An Empirical Analysis of the Effects of LBOs on Supermarket Pricing*, 50 J. FIN. 1095 (1995).

[112] See Michal Barzuza, *The State of State Anti-takeover Law*, 95 VA. L. REV. 1973 (2009).

[113] Indiana, Maryland, Massachusetts, Nevada, New Jersey, New York, North Carolina, Ohio, Pennsylvania, and Virginia.

[114] Professor Barzuza could only find cases in Arkansas, California, Kansas, Michigan, Minnesota, Oregon, and Texas that are still current and that accept *Unocal* and *Revlon*.

[115] Courts in Connecticut, Michigan and Ohio have refused to apply an entire fairness test in squeeze-out mergers.

[116] Barzuza, *supra* note 112.

that wanted protection from unwanted buyers. But there may be something else at work as well.

Looking back over the last thirty years of Delaware court jurisprudence, one is not struck with awe and admiration. One wonders about the court's batting record on results. There have been several cases in which the court has sanctioned poor deals—the Time acquisition of Warner, the Toys R Us buyout, and the Hewlett-Packard acquisition of Compaq—in the face of obvious problems. There have been cases in which the court has subjected good deals to years of litigation. Cinerama overpaid for Technicolor and had to suffer over twenty years of litigation from Technicolor shareholders to prove the point. The prices paid in the Trans Union and UOP takeovers were reasonable but the buyers had to pony up token price increases after multiple trials and hearings. And there are cases in which the court has blocked good deals to the detriment of the shareholders. The Airgas shareholders will not see $70 a share again for some time, if ever. Does the court intervene when it should and defer when it should? There have been notable published opinions that do not inspire confidence. But perhaps there is a deeper problem.

The legal doctrine developed in the Delaware cases over the thirty year period has become multi-layered and complex. It seems to expand with each new Delaware Supreme Court case. Under the first part of the *Unocal* two prong test, which itself is a threshold test for another test, we now have a three part test; under the second part of the *Unocal* test we have a two part qualifying test with a fall-back test. In controlling shareholder tender offers, we now have either a three part test for coercion or a unified test (as of the time of writing we do not know which will prevail). In deal protection provision cases we struggle with whether both the *Unocal* and *Blasius* tests attach. And in one of the newest and worst line of cases, the courts are applying *Revlon* rules to ordinary negotiated deals to monitor whether the selling board had an effective "market test" in place.[117]

Confusion abounds and judges and ex-judges of the Delaware court resort to law review articles to ask for and recommend clarification. The upper and lower courts do not seem to be on the same page. One sees a note of impatience in Delaware Supreme Court language overruling the Chancery Court when we, along with the lower court, are struggling with the new multiple part tests.[118] And a new confounding wrinkle is the spectacle of Chancellors disagreeing with and suggesting modification of Delaware Supreme Court precedent in lower court opinions.[119] The Delaware takeover law is, of course, a gold mine for academics, who write waves of one-hundred page plus articles recommending doctrinal

---

117 Lost is whether a failed market test, failing a threshold for the business judgment rule, can survive an entire fairness test.

118 Read the early *Cede* and *Technicolor* opinions or the first *Disney* opinion.

119 See, e.g., *Cox Communications, supra* (the unified test); Mercier v. Inter-Tel Inc., 929 A.2d 786 (Del. Ch. 2007) (limiting *Blasius).*

reconciliation and purity after each new major opinion. In the end, one has to question whether the complexity of the doctrine is detracting from the production of appropriate results.

Perhaps the most stunning illustration of the problems with the Delaware courts are footnotes in *Technicolor II* (or is it III?),[120] in which Justice Holland first takes pains to distinguish the case from the fictional case of *Jarndyce v. Jarndyce* in Dicken's *Bleak House* and second pens a self-congratulatory note on how good the Delaware courts are, citing articles by other Delaware court judges. The lady doth protest too much. The opinion itself has layer upon layer of analysis that is mind-numbing. We are sure these footnotes thrilled the weary litigants in the case who were simply interested in how much they had to pay or not pay.

The most telling indictment of Delaware doctrine comes in the work of sophisticated parties tasked with writing complete packages of law on the duty of boards of directors in acquisitions. One would include the drafters of the American Law Institute's Corporate Governance Project, of the ABA Model Business Corporation Act, of the United Kingdom Takeover Code, and of the European Commission's Directive on Takeover Bids. No doubt there are other groups. These groups are not driven by local protectionism. In each instance they have rejected Delaware jurisprudence on acquisitions and come up with systems of their own.

The ALI's Project is particularly instructive. Although necessarily influenced by Delaware law, the drafters pushed hard at its edges. The provisions of the project put a premium on the decisions of disinterested directors and shareholders.[121] The definition of "disinterested" is carefully and thoroughly considered. ALI, Principles of Corporate Governance: Analysis and Recommendations, §§ 1.15, 1.16 & 1.23. One comes to a similar conclusion when reading the latest edition of the ABA Model Business Corporation Act. There is again a heavy emphasis on the role of disinterested (*qualified*) directors and shareholders and the definition of "qualified" receives careful, reoccurring reevaluation.[122] ABA Model Bus. Corp. Act §§ 1.43 & 8.61 (2016 rev.).

---

[120] Cinerama, Inc. v. Technicolor, Inc., 663 A.2d 1156, 1180 n.34 (Del. 1995).

[121] The legal principles are divided by type of acquisition. For example, in arm's-length transactions the business judgment rule applies and appraisal is the exclusive remedy for complaining shareholders. In the appraisal action, the price accepted by a board is presumed to be fair. In controlling shareholder buyouts, approval by disinterested directors and by disinterested shareholders limits a shareholder to an appraisal remedy where the price negotiated by the directors gets deference. On defensive tactics in tender offers, the drafters rejected the enhanced scrutiny language in favor of reasonableness language and put the burden of proof on the complaining shareholder.

[122] The Model Act is less complete than the ALI Project. One should quibble, for example, with the drafters use of negligence style language and business judgment rule-style language in their duty of care sections combined with their earnest disclaimers in the Official Comments that they are neither using a negligence test nor codifying the business judgment rule. They also refused to consider whether to follow *Unocal* and *Revlon*.

The authors of this casebook suggest that the Delaware legislature step in with some codification of the rules that will escape the Delaware Supreme Court's reluctance to overrule some early cases so as to rationalize these multiple lines of analysis.

E. FIDUCIARY DUTY OF ACQUISITION CONSULTANTS AND ADVISORS

IN RE DAISY SYSTEMS CORPORATION

United States Court of Appeals, Ninth Circuit,1996.
97 F.3d 1171.

NELSON, CIRCUIT JUDGE.

... In 1988, Daisy, a public corporation specializing in the development of computer-aided engineering systems, sought to acquire Cadnetix, a public company that developed computer-aided and manufacturing design systems. Daisy's president and Chief Executive Officer, Dr. Norman Friedmann, approached Michael Tennenbaum, a senior managing director at Bear Stearns, for his assistance in the acquisition. Friedmann, who had never before been involved in the acquisition of a public company, reportedly asked Tennenbaum if Bear Stearns could analyze the Daisy/Cadnetix merger and the benefits the deal would confer upon Daisy shareholders. Tennenbaum maintained that the investment bank had adequate resources to analyze the transaction, and told Friedmann that Bear Stearns would charge Daisy $75,000 for the bank's services.

On May 5, 1988, Bear Stearns sent Daisy a letter outlining the terms of its retention; in it, Bear Stearns agreed to "assist [Daisy] as its exclusive financial advisor in connection with any Transaction with Cadnetix Corporation." Bear Stearns' services were to "include advice on valuation and structuring of the Transaction, and assisting [Daisy] in negotiations with Cadnetix." Daisy was obliged by the agreement to provide Bear Stearns with any information regarding either Daisy or Cadnetix that Bear Stearns "deem[ed] appropriate." The letter further stated that the bank would be using and relying upon this information "without independent verification ... by Bear Stearns," and that it was to assume no responsibility for the accuracy and completeness of any information provided by Daisy regarding Cadnetix. In addition to the $75,000 fee to which Bear Stearns was entitled, Daisy was to pay Bear Stearns 1 percent of the fair market value of the total consideration received by Cadnetix if the merger was consummated successfully.

Cadnetix, however, rejected Daisy's attempts to effect a friendly merger; consequently, Tennenbaum told Friedmann that Daisy should consider a hostile acquisition, and that it should "create[ ] more pressure" on Cadnetix by acquiring shares of the company.

On September 19, 1988, Tennenbaum advised the Daisy Board of Directors of Bear Stearns' analysis of the proposed acquisition of Cadnetix; this analysis included a discussion of acquisition strategies, price ranges for the acquisition, feasibility, financial analysis, and the availability of financing. At this meeting, the Daisy Board voted to engage in a hostile tender offer for Cadnetix. Friedmann stated that Tennenbaum told him that if Daisy could not otherwise fund the transaction, Bear Stearns would provide funding.

By letter dated September 22, 1988, Bear Stearns and Daisy amended the terms of Bear Stearns' retention; while this letter contained substantially the same provisions as those in the May 5 agreement, it further provided that, "Bear Stearns will act as dealer manager in any tender offer or exchange offer for securities of Cadnetix . . . and, subsequent to the approval of Bear Stearns' Commitment Committee, will assist the Company in obtaining financing, *if so required*." (emphasis added) Daisy was to pay Bear Stearns a fee of $250,000 "[e]ither for acting as Dealer/Manager . . . or upon any public report associating Bear Stearns with a hostile takeover of Cadnetix by Daisy," and was to give Bear Stearns the opportunity to be the "sole managing underwriter or exclusive agent" if Daisy chose to retain an investment banker or financial advisor for assistance in obtaining financing. The letter also stated that if Bear Stearns were to issue to Daisy any letters stating that the investment bank was "highly confident" that it could arrange the financing for the deal, Daisy would pay Bear Stearns 3/8 percent of the principal amount of the financing referred to in the letter, subject to a $100,000 minimum.

On September 30, 1988, Daisy announced its offer to purchase 51 percent of Cadnetix's shares at $8.00 per share; the offer was conditioned on Daisy's being able to obtain "sufficient financing on terms acceptable to [Daisy]." Bear Stearns then issued a letter stating that it was "highly confident" that $50 million of financing could be secured "under current market conditions." On October 12, 1988, the Cadnetix Board rejected the Daisy offer as inadequate. On October 17, 1988, Daisy offered $8.00 per share for 100% of Cadnetix stock; Bear Stearns issued yet another letter, stating that it was "highly confident" that $100 million of financing could be secured "under current market conditions." On October 24, 1988, Daisy raised its offer to $8.375 per share.

On October 31, 1988, Tennenbaum met with representatives of Daisy and Cadnetix and informed them that Bear Stearns intended to finance the transaction even if it was hostile. On November 6, however, Tennenbaum told the Commitment Committee that efforts to finance the transaction had been unsuccessful "due to the hostile nature of the transaction, the current turnaround of Daisy and general unwillingness to lend to high technology companies. Few banks actually reached the credit analysis stage."

Bear Stearns argues that on November 10, it committed to loan Daisy $130 million in connection with the October 24 offer. Kenney contends, however, that Tennenbaum's offer to loan Daisy $130 million, a commitment for which Daisy paid $975,000, was not limited to the October 24 offer. Cadnetix subsequently agreed to a friendly merger, and on November 10, an agreement between the companies was reached. Pursuant to the agreement, Daisy was to acquire Cadnetix in a one-step merger for $9.50 per share, payable with $6.50 in cash and $3.00 in debentures convertible into Daisy common stock. Bear Stearns contends that it was to be involved only in "giving 'advice on the terms of the debentures,' specifically the price and timing of the conversion features."

The companies later amended the details of their agreement to provide for a two-step merger. In the first stage, Daisy was to purchase 50.1 percent of Cadnetix's shares at $9.50 cash per share, and in the second, the remaining Cadnetix shares would be acquired for $3.78 cash per share and convertible Daisy debentures. The merger was to become effective on November 23, 1988, and the second stage was to be completed within 6 months of the acquisition. Bear Stearns contends that it was not asked to prepare a report or opinion on any part of the transaction.

Bear Stearns also argues that Daisy did not ask it for assistance in financing the second step of the merger. The bank maintains that one of Daisy's SEC filings made pursuant to the offer, in which Daisy states that the "management of Daisy presently intends to arrange at least $50 million of bank indebtedness which will be a liability, and possibly secured by the assets of New Daisy," lends support to the bank's contention that Daisy intended to finance the deal independently. Nonetheless, Bear Stearns contends that "on the chance that it would be asked to seek financing," it informed Daisy in early December 1988 that Daisy would need to submit detailed financial projections regarding the future prospects of the business in order to secure financing; it also "informed Daisy that it was imperative that Bear Stearns begin to search for financing as soon as possible."

Kenney contends that when Tennenbaum learned that Daisy was making its own attempts to secure financing, he discontinued Bear Stearns' efforts to obtain financing for the deal. Indeed, Tennenbaum stated that he told the Commitment Committee that "[Daisy] had misled us for several months and had by themselves been seeking the financing in order not to pay us a fee." Kenney maintains, however, that Daisy did not know that Bear Stearns was not actively seeking financing until its Chief Financial Officer contacted Tennenbaum and was told no more work would be done until another engagement letter was executed. Daisy's counsel informed Friedmann that Bear Stearns' merger success fee suggested that Bear Stearns was to continue its financing efforts; moreover, in an internal memo dated November 28, 1988, Bear Stearns confirmed its intention of arranging for financing for the second step in the acquisition. Nevertheless, Daisy and Bear Stearns executed yet another engagement letter in which the parties agreed to amend the terms of the September 22 agreement, and to provide for Bear Stearns' retention as "exclusive agent in connection with raising all financing necessary."

Bear Stearns contends that on April 18, 1989, it committed to contribute $15 million to a financing package for Daisy; the record indicates, however, that 2 days later, on April 20, 1989, the Bear Stearns Commitment Committee approved a $45 million bridge loan to Daisy. Tennenbaum told Daisy that the Committee had rejected the bridge loan proposal; at the same time, he informed Daisy that Heller Financial, Inc., would be willing to finance the second step of the transaction. Heller representatives stated that the pricing proposed by Bear Stearns on the Daisy loan "far exceeded what we would normally receive in any other type of transaction."

Kenney maintains that the lack of publicly disclosed financing caused Daisy's major customers to defer their orders, and that at the same time, competitors were attempting to lure key employees away from the company. Consequently, Kenney argues, Daisy failed to meet its sales projections and was unable to refinance the company. The company's condition continued to decline, and its creditors eventually placed it into involuntary bankruptcy. Kenney then was named as the company's Chapter 11 trustee. . . .[Ed.[123]]

[Ed.: Professional Malpractice Claim] . . . In order to establish a claim for professional negligence, a plaintiff must demonstrate: 1) the duty of the professional to use such skill, prudence and diligence as other members of his profession commonly possess and exercise; 2) a breach of that duty; 3) a proximate causal connection between the negligent conduct and the resulting injury; and 4) actual loss or damage resulting from the professional's negligence. *Jackson v. Johnson*, 5 Cal.App.4th 1350, 1355, 7 Cal.Rptr.2d 482 (1992).

Kenney argues that as Daisy's "exclusive financial advisor," Bear Stearns was obliged to assume a broad range of duties. The contours of these duties, Kenney maintains, can be determined by expert testimony.... Accordingly, Kenney's expert stated that as Daisy's "exclusive financial advisor," Bear Stearns should have assessed the risks and benefits of alternative structures for the transaction and the probable impact of the transaction on the market for the companies' stock, analyzed the effects of the transaction on Daisy and Cadnetix's business operations, determined financing alternatives and sources, analyzed operational impacts, and provided the necessary expertise to assess the feasibility of

[123] [Ed. As a result of the Daisy engagement, Bear Stearns earned a fee of approximately $2.7 million, of which $1.7 million was paid prior to the consummation of the acquisition.]

alternatives. That Bear Stearns failed to discharge these duties is, according to Kenney, indicated by its negligent advice to embark upon a hostile tender offer. Indeed, there were statements that hostile mergers are ill-advised in the high-tech industry, and even Tennenbaum admitted that financing the Daisy/Cadnetix deal was difficult due to the "hostile nature of the transaction" and the "general unwillingness to lend to high technology companies."

. . . The investment bank argues that the Daisy/Bear Stearns engagement letters establish the limits of Bear Stearns' duties to Daisy, and that the bank's primary function was to advise on valuation and structuring and assist in negotiations. Bear Stearns further argues that Kenney's vision of duty is expressly disclaimed by the terms of the engagement letters, which provide that Bear Stearns is not responsible for the accuracy of any of the information provided by Daisy; in addition, the bank maintains that in the absence of any evidence that Daisy in fact relied on trade custom, any evidence of that custom as to the appropriate professional duties cannot be used to contradict the express terms of the letter.

However, Bear Stearns' analysis misconstrues the terms of the engagement letters. While the investment bank argues that the engagement letters establish the outer boundaries of the professional duties owed Daisy, an examination of those letters demonstrates that Bear Stearns' argument overstates the reach of those agreements. The letters merely provide that Bear Stearns' assistance will "include advice on valuation and structuring"; they do not state that Bear Stearns' involvement in the transaction will be limited to those activities. . . .

The bank's contention that Daisy did not rely on the broad set of duties that Kenney now claims Bear Stearns should have assumed is also without support; the record demonstrates that Friedmann, Daisy's CEO, had no experience in acquiring public companies, and that he may have relied on Tennenbaum to provide him with assistance on a broad range of issues.

Thus, as Daisy's expert testimony established the appropriate duty of care in the investment banking community, and that interpretation of professional duty was not inconsistent with the express terms of any written agreements between Daisy and Bear Stearns, we accept that view of professional duty, and now look to whether there is any evidence that it was breached.

We have little difficulty concluding that genuine questions of fact exist as to whether any duty Bear Stearns owed Daisy was breached. While Bear Stearns relies on the fact that the engagement letters provided that the investment bank would not be held responsible for the accuracy of information, the letters absolved the bank of responsibility only with respect to the accuracy of information provided by Daisy. What is being challenged here, however, is the diligence of Bear Stearns' analysis. It is worth noting that Bear Stearns does not appear to argue that it conducted anything but a post-hoc analysis of the possibility of financing a hostile Daisy/Cadnetix deal; indeed, on November 6, several weeks after the "highly confident" letters had been issued, Tennenbaum told the Bear Stearns Commitment Committee that banks were generally unwilling to lend to high technology companies. . . .

[Ed.: Breach of Fiduciary Duty Claim] . . . In *Beery v. State Bar*, 43 Cal.3d 802, 239 Cal.Rptr. 121, 126–27, 739 P.2d 1289, 1294 (1987), the California Supreme Court cited *Barbara A. v. John G.*, 145 Cal.App.3d 369, 383, 193 Cal.Rptr. 422 (1983), for the proposition that "[t]he essence of a fiduciary or confidential relationship is that the parties do not deal on equal terms, because the person in whom trust and confidence is reposed and who accepts that trust and confidence is in a superior position to exert unique influence over the dependent party. . . ."

Contrary to the district court's holding, however, the parties' general degree of business sophistication is not at issue here; rather, what Kenney argues is that Daisy, whose Chief Executive Officer was unschooled in the niceties of public acquisitions, relied upon Bear Stearns to "undertake to do an analysis of [a Daisy/Cadnetix] merger." Thus, even though both parties were sophisticated corporations, the fact that Bear Stearns was retained to advise Daisy in a type of transaction with which Daisy had no experience suggests that the requisite degree of "superiority" may have existed. . . .

Having established that there may have existed between the parties a fiduciary relationship, we next direct our attention to whether there are any facts in the record that would support a claim for breach of fiduciary duty. . . . We think that there are.

Daisy points to the fact that Tennenbaum concealed the $45 million bridge loan as evidence of a breach of fiduciary duty. . . .

[Ed.: Negligent Misrepresentation Claim] . . . To prevail on a negligent misrepresentation claim, a plaintiff must provide evidence of the following: 1) a representation as to a material fact; 2) that the representation is untrue; 3) that the defendant made the representation without a reasonable ground for believing it true; 4) an intent to induce reliance; 5) justifiable reliance by the plaintiff who does not know that the representation is false; and, 6) damage. *Masters v. San Bernardino County Employees Retirement Ass'n*, 32 Cal.App.4th 30, 40 n.6, 37 Cal. Rptr.2d 860 (1995). Kenney rests his negligent misrepresentation claim against Bear Stearns on the bank's issuance of the highly confident letters and its alleged oral commitment to providing financing. For the reasons that follow, we reject those claims.

Kenney complains of Bear Stearns' ill-founded representations to Daisy—via the "highly confident" letters—that the market would support the Daisy/Cadnetix transaction; indeed, there is no indication Bear Stearns sufficiently analyzed market conditions before issuing the letters. Kenney argues that the letters were significant not because they detailed the particular terms under which a hostile acquisition could be financed, but rather because they were meant to communicate to Cadnetix Daisy's ability to consummate the deal under any circumstances, be they hostile or friendly, and to thereby force Cadnetix to negotiate.

This argument must fail. The terms of the letters make clear that the letters were expressions of confidence that financing could be obtained under certain specified conditions, and did not constitute guarantees that the deal could be financed regardless of the successive permutations it might take. Moreover, because the letters were conditioned upon "satisfaction of all the conditions set forth in the [October 17] offer to Purchase," any reliance upon them as being indicative of a general availability of financing clearly was unreasonable. . . . [T]he terms of the letters clearly are limited to the specific transactions noted therein.

Kenney maintains that although Bear Stearns' commitment to loan Daisy $130 million initially was made with respect to the October 24 offer, the terms of that loan could be modified so as to provide financing for any later deals agreed upon. Kenney also introduced evidence that industry custom suggests that where an investment bank has provided temporary financing, it will usually provide the client with some form of bridge financing as well.

The investment bank maintains, however, that given the fact that loan commitments must first be approved by the Commitment Committee and are subject to the payment of a fee, any reliance Daisy had upon these alleged oral representations was unreasonable. . . . We agree. To the extent that Tennenbaum's representations merely implied the possibility of Daisy securing long-term financing, such a representation, and accordingly, the terms of any implied loan agreement, were so vague as to render unjustifiable any reliance on them. . . .

FERNANDEZ, CIRCUIT JUDGE, concurring and dissenting:

It is impossible not to recognize that this is a case of biting off more than one can chew. Daisy was not satisfied with being a major player in the computer field; it decided to gobble up another major player—Cadnetix. It thought that it would then be an even bigger and more powerful company. Instead, it choked on the bite. Its trustee in bankruptcy is now looking for a deep pocket. Perhaps he has found it in the trousers of Bear Stearns.

The issue is close, but on the evidence presented it is just barely possible that a trier of fact will determine that Bear Stearns performed negligently and that the negligence led to the collapse of Daisy. That is so even though Daisy had designs on Cadnetix before it even contacted Bear

Stearns; that Daisy did not even seek Bear Stearns' advice for the deal it actually finally consummated; that Daisy did not seek financing help from Bear Stearns until its attempts at self help created an almost impossible timing situation; and, finally, that it was Daisy which failed to conduct its business in a way that allowed it to meet even in its own financial projections. Still, I suppose a reasonable trier of fact could determine that Bear Stearns is responsible for Daisy's debacle, and that is the summary judgment test. . . .

However, Kenney reaches too far when he says that the facts could possibly support a breach of fiduciary duty claim. The district court, with that perceptive and informed sententiousness that often characterizes the work of our district judges, said that:

> Merely because Bear Stearns was hired as an expert consultant to render financial services does not mean it was in a position of superiority in this relationship between two sophisticated business entities. Daisy's "complete" dependence on Bear Stearns, even if it is true, is unjustified and does not render Bear Stearns liable for an arms-length business transaction that has gone sour. In addition, the conclusory allegations that Daisy was somehow vulnerable to Bear Stearns or that Bear Stearns "exerted undue influence" over Daisy are unsupported. . . .

Just so. Nothing in this case suggests that there was any fiduciary relationship whatever between these sophisticated entities or that Kenney can honestly plead one. Kenney's attempt to clothe Daisy in the weeds of a poor put-upon consumer of professional services borders on the ludicrous; I suspect that it is only in conditions of litigation that Daisy's high-powered executives would be willing to say that they were mere lambs under the protection of the shepherds at Bear Stearns. Finally, while there is at least some indication of negligence on the part of Bear Stearns, there is no indication of a breach of fiduciary duty.

Thus, with some misgivings, I agree that there may have been negligence. But to leverage this action into a fiduciary duty case breaks down all barriers between mere negligence and breach of fiduciary duty. . . .

QUESTIONS

Can investment bankers rewrite their engagement letters to mitigate the case's effect? What will be the impact of representations attesting to a client's sophistication and knowledge about the contemplated transaction and of disclaimers of broad professional duties or the existence of a fiduciary relationship?

Does the contingent nature of the investment banker's fee affect its advice? Why did the investment banker not advise the purchaser to kill the deal when it turned hostile?

The Delaware Supreme Court, in language in a released and then withdrawn opinion, has stated that an investment bank supplying a fairness opinion does not have a fiduciary duty to shareholders. The relationship, the court noted, is "exclusively contractual." *Weinberger v. UOP*, No. 58–1981, available in 8 Del. J. Corp. L. 162 (Del. Feb. 9, 1982), withdrawn on reargument and later replaced by 457 A.2d 701 (Del. 1983) (en banc) (the shareholders dropped the claim against the bank after the court withdrew and before the court replaced the opinion).

What is the difference between a cause of action based on a breach of fiduciary duty and a cause of action based on professional negligence? Do shareholders have standing to sue directly under either cause of action or must they sue in a derivative action? The only published case in which a court has permitted shareholders to sue investment bankers directly for breach of fiduciary duty is the curious case of *Schneider v. Lazard Freres & Co.*, 552 N.Y.S. 571 (App. Div. 1990) (a special committee operating under their *Revlon* duties to auction the firm is an agent of the shareholders and the investment bank hired by the committee to advise it is a subagent of the shareholders).

NOTE: THE HISTORY OF THE DAISY SYSTEMS CASE

The *Daisy Systems* case went to trial in the spring of 1998. A jury found that, although the investment bank Bear Stearns owed a fiduciary duty to its client, Daisy Systems Corporation, that duty had not been breached. The jury did conclude that Bear Stearns owed Daisy Systems over $108 million for professional negligence. The award was 39 percent of the $277 million in total damages that Daisy had claimed. See Leslie P. Norton, *Costly Advice: A Federal Jury Finds Bear Stearns Liable for Part of a Failed Merger*, BARRON'S, May 25, 1998, at 13.

F. TAKEOVERS IN BANKRUPTCY: CLAIMS TRADING

In Chapter 11, a sale of assets under § 363 outside a plan of reorganization usually requires the active cooperation and support of the firm's management, the debtor-in-possession. See Chapter Two, Section C. Creditors that cannot convince a board to sell the assets to an active bidder and who want to force a sale have three options: (1) seek the appointment of a trustee to oust existing management,[124] (2) convert the Chapter 11 into a forced liquidation under Chapter 7,[125] or (3) propose and confirm a plan

[124] Bankruptcy Code § 1104. The creditors must show fraud or gross management to overcome a presumption in favor of continuing the existing management.

[125] The creditor must show that there is little prospect for a successful reorganization. Bankruptcy Code § 1112.

of reorganization that provides for the acquisition.[126] All three options are long shots. The issue gets more interesting still when a frustrated bidder purchases debt in the firm (known as claims trading), becomes a creditor and attempts to use its new position as a creditor to force the acquisition. In the straightforward case, the bidder, also known as a vulture, buys a majority of the so-called *fulcrum securities*, the lowest debt level at which the instruments show positive value. Fulcrum securities are, in essence, the equity-level securities of the company once reorganized, and the owner of the fulcrum securities is the new owner of the company post-bankruptcy. The bidder then argues in reorganization for a cancellation of the securities with lower priority (lower debt securities and all equity securities) and for an exchange of its debt securities for new equity securities, a majority of which it controls. There should be no objection to such a tactic, as long as the purchase of the fulcrum securities is not fraudulent (and the bidder does not take a fiduciary position as the head of a creditor committee that includes other creditors with adverse interests to those of the bidder). In less straightforward attempts, the bidder buys a blocking position in a class of claims and attempts to use the blocking position to force an acquisition. The bidder votes against the management plan as creditor (recall that it only takes one-third of the amount of the class to block confirmation), attempting to force a consideration of its competing plan. This approach can upset a bankruptcy judge. The classic case on such an attempt is the following.

IN RE ALLEGHENY INTERNATIONAL, INC.

United States Bankruptcy Court for the Western District of Pennsylvania, 1990.
118 Bankr. Rep. 282.

COSETTI, UNITED STATES BANKRUPTCY JUDGE.

. . . [W]e take up the saga, beginning on December 29, 1989, when the debtor filed the instant plan of reorganization. . . . The court approved the debtor's disclosure statement on February 5, 1990, setting the last day to ballot on the debtor's plan as March 30, 1990, at 5:00 P.M.

However, on January 24, 1990, near the conclusion of the hearings on the debtor's disclosure statement, Japonica filed its plan of reorganization (the "Japonica plan") and disclosure statement which mirrored and utilized in large part the debtor's material and organization. The court was urged by Japonica not to approve the debtor's disclosure statement until Japonica's disclosure statement could be approved and a joint ballot distributed. . . .

The Japonica plan offered cash of $6.42 with holdbacks, as compared to the debtor's proposed stock plan which offered $7.00 per share. Under

[126] The management has the exclusive right to file a plan for 120 days. Bankruptcy Code § 1121. The period may be extended or reduced "for cause." If the management plan fails, any creditor may file a competing plan.

the Japonica plan, Japonica would acquire control of the debtor. Although Japonica had indicated its interest in acquiring control of the debtor as early as July 1989, Japonica held no interest as a creditor or equity holder of the debtor until immediately prior to the filing of its proposed plan and disclosure statement. To qualify as a party in interest authorized to file a plan, Japonica purchased public subordinated debentures of the debtor with a face value of $10,000 for $2,712. At that time, the court was unaware that the purchase of claims would be the tactic used by Japonica to gain control.

On February 23, 1990, Japonica began purchasing claims of the secured bank lenders, Class 2.AI.2. This occurred after the debtor's disclosure statement was approved and the debtor's plan balloting had commenced. This was also after Japonica had proposed a plan and disclosure statement and had become a proponent of a plan. . . . Following the purchase of the claim of Continental, Japonica held 33.87 percent of the claims in Class 2.AI.2 enabling Japonica to block an affirmative vote by that class on the debtor's plan of reorganization. 11 U.S.C. § 1126(c). . . .Under the terms of the assignments by the aforementioned banks, Japonica caused the votes of the claims it purchased to be voted against the debtor's plan. . . .

Japonica also purchased claims from senior unsecured creditors in Class 4.AI.2. . . . Japonica caused the votes of these claims to be voted against the debtor's plan. Although Japonica purchased less than 1/3 of the claims in Class 4.AI.2, its negative votes were sufficient to defeat the debtor's plan in that class because of the large number of claims in Class 4.AI.2 that did not vote. . . .

Section 1126(e) of the Bankruptcy Code, 11 U.S.C. § 1126(e), empowers the court to "designate" (i.e., disqualify) the ballot of "any entity whose acceptance or rejection . . . was not in good faith or was not solicited or procured in good faith. . . ." However, the Bankruptcy Code does not define "good faith. . . ."

In the case at bar, Japonica, by acquiring a blocking position, has defeated the debtor's plan and can defeat any other plan and thereby obstruct a "fair and feasible reorganization." . . . Although Lederman testified that he voted against the plan for economic reasons, the court does not find the economic reasons offered by Japonica creditable. We find that Japonica acted "in aid of an interest other than an interest as a creditor. . . ." The overriding fact that causes this court to reach this conclusion is that Japonica chose to buy claims which gave it unique control over the debtor and the process. With one minor exception, Japonica purchased its claims—and became a creditor—after the debtor's disclosure statement was approved. Japonica knew what it was getting into when it purchased its claims. Japonica is a voluntary claimant. If Japonica was unsatisfied by the proposed distribution, it had the option of not becoming a creditor. Japonica could have proposed its plan without buying these claims.

Japonica's actions with respect to the purchase of claims were in bad faith. Notwithstanding Japonica's allegedly longstanding interest in the debtor, Japonica filed its plan of reorganization at the eleventh hour. Notwithstanding Japonica's allegedly longstanding interest in the debtor, Japonica did not purchase significant claims until the voting period on the debtor's plan. Japonica was also at this time a proponent of a plan. . . .Votes must be designated when the court determines that the "creditor has cast his vote with an 'ulterior purpose' aimed at gaining some advantage to which he would not otherwise be entitled in his position." *In re Gilbert*, 104 Bankr. at 216. . . . Japonica's stated purpose was to take over the debtor. To do so, it was necessary for Japonica to block confirmation of the debtor's plan of reorganization. Thus, the court concludes that Japonica's actions were for an ulterior motive.

Under Chapter 11, creditors and interest holders vote for or against a plan of reorganization, after adequate disclosure, if such vote is in their best economic interests. If, as in the instant case, an outsider to the process can purchase a blocking position, those creditors and interest holders are disenfranchised. If competing plans of reorganization are pending, the court must consider the preferences of the creditors and interest holders. If a plan proponent, such as Japonica, can purchase a blocking position, the votes of the other creditors and interest holders are rendered meaningless. Moreover, Japonica, who chose to become a creditor, should not have veto control over the reorganization process. The court does not believe that such a result was intended by Congress. Therefore, for all of the reasons stated above, the court designates the votes of Japonica pursuant to 11 U.S.C. § 1126(e) in Class 2.AI.2 and Class 4.AI.2. . . .

On April 14, 1989 Japonica announced a tender offer for all claims in Class 7.AI.1, the subordinated debt, and for certain of the claims in Class 5.CH.1, Chemetron general unsecured claims. . . . Through the tender offer, Japonica acquired approximately 62 percent of the claims in Class 7.AI.1 and 36 percent of the debentures in Class 5.CH.1. . . .

Japonica, a proponent of a plan, chose an "end run" around the bankruptcy process by purchasing through its public tender offer approximately 62 percent of a class. . . . Japonica did not receive this court's approval for its tender offer. As a plan proponent, Japonica could not have solicited acceptances until a disclosure statement had been approved. 11 U.S.C. § 1125(b). Japonica's action caused discriminatory treatment among members of the same class, in violation of 11 U.S.C. § 1123(a)(4). Those who accepted the Japonica tender offer received immediate cash. Those creditors who did not would receive their distribution at a later undetermined date, pursuant to the "official" Japonica plan. Those creditors would receive potentially more cash, but subject to an undesired holdback.

During this period, Japonica had incompatible and inconsistent roles. Japonica made an offer to purchase the claims of Class 7.AI.1. Japonica was also a plan proponent with an offer to that class. The court finds that Japonica acted in bad faith by offering to provide a settlement to a class of claimholders in the absence of a confirmed plan. By doing so, Japonica did not comply with the letter or the spirit of the Bankruptcy Code. . . .

The purpose of reorganization is to offer an opportunity to maximize results for all creditors and interest holders. . . .The purpose is to increase the pool of value for all creditors and shareholders. Here, Japonica clearly attempts to deprive creditors of the control premium by a manipulation of the reorganization process through the strategic purchase of claims. Acquiring claims with the clear purpose of achieving control of the debtor, thereby earning a control profit, does not maximize the result for all creditors. Such action manipulates the process. . . .

In 1991 the Advisory Committee on the Rules of Bankruptcy Procedure amended Rule 3001(e)(2) to allow claims to be traded without a bankruptcy judge's approval. The rule change led to a threefold increase in the trading of distressed debt. The court's role is limited in theory to an adjudication of disputes regarding transfers of claims and to questions on whether the court will recognize the votes on the claim transferred.

QUESTIONS

Does Rule 3001(e)(2) change the holding in *Allegheny*? Distressed debt investors, *vultures*, readily intervene in the management of the debtor and in the plan negotiations. In the Japonica reorganization, a vulture took the next step of attempting to buy the company by buying enough claims to block the debtor's plan and secure a favorable confirmation vote on its own proposed plan. Should we encourage, discourage, or be neutral on such a takeover?

IN RE DBSD NORTH AMERICA, INC., 634 F.3d 79 (2d Cir. 2011): ". . . DISH, although not a creditor of DBSD before its filing, had purchased the claims of various creditors with an eye toward DBSD's spectrum rights. As a provider of satellite television, DISH has launched a number of its own satellites, and it also has a significant investment in TerreStar Corporation, a direct competitor of DBSD's in the developing field of hybrid satellite/terrestrial mobile communications. . . .

Shortly after DBSD filed its plan disclosure, DISH purchased all of the First Lien Debt at its full face value of $40 million . . . . As DISH admitted, it bought the First Lien Debt not just to acquire a 'market piece of paper' but also to 'be in a position to take advantage of [its claim] if things didn't go well in a restructuring.' Internal DISH communications also promoted an 'opportunity to obtain a blocking position in the [Second Lien Debt] and control the bankruptcy process for this potentially strategic asset.' In the end, DISH (through a subsidiary) purchased only $111 million of the Second Lien Debt—not nearly enough to control that class—with the small size of its stake due in part to DISH's unwillingness to buy any claims whose prior owners had already entered into an agreement to support the plan . . . .

The Loan Syndications and Trading Association (LSTA), as *amicus curiae,* argues that courts should encourage acquisitions and other strategic transactions because such transactions can benefit all parties in bankruptcy. We agree. But our holding does not 'shut[ ] the door to strategic transactions,' as the LSTA suggests. Rather, it simply limits the methods by which parties may pursue them. [The claims purchaser] DISH had every right to propose for consideration whatever strategic transaction it wanted—a right it took advantage of here—and DISH still retained this right even after it purchased its claims. All that the bankruptcy court stopped DISH from doing here was using the votes it had bought to secure an advantage in pursuing that strategic transaction.

DISH argues that, if we uphold the decision below, 'future creditors looking for potential strategic transactions with chapter 11 debtors will be deterred from exploring such deals for fear of forfeiting their rights as creditors.' But our ruling today should deter only attempts to '*obtain* a blocking position' and thereby 'control the bankruptcy process for [a] potentially strategic asset' (as DISH's own internal documents stated). We leave for another day the situation in which a *preexisting* creditor votes with strategic intentions. . . . We emphasize, moreover, that our opinion imposes no categorical prohibition on purchasing claims with acquisitive or other strategic intentions. On other facts, such purchases may be appropriate. Whether a vote has been properly designated is a fact-intensive question that must be based on the totality of the circumstances, according considerable deference to the expertise of bankruptcy judges. Having reviewed the careful and fact-specific decision of the bankruptcy court here, we find no error in its decision to designate DISH's vote as not having been cast in good faith."

CHAPTER SEVEN

THE DISCLOSURE REQUIREMENTS OF THE FEDERAL SECURITIES ACTS AND STATE LAW

■ ■ ■

A. DISCLOSURE REQUIREMENTS OF THE FEDERAL SECURITIES ACTS

1. INTRODUCTION TO MANDATORY DISCLOSURE REQUIREMENTS UNDER FEDERAL SECURITIES LAW

In the United States, the disclosure obligation of publicly traded firms is defined from the ground up by the accumulation of a constantly growing body of specific federal rules. The aggregate effect of the federal rules constitutes our mandatory disclosure system. There are other sources of disclosure obligations for publicly traded firms. Most state corporate codes[1] include minimal disclosure obligations, as does Delaware case law, which affects over one-half of our NYSE listed companies. And our organized stock trading markets include disclosure obligations in their private listing contracts. But the details of the Securities Exchange Act of 1934 (the "Exchange Act"), now heavily laden with (and even, in some cases, superseded by)[2] a thick clothing of SEC administrative rules, are the dominate source of disclosure obligations for our publicly traded companies.

The SEC rules, adopted through the formal procedures of the Administrative Procedure Act,[3] have the force of law and are themselves multi-layered: They come in the form of "Regulations," which contain individual "Rules," which refer to "Forms" or "Schedules," which in turn contain "Items" (which often cross-reference other Regulations). SEC pronouncements on how to interpret the rules in light of specific facts come in "Interpretive Releases," "No-Action Letters," agency enforcement

---

[1] See, e.g., ABA Model Bus. Corp. Act § 16.20(a) (2016 rev.) (furnishing of annual financial statements to requesting shareholders). See also Marhart v. CalMat, 1992 WL 82365, at *3 (Del. Ch.) (duty of candor under Delaware law).

[2] Schedule A of the original Exchange Act has now been replaced by SEC Regulations.

[3] The SEC publishes proposals for new rules or amendments to existing rules, holds hearings, receives written comments, and then publishes a final version of the new or amended rule.

proceedings, *amicus* briefs filed with federal courts and miscellaneous public comments by agency officials.

No General Duty to Speak: In the United States there is no general over-arching legal duty to disclose material facts, plans, strategies or other information to the trading markets. The Supreme Court articulated the principle in 1980: "When an allegation of fraud is based upon nondisclosure, there can be no fraud *absent a duty to speak*. We hold that a duty to disclose does not arise from the mere possession of non-public market information."[4] A precise formulation of when the duty to speak arises under federal law is hazardous, however, with the writer more likely to have missed some technical wrinkle than not. Nevertheless, one reasonable classification of the duty to speak could be the following.

A duty to speak arises in two contexts, the second of which is, to some degree, under the control of the issuer. First, the Exchange Act, as heavily supplemented by SEC Regulations, affirmatively requires publicly traded firms to file periodic reports, such as annual reports and quarterly reports.[5] All publicly traded firms, whether or not they solicit proxies, are also required to send a proxy statement to their shareholders in anticipation of the firm's required annual meeting.

Second, an issuer must file public reports with the SEC on the occurrence of specified events: major corporate transactions (mergers and recapitalizations, for example),[6] special shareholder meetings, the announcement of a tender offer, a response to a tender offer, a share repurchase,[7] a public offering of securities, the purchase of over 5 percent of the registered stock of another firm, and rumors affecting stock price that are attributable to the leaks or trades of corporate insiders. In this second category of disclosure obligations, some of the disclosure requirements are in specific administrative regulations and schedules and some (when the firm repurchases a small percentage of its outstanding

---

[4] Chiarella v. United States, 445 U.S. 222, 234, 100 S.Ct. 1108, 63 L.Ed.2d 348 (1980) (emphasis added). See also In re Time Warner Inc. Securities Litig., 9 F.3d 259, 267 (2d Cir. 1993) ("[A] corporation is not required to disclose a fact merely because a reasonable investor would very much like to know that fact. Rather, an omission is actionable under the securities laws only when the corporation is subject to a duty to disclose the omitted facts.").

[5] The Exchange Act requires an issuer to file annual reports on Form 10–K, which must contain a full analysis of the issuer's business, audited financial statements, disclosures on pending legal proceedings, and a management discussion and analysis (MD & A) section. Exch. Act § 13(a)(2) & Exch. Act Rule 13a–1. The Exchange Act also requires issuers to file quarterly reports on Form 10–Q. Exch. Act § 13(a)(2) & Exch. Act Rule 13a–13.

[6] These are "current reports" on Form 8–K. Included in the disclosure requirements is the entry into or termination of a "material definitive agreement(s)," the acquisition or disposition of a significant amount of assets (not in the ordinary course of business), and changes in the control of the issuer. See Exch. Act Rule 13a–11. The material definitive agreement requirement does not include the entry into non-binding agreements such as letters of intent. See *Additional Form 8–K Disclosure Requirements and Acceleration of Filing Date*, SEC Rel. No. 34–49424, 2004 WL 1258060 (Mar. 16, 2004). Issuers have four business days to file after the date the event occurs.

[7] With separate rules for a self-tender offer, a going-private transaction and a general share buy-back.

shares on the open market, for example) are contained and defined only in the case law applying the open-textured language of Rule 10b–5, the general antifraud rule of the Exchange Act.[8]

If a firm chooses to speak to the trading markets, that is, when federal law does not require the statement, Rule 10b–5 applies to require that the statement be sufficiently complete so as not to mislead. Some refer to the statements in this category as *voluntary statements*.[9] This duty to be complete is a subset of, in essence, a third category of mandatory disclosure obligations often called the *half-truth rule*.

The Half-Truth Rule: Whenever a duty to speak attaches, usually as the result of an obligation to file reports with the SEC pursuant to a specific administrative regulation or schedule, an issuer must first satisfy the subject matter requirements of whatever statute, rule, regulation or schedule is appropriate. The specific information requested is presumed material. And second, the firm must satisfy a general obligation, known among securities practitioners as the half-truth rule, to "add . . . such further material information, if any, as may be necessary to make the required statements, in the light of the circumstances under which they are made[,] not misleading."[10] In other words, a "half-truth" or a partial disclosure of facts that are literally correct but misleading in light of facts that are concealed is as culpable as an affirmative misrepresentation.[11] A definition of materiality is crucial to the doctrine.

The half-truth rule appears in other contexts defined by case law precedent as well. If the duty to speak arises from case law under Rule 10b–5 or a similar general antifraud rule, a firm must disclose all material information with any other information necessary to make the information disclosed not misleading.[12] Thus a firm, when obliged to correct market rumors originating with statements or trades by insiders, for example, must disclose information sufficient to satisfy the half-truth rule. If the duty to speak is triggered by a firm's voluntary statements, the statements must be truthful and supplemented by other information necessary to make the statements not misleading.[13]

---

8 See, e.g., Elkind v. Liggett & Myers, Inc., 635 F.2d 156 (2d Cir. 1980). This obligation has several tentacles. For example, a company has an obligation to correct inaccurate third party statements if it is somehow enmeshed with those statements. The common case involves statements by a securities analyst after a private or exclusive firm briefing. In re Aldus Sec. Lit., 1993 WL 121478 (W.D. Wash.); Syntex Corp. Sec. Lit., 1993 WL 13939795 (N.D. Cal.); Colby v. Hologic, Inc., 817 F.Supp. 204 (D. Mass. 1993).

9 Some break the categories down differently. They would include all specific schedule requirements in one, break out insider trading or a firm trading in its own securities in two, and a duty to correct or update in three. Louis Loss & Joel Seligman, FUNDAMENTALS OF SECURITIES REGULATION 790 (1995).

10 Exch. Act Rule 12b–20; see also Sec. Act Rule 408(a) (the Securities Act analog).

11 See Dale E. Barnes, Jr. & Constance E. Bagley, *Great Expectations: Risk Management Through Risk Disclosure*, 1 STAN. J.L. BUS. & FIN. 155 (1994) (discussion of half-truth rule).

12 Sec. Act § 17(a)(2) & Sec. Act Rule 408(a); Exch. Act Rules 10b–5 (2) & 15cl–2(b).

13 Exch. Act Rule 10b–5(2).

The SEC occasionally seems to imply that the half-truth rule should be liberally applied to its Forms and Schedules. Under this view, the specific items requested in a Form or Schedule are presumed significant and material, a baseline for an appropriate filing, and a firm should add all other information that is material to investors to the baseline document. Those courts that have addressed the issue specifically, and there are not many, have refused to so read the language.

Courts have long recognized that the half-truth rule when applied to SEC Forms or Schedules cannot be pressed to its literal boundaries. In the context of specific disclosure Schedules, the half-truth doctrine, if read literally, could require an issuer to supplement any Schedule with all facts on the issuer material to investors regardless of the specific, identified items of information required by the Schedule. In theory, any non-public material information, although not covered by a specific item in a Form or Schedule, could, if disclosed, make a given annual or quarterly report, in a sense, more accurate or more complete and "not misleading." Whenever a moderate number of reasonably able investors are surprised by business developments that could not be gleaned from a reading of the historically-based SEC filings, and those developments were known at the time of the filing by one or more senior managers, one can make the argument that a firm's disclosure of that information would have made the filings "not misleading."[14] If the half-truth rule is so understood, all SEC required filings, whether periodic reports or event-triggered reports, would be expanded into occasions for a disclosure of all material facts on all business operations.

Courts seem to limit the doctrine to one requiring a disclosure only of facts that specifically contradict the statements in Forms or Schedules (or in press releases) rather than one requiring the issuer "to state every fact about stock offered that a prospective purchaser might like to know or that might, if known, tend to influence his decision."[15] Information that relates only to quantification, the gravity or significance of a public statement, apparently does not have to be disclosed. The First Circuit has noted, for example, that the half-truth rule

> does not mean that by revealing one fact about a product, one must reveal all others that, too, would be interesting, market-wise. . . . Disclosing that Polavision was being sold below cost was not misleading by reason of not saying how much below. Nor was it misleading not to report the number of sales, or that they were below expectations.[16]

---

[14] The temptation is strongest to so read the rule when the historical facts portray a company say, with a stolid consistent past earnings history, and the undisclosed information is a management-contemplated business strategy that portends a radical change of path.

[15] Otis & Co. v. SEC, 106 F.2d 579, 582 (6th Cir. 1939).

[16] Backman v. Polaroid Corp., 910 F.2d 10, 16 (1st Cir. 1990).

No doubt investors reading the "below cost" statement would be better informed if the statement was quantified—40 percent as opposed to 5 percent below cost is significant—or if the reason for the phenomenon were identified—lack of consumer demand as opposed to solvable problems in production. And, if better informed, investors would not have been so surprised, perhaps, by the later disclosure of the products' disastrous commercial failure. But the half-truth doctrine does not entitle investors to such information.

The courts' reluctance to interpret the half-truth rule broadly is understandable. First, it is curious at minimum (and perhaps a bit devious) for a federal agency, the SEC, to promulgate in excruciating detail pages and pages of lists of specific requirements and then, after a firm makes a several-hundred-page filing in accord with the lists, announce that the filing is not sufficient after the fact because the filing does not satisfy a general one-sentence rule containing a catch-all requirement for other material information. Moreover, the SEC's after-the-fact judgment usually brings with it a substantial risk of litigation exposure. In the details of its complex Schedules, the SEC has the opportunity and ought to ask for whatever information it wants with specificity.

Second, the defendants usually have a colorable business justification for delaying disclosure of the information in issue in the case. Courts find little or no guidance in the SEC language for dealing with these justifications, some of which have considerable appeal. With a narrow interpretation of the half-truth rule, courts avoid the problems.

Third, to some extent, the courts' practice is self-enforcing. As long as investors know of the courts' narrow definition and application of the half-truth rule, however crafted, they cannot claim to be misled by published Forms and Schedules. Investors should come to understand the limits of any firm disclosure and would themselves be at fault if they expect too much of firm reports in light of the courts' announced practice.[17]

It is worth noting that a class of cases exists in which the courts do appear to put a broad gloss on the half-truth obligation. The federal courts do read the half-truth language broadly if the duty to speak is triggered by firm or insider trading under Exchange Act Rule 10b–5. In such cases, all material information on the firm must be available to third parties on the opposite side of the trade. Here the firm's option is not to trade, or to disclose fully in the context of a trade. The distinction makes sense. The

---

[17] This illustrates that an important hidden component of most half-truth arguments (and this applies to the duty to update as well) is what the investment community reasonably understands (based on historical custom and usage) certain types of disclosures to mean. Investors understand that a disclosure of past earnings over five years is not a promise by managers to keep past business plans and strategies, which generated the historical earnings picture, more or less in place for the future (to continue the earnings trend). This is not an inherent truism, but the result of business custom and practice in our secondary trading markets. But an explicit projection of future earnings consistent with a past earnings pattern does imply that there will be no radical change in business plans. See, e.g., Weiner v. Quaker Oats Co., 129 F.3d 310 (1997).

ease of avoiding the disclosure obligation entirely (by not trading) is not replicated when a firm owes the SEC a periodic report, for example.

2. MATERIALITY

TSC INDUSTRIES, INC. V. NORTHWAY, INC.

Supreme Court of the United States, 1976.
426 U.S. 438, 96 S.Ct. 2126, 48 L.Ed.2d 757.

MR. JUSTICE MARSHALL delivered the opinion of the Court.

The proxy rules promulgated by the Securities and Exchange Commission under the Securities Exchange Act of 1934 bar the use of proxy statements that are false or misleading with respect to the presentation or omission of material facts. We are called upon to consider the definition of a material fact under those rules, and the appropriateness of resolving the question of materiality by summary judgment in this case.

* * *

The dispute in this case centers on the acquisition of petitioner TSC Industries, Inc., by petitioner National Industries, Inc. In February 1969 National acquired 34 percent of TSC's voting securities by purchase from Charles E. Schmidt and his family. Schmidt, who had been TSC's founder and principal shareholder, promptly resigned along with his son from TSC's board of directors. Thereafter, five National nominees were placed on TSC's board; and Stanley R. Yarmuth, National's president and chief executive officer, became chairman of the TSC board, and Charles F. Simonelli, National's executive vice president, became chairman of the TSC executive committee. On October 16, 1969, the TSC board, with the attending National nominees abstaining, approved a proposal to liquidate and sell all of TSC's assets to National. The proposal in substance provided for the exchange of TSC common and Series 1 preferred stock for National Series B preferred stock and warrants. On November 12, 1969, TSC and National issued a joint proxy statement to their shareholders, recommending approval of the proposal. The proxy solicitation was successful, TSC was placed in liquidation and dissolution, and the exchange of shares was effected.

This is an action brought by respondent Northway, a TSC shareholder, against TSC and National, claiming that their joint proxy statement was incomplete and materially misleading in violation of § 14(a) of the Securities Exchange Act of 1934 . . . and Rules 14a–3 and 14a–9 . . . promulgated thereunder. . . . The Rule 14a–9 claim, insofar as it concerns us, is that TSC and National omitted from the proxy statement material facts relating to the degree of National's control over TSC and the favorability of the terms of the proposal to TSC shareholders.

* * *

. . . In a suit challenging the sufficiency under § 14(a) and Rule 14a–9 of a proxy statement soliciting votes in favor of a merger, we held that there was no need to demonstrate that the alleged defect in the proxy statement actually had a decisive effect on the voting. So long as the misstatement or omission was material, the causal relation between violation and injury is sufficiently established, we concluded, if "the proxy solicitation itself . . . was an essential link in the accomplishment of the transaction." 396 U.S., at 385 . . . .

The question of materiality, it is universally agreed, is an objective one, involving the significance of an omitted or misrepresented fact to a reasonable investor. . . .

* * *

. . . As an abstract proposition, the most desirable role for a court in a suit of this sort, coming after the consummation of the proposed transaction, would perhaps be to determine whether in fact the proposal would have been favored by the shareholders and consummated in the absence of any misstatement or omission. But as we recognized in *Mills*, . . . such matters are not subject to determination with certainty. Doubts as to the critical nature of information misstated or omitted will be commonplace. And particularly in view of the prophylactic purpose of the Rule and the fact that the content of the proxy statement is within management's control, it is appropriate that these doubts be resolved in favor of those the statute is designed to protect. . . .

We are aware, however, that the disclosure policy embodied in the proxy regulations is not without limit. . . . Some information is of such dubious significance that insistence on its disclosure may accomplish more harm than good. The potential liability for a Rule 14a–9 violation can be great indeed, and if the standard of materiality is unnecessarily low, not only may the corporation and its management be subjected to liability for insignificant omissions or misstatements, but also management's fear of exposing itself to substantial liability may cause it simply to bury the shareholders in an avalanche of trivial information—a result that is hardly conducive to informed decisionmaking. . . .

The general standard of materiality that we think best comports with the policies of Rule 14a–9 is as follows: An omitted fact is material if there is a substantial likelihood that a reasonable shareholder would consider it important in deciding how to vote. This standard is fully consistent with *Mills'* general description of materiality as a requirement that "the defect have a significant *propensity* to affect the voting process." It does not require proof of a substantial likelihood that disclosure of the omitted fact would have caused the reasonable investor to change his vote. What the standard does contemplate is a showing of a substantial likelihood that, under all the circumstances, the omitted fact would have assumed actual significance in the deliberations of the reasonable shareholder. Put another way, there must be a substantial likelihood that the disclosure of the omitted fact would have been viewed by the reasonable investor as having significantly altered the "total mix" of information made available. . . .

* * *

The Court of Appeals concluded that two omitted facts relating to National's potential influence, or control, over the management of TSC were material as a matter of law. First, the proxy statement failed to state that at the time the statement was issued, the chairman of the TSC board of directors was Stanley Yarmuth, National's president and chief executive officer, and the chairman of the TSC executive committee was Charles Simonelli, National's executive vice president. Second, the statement did not disclose that in filing reports required by the SEC, both TSC and National had indicated that National "may be deemed to be a 'parent' of TSC as that term is defined in the Rules and Regulations under the Securities Act of 1933." . . . The Court of Appeals noted that TSC shareholders were relying on the TSC board of directors to negotiate on their behalf for the best possible rate of exchange with National. It then concluded that the omitted facts were material because they were "persuasive indicators that the TSC board was in fact under the control of National, and that National thus 'sat on both sides of the table' in setting the terms of the exchange." . . .

We do not agree that the omission of these facts, when viewed against the disclosures contained in the proxy statement, warrants the entry of summary judgment against TSC and National on this record. . . .

The proxy statement prominently displayed the facts that National owned 34 percent of the outstanding shares in TSC, and that no other person owned more than 10 percent. . . . It also prominently revealed that 5 out of 10 TSC directors were National nominees, and it recited the positions of those National nominees with National—indicating, among other things, that Stanley Yarmuth was president and a director of National, and that Charles Simonelli was executive vice president and a director of National. . . . These disclosures clearly revealed the nature of National's relationship with TSC and alerted the reasonable shareholder to the fact that National exercised a degree of influence over TSC. In view of these disclosures, we certainly cannot say that the additional facts that Yarmuth was chairman of the TSC board of directors and Simonelli chairman of its executive committee were, on this record, so obviously important that reasonable minds could not differ on their materiality.

Nor can we say that it was materially misleading as a matter of law for TSC and National to have omitted reference to SEC filings indicating that National "may be deemed to be a parent of TSC." As we have already noted, both the District Court and the Court of Appeals concluded, in denying summary judgment on the Rule 14a–3 claim, that there was a genuine issue of fact as to whether National actually controlled TSC at the time of the proxy solicitation. We must assume for present purposes, then, that National did not control TSC. On that assumption, TSC and National obviously had no duty to state without qualification that control did exist. If the proxy statements were to disclose the conclusory statements in the SEC filings that National "may be deemed to be a parent of TSC," then it would have been appropriate, if not necessary, for the statement to have included a disclaimer of National control over TSC or a disclaimer of knowledge as to whether National controlled TSC. The net contribution of including the contents of the SEC filings accompanied by such disclaimers is not of such obvious significance, in view of the other facts contained in the proxy statement, that their exclusion renders the statement materially misleading as a matter of law. . . .

* * *

The Court of Appeals also found that the failure to disclose two sets of facts rendered the proxy statement materially deficient in its presentation of the favorability of the terms of the proposed transaction to TSC shareholders. The first omission was of information, described by the Court of Appeals as "bad news" for TSC shareholders, contained in a letter from an investment banking firm whose earlier favorable opinion of the fairness of the proposed transaction was reported in the proxy statement. The second omission related to purchases of National common stock by National and by Madison Fund, Inc., a large mutual fund, during the two years prior to the issuance of the proxy statement.

* * *

The proxy statement revealed that the investment banking firm of Hornblower & Weeks-Hemphill, Noyes had rendered a favorable opinion on the fairness to TSC shareholders of the terms for the exchange of TSC shares for National securities. In that opinion, the proxy statement explained, the firm had considered, "among other things, the current market prices of the securities of both corporations, the high redemption price of the National Series B preferred stock, the dividend and debt service requirements of both corporations, the substantial premium over current market values represented by the securities being offered to TSC stockholders, and the increased dividend income." . . .

* * *

The closing price of the National warrants on November 7, 1969, was, as indicated in the proxy statement, $5.25. The TSC shareholders were misled, the Court of Appeals concluded, by the proxy statement's failure to disclose that in a communication two weeks after its favorable opinion letter, the Hornblower firm revealed that its determination of the fairness of the offer to TSC was based on the conclusion that the value of the warrants involved in the transaction would not be their current market price, but approximately $3.50. If the warrants were valued at $3.50 rather than $5.25, and the other securities valued at the November 7 closing price, the court figured, the apparent premium would be substantially reduced—from $3.23 (27 percent) to $1.48 (12 percent) in the case of the TSC preferred, and from $2.94 (22 percent) to $0.31 (2 percent) in the case of TSC common. . . .

It would appear, however, that the subsequent communication from the Hornblower firm, which the Court of Appeals felt contained "bad news," contained nothing new at all. At the TSC board of directors meeting held on October 16, 1969, the date of the initial Hornblower opinion letter, Blancke Noyes, a TSC director and a partner in the Hornblower firm, had pointed out the likelihood of a decline in the market price of National warrants with the issuance of the additional warrants involved in the exchange, and reaffirmed his conclusion that the exchange offer was a fair one nevertheless. The subsequent Hornblower letter, signed by Mr. Noyes, purported merely to explain the basis of the calculations underlying the favorable opinion rendered in the October 16 letter. "In advising TSC as to the fairness of the offer from [National]," Mr. Noyes wrote, "we concluded that the warrants in question had a value of approximately $3.50." . . . On its face, then, the subsequent letter from Hornblower does not appear to have contained anything to alter the favorable opinion rendered in the October 16 letter—including the conclusion that the securities being offered to TSC shareholders represented a "substantial premium over current market values."

The real question, though, is not whether the subsequent Hornblower letter contained anything that altered the Hornblower opinion in any way. It is, rather, whether the advice given at the October 16 meeting, and reduced to more precise terms in the subsequent Hornblower letter—that there might be a decline in the market price of the National warrants—had to be disclosed in order to clarify the import of the proxy statement's reference to "the substantial premium over current market values represented by the securities being offered to TSC stockholders." We note initially that the proxy statement referred to the substantial premium as but one of several factors considered by Hornblower in rendering its favorable opinion of the terms of exchange. Still, we cannot assume that a TSC shareholder would focus only on the "bottom line" of the opinion to the exclusion of the considerations that produced it.

TSC and National insist that the reference to a substantial premium required no clarification or supplementation, for the reason that there was a substantial premium even if the National warrants are assumed to have been worth $3.50. In reaching the contrary conclusion, the Court of Appeals, they contend, ignored the rise in price of TSC securities between early October 1969, when the exchange ratio was set, and November 7, 1969—a rise in price that they suggest was a result of the favorable exchange ratio's becoming public knowledge. When the proxy statement was mailed, TSC and National contend, the market price of TSC securities already reflected a portion of the premium to which Hornblower had referred in rendering its favorable opinion of the terms of exchange. Thus, they note that Hornblower assessed the fairness of the proposed transaction by reference to early October market prices of TSC preferred, TSC common, and National preferred. On the basis of those prices and a $3.50 value for the National warrants involved in the exchange, TSC and National contend that the premium was substantial. Each share of TSC preferred, selling in early October at $11, would bring National preferred stock and warrants worth $13.10—for a premium of $2.10, or 19 percent. And each share of TSC common, selling in early October at $11.63, would bring National preferred stock and warrants worth $13.25—for a premium of $1.62, or 14 percent. We certainly cannot say as a matter of law that these premiums were not substantial. And if, as we must assume in considering the appropriateness of summary judgment, the increase in price of TSC's securities from early October to November 7 reflected in large part the market's reaction to the terms of the proposed exchange, it was not materially misleading as a matter of law for the proxy statement to refer to the existence of a substantial premium.

There remains the possibility, however, that although TSC and National may be correct in urging the existence of a substantial premium based upon a $3.50 value for the National warrants and the early October market prices of the other securities involved in the transaction, the proxy statement misled the TSC shareholder to calculate a premium substantially in excess of that premium. The premiums apparent from early October market prices and a $3.50 value for the National warrants—19 percent on TSC preferred and 14 percent on TSC common—are certainly less than those that would be derived through use of the November 7 closing prices listed in the proxy statement—27 percent on TSC preferred and 22 percent on TSC common. But we are unwilling to sustain a grant of summary judgment to Northway on that basis. To do so we would have to conclude as a matter of law, first, that the proxy statement would have misled the TSC shareholder to calculate his premium on the basis of November 7 market prices, and second, that the difference between that premium and that which would be apparent from early October prices and a $3.50 value for the National warrants was material. These are questions we think best left to the trier of fact.

* * *

The final omission that concerns us relates to purchases of National common stock by National and by Madison Fund, Inc., a mutual fund. Northway notes that National's board chairman was a director of Madison, and that Madison's president and chief executive, Edward Merkle, was employed by National pursuant to an agreement obligating him to provide at least one day per month for such duties as National might request.[19] Northway contends that the proxy statement, having called the TSC shareholders' attention to the market prices of the securities involved in the proposed transaction, should have revealed substantial purchases of National common stock made by National and Madison during the two years prior to the issuance of the proxy statement.[20] In particular, Northway contends that the TSC shareholders should, as a matter of law, have been informed that National and Madison purchases accounted for 8.5 percent of all reported transactions in National common stock during the period between National's acquisition of the Schmidt interests and the proxy solicitation. The theory behind Northway's contention is that disclosure of these purchases would have pointed to the existence, or at least the possible existence, of conspiratorial manipulation of the price of National common stock, which would have had an effect on the market price of the National preferred stock and warrants involved in the proposed transaction. . . .

* * *

In short, while the Court of Appeals viewed the purchases as significant only insofar as they suggested manipulation of the price of National securities, and acknowledged the existence of a genuine issue of fact as to whether there was any manipulation, the court nevertheless required disclosure to enable the shareholders to decide whether there was manipulation or not.

The Court of Appeals' approach would sanction the imposition of civil liability on a theory that undisclosed information may *suggest* the existence of market manipulation, even if the responsible corporate officials knew that there was in fact no market manipulation. We do not agree that Rule 14a–9 requires such a result. Rule 14a–9 is concerned only with whether a proxy statement is misleading with respect to its presentation of material facts. If, as we must assume on a motion for summary judgment, there was no collusion or manipulation whatsoever in the National and Madison purchases—that is, if the purchases were made wholly independently for proper corporate and investment purposes, then by Northway's implicit acknowledgment they had no bearing on the soundness and reliability of

---

[19] Employed in 1967, Merkle initially received a salary of $2,500 per year (increased in 1968 to $12,000) and an option to purchase 10,000 shares of National common stock. App. 520, 522.

[20] In a table entitled "Statements of Consolidated Stockholders' Equity," the proxy statement indicated that National acquired approximately 83,000 shares of its own common stock in 1968 and 1969, while it sold approximately 67,000 shares under stock option plans, employment agreements, and warrants. *Id.*, at 324, 330. The proxy statement did not disclose that Madison acquired approximately 170,000 shares of National common during the two-year period, or that approximately one year prior to the proxy solicitation Madison acquired $2 million in National debentures convertible to common.

the market prices listed in the proxy statement,[22] and it cannot have been materially misleading to fail to disclose them.[23]

That is not to say, of course, that the SEC could not enact a rule specifically requiring the disclosure of purchases such as were involved in this case, without regard to whether the purchases can be shown to have been collusive or manipulative. We simply hold that if liability is to be imposed in this case upon a theory that it was misleading to fail to disclose purchases suggestive of market manipulation, there must be some showing that there was in fact market manipulation. . . .

* * *

In summary, none of the omissions claimed to have been in violation of Rule 14a–9 were, so far as the record reveals, materially misleading as a matter of law, and Northway was not entitled to partial summary judgment. . . .

QUESTIONS

1. On the question of the fairness opinion issued by the investment banking firm to the TSC board, it was clear that the opinion was an important part of the proxy statement, justifying the exchange ratio. Yet the opinion was vague, not revealing the amount of the premium found to be "fair." This case is yet another example of the slippery language used by investment bankers to dress up a pitiful product; they often say much less than they appear to say. Managers go along because they too are intent on "selling the deal" to shareholders. On the facts of the case, regardless of whether the investment banker's second letter, which was not disclosed to shareholders, qualified or just explained the earlier fairness opinion, which was disclosed, shouldn't shareholders of TSC have been told the amount of the exchange premium that the investment banker thought to be "substantial"? Is a 2 percent premium substantial? A 15 percent premium? A 25 percent premium? Apparently the language covered both a 14 percent and a 22 percent premium on the TSC common (and both a 19 percent and 27 percent premium on the TSC preferred).

---

[22] There has been no suggestion that the purchases in question would have any significance if there was in fact no manipulation or collusion, although there may perhaps be such a claim in another case. Nor is there any indication that manipulation or collusion are matters as to whose existence National might have been left in doubt at the time the proxy statement was issued. *Cf.* n.16, *supra*.

[23] In holding that the failure to disclose the National and Madison purchases violated Rule 14a–9 as a matter of law, the Court of Appeals not only found it unnecessary to consider whether there was in fact any collusion or manipulation, but also found it unnecessary to consider whether the purchases had any significant effect on the price of National common stock or, more pertinently, the price of the National preferred stock and warrants involved in the proposed transaction. Since we find the existence of a genuine issue of fact with respect to whether there was manipulation sufficient to bar summary judgment, it is unnecessary to consider the remaining aspects of the Court of Appeals' decision.

How credible is the court's position that shareholders would not focus on the "bottom line" premium in a fairness opinion?

Why were the predictions of a $3.50 warrant price at closing, which the bankers claim they used in the October fairness opinion and which were the basis for the TSC board's acceptance of the deal, not disclosed (along with the misleading November 7 market prices)? What was the reason for the difference between the value of the warrants on November 7 ($5.25) and the predicted value of the warrants at closing ($3.50)? Should not the fairness opinion have specifically disclosed and estimated the dilutive effect of the acquisition on the value of the warrants?

Note the timing problems in the fairness opinion. When the investment bankers wrote the fairness opinion on the exchange ratio of the stock swap, they compared existing market prices (taking into account the dilution effects of the swap) of the two firms and found that TSC shareholders would receive a premium. Once the deal was announced, it appears that National stock prices (including the warrants) declined and TSC stock prices rose. Does this suggest a reason for the investment bankers' letter of "clarification"?

2. The most interesting part of the case is perhaps the court's treatment of the stock purchases by National itself and by the Madison Mutual Fund. The proxy statement did detail the amount of National purchases but did not "call attention" to the purchases, presumably by stating the percentage of outstanding stock purchased. The proxy statement did not detail the Madison purchases at all.

The court reversed a summary judgment for the plaintiffs on the disclosure. The movant had to take the position that it should prevail even when admitting, for the sake of argument, that the purchases were not manipulative or collusive and had no effect on National stock prices. The court rejected the argument that voting shareholders had a right to judge for themselves the possibility of stock price manipulation. At the same time the court somewhat sheepishly admitted that the Securities and Exchange Commission could require such disclosures under its authority to pass rules detailing instances of fraud. This admission was a recognition by the court that stock dealings by insiders (here National's board chair was a director of Madison) and the firm itself are often of substantial interest to investors. The strict language of the materiality test in *TSC Industries*, often quoted, seems belied by the lenient holding on the specific facts of the case.

3. The case's real legacy is its separation of materiality from the potential effect on conduct. Information is material even if it would not change a reasonable investor's vote (and later decision to buy or sell) as long as a reasonable investor would like to have it. Is this sound policy? Reasonable investors want most all the information they can get. This very low threshold for materiality has led to some very odd decisions as courts work around the requirements of the *TSC Industries* language.

LEWIS V. CHRYSLER CORPORATION

United States Court of Appeals, Third Circuit, 1991.
949 F.2d 644.

NYGARD, CIRCUIT JUDGE.

* * *

In February 1988 Chrysler adopted a shareholder rights plan, commonly known as a "poison pill." . . .

* * *

In 1989, Chrysler amended the Plan to reduce the 30 percent threshold of an acquiring entity's beneficial ownership in Chrysler needed to trigger exercise of shareholder rights under the Plan to 20 percent. . . . The 1989 amendments also added an additional "flip-in" event. . . .

* * *

On December 14, 1990, Chrysler issued a press release which announced further amendments to the Plan. . . . This Release, which is the focus of appellants' federal securities fraud claim, read as follows:

* * *

> . . . Chrysler Corporation announced today it had been informed that Mr. Kirk Kerkorian had acquired in excess of nine percent of Chrysler's outstanding common stock.
>
> Chrysler said that Mr. Kerkorian's stock purchase was not solicited by the Company.
>
> * * *
>
> . . . Chrysler's Board of directors today adopted amendments to the Company's share purchase rights plan.
>
> * * *
>
> The Company said: "The amendments adopted today *are intended to enhance the ability of Chrysler's Board to act in the best interest of all the Company's shareholders if someone should seek to obtain a position of control or substantial influence over Chrysler.*"
>
> (Emphasis in amended complaint)

Appellant alleges that the amended Plan renders a substantial outside acquisition of Chrysler common stock economically unfeasible and prohibitively expensive; and that the Plan gives Chrysler's board unilateral power to block a takeover whether or not it would be in the stockholders' best interests, if the acquiror is unwilling to meet the personal demands of the board members. . . . Allegedly too, the last amendments to the Plan changed the nature of stockholders' investments in Chrysler . . . , chilled interest in Chrysler stock, deterred Kerkorian and other investors from making future purchases of common shares, and effectively caps the price at which Chrysler stock is traded . . . —all of which has or will cause economic damage to Chrysler stockholders. . . .

* * *

Appellant alleges another fraudulent statement is attributable to Chrysler management: allegedly, Chrysler board member Lutz was quoted on December 19, 1990, in *The Wall Street Journal* "as stating that stiffening the Poison Pill was the 'prudent thing to do' because he was not sure that Kerkorian's intentions would not be hostile to current management." . . .

* * *

. . . First, contrary to appellant's allegation . . . , the plain language of the Release did not portray the amended Plan as being in the shareholders' best interests. The Release said only that the amendments were "*intended to enhance the ability* of Chrysler's Board *to act in the best interest* of all the Company's shareholders *if someone should seek to obtain control . . . over Chrysler*." It did not pronounce upon the December 14, 1990, amendments in terms of shareholder interests—it said merely that the Plan was amended to give Chrysler's board of directors increased wherewithal to act in the shareholders' interest in the future. The Release did not inform investors that, by amending the Plan, Chrysler had or necessarily would ever act in shareholders' best interests.

* * *

Second, the Release did not impose on Chrysler a duty to disclose how the amended Plan benefits management. Chrysler's failure to say how management might use the amended Plan to its own advantage is not an actionable omission of material fact because the investing public is charged with "knowledge of information of which they reasonably should be aware", which includes "the 'universal' interest of corporate officers and directors in maintaining corporate control." *Warner Communications Inc. v. Murdoch,* 581 F.Supp. 1482, 1492 (D.Del.1984). Knowing that, and also the Release which accurately described the substance of the amendments, Chrysler shareholders cannot prevail on the theory they were misled about the possibility management might use the amended Plan to frustrate an outside effort to wrest control of the company.

The claim that Chrysler was obligated to disclose that the amendments benefitted management is, in effect, a claim that Chrysler misrepresented the amendments by failing to reveal management adopted them as part of its entrenchment scheme. While management motives in changing the Plan may have been self-serving as alleged, Chrysler's failure to disclose management's entrenchment scheme is not actionable under the federal securities laws.

"The unclean heart of a director is not actionable, whether or not it is 'disclosed', unless the impurities are translated into actionable deeds or omissions both objective and external." *Biesenbach* v. *Guenther,* 588 F.2d 400, 402 (3d Cir.1978). "[C]orporate officers and directors do not violate the federal securities laws by failing to disclose an entrenchment motive or scheme underlying their actions." *Warner Communications,* 581 F.Supp. at 1490. Indeed, "the decision to resist a takeover is within the scope of directors' state law fiduciary duties, and there is no federal securities law duty to disclose one's motives in undertaking such resistance." *Panter v. Marshall Field & Co.,* 646 F.2d 271, 290 (7th Cir.), *cert. denied,* 454 U.S. 1092, 102 S.Ct. 658, 70 L.Ed.2d 631 (1981). This is because "the general rule [is] that the federal securities laws do not impose a duty upon parties to publicly admit the culpability of their actions." *Warner Communications,* 581 F.Supp. at 1490.

The policy considerations underlying the general rule are as follows:

> First, in the absence of such a rule, parties would be placed in the untenable position of either publicly confessing their potential misconduct before their guilt is properly determined by a court, or incurring liability for damages resulting from their failure to disclose the misconduct. Second, absent such a rule, instances of misconduct which do not constitute securities fraud but which constitute violations of state law, would, nevertheless, often give rise to a 10b–5 claim for failure to disclose the misconduct. As a result, the state law claim would effectively be boot-strapped into a 10b–5 claim and brought into the federal courts for resolution, circumventing the federalism considerations underlying *Santa Fe Industries, Inc. v. Green* [citation omitted]. Third, the rule does not significantly impede the flow of material information to investors. The rule limits only the duty to publicly admit to misconduct; it does not limit a party's duty to disclose all material facts relating to the party's actions, including those that might relate to misconduct.

Id. Accordingly, appellant "may not 'bootstrap' a state law claim into a federal case 'by alleging that the disclosure philosophy of the statute obligates defendants to reveal either the culpability of their activities, or their impure motives for entering the allegedly improper transaction.'" *Kademian v. Ladish Co.,* 792 F.2d 614, 622 (7th Cir.1986).

For the same reasons, we reject appellant's argument that if the Release affirmatively portrayed the amendments as being in the shareholders' best interests, Chrysler became obligated to reveal that the Plan would facilitate management's entrenchment interests. *See Biesenbach,* 588 F.2d at 402 (management statement that transaction was in shareholders' interest when allegedly it was not does not support securities fraud claim); *see also Kademian,* 792 F.2d at 623–624 (no duty to disclose true purpose or motives for corporate transaction even following express statement of other purported reasons for same, as long as there has been no false allegation of factual matter).

Third, contrary to the allegation . . . , the Release did accurately describe the substance of the amendments' effects on shareholder and management rights under the Plan. Since shareholders are charged with knowledge that "companies almost invariably engage in defensive tactics when faced with an undesired takeover bid", *Warner Communications, Inc.,* 581 F.Supp. at 1492, we conclude the Release did not deceive investors about how Chrysler's board could use its rights under the amended Plan to thwart a takeover of the company and deprive Chrysler shareholders of the opportunity to sell their shares for a "control premium".

Fourth, Chrysler's failure to "disclose the cost to shareholders of the amendment" is not actionable under § 10(b) and Rule 10b–5. While "[t]he task of determining whether a given omission is material is especially difficult when the plaintiff alleges nondisclosure of 'soft' information . . . such as opinions, motives, intentions, or forward looking statements, such as projections, estimates and forecasts", *Craftmatic,* 890 F.2d at 642—and even though the ultimate materiality of an omission should not be decided as a matter of law unless "reasonable minds could not differ", *id.* at 641—nevertheless, we have no difficulty concluding as a matter of law that any management estimate of "the cost" to Chrysler shareholders of the amendments would not be material for § 10(b) and Rule 10b–5 purposes.

Pre-planned defensive strategies like the Plan "are inherently contingent in nature." *Warner Communications,* 581 F.Supp. at 1491. It follows that estimates of the amended Plan's financial effects on shareholder wealth would be wholly speculative and depend upon the Plan's actual operation in the context of some as yet undeveloped future attempt to acquire control of Chrysler in the face of the Plan. Understandably, Chrysler management never talked publicly about the amendments' future financial impact on shareholder wealth.

We hold that any prediction on December 14, 1990, of the Plan amendments' "cost to shareholders" would have been so speculative and unreliable as to be immaterial as a matter of law, and the failure to make such a prediction cannot be the basis for finding a securities fraud violation. *See Craftmatic,* 890 F.2d at 644. If Chrysler's board could be liable for that omission, then companies like Chrysler would be forced to either speculate on matters of future valuation, or else forgo any public announcement of important corporate developments like the Plan amendment in this case. We will not impose such a rule.

With respect to Director Lutz's alleged statement reported in *The Wall Street Journal,* we hold it does not constitute a § 10(b) or Rule 10b–5 violation. Lutz's statement, that the amendments were "prudent" in terms of management interests because Kerkorian might be "hostile to current management," cannot be a misrepresentation of material fact because Lutz's statement is consistent with appellant's allegations (which we must accept as true) that management's entrenchment motives prompted the amendments and they benefit *only* management. . . . In other words, Lutz's statement reflects rather than misrepresents the facts alleged. For the same reason, Lutz's omission to say the amendments "were prudent to protect the Company or its stockholders" . . . cannot be a fraud on the shareholders.

* * *

[The Court granted summary judgment for the defendants.]

3. PLEADING STANDARDS: THE PSLRA

As the ease of satisfying the materiality standard stimulated plaintiff's litigation, Congress attempted to rein in the resulting litigation explosion with tighter pleading standards set forth in the Private Securities Litigation Reform Act of 1995 (PSLRA).

FLAHERTY & CRUMRINE PREFERRED INCOME FUND, INC. V. TXU CORP.

United States Court of Appeals, Fifth Circuit, 2009.
565 F.3d 200.

BENAVIDES, CIRCUIT JUDGE:

Appellants . . . filed a securities fraud class action and individual fraud claims against Appellees TXU Corporation ("TXU") and its former CEO John Wilder ("Wilder") for allegedly making material misrepresentations and omissions of fact in connection with a self-tender offer to purchase certain convertible TXU securities (the "tender offer") in 2004. Specifically, Appellants alleged that Appellees fraudulently misrepresented the timing and magnitude of a planned stock repurchase program and dividend increase in order to induce the Appellants to participate in the tender offer. The district court dismissed Appellants' fraud claims alleged under Sections 10(b) and 14(e) of the Securities Exchange Act and SEC Rule 10b–5 . . . for failure to state a claim under the heightened pleading standards applicable to securities fraud claims. We affirm the judgment of the district court.

* * *

Appellants are three investment funds (F&C) and an individual plaintiff (Haiduk), all of whom owned convertible TXU securities called TXU Corporate Units (the "Corporate Units") and TXU Income PRIDES (the "PRIDES"). Both classes of securities were traded on the New York Stock Exchange and were convertible into TXU common stock.

Prior to the tender offer, Wilder, TXU's CEO, had implemented a three-phase restructuring program aimed at improving TXU's business. On May 18, 2004, approximately four months before the tender offer, TXU issued a press release outlining its view of the company's financial restructuring program. The press release indicated that TXU did not anticipate a dividend increase until 2006, when certain financial benchmarks were reached, but noted that TXU's Board of Directors (the "Board") might consider other relevant factors in determining when or if to authorize a dividend increase . . . .

On September 15, 2004, TXU announced that it was offering to purchase up to 11,433,285 outstanding Corporate Units and up to 8,700,000 outstanding PRIDES. Appellants collectively held 530,000 Corporate Units and 5,000 PRIDES prior to the tender offer. Investors holding the outstanding securities had the option to tender their securities to TXU or retain them, and Appellants were among the roughly 65% of investors who accepted the tender offer and sold their securities back to TXU. The price offered for the securities in the tender offer was $52.28 for each Corporate Unit and $52.39 for each PRIDE. The tender offer purchase price was determined by applying a factor to the twenty-day weighted average price of TXU common stock between September 20, 2004, and October 8, 2004. The tender price was higher than the market price for the securities at the time of the tender offer. The offer itself (as well as forms filed with the SEC and the associated press release) contained the following language concerning the dividend policy:

> . . . As a part of its capital management and restructuring program and considering current business and market conditions, TXU Corp.'s management is evaluating whether it should recommend to the TXU Corp. Board of Directors that they reevaluate TXU Corp.'s current common stock dividend policy. TXU Corp. cannot predict the outcome of management's evaluation, when, if at all, management would make a recommendation to the Board of Directors to change the current common stock dividend policy, or what management's recommendation might be. In addition to any recommendation from management, the Board of Directors may consider other relevant factors in determining if and when to make a change in TXU Corp.'s common stock dividend policy.

* * *

. . . On October 19, 2004, six days after the end of the tender offer period, TXU management provided materials to the Board proposing a change in dividend policy, and on October 21, 2004, management recommended a 350% increase of the annual dividend on common stock and a 400% increase in the stock repurchase program. . . . On October 22, 2004, the Board approved the dividend increase and the stock repurchase program. On October 25, 2004, TXU publicly announced its plan to increase the common stock dividend from $0.50 to $2.25 and to repurchase approximately 50 million shares of TXU common stock. Immediately following the announcement, the per-share value of TXU common stock jumped nearly 20%. The Corporate Units and the PRIDES experienced correlated increases in value.

* * *

Rule 12(b)(6) authorizes dismissal of a complaint for "failure to state a claim upon which relief can be granted." Fed.R.Civ.P. 12(b)(6). "To survive a Rule 12(b)(6) motion, the plaintiff must plead 'enough facts to state a claim to relief that is plausible on its face.'" *In re Katrina Canal Breaches Litig.*, 495 F.3d 191, 205 (5th Cir.2007) (quoting *Bell Atlantic Corp. v. Twombly,* 550 U.S. 544, 570, 127 S.Ct. 1955, 167 L.Ed.2d 929 (2007)).

Rule 9(b) states that "in alleging fraud or mistake, a party must state with particularity the circumstances constituting fraud or mistake." . . . This Circuit's precedent interprets Rule 9(b) strictly, requiring the plaintiff to "specify the statements contended to be fraudulent, identify the speaker, state when and where the statements were made, and explain why the statements were fraudulent." *Williams v. WMX Techs., Inc.*, 112 F.3d 175, 177 (5th Cir.1997) . . . .

In order to state a claim for fraud under Section 10(b) and Rule 10b–5 of the Securities Exchange Act, a plaintiff must allege, in connection with the purchase or sale of securities, (1) a misstatement or an omission (2) of a material fact (3) made with scienter (4) on which the plaintiffs relied (5) that proximately caused the plaintiff's injury. . . . The elements of a claim under Section 14(e), which applies to tender offers, are identical to the Section 10(b)/Rule 10b–5 elements. . . .

The Private Securities Litigation Reform Act ("PSLRA"), which governs federal securities fraud claims, requires that a plaintiff in a securities fraud case must, for "each act or omission alleged" to be false or misleading, "state with particularity facts giving rise to a strong inference that the defendant acted with the required state of mind." 15 U.S.C. § 78u–4(b)(2) . . . . The PSLRA also incorporates the Rule 9(b) requirements into the pleading standard for federal securities fraud claims. . . . Under the PSLRA, the court considers whether all the facts and circumstances, taken together, give rise to a strong inference of scienter. . . .

Scienter, in the context of securities fraud, is defined as "an intent to deceive, manipulate, or defraud or that severe recklessness in which the danger of misleading buyers or sellers is either known to the defendant or is so obvious that the defendant must have been aware of it." . . . "Severe recklessness is limited to those highly unreasonable omissions or misrepresentations that involve not merely simple or even inexcusable negligence, but an extreme departure from the standards of ordinary care."

. . . In *Tellabs,* the Supreme Court clarified the standard for pleading a "strong inference" of scienter. *Tellabs,* 127 S.Ct. at 2509–10. This Circuit has recently interpreted *Tellabs* as requiring a "three step approach to reviewing scienter allegations on a motion to dismiss a federal securities fraud case pursuant to the PSLRA":

> First, the allegations must, as in federal pleadings generally, be taken as true. Second, courts may consider documents incorporated in the complaint by reference and matters subject to judicial notice. The facts must be evaluated collectively, not in isolation, to determine whether a strong inference of scienter has been pled. Third, a court must take into account plausible inferences opposing as well as supporting a strong inference of scienter. The inference of scienter must ultimately be "cogent and compelling," not merely "reasonable" or "permissible."

Ind. Elec., 537 F.3d at 533 (citing *Tellabs,* 127 S.Ct. at 2509–10). . . .

Although we have stated that allegations of motive and opportunity standing alone will not suffice to meet the scienter requirement, motive and opportunity allegations may meaningfully enhance the strength of the inference of scienter. . . . We have rejected the group pleading approach to scienter and instead look to the state of mind of the individual corporate official or officials "who make or issue the statement (or order or approve it or its making or issuance, or who furnish information or language for inclusion therein, or the like) rather than generally to the collective knowledge of all the corporation's officers and employees acquired in the course of their employment." . . .

* * *

Although the timing of the dividend increase, which was recommended by TXU management just eight days after the close of the tender offer, is suspect, Appellants have not provided facts sufficient to support a "cogent and compelling" inference that Appellees made any statements intentionally or recklessly to mislead TXU's investors. In fact, it is not clear that Appellees ever issued a materially misleading statement or omission of fact concerning the dividend policy. The close proximity of the dividend increase to the end of the tender offer, though it provides some support for an inference of scienter, is not sufficient, without more, to establish a strong inference of the requisite intent. . . .

Appellants contend that they relied on the May 2004 press release which stated that a dividend increase was not likely until 2006 when certain financial benchmarks had been made, but reserved the right of the management to consider other factors in determining if and when to change the dividend policy. Appellants have not presented any evidence of scienter with regard to this statement. [Ed. We assume the Court means here that the appellants had not pled facts that support a claim of scienter.]

There is no evidence that at the time this statement was made in May 2004, TXU management, specifically Wilder, was aware or should have been aware that TXU planned to increase the dividend prior to the financial benchmarks being reached.

* * *

. . . [A]s this court stated in *Indiana Electric*, under *Tellabs*, we are obligated to consider inferences opposing the allegations of fraud. . . . Here, it can be inferred that Appellees had not made a final decision concerning a change in the dividend policy during the tender offer period, and were thus truthfully stating that the policy was under review. This constitutes a plausible nonculpable explanation of Appellees' actions. . . . TXU management did not recommend a dividend increase, nor did the Board approve one, until after the close of the tender offer. Given that TXU and Wilder did disclose that the dividend policy was "under review" during the tender offer period, the inference of non-fraudulent intent weighs in favor of the Appellees. Although it is a close question, the facts alleged support at most only a permissible inference of scienter. Taking into account all of the facts in the aggregate, as well as inferences opposing fraudulent intent, Appellants have failed to raise a strong inference that TXU, and specifically Wilder, acted with the intent to deceive, manipulate, or defraud or acted with severe recklessness in making statements concerning the dividend policy. . . .

* * *

The Fifth Circuit has passed down some extraordinary dismissals based on the pleading standards. In 2003, the Court affirmed a lower court dismissal of a shareholder suit against the two authors of the WorldCom $100 billion Ponzi scheme, Bernard J. ("Bernie") Ebbers (CEO) and Scott D. Sullivan (CFO). The opinion came down after WorldCom had fired the two, had announced it would take a $700 million write-off and would restate its financial statements to account for accounting irregularities, and had filed for bankruptcy. *Goldstein v. MCI WorldCom*, 340 F.3d 238 (5th Cir. 2003). Both defendants later went to jail,[18] but they beat the shareholder civil suit on a motion to dismiss.

4. DISCLOSURE OF AN ACQUIRER'S *PLANS* AND *PROJECTIONS*

It goes almost without saying that projections are an important part of all acquisitions. Participants negotiating an acquisition are necessarily

---

18 Scott Sullivan was sentenced to five years in prison as part of a plea deal requiring him to testify against Bernie Ebbers. He was released from prison in 2009. Bernie is serving a 25-year sentence in Oakdale Federal Correctional Institution in Oakdale, Louisiana. He is eligible for parole in July 2028.

projecting the post-acquisition value of a combined firm and comparing this figure with projections of the value of the constituent firms standing alone. Once a deal is announced, shareholders who must vote or tender their shares want to know the projections made by the managers of both constituent firms. Consider, however, the timing difficulties of any projections. A projection made to enable the chief executive officer to negotiate an agreement in principle will have assumptions about market value that will be stale when the board approves the acquisition agreement, to say nothing of when the proxy solicitation is mailed, when the shareholders vote, and when the deal is closed. If projections are disclosed, must they be continuously updated with the passage of time?

Legal standards aside, managers of the participants can be ambivalent about revealing their projections to their shareholders. On the one hand, the managers want to sell the deal by using the projections to justify their decision; on the other hand, the managers are uncomfortable with putting themselves on record for criticisms of, first, their negotiating skill in garnering a share of the anticipated gains from the acquisition and, second, their acceptance of projections that may turn out to have been wildly optimistic or pessimistic. The result of this conflict is a temptation for managers to establish two sets of books, contracting for projections designed for circulation to their shareholders and, at the same time, using in-house or unwritten projections to help negotiate the deal.

This schizophrenia has infected the Securities and Exchange Commission as well. The SEC knows that shareholders view the projections as significant but fears that managers will misuse projections and shareholders will misunderstand them (that is, overrate their importance). Moreover, the SEC is concerned that managers' misuse of projections would be difficult to police. A projection is only an opinion of future events, usually heavily qualified. When is a guarded opinion intentionally false or misleading? The *Virginia Bankshares* case below addresses the question. Congress added its voice on the matter in the Private Securities Litigation Reform Act of 1995, attempting to provide a safe harbor against litigation for some kinds of projections.

Known as the debate over *prospective* or *forward-looking information*, the SEC has been very active on the issue. Under the SEC rules and interpretative releases there are four categories of projections: (1) projections an issuer must create and disclose; (2) projections an issuer must disclose if created and available; (3) projections an issuer can voluntarily disclose, if in good faith and with a reasonable basis in fact; and finally, (4) projections an issuer cannot legally disclose even if created and available. Also important is the role of lawyers and accountants in recommending to clients that issuers avoid category type two and three disclosures.

As a result of the SEC's traditional suspicion of predictions, most lawyers advise their clients not to disclose publicly any predictions or projections (including valuations) unless legally required to do so. Thus, much of the litigation on projections in the reported case law in the past thirty years deals with when managers ought to have disclosed internal or outside expert's projections or valuations in their public statements and filings.

a. SEC Forms and Schedules: Disclosures of Forward-Looking Information Required of Firms Executing Acquisitions

Shareholder Voting and the Proxy Statement: We begin our inquiry on required disclosures of prospective information in acquisitions or reorganizations by examining Items 11 ("Authorization or Issuance of Securities Otherwise Than for Exchange"), 12 ("Modification or Exchange of Securities") and 14 ("Mergers, Consolidations, Acquisitions and Similar Matters") of Schedule 14A[19] ("Information Required in Proxy Statement"). There are three separate bits of language in the Items that appear to call for the disclosure of prospective information. Item 14, for example, calls for financial statements meeting the requirements of Article 11 of Regulation S–X. Article 11 requires *pro forma financial information* if significant business combinations are "probable." In essence, the pro forma financials present the combined financials of the two constituent corporations as if they had combined on the date of the last financial statements prepared by the surviving company. Thus, in a sense, the information is not prospective at all; it is historical in that the companies are combined as of a past date:

> Pro forma financial information should provide investors with information about the continuing impact of a particular transaction by showing how it might have affected historical financial statements if the transaction had been consummated at an earlier time. Such statements should assist investors in analyzing the future prospects of the registrant because they illustrate the possible scope of the change in the registrant's historical financial position and results of operations caused by the transaction.

Rule 11–02(a) of Reg. S–X.

At issue, however, are the obligations of the firms in an acquisition to adjust or footnote the pro forma financials if the pro formas do not accurately reflect what is likely to occur in the transaction. The SEC regulations on Article 11 contain some general language on the matter, requiring that pro formas be adjusted in light of the structure of any planned acquisition to "give effect to the range of possible results." Rule 11–02(b)(8) of Reg. S–X. These adjustments and, in lieu thereof, the

---

[19] Exchange Act Rule 14a–101.

footnotes to the pro formas *could* constitute a very valuable kind of prospective information for investors. Yet accountants read this language in Article 11 very narrowly. The dominant footnote to pro formas is a disclaimer! The disclaimer states that the pro formas are a "mechanical exercise." They are not an accurate indication of any real results in the acquisition, and they do not include any quantification of synergy gains and other savings that may occur in the acquisition. It is clear, then, that any investor reading the pro forma for information must have a very sophisticated knowledge of accounting principles to make sense of the numbers and qualifications.

Article 11 also has a little-used provision that allows a firm, if it so chooses, to file a "financial forecast" *in lieu of* a pro forma income statement. The forecast is a condensed income statement under Rule 11–03 of Regulation S–X. The financial forecast must cover a period of at least twelve months from the latest of (a) the most recent balance sheet included in the filing and (b) the estimated consummation date of the transaction. Rule 11–03(a)(1) of Reg. S–X Moreover, it must set out clearly "assumptions particularly relevant to the transaction and effects thereof." Rule 11–03(a)(3) of Reg. S–X. Although forecasts are very carefully regulated by generally accepted accounting principles—professional standards generated by accountants themselves—there is room in such forecasts to make predictions about the future results of an acquisition. In practice, accountants often advise firms not to use the forecast rule.

A second call for prospective information in Item 14 of Schedule 14A appears in subsection (b)(6). It comes the closest to asking for some concrete estimates:

> If a report, opinion or appraisal materially relating to the transaction has been received from an outside party, and is referred to in the proxy statement, furnish [a summary of the report, opinion or appraisal].

The requirement is readily avoidable, however. Parties to the transaction usually omit any reference to opinions and appraisal, even if available, in their proxy information statements.

A third call for prospective information appears in the tame language of Instruction 3 to Item 303(a) in Regulation S–K. Item 303 of Regulation S–K is incorporated by reference in Items 12 and 14 of Regulation 14A. The Instruction deals with the "Management's Discussion and Analysis" (MD&A) section of a firm's financial statements. The MD&A is text that helps readers understand the bare numbers in the financials themselves.[20] Instruction 3 requires that "[t]he discussion and analysis shall focus

[20] One of the purposes of the MD&A section is to enable "investors to see the company through the eyes of management." *Commission Guidance Regarding Management's Discussion and Analysis of Financial Condition and Results of Operations*, SEC Rel. 34–48960, 2003 WL 22996757, at *2 (Dec. 19, 2003).

specifically on material events and uncertainties known to management that would cause reported financial information not to be necessarily indicative of future operating results or of future financial condition." Major acquisition transactions would appear to qualify, but presumably such information would seem to be already contained in the pro forma financials.

What prospective information can a firm *voluntarily* choose to disclose that is not required? Instruction 7 to Item 303(a) in Regulation S–K provides the basic standard for the MD&A section of a firm's financials: "Any forward-looking information supplied is expressly covered by the safe harbor rule for projections. See Rule 175 under the Securities Act [17 CFR 230.175], Rule 3b–6 under the Exchange Act [17 CFR 240.3b–6] and Securities Act Release No. 6084 (June 25, 1979) (44 FR 38810)."

The SEC has defined "forward-looking information" in Securities Act Rule 175(c) as follows:

> (1) A statement containing a projection of revenues, income (loss), earnings (loss) per share, capital expenditures, dividends, capital structure or other financial items;
>
> (2) A statement of management's plans and objectives for future operations;
>
> (3) A statement of future economic performance contained in management's discussion and analysis of financial condition and results of operations included pursuant to Item 303 of Regulation S–K (§ 229.303 of this chapter) or Item 9 of Form 20–F; or Item 5 of Form 20–F[; and]
>
> (4) Disclosed statements of the assumptions underlying or relating to any of the statements described in paragraphs (c)(1), (2), or (3) of this section.

The Commission issued an interpretative release in May of 1989 emphasizing the distinction between prospective information that an issuer *must* disclose and forward-looking information that an issuer *may* disclose.[21] In the release, the SEC defines management obligations through a series of double negatives. First, management must determine whether the known trend or event is likely to occur. If management determines that it is not reasonably likely to occur, no disclosure is required. Second, if management cannot make a determination that the event is not likely to occur, disclosure is required unless management determines that a

[21] *Management's Discussion and Analysis of Financial Condition and Results of Operations; Certain Investment Company Disclosures*, SEC Rel. No. 33–6835, 1989 WL 1092885 (May 18, 1989).

material effect on the financial condition of the reporting company is not reasonably likely to occur.[22]

Stock Swaps and the Prospectus: Purchasing firms issuing securities as consideration in stock-for-stock mergers, stock-for-assets acquisitions or stock-for-stock tender offers, as noted in Chapter Two, are selling securities for the purposes of the Securities Act of 1933. Sec. Act Rule 145(a) and prelim. note thereto (asset sales and mergers). If a purchasing firm cannot qualify under an exemption to Securities Act registration, the firm must register the securities with the SEC and distribute the securities using a selling document referred to as a *prospectus*. The securities may be registered on a special Form S–4 registration statement for acquisitions or on the basic Form S–1 registration statement. Form S–4 follows the pattern established in the proxy regulations noted above. For example, Item 3(e) and (f) incorporates Item 301 of Regulation S–K and requires pro forma information on book value per share, cash dividends, and income per share, assuming the acquisition. Item 5 incorporates by reference Article 11 of Regulation S–X and requires pro forma financial statements. Item 303 of Regulation S–K on MD&A text applies as well. *E.g.*, Form S–4, Items 12(b)(3)(v), 13(a)(3)(v) & 14(h). Item 4(b) notes that "if a report, opinion or appraisal materially relating to the transaction has been received from an outside party, and such report, opinion, or appraisal is referred to in the prospectus . . . ," the issuer must include information on the details of the report.

Third-Party Tender Offers and Schedules TO and 14D–9: Schedule TO, the bidders' announcing document, and Schedule 14D–9, the targets' response, also follow the pattern discussed above for proxy statements on pro formas and the MD&A requirements. In addition, however, Regulation M–A has Item 1006(a)–(c) that requires a bidder to "state the purposes" of the tender offer including: "any plans, proposals or negotiations that relate to or would result in" a follow-up merger (a squeeze-out, for example), the subsequent sale of the target's assets (a bust-up, for example), any change in the board or management of the target, any change in the capitalization or dividend policy, any material change in corporate structure or business, and any plans to delist the target's securities. Targets, on the other hand, must state "reasons" for whatever recommendation they make to their shareholders in response to a tender offer, Item 4 of Schedule 14D–9[23] (referring to Reg. M–A, Item 1012(b)), and must disclose negotiations with other potential acquirers in Item 7 (referring to Reg. M–A, Item 1006(d)(1)). If the target has signed an agreement in principle with another acquirer,

[22] See also *Interpretation: Commission Guidance Regarding Management's Discussion and Analysis of Financial Condition and Results of Operations*, SEC Rel. No. 33–8350, 2003 WL 22996757 (Dec. 19, 2003).

[23] Exch. Act Rule 14d–101.

the target must disclose the details of the acquisition, including the acquirer's future plans for the target. Reg. M–A, Item 1006(d)(2).

Issuer Repurchases and Schedule TO: Schedule TO for issuer repurchases through a tender offer is similar to Schedule TO for third-party tender offers. Both require, for example, the issuer to disclose its plans and purposes. Item 6 of Schedule TO[24]. The novel disclosure provision is in Schedule 13E–3[25], on going-private transactions. Item 8 in the Schedule, referring to Item 1014 of Reg. M–A, requires a statement on the "fairness of the transaction" by the issuer. The Item also requires "reasonable detail" on the "material factors" behind the statement and, to the extent practicable, the "weight" assigned to each factor. Item 8 is supplemented by Item 9, referring to Item 1015 of Reg. M–A, on "reports, opinions, appraisals and negotiations." An issuer *must* disclose any report, opinion or appraisal from an "outside party" other than an opinion of counsel (fairness opinions from investment bankers, for example) that is "materially related" to the transaction, including those relating to the "fairness of the consideration" and those relating to the "fairness of the transaction." The Item also requires substantial detail on the content and authors of the reports. Items 8 and 9 are unique in the SEC forms and schedules, and apply only to going-private transactions. They are reflective of the internal conflicts of interest inherent in those transactions.

NOTE: THE OBLIGATION TO DISCLOSE INSIDE AND OUTSIDE "REPORTS, OPINIONS, AND APPRAISALS"

Most of the SEC schedules and forms require a purchaser to disclose its plans for the selling company and purposes for the acquisition.[26] The formulation of these plans and purposes is expensive, often involving much study and the retention of outside consultants, investment bankers, accountants and lawyers. If candidly offered in the SEC filings, this information could be very valuable indeed for other companies who, on the publication of the information, can use the information at no cost to make competitive bids for the selling firm. Shareholders of a purchaser will, no doubt, find the information useful in their deliberations but they also may find that they lose value when the same information encourages a second bidder to appear and outbid their company for the target. As a consequence, lawyers for most purchasers use a combination of two obscuring devices—the use of abstract, oblique, general language and the laundry list approach (list pages of possible past acquisition business alternatives with no assignment of probabilities to the various choices)—to avoid the true import of the disclosure obligation.

The rules on disclosing plans do not mention internal reports and projections. Most courts that have addressed the issue are reluctant to require

24 Exch. Act Rule 14d–100.

25 Exch. Act Rule 13e–100.

26 And, in self-tender offers, a purchaser's plans for itself.

firms to disclose internal reports and projections used in formulating the plans so disclosed. See *Walker, infra* Section A.4.c. Reports from paid consultants get explicit treatment, however. The only schedule or form that requires a purchaser to identify reports, opinions and appraisals from outside consultants is Schedule 13E–3 on going-private issuer repurchases. Schedule 13E–3, Items 8 & 9. The other schedules and forms require the disclosure of such reports only if a purchaser decides to mention them voluntarily. *E.g.*, Schedule 14A, Item 14(b)(6) (cross referencing Reg. M–A, Item 1015(b)); Form S–4, Item 4(b) (same). Case law on whether a purchaser must disclose outside reports under general antifraud provisions (such as Exchange Act Rule 10b–5) is in conflict. Compare *Flynn v. Bass Bros. Enter., Inc.*, 744 F.2d 978 (3d Cir. 1984), with *Radol v. Thomas*, 772 F.2d 244 (6th Cir. 1985), and *Starkman v. Marathon Oil Co.*, 772 F.2d 231 (6th Cir. 1985), *cert. denied*, 475 U.S. 1015, 106 S.Ct. 1195, 89 L.Ed.2d 310 (1986).[27]

QUESTION

When should a bidder have to disclose its valuation work on the target?

b. SEC Rules on Optional Disclosure of Projections

If disclosure is not required, issuers can decide to disclose forward-looking information anyway.[28] At issue is whether managers can or ought to use the encouragement from Instruction 7 to Item 303(a) of Regulation S–K on voluntary disclosures to give their official predictions of the firm's future health after an acquisition or reorganization. Such information is always of great interest to the investors/voters, but in practice, firms do not make such projections in their MD&A language. The legal risks are too great, despite the four safe harbors found in Exchange Act § 21E, Exchange Act Rule 3b–6, Securities Act § 27A and Securities Act Rule 175.

The four safe harbors permit a firm to disclose a short, specific list of projections in identified SEC filings. The SEC terms the disclosures *forward-looking information*. The safe harbors protect projections of "revenues, income (loss), earnings (loss) per share, capital expenditures, dividends, capital structure or other financial items," "a statement of management's plans and objectives for future operations," and a "statement of future economic performance" contained in the management's discussion and analysis (MD&A) section. Presumably each type of projection could be made about the business future of a surviving

---

[27] State law is also weighing in on the question. E.g., In re Pure Resources, Inc., Shareholders Litig., 808 A.2d. 421, 455 (Del. Ch. 2002) (disclosure of investment banker valuation report).

[28] Some predictions are so vague that the courts dismiss them as mere "puffery," which are not material because they cannot have misled a reasonable investor. See, e.g., Eisenstadt v. Centel Corp., 113 F.3d 738, 746 (7th Cir. 1997); San Leandro Emergency Medical Group Profit Sharing Plan v. Philip Morris Cos., Inc., 75 F.3d 801, 811 (2d Cir. 1996); Rabb v. General Physics Corp., 4 F.3d 286, 289–90 (4th Cir. 1993). The text deals with projections and predictions that are firm and specific enough to be material.

entity in an acquisition or reorganization. All the safe harbors also protect voluntary disclosures of "assumptions underlying" forward-looking statements as well as the statements themselves.

The interaction of the four safe harbors is complex. The largest safe harbors are Exchange Act § 21E and Securities Act § 27A—both added by the PSLRA—that protect written and oral forward-looking statements if they are "accompanied by meaningful cautionary statements" and made without "actual knowledge . . . that [they are] false or misleading."[29] The sections have several exemptions, however, and in some (but not all) of those exemptions one could apply the safe harbor rules that apply to annual and quarterly reports, Securities Act Rule 175 and Exchange Act Rule 3b–6. The two Rules protect an issuer's voluntary projections in the reports if made on a "reasonable basis" and "in good faith."[30] Moreover, if a forward-looking statement in the annual or quarterly reports does not come with a meaningful cautionary statement, the two safe harbors in the PSLRA would not apply, but technically the good faith/reasonable basis Rules could still apply. Some SEC filings may fall outside all the safe harbors; none of the safe harbors apply to tender offer filings, for example.

The two safe harbor Rules do not specifically require the disclosure of the assumptions that underlie the forward-looking statements; however, the SEC has taken the position in the past on Rules 175 and 3b–6 that "under certain circumstances the disclosure of the assumptions may be material to an understanding of the projected results . . . and key assumptions underlying a forward-looking statement are of such significance that their disclosure may be necessary in order for the statement to meet the reasonable basis and good faith standards embodied in the rule[s]." *Safe Harbor Rule for Projections*, SEC Rel. No. 33–6084, 1979 WL 181199 (July 5, 1979). The release may not survive current case law, however. See *Wielgos, infra* Section A.4.c.

The four safe harbors do not include, and therefore do not protect, projections of future stock prices or other market values of the survivor. However, this is the information probably most desired by selling firm shareholders who are deciding whether to vote on a transaction that will exchange their shares for stock in the survivor. Regardless, the note to Exchange Act Rule 14a–9, the general antifraud rule applicable to proxy statements, lists examples of projections that "may be misleading." The very first example is one including "predictions as to specific future market values." The SEC is generally very suspicious of broad predictions by firm managers on post-acquisition stock prices, believing that given half a

---

[29] See Helwig v. Vencor, 251 F.3d 540 (6th Cir. 2001) (applying the language). *Helwig* involved a hotly contested 7 to 6 *en banc* decision on when a firm must disclose "soft information"; the court's holding on pleadings standards was overruled by the Supreme Court case of Tellabs, Inc. v. Makor Issues and Rights, Ltd., 551 U.S. 308, 127 S.Ct. 2499, 168 L.Ed.2d 179 (2007).

[30] The Rules apply to forward-looking statements in the financial statements prepared in accordance with GAAP, for example.

chance, managers will imitate snake oil salesmen. The SEC fears that general exaggerated claims by managers are not susceptible to correction by after-the-fact litigation based on fraud.

In sum, the SEC provisions that allow but do not require disclosure of certain types of prospective information are used parsimoniously. Indeed, lawyers counsel their clients to disclose only that which is legally required if at all possible—and even then only at minimal levels.

NOTE: THE DUTY TO AMEND, CORRECT OR UPDATE PROJECTIONS

The *duty to amend* is found expressly in several of the disclosure schedules pertaining to stock acquisitions. Exchange Act Rule 13d–2 (disclosure of a purchase of more than 5 percent of a class of equity securities of an issuer), for example, requires a "promptly" filed amendment for any material changes in the facts disclosed in an original filing on Schedule 13D.[31] *In re Phillips Petroleum Sec. Litig.*, 881 F.2d 1236, 1245 (3d Cir. 1989). The duty to amend is an express direction to amend in the schedules, forms and rules. See also Exch. Act Rules 14d–6(d) (tender offers), 14d–9(b) (issuer responses to tender offers), 13e–3(e)(2) (going-private transactions), and 13e–4(e)(2) (issuer tender offers).

The *duty to correct* is the obligation of a filing company to correct promptly statements that it discovers were incorrect *when originally made.* See, e.g., *Gallagher v. Abbott Laboratories*, 269 F.3d 806, 810 (7th Cir. 2001) ("[A] statement may be 'corrected' only if it was *in*correct when made . . . .").

The *duty to update*, the most controversial of the three, is a general duty derived from Exchange Act Rule 10b–5 to supplement statements that were *accurate when originally made* (and hence do not have to be "corrected" per se) but that have become inaccurate or misleading due to *subsequent* or *intervening events*. There is disagreement among the federal circuit courts on whether the duty exists at all—the Seventh Circuit says no,[32] the First, Second and Third Circuit Courts[33] say yes.

---

[31] Exch. Act Rule 13d–101.

[32] Gallagher v. Abbott Laboratories, 269 F.3d 806, 808–10 (7th Cir. 2001) (noting the federal securities laws is a system of "periodic disclosure" and not "continuous disclosure"); Stransky v. Cummins Engine Co., 51 F.3d 1329, 1332 (7th Cir. 1995) ("Some have argued that a duty to update arises when a company makes a forward-looking statement—a projection—that because of subsequent events becomes untrue. . . . This court has never embraced such a theory, and we decline to do so now." (footnotes omitted)).

[33] E.g., Weiner v. Quaker Oats Co., 129 F.3d 310, 318 (3d Cir. 1997) ("[A] reasonable factfinder could determine that Quaker's statements regarding its total debt-to-total capitalization ratio guideline would have been material to a reasonable investor, and hence that Quaker had a duty to update such statements when they became unreliable"); In re Time Warner Sec. Litig., 9 F.3d 259, 267 (2d Cir. 1993) ("[A] duty to update opinions and projections may arise if the original opinions or projections have become misleading as the result of intervening events"); Backman v. Polaroid, 910 F.2d 10, 17 (1st Cir. 1990) ("[I]n special circumstances, a statement, correct at the time, may have a forward intent and connotation upon which parties may be expected to rely. If this is a clear meaning, and there is a change, correction, more exactly, further disclosure, may be called for.").

There is also disagreement on how to define the duty to update among those courts that recognize and apply that duty. First, those circuit courts accepting the doctrine have excluded "historical facts" from the class of statements that an issuer must update. The duty attaches to "forward-looking" statements only, explicit firm projections and predictions made in the public filings or statements. Second, there is disagreement over the relationship between the prior forward-looking statement and the subsequent event necessary to trigger the supplemental duty to speak. On the one hand, the Third Circuit seems to hold that there is a duty to update any time a subsequent fact, if assumed to have been true at the time of the original disclosure, would have had to have been disclosed with the original disclosure so as to make the original statement complete (and not misleading).[34] On the other hand, the First Circuit seems to hold that there is a duty to update any time a subsequent fact contradicts a specific earlier public statement, a much narrower standard. Indeed, if one can find a sense in which the earlier statement remains even technically true, there is no duty to update according to the First Circuit.

c. Case Law on Acquisition-Related Projections

VIRGINIA BANKSHARES, INC. V. SANDBERG

Supreme Court of the United States, 1991.
501 U.S. 1083, 111 S.Ct. 2749, 115 L.Ed.2d 929.

JUSTICE SOUTER delivered the opinion of the Court.

* * *

In December 1986, First American Bankshares, Inc., (FABI), a bank holding company, began a "freeze-out" merger, in which the First American Bank of Virginia (Bank) eventually merged into Virginia Bankshares, Inc., (VBI), a wholly owned subsidiary of FABI. VBI owned 85 percent of the Bank's shares, the remaining 15 percent being in the hands of some 2,000 minority shareholders. FABI hired the investment banking firm of Keefe, Bruyette & Woods (KBW) to give an opinion on the appropriate price for shares of the minority holders, who would lose their interests in the Bank as a result of the merger. Based on market quotations and unverified information from FABI, KBW gave the Bank's executive committee an opinion that $42 a share would be a fair price for the minority stock. The

---

34 In other words, is the subsequent fact, if assumed to have been in existence at the time of the original disclosure, material? Since the definition of materiality is broad in such a case, the duty to update is correspondingly broad. The standard explains not only *Weiner*, *supra* note 33, but the prior case of Greenfield v. Heublein, 742 F.2d 751 (3d Cir. 1984), *cert. denied,* 469 U.S. 1215, 105 S.Ct. 1189, 84 L.Ed.2d 336 (1985), which represents the flip side of the standard. In *Greenfield* the Third Circuit held that the defendant's public denial of any reason for activity in its stock did not have to be updated by an announcement of ongoing merger discussions because the discussions themselves were not "material." While the Supreme Court has rejected the *Greenfield* definition of materiality for preliminary merger discussions, the structure of the reasoning remains.

executive committee approved the merger proposal at that price, and the full board followed suit.

Although Virginia law required only that such a merger proposal be submitted to a vote at a shareholders' meeting, and that the meeting be preceded by circulation of a statement of information to the shareholders, the directors nevertheless solicited proxies for voting on the proposal at the annual meeting set for April 21, 1987. In their solicitation, the directors urged the proposal's adoption and stated they had approved the plan because of its opportunity for the minority shareholders to achieve a "high" value, which they elsewhere described as a "fair" price, for their stock.

* * *

We consider first the actionability *per se* of statements of reasons, opinion or belief. Because such a statement by definition purports to express what is consciously on the speaker's mind, we interpret the jury verdict as finding that the directors' statements of belief and opinion were made with knowledge that the directors did not hold the beliefs or opinions expressed, and we confine our discussion to statements so made. That such statements may be materially significant raises no serious question. . . . We think there is no room to deny that a statement of belief by corporate directors about a recommended course of action, or an explanation of their reasons for recommending it, can take on just that importance. Shareholders know that directors usually have knowledge and expertness far exceeding the normal investor's resources, and the directors' perceived superiority is magnified even further by the common knowledge that state law customarily obliges them to exercise their judgment in the shareholders' interest. . . . Naturally, then, the share owner faced with a proxy request will think it important to know the directors' beliefs about the course they recommend, and their specific reasons for urging the shareholders to embrace it.

* * *

. . . Such statements are factual in two senses: as statements that the directors do act for the reasons given or hold the belief stated and as statements about the subject matter of the reason or belief expressed. . . . Reasons for directors' recommendations or statements of belief are characteristically matters of corporate record subject to documentation, to be supported or attacked by evidence of historical fact outside a plaintiff's control. Such evidence would include not only corporate minutes and other statements of the directors themselves, but circumstantial evidence bearing on the facts that would reasonably underlie the reasons claimed and the honesty of any statement that those reasons are the basis for a recommendation or other action, a point that becomes especially clear when the reasons or beliefs go to valuations in dollars and cents.

It is no answer to argue, as petitioners do, that the quoted statement on which liability was predicated did not express a reason in dollars and cents, but focused instead on the "indefinite and unverifiable" term, "high" value, much like the similar claim that the merger's terms were "fair" to shareholders.[6] The objection ignores the fact that such conclusory terms in a commercial context are reasonably understood to rest on a factual basis that justifies them as accurate, the absence of which renders them misleading. Provable facts either furnish good reasons to make a conclusory commercial judgment, or they count against it, and expressions of such judgments can be uttered with knowledge of truth or falsity just like more definite statements, and defended or attacked through the orthodox evidentiary process that either substantiates their underlying justifications or tends to disprove their existence. . . . In this case, whether $42 was "high," and the proposal "fair" to the minority shareholders depended on whether provable facts about the Bank's assets, and about actual and potential levels of operation, substantiated a value that was above, below, or more or less at the $42 figure, when assessed in accordance with recognized methods of valuation.

Respondents adduced evidence for just such facts in proving that the statement was misleading about its subject matter and a false expression of the directors' reasons. Whereas the proxy statement described the $42 price as offering a premium above both book value and market price, the evidence indicated that a calculation of the book figure based on the appreciated value of the Bank's real estate holdings eliminated any such premium. The evidence on the significance of market price showed that KBW had conceded that the market was closed, thin and dominated by FABI, facts omitted from the statement. There was, indeed, evidence of a "going concern" value for the Bank in excess of $60 per share of common stock, another fact never disclosed. However conclusory the directors' statement may have been, then, it was open to attack by garden-variety evidence, subject neither to a plaintiff's control nor ready manufacture, and there was no undue risk of open-ended liability or uncontrollable litigation in allowing respondents the opportunity for recovery on the allegation that it was misleading to call $42 "high."

* * *

[6] Petitioners are also wrong to argue that construing the statute to allow recovery for a misleading statement that the merger was "fair" to the minority shareholders is tantamount to assuming federal authority to bar corporate transactions thought to be unfair to some group of shareholders. It is, of course, true that we said in Santa Fe Industries, Inc. v. Green, 430 U.S. 462, 479, 97 S.Ct. 1292, 1304, 51 L.Ed.2d 480 (1977), that " '[c]orporations are creatures of state law, and investors commit their funds to corporate directors on the understanding that, except where federal law expressly requires certain responsibilities of directors with respect to stockholders, state law will govern the internal affairs of the corporation,' " quoting Cort v. Ash, 422 U.S. 66, 84, 95 S.Ct. 2080, 2091, 45 L.Ed.2d 26 (1975). But § 14(a) does impose responsibility for false and misleading proxy statements. Although a corporate transaction's "fairness" is not, as such, a federal concern, a proxy statement's claim of fairness presupposes a factual integrity that federal law is expressly concerned to preserve. . . .

Under § 14(a), then, a plaintiff is permitted to prove a specific statement of reason knowingly false or misleadingly incomplete, even when stated in conclusory terms. In reaching this conclusion we have considered statements of reasons of the sort exemplified here, which misstate the speaker's reasons and also mislead about the stated subject matter (*e.g.*, the value of the shares). A statement of belief may be open to objection only in the former respect, however, solely as a misstatement of the psychological fact of the speaker's belief in what he says. . . .

The question arises, then, whether disbelief, or undisclosed belief or motivation, standing alone, should be a sufficient basis to sustain an action under § 14(a), absent proof by the sort of objective evidence described above that the statement also expressly or impliedly asserted something false or misleading about its subject matter. We think that proof of mere disbelief or belief undisclosed should not suffice for liability under § 14(a), and if nothing more had been required or proven in this case we would reverse for that reason.

On the one hand, it would be rare to find a case with evidence solely of disbelief or undisclosed motivation without further proof that the statement was defective as to its subject matter. While we certainly would not hold a director's naked admission of disbelief incompetent evidence of a proxy statement's false or misleading character, such an unusual admission will not very often stand alone, and we do not substantially narrow the cause of action by requiring a plaintiff to demonstrate something false or misleading in what the statement expressly or impliedly declared about its subject.

On the other hand, to recognize liability on mere disbelief or undisclosed motive without any demonstration that the proxy statement was false or misleading about its subject would authorize § 14(a) litigation confined solely to what one skeptical court spoke of as the "impurities" of a director's "unclean heart." . . . While it is true that the liability, if recognized, would rest on an actual, not hypothetical, psychological fact, the temptation to rest an otherwise nonexistent § 14(a) action on psychological enquiry alone would threaten just the sort of strike suits and attrition by discovery that *Blue Chip Stamps* sought to discourage. We therefore hold disbelief or undisclosed motivation, standing alone, insufficient to satisfy the element of fact that must be established under § 14(a).

* * *

JUSTICE SCALIA, concurring in part and concurring in the judgment.

As I understand the Court's opinion, the statement "In the opinion of the Directors, this is a high value for the shares" would produce liability if in fact it was not a high value and the Directors knew that. It would not produce liability if in fact it was not a high value but the Directors honestly believed otherwise. The statement "The Directors voted to accept the proposal *because* they believe it offers a high value" would not produce liability if in fact the Directors' genuine motive was quite different—except that it would produce liability if the proposal in fact did not offer a high value and the Directors knew that.

I agree with all of this. However, not every sentence that has the word "opinion" in it, or that refers to motivation for Directors' actions, leads us into this psychic thicket. Sometimes such a sentence actually represents facts as facts rather than opinions—and in that event no more need be done than apply the normal rules for § 14(a) liability. I think that is the situation here. In my view, the statement at issue in this case is most fairly read as affirming *separately* both the fact of the Directors' opinion *and* the accuracy of the facts upon which the opinion was assertedly based. It reads as follows:

> "The Plan of Merger has been approved by the Board of Directors because it provides an opportunity for the Bank's public shareholders to achieve a high value for their shares." App. to Pet. for Cert. 53a.

Had it read "because *in their estimation* it provides an opportunity, etc." it would have set forth nothing but an opinion. As written, however, it asserts both that the Board of Directors acted for a particular reason *and* that that reason is correct. This interpretation is made clear by what immediately follows: "The price to be paid is about 30 percent higher than the [last traded price immediately before announcement of the proposal]. . . . [T]he $42 per share that will be paid to public holders of the common stock represents a premium of approximately 26 percent over the book value. . . . [T]he bank earned $24,767,000 in the year ended December 31, 1986. . . ." *Id.* at 53a–54a. These are all facts that support—and that are obviously introduced for the *purpose* of supporting—the factual truth of the "because" clause, *i.e.*, that the proposal gives shareholders a "high value."

If the present case were to proceed, therefore, I think the normal § 14(a) principles governing misrepresentation of fact would apply.

* * *

WALKER V. ACTION INDUSTRIES, INC.

United States Court of Appeals, Fourth Circuit, 1986.
802 F.2d 703, *cert. denied* 479 U.S. 1065, 107 S.Ct. 952, 93 L.Ed.2d 1000 (1987).

EARVIN, CIRCUIT JUDGE:

* * *

On July 16, 1982, Action made a tender offer to purchase 15 percent of its common stock at $4.00 per share until August 6. In connection with the tender offer, Action issued a tender offer statement pursuant to rule 13e–4, which contained financial information on the corporation. Action's fiscal year runs from July through June. The tender offer statement disclosed audited financial statements for fiscal years 1979, 1980 and 1981. These figures revealed a net loss of $2,306,900 in fiscal 1979, net earnings of $372,900 in fiscal 1980, and net earnings of $731,200 in fiscal 1981. Because the 1982 fiscal year had just ended, audited financial statements for that year were not available. Action did disclose, however, unaudited, interim financial statements for fiscal 1982 through March 27, 1982, the end of Action's third fiscal quarter. These figures indicated a net loss of $4,014,900 as compared with net earnings of $1,037,600 for the same period in the previous year. In § 14B of the tender offer statement, Action also made disclosures entitled "Events Subsequent to March 27, 1982," which stated in part:

> The Company's fiscal year ended on June 26, 1982. Although financial statements have not yet been prepared or audited, the Company expects results from continuing operations to reflect a sales increase compared with the prior year. However, earnings from continuing operations are estimated to be somewhat lower than last year as a result of lower gross margins on sales and higher operating expenses.

In addition to financial statements, Action regularly prepared a number of other financial reports internally. On a weekly basis, Action prepared "work projections," which recorded actual orders and identified them as "firm" or "anticipated," depending on their likelihood of cancellation. Approximately monthly, Action prepared "gross sales forecasts." These reports projected monthly and quarterly sales based on the orders reflected in the weekly work projections. Action also tracked actual financial results in weekly "flash sales reports," which showed sales for the current week, month-to-date sales and quarter-to-date sales.

As early as May 1982, Action's internal financial reports indicated substantial increases in actual orders and projected sales for the first quarter of fiscal 1983 over the same period for fiscal 1982. As the July 16 tender offer grew nearer, and the first quarter of fiscal 1983 began, subsequent internal reports indicated even more substantial increases in actual orders and projected sales, as well as increases in actual sales over the prior year. Action, however, did not disclose the projected increases in sales or the increases in actual orders and sales in the tender offer statement, which was issued approximately twenty days into its first quarter of fiscal 1983.

* * *

On August 18, 1982, Action issued a press release regarding its year-end financial results for fiscal 1982. The press release and Action's audited financial statements, on which the press release was based, essentially confirmed the statements made in § 14B of the tender offer statement regarding the company's financial performance in fiscal 1982; sales were up but earnings were down. Between the time of the tender offer and the press release, Action's internal financial reports continued to indicate substantial increases in projected sales, and actual orders and sales, for the company's first quarter of fiscal 1983 and thereafter. As with the tender offer statement, however, Action refrained from disclosing such information in the press release. Walker read the press release and concluded that the company's prospects were not favorable. On September 21, he sold all of his Action shares on the open market at approximately $5.25 per share.

Action's stock traded as high as 7 1/8 per share on October 21. Then on October 28, Action issued a press release revealing its financial results for the first quarter of fiscal 1983 ending September 25, 1982. The release and accompanying unaudited, interim financial statements showed a 75% increase in sales, and net earnings of $1,467,600 compared with a net loss of $412,500, for the same period in the previous year. The following day, on October 29, Action stock traded as high as 9 7/8. By November 12, the stock reached 15 3/4 per share.

Subsequently, Walker brought suit against Action and three of its directors. Walker pursued a claim under rule 10b–5 alleging that defendants had a duty to disclose financial projections and actual orders and sales for fiscal 1983 in the tender offer statement and the August 18 press release. . . .

* * *

We turn first to Walker's argument that the district court should have instructed the jury that Action had a duty to disclose its financial projections. Historically, the Securities Exchange Commission (SEC) has discouraged the disclosure of financial projections and other "soft" information such as asset appraisals in proxy statements, tender offers and other disclosure documents on the ground that they were likely to mislead investors. . . . For example, in 1956 the SEC added a note to rule 14a–9 which listed "predictions as to specific future market values, earnings or dividends" as "examples of what, depending upon particular facts and circumstances, may be misleading" in proxy statements. . . .

The traditional SEC position, however, encountered substantial criticism in the early 1970s. . . . Then, in 1976, the SEC deleted earnings projections in the 14a–9 note from the list of potentially misleading disclosures. . . . In 1978, the SEC also adopted rule 175, which provides a "safe harbor" for "forward-looking statements" made in good faith. . . . Forward-looking statements are defined to include "a statement containing a projection of revenues, income (loss), earnings (loss) per share, capital expenditures, dividends, capital structure or other financial items." Rule 175, however, does not require the disclosure of financial projections. . . .

Thus, the SEC currently allows or permits disclosure of financial projections on a voluntary basis.

The circuits which have addressed whether there is a duty to disclose financial projections, and others of information such as asset appraisals, have reached varying results. These can be described as falling into three groups. First, the Seventh Circuit would appear to take the position that there is no duty to disclose financial projections.... Although the Second Circuit has not considered whether there is a duty to disclose financial projections, it has declined to recognize a duty to disclose asset appraisals.... Thus, it appears that the Second Circuit also would not impose a duty to disclose financial projections....

Second, the Third Circuit has held that "[c]ourts should ascertain the duty to disclose asset valuations and other soft information on a case by case basis." *Flynn v. Bass Brothers Enterprises, Inc.*, 744 F.2d 978, 988 (3d Cir.1984).... Whether there is duty to disclose soft information in a given case depends on a number of factors announced by the *Flynn* court.[9] ...

A third approach has been adopted by the Sixth Circuit. It has ruled that there is no duty to disclose financial projections unless they are "substantially certain." ... *See Starkman v. Marathon Oil Company,* 772 F.2d at 241–42.... While the Sixth Circuit's "substantially certain" test appears similar to the "case by case" approach announced by the Third Circuit in *Flynn,* the Sixth Circuit has rejected *Flynn* as, among other things, "uncertain and unpredictable." It should also be noted that the Sixth Circuit in applying its "substantially certain" test, has yet to impose a duty to disclose financial projections in any case.

The Ninth Circuit appears properly categorized with the Sixth....

... [W]e conclude that under the circumstances of this case Action had no duty to disclose its financial projections in the August 18 press release, for the reasons that follow.[11]

First, we note that Action made disclosures regarding its tender offer pursuant to rule 13e–4, which governs disclosures in the context of a corporation's tender offer for its own stock. Rule 13e–4 and its accompanying schedule 13E–4, ... require that certain information be disclosed. That information includes audited financial statements for the company's two most recent fiscal years and unaudited financial statements for the company's most recent quarter.... There is no requirement under

---

[9] The factors a court must consider in making such a determination are: the facts upon which the information is based; the qualifications of those who prepared or compiled it; the purpose for which the information was originally intended: its relevance to the stockholders' impending decision; the degree of subjectivity or bias reflected in its preparation; the degree to which the information is unique; and the availability to the investor of other more reliable sources of information....

[11] We do not specifically adopt any of the various positions held by the other circuits regarding whether a duty exists to disclose financial projections.

these regulations that financial projections be disclosed. Thus, the SEC has declined to impose expressly a duty to disclose such information in the context of 13e–4 tender offer statements. It follows that there was a similar absence of any express duty to disclose financial projections in the subsequent press release.

Second, the SEC has not imposed a duty to disclose financial projections in disclosure documents generally. As already noted, financial projections were discouraged by the SEC for approximately twenty years. Now, such disclosures are allowed or permitted. The transition from disclosure to permissive disclosure was heralded primarily by the SEC's modification of its regulations such as the adoption of voluntary disclosure provisions in Rule 175. We perceive the current SEC regulatory environment to be an experimental stage regarding financial projection disclosures. Respecting these evolutionary processes, we believe that a further transition, from permissive disclosure to required disclosure, should be occasioned by congressional or SEC adoption of more stringent disclosure requirements for financial projections, rather than by the courts.

Third, we are reluctant to recognize a duty to disclose financial projections in this case because of their uncertainty and their potential to mislead investors. Walker would have us impose a duty on Action to disclose its "gross sales forecasts," which projected monthly and quarterly sales. . . . Clearly, the projections were changing constantly, with each new one rendering the last incorrect. A disclosure of the May or June projections would have grossly understated subsequent projections. Furthermore, the projections failed to reflect accurately actual sales. . . . Most importantly, the quarter ended with an actual sales increase of 75 percent compared with over 129% projected. Net income, however, increased tenfold, a performance hardly forewarned by the projections. Because of the evident uncertainty and misleading nature of the projections, we deem it unwise to require their disclosure. Indeed, in light of the disparity between actual and projected sales, we wonder whether Walker also would have sued had the disclosures been made, alleging that the projections were overly optimistic. . . .

Finally, we believe that the projection disclosures sought by Walker are impractical. Action made its "gross sales forecasts" at least monthly and sometimes more frequently. Also, as described above, each forecast was substantially different. Because of the frequency and volatility of these projections, the imposition of a duty to disclose them would have required virtually constant statements by Action in order not to mislead investors. Under these circumstances, we deem the projection disclosures urged by Walker to be impractical, if not unreasonable.

For all of these reasons, we conclude that defendants did not have a duty to disclose Action's financial projections.[12] . . . We also note that our holding is not intended to discourage disclosures of financial projections. Indeed, we fully support voluntary disclosure as contemplated by Rule 175. Of course, it would appear prudent to release only those projections that are reasonably certain. . . . Furthermore, if a company undertakes projection disclosures, it must make the full disclosures necessary to avoid making the statements misleading. . . .

* * *

QUESTION

Should the standard for requiring the disclosure of projections be the same in a periodic report (an Annual Report on Form 10–K) as in a self-tender offer (a Schedule 13e–4)?

ASHER V. BAXTER INT'L INC.

United States Court of Appeals, Seventh Circuit, 2004.
377 F.3d 727.

EASTERBROOK, CIRCUIT JUDGE.

Baxter International, a manufacturer of medical products, released its second-quarter financial results for 2002 on July 18 of that year. Sales and profits did not match analysts' expectations. Shares swiftly fell from $43 to $32. This litigation followed; plaintiffs contend that the $43 price was the result of materially misleading projections on November 5, 2001, projections that Baxter reiterated until the bad news came out on July 18, 2002. Plaintiffs want to represent a class of all investors who purchased during that time either in the open market or by exchanging their shares of Fusion Medical Technologies. (Baxter acquired Fusion in a stock-for-stock transaction; plaintiffs think that Baxter juiced up the market price so that it could secure Fusion in exchange for fewer of its own shares.) . . .

Baxter's projection, repeated many times (sometimes in documents filed with the SEC, sometimes in press releases, sometimes in executives' oral statements), was that during 2002 the business would yield revenue growth in the "low teens" compared with the prior year, earnings-per-share growth in the "mid teens," and "operational cash flow of at least $500 million." . . . [Plaintiffs] say . . . that the projections were too rosy, and that Baxter knew it. That charges the defendants with stupidity as much as

---

[12] Stated another way, as a matter of law, defendants' failure to disclose the financial projections was not an omission of material facts, which were necessary under the circumstances to make the statements made not misleading.

with knavery, for the truth was bound to come out quickly, but the securities laws forbid foolish frauds along with clever ones.

* * *

Section 77z–2, which deals with statements covered by the Securities Act of 1933 (here, those in the registration statement and prospectus for the stock that Baxter exchanged for Fusion's shares) and § 78u–5, which deals with statements covered by the Securities Exchange Act of 1934 (here, the statements in Baxter's press releases, press conferences, and periodic filings) are identical in all significant respects, so from now on we mention only the former statute. The statutory safe harbor forecloses liability if a forward-looking statement "is accompanied by meaningful cautionary statements identifying important factors that could cause actual results to differ materially from those in the forward-looking statement" (§ 77z–2(c)(1)(A)(i)). The fundamental problem is that the statutory requirement of "meaningful cautionary statements" is not itself meaningful. What must the firm say? Unless it is possible to give a concrete and reliable answer, the harbor is not "safe"; yet a word such as "meaningful" resists a concrete rendition and thus makes administration of the safe harbor difficult if not impossible. It rules out a caution such as: "This is a for-ward-looking statement: caveat emptor." But it does not rule *in* any particular caution, which always may be challenged as not sufficiently "meaningful" or not pinning down the "important factors that could cause actual results to differ materially"—for if it *had* identified all of those factors, it would not be possible to describe the forward-looking statement itself as materially misleading. A safe harbor matters only when the firm's disclosures (including the accompanying cautionary statements) are false or misleadingly incomplete; yet whenever that condition is satisfied, one can complain that the cautionary statement must have been inadequate. The safe harbor loses its function. Yet it would be unsound to read the statute so that the safe harbor never works; then one might as well treat § 77z–2 and § 78u–5 as defunct.

Baxter provided a number of cautionary statements throughout the class period. This one, from its 2001 Form 10–K filing—a document to which many of the firm's press releases and other statements referred—is the best illustration:

> Statements throughout this report that are not historical facts are forward-looking statements. These statements are based on the company's current expectations and involve numerous risks and uncertainties. Some of these risks and uncertainties are factors that affect all international businesses, while some are specific to the company and the health care arenas in which it operates.
>
> Many factors could affect the company's actual results, causing results to differ materially, from those expressed in any

> such forward-looking statements. These factors include, but are not limited to, interest rates; technological advances in the medical field; economic conditions; demand and market acceptance risks for new and existing products, technologies and health care services; the impact of competitive products and pricing; manufacturing capacity; new plant start-ups; global regulatory, trade and tax policies; regulatory, legal or other developments relating to the company's Series A, AF, and AX dialyzers; continued price competition; product development risks, including technological difficulties; ability to enforce patents; actions of regulatory bodies and other government authorities; reimbursement policies of government agencies; commercialization factors; results of product testing; and other factors described elsewhere in this report or in the company's other filings with the Securities and Exchange Commission. Additionally, as discussed in Item 3—"Legal Proceedings," upon the resolution of certain legal matters, the company may incur charges in excess of presently established reserves. Any such change could have a material adverse effect on the company's results of operations or cash flows in the period in which it is recorded.
>
> Currency fluctuations are also a significant variable for global companies, especially fluctuations in local currencies where hedging opportunities are unreasonably expensive or unavailable. If the United States dollar strengthens significantly against mist foreign currencies, the company's ability to realize projected growth rates in its sales and net earnings outside the United States could be negatively impacted.
>
> The company believes that its expectations with respect to forward-looking statements are based upon reasonable assumptions within the bounds of its knowledge of its business operations, but there can be no assurance that the actual results or performance of the company will conform to any future results or performance expressed or implied by such forward-looking statements.

* * *

Before considering whether plaintiffs' objections defeat the safe harbor, we ask whether the cautionary statements have any bearing on Baxter's potential liability for statements in its press releases, and those its managers made orally. The press releases referred to, but did not repeat verbatim, the cautionary statements in the Form 10–K and other documents filed with the Securities and Exchange Commission. The oral statements did not do even that much. Plaintiffs say that this is fatal, because § 77z–2(c)(1)(A)(i) provides a safe harbor only if a written statement is "accompanied by" the meaningful caution; a statement published elsewhere differs from one that accompanies the press release. As for the oral statements: § 77z–2(c)(2)(A)(ii), a special rule for oral statements, provides a safe harbor only if the statement includes "that the actual results could differ materially from those projected in the forward-looking statement" and in addition:

> (i) the oral forward-looking statement is accompanied by an oral statement that additional information concerning factors that could cause actual results to differ materially from those in the forward-looking statement is contained in a readily available written document, or portion thereof;
>
> (ii) the accompanying oral statement referred to in clause (i) identifies the document, or portion thereof, that contains the additional information about those factors relating to the forward-looking statement; and
>
> (iii) the information contained in that written document is a cautionary statement that satisfies the standard established in paragraph (1)(A).

15 U.S.C. § 77z–2(c)(2)(B). When speaking with analysts Baxter's executives did not provide them with all of this information, such as directions to look in the 10–K report for the full cautionary statement. It follows, plaintiffs maintain, that this suit must proceed with respect to the press releases and oral statements even if the cautionary language filed with the SEC in registration statements and other documents meets the statutory standard.

If this were a traditional securities suit—if, in other words, an investor claimed to have read or heard the statement and, not having access to the truth, relied to his detriment on the falsehood—then plaintiffs' argument would be correct. But this is not a traditional securities claim. It is a fraud-on-the-market claim. None of the plaintiffs asserts that he read any of Baxter's press releases or listened to an executive's oral statement. Instead the theory is that other people (professional traders, mutual fund managers, securities analysts) did the reading, and that they made trades or recommendations that influenced the price. In an efficient capital market, all information known to the public affects the price and thus affects every investor. . . .

When markets are informationally efficient, it is impossible to segment information as plaintiffs propose. . . . Thus if the truth or the nature of a business risk is widely known, an incorrect statement can have no deleterious effect, and if a cautionary statement has been widely disseminated, that news too affects the price just as if that statement had been handed to each investor. If the executives' oral statements came to plaintiffs through professional traders (or analysts) and hence the price, then the cautions reached plaintiffs via the same route; market professionals are savvy enough to discount projections appropriately. Then § 77z–2(c)(2)(B) has been satisfied for the oral statements (and so too § 77z–2(c)(1)(A)(i) for the press releases). And if the cautions did not affect the price, then the market must be inefficient and the suit fails for that reason. So we take the claim as the pleadings framed it: the market for Baxter's stock is efficient, which means that Baxter's cautionary language must be treated as if attached to every one of its oral and written statements. That leaves the question whether these statements satisfy the statutory requirement that they adequately "identify [ ] important factors that could cause actual results to differ materially from those in the forward-looking statement".

The parties agree on two propositions, each with support in decisions of other circuits. First, "boilerplate" warnings won't do; cautions must be tailored to the risks that accompany the particular projections. Second, the cautions need not identify what actually goes wrong and causes the projections to be inaccurate; prevision is not required. . . . Unfortunately, these principles don't decide any concrete case—for that matter, the statutory language itself does not decide any concrete case. It is the result of a compromise between legislators who did not want any safe harbor (or, indeed any new legislation), and those who wanted a safe harbor along the lines of the old Rule 175 . . . that did not require any cautionary statements but just required the projection to have a reasonable basis. Rule 175 was limited to statements in certain documents filed with the SEC; proponents of the PSLRA wanted to extend this to all statements, including oral declarations and press releases. As is often the situation, a compromise enabled the bill to pass but lacks much content; it does not encode a principle on which political forces agreed as much as it signifies conflict about both the scope and the wisdom of the safe harbor. Compromises of this kind lack spirit. Still, the language was enacted, and we must make something of it.

Plaintiffs say that Baxter's cautions were boilerplate, but they aren't. Statements along the lines of "all businesses are risky" or "the future lies ahead" come to nothing other than caveat emptor (which isn't enough); these statements, by contrast, at least included Baxter-specific information and highlighted some parts of the business that might cause problems. For its part, Baxter says that mentioning these business segments demonstrates that the caution is sufficient; but this also is wrong, because then any issuer could list its lines of business, say "we could have problems in any of these," and avoid liability for statements implying that no such problems were on the horizon even if a precipice was in sight.

What investors would like to have is a full disclosure of the assumptions and calculations *behind* the projections; then they could apply their own discount factors. For reasons covered at length in *Wielgos,* however, this is not a sensible requirement.[Ed.35] Many of the assumptions and calculations would be more useful to a firm's rivals than

---

35 [Ed.] WIELGOS v. COMMONWEALTH EDISON CO., 892 F.2d 509, 513–15 (7th Cir. 1989) (Easterbrook, J.): [A firm disclosed voluntarily cost projections on nuclear power plants without disclosing internal work papers behind those projections. The Court affirmed a grant of a motion to dismiss. The following is the Court's discussion of Rule 175's reasonable basis test]:

> Forward-looking statements need not be correct. It is enough if they have a reasonable basis. . . .
>
> * * *
>
> Inevitable inaccuracy of a projection does not eliminate the safe harbor. . . . Rule 175 assumes that readers are sophisticated, can understand the limits of a projection—and that if any given reader does not appreciate its limits, the reactions of the many professional investors and analysts will lead to prices that reflect the limits of the information. . . . A belief that investors—collectively if not individually—can look out for themselves and ought to have information that may improve the accuracy of prices even if it turns out to be fallacious in a given instance underlies the very existence of Rule 175.
>
> Until 1978, when it adopted Rule 175, the SEC discouraged firms from making projections or commenting beyond the domain of 'hard' information, such as last year's sales. . . . It did this because statements about the future are less reliable than statements about the past. If you view investors as easily misled and unable to appreciate the uncertainty of predictions, you try to keep such information out of their hands. You will not succeed. Investors value securities because of beliefs about how firms will do tomorrow, not because of how they did yesterday. If enterprises cannot make predictions about themselves, then securities analysts, newspaper columnists, and charlatans have protected turf. There will be predictions aplenty outside the domain of the securities acts, predictions by persons whose access to information is not as good as the issuer's. When the issuer adds its information and analysis to that assembled by outsiders, the *collective* assessment will be more accurate even though a given projection will be off the mark.
>
> Convincing the SEC of the utility of projections is one thing, and convincing enterprises that they ought to make projections is another. What's in it for them? If all estimates are made carefully and honestly, half will turn out too favorable to the firm and the other half too pessimistic. In either case the difference may disappoint investors, who can say later that they bought for too much (if the projection was too optimistic) or sold for too little (if the projection turns out to be too pessimistic). Thus the role of a safe harbor: the firm is not liable despite error.
>
> Safe harbors are not necessarily enough. Harbors could be impossible to enter. Suppose the Commission were to require the issuer to reveal all of the data, assumptions, and methodology behind its projections, so that participants in the market could assess them fully and react appropriately. Data could be proprietary, secrets whose revelation to business rivals could damage the firm and its investors. Assumptions about the firm's own behavior could lead other firms to change theirs—for example, revealing the assumption that product line X will be discontinued at the end of the year could lead customers to stop buying it now or offer a rival a clue about how to capitalize. . . . The SEC therefore does not require the firm to reveal its data, assumptions, and methods. Rule 175(c)(4) *allows* the firm to reveal them, but their disclosure is not a condition of the safe harbor. Shelter without mandatory disclosure of the data and assumptions that may turn out to be important to evaluate the soundness depends on a belief that investors, collectively, are sophisticated. Readers may infer from what is said and what is omitted how reliable the estimate is. Firms that want to induce greater reliance may reveal more. Rule 175 leaves it to the issuer and the market to determine how much is revealed.
>
> * * *
>
> [In writing cautionary language] [i]ssuers need not "disclose" Murphy's Law or the Peter Principle, even though these have substantial effects on business. So too issuers need not estimate the chance that a federal agency will change its rules or tighten up on enforcement. Securities laws require issuers to disclose *firm-specific* information; investors and analysts combine that information with knowledge about the competition, regulatory conditions, and the economy as a whole to produce a value for stock. . . . Just as a firm needn't disclose that 50% of all new products vanish from the market within a short time, so Commonwealth Edison needn't disclose the hazards of its business, hazards apparent to all serious observers and most casual ones.

to its investors. Suppose, for example, that Baxter had revealed its sterility failure in the BioSciences Division, the steps it had taken to restore production, and the costs and prospects of each. Rivals could have used that information to avoid costs and hazards that had befallen Baxter, or to find solutions more quickly, and as Baxter could not have charged the rivals for this information they would have been able to undercut Baxter's price in future transactions. Baxter's shareholders would have been worse off. Similarly Baxter might have added verisimilitude to its projections by describing its sales policies and the lowest prices it would accept from major customers, but disclosing reservation prices would do more to help the customers than to assist the investors.

Another form a helpful caution might take would be the disclosure of confidence intervals. After saying that it expected growth in the low teens, Baxter might have added that events could deviate 5% in either direction (so the real projection was that growth would fall someplace between 8% and 18%); disclosure of the probability that growth will be under 10% (or over 16%) would have done much to avoid the hit stock prices took when the results for the first half of 2002 proved to be unexpectedly low. Baxter surely had developed internally some estimate of likely variance. Revealing the mean, median, and standard deviation of these internal estimates, and pinpointing the principal matters that could cause results to differ from the more likely outcome, could help to generate an accurate price for the stock. Knowledge that the mean is above the median, or that the standard deviation is substantial, would be particularly helpful to those professional investors whose trades determine the market price. (It might imply, for example, that as in *Wielgos* the firm was projecting what would happen if nothing unexpected happened; because some things always go wrong, investors could apply discounts.) Perhaps, however, a firm's data do not permit estimates to be stated in probabilities. If, for example, a major source of uncertainty for Baxter's business was how Congress would resolve the debate about Medicare coverage for prescription drugs, or whether a rival would manage to win the FDA's approval for a product that would compete with one of Baxter's most profitable items, it would be hard to reduce these chances to probabilities. Events such as these are discrete rather than continuous variables, so standard confidence intervals would be meaningless even if probabilities could be attached to the likely outcomes.

Whether or not Baxter could have made the cautions more helpful by disclosing assumptions, methods, or confidence intervals, none of these is required. The PSLRA does not require the *most* helpful caution; it is enough to "identify[ ] important factors that could cause actual results to differ materially from those in the forward-looking statement". This means that it is enough to point to the principal contingencies that could cause actual results to depart from the projection. The statute calls for issuers to reveal the "important factors" but not to attach probabilities to each potential bad outcome, or to reveal in detail what could go wrong; as we have said, that level of detail might hurt investors (by helping rivals) even as it improved the accuracy of stock prices. (Requiring cautions to contain elaborate detail also would defeat the goal of facilitating projections, by turning each into a form of registration statement. Undue complexity would lead issuers to shut up, and stock prices could become even less accurate. Incomplete information usually is better than none, because market professionals know other tidbits that put the news in context.) Moreover, "[i]f enterprises cannot make predictions about themselves, then securities analysts, newspaper columnists, and charlatans have protected turf. There will be predictions aplenty outside the domain of the securities acts, predictions by persons whose access to information is not as good as the issuer's. When the issuer adds its information and analysis to that assembled by outsiders, the *collective* assessment will be more accurate even though a given projection will be off the mark." *Wielgos,* 892 F.2d at 514 (emphasis in original).

Yet Baxter's chosen language may fall short. There is no reason to think—at least, no reason that a court can accept at the pleading stage, before plaintiffs have access to discovery—that the items mentioned in Baxter's cautionary language were those that at the time were the (or any of the) "important" sources of variance. The problem is not that what actually happened went unmentioned; issuers need not anticipate all sources of deviations from expectations. Rather, the problem is that there is no reason (on this record) to conclude that Baxter mentioned those sources of variance that (at the time of the projection) were the principal or important risks. For all we can tell, the major risks Baxter objectively faced when it made its forecasts were exactly those that, according to the complaint, came to pass, yet the cautionary statement mentioned none of them. Moreover, the cautionary language remained fixed even as the risks changed. When the sterility failure occurred in spring 2002, Baxter left both its forecasts and cautions as is. When Baxter closed the plants that (according to the complaint) were its least-cost sources of production, the forecasts and cautions continued without amendment. This raises the possibility—no greater confidence is possible before discovery—that Baxter omitted important variables from the cautionary language and so made projections more certain than its internal estimates at the time warranted. Thus this complaint could not be dismissed under the safe harbor, though we cannot exclude the possibility that if after discovery Baxter establishes that the cautions did reveal what were, *ex ante,* the major risks, the safe harbor may yet carry the day.

Baxter urges us to affirm the judgment immediately, contending that the full truth had reached the market despite any shortcomings in its cautionary statements. If this is so, however, it is hard to understand the sharp drop in the price of its stock. A "truth-on-the-market" defense is available in principle, as we discussed in *Flamm,* but not at the pleading stage. Likewise one must consider the possibility that investors looked at all of the projections as fluff and responded only to the hard numbers; on this view it was a reduction in Baxter's growth rate, not the embarrassment of a projection, that caused the price decline in July 2002; again it is too early in the litigation to reach such a conclusion. It would be necessary to ask, for example, whether the price rose relative to the rest of the market when Baxter made its projections; if not, that might support an inference that the projections were so much noise.

* * *

5. THE DUTY TO DISCLOSE PRE-SIGNING MERGER NEGOTIATIONS

BASIC, INC. V. LEVINSON

Supreme Court of the United States, 1988.
485 U.S. 224, 108 S.Ct. 978, 99 L.Ed.2d 194.

JUSTICE BLACKMUN delivered the opinion of the Court.

This case requires us to apply the materiality requirement of § 10(b) of the Securities Exchange Act of 1934, 48 Stat. 881, as amended, 15 U.S.C. § 78a *et seq.* (1934 Act), and the Securities and Exchange Commission's Rule 10b–5, promulgated thereunder, *see* 17 CFR § 240.10b–5 (1987), in the context of preliminary corporate merger discussions. . . .

* * *

Prior to December 20, 1978, Basic Incorporated was a publicly traded company primarily engaged in the business of manufacturing chemical refractories for the steel industry. As early as 1965 or 1966, Combustion Engineering, Inc., a company producing mostly alumina-based refractories, expressed some interest in acquiring Basic, but was deterred from pursuing this inclination seriously because of antitrust concerns it then entertained. . . . In 1976, however, regulatory action opened the way to a renewal of Combustion's interest. The "Strategic Plan," dated October 25, 1976, for Combustion's Industrial Products Group included the objective: "Acquire Basic Inc. $30 million." . . .

Beginning in September 1976, Combustion representatives had meetings and telephone conversations with Basic officers and directors, including petitioners here, concerning the possibility of a merger. During 1977 and 1978, Basic made three public statements denying that it was engaged in merger negotiations.[4] On December 18, 1978, Basic asked the

---

[4] On October 21, 1977, after heavy trading and a new high in Basic stock, the following news item appeared in the Cleveland Plain Dealer:

> "[Basic] President Max Muller said the company knew no reason for the stock's activity and that no negotiations were under way with any company for a merger. He said Flintkote recently denied Wall Street rumors that it would make a tender offer of $25 a

New York Stock Exchange to suspend trading in its shares and issued a release stating that it had been "approached" by another company concerning a merger. *Id.* at 413. On December 19, Basic's board endorsed Combustion's offer of $46 per share for its common stock, *id.* at 335, 414–416, and on the following day publicly announced its approval of Combustion's tender offer for all outstanding shares.

Respondents are former Basic shareholders who sold their stock after Basic's first public statement of October 21, 1977, and before the suspension of trading in December 1978. Respondents brought a class action against Basic and its directors, asserting that the defendants issued three false or misleading public statements and thereby were in violation of § 10(b) of the 1934 Act and of Rule 10b–5. Respondents alleged that they were injured by selling Basic shares at artificially depressed prices in a market affected by petitioners' misleading statements and in reliance thereon.

* * *

. . . The Court also explicitly has defined a standard of materiality under the securities laws, *see TSC Industries, Inc. v. Northway, Inc.,* 426 U.S. 438, 96 S.Ct. 2126, 48 L.Ed.2d 757 (1976), concluding in the proxy-solicitation context that "[a]n omitted fact is material if there is a substantial likelihood that a reasonable shareholder would consider it important in deciding how to vote." *Id.* at 449. . . . We now expressly adopt the *TSC Industries* standard of materiality for the § 10(b) and Rule 10b–5 context.

* * *

The application of this materiality standard to preliminary merger discussions is not self-evident. Where the impact of the corporate development on the target's fortune is certain and clear, the *TSC Industries* materiality definition admits straight-forward application. Where, on the other hand, the event is contingent or speculative in nature, it is difficult to ascertain whether the "reasonable investor" would have considered the omitted information significant at the time. Merger negotiations, because

---

> share for control of the Cleveland-based maker of refractories for the steel industry." App. 363.

On September 25, 1978, in reply to an inquiry from the New York Stock Exchange, Basic issued a release concerning increased activity in its stock and stated that

> "management is unaware of any present or pending company development that would result in the abnormally heavy trading activity and price fluctuation in company shares that have been experienced in the past few days." *Id.* at 401.

On November 6, 1978, Basic issued to its shareholders a "Nine Months Report 1978." This Report stated:

> "With regard to the stock market activity in the Company's shares we remain unaware of any present or pending developments which would account for the high volume of trading and price fluctuations in recent months." *Id.* at 403.

of the ever-present possibility that the contemplated transaction will not be effectuated, fall into the latter category.

* * *

Petitioners urge upon us a Third Circuit test for resolving this difficulty. . . . Under this approach, preliminary merger discussions do not become material until "agreement-in-principle" as to the price and structure of the transaction has been reached between the would-be merger partners. *See Greenfield v. Heublein, Inc.,* 742 F.2d 751, 757 (CA3 1984), *cert. denied,* 469 U.S. 1215, 105 S.Ct. 1189, 84 L.Ed.2d 336 (1985). By definition, then, information concerning any negotiations not yet at the agreement-in-principle stage could be withheld or even misrepresented without a violation of Rule 10b–5.

Three rationales have been offered in support of the "agreement-in-principle" test. The first derives from the concern expressed in *TSC Industries* that an investor not be overwhelmed by excessively detailed and trivial information, and focuses on the substantial risk that preliminary merger discussions may collapse: because such discussions are inherently tentative, disclosure of their existence itself could mislead investors and foster false optimism. . . . The other two justifications for the agreement-in-principle standard are based on management concerns: because the requirement of "agreement-in-principle" limits the scope of disclosure obligations, it helps preserve the confidentiality of merger discussions where earlier disclosure might prejudice the negotiations; and the test also provides a usable, bright-line rule for determining when disclosure must be made. . . .

None of these policy-based rationales, however, purports to explain why drawing the line at agreement-in-principle reflects the significance of the information upon the investor's decision. The first rationale, and the only one connected to the concerns expressed in *TSC Industries,* stands soundly rejected, even by a Court of Appeals that otherwise has accepted the wisdom of the agreement-in-principle test. "It assumes that investors are nitwits, unable to appreciate—even when told—that mergers are risky propositions up until the closing." *Flamm v. Eberstadt,* 814 F.2d, at 1175. Disclosure, and not paternalistic withholding of accurate information, is the policy chosen and expressed by Congress. We have recognized time and again, a "fundamental purpose" of the various securities acts, "was to substitute a philosophy of full disclosure for the philosophy of *caveat emptor* and thus to achieve a high standard of business ethics in the securities industry." . . .

The second rationale, the importance of secrecy during the early stages of merger discussions, also seems irrelevant to an assessment whether their existence is significant to the trading decision of a reasonable investor. To avoid a "bidding war" over its target, an acquiring firm often will insist that negotiations remain confidential, *see, e.g., In re Carnation*

Co., Exchange Act Release No. 22214, 33 SEC Docket 1025 (1985), and at least one Court of Appeals has stated that "silence pending settlement of the price and structure of a deal is beneficial to most investors, most of the time." *Flamm v. Eberstadt,* 814 F.2d, at 1177.

We need not ascertain, however, whether secrecy necessarily maximizes shareholder wealth—although we note that the proposition is at least disputed as a matter of theory and empirical research—for this case does not concern the *timing* of a disclosure; it concerns only its accuracy and completeness. We face here the narrow question whether information concerning the existence and status of preliminary merger discussions is significant to the reasonable investor's trading decision. Arguments based on the premise that some disclosure would be "premature" in a sense are more properly considered under the rubric of an issuer's duty to disclose. The "secrecy" rationale is simply inapposite to the definition of materiality.

The final justification offered in support of the agreement-in-principle test seems to be directed solely at the comfort of corporate managers. A bright-line rule indeed is easier to follow than a standard that requires the exercise of judgment in the light of all the circumstances. But ease of application alone is not an excuse for ignoring the purposes of the securities acts and Congress' policy decisions. Any approach that designates a single fact or occurrence as always determinative of an inherently fact-specific finding such as materiality, must necessarily be over-or underinclusive. In *TSC Industries* this Court explained: "The determination [of materiality] requires delicate assessments of the inferences a 'reasonable shareholder' would draw from a given set of facts and the significance of those inferences to him. . . ." 426 U.S., at 450, 96 S.Ct., at 2133. After much study, the Advisory Committee on Corporate Disclosure cautioned the SEC against administratively confining materiality to a rigid formula. Courts also would do well to heed this advice.

We therefore find no valid justification for artificially excluding from the definition of materiality information concerning merger discussions, which would otherwise be considered significant to the trading decision of a reasonable investor, merely because agreement-in-principle as to price and structure has not yet been reached by the parties or their representatives.

* * *

Even before this Court's decision in *TSC Industries,* the Second Circuit had explained the role of the materiality requirement of Rule 10b–5, with respect to contingent or speculative information or events, in a manner that gave that term meaning that is independent of the other provisions of the Rule. Under such circumstances, materiality "will depend at any given time upon a balancing of both the indicated probability that the event will occur and the anticipated magnitude of the event in light of the totality of the company activity." *SEC v. Texas Gulf Sulphur Co.,* 401 F.2d, at 849. . . .

In a subsequent decision, the late Judge Friendly, writing for a Second Circuit panel, applied the *Texas Gulf Sulphur* probability/ magnitude approach in the specific context of preliminary merger negotiations. After acknowledging that materiality is something to be determined on the basis of the particular facts of each case, he stated:

> "Since a merger in which it is bought out is the most important event that can occur in a small corporation's life, to wit, its death, we think that inside information, as regards a merger of this sort, can become material at an earlier stage than would be the case as regards lesser transactions—and this even though the mortality rate of mergers in such formative stages is doubtless high." *SEC v. Geon Industries, Inc.,* 531 F.2d 39, 47–48 (CA2 1976).

We agree with that analysis.[16]

Whether merger discussions in any particular case are material therefore depends on the facts. Generally, in order to assess the probability that the event will occur, a factfinder will need to look to indicia of interest in the transaction at the highest corporate levels. Without attempting to catalog all such possible factors, we note by way of example that board resolutions, instructions to investment bankers, and actual negotiations between principals or their intermediaries may serve as indicia of interest. To assess the magnitude of the transaction to the issuer of the securities allegedly manipulated, a factfinder will need to consider such facts as the size of the two corporate entities and of the potential premiums over market value. No particular event or factor short of closing the transaction need be either necessary or sufficient by itself to render merger discussions material.[17]

---

[16] The SEC in the present case endorses the highly fact-dependent probability/magnitude balancing approach of *Texas Gulf Sulphur.* It explains: "The *possibility* of a merger may have an immediate importance to investors in the company's securities even if no merger ultimately takes place." . . . The SEC's insights are helpful, and we accord them due deference. . . .

[17] To be actionable, of course, a statement must also be misleading. Silence, absent a duty to disclose, is not misleading under Rule 10b–5. "No comment" statements are generally the functional equivalent of silence. See *In re Carnation Co.,* Exchange Act Release No. 22214, 33 S.E.C. Docket 1025 (1985). See also New York Stock Exchange Listed Company Manual § 202.01, reprinted in 3 CCH Fed.Sec.L.Rep. ¶ 23,515 (1985) (premature public announcement may properly be delayed for valid business purpose and where adequate security can be maintained); American Stock Exchange Company Guide §§ 401–405, reprinted in 3 CCH Fed.Sec.L.Rep. ¶¶ 23,124A–23,124E (1985) (similar provisions).

It has been suggested that given current market practices, a "no comment" statement is tantamount to an admission that merger discussions are underway. *Flamm v. Eberstadt,* 814 F.2d, at 1178. That may well hold true to the extent that issuers adopt a policy of truthfully denying merger rumors when no discussions are underway, and of issuing "no comment" statements when they are in the midst of negotiations. There are, of course, other statement policies firms could adopt; we need not now advise issuers as to what kind of practice to follow, within the range permitted by law. Perhaps more importantly, we think that creating an exception to a regulatory

As we clarify today, materiality depends on the significance the reasonable investor would place on the withheld or misrepresented information. The fact-specific inquiry we endorse here is consistent with the approach a number of courts have taken in assessing the materiality of merger negotiations. Because the standard of materiality we have adopted differs from that used by both courts below, we remand the case for reconsideration of the question whether a grant of summary judgment is appropriate on this record.[20]

* * *

NOTE: WHAT TRIGGERS THE DUTY TO DISCLOSE?

The *Basic* case contained allegations that voluntary statements to the press violated Exchange Act Rule 10b–5. Footnote 17 in *Basic* notes that "silence, absent a duty to disclose, is not misleading." The question becomes: When does a participant in a preliminary merger discussion have a duty to disclose? The primary source of this duty comes from specific rules, forms, and schedules promulgated by the Securities and Exchange Commission. Some of the language in the regulations is very broad and could be read to impose a duty to disclose otherwise undisclosed preliminary merger negotiations. See, e.g., Sec. Act Rule 408 (registration statements);[36] Exch. Act Rule 12b–20 (periodic reports). Consider, for example, Item 303 of Regulation S–K, which is incorporated by reference into several disclosure statements. See Item 11(h) of Form S–1 (stock offerings); Item 13(a)(3) of Schedule 14A (proxy solicitations); Item 2 in Form 10–Q (quarterly reports required by the Exchange Act); and Item 7 in Form 10–K (annual reports required by the Exchange Act). Must a firm engaged in preliminary merger negotiations disclose them in its periodic reports, in any proxy solicitation (even if unrelated to the acquisition), or in any offering of securities (even if unrelated to the acquisition)? The SEC addressed some of these problems in the Release that follows. Note the Release's exceptions for registration statements, sales of a business segment, and a Schedule 14D–9.

---

scheme founded on a pro-disclosure legislative philosophy, because complying with the regulation might be "bad for business," is a role for Congress, not this Court. See also *id.* at 1182 (opinion concurring in the judgment and concurring in part).

[20] The Sixth Circuit rejected the District Court's narrow reading of Basic's "no development" statement, see n. 4, *supra*, which focused on whether petitioners *knew* of any reason for the activity in Basic stock, that is, whether petitioners were aware of leaks concerning ongoing discussions. . . . We accept the Court of Appeals' reading of the statement as the more natural one, emphasizing management's knowledge of developments (as opposed to leaks) that would explain unusual trading activity. . . .

[36] Sec. Act Rule 408(a): "In addition to the information expressly required to be included in a registration statement, there shall be added such further material information, if any, as may be necessary to make the required statements, in the light of the circumstances under which they are made, not misleading."

MANAGEMENT'S DISCUSSION AND ANALYSIS OF FINANCIAL CONDITION AND RESULTS OF OPERATIONS; CERTAIN INVESTMENT COMPANY DISCLOSURES

SEC Rel. No. 33–6835, 1989 WL 1092885, at *16–17 (May 18, 1989).

* * *

4. *Preliminary Merger Negotiations*

While Item 303 could be read to impose a duty to disclose otherwise nondisclosed preliminary merger negotiations, as known events or uncertainties reasonably likely to have material effects on future financial condition or results of operations, the Commission did not intend to apply, and has not applied, Item 303 in this manner. As reflected in the various disclosure requirements under the Securities Act and Exchange Act that specifically address merger transactions, the Commission historically has balanced the informational need of investors against the risk that premature disclosure of negotiations may jeopardize completion of the transaction.[50] In general, the Commission's recognition that registrants have an interest in preserving the confidentiality of such negotiations is clearest in the context of a registrant's continuous reporting obligations under the Exchange Act, where disclosure on Form 8–K of acquisitions or dispositions of assets not in the ordinary course of business is triggered by completion of the transaction.[51]

In contrast, where a registrant registers securities for sale under the Securities Act, the Commission requires disclosure of material probable acquisitions and dispositions of businesses, including the financial statements of the business to be acquired or sold.[52] Where the proceeds

[50] *See, e.g.,* Securities Exchange Act Release No. 16384 (November 29, 1979) (44 FR 70326, 70336) (considering these conflicting interests in adopting Item 7 of Schedule 14D–9, 17 CFR 240.101, which requires that the subject company of a public tender offer provide two levels of disclosure: (a) a statement as to whether or not "any negotiation [which would result in certain transactions or fundamental changes] is being undertaken or is underway . . . in response to the tender offer," which disclosure need not include "the possible terms of the transaction or the parties thereto" if in the registrant's view such disclosure would jeopardize the negotiations; and (b) a description of "any transaction board resolution, agreement in principle or a signed contract" relating to such transactions or changes.)

[51] Item 2 of Form 8–K, 17 CFR 249.308. *See also* Item 8 of Form 10–K, 17 CFR 249.310 (excluding pro forma financial information otherwise called for by Article 11 of Regulation S–X from the financial information required); Item 1 of Form 10–Q, 17 CFR 249.308a, and Rule 10–01 of Regulation S–X, 17 CFR 210.01. [Ed. The SEC amended Form 8–K in 2004 to require disclosure of entry into or termination of a "material definitive agreement." The new language requires disclosure of acquisition agreements on signing.]

With respect to the disposal of a segment of a business, however, Accounting Principles Board Opinion 30 requires that results of operations of the segment be reclassified as discontinued operations, and any estimated loss on disposal be recorded, as of the date management commits itself to a formal plan to dispose of the segment (*i.e.,* the "measurement data"). Filings, including periodic reports under the Exchange Act that contain annual or interim financial statements are required to reflect the prescribed accounting treatment as of the measurement date.

[52] Article 11 of Regulation S–X, 17 CFR 210.11–01 *et seq.* (generally requiring the provision of pro forma financial information where a significant acquisition or disposition "has occurred or is probable"). Entry into the continuous reporting system by registration under the Exchange Act also requires the provision of such pro forma financial information. Item 13 of Form 10, 17 CFR

from the sale of the securities being registered are to be used to finance an acquisition of a business, the registration statement must disclose the intended use of proceeds. Again, accommodating the need for confidentiality of negotiations, registrants are specifically permitted not to disclose in registration statements the identity of the parties and the nature of the business sought if the acquisition is not yet probable and the board of directors determines that the acquisition would be jeopardized.[53]

The Commission's interpretation of Item 303, as applied to preliminary merger negotiations, incorporates the same policy determinations. Accordingly, where disclosure is not otherwise required, and has not otherwise been made, the MD & A need not contain a discussion of the impact of such negotiations where, in the registrant's view, inclusion of such information would jeopardize completion of the transaction. Where disclosure is otherwise required or has otherwise been made by or on behalf of the registrant, the interests in avoiding premature disclosure no longer exist. In such case, the negotiations would be subject to the same disclosure standards under Item 303 as any other known trend, demand, commitment, event or uncertainty. These policy determinations also would extend to preliminary negotiations for the acquisition or disposition of assets not in the ordinary course of business.

* * *

NEW YORK STOCK EXCHANGE MANUAL

202.01 Internal Handling of Confidential Corporate Matters

Unusual market activity or a substantial price change has on occasion occurred in a company's securities shortly before the announcement of an important corporate action or development. Such incidents are extremely embarrassing and damaging to both the company and the Exchange since the public may quickly conclude that someone acted on the basis of inside information.

Negotiations leading to mergers and acquisitions, stock splits, the making of arrangements preparatory to an exchange or tender offer, changes in dividend rates or earnings, calls for redemption, and new contracts, products, or discoveries are the type of developments where the risk of untimely and inadvertent disclosure of corporate plans are most likely to occur. Frequently, these matters require extensive discussion and study by corporate officials before final decisions can be made. Accordingly,

---

249.210. *See also* Item 14 of Schedule 14A, 17 CFR 240.14a–101 (requiring Article 11 pro forma financial information and extensive other information about certain extraordinary transactions if shareholder action is to be taken with respect to such a transaction).

[53] Item 504 of Regulation S–K, 17 CFR 229.504, Instruction 6.

extreme care must be used in order to keep the information on a confidential basis.

Where it is possible to confine formal or informal discussions to a small group of the top management of the company or companies involved, and their individual confidential advisors where adequate security can be maintained, premature public announcement may properly be avoided. In this regard, the market action of a company's securities should be closely watched at a time when consideration is being given to important corporate matters. If unusual market activity should arise, the company should be prepared to make an immediate public announcement of the matter.

At some point it usually becomes necessary to involve other persons to conduct preliminary studies or assist in other preparations for contemplated transactions, *e.g.*, business appraisals, tentative financing arrangements, attitude of large outside holders, availability of major blocks of stock, engineering studies and market analyses and surveys. Experience has shown that maintaining security at this point is virtually impossible. Accordingly, fairness requires that the company make an immediate public announcement as soon as disclosures relating to such important matters are made to outsiders.

The extent of the disclosures will depend upon the stage of discussions, studies, or negotiations. So far as possible, public statements should be definite as to price, ratio, timing and/or any other pertinent information necessary to permit a reasonable evaluation of the matter. At a minimum, they should include those disclosures made to outsiders. Where an initial announcement cannot be specific or complete, it will need to be supplemented from time to time as more definitive or different terms are discussed or determined.

* * *

202.03 Dealing With Rumors or Unusual Market Activity

The market activity of a company's securities should be closely watched at a time when consideration is being given to significant corporate matters. If rumors or unusual market activity indicate that information on impending developments has leaked out, a frank and explicit announcement is clearly required. If rumors are in fact false or inaccurate, they should be promptly denied or clarified. A statement to the effect that the company knows of no corporate developments to account for the unusual market activity can have a salutary effect. It is obvious that if such a public statement is contemplated, management should be checked prior to any public comment so as to avoid any embarrassment or potential criticism. If rumors are correct or there are developments, an immediate candid statement to the public as to the state of negotiations or of development of corporate plans in the rumored area must be made directly and openly. Such statements are essential despite the business inconvenience which may be caused and even though the matter may not as yet have been presented to the company's Board of Directors for consideration.

* * *

202.04 Exchange Market Surveillance

The Exchange maintains a continuous market surveillance program through its Market Surveillance and Evaluation Division. An "on-line" computer system has been developed which monitors the price movement of every listed stock—on a trade-to-trade basis—throughout the trading session. The program is designed to closely review the markets in those securities in which unusual price and volume changes occur or where there is a large unexplained influx of buy or sell orders. If the price movement of a stock exceeds a predetermined guideline, it is immediately "flagged" and review of the situation is immediately undertaken to seek the causes of the exceptional activity. Under these circumstances, the company may be called by its Exchange representative to inquire about any company developments which have not been publicly announced but which could be responsible for unusual market activity. Where the market appears to reflect undisclosed information, the company will normally be requested to make the information public immediately. . . .

The Listing Agreement provides that a company must furnish the Exchange with such information concerning the company as the Exchange may reasonably require.

* * *

202.05 Timely Disclosure of Material News Developments

A listed company is expected to release quickly to the public any news or information which might reasonably be expected to materially affect the market for its securities. This is one of the most important and fundamental purposes of the listing agreement which the company enters into with the Exchange.

A listed company should also act promptly to dispel unfounded rumors which result in unusual market activity or price variations.

* * *

QUESTIONS

Under the testing requirements, could Basic's officers have responded to the press inquiries in October of 1977 with a "no comment"? Could Basic's officers have responded to the NYSE inquiry of September, 1978 with a "no comment"?

NOTE: FOOTNOTE 17 IN BASIC V. LEVINSON—*A CONFUSING BIT OF DICTA ON THE BUSINESS PURPOSE EXCEPTION*

The SEC and the Second Circuit have recognized the propriety of temporarily withholding material information when there are "good business reasons," so long as neither the firm nor insiders are trading during the period.[37] The risk of withholding material information is a later adverse judicial determination that the delay was in "bad faith."[38] The number of cases in which the business purpose test appears is very limited, however.[39] The exception may not be well known. In any event, casual dicta in a Supreme Court footnote may scuttle the exception anyway.

The Supreme Court has put the business purpose exception in doubt in a curious bit of dicta in its *Basic v. Levinson* opinion. The Court paraphrased with approval in dicta, early in footnote seventeen, a section of the New York Stock Exchange Listing Manual that contained, according to the Court, a license: "premature public announcements may properly be delayed for valid business purpose and where adequate security can be maintained." The paraphrasing was not accurate, but the Court's approval of what it thought the section meant is significant.[40] But later in the same footnote the Court gave the back of its hand to the same argument:

> We think that creating an exception to a regulatory scheme founded on a pro-disclosure legislative philosophy, because complying with the regulation might be "bad for business," is a role for Congress not this Court.

We are left with the two conflicting indications. Can firms argue a "valid business purpose" or is the "bad for business" argument only one for Congress? As noted in SEC Rel. 33–6835 above, the SEC has taken business concerns into account in its interpretation of Item 303 of Regulation S–K. Why can the Court not do the same for Exchange Act Rule 10b–5, largely a judicially-created creature?

---

[37] In the Matters of Investors Management Co., Inc., 44 SEC 633, 646, 1971 WL 120502 (1971); SEC v. Texas Gulf Sulphur, 401 F.2d 833, 850 n.12 (2d Cir.1968), *cert. denied*, SEC v. Coates, 394 U.S. 976, 89 S.Ct. 1454, 22 L.Ed.2d 756 (1969); see also Astor v. Texas Gulf Sulphur Co., 306 F.Supp. 1333, 1338–39 (S.D.N.Y. 1969) (granting a motion for summary judgment on the language). In *Texas Gulf Sulphur*, the court respected a claim that the disclosure of a drill sample revealing the existence of minerals would prejudice a mining firm's ability to buy land on which to mine. "We do not suggest that material facts must be disclosed immediately; the timing of disclosure is a matter for the business judgment of the corporate officers entrusted with the management of the corporation within the affirmative disclosure requirements promulgated by the exchanges and the SEC." 401 F.2d at 850 n.12.

[38] Financial Indus. Fund, Inc. v. McDonnell Douglas Corp., 474 F.2d 514, 519 (10th Cir. 1973).

[39] We have found only two federal district court cases that have applied the doctrine. State Teachers Retirement Bd. v. Fluor Corp., 500 F.Supp. 278, 293 (S.D.N.Y. 1980) (delay in announcing major construction contract); U.S. v. Koenig, 388 F.Supp. 670, 705 (S.D.N.Y. 1974) (delay in announcing recapitalizations plan).

[40] The NYSE does not have an explicit business purpose exception but the American Exchange Stock (AMEX) did at that time. The Supreme Court put the parenthetical note in the text behind the NYSE rule and merely cited the AMEX rule, however. NYSE Euronext acquired the AMEX in 2008.

The reasoning in the footnote has other trouble spots as well. Consider an analysis of what could have been in the Court's opinion in *Basic*. In the case, a corporation listed on the New York Stock Exchange was in very early merger negotiations and, due to leaks from unspecified sources, the negotiations were affecting the firm's stock price. An Exchange official made an official inquiry of the firm, permitted by the listing contract, and the firm was contractually obliged to give the Exchange an accurate response. As noted above, the Listing Manual specifically refers to market activity in a company's securities generated by rumors. The firm, however, responded to the Exchange's inquiry with an affirmative misrepresentation: "management is unaware of any present or pending company development that would result in the abnormally heavy trading activity and price fluctuation in company shares that have been experienced in the past few days." Management knew why the stock price was volatile, but it did not want to spoil the delicate negotiations with a press release. The Supreme Court found the misrepresentation actionable if material and then proceeded to define materiality in the context of the facts of the case.

In the latter part of footnote seventeen, the Court gives the business community some advice on what to do if a firm did not want to jeopardize merger talks with premature public disclosures. After stating that silence is not actionable absent a duty to disclose, the Court wrote that "no comment" statements are "*generally* the functional equivalent of silence." The Court seemed to imply that the defendant in the case, although obligated in its listing agreement to provide information to the NYSE, could have replied with a "no comment." The response would seem to be a violation of the listing agreement and run the risk of the NYSE sanctions but apparently the response would not by itself trigger a duty to speak under Rule 10b–5. In the background is the possibility that if the NYSE did sanction the firm, then shareholders could bring a derivative action against the board for their breach of fiduciary duty for getting on the wrong side of NYSE officials.

Moreover, there is the matter of the word "generally" in the Court's advice on the use of a "no comment" statement. At issue are the difficulties caused by a firm changing its pattern of public statements. All market participants understand that a "no comment" may sometimes itself be an admission, especially if a company had issued a series of explicit denials in response to prior inquiries about the same rumor and suddenly shifts to the "no comment" response when the query is repeated. If, at the time of the "no comment" reply, a firm still has no merger discussions under way, the "no comment" may be materially misleading and actionable because some in the investing public reasonably will consider the change in response to indicate that something is brewing. On the other hand, if merger discussions have just begun, a change in response may still mislead some. If, at the time of the "no comment," a firm had begun merger negotiations, the response is, to the dismay of the management in the midst of a difficult negotiation, and as noted by the Court, a premature public disclosure of a sensitive matter to some members of the public and, perhaps, misleading to others who take the response at its face value.

The Court acknowledged the problem, and concluded with an oblique hint: "There are, of course, other statement policies firms could adopt; we need not now advise issuers as to what kind of practice to follow, with the range permitted by law." What is the hinted practice? Full disclosure? But if so, why the reference to a "no comment" response at all? Or, perhaps, in the alternative, a practice of permanently responding to Exchange inquiries with a "no comment" unless a legal duty to speak otherwise attaches? The latter practice would appear to violate the firm's listing agreement with the NYSE. It would also reduce the total amount of information available to the public trading markets.

The Court could have taken another tack to respect the firm's obligation under its listing agreement to the New York Stock Exchange. The "no comment" advice would be inappropriate, and the firm, on an inquiry from the Exchange, would be expected to provide accurate information in accordance with its listing contract.

The Supreme Court put the ball in the NYSE's court and the NYSE had several possible responses. The NYSE could modify its listing requirements to comport with *Basic,* and respect a "no comment" response. The NYSE could keep its listing requirements in place and, in light of the Supreme Court language, simply adopt a lenient enforcement policy on "no comment" responses. Or the NYSE could understand Rule 10b–5 to be less demanding than its listing requirement and enforce NYSE requirements regardless of the Supreme Court's language. The NYSE has adopted the second approach.

QUESTION

Given the foregoing, what do you make of the following comment made by a publicly traded company in response to a press inquiry relating to a rumor involving that company negotiating to potentially acquire a competitor?

> "At any given time, the Company is evaluating possible acquisitions and divestitures in its pursuit of enhancing shareholder value."

PHILLIPS v. LCI INT'L INC., 190 F.3d 609 (4th Cir. 1999) (Motz, J.): [LCI was a long-distance telecommunications company with both residential and business customers. Qwest Communications, a competitor, had an extensive fiber-optic network but lacked a strong customer base. In October of 1997, the CEO of Qwest suggested to the CEO of LCI that the companies merge. The companies held meetings and started due diligence investigations. On December 11, Qwest proposed a stock swap merger but the LCI board rejected the offer as too low. When LCI reported its fourth quarter earnings on February 17, 1998, a reporter asked the LCI CEO about the company's future. The CEO responded that "We're not a company that's for sale." Two days later Qwest renewed its offer at a higher price and, by March 8, both boards had approved an acquisition agreement. The deal was announced on March 9. A shareholder suit was filed by those shareholders who sold their stock after February 17 and before March 9. The district court dismissed the suit and the circuit court affirmed.]

"Nevertheless, we agree with the district court that the stockholders' complaint fails to allege a misrepresentation of material fact. The complaint rests on mischaracterizations of the public record, exaggeration of a single statement, and isolation of that statement from its context and from the wealth of other information publicly available when it was made. . . .

* * *

. . . Thompson's statement itself belies the stockholders' contention that Thompson 'publicly denied any negotiations were ongoing[.]' . . . The sole asserted basis for the claim of securities fraud in this case is the purportedly fraudulent statement that: 'we're not a company that's for sale.' That statement does not 'publicly deny any ongoing negotiations.' Nor does it 'resemble' the Basic statements. . . . [I]n Basic, the company flatly denied any 'awareness' of any 'developments'—present or pending—that would affect the price or volatility of the company's stock and specifically denied that the merger 'negotiations were underway.'

Similarly, in the only other case that the stockholders cite in which shareholders of a publicly-held corporation were found to have stated a securities fraud claim solely on the basis of asserted misrepresentations about merger negotiations, corporate officers had repeatedly 'denied the existence of any merger negotiations' and stated that they 'were not currently engaged in any' such efforts. *In re Columbia Sec. Litig.*, 747 F.Supp. 237, 240 (S.D.N.Y. 1990). Thompson's 'we're not a company that's for sale' statement contains no equivalent blanket denial of awareness of any merger negotiations, let alone, any explicit assertion that the company was not presently engaged in such negotiations.

Nor do the remarks Thompson made in the post-merger interviews on March 9 provide support for the stockholders' assertion that his February 'not for sale' statement was materially false like the statements in Basic and Columbia. During the interviews, Thompson acknowledged that Qwest and LCI 'started talking a couple months ago . . . on a sincere basis,' which 'accelerated about three weeks ago.' That account tells us nothing about the truth or materiality of the 'not for sale' statement. Although the post-merger remarks could be consistent with a hiatus in negotiations after the December rejection and renewal of them with announcement of LCI's strong fourth quarter earnings, if interpreted in the light most favorable to the stockholders, the remarks certainly could support their allegation that merger negotiations were 'ongoing' when Thompson issued his February 'not for sale' statement. But that is all the post-merger remarks could do and thus they add nothing to the stockholders' case because, for purposes of evaluating the complaint, we assume that the stockholders' allegation as to 'ongoing' negotiations is true. The post-merger remarks simply do not transform Thompson's February statement into a flat denial of any merger negotiations like those in *Basic* and *Columbia*.

* * *

. . . A corporate officer's statement that the company was not 'for sale' or 'in play' is a good deal different from that officer's express denial of any merger negotiations.[Ed.[41]]"

WEINER v. QUAKER OATS CO., 129 F.3d 310 (3d Cir. 1997) (Pollack, J.): [Quaker Oats had, in its 1993 Annual Report, filed in October of 1993, noted that its "guideline" for the ratio of debt to equity was "in the upper–60 percent range." Quaker Oats repeated the statement in its Quarterly Report on Form 10–Q, filed in November of 1993 and in the 1994 Annual Report on Form 10–K, filed in September of 1994. Quaker Oats had begun negotiations to buy Snapple, beginning one of the most disastrous acquisitions of the 1990s, in spring 1994. By August Quaker's lawyers and accountants were conducting a due diligence investigation. Quaker announced the acquisition on November 2, 1994 and closed the acquisition by the end of the month. To finance the acquisition, Quaker had to incur significant amounts of new debt (a new $2.4 billion line of credit), raising its debt/equity ratio to around 80 percent. Analysts speculated that the managers of Quaker bought Snapple to releverage the company and thereby make Quaker a less attractive takeover target. Subsequent to the November 2nd announcement, the price of Quaker stock fell 10 percent. Angry holders of Quaker stock, who had purchased before the November 2nd announcement and, after the Snapple negotiations had begun, sued Quaker, primarily for a violation of Exchange Act Rule 10b–5.

The court reversed the district court's dismissal of the claim. Although noting that each of the statements on debt/equity ratios were correct when made, the Third Circuit held that "it was reasonable for an investor to expect that the company would make another such prediction if it expected the ratio to change markedly in the ensuing year."[42] It added that "Quaker had a duty to update such statements when they became unreliable."[43] In response to the defendant's claim that a supplementing disclosure on its debt/equity ratio would require the disclosure of the merger negotiations, the court stated, first, that Quaker could have projected an increase in the ratio and not tipped the market to its plans, and, second, if not, too bad.

---

[41] [Ed. For cases in which denials of merger discussions were actionable, see In re MCI Worldcom, Inc. Sec. Litig., 93 F.Supp.2d 276 (E.D.N.Y. 2000) (spokesperson said "no comment" but added a sentence implying her firm's lack of takeover intent); Buxbaum v. Deutsche Bank, 2000 WL 33912712, at *2 (S.D.N.Y.) ("everybody talks to everybody . . . there was no talk of a takeover").]

[42] 129 F.3d at 317.

[43] *Id.* at 318.

Citing the last sentence of footnote seventeen in *Basic* (discussed above), the court restated the Supreme Court's argument that the pro-disclosure philosophy is a recognized part of the securities laws and it was up to Congress, not the courts, to create an exception for sensitive merger negotiations.

In response to the defendant's argument that Quaker and Snapple did not even have a preliminary agreement on basic terms at the time of the voluntary November 2nd disclosure, the court replied, "Whatever the terms of the agreement may have been by the time of the purported false or misleading statements, it must by then have been clear to defendants that the merger would compel Quaker to take on sufficient debt to raise the total debt-to-total capitalization ratio to a level far higher than the 'upper–60 percent' range."

Also in issue was whether Quaker Oaks had a similar duty to update its earnings projections. The Third Circuit noted that there was no "per se" rule protecting earnings projections in the financials and that the annual and quarterly statements, if not updated, might have supported Rule 10b–5 liability.[44] The Third Circuit disagreed with the District Court's holding that the earnings statements were "vague expressions of optimism" and not material as a matter of law. The Third Circuit, however, held that the earnings projections had been superseded and were no longer "alive."]

6. GUN JUMPING: PRE-FILING ANNOUNCEMENTS

On October 19, 1999, the SEC adopted revisions to the registration, proxy and tender offer rules governing business combination transactions and shareholder communications.[45] An important part of the rule amendments substantially eliminated the severe limitations under the old rules on pre-transaction communication with shareholders. Under the new rules the parties to a business combination are permitted to communicate freely with analysts, investors and the public about a proposed transaction as long as the communications do not violate the various securities antifraud rules.[46]

The new rules largely eliminate the offense of "gun jumping" (communications prior to the filing of a registration statement necessary for stock swap mergers and exchange tender offers), largely eliminate the

---

[44] *Id.* at 320 n.11. The court did note, however, in a following footnote, in a sort of dicta on dicta comment, that a merger "almost certainly" would have had a "less direct and immediate" effect on earnings growth than a merger would have on a debt-capitalization ratio. *Id.* n.12. We are left to speculate on whether the difference on the facts is crucial.

[45] See *Regulation of Takeovers and Security Holder Communications*, SEC Rel. No. 33–7760, 1999 WL 969596 (Oct. 19, 1999). The SEC is continuing its efforts to liberalize pre-offering communications. *Securities Offering Reform*, SEC Rel. No. 33–8501, 2004 WL 2610458 (Nov. 3, 2004) (relaxing gun jumping rules in public offerings, particularly for "seasoned issuers").

[46] The rules include not only the general antifraud rules such as Exchange Act Rule 10b–5, but also, in the case of communications prior to the filing of a registration statement for stock swaps, the strict liability standard in § 12 of the Securities Act of 1933.

offense of an illegal, pre-filing proxy solicitation (communications to shareholders prior to the filing and dissemination of a proxy statement necessary for shareholder votes in mergers and asset sales), and eliminate the five-day rule for tender offer announcements (the requirement that a tender offeror file with the SEC within five days of an announcement containing a price). See Sec. Act Rule 165 (registration statements), Exch. Act Rule 14a–12 (proxy statements) and Exch. Act Rule 14d–2(b) (tender offer statements), respectively. In place of the old rules are requirements that at or prior to the time shareholders are actually provided with a proxy card or a letter of transmittal in a tender offer, shareholders must also be provided with the appropriate disclosure document containing the information mandated in the Schedules, whether it be a prospectus, tender offer statement or proxy statement.

All other written pre-transaction communications must be filed with the SEC on the date of their first use and must include a legend urging investors to read the formal disclosure document when it is released. The SEC staff stated, in the accompanying release, that the new filing requirement would apply to scripts used in communicating information to the public, slides shown to investors, and electronic communications in videos and CD-ROMs. See also SEC Reg. S–T, Rule 304 (Reg. S–T contains general rules and regulations for electronic filings with the SEC).

7. SECTION 13(d): DISCLOSING STOCK PURCHASES OF A PUBLIC CORPORATION OF MORE THAN 5 PERCENT

a. The Early Warning System

Section 13(d) of the Exchange Act provides that any person or group which becomes the beneficial owner of *more than five percent* of a class of equity securities of a publicly traded company must file a disclosure document under cover of Schedule 13D with the SEC, the publicly traded company in question, and each stock exchange on which the securities in question are listed. Filings must be made within 10 days after the purchase that pushes beneficial ownership over the five percent threshold.[47]

The policy behind Section 13(d) is twofold. First, its mandated disclosure alerts the market to the possibility that a given publicly traded company may soon be the subject of a takeover. Critics, of course, point out that such an early warning system also gives the prospective target company advance warning so that it can install a panoply of takeover defenses. Second, Section 13(d) prevents creeping acquisitions of public companies. Without Section 13(d), a bidder could attempt to make periodic

---

[47] In early 2014, momentum within Congress and the SEC to substantially shorten the 10-day filing window appeared to be building. However, to date no definitive action in this regard has occurred.

purchases of the target's stock through open market purchases that neither qualify as "tender offers" nor draw undue attention. Selling shareholders of the target, oblivious as to what was really happening, would sell their shares to the acquirer without receiving any control premium.

Disclosure in a Schedule 13D includes, among other information:

- The identity and background of the party or group making the filing;
- The source of funding used to purchase the shares;
- The number of shares of the security beneficially owned by the filer; and
- The purpose the purchase serves.

One of the most useful disclosures contained in a Schedule 13D is the filer's purpose for acquiring the shares in question. In particular, the filer must disclose any plans or proposals which relate to or would result in, among other things: (a) the acquisition or disposition of the issuer's securities by any person (such as a tender offer); (b) an extraordinary corporate transaction (such as a merger); and (c) any change in the present board of directors or management of the issuer (such as a hostile proxy contest to oust incumbent target directors from office).

Many who file Schedule 13D state that the purpose of their purchase is for "investment purposes only." Whether the market believes this statement has a lot to do with the person or entity making it. The market takes with a grain of salt such statements coming from well-known corporate raiders, many of whom make that disclosure only to change it later on through a well-timed amendment to their Schedule 13D. In fact, under Exchange Act Rule 13d–2(a), a filer must amend its Schedule 13D "promptly" if there is a material change to it (e.g., a material increase or decrease in the percentage of the class of securities beneficially owned).[48] Thus, if a filer changes its purpose in owning the shares in question, it must disclose this change relatively quickly.

Section 13(d) focuses on "*beneficial ownership*." Indeed, only those who "beneficially own" more than five percent of an issuer's equity securities must file a Schedule 13D. Under Exchange Act Rule 13d–3(a), a "*beneficial owner*" is any person who, directly or indirectly, through any contract,

---

[48] According to the SEC, "[n]o bright line test has been adopted in order to determine when an amendment to a Schedule 13D is 'prompt'." *In the Matter of Cooper Laboratories, Inc.*, SEC Rel. No. 34–22171, 1985 WL 548418, at *5 (June 26, 1985). The SEC has added that "[t]he determination of what constitutes 'promptly' under Regulation 13D-G is based upon the facts and circumstances surrounding the materiality of the change in information triggering the filing obligation and the filing person's previous disclosures. Any delay beyond the date the filing reasonably can be filed may not be prompt." *Amendments to Beneficial Reporting Requirements*, SEC Rel. No. 34–39538, 1998 WL 7449, at *3 n.14 (Jan. 12, 1998); see also *Cooper Laboratories*, 1985 WL 548418, at *5 ("Whether an amendment to a Schedule 13D is 'prompt' must be judged, at least in part, by the market's sensitivity to the particular change of fact triggering the obligation to amend, and the effect on the market of the filing person's previous disclosures.").

arrangement, understanding, relationship, or otherwise, has or shares either "*voting power*" over the shares in question and/or "*investment power*" over those shares. "Voting power" includes the power to vote, or to direct the voting of, the shares in question. "Investment power," by contrast, includes the power to dispose, or to direct the disposition, of those shares.

Because voting power and investment power over particular securities can be "shared" by more than one person or split between more than one person, it is possible for more than one person to be deemed the "beneficial owner" of the same securities at the same time; hence, more than one person may have to file a Schedule 13D with respect to those securities. In recognition of this, Exchange Act Rule 13d–4 allows any person to "expressly declare in any statement filed that the filing of such statement shall not be construed as an admission that such person is, for the purposes of sections 13(d) or 13(g) of the [Exchange] Act, the beneficial owner of any securities covered by the statement."

QUESTION

As noted above, Schedule 13D filings must be made within 10 days after the purchase that pushes beneficial ownership over the five percent threshold. Given today's technology, why on earth hasn't Congress acted to reduce the 10 day period? What do you suspect an acquirer is doing with respect to the target's shares during the 10–day window? Hint: it's not selling.

b. The Question of Remedy

What is the appropriate remedy with respect to a person or entity who either fails to file a Schedule 13D when required to do so or files a Schedule 13D in a tardy manner? Who is hurt by a late filing, and who is benefitted? Consider the following two cases.

RONDEAU V. MOSINEE PAPER CORP.

Supreme Court of the United States, 1975.
422 U.S. 49, 95 S.Ct. 2069, 45 L.Ed.2d 12.

MR. CHIEF JUSTICE BURGER delivered the opinion of the Court.

* * *

Respondent Mosinee Paper Corp. is a Wisconsin company engaged in the manufacture and sale of paper, paper products, and plastics. Its principal place of business is located in Mosinee, Wis., and its only class of equity security is common stock which is registered under § 12 of the Securities Exchange Act of 1934, 15 U.S.C. § 78*l*. At all times relevant to this litigation there were slightly more than 800,000 shares of such stock outstanding.

In April 1971 petitioner Francis A. Rondeau, a Mosinee businessman, began making large purchases of respondent's common stock in the over-the-counter market. Some of the purchases were in his own name; others were in the name of businesses and a foundation known to be controlled by him. By May 17, 1971, petitioner had acquired 40,413 shares of respondent's stock, which constituted more than 5 percent of those outstanding. He was therefore required to comply with the disclosure provisions of the Williams Act[1], by filing a Schedule 13D with respondent and the Securities and Exchange Commission within 10 days.[Ed.[49]] That form would have disclosed, among other things, the number of shares beneficially owned by petitioner, the source of the funds used to purchase them, and petitioner's purpose in making the purchases.

---

[1] The Williams Act added s 13(d) to the Securities Exchange Act of 1934, which has been further amended to provide in relevant part:

'(d)(1) Any person who, after acquiring directly or indirectly the beneficial ownership of any equity security of a class which is registered pursuant to section 78l of this title . . . is directly or indirectly the beneficial owner of more than 5 per centum of such class shall, within ten days after such acquisition, send to the issuer of the security at its principal executive office, by registered or certified mail, send to each exchange where the security is traded, and file with the Commission, a statement containing such of the following information, and such additional information, as the Commission may by rules and regulations prescribe as necessary or appropriate in the public interest or for the protection of investors—

'(A) the background and identity of all persons by whom or on whose behalf the purchases have been or are to be effected;

'(B) the source and amount of the funds or other consideration used or to be used in making the purchases, and if any part of the purchase price or proposed purchase price is represented or is to be represented by funds or other consideration borrowed or otherwise obtained for the purpose of acquiring, holding, or trading such security, a description of the transaction and the names of the parties thereto, except that where a source of funds is a loan made in the ordinary course of business by a bank, as defined in section 78c(a) (6) of this title, if the person filing such statement so requests, the name of the bank shall not be made available to the public;

'(C) if the purpose of the purchases or prospective purchases is to acquire control of the business of the issuer of the securities, any plans or proposals which such persons may have to liquidate such issuer, to sell its assets to or merge it with any other persons, or to make any other major change in its business or corporate structure;

'(D) the number of shares of such security which are beneficially owned, and the number of shares concerning which there is a right to acquire, directly or indirectly, by (i) such person, and (ii) by each associate of such person, giving the name and address of each such associate; and

'(E) information as to any contracts, arrangements, or understandings with any person with respect to any securities of the issuer, including but not limited to transfer of any of the securities, joint ventures, loan or option arrangements, puts or calls, guaranties of loans, guaranties against loss or guaranties of profits, division of losses or profits, or the giving or withholding of proxies, naming the persons with whom such contracts, arrangements, or understandings have been entered into, and giving the details thereof.' . . .

The Commission requires the purpose of the transaction to be disclosed in every Schedule 13D, regardless of an intention to acquire control and make major changes in its structure. . . .

[49] [Ed. A purchaser has to file a Schedule 13D in ten days unless she can qualify to file a Schedule 13G, which is filed yearly. A purchaser who has acquired securities in the "ordinary course of his business and not with the purpose nor with the effect of changing or influencing the control of the issuer" may file a 13G. Typical 13G filers are large institutional investors, such as mutual funds, that ordinarily have no interest in influencing or acquiring the public corporation in question.]

Petitioner did not file a Schedule 13D but continued to purchase substantial blocks of respondent's stock. By July 30, 1971, he had acquired more than 60,000 shares. On that date the chairman of respondent's board of directors informed him by letter that his activity had "given rise to numerous rumors" and "seems to have created some problems under the Federal Securities Laws. . . ." Upon receiving the letter petitioner immediately stopped placing orders for respondent's stock and consulted his attorney. On August 25, 1971, he filed a Schedule 13D which, in addition to the other required disclosures, described the "Purpose of Transaction" as follows:

> "Francis A. Rondeau determined during early part of 1971 that the common stock of the Issuer [respondent] was undervalued in the over-the-counter market and represented a good investment vehicle for future income and appreciation. Francis A. Rondeau and his associates presently propose to seek to acquire additional common stock of the Issuer in order to obtain effective control of the Issuer, but such investments as originally determined were and are not necessarily made with this objective in mind. Consideration is currently being given to making a public cash tender offer to the shareholders of the Issuer at a price which will reflect current quoted prices for such stock with some premium added."

Petitioner also stated that, in the event that he did obtain control of respondent, he would consider making changes in management "in an effort to provide a Board of Directors which is more representative of all of the shareholders, particularly those outside of present management . . . ." One month later petitioner amended the form to reflect more accurately the allocation of shares between himself and his companies.

On August 27 respondent sent a letter to its shareholders informing them of the disclosures in petitioner's Schedule 13D.[3] The letter stated that by his "tardy filing" petitioner had "withheld the information to which you [the shareholders] were entitled for more than two months, in violation of federal law." In addition, while agreeing that "recent market prices have not reflected the real value of your Mosinee stock," respondent's management could "see little in Mr. Rondeau's background that would qualify him to offer any meaningful guidance to a Company in the highly technical and competitive paper industry."

* * *

The Court of Appeals' conclusion that respondent suffered "harm" sufficient to require sterilization of petitioner's stock need not long detain us. The purpose of the Williams Act is to insure that public shareholders

---

[3] Respondent simultaneously issued a press release containing the same information. Almost immediately the price of its stock jumped to $19–$21 per share. A few days later it dropped back to the prevailing price of $12.50–$14 per share, where it remained.

who are confronted by a cash tender offer for their stock will not be required to respond without adequate information regarding the qualifications and intentions of the offering party. By requiring disclosure of information to the target corporation as well as the Securities and Exchange Commission, Congress intended to do no more than give incumbent management an opportunity to express and explain its position. The Congress expressly disclaimed an intention to provide a weapon for management to discourage takeover bids or prevent large accumulations of stock which would create the potential for such attempts. Indeed, the Act's draftsmen commented upon the "extreme care" which was taken "to avoid tipping the balance of regulation either in favor of management or in favor of the person making the takeover bid." . . .

The short of the matter is that none of the evils to which the Williams Act was directed has occurred or is threatened in this case. Petitioner has not attempted to obtain control of respondent, either by a cash tender offer or any other device. Moreover, he has now filed a proper Schedule 13D, and there has been no suggestion that he will fail to comply with the Act's requirement of reporting any material changes in the information contained therein.[9] . . . On this record there is no likelihood that respondent's shareholders will be disadvantaged should petitioner make a tender offer, or that respondent will be unable to adequately place its case before them should a contest for control develop. Thus, the usual basis for injunctive relief, "that there exists some cognizable danger of recurrent violation," is not present here. *United States v. W.T. Grant Co.*, 345 U.S. 629, 633 (1953). . . .

Nor are we impressed by respondent's argument that an injunction is necessary to protect the interests of its shareholders who either sold their stock to petitioner at predisclosure prices or would not have invested had they known that a takeover bid was imminent. . . . As observed, the principal object of the Williams Act is to solve the dilemma of shareholders desiring to respond to a cash tender offer, and it is not at all clear that the type of "harm" identified by respondent is redressable under its provisions. In any event, those persons who allegedly sold at an unfairly depressed price have an adequate remedy by way of an action for damages, thus negating the basis for equitable relief.[10] . . . Similarly, the fact that the second group of shareholders for whom respondent expresses concern have retained the benefits of their stock and the lack of an imminent contest for control make the possibility of damage to them remote at best. . . .

---

[9] Because this case involves only the availability of injunctive relief to remedy a § 13(d) violation following compliance with the reporting requirements, it does not require us to decide whether or under what circumstances a corporation could obtain a decree enjoining a shareholder who is currently in violation of § 13(d) from acquiring further shares, exercising voting rights, or launching a takeover bid, pending compliance with the reporting requirements.

[10] The Court was advised by respondent that such a suit is now pending in the District Court and class action certification has been sought. Although we intimate no views regarding the merits of that case, it provides a potential sanction for petitioner's violation of the Williams Act.

* * *

[JUSTICES MARSHALL, BRENNAN and DOUGLAS dissented.]

SEC v. FIRST CITY FINANCIAL CORP., LTD.

United States Court of Appeals, District of Columbia Circuit, 1989.
890 F.2d 1215.

SILBERMAN, CIRCUIT JUDGE.

Section 13(d) of the Securities Exchange Act of 1934 . . . requires any person who has directly or indirectly obtained the beneficial ownership of more than 5 percent of any registered equity security to disclose within 10 days certain information to the issuer, the exchanges on which the security trades, and to the Securities and Exchange Commission ("SEC"). The SEC charged appellants, First City Financial Corporation, Ltd. ("First City") and Marc Belzberg, with deliberately evading section 13(d) and its accompanying regulations in their attempted hostile takeover of Ashland Oil Company ("Ashland") by filing the required disclosure statement after the 10 day period. The district court concluded that appellants had violated the statute; it then enjoined them from further violations of section 13(d) and ordered them to disgorge all profits derived from the violation. *See SEC v. First City Financial Corp., et al.* 688 F.Supp. 705 (D.D.C.1988). We think that the district court's findings were not clearly erroneous and that the injunction and disgorgement orders were lawful and appropriate remedies for appellants' violations. We therefore affirm.

* * *

The SEC's case is based on its contention that on March 4, 1986 Marc Belzberg, a vice-president of First City, telephoned Alan ("Ace") Greenberg, the Chief Executive Officer of Bear Stearns, a large Wall Street brokerage firm, and asked Greenberg to buy substantial shares of Ashland for First City's account. Appellants claim that Greenberg "misunderstood" Belzberg: the latter intended only to recommend that Bear Stearns buy Ashland for its own account.

* * *

. . . [O]n March 4, Marc Belzberg telephoned Greenberg and engaged him in a short conversation that would be the centerpiece of this litigation. At his deposition, Greenberg described the conversation in the following manner:

> [Marc Belzberg] called me and said something to the effect that—something like, "It wouldn't be a bad idea if you bought Ashland Oil here," or something like that. And I took that to mean that we were going to do another put and call arrangement that we had

> done in the past. . . . I was absolutely under the impression I was buying at their risk and I was going to do a put and call.[4]

While Greenberg interpreted Marc Belzberg's call as an order to purchase Ashland stock on behalf of First City, Marc Belzberg later claimed that he intended only to recommend that Greenberg buy stock for himself, that is, for Bear Stearns, and that Greenberg apparently misunderstood Belzberg. Immediately after the phone call, Greenberg purchased 20,500 Ashland shares. If purchased for First City, those shares would have pushed First City's Ashland holdings above 5 percent and triggered the beginning of the 10 day filing period of section 13(d). In that event, First City would have been obliged to file a Schedule 13D disclosure statement on March 14 with the SEC.

Between March 4 and 14, Greenberg purchased an additional 330,700 shares of Ashland stock for First City costing more than $14 million. Greenberg called Marc Belzberg periodically during those ten days to discuss various securities, including Ashland. In these conversations, Greenberg reported to Marc Belzberg the increasing number of Ashland shares Greenberg had accumulated. According to Greenberg, Belzberg replied to these reports by saying, " 'Fine, keep going,' or something to that effect." Greenberg also characterized Belzberg's response as "grunt[ing]" approvingly. Belzberg did not squarely deny that testimony; he testified that he, Belzberg, said "uh-huh, I think it's cheap." Over the March 15–16 weekend, Marc Belzberg met with his father and uncles in Los Angeles to discuss Ashland. On Sunday, March 16, Samuel Belzberg decided that First City should continue to buy Ashland stock. Marc Belzberg then advised his father that Greenberg had accumulated a block of Ashland shares that "First City could acquire quickly." Samuel Belzberg later testified that he had no prior knowledge of the Greenberg purchases.

Returning to New York the next morning, March 17, Marc Belzberg called Greenberg and arranged a written put and call agreement for the 330,700 shares Bear Stearns had accumulated. During that conversation, Marc Belzberg did not mention a price to Greenberg. Several days later, Marc Belzberg received the written agreement with a "strike price," or the price Bear Stearns was charging First City, of $43.96 per share. This price was well below the then market price of $45.37; thus, the total March 17 put and call price was almost $500,000 below market. Marc Belzberg apparently expressed no surprise that Bear Stearns was charging almost

---

[4] Large investors sometimes purchase stock through "put and call agreements." Under these agreements, a broker such as Bear Stearns would purchase the stock subject to the agreement and place it in its own account. The agreement entitles the investor to "call" or purchase the shares from the broker for an agreed upon period at an agreed upon price, the cost to the broker plus interest and a small commission. At the same time, the broker has the right to "put" or sell the shares to the investor at the same price. As a result, the investor rather than the broker bears all of the market risks in buying the stock. The put and call agreements were developed apparently in response to the pre-merger notification requirements of the Hart-Scott-Rodino [Antitrust Improvements] Act [of 1976].

half a million dollars less than market value. He later testified that he believed that Bear Stearns was acting as a "Santa Claus" and that Greenberg was giving him "a bit of a break" to gain more business from First City in the future.

When Blumenstein, the officer responsible for ensuring First City's compliance with the federal securities laws, noticed the strike price, he immediately met with Marc Belzberg. Blumenstein recognized that the computation of the price reflected only the cost to Bear Stearns of acquiring the stock over the two week period before the written agreement (plus interest and commission), thus creating an inference that First City was the beneficial owner of the securities before March 17. After Blumenstein outlined the problem to Belzberg, the two men called Greenberg on a speakerphone. Belzberg later testified, "I informed Mr. Greenberg [during that conversation] that the letter [the written agreement] was incorrect, that I didn't care what the price of the stock was that he bought for himself, I didn't care what day he made the trades for himself, that I was buying stock from him as of today." Belzberg then testified that Greenberg said, "[Y]ou're right, the letter's wrong, I didn't read it before it went out, throw it out and I will send you a corrected copy." Greenberg, however, testified that Belzberg referred only to an error in the calculation of interest and not to the date on which First City acquired the stock. At the end of the conversation, Belzberg suggested he pay $44.00 per share, 4 cents per share higher than the original strike price but still $1.36, or a total of nearly $450,000, below the market price. At trial, Belzberg admitted to picking the $44 figure "out of the air" and that he "did not want the price [he] was paying to relate to [Greenberg's] cost." Between March 17 and 25, on Marc Belzberg's instructions, Greenberg bought another 890,100 Ashland shares on behalf of First City using several put and call agreements.

After these purchases, Samuel Belzberg sent a letter to Ashland's management, informing them of First City's holdings in their stock and proposing a friendly takeover of the company. Ashland rejected the offer, and on the morning of March 25 the company issued a press release disclosing that First City held between 8 and 9 percent of Ashland's stock. Almost immediately, the price of Ashland stock rose 10 percent to $52.25. The next day, on March 26, First City filed the Schedule 13D disclosure statement required by section 13(d). The statement indicated that First City had accumulated 9 percent of Ashland stock and intended to launch a tender offer for the remaining shares at $60 per share. The market price of Ashland stock then rose to $55, peaking at $55.75 per share the next day.

* * *

The district court found that Marc Belzberg and First City entered into an informal put and call agreement on March 4 and then deliberately violated the 10 day filing requirement of section 13(d). The district court, in an extensive opinion, relied primarily on First City's acknowledged ultimate purpose to take over Ashland, Greenberg's understanding of his March 4 telephone conversation with Marc Belzberg, the subsequent conversations between Belzberg and Greenberg, and the suspicious price of the March 17 written agreement. The court discounted Marc Belzberg's "misunderstanding" explanation as "self-serving, inconsistent with his later actions and [not] squar[ing] with the objective evidence." 688 F.Supp. at 712. Belzberg, to put it bluntly, was not credited. The court also refused to consider Greenberg's later testimony that there might have been an "honest misunderstanding" since Greenberg reached that conclusion based only on Belzberg's suggestions and statements. *See id.* at 720.

The district court permanently enjoined appellants from future violations of section 13(d) because they violated the statute deliberately, showed no "remorse," and were engaged in a business which presented opportunities to violate the statute in the future. *See id.* at 725–26. The court also ordered appellants to disgorge approximately $2.7 million, representing their profits on the 890,000 shares of Ashland stock acquired between March 14 and 25. The court reasoned that appellants were able to purchase these shares at an artificially low price due to their failure to make the section 13(d) disclosure on March 14. *See id.* at 726–28. Appellants appeal the district court's finding of violation as unsupported by the evidence and a product of judicial bias. They further contend that the district court abused its discretion in ordering the injunction and disgorgement remedies.

* * *

The district court directed disgorgement of profits, and appellants' challenge to this aspect of the order presents an issue of first impression—whether federal courts have the authority to employ that remedy with respect to section 13(d) violations and whether it is appropriate in this sort of case. Appellants also claim that the amount ordered disgorged is excessive. We reject both arguments and affirm the district court's order on these issues as well.

Appellants, by claiming that Congress did not explicitly authorize a monetary remedy for section 13(d) violations, misapprehend the source of the court's authority. Disgorgement is an equitable remedy designed to deprive a wrongdoer of his unjust enrichment and to deter others from violating the securities laws. . . . "Unless otherwise provided by statute, all the inherent equitable powers of the District Court are available for the proper and complete exercise of that jurisdiction." *Porter v. Warner Holding Co.,* 328 U.S. 395, 398, 66 S.Ct. 1086, 1089, 90 L.Ed. 1332 (1946); . . . We see no indication in the language or the legislative history of the 1934 Act that even implies a restriction on the equitable remedies of the district courts. . . . Disgorgement, then, is available simply because the relevant provisions of the Securities Exchange Act of 1934, sections 21(d) and (e), . . . vest jurisdiction in the federal courts.

Indeed, appellants concede that disgorgement is rather routinely ordered for insider trading violations despite a similar lack of specific authorizations for that remedy under the securities law. . . . But they seek to distinguish section 13(d) violations as a "technical" transgression of reporting rules that really do not cause injury. In contrast, they argue, insider trading under modern theory is tantamount to theft; an actual injury is inflicted on the individual or institution entitled to confidentiality. Section 13(d), however, is the pivot of the entire Williams Act regulation of tender offers.[21] To be sure, some may doubt the usefulness of that statute generally or the section 13(d) requirement specifically, but it is hardly up to the judiciary to second-guess the wisdom of Congress' approach to regulating takeovers. Suffice it for us to note that section 13(d) is a crucial requirement in the congressional scheme, and a violator, it is legislatively assumed, improperly benefits by purchasing stocks at an artificially low price because of a breach of the duty Congress imposed to disclose his investment position. The disclosure of that position—a holding in excess of 5 percent of another company's stock—suggests to the rest of the market a likely takeover and therefore may increase the price of the stock. Appellants circumvented that scheme, and the theory of the statute, by which we are bound, is that the circumventions caused injury to other market participants who sold stock without knowledge of First City's holdings. We therefore see no relevant distinction between disgorgement of inside trading profits and disgorgement of post-section 13(d) violation profits.

There remains, of course, the question of how the court measures those illegal profits. Appellants vigorously dispute the $2.7 million figure that the district court arrived at by simply calculating all of the profits First City realized (in its eventual sale back to Ashland) on the 890,000 shares First City purchased between March 14 and 25. . . . The SEC's claim to disgorgement, which the district court accepted, is predicated on the assumption that had First City made its section 13(d) disclosure on March 14, at the end of the statutory 10 day period,[22] the stock it purchased during the March 14–25 period would have been purchased in a quite different and presumably more expensive market. That hypothetical market would have been affected by the disclosure that the Belzbergs had taken a greater than 5 percent stake in Ashland and would soon propose a tender offer.

---

[21] According to the sponsor of the Williams Act, section 13(d) may be "the only way that corporations, their shareholders and others can adequately evaluate a tender offer or the possible effects of a change in substantial shareholdings." 113 Cong.Rec. 855 (January 18, 1967) (statement of Sen. Williams).

[22] The statute provides "within 10 days" but it is assured that First City would have waited until the end.

Since disgorgement primarily serves to prevent unjust enrichment, the court may exercise its equitable power only over property causally related to the wrongdoing. The remedy may well be a key to the SEC's efforts to deter others from violating the securities laws, but disgorgement may not be used punitively. . . . Therefore, the SEC generally must distinguish between legally and illegally obtained profits. . . .

If exact information were obtainable at negligible cost, we would not hesitate to impose upon the government a strict burden to produce that data to measure the precise amount of the ill-gotten gains. Unfortunately, we encounter imprecision and imperfect information. Despite sophisticated econometric modelling, predicting stock market responses to alternative variables is, as the district court found, at best speculative. Rules for calculating disgorgement must recognize that separating legal from illegal profits exactly may at times be a near-impossible task. . . .

Accordingly, disgorgement need only be a reasonable approximation of profits causally connected to the violation. In the insider trading context, courts typically require the violator to return all profits made on the illegal trades . . . and have rejected calls to restrict the disgorgement to the precise impact of the illegal trading on the market price. . . .

Although the SEC bears the ultimate burden of persuasion that its disgorgement figure reasonably approximates the amount of unjust enrichment, we believe the government's showing of appellants' actual profits on the tainted transactions at least presumptively satisfied that burden. Appellants, to whom the burden of going forward shifted, were then obliged clearly to demonstrate that the disgorgement figure was not a reasonable approximation. . . .

* * *

Placing the burden on the defendants of rebutting the SEC's showing of actual profits, we recognize, may result, as it has in the insider trader context, in actual profits becoming the typical disgorgement measure. But the line between restitution and penalty is unfortunately blurred, and the risk of uncertainty should fall on the wrongdoer whose illegal conduct created that uncertainty. . . .

* * *

QUESTIONS

1. Is the court correct in stating that First City made a "profit" by failing to file its Schedule 13D in a timely manner? Or is it more accurate to say that First City "saved" money through its tardy filing?

2. What was the point of the lower court enjoining First City from further violations of Exchange Act Section 13(d)? Are not all market participants—including First City—*already* required to obey the law?

3. Assume the prices of all other oil companies (industry participants) rose during the time between when First City should have filed its Schedule 13D and when it actually did file that Schedule. What "profits" would First City have had to disgorge if First City could have shown that the Ashland stock price remained flat during that time while those of the other oil companies rose? How hard is it to single out the impact that a particular event (or nonevent) has on the market price of a public company's stock?

4. Do you believe the court allowed the SEC to "reasonably approximate profits" rather than requiring specificity as a matter of professional courtesy extended by one branch of the government to another? Would the court have been so lenient towards non-governmental plaintiffs?

c. Criticisms of Section 13(d)

Section 13(d) offers target shareholders an *illusion* of benefit: Without § 13(d) the shareholders may sell their stock too cheaply in the face of a pending (but as of yet undisclosed) takeover. Yet, they may benefit as *buyers* in the same period. The gains and losses without the section should even out over time for those who are diversified. At issue is whether § 13(d)'s costs in reducing the likelihood of acquisitions are counterbalanced by its gains, increased takeover prices due to the target board's enhanced ability to bargain with potential bidders.

The Section reduces the likelihood of acquisitions for two reasons, and the same two reasons provide a target board with negotiating leverage over a bidder. First, critics of the Williams Act argue that the effect of § 13(d) is to reduce the incentives for investors to make investments that trigger the disclosure requirements of the Section, especially when there are significant search costs necessary in locating firms that are good buys. After the disclosure other parties can take a "free ride" on the disclosing purchaser's search costs and also jump in and buy target stock without compensating the disclosing purchaser.

The argument is strongest in light of Item 4 in Schedule 13D, requiring disclosure of the purpose behind a "more than 5 percent acquisition." A bidder intent on making a public tender offer in the near future will not want to trigger the disclosure requirement in § 13(d) in advance of the announcement of its tender offer. The earlier the bidder must disclose its plans, the more time other bidders will have to make competing offers and the more time target managers will have to erect takeover defenses to the bid. Indeed, one of the most effective defenses is the adoption by the incumbent managers of the strategic plan of the unwanted bidder—thus beating the bidder at its own game! Competitors and target managers have the benefit, free of cost, of the initial bidder's views, generated at considerable cost, on how best to change the operation of the target to maximize its worth.

A second, related argument against the Section focuses on the ability of the target to file lawsuits on the Section's requirements that are designed, not to vindicate rights under the Section, but to stall swiftly moving and unwanted takeover attempts. When a target board receives a Schedule 13D filing, it hires lawyers, who file with a federal judge within hours, a request for, first, a temporary restraining order (TRO) and, second, a preliminary injunction based on alleged violations of § 13(d). In response to a request for a TRO the judge, if impressed with the urgency of the situation and persuaded by the target's lawyers of the legitimacy of the allegations (even if the bidder's lawyers have, because of the short notice, not been able to attend the hearing), can grant a temporary injunction against the takeover. In a request for a preliminary injunction a judge can stop the takeover pending a full hearing on the merits of the claim. The target board hopes that even if a court ultimately rejects the target's allegations that the bidder has violated § 13(d), the court will have delayed the takeover during the proceedings. The delay is a powerful defense because it enables a target to erect defenses, encourages competitive bidders and stretches the financing behind the initial bidder's stock purchases.

Of course, target managers can use the threat of litigation and other defensive tactics to increase the price paid to target shareholders. It is an empirical question, which may change over time as sensibilities change, whether increased prices on deals that happen offset the losses from the deals that never happen but would have had § 13(d) not been in place.

The Section has effects beyond takeovers. At the margin, it discourages those who would mount proxy contests for control of the firm and reduces the monitoring activity of institutional investors. Since § 13(d) covers investors that form a *group* controlling over 5 percent of the target stock, plans for a proxy campaign must be disclosed *when the group first forms*, even if the group's campaign hasn't yet begun.[50] Congress defined a group as "two or more persons [who] act as a . . . group for the purpose of *acquiring, holding, or disposing* of securities of an issuer." Exch. Act § 13(d)(3). This language needs stretching to reach a consortium formed solely to solicit votes, but the SEC has so stretched it. The Commission defines a "group" to include "two or more persons who agree to act together for the purpose of acquiring, holding, *voting*, or disposing of equity securities." Exch. Act Rule 13d–5(b)(1). The courts have allowed the stretch and have also construed the group concept broadly. A group can be formed informally, without written documentation, and its existence can be proven by circumstantial evidence. Each member can file its own Schedule 13D, but each filing must identify all other group members and disclose all information about other filers which "the filing person knows or has reason to know." Exch. Act Rule 13d–1(k)(2).

The Section also discourages active monitoring of managers by institutional investors. Institutions that acquire a greater than 5 percent stake without the purpose or effect of "changing or influencing the control of the issuer" can file a bare bones Schedule 13G instead of a Schedule 13D. The 13G

50 See Bernard S. Black, *Next Steps in Corporate Governance Reform: 13(d) Rules and Control Person Liability*, 9 BANK & CORP. GOV. L. RPTR. 751 (1992).

is due forty-five days after the end of the year in which the more than 5 percent purchase was made. The Schedule 13G option offers scant comfort, however. The SEC has offered no solid guidance on what the elastic concept of "influencing control" means. Much of what shareholders might want to do, especially any effort to nominate and elect responsive directors, thus creates litigation risk if one tries to use Schedule 13G. The net effect is that no active more than 5 percent shareholder even tries to use Schedule 13G, and those who do use Schedule 13G have an incentive to stay passive.

d. Groups and Beneficial Ownership

Hedge funds have tested the limits of the group definition in Exchange Act Section 13(d)(3). First, the funds often act in *wolf packs*,[51] gathering to purchase stock in a target that they perceive to be mismanaged. When does simultaneous action become a group for the purposes of the Section? Second, the funds use sophisticated *swaps contracts* to buy the consequences of stock price appreciation but not the stock itself. When does such a contract constitute either *beneficial ownership* of the shares owned by a counter-party to hedge its exposure or a group agreement with a counter-party? The following case had both issues and demonstrated judges' current ambivalence over swaps contracts. Compare the views of the district court judge (very suspicious) and the concurring judge, Judge Winter (absent concrete proof, not suspicious), on the Court of Appeals.

CSX CORPORATION V. THE CHILDREN'S INVESTMENT FUND MANAGEMENT (UK) LLP

United States Court of Appeals, Second Circuit, 2011.
654 F.3d 276.

JON O. NEWMAN, CIRCUIT JUDGE:

* * *

The Children's Investment Fund Management ("TCI") and 3G Capital Partners ("3G") are hedge funds that entered into cash-settled total-return equity swap agreements referencing shares of CSX Corporation ("CSX"). They later sought to elect a minority slate of candidates to CSX's board of directors. Alleging that TCI and 3G ("the Funds") had failed to comply in a timely fashion with the disclosure requirements of section 13(d) of the Williams Act, . . . CSX brought the present action. It sought injunctions barring the Funds from any future violations of section 13(d) and preventing the Funds from voting CSX shares at the 2008 CSX annual shareholders' meeting.

* * *

TCI and 3G ("the Funds") are investment funds that in 2006 came to believe that CSX, a large railroad company, had unrealized value that a

[51] For more on wolfpacking, see Chapter Eleven, Section D.5.

change in corporate policy and perhaps management might unlock. The Funds purchased shares in CSX and entered into cash-settled total-return equity swaps referencing CSX stock. The Funds then engaged in a proxy fight with the management of CSX.

(a) *Cash-settled total-return equity swaps.* Total-return swaps are contracts in which parties agree to exchange sums equivalent to the income streams produced by specified assets. Total-return equity swaps involve an exchange of the income stream from: (1) a specified number of shares in a designated company's stock, and (2) a specified interest rate on a specified principal amount. The party that receives the stock-based return is styled the "long" party. The party that receives the interest-based return is styled the "short" party. These contracts do not transfer title to the underlying assets or require that either party actually own them. Rather, in a total-return equity swap, the long party periodically pays the short party a sum calculated by applying an agreed-upon interest rate to an agreed-upon notional amount of principal, as if the long party had borrowed that amount of money from the short party. Meanwhile, the short party periodically pays the long party a sum equivalent to the return to a shareholder in a specified company—the increased value of the shares, if any, plus income from the shares—as if the long party owned actual shares in that company.

As a result, the financial return to a long party in a total-return equity swap is roughly equivalent to the return when borrowed capital is used to purchase shares in the referenced company. Long swap positions can, therefore, be attractive to parties that seek to increase the leverage of their holdings without actually buying the shares. The short party's financial return, in turn, is equivalent to the return to someone who sold short and then lent out the proceeds from that sale. However, because of the inherent risks in short-equity positions—share value can be more volatile than interest rates—persons holding short positions in total-return equity swaps will usually choose to purchase equivalent numbers of shares to hedge their short exposure.

Total-return equity swaps may be "settled-in-kind" or "cash-settled." When an equity swap that is settled-in-kind terminates, the long party receives the referenced security itself, in exchange for a payment equal to the security's market price at the end of the previous payment period. When a cash-settled equity swap terminates, the short party pays the long party the sum of the referenced equity security's appreciation in market value and other net cash flows (such as dividend payments) that have occurred since the most recent periodic payment. If this sum is negative, then the short party receives the corresponding amount from the long party. Unlike swaps settled in kind, cash-settled swaps do not give the long party a right to acquire ownership of the referenced assets from the short party. In all other respects, settled-in-kind and cash-settled equity swaps are economically equivalent.

(b) *The transactions in the present case.* The swaps purchased by the Funds were cash-settled total-return equity swaps referencing shares of CSX. The Funds were the long parties, and several banks were the short parties. Although the swap contracts did not require the short parties—the banks—actually to own any CSX shares, the Funds understood that the banks most likely would hedge their short swap positions by purchasing CSX shares in amounts matching the number of shares referenced in the swaps, and the banks generally did so.

The Funds' trading in CSX shares and CSX-referenced swaps followed no consistent pattern. During some periods the Funds increased their holdings; during other periods they decreased them. Almost immediately after making its initial investment in CSX, TCI approached the company to negotiate "changes in policy and, if need be, management [that] could bring better performance and thus a higher stock price," . . . which would allow TCI to profit from its swap holdings. TCI later explored the possibility of a leveraged buyout ("LBO") of CSX, and informed other hedge funds of its interest in "altering CSX's practices in a manner that TCI believed would cause its stock to rise." . . . When it became clear that CSX had little interest in TCI's proposed policy changes or LBO proposals, TCI began preparations for a proxy contest to effectuate its desired policy and management changes at CSX.

There is no doubt that the Funds wanted to avoid disclosure under the Williams Act until a time they believed suitable. Thus, TCI took care to disperse its swaps among multiple counterparties so that no one particular counterparty would trigger disclosure under the Williams Act by purchasing as a hedge more than 5 percent of a class of CSX securities. TCI could not be certain how counterparties would vote their hedge shares but of course could vote the shares that it owned. When a proxy fight seemed likely, TCI decreased its swap holdings and purchased more CSX shares.

Meanwhile, the Funds engaged in various communications among themselves, with CSX's management, and with some of the banks. As early as November 2006, TCI had contacted CSX and two banks—one in December 2006, and the other in January 2007—about the possibility of a leveraged buyout. TCI also had communications with both Austin Friars, a hedge fund owned by Deutsche Bank, and with Deutsche Bank itself about CSX. TCI and 3G communicated between themselves at various times in 2007, but not until December 19, 2007, did they file a Schedule 13D with the SEC disclosing that they had formed a "group" by "enter[ing] into an agreement to coordinate certain of their efforts with regard [*sic*] (I) the purchase and sale of [various shares and instruments] and (ii) the proposal of certain actions and/or transactions to [CSX]." . . .

On January 8, 2008, the TCI–3G group proposed a minority slate of directors for the CSX board. . . . The vote on this proposal occurred at the June 25, 2008, CSX shareholders' meeting.

* * *

Section 13(d) provides in pertinent part:

> (1) Any person who, after acquiring directly or indirectly the beneficial ownership of any equity security of a class which is registered pursuant to section 78*l* of this title . . . , is directly or indirectly the beneficial owner of more than 5 per centum of such class shall, within ten days after such acquisition, [disclose to the issuer, the SEC, and the exchanges] a statement containing such of the following information, and such additional information, as the Commission may by rules and regulations, prescribe as necessary or appropriate in the public interest or for the protection of investors. . . .
>
> . . .
>
> (3) When two or more persons act as a partnership, limited partnership, syndicate, or other group for the purpose of acquiring, holding, or disposing of securities of an issuer, such syndicate or group shall be deemed a "person" for the purposes of this subsection.

* * *

SEC Rule 13d–5(b)(1) provides that the section 13(d) disclosure requirements apply to the aggregate holdings of any "group" formed "for the purpose of acquiring, holding, voting or disposing" of equity securities of an issuer. . . . This Rule tracks Section 13(d)(3) in all respects except that the Rule adds voting as a group for the purpose of triggering the disclosure provisions. . . . " '[T]he touchstone of a group within the meaning of section 13(d) is that the members combined in furtherance of a common objective.' " *Roth v. Jennings,* 489 F.3d 499, 508 (2d Cir.2007) (quoting *Wellman v. Dickinson,* 682 F.2d 355, 363 (2d Cir.1982)).

* * *

There are three kinds of groups that might be found in the present matter. One might consist of one or more long parties (the Funds) and one or more short counterparties that have hedged with shares (the banks). The second might consist of the Funds, *i.e.,* TCI and 3G. The third might consist of banks that have purchased shares as a hedge. Only the possibility of a group comprising TCI and 3G is at issue on this appeal.

* * *

These findings are insufficient for proper appellate review. Although the District Court found the existence of a group "with respect to CSX securities," the Court did not explicitly find a group formed for the purpose of acquiring CSX securities. Even if many of the parties' "activities" were the result of group action, two or more entities do not become a group within the meaning of section 13(d)(3) unless they "act as a . . . group for the purpose of acquiring . . . securities of an issuer." . . .

Moreover, because the District Court deemed the Funds, as long parties to cash-settled total-return equity swap agreements, to have a beneficial interest in shares acquired by hedging short parties to such agreements, the Court did not distinguish in its group finding between CSX shares deemed to be beneficially owned by the Funds and those owned outright by the Funds. However, with our current consideration of a group violation confined to CSX shares owned outright by the Funds, a precise finding, adequately supported by specific evidence, of whether a group existed for purposes of acquiring CSX shares outright during the relevant period needs to be made in order to facilitate appellate review, and we will remand for that purpose. . . . Only if such a group's outright ownership of CSX shares exceeded the 5 percent threshold prior to the filing of a section 13(d) disclosure can a group violation of section 13(d) be found.

* * *

. . . In *Treadway Companies, Inc. v. Care Corp.*, 638 F.2d 357 (2d Cir.1980), we held that "an injunction will issue for a violation of § 13(d) only on a showing of irreparable harm to the interests which that section seeks to protect." 638 F.2d at 380. We also said that "[t]he goal of § 13(d) is to alert the marketplace to every large, rapid aggregation or accumulation of securities . . . which might represent a potential shift in corporate control." *Id.* . . . Thus, the interests that section 13(d) protects "are fully satisfied when the shareholders receive the information required to be filed." *Treadway*, 638 F.2d at 380 . . . . Consequently, in *Treadway,* we held that because shareholders had received the required information four months before the proxy contest in that case, "there was no risk of irreparable injury and no basis for injunctive relief." 638 F.2d at 380. In the present matter, the Funds' section 13(d) disclosures occurred in December 2007, approximately six months before the June 25, 2008, shareholders' meeting. Therefore, following *Treadway,* we conclude that injunctive share "sterilization" was not available.

* * *

WINTER, CIRCUIT JUDGE, concurring:

* * *

The court viewed the economic role of such swaps as an underhanded means of acquiring or facilitating access to CSX stock that could be used to gain control through a proxy fight or otherwise. In my view, without an agreement between the long and short parties permitting the long party ultimately to acquire the hedge stock or to control the short party's voting of it, such swaps are not a means of indirectly facilitating a control transaction. Rather, they allow parties such as the Funds to profit from efforts to cause firms to institute new business policies increasing the value of a firm. If management changes the policies and the firm's value increases, the Funds' swap agreements will earn them a profit for their efforts. If management does not alter the policies, however, and a proxy fight or other control transaction becomes necessary, the swaps are of little value to parties such as the Funds. Absent an agreement such as that described above, such parties must then, as happened here, unwind the swaps and buy stock at the open market price, thus paying the costs of both the swaps and the stock.

* * *

In my view, cash-settled total-return equity swaps do not, without more, render the long party a "beneficial owner" of such shares with a potential disclosure obligation under Section 13(d). However, an agreement or understanding between the long and short parties to such a swap regarding the short party's purchasing of such shares as a hedge, the short party's selling of those shares to the long party upon the unwinding of the swap agreements, or the voting of such shares by the short parties renders the long party a "beneficial owner" of shares purchased as a hedge by the short party.

* * *

To reiterate, the swap agreements in the instant case do not obligate short parties to purchase shares as a hedge, to sell such shares either at a particular time or to the long party, or to vote those shares as the long party desires. The issue here is whether, under Rule 13d–3(a), such swaps accord the long party investment or voting power over the hedge shares when the short party purchases referenced shares as a hedge.

* * *

. . . Absent an agreement or informal understanding committing the banks to buy shares to hedge their CSX-referenced swaps or to sell those shares to the long party when the swaps terminated, the Funds possessed only the power to predict with some confidence the purchase of those shares as a hedge, not the power to direct such a purchase, much less to direct those shares' disposition. The long counterparties' act of entering into a swap, therefore, falls well short of "directing" the short counterparties to purchase the stock.

* * *

That a short party's self-interest predisposes it to vote in favor of positions taken by a prospective long counterparty is insufficient, on its own, to show a transfer of voting power to the long counterparty for purposes of Section 13(d) and Rule 13d–3(a)(1). To hold otherwise would distort both the term "beneficial owner" and the word "power." A short party's self-interest is not an obligation to vote as the long party would desire. Nor is it a right in the long party to compel the short party to vote in a particular way. Indeed, were another putative acquirer to appear in competition with the long party, the long party might well find that the short party's self-interest was now at odds with its own. . . .

* * *

Rule 13d–5(b)(1) provides that the Section 13(d) disclosure requirements apply to the aggregate holdings of any "group" formed "for the purpose of acquiring, holding, voting or disposing" of those securities. . . .

* * *

. . . The Rule does not encompass all "concerted action" with an aim to change a target firm's policies even while retaining an option to wage a proxy fight or engage in some other control transaction at a later time. Indeed, the Rule does not encompass "concerted action" with a change of control aim that does not involve one or more of the specified acts.

* * *

B. INSIDER TRADING IN ADVANCE OF ACQUISITIONS

1. SEC RULES 10b–5 AND 14e–3

UNITED STATES V. O'HAGAN[52]

Supreme Court of the United States, 1997.
521 U.S. 642, 117 S.Ct. 2199, 138 L.Ed.2d 724.

JUSTICE GINSBURG delivered the opinion of the Court.

* * *

Respondent James Herman O'Hagan was a partner in the law firm of Dorsey & Whitney in Minneapolis, Minnesota. In July 1988, Grand Metropolitan PLC (Grand Met), a company based in London, England, retained Dorsey & Whitney as local counsel to represent Grand Met regarding a potential tender offer for the common stock of the Pillsbury Company, headquartered in Minneapolis. Both Grand Met and Dorsey & Whitney took precautions to protect the confidentiality of Grand Met's tender offer plans. O'Hagan did no work on the Grand Met representation. Dorsey & Whitney withdrew from representing Grand Met on September 9, 1988. Less than a month later, on October 4, 1988, Grand Met publicly announced its tender offer for Pillsbury stock.

On August 18, 1988, while Dorsey & Whitney was still representing Grand Met, O'Hagan began purchasing call options for Pillsbury stock.

[52] One of your co-authors, Professor Haas, represented Grand Met in its hostile takeover of The Pillsbury Company while an associate attorney at New York's Cravath, Swaine & Moore.

Each option gave him the right to purchase 100 shares of Pillsbury stock by a specified date in September 1988. . . . By the end of September, he owned 2,500 unexpired Pillsbury options, apparently more than any other individual investor. . . . O'Hagan also purchased, in September 1988, some 5,000 shares of Pillsbury common stock, at a price just under $39 per share. When Grand Met announced its tender offer in October, the price of Pillsbury stock rose to nearly $60 per share. O'Hagan then sold his Pillsbury call options and common stock, making a profit of more than $4.3 million.

The Securities and Exchange Commission (SEC or Commission) initiated an investigation into O'Hagan's transactions, culminating in a 57–count indictment. The indictment alleged that O'Hagan defrauded his law firm and its client, Grand Met, by using for his own trading purposes material, nonpublic information regarding Grand Met's planned tender offer. . . .[1] . . . A jury convicted O'Hagan on all 57 counts, and he was sentenced to a 41–month term of imprisonment.

* * *

In pertinent part, § 10(b) of the Exchange Act provides:

> "It shall be unlawful for any person, directly or indirectly, by the use of any means or instrumentality of interstate commerce or of the mails, or of any facility of any national securities exchange—
>
> . . . .
>
> "(b) To use or employ, in connection with the purchase or sale of any security registered on a national securities exchange or any security not so registered, any manipulative or deceptive device or contrivance in contravention of such rules and regulations as the [Securities and Exchange] Commission may prescribe as necessary or appropriate in the public interest or for the protection of investors." 15 U.S.C. § 78j(b).

The statute thus proscribes (1) using any deceptive device (2) in connection with the purchase or sale of securities, in contravention of rules prescribed by the Commission. The provision, as written, does not confine its coverage to deception of a purchaser or seller of securities . . . ; rather,

---

[1] As evidence that O'Hagan traded on the basis of nonpublic information misappropriated from his law firm, the Government relied on a conversation between O'Hagan and the Dorsey & Whitney partner heading the firm's Grand Met representation. That conversation allegedly took place shortly before August 26, 1988. . . . O'Hagan urges that the Government's evidence does not show he traded on the basis of nonpublic information. O'Hagan points to news reports on August 18 and 22, 1988, that Grand Met was interested in acquiring Pillsbury, and to an earlier, August 12, 1988, news report that Grand Met had put up its hotel chain for auction to raise funds for an acquisition. . . . O'Hagan's challenge to the sufficiency of the evidence remains open for consideration on remand.

the statute reaches any deceptive device used "in connection with the purchase or sale of any security."

Pursuant to its § 10(b) rulemaking authority, the Commission has adopted Rule 10b–5, which, as relevant here, provides:

> "It shall be unlawful for any person, directly or indirectly, by the use of any means or instrumentality of interstate commerce, or of the mails or of any facility of any national securities exchange,
>
> "(a) To employ any device, scheme, or artifice to defraud, [or]
>
> . . . .
>
> "(c) To engage in any act, practice, or course of business which operates or would operate as a fraud or deceit upon any person,
>
> "in connection with the purchase or sale of any security." 17 CFR § 240.10b–5 (1996).

Liability under Rule 10b–5, our precedent indicates, does not extend beyond conduct encompassed by § 10(b)'s prohibition. *See Ernst & Ernst v. Hochfelder*, 425 U.S. 185, 214, 96 S.Ct. 1375, 1391, 47 L.Ed.2d 668 (1976) (scope of Rule 10b–5 cannot exceed power Congress granted Commission under § 10(b)); *see also Central Bank of Denver, N.A. v. First Interstate Bank of Denver, N. A.*, 511 U.S. 164, 173, 114 S.Ct. 1439, 1446, 128 L.Ed.2d 119 (1994) ("We have refused to allow [private] 10b–5 challenges to conduct not prohibited by the text of the statute.").

Under the "traditional" or "classical theory" of insider trading liability, § 10(b) and Rule 10b–5 are violated when a corporate insider trades in the securities of his corporation on the basis of material, nonpublic information. Trading on such information qualifies as a "deceptive device" under § 10(b), we have affirmed, because "a relationship of trust and confidence [exists] between the shareholders of a corporation and those insiders who have obtained confidential information by reason of their position with that corporation." *Chiarella v. United States*, 445 U.S. 222, 228, 100 S.Ct. 1108, 1114, 63 L.Ed.2d 348 (1980). That relationship, we recognized, "gives rise to a duty to disclose [or to abstain from trading] because of the 'necessity of preventing a corporate insider from . . . tak[ing] unfair advantage of . . . uninformed . . . stockholders.'" *Id.*, at 228–229, 100 S.Ct., at 1115 (citation omitted). The classical theory applies not only to officers, directors, and other permanent insiders of a corporation, but also to attorneys, accountants, consultants, and others who temporarily become fiduciaries of a corporation. *See Dirks v. SEC*, 463 U.S. 646, 655 n.14, 103 S.Ct. 3255, 3262, 77 L.Ed.2d 911 (1983).

The "misappropriation theory" holds that a person commits fraud "in connection with" a securities transaction, and thereby violates § 10(b) and Rule 10b–5, when he misappropriates confidential information for securities trading purposes, in breach of a duty owed to the source of the information. Under this theory, a fiduciary's undisclosed, self-serving use of a principal's information to purchase or sell securities, in breach of a duty of loyalty and confidentiality, defrauds the principal of the exclusive use of that information. In lieu of premising liability on a fiduciary relationship between company insider and purchaser or seller of the company's stock, the misappropriation theory premises liability on a fiduciary-turned-trader's deception of those who entrusted him with access to confidential information.

The two theories are complementary, each addressing efforts to capitalize on nonpublic information through the purchase or sale of securities. The classical theory targets a corporate insider's breach of duty to shareholders with whom the insider transacts; the misappropriation theory outlaws trading on the basis of nonpublic information by a corporate "outsider" in breach of a duty owed not to a trading party, but to the source of the information. The misappropriation theory is thus designed to "protec[t] the integrity of the securities markets against abuses by 'outsiders' to a corporation who have access to confidential information that will affect th[e] corporation's security price when revealed, but who owe no fiduciary or other duty to that corporation's shareholders." *Ibid.*

In this case, the indictment alleged that O'Hagan, in breach of a duty of trust and confidence he owed to his law firm, Dorsey & Whitney, and to its client, Grand Met, traded on the basis of nonpublic information regarding Grand Met's planned tender offer for Pillsbury common stock. . . . This conduct, the Government charged, constituted a fraudulent device in connection with the purchase and sale of securities.[5]

* * *

We agree with the Government that misappropriation, as just defined, satisfies § 10(b)'s requirement that chargeable conduct involve a "deceptive device or contrivance" used "in connection with" the purchase or sale of securities. . . .[6]

* * *

. . . Although informational disparity is inevitable in the securities markets, investors likely would hesitate to venture their capital in a market where trading based on misappropriated nonpublic information is unchecked by law. An investor's informational disadvantage vis-a-vis a

5 The Government could not have prosecuted O'Hagan under the classical theory, for O'Hagan was not an "insider" of Pillsbury, the corporation in whose stock he traded. Although an "outsider" with respect to Pillsbury, O'Hagan had an intimate association with, and was found to have traded on confidential information from, Dorsey & Whitney, counsel to tender offeror Grand Met. Under the misappropriation theory, O'Hagan's securities trading does not escape Exchange Act sanction, . . . simply because he was associated with, and gained nonpublic information from, the bidder, rather than the target.

6 Under the misappropriation theory urged in this case, the disclosure obligation runs to the source of the information, here, Dorsey & Whitney and Grand Met. . . .

misappropriator with material, nonpublic information stems from contrivance, not luck; it is a disadvantage that cannot be overcome with research or skill. . . .

In sum, considering the inhibiting impact on market participation of trading on misappropriated information, and the congressional purposes underlying § 10(b), it makes scant sense to hold a lawyer like O'Hagan a § 10(b) violator if he works for a law firm representing the target of a tender offer, but not if he works for a law firm representing the bidder. . . .[9] . . . .

* * *

We consider next the ground on which the Court of Appeals reversed O'Hagan's convictions for fraudulent trading in connection with a tender offer, in violation of § 14(e) of the Exchange Act and SEC Rule 14e–3(a). A sole question is before us as to these convictions: Did the Commission, as the Court of Appeals held, exceed its rulemaking authority under § 14(e) when it adopted Rule 14e–3(a) without requiring a showing that the trading at issue entailed a breach of fiduciary duty? We hold that the Commission, in this regard and to the extent relevant to this case, did not exceed its authority.

The governing statutory provision, § 14(e) of the Exchange Act, reads in relevant part:

> "It shall be unlawful for any person . . . to engage in any fraudulent, deceptive, or manipulative acts or practices, in connection with any tender offer. . . . The [SEC] shall, for the purposes of this subsection, by rules and regulations define, and prescribe means reasonably designed to prevent, such acts and practices as are fraudulent, deceptive, or manipulative." 15 U.S.C. § 78n(e).

Section 14(e)'s first sentence prohibits fraudulent acts in connection with a tender offer. This self-operating proscription was one of several provisions added to the Exchange Act in 1968 by the Williams Act, 82 Stat. 454. The section's second sentence delegates definitional and prophylactic rulemaking authority to the Commission. Congress added this rulemaking delegation to § 14(e) in 1970 amendments to the Williams Act. . . .

* * *

[9] As noted earlier, however, . . . the textual requirement of deception precludes § 10(b) liability when a person trading on the basis of nonpublic information has disclosed his trading plans to, or obtained authorization from, the principal—even though such conduct may affect the securities markets in the same manner as the conduct reached by the misappropriation theory. Contrary to [the dissent's] suggestion . . . , the fact that § 10(b) is only a partial antidote to the problems it was designed to alleviate does not call into question its prohibition of conduct that falls within its textual proscription. Moreover, once a disloyal agent discloses his imminent breach of duty, his principal may seek appropriate equitable relief under state law. Furthermore, in the context of a tender offer, the principal who authorizes an agent's trading on confidential information may, in the Commission's view, incur liability for an Exchange Act violation under Rule 14e–3(a).

Relying on § 14(e)'s rulemaking authorization, the Commission, in 1980, promulgated Rule 14e–3(a). That measure provides:

> "(a) If any person has taken a substantial step or steps to commence, or has commenced, a tender offer (the 'offering person'), it shall constitute a fraudulent, deceptive or manipulative act or practice within the meaning of section 14(e) of the [Exchange] Act for any other person who is in possession of material information relating to such tender offer which information he knows or has reason to know is nonpublic and which he knows or has reason to know has been acquired directly or indirectly from:
>
> "(1) The offering person,
>
> "(2) The issuer of the securities sought or to be sought by such tender offer, or
>
> "(3) Any officer, director, partner or employee or any other person acting on behalf of the offering person or such issuer, to purchase or sell or cause to be purchased or sold any of such securities or any securities convertible into or exchangeable for any such securities or any option or right to obtain or to dispose of any of the foregoing securities, unless within a reasonable time prior to any purchase or sale such information and its source are publicly disclosed by press release or otherwise." 17 CFR § 240.14e–3(a) (1996).

As characterized by the Commission, Rule 14e–3(a) is a "disclose or abstain from trading" requirement. . . . The Second Circuit concisely described the rule's thrust:

> "One violates Rule 14e–3(a) if he trades on the basis of material nonpublic information concerning a pending tender offer that he knows or has reason to know has been acquired 'directly or indirectly' from an insider of the offeror or issuer, or someone working on their behalf. Rule 14e–3(a) is a disclosure provision. It creates a duty in those traders who fall within its ambit to abstain or disclose, *without regard to whether the trader owes a pre-existing fiduciary duty* to respect the confidentiality of the information. *United States v. Chestman*, 947 F.2d 551, 557 (1991) (en banc) (emphasis added), *cert. denied*, 503 U.S. 1004, 112 S.Ct. 1759, 118 L.Ed.2d 422 (1992). . . .

* * *

We need not resolve in this case whether the Commission's authority under § 14(e) to "define . . . such acts and practices as are fraudulent" is broader than the Commission's fraud-defining authority under § 10(b), for we agree with the United States that Rule 14e–3(a), as applied to cases of this genre, qualifies under § 14(e) as a "means reasonably designed to prevent" fraudulent trading on material, nonpublic information in the tender offer context.[17] A prophylactic measure, because its mission is to prevent, typically encompasses more than the core activity prohibited. . . . We hold, accordingly, that under § 14(e), the Commission may prohibit acts, not themselves fraudulent under the common law or § 10(b), if the prohibition is "reasonably designed to prevent . . . acts and practices [that] are fraudulent." 15 U.S.C. § 78n(e). . . .

* * *

. . . [I]t is a fair assumption that trading on the basis of material, nonpublic information will often involve a breach of a duty of confidentiality to the bidder or target company or their representatives. The SEC, cognizant of the proof problem that could enable sophisticated traders to escape responsibility, placed in Rule 14e–3(a) a "disclose or abstain from trading" command that does not require specific proof of a breach of fiduciary duty. That prescription, we are satisfied, applied to this case, is a "means reasonably designed to prevent" fraudulent trading on material, nonpublic information in the tender offer context. . . .

* * *

[JUSTICES SCALIA and THOMAS wrote separate opinions concurring in part and dissenting in part.]

NOTE: INSIDER TRADING IN ADVANCE OF ACQUISITION ANNOUNCEMENTS

The 1986 insider trading scandal involving Ivan Boesky and his cohorts in investment banking firms and Wall Street law firms, all of whom traded in target stock in advance of tender offer announcements, focused the public on what traders already knew.[53] See Douglas Frantz, LEVINE & CO. (1987) (describing the scandal and its prosecution; a good read). There is a substantial run-up in the stock price of acquisition targets before the public announcement of any acquisition. A 1987 SEC study found,[54] for example, that, on average in

---

[17] We leave for another day, when the issue requires decision, the legitimacy of Rule 14e–3(a) as applied to "warehousing," which the Government describes as "the practice by which bidders leak advance information of a tender offer to allies and encourage them to purchase the target company's stock before the bid is announced." . . . As we observed in *Chiarella*, one of the Commission's purposes in proposing Rule 14e–3(a) was "to bar warehousing under its authority to regulate tender offers." 445 U.S., at 234, 100 S.Ct., at 1117–1118. The Government acknowledges that trading authorized by a principal breaches no fiduciary duty. . . . The instant case, however, does not involve trading authorized by a principal; therefore, we need not here decide whether the Commission's proscription of warehousing falls within its § 14(e) authority to define or prevent fraud.

[53] Just as Boesky's tipper, Dennis Levine, used the Bahamian branch of a Swiss bank, many of these trades involve off-shore accounts and stretch the enforcement powers of the SEC.

[54] SEC, Report From the Office of Chief Economist, *Stock Trading Before the Announcement of Tender Offers: Insider Trading or Market Anticipation*? (Feb. 24, 1987).

tender offers from 1981 to 1985, close to 30 percent of any tender offer premium was reflected in the target stock price before the public announcement of the acquisition. On friendly, negotiated deals, the norm today, the average run-up in the data period was close to 50 percent! Average trading volume in the target increased about 10 days before the announcement and surged to five times normal on the day before the announcement. These run-ups continue today.

The SEC study noted, however, that insider trading is but one source of the stock price run-ups. Some of the run-up is due to speculation from Schedule 13D filings (although this does not explain the run-ups before stock swap mergers) and some of the run-up is "street talk." Some street talk may originate with insiders but much of it comes from the sleuthing done by professional traders, arbitrageurs, "shark watchers," and Wall Street reporters. See William S. Cohen, *Gambling with the Future*, N.Y. TIMES, Aug. 12, 1986, at D8 (describing an army of traders, arbitrageurs and stock analysts quick to spot unusual activity of corporate executives). But there can be little doubt that acquisitions are a major stimulus for a substantial level of illegal insider trading activity.

2. SECTION 16(b) OF THE EXCHANGE ACT: A TRAP FOR LOSING BIDDERS

Exchange Act Rule 10b–5 did not extend to insider trading until the SEC's administrative decision in *In the Matter of Cady, Roberts & Co.*, 40 S.E.C. 907, 1961 WL 60638 (1961). Until that time the only congressional language on insider trading was contained in Exchange Act Section 16. Section 16(a) imposes a reporting obligation on officers, directors, and more than 10–percent shareholders who must file with the SEC forms that detail their holdings of and transactions in the issuer's stock. Such persons are referred to as *reporting persons*.

Reporting persons, in Section 16(b), are obliged to remit to the issuer any *profits* realized by buying and selling the issuer's securities in any period of *less* than six months.[55] Known as the *short swing profits* rule, the section stops the use of insider information by perverting all profitable short turnaround trading by reporting persons. The Section also prevents reporting persons from selling short issuer stock (selling stock they have borrowed and do not own) and regulates "sales against the box" (shorting stock by those who own shares long (for their own account)).

Importantly, a bidder typically owns some target company shares before launching its bid. Sometimes the number of shares is substantial. Should that bidder lose out to a competing bidder, the now jilted bidder typically seeks to liquidate its position in target shares. Often, the jilted bidder tenders the target shares it owns into any tender offer commenced by the winning bidder. Other times the jilted bidder must give up its shares

---

55 While selling at a *loss* is not proscribed by Section 16(b), such selling is prohibited by Exchange Act Rule 10b–5 if it is done on the basis of material, non-public information.

in connection with a merger between the winning bidder and the target in exchange for merger consideration. Should the jilted bidder's purchase of target shares have occurred less than six months before those shares are purchased through the tender offer or converted into the right to receive merger consideration, the target could seek to force the jilted bidder to forfeit back to the target any profit it makes as a result under Section 16(b). With that in mind, consider the following case.

TEXAS INT'L AIRLINES V. NAT'L AIRLINES, INC.

United States Court of Appeals, Fifth Circuit, 1983.
714 F.2d 533, *cert. denied,* 465 U.S. 1052, 104 S.Ct. 1326, 79 L.Ed.2d 721 (1984).

JOHNSON, CIRCUIT JUDGE:

Texas International (TI) appeals the grant of summary judgment for National Airlines (National) holding TI liable to National under section 16(b) of the Securities Exchange Act of 1934 (the Exchange Act) for the "short swing profits" made on the sale of 121,000 shares of National common stock. . . .

* * *

On March 14, 1979, during an attempt by TI to gain control of National, TI purchased 121,000 shares of National common stock in open market brokerage transactions. On March 14, the date of the purchase, TI was a beneficial owner of more than ten percent of National's common stock. On July 28, 1979, within six months of the March 14 purchase, TI and Pan American World Airways, Inc. (Pan Am) entered into a stock purchase agreement whereby TI agreed to sell 790,700 shares of National common stock to Pan Am [the winning bidder for National] at $50 per share. The closing was held on July 30, 1979. Under the matching rules of section 16(b) the 790,700 shares sold by TI on July 28, 1979 are deemed to include the 121,000 shares purchased by TI in March.

On September 6, 1978, National and Pan Am had entered into a merger agreement which provided for the merger of National into Pan Am contingent upon certain conditions and, in connection with the merger, for the exchange by Pan Am of not less than $50 in cash for each share of National common stock, other than the shares held by Pan Am. On May 16, 1979, National stockholders approved the merger agreement dated September 6, 1978, as amended. TI, as a National stockholder, stood to receive $50 per share for its National stock if and when the merger closed. For whatever reason, TI decided not to wait until the merger went through to negotiate for the disposition of its holdings to Pan Am. It was not until after the July 28, 1979 sale by TI of its National stock to Pan Am that the National-Pan Am merger was effectuated.

* * *

TI urges this Court to create an exception to automatic section 16(b) liability in cases where a defendant can prove that, notwithstanding its ownership of over ten percent of the stock of the issuer, the defendant had no access to inside information concerning the issuer. According to TI, the classic example of such a case is a sale of stock in the hostile takeover context. Application of section 16(b) in this type of case, argues TI, does not serve congressional goals—Congress intended short-swing profits to be disgorged only when the particular transaction serves as a vehicle for the realization of these profits based upon access to inside information.

TI's argument is unsupported by the legislative history of section 16(b). Although the abuse Congress sought to curb was speculation by stockholders with inside information, "the only method Congress deemed effective to curb the evils of insider trading was a *flat rule* taking the profits out of a *class of transactions* in which the possibility of abuse was believed to be intolerably great." *Kern County,* 93 S.Ct. at 1473 (emphasis added). . . .

* * *

In *Kern County* the Supreme Court approved an extremely narrow exception to the objective standard of section 16(b). The Court held that when a transaction is "unorthodox" or "borderline," the courts should adopt a pragmatic approach in imposing section 16(b) liability which considers the opportunity for speculative abuse, *i.e.*, whether the statutory "insider" had or was likely to have access to inside information.

TI engages in an analogy between the hostile and adversary situation that existed between the target company and the putative insider in *Kern County* and the adversary relationship between TI and National in the instant case. Even assuming the alleged parallelism between the adversary situations in the two cases and assuming that TI could prove that it neither had nor was likely to have access to inside information by virtue of its statutory "insider" status, no valid basis for an exception to section 16(b) liability on these facts is perceived. The Supreme Court in *Kern County* inquired into whether the transaction had the potential for abuse of inside information only because the transaction fell under the rubric of "unorthodox" or "borderline."[9] In *Kern County,* Occidental, a shareholder in Kern County Land Company (Old Kern) converted its shares in Old Kern into shares of the acquiring corporation pursuant to a merger. [The winning bidder in *Kern County* executed a second-stage stock swap merger to eliminate the share block in the target held by the losing bidder.] The Supreme Court clearly distinguished the unorthodox transaction—a conversion of securities—before it from the traditional cash-for-stock

[9] The Court, in a nonexhaustive list, enumerated certain transactions which are unorthodox: stock conversions, exchanges pursuant to mergers and other corporate reorganizations, stock reclassifications, and dealings in options, rights, and warrants. *Kern County,* 93 S.Ct. at 1744 n. 24.

transaction in the instant case: "traditional cash-for-stock transactions . . . are clearly within the purview of § 16(b)." *Kern County,* 93 S.Ct. at 1744.

TI lays frontal attack on the unorthodox transaction test as fundamentally flawed, principally because the form of consideration received—cash or stock—has nothing to do with whether inside information was or might have been used. What this attack fails to consider, however, is the significance of the factor of voluntariness in the Supreme Court's decision. The Court's sole concern was not that cash-for-stock sales present a greater opportunity for abuse of inside information than do stock-for-stock sales. Rather, language in the Supreme Court's opinion indicates that traditional cash-for-stock sales were excluded from the concept of unorthodox transactions because of their voluntary nature. . . .

. . . In the instant case, TI voluntarily entered into the stock purchase agreement with Pan Am before the National-Pan Am merger was effectuated. Despite the alleged lack of access to inside information and therefore the possibility of speculative abuse, the volitional character of the exchange is sufficient reason to trigger applicability of the language of section 16(b). For whatever reason, after the National-Pan Am merger had been approved, TI decided to take the initiative for the course of subsequent events into its own hands rather than wait for the merger to become accomplished. These circumstances do not warrant the creation of an exception to automatic section 16(b) liability.

* * *

GARZA, CIRCUIT JUDGE, dissenting:

* * *

. . . Texas International (TI) correctly argues that there are many similarities between the present case and that presented to the Supreme Court in *Kern County.* The putative "insider" in both cases was a party seeking to institute a "hostile" takeover of the issuer. It is evident from the record in this case that in both cases the party seeking takeover had no "inside information" upon which it could obtain short swing profits. In both cases the statutory stockholder failed in its attempt to take over the target company. The Supreme Court recognized in *Kern County* that after the merger agreement was approved, Occidental had no choice but to take action to protect its own interest.

In this case TI moved to protect its own interest when it agreed to sell its stock to the takeover company, Pan American World Airways, Inc. (Pan Am), after it became apparent that TI had lost the takeover battle. Unfortunately for TI, the sale took place forty-eight days before the statutory period had run.

Admittedly, the forced merger present in *Kern County* distinguishes that case from the present one. However, the facts of this case present a scenario which favors extension of the "unorthodox" exception.

Like Occidental, no one can argue that TI actually made use of inside information to obtain any short swing profits. The reason for the existence of § 16(b) is in no way promoted by its application to the present transaction. Furthermore, TI's sale of stock was to the parent corporation for the purpose of protecting its own interests and cooperating in the merger transaction which Pan Am was attempting to effectuate.

The record clearly evidences that at the time of the sale by TI to Pan Am, no present or past shareholders of National Airlines had in any way been monetarily damaged by TI's purchase and sale of stock. In fact, it can be argued that the attempted takeover of National by TI helped to increase the value of National Airlines' stock. TI did not receive a higher price for the stock than any other shareholder. ALL shareholders of National Airlines received $50 per share.

Application of § 16(b) in this case serves only to permit Pan Am to avoid that portion of its contract with TI in which it agreed to pay $50 per share. The award in this case is nothing more than a "windfall" to Pan Am as the successor of National Airlines.

* * *

I agree that if Occidental in *Kern County* or TI in this case had sold its shares after the merger agreement to a third party, § 16(b) would have been clearly implicated. On the other hand, such is not the case if the sale was to the takeover company itself and the statutory insider, TI, received no more than any other shareholder of the issuer. . . .

* * *

STERMAN v. FERRO CORP., 785 F.2d 162 (6th Cir.1986): ". . . The facts giving rise to this cause of action are basically undisputed. Between early 1981 and November 1982 defendant Crane Co. (Crane), through its chairman Thomas Evans (Evans), acquired 1,733,220 (or 22.4 percent) shares of Ferro Corporation (Ferro) common stock at prices ranging from $22 to $27 per share.

. . . In late spring of 1982, at the request of the board of directors, . . . Rosenthal (a Ferro director and acquaintance of Evans . . .) arranged a November 3, 1982 meeting . . . to discuss a possible repurchase of the Ferro stock held by Crane.

. . . Tentatively, the parties reached accord at a repurchase price of $30 per share plus a $.30 per share dividend payable on December 10, 1982 to all shareholders of record as of the close of business on November 15, 1982. . . .

Shortly after the November 3, 1982 meeting but prior to any action by Ferro's board of directors, Evans telephoned Rosenthal to advise him that, upon reconsideration, Crane could not agree to the discussed $30.30 per share price of Ferro Stock because of the short swing profit liability which would attach to the transaction. . . .

On November 8, 1982, the Ferro board of directors convened to consider the proposed offer of repurchase as negotiated by Rosenthal. The board of directors duly approved the offer of repurchase authorizing the payment of $31.03 per share of stock. The transaction resulted in an additional payment to Crane of $1,260,975, the precise amount of the short swing profit liability required to be paid to Ferro in satisfaction of the Section 16(b) liability that attached to the repurchase of the Ferro shares by Crane.

The transaction was finalized on November 8, 1982 whereupon Ferro demanded a return of Crane's adjusted short swing profits. On November 11, 1982, Crane delivered a check to Ferro in the amount of $1,260,975, thereby discharging its 16(b) liability.

Plaintiffs brought suit against Ferro, ten individual directors of Ferro and Crane alleging that the transaction constituted an illegal waiver of short swing profits. . . .

* * *

A review of the record discloses compliance with the statute. It is apparent that the pricing of the transaction was structured in a manner to accommodate a Section 16(b) liability. The Section 16(b) liability was, in fact, discharged by an appropriate cash payment to Ferro at the close of the transaction. However, to be culpable under Section 16(b), there must have been an attempt to *avoid* payment of the short swing profits imposed thereby. Moreover, the Supreme Court has determined that a Section 16(b) violation does not necessarily attach where the parties have intentionally structured their transaction to accommodate the liability imposed by the statute:

> Liability cannot be imposed simply because the investor structured his transaction with the intent of avoiding liability under § 16(b). The question is, rather, whether the method used to "avoid" liability is one permitted by the statute.

Reliance Electric Co. v. Emerson Electric Co., 404 U.S. at 422, 92 S.Ct. at 599.

Accordingly, this court finds no violation of Section 16(b) of the Act."

NOTE: THE SHORT-SWING PROFIT RULE'S APPLICATION TO SHARES EXCHANGED BY OFFICERS AND DIRECTORS IN MERGERS

Another troublesome application of § 16(b) is the Section's effect on the stock holdings of officers and directors of a target corporation that were included in a stock swap acquisition. If the officers and directors acquired shares within six months of the acquisition, did the acquisition trigger the short-swing profit restitution remedy of § 16(b) of the Exchange Act? Moreover, does the Section apply to the conversion of target equity securities held by officers and directors of the acquirer?

In 1996, the SEC promulgated Exchange Act Rule 16b–3, exempting transfers by officers and directors (but not more than 10–percent shareholders) of equity securities to the issuer if the transaction was approved by a disinterested board or ratified by a firm's shareholders. Could shares held by officers and directors of a target and converted in a merger into securities of an acquiring company or into cash qualify as exempt under the Rule? In a January 12, 1999 interpretative letter, the SEC answered in the affirmative. *Skadden, Arps, Slate, Meagher & Flom*, SEC No-Action Letter, Fed. Sec. L. Rep. (CCH) ¶ 77,515, 1999 WL 35771026 (Jan. 12, 1999). The target board or shareholders can ratify dispositions of target shares by target officers and directors and, if the holders are or became officers or directors in the acquirer and received acquirer shares, the acquiring board or shareholders also have to ratify the disposition.

C. STATE LAW

Under general principles of fiduciary duty defined in the state courts, a board has an obligation to make proper disclosures to its shareholders in anticipation of a shareholder vote. While most of the disclosure obligations in federal law are contained in detailed forms, schedules and rules, the state law duty is an opened-ended general obligation. As noted in the case below, the disclosure obligation in state law comes from both the directors' general fiduciary duty to shareholders and the separate doctrine of *equitable fraud*. As a consequence, state courts use federal case law, applying the open-ended federal antifraud sections and rules, Exchange Act Rule 10b–5 in particular, as precedent. See, e.g., *Skeen v. Jo-Ann Stores*, 750 A.2d 1170 (Del. 2000) (notice to minority shareholders in a squeeze-out was sufficient); *Zirn v. VLI Corp.*, 681 A.2d 1050 (Del. 1996) (notice on merger was insufficient).

Of particular interest is the position of the Delaware courts requiring disclosure of work papers behind fairness opinions from financial advisors. Consider the following case[56]:

---

[56] See also *In re Netsmart Technologies, Inc. Shareholders Litig.*, 924 A.2d 171, 203–05 (Del. Ch. 2007) (holding that when an investment banker's endorsement of the fairness of a transaction is touted to shareholders, the valuation methods used to arrive at that opinion as well

IN RE PURE RESOURCES, INC., SHAREHOLDERS LITIGATION

Court of Chancery of Delaware, 2002.
808 A.2d 421.

STRINE, VICE CHANCELLOR:

* * *

As their other basis for attack, the plaintiffs argue that neither of the key disclosure documents provided to the Pure stockholders—the S–4 Unocal issued in support of its Offer and the 14D–9 Pure filed in reaction to the Offer—made materially complete and accurate disclosure. The general legal standards that govern the plaintiffs' disclosure claims are settled.

In circumstances such as these, the Pure stockholders are entitled to disclosure of all material facts pertinent to the decisions they are being asked to make. In this case, the Pure stockholders must decide whether to take one of two initial courses of action: tender and accept the Offer if it proceeds or not tender and attempt to stop the Offer. If the Offer is consummated, the non-tendering stockholders will face two subsequent choices that they will have to make on the basis of the information in the S–4 and 14D–9: to accept defeat quietly by accepting the short-form merger consideration in the event that Unocal obtains 90% and lives up to its promise to do an immediate short-form merger or seek to exercise the appraisal rights described in the S–4. I conclude that the S–4 and the 14D–9 are important to all these decisions, because both documents state that Unocal will effect the short-form merger promptly if it gets 90%, and shareholders rely on those documents to provide the substantive information on which stockholders will be asked to base their decision whether to accept the merger consideration or to seek appraisal.

As a result, it is the information that is material to these various choices that must be disclosed. In other words, the S–4 and the 14D–9 must contain the information that "a reasonable investor would consider important in tendering his stock," including the information necessary to make a reasoned decision whether to seek appraisal in the event Unocal effects a prompt short-form merger. In order for undisclosed information to be material, there must be a "substantial likelihood that the disclosure of the omitted fact would have been viewed by the reasonable stockholder as having significantly altered the 'total mix' of information made available."

The S–4 and 14D–9 are also required "to provide a balanced, truthful account of all matters" they disclose. Related to this obligation is the requirement to avoid misleading partial disclosures. When a document

as the key inputs and range of ultimate values generated by those analyses must also be fairly disclosed).

ventures into certain subjects, it must do so in a manner that is materially complete and unbiased by the omission of material facts.

* * *

First and foremost, the plaintiffs argue that the 14D–9 is deficient because it does not disclose *any* substantive portions of the work of First Boston and Petrie Parkman on behalf of the Special Committee, even though the bankers' negative views of the Offer are cited as a basis for the board's own recommendation not to tender. Having left it to the Pure minority to say no for themselves, the Pure board (the plaintiffs say) owed the minority the duty to provide them with material information about the value of Pure's shares, including, in particular, the estimates and underlying analyses of value developed by the Special Committee's bankers. This duty is heightened, the plaintiffs say, because the Pure minority is subject to an immediate short-form merger if the Offer proceeds as Unocal hopes, and will have to make the decision whether to seek appraisal in those circumstances.

In response, the Pure director-defendants argue that the 14D–9 contains a great deal of financial information, including the actual opinions of First Boston and Petrie Parkman. They also note that the S–4 contains historical financial information about Pure's results as well as certain projections of future results.[57] As such, they claim that disclosure of more detailed information about the banker's views of value, while interesting, would not have been material. Furthermore, the Special Committee argues that disclosure could be injurious to the minority. Because the Special Committee still hopes to secure a better price at the negotiating table, they are afraid that disclosure of their bankers' range of values will hamper their bargaining leverage. . . .

This is a continuation of an ongoing debate in Delaware corporate law, and one I confess to believing has often been answered in an intellectually unsatisfying manner. Fearing stepping on the SEC's toes and worried about encouraging prolix disclosures, the Delaware courts have been reluctant to require informative, succinct disclosure of investment banker analyses in circumstances in which the bankers' views about value have been cited as justifying the recommendation of the board. But this reluctance has been accompanied by more than occasional acknowledgement of the utility of such information, an acknowledgement that is understandable given the substantial encouragement Delaware case law has given to the deployment of investment bankers by boards of directors addressing mergers and tender offers.

* * *

57 Because Pure's historical financial results and projected results were disclosed in the S–4, it would not add materially to the mix of information for the 14D–9 to simply repeat them.

In my view, it is time that this ambivalence be resolved in favor of a firm statement that stockholders are entitled to a fair summary of the substantive work performed by the investment bankers upon whose advice the recommendations of their board as to how to vote on a merger or tender rely. I agree that our law should not encourage needless prolixity, but that concern cannot reasonably apply to investment bankers' analyses, which usually address the most important issue to stockholders—the sufficiency of the consideration being offered to them for their shares in a merger or tender offer. Moreover, courts must be candid in acknowledging that the disclosure of the banker's "fairness opinion" alone and without more, provides stockholders with nothing other than a conclusion, qualified by a gauze of protective language designed to insulate the banker from liability.

The real informative value of the banker's work is not in its bottom-line conclusion, but in the valuation analysis that buttresses that result. This proposition is illustrated by the work of the judiciary itself, which closely examines the underlying analyses performed by the investment bankers when determining whether a transaction price is fair or a board reasonably relied on the banker's advice. Like a court would in making an after-the-fact fairness determination, a Pure minority stockholder engaging in the before-the-fact decision whether to tender would find it material to know the basic valuation exercises that First Boston and Petrie Parkman undertook, the key assumptions that they used in performing them, and the range of values that were thereby generated. After all, these were the very advisors who played the leading role in shaping the Special Committee's finding of inadequacy.

The need for this information is heightened here, due to the Pure board's decision to leave it up to the stockholders whether to "say no." Had the Pure board taken steps to stop the Offer itself, the Special Committee's desire to conceal the bankers' work during ongoing negotiations might make some sense. But Unocal has not even made a counter-offer to the Committee. Thus, the Special Committee's reserve price is not the issue, it is that of the stockholders that counts, and they deserve quality information to formulate it. Put differently, disclosure of the bankers' analyses will not reveal the stockholders' reserve price, but failure to disclose the information will deprive the stockholders of information material to making an informed decision whether the exchange ratio is favorable to them. In this regard, it is notable that the 14D–9 discloses the Special Committee's overture to increase the exchange ratio. Because this was the Special Committee's first offer, it is likely seen by Unocal as negotiable and as setting a frame on further discussions. Since the Special Committee has already tipped its hand in this way, I fail to see the danger of arming the stockholders who must actually decide on the Offer with the advice of the bankers who were hired at very expensive rates to protect their interests.

Although there are other reasons why I find this type of information material, one final policy reason will suffice for now. When controlling stockholders make tender offers, they have large informational advantages that can only be imperfectly overcome by the special committee process, which almost invariably involves directors who are not involved in the day-to-day management of the subsidiary. The retention of financial advisors by special committees is designed to offset some of this asymmetry, and it would seem to be in full keeping with that goal for the minority stockholders to be given a summary of the core analyses of these advisors in circumstances in which the stockholders must protect themselves in the voting or tender process. That this can be done without great burden is demonstrated by the many transactions in which meaningful summary disclosure of bankers' opinions are made, either by choice or by SEC rule.[63]

For all these reasons, I conclude that the plaintiffs have shown a reasonable probability of success on their claim that the 14D–9 omits material information regarding the First Boston and Petrie Parkman analyses.

* * *

[63] In certain going private transactions, the SEC requires that the entire investment banker board presentation books be made public as an exhibit. This requirement has hardly had a deal-stopping effect.

CHAPTER EIGHT

ACCOUNTING AND TAX ISSUES IN MERGERS AND ACQUISITIONS

■ ■ ■

Whenever two firms combine or one firm otherwise purchases a significant amount of stock in another, the transaction raises accounting and tax issues. How does the surviving or acquiring firm account for the transaction in its financial statements? Do the participants in the transaction (which include both the constituent firms and their investors) recognize and realize taxable gain or loss under federal income tax statutes? The promulgators of accounting and tax rules relevant to mergers and acquisitions have necessarily diverged from the path taken by states in drafting and interpreting their corporation codes. In Chapter Two we noted that state codes began with a tripartite division—mergers, sales of all or substantially all of a firm's assets, and stock sales—and states have refused (with the exception of California) to protect the integrity of the distinctions when clever lawyers designed asset and stock acquisitions to avoid the shareholder rights requirements of the classic merger provisions (e.g., voting and appraisal rights). Drafters of accounting rules and tax rules also begin with a basic classification system. Transactions in one category receive different accounting or tax treatment from transactions in another. Yet unlike state officials, these rule-makers have taken steps to preserve the integrity of the basic classifications.

Accounting and tax rules thus have two parts—first, a basic classification system and second, a series of rules designed to stop clever planners from avoiding the effects of the basic system. While the rule-makers aim to preserve the integrity of the basic distinction, accountants and lawyers aim to find crevices in the rules and statutes that may frustrate the basic distinctions and generate preferred outcomes for their clients. The rule-makers have the harder job, looking ahead to anticipate avoidance schemes, and the professional planners are often one step ahead of the drafters. To exacerbate the inequality, the rule-makers are on the public payroll, where pay and experience are often modest, and the planners are paid handsomely, attracting some of the country's finest minds. As a consequence, the drafters often look not ahead but behind, reacting to schemes. In a constantly evolving set of rules, yesterday's tricks produce today's rules, and today's tricks generate tomorrow's rules.

A. ACCOUNTING FOR MERGERS AND ACQUISITIONS

1. INTRODUCTION TO FINANCIAL STATEMENTS

Managerial accounting focuses on information produced for internal use in varied contexts such as pricing, budgeting and inventory planning. In comparison, *financial accounting* reports the overall financial position of the enterprise at certain points in time (for example, quarterly or annually), and the information is relied upon primarily by external users such as lenders, labor unions, regulators, investment analysts and investors. One of those financial accounting measures discussed below, *earnings per share*, is used in evaluating the profitability impacts of merger and acquisition transactions. Another measure of enterprise profitability used by analysts is so-called "EBITDA," an acronym for a cash flow measure derived from financial accounting earnings, but before interest, tax, depreciation, and amortization expenses are considered. Financial accounting information provides the foundations of such analyses, and therefore is the focus of this chapter.

Financial accounting information must be reliable, accurately and neutrally reflecting the underlying transactions of the enterprise. To ensure reliability, management must adopt appropriate internal control and reporting systems.[1] Accounting information must also be relevant, capable of making a difference in decisions by potential users of the information. Financial accounting information should be reported in a consistent manner from reporting period to reporting period. Furthermore, financial accounting information should be based on common principles that make the basis for the information *comparable* from enterprise to enterprise. In that regard, reference is frequently made to *generally accepted accounting principles* or *GAAP*. In the United States GAAP has been largely determined by the private sector (principally the accounting profession) through pronouncements of the Financial Accounting Standards Board ("FASB") (a non-profit organization comprised of members from professional accounting firms, as well as industry members), which in 1973 replaced its predecessor, the Accounting Principles Board ("APB"), created by the American Institute of Certified Public Accountants. However, for publicly traded companies the Securities and Exchange Commission ("SEC"), principally through the Office of the Chief Accountant, works with the accounting profession and the FASB to develop accounting standards for reporting companies. While the SEC has statutory authority to prescribe the accounting principles utilized in reports filed with it, it has generally relied on the accounting profession to develop such rules. However, in some areas, most notably Regulation S–X,

1 See Sarbanes-Oxley Act of 2002, § 404.

the SEC has specified the type of financial information that must be supplied by a reporting company.

In the United States, business entities produce general-purpose financial statements that are intended to provide information on the financial condition of the entity. The financial statements include an *earnings statement* (income statement or profit and loss statement) which reflects operating performance of the entity for a specific period of time, generally one year; *balance sheet* (a statement of financial position), which reflects the assets, liabilities, and owners' equity of the entity as of a specific moment or "snapshot" in time (e.g., December 31st); and a *statement of cash flows*, which reflects the cash inflows and outflows of the entity for the period. The statements, together often referred to as the *financials* of a firm, are prepared using accounting procedures derived from the British system that have evolved gradually over time as a matter of professional custom and practice.

The balance sheet is a snapshot description of the firm at a single point in time. It is divided into two sides: on the left are shown assets, on the right are shown liabilities and stockholders' equity (or net worth).[2] Both sides are always in balance. In the asset column a firm lists all the goods and property owned as well as claims it has against others yet to be collected. Under liabilities the firm lists all debts due. Under stockholders' equity the firm lists the amount the stockholders would divide if the firm were liquidated at its balance sheet, or "book," value.

The mistake a layperson can make is in equating the total equity or net worth figure in a balance sheet's lower right corner with a firm's actual value. Since assets are not carried at current market values, and there is no market value assigned to the firm's reputation or name, the net worth category cannot accurately reflect the market value of the firm.[3] Profitable companies often show a very low net book value when compared to the market price of their shares, and manufacturing companies in declining industries, railroads and steel, for example, may show a very high book value per share. Insurance companies, banks, and investment companies, because their assets are largely liquid (cash, accounts receivable and marketable securities), may show a book value that is a fair indication of market value.

---

2 In the tables of this section (see Table 1), the linear form of balance sheet appears. The text describes the tabular form. In the linear form, assets, liabilities and equity follow each other down the page. A subtotal for assets equals a subtotal for liabilities and equity.

3 First—with some exceptions for cash, accounts receivable, and marketable securities—historical cost, rather than current fair value, is reported for assets. In a declining industry book value may overstate the value of assets. By contrast, for assets purchased long ago the book value may understate the current fair value. Second, the balance sheet amounts may not include valuable assets, such as internally developed goodwill, going concern value, or important innovations, or may exclude liabilities such as certain lease obligations, substituting footnote disclosures that are consequently a critical part of the financial statements.

The income statement is less a snapshot than a movie of a firm's activities; it shows the record of a firm's operation activities for a period of time and answers the question: Did the company turn a profit over that period of time or not? An income statement matches the amounts received from selling goods and services and other items of income (the sale of capital assets, for example) against all the costs and outlays incurred in order to operate the company. The result, therefore, is a net profit or a net loss for the time period in question (e.g., a year). The costs incurred usually consist of the cost to the firm of goods sold; overhead expenses such as wages and salaries, rent, supplies, and depreciation; interest on money borrowed; and taxes owed.

The mistake a layperson can make is in believing that the net income figure at the bottom of an income statement is, without additional analysis, an accurate rendition of the past profitability of a firm relative to other firms and an accurate predictor of how the company will do in the near future. First, an income statement reports past results and is of limited aid in forecasting future profitability. Indeed, with a fast-growing company the focus of analysts in predicting the future price of a stock is often not on *trailing* earnings but rather on *future* (or *projected*) earnings. Second, the income statement can report non-cash expenditures (such as depreciation of buildings and equipment) that decrease earnings but not cash flow (hence the usefulness of the EBITDA analysis discussed above). Third, it would be rare for a public company to report on a simple cash receipts-and-expenditures basis. Consequently, the accrual method of accounting[4] is employed, and it permits some latitude (and potential abuses) in the timing of revenue recognition and the deduction of costs.

The statement of cash flows (also known as the statement of changes in financial position and cash flow from operations, the sources and uses of funds statement, the statement of changes in financial position, and the funds statement) presents changes in a firm's financial position that are normally generated from operations and summarizes the financing and investing activities of the firm for the same period. The statement adds the cash balance at the beginning of the year, the cash generated from operations, the cash raised from the issuance of debt or capital stock, and the cash raised from the sale of fixed assets, and subtracts the distributions of cash to shareholders in dividends, the cash paid in the redemption of debt or stock, and the cash acquisition price of fixed assets. The result is a cash balance at the end of the year. It is hoped that the firm is generating a positive cash flow. The mistake made by a layperson is the assumption that a firm disclosing a net profit on its income statement is healthy. The

---

4 Under the accrual basis of accounting, "revenues are recognized when earned and are matched up with the expenses associated with them. Matching is done without regard to the actual timing of cash receipts or payments." Jeffrey J. Haas, CORPORATE FINANCE 36 (1st ed. 2014).

statement of cash flows may indicate the contrary, and a history of negative cash flows is usually a precursor of trouble.

NOTE: DON'T LOOK LIKE A DUMMY TO YOUR CLIENT

When business clients complain about their lawyer's lack of sophistication about business matters, the source of many of their complaints is their lawyer's ignorance about financials. Avoid these mistakes to not look like a dummy: (1) Accounting financials are not the same as tax financials. The rules are different in substantial respects and, when discretion is available, the incentives are different on how to shade the numbers. In accounting financials, an accountant wants to maximize earnings (favor capitalization over expensing[5]); in tax financials an accountant wants to minimize earnings (favor expensing over capitalization) to reduce taxes. Accounting financials are subject to public disclosure requirements; tax financials are not. (2) In accounting financials, (a) equity (or book value) is not usually an accurate measure of fair market value and (b) net earnings are not usually an accurate measure of on-going profitability. (See above.) (3) Auditors do not certify or guarantee the accuracy of the numbers on accounting financials, as those numbers come from company management (particularly the chief financial officer (CFO) or controller (chief accounting officer)). Auditors certify that the financials were prepared according to GAAP, which is much more limited. It has been common, for example, for auditors to give clean audits to companies that then declare bankruptcy in a cacophony of fraud accusations (WorldCom and Enron, for example). (4) Tax, and to a lesser extent accounting, rules drive acquisition planning. Tax planning limits cash payments to the government; accounting rules make the company look more attractive to investors (efficient market theorists will wince here; business people will not).

2. INTRODUCTION TO ACCOUNTING ISSUES IN INTERCOMPANY OWNERSHIP

In this section we will examine the accounting procedures used to report various levels of ownership of another firm. We use a common set of hypothetical accounting statements to illustrate the reporting consequences of each alternative. The companies are called Acquirer and Target, and the balance sheets for the two companies are presented in Table 1 as of 12/31/Yr 0, assuming no preexisting interrelationship. In Table 2 the hypothetical earnings statements of the two companies appear for the subsequent year (Year One), assuming that Acquirer has no interest in Target at any point during the year.

---

[5] "Expensing" a cost means the entire amount of the cost is included on the income statement and subtracted from revenue when determining profit or loss. By contrast, "capitalizing" a cost means that accountants have determined that the cost is a capital asset that must be included on the firm's balance sheet. That amount will be depreciated over its useful life, and only the yearly amount of depreciation expense will be included on the income statement and subtracted from revenue when determining profit or loss. Expensing a cost, therefore, reduces firm profitability in the year in which the cost is expensed when compared to capitalizing that cost.

Table 1
Hypothetical Balance Sheets
Independent Companies
as of 12/31/Yr 0

	Acquirer	Target
Current assets	$300	$50
Noncurrent assets	200	100
Total assets	$500	$150
Liabilities	$150	$25
Stated capital (common $1 par)[6]	75	40
Capital surplus	125	60
Retained earnings	150	25
Total liabilities and equities	$500	$150

Table 2
Hypothetical Earnings Statements
Independent Companies
for the Year Ending 12/31/Yr 1

	Acquirer	Target
Sales	$600	$200
Cost:		
Cost of goods sold	300	100
Expenses	100	40
Depreciation	80	30

[6] Assume Acquirer was originally capitalized by selling $1 par value common for $2.67 and Target was originally capitalized by selling $1 par value common for $2.50. Thus each share of stock sold results in $1.00 in stated capital (for a total of $1.00 times the number of shares outstanding, $75 and $40 respectively) and $1.67 and $1.50 of capital surplus (for a total of these amounts times the number of shares sold, $125 and $60 respectively). Acquirer has 75 shares outstanding, and Target has 40 shares outstanding. The examples will include par value on common stock because those who author the Delaware Corporate Code stubbornly refuse to follow most of the other state legislatures in updating the old legal capital statutes to eliminate par value for shares. Since Delaware's Code is relevant to a majority of large-scale acquisitions, par value is respected in the balance sheets of the examples. Del. Gen. Corp. L. § 154. Most states combine the paid-in capital accounts into one capital stock category and prohibit distributions that make a firm insolvent. ABA Model Bus. Corp. Act §§ 6.21, Off. Cmt. 1, & 6.40(c)(1) (2016 rev.).

Taxes	40	10
Total costs	520	180
Net earnings	$ 80	$ 20

The examples that follow necessarily simplify economic reality somewhat. In fact, whenever one company acquires any part of another, many economic relationships change. The buyer may finance the investment by borrowing, by issuing stock, by selling other assets of the firm, and so on. In each of the examples that follow, the assumption is that the acquiring firm issues new common stock sufficient to acquire the desired percentage of the target. We assume that the shares of the acquirer sell for $3 per share and the shares of the target sell for $3.75. These assumptions are arbitrary and consciously ignore many issues. For example, the very act of acquiring shares in another company may affect the value of both the acquirer's shares and the target's shares. When one company purchases the whole of a second, for example, the per share price paid by the acquiring company for the selling company is typically 25 to 50 percent over the recent trading price of the selling company stock (i.e., the acquirer pays a control premium) and the trading price of the acquiring company's stock often drifts downward a bit. We ignore such issues in the examples below.

The three basic accounting methods are tied to the level of ownership achieved by the acquirer. They are: the cost method for ownership of 20 percent or less, when no significant influence of investor over the target company exists; the equity method for ownership of greater than 20 percent but less than 50 percent, when significant influence exists; and the consolidation method for ownership of greater than 50 percent.

3. COST METHOD: ACQUISITIONS OF LESS THAN 20 PERCENT OF TARGET'S OUTSTANDING COMMON STOCK

Assume that Acquirer buys 10 percent (four shares) of Target at a cost of $15. To raise the $15, Acquirer sells five shares of its own stock in the open market. Accountants reflect the shares of Target that Acquirer owns as an asset on its balance sheet and will initially be reported at cost, $15. Table 3 reflects the balance sheet for Acquirer before and after this transaction.

Two principal financial accounting issues arise: (1) When and how should Acquirer's income statement reflect the earnings of Target? (2) How should Acquirer's balance sheet reflect the investment in Target?

With respect to the first issue, income statement presentation, under the *cost method* of accounting the separate accounting identity of Target is respected and Acquirer reports income from Target's operations only when and if dividends are distributed by Target to Acquirer. Dividends from Target in excess of its earnings subsequent to the acquisition date are a return of Acquirer's investment and reduce the reported amount of the investment. When Acquirer sells the stock of Target, Acquirer will record, as gain or loss on its income statement, the difference between the cost basis of the investment (as adjusted for any dividends in excess of earnings) and its sales price. However, as discussed in the following paragraphs, unrealized holding gains and losses of certain equity securities must also be included in current earnings.

Table 3
Cost Method
Acquirer Balance Sheets
Reflecting 10 Percent Interest in Target
as of 12/31/Yr 0

	Before Buying 10% of Target	After Issuing Stock and Buying 10% of Target
Current assets	$300	$300
Investment in Target		15
Noncurrent assets	200	200
Total assets	$500	$515
Liabilities	$150	$150
Stated capital	75	80
Capital surplus	125	135
Retained earnings	150	150
Total liabilities and equities	$500	$515

As Year One progresses, Acquirer and Target generate the earnings reflected in Table 2. Because Acquirer now owns 10 percent of Target, Target's profitability has favorable economic implications for Acquirer. However, Target's profits will only affect Acquirer's financial statements to the extent that Target declares dividends. The declaration of a dividend on common shares is a voluntary act of Target's board of directors. Since Acquirer does not control Target, Acquirer cannot direct Target to declare dividends, and therefore Acquirer's economic benefit from Target's earnings is uncertain until dividends are declared.[7] Once declared, the dividends become legal obligations of Target, and Acquirer must reflect them as income. Table 4 shows three earnings statements for Acquirer—before buying 10 percent of Target, after buying 10 percent but assuming no dividend is declared, and after buying 10 percent assuming a dividend of $0.50 per share is declared. Earnings in the first two cases are identical. Only in the third case do net earnings change. While the dividend is $2.00, net earnings rise by less than $2.00, because the dividend is taxable.[8]

Table 4
Cost Method
Earnings Statements of Acquirer
Reflecting 10 Percent Interest in Target
for the Year Ending 12/31/Yr 1

	Before Buying 10% of Target	After Buying 10% of Target: Target Does Not Declare Dividend	After Buying 10% of Target: Target Declares Dividend
Sales	$600	$600	$600
Dividend Income	—	—	2
			$602
Costs:			
Cost of goods	$300	$300	$300
Expenses	100	100	100
Depreciation	80	80	80
Taxes	40	40	41
	$520	$520	$521
Net earnings	$ 80	$ 80	$ 81

The earnings statement is also affected by realized gains and losses on the sale of investment interests. A company recognizes gain or loss in a completed transaction. Borrowing from tax concepts, accountants record the gain or loss as the difference between the cost basis of the investment (its purchase price with modifications) and its sale price.

7 In fact, dividends are theoretically income to the investor only to the extent Target has earnings after the investor purchases its ownership interest. The accounting and tax issues of this distinction are beyond the scope of this discussion.

8 In fact, dividends are taxed at special rates. In this series of examples, details of taxation are ignored and tax is assumed at a constant 40 percent.

With respect to the second issue of balance sheet presentation, the accounting nomenclature for the investment is determinative. Accounting Standards Codification (*ASC*) 320–10 (FASB Statement 115), *Investments—Debt and Equity Securities—Overall*. The rule characterizes equity securities that are bought and held principally for the purpose of selling them in the near term as *trading securities*. Trading is the active and frequent buying and selling of securities with the objective of producing profits on short-term differences in price. Equity investments that are not classified as trading securities are *available-for-sale* securities. Most strategic investments in companies like Target would fall into this category unless a greater stake in target is acquired. However, ASC 320–10 does not apply to investments in equity securities unless the fair value is *readily determinable*, with reference to bid-and-asked quotations that are currently available on a securities exchange registered with the SEC or in the over-the-counter market. The rule might not therefore govern venture capital investments in closely-held companies and partnerships. Furthermore, equity securities for which sale is restricted by governmental (e.g., Securities Act Rule 144) or contractual requirement are not considered to have a readily determinable fair value unless the requirement terminates within one year.

Once the ASC 320–10 (FAS 115) categories are determined, the rest of the accounting treatment falls into place.

Fair Market Value or Cost Basis: If ASC 320–10 does not apply to an equity investment (an *excluded investment*), it is reported on the balance sheet at the original acquisition cost with adjustment only for other than temporary impairment of value (e.g., a series of operating losses of an investee or other factors may indicate that a decrease in value has occurred which is other than temporary and should be recognized).

Current or Non-Current Assets: Under ASC 320–10, trading securities are classified as current assets on the balance sheet. Unrealized holding gains and losses are included in current earnings. Under ASC 320–10, available-for-sale securities are classified as either current or noncurrent assets. If the investment in target is a marketable security representing the investment of cash available for current operations, the stock would be classified as a current asset. In the more likely case of a strategic investment in target, the stock would be classified as a noncurrent asset. Dividend income, as well as realized gains and losses, are included in earnings.

On cost basis investments, unrealized holding gains and losses are generally excluded from earnings, but reported as a separate component of shareholders' equity until realized. If an available-for-sale security suffers a decline in fair value below cost that is other than temporary, the cost basis is written down to fair value, and the amount of the write-down is included in earnings, accounted for as a realized loss. Subsequent increases in the fair value do not increase the previously written-down cost basis and are included in the separate component of shareholders' equity. Subsequent decreases in fair value, if temporary, are also included in the separate component of shareholders' equity.

4. EQUITY METHOD: ACQUISITIONS OF 20 PERCENT TO 50 PERCENT OF TARGET'S OUTSTANDING STOCK

Accountants use the equity method most frequently to account for an ownership interest of 20 percent to 50 percent in another firm. Paragraph 6 of Accounting Principles Board (APB) (Opinion 18) (now in ASC 323–10 and 325–20) compares the equity and cost methods:

a. *The cost method.* An investor records an investment in the stock of an investee at cost, and recognizes as income dividends received that are distributed from net accumulated earnings of the investee since the date of acquisition by the investor. The net accumulated earnings of an investee subsequent to the date of investment are recognized by the investor only to the extent distributed by the investee as dividends. Dividends received in excess of earnings subsequent to the date of investment are considered a return of investment and are recorded as reductions of cost of the investment. A series of operating losses of an investee or other factors may indicate that a decrease in value of the investment has occurred which is other than temporary and should accordingly be recognized.

b. *The equity method.* An investor initially records an investment in the stock of an investee at cost, and adjusts the carrying amount of the investment to recognize the investor's share of the earnings or losses of the investee after the date of acquisition. The amount of the adjustment is included in the determination of net income by the investor, and such amount reflects adjustments similar to those made in preparing consolidated statements including adjustments to eliminate intercompany gains and losses, and to amortize, if appropriate, any difference between investor cost and underlying equity in net assets of the investee at the date of investment. The investment of an investor is also adjusted to reflect the investor's share of changes in the investee's capital. Dividends received from an investee reduce the carrying amount of the investment. A series of operating losses of an investee or other factors may indicate that a decrease in value of the investment has occurred which is other than temporary and which should be recognized even though the decrease in value is in excess of what would otherwise be recognized by application of the equity method.

As noted in ASC 323–10–35 (paragraph 10 of APB Opinion 18), while the cost method recognizes earnings only on the receipt of dividends, the equity method links the investor's financial statements more directly to those of the investee:

> 10. Under the equity method, an investor recognizes its share of the earnings or losses of an investee in the periods for which they are reported by the investee in its financial statements rather than in the period in which an investee declares a dividend. An investor adjusts the carrying amount of an investment for its share of the earnings or losses of the investee subsequent to the date of investment and reports the recognized earnings or losses in income. Dividends received from an investee reduce the carrying amount of the investment. Thus, the equity method is an appropriate means of recognizing increases or decreases measured by generally accepted accounting principles in the economic resources underlying the investments. Furthermore, the equity method of accounting more closely meets the objectives of accrual accounting than does the cost method since the investor recognizes its share of the earnings and losses of the investee in the periods in which they are reflected in the accounts of the investee.

Accountants generally tie the distinction between the two methods to the percentage of the investee owned—the cost method below 20 percent and the equity method from 20 percent to 50 percent. But the real issue theoretically is control and influence by the investor, as discussed in ASC 323–10 (Paragraph 12 of APB Opinion 18):

> 12. The equity method tends to be most appropriate if an investment enables the investor to influence the operating and financial decisions of the investee. The investor then has a degree of responsibility for the return on its investment, and it is appropriate to include in the results of operations of the investor its share of the earnings or losses of the investee. Influence tends to be more effective as the investor's percent of ownership in the voting stock of the investee increases. Investments of relatively small percentages of voting stock of an investee tend to be passive in nature and enable the investor to have little or no influence on the operations of the investee.

Thus, while the 20 percent cutoff is presumptive, cases can be found where circumstances lead to presumed control at lower levels of ownership or a lack of control at higher levels, though neither is common.

To illustrate the application of the equity method: Assume Acquirer purchased 30 percent (12 shares) of Target and financed the purchase price of $45 by issuing 15 shares of Acquirer stock for $3 per share. The stock has a par value of $1 per share. Table 5 presents the Year 0 balance sheet, and Table 6 presents the Year 1 earnings statement.

Table 5
Equity Method
Acquirer Financials
Balance Sheet
as of 12/31/Yr 0

	Before Buying 30% of Target	After Buying 30% of Target
Current assets	$300	$300
Investment in target	—	45
Noncurrent assets	200	200
Total assets	$500	$545
Liabilities	$150	$150
Stated capital	75	90
Capital surplus	125	155
Retained earnings	150	150
Total liabilities and equity	$500	$545

Table 6
Equity Method
Acquirer Financials
Earnings Statement
for Year Ending 12/31/Yr 1

	Before Buying 30% of Target	After Buying 30% of Target
Sales	$600	$600
Costs:		
Costs of goods	300	300
Expenses	100	100

Depreciation	80	80
Taxes	40	40
	$520	$520
Operating earnings	$ 80	$ 80
Equity in earnings of affiliate[9]	—	6
Net earnings	$ 80	$ 86

Under the cost method, requiring that companies use the lower of cost or market accounting may lead to a carrying value below cost, but the carrying value never exceeds cost. In the equity method the carrying value may exceed cost. For Acquirer, the investment in Target at the end of Year One would be increased by its $6 share in Target's earnings, to $51 on the balance sheet. Target's act of making a dividend payment would reduce Acquirer's carrying value of the investment in Target. A dividend payment of $3, for example, would reduce the $51 to $48 on the Year 1 balance sheet, although Acquirer would add the $3 to its current assets column. Conceptually, when Target generates earnings, its economic resources are increased, and an increase in Acquirer's assets reflects the gain. When Target pays a dividend, it is distributing part of those resources.

5. CONSOLIDATIONS: ONE COMPANY ACQUIRES OVER 50 PERCENT OF THE STOCK OF ANOTHER

When one company owns more than 50 percent of another, accountants *consolidate* the financial statements of the two companies into one combined set of statements. See FAS 94, *Consolidation of All Majority-Owned Subsidiaries.* Accounting Principles Board Opinion 16, *Business Combinations,* from the time of its release in 1970 until July 2001, provided for the use of two alternative bases of accounting for changes in corporate control—*purchase* accounting and *pooling of interests* accounting. The financial statements of the acquirer differed markedly, depending on whether the acquisition received purchase or pooling treatment. The FASB voted in April of 1999 to phase out pooling so that the purchase method would be the only permissible approach. In July 2001, the FASB issued two final statements on this matter, FASB Statement 141 *Business Combinations* (later superseded by FAS 141(R), a 2007 revision) and FASB Statement 142 *Goodwill and Other Intangible Assets.* In FAS 141(R) (see ASC 805), the FASB ruled that only the purchase method of accounting is permitted for business combinations initiated after June 30, 2001. In FAS 142 (see ASC 350), mandatory amortization of goodwill is abolished, but

[9] The equity in earnings is 30 percent of Target's earnings, as disclosed in Table 2. In this example the potential tax consequences are ignored.

goodwill is subject to a write down to fair value if, under certain conditions, the fair value of the goodwill appears to be impaired.

Under purchase accounting, accountants treat the acquisition of one firm by another as an arm's-length purchase and sale between disinterested parties. Accountants deem the transaction price to reflect, at minimum, the market value of the combination of assets and liabilities being acquired. The surviving firm allocates that market value among all the assets and liabilities of the new firm, and a new basis of valuation arises for accounting in the future. The target's book values are not relevant.[10] The surviving company's balance sheet carries the target assets at their current fair market values. Accountants treat the entire transaction prospectively; that is, they "step-up" or "step-down" assets to their fair market values. If the acquisition price exceeds a reasonable determination of the fair market cost of all target assets, the acquirer recognizes the excess as *goodwill*.[11]

Prior to FAS 142, goodwill was *amortized* for financial accounting purposes over no longer than forty years, and that amortization decreased the reported earnings of the surviving enterprise over the reporting period.[12] Under the old rule the mandatory amortization of purchased goodwill could make the pooling accounting alternative more attractive to the Acquirer. Under ASC 350 (FAS 142), mandatory amortization of goodwill has been supplanted by a write down of goodwill only in the event of a demonstrated impairment of its fair value, so the immediate impact on earnings is postponed or, optimally, eliminated.[13] Examples of events or circumstances that would require goodwill to be tested for impairment include a current-period operating or cash flow loss for a reporting unit combined with a history of operating or cash flow losses or a forecast of continuing losses, a significant adverse change in one or more of the

[10] The lack of symmetry is remarkable in that the other assets and liabilities of Acquirer remain at historical cost amounts and are not adjusted to reflect their market values; this is why it is so critical to have principles for determining which of the two combining companies is the acquirer. Consequently, all pertinent facts are examined in determining which party is considered to be the acquirer, including relative voting power in the combined enterprise, composition of the board of directors and senior management, and which company received a premium as an inducement for the combination.

[11] If Acquirer acquires the assets at a bargain price, below target's historical cost, the "negative goodwill" is eliminated by reducing the historical cost of certain of target's assets, to zero if necessary.

[12] *Amortization* is the expensing off the income statement of a portion of the value of an asset listed on a firm's balance sheet. Under the old rule, in each year after an acquisition, Acquirer had to charge at least 1/40th of the goodwill account created by the acquisition against its earnings, reducing reported net profits in each of those forty years.

[13] The test for writing down goodwill based on impairment was simplified in Accounting Standards Update (ASU) 2017–04, *Intangibles—Goodwill and Other (Topic 350): Simplifying the Test for Goodwill Impairment.* Under the simplification, if a reporting unit's carrying amount exceeds its fair value, an entity will record an impairment charge based on that difference. The impairment charge will be limited to the amount of goodwill allocated to that reporting unit. The simplification takes effect December 19, 2019 for publicly traded companies, although voluntary early adoption is available.

assumptions or expectations used in the most recent determination of the fair value of a reporting unit (e.g., introduction of competing products, loss of a customer or customer group, unplanned cost increases, product or technology obsolescence, loss of key personnel, and significant change in strategy or restructuring), or a change in legal factors or actions of a regulator.

Table 7 presents a simple case of purchase method accounting in a consolidation. Acquirer buys Target for $150 and raises the money by selling 50 new shares of Acquirer stock to members of the public, a purchase transaction, then uses the cash proceeds to purchase all the Target company stock. Assume that Acquirer issues capital stock with a par value of $50 and a market value of $150 in completing its acquisition of the subsidiary. The difference between the acquisition price, $150, and the book value of the Target, $125, is assumed to be goodwill or going-concern value. Book value of individual assets is assumed to be their market value in the transaction.[14]

Accountants prepare the earnings statement of the consolidated firm in Panel B by simply adding across. Accountants also use this method for all the entries in the balance sheet in Panel A except the owners' equity section and for the recognition of $25 of goodwill in the asset section. Before the acquisition, the parties to a transaction set the total consolidated sum of common stock and paid-in-capital and retained earnings ($125 + $225 + $150 = $500) for the combined entity in the owner's equity section and do not change the accounts with the acquisition.[15] The acquisition itself results in an elimination of the $150 cash account reflecting the proceeds of the stock sale and the addition of accounts containing the assets (including goodwill) and liabilities of Target, which net $120.

---

[14] Moreover, this example assumes that Acquirer purchases 100 percent of Target and that Acquirer and Target do not do business with each other. Neither one is a customer of the other, and no liabilities exist between them.

[15] After the stock sale but before the acquisition, Acquirer's equity section equals the sum of the pre-stock sale figures ($75 + $125 + $150 = $350) and the allocated proceeds of the stock sale, which add $50 to the $75, $100 to the $125, $0 to the $150, and $150 to the $350 total.

Table 7

Financial Statements Given 100 Percent Ownership
$150 Acquisition Price

Panel A
Post-combination

	Before Combination		Combined Firm
	Acquirer	Target	Purchase
Current assets	$300	$50	$350
Noncurrent assets	200	100	300
Goodwill			25
Total assets	$500	$150	$675
Liabilities	$150	$25	$175
Stated capital	75	40	125
Surplus capital	125	35	225[16]
Retained earnings	150	50	150
Total liabilities and equity	$500	$150	$675

Panel B
Earnings Statement
for the Year Ending 12/31/Yr 1

	Pre-combination		
	Acquirer	Target	Consolidated
Sales	$600	$200	$800
Costs:			
Cost of goods	300	100	400
Expenses	100	40	140
Depreciation	80	30	110

16 Surplus capital is a residual figure. Here it is Acquirer's surplus capital ($125) plus the excess of new Acquirer stock at market ($150) over its par value ($50).

Taxes	40	10	50
	520	180	700
Net earnings	$ 80	$ 20	$100

Note in Table 7 that accountants recognize goodwill in a purchase[17] and that the purchase method eliminates retained earnings of the Target before acquisition. Under ASC 350 (FAS 142), amortization of goodwill is not required unless its value is impaired.

Table 8

Purchase Accounting

Assets with Market Values in Excess of Book Value

	Before Combination			Consolidated
	Acquirer[18]	Target		
		Book	Market	
Cash and accounts receivable	$75	$10	$10	$85
Inventories	100	20	35[19]	135
Notes receivable	125	20	25[20]	150
Noncurrent assets	200	100	105[21]	305
Goodwill			15[22]	15
Total assets	$500	$150	$190	$690

[17] The recognition of goodwill was a substantial handicap to using the purchase method when pooling was an option, because goodwill had to be amortized like any other intangible asset, typically using the straight-line method over forty years (1/40th of the amount is deducted from earnings each year after the acquisition for forty years). The required amortization of goodwill in purchase accounting reduced the net earnings of the Acquirer, as compared with the pooling method of accounting that completely ignored goodwill.

[18] The initial values shown for Acquirer are the values before the actual acquisition occurs. Thus, they do not reflect the issuance of the $165 in common stock for cash or the use of the $165 to acquire the shares of the target.

[19] Inventory values are in excess of book value because of inflation (or the target uses the "last-in first-out" (LIFO) method of accounting for inventory).

[20] Notes receivable valued at market exceeds book value because of a decrease in interest rates, as prices of outstanding debt securities increase when interest rate decline (and vice versa).

[21] Noncurrent assets are in excess of book because depreciation patterns have not perfectly matched rates of decline in market value, i.e., depreciation expense has exceeded actual depreciation of assets.

[22] The goodwill reflects the target company's ability to earn above-normal returns due, for example, to the skill and training of employees, established business relations, reputation, etc. The monetary measure of goodwill is the difference between the purchase price paid by Acquirer and the estimated fair value of Target's assets and liabilities.

Liabilities	$150	$25	$25	$175
Stated capital	75	40	165[23]	130[24]
Surplus capital	125	35		235
Retained earnings	150	50	___	150
Total liabilities and equity	$500	$150	$190	$690

To add a level of sophistication to our example, we must relax an assumption. In Table 7 the Acquirer bought the Target for $150, although the market value and book value of its assets were equal, at a net $125, and we assumed the difference was goodwill. The assumption that the purchase price (or market value) of the identifiable assets and liabilities equaled book value is more often false than true. Table 8 reflects situations where the excess of the purchase price over the book value of the acquired firm is not solely a reflection of goodwill, but the excess can be tied directly and allocated to identifiable assets and liabilities. In the table, Acquirer pays $165 for a firm with a book value of $125. The details of the example are characterized in the notes to Table 8.

NOTE: ACCOUNTING RULES' EFFECT ON THE SIZE OF AN ACQUISITION

In general, the nature of the transaction and the nature (size) of the ownership interest determine the accounting treatment for an investment in another company. Many investors hold 19 percent of another company to avoid the accounting difficulties associated with the equity method. For start-up companies that will generate accounting losses for a few years, investors can avoid reporting a share of those losses by owning less than 20 percent. On the other hand, an investor may prefer to own over 20 percent of a non-dividend-paying profitable corporation.

Similar concerns arise in the neighborhood of 50 percent ownership. Many companies own exactly 50 percent of joint ventures and accordingly use the equity method. This may reflect the economic reality of shared ownership and decision making, but it may also reflect a desire not to consolidate the investee's debt. Effectively the equity method allows *off-balance-sheet financing* because the one line "investment in equity companies" reflects only the adjusted cost basis of the investment. Table 9 shows the potential impact of this off-balance-sheet financing. Note that debt to total assets is 33 percent ($5,000/$15,000) for the investor and 67 percent ($40,000/$60,000) for the

[23] In the market valuation of the Target, the notion of allocating the value between par value, surplus capital, and retained earnings is not useful. These items have no separable values. Collectively, they represent the total value of the firm.

[24] The combined firm will reflect the actual number of shares outstanding after the combination. In our example, the firm sold 55 shares with par value of $55 and market value of $165 to finance the purchase. When the $55 par value is added to the $75 in existing stated capital, the result is $130.

investee. Yet only the investor financials are disclosed publicly. If the investor had consolidated its financials with those of the subsidiary, the effect of the heavy indebtedness at the investee level would be reflected by a debt to total assets of 69 percent ($45,000/$65,000) (if minority interest is treated as equity) in the investor's financials.

Are investors misled by off-balance-sheet financing? This remains an open question. Some investors use computer screening programs to select companies with certain attributes, and under the equity method the investor would show low debt-to-equity ratios and high profitability (earnings/sales), since the earnings statement reflects only the investee profit, not sales. On the other hand, the footnotes to the financials and other disclosures of the investor would assist an analyst in developing a more complete picture.

Table 9

Off-Balance-Sheet Financing

The Equity Method v. Consolidation

	Equity Method		Consolidated Method
	Investor	Subsidiary	Investor
Current assets	$1,000	$20,000	$21,000
Noncurrent assets	4,000	40,000	44,000
Equity in investee	10,000		
Total assets	$15,000	$60,000	$65,000
Current liabilities	5,000	20,000	25,000
Noncurrent liabilities	0	20,000	20,000
Minority interest			10,000
Owner's equity	10,000	20,000	10,000
Total liabilities and equity	$15,000	$60,000	$65,000

NOTE: HISTORICAL ACCOUNT OF POOLING ACCOUNTING

On April 21, 1999, the FASB announced that it would eliminate pooling of interests as a method of accounting for business combinations. The announcement stirred up immediate debate about the effect that elimination of pooling would have upon the intangible asset called "goodwill." Under the pooling method, popular over the previous thirty years, goodwill was not recognized and had no effect upon future earnings. Purchase accounting, on the other hand, recognized goodwill and amortized it over a period of forty years, decreasing future reported earnings. Technology companies were particularly critical of the change, arguing that it would adversely affect the value of their companies as acquisition targets.[25] The compromise solution, in place by July 2001, was to recognize goodwill but to eliminate the mandatory write-down requirement for goodwill.

The pooling method of accounting treated the combined enterprise as a merger of the separate interests of the acquirer and the target, rather than as an arm's-length transfer of assets at market value. The predominant feature of a pooling involved the exchange of shares of stock rather than cash, and the prior shareholders of the separate companies continued as shareholders in the combined company. The book values of the separate enterprises were retained and consolidated into the surviving entity. Since the book value of the target's assets carried over without change, no goodwill was created. The only changes on the balance sheet occurred in the owners' capital section, where the capital stock and paid-in-capital accounts of the combined entity reflected the actual outstanding shares after the combination. Accountants also restated the financial statements of prior years as though the companies had always been together.

Parties preferred to use the pooling method over the purchase method when both options were available. The availability of pooling then is necessary to understanding the structure of many transactions closed before 2001. Generally, in a purchase, the asset values of the combined entity are higher than when using pooling treatment, lowering the net earnings and earnings per share (EPS). Only in a purchase is goodwill recognized, and until 2001 the amortization of goodwill had the effect of continuing to reduce earnings until it was fully amortized, usually over a period of forty years. Thus, management concerned about maximizing earnings as reported on future income statements preferred pooling when goodwill was large or when the carrying value of the acquired assets was well below market value. Goodwill is often the largest dollar factor in business combinations. For example, the goodwill asset created by the $7.5 billion AT&T-NCR merger, which occurred in the early 1990s, was approximately $5.7 billion, amounting to a forty-year annual charge against earnings of approximately $114 million.

First, although higher book earnings in a pooling may have been attractive to managers, there were undesirable tax consequences. Taxes on future earnings were higher under pooling and not fully offset by the tax deduction for amortized goodwill. Second, with assets reported at below-market values under pooling, asset sales generated higher recognized gains. Finally, where there was no goodwill in the transaction, a purchase had the advantage of adding in the target's earnings only after the acquisition (in pooling the target's earnings before the acquisition are added to the acquirer's pre-acquisition earnings), which typically caused favorable year-to-year earnings comparisons.

---

[25] Technology companies' market value was, in the late nineties, greatly in excess of their book value. Intellectual property developed in-house at low cost was, on the market, worth thirty to forty times book value, which was cost. Firms buying technology companies had to record huge goodwill amounts under the purchase method.

More important, perhaps, is that an acquirer's decision to use pooling or purchase accounting was inexorably tied to its decision to seek tax-free status for the exchange. An acquisition using the pooling method of accounting was usually a tax-free exchange, while an acquisition using the purchase method of accounting was often (but not always) a taxable exchange. However, the tax and accounting rules were not coterminous; a tax-free acquisition did occasionally fail the pooling requirements and a rare taxable acquisition did constitute a pooling. In a tax-free exchange the acquirer had a carryover tax basis in the acquired assets. In taxable exchanges the acquirer had a step-up in the tax basis of the acquired assets equal to the purchase price.

Since, given a choice, participants in an acquisition preferred to use the pooling method of accounting, the Financial Accounting Standards Board had to anticipate the ingenuity of planners' attempts to take an acquisition that would otherwise have used the purchase method of accounting and transform it into an acquisition that, at least in part, could use the pooling method of accounting. In an effort to prohibit such end runs, APB Opinion 16 established a set of twelve criteria under which pooling treatment could be used, ensuring that a pooling truly represented long-term combinations at both the shareholder and firm levels of the separate companies. The requirements for pooling treatment affected the structure of many acquisitions. With limited exceptions for fractional shares and dissenting shareholders, the target common shareholders could receive only common stock in the surviving enterprise, and there could be no pro rata distribution of cash. These requirements reflected the premise that the surviving enterprise was a continuation of the two separate enterprises, and the target shareholders continued their undisturbed investment in the form of stock of the surviving entity. Again, pooling rules are now of historical interest only, as the purchase rules are the only rules utilized today.

NOTE: GOODWILL GAMES

The accounting differences in the amortization rules apply to various intangible assets, including goodwill, and the difference between expensing and amortizing target costs have led accountants to manage their numbers aggressively allocating amount values to target costs and assets to maximize future reported earnings. There are several notable techniques. First, *eliminate amortization.* The cost of an acquired intangible asset recognized separately from goodwill is amortized over the asset's useful economic life. Some types of assets can be said to have infinite life, others more limited lives. *Allocating* amounts to those with infinite life, goodwill included, reduces amortization charges. The practice backfired in 2000 and 2001, however, as large portions of acquisition price allocated to goodwill became "impaired" when Nasdaq stock prices fell dramatically. Technology firms, having acquired numerous other high-tech businesses, were forced to take huge, historic write-offs to earnings. Such firms then had to use technique two, the *big bath.* In the big bath, firms take one-time, extraordinary charges to current earnings in an effort to protect a robust record of future earnings statements. The one-time write downs protect the following years' earnings statements. The firms supplement the technique with *unaudited pro forma earnings statements* that exclude the effect of the one-time charges in the current year.[26] Investors are encouraged to ignore the GAAP earnings statement in favor of the pro forma one. The technique works with goodwill write-offs and with the target's research and development costs (R & D). ASC 730 (FAS 2), *Accounting for Research and Development Costs*, permits acquiring firms to write off costs assigned to target assets that have "no alternative future uses." Acquiring firms allocate large amounts to target R & D, declare the R & D unusable and write off the amount in the year immediately after the acquisition. Subsequent years' income statements then look rosy by comparison.

Finally, there is the *capitalization of acquisition merger costs* game. Opposite of the practice of those who prepare tax returns, an accountant seeks to capitalize merger costs rather than expense them against earnings (reducing EPS). When AOL purchased Time Warner, AOL capitalized $1.3 billion of what it called "merger-related costs." The costs were associated with layoffs ($880 million in severance payments) and the other costs of closing businesses at former Time Warner locations. Instead of writing off the expenses as special charges to earnings, AOL recognized the costs as assumed liabilities in the purchase (part of the purchase price) and added them to goodwill recorded in the merger. Critics charge that the costs were not all directly related to the merger. They note that many of the layoffs, for example, were the result of efficiency considerations and would have happened had the merger not been announced.

NOTE: ACQUISITION ACCOUNTING AS A PONZI SCHEME—THE WORLDCOM EXAMPLE

Bernard J. ("Bernie") Ebbers, the chief executive of WorldCom, built a multi-billion dollar company on over sixty-five acquisitions. The largest was a $37 billion acquisition of MCI. When the Justice Department blocked a $129 billion acquisition of Sprint on antitrust grounds, WorldCom died. We now

26 The SEC permits public companies to present non-GAAP financial measures in their public disclosures generally, as well as the periodic reports and registration statements they file with the SEC pursuant to the Securities Exchange Act of 1934 and the Securities Act of 1933, respectively. However, to ensure that investors are provided with information that is not misleading, such companies must comply with Regulation G and Item 10(e) of Regulation S-K when doing so. Regulation G, which was adopted by the SEC based on a directive found in § 401(b) of the Sarbanes-Oxley Act of 2002, covers all public disclosures by public companies that contain non-GAAP financial measures, including press releases, investor presentations and conference calls, whether such disclosures are made in print, orally, telephonically, by webcast or by broadcast. Item 10(e) of Regulation S-K governs all filings with the SEC under the Securities Act and the Exchange Act and prohibits the presentation of non-GAAP financial measures on the face of a registrant's financial statements or in the accompanying notes, as well as on the face of any pro forma financial information required to be disclosed pursuant to Regulation S-X. Item 10(e) typically applies to the Summary Financial Information, Selected Historical Financial Information, Management's Discussion and Analysis and any other sections of prospectuses and periodic reports that contain non-GAAP financial measures. Certain provisions of Item 10(e) also apply to earnings releases that are required to be furnished to the SEC pursuant to Item 2.02 of Form 8–K. For more on the use of non-GAAP financial measures, see generally *Conditions for Use of Non-GAAP Financial Measures*, SEC Rel. No. 33–8176, 2003 WL 161117 (Jan. 22, 2003) (final rules); SEC, *Non-GAAP Financial Measures: Questions and Answers of General Applicability* (Oct. 17, 2017) (avail. at https://www.sec.gov/divisions/corpfin/guidance/nongaapinterp.htm).

know that WorldCom needed acquisitions to survive because it used acquisition accounting gimmicks to keep its earnings up. As the company grew, it needed larger and larger acquisitions to maintain the ruse. It was a Ponzi scheme,[27] and all such schemes ultimately fail.

WorldCom was a poorly run company. It did not consolidate its many acquired companies into a viable single company and its core business was barely growing or losing ground. Through the use of accounting maneuvers tied to acquisitions, WorldCom reported ever-higher per share profits. It was a bubble gum and band-aid operation.

With a high price to earnings (p/e) ratio, WorldCom purchased companies with lower ratios. Since WorldCom used its stock in the acquisition, the acquisitions automatically increased WorldCom's per-share earnings. When investors used the higher WorldCom p/e ratio on the new assets, WorldCom stock price rose. Moreover, WorldCom used acquisition accounting gimmicks to hide expenses and increase profits.

what it did

First, it perfected the "big bath," subtracting many millions and even billions of dollars from its profits in a single year in write downs of assets. The result was bigger losses in the current quarter but smaller ones in future quarters, so that its profit picture seemed to be improving. Moreover, some of the write-downs, particularly those for research and development, were reversible and created a "cookie jar" of earnings reserves that the company could tap when needed. Second, it converted target company expenses to capital charges. It reduced the book value of hard assets of MCI, for example, which had to be depreciated, by $3.4 billion and allocated the amount to acquisition goodwill, amortized (under the rules in place) over a much longer time. The result was a significant reduction in the charges against earnings. The maneuver increased per-share earnings by 14 cents. Third, each deal came with window dressing opportunities. WorldCom could ask a target to slow its sales and collect bills after the deal closed so as to increase post-acquisition revenue figures and so on.

With each acquisition came a boost to earnings from post-acquisition accounting. And the boosts hid the dismal condition of the business. When the Sprint deal fell apart in June of 2000, WorldCom was heavy with expenses from poor planning. The company's debt was rising and its revenue was falling. Its total cash flow was dropping. With no acquisitions to shore up the income statement, its managers resorted to purer forms of accounting fraud, expenses were simply not reported and bogus revenues were. In 2000, for example, desperate WorldCom managers improperly reduced expenses by more than $3.8 billion. The fraud was exposed for what it was in 2002, when WorldCom

27 In a Ponzi scheme, a promoter raises money with promises of high returns on a non-existent business. Early investors are paid with money raised from later investors. As long as the new money raised exceeds the money owed to early investors, the scheme survives. But the need for new money increases exponentially until the obligation gets too large to meet. The house of cards then collapses.

filed for bankruptcy, one of the largest bankruptcies in American history.[28] WorldCom had to restate revenue in 2001 and 2002 of close to $11 billion. It also had to take writedowns of acquisitions goodwill over $80 billion, the largest in history. Shareholders lost $180 billion on the company's stock from its peak stock price in 2000. The successor to WorldCom, MCI, received the largest fine ever levied by the SEC to that time, $500 million. We also discovered that Bernie Ebbers, the CEO of WorldCom, had borrowed more than $400 million from the company that he would never pay back. Mr. Ebbers is currently serving a 25-year sentence in Oakdale Federal Correctional Institution in Oakdale, Louisiana. He is eligible for parole in July 2028.

B. TAX TREATMENT OF MERGERS, ACQUISITIONS, AND REORGANIZATIONS

1. INTRODUCTION TO THE TRANSACTIONAL BASE OF OUR FEDERAL INCOME TAX

The federal income tax code taxes gains and losses on held property only when they are "[g]ains derived from dealings in property." Internal Revenue Code (I.R.C.) § 61(a)(3). The basic calculation of gain or loss is contained in I.R.C. § 1001(a):

> The gain from the sale or other disposition of property shall be the excess of the amount realized therefrom over the adjusted basis provided in section 1011 for determining gain, and the loss shall be the excess of the adjusted basis provided in such section for determining loss over the amount realized.

The two important numbers, then, are the sale price and the *basis*; sale price minus basis equals *realized gain or loss.*

An original basis is often the cost of the property when first acquired by the taxpayer. An *adjusted basis* is the taxpayer's original basis with adjustments downward for depreciation and similar tax allowances and adjustments upward to reflect improvements or other capital outlays.

Not all exchanges are taxable events, however. For example, assume a taxpayer buys a share of convertible preferred stock for $100. The conversion right gives the taxpayer the option of exchanging her share of preferred stock for one share of the firm's common stock. Exercising the conversion right, even if the value of the common received at the time of conversion is $200, is not a taxable "sale or disposition" of the preferred stock. See Rev. Rule 57–535, 1957–2 C.B. 513. The conversion is not a *tax realization event* because there is not a sufficient change in the form of ownership. Moreover, even if there is a sufficient change in the form of

---

[28] See Dale A. Oesterle, *Year 2002: The Year of the Telecom Meltdown*, 2 J. TELE. & HIGH TECH. L. 413 (2003) (telecom companies lost 95 percent of the their total capitalization in a single year).

ownership to realize gain, the tax code may expressly exempt the gain from taxation; the realized gain is *not recognized* at that time. The tax-free status of most acquisitive reorganizations comes from an exemption from recognition for realized gains in the transaction.

An original basis can be a *substituted* (or *carry-over*) *basis* if the property in question is acquired in an exchange that is either not a taxable "sale or disposition" (the gain is not realized) or one in which the realized gains from an otherwise taxable event are, by statutory exception, not recognized. In our earlier example of the convertible security, the taxpayer takes a substituted basis in the new common stock equal to her old adjusted basis in the preferred stock—$100 (not $200, the value of the common at the time of conversion). Not realizing a tax on the $100 gain is not a tax waiver but rather a *tax deferral*; the Internal Revenue Service will collect the tax on the $100 appreciation when the common stock is sold later in a taxable transaction.

In mergers, acquisitions, and reorganizations, shareholders of constituent corporations often exchange one investment instrument for another. An acquired firm shareholder can exchange acquired firm shares for shares in the acquirer or for cash, for example. Each of these events is taxable to the acquired firm shareholder under I.R.C. § 1001(a) unless there is an applicable statutory exception that permits non-recognition of the gain realized. Moreover, in these acquisitive transactions, corporations as well as shareholders may exchange one form of investment for another. An acquired firm may exchange its assets for cash. Since corporations are taxed, as well as individuals, each of the events is also taxable to the acquired firm under § 1001(a) unless we can qualify it under a statutory exception.

I.R.C. §§ 354(a)(1) and 361 contain the statutory exception for selected transactions, known as *tax-free reorganizations*. Those two sections incorporate definitions found in I.R.C. § 368. The dividing line between taxable and tax-free reorganizations is generally whether the acquirer is paying with cash or stock consideration in the deals.

2. TAXABLE ACQUISITIONS: CASH DEALS

In a taxable stock acquisition or a taxable reverse triangular merger, the acquiring firm (A) buys the stock of a target corporation (T) for cash (or a combination of cash, notes, and other consideration). T's shareholders recognize gain or loss on their sale of their stock, measured by the difference between their amount realized and their stock basis, and A takes a cost basis in the T stock it acquires. T, as a subsidiary of A, retains its tax attributes, including the historical basis in its assets, earnings and profits. I.R.C. § 382 limits the use of T's net operating losses (NOLs), however, assuming it has any. Importantly, A, if it has purchased over 80 percent of

T's stock, may make a *Section 338 election* to treat the acquisition under the tax code as an acquisition of T's assets followed by a liquidation of T.

In a taxable asset acquisition, followed by liquidation, T's shareholders receive cash or notes and T's assets and selected liabilities transfer to A. T recognizes gain or loss on the transaction since it is selling its assets and pays a corporate-level tax. T shareholders recognize a gain on the residual amount received in connection with the liquidation and pay a capital gains tax. A takes the assets with a cost basis and does not succeed to any of T's tax attributes. *Cash mergers, other than reverse triangular mergers, are treated as asset acquisitions*. The parties allocate the purchase price among the various tangible and intangible assets sold, and the allocation determines the amount and character of the seller's gain or loss and the buyer's cost basis in each asset (for computing depreciation and amortization deductions and gain or loss on a subsequent disposition of the assets by A). Liabilities assumed by the buyer are included in the total purchase price.

I.R.C. §§ 1060 and 197 restrict the parties ability to make strategic purchase price allocations.[29] The parties must first value each tangible and intangible asset (excluding goodwill and going concern value) in seven classes in a descending order of priority, and if the price paid exceeds the aggregate fair market value of these assets, the excess is allocated to goodwill and going concern value. The amount allocated to an asset may not exceed its fair market value. The U.S. Treasury Department may contest any written agreement between the parties on the allocations.

NOTE: SOME SIGNIFICANT PLANNING CHOICES FOR TAXABLE STOCK ACQUISITIONS

The tax code is layered and complex, offering tax planners a variety of methods to reduce taxes on any given taxable transaction. The following options are just a few of the many available and give you a sense of the importance of retaining a knowledgeable expert.

Election of a Stock Acquisition Form: If target shareholders refuse to accept stock as consideration, or if the target is a subsidiary of another corporation, or the acquiring corporation does not want to put a large block of its stock in the hands of one corporate shareholder, then a taxable acquisition is the result. In taxable acquisitions, stock acquisitions are more common than asset acquisitions or statutory mergers. Acquisitions of assets for cash or statutory mergers in which the target shareholders are cashed out subject the

[29] It is desirable for the buyer to allocate as much as possible of the purchase price to assets that are depreciable over the shortest period (e.g., inventory and depreciable equipment). There are a complex series of Treasury Regulations aimed at curbing extreme allocations to assets with fast amortization rates. Moreover, § 197 on intangible assets eliminates the old strategy of allocating a large portion of the purchase price to covenants not to compete (minimizing goodwill). Covenants not to compete acquired as part of an acquisition (including a stock acquisition) now must be amortized over fifteen years. Buyers can still gain advantage by using consulting contracts (amortized over the term of the contract) rather than covenants not to compete.

target shareholders to a double tax. There is a corporate-level tax (a corporate tax on the consideration received in excess of the corporation's basis in the assets transferred) and a shareholder-level tax (a personal tax on the consideration received in excess of the shareholder's basis in his or her shares). A taxable stock acquisition, on the other hand, results in only a shareholder-level tax. There is no corporate-level tax.

The tax benefit to the buyer in an asset purchase, a step-up in the tax basis of the acquired assets, is not generally sufficient to offset the additional tax cost to the target and its shareholders. Thus, a buyer in an asset sale receives a reduction in future tax (on, for example, depreciation) equal to a maximum of 21 percent of the step-up basis while the target and its shareholders together suffer an immediate tax at a combined rate of about 50 percent (21 percent corporate tax plus 37 percent individual tax on the residual 79 percent[30]) of the taxable gain represented by the step-up amount. The maximum tax to target shareholders in a stock sale is 37 percent (or a bit higher if social security and Medicare taxes are added). In special circumstances, a taxable asset acquisition may be preferable, however.[31]

The disadvantage of taxable asset acquisitions was narrowed by the Revenue Reconciliation Act of 1993 (RRA). The RRA added § 197 on intangible assets to the Internal Revenue Code. The section reverses previous law and, in § 197(a) and (d)(1)(A), provides for the amortization of goodwill over a 15-year period.[32] Prior to the RRA, goodwill and going-concern value were not amortizable at all, and any amounts attributable to goodwill could only be recovered upon liquidation or sale of the business. Consequently, buyers fought to avoid any purchase price allocation to goodwill. Today, § 197 treatment is generally available only if a transaction is treated as a taxable asset purchase. A stock purchase will not lead to § 197 treatment of goodwill because no amortizable basis is assigned to assets. In essence, § 197 allows the purchaser to recover, through the amortized goodwill deductions, some of the corporate-level tax levied on the target in taxable asset acquisitions.

Sale of Stock of a Subsidiary with a Bootstrap Dividend: A corporation that receives dividends from other domestic (and some foreign) corporations is allowed a *dividends-received deduction* computed as 70, 80, or 100 percent of the dividend (the percentage being determined primarily by the degree of ownership in the distributing corporation; see I.R.C. § 243). A *bootstrap dividend* plan takes advantage of the dividends-received deduction through the declaration of a dividend *prior* to a sale of subsidiary stock, wagering that much of the dividend income will be eliminated by the dividends-received deduction.

---

30 The top tax rates of 37 percent for individuals and 21 percent for corporations were used. Effective tax rates, rates actually paid once deductions and credits are netted out, are, of course, much lower.

31 A taxable asset acquisition is preferable to a taxable stock acquisition if the target has loss carryovers that can offset its gain, if the target has a loss on the assets, if the target is an 80 percent-owned subsidiary and the parent's basis in the target's stock is the same as the target's basis in its own assets, or if the target has been an S Corporation for over ten years.

32 Do not confuse amortizing goodwill in accounting, which is bad—it reduces earnings—with amortizing goodwill in taxation, which is good—it reduces taxes owed.

The dividend becomes part of the sales price, in that the acquirer is purchasing the subsidiary sans the cash needed to pay the dividend. This planning tool involves some technical care and the overall structure has been given a mixed reception by the courts; the timing of the dividend declaration versus the stock sale is a critical factor. See, e.g., *Waterman Steamship Corp. v. Commissioner*, 4[illegible] F.2d 1185 (5th Cir. 1970) (finding that the dividend was in substance part of the sales price and denying a dividends-received deduction); *TSN Liquidating Corp. v. U.S.*, 624 F.2d 1328 (5th Cir. 1980) (respecting the dividend characterization); *Litton Industries, Inc. v. Commissioner*, 89 T.C. 1086 (1987) (respecting the dividend characterization). See generally *Nondividend Payments Disguised as Dividends*, FED. TAX COORDINATOR ¶ D–2220 (2d Ed. 2017).

Sale of Stock with an I.R.C. § 338 Election: A stock sale does not affect the adjusted basis of the assets held by target. A pure asset sale, on the one hand, can provide the purchaser with a fair market value adjusted basis in purchased assets, but on the other hand, can be cumbersome, involving numerous documents of transfer, transfer fees, third-party approvals, and other complications. In response I.R.C. § 338 generally permits a *sale of stock* to be treated as a *sale of assets* for income tax purposes, although only shares of stock are changing hands. If an asset purchase is otherwise desirable, an I.R.C. § 338 election can simplify the mechanics of the acquisition while producing equivalent income tax consequences. However, the I.R.C. § 338 election does not generally offer a better income tax result than a simple stock sale because it generates an immediate tax liability that must be paid by target. While target, in the hands of acquirer, now has a purchase price adjusted basis in its assets, the result required immediate recognition of gain or loss and payment of tax. In the absence of special circumstances, the purchasing corporation would usually not choose to incur the immediate tax.

Sale of Stock with I.R.C. § 338(h)(10) Election: In the I.R.C. § 338 election discussed above, two layers of tax are imposed. First, target computes gain or loss on the sale of its assets through the deemed sale produced by the I.R.C. § 338 election. Second, the seller of the shares computes gain or loss on the shares sold by subtracting the adjusted basis of the shares from the sales price. Although I.R.C. § 338 may offer little advantage under the current corporate income tax provisions, I.R.C. § 338(h)(10) has continued vitality.

The I.R.C. § 338(h)(10) election is made jointly by the seller and purchaser, and can be made only if target is part of an affiliated group of corporations (generally speaking, it must be at least an 80 percent-owned subsidiary of another corporation) or is an S corporation. If the I.R.C. § 338(h)(10) election is made, two results follow. First, target can be included as a member of a consolidated group that includes the selling corporation, so that the gains and losses from the deemed asset sale could be combined with other losses, income, or credits of the consolidated group. Second, no gain or loss is recognized on the sale of the stock of target. In many cases, the only gain or loss recognized is that produced by the deemed asset sale so only one layer of tax is imposed.

Liquidating the Target—The I.R.C. § 332 Alternative: The I.R.C. § 338(h)(10) election permits the sale of a subsidiary's stock to be treated as a sale of assets, but without the need for conveyancing and transfer documents for the assets "transferred." If the seller is not troubled by the need for conveyancing and transfer documents, and indeed, if the purchaser insists on receiving a transfer of assets, rather than taking stock in the subsidiary, a similar income tax result can be achieved by first liquidating the subsidiary into the parent corporation and then selling the assets to the purchaser. The liquidation of an 80 percent-controlled subsidiary is generally not a taxable event to either the subsidiary or the parent corporation. The parent corporation receives the subsidiary's basis in each of the assets received; the parent corporation's basis in the subsidiary's stock is irrelevant. As with an I.R.C. § 338(h)(10) election, the parent corporation's gain or loss on the sale of the assets will be determined with reference to the subsidiary's adjusted basis in the assets. Since the parent need not sell all of the assets to the purchasing party, this approach may be preferable to an I.R.C. § 338(h)(10) election if the target holds assets that the acquirer does not want.

3. TAX-FREE REORGANIZATIONS: STOCK DEALS

I.R.C. § 354(a)(1) provides for the tax-free treatment of investors[33] who exchange stock or securities of one corporation for stock or securities of another corporation if both corporations are "parties" to a reorganization as defined in I.R.C. § 368(b). I.R.C. § 361 provides for the tax-free treatment of a transferor corporation in a statutory reorganization defined in I.R.C. § 368(a)(1).[34] Thus if the detailed provisions of § 368 are met by a transaction, the participants avoid a tax at *both* the corporate and the shareholder level. The unifying theme of the section is "continuity of interest;" that is, Congress provides tax-free treatment to corporate reorganizations only if, after the transaction, participating shareholders in both constituent firms can be said to continue to hold their investments in the surviving firm in a form materially similar to the form of their pre-transaction investments.[35] The ostensible rationale for non-recognition treatment of qualifying reorganizations is that the transaction does not change the position of the participants enough to warrant an immediate imposition of a tax.

Viewed through an income tax lens, the structure of mergers and acquisitions is therefore often divided into *taxable* transactions, on the one hand, and *tax-free* or *tax-deferred* transactions, on the other hand. In the absence of special factors (such as a tax-exempt seller or stock purged of its built-in gain under I.R.C. § 1014 on account of the death of a shareholder),

---

[33] With an exception for *boot*, money or other property received in addition to stock, which is taxed as a dividend or as a capital gain. I.R.C. § 356.

[34] If an acquirer issues shares in exchange for assets or shares of the target, the issuance and transfer is not a taxable event. I.R.C. § 1032.

[35] There is a continuity of shareholder interest requirement *and* a continuity of business enterprise requirement. See Treas. Reg. § 1.368–1, *infra* Section B.3.

the tax-deferred label is more accurate for the latter category of transactions. A consequence of tax-free reorganization treatment is a *substituted* or *carryover* adjusted basis for stock or assets received by a party to the reorganization that preserves the built-in gain or loss in the asset, postponing the tax until a resale of the stock or assets.[36]

The reorganizations covered by § 368 are commonly divided into four groups: (1) *acquisitive* or *amalgamating* reorganizations in which two or more corporations are combined, (2) *divisive* reorganizations in which a single corporation subdivides, (3) *single-party reorganizations* in which a firm changes its capital structure or its place of incorporation, and (4) bankruptcy reorganizations. The amalgamating reorganizations can qualify under subsections (a)(1)(A) through (C) and in some cases (D) of § 368; the divisive reorganizations include the remainder of the (a)(1)(D) reorganizations (and some that are covered in § 355 as well); the single-party reorganizations qualify under (a)(1)(E) and (F) of § 368; and the bankruptcy reorganizations qualify under (a)(1)(G) of § 368. Special rules for triangular mergers are contained in (a)(2)(D) and (E) of § 368. It is common for tax practitioners to label tax-free transactions by the qualifying § 368(a)(1) subsection—an *A Reorganization* (or *A Reorg*) is a transaction that qualifies under § 368(a)(1)(A), for example.

An A Reorganization (or A Reorg) is a statutory merger or consolidation. Although not expressly required by statute, the IRS requires that at least 50 percent of the consideration received by the acquired firm shareholders be stock in the acquiring corporation. Rev. Proc. 77–37, 1977–2 C.B. 568. In hybrid Type A reorgs, the corporate acquirer uses a controlled subsidiary.[37]

A *B Reorganization* (or *B Reorg*) is a stock-for-stock acquisition. The acquiring firm exchanges its voting stock (and nothing else[38]) for control of a target, usually an 80 percent or larger block of the voting stock of the target corporation.[39] Other consideration—cash—may be paid for non-stock interests—debt instruments—in the target. A *C Reorganization* (or *C Reorg*) is a stock-for-assets acquisition. The acquiring firm exchanges its voting stock for "substantially all" of the assets of the target. "Substantially all" is defined, much more restrictively than it is defined in state corporate

[36] See I.R.C. §§ 358, 362(b), & 1032.

[37] The parent steps up the basis in its subsidiary's stock by the net inside basis (basis less liabilities assumed) of the target company's assets.

[38] The "solely for voting stock" language has caused interpretative struggles. See, e.g., C.E. Graham Reeves, 71 TC 727 (1979) (6 judge plurality majority, 5 dissents, 2 concurring), *rev'd sub nom.* Chapman v. CIR, 618 F.2d 856, *vacated* 618 F.2d 856 (1st Cir. 1980). The stock can be either the stock of a subsidiary or a parent but not both. Moreover, the stock may be preferred, even the debt-like (*nonqualified*) preferred.

[39] The section defines control as the ownership of stock possessing at least 80 percent of the total combined voting power, plus at least 80 percent of the total number of shares of all other classes of stock. The 80 percent rule explains the often seen public tender offer condition of an 80 percent tender of the target's voting shares.

codes, as 90 percent of the fair market value of the net assets and 70 percent of the fair market value of the gross assets of the target. Rev. Proc. 77–37, 1977–2 C.B. 568. Note that the assumption of target firm liabilities in the asset acquisition does not necessarily disqualify the transaction.[40] The target must liquidate and distribute the acquiring firm stock to its shareholders. I.R.C. § 368(a)(2)(G)(i). A *triangular asset acquisition* qualifies under § 368(a)(2)(C); a subsidiary may acquire the assets of the target in exchange for voting stock in the parent.[41]

An extension and modification of an A Reorg (including also elements of B and C Reorgs) are the two sections on triangular acquisitions. Section 368(a)(2)(D) permits *forward triangular mergers* in which the target corporation merges into a subsidiary controlled by a parent corporation. The shareholders of the target must receive at least 50 percent of the acquisition consideration in the form of stock of the parent corporation and "substantially all" (see Rev. Proc. 77–37, *infra* Section B.3) of the properties of the target must end up in the controlled subsidiary. Also important for mergers is § 368(a)(2)(E) that permits *reverse triangular mergers* in which the subsidiary controlled by a parent corporation merges into the target corporation.[42] The shareholders of the target must receive voting stock in the parent corporation and the parent must end up with control of the target. In practice, this means that at least 80 percent of the purchase price must be paid in voting stock of the parent. In both reverse and forward triangular mergers, the target's assets end up in a controlled subsidiary of the parent and the shareholders of the target become shareholders of the parent. The major difference between the forward and reverse rules is that in a forward a planner may use a much wider range of consideration (non-voting stock, for example). These two acquisitions are the most common forms of tax-free reorganization for publicly traded companies.[43]

---

[40] Target liabilities assumed by the acquirer are ignored if no consideration other than voting stock is used. If any other form of consideration (*boot*) is used, voting stock must be exchanged for assets of target, the fair market value of which is at least 80 percent of the fair market value of all of the property of target and debts assumed are treated as money paid for the property. I.R.C. § 368(a)(2)(B). Even a modest level of debt can exceed the 20 percent limit, making the exception of limited use. The money or other property to which the 20 percent rule is applied can include money or other property paid to acquire toehold positions in target unless the stock was, for example, "purchased several years ago in an unrelated transaction." See Treas. Reg. § 1.368–2(d)(4)) (Example 1).

[41] These rules can be extraordinarily complex. A 2001 IRS Revenue Ruling, the Double Merger Ruling, 2001–42, 2001–2 C.B. 321, provides a road map to eliminate the 20 percent limitation on cash or other non-stock consideration in a tax-free reverse triangular merger and eliminates the requirement that in such an acquisition the acquirer must acquire "substantially all" of the assets of the target. The technique requires back-to-back mergers, a reverse triangular merger followed by either an upstream merger of the sub into the parent or a sideways merger of the acquired sub into another sub. The IRS collapses the mergers together and qualifies the package as an A reorganization. An A Reorg does not suffer the 20 percent boot limitation.

[42] The planners may elect, as the parent's basis in the acquired subsidiary stock, the target's inside net asset basis (basis less assumed liabilities) rather than take a carry-over basis from the target shareholders.

[43] Forward or reverse triangular mergers that cannot qualify under § 368(a)(2)(D) or (E) can still qualify as a C or B Reorg.

Since the statutory development of tax-free reorganizations has been haphazard, there are different technical requirements for each type of reorganization and the technical differences can drive the form chosen. For example, if the acquiring firm wants to use cash as well as its voting stock for consideration in the acquisition, the most lenient form for using cash is an A Reorg (up to 50 percent of the purchase price), followed by a C Reorg (up to 20 percent of the purchase price). It cannot use a B Reorg.

QUESTIONS ON TRIANGULAR DEALS

As noted, triangular acquisitions are very popular, but both tax-free forms under § 368(a)(2)(D) (forward triangular) and (E) (reverse triangular) must meet the substantially all test of a C Reorg. This limits the planners' ability to strip-off unwanted assets before the merger (*pre-tailoring*), something planners can do in an A or B Reorg. Why do we have such a requirement for tax-free triangular deals? In § 368(a)(2)(D), deals planners can use a wider range of consideration. Target shareholders can receive non-voting stock in the parent and can receive cash and debt securities of either the acquisition subsidiary or the parent, limited only by the general continuity of interest requirement (unlike in B Reorgs, C Reorgs and 368(a)(2)(D)s[44]). A § 368(a)(2)(D) (reverse triangular) avoids the requirement in a B Reorg that only voting stock (the solely rule) can be used as consideration. Does all this make any economic sense?

Single firm reorganizations may qualify under D, E or F.

A *D reorganization* is described as a transfer by a corporation of all or part of its assets to another controlled corporation. Immediately after the transfer, the transferor, one or more of its shareholders, or any combination thereof, must control the corporation to which the assets are transferred. The most common divisive reorganization for public corporations is the *spin-off*. In a spin-off the corporation places the assets of a business unit (such as a division) in a newly-formed subsidiary. The corporation then distributes stock of the subsidiary to its shareholders pro rata in a manner that resembles a dividend for state law purposes. At the conclusion of the transaction, the same shareholders own shares of the original corporation (sans the subsidiary) plus shares of the former subsidiary (now a stand-alone corporation), and both companies may now be publicly traded as separate stocks.

In the *split-off* transaction, the stock of the subsidiary is not distributed pro rata, but is instead distributed only to some of the distributing corporation's shareholders in complete redemption of their

---

44 In § 368(a)(2)(E), voting stock of the parent must be exchanged for at least 80 percent control of the stock of the acquired corporation; the other 20 percent can be acquired for any other types of consideration.

stock. At the conclusion of the transaction, one group of shareholders owns the distributing corporation and another group of shareholders owns the distributed corporation. This technique is often employed to split corporate assets, on a tax-free basis, among feuding shareholders in a closely-held corporation.

The *split-up* transaction involves the creation of multiple subsidiaries, the stock of which is distributed to all of the shareholders in liquidation of the original corporation, which ceases to exist. A regulator, for example, might require the split-up of a public corporation for antitrust purposes.

An *E Reorganization* involves a single corporation and is defined in the Internal Revenue Code simply as "a recapitalization." It is very flexible, and the regulations permit the issuance of preferred shares to bondholders,[45] the surrender of preferred stock for no par value common stock, the issuance of preferred stock for outstanding common stock, and the exchange of preferred stock with various rights for a new issue of common stock having no such rights. An *F Reorganization* is "a mere change in identity, form, or place of organization of one corporation, however effected." This provision is helpful in changing the place of incorporation. A Nevada corporation can be merged into a newly-formed Delaware shell, and while that would qualify as an A Reorganization, it also will qualify as an F Reorganization. An advantage of F Reorganization status over A Reorganization status lies in avoiding certain limitations on the use of corporate attributes, such as net operating losses.

G Reorganizations are insolvency reorganizations. Covered is a transfer by a corporation of all or part of its assets to another corporation in a Chapter 11 bankruptcy or similar case, but only if, in pursuance of the plan of reorganization, stock or securities of the corporation to which the assets are transferred are distributed in a transaction which qualifies under § 354, 355 or 356.

NOTE: SECTION 351 TAX-FREE DEALS

As if this were not all complicated enough, another section, § 351 on contributions to a corporation, can be used to effect a tax-free business combination. In a simple tax-free § 351 merger, the acquiring firm shareholders and the target firm shareholders exchange all their shares for stock in a new shell company.[46] The advantage? There is no continuity of ownership requirement restricting the amount of non-taxable consideration (non-voting forms of acquirer stock) that target shareholder can receive. Target

[45] With the issuance of stock to bondholders or bonds for bonds, the corporation must consider the income generated from the cancellation of indebtedness. See I.R.C. § 108(e)(10).

[46] This is often done as a *horizontal double dummy* deal in which the target and the acquirer merge into separate shell subsidiaries of a parent shell company, with the target shareholders and acquirer shareholders taking stock in the parent shell company.

shareholders may also receive taxable boot, cash, in the deal. The IRS has blown both hot and cold on such deals.

INTERNAL REVENUE CODE § 368

(1999).

(a) Reorganization—

(1) For purposes of parts I and II and this part, the term "reorganization" means—

(A) a statutory merger or consolidation;

(B) the acquisition by one corporation, in exchange solely for all or a part of its voting stock (or in exchange solely for all or a part of the voting stock of a corporation which is in control of the acquiring corporation) of stock of another corporation if, immediately after the acquisition, the acquiring corporation has control of such other corporation (whether or not such acquiring corporation had control immediately before the acquisition);

(C) the acquisition by one corporation, in exchange solely for all or a part of its voting stock (or in exchange solely for all or a part of the voting stock of a corporation which is in control of the acquiring corporation), of substantially all of the properties of another corporation, but in determining whether the exchange is solely for stock the assumption by the acquiring corporation of a liability of the other, or the fact that property acquired is subject to a liability, shall be disregarded;

(D) a transfer by a corporation of all or a part of its assets to another corporation if immediately after the transfer the transferor, or one or more of its shareholders (including persons who were shareholders immediately before the transfer), or any combination thereof, is in control of the corporation to which the assets are transferred; but only if, in pursuance of the plan, stock or securities of the corporation to which the assets are transferred are distributed in a transaction which qualifies under section 354, 355, or 356;

(E) a recapitalization;

(F) a mere change in identity, form, or place of organization of one corporation, however effected; or

(G) a transfer by a corporation of all or part of its assets to another corporation in a title 11 or similar case; but only if, in pursuance of the plan, stock or securities of the corporation to which the assets are transferred are distributed in a transaction which qualifies under section 354, 355, or 356.

(2) SPECIAL RULES RELATING TO PARAGRAPH (1)

* * *

(D) USE OF STOCK OF CONTROLLING CORPORATION IN PARAGRAPH (1)(A) AND (1)(G) CASES—The acquisition by one corporation, in exchange for stock of a corporation (referred to in this subparagraph as "controlling corporation") which is in control of the acquiring corporation, of substantially all of the properties of another corporation shall not disqualify a transaction under paragraph (1)(A) or (1)(G) if—

(i) no stock of the acquiring corporation is used in the transaction, and

(ii) in the case of a transaction under paragraph (1)(A), such transaction would have qualified under paragraph (1)(A) had the merger been into the controlling corporation.

(E) STATUTORY MERGER USING VOTING STOCK OF CORPORATION CONTROLLING MERGED CORPORATION—A transaction otherwise qualifying under paragraph (1)(A) shall not be disqualified by reason of the fact that stock of a corporation (referred to in this subparagraph as the "controlling corporation") which before the merger was in control of the merged corporation is used in the transaction, if—

(i) after the transaction, the corporation surviving the merger holds substantially all of its properties and of the properties of the merged corporation (other than stock of the controlling corporation distributed in the transaction); and

(ii) in the transaction, former shareholders of the surviving corporation exchanged, for an amount of voting stock of the controlling corporation, an amount of stock in the surviving corporation which constitutes control of such corporation.

* * *

(G) DISTRIBUTION REQUIREMENT FOR PARAGRAPH (1)(C)

(i) IN GENERAL—A transaction shall fail to meet the requirements of paragraph (1)(C) unless the acquired corporation distributes the stock, securities, and other properties it receives, as well as its other properties, in pursuance of the plan of reorganization. For purposes of the preceding sentence, if the acquired corporation is liquidated pursuant to the plan of reorganization, any distribution to its creditors in connection with such liquidation shall be treated as pursuant to the plan of reorganization.

* * *

TREAS. REG. § 1.368–1

26 C.F.R. § 1.368–1 (2011).

Purpose and scope of exception of reorganization exchanges.

* * *

(b) *Purpose.* Under the general rule, upon the exchange of property, gain or loss must be accounted for if the new property differs in a material particular, either in kind or in extent, from the old property. The purpose of the reorganization provisions of the Code is to except from the general rule certain specifically described exchanges incident to such readjustments of corporate structures made in one of the particular ways specified in the Code, as are required by business exigencies and which effect only a readjustment of continuing interest in property under modified corporate forms. Requisite to a reorganization under the Code are a continuity of the business enterprise through the issuing corporation under the modified corporate form as described in paragraph (d) of this section, and (except as provided in section 368(a)(1)(D)) a continuity of interest as described in paragraph (e) of this section. . . . The continuity of business enterprise requirement is described in paragraph (d) of this section. . . . In order to exclude transactions not intended to be included, the specifications of the reorganization provisions of the law are precise. Both the terms of the specifications and their underlying assumptions and purposes must be satisfied in order to entitle the taxpayer to the benefit of the exception for the general rule. . . .

* * *

(d) *Continuity of business enterprise–*

(1) *General rule.* Continuity of business enterprise (COBE) requires that the acquiring corporation (P) . . . either continue the acquired corporation's (T's) historic business or use a significant portion of T's historic business assets in a business. . . . The policy underlying this general rule, which is to ensure that reorganizations are limited to readjustments of continuing interests in property under modified corporate form, provides the guidance necessary to make these facts and circumstances determinations.

* * *

(5) *Examples.* . . .

* * *

Example 5. T manufactures farm machinery and P operates a lumber mill. T merges into P. P disposes of T's assets immediately after the merger as part of the plan of reorganization. P does not continue T's farm machinery manufacturing business. Continuity of business *enterprise* is lacking. . . .

* * *

(e) *Continuity of interest–*

(1) *General rule.* (i) The purpose of the continuity of interest requirement is to prevent transactions that resemble sale from qualifying for nonrecognition of gain or loss available to corporate reorganizations. Continuity of interest requires that in substance a substantial part of the value of the proprietary interests in the target corporation be preserved in the reorganizations. A proprietary interest in the target corporation is preserved if, in a potential reorganization, it is exchanged for a proprietary interest in the issuing corporation . . . , it is exchanged by the acquiring corporation for a direct interest in the target corporation enterprise, or it otherwise continues as a proprietary interest in the target corporation. However, a proprietary interest in the target corporation is not preserved if, in connection with the potential reorganization, it is acquired by the issuing corporation for consideration other than stock of the issuing corporation, or stock of the issuing corporation furnished in the exchange for a proprietary interest in the target corporation in the potential reorganization is redeemed. . . .

* * *

REV. PROC. 77–37, 1977–2 C.B. 568, 1977 WL 42722, § 3.02

The "continuity of interest" requirement of § 1.368–1(b) of the Income Tax Regulations is satisfied if there is continuing interest through stock ownership in the acquiring or transferee corporation (or a corporation in "control" thereof within the meaning of § 368(c) of the Code) on the part of the former shareholders of the acquired or transferor corporation which is equal in value, as of the effective date of the reorganization, to at least 50 percent of the value of all of the formerly outstanding stock of the acquired or transferor corporation as of the same date. It is not necessary that each shareholder of the acquired or transferor corporation receive in the exchange stock of the acquiring or transferee corporation, or a corporation in "control" thereof, which is equal in value to at least 50 percent of the value of his former stock interest in the acquired or transferor corporation, so long as one or more of the shareholders of the acquired or transferor corporation have a continuing interest through stock ownership in the acquiring or transferee corporation (or a corporation in "control" thereof) which is, in the aggregate, equal in value to at least 50 percent of the value of all of the formerly outstanding stock of the acquired or transferor corporation. Sales, redemptions, and other dispositions of stock occurring prior or subsequent to the exchange which are part of the plan of reorganization will be considered in determining whether there is a 50 percent continuing interest through stock ownership as of the effective date of the reorganization.

[In January of 1998, the IRS modified the Rev. Proc. to allow shareholders of the seller to sell stock both before and after the reorganization. An acquisition can qualify as a tax-free reorganization even if shareholders of the seller sell their shares to strangers (not the acquired corporation) before the acquisition or sell all of the buyer's stock received in the acquisition immediately after the transaction, so long as they do not too quickly resell the stock to the buyer (in a redemption or repurchase) or to a corporation affiliated with the buyer. Treas. Reg. §§ 1.368–1(e) & 1.368–2 (amended 1998 and 2000).]

Treasury Regulation § 1.368–1(d) imposes a *continuity of business enterprise* requirement (known by tax practitioners as the COBE) on top of the statutory definitions. The requirement is satisfied if the buyer either continues the historical business of the seller or uses in its business a significant portion of the seller's historical assets. Why should tax collectors care whether the buyer continues the seller's business? The Department of Treasury provided an answer in the following release. Is it persuasive?

T.D. 7745, 1981–1 C.B. 134, 1980 WL 111151

. . . Continuity of Business Enterprise Requirement for Corporate Reorganizations

* * *

Overall Policy Considerations

* * *

An exception to the general rule of gain or loss recognition is contained in the reorganization provisions—sections 354 through 368—of the Code. As stated in § 1.1002–1(c), the underlying assumption of any tax-free exchange "is that the new property is substantially a continuation of the old investment still unliquidated" and, with respect to corporate reorganizations, nonrecognition results because "the new enterprise, the new corporate structure, and the new property are substantially continuations of the old still unliquidated." . . .

. . . A necessary corollary to this continuity of interest requirement is that the interest retained represent a link to *T's* business or its business assets. The continuity of business enterprise requirement ensures that tax-free reorganizations effect only a readjustment of the *T* shareholders' continuing interest in *T's* property under a modified corporate form. *See* § 1.368–1(b).[Ed.[47]] Absent such a link between *T's* shareholders and *T's* business or assets there would be no reason to require *T's* shareholders to

[47] [Ed. See the examples in Reg. § 1.368–1(d)(5). Example 1 illustrates that an acquirer need only continue one of the seller's lines of business.]

retain a continuing stock interest in *P*. If the shareholders' link to *T's* business or its assets is broken by, for example, a sale of *T's* business to an unrelated party as part of the overall plan of reorganization, the interest received in *P* is no different than an interest in any corporation. An exchange of stock without a link to the underlying business or business assets resembles any stock for stock exchange and, as such, is a taxable event. Thus, it is not enough that the shareholders' investment remains in corporate solution. . . .

* * *

NOTE: ADVANCE RULINGS FROM THE IRS

A company planning a tax-free reorganization is not usually content with an opinion from their tax lawyers. It seeks an advance ruling from the IRS that the planned acquisition qualifies as tax-free. A company often, therefore, requests a *private letter ruling* from the IRS (also known as a *comfort ruling*). Some deals are conditioned on a favorable ruling. The ruling is binding on the IRS if the facts described by the company are accurate and do not change. Obtaining a ruling takes time, however. A company has a preliminary conference with an IRS official, files a formal request and receives a preliminary response in roughly three weeks. The response may call for additional information. Appeals may be made to supervisors. The entire process can take five or six months and provides a lucrative living for lawyers specializing in the procedure. If the IRS refuses approval, a company must decide whether courts will rule the transaction tax-free if the company contests the IRS position. Most companies do not, given the time delays of litigation and the negative public exposure that comes from bucking the IRS.

If a deal time schedule will not accommodate a ruling request (or because the deal falls into a category of deals on which the IRS will not rule), the deals will be conditioned upon receiving a satisfactory opinion of counsel. A tax opinion from counsel can come in several gradations. The opinions are normally based on stated assumptions or on management representations that the elements and circumstances that would have been required for a favorable ruling from the IRS exist. An attorney may state that a transaction "will" be treated by the IRS as tax-free; "should" be treated as tax-free; or "is more likely than not" to be treated as tax-free. Attorneys worrying about malpractice liability joust with clients attempting to force stronger opinions ("Stand up for your advice!"). In any event, any malpractice payments pale in comparison to the tax liability owed in a taxable deal.

The essence of a tax-free reorganization is that in exchange for the elimination of current tax payments by the selling firm and its shareholders, both the purchasing firm and the selling firm shareholders take a lower basis in assets involved in the transaction. The lower basis means higher taxes for the parties later when the assets are sold to another party in a subsequent transaction. The tax consequences of qualifying as a tax-free reorganization are best understood by example.

Assume the following facts: Corporation T has 100 shares of stock outstanding, all of which are owned by Tim. Each share has a fair market value of $1,000 and an adjusted basis of $100 (the 100 shares are worth $100,000 with a basis of $10,000). T Corp. owns assets with a combined fair market value of $120,000 and a combined adjusted basis of $50,000, and has outstanding $20,000 in liabilities. Corporation P is a publicly held corporation that has more than 100,000 shares of common voting stock outstanding. P Corp. is going to acquire T Corp. for $100,000 in value, the consideration for which will be either 1,000 shares of P common voting stock, each with a value of $100, or $100,000 in cash.

A Reorganization: T Corp. is merged into P Corp.[48] P Corp. becomes the owner of all the assets and liabilities previously owned by T Corp. as a matter of law and T Corp. ceases to exist as an entity. Tim's stock in T Corp. is cancelled, and P Corp. issues Tim 1,000 shares of its common voting stock.[49] Tim realizes a gain of $90,000 on the exchange of his T stock for P stock (the value of the P Corp. stock received minus his adjusted basis); but under I.R.C. § 354(a), none of that gain is recognized.[50] Tim's basis in the 100 shares of P stock is a carry-over basis of $10,000, the same as his basis in his cancelled T stock. I.R.C. § 358(a). P Corp. recognizes no income by virtue of acquiring the assets of T. I.R.C. § 1032. P's basis in the acquired assets is $50,000, the same as T's basis in the property. I.R.C. § 362(b). T recognizes no gain because of the transfer of its property to P or because P assumed T's $20,000 in liabilities. I.R.C. §§ 357(a) & 361(a).

Taxable Merger: Assume a cash merger acquisition: P Corp. purchases all of T Corp.'s assets for $100,000 in cash.[51] The transaction is accomplished by a forward statutory merger of T into P in which Tim receives $100,000 in cash for his canceled T stock. P takes a *stepped-up*

---

[48] If instead P Corp. drops down a subsidiary and T Corp. merges into the subsidiary—a forward triangular merger—and Tim receives stock in P Corp., § 368(a)(2)(D) applies with the same results.

[49] If, instead of issuing 1,000 shares of common stock, P issues 700 shares of common voting stock plus a bond with a fair market value and principal amount of $30,000, the $30,000 bond will constitute boot, and Tim will recognize $30,000 of his $90,000 realized gain. I.R.C. §§ 354(a) & 356(a). Tim's basis in the 700 shares of P stock is his basis in the cancelled T stock ($10,000), less the fair market value of the boot received in the exchange ($30,000), plus the gain he recognized on the exchange ($30,000). I.R.C. § 358(a)(1). Thus, Tim's basis in the 150 shares of T stock is $10,000. His basis in the $30,000 bond is its fair market value of $30,000. I.R.C. § 358(a)(2).

[50] A *realized* gain requires a report to the IRS; a *recognized* gain generates a tax. So an event in which a gain is realized and unrecognized is an event in which a tax is excused.

[51] The equivalence of the purchase price in the tax-free and taxable exchanges is artificial, for institutional purposes. In a taxable exchange, P will pay more and Tim will demand more. P gets the tax benefit of a stepped-up basis and Tim must pay taxes. The deal will close at, say, $105,000 cash. Since P's benefit is often smaller than Tim's cost, the aggregate position of both parties in the taxable exchange is inferior to that in the tax-free exchange.

basis in T's assets equal to the purchase price, plus any T liabilities transferred to P and T's expenses of the transaction, $120,000. T Corp. realizes and recognizes a tax on its gain or loss in its assets (including goodwill), in this case $70,000. The gain or loss on each asset is either ordinary income or capital gains in character, depending on the nature of each asset sold (assume a tax of around $10,000). Tim recognizes any gain or loss realized on the disposition of his T shares—the excess of the cash and fair market value of property received over his basis in T stock, around $80,000.[52] The benefit to P of any step-up in basis in T's assets is that on a resale of the assets, P will realize less gain or a greater loss. P may also benefit if part of the consideration that it pays in an acquisition is allocated to deductible items that can be immediately expensed, such as salary for Tim rather than to the purchase price of the acquired assets. See Rev. Rul. 69–6, 1969–1 C.B. 104.

B Reorganization: In a stock-for-stock acquisition, Tim exchanges his 100 shares of T for 1,000 shares of common voting stock of P. Tim realizes a gain of $90,000 on the exchange; but under I.R.C. § 354(a), none of that gain is recognized. Tim's basis in the 1,000 shares of P stock is $10,000, the same as his basis in the T stock. I.R.C. § 358(a). P recognizes no income when it acquires the T stock. I.R.C. § 1032. P's basis in the 100 shares of T stock is $10,000, the same as the pre-transaction basis of Tim in that stock. I.R.C. § 362(b).

Taxable Stock Acquisition: In a cash-for-stock acquisition, Tim exchanges his T Corp. stock for $100,000 in cash from P Corp. Tim realizes and recognizes any gain or loss realized on the sale of the T shares, $90,000. P's basis in the T shares purchased is stepped up equal to the purchase price paid by P for the shares plus the expenses of the acquisition. T's basis in its assets, however, does not change as a result of P's purchase of the T stock (unless P makes a so-called § 338 election, see Note below).[53]

C Reorganization: In a stock-for-assets acquisition, T Corp. transfers all of its assets and liabilities to P in exchange for 1,000 shares of P Corp. common voting stock, and shortly thereafter, pursuant to the plan of

---

[52] Tim will net $90,000 with a basis of $10,000, because $10,000 of the purchase price is applied to T Corp.'s tax liability. If P gives Tim notes rather than cash, Tim may report the gain on the installment method (postponing the tax), so long as the P notes are not readily tradable and the notes otherwise meet the requirements of the installment method. In general this means that Tim will report a proportionate part of his total gain on the sale each time he collects a part of the purchase price for his stock (represented by payments on the notes). The installment method does not apply if Tim's stock is traded on an "established securities market." Moreover, I.R.C. § 453A imposes an annual interest charge on Tim's tax liability deferred by the installment method to the extent that the face amount of his receivables exceeds $5 million. The section also triggers immediate gain recognition on any installment receivable (in sales of over $150,000) to the extent that Tim uses the receivable as direct security for his own debts.

[53] T's ability to use thereafter its net operating loss, capital loss, and tax credit carry-forwards may be limited by I.R.C. §§ 269, 383, and 384, and perhaps by the separate return limitation year (SRLY) rules of the consolidated return regulations. T's other tax attributes are not affected by the purchase of T's stock.

reorganization, T Corp. liquidates.[54] T realizes a gain of $70,000 on the exchange of assets for P stock plus the assumption by P of T's liabilities; but under I.R.C. § 361(a), none of that gain is recognized. T does not recognize any gain because P assumed T's $20,000 in liabilities. I.R.C. §§ 357(a) & 361(a). P recognizes no gain on the exchange of its common stock for T's assets. I.R.C. § 1032. P's basis in the acquired assets is $50,000, the same as T's basis in the property. I.R.C. § 362(b). T will not recognize a gain on distributing those 1,000 shares of P stock to Tim. I.R.C. § 361(c). Tim will realize a gain of $90,000 because of the liquidation of T, but that gain will not be recognized. I.R.C. § 354(a). Tim's basis in the 1,000 shares of P stock will be $10,000, the same as his basis in the T stock cancelled on the liquidation of T. I.R.C. § 358(a).

Taxable Asset Acquisition: In a cash-for-assets acquisition, P Corp. purchases all of T Corp.'s assets for $100,000 in cash and assumes the $20,000 in liabilities. P takes a basis in T's assets equal to $120,000 (the purchase price plus the liabilities assumed). T recognizes gain on the transaction of $70,000 (assume a tax of around $10,000). If T liquidates, Tim recognizes gain on the excess of the cash or property received (approximately $90,000 once T pays its tax) over his basis in T stock, around $80,000.

NOTE: WHY USE A TAXABLE EXCHANGE?

When should parties favor a taxable transaction? Considering the time value of money, if income tax consequences were the sole consideration, it would seem that the opportunity to defer income taxes into future years would channel most acquisitions into a tax-free structure. An investor could take the tax money not paid to the government and invest it, keeping the returns until such time as the tax is due. Granted, a taxable transaction produces a cost (fair market value) adjusted basis to be used by acquirer (see I.R.C. § 1012) rather than a substituted basis. However, a taxable transaction can require the payment of tax by target in the year of disposition while the income tax benefits of the cost basis may be realized by acquirer only in future years through cost recovery (i.e., depreciation or amortization) deductions and subsequent taxable dispositions of the assets.

There may be business reasons for a taxable exchange—the target shareholders may not accept voting stock in the purchaser. Even if the target's

[54] To see the effect of cash in the transaction, called *boot* by tax practitioners, assume that T Corp. transfers all of its assets and liabilities to P Corp. in exchange for 900 shares of P common voting stock plus $10,000 cash, and T promptly distributes the stock and the cash to its shareholder, Tim, in liquidation. Again, T realizes a gain of $50,000 on the exchange of assets for P stock. Even though T received $10,000 cash, it will not recognize any of its gain. I.R.C. § 361(b)(1). P's basis in the assets transferred from T is $50,000, the same as T's basis in the assets. I.R.C. § 362(b). Tim realizes a gain of $90,000 when T is liquidated. This gain is recognized to the extent of the $10,000 boot received. I.R.C. §§ 354(a) and 356(a). Tim's basis in the 900 shares of P stock that he received on T's liquidation is equal to his basis in the T stock that he surrendered ($10,000), plus the gain he recognized on the exchange ($10,000), less the amount of money he received ($10,000). I.R.C. § 358(a)(1). Thus, Tim's basis in the 900 shares of P stock is $10,000.

shareholders would take an equity stake in the survivor, the acquirer might prefer to pay in cash or debt securities. The acquirer might desire the financial leverage, deal flexibility, lack of equity dilution, as well as income tax deductions for the interest on the acquisition financing. Moreover, the acquirer may fear a negative impact on its stock price when it offers stock. Studies have found that announcement returns to bidding firms who make cash offers are higher than when stock offers are made. See, e.g., Steven J. Brown & Michael Ryngaert, *The Mode of Acquisition in Takeovers: Taxes and Asymmetric Information*, 19 J. of FIN. 653 (June 1991). Academics claim that a bidder with private information about the value of its assets only offers stock when its shares are overvalued by target shareholders. Recognizing this adverse selection, target shareholders reduce their estimate of the bidder's value. Thus, without some benefit in stock over cash as a means of payment, a "lemons" problem arises for stock offers, and bidders only choose cash offers. There also may be pure tax reasons for structuring a transaction as a taxable exchange. They are rare, however.[55]

Some acquisitions can combine taxable and tax-free exchanges and make everyone happy. When Procter & Gamble bought Gillette in 2005, it used a novel two-step deal, tax-free on the first step, taxable on the second. In the first step, P & G exchanged .975 of its shares for each Gillette share. Large holders of Gillette stock, such as Berkshire Hathaway, paid no tax (Berkshire could have faced a $1.5 billion tax bill if the sale of its stock was taxable; it would pay a corporate rate of 35 percent in effect at that time on the sales). The new stock issued to Gillette, however, would dilute the value of the P & G shares and slash earnings per share. In the second step, P & G announced that it would follow up the stock exchange with an $18 to $22 billion stock buy-back program over the next 12 to 18 months. The result is the same as if P & G had paid for Gillette with a package of sixty percent stock and forty percent cash. Tax-exempt pension funds or others who want to cash out can sell in the open market during the buy-back period. P & G purchases will prop up the share price.

4. THE POLICY DEBATE ON TAX-FREE REORGANIZATIONS

AMERICAN LAW INSTITUTE, FEDERAL INCOME TAX PROJECT, SUBCHAPTER C: PROPOSALS ON CORPORATE ACQUISITIONS AND DISPOSITIONS AND REPORTER'S STUDY OF CORPORATE DISTRIBUTIONS

30–33 (1982).

Corporate acquisitions are classified and differently treated for purposes of financial accounting, corporate law, and securities regulation,

[55] If a target has net operating loss carry-forwards or tax credits that are about to expire, a taxable transaction structured to enable use of the carry-forwards may make sense. Similarly, a corporation may want to split off a lackluster division to produce a recognized tax loss to offset other income.

as well as income taxation, and classification for tax purposes is often criticized for being in conflict with the classification for these other purposes.

One kind of conflict is simply a matter of different criteria for making apparently analogous classifications. . . .

It is not clear, however that this kind of conflict is very serious or that there is any feasible way to eliminate it. The purposes and uses of financial reporting are quite different from those of tax accounting, and while different criteria may produce administrative complications, there is no reason to assume they could be eliminated while responding adequately to those different purposes. . . .

A more serious kind of conflict arises because tax classification depends on taking particular corporate procedural steps, which may sometimes be impossible or inconvenient for nontax reasons. The tax law offers a different set of tax consequences, for example, for a stock purchase than for an asset purchase, but in a particular situation it may be inconvenient or impossible to deal individually with shareholders for the purchase of their shares, or to have a corporate sale of assets, and a conflict then may emerge between what is convenient and feasible as a matter of corporate procedure and what is most desirable from a tax standpoint. Corporation P might wish to acquire X, for example, on a carryover basis, by purchasing its stock, in order to avoid immediate taxes on depreciation recapture. But an asset acquisition might be more convenient than a stock purchase because the latter requires direct dealing with a multitude of individual shareholders. . . .

The main explicit distinction in the classification of acquisitions under existing law is between reorganizations and purchases. But from a functional standpoint, focusing on the computation of corporate taxable income, a more fundamental differentiation exists between all acquisitions in which basis and other tax attributes carry over in the acquisition transaction so that the computation of taxable income from conduct of the acquired business is uninterrupted by the acquisition, and others in which tax attributes do not carry over and there is a fresh start in computing taxable income from the acquired business on the basis of cost in the acquisition transaction itself. It is convenient to call the former "carryover-basis" acquisitions and the latter "cost-basis" acquisitions. Reorganizations fall in the category of carryover-basis acquisitions. . . .

There are affirmative reasons for preserving both cost-basis and carryover-basis modes of treatment of potential corporate income tax liabilities in an acquisition transaction, and for preserving effective taxpayer choice between them for a substantial number of kinds of transactions.

First, cost-basis treatment makes sense because it enables a corporate purchaser of assets to buy those assets without entanglement in the tax history of the prior owner, just as corporate law makes it possible, generally, to purchase assets without assuming financial and continuing business obligations of the seller. Furthermore, cost-basis treatment enables a purchaser to buy from a prior corporate owner on just the same terms, so far as its own taxes are concerned, as from an unincorporated seller or from a larger corporation for which the assets are not substantially all its assets, or from several different sellers.

Moreover, it seems perfectly feasible, as a condition to cost-basis treatment, to insist on an adequate accounting for previously unrealized corporate tax liabilities by the old corporate owner. Present law shows the way to do that in the case of depreciation recapture. Present law fails to require an adequate accounting for some other sorts of gains, such as inventory appreciation, and so cost-basis acquisitions now provide a way of causing those gains to escape corporate income tax altogether. But the remedy for these abuses is to require a more adequate accounting by the transferor, not to ban cost-basis acquisitions. . . .

Second, carryover-basis treatment makes sense because it provides a way to preserve the flow of corporate tax revenues without imposing a barrier against economically desirable changes in ownership. A corporation may have very substantial unrealized gains, but a shortage of cash with which to pay any current tax on them. A purchaser may also be without cash to provide for payment of such taxes. Just as corporate law and procedure provide for the acquisition of assets subject to financial and business obligations, so that an acquisition will not necessarily require the raising of funds to pay them off, so carryover-basis tax treatment makes it possible in effect to conduct an acquisition subject to ongoing corporate income tax liabilities.

Moreover, the possibility of carryover-basis treatment does not seem to entail compromise of any important government interest. Carryover of losses and deferral of tax on gain are the advantages that taxpayers . . . may secure from carryover-basis treatment. But neither of these imposes a cost on the government that warrants prohibition of carryover treatment.

Carryover of losses is subject to special limitations, under existing law, applicable to both reorganizations and stock purchases. Sections 269, 382. Those limitations are imperfect in some respects, and the policies underlying them are debatable. . . . But the strategy of dealing specially with carryover of losses is essentially sound; any general restriction on carryover treatment would be both unnecessary and insufficient to deal with the special problems of loss carryovers.

If net undeducted losses are subjected to special limitations, then the primary issue in allowing carryover treatment is one of deferral or acceleration of tax on net unrealized gains. If one takes the view that previously unrealized gains should always be taxed as soon as possible whenever any kind of transaction presents a feasible occasion for taxation, then carryover-basis treatment of a corporate acquisition will appear as unjustified deferral. But one may start from the observation that the corporate income tax is generally imposed on profits realized from corporate operations, not on the excess over basis of value that reflects expectations of future profits. This is the general case even when individual shareholders realize their share of that value by selling their stock. Carryover-basis treatment of a corporate stock acquisition is just an extension of that general pattern to cases in which all or a major part of the shares of a corporation are sold to a corporate transferee. Carryover treatment of asset acquisitions involves a further extension to cases in which essentially the same result is achieved by a corporate asset transfer. In such cases the corporate transferor will only avoid tax if it makes distributions that subject its shareholders to whatever taxes they would have incurred on a direct sale or exchange of their shares. Against this background, any attempt to insist on cost-basis treatment of acquisition transactions would represent an unjustified acceleration of corporate income-tax liabilities, not elimination of unjustified deferral.

Third, the reasons for preserving both carryover and cost-basis treatment also support the notion of taxpayer choice between them. The reasons have to do with either treatment being adequate—or being able to be made adequate—from the government's standpoint, and each being able to meet certain different needs of taxpayers in particular situations. Since the taxpayer parties to an acquisition will be best able to determine the relative magnitude of those needs, it makes sense to give them a choice in determining the mode of tax treatment. . . .

The trouble with present law is not that tax classification of acquisitions is effectively elective, but that the election is tied unnecessarily to matters of corporate procedure. The solution to the trouble is to make tax classification explicitly elective and as independent as possible of corporate procedural considerations. While the reasons for electivity in tax classification are analogous to some of the reasons for electivity in matters of corporate procedure, there is no compelling reason to tie the two together. Indeed any such tie-in has the effect of arbitrarily limiting free electivity in cases in which tax and corporate procedural considerations conflict. Simple and explicit procedures should be provided, therefore, whereby any acquisition that would otherwise be a cost-basis acquisition can be classified as a carryover-basis acquisition, and vice versa, if all affected corporate parties consent to that change in classification. . . .

NOTE: 1985 SENATE FINANCE COMMITTEE STAFF REFORM PROPOSAL

The ALI proposal was one of several offered in the 1980s to reform the treatment of corporate acquisitions. The complexity of the reorganization rules and the different tax results for equivalent deals (for example, a stock sale has one level of tax and a corporate asset sale followed by a liquidation has two levels of tax) sparked the interest. The high water mark of the proposals was when the Staff of the Senate Finance Committee submitted a preliminary report, proposing to replace the Type A, B, and C acquisitive-reorganization rules (and the related triangular-acquisition rules) with a single elective non-recognition/carryover-basis system at the corporate level. The present system of transaction specific rules would have been replaced with an election regime keyed to the parties' decision to preserve basis for the acquired corporate assets by electing carry-over basis treatment, regardless of the type of consideration paid. The staff's final report was issued in 1985 and contained draft statutory language.[56] The proposals were never formally introduced and no subsequent proposals have been seriously considered. Why?

STEVEN A. BANK, MERGERS, TAXES AND HISTORICAL REALISM

75 TUL. L. REV. 1, 73–78 (2000).

* * *

. . . [T]he government adopted two basic principles that served as the theoretical underpinnings of a realization compromise: (1) capital appreciation was considered taxable, but only when actually realized in a sale or exchange; and (2) gains that were technically, but not actually, realized, were deferred rather than exempted from tax altogether.

* * *

Once a realization requirement was adopted, the principal concern was to interpret it so as to preserve a distinction between paper and real gains. . . .

* * *

. . . [T]he reorganization provision was a product of the realization compromise. . . .

* * *

There were two features meriting per se nonrecognition treatment for reorganizations, mergers, and consolidations. First, the stockholders in such transactions continued their investments, rather than cashing them out, to the extent that they received stock in the combined venture. In both a merger and a consolidation, the resulting entity was considered to be a

[56] Staff of Senate Finance Comm. Report on the Reform and Simplification of Income Taxation of Corporations, S.Rep. No. 85, 98th Cong., 1st Sess.

combination of the assets and liabilities of the constituent parties. Stock in this entity would thus represent the former target shareholder's continuing investment in the property of the disappearing corporation. As one contemporary practitioner explained:

> The fundamental principle then recognized ... was that where a taxpayer's investment in a business conducted in corporate form was not terminated by intercorporate adjustments and exchanges, but was continued, though in different corporate form, it was unjust and unwise to treat him as though he had sold out and taken his profit or loss, even though technically there was a closed transaction.

While a general property exchange may or may not, depending upon the underlying facts, involve a continuing investment, a shareholder receiving stock in a reorganization, merger, or consolidation by definition continued his or her investment.

There were, of course, transactions that appeared to test this general principle. For example, a shareholder of a corner grocery store "may feel, quite rightly, that he has [']sold out' for the near-equivalent of cash" when the store is merged into a large national grocery chain, but this is not precisely true. . . . [T]he shareholders would still hold an interest in the assets of the corner grocery store. This interest, of course, has been diluted to some extent because the former corner grocery store shareholders no longer hold an exclusive interest in the assets of the store. To measure the extent to which the shareholders have truly sold out their investment, however, the government would have to look through the stock to the assets. This would be a difficult task in any event, but practically impossible in the case of a large public corporation. Instead of measuring such partial implicit disinvestments, Congress chose an "all-or-nothing approach." Unless former target shareholders received cash or other property not constituting an equity interest in the surviving or resulting corporation, they were treated as if they had continued their investment in its entirety.

Second, reorganizations not only posed a high risk of taxing paper or theoretical gains, but also posed a substantial risk that such gains were based on "fictitious" or inaccurate values. In the closely held corporation context, this problem was readily apparent as a practical matter. There is no easy reference for determining the fair market value of the stock of the acquiring corporation. While the parties surely have arrived at their own respective estimates in determining whether to enter into the transaction, there are few reliable measures by which to judge such estimates. Even independent appraisers are limited in their estimations in the absence of comparable sales. Through protracted litigation and administrative proceedings, government appraisers are likely to lose what is an uphill battle from the start. Moreover, the conceptual difficulties in arriving at a "true" value are equally as great. A taxpayer's investment in closely held corporation stock is generally recouped more through salaries and, to a lesser extent, dividends, than sale or liquidation proceeds. Thus, the "value" of the stock may represent a gain that not only will never be realized but also a gain that does not represent the taxpayer's measure of the investment's profitability.

These conceptual difficulties would not be overcome by limiting the taxation of reorganizations, mergers, and consolidations to exchanges of publicly traded stocks and securities. While isolated exchanges of public stocks and securities fail to cause even a ripple in a stock's trading price, mergers and acquisitions often involve wholesale changes in ownership of a corporation's stock. Such massive changes may produce intense fluctuations in the prices of the respective stocks. At the time the reorganization provision was first adopted, it was not always clear that even publicly traded stock or securities could be sold after the transaction for the listed price. . . . The problem is that, while a public market may exist after a reorganization, it "is usually a temporary, excited, manipulated market." Any value obtained may be artificially inflated, and it becomes difficult as a conceptual matter to distinguish between the real gain and the temporary gain in the stock's value. . . .

Even today, reorganizations and other similar transactions routinely produce pre-and post-merger fluctuations in even the most widely traded of shares. These wide swings were shaky evidence of profit or taxable income for contemporary courts. . . . The alternative was to end up with some transactions being taxed and others being deferred, depending upon a court's view of the state of the market for the corporation's shares.

Thus, the reorganization provision was enacted in 1918 in a compromise over two competing models of the taxation of capital investments. The accretion model suggested annual taxation of increases in value, while the consumption model favored no taxation at all on increases in value or on proceeds that were reinvested rather than consumed. Observers feared the taxation of paper gains under the former and the indefinite deferral of taxes under the latter. At a time when the legal outcome of the taxation of capital gains and stock dividends was still uncertain, Congress struck a compromise that exempted capital gains from taxation until the occurrence of a definite realization event. While a realization event was relatively easy to spot when property was sold for cash, it was more difficult in the case of property exchanges. As a result, Congress taxed property exchanges as a general rule, while exempting those, such as like-kind exchanges or reorganizations, that were most likely not to represent the termination of the taxpayer's investments and therefore the taxation of which would most likely measure only paper rather than real gains. . . . [A]s with all compromises, logical consistency was stretched to some degree. On the whole, however, the reorganization provision was important in securing the popular and legal acceptance of the realization compromise.

* * *

Many will likely attack the modern relevance of any rationale that relies on the understanding of concepts such as realization and the taxation of capital appreciation. . . . The realization concept, while strongly supported by the legislature in the 1918 Act and later by the Court in *Eisner v. Macomber*, [252 U.S. 189 (1920),] was scaled back considerably in the reorganization cases decided during the 1920s. Eventually, it was stripped of its status as a constitutional requirement. Subsequent judicial decisions have further eroded the realization requirement by permitting seemingly minor changes to trigger gain or loss. While such decisions do not preclude the legislative reaffirmation of a strong realization requirement, no such action appears to be forthcoming. . . .

Moreover, any uncertainty about the taxation of capital gains has long since dissipated. When the 1918 Act was enacted, anti-capital gains taxation sentiments combined with sympathetic judicial precedent to form an effective argument against taxing such gains. In *Eisner v. Macomber*, the Court fueled the debate by declaring that income included the "profit gained through a sale or conversion of capital assets," while later appearing to contradict itself with the statement that "enrichment through increase in value of capital investment is not income." Around the same time, a federal district court issued an opinion holding that the taxation of gain on the sale of a capital asset was unconstitutional. By 1921, however, the Supreme Court had resolved the question by declaring, in a series of four cases, that income included capital appreciation. While subsequent legislatures have differed over the application of special reduced rates to the taxation of capital gains, few currently dispute the government's power to tax such gains to the full extent of other income.

Despite the apparent change in our conceptual understanding of realization and capital gains, it is too simplistic to dismiss the realization compromise rationale as a victim of changed circumstances. . . . [T]he debate between accretion-and consumption-based tax models endures. . . .

* * *

. . . [T]he "deep-rooted" political and popular opposition to the taxation of paper gains has continued unabated since the 1918 Act. . . .

* * *

Thus, the current system of taxing property exchanges, as well as the popular and scholarly commentary surrounding this system, continues to reflect a compromise between the accretion and consumption tax models. In the context of this compromise, the retention of the tax-free reorganization is more easily justified as a conceptual and political matter.

The taxation of such continuing investments would measure income when any gains are still perceived to be paper or artificial. If this per se rule is inaccurate in a particular case, so that a taxpayer sells his or her newly received shares in the acquiring corporation rather than retaining them, then the realization requirement will detect a termination of investment and impose the appropriate tax. On the whole, therefore, the tax-free reorganization provisions protect against the current taxation of paper gains while preserving such gains for taxation upon an actual termination of the investment. . . .

5. WHEN ARE ACQUISITIONS DRIVEN PURELY BY TAX AVOIDANCE?

If the ongoing tax obligations of two independent firms are reduced when the firms combine, the parties can divide the gains created by the savings in an acquisition. Congress intended the tax-free reorganization provisions to remove tax as a reason for discouraging mergers that had *legitimate* business justifications; Congress did not intend the provisions to justify mergers based on tax avoidance. The United States Treasury suffers a loss whenever purely tax-driven acquisitions occur. In many ways the problem is similar to the problems of opportunistic behavior we studied in Chapter Three, with the United States Treasury in the position of pre-existing creditors, employees, and tort claimants. As clever planners discover new methods of minimizing taxes through acquisitions, Congress responds by amending the tax code to stop the new practices. From 1986 to 1998, for example, Congress amended the code every year (with a few exceptions) to stop perceived loopholes in tax law applicable to acquisitions. Congress' and the Treasury's efforts to stop purely tax-driven acquisitions have been focused on three issues: first, the post-acquisition survival of tax attributes, particularly net operating loss carry-backs and carry-forwards; second, the use of debt in highly-leveraged acquisitions; and third, attempts by U.S. corporations to "redomicile" in or "expatriate" to a more tax-friendly country through so-called "inversion" deals.

a. Survival of Tax Attributes in an Acquisition: NOLs

The tax code operates on an artificial one-year accounting system. If a corporation is profitable one year, making $10 million, and loses $5 million the next, without special averaging rules it must pay tax on $10 million in one year and no tax in the next. A firm making the same aggregate profits in the two-year period, $2.5 million each year, will pay taxes on only a total of $5 million dollars. Congress has designed, in I.R.C. § 172, a net operating loss (NOL) carryover provision that allows a corporation to average its losses with its profits in both the three prior years and the fifteen years subsequent. The carryover provisions have generated two controversies with respect to acquisitions.

First, can a firm that has been consistently losing money sell its NOLs? In a typical scenario a struggling corporation showing net losses on its income statement for some time will generate net operating losses that it cannot use. It has no profits in prior years and is unlikely to generate profits in subsequent years. Can it combine with a firm that is profitable and use its NOLs to offset the taxable income of the profitable firm? Congress' answer is contained in the Tax Reform Act of 1986, which includes I.R.C. § 382. The conference committee report explaining the provision is presented below.

Second, can NOLs help fund a leveraged acquisition? In a typical case, a leveraged buyout group borrows funds to buy an otherwise profitable firm. After the acquisition the buyout group leverages the firm to refinance the buyout debt, causing the firm to show large losses. Can the firm carry back these losses to prior years, when the firm was showing a profit, and claim a refund of the taxes the firm paid in those years? Section 172(b)(1)(E) in the Revenue Reconciliation Act of 1989 is Congress' answer. The House committee report on the section follows the conference committee report on I.R.C. § 382 below.

TAX REFORM ACT OF 1986

H.R. Conf. Report No. 99–841 (Sept. 18, 1986), 1986 WL 31988

* * *

The [Act] alters the character of the special limitations on the use of NOL carryforwards. . . . After an ownership change, as described below, the taxable income of a loss corporation available for offset by pre-acquisition NOL carryforwards is annually limited to a prescribed rate times the value of the loss corporation's stock immediately before the ownership change. In addition, NOL carryforwards are disallowed entirely unless the loss corporation satisfies continuity-of-business enterprise requirements for the two-year period following any ownership change. . . . [T]he [Act] applies similar rules to carryforwards other than NOLs, such as net capital losses and excess foreign tax credits.

OWNERSHIP CHANGE

. . . [T]he special limitations apply after any ownership change. An ownership change occurs, in general, if the percentage of stock of the new loss corporation owned by any one or more 5–percent shareholders[Ed.[57]] . . . has increased by more than 50 percentage points relative to the lowest percentage of stock of the old loss corporation owned by those 5–percent shareholders at any time during the testing period (generally a three-year period). The determination of whether an ownership change has occurred is made by aggregating the increases in percentage ownership for each 5–

[57] [Ed. All less than five percent shareholders are aggregated and treated as one five percent shareholder.]

percent shareholder whose percentage ownership has increased during the testing period. . . . The determination of whether an ownership change has occurred is made after any owner shift involving a 5–percent shareholder or any equity structure shift.

* * *

An equity structure shift is defined [in the Act] as any tax-free reorganization within the meaning of section 368, other than a divisive reorganization or an "F" reorganization. In addition, to the extent provided in regulations, the term equity structure shift will include other transactions, such as public offerings not involving a 5–percent shareholder or taxable reorganization-type transactions *(e.g.,* mergers or other reorganization-type transactions that do not qualify for tax-free treatment due to the nature of the consideration or the failure to satisfy any of the other requirements for a tax-free transaction).

* * *

EFFECT OF OWNERSHIP CHANGE

For any taxable year ending after the change date *(i.e.,* the date on which an owner shift resulting in an ownership change occurs or the date of the reorganization in the case of an equity structure shift resulting in an ownership change), the amount of a loss corporation's taxable income that can be offset by a pre-change loss . . . cannot exceed the section 382 limitation for such year. The section 382 limitation for any taxable year is generally the amount equal to the value of the loss corporation immediately before the ownership change multiplied by the long-term tax-exempt rate (described below).

* * *

The value of a loss corporation is generally the fair market value of the corporation's stock (including preferred stock described in section 1504(a)(4)) immediately before the ownership change. . . .

* * *

The long-term tax-exempt rate is defined as the highest of the Federal long-term rates determined under section 1274(d), as adjusted to reflect differences between rates on long-term taxable and tax-exempt obligations, in effect for the month in which the change date occurs or the two prior months. . . . The long-term tax-exempt rate will be computed as the yield on a diversified pool of prime, general obligation tax-exempt bonds with remaining periods to maturity of more than nine years.[Ed.[58]]

The use of a rate lower than the long-term Federal rate is necessary to ensure that the value of NOL carryforwards to the buying corporation is

[58] [Ed. For example, the long-term tax exempt rate for ownership changes was 2.18 percent for the month of March 2018.]

not more than their value to the loss corporation. Otherwise there would be a tax incentive to acquire loss corporations. If the loss corporation were to sell its assets and invest in long-term Treasury obligations, it could absorb its NOL carryforwards at a rate equal to the yield on long-term government obligations. Since the price paid by the buyer is larger than the value of the loss company's assets (because the value of NOL carryforwards are taken into account), applying the long-term Treasury rate to the purchase price would result in faster utilization of NOL carryforwards by the buying corporation. . . .

* * *

Following an ownership change, a loss corporation's NOL carryforwards . . . are subject to complete disallowance . . . , unless the loss corporation's business enterprise is continued at all times during the two-year period following the ownership change. If a loss corporation fails to satisfy the continuity of business enterprise requirements, no NOL carryforwards would be allowed to the new loss corporation for any post-change year. This continuity of business enterprise requirement is the same requirement that must be satisfied to qualify a transaction as a tax-free reorganization under section 368. . . .

* * *

Examples: (1) Assume the shareholders of A and T are either a single person, a single corporation, or a public group of less than five percent shareholders. T, a profitable corporation, merges into A, a loss corporation. The shareholders of T take sixty percent of A's stock. Section 382 is triggered by both an equity-structure and an owner shift. T shareholders have increased their ownership interest from zero to sixty percent. (2) A, a loss corporation, buys all of the stock in T, a profitable corporation, using A voting stock as consideration. After the transaction, the shareholders of T own fifty-one percent of A. Section 382 applies.[59]

NOTE: FEDERAL TAKEOVERS EXEMPTED FROM I.R.C. § 382

The financial meltdown in the fall of 2008 led to the federal government's bailout or takeover of many of the country's major financial institutions. Treasury issued a series of notices on I.R.C. § 382 designed to preserve tax

---

[59] In 1987 Congress buttressed § 382 with § 384, preventing parties in an acquisition from blending pre-acquisition losses from one company with pre-acquisition built-in-gains from the other. Otherwise the surviving firm could realize the gains after the acquisition, by selling the items with built in capital gains from one firm, and use the losses from the other to eliminate the tax. Section 384 prevents this blending by segregating the built-in-gain items for a five-year quarantine period. Example: A purchases all of the stock of T for cash. Section 382 does not apply to A because there is no ownership change in A. Section 384 does apply and any losses realized by A within five years on asset sales cannot be used in the A/T consolidated return to shelter T's built in pre-acquisition gains on asset sales.

losses sustained by the financial institutions that had taken government funds in exchange for stock (often senior preferred and warrants).[60] The notices, among other things, waived an ownership change on federal takeovers and waived the built-in loss limitations for banks. In other words, Treasury neutered § 382 whenever the federal government provided bailout funds in exchange for stock. Congress solved the questionable legal status of the Treasury notices by adding § 382(n) in 2009, providing that the § 382 limits do not apply to an ownership change that results from a restructuring required under a loan agreement from the Treasury under the Economic Stabilization Act of 2008. The waiver is not available if, after an ownership change, any person (other than a voluntary employee beneficiary association) owns more than fifty percent of the voting control of the stock of the firm.

OMNIBUS BUDGET RECONCILIATION ACT OF 1989

House Ways and Means Comm. Rep. No. 101–247 on P.L. 101–239,
1989 WL 168143 (Sept. 20, 1989).

[The Report describes the operation of § 172(b)(1)(E) and (h) limiting the deductibility of net operation loss carrybacks generated by interest deductions on debt issued in leveraged buyouts.]

* * *

Corporate equity reduction transaction

A corporate equity reduction transaction ("CERT") means either a major stock acquisition or an excess distribution. A major stock acquisition is an acquisition by a corporation (or any group of persons acting in concert with such corporation) of at least 50 percent of the vote or value of the stock of another corporation. . . .

An excess distribution is the excess of the aggregate distributions and redemptions made by a corporation during the taxable year with respect to its stock . . . , over 150 percent of the average of such distributions and redemptions for the preceding 3 taxable years. . . . Notwithstanding the above, a distribution or redemption (or series thereof) is not treated as an excess distribution if it does not exceed 10 percent of the value of the corporation's outstanding stock . . . measured at the beginning of the corporation's taxable year.

Limitation of net operating loss carryback

If a C corporation has an NOL in the taxable year in which it is involved in a CERT or in the following 2 taxable years, the corporation may be limited in its ability to carry back some portion of the loss. . . . Any portion of an NOL that cannot be carried back due to the operation of this provision may be carried forward to the corporation's future taxable years, as otherwise provided under present law.

---

60 See, e.g., *Treasury Notice* 2008–83, 2008–42 IRB 905.

The portion of the corporation's NOL carryback that is limited is the lesser of (1) the corporation's interest expense that is allocable to the CERT, or (2) the excess of the corporation's interest expense in the loss limitation year over the average of the corporation's interest expense for the three taxable years prior to the taxable year in which the CERT occurred. If the lesser of these two amounts is less than $1 million, the provision does not apply. . . .

* * *

If a corporation avoids the traps of § 382 or § 172(b)(1)(E), it still may find its losses limited by § 269 or by the regulations issued under § 1501. Section 269 applies if the principal purpose of an acquisition is the evasion or avoidance of Federal income tax. Under this Section, the Commissioner has the power to deny any deduction, credit or allowance. The regulations under § 1501 apply to shareholders electing to file a consolidated tax return. The *separate return limitation year* (or *SRLY*) rule in the regulations limits the use of net operating losses by newly-added members in a group of affiliated companies.[61]

b. Leverage in Acquisitions and the Corporate Tax System

STAFF REPORT, FEDERAL INCOME TAX ASPECTS OF CORPORATE FINANCIAL STRUCTURES

Joint Comm. on Taxation 6–7, 15–17, 53–58 (Jan. 18, 1989).

* * *

. . . *Corporate Restructurings that Affect Debt and Equity*

There are a variety of transactions that affect the level of debt and equity in the corporate sector. Many of these transactions involve mergers and acquisitions, others do not; they all share the common trait that they may serve to reduce equity or increase debt in the corporate sector. What follows is a brief description of a few transactions and financing methods that may be of particular interest from a tax policy perspective.

Acquisitions.—Acquisitions for which the target shareholders receive cash in exchange for their shares, and in which the funding for the acquisition is provided by new debt issues or retained earnings of the acquiror, serve to reduce the level of corporate equity and generally to increase the level of debt relative to equity in the corporate sector. The acquisition process may take many forms, hostile or friendly, and may be

---

[61] The SRLY limitation does not apply if a firm becomes a member within six months of a § 382 change of ownership date, however.

relatively simple or involve any of the more complex maneuverings that have generated so much publicity.

Leveraged buyouts.—Leveraged buyouts are a particular form of debt-financed acquisition in which the acquiring group finances the acquisition of an existing target corporation, or a division or subsidiary of an existing company, primarily with debt secured by the assets or stock of the target corporation. Such an acquisition often produces unusually high debt to equity ratios (sometimes greater than ten to one) in the resulting company. The management of the target corporation frequently obtains a significant portion of the equity in the resulting company. The acquired corporation sometimes is taken private and, therefore, is no longer subject to the reporting requirements that apply to public corporations. It is common, however, sometimes after major asset sales or restructurings by the leveraged company, for the private company eventually to go public again, sometimes with a new infusion of equity.

Leveraged ESOPs.—An employee stock ownership plan (ESOP) is a type of tax-qualified pension plan that is designed to invest primarily in the securities of the employer maintaining the plan and that can be used as a technique of corporate finance. An ESOP that borrows to acquire employer securities is referred to as a leveraged ESOP. ESOPs may be used to effect a takeover and to defend against a hostile takeover. The Code contains numerous tax incentives designed to encourage the use and establishment of ESOPs and to facilitate the acquisition of employer securities by ESOPs through leveraging. Because of these tax benefits, use of an ESOP can result in a lower cost of borrowing than would be the case if traditional debt or equity financing were used. Despite the tax advantages, ESOPs may not be attractive in all cases because the rules relating to leveraged ESOPs require that some transfer of ownership to employees occur and may place limitations on the terms of the leveraging transaction. To the extent that ESOPs make leveraging more attractive, they may increase the degree of leverage in the economy.

Debt-for-equity swaps.—A corporation may exchange new debt for existing equity in the company. This transaction increases the degree of leverage of the corporation.

Redemptions of stock.—It has become increasingly common, particularly for large public corporations, to buy back their own shares. These repurchases of shares by the corporation will reduce outstanding equity and, particularly if financed by issues of debt, increase leverage.

Extraordinary distributions.—The quarterly or annual dividend has long been the prototypical method for distributing corporate earnings to equity investors. Sometimes a distribution amounting to a very large percentage of the value of the firm will be made to shareholders. This extraordinary distribution may be financed by debt and often is used in defensive restructurings in an attempt to avoid a takeover. [Ed. This is known as a *leveraged recapitalization* or *leveraged recap* for short.] The resulting corporate financial structure may be highly leveraged. . . .

* * *

II. PRESENT LAW TAX RULES

A. *Treatment of Corporations and Their Investors*

Under present law, corporations and their investors are generally separate taxable entities. The tax treatment of the corporation and the investor may vary depending upon whether the investor's interest in the corporation is considered debt or equity.

1. *Treatment of debt versus equity at the corporate level*

If a corporation earns a return on its assets and distributes that return to investors, the tax treatment of the corporation will depend on the characterization of the investors' interests in the corporation as debt or equity. Returns from corporate assets that are paid to debtholders are not taxed at the corporate level because interest payments generally are deductible for purposes of computing taxable income. Conversely, returns from corporate assets that are paid out as distributions with respect to stock (e.g., dividend distributions) are subject to corporate-level tax because distributions with respect to stock generally are not deductible by a corporation.

The characterization of an investor's investment as debt or equity also affects the tax treatment of the issuing corporation if the interest is retired either at a premium or at a discount. A premium paid by a corporation to redeem stock is not deductible, whereas a premium paid to retire debt is deductible. If stock is redeemed for a price less than the issue price, the issuing corporation recognizes no income, whereas if debt is retired at a discount, the corporation recognizes income from the discharge of indebtedness.

2. *Treatment of debt versus equity at the investor level*

a. *U.S. individuals*

Individual shareholders are, in general, taxed on the return from corporate assets only when amounts are distributed with respect to their stock (e.g., dividend distributions) or when gain is realized from a sale or other disposition of their shares. Thus, individual-level tax generally is deferred to the extent management of the corporation chooses to invest earnings rather than distribute them. At present, individual shareholders are taxed at a maximum rate of 28 percent on both dividend distributions and on gains from the sale or other disposition of stock [Ed.: now 20 percent on dividend distributions and 15 percent or, for individuals in the top income tax bracket, 20 percent on stock sales, if stock has been held more than one year.[62]]

The full amount of a dividend distribution is subject to the individual-level tax.[16] Distributions with respect to stock that exceed corporate earnings and profits, and thus are not dividends, are treated as a tax-free return of capital that reduces the shareholder's basis in the stock. Distributions in excess of corporate earnings and profits that exceed a shareholder's basis in the stock are treated as amounts received in exchange for the stock and, accordingly, are taxed to the shareholder as capital gain (currently taxed at the same rate as ordinary income). In the case of a sale or other disposition of stock, a shareholder recovers basis in the stock tax-free and is subject to tax only on gain (i.e., the excess of the amount received over basis). If an individual shareholder retains stock until death, any appreciation that occurred before death will permanently escape investor-level income tax.

Individual debtholders are, in general, taxed on interest received periodically as paid, on original issue discount as accrued, and on market discount upon the sale or disposition of the debt instrument. Such interest income is currently taxed at a maximum rate of 28 percent [Ed.: now 37 percent]. Individual debtholders are also subject to tax at a 28–percent maximum rate on gain from the sale or other disposition of debt (i.e., the excess of the amount received over basis) [Ed.: now 20 percent after cost indexation if held for one year]. If an individual debtholder retains debt until death, the appreciation that occurred before death generally will permanently escape investor-level income tax.

b. U.S. corporations

Corporate shareholders, like individual shareholders, are, in general, taxed on the return from the assets of the corporation in which they own stock only when amounts are distributed with respect to their stock (e.g., dividend distributions) or when gain is realized from a sale or other disposition of their shares. Thus, tax generally is deferred to the extent management of the distributing corporation chooses to invest earnings rather than distribute them.

If corporate income is distributed as a dividend, corporate shareholders are entitled to a dividends received deduction based on the ownership of the distributing corporation by the corporate shareholder. Under present law, corporations owning less than the portfolio threshold of 20 percent of the stock of a distributing corporation (by vote and value) are entitled to a deduction equal to 70 percent of the dividends received from a domestic corporation. Corporations owning at least 20 percent of the

62 [Ed. How does this affect the basic analysis of the Report?]

16 A distribution is treated as a dividend to the extent it does not exceed the current or accumulated earnings and profits of the distributing corporation.

payor's stock are entitled to an 80 percent deduction and corporations owning 80 percent or more may be entitled to a 100 percent deduction. Because the maximum rate of tax on income received by a corporation is 34 percent [Ed.: now 21 percent], the maximum rate of tax on dividends received by a corporation is generally 10.2 percent (30 percent of the amount of the dividend times 34 percent [Ed.: now 21 percent]).[21]

At present, corporate shareholders are taxed at a maximum rate of 34 percent on gains from the sale or other disposition of stock (i.e., the excess of the amount realized over basis).

Corporate debtholders are, in general, taxed on interest received periodically as such interest is paid or accrued, on original issue discount as accrued, and on market discount upon the sale or disposition of the debt instrument. Such interest income is currently taxed at a maximum rate of 34 percent [Ed.: now 21 percent]. Corporate debtholders are also subject to tax at a 34 percent maximum rate [Ed.: now 21 percent] on gains from the sale or other disposition of the debt (*i.e.*, the excess of the amount realized over basis). . . .

* * *

IV. POLICY ISSUES

The recent wave of debt-financed mergers and acquisitions, both friendly and hostile, and the significant changes in patterns of corporate financing and distributions raise a number of public policy issues, including: (1) does the tax system encourage corporate debt financing relative to equity financing . . .

A. *Tax Advantage of Debt Versus Equity*

The total effect of the tax system on the incentives for corporations to use debt or equity depends on the interaction between the tax treatment at the shareholder and corporate levels.

The case of no income taxes.—In a simple world without taxes or additional costs in times of financial distress, economic theory suggests that the value of a corporation, as measured by the total value of the outstanding debt and equity, would be unchanged by the degree of leverage of the firm.[88] This conclusion explicitly recognizes that debt issued by the

---

[21] In the case of certain "extraordinary dividends," the effective rate of tax may be as high as the maximum corporate rate of 34 percent [Ed. now 21 percent], imposed at the time of the sale or disposition of the underlying stock (sec. 1059).

As with individual shareholders, distributions with respect to stock that exceed the distributing corporation's earnings and profits, and thus are not dividends, are treated as a tax-free return of capital that reduces the shareholder's basis in the stock. Distributions in excess of the distributing corporation's earnings and profits that exceed a shareholder's basis in the stock are treated as amounts received in exchange for the stock and accordingly are taxed to the shareholder as capital gain (currently taxed at the same rate as ordinary income).

[88] Franco Modigliani and Merton Miller, "The Cost of Capital, Corporation Finance, and the Theory of Investment," *American Economic Review*, June 1958, pp. 261–97. Updated versions of this argument require only that market prices adjust so that there remain no available,

corporation represents an ownership right to future income of the corporation in a fashion similar to that of equity. In this simple world there would be no advantage to debt or to equity and the debt-equity ratio of the firm would not affect the cost of financing investment.

Effect of corporate income tax

Tax advantages

Taxes greatly complicate this analysis. Since the interest expense on debt is deductible for computing the corporate income tax while the return to equity is not, the tax at the corporate level provides a strong incentive for debt rather than equity finance.

The advantages of debt financing can be illustrated by comparing two corporations with $1,000 of assets that are identical except for financial structure: the first is entirely equity financed; while the second is 50–percent debt financed. Both corporations earn $150 of operating income. The all-equity corporation pays $51 in corporate tax and retains or distributes $99 of after-tax income ($150 less $51). Thus, as shown in Table IV-A, the return on equity is 9.9 percent ($99 divided by $1,000).

Table IV-A.—Effect of Debt Financing on Returns to Equity Investment

Item	All-equity corporation	50-percent debt-financed corporation
Beginning Balance Sheet:		
Total assets	$1,000	$1,000
Debt	0	500
Shareholders' equity	1,000	500
Income Statement		
Operating income	150	150
Interest expense	0	50
Taxable income	150	100
Income tax	51	34

unexploited arbitrage profits. *See* Stephen Ross, "Comment on the Modigliani-Miller Propositions," *Journal of Economic Perspectives*, Fall 1988, pp. 127–33, for a nontechnical discussion of this point. [Ed. Modigliani's and Miller's theory on capital structure is known as the "Irrelevance Theory."]

Income after corporate tax	99	66
Return on Equity[1] (percent)	9.9	13.2

The leveraged corporation is financed by $500 of debt and $500 of stock. If the interest rate is 10 percent, then interest expense is $50 (10 percent times $500). Taxable income is $100 after deducting interest expense. The leveraged corporation is liable for $34 in corporate tax (34 percent times $100) and distributes or retains $66 of after-tax income ($100 less $34). Consequently, the return on equity is 13.2 percent ($66 divided by $500). Thus, as shown in Table IV-A, increasing the debt ratio from zero to 50 percent increases the rate of return on equity from 9.9 to 13.2 percent.

This arithmetic demonstrates that a leveraged corporation can generate a higher return on equity (net of corporate income tax) than an unleveraged company or, equivalently, that an unleveraged company needs to earn a higher profit before corporate tax to provide investors the same return net of corporate tax as could be obtained with an unleveraged company. More generally, the return on equity rises with increasing debt capitalization so long as the interest rate is less than the pre-tax rate of return on corporate assets. This suggests that the Code creates an incentive to raise the debt-equity ratio to the point where the corporate income tax (or outstanding equity) is eliminated.

Costs of financial distress

With higher levels of debt the possibility of financial distress increases, as do the expected costs to the firm which occur with such distress. These additional costs include such items as the increase in the costs of debt funds; constraints on credit, expenditure or operating decisions; and the direct costs of being in bankruptcy. These expected costs of financial distress may, at sufficiently high debt-equity ratios, offset the corporate tax advantage to additional debt finance.

Effect of shareholder income tax

The above analysis focuses solely on the effect of interest deductibility at the corporate level. Shareholder-level income taxation may offset to some degree the corporate tax incentive for corporate debt relative to equity.

Shareholder treatment of debt and equity

The conclusion that debt is tax favored relative to equity remains unchanged if interest on corporate debt and returns on equity are taxed at the same effective rate to investors [Ed. No longer true; interest is taxed at a maximum of 37 percent, dividends at a maximum of 20 percent. Does the

[1] Return on equity is computed as income after corporate tax divided by beginning shareholders' equity.

lower rate on dividends offset the lack of deductibility of dividend payments at the firm level? No, but the advantage of debt has been substantially reduced]. In this case, the returns to investors on both debt and equity are reduced proportionately by the income tax; the advantage to debt presented by corporate tax deductibility remains. One noteworthy exception exists if the marginal investments on both debt and equity are effectively tax-exempt.[89] Given the previously documented importance of tax-exempt pension funds in the bond and equity markets, this case may be of some importance.

Shareholder level tax treatment of equity

In general, returns to shareholders and debtholders are not taxed the same. Although dividends, like interest income, are taxed currently, equity income in other forms may reduce the effective investor-level tax on equity below that on debt. First, the firm may retain earnings and not pay dividends currently. In general, the accumulation of earnings by the firm will cause the value of the firm's shares to rise.[90] Rather than being taxed currently on corporate earnings, a shareholder will be able to defer the taxation on the value of the retained earnings reflected in the price of the stock until the shareholder sells the stock. Thus, even though the tax rates on interest, dividends, and capital gains are the same [Ed.: no longer—dividends are taxed at a maximum 20 percent, interest at up to 37 percent], the ability to defer the tax on returns from equity reduces the effective rate of individual tax on equity investment below that on income from interest on corporate debt.[91]

Other aspects of capital gain taxation serve to reduce further the individual income tax on equity. Since tax on capital gain is normally triggered after a voluntary recognition event (*e.g.*, the sale of stock), the taxpayer can time the realization of capital gain income when the effective rate of tax is low. The rate of tax could be low if the taxpayer is in a low or zero tax bracket because other income is abnormally low, if other capital losses shelter the capital gain, or if changes in the tax law cause the statutory rate on capital gains to be low [Ed.: which is now the case, capital

---

[89] Merton Miller and Myron Scholes "Dividends and Taxes," *Journal of Financial Economics*, 1978, pp. 333–364 suggest that certain nuances of the Tax Code may render otherwise taxable investors untaxed on the margin between interest and equity. For example, if a taxpayer has investment interest expense that cannot be deducted because it exceeds current investment income to the taxpayer, any additional dividends is effectively sheltered from tax by additional interest deductions. Daniel Feenberg "Does the Investment Interest Limitation Explain the Existence of Dividends?" *Journal of Financial Economics*, 1981 presents evidence that this argument was unlikely to be important for most individual investors. However, the reduction in the deductibility of consumer interest by the 1986 Act may increase the plausibility of this argument.

[90] Alan Auerbach "Wealth Maximization and the Cost of Capital," *Quarterly Journal of Economics*, 1979, pp. 488–500 argues that, for mature firms, a dollar of retained earnings will cause the value of the firm to increase by less than a dollar.

[91] Before the 1986 Act, the 60 percent capital gain exclusion caused a further reduction in the effective rate of tax on equity investment.

gains are taxed at a maximum 20 percent]. Perhaps most important, the step up in the adjusted tax basis of the stock upon the death of the shareholder may permit the shareholder's heirs to avoid tax completely on capital gains. For all these reasons, the effective rate of tax on undistributed earnings may be already quite low.

Corporations can distribute their earnings to owners of equity in forms that generally result in less tax to shareholders than do dividend distributions. Share repurchases have become an important method of distributing corporate earnings to equity holders. When employed by large publicly traded firms, repurchases of the corporation's own shares permit the shareholders to treat the distribution as a sale of stock (i.e., to obtain capital gain treatment, and recover the basis in the stock without tax).[92] The remaining shareholders may benefit because they have rights to a larger fraction of the firm and may see a corresponding increase in the value of their shares.[93] Thus, less individual tax will generally be imposed on a $100 repurchase of stock than on $100 of dividends. In addition, share repurchases allow shareholders to choose whether to receive corporate distributions by choosing whether to sell or retain shares, so as to minimize tax liability.[94]

Acquisitions of the stock of one corporation for cash or property of another corporation provides a similar method for distributing corporate earnings out of corporate solution with less shareholder tax than through a dividend. The target shareholders generally treat the acquisition as a sale and recover their basis free of tax. For purposes of analyzing the individual tax effect of corporate earnings disbursements, this transaction can be thought of as equivalent to a stock merger of the target with the acquiror followed by the repurchase of the target shareholders' shares by the resulting merged firm. The result is similar to the case of a share repurchase in that cash is distributed to shareholders with less than the full dividend tax, except that two firms are involved instead of one.

Since dividends typically are subject to more tax than other methods for providing returns to shareholders, the puzzle of why firms pay dividends remains. [Ed. Dividends are taxed at a maximum 20 percent, while capital gains are taxed at 15 percent or, for individuals in the top income tax bracket, 20 percent; capital gains can still be deferred however.]

---

92 Sec. 302 governs the treatment of stock redemptions and may cause some repurchases to be treated as dividends.

93 If a dollar of repurchases by the firm reduces the value of the equity by one dollar, the remaining shareholders are no worse off; if the repurchase reduces the value by less than a dollar (perhaps because the normally higher shareholder tax on dividends is avoided) the remaining shareholders are made better off. *See*, Auerbach, *supra*.

94 Some have proposed that the taxation of share repurchases follow the taxation of dividend distributions at the investor level. One method by which this could be done is to treat the repurchase as a pro rata dividend to all shareholders followed by a pro rata sale of shares of the selling shareholders to the remaining shareholders. See, Chirelstein, "Optional Redemptions and Optional Dividends: Taxing the Repurchase of Common Shares," 78 *Yale Law Journal* 739 (1969).

Because dividends are paid at the discretion of the firm, it appears that firms cause their shareholders to pay more tax on equity income than is strictly necessary.[95] Until a better understanding of corporate distribution policy exists, the role of dividend taxation on equity financing decisions remains uncertain.

To summarize, although the current taxation of dividends to investors is clearly significant, there are numerous reasons why the overall individual tax on equity investments may be less than that on interest income from debt. Since the effective shareholder tax on returns from equity may be less than that on debt holdings, the shareholder tax may offset some or all of the advantage to debt at the corporate level.

Interaction of corporate and shareholder taxation

With shareholders in different income tax brackets, high tax rate taxpayers will tend to concentrate their wealth in the form of equity and low tax rate taxpayers will tend to concentrate their wealth in the form of debt. The distribution of wealth among investors with different marginal tax rates affects the demand for investments in the form of debt or equity. The interaction between the demand of investors, and the supply provided by corporations, determines the aggregate amount of corporate debt and equity in the economy.

At some aggregate mix between debt and equity, the difference in the investor-level tax on income from equity and debt may be sufficient to offset completely, at the margin, the apparent advantage of debt at the corporate level. Even if the difference in investor tax treatment of debt and equity is not sufficient to offset completely the corporate tax advantage, the advantage to debt may be less than the corporate-level tax treatment alone would provide.

Some believe that, because the top personal tax rate was reduced below the top corporate tax rate in the 1986 Act [Ed. This was reversed in 1993 and later changed in 2017; at present, the corporate rate can reach 21 percent while the individual rate can reach 37 percent] and because the share of wealth held by tax-exempt entities is substantial, the tax advantage of debt at the corporate level outweighs its disadvantages to investors.[96] They would argue that changes in tax law have provided the motive force in the drive toward higher leverage. However, given that the observed changes in corporate financial behavior began well before 1986, the changes due to the 1986 Act may be of relatively little importance in determining changes in leverage and acquisition behavior. The individual

---

[95] The trends outlined in Part I.A demonstrate that corporations are shifting away from dividends as the predominant method for distributing income.

[96] Merton Miller, "The Modigliani-Miller Propositions After Thirty Years," *Journal of Economic Perspectives*, Fall 1988, pp. 99–120. Also see the discussion of corporate integration in part V.A.1 of this pamphlet, *infra*, for a numerical analysis of various possible total tax effects and the effect of the Tax Reform Act of 1986.

rate reductions in the Economic Recovery Tax Act of 1981, some respond, started the shift toward more debt in corporate structures and the 1986 Act merely provided another push in that direction.

Implications for policy

The analysis above suggests that any policy change designed to reduce the tax incentive for debt must consider the interaction of both corporate and shareholder taxes. For example, proposals to change the income tax rates for individuals or corporations will change the incentive for corporate debt. Likewise, proposals to change the tax treatment of tax-exempt entities may alter the aggregate mix and distribution of debt and equity.

In addition, proposals to reduce the bias toward debt over equity, for example, by reducing the total tax on dividends, must confront the somewhat voluntary nature of the dividend tax. Since the payment of dividends by corporations generally is discretionary and other means exist for providing value to shareholders with less tax, corporations can affect the level of shareholder level tax incurred. Until a better understanding of the determinants of corporate distribution behavior exists, the total impact of policies designed to reduce the bias between debt and equity are uncertain.

COMMENT: INTEGRATED EFFECTS OF CORPORATE DEBT FINANCING ON TAX COLLECTIONS

Although the tax rates have changed since the Staff Report was written in 1989, the Report still makes a valuable point. Any analysis of the effect of leverage on tax collections must include more than an argument on the corporate tax rates; it must integrate the tax effect at the corporate and shareholder level. With the new rules on dividend rates, debt is still better than dividends if the payments at the shareholder level occur at the same time (interest or dividends). However, delayed dividend payments are the norm so the advantage dissipates as the time for receiving dividends (or selling stock) lengthens. In sum, there is not a substantial reason to do leveraged deals solely to cheat the tax man; other business reasons will dwarf the tax rationale. Moreover, the issue gets more complicated with a transactional analysis (as opposed to a debt/equity static analysis as is contained in the Staff Report). As the next article illustrates, leveraged acquisitions that increase debt can also *increase* tax collections:

MICHAEL C. JENSEN, STEVEN KAPLAN & LAURA STIGLIN, EFFECTS OF LBOS ON TAX REVENUES OF THE U.S. TREASURY

42 TAX NOTES 727–733 (Feb. 6, 1989).

We examine the tax effects of leveraged buyouts (LBOs) in which a group of investors (including managers) take a company private, a topic that is receiving increasing attention from legislators, the business community, and the press. In examining the tax implications of these transactions, many observers have focused on the interest deductibility of the debt used to finance them. It has been noted that LBO firms' increased debt payments generate sufficient tax deductions to ensure that many of them do not pay income taxes in the period immediately following the LBO. Some argue these transactions are being subsidized by the Federal taxpayer in the sense that they cause net losses of tax revenues to the U.S. Treasury. Our analysis, based on current tax law and data from buyouts in the period 1979 through 1985, indicates these arguments are incorrect; Treasury revenues from LBO firms increase on average by about 61 percent over the prebuyout payments. Our estimates indicate that at a total dollar volume of LBO transactions of $75 billion per year, the Treasury gains about $9 billion in the first year and about $16.5 billion per year in present value of future net tax receipts.

What often has been overlooked is the fact that there are five ways in which LBOs can generate incremental revenues to the U.S. Treasury. First, because they create substantial realized capital gains for shareholders, LBOs give rise to increased capital gains taxes. Second, LBO firms realize significant increases in operating income, which are also taxable. Third, many of the creditors who finance LBOs are taxed on the interest income from LBO debt payments. Fourth, LBO firms contribute to tax revenues by using capital more efficiently. Finally, many LBO firms sell off assets, triggering additional corporate taxes on the capital gains. Offsetting these incremental revenue gains are increased interest deductions on the large debt commonly incurred, and lower tax revenues on dividends, because LBOs generally do not pay dividends on common equity.

* * *

Because the RJR-Nabisco LBO by Kohlberg, Kravis and Roberts is so large, and involved such heated bidding, it has attracted much attention and controversy. Along with this have come accusations that the gains to shareholders are at the expense of Treasury.[8] Table Three contains our estimates of the implications of the transaction for the U.S. Treasury, which indicate Treasury is highly likely to gain rather than lose tax revenues. In prevent value terms, the increased revenue for Treasury is

---

[8] *Time* magazine, for example, in its cover story of December 5, 1988, "A Game of Greed," claims the U.S. taxpayers will lose between $2 and $5 billion in the long run, p. 69.

$3.76 billion, $3.28 billion of which it will likely gain in the year following the buyout. These payments are more than eight times higher than the approximately $370 million in Federal taxes paid by RJR-Nabisco in 1987.[9] Indeed, at a rate of $370 million per year, the total present value of RJR-Nabisco's tax payments into perpetuity is only $3.7 billion, just slightly higher than the first year's tax revenues induced by the buyout.

* * *

The typical LBO is more beneficial to the U.S. Treasury than many observers realize. Increased interest deductions and foregone dividend payments clearly have the potential to reduce tax revenues. However, the large capital gains that result from LBOs, increases in their operating income and capital efficiency, enhanced creditor income, and taxes on asset sales have the potential to increase tax revenues. The net effect of these tax changes varies across transactions; some LBOs may result in tax revenue reductions, while others may generate new tax revenues. As the examples in our tables show, however, the preponderance of evidence indicates that in the aggregate, these transactions generate revenue gains for Treasury.

Based on the data from transactions over $50 million in the period 1979 through 1985, on average, LBO transactions increase tax revenues to the U.S. Treasury by $110 million on a present value basis, and by $59.4 million in the year after the buyout. The present value of gains translates to a permanent equivalent annual increase of approximately $11 million on average, or a 61–percent increase in taxes per buyout firm. Our conservative assumptions in Table 2, which we believe understate Treasury revenues, indicate that even in those circumstances, Treasury is likely to break even. Our application of the analysis to the RJR-Nabisco transaction indicates contrary to popular views, that the transaction will enrich Treasury by over $3 billion, whether viewed from a short-or long-term perspective.

Policies that restrict LBO transactions likely will reduce future tax revenues received by Treasury. At a total volume of $75 billion per year, LBO transactions are generating about $16.5 billion in present value of tax revenues for the Treasury per year, and on a current account basis, they generate approximately $9 billion per year. It appears that from a narrow tax policy perspective, great care should be taken in adopting policies that discourage LBO transactions.

---

[9] Total taxes paid by RJR-Nabisco in 1987 were $682 million, but $313 million of this were "foreign and other" taxes.

ALVIN C. WARREN, JR., RECENT CORPORATE RESTRUCTURING AND THE CORPORATE TAX SYSTEM

42 TAX NOTES 715–20 (Feb. 6, 1989).

. . . REDUCING THE TAX DISADVANTAGE OF EQUITY

1. **Integration Proposals.** The third principal means of eliminating the problem identified above is to reduce the tax disadvantage of new equity finance by integrating the individual and corporate income taxes. In very general terms, such integration could be accomplished by allowing either a corporate deduction for dividends or a shareholder credit for corporate taxes paid with respect to distributed earnings. The House of Representatives' version of the Tax Reform Act of 1986 included a phased-in partial deduction for dividends. Under either dividend deduction or shareholder credit integration, the corporate income tax would become a withholding tax on distributions to suppliers of corporate capital, functioning as an adjunct to shareholder or debtholder income taxation.

2. **Advantages.** Integration is a massive subject that has long been on the agenda of the congressional tax-writing committees and various Administrations. Adoption of an integrated system would eliminate many of the defects in our corporate tax system, including the one under discussion, primarily because debt would no longer be treated significantly differently from equity. The ability to avoid future corporate taxes by making nontaxed nondividend distributions would be eliminated to the extent such distributions were subject to the shareholder credit mechanism.

Integration also would subject U.S. companies to a tax regime that was similar to that of many other industrialized nations, a number of which have implemented partial integration systems in recent years. Finally, integration, particularly of the shareholder credit variety, would permit explicit congressional decisions about the appropriate treatment of distributees who might not otherwise be taxable. If, for example, it were decided that corporate income distributed to charitable institutions, pension funds, and foreign shareholders should not go completely untaxed, the shareholder credit could be made nonrefundable. In short, integration is the most ideal long-run solution to both the particular problem posed by recent corporate restructurings and the urgent need to reform the corporate tax system more generally.

3. **Disadvantages.** Like many long-run solutions, integration has certain short-run disadvantages. For example, immediate, full enactment of a dividend deduction would undoubtedly generate significant revenue losses. Such an enactment also might allow current shareholders to reap the full benefit of any windfall gains due to capitalization of taxes. But, there is no need to enact integration in one fell swoop. It could easily be phased in, as was the 1985 House legislation. And the possibility of positive

windfall gains in the stock markets might well give Congress more flexibility to consider adopting limitations on interest deductions, which could have the opposite effect on share prices if enacted by themselves.

* * *

It would probably be easiest to accomplish these results, as well as equivalent treatment of debt and equity, in a shareholder credit system that also required withholding on corporate interest payments, together with a nonrefundable credit for nontaxable debtholders.[23] To the extent of integration, *the result would be that all income earned on corporate assets, however financed, would always be taxed once,* a result that is certainly not achieved today. Such a regime might well not have the negative revenue implications generally associated with integration. There would, of course, be important design issues to be resolved in treating debt and equity equivalently, including the appropriate taxation of financial intermediaries.

* * *

NOTE: CONGRESS' ATTACK ON INTEREST DEDUCTIONS IN LEVERAGED ACQUISITION FINANCING

The tax rules are not totally silent on the deduction of interest payments incurred in acquisition financing. As we have already seen, under § 172(1)(b)(E), net operating losses generated by increased interest deductions as the result of leveraged acquisition may not be carried back against income generated by the target in prior profitable years. Moreover, if parties to an acquisition attempt to use the debt instruments that for all practical purposes are equity instruments, the Internal Revenue Service may disallow the interest deductions. Congress, in § 385(a), gave the Secretary of the Treasury the power to pass regulations classifying equity and debt instruments.[63] Finally, after several decades of aborted attempts,[64] the IRS issued final and

---

[23] Shareholder credit integration has exactly the same effect as a dividend or interest deduction, coupled with withholding. . . .

[63] I.R.C. § 385(b) provides a nonexclusive list of factors that the regulations may take into account in making the determination: (1) whether there is an unconditional promise to pay, on demand or on a specified date, a certain sum and to pay a fixed rate of interest, (2) whether the instrument is subordinated or preferred to any other corporate debt, (3) the issuer's debt-equity ratio, (4) whether the instrument is convertible into equity, and (5) the relationship between the issuer's stock and the instrument. In 1989 Congress amended § 385(a) to permit future regulations to treat an instrument as a hybrid, part stock and part equity, for tax purposes.

[64] Lacking IRS regulations over so many years, the courts had no choice but to utilize a general list of factors that weigh in favor of debt treatment for a given instrument: (1) a fixed maturity date not too far removed, (2) an unconditional obligation to pay, (3) a fixed rate of interest, (4) rights in the holder, such as acceleration, that accrue on default, (5) the absence of convertibility into equity, of voting power or other forms of voice in management; and of any participation in distributions of capital surplus, (6) the ability of the issuer at the time of issuance to meet anticipated repayment obligations, (7) a reasonable debt-equity ratio upon issuance, (8) the subordination of other debt instruments to it, and (9) the holder's acting like a creditor by taking

certain temporary rules in October 2016,[65] largely out of concern for so-called *inversion deals* that utilize *earnings stripping* (both discussed *infra*). Congress, apparently impatient with the IRS' attempts to pass the aforementioned regulations, amended § 163 to reclassify zero coupon debentures and pay-in-kind (PIK) securities, both often used in acquisition financing. Section 279 of the Code "expressly limits" the interest deductions allowable for acquisition debt, but the section has proven to be largely toothless for modern acquisitions.

Section 163(e), (i) and (l) on Original Issue Discount Instruments (OIDs): In 1989 Congress took steps to re-characterize the tax treatment of two special debt instruments used in leveraged acquisition financing: *zero coupon* debentures and *pay-in-kind* (PIK) debentures. Recall that traditional debt instruments are issued at a price approximately equal to their final redemption price, with the return to the holder taking the form of periodic interest payments. Zero coupon debentures are original issue discount instruments (OIDs) that eliminate periodic interest payments. They are issued at prices well below their final redemption price, and the return to a holder is the appreciation at the time of redemption. A PIK debenture requires the issuer to pay periodic interest in the form of additional debt (*bunny* debentures) or equity instruments of the issuer. Issuers use both instruments to finance leveraged acquisitions when the cash flow position of the surviving firm will be, for a time, very tight.

Before 1989, OID and bunny debentures were generally treated as interest income to the holder and were deductible by the issuer in equal installments over the life of the instrument (on a constant-yield basis). If the PIK payments were in stock, the fair market value of the stock was treated as interest currently paid, giving the issuer a deduction and the holder income for that amount. Section 163(e)(5) and (i), enacted in December 1989, limits interest deductions for high-yield zero coupon debentures and PIK debentures. If either instrument qualifies as an applicable high-yield discount obligation (AHYDO), then the issuer's interest deductions are deferred until cash is actually paid and are in some cases partially eliminated. The interest is

---

steps to protect his rights. For collections of decided cases on the debt-equity determination, see William T. Plumb, *The Federal Income Tax Significance of Corporate Debt: A Critical Analysis and a Proposal*, 26 TAX L. REV. 369 (1971); Boris I. Bittker & James S. Eustice, FEDERAL INCOME TAXATION OF CORPORATIONS AND SHAREHOLDERS ¶ 4.05 (Debt Versus Equity: Problems in Classification) (2014 rev. Thomson Reuters).

[65] See Treas. Reg. §§ 1.385–1, 1.385–2, 1.385–3, 1.385–3T & 1.385–4T (2016) (collectively, the "Section 385 Regulations"). Paragraph (b) of § 1.385–1 provides the general rule for determining the treatment of an interest based on provisions of the I.R.C., including the factors prescribed under the common law. See *supra* note 64. Paragraphs (c), (d) and (e) of § 1.385–1 provide definitions and rules of general application for purposes of the Section 385 Regulations. Section 1.385–2 provides additional guidance regarding the application of certain factors in determining the federal tax treatment of an interest in a corporation that is held by a member of the corporation's expanded group. Section 1.385–3 sets forth additional factors that, when present, control the determination of whether an interest in a corporation that is held by a member of the corporation's expanded group is treated (in whole or in part) as stock or indebtedness. Section 1.385–3T(f) provides rules on the treatment of debt instruments issued by certain partnerships. Section 1.385–4T provides rules regarding the application of the factors set forth in § 1.385–3 and the rules in § 1.385–3T to transactions described in those sections as they relate to consolidated groups.

nevertheless reported by the holder as income as it accrues under the regular OID rules. A debenture is an AHYDO if it is issued by a corporation with a maturity date more than five years from issuance, has a yield to maturity of at least five percentage points over the application federal rate (AFR)[66] in effect for the month in which the debenture is issued, and has a "significant original issue discount" (using a series of complex measurements). Section 163(i) treats PIK debenture interest in the same fashion as OID. If a PIK debenture pays interest in the form of bunny debentures, for example, the interest is treated as paid at the maturity date of the bunny debentures. In 1997 Congress eliminated deductions for any interest paid or accrued on PIK debentures that are payable in equity of the issuer.

OMNIBUS BUDGET RECONCILIATION ACT OF 1989

H.R. Conf. Rep. No.101–386 (Nov. 21, 1989), 1989 WL 168141.

* * *

Original issue discount ('OID') is the excess of the stated redemption price at maturity over the issue price of a debt instrument. The issuer of a debt instrument with OID generally accrues and deducts the discount, as interest, over the life of the obligation even though the amount of such interest is not paid until the debt matures. The holder of such a debt instrument also generally includes the OID in income as it accrues as interest on an accrual basis.

* * *

. . . [T]he conferees believe that a portion of the return on certain high-yield OID obligations is similar to a distribution of corporate earnings with respect to equity. Thus, the conference agreement bifurcates the yield on applicable instruments, creating an interest element that is deductible when paid and a return on equity element for which no deduction is granted and for which the dividends received deduction may be allowed.

* * *

A portion of the OID ('the disqualified portion') on an applicable instrument is afforded special treatment. The issuer is allowed no deduction with respect to the disqualified portion. The holder, however, is allowed a dividends received deduction for that part of the disqualified portion that would have been treated as a dividend had it been distributed by the issuing corporation with respect to stock.

In general, the disqualified portion of OID is the portion of the total return on the obligation that bears the same ratio to the total return as the disqualified yield bears to the total yield to maturity on the instrument. The term 'disqualified yield' means that portion of the yield that exceeds

[66] The AFR is determined by the Treasury. For example, the AFR for March 2018 was 2.55 percent for obligations with a term of three to nine years ("mid-term"), with interest compounded semi-annually.

the applicable Federal rate for the month in which the obligation is issued (the 'AFR') plus [five] percentage points. If the yield to maturity on the obligation determined by disregarding the OID exceeds the AFR plus [five] percentage points, then the disqualified portion is the entire amount of the OID. . . . The remainder of the OID on the instrument (the portion other than the disqualified portion) is not deductible until paid in property other than stock or obligations of the issuer.

* * *

Section 279 General Limits on Acquisition Indebtedness: In October 1969 Congress attempted to impose, through I.R.C. § 279, a general interest deduction ceiling on acquisition financing. Congress designed the section to catch financing peculiar to the conglomerate merger wave of the late sixties, which made heavy use of convertible subordinated debt instruments. The wave had largely passed by the time the section became effective, and modern leveraged acquisitions use much more imaginative financing techniques.

The section, as is, prevents debtors from deducting interest paid or incurred on qualifying debt in a given year to the extent that the interest exceeds $5 million, less any interest paid on non-qualifying acquisition debt. Debt is subject to the deduction disallowance only if it is (1) issued as consideration in an acquisition of stock or two-thirds of the assets of another firm, (2) subordinated to trade creditors or any substantial amount of other unsecured debt, (3) convertible (directly or indirectly) into stock of the issuer, and (4) issued when the debtor is thinly capitalized (its debt-to-equity ratio exceeding two-to-one or its average earnings not exceeding three times the annual interest to be paid).

There are several common methods of avoiding the provision. The debtor issues nonconvertible debt, issues combined units of its subordinated debt and its common stock, issues debt subordinated only to secured debt, uses a holding company to issue debt implicitly subordinated by law to a subsidiary's unsecured debt, or has the target firm adopt the debt (causing the transaction to be treated as a redemption). Thus, the section is easily avoided by modern planners.

Congress has yet to pass proposals that would remedy the section's many loopholes. The proposals demonstrate the potential breadth of such an approach, however. A 1987 House bill proposed a $5-million-per-year ceiling on the interest deduction for debt arising in any acquisition of 50 percent or more of a target firm's stock, regardless of whether the debt was subordinated or issued with conversion privileges. See Omnibus Budget Reconciliation Act of 1987, Conference Committee Report No. 100–495,

995–96 (Dec. 21, 1987).[67] The provision would have applied to normal bank financing incurred without an equity kicker. A second proposal would impose interest deductions for debt used to finance hostile asset and stock acquisitions. *Id.* at 970.

NOTE: 2017 TAX REFORM EFFORTS AND POSSIBLE IMPACT ON LEVERAGED BUYOUTS AND PRIVATE EQUITY DEALS

Republican tax reform efforts of 2017 could have an adverse impact on leveraged buyouts and private equity deals. The Tax Cuts and Jobs Act of 2017 ("TCJA") caps the amount of interest expense that companies can deduct from their taxes at 30 percent of "adjusted taxable income." I.R.C. § 163(j). Before January 1, 2022, "adjusted taxable income" consists of taxable income *without regard to* (1) items of income or loss not allocable to the trade or business, (2) any business interest or business interest income, (3) any net operating loss under I.R.C. § 172, (4) any deduction for certain pass-through income under I.R.C. § 199A, and, *importantly*, (5) any deduction for depreciation, amortization or depletion. On or after January 1, 2022, "adjusted taxable income" is calculated the same way *but without* the adjustment for depreciation, amortization and/or depletion. Thus, the Act presents challenges to private equity firms that pursue strategies that entail loading up acquired firms with debt in order to boost returns.

The interest expense cap is designed to offset, in part, lost tax revenues relating to the reduction in the corporate income tax from 35 percent down to 21 percent. Analysts at both Goldman Sachs and Morgan Stanley anticipate that, even with the interest deduction cap, the proposed corporate tax reduction would have a net positive impact of more than 100 basis points (1 percent) on private equity internal rates of return, the key measure of profitability for private equity investments.[68]

Private equity firms must be cognizant of these potential tax changes. If implemented, private equity firms will likely avoid targets with cyclical earnings. During down cycles, the ability of those targets to take advantage of a lower corporate income tax rate as well as deduct interest payments will be diminished. Thus, private equity firms should favor targets with more consistent earnings. Moreover, given the definition of "adjusted taxable income," private equity firms will likely favor firms that are less capital-intensive (and thus have lower depreciation charges) as potential targets.

c. Tax-Driven "*Inversion*" Deals

Before the Tax Cuts and Jobs Act of 2017 ("TCJA"), the U.S. federal corporate income tax rate of 35 percent[69] was one of the highest in the

---

[67] Available at https://www.finance.senate.gov/imo/media/doc/crpt100-495.pdf.

[68] See Aaron Back, *Tax Reform is a Game Changer for Buyouts*, WALL ST. J. (Nov. 27, 2017) (avail. at https://www.wsj.com/articles/tax-reform-is-a-game-changer-for-buyouts-1511794152?-mg=prod/accounts-wsj).

[69] This rate was reduced to 21 percent by the TCJA.

industrialized world. According to the Organization for Economic Cooperation and Development ("OECD"), before the TCJA the U.S. clocked in with the highest—by far—combined federal, state and local corporate tax rate (38.9 percent) among any of the OECD member countries:

10 OECD Member Countries with Highest Combined Corporate Tax Rate[70]

Member Country	Combined Corp. Tax Rate (%)
U.S.	38.9
France	34.4
Belgium	34.0
Germany	30.2
Australia	30.0
Mexico	30.0
Japan	29.9
Portugal	29.5
Luxembourg	27.8
Italy	27.8

10 OECD Member Countries with Lowest Combined Corporate Tax Rate[71]

Member Country	Combined Corp. Tax Rate (%)
Finland	20.0
Iceland	20.0
Turkey	20.0
Czech Republic	19.0
Poland	19.0
Slovenia	19.0
United Kingdom	19.0
Latvia	15.0
Ireland	12.5
Hungary	9.0

[70] See OECD Tax Database, avail. at http://stats.oecd.org/index.aspx?DataSetCode=TABLE_II1 (visited Nov. 26, 2017).

[71] *Id.*

The pre-2018 disparity in corporate tax rates led many U.S. companies, particularly those with multinational operations and hordes of cash (estimated at $2.1 trillion in 2015[72]) sitting overseas,[73] to seek to *redomicile* in (or, in the parlance of the IRS, *expatriate* to) a more tax-friendly location through so-called *inversion* deals. This, in turn, caused consternation and sabre rattling among members of the U.S. government who believed inversions, as a matter of public policy, displayed a lack of "economic patriotism."[74] Moreover, these critics viewed inversions as unfair to U.S. taxpayers, as those taxpayers would have to pay more in income taxes to offset the revenue decline in corporate taxes. Treasury Secretary Jacob Lew in particular heavily criticized U.S. corporations that redomiciled because they continued to operate from U.S. soil and benefit from U.S. legal protections, infrastructure and basic research.[75]

i. A Long History

The first inversion of note occurred in 1983 when McDermott Inc., a company incorporated in the U.S., merged with its existing Panamanian subsidiary, McDermott International. The IRS became keenly interested in inversions when U.S. companies began merging into non-U.S. shell corporations formed solely for the purpose of effecting an inversion. By 1993, when Helen of Troy Limited merged into a newly-formed Bermuda shell corporation for the sole purpose of avoiding U.S. taxes, the IRS decided to act. In 1996 the IRS issued the first comprehensive set of anti-inversion regulations under the auspices of I.R.C. § 367(a). See Treas. Reg. §§ 1.367(a)–1 through 1.367(a)–8.

Had they been in place, the 1996 regulations would have caused the Helen of Troy Limited inversion transaction to be fully taxable to its U.S. shareholders. However, in situations where U.S. shareholders represent only a minority of all shareholders of a publicly traded multinational corporation, or where U.S. shareholders either have a small or zero gain in their shares, the steps taken by the IRS provided very little deterrent to inversion deals. As a result, Tyco International moved to Bermuda in 1997,

---

72 See Richard Rubin, *U.S. Companies Are Stashing $2.1 Trillion Overseas to Avoid Taxes*, BLOOMBERG (Mar. 4, 2015) (avail. at http://tinyurl.com/pv2azxw).

73 Prior to the TCJA, profits earned overseas by U.S. conglomerates were subject to the 35 percent U.S. corporate income tax rate when those profits were brought back (*repatriated*) into the U.S. to the parent corporation. This resulted in many U.S. conglomerates leaving large amounts of money offshore (*foreign trapped earnings*)—the so-called *cash lock-out effect*. Of course, U.S. multinationals did not intend to repatriate all of their offshore cash, but instead intended to use some of it purely for overseas purposes. This cash is known as *permanently reinvested earnings*, or PRE. The TCJA taxes repatriated cash assets from overseas at a one-time low rate of only 15.5 percent.

74 John D. McKinnon, *Lew Urges Congress to Curb Inversions*, WALL ST. J., Sept. 9, 2014, at B3 (quoting former Treasury Secretary Jacob Lew).

75 See John D. McKinnon, *Obama Urges Action to Limit "Inversions,"* WALL ST. J., July 16, 2014, at B1.

Fruit of the Loom moved to the Cayman Islands in 1998 and Ingersoll-Rand moved to Bermuda in 2001.

Inversion deals, particularly in the pharmaceutical industry, have been aggressively pursued much to the dismay of the U.S. government. From 2008 through 2015, 28 U.S. corporations have used the inversion strategy, compared with around the same number over the 25 preceding years.[76] Recent deals have involved Mylan, Inc., Medtronic Inc., Burger King Worldwide Inc., Steris Corp., Horizon Pharma and Forest Laboratories, among others.

ii. Congress' First Entry into the Fray

In 2004 Congress enacted I.R.C. §§ 7874 and 4985 in order to diminish the appeal of tax-driven inversion deals. These anti-inversion provisions are carefully tailored to penalize inversions primarily motivated by tax avoidance but not those motivated by substantive business reasons. They are directly targeted at the taxation of U.S. corporations and their directors, officers and significant shareholders. In extreme cases, these provisions treat a foreign acquirer as if it were a U.S. company for U.S. tax purposes.

a) I.R.C. § 7874

Section 7874 penalizes inversions when (i) the foreign acquiring corporation completes the direct or indirect acquisition of substantially all of the properties held directly or indirectly by a U.S. corporation, (ii) former shareholders of a U.S. corporation end up owning more than a specified percentage of stock of the foreign acquiring corporation (the "Ownership Test") and (iii) the foreign acquiring corporation's "expanded affiliate group" or "EAG" does not have "substantial business activities" in the foreign acquiring corporation's country of incorporation when compared with the total business activity of the EAG (the "Substantial Business Activities Test").

The Ownership Test has a 60 percent and 80 percent trigger. If former shareholders of the U.S. corporation end up owning at least 60 percent but less than 80 percent of the stock of the foreign corporation post transaction (measured based on either voting power or value), and the foreign corporation fails the Substantial Business Activities Test, then the foreign corporation is treated as a "surrogate foreign corporation." As a result, certain gain that the U.S. target corporation recognizes in the inversion and certain post-transaction income and gain are taxable in full at the maximum U.S. corporate tax rate. Moreover, any offsets for losses, credits or other tax attributes are disregarded in this context.

---

[76] See Congressional Budget Office, *An Analysis of Corporate Inversions*, 6 (Sept. 2017) (avail. at https://www.cbo.gov/system/files/115th-congress-2017-2018/reports/53093-inversions.pdf).

The Ownership Test's 80 percent trigger carries even stiffer tax consequences. If former shareholders of a U.S. corporation receive 80 percent or more of the stock of the foreign acquiring corporation (again, measured based on either voting power or value), and the foreign acquiring corporation fails the Substantial Business Activities Test, then the foreign acquiring corporation will be treated as a U.S. corporation for all U.S. tax purposes.

Not surprisingly, U.S. companies have attempted to avoid application of § 7874 by attempting to dilute the percentage of shares of the foreign acquirer ultimately owned by the former U.S. shareholders. Section 7874, however, contains a "kick out" provision that disregards certain shares in the foreign acquirer for purposes of the Ownership Test. Specifically excluded from the calculation are shares of the foreign acquirer (a) held by any member of its EAG (including treasury shares held by the foreign acquirer itself) and (b) sold in a public offering related to the acquisition of the U.S. corporation (e.g., an offering designed to provide funding for the deal). The IRS later subjected shares sold in private placements to the "kick out" provision as well. See IRS Notice 2009–78, 2009 WL 2960713 (Sept. 17, 2009).

As mentioned above, the Substantial Business Activities Test measures the foreign acquirer's business activities in the jurisdiction in which it was incorporated against the overall business activities of its EAG. The IRS and Treasury Department implemented final regulations in 2015 that employ a "bright line" test to determining whether the Substantial Business Activities Test is passed. See *Substantial Business Activities*, T.D. 9720, 80 FR 31837–01, 2015 WL 3489208 (June 4, 2015). The test focuses on the EAG's assets, employees and sales. Importantly, only certain types of assets, employees and sales qualify for purposes of the test. Specifically, a foreign acquirer will be deemed to pass the Substantial Business Activities Test if (a) after the acquisition, EAG qualified employees based in the country of incorporation accounted for at least 25 percent of total EAG qualified employees (as measured by headcount and compensation), (b) after the acquisition, the total value of EAG qualified assets located in the country of incorporation represented at least 25 percent of the total value of all EAG qualified assets, and (c) during a 12-month testing period, EAG qualified sales in the country of incorporation accounted for at least 25 percent of total EAG qualified sales.

b) I.R.C. § 4985

While § 7874 targets U.S. corporations engaged in certain inversions, § 4985 targets corporate insiders entitled to stock-based compensation. Thus, the Section makes corporate insiders think twice before approving an inversion. Specifically, the Section imposes a 15 percent excise tax on any gain on stock-based compensation held by or for the benefit of any "disqualified individual" of an "expatriated corporation" during a 12-month period beginning on the date that is six months prior to the expatriation date. "Disqualified individuals" are generally corporate insiders, while an "expatriated corporation" includes inverted U.S. corporations surpassing at least the 60 percent trigger of the Ownership Test discussed above.

iii. Use of "Earnings Stripping"

As a result of §§ 7874 and 4985, the only inversion "free lunch" occurs when a U.S. target corporation is acquired by a larger foreign acquirer that has an established foreign trade or business. However, few U.S. corporations would view giving up their independence in exchange for escaping U.S. taxation as a good trade-off. Instead, U.S. corporations are acquiring foreign companies and redomiciling overseas in the process.

In order to reduce their U.S. tax bills, the former U.S. corporations then engage in *earnings stripping*, a process whereby profits earned by their U.S. subsidiaries are shipped offshore in the form of untaxed interest payments. This requires the U.S. subsidiaries to incur substantial amounts of debt from foreign lenders affiliated with their foreign parents. As a result, the subsidiaries may shelter up to 50 percent of their U.S. taxable income due to the interest payments they make to the lenders. These lenders are carefully chosen so that they do not qualify as controlled foreign corporations for U.S. tax purposes. However, as noted *infra*, earnings stripping has lost some of its appeal due to the Tax Cuts and Jobs Act of 2017, as the TCJA caps the ability of U.S. subsidiaries to deduct interest payments to their parents.

iv. Treasury Responds

Not willing to wait for Congressional action, in 2014 the IRS and the Treasury Department issued Notice 2014–52, 2014 WL 4715633 (Sept. 24, 2014). Among other things, Notice 2014–52 curbs tax efficient access to a U.S. target's offshore trapped cash to finance inversions, including where that cash is to be loaned to the foreign acquirer. This is particularly painful to U.S. multinationals which had been facing mounting pressure from shareholders to utilize their offshore earnings. As a result, Medtronic Inc.'s proposed inversion with Coviedien PLC had to be rethought. Medtronic, which had planned on using $13.5 billion in trapped cash to help finance the deal, decided instead to incur $16 billion in debt to help finance the deal in response to the new regulations. Other U.S. companies, including Salix Pharmaceuticals and AbbVie Inc., scrapped their inversion deals completely. AbbVie was forced to pay a $1.6 billion break up fee to Shire PLC as a result.

In April 2016, the Treasury Department issued two new rules that targeted both inversion deals and earnings stripping. See *Inversions and Related Transactions*, T.D. 9761, 81 FR 20858–01, 2016 WL 1378603 (Apr. 8, 2016). The first rule (the "Stock Attribution Rule") was designed to crack down on so-called "serial inverters"—U.S. companies that invert by acquiring a foreign company that has previously inverted or expanded its size through acquisitions of U.S. corporations. The rule applies retroactively and disregards three years' of past mergers with U.S. corporations in determining a foreign company's size. Stock that was accumulated through a foreign company's deals with U.S. corporations within those three years can no longer count towards the necessary book value to meet an inversion threshold. As a result, the Treasury can ignore a foreign company's actual size for tax purposes, which makes inversion a less viable financial option for U.S. companies.

The second rule targets earnings stripping, which is frequently a consequence of an inversion. This rule gives the IRS flexibility to reclassify certain transactions between parent and subsidiary companies as an exchange of equity instead of interest on debt. As a result, former tax deductible interest payments may be reclassified as taxable dividends. The rule is designed to prevent companies from receiving tax breaks for debt that does not actually finance new investment in the U.S.

The Stock Attribution Rule, however, is in limbo. It was challenged in federal court in 2016 by the U.S. Chamber of Commerce and the Texas Association of Business. The plaintiffs alleged that the Rule was "arbitrary and capricious" and was instated without notice and opportunity for comment. Indeed, the Rule was simultaneously issued as a temporary regulation effective immediately and as a proposed regulation subject to notice and comment. Siding with the plaintiffs, the U.S. District Court for Western Texas granted their motion for summary judgment, holding that the temporary nature of the Rule did not excuse the IRS from complying with the notice and comment period under the Administrative Procedures Act before it was instated. See *Chamber of Commerce v. I.R.S.*, 2017 WL 4682049, at *7–8 (W.D. Tex.).

v. The Tax Cuts and Jobs Act of 2017: Congress' Second Entry into the Fray

While members of both houses of Congress have sought to prevent inversion deals the primary purpose of which is the avoidance of U.S. taxes, no consensus has been reached on exactly what to do. Democrats and Republicans generally agree that tax-avoidance inversions should be prevented. Democrats, however, want to pass inversion-specific legislation and, importantly, make it retroactive in order to capture previously announced and even closed transactions. Republicans, by contrast, hope that the TCJA will largely take care of the problem. They may be right.

The TCJA reduces the federal corporate income tax rate from 35 percent down to only 21 percent. Moreover, under the Act repatriated money (cash assets) from overseas will be a taxed at a one-time low rate of only 15.5 percent. Republicans believe that the lower federal corporate income tax rate will make the U.S. more competitive with the world, thus encouraging U.S. companies to stay in the U.S. Moreover, they believe that internationally held money will come flooding back into the U.S. based on the low rate on repatriated money. So far, so good. In early 2018, Apple, Inc. announced it would repatriate $252 billion in cash to the U.S., resulting in a one-time tax payment of $38 billion to the U.S. Government. It also announced that it would create 20,000 new U.S. jobs over the next five years. Similarly, Cisco announced that it would repatriate $67 billion in cash to the U.S. and spend the bulk of it on increased dividends to shareholders and stock buybacks.

While the TCJA is off to a good start in accomplishing its objectives, the ultimate irony may be its impact on many currently inverted companies. Those that rely heavily on earnings stripping—intercompany debt that causes U.S. subsidiaries to make large interest payments to their offshore parents—will see their subsidiaries' ability to deduct interest payments capped under the TCJA. Specifically, interest is capped at 30 percent of a subsidiary's "adjusted taxable income."[77] I.R.C. § 163(j). Moreover, the TCJA imposes a new "base erosion and anti-abuse" tax ("BEAT") on large corporations. I.R.C. § 59A. BEAT operates as a limited scope alternative minimum tax, by adding back to taxable income certain deductible payments made to related foreign persons. The minimum rate is 5 percent in 2018, but rises to 10 percent in 2019 and 12.5 percent in 2026. The BEAT minimum tax is due if the BEAT tax amount is greater than the regular corporate tax owed in a given a year. While experts do not believe the tax hit to inverted companies will cause them to return to the U.S., at least the U.S. taxes their subsidiaries do pay will be closer to those paid by non-inverted U.S. companies going forward.[78]

d. Miscellaneous Tax Provisions Relevant to Acquisitions: Golden Parachutes, Greenmail, Poison Pills, and Acquisition Expenses

Congress is slowly accumulating a series of provisions tucked in various places in the tax code that affect defensive tactics in acquisitions. Two such provisions, on golden parachutes and greenmail, are noted below. More importantly, the IRS, backed by the Supreme Court, has taken a tough stance on deductibility of acquisition fees and expenses.

i. Golden Parachutes: §§ 280G and 4999

Golden parachutes are severance-related agreements between corporations and their key personnel under which the corporation agrees to pay the employees certain amounts in the event that a "change of

[77] See *supra* Section B.5.b (Note: 2017 Tax Reform Efforts and Possible Impact on Leveraged Buyouts and Private Equity Deals).

[78] See Jonathan D. Rockoff & Nina Trentmann, *Higher Taxes Await "Inverted" Companies,* WALL ST. J., Feb. 12, 2018, at A1.

control"[79] of the corporation occurs. Most golden parachutes require a "double trigger" to activate payments: (a) a change of control must occur and (2) the executive must be terminated.[80] The vast majority of companies define termination as involuntary or "constructive"—for example, a reduction in pay or a demotion. Typically, golden parachute agreements prescribe a maximum time period of two years between the date on which a change of control occurs and the termination of the executive, for purposes of triggering payments.[81]

The use of golden parachutes is highly controversial. Proponents believe golden parachutes facilitate the hiring and retention of key employees and allow those employees to remain objective if their corporation is involved in a merger or takeover. In addition, they point out that golden parachutes can discourage a takeover in the first place, as parachutes force an acquirer to indirectly satisfy their payment and other obligations in addition to paying the overall purchase price to acquire the target.

Opponents of golden parachutes, by contrast, point to the handsome compensation packages key employees already receive. While some severance makes sense in the event key employees are terminated following a change of control, critics argue golden parachute payments have been grossly excessive—often three times the employee's previous year's salary and bonus. Opponents further highlight that executive officers have fiduciary obligations to act in the best interests of the corporation in the context of a proposed sale, and thus financial incentives to do so in the form of golden parachutes are not necessary. In addition, opponents disagree that golden parachutes discourage takeovers given that

---

79 While there is no standard definition of "change of control," the definition normally covers the numerous ways in which control of corporate management can change. Thus, stock purchases, mergers, consolidations, asset purchases, material changes in the composition of the board of directors over a specified period of time, and corporate liquidations are typically covered.

80 In the case of a single trigger, a corporation will owe payments solely because a change of control has occurred. That is, the corporation must make payments if it has been acquired *even if* the key employee in question has not lost his or her job. Public companies rarely have single trigger provisions as they do not serve the purpose behind golden parachutes of retaining key employees in the face of an acquisition of their corporation. Moreover, institutional shareholders and proxy advisory services (such as Institutional Shareholder Services ("ISS")) frown on single trigger provisions. Nevertheless, even though double triggers are the norm, examples of public companies using single trigger golden parachutes do exist. Matthew Shattock, the CEO of Beam, Inc., the liquor producer, received almost $20.9 million from previously unvested stock options and stock awards as a result of Beam's April 2014 sale to Suntory Holdings, Inc.—despite the fact that Shattock remained CEO of Beam (renamed Beam Suntory Inc.). C. Larry Pope, the CEO of Smithfield Foods Inc., similarly received approximately $18 million when Smithfield Foods, the pork producer, was sold to a Chinese buyer in 2013. Mr. Pope remained the CEO of Smithfield Foods, now a subsidiary of WH Group Ltd., after the transaction.

81 Termination is, indeed, a possibility. A strategic acquirer typically already has a full complement of its own key executives, such as a CEO and CFO, and thus does not need a second set. A financial acquirer, by contrast, may believe target management has underperformed and intends to replace it with a more competent management team. An executive at a target company who feels financially secure is less likely to oppose a good deal for his or her company. Golden parachutes provide that security.

the costs associated with golden parachutes are trivial when compared to the overall cost to acquire a target.

In the Tax Reform Act of 1984, Congress imposed tax penalties for excess golden parachutes payments. Minor amendments in the Tax Reform Act of 1986 and the Technical and Miscellaneous Revenue Act of 1988, as well as the Treasury regulations adopted in 2003, complete the present picture. See Tres. Reg. § 1.208G–1. Section 280G disallows a deduction to the firm for, and Section 4999 imposes a 20 percent nondeductible excise tax on the recipient of, any "excess parachute payment." In general, payments with a present value equal to or exceeding three times an individual's base salary are "excess" payments. See I.R.C. § 280G(b)(2)(A)(ii).

More than half of the golden parachute arrangements do not cap parachute payments to the legislated ceiling of three times a "base amount." When payments are greater, the excess over the base amount is nondeductible by the corporation and is subject to an excise tax payable by the executive. About 33 percent of companies gross up executives for any excise taxes due on parachute payments. These results suggest that companies are placing less emphasis on tax consequences when designing change of control arrangements.

IRS PROPOSED REGULATIONS, GOLDEN PARACHUTES § 1.280G–1[82]

54 Fed.Reg. 19390, 1989 WL 304387 (May 5, 1989).

* * *

In applying the golden parachute provisions, the first step is to identify payments that constitute "parachute payments." Section 280G(b)(2)(A) defines a "parachute payment" as any payment that meets all of the following four conditions: (a) the payment is in the nature of compensation; (b) the payment is to, or for the benefit of, a disqualified individual; (c) the payment is contingent on a change in the ownership of a corporation, the effective control of a corporation, or the ownership of a substantial portion of the assets of a corporation ("change in ownership or control"); and (d) the payment has . . . an aggregate present value of at least three times the individual's base amount.

For this purpose, an individual's base amount is, in general, the individual's average annualized includible compensation for the most recent five taxable years ending before the change in ownership or control.

* * *

[82] The proposed regulations were rewritten in a question/answer format and adopted in 2003.

Once payments are identified as "parachute payments", the next step is to determine any "excess" portion of the payments. Section 280G(b)(1) defines the term "excess parachute payment" as an amount equal to the excess of any parachute payment over the portion of the disqualified individual's base amount that is allocated to such payment. . . .

Generally, excess parachute payments may be reduced by certain amounts of reasonable compensation. Section 280G(b)(4)(B) provides that except in the case of securities violation parachute payments, the amount of an excess parachute payment is reduced by any portion of the payment that the taxpayer establishes by clear and convincing evidence is reasonable compensation for personal services actually rendered by the disqualified individual before the date of change in ownership or control. . . .

* * *

Section 280G(b)(5) provides an exemption for payments with respect to certain corporations. Pursuant to that section, the term "parachute payment" does not include any payment made to a disqualified individual with respect to a corporation which, immediately before the change in ownership or control, was a small business corporation. In addition, the term "parachute payment" does not include any payment made with respect to a corporation if, immediately before the change in ownership or control, no stock in the corporation was readily tradable on an established securities market (or otherwise) and certain shareholder approval requirements are met with respect to the payment. . . .

* * *

To be a parachute payment, a payment must be made to (or for the benefit of) a "disqualified individual." Section 280G(c) defines the term "disqualified individual" to include any individual who (a) is an employee or independent contractor who performs personal services for a corporation, and (b) is an officer, shareholder, or highly-compensated individual. . . .

Section 280G(c) provides that a "highly-compensated individual" with respect to a corporation only includes an individual who is (or would be if the individual were an employee) a member of the group consisting of the highest paid one percent of the employees of the corporation or, if less, the 250 highest paid employees of the corporation. . . .

* * *

NOTE: CORPORATIONS TAKING TARP FUNDS AND SHAREHOLDER SAY ON PAY

Section 302(b) of the Emergency Economic Stabilization Act of 2008 (the "EESA") amended Section 280G by expanding the definition of a parachute payment to include additional forms of severance payments made to a covered executive of a company participating in the Troubled Asset Relief Program (commonly known as "TARP"). A covered executive is a CEO, CFO or one of the other three highest paid employees in the firm. The limits of § 280G now apply to severance payments for such executives made on involuntary terminations by the firm or on bankruptcy, liquidation or receivership of the company. Congress did not want TARP funds going into the pockets of fired, high priced executives.

NOTE: SHAREHOLDER SAY ON PAY

Section 951 of the Dodd-Frank Wall Street Reform and Consumer Protection Act of 2010 ("Dodd-Frank) requires advisory votes of shareholders about executive compensation and golden parachutes. This Section also requires specific disclosure of golden parachutes in merger proxies. It further requires institutional investment managers subject to Exchange Act § 13(f) to report at least annually how they voted on these advisory shareholder votes.

Thus, shareholders today now have an advisory vote on golden parachute agreements, and they have been using it to their advantage. For example, shareholders holding a majority of the shares of oil refiner Valero Energy Corp., media company Gannett Co., commercial landlord Boston Properties Inc. and dairy and soy producer Dean Foods Co. voted in favor of preventing key executives' unvested stock awards tied to future performance from automatically vesting in the event of a merger. While the votes are nonbinding, they represent a clear sign that shareholders are pushing back on overly generous golden parachute agreements. Corporate boards, therefore, are under pressure from shareholders as well as regulators to consider shareholder views when crafting executive pay packages.

ii. Greenmail: § 5881

OMNIBUS BUDGET RECONCILIATION ACT OF 1987[83]

Conference Comm. Rep. No. 100–495, 970–71 (Dec. 21, 1987).

* * *

R

Act:

[*Greenmail excise tax*] [T]he [House] bill provides that a person who receives "greenmail" is subject to a non-deductible 50–percent excise tax on any gain realized on such receipt. Greenmail is defined as any consideration paid by a corporation in redemption of its stock if such stock has been held by the shareholder for less than two years and the

[83] Available at https://www.finance.senate.gov/imo/media/doc/crpt100-495.pdf.

shareholder (or any related person or person acting in concert with the shareholder) made or threatened a public tender offer for stock in the corporation during that period.

* * *

The conference agreement adopts . . . the House bill provision imposing an excise tax on greenmail, with certain modifications . . . .

The greenmail excise tax does not apply if, prior to the redemption, the redeeming corporation offered to purchase the stock of other shareholders for the same consideration and on the same terms that it redeemed the stock of the taxpayer. The provision is intended to apply where a taxpayer otherwise subject to the provision sells his stock to an entity related to the issuing corporation (*e.g.*, a controlled subsidiary).

* * *

On December 18, 1991, the Internal Revenue Service published in the Federal Register its final regulations on excise tax payments relating to income realized through the receipt of greenmail. See IRS, *Excise Tax Relating to Gain or Other Income Realized By Any Person on Receipt of Greenmail*, 56 FR 65684–02, 1991 WL 11000253 (Dec. 18, 1991). The IRS defines greenmail as "any consideration transferred by a corporation (or any person acting in concert with the corporation) to directly or indirectly acquire stock of the corporation from any shareholder" under certain defined conditions. Treas. Reg. § 156.5881–1(b). First, the shareholder must have held the stock for less than two years prior to the repurchase agreement. Second, the shareholder must have "made or threatened to make a public tender offer for stock of the corporation at some time during the two-year period ending on the date of the acquisition of the stock by the corporation." Third, the stock repurchase must have been "pursuant to an offer that was not made on the same terms to all shareholders." *Id.*

QUESTION

Why is a charter amendment that prohibits managers from paying greenmail often part of a shark repellant, antitakeover package of charter amendments?

States like New York have attempted to clamp down on greenmail practices by adopting anti-greenmail statutes. Consider Section 513(c) of the New York Business Corporation Law:

> (c) No domestic corporation . . . shall purchase or agree to purchase more than ten percent of the stock of the corporation from a shareholder for more than the market value thereof unless such purchase or agreement to purchase is approved by the affirmative vote of the board of directors and a majority of the votes of all

outstanding shares entitled to vote thereon at a meeting of shareholders unless the certificate of incorporation requires a greater percentage of the votes of the outstanding shares to approve.

The provisions of this paragraph shall not apply when the corporation offers to purchase shares from all holders of stock or for stock which the holder has been the beneficial owner of for more than two years.

For all intents and purposes, New York's provision puts the kibosh on greenmail payments by New York corporations. Could you image the board and senior executives of a New York corporation actually asking their shareholders to approve greenmail payments so that they can keep their jobs!

iii. Excise Tax on Terminating Overfunded Pension Plans

def:

In the 1980s, defined benefit pension plans grew fat from stock market run-ups, and financial takeover wizards used the plans to fund their acquisitions. A defined benefit pension plan is a promise to pay retiring workers a stated accrued sum, usually in the form of an annuity with monthly payments, determined on the basis of a formula tied to salary on retirement.[84] In a defined benefit plan, a sponsoring employer has to contribute cash and securities to fund the plan equal to the present value of the future pension claims. Actuarial calculations, estimates based on anticipated investment return on plan assets, mortality of workers, turnover of employees and anticipated salary level set an employer's annual contribution. If the actual investment return on plan assets exceeds estimates, the plan is overfunded. In the '80s financial buyers would buy the firm, terminate the overfunded plan, put a new pension plan in place, and use the surplus funds to pay back acquisition financing. When Ronald Perelman took over Revlon in 1985, he took control of over $100 million in surplus pension fund assets. Charles Hurwitz used the $55 million in pension surplus to fund his takeover of Pacific Lumber. The tactic even gets a mention in the movie *Wall Street* as Gordon Gecko attempts to liquidate Blue Star Airline.

Embittered employees sued in federal court and lobbied Congress for assistance. Employees claimed that under ERISA any surplus in a defined benefit plan rightfully belonged to the employees, not a firm or its successors. The federal courts found for the corporate defendants[85] and Congress has not changed the statute, maintaining the distinction between defined benefit and defined contribution plans. But Congress, anxious to stop financial takeovers, did amend the tax code in 1990 to slap firms with a whopping 50 percent excise tax on reversions of pension funds under

---

[84] A defined contribution plan (e.g., a "401K" plan), on the other hand, is an employer's promise to pay workers at retirement whatever amounts have accumulated in the workers' individual accounts from the returns on both employee and employer yearly payments.

[85] Shepley v. New Coleman Holdings, 174 F.3d 65 (2d Cir. 1999) (citing dicta in Hughes Aircraft Co. v. Jacobson, 525 U.S. 432, 119 S.Ct. 755, 761, 142 L.Ed.2d 881 (1999)).

terminated plans. I.R.C. § 4980(d). Pension terminations died. A firm is better off letting the surplus lie and reducing its future pension contribution obligations.

Clever tax lawyers have resurrected the technique. They note that Congress reduced the excise tax to only 20 percent if a firm replaced a terminated plan with a "replacement plan" that contains at least one-quarter of the old plan's surplus. So when Dillard's acquired Mercantile Stores in 1999, it terminated a pension plan and took the $194 million surplus, allocated 25 percent to a new plan, paid a 20 percent excise tax and used the remaining $117 million to retire acquisition financing. Companies facing bankruptcy are also using the strategy: Montgomery Ward and Edison Brothers Stores terminated pension plans to pay creditors. They added another twist, however. In the years before terminating a pension plan, a financially strapped firm will take steps to increase the surplus by freezing or even reducing plan benefits. In the two years before Ward's termination of its plan, it converted its plan to a "cash balance" version to reduce costs and build surplus more rapidly.

iv. Deductibility of Acquisition Fees and Expenses

INDOPCO, INC. V. COMMISSIONER

Supreme Court of the United States, 1992.
503 U.S. 79, 112 S.Ct. 1039, 117 L.Ed.2d 226.

JUSTICE BLACKMUN delivered the opinion of the Court.

In this case we must decide whether certain professional expenses incurred by a target corporation in the course of a friendly takeover are deductible by that corporation as "ordinary and necessary" business expenses under § 162(a) of the federal Internal Revenue Code.

. . . Petitioner INDOPCO, Inc., formerly named National Starch and Chemical Corporation and hereinafter referred to as National Starch, is a Delaware corporation that manufactures and sells adhesives, starches, and specialty chemical products. In October 1977, representatives of Unilever United States, Inc., also a Delaware corporation (Unilever), expressed interest in acquiring National Starch, which was one of its suppliers, through a friendly transaction. National Starch at the time had outstanding over 6,563,000 common shares held by approximately 3,700 shareholders. The stock was listed on the New York Stock Exchange. . . .

* * *

In November 1977, National Starch's directors were formally advised of Unilever's interest and the proposed transaction. At that time, Debevoise, Plimpton, Lyons & Gates, National Starch's counsel, told the directors that under Delaware law they had a fiduciary duty to ensure that the proposed transaction would be fair to the shareholders. National Starch thereupon engaged the investment banking firm of Morgan Stanley & Co., Inc., to evaluate its shares, to render a fairness opinion; and generally to assist in the event of the emergence of a hostile tender offer.

Although Unilever originally had suggested a price between $65 and $70 per share, negotiations resulted in a final offer of $73.50 per share, a figure Morgan Stanley found to be fair. Following approval by National Starch's board and the issuance of a favorable private ruling from the Internal Revenue Service that the transaction would be tax-free under § 351 for those National Starch shareholders who exchanged their stock for Holding preferred, the transaction was consummated in August 1978.

Morgan Stanley charged National Starch a fee of $2,200,000, along with $7,586 for out-of-pocket expenses and $18,000 for legal fees. The Debevoise firm charged National Starch $490,000, along with $15,069 for out-of-pocket expenses. National Starch also incurred expenses aggregating $150,962 for miscellaneous items—such as accounting, printing, proxy solicitation, and Securities and Exchange Commission fees—in connection with the transaction. No issue is raised as to the propriety or reasonableness of these charges.

On its federal income tax return for its short taxable year ended August 15, 1978, National Starch claimed a deduction for the $2,225,586 paid to Morgan Stanley, but did not deduct the $505,069 paid to Debevoise or the other expenses. Upon audit, the Commissioner of Internal Revenue disallowed the claimed deduction and issued a notice of deficiency. Petitioner sought redetermination in the United States Tax Court, asserting, however, not only the right to deduct the investment banking fees and expenses but, as well, the legal and miscellaneous expenses incurred.

* * *

Section 162(a) of the Internal Revenue Code allows the deduction of "all the ordinary and necessary expenses paid or incurred during the taxable year in carrying on any trade or business." 26 U.S.C. § 162(a). In contrast, § 263 of the Code allows no deduction for a capital expenditure—an "amount paid out for new buildings or for permanent improvements or betterments made to increase the value of any property or estate." 26 U.S.C. § 263(a)(1). The primary effect of characterizing a payment as either a business expense or a capital expenditure concerns the timing of the taxpayer's cost recovery: While business expenses are currently deductible, a capital expenditure usually is amortized and depreciated over the life of the relevant asset, or, where no specific asset or useful life can be ascertained, is deducted upon dissolution of the enterprise. *See* 26 U.S.C. §§ 167(a) and 336(a); Treas. Reg. § 1.167(a), 26 CFR § 1.167(a) (1991). Through provisions such as these, the Code endeavors to match expenses with the revenues of the taxable period to which they are properly attributable, thereby resulting in a more accurate calculation of net income for tax purposes. . . .

* * *

. . . [W]e conclude that National Starch has not demonstrated that the investment banking, legal, and other costs it incurred in connection with Unilever's acquisition of its shares are deductible as ordinary and necessary business expenses under § 162(a).

Although petitioner attempts to dismiss the benefits that accrued to National Starch from the Unilever acquisition as "entirely speculative" or "merely incidental," . . . the Tax Court's and the Court of Appeals' findings that the transaction produced significant benefits to National Starch that extended beyond the tax year in question are amply supported by the record. For example, in commenting on the merger with Unilever, National Starch's 1978 "Progress Report" observed that the company would "benefit greatly from the availability of Unilever's enormous resources, especially in the area of basic technology." . . . Morgan Stanley's report to the National Starch board concerning the fairness to shareholders of a possible business combination with Unilever noted that National Starch management "feels that some synergy may exist with the Unilever organization given a) the nature of the Unilever chemical, paper, plastics and packaging operations . . . and b) the strong consumer products orientation of Unilever United States, Inc." . . .

In addition to these anticipated resource-related benefits, National Starch obtained benefits through its transformation from a publicly held, freestanding corporation into a wholly owned subsidiary of Unilever. The Court of Appeals noted that National Starch management viewed the transaction as "swapping approximately 3500 shareholders for one." . . . Following Unilever's acquisition of National Starch's outstanding shares, National Starch was no longer subject to what even it terms the "substantial" shareholder-relations expenses a publicly traded corporation incurs, including reporting and disclosure obligations, proxy battles, and derivative suits. . . . The acquisition also allowed National Starch, in the interests of administrative convenience and simplicity, to eliminate previously authorized but unissued shares of preferred and to reduce the total number of authorized shares of common from 8,000,000 to 1,000. . . .

Courts long have recognized that expenses such as these, " 'incurred for the purpose of changing the corporate structure for the benefit of future operations[,] are not ordinary and necessary business expenses.' " . . .

* * *

A.E. STALEY MFG. CO. v. COMMISSIONER, 119 F.3d 482 (7th Cir. 1997): [The Seventh Circuit reversed the Tax Court and held that a corporation could deduct (and need not capitalize) fees paid to investment bankers in connection with unsuccessful efforts to fend off a hostile takeover. In doing so, the court distinguished friendly takeovers from hostile takeovers. It asserted that in friendly takeovers a corporation aimed such expenditures at advancing the long-run benefit of the company. In hostile takeovers, by contrast, a corporation's expenditures provided no long-run benefit to the company. The costs incurred in defense "seek to preserve the status quo, not to produce future benefits." Once the hostile offer became inevitable (turned friendly), however, the target had to capitalize those expenditures facilitating the takeover.]

CHAPTER NINE

PROTECTING CONSUMER INTERESTS IN MERGERS AND ACQUISITIONS: THE CLAYTON ACT

■ ■ ■

As we saw in Chapter Three, acquisitions can impose costs on members of the public that may not be internalized by the parties to the transaction. Indeed, the parties to a transaction not only may be indifferent to the public interest but may in fact profit from public injury. They argue that a merger creates value simply because the market value of the combined firm (plus the value of any non-stock consideration) is greater than the combined market values of the constituent firms before the deal is announced. However, that argument is incomplete without an investigation of the effect of the merger on other public interests (the externalities). In earlier chapters we covered laws that regulate acquisitions to promote various aspects of the public interest—laws that relate to the health of our capital trading markets, to the collection of public taxes, to the preservation of a clean environment, to the goal of full employment, and to the compensation of tort victims. We have yet to cover, however, laws that protect consumers.

A. THE CLAYTON ACT

Consumer protection in acquisitions has been a central part of the American legal landscape since the late 1800s. Industrial combinations after the Civil War demonstrated one form of opportunistic behavior in acquisitions: two competing firms combine, creating a single firm that has enough market power to engage in noncompetitive pricing, or enough size to collude with other major firms to fix prices through express or tacit agreements. The surviving firm in such a combination may be more profitable than the two constituent firms standing separately, but this occurs at the expense of their consumers. The firms, in bargaining over the merger price, simply split the expected gains created by monopolistic or oligopolistic pricing behavior. A 1914 federal antitrust statute known as the Clayton Antitrust Act ("Clayton Act"), 15 U.S.C. § 12–27, and state antitrust statutes modeled after the Clayton Act, are designed to deter such acquisitions.[1] (There is, it should be noted, a special statute for research

[1] Some state laws on anti-competitive mergers predate the Sherman Act. E.g., Colo. Const. Art. XV, §§ 13–15 (from 1876) (on railroad consolidations).

and development joint ventures that is less confining to these combinations than the Clayton Act would be if it applied.[2])

The Clayton Act expands on the general prohibitions of the Sherman Antitrust Act of 1890 ("Sherman Act"), 15 U.S.C. §§1–7,[3] and is intended to stop anti-competitive problems in their incipiency by *regulating acquisitions*. Section 7 of the Clayton Act, 15 U.S.C. § 18, prohibits any merger or acquisition of stock or assets "where in any line of commerce or in any activity affecting commerce in any section of the country, the effect of such acquisition may be substantially to lessen competition, or to tend to create a monopoly." Section 15 of the Clayton Act empowers the U.S. Attorney General, and § 13(b) of the Federal Trade Commission Act of 1914 ("FTC Act") empowers the Federal Trade Commission ("FTC") to seek a court order enjoining consummation of a merger that would violate § 7. In addition, the FTC may seek a cease and desist order in an administrative proceeding against a merger under either § 11 of the Clayton Act or § 5 of the FTC Act, or both. Private parties may also seek injunctive relief under 15 U.S.C. § 26.

---

[2] The National Cooperative Research and Production Act of 1993 ("NCRPA"), 15 U.S.C. §§ 4301–06, clarifies the substantive application of the U.S. antitrust laws to joint research and development ("R & D") activities and joint production activities. (The NCRPA was previously named the National Cooperative Research Act of 1984 ("NCRA"), but the NCRA name and much of its substance was amended through the National Cooperative Production Amendments of 1993 (the "Amendments")). Originally drafted to encourage research and development by providing a special antitrust regime for research and development joint ventures, the NCRPA requires U.S. courts to judge the competitive effects of a challenged joint R & D or joint production venture, or a combination of the two, in properly defined relevant markets and under a rule-of-reason standard. The statute specifies that the conduct "shall be judged on the basis of its reasonableness, taking into account all relevant factors affecting competition, including, but not limited to, effects on competition in properly defined, relevant research, development, product, process, and service markets." 15 U.S.C. § 4302. The NCRPA also establishes a voluntary procedure pursuant to which the U.S. Attorney General and the Federal Trade Commission ("FTC") may be notified of a joint R & D or production venture. The statute limits the monetary relief that may be obtained in private civil suits against the participants in a notified venture to actual rather than treble damages, if the challenged conduct is within the scope of the notification. With respect to joint production ventures, the Amendments provide that the benefits of the limitation on recoverable damages for claims resulting from conduct within the scope of a notification are not available unless "(1) the principal facilities for the production are located within the United States or its territories, and (2) each person who controls any party to such venture (including such party itself) is a United States person, or a foreign person from a country whose law accords antitrust treatment no less favorable to United States persons than to such country's domestic persons with respect to participation in joint ventures for production." 15 U.S.C. § 4306.

[3] The Sherman Act is broad and sweeping in scope. According to § 1 of the Act, "[e]very contract, combination in the form of trust or otherwise, or conspiracy, in restraint of trade or commerce among the several States, or with foreign nations, is declared to be illegal." Section 2 goes even further, prohibiting monopolies or attempts at monopolization affecting any aspect of interstate trade or commerce. It also makes such acts a felony. The injured party may be the federal government, an individual state or a private party. That party is entitled to treble damages, i.e., three times the amount of injury that it has suffered. The Sherman Act has potential international implications as well. See 15 U.S.C. § 6A.

CLAYTON ACT, § 7

15 U.S.C. § 18.

Section 7. Acquisition by one corporation of stock of another

No person engaged in commerce or in any activity affecting commerce shall acquire, directly or indirectly, the whole or any part of the stock or other share capital and no person subject to the jurisdiction of the Federal Trade Commission shall acquire the whole or any part of the assets of another person engaged also in commerce or in any activity affecting commerce, where in any line of commerce or in any activity affecting commerce in any section of the country, the effect of such acquisition may be substantially to lessen competition, or to tend to create a monopoly.

* * *

This section shall not apply to persons purchasing such stock solely for investment and not using the same by voting or otherwise to bring about, or in attempting to bring about, the substantial lessening of competition. Nor shall anything contained in this section prevent a corporation engaged in commerce or in any activity affecting commerce from causing the formation of subsidiary corporations for the actual carrying on of their immediate lawful business, or the natural and legitimate branches or extensions thereof, or from owning and holding all or a part of the stock of such subsidiary corporations, when the effect of such formation is not to substantially lessen competition.

* * *

The responsibility for prosecuting violations of the Clayton Act is vested in both the United States Department of Justice ("DOJ") and the Federal Trade Commission ("FTC").[4] The DOJ and the FTC have jointly

---

[4] The role of agencies adds a political dimension to antitrust enforcement, with skeptics believing that Democrats enforce antitrust laws vigorously while Republicans do not. It is certainly true that during the years of the Reagan presidency (1981–1988) and George H. W. Bush presidency (1989–1992), the agencies rarely challenged acquisitions. During the Clinton presidency (1993–2000), the winds shifted. In 1994 the Justice Department attacked Microsoft's acquisition of Intuit and killed the deal. In 1996 the FTC challenged Rite Aid's deal with Revco and in 1997 challenged Staples' merger with Office Depot, stopping both deals. The Staples-Office Depot challenge stunned lawyers and hurt arbitrageurs, who had been betting millions on the deal on the advice of their lawyers. Although both Staples and Office Depot were in the retail office products business, there was little geographic overlap in their sales territories and both chains had a history of discount pricing. The CEOs argued that the merger would bring $4 billion of projected cost savings that would be passed back to customers. Even though Staples agreed to divest 63 stores overlapping markets, the FTC refused to settle and won a preliminary injunction in federal court. The judge found the pricing behavior of the parties changed in those areas in which they did have competing stores. At the same time, however, the FTC approved a $14 billion merger of Boeing and McDonnell Douglas Corporation (the numbers one and two U.S. airplane manufacturers) on efficiency grounds.

President George W. Bush (2001–2008) was focused on price fixing, asserting that everything evolves into price fixing over time (if it evolves at all). President Obama (2009–2016) believed that antitrust enforcement under President George W. Bush may have been the weakest of any

issued *Horizontal Merger Guidelines* which detail when the agencies will prosecute violations of the Clayton Act.[5]

HORIZONTAL MERGER GUIDELINES, U.S. DEPARTMENT OF JUSTICE AND THE FEDERAL TRADE COMMISSION

August 19, 2010 (updated June 25, 2015).

1. Overview

These Guidelines outline the principal analytical techniques, practices, and the enforcement policy of the Department of Justice and the Federal Trade Commission (the "Agencies") with respect to mergers and

---

administration in the last half century. See Ronan P. Harty, Howard A. Shelanski & Jesse Solomon, *Merger Enforcement Across Political Administrations in the United States*, Concurrences No. 2–2012, at 1 (avail. at www.concurrences.com) (hereinafter *Concurrences*).

More useful metrics are the number of transactions reported to the agencies under the Hart-Scott-Rodino Antitrust Improvements Act of 1976 ("HSR Act") and the number of "second requests" for additional information the agencies sent to transaction participants during each presidency. In terms of reportable transactions, not surprisingly those rose dramatically during times of economic boom and fell considerably during times of economic bust. On average per year, there were 1,682 (Reagan), 2,065 (G.H.W. Bush), 3,506 (Clinton), 1,671 (G.W. Bush) and 1,423 (Obama, through Sept. 30, 2016) reported transactions under the HSR Act. In terms of "second requests" made by the agencies for additional information from transaction participants, on average per year there were 62 (Reagan), 65 (G.H.W. Bush), 100 (Clinton), 48 (G.W. Bush) and 47 (Obama, through Sept. 30, 2016). In terms of the highest percent of "second requests" relative to the number of reportable transactions, the results are a bit surprising: Reagan (5.3%), G.H.W. Bush (3.7%), Obama (3.5%, through Sept. 30, 2016), Clinton (3.2%), and G.W. Bush (3.1%). In terms of the percentage of reportable transactions the agencies actually *challenged*, the results are as follows: Obama (2.9% through Sept. 30, 2015), G.W. Bush (2.0%), Clinton (1.7%), G.H.W. Bush (1.2%) and Reagan (1.1%).

The first year of President Donald Trump's presidency saw the agencies pass on challenging the $13.7 billion merger between Amazon.com Inc. and Whole Foods Market, Inc. However, in late 2017 the agencies challenged the $84.5 billion merger between AT&T and Time Warner, a surprise move given that the two companies did not compete directly against one another (the merger would be a vertical merger). Ultimately, therefore, it is tough to generalize on antitrust enforcement and politics: "Political rhetoric about levels of antitrust enforcement [is] . . . unlikely to tell us much about a particular administration's seriousness about competition policy . . . ." *Concurrences* at 9.

[5] The case law on the Clayton Act analyzes mergers in three categories: horizontal (between competitors), vertical (between suppliers and those they supply), and conglomerate (between firms in unrelated markets). The law is the most developed on horizontal mergers, has recently reversed field on vertical mergers, and is uncertain when applied to conglomerates.

The law covering vertical mergers has undergone considerable change in recent years. Recently both courts and the DOJ have reversed field and questioned the fundamental notion that vertical mergers are in fact anticompetitive. Several courts have highlighted the potential efficiency gains from a vertical combination and have rejected the idea that an acquisition by a supplier of an outlet for its products, foreclosing the supplier's competitors from a segment of the market, necessarily leads to increased market power. The DOJ's 1982 guidelines that still govern vertical mergers state that the DOJ is unlikely to challenge a vertical merger unless the relevant market is highly concentrated (an Herfindahl-Hirschman Index ("HHI") of over 1,000 (see *infra* note 9 and accompanying text for HHI description)). Under the Clinton Administration, the DOJ challenged three vertical mergers in telecommunications but withdrew all three challenges when the parties modified their deals to address the Department's concerns.

Prosecutions of conglomerate mergers are rare, perhaps because such mergers are no longer fashionable and because of the implicit recognition that the legal case against them has always been thin. The DOJ does not even mention conglomerate mergers in any of its prosecution guidelines.

The prosecution of horizontal mergers under the guidelines excerpted in the text remains the most important part of the Clayton Act enforcement program.

acquisitions involving actual or potential competitors ("horizontal mergers") under the federal antitrust laws.[1] The relevant statutory provisions include Section 7 of the Clayton Act, 15 U.S.C.A. § 18, Sections 1 and 2 of the Sherman Act, 15 U.S.C.A. §§ 1, 2, and Section 5 of the Federal Trade Commission Act, 15 U.S.C.A. § 45. Most particularly, Section 7 of the Clayton Act prohibits mergers if "in any line of commerce or in any activity affecting commerce in any section of the country, the effect of such acquisition may be substantially to lessen competition, or to tend to create a monopoly."

* * *

These Guidelines describe the principal analytical techniques and the main types of evidence on which the Agencies usually rely to predict whether a horizontal merger may substantially lessen competition. They are not intended to describe how the Agencies analyze cases other than horizontal mergers. These Guidelines are intended to assist the business community and antitrust practitioners by increasing the transparency of the analytical process underlying the Agencies' enforcement decisions. They may also assist the courts in developing an appropriate framework for interpreting and applying the antitrust laws in the horizontal merger context.

These Guidelines should be read with the awareness that merger analysis does not consist of uniform application of a single methodology. Rather, it is a fact-specific process through which the Agencies, guided by their extensive experience, apply a range of analytical tools to the reasonably available and reliable evidence to evaluate competitive concerns in a limited period of time. . . .

The unifying theme of these Guidelines is that mergers should not be permitted to create, enhance, or entrench market power or to facilitate its exercise. For simplicity of exposition, these Guidelines generally refer to all of these effects as enhancing market power. A merger enhances market power if it is likely to encourage one or more firms to raise price, reduce output, diminish innovation, or otherwise harm customers as a result of diminished competitive constraints or incentives. In evaluating how a merger will likely change a firm's behavior, the Agencies focus primarily on how the merger affects conduct that would be most profitable for the firm.

A merger can enhance market power simply by eliminating competition between the merging parties. This effect can arise even if the

---

[1] These Guidelines replace the Horizontal Merger Guidelines issued in 1992, revised in 1997. They reflect the ongoing accumulation of experience at the Agencies. The Commentary on the Horizontal Merger Guidelines issued by the Agencies in 2006 remains a valuable supplement to these Guidelines. These Guidelines may be revised from time to time as necessary to reflect significant changes in enforcement policy, to clarify existing policy, or to reflect new learning. These Guidelines do not cover vertical or other types of non-horizontal acquisitions.

merger causes no changes in the way other firms behave. Adverse competitive effects arising in this manner are referred to as "unilateral effects." A merger also can enhance market power by increasing the risk of coordinated, accommodating, or interdependent behavior among rivals. Adverse competitive effects arising in this manner are referred to as "coordinated effects." In any given case, either or both types of effects may be present, and the distinction between them may be blurred.

These Guidelines principally describe how the Agencies analyze mergers between rival suppliers that may enhance their market power as sellers. Enhancement of market power by sellers often elevates the prices charged to customers. For simplicity of exposition, these Guidelines generally discuss the analysis in terms of such price effects. Enhanced market power can also be manifested in non-price terms and conditions that adversely affect customers, including reduced product quality, reduced product variety, reduced service, or diminished innovation. Such non-price effects may coexist with price effects, or can arise in their absence. When the Agencies investigate whether a merger may lead to a substantial lessening of non-price competition, they employ an approach analogous to that used to evaluate price competition. Enhanced market power may also make it more likely that the merged entity can profitably and effectively engage in exclusionary conduct. Regardless of how enhanced market power likely would be manifested, the Agencies normally evaluate mergers based on their impact on customers. The Agencies examine effects on either or both of the direct customers and the final consumers. The Agencies presume, absent convincing evidence to the contrary, that adverse effects on direct customers also cause adverse effects on final consumers.

Enhancement of market power by buyers, sometimes called "monopsony power," has adverse effects comparable to enhancement of market power by sellers. The Agencies employ an analogous framework to analyze mergers between rival purchasers that may enhance their market power as buyers.

* * *

4. Market Definition

When the Agencies identify a potential competitive concern with a horizontal merger, market definition plays two roles. First, market definition helps specify the line of commerce and section of the country in which the competitive concern arises. In any merger enforcement action, the Agencies will normally identify one or more relevant markets in which the merger may substantially lessen competition. Second, market definition allows the Agencies to identify market participants and measure market shares and market concentration. The measurement of market shares and market concentration is not an end in itself, but is useful to the extent it illuminates the merger's likely competitive effects.

* * *

5. Market Participants, Market Shares, and Market Concentration

The Agencies normally consider measures of market shares and market concentration as part of their evaluation of competitive effects. . . .

* * *

5.2 Market Shares

The Agencies normally calculate market shares for all firms that currently produce products in the relevant market, subject to the availability of data. The Agencies also calculate market shares for other market participants if this can be done to reliably reflect their competitive significance.

* * *

5.3 Market Concentration

Market concentration is often one useful indicator of likely competitive effects of a merger. In evaluating market concentration, the Agencies consider both the post-merger level of market concentration and the change in concentration resulting from a merger. Market shares may not fully reflect the competitive significance of firms in the market or the impact of a merger. They are used in conjunction with other evidence of competitive effects. . . .

* * *

The Agencies often calculate the Herfindahl-Hirschman Index ("HHI") of market concentration. The HHI is calculated by summing the squares of the individual firms' market shares,[9] and thus gives proportionately greater weight to the larger market shares. When using the HHI, the Agencies consider both the post-merger level of the HHI and the increase in the HHI resulting from the merger. The increase in the HHI is equal to twice the product of the market shares of the merging firms.[10]

Based on their experience, the Agencies generally classify markets into three types:

---

[9] For example, a market consisting of four firms with market shares of thirty percent, thirty percent, twenty percent, and twenty percent has an HHI of 2600 ($30^2 + 30^2 + 20^2 + 20^2 = 2600$). The HHI ranges from 10,000 (in the case of a pure monopoly) to a number approaching zero (in the case of an atomistic market). Although it is desirable to include all firms in the calculation, lack of information about firms with small shares is not critical because such firms do not affect the HHI significantly.

[10] For example, the merger of firms with shares of five percent and ten percent of the market would increase the HHI by 100 ($5 \times 10 \times 2 = 100$).

- Unconcentrated Markets: HHI below 1500
- Moderately Concentrated Markets: HHI between 1500 and 2500
- Highly Concentrated Markets: HHI above 2500

The Agencies employ the following general standards for the relevant markets they have defined:

- *Small Change in Concentration.* Mergers involving an increase in the HHI of less than 100 points are unlikely to have adverse competitive effects and ordinarily require no further analysis.
- *Unconcentrated Markets.* Mergers resulting in unconcentrated markets are unlikely to have adverse competitive effects and ordinarily require no further analysis.
- *Moderately Concentrated Markets.* Mergers resulting in moderately concentrated markets that involve an increase in the HHI of more than 100 points potentially raise significant competitive concerns and often warrant scrutiny.
- *Highly Concentrated Markets.* Mergers resulting in highly concentrated markets that involve an increase in the HHI of between 100 points and 200 points potentially raise significant competitive concerns and often warrant scrutiny. Mergers resulting in highly concentrated markets that involve an increase in the HHI of more than 200 points will be presumed to be likely to enhance market power. The presumption may be rebutted by persuasive evidence showing that the merger is unlikely to enhance market power.

The purpose of these thresholds is not to provide a rigid screen to separate competitively benign mergers from anticompetitive ones, although high levels of concentration do raise concerns. Rather, they provide one way to identify some mergers unlikely to raise competitive concerns and some others for which it is particularly important to examine whether other competitive factors confirm, reinforce, or counteract the potentially harmful effects of increased concentration. The higher the post-merger HHI and the increase in the HHI, the greater are the Agencies' potential competitive concerns and the greater is the likelihood that the Agencies will request additional information to conduct their analysis.

* * *

10. Efficiencies

Competition usually spurs firms to achieve efficiencies internally. Nevertheless, a primary benefit of mergers to the economy is their potential to generate significant efficiencies and thus enhance the merged firm's ability and incentive to compete, which may result in lower prices, improved quality, enhanced service, or new products. For example, merger-generated efficiencies may enhance competition by permitting two ineffective competitors to form a more effective competitor, e.g., by combining complementary assets. In a unilateral effects context, incremental cost reductions may reduce or reverse any increases in the merged firm's incentive to elevate price. Efficiencies also may lead to new or improved products, even if they do not immediately and directly affect price. . . .

The Agencies credit only those efficiencies likely to be accomplished with the proposed merger and unlikely to be accomplished in the absence of either the proposed merger or another means having comparable anticompetitive effects. These are termed merger-specific efficiencies. . . .

* * *

The Agencies will not challenge a merger if cognizable efficiencies are of a character and magnitude such that the merger is not likely to be anticompetitive in any relevant market. . . .

In the Agencies' experience, efficiencies are most likely to make a difference in merger analysis when the likely adverse competitive effects, absent the efficiencies, are not great. Efficiencies almost never justify a merger to monopoly or near-monopoly. . . .

* * *

11. Failure and Exiting Assets

Notwithstanding the analysis above, a merger is not likely to enhance market power if imminent failure, as defined below, of one of the merging firms would cause the assets of that firm to exit the relevant market. This is an extreme instance of the more general circumstance in which the competitive significance of one of the merging firms is declining: the projected market share and significance of the exiting firm is zero. If the relevant assets would otherwise exit the market, customers are not worse off after the merger than they would have been had the merger been enjoined.

The Agencies do not normally credit claims that the assets of the failing firm would exit the relevant market unless all of the following circumstances are met: (1) the allegedly failing firm would be unable to meet its financial obligations in the near future; (2) it would not be able to reorganize successfully under Chapter 11 of the Bankruptcy Act; and (3) it has made unsuccessful good-faith efforts to elicit reasonable alternative offers that would keep its tangible and intangible assets in the relevant market and pose a less severe danger to competition than does the proposed merger.

Similarly, a merger is unlikely to cause competitive harm if the risks to competition arise from the acquisition of a failing division. The Agencies do not normally credit claims that the assets of a division would exit the relevant market in the near future unless both of the following conditions are met: (1) applying cost allocation rules that reflect true economic costs, the division has a persistently negative cash flow on an operating basis, and such negative cash flow is not economically justified for the firm by benefits such as added sales in complementary markets or enhanced customer goodwill; and (2) the owner of the failing division has made unsuccessful good-faith efforts to elicit reasonable alternative offers that would keep its tangible and intangible assets in the relevant market and pose a less severe danger to competition than does the proposed acquisition.

* * *

QUESTIONS

How do personnel in the Department of Justice acquire the general expertise and deal-specific information to make sound, sensible decisions on "efficiencies"? Who should control the agency's decision, lawyers or economists?

MIDWESTERN MACHINERY, INC. V. NORTHWEST AIRLINES, INC.

United States Court of Appeals, Eighth Circuit, 1999.
167 F.3d 439.

BEAM, CIRCUIT JUDGE.

* * *

In January 1986, Northwest Airlines (Northwest) reached an agreement with Republic Airlines (Republic) whereby the two airlines would merge. At the time of merger, Northwest and Republic were respectively the nation's eighth and ninth largest airlines and the two largest operators at the Minneapolis-St. Paul International Airport. The merger was approved by the Department of Transportation, the reviewing agency at the time, but no antitrust immunity was granted for the transaction. After the merger was completed in August 1986, all of Republic's stock was turned in and extinguished, and Republic ceased to exist as a separate entity.

The plaintiffs, . . . all frequent travelers on Northwest since the merger, brought this action in June 1997, alleging a violation of section seven of the Clayton Act (hereinafter section seven). 15 U.S.C. § 18. . . .

* * *

Northwest argues, consistent with the district court opinion, that when the two airlines became fully merged, no section seven claim is possible since all of Republic's stock is turned in and extinguished. In essence, Northwest argues that no Republic stock or assets are left to substantially lessen competition. We hold that a section seven cause of action can exist even though a merger occurs and two corporations effectively become one. . . .

. . . We are guided by the plain language of section seven of the Clayton Act which prohibits acquisitions of the "*whole or any part* of the stock" or assets of a company, where the effect may be to substantially lessen competition or tend to create a monopoly. 15 U.S.C. § 18 (emphasis added). The language of section seven expressly provides for a claim even when all ("whole") of the stock or assets are acquired. The existence of a section seven claim does not rise or fall with the percentage of the corporation acquired—whether it be a merger of all or acquisition of only part. . . . Thus, although the merger of Republic and Northwest resulted in the acquisition of all of Republic's stock and assets, it did not cut-off a section seven claim.

As noted, after the merger was completed, Republic's stock was turned in and extinguished. Northwest views this action as significant for purposes of section seven. If extinguishing stock eliminated section seven claims, corporations could seek to use this approach as an antitrust shelter and the speed at which it is accomplished would control the existence of a claim. The plain language of section seven does not support such a result. The district court's concern that it could not "conceive" of how Republic's stock or assets could be used to substantially lessen competition and thereby violate section seven centers around the fact that the two corporate entities are no longer distinct, and therefore the use of Republic's stock or assets is unclear and difficult to trace. However, this is a matter for discovery, proof, summary judgment or trial and not a matter for decision on a motion to dismiss. Midwestern's complaint should not be dismissed simply because Northwest acquired all of the assets of Republic and then Republic's stock was turned in and extinguished.

* * *

F.T.C. v. WHOLE FOODS MARKET, INC.

United States Court of Appeals, District of Columbia Circuit, 2008.
548 F.3d 1028.

BROWN, CIRCUIT JUDGE.

The FTC sought a preliminary injunction, under 15 U.S.C. § 53(b), to block the merger of Whole Foods and Wild Oats. It appeals the district court's denial of the injunction. I conclude the district court should be reversed, though I do so reluctantly, admiring the thoughtful opinion the district court produced under trying circumstances in which the defendants were rushing to a financing deadline and the FTC presented, at best, poorly explained evidence. . . .

Whole Foods Market, Inc. ("Whole Foods") and Wild Oats Markets, Inc. ("Wild Oats") operate 194 and 110 grocery stores, respectively, primarily in the United States. In February 2007, they announced that Whole Foods would acquire Wild Oats in a transaction closing before August 31, 2007. They notified the FTC, as the Hart-Scott-Rodino Act required for the $565 million merger, and the FTC investigated the merger through a series of hearings and document requests. On June 6, 2007, the FTC sought a temporary restraining order and preliminary injunction to block the merger temporarily while the FTC conducted an administrative proceeding to decide whether to block it permanently under § 7 of the Clayton Act. . . .

The FTC contended Whole Foods and Wild Oats are the two largest operators of what it called premium, natural, and organic supermarkets ("PNOS"). Such stores "focus on high-quality perishables, specialty and natural organic produce, prepared foods, meat, fish[,] and bakery goods; generally have high levels of customer services; generally target affluent and well educated customers [and] . . . are mission driven with an emphasis on social and environmental responsibility." . . . In eighteen cities, asserted the FTC, the merger would create monopolies because Whole Foods and Wild Oats are the only PNOS. To support this claim, the FTC relied on emails Whole Foods's CEO John Mackey sent to other Whole Foods executives and directors, suggesting the purpose of the merger was to eliminate a competitor. In addition the FTC produced pseudonymous blog postings in which Mr. Mackey touted Whole Foods and denigrated other supermarkets as unable to compete. The FTC's expert economist, Dr. Kevin Murphy, analyzed sales data from the companies to show how entry by various supermarkets into a local market affected sales at a Whole Foods or Wild Oats store.

On the other hand, the defendants' expert, Dr. David Scheffman, focused on whether a hypothetical monopolist owning both Whole Foods and Wild Oats would actually have power over a distinct market. He used various third-party market studies to predict that such an owner could not raise prices without driving customers to other supermarkets. In addition, deposition testimony from other supermarkets indicated they regarded Whole Foods and Wild Oats as critical competition. Internal documents from the two defendants reflected their extensive monitoring of other supermarkets' prices as well as each other's.

* * *

In this case, however, the FTC itself made market definition key. It claimed "[t]he operation of premium natural and organic supermarkets is a distinct 'line of commerce' within the meaning of Section 7," and its theory of anticompetitive effect was that the merger would "substantially increase concentration in the operation of [PNOS]." . . .

Thus, the FTC assumed the burden of raising some question of whether PNOS is a well-defined market. As the FTC presented its case, success turned on whether there exist core customers, committed to PNOS, for whom one should consider PNOS a relevant market. The district court assumed "the 'marginal' consumer, not the so-called 'core' or 'committed' consumer, must be the focus of any antitrust analysis." . . . To the contrary, core consumers can, in appropriate circumstances, be worthy of antitrust protection. *See* Horizontal Merger Guidelines § 1.12, 57 Fed.Reg. at 41,555 (explaining the possibility of price discrimination for "targeted buyers"). The district court's error of law led it to ignore FTC evidence that strongly suggested Whole Foods and Wild Oats compete for core consumers within a PNOS market, even if they also compete on individual products for marginal consumers in the broader market. . . .

A market "must include all products reasonably interchangeable by consumers for the same purposes." . . . Whether one product is reasonably interchangeable for another depends not only on the ease and speed with which customers can substitute it and the desirability of doing so, . . . but also on the cost of substitution, which depends most sensitively on the price of the products. A broad market may also contain relevant submarkets which themselves "constitute product markets for antitrust purposes." . . . "The boundaries of such a submarket may be determined by examining such practical indicia as industry or public recognition of the submarket as a separate economic entity, the product's peculiar characteristics and uses, unique production facilities, distinct customers, distinct prices, sensitivity to price changes, and specialized vendors." . . .

To facilitate this analysis, the Department of Justice and the FTC developed a technique called the SSNIP ("small but significant non-transitory increase in price") test, which both Dr. Murphy and Dr. Scheffman used. In the SSNIP method, one asks whether a hypothetical monopolist controlling all suppliers in the proposed market could profit from a small price increase. Horizontal Merger Guidelines § 1.11, 57 Fed.Reg. at 41,560–61. If a small price increase would drive consumers to an alternative product, then that product must be reasonably substitutable for those in the proposed market and must therefore be part of the market, properly defined. . . .

Experts for the two sides disagreed about how to do the SSNIP of the proposed PNOS market. Dr. Scheffman used a method called critical loss analysis, in which he predicted the loss that would result when marginal customers shifted purchases to conventional supermarkets in response to a SSNIP. . . . He concluded a hypothetical monopolist could not profit from a SSNIP, so that conventional supermarkets must be within the same market as PNOS. In contrast, Dr. Murphy disapproved of critical loss analysis generally, preferring a method called critical diversion that asked how many customers would be diverted to Whole Foods and how many to conventional supermarkets if a nearby Wild Oats closed. Whole Foods's internal planning documents indicated at least a majority of these customers would switch to Whole Foods, thus making the closure profitable for a hypothetical PNOS monopolist. One crucial difference between these approaches was that Dr. Scheffman's analysis depended only on the *marginal* loss of sales, while Dr. Murphy's used the *average* loss of customers. Dr. Murphy explained that focusing on the average behavior of customers was appropriate because a core of committed customers would continue to shop at PNOS stores despite a SSNIP.

In appropriate circumstances, core customers can be a proper subject of antitrust concern. In particular, when one or a few firms differentiate themselves by offering a particular package of goods or services, it is quite possible for there to be a central group of customers for whom "only [that package] will do." *United States v. Grinnell Corp.,* 384 U.S. 563, 574, 86 S.Ct. 1698, 16 L.Ed.2d 778 (1966); see also *United States v. Phillipsburg Nat'l Bank & Trust Co.,* 399 U.S. 350, 360, 90 S.Ct. 2035, 26 L.Ed.2d 658 (1970) ("[I]t is the *cluster* of products and services . . . that as a matter of trade reality makes commercial banking a distinct" market.). What motivates antitrust concern for such customers is the possibility that "fringe competition" for individual products within a package may not protect customers who need the whole package from market power exercised by a sole supplier of the package. . . .

Such customers may be captive to the sole supplier, which can then, by means of price discrimination, extract monopoly profits from them while competing for the business of marginal customers. . . . Not that prices that segregate core from marginal consumers are in themselves anticompetitive; such pricing simply indicates the existence of a submarket of core customers, operating in parallel with the broader market but featuring a different demand curve. . . . Sometimes, for some customers a package provides "access to certain products or services that would otherwise be unavailable to them." . . . Because the core customers require the whole package, they respond differently to price increases from marginal customers who may obtain portions of the package elsewhere. Of course, core customers may constitute a submarket even without such an extreme difference in demand elasticity. After all, market definition focuses on what products are *reasonably* substitutable; what is reasonable must ultimately be determined by "settled consumer preference." . . .

In short, a core group of particularly dedicated, "distinct customers," paying "distinct prices," may constitute a recognizable submarket, . . . whether they are dedicated because they need a complete "cluster of products," . . . because their particular circumstances dictate that a product "is the only realistic choice," . . . or because they find a particular product "uniquely attractive[.]" For example, the existence of core customers dedicated to office supply superstores, with their "unique combination of size, selection, depth[,] and breadth of inventory," was an important factor distinguishing that submarket. . . . As always in defining a market, we must "take into account the realities of competition." . . .

The FTC's evidence delineated a PNOS submarket catering to a core group of customers who "have decided that natural and organic is important, lifestyle of health and ecological sustainability is important." . . . It was undisputed that Whole Foods and Wild Oats provide higher levels of customer service than conventional supermarkets, a "unique environment," and a particular focus on the "core values" these customers espoused. . . . The FTC connected these intangible properties with concrete aspects of the PNOS model, such as a much larger selection of natural and organic products, . . . and a much greater concentration of perishables than conventional supermarkets . . . .

Further, the FTC documented exactly the kind of price discrimination that enables a firm to profit from core customers for whom it is the sole supplier. Dr. Murphy compared the margins of Whole Foods stores in cities where they competed with Wild Oats. He found the presence of a Wild Oats depressed Whole Foods's margins significantly. Notably, while there was no effect on Whole Foods's margins in the product category of "groceries," where Whole Foods and Wild Oats compete on the margins with conventional supermarkets, the effect on margins for perishables was substantial. Confirming this price discrimination, Whole Foods's documents indicated that when it price-checked conventional supermarkets, the focus was overwhelmingly on "dry grocery," rather than on the perishables that were 70% of Whole Foods's business. Thus, in the high-quality perishables on which both Whole Foods and Wild Oats made most of their money, they competed directly with each other, and they competed with supermarkets only on the dry grocery items that were the fringes of their business.

Additionally, the FTC provided direct evidence that PNOS competition had a greater effect than conventional supermarkets on PNOS prices. Dr. Murphy showed the opening of a new Whole Foods in the vicinity of a Wild Oats caused Wild Oats's prices to drop, while entry by non-PNOS stores had no such effect. Similarly, the opening of Earth Fare stores (another PNOS) near Whole Foods stores caused Whole Foods's prices to drop immediately. The price effect continued, while decreasing, until the Earth Fare stores were forced to close.

Finally, evidence of consumer behavior supported the conclusion that PNOS serve a core consumer base. Whole Foods's internal projections, based on market experience, suggested that if a Wild Oats near a Whole Foods were to close, the majority (in some cases nearly all) of its customers would switch to the Whole Foods rather than to conventional supermarkets. Since Whole Foods's prices for perishables are higher than those of conventional supermarkets, such customers must not find shopping at the latter interchangeable with PNOS shopping. They are the core customers. Moreover, market research, including Dr. Scheffman's own studies, indicated 68% of Whole Foods customers are core customers who share the Whole Foods "core values." . . .

Against this conclusion the defendants posed evidence that customers "cross-shop" between PNOS and other stores and that Whole Foods and Wild Oats check the prices of conventional supermarkets. . . . But the fact that PNOS and ordinary supermarkets "are direct competitors in some submarkets . . . is not the end of the inquiry[.]" . . . Of course customers cross-shop; PNOS carry comprehensive inventories. The fact that a customer might buy a stick of gum at a supermarket or at a convenience store does not mean there is no definable groceries market. Here, cross-shopping is entirely consistent with the existence of a core group of PNOS customers. Indeed, Dr. Murphy explained that Whole Foods competes actively with conventional supermarkets for dry groceries sales, even though it ignores their prices for high-quality perishables.

* * *

In sum, the district court believed the antitrust laws are addressed only to marginal consumers. This was an error of law, because in some situations core consumers, demanding exclusively a particular product or package of products, distinguish a submarket. The FTC described the core PNOS customers, explained how PNOS cater to these customers, and showed these customers provided the bulk of PNOS's business. The FTC put forward economic evidence—which the district court ignored—showing directly how PNOS discriminate on price between their core and marginal customers, thus treating the former as a distinct market. Therefore, I cannot agree with the district court that the FTC would never be able to prove a PNOS submarket. This is not to say the FTC has in fact proved such a market, which is not necessary at this point. To obtain a preliminary injunction under § 53(b), the FTC need only show a likelihood of success sufficient, using the sliding scale, to balance any equities that might weigh against the injunction. . . .

* * *

TATEL, CIRCUIT JUDGE, concurring in the judgment.

. . . Specifically, I believe the district court overlooked or mistakenly rejected evidence supporting the FTC's view that Whole Foods and Wild Oats occupy a separate market of "premium natural and organic supermarkets."

* * *

I agree with the district court that this " 'case hinges'—almost entirely—'on the proper definition of the relevant product market,' " for if a separate natural and organic market exists, "there can be little doubt that the acquisition of the second largest firm in the market by the largest firm in the market will tend to harm competition in that market." . . . But I respectfully part ways with the district court when it comes to assessing the FTC's evidence in support of its contention that Whole Foods and Wild Oats occupy a distinct market. As the Supreme Court explained in *Brown Shoe Co. v. United States:* "The outer boundaries of a product market are determined by the reasonable interchangeability of use or the cross-elasticity of demand between the product itself and substitutes for it." 370 U.S. at 325, 82 S.Ct. 1502. In this case the FTC presented a great deal of credible evidence—either unmentioned or rejected by the district court—suggesting that Whole Foods and Wild Oats are not "reasonabl[y] interchangeab[le]" with conventional supermarkets and do not compete directly with them.

To begin with, the FTC's expert prepared a study showing that when a Whole Foods opened near an existing Wild Oats, it reduced sales at the Wild Oats store dramatically. . . . By contrast, when a conventional supermarket opened near a Wild Oats store, Wild Oats's sales were virtually unaffected. . . . This strongly suggests that although Wild Oats customers consider Whole Foods an adequate substitute, they do not feel the same way about conventional supermarkets. . . .

The FTC also highlighted Whole Foods's own study-called "Project Goldmine"—showing what Wild Oats customers would likely do after the proposed merger in cities where Whole Foods planned to close Wild Oats stores. According to the study, the average Whole Foods store would capture most of the revenue from the closed Wild Oats store, even though virtually every city contained multiple conventional retailers closer to the shuttered Wild Oats store. . . . This high diversion ratio further suggests that many consumers consider conventional supermarkets inadequate substitutes for Wild Oats and Whole Foods. . . .

Several industry studies predating the merger also suggest that Whole Foods and Wild Oats never truly competed with conventional supermarkets. . . . In addition, Wild Oats's former CEO, Perry Odak, explained in a deposition why conventional stores have difficulty competing with Whole Foods and Wild Oats: if conventional stores offer a lot of organic products, they don't sell enough to their existing customer base, leaving the stores with spoiled products and reduced profits. But if conventional stores offer only a narrow range of organic products, customers with a high demand for organic items refuse to shop there. Thus, "the conventionals have a very difficult time getting into this business." . . .

In addition to all this direct evidence that Whole Foods and Wild Oats occupy a separate market from conventional supermarkets, the FTC presented an enormous amount of evidence of "industry or public recognition" of the natural and organic market "as a separate economic entity"—one of the "practical indicia" the Supreme Court has said can be used to determine the boundaries of a distinct market. . . . For example, dozens of record studies about the grocery store industry—including many prepared for Whole Foods or Wild Oats—distinguish between "traditional" or "conventional" grocery stores on the one hand and "natural food" or "organic" stores on the other. . . . Moreover, record evidence indicates that the Whole Foods and Wild Oats CEOs both believed that their companies occupied a market separate from the conventional grocery store industry. . . . As Judge Bork explained, this evidence of " 'industry or public recognition of the submarket as a separate economic' unit matters because we assume that economic actors usually have accurate perceptions of economic realities." . . .

The FTC also presented strong evidence that Whole Foods and Wild Oats have "peculiar characteristics" distinguishing them from traditional supermarkets, another of the "practical indicia" the Supreme Court has said can be used to determine the boundaries of a distinct market. . . . Most important, unlike traditional grocery stores, both Whole Foods and Wild Oats carry only natural or organic products. . . .

Insisting that all this evidence of a separate market is irrelevant, Whole Foods and the dissent argue that the FTC's case must fail because the record contains no evidence that Whole Foods or Wild Oats charged higher prices in cities where the other was absent—i.e., where one had a local monopoly on the asserted natural and organic market—than they did in cities where the other was present. This argument is both legally and factually incorrect.

As a legal matter, although evidence that a company charges more when other companies in the alleged market are absent certainly indicates that the companies operate in a distinct market, . . . that is not the *only* way to prove a separate market. . . . Furthermore, even if the FTC could *prove* a section 7 violation only by showing evidence of higher prices in areas where a company had a local monopoly in an alleged market, the FTC need not *prove* a section 7 violation to obtain a preliminary injunction; rather, it need only raise "serious, substantial" questions as to the merger's legality. . . . See [*Hosp. Corp. of Am. v. FTC,* 807 F.2d 1381, 1389 (7th Cir. 1986)] (stating that "[a]ll that is necessary" to prove a section 7 case "is that the merger create an appreciable danger of [higher prices] in the future"). . . . Moreover, the Merger Guidelines—which "are by no means to be considered binding on the court," . . . specify how the FTC decides which cases to bring, "*not* . . . how the Agency will conduct the litigation of cases that it decides to bring[.]" . . .

In any event, the FTC did present evidence indicating that Whole Foods and Wild Oats charged more when they were the only natural and organic supermarket present. The FTC's expert looked at prices Whole Foods charged in several of its North Carolina stores before and after entry of a regional natural food chain called Earth Fare. Before any Earth Fare stores opened, Whole Foods charged essentially the same prices at its five North Carolina stores, but when an Earth Fare opened near the Whole Foods in Chapel Hill, that store's prices dropped 5% below those at the other North Carolina Whole Foods. Prices at that store remained lower than at the other Whole Foods in North Carolina for nearly a year, until just before the Earth Fare closed. . . . Whole Foods followed essentially the same pattern when an Earth Fare opened near its stores in Raleigh and Durham—the company dropped prices at those stores but nowhere else in North Carolina. . . . The FTC's expert presented similar evidence regarding Whole Foods's impact on Wild Oats's prices, showing that a new Whole Foods store opening near a Wild Oats caused immediate and lasting reductions in prices at that Wild Oats store compared to prices at other Wild Oats stores. . . . In addition to this quantitative evidence, the FTC pointed to Whole Foods CEO John Mackey's statement explaining to the company's board why the merger made sense: "By buying [Wild Oats] we will . . . avoid nasty price wars in [several cities where both companies have stores]." . . .

The dissent raises two primary arguments against this pricing evidence. First, it relies on a study by Whole Foods's expert to conclude that Whole Foods's prices remain steady regardless of the presence or absence of a nearby Wild Oats, calling this "all-but-dispositive price evidence." . . . In fact, this study is all-but-meaningless price evidence because it examined Whole Foods's pricing on a single day several months *after* the company announced its intent to acquire Wild Oats; this gave the company every incentive to eliminate any price differences that may have previously existed between its stores based on the presence of a nearby Wild Oats, not only to avoid antitrust liability, but also because the company was no longer competing with Wild Oats. . . .

* * *

KAVENAUGH, CIRCUIT JUDGE, dissenting.

The Federal Trade Commission has sought a preliminary injunction to block the Whole Foods-Wild Oats merger as anticompetitive under § 7 of the Clayton Act. As in many antitrust cases, the analysis comes down to one issue: market definition. Is the relevant product market here *all* supermarkets? Or is the relevant product market here only so-called "organic supermarkets"? If the former, as Whole Foods argues, the Whole Foods-Wild Oats merger would be lawful because it would not lessen competition in the broad market of all supermarkets: Whole Foods and Wild Oats together operate about 300 of the approximately 34,000 supermarkets in the United States. If the latter, as the FTC contends, the merger may be unlawful: Whole Foods and Wild Oats are the only significant competitors in the alleged organic-store market and their merger would substantially lessen competition in such a narrowly defined market.

More than a year ago, after a lengthy evidentiary hearing and in an exhaustive and careful opinion, the District Court found that the record evidence overwhelmingly supports the following conclusions: Whole Foods competes against all supermarkets and not just so-called organic stores; the relevant market for evaluating this merger for antitrust purposes is all supermarkets; and the merger of Whole Foods and Wild Oats would not substantially lessen competition in a market that includes all supermarkets. The court therefore denied the FTC's motion for a preliminary injunction.

Also more than a year ago, a three-judge panel of this Court unanimously denied the FTC's request for an injunction pending appeal, thereby allowing the Whole Foods-Wild Oats deal to close. Since then, the merged entity has shut down, sold, or converted numerous Wild Oats stores and otherwise effectuated the merger through many changes in supplier contracts, leases, distribution, and the like.

The Court's splintered decision in this case seeks to unring the bell. In my judgment, this Court got it right a year ago in refusing to enjoin the merger, and there is no basis for a changed result now. Both a year ago and now, the same central question has been before the Court in determining whether to approve an injunction: whether the FTC demonstrated the necessary "likelihood of success" on its § 7 case. A year ago, the Court said no. Now, the Court says yes. The now-merged entity, the industry, and consumers no doubt will be confused by this apparent judicial about-face.

* * *

By seeking to block a merger without a sufficient showing that so-called organic stores constitute a separate product market and that the merged entity could impose a significant and nontransitory price increase, the FTC's position—which Judge Brown and Judge Tatel largely accept—calls to mind the bad old days when mergers were viewed with suspicion regardless of their economic benefits. . . . I would not turn back the clock. I agree with and would affirm the District Court's excellent decision denying the FTC's motion to enjoin the merger of Whole Foods and Wild Oats. . . .

Section 7 of the Clayton Act prohibits mergers "where in any line of commerce or in any activity affecting commerce in any section of the country, the effect of such acquisition may be substantially to lessen competition, or to tend to create a monopoly." . . . The Horizontal Merger Guidelines jointly promulgated by two Executive Branch agencies (the Department of Justice and the FTC) implement that statutory directive and recognize that the key initial step in the analysis is proper product-market definition. . . . Proper product-market analysis focuses on products' interchangeability of use or cross-elasticity of demand. A product "market can be seen as the array of producers of substitute products that could control price if united in a hypothetical cartel or as a hypothetical monopoly." . . . In the merger context, the inquiry therefore comes down to whether the merged entity could profitably impose a "small but significant and nontransitory increase in price" typically defined as five percent or more. If the merged entity could profitably impose at least a five percent price increase (because the price increase would not cause a sufficient number of consumers to switch to substitutes outside of the alleged product market), then there is a distinct product market and the proposed merger likely would substantially lessen competition in that market, in violation of § 7 of the Clayton Act.

* * *

Consistent with the statute, the Executive Branch's Merger Guidelines, and Judge Hogan's convincing opinion in *Staples*, the District Court here carefully analyzed the economics of supermarkets, including so-called organic supermarkets. The court considered whether Whole Foods charged higher prices in areas without Wild Oats than in areas with Wild Oats. After an evidentiary hearing and based on a painstaking review of the evidence in the record, the court concluded that "Whole Foods prices are essentially the same at all of its stores in a region, regardless of whether there is a Wild Oats store nearby." . . . That factual conclusion was supported by substantial evidence offered by Dr. Scheffman, Whole Foods's expert, and by the lack of any credible evidence to the contrary.

Dr. Scheffman analyzed Whole Foods's actual prices across stores and concluded that "there is no evidence that [Whole Foods'] and [Wild Oats'] price[s] [are] higher" where they face no competition from so-called organic supermarkets compared with where they do face such competition. . . . At a regional level, his studies revealed that only a "very small percentage" of products vary in price within a region, indicating that "prices are set across broad geographic areas." . . . He also analyzed prices at the individual store level, examining how many products sold at a specific store have prices that differ from the most common price in the region. He found that "differences in prices across stores are generally very small (less than one half of one percent) and there is no systematic pattern as to the presence or absence of [organic-supermarket] competition." . . .

Moreover, the record evidence in this case does not show that Whole Foods changed its prices in any significant way in response to exit from an area by Wild Oats. In the four cases where Wild Oats exited and a Whole Foods store remained, there is no evidence in the record that Whole Foods then raised prices. Nor was there any evidence of price increases after Whole Foods took over two Wild Oats stores.

* * *

In the absence of any evidence in the record that Whole Foods was able to (or did) set higher prices when Wild Oats exited or was absent, the District Court correctly concluded that Whole Foods competes in a market composed of all supermarkets, meaning that "all supermarkets" is the relevant product market and that the Whole Foods-Wild Oats merger will not substantially lessen competition in that product market.

In addition to the all-but-dispositive price evidence,[2] the District Court identified other factors further demonstrating that the relevant market consists of all supermarkets.

The record shows that Whole Foods makes site selection decisions based on all supermarkets and checks prices against all supermarkets, not only so-called organic supermarkets. . . . The point here is simple: Whole Foods would not examine the locations of and price check conventional grocery stores if it were not a competitor of those stores. Whole Foods does not price check Sports Authority; Whole Foods does price check Safeway.

The record also demonstrates that conventional supermarkets and so-called organic supermarkets are aggressively competing to attract customers from one another. After reviewing a wide variety of industry information and trade journals, Dr. Scheffman concluded that " '[o]ther' supermarkets are competing vigorously for the purchases made by shoppers at [Whole Foods] and [Wild Oats]." . . . Whole Foods "recognizes the fact that it has to appeal to a significantly broader group of consumers than organic and natural focused consumers." . . . The record shows that Whole Foods has made progress: Most products that Whole Foods sells are not organic. Conversely, conventional supermarkets have shifted towards "emphasizing fresh, 'natural' and organic" products. . . . "[M]ost of the major chains and others are expanding into private label organic and natural products." . . .

So the dividing line between "organic" and conventional supermarkets has blurred. . . . This is an industry in transition, and Whole Foods has pioneered a product differentiation that in turn has caused other supermarket chains to update their offerings. These are not separate product markets; this is a market where all supermarkets including so-called organic supermarkets are clawing tooth and nail to differentiate themselves, beat the competition, and make money.

* * *

In the end, the FTC's case is weak and seems a relic of a bygone era when antitrust law was divorced from basic economic principles. The record does not show that Whole Foods priced differently based on the presence or absence of Wild Oats in the same area. The reason for that and

---

[2] Judge Tatel's opinion disparages the evidence about Whole Foods's prices, calling it "all-but-meaningless" and implicitly suggesting that Whole Foods manipulated its prices just for the expert study. . . . But Judge Tatel offers no evidence for that suggestion.

the conclusion that follows from that are the same: Whole Foods competes in an extraordinarily competitive market that includes all supermarkets, not just so-called organic supermarkets. The merged entity thus could not exercise market power such that it could profitably impose a significant and nontransitory price increase. Therefore, there is no sound legal basis to block this merger.

* * *

GINSBURG, CIRCUIT JUDGE, with whom CHIEF JUDGE SENTELLE joins, concurring in the denial of rehearing en banc:

I concur in the denial of rehearing en banc because, there being no opinion for the Court, that judgment sets no precedent beyond the precise facts of this case. . . .

Nearly two years following the FTC's vigorous dispute of Whole Food's acquisition of Wild Oats, the food fight was over. The FTC and Whole Foods settled the case, with Whole Foods agreeing to sell the Wild Oats and Alfalfa brands, thirteen functioning stores, and the leases and assets of another nineteen closed stores. Under the settlement Whole Foods turned the assets over to a neutral Divestiture Trustee, who had to keep the offers open for twelve months. At the end of the twelve months, the Trustee had sold only three stores and still held the brands.

In 2017, Whole Foods itself was acquired by Amazon.com Inc. in a $13.7 billion merger. The $42 per share price that Amazon paid represented a premium of about 27 percent above where Whole Foods' shares were trading pre-announcement. The deal, which closed on August 27, 2017, represented Amazon's largest acquisition to date. In the FTC's first major test during the presidency of Donald Trump, the FTC greenlighted the transaction despite the fact that President Trump had criticized Amazon.com in the recent past.[6] Bruce Hoffman, an acting director at the FTC, said in a statement that the agency looked at the "proposed acquisition to determine whether it substantially lessened competition." He added that the FTC "decided not to pursue this matter further." Amazon, through its purchase of Whole Foods, will have a 2 percent share of the $600 billion a year U.S. grocery market, while Walmart holds more than 20 percent and Kroger has 7 percent.

---

[6] In late 2017, however, in a surprise move the DOJ challenged the $84.5 billion merger between AT&T and Time Warner. The move was a surprise because the two companies did not compete directly against one another—the merger would be a vertical merger. Similar mergers had passed regulatory muster for the past four decades, most notably Comcast's merger with NBC in 2011 and Time Warner's merger with AOL in 2000.

QUESTIONS

1. Consider the disagreements among the four *Whole Foods* judges, three circuit court judges and a district court judge, on how to sift the evidence in the case under a Section 7 standard. Are law judges in general jurisdiction courts the best decision makers in such a case?

2. In light of the Amazon merger with Whole Foods, do you believe our antitrust laws are prepared to address the dynamic changes instituted by giants like Google, Facebook and Amazon? Why or why not?

The longest running antitrust battle (and perhaps saddest for the two companies involved) stems from the two ill-fated merger attempts between office products superstores Staples, Inc. and Office Depot, Inc. The first attempt—a proposed $4 billion merger between the two companies—occurred in 1997. The FTC sought to block the merger, arguing that the business combination would give the combined company near-monopoly pricing power. The FTC's argument was considered controversial in antitrust circles because the combined company would control only 6 to 8 percent of the overall office products market. Nevertheless, the FTC convinced the District Court of the D.C. Circuit to issue a preliminary injunction against the deal, effectively killing it. The Court accepted the FTC's argument that office supply superstores constitute a unique market segment and that allowing two of the three major competitors in the field to combine would permit the combined company, with more than 1,100 stores and $11 billion in annual sales, to raise prices with impunity. See *FTC v. Staples, Inc.*, 970 F. Supp. 1066 (D.D.C. 1997).

The two companies' most recent attempt to combine occurred in early 2015. They believed their new $6.3 billion merger proposal would pass antitrust scrutiny given how the market for their products had changed over the last two decades. In particular, they pointed to the increased competition they faced from Amazon.com Inc.'s "Amazon Business" venture. The Court, however, refused to buy into that argument.

F.T.C. V. STAPLES, INC.

United States District Court, District of Columbia, 2016.
190 F. Supp.3d 100.

EMMET G. SULLIVAN, UNITED STATES DISTRICT JUDGE.

I. Introduction

. . . Defendant Staples Inc. ("Staples") and Defendant Office Depot, Inc. ("Office Depot") (collectively "Defendants") argue they are like "penguins on a melting iceberg," struggling to survive in an increasingly digitized world and an office-supply industry soon to be revolutionized by new entrants like [Amazon.com Inc.'s] Amazon Business. . . . Charged with enforcing antitrust laws for the benefit of American consumers, the Federal

Trade Commission ("FTC") and its co-plaintiffs, the Commonwealth of Pennsylvania and the District of Columbia, commenced this action in an effort to block Defendants' proposed [$6.3 billion] merger and alleged that the merger would "eliminat[e] direct competition between Staples and Office Depot" resulting in "significant harm" to large businesses that purchase office supplies for their own use.... The survival of Staples' proposed acquisition of Office Depot hinges on two critical issues: (1) the reliability of Plaintiffs' market definition and market share analysis; and (2) the likelihood that the competition resulting from new market entrants like Amazon Business will be timely and sufficient to restore competition lost as a result of the merger.

* * *

This antitrust case involved an extraordinary amount of work. As a result of the . . . FTC's investigation and seven weeks of discovery, more than fifteen million pages of documents were produced, more than seventy depositions around the country were taken, and five expert reports were completed. . . .

At the conclusion of Plaintiffs' case, Defendants chose not to present any fact or expert witnesses, arguing that Plaintiffs failed to establish their *prima facie* case. . . .

* * *

II. Background

A. Overview

. . . Companies that purchase office supplies for their own use operate in what the industry refers to as the B-to-B space. B-to-B customers prefer to work with one vendor that can meet all of the companies' office supply needs. . . .

To establish a primary vendor relationship, companies in the B-to-B space request proposals from national suppliers like Staples and Office Depot. . . . The request for proposal ("RFP") process typically results in a multi-year contract with a primary vendor that guarantees prices for specific items, includes an upfront lump-sum rebate, and a host of other services. . . . Because the office supplies consumed by large companies are voluminous, such companies typically pay only half the price for basic supplies as compared to the average retail consumer. . . .

B. Defendants Staples and Office Depot

Established as big-box retail stores in the 1980s, Defendants are the primary B-to-B office supply vendors in the United States today. . . . Plaintiffs allege that Defendants sell and distribute upwards of seventy-nine percent of office supplies in the B-to-B space. . . . Since the 2013 merger of Office Depot and Office Max, Defendants consistently engage in head-to-head competition with each other for B-to-B contracts. . . .

* * *

Staples' "commercial" and Office Depot's "business solutions" segments focus on the B-to-B contracts at issue in this case. While both companies serve businesses of all sizes, this case focuses on large B-to-B customers, defined by Plaintiffs as those that spend $500,000 or more per year on office supplies. . . . Approximately 1200 corporations in the United States are included in this alleged relevant market. . . . .

* * *

Regional and local office supply vendors exist throughout the country. . . . However, they typically do not bid for large B-to-B contracts. . . .

* * *

III. Legal Standards

A. The Clayton Act

Section 7 of the Clayton Act prohibits mergers or acquisitions "the effect of [which] may be substantially to lessen competition, or to tend to create a monopoly," in any "line of commerce or in any activity affecting commerce in any section of the country." 15 U.S.C. § 18. When the FTC has "reason to believe that a corporation is violating, or is about to violate, Section 7 of the Clayton Act," it may seek a preliminary injunction under Section 13(b) of the FTC Act to "prevent a merger pending the Commission's administrative adjudication of the merger's legality." *F.T.C. v. Staples, Inc.*, 970 F.Supp. 1066, 1070 (D.D.C.1997) (citing 15 U.S.C. § 53(b)); *see also Brown Shoe v. U.S.*, 370 U.S. 294, 317, 82 S.Ct. 1502, 8 L.Ed.2d 510 (1962) ("Congress saw the process of concentration in American business as a dynamic force; it sought to ensure the Federal Trade Commission and the courts the power to brake this force ... before it gathered momentum.") "Section 13(b) provides for the grant of a preliminary injunction where such action would be in the public interest—as determined by a weighing of the equities and a consideration of the Commission's likelihood of success on the merits." *F.T.C. v. Heinz Co.*, 246 F.3d 708, 714 (D.C.Cir.2001) (citing 15 U.S.C. § 53(b)).

B. Section 13(b) Standard for Preliminary Injunction

The standard for a preliminary injunction under Section 13(b) requires plaintiffs to show: (1) a likelihood of success on the merits; and (2) that the equities tip in favor of injunctive relief. *FTC v. Cardinal Health*, 12 F.Supp.2d 34, 44 (D.D.C.1998). To establish a likelihood of success on the merits, the government must show that "there is a reasonable probability that the challenged transaction will substantially impair competition." *Staples*, 970 F.Supp. at 1072 (citation omitted) (internal quotation marks omitted). "Proof of actual anticompetitive effects is not required; instead, the FTC must show an appreciable danger of future coordinated interaction based on predictive judgment." *F.T.C. v. Arch Coal, Inc.*, 329 F.Supp.2d 109, 116 (D.D.C.2004) (internal quotations omitted).

* * *

. . . As reflected by this standard, Congress' concern regarding potentially anticompetitive mergers was with "probabilities, not certainties." *Brown Shoe Co.*, 370 U.S. at 323, 82 S.Ct. 1502 (other citations omitted).

* * *

C. *Baker Hughes* Burden-Shifting Framework

In *United States v. Baker Hughes, Inc.*, 908 F.2d 981, 982–83 (D.C.Cir.1990), the U.S. Court of Appeals for the D.C. Circuit established a burden-shifting framework for evaluating the FTC's likelihood of success on the merits. . . . The government bears the initial burden of showing the merger would result in "undue concentration in the market for a particular product in a particular geographic area." *Baker Hughes*, 908 F.2d at 982. Showing that the merger would result in a single entity controlling such a large percentage of the relevant market so as to significantly increase the concentration of firms in that market entitles the government to a presumption that the merger will substantially lessen competition. *Id.*

The burden then shifts to the defendants to rebut the presumption by offering proof that "the market-share statistics [give] an inaccurate account of the [merger's] probable effects on competition in the relevant market." *Heinz*, 246 F.3d at 715 (quoting *United States v. Citizens & S. Nat'l Bank*, 422 U.S. 86, 95 S.Ct. 2099, 45 L.Ed.2d 41 (1975) (alterations in original)). "The more compelling the prima facie case, the more evidence the defendant must present to rebut it successfully." *Baker Hughes*, 908 F.2d at 991. "A defendant can make the required showing by affirmatively showing why a given transaction is unlikely to substantially lessen competition, or by discrediting the data underlying the initial presumption in the government's favor." *Id.*

"If the defendant successfully rebuts the presumption, the burden of producing additional evidence of anticompetitive effect shifts to the government, and merges with the ultimate burden of persuasion, which remains with the government at all times." *Id.* at 983. . . .

IV. Discussion

* * *

A. Legal principles considered when defining a relevant market

. . . To consider whether the proposed merger may have anticompetitive effects, the Court must first define the relevant market based on evidence proffered at the evidentiary hearing. *See United States v. Marine Bancorp.*, 418 U.S. 602, 618, 94 S.Ct. 2856, 41 L.Ed.2d 978 (1974) . . . .

Two components are considered when defining a relevant market: (1) the geographic area where Defendants compete; and (2) the products and services with which the defendants' products compete. . . . The parties agree that the United States is the relevant geographic market. . . . The parties vigorously disagree, however, about how the relevant product market should be defined.

. . . [A] product market includes all goods that are reasonable substitutes, even where the products are not entirely the same. Two factors contribute to an analysis of whether goods are "reasonable substitutes": (1) functional interchangeability; and (2) cross-elasticity of demand.

As the following discussion demonstrates, the concepts of cluster and targeted markets are critical to defining the market in this case.

a. Consumable office supplies as cluster market

Cluster markets allow items that are not substitutes for each other to be clustered together in one antitrust market for analytical convenience. . . . The Supreme Court has made clear that "[w]e see no barrier to combining in a single market a number of different products or services where that combination reflects commercial realities." *United States v. Grinnell Corp.*, 384 U.S. 563, 572, 86 S.Ct. 1698, 16 L.Ed.2d 778 (1966).

Here, Plaintiffs allege that items such as pens, file folders, Post-it notes, binder clips, and paper for copiers and printers are included in this cluster market. . . . Although a pen is not a functional substitute for a paperclip, it is possible to cluster consumable office supplies into one market for analytical convenience. . . . Defining the market as a cluster market is justified in this case because "market shares and competitive conditions are likely to be similar for the distribution of pens to large customers and the distribution of binder clips to large customers." . . .

b. Large B-to-B customers as target market

Another legal principle relevant to market definition in this case is the concept of a "targeted" or "price discrimination" market. According to the Merger Guidelines:

> When examining possible adverse competitive effects from a merger, the Agencies consider whether those effects vary significantly for different customers purchasing the same or similar products. Such differential impacts are possible when sellers can discriminate, e.g., by profitably raising price to certain targeted customers but not to others. [. . .]
>
> When price discrimination is feasible, adverse competitive effects on targeted customers can arise, even if such effects will not arise

for other customers. A price increase for targeted customers may be profitable even if a price increase for all customers would not be profitable because too many other customers would substitute away.

U.S. Dep't of Justice & FTC Horizontal Merger Guidelines § 3 (2010) (hereinafter Merger Guidelines).

Defining a market around a targeted consumer, therefore, requires finding that sellers could "profitably target a subset of customers for price increases . . ." *See* [*FTC v. Sysco Corporation*, 113 F.Supp.3d 1, 38 (D.D.C. 2015)] (citing Merger Guidelines Section 4.1.4.). This means that there must be differentiated pricing and limited arbitrage. . . .

B. Application of relevant legal principles to Plaintiffs' market definition

The concepts of cluster and targeted markets inform the Court's critical consideration when defining the market in this case: the products and services with which the Defendants' products compete. . . . The parties vigorously disagree on how the market should be defined. . . . Plaintiffs argue that the relevant market is a cluster market of "consumable office supplies" which consists of "an assortment of office supplies, such as pens, paper clips, notepads and copy paper, that are used and replenished frequently." . . . Plaintiffs' alleged relevant market is also a targeted market, limited to B-to-B customers, specifically large B-to-B customers who spend $500,000 or more on office supplies annually. . . .

Defendants, on the other hand, argue that Plaintiffs' alleged market definition is wrong because it is a "gerrymandered and artificially narrow product market limited to *some*, but not all, consumable office supplies sold to only the most powerful companies in the world." . . . In particular, Defendants insist that ink and toner must be included in a proper definition of the relevant product market. . . . Defendants also argue that no evidence supports finding sales to large B-to-B customers as a distinct market. . . .

1. *Brown Shoe* "Practical Indicia"

The *Brown Shoe* practical indicia support Plaintiffs' definition of the relevant product market. The *Brown Shoe* "practical indicia" include: (1) industry or public recognition of the market as a separate economic entity; (2) the product's peculiar characteristics and uses; (3) unique production facilities; (4) distinct customers; (5) distinct prices; (6) sensitivity to price changes; and (7) specialized vendors. *Brown Shoe*, 370 U.S. at 325, 82 S.Ct. 1502. Courts routinely rely on the *Brown Shoe* factors to define the relevant product market. . . .

The most relevant *Brown Shoe* indicia in this case are: (a) industry or public recognition of the market as a separate economic entity; (b) distinct prices and sensitivity to price changes; and (c) distinct customers that require specialized vendors that offer value-added services, including: (i) sophisticated information technology (IT) services; (ii) high quality customer service; and (iii) expedited delivery.

* * *

2. Expert testimony of Dr. Carl Shapiro and the Hypothetical Monopolist Test

In addition to the *Brown Shoe* factors, the Court must consider the expert testimony offered by Plaintiffs in this case. The parties agree that the main test used by economists to determine a product market is the hypothetical monopolist test. ("HMT"). . . . This test queries whether a hypothetical monopolist who has control over the products in an alleged market could profitably raise prices on those products. . . . ("The key question is whether a hypothetical monopolist in the alleged market profitably could impose a small but significant and non-transitory increase in price ("SSNIP")") . . . . If so, the products may comprise a relevant product market. . . . The SSNIP is generally assumed to be "five percent of the price paid by customers for the products or services to which the merging firms contribute value." Merger Guidelines § 4.1.2.

[Plaintiff's expert, Dr. Carl Shapiro, a Professor of Business Strategy at the Haas School of Business at the University of California at Berkley,] . . . points out that Staples and Office Depot's head-to-head competition "tells us that a *monopoly* provider of consumable office supplies would charge significantly more to large customers than Staples and Office Depot today charge these same customers." . . . Dr. Shapiro also highlights the record evidence that demonstrates Defendants compete "fiercely" for business in the large B-to-B space. . . . Dr. Shapiro concludes that such competition implies that "the elimination of competition would lead to a significant price increase to large customers, which in turn implies that the HMT is satisfied." . . .

* * *

In sum, Dr. Shapiro's expert report and testimony, as well as the testimony of the corporate representatives, supports Plaintiffs' definition of the relevant market as the sale and distribution of consumable office supplies to large B-to-B customers.

C. Defendants' arguments in opposition to Plaintiffs' alleged market

Defendants make two primary arguments in response to Plaintiffs' alleged market. First, although Defendants do not explicitly discuss the *Brown Shoe* practical indicia, they argue that exclusion of ink and toner, as well as "beyond office supplies" or "BOSS" products[Ed.7] from the alleged market, is error. . . . Second, Defendants argue that no evidence supports Plaintiffs' contention that large B-to-B customers should be treated as a separate market. . . .

1. Exclusion of ink, toner and BOSS from alleged market is proper

Defendants' principal challenge to Plaintiffs' alleged market centers on the exclusion of ink, toner and BOSS from the alleged relevant market. . . .

* * *

Competition for the sale of ink and toner has increased due to the "recent and rapid" rise of Managed Print Services ("MPS"). . . . MPS vendors like Xerox, Hewlett-Packard, Lexmark, and Ricoh provide a bundle of services that includes sale of ink and toner in addition to service and maintenance of printers and copiers. . . . There is ample record evidence to show that ink, toner, and other adjacent BOSS items are properly excluded from the relevant market because they are subject to distinct competitive conditions. For example, some large companies are shifting all of their ink and toner business to an MPS. . . . Other large companies are disaggregating ink and toner purchases between their primary vendor and an MPS. . . . Many companies hold separate sourcing events for ink and toner. . . . The same is true of other BOSS items. . . .

* * *

Here, the record evidence shows that large B-to-B customers do not view any alternative sources for bulk procurement of basic office supplies that would retain the current competitive conditions of the market. . . . In contrast, large B-to-B customers not only view alternative vendors for ink, toner and BOSS as adequate, they increasingly contract with MPS, furniture, and janitorial companies for their primary purchase of these distinct products. . . .

In sum, inclusion of ink, toner and BOSS items by large companies in the bundle of goods they want to have the **option** of purchasing through their primary vendor does not mean that those goods are subject to the same competitive conditions.

* * *

2. Antitrust laws exist to protect competition, not a particular set of consumers

Defendants' second primary argument in opposition to Plaintiffs' proposed relevant market is that "there is no evidence to support Plaintiffs'

---

7 [Ed. "BOSS" products would include janitorial and sanitation ("jan/san") products as well as break room supplies and furniture.]

claim that large B-to-Bs should be treated as a separate market." . . . Defendants maintain that Plaintiffs' attempt to protect "mega companies" is misplaced . . . .

Antitrust laws exist to protect competition, even for a targeted group that represents a relatively small part of an overall market. . . . Indeed, the Supreme Court has recognized that within a broad market, "well-defined submarkets may exist which, in themselves, constitute product markets for antitrust purposes." *Brown Shoe Co.*, 370 U.S. at 325, 82 S.Ct. 1502, (1962) . . . .

. . . There is overwhelming evidence in this case that large B-to-B customers constitute a market that Defendants could target for price increases if they are allowed to merge. Significantly, Defendants themselves used the proposed merger to pressure B-to-B customers to lock in prices based on the expectation that they would lose negotiating leverage if the merger were approved. . . . ("This offer is time sensitive. If and when the purchase of Office Depot is approved, Staples will have no reason to make this offer."); . . . ("[The merger] will remove your ability to evaluate your program with two competitors. There will only be one."); . . . ("Today, the FTC announced 45 days for its final decision. You still have time! You would be able to leverage the competition, gain an agreement that is grandfathered in and drive down expenses!").

D. Conclusions regarding the definition of the relevant market

The "practical indicia" set forth by the Supreme Court in *Brown Shoe* and Dr. Shapiro's expert testimony support the conclusion that Plaintiffs' alleged market of consumable office supplies (a cluster market) sold and distributed by Defendants to large B-to-B customers (a targeted market) is a relevant market for antitrust purposes. The *Brown Shoe* factors support Plaintiffs' argument that the sale and distribution of consumable office supplies to large B-to-B customers is a proper antitrust market because the evidence supports the conclusion that: (1) there is industry or public recognition of the market as a separate economic entity; (2) B-to-B customers demand distinct prices and demonstrate a high sensitivity to price changes; and (3) B-to-B customers require specialized vendors that offer value-added services. Dr. Shapiro's unrebutted testimony also supports Plaintiffs' alleged market definition because, in his opinion, "the elimination of competition would lead to a significant price increase to large customers," which implies the HMT is satisfied. . . .

E. Analysis of the Plaintiffs' arguments relating to probable effects on competition based on market share calculations

Having concluded that Plaintiffs have carried their burden of establishing that the sale and distribution of consumable office supplies to large B-to-B customers in the United States is the relevant market, the

Court now turns to an analysis of the likely effects of the proposed merger on competition within the relevant market. . . .

The Plaintiffs can establish their *prima facie* case by showing that the merger will result in an increase in market concentration above certain levels. . . . "Market concentration is a function of the number of firms in a market and their respective market shares." . . . The Herfindahl-Hirschmann Index ("HHI") is a tool used by economists to measure changes in market concentration. Merger Guidelines § 5.3. HHI is calculated by "summing the squares of the individual firms' market shares," a calculation that "gives proportionately greater weight to the larger market shares." . . . An HHI above 2,500 is considered "highly concentrated"; a market with an HHI between 1,500 and 2,500 is considered "moderately concentrated"; and a market with an HHI below 1,500 is considered "unconcentrated". . . . A merger that results in a highly concentrated market that involves an increase of 200 points will be presumed to be likely to enhance market power." . . .

1. Concentration in the sale and distribution of consumable office supplies to large B-to-B customers

Dr. Shapiro estimated Defendants' market shares by using data collected from Fortune 100 companies ("Fortune 100 sample" or "Fortune 100"). . . .

Defendants' market share of the Fortune 100 sample as a whole is striking: Staples captures 47.3 percent and Office Depot captures 31.6 percent, for a total of 79 percent market share. . . . The pre-merger HHI is already highly concentrated in this market, resting at 3,270. . . . Put another way, Staples and Office Depot currently operate in the relevant market as a "duopoly with a competitive fringe." . . . If allowed to merge, the HHI would increase nearly 3,000 points, from 3,270 to 6,265. . . . This market structure would constitute one dominant firm with a competitive fringe. . . . Staples' proposed acquisition of Office Depot is therefore presumptively illegal because the HHI increases more than 200 points and the post-merger HHI is greater than 2,500. . . .

* * *

. . . The Court rejects Defendants' arguments in opposition to Dr. Shapiro's market analysis . . . . Nevertheless, to strengthen their *prima facie* case, Plaintiffs presented additional evidence of harm, which the Court analyzes next.

H. Plaintiffs' evidence of additional harm

Sole reliance on HHI calculations cannot guarantee litigation victories. . . . Plaintiffs therefore highlight additional evidence, including bidding data ("bid data"), ordinary course documents, and fact-witness testimony. This additional evidence substantiates Plaintiffs' claim that this merger, if consummated, would result in a lessening of competition.

* * *

I. Defendants' response to Plaintiffs' *prima facie* case

Defendants' sole argument in response to Plaintiffs' *prima facie* case is that the merger will not have anti-competitive effects because Amazon Business, as well as the existing patchwork of local and regional office supply companies, will expand and provide large B-to-B customers with competitive alternatives to the merged entity. . . . Plaintiffs argue that there is no evidence that Amazon or existing regional players will expand in a timely and sufficient manner so as to eliminate the anticompetitive harm that will result from the merger. . . . For the reasons discussed below, Defendants' argument that Amazon Business and other local and regional office supply companies will restore the competition lost from Office Depot is inadequate as a matter of law.

"The prospect of entry into the relevant market will alleviate concerns about adverse competitive effects only if such entry will deter or counteract any competitive effects of concern so the merger will not substantially harm customers." Merger Guidelines § 9. Even in highly concentrated markets, Plaintiffs' *prima facie* case may be rebutted if there is ease of entry or expansion such that other firms would be able to counter any discriminatory pricing practices. *Cardinal Health*, 12 F.Supp.2d at 54–55. Defendants carry the burden of showing that the entry or expansion of competitors will be "timely, likely and sufficient in its magnitude, character, and scope to deter or counteract the competitive effects of concern." *H&R Block*, 833 F.Supp.2d at 73. The relevant time frame for consideration in this forward looking exercise is two to three years. . . .

1. Amazon Business

Defendants seize on Amazon's lofty vision for Amazon Business to be the "preferred marketplace for all professional, business and institutional customers worldwide" to support their contention that Amazon not only wants to take over the office supply industry, but desires to "take over the world." . . . [Amazon Business was launched just over one year ago, in April 2015. Amazon Business is a "top priority" for Amazon, . . . and a "must win" opportunity. . . .] The Court's unenviable task is to assess the likelihood that Amazon Business will, within the next three years, replace the competition lost from Office Depot in the B-to-B space as a result of the proposed merger.

Amazon Business has a number of impressive strengths. For example, Amazon Business already enjoys great brand recognition and its consumer marketplace has a reputation as user-friendly, innovative and reliable. Amazon Business' strategy documents also reveal a number of priorities that, if successful, may revolutionize office supply procurement for large companies. . . . .

However, several significant institutional and structural challenges face Amazon Business. Plaintiffs point to a long list of what they view as Amazon Business' deficiencies, including, but not limited to: (1) lack of RFP experience; (2) no commitment to guaranteed pricing [redacted text]; (3) lack of ability to control third-party price and delivery; (4) inability to provide customer-specific pricing; (5) a lack of dedicated customer service agents dedicated to the B-to-B space; (6) no desktop delivery; (7) no proven ability to provide detailed utilization and invoice reports; and (8) lack of product variety and breadth. . . . Although Amazon Business may successfully address some of these alleged weaknesses in the short term, the evidence produced during the evidentiary hearing does not support the conclusion that Amazon Business will be in a position to restore competition lost by the proposed merger within three years.

First, despite entering the office supply business fourteen years ago, large B-to-B customers still do not view Amazon Business as a viable alternative to Staples and Office Depot. . . .

* * *

Second, Amazon Business' marketplace model is at odds with the large B-to-B industry. Similar to Amazon's consumer marketplace, half of all sales on Amazon Business are serviced by Amazon directly, while the other half are serviced by third-party sellers. . . . Amazon does not control the price or delivery offered by third-party sellers. . . . Absent these features, which are fundamental to the current office supply industry for large B-to-B customers, the record is devoid of evidence to support the proposition that large business would shift their entire office supply spend to Amazon Business in the next three years.

Finally, although Amazon Business' 2020 revenue projection is an impressive $[redacted text], only [redacted text] percent of that is forecast to come from the sale of office supplies. . . . This level of revenue for office supplies would give Amazon Business only a very small share in the relevant market. . . . .

* * *

J. Weighing the Equities

Although Plaintiffs are entitled to a presumption in favor of injunctive relief for the reasons discussed, Section 13(b)'s "public interest" standard still requires the Court to weigh the public and private equities of enjoining the merger. *Heinz*, 246 F.3d at 726. The public interests to be considered include: (1) the public interest in effectively enforcing antitrust laws; and (2) the public interest in ensuring that the FTC has the ability to order effective relief if it succeeds at the merits trial. *See e.g. Sysco*, 113

F.Supp.3d at 86. Both factors weigh in favor of granting Plaintiffs' Motion for Preliminary Injunction.

First, the "principle public equity weighing in favor of issuance of preliminary injunctive relief is the public interest in the effective enforcement of the antitrust laws." *Swedish Match*, 131 F.Supp.2d at 173. Because the law is clear that this merger is likely to lessen competition in the relevant market, it is in the public's interest for the merger to be enjoined. Second, preserving the FTC's ability to order effective relief after the administrative hearing also weighs in favor of enjoining the proposed merger. As discussed at some length during the parties' summations, it is "impossible to recreate pre-merger competition" if the parties are allowed to merge pending the administrative hearing. *Sysco*, 113 F.Supp.3d at 87 (quoting *Swedish Match*, 131 F.Supp.2d at 173); . . . Thus, the second public interest consideration also weighs in favor of enjoining the merger.

* * *

V. Conclusion

. . . The Court concludes that Plaintiffs have met their burden of showing by a "reasonable probability" that Staples' acquisition of Office Depot would lessen competition in the sale and distribution of consumable office supplies in the large B-to-B market in the United States. The evidence offered by Defendants to rebut Plaintiffs' showing of likely harm was inadequate as a matter of law. Plaintiffs have therefore carried their ultimate burden of showing that they are likely to succeed in proving, after a full administrative hearing on the merits, that the proposed merger "may be substantially to lessen competition, or to tend to create a monopoly" in violation of Section 7 of the Clayton Act.

For the reasons discussed herein, Plaintiffs' Motion for Preliminary Injunction is GRANTED. . . .

SO ORDERED.

QUESTION

How horrified must the attorneys for the defendants have been when they discovered that, while the FTC was reviewing the proposed merger, their clients attempted to pressure B-to-B customers to "lock in" prices based on the expectation that those customers would lose negotiating leverage if the merger were approved?!! The writing was on the wall when Staples sent their B-to-B customers offers that were "time sensitive," noting that "[i]f and when the purchase of Office Depot is approved, Staples will have no reason to make this offer." Yikes!

CLAYTON ACT, § 8

15 U.S.C. § 19.

Section 8. Interlocking directorates and officers

(a)(1) No person shall, at the same time, serve as a director or officer in any two corporations (other than banks, banking associations, and trust companies) that are—

(A) engaged in whole or in part in commerce; and

(B) by virtue of their business and location of operation, competitors, so that the elimination of competition by agreement between them would constitute a violation of any of the antitrust laws;

if each of the corporations has capital, surplus, and undivided profits aggregating more than $10,000,000[Ed.[8]] as adjusted pursuant to paragraph (5) of this subsection.

(2) Notwithstanding the provisions of paragraph (1), simultaneous service as a director or officer in any two corporations shall not be prohibited by this section if—

(A) the competitive sales of either corporation are less than $1,000,000,[Ed.[9]] as adjusted pursuant to paragraph (5) of this subsection;

(B) the competitive sales of either corporation are less than 2 per centum of that corporation's total sales; or

(C) the competitive sales of each corporation are less than 4 per centum of that corporation's total sales.

For purposes of this paragraph, "competitive sales" means the gross revenues for all products and services sold by one corporation in competition with the other, determined on the basis of annual gross revenues for such products and services in that corporation's last completed fiscal year. For the purposes of this paragraph, "total sales" means the gross revenues for all products and services sold by one corporation over that corporation's last completed fiscal year.

(3) The eligibility of a director or officer under the provisions of paragraph (1) shall be determined by the capital, surplus and undivided profits, exclusive of dividends declared but not paid to stockholders, of each corporation at the end of that corporation's last completed fiscal year.

(4) For purposes of this section, the term "officer" means an officer elected or chosen by the Board of Directors.

---

8 [Ed. For 2018, the number is set at $34,395,000.]

9 [Ed. For 2018, the number is set at $3,439,500.]

(5) For each fiscal year commencing after September 30, 1990, the $10,000,000 and $1,000,000[Ed.[10]] thresholds in this subsection shall be increased (or decreased) as of October 1 each year by an amount equal to the percentage increase (or decrease) in the gross national product . . . .

* * *

Section 8 provides that no person shall, at the same time, serve as a director or officer in any two corporations that are *competitors*, such that elimination of competition by agreement between them would constitute a violation of the antitrust laws. It was designed to "nip in the bud incipient violations of the antitrust laws by removing the opportunity or temptation to such violations through interlocking directorates." *U.S. v. Sears, Roebuck & Co.*, 111 F. Supp. 614, 616 (S.D.N.Y. 1953). However, there are several "safe harbors" which render § 8 inapplicable under certain circumstances. These include when the size of the corporations, or the size and degree of competitive sales between them, are below certain dollar thresholds. Based on 2017 thresholds, competitor corporations are now subject to § 8 if each one has capital, surplus and undivided profits aggregating more than $32,914,000; however, neither corporation is covered if the competitive sales of either corporation are less than $3,291,400. Other exceptions preventing the applicability of § 8 may be available (e.g., based on the percentage of competitive sales relative to total sales) even when the dollar thresholds are exceeded.

Section 8 is typically enforced by governmental regulators, although a limited private right of action exists.[11] The FTC's remedy for a § 8 violation is injunctive relief—an order to cease and desist, as the Section itself does

---

[10] [Ed. For 2018, the numbers are set at $34,395,000 and $3,439,500, respectively.]

[11] The Seventh Circuit chilled shareholder derivative suits alleging Section 8 violations in Robert F. Booth Trust v. Crowley, 687 F.3d 314 (7th Cir. 2012). Sears, Roebuck & Co., the company at issue, inherited directors from the board of Kmart Corp. following a 2005 merger. One of those directors was also on the boards of AutoNation, Inc. and AutoZone, Inc., both competitors of Sears. Another of the directors also served on the board of Jones Apparel Group, Inc., another Sears' competitor. Shareholders of Sears filed a shareholders' derivative action against Sears in 2010, alleging violations of Section 8. Pursuant to a proposed settlement, one of the contested directors would step down from the Sears' board and Sears would pay $925,000 of the plaintiffs' legal fees. Another Sears' shareholder sought to intervene to oppose the settlement, arguing that the settlement would deprive Sears of a competent director and the payment of plaintiffs' legal fees smelled like a shake down. After the District Court denied the shareholder's attempt to intervene, he appealed to the Seventh Circuit.

On appeal, the Seventh Circuit ordered the District Court to end this "feeble" case and enter judgments for the defendants, as "the only goal of this suit appears to be fees for plaintiffs' lawyers." *Id.* at 319. It noted that private antitrust litigation is available only "to suits by those parties for whose benefit the laws were enacted." *Id.* at 317. Indeed, Section 8 was designed to protect consumers, not shareholders, from the risk that "producers will cooperate and raise prices to the detriment of consumers." *Id.* The Court held that neither Sears nor the plaintiff-shareholders suffered any cognizable antitrust injury: "It is an abuse of the legal system to cram unnecessary litigation down the throat of firms whose directors serve on multiple boards, and then use the high cost of antitrust suits to extort settlements (including undeserved attorneys' fees) from targets." *Id.* at 319–20.

not provide for civil penalties or other monetary relief. Once the FTC staff raises concerns about the existence of an interlocked director or officer, that director or officer typically resigns voluntarily. This, in turn, causes public embarrassment to the companies involved, thus deterring other companies from engaging in similar conduct. "A resignation that eliminates the interlock may effectively bring each company back into compliance with Section 8 and may lead the [FTC] to determine that there is no need for any further action where there is little risk of recurrence." Debbie Feinstein, *Have a Plan to Comply with the Bar on Horizontal Interlocks*, Federal Trade Comm'n (Jan. 23, 2017).[12] However, a potentially greater concern with an interlocked director or officer lies with the potential for a violation of the Sherman Act—i.e., price fixing, bid-rigging and the like. Interlocked directors and officers raise the eyebrows of government regulators who may dig deeper and discover violations under the Sherman Act. The Sherman Act provides for harsher penalties, including criminal penalties and fines and treble damages for private litigants.

Historically, the FTC has generally relied on self-policing to prevent § 8 violations and, as a result, litigated § 8 cases are rare—the last case was begun in 1978! Nevertheless, the FTC staff still looks out for § 8 violations and commences investigations when warranted. For example, in 2009 an FTC investigation focused on the relationship between Google and Apple. It led to the voluntary resignations of Google CEO Eric Schmidt from Apple's board and of former Genentech CEO Arthur Levinson from the board of Google. An FTC investigation in 2010 into Amazon.com Inc.'s relationship with Google led to the resignation of acclaimed venture capitalist John Doerr, who served on the boards of both companies, from the Amazon board.

In 2016, the DOJ caused the restructuring of the $1.5 billion transaction between Tullett Prebon Group Ltd. (Tullett Prebon) and ICAP plc due to § 8 concerns with the original transaction structure. That structure would have resulted in ICAP owning 19.9 percent of Tullett Prebon and having the right to nominate one member to the Tullett Prebon board of directors. The DOJ had serious § 8 concerns about ICAP's ability to nominate a Tullet Prebon board member given that ICAP and Tullett Prebon would continue to compete against one another after the transaction. It believed the original structure would have created "a cozy relationship among competitors."[13] The transaction as revised resulted in ICAP not owning any part of Tullett Prebon post-closing and gave ICAP no right to nominate a member to the Tullett Prebon board.

---

[12] Available at https://www.ftc.gov/news-events/blogs/competition-matters/2017/01/have-plan-comply-bar-horizontal-interlocks.

[13] Press Release, U.S. Department of Justice, *Tullett Prebon and ICAP Restructure Transaction after Justice Department Expresses Concerns about Interlocking Directorates* (July 14, 2016).

FTC staff monitoring of director interlocks is particularly troubling for Silicon Valley, where corporate executives and venture capitalists often sit concurrently on the boards of companies that have joint marketing and development agreements while competing head-to-head with each other in other markets. Private equity firms, which typically place officers on the boards of their portfolio companies, also should be wary of § 8 if any of those companies are horizontal competitors.

Section 8 also has defensive implications for takeover battles. For example, Genzyme asserted a § 8 violation in connection with a proxy fight with Carl Icahn. Icahn Partners L.P. owned a minority interest in Genzyme. Thus, when Carl Icahn nominated himself and three associates to the Genzyme board, Genzyme highlighted the fact that Icahn Partners L.P. already held two board seats at Biogen, a main competitor of Genzyme. Therefore, the election of Icahn and his associates to the Genzyme board would result in a per se violation of § 8.

B. PRICE FIXING AMONG BIDDERS

FINNEGAN V. CAMPEAU CORP.

United States Court of Appeals, Second Circuit, 1990.
915 F.2d 824, *cert. denied*, 499 U.S. 976, 111 S.Ct. 1624, 113 L.Ed.2d 721 (1991).

CARDAMONE, CIRCUIT JUDGE:

* * *

. . . In March 1988 Federated was "put into play," that is, offered for sale to the highest bidder and a battle for its control between Macy's and Campeau began. At first the rival bidders pushed up the price of Federated stock with each submitting a bid one step higher than the other. In April 1988 it dawned on the contestants that constantly raising the price of the target company was economically disadvantageous for them. Consequently, they allegedly reached an understanding under which Macy's agreed to withdraw its latest bid and allow Campeau to acquire Federated. In exchange, Campeau agreed to permit Macy's to purchase two Federated divisions—I. Magnin and Bullock's Wilshire—and to pay Macy's $60 million to cover its legal and investment banking expenses. The difference between the $73.50 a share ultimately paid by Campeau to acquire Federated and Macy's withdrawn bid of $75.51 amounted to about $172 million. Whether Campeau's purchase was worth the price it had to pay is questionable in light of Campeau's present insolvent condition and Federated's Chapter 11 petition filed in the United States Bankruptcy Court in Cincinnati, Ohio. . . .

In his complaint Finnegan charges that the agreement between Macy's and Campeau constitutes a conspiracy in violation of § 1 of the Sherman Act (Act), 15 U.S.C. § 1 (1988). Specifically, he asserts that Macy's and

Campeau conspired to "refrain[ ] from bidding against each other for the purchase of the shares of common stock of Federated in order to suppress [sic], . . . and eliminate competition in the market for Federated common stock and to cause the sale of said shares at a price lower than a competitive price." . . .

* * *

. . . Although the Williams Act, 82 Stat. 454, *codified* at 15 U.S.C. §§ 78m(d)–(e) & 78n(d)–(f) (1988), does not foreclose all antitrust claims arising in the context of market manipulation, we hold that the Sherman Act is implicitly repealed in the circumstances of the case at bar.

The three seminal Supreme Court cases, *Silver v. New York Stock Exchange,* 373 U.S. 341 (1963), *Gordon v. New York Stock Exchange,* 422 U.S. 659 (1975), and *United States v. National Association of Securities Dealers,* 422 U.S. 694 (1975), establish the rules for implied revocation of the antitrust laws in the field of securities regulation. To begin with, repeal "by implication is not favored and not casually to be allowed. Only where there is a 'plain repugnancy between the antitrust and regulatory provisions' will repeal be implied." *Gordon,* 422 U.S. at 682 (quoting *Philadelphia Nat'l Bank,* 374 U.S. at 350–51). The holdings in *Silver* and *Gordon* teach that antitrust laws do not come into play when they would prohibit an action that a regulatory scheme permits. . . .

* * *

Section 14(d) of the statute grants to the SEC the authority to prescribe substantive rules and regulations setting forth information necessary to protect shareholders of target companies. Under § 14(d), a bidder for a public company whose shares are registered with the SEC under the 1934 Act must file a Schedule 14D–1[Ed.[14]] with the SEC on the date of the commencement of the tender offer. The disclosure requirements of Schedule 14D–1 and the language of the Williams Act contemplate agreements between bidders. Item 7 of Schedule 14D–1 reads:

> *Contracts, Arrangements, Understandings or Relationships with Respect to the Subject Company's Securities.* Describe any contract, arrangement, understanding or relationship . . . between the bidder . . . and any person with respect to any securities of the subject company (including . . . joint ventures . . .), naming the persons with whom such contracts, arrangements, understandings or relationships have been entered into. . . .

17 C.F.R. § 240.14d–100 (1989).

Further, § 14(d)(2) of the 1934 Act, 15 U.S.C. § 78n(d)(2) (1988), reads:

---

[14] [Ed. Schedule 14D–1 is now referred to as Schedule TO.]

> When two or more persons act as a partnership, limited partnership, syndicate, or other group for the purpose of acquiring, holding, or disposing of securities of an issuer, such syndicate or group shall be deemed a "person" for purposes of this subsection.

Because disclosure is the means by which Congress sought to protect target shareholders, the prior provisions make clear that once information regarding an agreement between rival bidders has been revealed in a filing, the target company's shareholders have received the protection Congress and the SEC designed for them and there has been compliance with the Williams Act.

Recognizing the logical implication of the word "group" as anticipating the sort of bid made by Macy's and Campeau, appellant contends that these provisions authorize only those agreements made by bidders prior to engaging in a contest for control of a target company, not agreements made by rival bidders during the bidding process such as was the case here. We are unable to agree with this view because neither the Williams Act nor the SEC regulations make a distinction between joint bids made by parties prior to entering a battle for control of the target and those made by parties who are rival bidders at the outset. We would think the SEC justified in deeming an agreement such as that alleged here to be a joint bid and to require the parties to file amendments to their existing filings under Schedule 14D–1, *see* 17 C.F.R. § 240.14d–3(b) (1990). Further, joint bids are not that uncommon. For example, in 1984, Reliance Financial Services Corporation and Fisher Brothers jointly offered to purchase Walt Disney Productions, and Waste Management, Inc. and Genstar made a joint offer for SCA Services, Inc. . . .

Congress drafted the Williams Act with language allowing joint bids for target companies and the SEC promulgated a regulation—Regulation 14D–1, 17 C.F.R. §§ 240.14d–1 through 240.14d–101 (1990)—that requires disclosure of agreements between bidders. In order for § 14(d) and the accompanying SEC regulation to function as intended, such agreements cannot be subject to suit under the antitrust laws; to permit such a suit would foster a direct conflict between the securities and antitrust laws. . . . We cannot presume that Congress has allowed competing bidders to make a joint bid under the Williams Act and the SEC's regulations and taken that right away by authorizing suit against such joint bidders under the antitrust laws.

The SEC also has the power to regulate tender offers under the antifraud provision of the same statute. Among the sections added to the 1934 Act by the Williams Act was § 14(e), 15 U.S.C. § 78n(e) (1988), which made it "unlawful for any person . . . to engage in any fraudulent, deceptive, or manipulative acts or practices, in connection with any tender offer. . . ." . . . .

* * *

The SEC is able to regulate agreements between bidders by virtue of its authority to define fraudulent, deceptive or manipulative practices and to prescribe means to prevent such practices. 15 U.S.C. § 78n(e). Through its power to prohibit fraudulent activity, the SEC has supervisory authority over the submission of joint bids or other agreements in the corporate auction contest. . . . Although such agreements are not defined as deceptive practices under the regulations, the fact that they must be disclosed under Regulation 14D–1 clearly implies that the SEC contemplated their existence. That the SEC has chosen not to prohibit agreements between rival bidders as fraudulent or manipulative practices once shareholders are properly informed of them, does not reduce the SEC's supervisory authority over such agreements.

Consequently, because the SEC has the power to regulate bidders' agreements under § 14(e), . . . and has implicitly authorized them by requiring their disclosure under Schedule 14D–1 as part of a takeover battle, . . . to permit an antitrust suit to lie against joint takeover bidders would conflict with the proper functioning of the securities laws.

A further though lesser conflict may also be seen between the antitrust laws and the Williams Act. It surfaces in the legislative policy of maintaining neutrality among bidders, shareholders and target company management. Congress realized "that takeover bids should not be discouraged because they serve a useful purpose in providing a check on entrenched but inefficient management." S.Rep. No. 550, 90th Cong., 1st Sess. 3–4 (1967). If the antitrust laws were applied to prohibit agreements between rival bidders, it would discourage potential bidders from making a tender offer. Once more than one bidder entered the fray for control of a target company, the shareholders of that company could use the antitrust laws to force a fight to the last ditch, notwithstanding that the bidders could agree on terms more advantageous to themselves. Certainly this would discourage takeover activity—an end Congress sought to avoid in enacting the Williams Act. . . .

* * *

Here, the application of the antitrust laws would upset the balance among incumbent management, target shareholders and bidders which Congress sought to achieve through the Williams Act. Allowing antitrust suits to rule out agreements between rival bidders would give target shareholders undue advantage in the takeover context and discourage such activity. Fewer takeover attempts ultimately favor incumbent management whose entrenched position is thereby less subject to challenge. . . .

* * *

QUESTION

State law prohibits agreements among rug buyers at estate auctions that "chill the bid" (e.g., "You bid only on rug A, I will only bid on rug B"). See 7A C.J.S. Auctions and Auctioneers § 14 (Chilling the Bid) (1980). Why should we treat rival bidders for corporations any differently? Indeed, collusive bidding by rival bidders in bankruptcy permits a bankruptcy court to avoid the sale or recover damages. Bankr. Code, 11 U.S.C. § 363(n).

C. PRE-MERGER NOTIFICATION: THE HART-SCOTT-RODINO ANTITRUST IMPROVEMENTS ACT OF 1976

In 1976 Congress added § 7A to the Clayton Act to give antitrust agencies an opportunity to determine whether a *proposed* acquisition might violate the Clayton Act.[15] Title II of the Act, called the Hart-Scott-Rodino Antitrust Improvements Act of 1976, requires firms planning an acquisition to file a merger notice with the Department of Justice and the Federal Trade Commission. The Act has a low notification threshold, significantly affecting the timing of acquisitions by imposing a waiting period before any qualifying merger could be consummated. The HSR has a "size of person" test and a "size of transaction" test serving as triggers to notification. The statutory language and supporting regulations are a very complex package. To aid filers, the Federal Trade Commission has issued a series of Guides. A portion of Guide I is reproduced below.

INTRODUCTORY GUIDE I—WHAT IS THE PREMERGER NOTIFICATION PROGRAM? AN OVERVIEW

Federal Trade Commission, March 2009.

* * *

The Act requires that parties to certain mergers or acquisitions notify the Federal Trade Commission and the Department of Justice (the "enforcement agencies") before consummating the proposed acquisition. The parties must wait a specific period of time while the enforcement agencies review the proposed transaction. . . .

* * *

In general, the Act requires that certain proposed acquisitions of voting securities, non-corporate interests ("NCI") or assets be reported to the FTC and the DOJ prior to consummation. The parties must then wait a specified period, usually 30 days (15 days in the case of a cash tender

---

[15] HSR was Congress' response to the case of El Paso Natural Gas Co. v. U.S., 410 U.S. 962, 93 S.Ct. 1440, 35 L.Ed.2d 697 (1973), a case that ended with an order to divest over seventeen years after the deal had closed. El Paso made an estimated $170 million in illegal profits during the prolonged review.

offer or a bankruptcy sale), before they may complete the transaction. Much of the information needed for a preliminary antitrust evaluation is included in the notification filed with the agencies by the parties to proposed transactions and thus is immediately available for review during the waiting period.

Whether a particular acquisition is subject to these requirements depends upon the value of the acquisition and the size of the parties, as measured by their sales and assets. Small acquisitions, acquisitions involving small parties and other classes of acquisitions that are less likely to raise antitrust concerns are excluded from the Act's coverage.

If either agency determines during the waiting period that further inquiry is necessary, it is authorized by Section 7A(e) of the Clayton Act to request additional information or documentary materials from the parties to a reported transaction (a "second request"). A second request extends the waiting period for a specified period, usually 30 days (ten days in the case of a cash tender offer or a bankruptcy sale), after all parties have complied with the request (or, in the case of a tender offer or a bankruptcy sale, after the acquiring person complies). This additional time provides the reviewing agency with the opportunity to analyze the submitted information and to take appropriate action before the transaction is consummated. If the reviewing agency believes that a proposed transaction may violate the antitrust laws, it may seek an injunction in federal district court to prohibit consummation of the transaction.

The Program has been a success. Compliance with the Act's notification requirements has been excellent, and has minimized the number of post-merger challenges the enforcement agencies have had to pursue. In addition, although the agencies retain the power to challenge mergers post-consummation, and will do so under appropriate circumstances, the fact that they rarely do has led many members of the private bar to view the Program as a helpful tool in advising their clients about particular acquisition proposals.

The Rules, which govern compliance with the Program, are necessarily technical and complex. We have prepared Guide I to introduce some of the Program's specially defined terms and concepts. This should assist you in determining if proposed business transactions are subject to the requirements of the Program.

II. DETERMINING REPORTABILITY

The Act requires persons contemplating proposed business transactions that satisfy certain size criteria to report their intentions to the enforcement agencies before consummating the transaction. If the proposed transaction is reportable, then both the acquiring person and the person whose business is being acquired must submit information about their respective business operations to the enforcement agencies and wait a specific period of time before consummating the proposed transaction. During that waiting period, the enforcement agencies review the antitrust implications of the proposed transaction. Whether a particular transaction is reportable is determined by application of the Act, the Rules, and formal and informal staff interpretations.

As a general matter, the Act and the Rules require both acquiring and acquired persons to file notifications under the Program if all of the following conditions are met:

1. As a result of the transaction, the acquiring person will hold an aggregate amount of voting securities, NCI and/or assets of the acquired person valued in excess of $200 million (as adjusted)[2], regardless of the sales or assets of the acquiring and acquired persons; or
2. As a result of the transaction, the acquiring person will hold an aggregate amount of voting securities, NCI and/or assets of the acquired person valued in excess of $50 million (as adjusted) but is $200 million (as adjusted) or less; and
3. One person has sales or assets of at least $100 million (as adjusted); and
4. The other person has sales or assets of at least $10 million (as adjusted).

* * *

D. Notification Thresholds

An acquisition that will result in a buyer holding more than $50 million (as adjusted) worth of the voting securities of another issuer crosses the first of five staggered "notification thresholds." The rules identify four additional thresholds: voting securities valued at $100 million (as adjusted) or greater but less than $500 million (as adjusted); voting securities valued at $500 million (as adjusted) or greater; 25 percent of the voting securities of an issuer, if the 25 percent (or any amount above 25% but less than 50%) is valued at greater than $1 billion (as adjusted);and 50 percent of the voting securities of an issuer if valued at greater than $50 million (as adjusted).

The thresholds are designed to act as exemptions to relieve parties of the burden of making another filing every time additional voting shares of the same person are acquired. As such, when notification is filed, the

---

[2] The 2000 amendments to the Act require the Commission to revise certain thresholds annually based on the change in the level of gross national product. A parenthetical "(as adjusted)" has been added where necessary throughout the Rules (and in this guide) to indicate where such a change in statutory threshold value occurs. The term "as adjusted" is defined in subsection 801.1(n) of the Rules and refers to a table of the adjusted values published in the Federal Register notice titled "Revised Jurisdictional Thresholds for Section 7A of the Clayton Act." The notice contains a table showing adjusted values for the rules and is published in January of each year.

acquiring person is allowed one year from the end of the waiting period to cross the threshold stated in the filing. If within that year the person reaches the stated threshold (or any lower threshold), it may continue acquiring voting shares up to the next threshold for five years from the end of the waiting period. For example, if you file to acquire $100 million (as adjusted) of the voting securities of Company B and cross that threshold within one year, you would be able to continue to acquire voting securities of Company B for a total of five years without having to file again so long as your total holding of Company B's voting securities did not exceed either $500 million (as adjusted) or 50 percent, *i.e.*, additional notification thresholds. Once an acquiring person holds 50 percent or more of the voting securities of an issuer, all subsequent acquisitions of securities of that issuer are exempt.

These notification thresholds apply only to acquisitions of voting securities. The 50 percent threshold is the highest threshold regardless of the corresponding dollar value.

E. Exempt Transactions

In some instances, a transaction may not be reportable even if the size of person and the size of transaction tests have been satisfied. The Act and the Rules set forth a number of exemptions, describing particular transactions or classes of transactions that need not be reported despite meeting the threshold criteria. For example, certain acquisitions of assets in the ordinary course of a person's business are exempted, including new goods and current supplies (*e.g.*, an airline purchases new jets from a manufacturer, or a supermarket purchases its inventory from a wholesale distributor). The acquisition of certain types of real property also would not require notification. These include certain new and used facilities, not being acquired with a business, unproductive real property (*e.g.*, raw land), office and residential buildings, hotels (excluding hotel casinos), certain recreational land, agricultural land and retail rental space and warehouses. In addition, the acquisition of foreign assets would be exempt where the sales in or into the U.S. attributable to those assets were $50 million (as adjusted) or less. Once it has been determined that a particular transaction is reportable, each party must submit its notification to the FTC and the DOJ. In addition, each acquiring person must pay a filing fee to the FTC for each transaction that it reports (with a few exceptions, *see* IV below).

III. THE FORM

The Notification and Report Form ("the Form") solicits information that the enforcement agencies use to help evaluate the antitrust implications of the proposed transaction. . . .

A. Information Reported

In general, a filing party is required to identify the persons involved and the structure of the transaction. The reporting person also must provide certain documents such as balance sheets and other financial data, as well as copies of certain documents that have been filed with the Securities and Exchange Commission. In addition, the parties are required to submit certain planning and evaluation documents that pertain to the proposed transaction.

* * *

E. Confidentiality

Neither the information submitted nor the fact that a notification has been filed is made public by the agencies except as part of a legal or administrative action to which one of the agencies is a party or in other narrowly defined circumstances permitted by the Act. However, in response to inquiries from interested parties who wish to approach the agencies with their views about a transaction, the agencies may confirm which agency is handling the investigation of a publicly announced merger. The fact that a transaction is under investigation also may become apparent if the agencies interview third parties during their investigation.

* * *

V. THE WAITING PERIOD

After filing, the filing parties must then observe a statutory waiting period during which they may not consummate the transaction. The waiting period is 15 days for reportable acquisitions by means of a cash tender offer, as well as acquisitions subject to certain federal bankruptcy provisions, and 30 days for all other types of reportable transactions. The waiting period may be extended by issuance of a request for additional information and documentary material. Any waiting period that would end on a Saturday, Sunday or legal public holiday will expire on the next regular business day.

* * *

VIII. SECOND REQUESTS

Once the investigating agency has clearance to proceed, it may ask any or all persons to the transaction to submit additional information or documentary material to the requesting agency. The request for additional information is commonly referred to as a "second request." As discussed above, although both agencies review each Form submitted to them, only one agency will issue second requests to the parties in a particular transaction.

A. Information Requested

Generally, a second request will solicit information on particular products or services in an attempt to assist the investigative team in examining a variety of legal and economic questions. A typical second request will include interrogatory-type questions as well as requests for the production of documents. A model second request has been produced jointly by the FTC and DOJ for internal use by their attorneys and is contained in Guide III.[Ed.[16]] . . .

* * *

C. Extension of the Waiting Period

The issuance of a second request extends the statutory waiting period until 30 days (or in the case of a cash tender offer or certain bankruptcy filings, 10 days) after both parties are deemed to have complied with the second request (or in the case of a tender offer and bankruptcy, until after the acquiring person has complied). During this time, the attorneys investigating the matter may also be interviewing relevant parties and using other forms of compulsory process to obtain information.

* * *

IX. AGENCY ACTION

After analyzing all of the information available to them, the investigative staff will make a recommendation to either the Commission or the Assistant Attorney General (depending on which agency has clearance).

A. No Further Action

If the staff finds no reason to believe competition will be reduced substantially in any market, it will recommend no further action. Assuming that the agency concurs in that recommendation, the parties are then free to consummate their transaction upon expiration of the waiting period. As with a decision not to issue a second request, a decision not to seek injunctive relief at that time does not preclude the enforcement agencies from initiating a post-merger enforcement action at a later time.

B. Seeking Injunctive Relief

If the investigative staff believes that the transaction is likely to be anticompetitive, it may recommend that the agency initiate injunction proceedings in U.S. district court to halt the acquisition. If the Commission

---

[16] [Ed. Guide III: *A Model Request for Additional Information and Documentary Material (Second Request)* contains materials designed for the attorneys of the antitrust enforcement agencies in preparing requests for additional information. It provides an example of what transaction parties might expect if either enforcement agency issues a second request. The model "second request" may be found at https://www.ftc.gov/enforcement/premerger-notification-program/statute-rules-formal-interpretations/premerger.]

or the Assistant Attorney General concurs in the staff's recommendation, then the agency will file suit in the appropriate district court. . . .

C. Settlements

During an investigation, the investigative staff may, if appropriate, discuss terms of settlement with the parties. The staff of the FTC is permitted to negotiate a proposed settlement with the parties; however, it must then be presented to the Commission, accepted by a majority vote, and placed on the public record for a notice and comment period before it can be made final. A proposed settlement negotiated by DOJ staff must be approved by the Assistant Attorney General and also placed on the public record for a notice and comment period before it will be entered by a district court pursuant to the provisions of the Antitrust Procedures and Penalties Act, 15 U.S.C. § 16(b)–(h).

X. FAILURE TO FILE

A. Civil Penalties

If you consummate a reportable transaction without filing the required prior notification or without waiting until the expiration of the statutory waiting period, you may be subject to civil penalties. The Act provides that "any person, or any officer, director or partner thereof" shall be liable for a penalty of up to $16,000 a day[Ed.[17]] for each day the person is in violation of the Act. The enforcement agencies may also obtain other relief to remedy violations of the Act, such as an order requiring the person to divest assets or voting securities acquired in violation of the Act.

* * *

C. Deliberate Avoidance

The Rules specifically provide that structuring a transaction to avoid the Act does not alter notification obligations if the substance of the transaction is reportable. For example, the agencies will seek penalties where the parties split a transaction into separate parts that are each valued below the current filing threshold in order to avoid reporting the transaction, but the fair market value of the assets being acquired is actually above the threshold.

* * *

The FTC revises the threshold amounts annually to account for changes in the gross national product. The 2018 announcement, for

[17] [Ed.: For 2018, the maximum civil penalty is $41,484 per day. The significant penalty increase stems from the Federal Civil Penalties Inflation Adjustment Act Improvements Act of 2015 ("IAAI Act") (yes, the name uses "Act" twice!), which requires federal agencies (including the FTC) to adjust civil penalties for violations of any acts that those agencies are tasked to enforce. Annual adjustments must be made each January.]

example, notes that in the basic test, transactions valued at greater than $337.6 million are reportable without regard to the size of person test. In the size of transaction test the acquiring person must hold, as a result of the transaction, an aggregate total amount of voting securities, assets and/or interests in non-corporate entities of the acquired person valued in excess of $84.4 million; and in the size of person test the acquiring person or the acquired person has annual net sales or total assets of $16.9 million or more and the other person has annual net sales or total assets of $168.8 million or more.

While it is inconceivable to think that well-counseled, sophisticated parties would fail to file HSR Notification and Report Forms when required, such failures (by lesser mortals) do, in fact, occur:

U.S. v. BLAVATNIK.[18] The U.S. alleged that investor (and repeat HSR offender) Len Blavatnik, via his company Access Industries, violated the HSR Act by failing to report voting shares valued at approximately $228 million that he acquired in a California start-up company, TangoMe, in August 2014. Before acquiring the TangoMe shares, neither Access nor Mr. Blavatnik conducted any HSR review of the proposed acquisition or consulted with HSR counsel to determine whether an HSR filing was required. They failed to do so notwithstanding their previous commitments to do so, which were made in connection with Mr. Blavatnik's *prior* HSR violation in 2010 for his failure to file for a reportable acquisition of LyondellBasell shares. Under the terms of a proposed final judgment filed at the same time as the complaint, Mr. Blavatnik agreed to pay a $656,000 civil penalty to resolve the lawsuit. On July 12, 2016, the court entered the final judgment.

U.S. v. VA PARTNERS I, LLC.[19] The complaint alleged that certain ValueAct Capital entities—VA Partners, LLC, ValueAct Master Capital Fund, L.P., and ValueAct Co-Invest International, L.P.—violated the reporting and waiting period requirements of the HSR Act. ValueAct, an activist investment firm, purchased over $2.5 billion of Halliburton and Baker Hughes voting securities without complying with the HSR Act's notification requirements. According to the complaint, ValueAct purchased these shares with the intent to influence the companies' business decisions as the Halliburton-Baker Hughes merger unfolded. Therefore, ValueAct could not rely on the limited "investment-only" exemption to the HSR notification requirements. Under the terms of a proposed final judgment filed July 12, 2016, ValueAct agreed to pay a civil penalty of $11 million to resolve the lawsuit. On November 1, 2016, the court entered the final judgment.

[18] No. 1:15-cv-01631 (D.D.C. filed Oct. 6, 2015).

[19] No. 3:16-cv-01672 (N.D. Cal. filed Apr. 4, 2016).

U.S. v. CALEDONIA INVESTMENTS PLC.[20] The complaint alleged that Caledonia Investments plc failed to report its purchase of voting shares in the helicopter services company Bristow Group, Inc. in 2014, which resulted in Caledonia holding Bristow shares valued at approximately $111 million. The complaint alleged that in June 2008, Caledonia first acquired voting shares in Bristow and reported its purchase as required under the HSR Act. In February 2014, however, Caledonia acquired *additional shares* of Bristow. Although the HSR Act allows a company that has reported an initial purchase of voting shares to purchase additional voting shares from the same issuer up to the next highest reporting threshold over a five-year period following the initial purchase, Caledonia's 2014 purchase of voting shares in Bristow fell outside the five-year period following its initial purchase. Caledonia failed to report this purchase, as required under the HSR Act. Under the terms of a proposed final judgment filed at the same time as the complaint, Caledonia agreed to pay a $480,000 civil penalty to resolve the lawsuit. On November 15, 2016, the court entered the final judgment.

1. THE HSR NOTIFICATION AND REPORT FORM

The HSR Notification and Report Form is extensive, containing nine items. Since the FTC first promulgated the HSR rules in 1978, those items have been amended multiple times. The requirements for combining firms are searching and include a detailed identification of the business and ownership of both constituents, a description of the transaction, and other miscellany (information about subsidiaries, for example). Some of the items, such as those that require the attachment of SEC filings, are of marginal relevance and all are in the public record. The parties may submit their HSR Forms on DVD (containing searchable PDF documents and MS Excel spreadsheets), although their cover letter, certification and affidavit must still be provided in hard copy form.

The most controversial item of the HSR Form is Item 4(c), which calls for the acquiring party to submit all studies or analyses that were prepared by or for any officer or director, which were for the purpose of analyzing or evaluating the acquisition with respect to various issues relating to competitive effects.[21] The requirement is controversial as filing parties worry about protecting attorney-client privilege and the exposure of confidential documents from investment bankers and management consultants. See Robert S. Schlossberg & Harry T. Robins, *Hart-Scott-*

---

[20] No. 1:16-cv-01620 (D.D.C. filed Aug. 16, 2016).

[21] The government can gain access to internal memos written by people who never assumed their words would be made public. The result can be the discovery of a classic smoking gun document. In Microsoft's 1994 proposal to merge with Intuit Corporation, the Justice Department had documents written by the CEO of Intuit labeling Microsoft as "Godzilla" and predicting that the deal would leave "one clear option" for financial software and eliminate a "bloody [market] share war." The Justice Department challenged the deal and it collapsed.

Rodino Merger Investigations: A Guide for Safeguarding Business Secrets, 56 BUS. LAW. 943 (2001).

The FTC has interpreted Item 4(c) broadly and takes the requirement very seriously. In 1996 the FTC and Automatic Data Processing, Inc. agreed to settle for $2.97 million a charge that ADP had not complied with Item 4(c).[22] *United States v. Automatic Data Processing*, 1996–1 Trade Cas. (CCH) ¶ 71,361, 1996 WL 224758 (D.D.C. 1996). Most parties to acquisitions now warn all their inside and outside consultants about the potential for Item 4(c) exposure of consultants' reports and try to avoid preparing reports that will satisfy the criteria of Item 4(c), or they try to sanitize[23] any reports that are prepared. In 2011 the FTC amended its rules to make explicit its views on the breath of Item 4(c). The new rules, adding new Item 4(d) to the form, specifically require the submission of confidential information prepared by third party advisors with 4(c) content and documents analyzing synergies and/or efficiencies of a transaction.

2. THE HSR WAITING PERIOD

The HSR waiting period has a significant effect on acquisition planning. If delay is a major concern of an acquiring party, the Act can significantly burden the acquisition or tip off a target firm to an unwanted bid long before notice may be required under the federal securities acts. Once the Federal Trade Commission and the Department of Justice receive complete filings, the initial waiting period begins to run, which lasts fifteen days for cash tender offers and thirty days for all other types of acquisitions. If, upon a review of the completed filings of the constituent parties, the reviewing agencies determine that the proposed transaction has no anti-competitive effects, they must grant an early termination of the waiting period, if the parties so request. If an agency grants early termination, the names of the filing parties and the target are published, but the contents of the filings are not. For most transactions the agencies complete their antitrust review within two weeks and terminate the waiting period soon thereafter.[24]

---

22 The amount represented $10,000 for each day that ADP failed to provide the documents necessary to fulfill the requirements of Item 4(c). For 2018, the daily civil penalty increased to a maximum of $41,484.

23 Sanitize means to eliminate blustery or overblown language about the competitive effects of an acquisition. Purchasers prefer to understate such effects.

24 Although Congress did not envision the Act as a source of government revenue, the hefty filing fees coupled with the breadth of the Act's coverage provide significant funds for the government's coffers. The fee is in essence a transaction tax. The fees now provide a substantial portion of the revenue of the Antitrust Divisions of both the DOJ and the FTC. Originally the filing fee was a flat $45,000. The 2000 amendments reduced the number of deals covered but increased the fees for larger acquisitions. The fee schedule in place for 2018 is three-tiered: (1) for transactions valued at more than $84.4 million, but less than $168.8 million, the filing fee is $45,000; (2) for transactions valued at $168.8 million or more, but less than $843.9 million, the filing fee is $125,000; and (3) for transactions valued at $843.9 million or more, the filing fee is $280,000. The trigger amounts will be adjusted annually to reflect the percentage change in the gross national product from the previous year.

Before the expiration of the waiting period, the FTC or the DOJ may request additional documents or information (the feared or dreaded "Second Request"[25]), which automatically extends the initial waiting period until the requesting agency obtains "substantial compliance" with the request.[26] Upon receipt of the additional information, an additional waiting period begins to run and expires at the end of the 10th day for cash tender offers, and the 30th day for all others. Thus, the Act favors cash tender offers in contested acquisitions. A person making a cash tender offer may be free to purchase shares fifteen to thirty-five days in advance of a person making an exchange tender offer. This bias in favor of cash-for-stock acquisitions, and in favor of three-step transactions that use cash tender offers in the second stage, is substantial.[27]

The initial Hart-Scott-Rodino filing and any Second Request filings are confidential. Thus the pre-merger data are exempt from the Freedom of Information Act. There are two exceptions. First, statutory grants of early termination are published in the Federal Register.[28] The public announcements of early terminations have become significant news events. Second, information may be made public in an administrative or judicial proceeding, or disclosed to Congress or to a duly authorized committee or subcommittee of Congress. The FTC and DOJ staffs have agreed that parties will receive ten days advance notice of such disclosures when possible or, at minimum, be given time to seek a protective order. The Hart-Scott-Rodino filings are not, without a protective order, exempt from discovery requests in litigation. There is nothing that limits the rights of a party in a private action challenging the proposed acquisition to gain access to the filings and accompanying documents through civil discovery proceedings. Two federal circuit courts of appeal have held, however, that state attorneys general, as members of the public, cannot obtain the materials. See, e.g., *Lieberman v. FTC*, 771 F.2d 32 (2d Cir. 1985).

---

[25] The agencies use the Second Request process to create a new discovery mechanism, unconstrained by the Federal Rules of Civil Procedure and free of any oversight by any neutral arbiter. The requests can be highly intrusive and very expensive. The agencies, in response to substantial criticism over the process, have undertaken a variety of modest reforms. See William J. Baer, *Reflections on Twenty Years of Merger Enforcement Under the Hart-Scott-Rodino Act*, 65 ANTITRUST L. J. 825, 845–46 (1997) (discussing an expedited clearance procedure, a model Second Request, and an internal appeal from staff decisions).

[26] In practice "substantial compliance," according to the agencies, is equal to "absolute compliance." See, e.g., 43 Fed. Reg. 33,450, 33,509 (1978).

[27] The Act's waiting period can also affect *competing* cash tender offers. In 1981 Mobil Corporation and DuPont both bid for Conoco, then the nation's ninth largest oil company. The HSR review process was scheduled to end on different dates for each player; DuPont's would close a week earlier. To make matters worse, Mobil got a Second Request and DuPont did not. With the Second Request, Mobil had to ask institutional investors and arbs not to tender to DuPont and to wait for Mobil's bid, in essence to take the risk of the Justice Department's antitrust review. Investors tendered to DuPont and the battle was over.

[28] This is odd given the confidentiality of HSR notifications. Since the vast majority of filings request and receive early terminations, most acquisitions are now a matter of public record.

The Act creates significant disincentives for hostile acquisitions. First, the Act creates additional filing burdens in hostile tender offers. Although the waiting period for hostile tender offers begins when the acquirer files its report (for all other acquisitions *both* parties to the transaction must file reports to start the waiting period), HSR Premerger Notification Rule 801.30(b)(2) requires a *target* to file a report within ten days of a cash tender offer and within fifteen days of an exchange tender offer. Rule 803.5 requires that the acquirer's filing include an affidavit that the acquirer has notified the target of the transaction. So, on the day of the announcement of the tender offer, a bidder, intent on minimizing any advance notice to a target, must file a Hart-Scott-Rodino report with antitrust officials and notify the target of the filing. Of course, the tender offeror cannot buy any securities tendered until the waiting period expires without action by the FTC or the DOJ. Thus, all tender offers must necessarily be conditioned on the expiration of the HSR waiting period.[29]

Second, and more damaging perhaps, the Act's thirty-day waiting period significantly impacts street sweeps and other large-scale confidential stock acquisitions. The required waiting period in HSR, with its additional requirement of notice to the target at the *commencement* of the applicable period, stops any lightning-quick acquisitions. Consider, for example, the poor fit of the HSR with § 13(d) of the Williams Act. Under the Williams Act, an acquirer has ten days after the date of purchase to file a notice with the target (which allows the acquirer to purchase significantly more than the 5 percent triggering amount before notice). Under the HSR, an acquirer must notify the target at least thirty days (fifteen if the purchase is through a cash tender offer) *before* it can purchase stock that triggers the Act. The overlap catches purchases of stock that constitute more than 5 percent of the outstanding voting stock of the target whenever the stock acquired is valued at over $84.4 million and the purchaser's total value is over $168.8 million.[30]

Parties intent on avoiding early disclosure under HSR have attempted, with limited success, to use a variety of techniques to avoid making a filing until they must otherwise file under § 13(d) of the Exchange Act. First, some acquirers have attempted to avoid buying the stock. For example, the selling shareholder agrees to a "lock-up" option; that is, she agrees to sell her holdings at a fixed price after the HSR waiting period expires. A broker agrees to reciprocal put and call options with the bidder in which the bidder gains the right to buy shares at a fixed price after the waiting period expires, and the broker gains the right to sell shares to the bidder after the waiting period expires. The FTC takes the

---

[29] A typical tender offer condition would read as follows: "Any waiting periods under the Hart-Scott-Rodino Antitrust Improvements Act of 1976, as amended, applicable to the purchase of Shares pursuant to the Offer must have expired or been terminated."

[30] Amounts applicable for 2018.

position that these options are not legitimate methods of delaying a Hart-Scott-Rodino filing.

Second, acquirers have claimed exemptions under the Act for acquisitions of up to 10 percent of their targets' securities for "investment only." At issue is how serious a bidder must be about a takeover before it loses the investment exemption. Can an investor buy up to 10 percent under the exemption with an intent to "test the waters" for a possible takeover attempt? On the other hand, a bidder could take the opposite approach, filing HSR notices on many targets in the hopes of disguising its intention to buy any one of them. Some bidders, for example, have filed well in advance of any firm intention to move on any particular target by (1) identifying several possible targets and filing on each (it must have a "good faith intention" to pass the reporting threshold on each), (2) waiting for the market effects of its announcement to dissipate (a filing is good for one year), and then (3) announcing a tender offer for one target.

The third method of avoidance is the formation of a partnership acquisition vehicle in which two partners hold 49 percent of the equity and a third partner holds 2 percent of the equity. Under the present Act and rules, the Size-of-Person test of a partnership is applied only to partners who "control" the partnership by having the right to over 50 percent of the profits. If the partnership is newly-formed and has no controlling partner, it can make an acquisition without reporting if the total assets of the partnership are less than $10 million, after netting out the assets to be used in the acquisition. After the acquisition one of the partners buys out the others; this second acquisition of the entire partnership is not itself reportable. The FTC has attacked such partnerships on the grounds that the nominal partner was not independent or that there was no reason for the structure other than avoidance of filing obligations. E.g., *U.S. v. Tengelmann Warenhandelsgesellschaft,* 1989–1 Trade Cas. (CCH) ¶ 68,623, 1989 WL 90361 (D.D.C. 1989).

Outright evasion is the fourth method of avoidance. The acquirer just refuses to file the required Hart-Scott-Rodino Act notice, filing the notice instead when it files its Williams Act material and absorbing the Hart-Scott-Rodino Act penalties as a cost of the acquisition. Noncompliance may subject the violator to up to $41,484[31] in penalties for each day in violation of the Act. § 7A(g)(1). The FTC's recent vigilance has caused this approach to lose much of its luster, however. In February of 1997, the FTC forced a German automotive and diesel engine parts manufacturer, Mahle GmbH, to pay a civil penalty in excess of $5 million for their failure to file a pre-merger notification. And one year earlier to the month, Sara Lee agreed to pay $3.1 million to settle charges that it violated HSR. Three other recent examples appear earlier in this Section C.

---

[31] This is the maximum daily amount set for 2018. An annual adjustment is made by the FTC each January.

Parties impatient with the waiting period have also attempted to turn control of the target over to the buyer during the period. The DOJ and FTC take a very dim view of the practice as is seen in the *Computer Associates* case that follows the *American Stores* case below.

The most startling aspect of the Act is the poor correlation of its provisions with its ostensible purpose. Very few of the Hart-Scott-Rodino filings result in action by the FTC or the DOJ. Moreover, when one of the government agencies does take corrective action, inducing parties to modify the terms of a proposed merger to comport with the Clayton Act, the settlement does not preclude future suits. The government reserves the right to sue if it should change its mind, and in the *California v. American Stores Co.* case below, the Supreme Court held that negotiated settlements between the federal government and constituent parties to a merger prompted by a Hart-Scott-Rodino Act filing do not divest private plaintiffs from suing to set aside a merger.

CALIFORNIA V. AMERICAN STORES CO.

Supreme Court of the United States, 1990.
495 U.S. 271, 110 S.Ct. 1853, 109 L.Ed.2d 240.

JUSTICE STEVENS delivered the opinion of the Court.

By merging with a major competitor, American Stores Co. (American) more than doubled the number of supermarkets that it owns in California. The State sued, claiming that the merger violates the federal antitrust laws and will harm consumers in sixty-two California cities. The complaint prayed for a preliminary injunction requiring American to operate the acquired stores separately until the case is decided, and then to divest itself of all of the acquired assets located in California. . . .

American operates over 1,500 retail grocery stores in forty States. Prior to the merger, its 252 stores in California made it the fourth largest supermarket chain in that State. Lucky Stores, Inc. (Lucky), which operated in seven Western and Midwestern States, was the largest, with 340 stores. The second and third largest, Von's Companies and Safeway Stores, were merged in December 1987. . . .

On March 21, 1988, American notified the Federal Trade Commission (FTC) that it intended to acquire all of Lucky's outstanding stock for a price of $2.5 billion. The FTC conducted an investigation and negotiated a settlement with American. On May 31, it simultaneously filed both a complaint alleging that the merger violated § 7 of the Clayton Act and a proposed consent order disposing of the § 7 charges subject to certain conditions. Among those conditions was a requirement that American comply with a "Hold Separate Agreement" preventing it from integrating the two companies' assets and operations until after it had divested itself of several designated supermarkets. American accepted the terms of the

FTC's consent order. In early June, it acquired and paid for Lucky's stock and consummated a Delaware "short form merger." . . . Thus, as a matter of legal form American and Lucky were merged into a single corporate entity on June 9, 1988, but as a matter of practical fact their business operations have not yet been combined.

On August 31, 1988, the FTC gave its final approval to the merger. The next day California filed this action in the United States District Court for the Central District of California. . . .

* * *

If we assume that the merger violated the antitrust laws, and if we agree with the District Court's finding that the conduct of the merged enterprise threatens economic harm to California consumers, the literal text of § 16 is plainly sufficient to authorize injunctive relief, including an order of divestiture, that will prohibit that conduct from causing that harm. . . .

* * *

JUSTICE KENNEDY, concurring.

. . . I write further to note that both the respondents and various interested labor unions, the latter as *amici curiae*, have argued for a different result on the basis of the Hart-Scott-Rodino Antitrust Improvements Act of 1976 (Clayton Act § 7A, as added and amended), 15 U.S.C. § 18a. . . . Although I do not believe that § 7A is controlling as an interpretation of the earlier enacted § 16, it may be of vital relevance in determining whether to order divestiture in a particular case.

Section 7A enables the Federal Government to review certain transactions that might violate § 7 before they occur. The provision, in brief, requires those contemplating an acquisition within its coverage to provide the Federal Trade Commission (FTC) with the information necessary for determining "whether such acquisition may, if consummated, violate the antitrust laws." 15 U.S.C. § 18a(d)(1). During the mandatory waiting period that follows the submission of this information, see § 18a(b)(1), the agency may decide, as it did in this case, to negotiate a settlement intended to eliminate potential violations. . . . The procedure may resolve antitrust disputes in a manner making it easier for businesses and unions to predict the consequences of mergers and to conform their economic strategies in accordance with the probable outcome.

The respondents, and the unions in their brief as *amici,* argue that a State or private person should not have the power to sue for divestiture under § 16 following a settlement approved by the FTC. They maintain that the possibility of such actions will reduce the Federal Government's negotiating strength and destroy the predictability that Congress sought to provide when it enacted § 7A. It is plausible, in my view, that allowing suits under § 16 may have these effects in certain instances. But the respondents and unions have identified nothing in § 7A that contradicts the Court's interpretation of § 7 and § 16. Section 7A, indeed, may itself contain language contrary to their position. *See, e.g.,* 15 U.S.C. § 18a(i)(1). Although Congress might desire at some point to enact a strict rule prohibiting divestiture after a negotiated settlement with the FTC, it has not done so yet.

The Court's opinion, however, does not render compliance with the Hart-Scott-Rodino Antitrust Improvements Act irrelevant to divestiture actions under § 16. The Act, for instance, may bear upon the issue of laches. By establishing a time period for review of merger proposals by the FTC, § 7A may lend a degree of objectivity to the laches determination. Here the State received the respondents' § 7A filings in mid-April 1988, and so had formal notice of the parties' intentions well before completion of the merger or the settlement with the FTC. It elected not to act at that time, but now seeks a divestiture which, the facts suggest, would upset labor agreements and other matters influenced in important ways by the FTC proceeding. These considerations should bear upon the ultimate disposition of the case. As the Ninth Circuit stated:

> "California could have sued several months earlier and attempted to enjoin the merger before the stock sale was completed. The Attorney General chose not to do so. California must accept the consequences of his choice." 872 F.2d 837, 846 (1989).

With the understanding that these consequences may include the bar of laches, I join the Court's decision.

American Stores ultimately settled the dispute with the Attorney General of California by disposing of 152 of its 175 southern California Alpha Beta stores (American's California subsidiary) and nine of its newly-acquired southern California Lucky stores and most of the related Alpha Beta support facilities. The Tax Court then held that American could not deduct its legal fees and costs incurred in defending the state antitrust suit. *American Stores Co. v. Commissioner*, 114 T.C. 458 (2000).

UNITED STATES V. COMPUTER ASSOCIATES INT'L, INC.

Department of Justice Antitrust Division, June 18, 2002.
67 Fed. Reg. 41,472, 2002 WL 1310208.

Proposed Final Judgment and Competitive Impact Statement

* * *

After this suit was filed, the United States and Defendants reached a proposed settlement that eliminates the need for a trial in this case. The proposed Final Judgment remedies the Section 1 violation by prohibiting CA in future acquisitions from agreeing on prices, approving customer contracts, and misusing competitively sensitive bid information. CA and Platinum would also agree to pay a $638,000 civil penalty to resolve the HSR Act violation.

* * *

CA is a Delaware corporation with its principal place of business in Islandia,, New York. CA develops, markets, and supports software products for a variety of computers and operating systems, including systems management software for computers that use IBM's OS/390, VSE and VM operating systems ("mainframe computers"). Systems management software products are used to help manage, control, or enhance the performance of mainframe computers. CA, in its 1998 fiscal year, reported revenues in excess of $4.7 billion.

Platinum was a Delaware corporation with its principal place of business in Oakbrook Terrace, Illinois. Platinum, like CA, was a leading vendor of mainframe systems management software products. In addition to its software business, Platinum offered computer consulting services, including Y2K remediation services. In its fiscal year 1998, Platinum reported revenues of about $968 million.

Prior to March 1999, Platinum aggressively competed with CA in the development and sale of numerous software products, including mainframe systems management software products. On March 29, 1999, CA and Platinum announced the Merger Agreement, pursuant to which CA would purchase all issued and outstanding shares of Platinum through a $3.5 billion cash tender offer. Thereafter, CA and Platinum filed the pre-acquisition Notification and Report Forms required by the HSR Act.

After reviewing the parties' HSR filings, DOJ opened an investigation that led to the filing of a Complaint on May 25, 1999, alleging that CA's proposed acquisition of Platinum would eliminate substantial competition and result in higher prices in certain mainframe systems management software markets. . . . Simultaneously with the filing of the Complaint, the parties reached an agreement that allowed CA and Platinum to go forward with the merger, provided that CA sell certain Platinum mainframe systems management software products and related assets. The HSR waiting period expired on May 25, 1999. Three days later, CA announced that it had accepted for payment all validly tendered Platinum shares and the Defendants thereafter consummated the merger. Platinum survived the merger and is now a wholly-owned subsidiary of CA.

* * *

CA, during the HSR waiting period, took operational control over Platinum's ability to price its products and services, set other terms and conditions of sale, enter into fixed-price contracts over 30 days, and offer Y2K remediation services.

* * *

C. CA's Exercise of Operational Control Over Platinum Violated the HSR Act

* * *

Prior to enactment of the HSR Act, the DOJ and FTC often investigated anticompetitive "midnight mergers" that had been consummated with no public notice. The merged entity thereafter had the incentive to delay litigation so that substantial time 'elapsed before adjudication and attempted relief. During this extended time, consumers were harmed by the reduction in competition between the acquiring and acquired firms and, if after adjudication, the court found that the merger was illegal, effective relief was difficult to achieve. The HSR Act was designed to strengthen antitrust enforcement by preventing the consummation of large mergers before they were investigated by the enforcement agencies. In particular, the HSR Act prohibits certain acquiring parties from consummating a merger before a prescribed waiting period expires. The HSR waiting period remedies the problem of "midnight mergers" by keeping the parties separate, thereby preserving their status as independent economic actors during the antitrust investigation. The legislative history of the HSR Act makes this plain. Congress was concerned that competition existing before the merger should be maintained to the extent possible pending review by the antitrust enforcement agencies and the court. Consistent with this purpose, an acquiring person may not, after signing a merger agreement, exercise operational or management control of the to-be-acquired person's business.

* * *

Merger agreements typically contain "interim covenants" limiting the to-be-acquired person's operations during the pre-consummation period. The Merger Agreement between CA and Platinum contained a covenant typically found in most merger agreements that Platinum would continue to operate its business in the ordinary course of business. Such "ordinary course" provisions do not violate the HSR Act.

The Merger Agreement also contained many other customary covenants, including Platinum's agreement that it would not, without the prior written approval of CA: (1) Declare or pay dividends or distributions of its stock; (2) issue, sell, pledge, or encumber its securities; (3) amend its organizational documents; (4) acquire or agree to acquire other businesses; (5) mortgage or encumber its intellectual property or other material assets outside the ordinary course; (6) make or agree to make large new capital expenditures; (7) make material tax elections or compromise material tax liabilities; (8) pay, discharge or satisfy any claims or liabilities outside the ordinary course; and (9) commence lawsuits other than routine collection of bills. The purpose of these standard provisions is to prevent a to-be-acquired person from taking actions that could seriously impair the value of what the acquiring firm had agreed to buy. While these customary provisions limited Platinum's ability to make certain business decisions without CA's consent, they were also reasonable and necessary to protect the value of the transaction and did not constitute the HSR Act violation.

The Merger Agreement, however, did not stop with these customary covenants, but went further to impose extraordinary conduct of business limitations enabling CA to exercise operational control over significant aspects of Platinum's business. These 18a(b)(I), (e). The enforcement agency may grant early termination of the waiting period. 15 U.S.C. 18a(b)(2), and often does when the merger poses no competitive problems restrictions and CA's exercise of operational control went far beyond ordinary and reasonable pre-consummation covenants and constituted a violation of the HSR Act. In the pre-merger context, an acquiring person may not exercise operational control of the to-be acquired person's business. This is what CA did in this case.

Platinum, immediately upon executing the Merger Agreement, transferred to CA operational control of substantial aspects of its business, including the right to set prices and other terms of customer contracts, enter into certain consulting services contracts, account for revenues, and participate at trade shows. To ensure compliance with the Merger Agreement's business restrictions, Platinum's CEO, COO, and CFO were personally liable if the restrictions were not observed. Moreover, a CA Divisional Vice President occupied an office at Platinum's Illinois headquarters where he reviewed proposed Platinum customer contracts and exercised authority to approve or reject contracts. In effect, the decision-making authority with respect to these business activities resided with CA's management, not Platinum's. Further exercising its operational control, CA obtained Platinum's competitively sensitive customer information without any restriction as to its use by CA or its dissemination within CA. This conduct demonstrates that CA and Platinum did not adhere to the requirement of the HSR Act that they remain separate and independent economic entities during the waiting period.

Both CA and Platinum were in violation of the HSR Act from March 29, 1999, the date on which the Merger Agreement was executed, through May 25, 1999, the day on which CA, Platinum, and DOJ agreed to a consent decree resolving DOJ's antitrust concerns.

* * *

Under section (g)(1) of the HSR Act, 15 U.S.C. 18a(g)(1), any person who fails to comply with the Act shall be liable to the United States for a civil penalty of not more than $11,000[Ed.[32]] for each day during which such person is in violation of the Act. As the Stipulation and proposed Final Judgment indicate, Defendants have agreed to pay civil penalties totaling $638,000 within 30 days of the Final Judgment. While the United States was prepared to seek civil penalties totaling $1,267,000 at trial, the uncertainties inherent in any litigation led to acceptance of $638,000 as an appropriate civil penalty for settlement purposes. Moreover, this civil penalty should be sufficient to deter CA and other acquiring persons from exercising operational control over a to-be-acquired person during the HSR waiting period.

* * *

[32] [Ed. For 2018, the maximum civil penalty is $41,484 per day. The FTC makes annual adjustments each January.]

CHAPTER TEN

ISSUES IN INTERNATIONAL ACQUISITIONS

■ ■ ■

Cross-border mergers in terms of aggregate U.S. dollar deal volumes peaked in 2007, sagged significantly in 2009, and in 2011 grew back to 2008 levels. After a slight dip in 2012, aggregate U.S. dollar deal volumes grew each year from 2013–2016, with 2015 and 2016 experiencing double digit growth. Aggregate U.S. dollar deal volume in 2016 was approximately USD $1.35 trillion, an astounding number, with the average deal size just north of USD $140 million. Growth in 2016 affected all regions, with European aggregate U.S. dollar deal volume up 30 percent, inward North America up 22 percent, Japan up 100 percent and the Indian subcontinent up 50 percent, in each case over 2015 numbers.[1]

The cross-border market is now a permanent part of any healthy M & A practice. The Big Four accounting firms have developed an international network of offices to advise clients in international acquisitions and large U.S. law firms are racing to develop foreign affiliates or foreign contacts to stay competitive with the accounting firms. Buyers and sellers must consult legal counsel familiar with the foreign laws that may apply, and this Chapter cannot cover most of the issues that parties to international acquisitions will face. Rather, the text highlights some penetrating problems presented by international acquisitions that are not presented by domestic acquisitions.

A. FOREIGN ACQUISITIONS OF UNITED STATES CORPORATIONS

1. ACQUISITIONS THAT "IMPAIR NATIONAL SECURITY"—THE EXON-FLORIO AMENDMENT

a. Introduction and Overview

Congress passed the Exon-Florio Amendment as part of the Omnibus Trade and Competitiveness Act of 1988. The Amendment modifies § 721 of the Defense Production Act of 1950 (the "DPA"). Congress passed the Amendment in the wake of Fujitsu, Ltd.'s (a Japanese company) attempted

[1] See generally OECD, Global Forum on International Investing, *Cross-Border M&A on the Rise: Recovery or a Warning of Another FDI Crash?* (Mar. 6, 2017), avail. at https://www.oecd.org/investment/globalforum/2017-GFII-Background-Note-MA-trends.pdf.

takeover of Fairchild Semiconductor Corporation in early 1987. Fujitsu's acquisition, coming on the heels of Sir James Goldsmith's raid on the Goodyear Tire and Rubber Company, stirred great controversy on Capitol Hill. If successful, the takeover would have made "Fujitsu the leading semiconductor firm in the world, while Fairchild's defense-electronics subsidiary provided more than $100 million of high-speed circuitry annually to the defense community." Martin Tolchin & Susan J. Tolchin, *Selling Our Security: The Erosion of America's Assets* 48 (1992) (a protectionist's view of the issue).

Ironically, Fairchild was owned by Schlumberger, a private French concern. Fujitsu's acquisition, therefore, would have shifted ownership only to another foreign company. Still, Fairchild represented itself as an "American" company and the leader in semiconductor technology. Because of the quantity and nature of Fairchild's defense contracts, Defense Department officials and Commerce Secretary Malcolm Baldridge both publicly opposed the deal. Faced with such heavy odds, Fujitsu eventually withdrew its offer but left as its legacy a new piece of legislation, the 1988 Exon-Florio Amendment. Defense Department officials had come to realize that the government had no legal authority to restrict foreign acquisitions of American businesses and believed that this lack of authority threatened national security.

Similarly, Thompson's failed attempt to purchase the missile division of bankrupt LTV Corp. in the summer of 1992, another acquisition that generated great controversy in Congress (the French government owns 60 percent of Thompson), led to the 1992 Byrd-Exon amendment which added subsection (b) to Exon-Florio. The public notoriety of the effort of a company owned by the government of Dubai, Dubai Ports World, to buy control of the container operations of six major ports in the United States[2] led Congress to pass the Foreign Investment and National Security Act of 2007, rewriting the Exon-Florio language.

---

[2] DP World purchased control of Peninsular and Oriental Steam Navigation Company, a U.K. firm that managed container port facilities in six major U.S. ports. The Committee on Foreign Investment in the United States "(CFIUS") approved the transaction. A bipartisan congressional coalition called for a second review of the transaction and threatened legislative action to unwind the deal. They fed off public concerns that terrorists could smuggle nuclear devices (or other weapons) through an Arab controlled port. When a House subcommittee voted favorably on legislation to block the deal, DP World capitulated, selling the port operations to a subsidiary of a U.S. company.

b. Statutory Authority for CFIUS and Presidential Review

AUTHORITY TO REVIEW CERTAIN MERGERS, ACQUISITIONS, AND TAKEOVERS

50 U.S.C. § 2170.

(a) Definitions—For purposes of this section, the following definitions shall apply:

(1) COMMITTEE; CHAIRPERSON—The terms "Committee" and "chairperson" mean the Committee on Foreign Investment in the United States and the chairperson thereof, respectively.

(2) CONTROL—The term "control" has the meaning given to such term in regulations which the Committee shall prescribe.

(3) COVERED TRANSACTION—The term "covered transaction" means any merger, acquisition, or takeover that is proposed or pending after August 23, 1988, by or with any foreign person which could result in foreign control of any person engaged in interstate commerce in the United States.

(4) FOREIGN GOVERNMENT-CONTROLLED TRANSACTION—The term "foreign government-controlled transaction" means any covered transaction that could result in the control of any person engaged in interstate commerce in the United States by a foreign government or an entity controlled by or acting on behalf of a foreign government.

(5) CLARIFICATION—The term "national security" shall be construed so as to include those issues relating to "homeland security", including its application to critical infrastructure.

(6) CRITICAL INFRASTRUCTURE—The term "critical infrastructure" means, subject to rules issued under this section, systems and assets, whether physical or virtual, so vital to the United States that the incapacity or destruction of such systems or assets would have a debilitating impact on national security.

(7) CRITICAL TECHNOLOGIES—The term "critical technologies" means critical technology, critical components, or critical technology items essential to national defense, identified pursuant to this section, subject to regulations issued at the direction of the President, in accordance with subsection (h).

(8) LEAD AGENCY—The term "lead agency" means the agency, or agencies, designated as the lead agency or agencies pursuant to subsection (k)(5) for the review of a transaction.

(b) National Security Reviews and Investigations—

(1) NATIONAL SECURITY REVIEWS—

(A) IN GENERAL—Upon receiving written notification under subparagraph (C) of any covered transaction, or pursuant to a unilateral notification initiated under subparagraph (D) with respect to any covered transaction, the President, acting through the Committee—

(i) shall review the covered transaction to determine the effects of the transaction on the national security of the United States; and

(ii) shall consider the factors specified in subsection (f) for such purpose, as appropriate.

(B) CONTROL BY FOREIGN GOVERNMENT—If the Committee determines that the covered transaction is a foreign government-controlled transaction, the Committee shall conduct an investigation of the transaction under paragraph (2).

(C) WRITTEN NOTICE—

(i) IN GENERAL—Any party or parties to any covered transaction may initiate a review of the transaction under this paragraph by submitting a written notice of the transaction to the Chairperson of the Committee.

* * *

(D) UNILATERAL INITIATION OF REVIEW—Subject to subparagraph (F), the President or the Committee may initiate a review under subparagraph (A) of—

(i) any covered transaction;

* * *

(E) TIMING—Any review under this paragraph shall be completed before the end of the 30-day period beginning on the date of the acceptance of written notice under subparagraph (C) by the chairperson, or beginning on the date of the initiation of the review in accordance with subparagraph (D), as applicable.

(F) LIMIT ON DELEGATION OF CERTAIN AUTHORITY—The authority of the Committee to initiate a review under subparagraph (D) may not be delegated to any person, other than the Deputy Secretary or an appropriate Under Secretary of the department or agency represented on the Committee.

(2) NATIONAL SECURITY INVESTIGATIONS—

(A) IN GENERAL—In each case described in subparagraph (B), the Committee shall immediately conduct an investigation of the effects of a covered transaction on the national security of the United

States, and take any necessary actions in connection with the transaction to protect the national security of the United States.

(B) APPLICABILITY—Subparagraph (A) shall apply in each case in which—

(i) a review of a covered transaction under paragraph (1) results in a determination that—

(I) the transaction threatens to impair the national security of the United States and that threat has not been mitigated during or prior to the review of a covered transaction under paragraph (1);

(II) the transaction is a foreign government-controlled transaction; or

(III) the transaction would result in control of any critical infrastructure of or within the United States by or on behalf of any foreign person, if the Committee determines that the transaction could impair national security, and that such impairment to national security has not been mitigated by assurances provided or renewed with the approval of the Committee, as described in subsection (l), during the review period under paragraph (1); or

(ii) the lead agency recommends, and the Committee concurs, that an investigation be undertaken.

(C) TIMING—Any investigation under subparagraph (A) shall be completed before the end of the 45-day period beginning on the date on which the investigation commenced.

(D) EXCEPTION—

(i) IN GENERAL—Notwithstanding subparagraph (B)(i), an investigation of a foreign government-controlled transaction described in subclause (II) of subparagraph (B)(i) or a transaction involving critical infrastructure described in subclause (III) of subparagraph (B)(i) shall not be required under this paragraph, if the Secretary of the Treasury and the head of the lead agency jointly determine, on the basis of the review of the transaction under paragraph (1), that the transaction will not impair the national security of the United States.

(ii) NONDELEGATION—The authority of the Secretary or the head of an agency referred to in clause (i) may not be delegated to any person, other than the Deputy Secretary of the Treasury or the deputy head (or the equivalent thereof) of the lead agency, respectively.

* * *

(d) Action by the President

(1) IN GENERAL—Subject to paragraph (4), the President may take such action for such times as the President considers appropriate to suspend or prohibit any covered transaction that threatens to impair the national security of the United States.

* * *

(4) Findings of the President—The President may exercise the authority conferred by paragraph (1), only if the President finds that—

(A) there is credible evidence that leads the President to believe that the foreign interest exercising control might take action that threatens to impair the national security; and

(B) provisions of law, other than this section and the International Emergency Economic Powers Act, do not, in the judgment of the President, provide adequate and appropriate authority for the President to protect the national security in the matter before the President.

(5) Factors to be considered—For purposes of determining whether to take action under paragraph (1), the President shall consider, among other factors each of the factors described in subsection (f) of this section, as appropriate.

(e) Actions and findings nonreviewable—The actions of the President under paragraph (1) of subsection (d) of this section and the findings of the President under paragraph (4) of subsection (d) of this section shall not be subject to judicial review.

(f) Factors to be considered—For purposes of this section, the President or the President's designee may, taking into account the requirements of national security, consider—

(1) domestic production needed for projected national defense requirements,

(2) the capability and capacity of domestic industries to meet national defense requirements, including the availability of human resources, products, technology, materials, and other supplies and services,

(3) the control of domestic industries and commercial activity by foreign citizens as it affects the capability and capacity of the United States to meet the requirements of national security,

(4) the potential effects of the proposed or pending transaction on sales of military goods, equipment, or technology to any country—

(A) identified by the Secretary of State—

(i) under section 6(j) of the Export Administration Act of 1979 as a country that supports terrorism;

(ii) under section 6(l) of the Export Administration Act of 1979, as a country of concern regarding missile proliferation; or

(iii) under section 6(m) of the Export Administration Act, as a country of concern regarding the proliferation of chemical and biological weapons;

(B) identified by the Secretary of Defense as posing a potential regional military threat to the interests of the United States; or

(C) listed under section 309(c) of the Nuclear Non-Proliferation Act of 1978 on the "Nuclear Non-Proliferation-Special Country List" (15 C.F.R. Part 778, Supplement No. 4) or any successor list;

(5) the potential effects of the proposed or pending transaction on United States international technological leadership in areas affecting United States national security;

(6) the potential national security-related effects on United States critical infrastructure, including major energy assets;

(7) the potential national security-related effects on United States critical technologies;

(8) whether the covered transaction is a foreign government-controlled transaction, as determined under subsection (b)(1)(B) of this section;

(9) as appropriate, and particularly with respect to transactions requiring an investigation under subsection (b)(1)(B) of this section, a review of the current assessment of—

(A) the adherence of the subject country to nonproliferation control regimes, including treaties and multilateral supply guidelines, which shall draw on, but not be limited to, the annual report on "Adherence to and Compliance with Arms Control, Nonproliferation and Disarmament Agreements and Commitments" required by section 2593a of Title 22;

(B) the relationship of such country with the United States, specifically on its record on cooperating in counter-terrorism efforts, which shall draw on, but not be limited to, the report of the President to Congress under section 7120 of the Intelligence Reform and Terrorism Prevention Act of 2004; and

(C) the potential for transshipment or diversion of technologies with military applications, including an analysis of national export control laws and regulations;

(10) the long-term projection of United States requirements for sources of energy and other critical resources and material; and

(11) such other factors as the President or the Committee may determine to be appropriate, generally or in connection with a specific review or investigation.

* * *

(k) Committee on Foreign Investment in the United States—

(1) ESTABLISHMENT—The Committee on Foreign Investment in the United States, established pursuant to Executive Order No. 11858, shall be a multi agency committee to carry out this section and such other assignments as the President may designate.

(2) MEMBERSHIP—The Committee shall be comprised of the following members or the designee of any such member:

(A) The Secretary of the Treasury.

(B) The Secretary of Homeland Security.

(C) The Secretary of Commerce.

(D) The Secretary of Defense.

(E) The Secretary of State.

(F) The Attorney General of the United States.

(G) The Secretary of Energy.

(H) The Secretary of Labor (nonvoting, ex officio).

(I) The Director of National Intelligence (nonvoting, ex officio).

(J) The heads of any other executive department, agency, or office, as the President determines appropriate, generally or on a case-by-case basis.

(3) CHAIRPERSON—The Secretary of the Treasury shall serve as the chairperson of the Committee.

(4) ASSISTANT SECRETARY FOR THE DEPARTMENT OF THE TREASURY—There shall be established an additional position of Assistant Secretary of the Treasury, who shall be appointed by the President, by and with the advice and consent of the Senate. The Assistant Secretary appointed under this paragraph shall report directly to the Undersecretary of the Treasury for International Affairs. The duties of the Assistant Secretary shall include duties related to the Committee on Foreign Investment in the United States, as delegated by the Secretary of the Treasury under this section.

* * *

Neither Congress nor the Administration has attempted to define the term *national security*. Treasury Department officials have indicated, however, that during a review or investigation each CFIUS member is expected to apply that definition of national security that is consistent with the representative agency's specific legislative mandate. Congress, in the Foreign Investment and National Security Act of 2007 ("FINSA"), broadened the concept of national security to include, "those issues relating to 'homeland security,' including its application to critical infrastructure."[3] CFUIS does appear to reference definitions from other statutes and regulations, however. The Patriot Act of 2001, 42 U.S.C. § 5195c(e), contains a definition of critical infrastructures for the Department of Homeland Security, a member of CFIUS. There is also a regulation defining "critical technologies" under U.S. export control regulations. See 31 C.F.R. § 800.209.

In any event, the definition of national security is the dividing line that separates legitimate national security protections from rank economic protectionism. The first excerpt below introduces you to this complex, interwoven political and economic issue.

QUESTION

FINSA requires that Treasury report to Congress on investments by entities controlled by a foreign government whenever the government complies with any boycott of Israel. Pub. L. No. 110–49, § 7(c). How do such acquisitions impair U.S. national security?

JEREMY DAVID SACKS, MONOPSONY AND THE ARCHERS: RETHINKING FOREIGN ACQUISITIONS AFTER *THOMSON-LTV*[4]

25 L. & POL'Y INT'L BUS. 1019, 1046–51 (1994).

Unfortunately, it is not always easy to decide what goods are vital to national security and what products are not. As Amy Borrus of Business

---

3 Are sovereign wealth funds' investments in the privatization of toll roads covered?

4 [Ed.: In 1992, Thomson, a French firm, attempted to purchase LTV Corporation's missiles and aerospace divisions using its U.S. subsidiary, Thomson-CSF. The French government owns approximately 60 percent of Thomson and protects the firm from domestic competitors. Both Congress and the outgoing Bush administration were prepared to block the transaction on national security grounds under the Exon-Florio Amendment. House defense committees and subcommittees publicly opposed the acquisition and the Senate eventually voted ninety-three to four against the deal. CFIUS undertook a formal investigation and rumors spread that it was going to recommend to President Bush that he block the acquisition. The European Community complained, warning such an action could have negative effects on U.S.-EC trade. Thomson withdrew its CFIUS notification and sought to restructure the deal within U.S. security constraints. After more negotiation, Thomson announced that it had decided to withdraw its offer for LTV missiles. Loral, an American company, eventually bought the missile division while the Carlyle Group and Northrop purchased the aircraft business. Lockheed later bought most of Loral. Ironically, Loral stood accused in 1998 for letting secret missile technology fall into the hands of the Chinese. President Clinton had approved (some say under the influence of campaign

Week couched the issue, "the problem is where to draw the line between benign foreign investment and acquisitions that endanger U.S. control of key technologies," such as those identified by the Pentagon in its study. "Prohibiting all foreign acquisitions of U.S. defense companies could backfire. Military readiness does not demand that Americans own every widget maker that sells to the Pentagon. . . . Foreign ownership may even be beneficial if it brings new technology or bolsters a financially ailing U.S. company." Further benefits brought by direct foreign investment include financing of 16.5 percent of the Treasury debt, providing needed capital to supplement the low domestic savings rate, and creating jobs and increasing competition.

Still, where do policymakers draw the line? An analysis of three of the main camps engaged in the debate points to a synthesis of their views, one which also hints at needed changes in the Exon-Florio regime. The first paradigm, that espoused by Secretary of Labor Robert Reich, ostensibly values foreign investment in general but acknowledges the dangers that unfair trade poses to key sectors of the U.S. economy, such as defense. Earlier a partisan of preservationist policies designed to shield larger segments of the domestic economy, Reich now advocates a more open attitude to foreign direct investment: "the underlying predicament is not that the Japanese [or the French] are exploiting our discoveries but that we can't turn basic inventions into new products nearly as fast or as well as they can." Latching onto the idea of technical training and experience, Reich welcomes investment if it provides this needed foundation for U.S. workers, allowing them in turn to exploit this training by turning technology into consumer durables in the United States through entrepreneurial enterprise.

Reich is not blind to the raw political choices that underpin his prescription; he wants foreigners to train U.S. workers because such apprenticeship will produce a better-skilled U.S. workforce. However, Reich recommends that the government preserve key industries, so that they can serve U.S. national security and provide a technological basis for his desired entrepreneurial revolution. The United States' "interest lies in ensuring that Americans get at least a fair share" of technological experience. Doing so may entail subsidizing "corporations that undertake more of their complex production in America," even if they are Japanese flagship firms. To critics of this recommendation, Reich aptly notes that we

> have been willing to subsidize business indirectly, through a wide array of devices (quotas on foreign imports, government procurement contracts, tax breaks, anti-trust exemptions) that are often relatively covert and whose purposes are sometimes only tangentially related to the public interest. Far better to do it

---

contributions from the Chinese) a joint venture of Loral and the Chinese government to place weather satellites in orbit. Loral eventually paid a $20 million fine to settle the charges.]

directly, and for a reason crucial to our continued economic prosperity and military security.

While Reich is correct in assuming that these decisions directly bear on military security and in uncovering the many hidden subsidies provided by U.S. taxpayers, his notion of subsidizing a Japanese firm for its U.S. production line is a bit foggy. As Mickey Kaus notes, "though IBM may see itself as a cosmopolitan corporation, with no particular national loyalties, that doesn't seem to be how Fujitsu sees itself." [F]irms like Fujitsu and Thomson have a vast wealth of home government support and banking connections to draw upon in capturing market share for their companies; U.S. firms generally do not. Susan and Martin Tolchin, representatives of the second paradigm of trade policy, say as much. The Tolchins note that Fujitsu's attempted takeover of Fairchild should not have been welcomed, as Reich claims, but was rightly opposed. "The U.S. semiconductor industry's steep loss of market share in the 1980's . . . resulted in large measure from the gains made by Japanese competitors supported by government subsidies." If the U.S. firms, providing jobs to U.S. workers, were effectively destroyed by Japanese firms with government subsidies, why should the U.S. government subsidize those same firms a second time? After all, they already effectively excluded U.S. firms from the international market.

The Tolchins support what Reich pejoratively calls "techno-nationalism:" they call for a large-scale U.S. government-led campaign to target key industries, whether in the defense field or not, for support and preservation. While some of their recommendations, such as revamping domestic antitrust laws which hinder U.S. competitiveness, aim to use the market to pick the winner in a competitive contest, others smack of too much trust in planning as an answer to U.S. industry's problems.

While defense firms are more deserving of protection from foreign buyers on political grounds, commercial firms are not. Government has never proven itself better than a working market mechanism at picking "winners" and "losers" in the commercial world. Even Japan's Ministry for International Trade and Investment (MITI) has picked some notorious losers, including Sony's Betamax videocassette system. Its "fifth-generation computer project, so feared in the early 1980's, closed up shop recently, left in the dust by the private sector's pace of innovation. Similarly, Japan's high-definition television effort seems to have bet on yesterday's technology." Indeed, high-tech industries by themselves may not be any more worthy of protection on economic grounds than a widget maker: "Paul Krugman of MIT, though a pioneer of the new [interventionist] theories, says the claim that the social returns to high-tech industries significantly exceed the private returns is 'at best unsupported by the evidence.' " Yet if these industries are central to a nation's defense, then the economic argument placing "social returns" at the apex of values may be overridden by national security concerns.

Theodore Moran offers a third paradigm which can reconcile the need for national security protection with the general notion that functioning competitive markets and the price mechanism best create and distribute wealth. In testimony before a Senate panel, Moran outlined the problem. First, the United States should be in favor of foreign investment, even by acquisition, since it "provides substantial benefits to the host country in the form of managerial skill, productivity efficiency, financial resources, and (perhaps) new technology." Still, there are exceptions to this general liberal attitude. When direct foreign investment becomes a national security threat, the government should stop the purchase. Moran applies a concentration test to judge when the line is crossed, asking how many alternative suppliers remain for a product and if there are comparable substitutes. In general, "if more than four suppliers (four companies and/or four home governments) control more than 50 percent of the market, the suppliers are unlikely to be able to impose conditions on the use of their products, inputs, or technologies even if they try to coordinate efforts to do so."

In the Thomson case,

> for each of [the] principal LTV missile systems, the LTV acquisition by Thomson-CSF represents the transference of quasi-monopoly power from one sovereign domain to another. This will require America to seek French acquiescence as we try to pursue our own economic or foreign policy interests with these products or technologies around the world.

Yet Thomson was an "easy" case; as a prime defense contractor, it bore directly on national security concerns. Still, Moran insists that his concentration test is equally applicable to "military acquisitions, to dual-use acquisitions, and to critical civilian acquisitions." Blending the Tolchins' notion of economic security with Reich's understanding that foreign investment is inherently beneficial, Moran sets up a test mechanism that is applicable to all acquisitions.

* * *

A January 2008 Executive Order by President George W. Bush laid out the role of the President in evaluating covered transactions. The President will step in when the Committee: (1) recommends that the President suspend or prohibit the transactions; (2) is unable to reach a decision; or (3) asks the President to decide.

At its core, the CFIUS review process now consists of four steps: (1) a triggering event for review (usually a voluntary filing by an interested party); (2) an initial thirty day *National Security Review* of the transaction; (3) a determination to either cease any further action or proceed to a forty-five day continuation of a *National Security Investigation*; and (4) in the event of a forty-five day investigation, an announcement by the President within fifteen days of a final decision of a CFIUS recommendation.

Certain transactions automatically require the second stage review,[5] particularly those involving acquisitions made by *sovereign wealth funds*. A sovereign wealth fund is an investment fund or entity controlled by a foreign government. It is commonly established from the balance of payment surpluses, official foreign currency operations, the proceeds of privatizations, government transfer payments, fiscal surpluses and/or receipts resulting from resource exports. According to the Sovereign Wealth Fund Institute, in 2017 the three largest funds in terms of assets under management where Norway's Government Pension Fund—Global ($1 trillion), UAE's Abu Dhabi Investment Authority ($828 billion) and China's China Investment Corporation ($814 billion).[6]

According to CFIUS's Annual Report to Congress (2015), between 2009 and 2015 companies filed 770 notices of transactions that CFIUS determined were covered transactions. Of those, about three percent were withdraw during the review stage, seven percent were withdrawn during the investigation stage and 40 percent resulted in an investigation. From 2013 to 2015, 40 cases (10 percent) resulted in the use of legally binding mitigation measures, ranging from national security agreements to letters of assurance.[7] In 2015, CFIUS mitigation measures were applied to 11 different covered transactions (8 percent of total 2015 transactions). One transaction resulted in successful litigation *against* the U.S. government. See *Ralls Corp. v. CFIUS*, 758 F.3d 296 (D.C. Cir. 2014) (*infra* Section A.1.c). Some question whether CFIUS is a serious impediment to foreign acquisitions.[8] Deal professionals believe, however, that the prospect of a CFIUS review has a significant chilling effect on investments by Chinese companies, in general, and Chinese sovereign wealth funds, in particular, in the United States.

The growth of interest by sovereign wealth funds in United States companies has many wondering whether the CFIUS system is up to the

---

5 Unless senior CFIUS officials conclude that the transactions, after a review, will not impair the national security of the U.S.

6 While these numbers are large, they should be put into context. U.S.-based Vanguard Group, a mutual fund family consisting of approximately 175 U.S. funds and 195 non-U.S. funds, had approximately *$4.5 trillion* in global assets under management as of September 17, 2017.

7 The measures required the businesses to take specific and verifiable actions including the establishment of a Corporate Security Committee and the position of a security office, reporting obligations to a government agency, and, in the case of a sovereign wealth fund, a promise that the fund will be a passive investor.

8 See. e.g., David Zaring, *CFIUS as a Congressional Notification Service*, 83 S. CAL. L. REV. 81 (2009) ("The actual practice of the Committee shows that, although apparently a hurdle that foreign acquirers rather fear, it rarely interferes with foreign acquisitions—and when it does interfere, it does so in a pro forma manner.").

task of regulating these investments. The author of the following excerpt suggests that the CFIUS process is too heavy handed.

PAUL ROSE, SOVEREIGNS AS SHAREHOLDERS

87 N.C. L. REV. 83 (2008).

* * *

A number of concerns remain with the CFIUS process, however, which suggest that the risk of heavy-handed application of CFIUS is greater than the risk of political exploitation of [sovereign wealth funds (SWFs))] by sponsoring sovereigns. First, even for transactions that are not reviewed, CFIUS already adds substantial transaction costs to any significant SWF transaction involving a U.S. entity. Aside from the added costs to the SWF and the issuer of legal advisors that help the parties navigate the CFIUS process, CFIUS also creates potentially costly delays if the transaction is reviewed. By requiring officials to affirmatively sign off on a decision not to investigate, FINSA creates pressure to investigate which will undoubtedly increase the average time for review of SWF deals.

The CFIUS process also raises the possibility of political mischief. The FINSA amendments to the CFIUS process created broad and arguably political tests that may not be directly related to the transaction itself and that may result in transaction approval being tied to political concerns. For example, CFIUS is required to consider: (a) "the adherence of the [SWF's] subject country to nonproliferation control regimes"; (b) "the relationship of such country with the United States," specifically regarding its record of cooperating with counter-terrorism efforts; and (c) "the potential for transshipment or diversion of technologies with military applications, including an analysis of national export control laws and regulations."

Politicization of the CFIUS process can also result from both private and governmental activities outside of CFIUS. Private parties have repeatedly used the CFIUS process to achieve private gains . . . .

* * *

. . . In June 2005, [the Chinese National Offshore Oil Corporation (CNOOC)], a state-controlled company, made an unsolicited, all-cash, $18.5 billion bid for Unocal Oil Company. The bid followed a $16.5 billion bid in cash and stock by Chevron. The bid expectedly raised political concerns. In July, the U.S. House of Representatives voted 398–15 for a resolution asking President Bush to block the transaction as a threat to national security. Chevron then increased its bid to approximately $17 billion. Unocal asked CNOOC to sweeten its bid to compensate for the inevitable delays as the Bush administration conducted a lengthy review of the acquisition. CNOOC declined to increase its offer unless Unocal agreed to pay the costs of terminating the Chevron transaction and "lobby for the deal in the US Congress." Unocal declined, and CNOOC withdrew its bid.

* * *

As made clear in the foregoing examples, the key to success of private efforts to exploit the CFIUS process is the encouragement of congressional involvement, which was enhanced through the FINSA amendments. FINSA provides for enhanced congressional oversight . . . . As practitioners have argued, "[s]uch broad ranging, transaction-by-transaction Congressional involvement in the potentially explosive issue of foreign investment can only raise the risk of political mischief, particularly where US constituents have an interest in opposing a competing foreign investor." The danger in the CFIUS process is that political abuse is easily masked as the furtherance of a legitimate task and the protection of national security. The risk of such political or protectionist measures, however, is less investment in the United States. For example, the head of China Investment Corp. warned that his $200 billion SWF will avoid investing in countries that use national security as an excuse for protectionism: "If an economy will use national security as a criteria [sic] for entry of sovereign wealth funds, we will be reluctant to tap the market because you are not sure what will happen . . . . [N]ational security should not be an excuse for protectionism."

* * *

FINSA will successfully discourage political investment by SWFs. However, FINSA may also have the unintended effect of discouraging active sovereign investors and perhaps even some passive sovereign investors, unless experience with the CFIUS process eases SWF concerns that CFIUS will be politicized.

* * *

QUESTION ON RECIPROCITY

Many of the sovereign wealth funds hold government funds in countries that do not have rules that allow U.S. companies to invest in those countries' domestic corporations as easily as they can invest in our companies. For example, China has a basic rule against foreign acquisitions of more than 50 percent of any of their own companies. A reciprocity rule would give CFIUS the same power to stop acquisitions of our companies whenever U.S. companies could not make the same kind of acquisitions in China (or any other country that prevents or inhibits acquisitions by U.S. companies). Should we demand reciprocity (or mutuality) and enable CFIUS to enforce those rules?

NOTE: THE EFFECT OF EXON-FLORIO ON HOSTILE ACQUISITIONS AND ACQUISITION TIMING

Regardless of whether the transaction is friendly or hostile, Exon-Florio adds strategic considerations to acquisitions in national security-sensitive industries. In a friendly deal, a third-party business competitor, while lacking standing to file a notice itself, can appeal to the President or members of Congress to put pressure on member agencies to trigger a review of a transaction, whether completed or proposed. For hostile tender offers, the amendment imposes a significant burden on bidders while providing a significant defense to targets.

Most hostile bidders, therefore, will choose to commence their tender offers and immediately file with CFIUS before closing the offers. A bidder could structure the transaction so that the offer is conditional upon no actual or threatened investigation by CFIUS and no prohibitive action by the President. A bidder could choose not to so condition an offer if only limited assets or business segments have national security implications and those assets or segments are not central to the acquisition and could be divested easily, if necessary. This post-announcement CFIUS filing preserves secrecy and, at the same time, gives bidders the option of not being contractually committed to purchase securities from shareholders if the President stops the acquisition.[9] A favorable CFIUS opinion also forecloses an investigation and divestiture order in the future, eliminating the possibility that the bidder will have to divest later, possibly at unfavorable prices.

Target companies in hostile bids have a number of strategic choices under the Exon-Florio amendment. The amendment has added a new term to the takeover defense arsenal—the "Pentagon ploy."[10] In a Pentagon ploy, the target board lobbies the Department of Defense or one of the ten other agencies in CFIUS for support in the target's push for a formal CFIUS investigation.[11]

---

[9] Some hostile bidders will be tempted to not contact or file notice with CFIUS until the acquisition closes. A bidder ought to pursue this strategy only if highly confident that, if investigated, the transaction would survive scrutiny under Exon-Florio. If the bidder miscalculates, it risks an investigation while the tender offer is underway, resulting in unplanned substantial delays and an order either prohibiting consummation of the transaction or requiring divestiture of the bidder's investment.

[10] In a related ploy, a firm can use the U.S. export control laws and regulations that prevent the transfer of technical data from a defense contractor to a foreigner. E.g., Arms Export Control Act of 1976, 22 U.S.C. § 2751 et seq. The Export Administration Regulations and the International Traffic in Arms Regulations, enforced by the Secretary of State and the Secretary of Commerce, respectively, treat the acquisition of a U.S. corporation by a non-U.S. corporation as an export of the technology of the U.S. to the nation of the acquirer. E.g., Export Administration Regulations, 15 C.F.R. § 768 (1989); International Traffic in Arms Regulations, 22 C.F.R. § 121 (1988).

[11] The 1990 BTR/Norton transaction illustrates the use of the defense. Norton, hoping to trigger a forty-five day probe under Exon-Florio, made aggressive appeals to the CFIUS agencies, both directly and through Congress, giving them exaggerated claims of national security threats. BTR, a British conglomerate, made a hostile bid to acquire the Norton Co., a Worcester, Mass.-based maker of abrasives, ceramics, and engineering materials that holds several classified Defense Department contracts. Norton's management enlisted the help of the Massachusetts governor, the state legislature, local officials, grass-roots employee groups, and 120 members of Congress (including the entire Massachusetts delegation), all of whom asked President George Bush to block the deal, ostensibly on national security grounds. CFIUS staff officials originally recommended against a formal investigation but, because of the unprecedented political pressure,

The agencies all have representatives on CFIUS who will vote on whether to conduct a formal investigation and, ultimately, on whether to recommend to the President that he or she stop the attempted takeover. The Defense Department is often a target's best choice to lobby. Not only is the Defense Department very influential in CFIUS, but the Department itself can also block some acquisitions by threatening to revoke a target's security clearance as a defense contractor,[12] significantly devaluing the firm by diminishing its earning potential so that it is an unattractive choice to a buyer. If a target firm cannot use the Pentagon ploy because it does not have a division engaged in defense industry contracting (a "black program" division), the target itself can acquire a third party defense contractor to defeat a foreign takeover—the so-called "Pentagon Defense."[13]

In any event, a target firm can file a notice for Exon-Florio review as a tactic to delay a hostile acquisition. A target's objective may be to trigger a formal investigation—whether it is warranted or not—so that the target will have as much as ninety days to bolster its defenses or encourage a bid from a more congenial suitor.[14] Statistics reveal that CFIUS is more likely to conduct a formal investigation if the attempted takeover is hostile rather than friendly. The delay from a CFIUS investigation can also create problems with the bidder's financing or increase the acquisition price due to additional speculation in the target's stock.

The problem with these defenses is that a target may disable itself from accepting a higher offer from an initially hostile bidder. A higher offer will not itself derail a CFIUS review once it has begun, and the target's national security complaint language may come back to complicate the now friendly deal.

CFIUS nonetheless launched a formal investigation. Although the President ultimately decided not to intervene in the possible acquisition of Norton, BTR had withdrawn its bid by then and Norton agreed to merge with France's Compagnie de Saint Gobain. The bid by Saint Gobain, France's seventh-largest company at the time, was at a slightly higher price. More important, perhaps, was that it included five-year employment contracts for twelve Norton executives and a seven-year contract for Norton's chairman, John Nelson, who quickly disavowed any national security concerns based on French ownership of the company. BTR Chairman John Cahill mused, "I guess Norton prefers the tricolor to the Union Jack." Many of those legislators who had helped Norton against BTR on less parochial grounds were left, according to a *Washington Post* reporter, "feeling had." Fullerton & Knee, *Running For Cover Under The Flag*, LEGAL TIMES (Jan. 6, 1992), pp. 20–21.

[12] Under the Defense Industrial Security Program, foreign-owned companies generally are prohibited from obtaining the security clearance necessary to compete for government contracts. See Melvin Rishe, *Foreign Ownership, Control or Influence: The Implications for United States Companies Performing Defense Contracts*, 20 PUB. CONT. L. J. 143 (1991).

[13] Similar defensive techniques have been employed through the purchase of insurance companies and radio or television stations, where government approval of such acquisitions is a prerequisite to the completion of a tender offer.

[14] There may be ways to delay the commencement and running of the statutory thirty-day review period.

NOTE: THE URANIUM ONE TRANSACTION BECOMES A POLITICAL FOOTBALL

Perhaps no other CFIUS covered transaction has become more of a political football than the Uranium One deal. Completed during 2010, the deal allowed JSC Atomredmetzoloto, or ARMZ, the mining arm of Rosatom, the Russian nuclear energy agency, to acquire a controlling stake in Uranium One, a Canadian-based company. At the time, Uranium One had two licensed mining operations in Wyoming which covered, according to the Nuclear Regulatory Commission (NRC), about 20 percent of the then licensed uranium in-situ recovery production capacity in the U.S. Uranium One also had exploration projects in the States of Arizona, Colorado and Utah.

To consummate the deal, ARMZ needed to notify CFIUS and await its review due to the obvious national security concerns raised by the acquisition. Of course, it is impossible to know what the deliberations of the CFIUS members were. Secretary of State Hillary Clinton could have objected to the sale,[15] as could the other voting members. But objections—even if they existed—would not have stopped the sale, as only President Obama had the power to suspend or prohibit this covered transaction. And he did not.

Additionally, the NRC had to approve the transfer of two uranium recovery licenses in Wyoming from Uranium One to ARMZ. While the NRZ approved the transfer on November 24, 2010, its approval did not allow uranium produced at either facility to be exported to Russia. Before export would be allowed, ARMZ would have to apply for and obtain an export license from the NRZ and commit to use the material only for "peaceful purposes" in accordance with Section 123 of the U.S. Atomic Energy Act of 1954. However, in 2012 the NRC did agree to amend the export license of RSB Logistics Services to allow the Kentucky shipping company to export uranium to Canada from various sources. Those sources included a Uranium One site in Wyoming. The amendment allowed RSB to ship uranium to a conversion plant in Canada and then back to the U.S. for further processing. Before Canada can export any U.S. uranium to any other country besides the U.S., it is required to obtain U.S. approval.

Although Uranium One once held 20 percent of licensed uranium in-situ recovery production capacity in the U.S., that has dropped to an estimated 10 percent in 2017. However, that drop is misleading. Back in 2010, there were only four in-situ licensed uranium facilities. Currently, there are 10 such facilities. In terms of actual domestic uranium *production*, Uranium One has been responsible for no more than 5.9 percent according to a September 2017 report by the U.S. International Trade Commission.

---

[15] Jose Fernandez, a former assistant secretary of state, told the *New York Times* in 2015 that he represented the State Department on CFIUS. While not referring specifically to the Uranium One deal, he commented that "Mrs. Clinton never intervened with me on any C.F.I.U.S. matter." Jo Becker & Mike McIntire, *Cash Flowed to Clinton Foundation Amid Russian Uranium Deal*, N.Y. TIMES (Apr. 25, 2015) (avail. at https://www.nytimes.com/2015/04/24/us/cash-flowed-to-clinton-foundation-as-russians-pressed-for-control-of-uranium-company.html).

Hillary Clinton's role in the Uranium One sale, and the transaction's link to the Clinton Foundation, first became an issue in 2015. At that time, news organizations received advance copies of the book CLINTON CASH: THE UNTOLD STORY OF HOW AND WHY FOREIGN GOVERNMENTS AND BUSINESSES HELPED MAKE BILL AND HILLARY CLINTON RICH, by Peter Schweizer, a former fellow at a conservative think tank. Later, the *New York Times* detailed how the Clinton Foundation had received millions of dollars in donations from investors in Uranium One.[16] The Clinton Foundation failed to publicly disclose those donations, even though Hillary Clinton had an agreement with the White House that the Foundation would disclose the identities of all contributors.

The *Times* also wrote that former President Bill Clinton spoke at a conference in Moscow on June 29, 2010—which was after the Uranium One deal was announced but before it was approved by CFIUS in October 2010. The organizer of the conference, the Russian-based Renaissance Capital Group, paid Mr. Clinton a handsome $500,000 speaking fee. According to the *Times*, Renaissance Capital has "ties to the Kremlin" and its analysts "talked up Uranium One's stock, assigning it a 'buy' rating and saying in a July 2010 research report that it was 'the best play' in the uranium markets."[17]

Hillary Clinton's involvement in the Uranium One deal took center stage during the 2016 U.S. Presidential election. Then candidate Donald Trump accused Mrs. Clinton in her role as Secretary of State of giving away U.S. uranium rights to the Russians and claimed that it was done in exchange for donations to the Clinton Foundation. Since then, two U.S. House of Representative committees have stated that they will investigate the Obama administration's approval of the Uranium One deal. Will we ever know the answer to whether Hillary Clinton was personally involved in the Uranium One deal? Was it "pay-for-play"? While we may never know the answers, the deal does make for interesting political intrigue.

c. Judicial Review

What ability, if any, do the courts have to review the national security recommendations and determinations of CFIUS and the President? Until recently, the universal answer had been "none." Does the following decision change the answer? If so, to what degree?

RALLS CORP. V. COMMITTEE ON FOREIGN INVESTMENT IN THE UNITED STATES

United States Court of Appeals for the District of Columbia Circuit, 2014.
758 F.3d 296.

KAREN LECRAFT HENDERSON, CIRCUIT JUDGE.

In March 2012, Appellant Ralls Corporation (Ralls) purchased four American limited liability companies (Project Companies) previously

---

16 See *id.*

17 *Id.*

formed to develop windfarms in north-central Oregon. The transaction quickly came under scrutiny from the Committee on Foreign Investment in the United States (CFIUS), an Executive Branch committee created by the Defense Production Act of 1950 (DPA) . . . and chaired by the Secretary of the U.S. Treasury Department (Treasury Secretary) . . . . Although Ralls is an American corporation, the transaction fell within the ambit of the DPA because both of Ralls's owners are Chinese nationals. CFIUS determined that Ralls's acquisition of the Project Companies threatened national security and issued temporary mitigation orders restricting Ralls's access to, and preventing further construction at, the Project Companies' windfarm sites. The matter was then submitted to the President, who also concluded that the transaction posed a threat to national security. He issued a Presidential Order that prohibited the transaction and required Ralls to divest itself of the Project Companies. Ralls challenged the final order issued by CFIUS (CFIUS Order) and the Presidential Order in district court, alleging, *inter alia*, that the orders violate the Due Process Clause of the Fifth Amendment to the United States Constitution because neither CFIUS nor the President (collectively, with Treasury Secretary and CFIUS Chairman Jacob Lew, Appellees) provided Ralls the opportunity to review and rebut the evidence upon which they relied. The district court dismissed Ralls's . . . due process challenge to the Presidential Order for failure to state a claim. For the reasons set forth below, we reverse.

I. BACKGROUND

A. Statutory and Regulatory Framework

This case involves Executive Branch review of a business transaction under section 721 of the DPA, also known as the "Exon-Florio Amendment." As amended, section 721 of the DPA directs "the President, acting through [CFIUS]," to review a "covered transaction to determine the effects of the transaction on the national security of the United States." 50 U.S.C. app. § 2170(b)(1)(A). Section 721 defines a covered transaction as "any merger, acquisition, or takeover by or with any foreign person which could result in foreign control of any person engaged in interstate commerce in the United States." *Id.* § 2170(a)(3).

Review of covered transactions under section 721 begins with CFIUS. As noted, CFIUS is chaired by the Treasury Secretary and its members include the heads of various federal agencies and other high-ranking Government officials with foreign policy, national security and economic responsibilities.[2] *See id.* § 2170(k)(2), (3). CFIUS review is initiated in one

[2] CFIUS includes the Secretaries of Treasury, Homeland Security, Commerce, Defense, State and Energy; the Secretary of Labor and the Director of National Intelligence, who participate as non-voting, *ex officio* members; the United States Attorney General; and other officials as the President deems appropriate. 50 U.S.C. app. § 2170(k)(2). The President also appointed the United States Trade Representative and the Director of the Office of Science and Technology Policy to CFIUS and directed several White House officials, among others, to participate as observers. . . .

of two ways. First, any party to a covered transaction may initiate review, either before or after the transaction is completed, by submitting a written notice to the CFIUS chairman. . . . Alternatively, CFIUS may initiate review *sua sponte*. . . . The CFIUS review period lasts thirty days, during which CFIUS considers the eleven factors set forth in 50 U.S.C. app. § 2170(f) to assess the transaction's effect on national security.[4] *See id.* § 2170(b)(1)(A)(ii), (E).

During its review, if CFIUS determines that "the transaction threatens to impair the national security of the United States and that threat has not been mitigated," it must "immediately conduct an investigation of the effects of [the] covered transaction on the national security . . . and take any necessary actions in connection with the transaction to protect the national security." *Id.* § 2170(b)(2)(A), (B). CFIUS is given express authority to "negotiate, enter into or impose, and enforce any agreement or condition with any party to the covered transaction in order to mitigate any threat to the national security of the United States that arises as a result of the covered transaction." *Id.* § 2170(l)(1)(A). The investigation period lasts no more than forty-five days. *See id.* § 2170(b)(2)(C). If CFIUS determines at the end of an investigation that the national security effects of the transaction have been mitigated and that the transaction need not be prohibited, action under section 721 terminates and CFIUS submits a final investigation report to the Congress. *See id.* § 2170(b)(3)(B); 31 C.F.R. § 800.506(d).

If CFIUS concludes at the end of its investigation that a covered transaction should be suspended or prohibited, it must "send a report to the President requesting the President's decision," which report includes, *inter alia*, information regarding the transaction's effect on national security and CFIUS's recommendation. 31 C.F.R. § 800.506(b), (c). Once CFIUS's report is submitted to the President, he has fifteen days to "take such action for such time as the President considers appropriate to suspend

[4] The eleven factors include "(1) domestic production needed for projected national defense requirements, (2) the capability and capacity of domestic industries to meet national defense requirements, including the availability of human resources, products, technology, materials, and other supplies and services, (3) the control of domestic industries and commercial activity by foreign citizens as it affects the capability and capacity of the United States to meet the requirements of national security, (4) the potential effects of the proposed or pending transaction on sales of military goods, equipment, or technology to [certain] countries . . . (5) the potential effects of the proposed or pending transaction on United States international technological leadership in areas affecting United States national security; (6) the potential national security-related effects on United States critical infrastructure, including major energy assets; (7) the potential national security-related effects on United States critical technologies; (8) whether the covered transaction is a foreign government-controlled transaction, as determined under subsection (b)(1)(B) of this section; (9) as appropriate, and particularly with respect to transactions requiring an investigation under subsection (b)(1)(B) of this section, a review of the current assessment of [the foreign country's relationship and cooperation with the United States]; (10) the long-term projection of United States requirements for sources of energy and other critical resources and material; and (11) such other factors as the President or [CFIUS] may determine to be appropriate, generally or in connection with a specific review or investigation." 50 U.S.C. app. § 2170(f).

or prohibit any covered transaction that threatens to impair the national security of the United States." 50 U.S.C. app. § 2170(d)(1), (2). The President may exercise his authority under section 721 only if he finds that

> there is credible evidence that leads [him] to believe that the foreign interest exercising control might take action that threatens to impair the national security; and . . . provisions of law, other than [section 721] and the International Emergency Economic Powers Act, do not, in the judgment of the President, provide adequate and appropriate authority for the President to protect the national security in the matter before the President.

Id. § 2170(d)(4). Significantly, the statute provides that "[t]he actions of the President under paragraph (1) of subsection (d) of this section and the findings of the President under paragraph (4) of subsection (d) of this section shall not be subject to judicial review." *Id.* § 2170(e). In deciding whether to suspend or prohibit a transaction, the President is directed to consider, "among other factors, each of the factors described in subsection (f) of this section, as appropriate." *Id.* § 2170(d)(5); *see supra* note 4.

B. Factual Background

Ralls is an American company incorporated in Delaware with its principal place of business in Georgia. Ralls is owned by two Chinese nationals, Dawei Duan and Jialiang Wu. Duan is the chief financial officer of Sany Group (Sany), a Chinese manufacturing company, and, at the time of the transaction at issue, Wu was a Sany vice-president and the general manager of Sany Electric Company, Ltd. (Sany Electric). Ralls's amended complaint asserts that "Ralls is in the business of identifying U.S. opportunities for the construction of windfarms in which the wind turbines of Sany Electric, its affiliate, can be used and their quality and reliability demonstrated to the U.S. wind industry in comparison to competitor products.". . .

In March 2012, Ralls purchased the Project Companies, which are four American-owned, limited liability companies: Pine City Windfarm, LLC; Mule Hollow Windfarm, LLC; High Plateau Windfarm, LLC; and Lower Ridge Windfarm, LLC. The Project Companies were originally created by an Oregon entity (Oregon Windfarms, LLC) owned by American citizens to develop four windfarms in north-central Oregon (collectively, Butter Creek projects). Before Ralls acquired them, each of the Project Companies had acquired assets necessary for windfarm development, including

> easements with local landowners to access their property and construct windfarm turbines; power purchase agreements with the local utility, PacifiCorp; generator interconnection agreements permitting connection to PacifiCorp's grid; transmission interconnection agreements and agreements for the management and use of shared facilities with other nearby

windfarms; and necessary government permits and approvals to construct five windfarm turbines at specific, approved locations. . . .

The Butter Creek project sites are located in and around the eastern region of a restricted airspace and bombing zone maintained by the United States Navy (Navy). Three of the windfarm sites are located within seven miles of the restricted airspace while the fourth—Lower Ridge—is located within the restricted airspace. After the Navy urged Ralls to move the Lower Ridge site "to reduce airspace conflicts between the Lower Ridge wind turbines and low-level military aircraft training," . . . Ralls relocated the windfarm but it remains within the restricted airspace.

Ralls's complaint alleges that Oregon Windfarms, LLC, has developed nine other windfarm projects (Echo Projects) in the same general vicinity as the Butter Creek projects and that all nine use foreign-made wind turbines. According to Ralls, seven turbines used by the Echo Projects are located within the restricted airspace and one of the nine Echo Projects—Pacific Canyon—is currently owned by foreign investors. In addition, Ralls claims that there are "dozens if not hundreds of existing turbines in or near the western region of the restricted airspace" that "are foreign-made and foreign-owned." . . . The Appellees conceded at oral argument that there are other foreign-owned wind turbines near the restricted airspace. . . .

On June 28, 2012,[6] Ralls submitted a twenty-five-page notice to CFIUS informing it of Ralls's March acquisition of the Project Companies.[7] The notice explained why Ralls believed the transaction did not pose a national security threat. CFIUS initiated its review pursuant to 50 U.S.C. app. § 2170(b)(1). During the thirty-day review period, Ralls responded to several questions posed by CFIUS and gave a presentation to CFIUS officials. . . .

CFIUS determined that Ralls's acquisition of the Project Companies posed a national security threat and on July 25 it issued an Order Establishing Interim Mitigation Measures (July Order) to mitigate the threat. The July Order required Ralls to (1) cease all construction and operations at the Butter Creek project sites, (2) "remove all stockpiled or stored items from the [project sites] no later than July 30, 2012, and shall not deposit, stockpile, or store any new items at the [project sites]" and (3) cease all access to the project sites. . . . Five days later, July 30, CFIUS launched an investigation under 50 U.S.C. app. § 2170(b)(2).

Three days into its investigation, on August 2, CFIUS issued an Amended Order Establishing Interim Mitigation Measures (CFIUS Order). In addition to the July Order restrictions, the CFIUS Order prohibited

---

6 Unless otherwise indicated, all events occurred in 2012.

7 Ralls conceded in district court that it submitted the notice only after CFIUS informed it that the Defense Department intended to file a notice triggering CFIUS review if Ralls did not file first.

Ralls from completing any sale of the Project Companies or their assets without first removing all items (including concrete foundations) from the Butter Creek project sites, notifying CFIUS of the sale and giving CFIUS ten business days to object to the sale. The CFIUS Order remained in effect "until CFIUS concludes action or the President takes action under section 721" or until express "revocation by CFIUS or the President." . . . Neither the July Order nor the CFIUS Order disclosed the nature of the national security threat the transaction posed or the evidence on which CFIUS relied in issuing the orders. On September 13, the investigation period ended and CFIUS submitted its report (including its recommendation) to the President, requesting his decision.

On September 28, the President issued an "Order Regarding the Acquisition of Four U.S. Wind Farm Project Companies by Ralls Corporation" (Presidential Order). The Presidential Order stated that "there is credible evidence that leads [the President] to believe that Ralls . . . might take action that threatens to impair the national security of the United States" and that "[p]rovisions of law, other than section 721 and the International Emergency Economic Powers Act . . . do not, in [the President's] judgment, provide adequate and appropriate authority for [the President] to protect the national security in this matter." . . . In light of the findings, the Presidential Order directed that the transaction be prohibited. "In order to effectuate" the prohibition, the Presidential Order required Ralls to, *inter alia,* (1) divest itself of all interests in the Project Companies, their assets and their operations within ninety days of the Order, (2) remove all items from the project sites "stockpiled, stored, deposited, installed, or affixed thereon," (3) cease access to the project sites, (4) refrain from selling, transferring or facilitating the sale or transfer of "any items made or otherwise produced by the Sany Group to any third party for use or installation at the [project sites]" and (5) adhere to restrictions on the sale of the Project Companies and their assets to third parties. . . . The Presidential Order also "revoked" both orders issued by CFIUS. . . .

It is undisputed that neither CFIUS nor the President gave Ralls notice of the evidence on which they respectively relied nor an opportunity to rebut that evidence. *See infra* note 19.

C. District Court Proceedings

Approximately two weeks before the Presidential Order issued, Ralls filed suit against CFIUS and its then-chairman, Treasury Secretary Timothy Geithner, in district court. Ralls sought to invalidate the CFIUS Order and to enjoin its enforcement, claiming that . . . the Order deprived Ralls of its constitutionally protected property interests in violation of the Due Process Clause of the Fifth Amendment to the United States Constitution. . . .

After the President issued the Presidential Order on September 28, Ralls amended its complaint to add claims challenging the Presidential Order and naming the President as a defendant. The amended complaint ... challenged the constitutionality of both orders, under the Fifth Amendment Due Process Clause .... CFIUS and the President moved to dismiss Ralls's complaint for lack of subject-matter jurisdiction, which motion the district court granted in part and denied in part in February 2013. The court ... concluded that section 721 [did not bar] ... judicial review of ... Ralls's due process challenge ....

Shortly thereafter, the Appellees moved to dismiss Ralls's due process claim attacking the Presidential Order for failure to state a claim under Federal Rule of Civil Procedure 12(b)(6). The district court eventually granted the motion in October 2013. In dismissing Ralls's remaining due process claim, it first determined that the Presidential Order did not deprive Ralls of a constitutionally protected property interest. Although the court acknowledged that Ralls had "entered into a transaction in March 2012 through which it obtained certain property rights under state law," ... it nonetheless found that Ralls had no constitutionally protected interest because Ralls "voluntarily acquired those state property rights subject to the known risk of a Presidential veto" and "waived the opportunity ... to obtain a determination from CFIUS and the President before it entered into the transaction[.]" ... The court then concluded that, even if Ralls had a constitutionally protected property interest, the Appellees provided Ralls with due process. According to the court, CFIUS informed Ralls in June 2012 that the transaction had to be reviewed and gave Ralls the opportunity to submit evidence in its favor in its notice filing and during follow-up conversations with—and a presentation to—CFIUS officials.

Ralls timely appealed the district court's Rule 12(b)(6) dismissal of its due process challenge to the Presidential Order ....

II. DUE PROCESS CLAIM

Our first order of business is to satisfy ourselves that we have jurisdiction to review the dismissal of Ralls's due process challenge to the Presidential Order.... The Appellees argue, first, that section 721 expressly deprives us of jurisdiction of the due process claim and, second, that the claim is non-justiciable. Rejecting the Appellees' two jurisdictional challenges, we then treat the merits.

A. Statutory Bar to Judicial Review

As noted, the DPA provides that

> [t]he actions of the President under paragraph (1) of subsection (d) of this section and the findings of the President under paragraph (4) of subsection (d) of this section shall not be subject to judicial review.

50 U.S.C. app. § 2170(e). The "actions of the President" referred to are "such action[s] for such time as the President considers appropriate to suspend or prohibit any covered transaction that threatens to impair the national security of the United States." *Id.* § 2170(d)(1). The President's "findings" under subsection (d) of paragraph (4) include his determination that (1) there is "credible evidence that leads [him] to believe that the foreign interest exercising control might take action that threatens to impair the national security" and (2) other provisions of law do not give him adequate authority to protect the national security. *Id.* § 2170(d)(4).

The Supreme Court has long held that a statutory bar to judicial review precludes review of constitutional claims only if there is "clear and convincing" evidence that the Congress so intended. . . . Our precedent makes clear that the "particularly rigorous" clear-and-convincing standard applies to both facial and as-applied constitutional claims. . . . In applying the clear-and-convincing evidence standard, we examine both the text of the statute and the legislative history for evidence of congressional intent to bar judicial review of constitutional claims.

* * *

. . . [T]he Appellees argue that section 2170(e) bars our review of Ralls's due process claim. According to the Appellees, the text of the provision—which precludes judicial review of "actions of the President under paragraph (1) of subsection (d)," 50 U.S.C. app. § 2170(e)—bars judicial review of *all* actions taken by the President under the statute, including "the President's choice not to provide Ralls with more notice than it had already received, his decision not to confide in Ralls his national security concerns, and his judgment about the appropriate level of detail with which to publicly articulate his reasoning." . . .

. . . [T]he Appellees also submit that we may infer from current and former congressional oversight provisions in the statute—and the portions of legislative history pertaining to them—that the Congress intended any review of the President's actions under the DPA to occur in the halls of the Congress, not in the courtrooms of the judiciary. They first point to legislative history relating to a now-superseded provision of the DPA requiring the President to "immediately transmit" to the Congress "a written report of the President's determination of whether or not to take action under subsection (d)." 50 U.S.C. app. § 2170(g) (1993). The legislative history indicates that this provision was intended to help the "Congress and the public develop an understanding of the policies underlying Presidential determinations, and hold the President accountable for actions under the Exon-Florio Amendment." H.R. Conf. Rep. 102–966, at 731–32 (1992). They also cite former section 2170(k), which required the President, "[i]n order to assist the Congress in its oversight responsibilities," to furnish to the Congress a quadrennial report regarding foreign countries' efforts to acquire U.S. companies involved in "critical technologies" or to "obtain commercial secrets related to critical technologies" therefrom. 50 U.S.C. app. § 2170(k) (1993). Under the current DPA, the President's suspension or prohibition of a covered transaction, as well as the President's critical technology assessment, are memorialized in a single annual report that is submitted to the Congress. *See* 50 U.S.C. app. § 2170(m). Finally, the Appellees direct our attention to the Foreign Investment and National Security Act of 2007 (FINSA), Pub. L. No. 110–49, 121 Stat. 246, which amended portions of section 721 of the DPA. According to a Senate report, the purpose of FINSA is "to strengthen Government review and oversight of foreign investment in the United States" and "to provide for enhanced Congressional oversight with respect thereto." S. Rep. No. 109–264, at 1 (2006). FINSA purported to accomplish this objective by increasing oversight of CFIUS.[12]

We conclude that neither the text of the statutory bar nor the legislative history of the statute provides clear and convincing evidence that the Congress intended to preclude judicial review of Ralls's procedural due process challenge to the Presidential Order. First, the text does not preclude judicial review of Ralls's as-applied constitutional claim by barring review of all "actions of the President under paragraph (1) of subsection (d)." 50 U.S.C. app. § 2170(e). We think the most natural reading, given its reference to subsection (d)(1), is that courts are barred from reviewing final "action[s]" the President takes "*to suspend or prohibit* any covered transaction that threatens to impair the national security of the United States." *Id.* § 2170(d)(1) (emphasis added). The text does not, however, refer to the reviewability of a constitutional claim challenging the *process* preceding such presidential action. . . .

The Appellees' reliance on legislative history and congressional oversight provisions is equally unavailing. To begin with, there is no legislative history expressly addressing judicial review of constitutional claims arising from the President's implementation of section 721. . . .

. . . Even if the absence of express legislative history were not conclusive, the nature of congressional oversight currently provided for in the DPA does not demonstrate that the Congress intended to withhold a judicial forum for a due process claim challenging the procedure followed by the President. Congressional oversight of the President under the current version of the statute consists of an annual, *ex post* review of "decisions or actions by the President" taken under section 721 and the President's assessment of foreign efforts to acquire critical technologies. 50 U.S.C. app. § 2170(m)(2), (3). We hardly think that, by reserving to itself

[12] Among other changes, FINSA requires CFIUS to submit more detailed notices and reports to the Congress upon completion of individual reviews and investigations, *see* 50 U.S.C. app. § 2170(b)(3), (m), and provide prompt notice of the results of its review or investigation to the parties to a covered transaction, *see id.* § 2170(b)(6). FINSA also requires any agency acting on behalf of CFIUS to make detailed reports to CFIUS regarding "any agreement entered into or condition imposed" by the agency. *See id.* § 2170(l)(3)(B)(i).

such limited review of presidential actions and critical technology assessments, the Congress intended to abrogate the courts' traditional role of policing governmental procedure for constitutional infirmity and perform that function itself. . . .

B. Justiciability

The Appellees also argue that *Ralls's* due process challenge to the Presidential Order raises a non-justiciable political question. . . . "The political question doctrine is essentially a function of the separation of powers and excludes from judicial review those controversies which revolve around policy choices and value determinations constitutionally committed for resolution to the halls of Congress or the confines of the Executive Branch." *El-Shifa Pharm. Indus. Co. v. United States*, 607 F.3d 836, 840, 391 U.S. App. D.C. 51 (D.C. Cir. 2010) (*en banc*) (quotation marks and citation omitted); *see also Schneider v. Kissinger*, 412 F.3d 190, 193, 366 U.S. App. D.C. 408 (D.C. Cir. 2005) ("The courts lack jurisdiction over political decisions that are by their nature committed to the political branches to the exclusion of the judiciary. . ." (quotation marks omitted)).

The framework to determine if a complaint presents a non-justiciable political question is set forth in *Baker v. Carr*, 369 U.S. 186 . . . (1962). Under *Baker*, the political question doctrine bars a court from considering a claim when

> [p]rominent on the surface of [the] case . . . is found a [1] textually demonstrable constitutional commitment of the issue to a coordinate political department; or [2] a lack of judicially discoverable and manageable standards for resolving it; or [3] the impossibility of deciding without an initial policy determination of a kind clearly for non-judicial discretion; or [4] the impossibility of a court's undertaking independent resolution without expressing lack of the respect due coordinate branches of government; or [5] an unusual need for unquestioning adherence to a political decision already made; or [6] the potentiality of embarrassment from multifarious pronouncements by various departments on one question.

Id. at 217 . . . . Because "[t]he *Baker* analysis lists the six factors in the disjunctive, not the conjunctive," the Court "need only conclude that one factor is present, not all," to apply the political question doctrine. . . .

Although "[m]atters intimately related to foreign policy and national security are rarely proper subjects for judicial intervention," . . . "it is error to suppose that every case or controversy which touches foreign relations lies beyond judicial cognizance," *Baker*, 369 U.S. at 211 . . . . Indeed, "the judiciary is the ultimate interpreter of the Constitution [and,] in most instances, claims alleging its violation will rightly be heard by the courts." *El-Shifa*, 607 F.3d at 841–42 . . . . Thus, we do not automatically decline to adjudicate legal questions if they may implicate foreign policy or national security. Instead, we "must conduct 'a discriminating analysis of the particular question posed' in the 'specific case' before the court to determine whether the political question doctrine prevents a claim from going forward." *Id.* at 841 (quoting *Baker*, 369 U.S. at 211).

* * *

But the Appellees contend . . . that "Ralls asks this Court to decide whether and how the President must engage a would-be foreign investor in deliberations on the question of the national security risk a transaction poses, when and if the President must reveal his thinking, and in what level of detail." . . . "[S]uch a determination," they argue, "calls for non-judicial discretion, is constitutionally committed to the Executive Branch, and offers no judicially discoverable or manageable standards." . . .

We disagree. First, Ralls's due process claim does *not* challenge (1) the President's determination that its acquisition of the Project Companies threatens the national security or (2) the President's prohibition of the transaction in order to mitigate the national security threat. . . . Instead, Ralls asks us to decide whether the Due Process Clause entitles it to have notice of, and access to, the evidence on which the President relied and an opportunity to rebut that evidence before he reaches his non-justiciable (and statutorily unreviewable) determinations. *See infra* note 19. We think it clear, then, that Ralls's due process claim does not encroach on the prerogative of the political branches, does not require the exercise of non-judicial discretion and is susceptible to judicially manageable standards. To the contrary, and as the Supreme Court recognized long ago, interpreting the provisions of the Constitution is the role the Framers entrusted to the judiciary. . . .

C. The Merits

* * *

. . . The gravamen of *Ralls's* challenge to the Presidential Order is that the President deprived it of its constitutionally protected property interests in the Project Companies and their assets without due process of law. The Due Process Clause of the Fifth Amendment provides that "[n]o person shall be . . . deprived of life, liberty, or property, without due process of law." U.S. Const. amend. V. "The first inquiry in every due process challenge is whether the plaintiff has been deprived of a protected interest in 'property' or 'liberty.' " *Am. Mfrs. Mut. Ins. Co. v. Sullivan*, 526 U.S. 40, 59 . . . (1999). If the plaintiff has been deprived of a protected interest, we then consider whether the procedures used by the Government in effecting the deprivation "comport with due process." *Id.*

1. Constitutionally Protected Property Interest

* * *

The district court found, and the Appellees do not dispute, that Ralls possessed state law property interests when it acquired 100% ownership of the Project Companies and their assets, including local easements permitting the construction of wind turbines, power purchase and generator interconnection agreements with the local utility, transmission interconnection and management agreements with nearby windfarms and the necessary permits and approvals to construct wind turbines. . . . We agree with the district court on this score—there can be no doubt that Ralls's interests in the Project Companies and their assets constitute "property" under Oregon law. . . .

In the usual case, the fact that the property interest is recognized under state law is enough to trigger the protections of the Due Process Clause. . . . Yet here, the district court concluded that Ralls's state law property interests were *not* constitutionally protected because Ralls (1) acquired its property interests "subject to the known risk of a Presidential veto" and (2) "waived the opportunity . . . to obtain a determination from CFIUS and the President before it entered into the transaction." . . . The Appellees take up this mantle on appeal . . . .

We reject the rationale used by the district court and advocated by the Appellees. First, we disagree with the notion that Ralls's state-law property interests are too contingent for constitutional protection. Ralls's state-law property rights fully vested upon the completion of the transaction, meaning due process protections necessarily attached. There is nothing "contingent" about the interests Ralls obtained under state law, and the Appellees offer no legal support—other than the district court order—for the proposition that the nature of a property interest recognized under *state* law is affected by potential *federal* deprivation. As *Ralls* aptly notes, the Federal Government cannot evade the due process protections afforded to state property by simply "announcing that future deprivations of property may be forthcoming." . . .

* * *

. . . [T]he district court concluded that Ralls received adequate process because it was notified that the transaction was subject to review and was given an opportunity to present evidence in its favor in both its voluntary notice filing and during follow-up conversations with—and a presentation to—CFIUS officials. In light of the Appellees' substantial interest in protecting national security, the court determined that no additional process was required. . . .

The Appellees make a similar argument in their brief, arguing that Ralls's ability to submit written arguments, meet with CFIUS officials in person, answer follow-up questions and receive advance notice of the

Appellees' intended action constitutes sufficient process in light of the national security interests at stake. . . . Finally, the Appellees assert that Ralls cannot "utilize this Court to force disclosure of the President's thinking on sensitive questions in discretionary areas and obtain otherwise forbidden judicial review." . . . And, even if such process *is* required, the Appellees requested—for the first time during oral argument—that we remand so that the district court can consider whether disclosure of certain unclassified information is nonetheless shielded by executive privilege.

We conclude that the Presidential Order deprived Ralls of its constitutionally protected property interests without due process of law. . . . [D]ue process requires, at the least, that an affected party be informed of the official action, be given access to the unclassified evidence on which the official actor relied and be afforded an opportunity to rebut that evidence. . . . Although the Presidential Order deprived Ralls of significant property interests—interests, according to the district court record, valued at $6 million—Ralls was not given any of these procedural protections at any point. . . . [T]his lack of process constitutes a clear constitutional violation, notwithstanding the Appellees' substantial interest in national security and despite our uncertainty that more process would have led to a different presidential decision. . . . [A] substantial interest in national security supports withholding only the *classified* information but does not excuse the failure to provide notice of, and access to, the unclassified information used to prohibit the transaction.[19] . . . That Ralls had the opportunity to present evidence to CFIUS and to interact with it, then, is plainly not enough to satisfy due process because Ralls never had the opportunity to tailor its submission to the Appellees' concerns or rebut the factual premises underlying the President's action. . . .

* * *

The Appellees' argument that we should refrain from requiring disclosure of the President's thinking on sensitive questions is off-base. Our conclusion that the procedure followed in issuing the Presidential Order violates due process does not mean the President must, in the future, disclose his thinking on sensitive questions related to national security in reviewing a covered transaction. We hold only that Ralls must receive the procedural protections we have spelled out before the Presidential Order prohibits the transaction. The DPA expressly provides that CFIUS acts on behalf of the President in reviewing covered transactions, *see* 50 U.S.C. app. § 2170(b)(1)(A) (review conducted by "President, acting through [CFIUS]"), and the procedure makes clear that the President acts only after

---

19 Because the record did not reflect whether the evidence relied on was classified, unclassified or both, we issued an order before oral argument requesting that the Government be prepared to discuss the nature of the evidence reviewed by CFIUS and the President. Responding to our inquiry at oral argument, the Appellees' counsel stated that CFIUS and the President relied on both classified and unclassified evidence.

reviewing the record compiled by CFIUS and CFIUS's recommendation, *see* 31 C.F.R. § 800.506(b), (c). Adequate process at the CFIUS stage, we believe, would also satisfy the President's due process obligation. . . .

In sum, we conclude that Ralls possesses substantial property interests and that the Presidential Order deprives Ralls of its interests without due process of law.

* * *

. . . We remand to the district court with instructions that Ralls be provided the requisite process set forth herein, which should include access to the unclassified evidence on which the President relied and an opportunity to respond thereto. . . . Should disputes arise on remand—such as an executive privilege claim—the district court is well-positioned to resolve them.

* * *

So ordered.

QUESTION

Would CFIUS or President Obama have shown such concern if, in the preceding case, the two owners of Ralls Corporation had been Italian nationals rather than Chinese nationals? While U.S. administrations are vocal about China being a "friend and ally," do actions speak louder than words?

Close scrutiny of investment from China has continued into the Trump Administration. In September 2017, President Trump blocked an attempt by Chinese government-backed Canyon Bridge Capital Partners to buy Lattice Semiconductor Corp. after CFIUS recommended against the deal. In early 2018, CFIUS refused to approve the attempt by Ant Financial Services Group to acquire MoneyGram International, Inc. Ant is controlled by Chinese billionaire Jack Ma, the founder of e-commerce giant Alibaba Group Holding Ltd. Ironically, Mr. Ma appeared to be on President Trump's good side—at a high-profile meeting about a year earlier with then President-Elect Trump, Mr. Ma had promised the creation of one million U.S. jobs!

Other Chinese deals have been caught up in the CFIUS approval web. In early 2018 both HNA Group Co.'s proposed acquisition of a controlling stake in SkyBridge Capital and China Oceanwide Holdings Group Co.'s proposed acquisition of Genworth Financial Inc. were being held up by CFIUS.

The oddest CFIUS China-related intervention didn't even directly involve China! In March 2018, CFIUS ordered Qualcomm Inc. to postpone its scheduled shareholder meeting for 30 days to give it an opportunity to review *Singapore-based* rival Broadcom Ltd.'s proposed $117 billion hostile takeover of Qualcomm. In an unusual move, Qualcomm had unilaterally raised national security concerns with CFIUS (and anyone else who would listen!) in an effort to thwart Broadcom's hostile bid (i.e., as a takeover defense).[18] Broadcom had pushed to replace six of Qualcomm's 11 directors in order to help consummate the takeover. CFIUS later recommended against the deal, arguing that it could have had implications for the U.S.'s broader technological competition *with China* (huh?).[19] President Donald Trump, citing national security concerns, officially quashed the deal soon thereafter. Ironically, prior to launching its attempted takeover of Qualcomm, Broadcom had announced its plans to "redomicile" in the U.S.[20] Had it been able to follow through sooner, CFIUS review would have been rendered moot.

Other federal agencies have gotten into the China bashing act. In early 2018, the Securities and Exchange Commission voted against the sale of the Chicago Stock Exchange (CHX) to North America Casin Holdings Inc., a company that had Chinese investors, despite the SEC's staff having recommended approval of the deal only six months earlier. In fact, CFIUS itself had previously approved the deal. The SEC's rejection capped a two-year battle over a deal that drew strong opposition in Congress. The SEC was worried that the CHX would run afoul of rules limiting the control that any one shareholder could exert over an exchange. It was also concerned about accessing records of owners based in China during regulatory reviews. Even though the CHX handled *less than 1 percent of U.S. securities trading volume*, other critics argued that allowing a Chinese-backed group to take a major stake in a U.S. stock exchange would create a "backdoor for the Chinese government to influence American financial infrastructure."[21] The paranoia is, indeed, palpable! The two parties to the proposed deal ultimately terminated it voluntarily rather than fight the SEC in court.

---

[18] The move was unusual because normally both parties to a deal jointly file for CFIUS review. Here, not only was the filing done solely by Qualcomm, but a deal hadn't even been signed up in the first place! See Ted Greenwald, Kate O'Keeffe and Tripp Mickle, *Qualcomm Pursued Unusual Strategy*, WALL ST. J., Mar. 14, 2018, at B1.

[19] Qualcomm was developing the next-generation wireless communications technology known as 5G, a technology the Trump Administration considered a national priority. China's tech juggernaut, Huawei Technologies Co., was also working on 5G. Broadcom had a reputation of emphasizing cost discipline over research and development. Therefore, there were legitimate concerns that Qualcomm's push towards 5G could be hampered if the takeover launched by the frugal Broadcom was successful, thus giving China an advantage in the race to 5G technology. See *id.* The *Wall Street Journal* summed up the mess this way: "The confluence of corporate self-interest and geopolitical considerations not only enabled Qualcomm to turn the tables on Broadcom, but canonized [Qualcomm] as a sort of national champion essential to battling China's might in the next-generation wireless communications techonology known as 5G." *Id.*

[20] Broadcom was originally a U.S. company prior to being acquired by Singapore-based Avago Technologies Ltd. in 2016. Avago then changed its name to Broadcom. About half of Broadcom's employees were still based in the U.S. at the time of its bid for Qualcomm. See *id.*

[21] Dave Michaels, *SEC Blocks Sale of Exchange to Chinese*, WALL ST. J., Feb. 16, 2018, at B1.

2. FEDERAL LEGISLATION SPECIFIC TO FOREIGN ACQUISITIONS IN PARTICULAR INDUSTRIES OR ASSETS

The United States Congress[22] has passed a series of laws that regulate foreign ownership (and therefore foreign acquisitions of domestic businesses) in specific industries. The following list of legislative acts focuses only on those that restrict not only the activity of foreign entities but also the activity of domestic entities (those incorporated in the United States) owned by foreign citizens or entities.[23] The list is not exhaustive.[24]

The Foreign Bank Supervision Enhancement Act of 1991 establishes special clearance and oversight criteria for foreign-owned banks that do business in the United States. 12 U.S.C. § 3105(d). The Bank Holding Company Act requires that foreign investors obtain Federal Reserve Board approval if they seek to control twenty-five percent or more of any class of voting securities of a domestic bank or bank holding company. 12 U.S.C. § 1841. The Federal Aviation Act of 1958, as amended, prohibits foreign citizens from owning more than a 25 percent voting interest in a United States "air carrier." 49 U.S.C. § 40102(a)(2) & (15)(C). The Act also requires that the president and at least two-thirds of the board of directors and other managing officers are citizens of the United States. § 40102(a)(15)(C).[25] The Federal Communications Act of 1934 bars foreign persons, entities or governments and United States entities controlled by foreign interests from possessing a broadcast or common carrier license unless the FCC determines it will serve the "public interest."[26] 47 U.S.C. § 310(b). The Merchant Marine Act of 1920 provides that merchandise moving between United States ports must be transported on United States built, owned and

[22] Some states, notably California, Iowa, New Mexico and Pennsylvania, may also restrict foreign ownership of certain types of property and the exploitation of natural resources by foreign investors.

[23] There are numerous acts that restrict the operation of foreign companies but allow free rein to foreign companies operating through domestic subsidiaries. See, e.g., Outer Continental Shelf Lands Act, 43 U.S.C. §§ 1331–1356; Mining Law of 1987, 30 U.S.C. § 22; Federal Power Act, 16 U.S.C. § 797(a); Geothermal Steam Act of 1970, 30 U.S.C. § 1015. This means, of course, that the form of the acquisition is critical. For example, stock acquisitions or reverse triangular mergers of American domestic airline companies are possible whereas forward triangular mergers or assets acquisitions are not under legislative acts.

[24] The restrictions on foreign acquisitions of companies involved in the defense industry are the subject of the previous section. Notes in the section also mention the problems of acquiring companies that have a security clearance or a sensitive, controlled technology.

[25] The Department of Transportation will review investments below the threshold and block the investment if a foreign investor will acquire effective control of the U.S. airline. See 14 C.F.R. § 399.88 (2001).

[26] The FCC abides by a World Trade Organization directive and allows foreign ownership when, among other considerations, the foreign company's home country has reciprocal rules for U.S. companies and the foreign company has no history of anti-competitive behavior. See 12 F.C.C.R. 7847, 7849–50 (1997), 1997 WL 298237.

registered vessels. 46 U.S.C. § 55102(b).[27] The Coast Guard Authorization Act of 1989 limits direct or indirect foreign investment in our commercial fishing industry. 46 U.S.C. § 12103(b). The Mineral Lands Leasing Act of 1920 allows the Secretary of the Interior to grant federal leases to develop natural resources in the United States to companies with larger than 10 percent foreign ownership only if United States citizens can obtain similar licenses or leases from the home governments of the foreign interests. 30 U.S.C. § 181. The Atomic Energy Act of 1954 effectively bars foreign ownership of companies that operate in the nuclear power industry, 42 U.S.C. § 2133(d), and foreign ownership of companies that mine uranium on public lands. 42 U.S.C. § 2097.

NOTE: BRITISH AIRWAYS ACQUISITION OF USAIR

Our changing view on domestic ownership requirements is well illustrated by developments in the airline industry. In the summer of 1992, British Airways began the most ambitious effort by a foreign entity to acquire a domestic airline in American aviation history at that time. On July 21, 1992, British Airways announced its intention to purchase 21 percent of the voting shares and 44 percent of the equity of USAir, a major American air carrier, for $750 million. The initial proposal would have given British Airways a substantial voice in the management of USAir: 75 percent of the new USAir board of directors would have consisted of Americans but a supermajority vote of 80 percent of the USAir board would have been required for any major policy to pass. Under the initial plan, the British minority would have to be included on all major corporate decisions. Shortly thereafter, the companies filed with the Department of Transportation (DOT) for approval of the proposed transaction. The deal ran into heavy opposition from labor unions and other domestic airlines. The DOT hesitated, arguing that foreign control of four members of the USAir board would amount to foreign control of USAir. Thus, on January 21, 1993, British Airways withdrew its first proposal and announced a second proposal.

British Airways proposed to purchase a new series of USAir shares for $300 million. The shares would be convertible to common stock and would immediately convey 19.9 percent of the voting interest in USAir to British Airways. Upon shareholder approval of the agreement, that interest would rise to 21.8 percent. Thus, the initial stake was more than one percent lower than the stake proposed in the first takeover effort. Of greater importance was the revised composition of the board of directors. Under the new proposal, British Airways would control only three, not four, of the USAir directors, so that British Airways would not hold the veto power it would have acquired under the first proposal. In the second stage of British Airways' second proposal, they proposed to purchase $200 million of preferred stock in USAir through an option, exercisable within three years of the first step. Then, in the third stage,

[27] The Secretary of the Treasury may suspend the requirement for citizens and entities of other countries by granting reciprocal treatment in extraordinary circumstances. 19 C.F.R. § 4.8 (2011).

within two more years, British Airways proposed to buy $250 million worth of additional preferred stock. After all three stages there would end up being a 32.4 percent voting interest in British hands, a violation of the threshold standard of the Federal Aviation Act. Without granting permission to go beyond the initial $300 million stock purchase, the DOT announced its approval of the second British Airways proposal on March 15, 1993.[28] Secretary of Transportation Pena announced that approval of the second two stages of the acquisition would be contingent on the British government's cooperation in negotiating a bilateral treaty between the United States and Great Britain on mutual aviation access rights. By 1996, the deal began to unravel. British Airways announced plans for a strategic alliance with American Airlines, instructed its three directors to resign from the USAir (now US Airways) board, and stated that it would sell its now 24.9 percent stock holding in US Air. US Airways sued the directors for breach of fiduciary duty. By 1997, British Airways had sold its US Airways stock for a profit of $200 million. US Airways was ultimately acquired by American Airlines in April 2015.

With intra-national airline consolidation seemingly exhausted, the next big airline industry push is for cross-border airline consolidation. However, governments around the world would have to relax or eliminate their restrictions on foreign ownership, something not likely to occur quickly (if at all). Taking matters into their own hands, airlines around the world have formed strategic alliances. These include the "One World" alliance consisting of 15 airline participants (including American Airlines, British Airways, Japan Airlines and Qantas), the "Star" alliance consisting of 29 participants (including United Airlines, Air China, Lufthansa and LOT Polish Airlines) and the "Sky Team" alliance consisting of 20 participants (including Delta Air Lines, Air France, Aeroflot and Korean Airlines).

Numerous federal laws also establish specific disclosure requirements for foreign investors. Again, the following list is not exhaustive. The best known is the International Investment and Trade in Services Survey Act of 1976. The Act requires U.S. corporations to report to the Bureau of Economic Affairs within thirty days of the quarter in which the deal closed by a foreign person or entity of a 10 percent or larger voting equity interest if the corporation has annual sales, assets or net income of greater than $60 million. 22 U.S.C. § 3101–3108. The Act also requires reports when an existing U.S. company that has a foreign investor who holds 10 percent or more of its voting stock acquires additional U.S. businesses. The Act has annual reporting requirements for companies with a majority owner that is foreign and that have total assets, total sales, or gross operating review

[28] A report issued by the U.S. General Accounting Office ("GAO") on January 8, 1993, shortly before British Air announced its second proposal, may have influenced the DOT. The GAO report reviewed the rationale behind the limits on foreign ownership of domestic air carriers and concluded that limits on foreign ownership are rooted in obsolete concerns over national security and trade protection.

of over $120 million.[29] The Foreign Investment and Real Property Tax Act of 1989 gives the Secretary of the Treasury the power to require reporting by foreign persons or entities holding direct investments in U.S. real estate having an aggregate fair market value in excess of $50,000. 26 U.S.C. § 6039C. The Agricultural Foreign Investment Disclosure Act of 1978 requires foreign persons or entities or domestic entities in which a foreigner has an interest to file a report within ninety days before purchasing an interest in U.S. farming, ranching or timberland. 7 U.S.C. §§ 3501–3508. There are also a series of tax acts, most notably the Tax Equity and Fiscal Responsibility Act of 1982, that contain special provisions for foreign corporations or U.S. corporations controlled by foreign interests.[30]

NOTE: THE BCCI SCANDAL

The most famous prosecution under a foreign ownership disclosure statute involved Clark Clifford, a former Secretary of Defense and a confidant to all Democratic Presidents from Harry S. Truman to Jimmy Carter.[31] The Justice Department brought criminal charges and the United States Federal Reserve Board brought civil charges against Clifford and Robert Altman (husband of Lynda Carter, the original 1970's T.V. "Wonder Woman") claiming they misrepresented the ownership of two American banks, First American Bankshares, Inc. and National Bank of Georgia. In fact, a Luxembourg bank holding company run by Arabs, BCCI Holdings, controlled both American banks. Moreover, Clifford and Altman had turned a $10 million profit in speculating in bank stock, with their grubstake a large no-interest loan from BCCI. The principals of BCCI were crooks (engaged in drug trafficking and money laundering) and when the company went bankrupt it hurt investors all around the world, including those in the two American bank subsidiaries. A court acquitted Altman of the criminal charges and the government dropped the criminal charges against Clifford. Clifford and Altman settled with the Federal Reserve Board for $5 million.

3. OTHER COUNTRIES' INVESTMENT BARRIERS

Other countries have a host of investment regulatory regimes that require specific government approvals as a precondition for direct investment through acquisition of a domestic company or otherwise. In socialist countries, domestic law typically requires foreign investors to use a joint venture with domestic partners or entities to guarantee domestic

---

29 Filing every other year is required of companies that meet a $40 million trigger.

30 See also the Tax Reform Act of 1986, the Revenue Reconciliation Act of 1990, the Omnibus Budget Reconciliation Act of 1933 and the Taxpayer Relief Act of 1997 (each with expanded foreign reporting requirements and special provisions on the taxation of foreign controlled entities).

31 Among many other things, he accompanied Truman on trips to negotiate with Churchill and Stalin at the conclusion of WWII and advised the Kennedy family on whether Edward's expulsion from Harvard would disqualify him from running for the Senate. Truman offered Clifford a Supreme Court appointment and Lyndon Johnson offered him the Attorney General position. He turned both down.

participation in ownership and control of a company. Initially, the joint ventures were solely based on contract (contractual joint ventures). When China's government opened the country to limited foreign investment in 1979, its regulations on foreign direct investment,[32] the model for most socialistic countries, created equity joint ventures (legal entities). China limited foreign investment to joint ventures in certain industries, with foreign interests relegated to a minority position. Cuba has a similar provision. Today, China has moved to allowing foreign wholly owned corporate entities.

Almost every nation prohibits foreign investment in certain sectors. Both developed and developing nations limit investment in industries crucial to national security.[33] Outside of the defense industry there is a range of approaches with varying degrees of limiting foreign investors. A scale that goes from the least degree of restrictions to the most degree of restrictions on foreign investors begins with exporting developed countries, such as New Zealand and the United Kingdom[34], which have scattered but minimal prohibitions; progresses through developed countries with statist tendencies, such as France[35] and Canada; continues with developing countries, such as India, that attempt to control, often through outright state ownership, the production and distribution of most of their domestic resources[36]; and ends with communist economies, which do not respect the notion of private property.[37] Popular protected sections include, from most popular to least popular, a country's most important natural resources (petroleum), a country's agriculture (rice growers), a country's infrastructure (railroads, communications and electricity), and a country's self-defined "key industries" (iron and steel, aeronautics, high-tech).

Most countries also have equity percentage limitations for some industries. Mandatory joint venture rules usually limit foreign investment to 49 percent of the company. Investors have found, however, that host governments will waive equity limitations if they are anxious to secure the investment. Companies with technology, companies willing to locate a plant in needy areas, companies willing to do local research and

---

[32] Law of the People's Republic of China on Joint Venture Using Chinese and Foreign Investment of 1979.

[33] U.K., Germany and France all sanction government intervention in mergers that affect national security.

[34] The U.K. has special rules for acquisitions of control of financial service businesses and airlines, for example.

[35] The French government must approve, in addition to investments in businesses that involve national security, investments in financial or insurance companies, press and broadcasting industries, gaming and casinos and private security services, for example. Italy, Luxembourg, Netherlands, and Spain have a similarly long list.

[36] India permits foreign acquisitions only if "in the national interest." Even so, a majority ownership in acquired companies must remain in Indian hands.

[37] There can be dramatic movement by a country on the scale. Until the early 1980s, Mexico made foreign investment very difficult with mandatory review by various ministries and agencies, joint venture requirements, restrictions on acquisitions, and the like. By 1994 Mexico, having suffered through a severe financial crisis, had removed nearly all of its restrictions.

development, and companies willing to train domestic workers and their families may find that they are able to avoid joint venture mandates. This means, of course, that host countries must have a government agency or official that screens foreign direct investment to determine which companies can avoid joint venture mandates.

Finally, some countries that allow foreign investment in identified sectors may still prohibit acquisitions of domestic companies in those sectors. Some governments apparently fear the loss of an existing domestic company but are nevertheless comfortable with the creation of a new foreign-owned company.

4. INTERNATIONAL AGREEMENTS ON FOREIGN DIRECT INVESTMENT

The nature of the rules that ought to govern foreign investment has been a subject of frequent debate among developed countries (the United States and France; the United States and Japan) and among developed and developing countries (the North-South debate in the United Nations). Among developed countries the cry is for reciprocity and fairness; among developed and developing countries the debate is far more complicated. These tensions are revealed in the international negotiations over failed multilateral agreements on investment control laws. The Organisation of Economic Co-operation and Development (OECD) failed to pass a Multilateral Investment Agreement (MIA) in 1997 and the World Trade Organization failed to negotiate an MIA in the Doha round of trade talks in 2004. The following text of remarks is a sample of the disagreements that wrecked both agreements.

AMERICAN SOCIETY OF INTERNATIONAL LAW PROCEEDINGS (MAURITS LUGARD ED., APRIL 9–12, 1997), IMPLEMENTATION, COMPLIANCE AND EFFECTIVENESS: TOWARD AN EFFECTIVE INTERNATIONAL INVESTMENT REGIME

91 AM. SOC'Y INT'L L. PROC. 485 (1997).

REMARKS BY KENNETH J. VANDEVELDE:

This unquestionably is the most interesting period for international investment law since the debates over the New International Economic Order of the early 1970s. And it is clearly the most productive period for international investment law in history. We now have a network of some 1,200 bilateral investment treaties, the majority negotiated in the past half-decade, involving about 160 countries in every region of the world; a number of regional or sectoral agreements, such as the North American Free Trade Agreement (NAFTA) and the Energy Charter Treaty; and the prospect in the very near future of the first multilateral agreement on investment,[Ed.[38]] now being drafted under the auspices of the Organisation for Economic Co-operation and Development (OECD).[Ed.[39]]

This network of investment treaties is striking with respect to both the number of treaties and the uniformity of their provisions. Quite clearly, there is an emerging consensus in the international community with respect to the desirability of transfrontier investment flows and the nature of the legal regime that should apply to such flows.

To the casual observer, the wonder might be that it has taken so long for an international investment regime to emerge. After all, the United States has been negotiating bilateral trade agreements since the American Revolution, and there has been a multilateral agreement on trade, the General Agreement on Tariffs and Trade (GATT), for a half-century. Why should international investment lag so far behind international trade?

Much of the answer lies in the comparative political economy of trade and investment. Historically, the magnitude of international trade dwarfed international investment flows, with the result that the practical need for law was greater in the case of trade than in the case of investment. Further, while all states engage in trade as both exporters and importers and, therefore, have a shared interest in a legal regime for trade, until recently the number of states that exported significant amounts of capital and thus had a substantial interest in developing a legal regime for investment was quite small. Finally, in the period following the Second World War, when the modern international trade regime was emerging, by far the most important form of foreign investment was foreign direct investment, that is, investment through which the investor attempts to control the enterprise.

Because foreign direct investment entails foreign control over the means of production, it is far more likely than portfolio investment or trade to engender ideologically inspired political opposition to a treaty regime that might encourage and protect such investment. Foreign direct investment often was seen by developing countries as a form of economic

[38] [Ed.: In May of 1997, a drafting group presented its draft to the OECD Ministerial Council. The Council dropped the draft in October of 1998 when the French withdrew from the negotiations. The Australians and Canadians were also balking. The French response was due to pressure from French film and television companies who feared the effects of foreign owners in their industries and from pressure from a variety of labor and citizen interest groups (non-governmental organizations (NGOs)). For an example of the criticism, see William Crane, *Corporations Swallowing Nations: The OECD and the Multilateral Agreement on Investment,* 9 COLO. J. INTL. ENVTL. L. & POLY. 429 (1998). There are many nuances to this story. The NGOs from many countries mobilized very early against the agreement when someone leaked the draft by placing it on the Internet which resulted in comments on the draft being bounced from one chat room to another. The city council of Boulder, Colorado, which prides itself on having a foreign policy, passed a resolution severely condemning the agreement.]

[39] [Ed.: The 35-country member OECD spans the globe, from North and South America to Europe and Asia-Pacific. Members include many of the world's most advanced countries but also emerging countries like Mexico, Chile and Turkey. The OECD also works closely with emerging economies like the People's Republic of China, India and Brazil and developing economies in Africa, Asia, Latin America and the Caribbean.]

colonialism, a view that was strongly encouraged by the socialist countries, with the result that it became impossible to forge any consensus on the proper international regime for the protection of investment. The division between the developed countries and the rest of the world was perhaps best illustrated by the votes in the UN General Assembly during the 1970s on the Declaration on a New International Economic Order and the Charter of Economic Rights and Duties of States.

Since the beginning of the decade, however, there has been a dramatic transformation in attitudes toward an international investment regime. The division between developed and developing countries has been replaced by a consensus, and that consensus has produced the emerging regime.

The roots of the change are many. The debt crisis of the early 1980s forced private lenders to reduce their loans to developing countries, while economic recession and budget deficits in the developed countries reduced the availability of capital from public sources. The U.S. Government budget deficits in particular were financed by foreign borrowing, and thus siphoned off much of the remaining available capital. The result was a worldwide shortage of investment capital for developing countries. Indeed, the net flow of private capital to developing countries in the 1980s was only 60 percent of what it was during the late 1970s. At the same time, the phenomenal growth of the eight high-performing Asian economies—Hong Kong, Indonesia, Japan, the Republic of Korea (South Korea), Malaysia, Singapore, Taiwan and Thailand—seemed to provide a blueprint for economic development, which was based in part on high levels of private investment. The collapse of the socialist economies in the late 1980s undermined the socialist critique of foreign investment and the models of economic growth based on central planning. Developing countries came to the realization that their dream of economic development might well depend upon their ability to provide a favorable climate for foreign investment, but that they would have to compete for such investment.

The result is that there now exists a broad international consensus in support of an international investment regime. We gather today to discuss how to make the regime an effective one.

The threshold question, of course, is "effective for what purpose?" The existing agreements proclaim as their purpose the liberalization of international investment.

Classic liberalism rests on the belief that the protection of the existing distribution of property combined with deference to market-based reallocations of wealth will maximize productivity. A liberal investment regime thus has two elements: investment security, that is, the protection of private investment, and investment neutrality, that is, the removal of political barriers to the transfrontier movement of investment.

Governments practice investment neutrality by declining to intervene in market allocations of capital, while they provide investment security by enforcing and protecting those same allocations. Let me just assert dogmatically, since in the limited time available I cannot demonstrate this proposition, that the texts of the existing treaties suggest that neither the developed nor the developing states have sought to achieve both investment neutrality and investment security.

The dominant interest of the capital-exporting states has been to establish investment security—that is, to protect existing investment as well as future investment, if any should be established, against expropriation, currency exchange controls and a variety of other injuries host states can inflict.

. . . I think it is clear, however, that, if the purpose of an international investment regime is genuinely to liberalize investment flows, then future treaties must go much further in promoting investment neutrality, that is, in providing an accessible and level playing field for all investors.

For capital-importing states, the goal has been neither investment security nor investment neutrality, but economic development. While neoclassical economics links increased productivity with a liberalized international economy, economic development requires more than growth. Genuine economic development rests not only on increased production but on an equitable distribution of wealth. The production of wealth seems unquestionably to require increased capital formation, which in many cases will necessitate the attraction of foreign investment. At the same time, many developing countries fear that the desired distribution of wealth will occur only if they can appropriately regulate the investment. Such attempts at regulation, however, have the potential to undermine both investment neutrality and investment security—particularly if, as seems almost inevitable, the regulatory process is captured by parochial interests.

In prior decades, developing countries that were concerned about retaining their regulatory prerogatives did so by refusing to negotiate investment treaties or, at a minimum, by reserving in any treaty they did conclude the right to screen out certain investments that they thought would be inconsistent with their developmental or other objectives. As more and more countries have chosen to negotiate one or more investment treaties, developing countries increasingly have committed themselves to providing security for foreign investment while continuing to insist upon the right to exclude investment from their territories or to impose performance requirements on investment as a condition of permitting its entry, thus abjuring any claim to investment neutrality.

If the capital-exporting countries begin to insist upon true liberalization, then the developing countries may find that the abandonment of screening will be added to the price of admission to the emerging international investment regime. We will have achieved a liberal investment regime, but only time will tell the extent to which liberalization will bring either increased productivity or the desired distribution of wealth. If liberalization fails to meet either objective, then one must question how long the current consensus will endure or how stable the new investment regime will be. In short, an effective international investment regime may be one characterized not just by liberalization but by sustainable liberalization.

The task before those committed to advancing international investment thus is twofold: to develop a regime that will ensure the security of foreign investment and lower the political barriers to future investment flows, while at the same time promoting the long-term durability of that regime. The regime must be one that promotes both liberalization and economic development. . . .

* * *

REMARKS BY DAVID H. SMALL:

* * *

What will this [OECD Multi-lateral Agreement on Investment (MAI)] do? The new regime will, on a multilateral basis, perform the traditional function of most bilateral investment treaties (BITs), i.e., provide legal security for existing investments. However, it will do more, going beyond the scope of most BITs.

Unlike most BITs, but like the OECD Codes, the MAI will also deal with the pre-establishment phase, applying the requirement of nondiscriminatory treatment, national treatment[Ed.[40]] and most-favored-nation (MFN),[Ed.[41]] to market access and the making of investments. Unlike the Codes, the MAI will combine this with binding state-state and investor-state dispute settlement. This has been done already among more limited parties or for more limited investment spheres, by the North American Free Trade Agreement (NAFTA), the Energy Charter Treaty and U.S. BITs and by the General Agreement on Trade in Services (GATS) ("mode three" service provision under GATS is, essentially, operation of an investment in a service industry), though GATS dispute settlement is limited to state-state. The MAI will be the second time an OECD-based regime does not rely solely on peer pressure to assure its effectiveness. (The first was the OECD shipbuilding agreement.)

---

[40] [Ed.: The national treatment principle forbids a country from differentiating between goods produced by foreign and domestic companies with respect to internal taxes and all other domestic laws and regulations affecting local sale, purchase, transportation, distribution, and use.]

[41] [Ed.: The MFN obligation obliges countries to treat each other no worse than they treat any other country. MFN clauses commit the signatories to extend to each other any concession subsequently ceded to any other state.]

The MAI will also go beyond previous instruments in some of its particular provisions, such as disciplines on privatization and monopolies.

The MAI will not afford unlimited rights of establishment: Governments will be able to list exceptions to national treatment and other obligations in this regard. There will be a liberalization negotiation in which the governments will be discussing their exceptions lists. . . . The general obligations with respect to establishment will be nondiscrimination, national treatment and MFN. We will have the top-down approach, unlike the GATS, under which countries only accept commitments for the sectors they list. In the MAI, parties must specifically negotiate acceptance of exceptions or reservations.

There will be a discipline to address performance requirements in a way that goes beyond the list in the Trade Related Investment Measures Agreement (TRIMs)[Ed.[42]]. The TRIMs covers only trade-related investment measures, but the MAI will cover nontrade performance requirements as well, such as local equity or joint-venture partner requirements. This will be one of the major accomplishments of MAI.[Ed.[43]]

* * *

REMARKS BY AMY L. CHUA:

* * *

. . . First, why have there been cycles in Latin America and Southeast Asia? That is, what are the pressures that have repeatedly caused developing countries to move away from the free market, especially since nationalization and state-interventionist policies have historically, and repeatedly, been such failures (under any number of economic indicators)? Part of the answer has to do with something I am sure you are all aware of. That is, in the past, free-market, pro-foreigner regimes in the developing

---

[42] [Ed.: Led by the United States, the developed countries negotiated the TRIMs agreement through the General Agreement on Tariffs and Trade (GATT) process in the Uruguay Round. Violations of the agreement include rules that force foreign-owned firms to obtain products from local sources or limit their ability to import product and rules that tie approval to do business for foreign-owned firms on their generation of an excess of foreign exchange from exports or on quotas favoring exports. Most developing countries in GATT have not joined the TRIMs accord. The failure of the OECD to negotiate an investment protocol may lead some countries, such as Japan, to negotiate such an agreement through the World Trade Organization, the successor to GATT.]

[43] [Ed.: Under the draft agreement a country could not require an investor from another signatory country to "establish a joint venture with domestic participation" or to "achieve a minimum level of domestic equity ownership." This proved to be the agreement's undoing as first the French and later the Australians withdrew from the negotiations. The French were concerned that they were giving up too much control over their economy. Specifically, they could not sustain their domestic ownership regimes in their film and television industries under the agreement. The MAI did provide that all signatory countries could list industries that were exempt from the agreement's provisions (so-called "country-specific exceptions"), so France could have simply listed its film and television industries as protected. Why this option was not palatable is unclear. Perhaps the French were not happy with the "standstill" and "rollback" obligations that attach to the exceptions. The standstill obligation requires signatory nations to not add to their list of exceptions established on the date of signing and the rollback obligation entreats but does not require nations to reduce the exceptions on their list.]

world repeatedly benefited the foreign investors far more than the local populations. In fact, in the past, during periods of economic liberalization, the vast majority of Mexicans, or Peruvians, or Indonesians or Malays experienced little or no benefit from a liberalized market. As a result, politicians (often themselves from the elite classes) found that they could whip up populist support for themselves by playing on these antiforeigner sentiments. And in fact, in case after case, leaders in the developing world came to power on explicitly antiforeigner, anti-imperialist, anti-free-market platforms. This was true of Juan Peron in Argentina, Getulio Vargas in Brazil, Jose Batlle y Ordonez in Uruguay, Salvador Allende in Chile, Sukarno in Indonesia and U Nu in Burma (now Myanmar), among others.

But that is only part of the explanation. There is another equally important dynamic going on that is internal to developing countries. Free-market policies in the developing world (including liberalized foreign-investment regimes) have tended to benefit disproportionately not just Western foreigners but certain resented *internal foreigners* (this is the term I am going to use for economically dominant ethnic minorities in these countries), vis-a-vis the rest of the population.

Who are these internal foreigners? In Southeast Asia I'm referring principally to the Chinese. In countries such as Malaysia, Indonesia, the Philippines, Thailand and Vietnam, during free-market periods the Chinese minority, . . . who make up much of the commercial class in these countries, prosper disproportionately. In stark contrast, the predominantly rural "indigenous" majorities in these countries basically remain impoverished, experiencing little or no benefit from the free market. The Chinese are not the only entrepreneurial minority in Southeast Asia. In Myanmar (as well as East Africa and the Caribbean), historically it was the very small Indian minority who tended to become economically dominant under free-market conditions, relative to the indigenous majority. In Sri Lanka it was the Tamil minority, as opposed to the Sinhalese.

Accordingly, in Southeast Asia, these movements against the free market—in favor of restrictive investment policies, nationalization and redistribution—historically have been far more expressions of ethnic nationalism than of Marxism or socialism. Unlike the experience of the former Soviet Union or China, during these antimarket periods in Southeast Asia there has really never been an attempt to eliminate private property or to level the class structure (Vietnam is the exception). Rather, in these countries, antimarket movements have principally been attempts by certain "indigenous" groups to reclaim resources and economic power from other groups identified as "foreigners." And again these foreigners include not only Western "imperialist" foreigners but also these "foreigners within."

* * *

To summarize, in country after country in Southeast Asia and Latin America, liberal, market-oriented policies have distributed their benefits disproportionately to Western foreigners and to certain resented internal foreigners; as a result, these market policies have fueled backlash reactions culminating in the return of xenophobic, antiliberal economic programs.

* * *

The solution is certainly not to scrap the market—there is no question that the market and foreign capital will have to be part of any developing country's long-term solution. Rather, the point is that today's foreign investment treaties and marketization programs, to be effective, to last, to be sustainable, are going to have to focus in a way they never have on the problems of nationalism and ethnicity in the developing world.

* * *

First, . . . in developing countries some foreign ownership restrictions may well make sense in certain sectors, for example, highly sensitive, high-profile sectors, such as oil in Mexico, teak in Myanmar and silver in Peru. These are sectors with symbolic value, sectors with a history of nationalization and renationalization. Foreign investors and the international community should realize that, in the long run, it will be the presence of indigenous owners along with the foreign owners that safeguards the sustainability of liberal investment regimes.

Second, perhaps foreign investment treaties, whether bilateral or multilateral, should address in an effective way the possibility of holding Western investors to higher environmental and labor standards. For example, when 8,000 Costa Rican workers are sterilized because U.S. companies such as Chiquita and Dow Chemical used chemicals that were banned in the United States, you have a recipe for backlash against foreign investment.

Finally, I want to address performance requirements. Again, in the context of developing countries, states with emerging economies should think seriously about requiring major foreign investors to undertake projects intended to benefit the general population. . . . Along these lines, governments of developing countries could perhaps work with economists to come up with ways to require foreign investors to put in water purification plants, hospitals or much-needed infrastructure, with a view to long-term efficiency and development.

Other methods would be appropriate for trying to handle the even more difficult problem of market-triggered backlash against the internal ethnic foreigner. Employee participation schemes, intended to disperse the benefits of the market, have been successful enough in Chile (the Endesa privatization) and in the United States (the United Airlines Employee Stock Ownership Plan[Ed.[44]]) to warrant attention to such strategies. . . .

The problem, of course, with all these suggestions is that they entail short-run efficiency costs; in the short run, they make it marginally less desirable for foreign investors to invest in emerging economies. But the international community as well as foreign investors should realize that such short-term costs may be necessary to ensure the long-term stability of an effective international investment regime.

B. EXTRA-TERRITORIAL APPLICATION OF UNITED STATES LAWS TO FOREIGN ACQUISITIONS

1. FEDERAL SECURITIES LAWS

The general rule is that foreigners selling or buying securities abroad are not covered by our federal securities acts. SEC Regulation S, Rule 901. The rule also applies to United States citizens or residents that buy or sell abroad as long as the offer and sale are entirely offshore. See generally SEC Regulation S, Rules 903 & 904. Many foreign companies, even those that sold their shares exclusively in foreign markets, have some United States shareholders. The shares have migrated to the United States even though they were purchased abroad. Some of the shareholders are directly owned by United States citizens and some are owned beneficially as, for example, American Depositary Shares (ADRs).[45] When those companies are the target of a tender offer or a party to a negotiated acquisition, those shareholders are affected. Do the federal securities laws now apply?

---

[44] [Ed.: United's ESOP has not reduced labor/management tensions to the extent promised. Why? Pilots, for example, found that salary concerns still dominate their stock returns.]

[45] ADRs are negotiable receipts tradable on U.S. stock exchanges and, in limited cases, over-the-counter (OTC). They are designed to facilitate trading in foreign securities by U.S. investors, as ADRs trade in U.S. dollars and dividends are received by investors in U.S. dollars. Each ADR represents an interest in an American Depositary Share (ADS). Each ADS, in turn, typically represents a specified number of ordinary shares (common stock) of a foreign company held in trust by the foreign branch of a U.S. bank. Because ordinary shares of foreign companies often trade below $1.00 per share, and given the aversion of most U.S. investors to so-called "penny stocks" (i.e., stocks trading below $1.00 per share), ADR facilities typically bunch multiple ordinary shares into a single ADS to ensure the trading price of the related ADR is above $1.00 per share. When a given foreign company actively participates in the creation of an ADR facility, the facility is a *sponsored facility*. When other enterprising individuals (e.g., a broker-dealer seeking to establish a trading market in the shares of a foreign company) take it upon themselves to establish an ADR facility without the consent (i.e., contractual commitment) of the foreign company in question, the facility is an *unsponsored facility*. ADRs of sponsored facilities generally trade on stock exchanges, while those of unsponsored facilities trade OTC. Indeed, U.S. stock exchanges refuse to list ADRs of unsponsored facilities because of the lack of support from the foreign companies to which they relate. See generally SEC, *Investor Bulletin: American Depositary Receipts* (Aug. 2012) (avail. at https://www.sec.gov/investor/alerts/adr-bulletin.pdf). Examples of foreign companies with ADRs trading in the U.S. include Siemens A.G. (ticker: SI), AstraZeneka PLC (ticker: AZN) and British American Tobacco (ticker: BTI).

SECURITIES AND EXCHANGE COMMISSION, CROSS-BORDER TENDER AND EXCHANGE OFFERS, BUSINESS COMBINATIONS AND RIGHTS OFFERINGS

SEC Rel. Nos. 33–7759 & 34–42054, 1999 WL 969592, at *2–3 (Oct. 26, 1999).[46]

* * *

A. Summary of Amendments

U.S. security holders are often excluded from tender and exchange offers, business combinations and rights offerings[Ed.[47]] involving foreign private issuers.[Ed.[48]] It is very common for bidders to exclude U.S. security holders from these transactions to avoid the application of the U.S. securities laws, particularly when U.S. security holders own a small amount of the securities of the foreign private issuer.[Ed.[49]] When bidders exclude U.S. security holders from tender or exchange offers, they deny U.S. security holders the opportunity to receive a premium for their securities and to participate in an investment opportunity. Similarly, when issuers exclude U.S. security holders from participation in rights offerings, U.S. security holders lose the opportunity to purchase shares at a possible discount from market price. U.S. investors must react to these transactions, which may significantly affect their existing investment in the foreign private issuer, without the disclosure or other protections afforded by U.S. or foreign law.

Today, the Commission is adopting exemptive rules [Ed.[50]] that are intended to encourage issuers and bidders to extend tender and exchange offers, rights offerings and business combinations to the U.S. security holders of foreign private issuers. The purpose of the exemptions adopted

---

46 The SEC adopted a number of amendments to the cross-border tender offer rules in 2008. See *Commission Guidance and Revisions to the Cross-Border Tender Offer, Exchange Offer, Rights Offerings, and Business Combination Rules and Beneficial Ownership Reporting Rules for Certain Foreign Institutions*, SEC Rel. No. 34–58597, 2008 WL 4287201 (Oct. 9, 2008). The amendments did not change the basic rules in the 1999 release. However, they did: (1) codify positions previously taken by the SEC staff in interpretative releases; (2) expand methods of calculating beneficial ownership; and (3) expressly waive rules on purchases outside a Tier II tender offer. The changes are noted in the Editor's Notes where appropriate.

47 [Ed.: In a rights offering, existing shareholders receive stock options in the firm, usually with the strike or exercise price lower than the market price of the stock. Firms use rights offerings to raise more capital from existing shareholders, often as a last resort after other financing sources refuse to provide financing.]

48 [Ed.: A "foreign private issuer" is defined as any foreign company except one that has (1) 50 percent or more of its outstanding voting securities held by United States residents and (2) either (a) United States residents or citizens as a majority of its executive officers and directors, (b) more than 50 percent of its assets in the United States, or (c) its business administered in the United States. See Sec. Act Rule 405 and Exch. Act Rule 3b–4.]

49 [Ed.: Based on a sample of thirty-one tender offers compiled in 1997 by the U.K. Takeover Panel (the entity that regulates tender offers in the United Kingdom), when the U.S. ownership of the target was less than 15 percent (thirty offers), the bidders excluded U.S. persons in all of the offers. When the U.S. ownership was more significant, such as 38 percent (one offer), the bidders included U.S. persons.]

50 [Ed.: See Sec. Act Rules 800 to 802 and Exch. Act Rules 13e–3(g)(6), 13e–4(h)(8) & (i), 14d–1(c) & (d) and 14e–5(b)(11) & (12).]

today is to allow U.S. holders to participate on an equal basis with foreign security holders. In the past, some jurisdictions have permitted exclusion of U.S. holders despite domestic requirements to treat all holders equally on the basis that it would be impracticable to require the bidder to include U.S. holders. The rules adopted today are intended to eliminate the need for such disadvantageous treatment of U.S. investors.

The exemptions balance the need to provide U.S. security holders with the protections of the U.S. securities laws against the need to promote the inclusion of U.S. security holders in these types of cross-border transactions. The specific exemptions are:

- Tender offers for the securities of foreign private issuers will be exempt from most provisions of the Exchange Act and rules governing tender offers when U.S. security holders hold 10 percent or less of the subject securities.[Ed.[51]] In addition to bidders, the subject company, or any officer, director or other person who otherwise would have an obligation to file Schedule 14D–9 also may rely on the exemption. We refer to this exemptive relief in this release as the "Tier I" exemption.[Ed.[52]]

---

[51] [Ed.: The 10 percent figure is calculated after excluding from the numbers securities held by the offeror in an exchange offer or business combination. To determine United States citizenship, an offeror must "look through" the record ownership of certain brokers, dealers, banks or nominees holding securities of the subject company for the accounts of their customers to determine the percentage of the securities held in nominee accounts that have U.S. addresses. The 2008 release relaxed the time period applicable to the look-through rule. See Sec. Act Rule 800(h) (definition of "US holder").

The SEC, concerned with the problems of a hostile bidder's difficulty in ascertaining the citizenship of target shareholders, gave hostile bidders a safe harbor. Hostile bidders may assume a level of U.S. ownership based on the average daily trading volume of the securities sought:

> [A] third-party bidder in an unsolicited or "hostile" tender offer may rely upon a presumption that the U.S. ownership percentage limitations of the Tier I, Tier II and Rule 802 exemptions are not exceeded unless:
>
> (1) the aggregate trading volume of the subject class of securities on all national securities exchanges in the United States, on the NASDAQ market or on the OTC market, as reported to the NASD, over the 12-calendar-month period ending 30 days before commencement of the offer, exceeds 10 percent in the case of Tier I offers and Rule 802, and 40 percent in the case of Tier II offers, of the worldwide aggregate trading volume of that class of securities over the same period;
>
> (2) the most recent annual report or other informational form filed or submitted by the issuer or security holders to securities regulators in its home jurisdiction or elsewhere (including with the Commission) indicates that U.S. holdings exceed the applicable threshold; or
>
> (3) the bidder knows or has reason to know from other sources that the level of U.S. ownership of the subject class exceeds the thresholds.

1999 WL 969592, at *23. The 2008 rules permit friendly bidders to use the safe harbor if a calculation of beneficial owners is otherwise too difficult.]

[52] [Ed.: The SEC later explained:

> Under the Tier I exemption adopted today, eligible issuer and third-party tender offers will not be subject to Rules 13e–3, 13e–4, Regulation 14D or Rules 14e–1 and 14e–2. These provisions contain disclosure, filing, dissemination, minimum offering period, withdrawal rights and proration requirements that are intended to provide security holders with equal treatment and adequate time and information to make a decision

- When U.S. security holders hold 40 percent or less of the class of securities of the foreign private issuer sought in the offer, limited tender offer exemptive relief will be available to bidders to eliminate frequent areas of conflict between U.S. and foreign regulatory requirements. We refer to this exemptive relief in this release as the "Tier II" exemption. The Tier II exemption represents a codification of current exemptive and interpretive positions.[Ed.[53]]
- Under new Securities Act exemptive Rule 801, equity securities issued in rights offerings by foreign private issuers will be exempt from the registration requirements of the Securities Act, if U.S. security holders own 10 percent or less of the issuer's securities that are the subject of the rights offering.
- Under new Securities Act exemptive Rule 802, securities issued in exchange offers for foreign private issuers' securities and securities issued in business combinations involving foreign private issuers will be exempt from the registration requirements of the Securities Act and the qualification requirements of the Trust Indenture Act, if U.S.

---

whether to tender into the offer. The Tier I exemption provides that tender offers for the securities of foreign private issuers are exempt from these U.S. tender offer requirements, so long as:

- U.S. security holders hold 10 percent or less of the class of securities sought in the tender offer; . . .
- U.S. security holders participate in the offer on terms at least as favorable as those offered to any other holders (United States citizens can be provided with an appropriate cash alternative to whatever is offered to shareholder abroad); and
- Bidders provide U.S. security holders with the tender offer circular or other offering documents, in English, on a comparable basis to that provided to other security holders.

The exemption is available to U.S. and foreign bidders. The domicile or reporting status of the bidder is not relevant. Instead of complying with the U.S. tender offer rules, a bidder taking advantage of the exemption will comply with any applicable rules of the foreign subject company's home jurisdiction or exchange.

1999 WL 969592, at *5–6.]

[53] [Ed.: The SEC later explained:

We are [exempting foreign issuers from the United States rules on] All-Holders/Best Price provisions [a bidder may divide its offer into separate offers, for example], notice of extensions, prompt payment, and the interpretation regarding a waiver or reduction of minimum conditions as proposed. Under our interpretation on changes to the minimum condition, we will not object if bidders meeting the requirements for the Tier II exemption reduce or waive the minimum acceptance condition without extending withdrawal rights during the remainder of the offer (unless an extension is required by Rule 14e–1), [under specified conditions]. . . .

1999 WL 969592, at *11. The 2008 release continues to expand the exemptions for U.S. tender offer rules, permitting eligible bidders to conduct multiple non-U.S. tender offers in parallel with a U.S. offer, to suspend withdrawal rights while securities are counted, to conduct a subsequent offering, to terminate the initial offer period in advance of a scheduled expiration date and to purchase securities outside of the offer.]

security holders hold 10 percent or less of the subject class of securities.[Ed.[54]]

- Tender offers for the securities of foreign private issuers will be exempt from new Rule 14e–5 (formerly Rule 10b–13) of the Exchange Act, which prohibits a bidder from purchasing securities otherwise than pursuant to the tender offer. This exemption will allow purchases outside the tender offer during the offer when U.S. security holders hold 10 percent or less of the subject securities.

The U.S. anti-fraud and anti-manipulation rules and civil liability provisions will, however, continue to apply to these transactions. Certain commentators believed that this liability will remain a hurdle to including U.S. security holders, particularly in view of the amount of litigation in the United States and the ability of subject companies to institute litigation as a defensive measure. However, in a transaction eligible for the exemptions adopted today, many of the disclosure and procedural protections of the federal securities laws will not be available. Therefore, it is necessary that the anti-fraud provisions continue to provide a basic level of protection for U.S. security holders participating in these transactions. The application of these provisions, however, may be different in the context of foreign disclosure requirements and practices. The Commission considers the information that is required to be disclosed by a form or schedule generally to be important in investment decisions. However, the omission of the information called for by U.S. forms in the context of foreign disclosure requirements and practices would not necessarily violate the U.S. disclosure requirements. An antifraud action could be brought by the Commission and investors if the omitted information is material in the context of the transaction and the disclosure provided is misleading as a result of the omission of the information.

* * *

QUESTIONS

1. Do the multiple exemptions from U.S. rules for foreign tender offers (from the all holders, fair price and exclusivity rules, among others) suggest that those rules might be relaxed for U.S. tender offers as well?

---

54 [Ed.: Under Securities Act Rules 801 and 802, the terms and conditions of the offer must be at least as favorable for U.S. security holders as foreign holders. These Rules do not mandate that specific information be sent to U.S. security holders. Instead, when any document, notice or other information is provided to offerees, copies (translated into English) must be provided to U.S. security holders in a similar manner. The documents must include a legend regarding the foreign nature of the transaction and the issuer's disclosure practices. The legend also must state that investors may have difficulty in enforcing rights against the issuer and its officers and directors.]

2. Is the 10 percent threshold in the Tier 1 exemption high enough to prompt bidders to expose themselves to liability in the U.S. in order to make their offers available to a relatively small group of U.S. shareholders?

The Antifraud Provisions of the Federal Securities Law: Minorco, a Luxemburg company controlled by two leading South African gold production companies, attempted a hostile takeover of a British company, Consolidated Gold Fields, in 1988. Gold Fields sought to block the takeover on antitrust grounds in courts in the U.S., Britain, South Africa, Australia and the EU. The challenges failed everywhere except in the U.S. where a federal district judge enjoined the transactions as violating federal antitrust and securities acts. Below is the section of the Second Circuit opinion dealing with the securities law questions in the case. Note how Minorco consciously attempted to avoid engaging in any conduct in the U.S. Moreover, Consolidated Gold Fields may have been violating British law by instituting a lawsuit in the U.S.[55] A 2010 Supreme Court opinion, *Morrison v. National Australia Bank LTD.*, 561 U.S. 247, 130 S.Ct. 2869 (2010), abrogates the effects test used in the case but may not affect the holding on the facts. See the SEC Release following the case.

CONSOLIDATED GOLD FIELDS PLC V. MINORCO, S.A.

United States Court of Appeals, Second Circuit, 1989.
871 F.2d 252, *cert. dismissed*, 492 U.S. 939 (1989).

JON O. NEWMAN, CIRCUIT JUDGE:

* * *

Gold Fields is a British corporation with significant holdings in the United States. It is engaged primarily in the exploration, mining, and sale of natural resources, especially gold. Half of Gold Fields' $2.4 billion in assets are located in the United States. . . .

Minorco is a Luxembourg corporation, whose principal assets are shareholdings in companies engaged in natural resource production and exploration, including a 29.9 percent interest in Gold Fields. . . .

In October 1988, Minorco commenced its offer for the 70 percent of Gold Fields' stock it does not already own. Of the 213,450,000 Gold Fields shares outstanding, approximately 5,300,000 (2.5 percent) are held by United States residents. Of these shares, approximately 50,000 shares are held directly by residents, 3.1 million shares are held indirectly through nominee accounts in the United Kingdom, and about 2.15 million shares are owned through the ownership of American Depository Receipts (ADR's), documents that indicate ownership by an American of a specific

---

[55] The British City Code on Takeovers and Mergers enjoins target companies from taking action to frustrate a bid.

number of shares in a foreign corporation held of record by a United States depository bank. The ADR depositories also have nominees in the United Kingdom.

In its offering documents, Minorco stated that the offer "is not being made directly or indirectly in, or by use of the mails or by any means or instrumentality of interstate or foreign commerce or of any facilities of a national securities exchange of, the United States of America, its possessions or territories or any area subject to its jurisdiction or any political sub-division thereof." Minorco sent the offering documents to the United Kingdom nominees for United States resident shareholders. Minorco did not mail offering documents to the United States resident shareholders who own Gold Fields shares directly, but the documents stated that Minorco would accept tenders from United States residents as long as the acceptance form was sent to Minorco from outside the United States. [Ed.: The antitrust analysis is omitted.]

* * *

. . . Gold Fields alleges that Minorco violated the anti-fraud provisions of the securities laws by making false and misleading statements about the extent to which Minorco is controlled by South African corporations and individuals. Gold Fields shareholders would want to be aware of these South African ties because, according to cross-appellant, such associations would make it difficult for Gold Fields to continue business operations in certain countries.

The anti-fraud laws of the United States may be given extraterritorial reach whenever a predominantly foreign transaction has substantial effects within the United States.[Ed.[56]] *See Schoenbaum v. Firstbrook*, 405 F.2d 200 (2d Cir.), reh'g on other grounds, 405 F.2d 215 (in banc), cert. denied, 395 U.S. 906, 89 S.Ct. 1747, 23 L.Ed.2d 219 (1969); Restatement (Third) of the Foreign Relations Law of the United States s 402(1)(c) (1987) [hereinafter "Third Restatement"]. . . .

In applying the so-called "effects" test enunciated in Schoenbaum, the District Court determined that the number of Americans holding stock in the allegedly defrauded British company was "insignificant" and that Minorco had taken "whatever steps it could to assure that the tender offer documents would not reach Gold Fields ADR holders." 698 F.Supp. 487 (S.D.N.Y.1989). Because Minorco had sent the offering documents to British nominees of American shareholders, the District Court concluded that the transaction between Minorco and Gold Fields had only indirect effects on a relatively small number of Americans. . . .

In this case, the District Court should have asserted jurisdiction once it noted that Minorco knew that the British nominees were required by law

56 [Ed.: The case is no longer good law. See Morrison v. Nat'l Australian Bank Ltd., 561 U.S. 247, 130 S.Ct. 2869 (2010).]

to forward the tender offer documents to Gold Fields' shareholders and ADR depository banks in the United States. This "effect" (the transmittal of the documents by the nominees) was clearly a direct and foreseeable result of the conduct outside the territory of the United States. Third Restatement, *supra*, s 402(1)(c). . . . Congress intended American anti-fraud laws to apply to a transaction . . . where American residents representing 2.5 percent of Gold Fields' shareholders owned 5.3 million shares with a market value of about $120 million.

* * *

. . . [T]he American shareholders in Gold Fields ADR's hold direct interests in the allegedly defrauded company. We therefore conclude that the District Court should have exercised subject matter jurisdiction over plaintiffs' fraud claims.

The SEC, which filed a brief as amicus curiae supporting subject matter jurisdiction over the fraud claims, nevertheless urges us to direct the District Court to abstain, for reasons of international comity, from enjoining the tender offer worldwide pending corrective disclosure.[7] We decline this suggestion and instead remand the fraud claims to the District Court for further proceedings. It is a settled principle of international and our domestic law that a court may abstain from exercising enforcement jurisdiction when the extraterritorial effect of a particular remedy is so disproportionate to harm within the United States as to offend principles of comity. . . . In determining whether a particular enforcement measure is "reasonably related to the laws or regulations to which they are directed," Third Restatement, supra, s 431(2), the American court may take note, for example, of "connections . . . between the regulating state and the person principally responsible for the activity to be regulated" as well as "the extent to which another state may have an interest in regulating the activity." . . . We decline to conduct this inquiry, however, because the record in the District Court is insufficiently developed for us to determine whether plaintiffs' requested remedy for the fraud violations—corrective disclosure of Minorco's ties to South African interests—is warranted. Now that we have determined that the District Court has jurisdiction over the fraud claims, Judge Mukasey should proceed to the merits and, if plaintiffs prevail, conduct additional factfinding to determine whether an appropriate remedy, consistent with comity principles, may be fashioned in this case.

* * *

---

[7] The Commission's amicus brief expressed the view that certain other remedies, such as a requirement of corrective disclosure, would have a narrower extraterritorial effect than the remedy of an injunction pending corrective disclosure. The Commission took no position on such other remedies. If the disclosure is to be informative at a meaningful time, it is not readily apparent why the Commission perceives a difference between an injunction pending disclosure and a disclosure requirement. [Ed.: The court amended the note, 890 F.2d 569 (1989), after an entreaty by the SEC.]

SECURITIES AND EXCHANGE COMMISSION, STUDY ON EXTRATERRITORIAL PRIVATE RIGHTS OF ACTION

SEC Release No. 34–63174, 2010 WL 4196006 (Oct. 25, 2010).

I. Introduction

In a recent decision in *Morrison v. National Australia Bank,* 130 S. Ct. 2869 (2010), the Supreme Court significantly limited the extraterritorial scope of Section 10(b) of the Exchange Act. In the Dodd-Frank Act, Congress restored the ability of the Commission and the United States to bring actions under Section 10(b) in cases involving transnational securities fraud. Congress further directed the Commission to conduct a study to determine whether, and to what extent, private plaintiffs should also be able to bring such actions. . . .

II. Background

In *Morrison,* the Supreme Court considered "whether § 10(b) of the Securities Exchange Act of 1934 provides a cause of action to foreign plaintiffs suing foreign and American defendants for misconduct in connection with securities traded on foreign exchanges." The text of the Exchange Act had been silent as to the transnational reach of Section 10(b). In a decision issued on June 24, 2010, the Supreme Court said: "When a statute gives no clear indication of an extraterritorial application, it has none." *Morrison,* 130 S. Ct. at 2878. "[T]here is no affirmative indication in the Exchange Act that § 10(b) applies extraterritorially," the Court found, "and we therefore conclude that it does not." *Id.* at 2883.Thus, the Court concluded, "it is in our view only transactions in securities listed on domestic exchanges, and domestic transactions in other securities, to which § 10(b) applies." *Id.* at 2884 (footnote omitted). The Court summarized the test as follows:

> Section 10(b) reaches the use of a manipulative or deceptive device or contrivance only in connection with the purchase or sale of a security listed on an American stock exchange, and the purchase or sale of any other security in the United States.

Id. at 2888.

The *Morrison* decision rejected long-standing precedents in most federal courts of appeals that applied some variation or combination of an "effects" test and a "conduct" test to determine the extraterritorial reach of Section 10(b) of the Exchange Act. . . . The effects test centered its inquiry on whether domestic investors or markets were affected as a result of actions occurring outside the United States. . . . By contrast, the conduct test focused "on the nature of [the] conduct within the United States as it relates to carrying out the alleged fraudulent scheme." . . .

On July 21, 2010, less than a month after the decision in *Morrison,* President Obama signed the Dodd-Frank Act. Section 929P of the Dodd-

Frank Act amended the Exchange Act to provide that the United States district courts shall have jurisdiction over an action brought or instituted by the Commission or the United States alleging a violation of the antifraud provisions of the Exchange Act involving:

> (1) conduct within the United States that constitutes significant steps in furtherance of the violation, even if the securities transaction occurs outside the United States and involves only foreign investors; or
>
> (2) conduct occurring outside the United States that has a foreseeable substantial effect within the United States.[Ed.[57]]

Under section 929Y of the Dodd-Frank Act, the Commission is required to conduct a study to determine whether *private* rights of action should be similarly extended. . . .

III. Request for Comments

Section 929Y(a) of the Dodd-Frank Act directs the Commission to solicit public comment on whether the scope of the antifraud provisions of the Exchange Act in cases of transnational securities fraud should be extended to private rights of action to the same extent as that provided to the Commission by Section 929P, or to some other extent.[Ed.[58]] Section 929Y(b) directs that the study shall consider and analyze, among other things—

> (1) the scope of such a private right of action, including whether it should extend to all private actors or whether it should be more limited to extend just to institutional investors or otherwise;
>
> (2) what implications such a private right of action would have on international comity;
>
> (3) the economic costs and benefits of extending a private right of action for transnational securities frauds; and
>
> (4) whether a narrower extraterritorial standard should be adopted.

Accordingly, we request comment on these issues and questions. We also encourage commenters to:

---

[57] [Ed.: With respect to U.S. Government and Commission actions, the Dodd-Frank Act largely codified the long-standing appellate court interpretation of the law that had existed prior to the Supreme Court's decision in *Morrison* by setting forth an expansive conducts and effects test, and providing that the inquiry is one of subject matter jurisdiction. The Dodd-Frank Act made similar changes to the Securities Act of 1933 and the Investment Advisers Act of 1940.]

[58] [Ed.: Section 929Y(a) of the Dodd-Frank Act provides that the Commission "shall solicit public comment and thereafter conduct a study to determine the extent to which private rights of action under the antifraud provisions of the Securities Exchange Act of 1934 (15 U.S.C. 78u–4) should be extended to cover: conduct within the United States that constitutes a significant step in the furtherance of the violation, even if the securities transaction occurs outside the United States and involves only foreign investors; and conduct occurring outside the United States that has a foreseeable substantial effect within the United States."]

- Propose the circumstances, if any, in which a private plaintiff should be allowed to pursue claims under the antifraud provisions of the Exchange Act with respect to a particular security where the plaintiff has purchased or sold the security outside the United States. Does it make a difference whether the security was issued by a U.S. company or by a non-U.S. company? Does it make a difference whether the security was purchased or sold on a foreign stock exchange or whether it was purchased or sold on a non-exchange trading platform or other alternative trading system outside of the United States? Does it make a difference whether the company's securities are traded exclusively outside of the United States?
- If you disagree with extending the test set forth in Section 929P to private plaintiffs, what other test would you propose?
- Should there be an effects test, a conduct test, a combination of the two, or another test?

* * *

- In *Morrison,* the Supreme Court held that in the case of securities that are not listed on an American stock exchange, Section 10(b) only reaches the use of a manipulative or deceptive device or contrivance in connection with the purchase or sale of a security *in the United States*. Address the criteria for determining where a purchase or sale can be said to take place in various transnational securities transactions. Discuss the degree to which investors know, when they place a securities purchase or sale order, whether the order will take place on a foreign stock exchange or on a non-exchange trading platform or other alternative trading system outside of the United States.

* * *

QUESTIONS

The effects test in *Consolidated Gold Fields* does not survive the language of *Morrison*. Does the Dodd-Frank provision resurrect it for SEC actions? Or is such a provision on court jurisdiction distinguishable from and not determinative of doctrine on the extraterritorial reach of the securities statutes? Does the holding on the facts in *Consolidated Gold Fields* comport with the new transaction test of *Morrison*? Note the role of the ADRs.

2. ANTITRUST LAWS

The Clayton Act and the Sherman Act present two categories of international issues: First, when do United States antitrust rules apply to overseas anticompetitive acquisitions that have some effect on U.S. *domestic* markets? Second, when do United States antitrust rules apply to acquisitions in the United States that affect overseas markets? The language of the Clayton Act itself gives no guidance so first the federal courts and later the Department of Justice in its Enforcement Guidelines have attempted to provide answers.

DEPARTMENT OF JUSTICE AND FEDERAL TRADE COMMISSION, ANTITRUST GUIDELINES FOR INTERNATIONAL ENFORCEMENT AND COOPERATION (JAN. 3, 2017)

Since the 1995 release of the Antitrust Enforcement Guidelines for International Operations, trade between the United States and other countries has expanded at a tremendous rate. With this expansion, the federal antitrust laws have played an increasingly important role in protecting consumers and businesses purchasing in U.S. import commerce and exporters selling in U.S. export commerce from anticompetitive conduct. In addition, anticompetitive conduct—from price-fixing cartels to competition-reducing mergers and monopolization—increasingly is subject to investigation and, in some cases, remedial action by foreign authorities.

The Department of Justice (the "Department") and the Federal Trade Commission (the "Commission" or "FTC") (collectively the "Agencies") are charged with enforcement of the federal antitrust laws, an essential component of which is the application of these laws to foreign commerce. Moreover, the Agencies cooperate on their antitrust enforcement with foreign authorities wherever appropriate.

In furtherance of that enforcement and in recognition of the role of international cooperation, the Agencies issue these Antitrust Guidelines for International Enforcement and Cooperation ("International Guidelines"), which replace the 1995 Antitrust Enforcement Guidelines for International Operations. The International Guidelines provide updated guidance to businesses engaged in international activities on questions that concern the Agencies' international enforcement policy as well as the Agencies' related investigative tools and cooperation with foreign authorities.

Many nations share our faith in the value of competition, and as of 2017, over 130 jurisdictions have enacted antitrust laws as a means to ensure open and free markets, promote consumer welfare, and prevent conduct that impedes competition. Accordingly, the Agencies have expanded their efforts and committed greater resources to building and maintaining strong relationships with foreign authorities to promote greater policy engagement.

* * *

2.4 Hart-Scott-Rodino Antitrust Improvements Act of 1976

Title II of the Hart-Scott-Rodino Antitrust Improvements Act of 1976 "HSR Act") facilitates the Agencies' enforcement of the antitrust laws with respect to anticompetitive mergers and acquisitions. It requires that persons provide notice to the Agencies of certain proposed mergers or acquisitions and imposes a waiting period on these mergers or acquisitions. Transactions are subject to these requirements only if they meet certain conditions, including minimum size thresholds. Some transactions are explicitly exempted from these requirements by the statute's text. The HSR Act and the Hart-Scott-Rodino Premerger Notification Rules ("HSR Rules") exempt from the notification requirements certain international transactions (typically those having little nexus to U.S. commerce) that otherwise meet the statutory thresholds. Transactions not subject to the HSR Act's notification and waiting period requirements may still be subject to the Sherman Act, the FTC Act, or the Clayton Act, and the Agencies may seek to block or undo an anticompetitive merger or acquisition or seek other equitable relief when any of those statutes applies.

* * *

3. Agencies' Application of U.S. Antitrust Law to Conduct Involving Foreign Commerce

In making investigative and enforcement decisions, the Agencies focus on whether there is a sufficient connection between the anticompetitive conduct and the United States such that the federal antitrust laws apply and the Agencies' enforcement would redress harm or threatened harm to U.S. commerce and consumers. . . . If the Agencies determine that a sufficient connection exists, the Agencies generally will proceed in the normal course, subject to the considerations described in Chapter 4 and principles of prosecutorial discretion.

It is well established that the federal antitrust laws apply to foreign conduct that has a substantial and intended effect in the United States. In 1982, Congress reaffirmed the applicability of the antitrust laws to conduct involving foreign commerce when it passed the [Foreign Trade Antitrust Improvements Act of 1982 (FTAIA)], which added Section 6a to the Sherman Act and Section 5(a)(3) to the [Federal Trade Commission Act (FTC Act)]. These provisions clarify whether the antitrust laws reach conduct—regardless of where it takes place—that involves trade or commerce with foreign nations. . . .

* * *

Although the FTAIA clarified the reach of the Sherman Act and the FTC Act, it did not address the reach of the Clayton Act. Nevertheless, the Agencies would apply the principles outlined below when making enforcement decisions regarding mergers and acquisitions involving trade or commerce with foreign nations.

3.1 Conduct Involving Import Commerce

In general, the proscriptions in the Sherman Act and the FTC Act apply to conduct subject to Congress' constitutional power "to regulate commerce with foreign nations," among other things. The FTAIA places "conduct involving trade or commerce (other than import trade or import commerce) with foreign nations" beyond the reach of these statutes, unless the conduct satisfies the FTAIA's effects exception described below. The parenthetical language, however, excludes from the FTAIA's operation conduct involving import trade and import commerce. This provision is commonly referred to as the "import commerce exclusion." As a result of this exclusion, conduct involving U.S. import commerce, like conduct involving commerce within the United States, is "subject to the Sherman Act's [or FTC Act's] general requirements for effects on commerce, not to the special requirements spelled out in the FTAIA."

The import commerce exclusion does not apply to conduct merely because those participating in the conduct are also engaged in import commerce. Rather the conduct being challenged must itself involve import commerce. Conversely, the import commerce exclusion may apply to conduct even if the participants themselves do not act as importers. For example, a firm cannot escape liability for unreasonably restraining or monopolizing import commerce by outsourcing the delivery of its product to the United States.

Conduct may "involve" import commerce even if it is not directed specifically or exclusively at import commerce and even if the import commerce involved constitutes a relatively small portion of the worldwide commerce involved in the anticompetitive conduct.

Illustrative Example A

Situation: Corporation 1 and Corporation 2 have factories in Country Alpha where they manufacture Widget X. Corporation 1 and Corporation 2 agree to charge higher prices for Widget X. They sell Widget X to customers around the world, including in the United States.

Discussion: Corporation 1 and Corporation 2 manufacture Widget X outside the United States and sell Widget X in or for delivery to the United States. Thus their conspiracy to fix the price of Widget X is conduct involving U.S. import commerce. Accordingly, the conduct is prohibited by Section 1 of the Sherman Act as a conspiracy in restraint of "trade . . . with foreign nations," and Section 6a would not exempt this conspiracy from the antitrust laws. The circumstance that the price-fixing agreement concerned worldwide sales and did not specifically identify sales into the United States would not change the analysis. Likewise, even if the sales of Widget X in import commerce were a relatively small proportion or dollar amount of the price-fixed goods sold worldwide, the analysis would remain unchanged.

* * *

3.2 Conduct Involving Non-Import Foreign Commerce

The FTAIA initially places conduct involving non-import foreign commerce, which means U.S. export commerce and wholly foreign commerce, outside the reach of the Sherman Act and FTC Act. What is commonly referred to as the FTAIA's "effects exception" brings such conduct back within the reach of the Acts if the conduct has a direct, substantial, and reasonably foreseeable effect on commerce within the United States, U.S. import commerce, or the export commerce of a U.S. exporter, and that effect gives rise to a claim. Whether an alleged effect on such commerce is direct, substantial, and reasonably foreseeable is a question of fact. An effect on commerce is "direct" if there is a reasonably proximate causal nexus, that is, if the effect is proximately caused by the alleged anticompetitive conduct. In other words, an effect is direct if, in the natural or ordinary course of events, the alleged anticompetitive conduct would produce an effect on commerce. The substantiality requirement does not provide a minimum pecuniary threshold, nor does it require that the effects be quantified. Finally, the "reasonable foreseeability" requirement is an objective test, requiring that the effect be foreseeable to "a reasonable person making practical business judgments."

* * *

Illustrative Example D

Situation: Company 1 and Company 2 are located in Country Alpha, where they extract Mineral X. Company 3 is located in the United States, where it extracts Mineral X. Company 3 is able to meet the entire U.S. demand for Mineral X and does so. Company 1 and Company 2 supply the rest of the world with Mineral X, but not the United States. By mutual agreement, Company 1 and Company 2 reduce their sales of Mineral X, significantly driving up the price of Mineral X outside the United States. Because of the increased price for Mineral X outside the United States, Company 3 begins to export much of the U.S. supply of Mineral X. No other firms replace Company 3's diverted sales, and the price of Mineral X rises inside the United States.

Discussion: Company 1 and Company 2's conspiracy to reduce their sales of Mineral X outside the United States is conduct involving wholly foreign commerce. Such conduct would fall within the reach of the Sherman Act if it has a direct, substantial, and reasonably foreseeable effect on U.S. interstate commerce in Mineral X. Here, the conspiracy had the effect of raising prices on interstate sales of Mineral X. That effect appears to be direct, substantial, and reasonably foreseeable.

The FTAIA's effects exception also requires that the effect on commerce within the United States, U.S. import commerce, or the export commerce of a U.S. exporter "gives rise to" a claim under the antitrust laws. In a damages action brought under the antitrust laws, this provision requires that the effect on U.S. commerce be an adverse one and that the effect proximately cause the plaintiff's antitrust injury. It is therefore appropriate for courts to distinguish among damages claims based upon the underlying transaction that forms the basis of the injury to ensure that each claim redresses injury consistent with the requirements of the antitrust laws, including the FTAIA. For example, when anticompetitive conduct affects commerce around the world, a plaintiff whose antitrust injury arises from that conduct's effect on U.S. import commerce may recover damages for that injury, but a plaintiff that suffers a foreign injury that is independent of, and not proximately caused by, the conduct's effect on U.S. commerce cannot recover damages under the U.S. antitrust laws.

Similarly, when the United States is a plaintiff seeking damages under Section 4A of the Clayton Act for injury to its business or property, the United States must establish that the alleged conduct's effect on U.S. commerce proximately caused the injury to the United States' business or property.

Civil actions for equitable relief brought by the Agencies or criminal enforcement actions brought by the Department, on behalf of the United States, do not seek to redress a pecuniary injury to the government. Instead, such actions are brought by the sovereign to enjoin or prosecute a violation of its laws. In such cases, a direct, substantial, and reasonably foreseeable effect on U.S. commerce would give rise to the sovereign's claim.

Thus, as a result of the effects exception's "gives rise to" provision, the Sherman Act can apply and not apply to the same conduct, depending upon the circumstances, including the plaintiff bringing the claim, the nature of the claim, and the injury underlying the claim.

* * *

4. Agencies' Consideration of Foreign Jurisdictions

4.1 Comity

In enforcing the federal antitrust laws, the Agencies consider international comity. Comity itself reflects the broad concept of respect among co-equal sovereign nations and plays a role in determining "the recognition which one nation allows within its territory to the legislative, executive or judicial acts of another nation." In determining whether to investigate or bring an action, or to seek particular remedies in a given case, the Agencies take into account whether significant interests of any foreign sovereign would be affected.

A decision to take an investigative step or to prosecute an antitrust action under the federal antitrust laws represents a determination that the importance of antitrust enforcement outweighs any relevant foreign policy concerns. That determination is entitled to deference. Some courts have undertaken a comity analysis in disputes between private parties.

In performing this comity analysis, the Agencies consider a number of relevant factors. The relative weight given to each factor depends on the facts and circumstances of each case. Among other things, the Agencies weigh: the existence of a purpose to affect or an actual effect on U.S. commerce; the significance and foreseeability of the effects of the anticompetitive conduct on the United States; the degree of conflict with a foreign jurisdiction's law or articulated policy; the extent to which the enforcement activities of another jurisdiction, including remedies resulting from those enforcement activities, may be affected; and the effectiveness of foreign enforcement as compared to U.S. enforcement.

An investigation or enforcement action by a foreign authority will not preclude an investigation or enforcement action by either the Department or the Commission. Rather, the Agency will determine whether, in light of actions by the foreign authority, investigation or enforcement is warranted to address harm or threatened harm to U.S. commerce and consumers from anticompetitive conduct. In cases in which an Agency opens an investigation or brings an enforcement action concerning conduct under investigation by a foreign authority, it may coordinate with that authority.

* * *

4.2 Consideration of Foreign Government Involvement

In some instances, a foreign government may be involved in anticompetitive conduct that involves or affects U.S. commerce. In determining whether to conduct an investigation or to file an enforcement action in cases in which foreign government involvement is known or suspected, the Agencies consider four legal doctrines that lie at the intersection of government action and the antitrust laws: (1) foreign sovereign immunity[Ed.[59]]; (2) foreign sovereign compulsion[Ed.[60]]; (3) act of state[Ed.[61]]; and (4) petitioning of sovereigns[Ed.[62]].

* * *

5. International Cooperation

Effective enforcement of the U.S. antitrust laws in a global economy benefits from cooperation with foreign authorities. The Agencies are committed to cooperating with foreign authorities on both policy and investigative matters. This cooperation contributes to convergence on substantive enforcement standards that seek to advance consumer welfare, based on sound economics, procedural fairness, transparency, and non-discriminatory treatment of parties. The Agencies' international policy work and case cooperation are closely connected. As noted above, consistent approaches to competition law, policy, and procedures across jurisdictions facilitate case cooperation among competition authorities. Moreover, through case cooperation, the Agencies and cooperating authorities often raise important substantive and procedural issues as they arise in practice, which can lead to greater convergence in substantive analysis and procedures. . . .

International case cooperation helps agencies investigating a particular matter to identify issues of common interest, gain a better understanding of relevant facts, and achieve consistent outcomes. Cooperation can yield better results for competition and promote efficiency for both cooperating agencies and subjects of an investigation. It can improve substantive analyses and procedures, and ensure that investigations and remedies are as consistent and predictable as possible, which improves outcomes, and reduces uncertainty and expense to firms

---

[59] [Ed.: In civil cases, the Foreign Sovereign Immunities Act of 1976 ("FSIA") provides the "sole basis for obtaining jurisdiction over a foreign state in the courts of this country." FSIA shields foreign states from the civil jurisdiction of the courts of the United States, subject to certain enumerated exceptions and to treaties in place at the time of FSIA's enactment.]

[60] [Ed.: Courts have recognized a limited defense against application of the U.S. antitrust laws when a foreign sovereign compels the very conduct that the U.S. antitrust laws would prohibit. If it is possible, however, for a party to comply with both the foreign law and the U.S. antitrust laws, the existence of the foreign law does not provide any legal excuse for actions that do not comply with U.S. law. Similarly, that conduct may be lawful, approved, or encouraged in a foreign jurisdiction does not, in and of itself, bar application of the U.S. antitrust laws—even when the foreign jurisdiction has a strong policy in favor of the conduct in question.]

[61] [Ed.: The act of state doctrine prevents courts from declaring invalid the official act of a foreign sovereign performed within its own territory. Applying this doctrine, courts decline to adjudicate claims or issues that would require the court to judge the validity of the sovereign act of a foreign state in its own territory. This doctrine is rooted in considerations of international comity and the separation of powers.]

[62] [Ed.: A genuine effort to obtain or influence action by governmental entities in the U.S. falls outside the scope of the Sherman Act, even if the intent or effect of that effort is to restrain or monopolize trade. The Agencies, therefore, will not challenge under the antitrust laws genuine efforts to obtain or influence action by foreign government entities. However, the Agencies will not exercise this discretion when faced with "sham" activities, in which petitioning ostensibly directed toward influencing governmental action, is a mere sham to cover an attempt to interfere directly with the business relationships of a competitor.]

doing business across borders. When either Agency reviews a case that raises possible competitive concerns in jurisdictions outside of the United States, it may consult with the relevant foreign authorities about the matter and coordinate and cooperate with those authorities conducting parallel investigations. . . . [C]ooperation can include a broad range of practices, from initiating informal discussions and informing cooperating authorities of the different stages of their investigations, to engaging in detailed discussions of substantive issues, exchanging information, conducting interviews at which two or more agencies may be present, and coordinating remedy design and implementation, as relevant and appropriate.

* * *

5.1.5 Remedies

The Agencies seek remedies that effectively address harm or threatened harm to U.S. commerce and consumers, while attempting to avoid conflicts with remedies contemplated by their foreign counterparts. An Agency will seek a remedy that includes conduct or assets outside the United States only to the extent that including them is needed to effectively redress harm or threatened harm to U.S. commerce and consumers and is consistent with the Agency's international comity analysis.

When multiple authorities are investigating the same transaction or same conduct, the Agencies may cooperate with other authorities, to the extent permitted under U.S. law, to facilitate obtaining effective and non-conflicting remedies. Cooperation also may facilitate the development of a proposed remedies package that comprehensively addresses the concerns of multiple authorities. In some circumstances, cooperation may result in one authority closing an investigation without remedies after taking another authority's remedies into account.

Sections 802.50 and .51 of the Hart-Scott-Rodino Pre-merger Notification Rules provide an exemption from the filing requirement for acquisitions of the assets and securities of a foreign target. The exemption depends on the absence of sales or assets in the United States in excess of $50 million.

QUESTION

If two exporting United States firms merge to monopolize a consumer market in a *foreign* country, should the Clayton Act apply?

NOTE: CONFLICTS WITH OUR TRADING PARTNERS

The application of U.S. antitrust principles to international companies has generated deep conflict with some of our trading partners and our principal allies. One of the most bitterly protested exercises of American antitrust jurisdiction was the *Uranium* litigation. *In re Uranium Antitrust Litigation*, 480 F.Supp. 1138 (N.D. Ill. 1979), *aff'd* on jurisdiction, 617 F.2d 1248 (7th Cir. 1980). The British responded with the following act.

UNITED KINGDOM PROTECTION OF TRADING INTERESTS ACT OF 1980

(1980 c.11).

Under § 1 of the Act, the Secretary of State may order:

> . . . a person in the United Kingdom who carries on business there . . . [not to comply with any] measures [that] have been or are proposed to be taken [under foreign law for the purpose of] regulating or controlling international trade . . . [if] those measures, insofar as they apply. . . to things done or to be done outside the territorial jurisdiction of [the issuing country] . . . by [the person] carrying on business in the United Kingdom, are damaging or threaten to damage the trading interest of the United Kingdom. . . .

The Secretary's orders may be special or general (*e.g.*, he may interdict all orders emanating from a specified matter pending abroad), absolute or conditional, and may be annulled by Parliament. The Secretary may require any person in Britain or carrying on business there to inform him of any measure potentially subject to his interdiction. A failure to comply with a Secretary's order is punishable by fine, except as to acts of non-compliance by non-citizens of Britain or by foreign corporations done outside the United Kingdom (Section 3 of the Act).

While apparently the "measures" which the Secretary may interdict do not include "judgments" of foreign courts, they do include all regulations and orders of administrative agencies (*e.g.*, a cease and desist order by the Federal Trade Commission), and possibly all intermediate court orders such as temporary restraining orders and preliminary injunctions.

Section 2 of the Act confers authority on the Secretary of State to bar compliance with certain judicial or administrative orders to produce commercial documents located outside the territory of the issuing authority or to furnish documentary evidence. Section 4 limits the authority of British courts to assist foreign courts in obtaining evidence in Great Britain and Section 5 prohibits those courts from entertaining any proceeding to recover sums payable under a foreign judgment if the latter calls for "multiple damages" or pertains to a restraint of competition. That section also bars registration of such judgments in Britain and is retroactive.

Lastly, Section 6 of the Act contains the so-called "claw-back" provision as follows:

(1) This section applies where a court of an overseas country has given a judgment for multiple damages [*i.e.* a "judgment for an amount arrived at by doubling, trebling or otherwise multiplying a sum assessed as compensation"] against—

(a) a citizen of the United Kingdom and Colonies; or

(b) a body corporate incorporated in the United Kingdom or in a territory outside the United Kingdom for whose international relations Her Majesty's Government in the United Kingdom are responsible; or

(c) a person carrying on business in the United Kingdom, (in this section referred to as a "qualifying defendant") and an amount on account of the damages has been paid by the qualifying defendant either to the party in whose favor the judgment was given or to another party who is entitled as against the qualifying defendant to contribution in respect of the damages.

(2) Subject to subsections (3) and (4) below, the qualifying defendant shall be entitled to recover from the party in whose favor the judgment was given so much of the amount referred to in subsection (1) above as exceeds the part attributable to compensation.

(3) Subsection (2) above does not apply where the qualifying defendant is an individual who was ordinarily resident in the overseas country at the time when the proceedings in which the judgment was given were instituted or a body corporate which had its principal place of business there at that time.

(4) Subsection (2) above does not apply where the qualifying defendant carried on business in the overseas country and the proceedings in which the judgment was given were concerned with activities exclusively carried on in that country.

(5) A court in the United Kingdom may entertain proceedings on a claim under this section notwithstanding that the person against whom the proceedings are brought is not within the jurisdiction of the court.

(6) The reference in subsection (1) above to an amount paid by the qualifying defendant includes a reference to an amount obtained by execution against his property or a company which (directly or indirectly) is wholly owned by him.

* * *

QUESTION

If an American company controlling 40 percent of a relevant U.S. market purchases in a London closing a U.K. company whose exports are 20 percent of the same market, but whose productive assets are all located in the U.K., and the FTC attempts to enjoin the acquisition, is the order interdictable?

General antitrust regulation in the European Union is contained in Articles 81 to 83 of the EU treaty. The Council of the European Communities, pursuant to authority under Article 83, has adopted a *Merger Control Regulation* (*MCR*). The European Commission has promulgated horizontal, conglomerate, and vertical merger guidelines under the MCR.

MARK LEDDY, CHRISTOPHER COOK, JAMES ABELL, GEORGINA ECLAIR-HEATH, TRANSATLANTIC MERGER CONTROL: THE COURTS AND THE AGENCIES

43 CORNELL INT'L L.J. 25 (2010).

* * *

European competition enforcement is based on an administrative system in which the European Commission (the Commission) has a broad duty "to apply, in competition matters, the principles laid down by the Treaty and to guide the conduct of undertakings in light of those principles." In the field of merger control, this duty requires the Commission to investigate and hand down decisions clearing, prohibiting, or undoing notified transactions, according to the procedure set out in Regulation 139/2004 (the EC Merger Regulation). In merger cases, the Commission thus serves as investigator, prosecutor, and judge.

Having these roles vested in a single authority is acceptable only if effective due process safeguards and checks and balances constrain the administration's power. As discussed below, since 2002 the Commission has put in place a number of internal measures that have undoubtedly contributed to sounder decision-making. Even with the best of intentions, however, an administrative system will only meet basic standards of fairness and predictability if an independent tribunal oversees the decision maker.

In the EU, the General Court (formerly the Court of First Instance) and the Court of Justice of the European Union (the Court of Justice) (together, the EU Courts) provide this check on the Commission. Merger decisions taken by the Commission may be challenged before the General Court, and decisions of the General Court may be further appealed on points of law to the Court of Justice. The EU Courts may annul Commission decisions where they find "lack of competence, infringement of an essential procedural requirement, infringement of the Treaty or of any rule of law relating to its application, or misuse of powers." Any natural or legal person may challenge a Commission decision that directly addresses or individually affects them.

The EU Courts do not have unfettered discretion when reviewing Commission merger clearance or prohibition decisions. The EU Courts cannot engage in a de novo review of the facts and cannot substitute their views for those of the Commission. The EU system instead revolves around the "cornerstone of error." While the EU Courts may scrutinize the Commission's factual analysis and are the ultimate arbiters with regard to matters of law, the Commission has traditionally enjoyed a "margin of discretion" in relation to complex economic matters, which are often at the heart of merger control decisions. In this area, the role of the EU Courts is limited to "restrained control," whereby the courts verify only whether the relevant procedural rules have been complied with, whether the statement of the reasons for the decision is adequate, "whether the facts have been accurately stated and whether there has been any manifest error of appraisal or misuse of powers."

Notwithstanding these stated limitations, in recent years the EU Courts have increasingly demonstrated a willingness to engage in rigorous and detailed scrutiny of the Commission's use of evidence in complex cases. Thus, while in theory the EU merger control regime envisages a delicate institutional balance in which the Commission and the EU Courts each focus on their primary function of competition policy enforcement and judicial review respectively, in practice the situation is not always so clear cut.

* * *

In the EU, appeals have been brought in only about forty of the approximately 4,000 Commission merger decisions since the Merger Regulation entered into force in 1990. Nonetheless, these decisions have had a disproportionately large impact on the development of EU merger control. In particular, landmark judgments of 2002 in Airtours, Schneider, and Tetra Laval led directly to a substantial overhaul of the European Commission's internal structure and decision-making practice. More recently, the General Court's judgment in Impala has raised the standard of care required of the Commission even in clearance decisions.

* * *

KEVIN ARQUIT, KEYNOTE ADDRESS, SYMPOSIUM FEB. 27, 2009

43 CORNELL INT'L L.J. 1 (2010).

* * *

Now, in the most general terms, I would like to give you a flavor of the conventional wisdom regarding the different approaches to antitrust. In the United States, merger policy has followed a consistent approach since 1984, when formal guidelines were implemented. Those guidelines, instituted more than twenty-five years ago, are reflective of a fairly stable policy; they are very flexible, and they allow for changes around the margins.

The 1984 guidelines reflect a theoretic approach, known as the "Chicago School of Economics." The essential premise of the Chicago School is that we do not know an awful lot about how humans actually behave, but we know, basically, how the rational person thinks. And so the doctrine is based on a theory of rational choice. The approach of the merger guidelines, and the Chicago School, accepts as a premise that individuals and firms will make rational choices. And by rational choices, what they mean is that firms, armed with adequate information, will make decisions based on their informed self-interest.

In other words, firms will make profit-maximizing decisions. This is essentially the underpinning of both U.S. merger guidelines and the entirety of U.S. merger analysis. What flows from this is the notion that competition and free markets provide the best products, the cheapest products, the highest quality products, and the most choice. There is a corollary to this, that while markets may temporarily suffer from distortions, they will quickly self-correct. There are those who would characterize this as representing a minimalist school of thought.

By extension, government intervention is something that should come about rarely, and, when it does occur, it should be minimal. And I think that, even as of a year ago, the majority of commentators would have generally agreed that the United States had gotten it right when it comes to how mergers are analyzed. Judge Richard Posner noted that the intellectual journey for how we view mergers has basically come to an end and that the merger guidelines offer a modest vindication of the Chicago School. All this could lead one to conclude that the U.S. approach is one essentially on cruise control, on settled presumptions to bring about the best results.

Without going into great depth, historically, the European approach to antitrust has had different underpinnings. At a very basic level, there has been less confidence in Europe that markets always get it right. There is more of a feeling that the government should step in, at least occasionally, and that it is independently important to maintain certain market structures.

* * *

The Europeans have responded in several ways to the difference in approach. . . . But nonetheless, through a series of steps over the last ten to fifteen years, it is fair to say that European merger policy has, in fact, moved closer to U.S. merger policy. The European Commission now, and has actually for several years, had a set of merger guidelines. Their test is one that focuses on impediments to effective competition as opposed to just pure dominance. They recognize efficiency. These are all steps suggesting increased convergence with the U.S. approach.

* * *

We can debate whether the changes in Europe are the result of regulators seeing the light and the brilliance of American ideas or whether it is really the response to a series of stinging defeats that the Commission suffered before the European courts, after blocking some transactions a few years ago. My own view is that the latter served as the predominant cause. . . .

* * *

I would note that the objectives of the European law are somewhat different from ours. European antitrust law is meant to facilitate integration into the common market. This has led some U.S. critics to say, and I think largely these are unfounded criticisms, that the Europeans are fond of picking national champions. The argument is that the Europeans select winners as a means of protecting the common market, and that specific firms are selected and provided breaks that allow them to have a leg up when it comes to competing with the rest of the world. In short, critics claim that the European system tends to protect competitors more than competition, whereas, under the U.S. regime, if you protect competition, you let the winners and losers fall where they may.

Now, these differences, for the most part, do not really impact very many transactions because this is kind of nuance stuff. But, when it does lead to different results, the fur flies. There have been a couple of circumstances over the past few years where identical transactions in the United States and Europe were looked at by both regimes because they were transactions with world-wide implications. One of these was the Boeing-McDonnell Douglas merger.

The United States took a look at it, and chose not to take any enforcement action, even though Boeing and McDonnell Douglas were two of only three civilian large aircraft manufacturers. The United States' enforcers reached out and talked to the airlines, only to have the airlines respond that they did not care about the merger because McDonnell

Douglas "can no longer exert competitive influence in the worldwide market for commercial aircraft." Note that post-merger, the only remaining player out there would be Airbus. Meanwhile, over in Europe, the European Commission took a different view.

Now, there are cynics who say: "well, maybe the only difference is that Boeing and McDonnell Douglas are American companies and Airbus is a European company. That led to the different results on different sides of the ocean." The American point of view was that the European Commission was not worried about the merger. The European Commission worried about making sure that Airbus would be able to survive in the post-merger world. Because Boeing had a series of exclusive contracts with U.S. airplane manufacturers, the Commission determined that because so much of the market would be tied up and not available to Airbus, the merger could only go through if the exclusivity clauses were lifted to give Airbus the chance to compete for those contracts.

In other words, behavioral relief was required by the European Commission as a condition for allowing the deal to go through. There was, however, some static at the time—non-trivial static—from the United States that the concerns raised were little more than a device used by the Europeans to favor their own national champion as opposed to making a decision on the competitive merits. While one could infer such motives, I believe it is also the case that the European Commission decision is reconcilable with its precedent.

The transaction that caused a lot more static, which still reverberates to this day, was the proposed GE-Honeywell combination. General Electric and Honeywell agreed to merge several years ago. The only identified overlaps between GE and Honeywell had to do with some fairly minor, smaller aircraft engines. And those issues were resolved in the United States pretty quickly. The companies agreed to spin off the overlapping business to somebody else.

Yet, over in Europe, the European Commission decided to ban the transaction outright. In other words, they said, "There's no fix here. You're just not going to do this." What did they base that result on? To some degree their analysis mirrored the U.S. approach. But, in addition to that, they saw General Electric as a huge financing operation with all kinds of capital. Moreover, GE had a subsidiary that was a big purchaser of airplanes and also a big aircraft engine maker. Honeywell makes avionics—the instruments that go in the airplanes—as well as landing systems and the like.

The United States' view was that the whole point of the merger was to allow for such efficiencies, fully recognizing that, after the merger, the combined entity would very likely be the preferred choice of customers—airlines. The fact that customers would be able to go to one source, to purchase an integrated package that includes engines, airline instruments, landing systems, and the like was seen as the benefit flowing from the transaction. To the Europeans, the likelihood of this occurrence provided the very reason to stop the deal. It goes back to the idea about dictating market structure versus looking solely at the state of competition.

Frankly, I think that the U.S. criticisms of the Europeans were largely unfounded. Some in the United States had picked up on the public relations value of saying things that made nice sound bites, but which oversimplified the European analysis. Regardless of which enforcer was right or wrong, it was a common conclusion that as a result of the merger, GE would be able to offer different mix-and-match packages to its consumers.

The concern in Europe was not that these packages would be forced on consumers—by consumers, I mean the airlines here—but that the airlines would actually want the packages. That is, the airlines would want the packages so much that they would no longer have any interest in dealing with the stand-alone companies that had theretofore competed with GE and Honeywell. The Europeans disapproved of this arrangement because the GE offer would be so attractive that airlines would move their business to the combined GE-Honeywell firm. As a result, the stand-alone companies would not have adequate resources left to engage in research and development. Ultimately, the other competitors would slowly shrink into oblivion, with the result that the market would be left with one dominant firm.

So, the European Commission blocked the deal. The decision was appealed through the European courts, and several years later, it was affirmed on certain grounds but not others. But the relevant point for discussion today is that the deal was blocked, notwithstanding the fact that the United States had approved it earlier. And, following the EU's rejection, there was much made of the difference between fairness considerations in Europe versus the pure efficiency approach of the United States.

* * *

QUESTION

For companies with international operations, the State that applies the most restrictive antitrust standard for mergers will get the most attention of the transaction planners. Where is the focus of attention today? Europe or the United States?

C. COMPARATIVE TAKEOVER LAW

After fifteen years of failed negotiations, the European Union (EU) adopted a Takeover Directive on April 21, 2004. The initial objective of the

Takeover Directive was to harmonize EU member states' takeover laws through the adoption of a pan-European Takeover code (modeled on the United Kingdom's City Code on Takeovers and Mergers (*Takeover Code*)). The Takeover Directives' harmonizing effect was substantially curtailed by political concessions, known as the Portuguese compromise, that made the adoption of the rules limiting the use of takeover defenses optional (*the board neutrality rule*). See Article 12.

The theory of the U.K. Takeover Code and the Takeover Directive is to, on the one hand, disable takeover defenses accomplished without a shareholder vote (poison pill plans) and, on the other hand, to force bidders to offer to buy all the shares of a target at once (either in a mandatory, article 5, or voluntary bid, articles 6 to 11), at one price. There are no partial bids.[63] Moreover, once a bidder acquires ninety percent, it triggers crossing options; the company has a call option to squeeze-out all remaining minority shareholders at the takeover price and the minority shareholders have a put option to force the company to buy their shares, a sell-out, at the same price.

DIRECTIVE 2004/25/EC OF THE EUROPEAN PARLIAMENT AND COUNCIL OF 21 APRIL 2004 ON TAKEOVER BIDS

* * *

Article 2

Definitions

1. For the purposes of this Directive:

(a) 'takeover bid' or 'bid' shall mean a public offer (other than by the offeree company itself) made to the holders of the securities of a company to acquire all or some of those securities, whether mandatory or voluntary, which follows or has as its objective the acquisition of control of the offeree company in accordance with national law;

* * *

Article 3

General principles

1. For the purpose of implementing this Directive, Member States shall ensure that the following principles are complied with:

(a) all holders of the securities of an offeree company of the same class must be afforded equivalent treatment; moreover, if a person acquires control of a company, the other holders of securities must be protected;

---

63 Other countries using the U.K. Takeover Code have provided for partial bids under strict regulations. See, e.g., New Zealand Takeover Code, Rules 9–14. Some claim a partial offer is possible under the U.K. Takeover Code as well.

* * *

Article 5

Protection of minority shareholders, the mandatory bid and the equitable price

1. Where a natural or legal person, as a result of his/her own acquisition or the acquisition by persons acting in concert with him/her, holds securities of a company as referred to in Article 1(1) which, added to any existing holdings of those securities of his/hers and the holdings of those securities of persons acting in concert with him/her, directly or indirectly give him/her a specified percentage of voting rights in that company, giving him/her control of that company, Member States shall ensure that such a person is required to make a bid as a means of protecting the minority shareholders of that company. Such a bid shall be addressed at the earliest opportunity to all the holders of those securities for all their holdings at the equitable price as defined in paragraph 4.

2. Where control has been acquired following a voluntary bid made in accordance with this Directive to all the holders of securities for all their holdings, the obligation laid down in paragraph 1 to launch a bid shall no longer apply.

* * *

4. The highest price paid for the same securities by the offeror, or by persons acting in concert with him/her, over a period, to be determined by Member States, of not less than six months and not more than twelve before the bid referred to in paragraph one shall be regarded as the equitable price. If, after the bid has been made public and before the offer closes for acceptance, the offeror or any person acting in concert with him/her purchases securities at a price higher than the offer price, the offeror shall increase his/her offer so that it is not less than the highest price paid for the securities so acquired.

* * *

Article 6

Information concerning bids

* * *

2. Member States shall ensure that an offeror is required to draw up and make public in good time an offer document containing the information necessary to enable the holders of the offeree company's securities to reach a properly informed decision on the bid. Before the offer document is made public, the offeror shall communicate it to the supervisory authority. When it is made public, the boards of the offeree company and of the offeror shall communicate it to the representatives of their respective employees or, where there are no such representatives, to the employees themselves.

* * *

3. The offer document referred to in paragraph 2 shall state at least:

(a) the terms of the bid;

(b) the identity of the offeror and, where the offeror is a company, the type, name and registered office of that company;

(c) the securities or, where appropriate, the class or classes of securities for which the bid is made;

(d) the consideration offered for each security or class of securities and, in the case of a mandatory bid, the method employed in determining it, with particulars of the way in which that consideration is to be paid;

(e) the compensation offered for the rights which might be removed as a result of the breakthrough rule laid down in Article 11(4), with particulars of the way in which that compensation is to be paid and the method employed in determining it;

(f) the maximum and minimum percentages or quantities of securities which the offeror undertakes to acquire;

(g) details of any existing holdings of the offeror, and of persons acting in concert with him/her, in the offeree company;

(h) all the conditions to which the bid is subject;

(i) the offeror's intentions with regard to the future business of the offeree company and, in so far as it is affected by the bid, the offeror company and with regard to the safeguarding of the jobs of their employees and management, including any material change in the conditions of employment, and in particular the offeror's strategic plans for the two companies and the likely repercussions on employment and the locations of the companies' places of business;

(j) the time allowed for acceptance of the bid;

(k) where the consideration offered by the offeror includes securities of any kind, information concerning those securities;

(l) information concerning the financing for the bid;

(m) the identity of persons acting in concert with the offeror or with the offeree company and, in the case of companies, their types, names, registered offices and relationships with the offeror and, where possible, with the offeree company;

(n) the national law which will govern contracts concluded between the offeror and the holders of the offeree company's securities as a result of the bid and the competent courts.

* * *

Article 7

Time allowed for acceptance

1. Member States shall provide that the time allowed for the acceptance of a bid may not be less than two weeks nor more than 10 weeks from the date of publication of the offer document. Provided that the general principle laid down in Article 3(1)(f) is respected, Member States may provide that the period of ten weeks may be extended on condition that the offeror gives at least two weeks' notice of his/her intention of closing the bid.

* * *

Article 9

Obligations of the board of the offeree company

* * *

2. During the period referred to in the second subparagraph, the board of the offeree company shall obtain the prior authorization of the general meeting of shareholders given for this purpose before taking any action, other than seeking alternative bids, which may result in the frustration of the bid and in particular before issuing any shares which may result in a lasting impediment to the offeror's acquiring control of the offeree company.

Such authorization shall be mandatory at least from the time the board of the offeree receives the information referred to in the first sentence of Article 6(1) concerning the bid and until the result of the bid is made public or the bid lapses. Member States may require that such authorisation be obtained at an earlier stage, for example as soon as the board of the offeree company becomes aware that the bid is imminent.

3. As regards decisions taken before the beginning of the period referred to in the second subparagraph of paragraph two and not yet partly or fully implemented, the general meeting of shareholders shall approve or confirm any decision which does not form part of the normal course of the company's business and the implementation of which may result in the frustration of the bid.

* * *

Article 11

Breakthrough

* * *

2. Any restrictions on the transfer of securities provided for in the articles of association of the offeree company shall not apply vis-à-vis the offeror during the time allowed for acceptance of the bid laid down in Article 7(1).

Any restrictions on the transfer of securities provided for in contractual agreements between the offeree company and holders of its securities, or in contractual agreements between holders of the offeree company's securities entered into after the adoption of this Directive, shall not apply vis-à-vis the offeror during the time allowed for acceptance of the bid laid down in Article 7(1).

3. Restrictions on voting rights provided for in the articles of association of the offeree company shall not have effect at the general meeting of shareholders which decides on any defensive measures in accordance with Article 9.

Restrictions on voting rights provided for in contractual agreements between the offeree company and holders of its securities, or in contractual agreements between holders of the offeree company's securities entered into after the adoption of this Directive, shall not have effect at the general meeting of shareholders which decides on any defensive measures in accordance with Article 9.

Multiple-vote securities shall carry only one vote each at the general meeting of shareholders which decides on any defensive measures in accordance with Article 9.

4. Where, following a bid, the offeror holds 75 percent or more of the capital carrying voting rights, no restrictions on the transfer of securities or on voting rights referred to in paragraphs two and three nor any extraordinary rights of shareholders concerning the appointment or removal of board members provided for in the articles of association of the offeree company shall apply; multiple-vote securities shall carry only one vote each at the first general meeting of shareholders following closure of the bid, called by the offeror in order to amend the articles of association or to remove or appoint board members.

To that end, the offeror shall have the right to convene a general meeting of shareholders at short notice, provided that the meeting does not take place within two weeks of notification.

5. Where rights are removed on the basis of paragraphs two, three, or four and/or Article 12, equitable compensation shall be provided for any loss suffered by the holders of those rights. The terms for determining such compensation and the arrangements for its payment shall be set by Member States.

6. Paragraphs 3 and 4 shall not apply to securities where the restrictions on voting rights are compensated for by specific pecuniary advantages.

* * *

Article 12

Optional arrangements

1. Member States may reserve the right not to require companies as referred to in Article 1(1) which have their registered offices within their territories to apply Article 9(2) and (3) and/or Article 11.

* * *

Article 15

The right of squeeze-out

* * *

2. Member States shall ensure that an offeror is able to require all the holders of the remaining securities to sell him/her those securities at a fair price. Member States shall introduce that right in one of the following situations:

(a) where the offeror holds securities representing not less than 90 percent of the capital carrying voting rights and 90 percent of the voting rights in the offeree company, or

(b) where, following acceptance of the bid, he/she has acquired or has firmly contracted to acquire securities representing not less than 90 percent of the offeree company's capital carrying voting rights and 90 percent of the voting rights comprised in the bid.

In the case referred to in (a), Member States may set a higher threshold that may not, however, be higher than 95 percent of the capital carrying voting rights and 95 percent of the voting rights.

* * *

4. If the offeror wishes to exercise the right of squeeze-out he/she shall do so within three months of the end of the time allowed for acceptance of the bid referred to in Article 7.

5. Member States shall ensure that a fair price is guaranteed. That price shall take the same form as the consideration offered in the bid or shall be in cash. Member States may provide that cash shall be offered at least as an alternative.

Following a voluntary bid, in both of the cases referred to in paragraph 2(a) and (b), the consideration offered in the bid shall be presumed to be fair where, through acceptance of the bid, the offeror has acquired securities representing not less than 90 percent of the capital carrying voting rights comprised in the bid.

Following a mandatory bid, the consideration offered in the bid shall be presumed to be fair.

Article 16

The right of sell-out

* * *

2. Member States shall ensure that a holder of remaining securities is able to require the offeror to buy his/her securities from him/her at a fair price under the same circumstances as provided for in Article 15(2).

* * *

NOTE: THE U.K. TAKEOVER CODE

The U.K. Takeover Code is administered by a Panel on Takeovers and Mergers. Members of the Panel come mainly from the financial and business community and have expertise in acquisitions. The Panel protects the interests of shareholders and does not decide on the merits of an offer. Like the EU Takeover Directive, the Takeover Code contains a statement of general principles and a collection of specific rules. Like the Takeover Directive, the Code has a mandatory offer rule for acquisitions of thirty percent or more of the voting stock in a company and a squeeze-out rule (compulsory acquisition rule) enabling a bidder that has acquired ninety percent or more of a target's voting shares to claim the rest. Unlike the Directive, the Code has a mandatory board neutrality rule; a target board may not take defensive actions without explicit shareholder approval. The bidder must pay a minimum price set at the highest price it has paid for stock of the target within three months of the commencement of the offer or for stock purchased outside the offer.

QUESTIONS

Is this a better system than the U.S. system (assuming a country does not opt out of Articles 9 and 11)? Note that the U.K., the model for the EU Directive, does not have as many takeovers as we do in the States. We are viewed as more "takeover friendly". Why is this?

CHAPTER ELEVEN

SHAREHOLDER ACTIVISM

■ ■ ■

A. OVERVIEW

Hostile takeovers are extremely expensive to mount and, in terms of success, risky propositions at best. This is especially true given how the Delaware courts have continually upheld target company takeover defenses under the *Unocal* standard. As a result, deals that start out in a hostile manner must, by necessity, end in a negotiated manner if they are to succeed. This reality has caused many *activist shareholders* (today's politically correct name for corporate raiders[1]) to pivot in order to achieve their goals for target companies. Today, these activists are often able to achieve their goals at only a fraction of the cost of a full-fledged takeover, despite holding only a small equity stake (often less than 10 percent[2]) in target companies.

Who are these "activist shareholders"? Some are traditional players, such as T. Boone Pickens, Jr., Carl Icahn and Ronald Perelman. The newer kids on the block operate typically through private equity and hedge funds. They include Daniel Loeb (Third Point Management), Bill Ackman (Pershing Square), Ralph Whitworth (Relational Investors), Steve Cohen (SAC Capital Advisors), Nelson Peltz (Trian Fund Management), Barry Rosenstein (Jana Partners), Jeffrey Smith (Starboard Value LP) and Leon Cooperman (Omega Advisors).

The goal of these activists is to put public pressure on target company management in order to induce changes which the activists believe will enhance shareholder value. The changes they seek include, among others, the redemption of the company's poison pill, divestiture of certain key assets and businesses, distribution of excess cash (in the form of increased dividends and/or stock repurchase programs), spin-offs of subsidiaries and, of course, the sale of the entire company. Table 1 sets forth several recent attempts by activists to influence publicly traded companies.

---

1 See Rob Copeland, *Returns from Activist Hedge Funds Are Causing a Stir*, WSJ.COM (July 7, 2014) (avail. at http://online.wsj.com/articles/returns-from-activist-hedge-funds-are-causing-a-stir-1404773120?KEYWORDS=valeant+pershing+square).

2 According to one study, the median activist shareholder stake in a target company is 6.3 percent. See Alon Brav, Wei Jiang & Hyunseob Kim, *Hedge Fund Activism: A Review (February 12, 2010)*, 16 (avail. at SSRN: https://ssrn.com/abstract=1551953).

Activist Target Company Year	Change Requested—Outcome
Trian Fund Mgt. Proctor & Gamble Co. 2017	Streamline businesses and bring in outside talent. After one of the most expensive proxy fights in history, and with the voting essentially ending in a tie (nearly 2 billion votes were cast), P&G agrees to expand its board by 2 seats, adding Trian's Nelson Peltz and Joseph Jimenez, CEO of Novartis AG.
Third Point LLC Nestlé SA 2017	Sell noncore assets, including Nestlé's 23 percent stake in L'Oréal SA; innovate core business; set profit margin target. Profit margin target of 17.5–18.5 percent set for 2020; previously announced share buyback program to be accelerated; but stake in L'Oréal SA to be retained, not sold.
Starboard Value Yahoo! Inc. 2016	Sought to overthrow entire board and force sale of Yahoo's core business. Yahoo agreed to reshape its board by adding 4 new independent directors nominated by Starboard (including Starboard's Jeffrey Smith). Smith joined the board's "strategic review committee" to oversee the auction of Yahoo's core business. Business ultimately sold for $4.48 billion to Verizon in 2017.
Icahn Enterprises Apple Inc. 2016	Use Apple's excess cash to repurchase shares of common stock. Apple launched $60 billion share repurchase program, but successfully resisted Icahn's request for additional share repurchases. Apple later increased share repurchase program to $90 billion.
Third Point LLC	Replace CEO Ruprecht with more innovative CEO with global vision; reduce pay and perquisites for Ruprecht and board members.

Sotheby's 2014	Ruprecht remains CEO and Chair, but board expands from 13 to 15 members with Third Point entitled to place 3 nominees (including Third Point's Daniel Loeb) on Sotheby's slate of nominees; poison pill redeemed so that Third Point's ownership can grow beyond the poison pill's 15 percent trigger.
Icahn Enterprises eBay, Inc. 2014	Spin off eBay's lucrative PayPal subsidiary and add 2 new directors to eBay's board. Overture rebuffed, but eBay agrees to add one mutually acceptable new independent director to eBay's board. In 2015, eBay "unilaterally" decides to spin off PayPal subsidiary giving Icahn no credit.
Pershing Square Herbalife Ltd. 2012	Arguing that the emperor wears no clothes, Pershing shorts large numbers of Herbalife's stock. It webcasts a public presentation concluding that Herbalife's business model is a "sham" and "pyramid scheme," arguing that the company should be subject to regulatory reform or even shutdown. Herbalife's stock price plummets initially but makes come back; stock price subject to increased volatility ever since. After five year battle, and with Herbalife engaging in stock buybacks in order to pressure Pershing's short position, Pershing ultimately capitulates by covering its position at a loss of about 3 percent of its *entire capital*. Pershing investors are *very unhappy*.

Activist funds use some of the typically billions of dollars of assets under management to purchase small stakes in publicly traded target companies. Then, as part of a coordinated publicity campaign, they write sharply worded letters using their "poison pens"[3] and send them to the CEOs of the targets (as well as make them publicly available to create pressure on the target) in order to push their activist agenda. Often, other shareholders of the target join in on the call for change, thus increasing pressure on target management to embrace it. Sometimes, but not always,

---

3 For example, Daniel Loeb's Third Point LLC hedge fund took a 1.25 percent stake (U.S. $3.5 billion) in Nestlé SA in June 2017. In a June 25, 2017 letter to investors, Loeb wrote with respect to Nestlé: "It is rare to find a business of Nestlé's quality with so many avenues for improvement." He added that Nestlé had "fallen behind over the past decade" and "has remained stuck in its old ways." Loeb's letter is available at http://www.marketfolly.-com/2017/06/third-point-takes-nestle-stake-letter.html.

the target CEO will meet with the activist shareholder, listen to the activist's agenda and agree to pursue some or even all of that agenda. However, many CEOs view the activists as opportunists looking to make a quick buck and, therefore, firmly rebuff their overtures.

B. TODAY'S ACTIVISM VERSUS PAST ACTIVISM

How is shareholder activism today distinguished from the activism of institutions that has been occurring since the 1960s? Commentators Alon Brav, Wei Jiang and Hyunseob Kim explain:

> Hedge fund activism distinguishes itself from other institutional activism in a number of aspects. First, hedge fund managers have stronger financial incentives to make profits. Hedge funds generally receive a significant proportion (e.g., 20%) of excess returns as performance fees on top of fixed management fees. Moreover, the managers of hedge funds invest a substantial amount from their personal wealth into their own funds. This strong incentive for high investment returns in the compensation structure contrasts with that of mutual fund or pension fund managers, which usually does not allow managers to capture a significant portion of (excess) returns.
>
> Second, hedge funds are lightly regulated since they are not widely available to the public but only to institutional clients and a limited number of wealthy individuals. Therefore, hedge funds are not subject to strict fiduciary standards (such as those embodied in ERISA), and this in turn allows them to have much more flexibility to intervene in the invested companies. For example, since the law does not require hedge funds to maintain diversified portfolios as required for some other institutional investors, they can take large and concentrated stakes in target firms more easily. Further, they can use derivative securities or trade on margin to hedge or leverage their stakes with a given capital. These are important advantages for activist shareholders to have influence over the target firms' management.
>
> Third, hedge funds face fewer conflicts of interest than some other institutional investors, such as mutual funds and pension funds, who often have other business relations with the invested companies or have non-financial agendas and goals. Hedge fund managers rarely face [these] . . . conflicts. Lastly, hedge funds usually have lock-up provisions that restrict the investors from withdrawing their principal. Given that hedge fund activists invest in target firms for more than a year on average to pursue their strategies, this feature affords the managers an extended flexibility to focus on intermediate and long-term activist objectives.

> To summarize, hedge fund activists are a new breed of shareholder activists that are equipped with more suitable financial incentives and organizational structures for pursuing activism agendas than earlier generations of institutional activists. Not surprisingly, they turn out to be successful in facilitating significant changes in corporate governance and operations of target firms, and in turn achieving the goal of improving value for both the firms' shareholders and their own investors.[4]

These same commentators also note that today's activists differ from those of the past based on the characteristics of the target companies against which they agitate:

> Hedge fund activists tend to target "value" firms that have low valuations compared to "fundamentals." In addition, activist hedge funds are more likely to target firms that have sound operating cash flows, but low (sales) growth rates, leverage, and dividend payout ratios. Therefore, one can characterize the targets as "cash-cows" with low growth potentials that may suffer from the agency problem of free cash flow .... This characterization of target firms differentiates hedge fund activism from earlier shareholder activism, which tended to target companies that had poor operating performance. The target firms are generally smaller than comparable firms. Hedge funds target small firms partly because they can accumulate a significant ownership more easily with a given amount of capital. Related to this point, the targets of hedge fund activism exhibit relatively high trading liquidity, institutional ownership, and analyst coverage. Essentially, these characteristics allow the activist investors to accumulate significant stakes in the target firms quickly without adverse price impact, and to get more support for their agendas from fellow sophisticated investors. Lastly, target companies tend to have weaker shareholder rights than comparable firms, consistent with the argument that hedge fund activists target poorly-governed firms where the potential for value improvement is higher.[5]

C. PERFORMANCE

Do activist strategies provide superior returns over time? At least two activist indices indicate that the answer is "yes." The first index, the Activist Insight Index (AI Index) created by Activist Insight, is comprised of the performances of over 40 activist-focused hedge funds from around

---

[4] Alon Brav, Wei Jiang & Hyunseob Kim, *Hedge Fund Activism: A Review* (Feb. 12, 2010), 2–3 (avail. at SSRN: https://ssrn.com/abstract=1551953).

[5] *Id.* at 4.

the globe. While the AI Index did not fare well against the MSCI world index in 2006–2007, and its performance essentially equaled that of the MSCI world index in 2009 and the first quarter of 2012, the AI Index consistently outperformed the MSCI world index in the years following the global financial crisis of 2008. The outperformance was most pronounced in 2010, when the average activist-focused fund returned 20.54 percent, outperforming the MSCI world index by 10.99 percentage points. The outperformance is even greater when taking into consideration that the MSCI world index does not factor in fees that would be incurred by traders pursuing an investment strategy that follows that index. It is also worth noting that the top performing activist-focused funds produced an average return of 53.04 percentage points greater than that of the MSCI world index between 2006 and 2011.[6]

The second activist index, the Novus Activist Portfolio (NAP) (comprised of the performances of approximately 60 activist managers), has returned 10.7 percent annualized from March 2004 through year end 2016. This compares very favorably with the 7.6 percent annualized return for the S&P 500 during that same time period. However, from June 2015 through year end 2016, the NAP underperformed the S&P 500 by almost 8 percent, with most of the underperformance occurring in the second half of 2015.[7]

Other research highlights the problems activists have had in recent years. FactSet Research Systems Inc. looked at 175 activist campaigns that launched between 2012 and 2016. In doing so, FactSet compared companies where activists won their campaigns with companies where activists lost or withdrew their demands. One year after a campaign ended, shares of companies where activists were successful had a median *loss* of 0.7 percent, and two years out the loss grew to 2.4 percent. However, the shares of companies that fended off activists' advances had a median *gain* of 9 percent one year following a campaign, while the median gain grew to 10.5 percent two years following a campaign.[8] Perhaps activists are running out of easy targets?

D. ACTIVIST STRATEGIES

The following is an overview of the various strategies activists pursue to achieve their agendas.

---

[6] See *Feature: Activism Outperforms*, ACTIVISM MONTHLY, Volume 1, Issue 1 (Nov. 2012) (avail. at http://www.activistinsight.com/research/November%202012%20Newsletter.pdf).

[7] See Novus, *Analyzing Activist Investor Performance in 2016* (Feb. 24, 2017) (avail. at https://www.novus.com/blog/analyzing-activist-investor-performance-2016/).

[8] See Ryan Derousseau, *Do Shareholders Win When Activists Win?*, FORTUNE.COM (Oct. 14, 2017) (avail. at http://fortune.com/2017/09/25/peltz-icahn-ackman-clx-hlf-stock/).

1. TROJAN HORSE

If an activist's external pressure is not enough to effectuate change, the activist often seeks to influence corporate decision-making from the *inside* via the so-called *Trojan Horse* strategy. Accordingly, the activist will nominate one or more (but typically less than a majority) of individuals sympathetic to the activist's goals to run against an equal number of the target's incumbent directors in a contested election of directors. The activist's slate of directors is known as a *short slate*, as its candidates seek less than a majority of seats on the target's board of directors. If the activist is successful in obtaining one or more board seats, it thereafter can legitimately pursue its agenda for change from the inside.

Pushing a short slate has certain key advantages over seeking majority board control. First, unlike the election of a majority of new directors to the board, the election of a short slate will not trigger change in control provisions in golden parachute agreements with key executives of the target. Thus, those executives will not be entitled to additional compensation or have their stock awards immediately vest if a short slate is elected. Second, it generally is easier to convince proxy advisory firms, such as Institutional Shareholder Services (ISS), and institutional investors to vote for the activist's slate of director nominees if that slate is a short slate. Electing one or two gadflies to the board to push an activist's agenda is a far cry from the dramatic step of ousting a majority or even all of the directors. Indeed, it is not easy for an activist generally to convince other shareholders and proxy advisory firms that it deserves *control* of the target board at a time when it does not own a controlling stake, as typically only those with a controlling stake deserve the keys to the kingdom. However, if an activist has a sound operational plan for the target and the ability to demonstrate why its plan is substantially better than the existing board's plan, it has a shot at ousting a majority of the existing board.

It is worth noting that ousting a majority or even the entire board of directors of a target company has become somewhat easier over the last 15 years. The vast majority of all publicly traded companies now put all of their directors up for reelection annually, as instances of staggered or classified boards of directors are less frequent. In the year 2000, 300 of the 500 companies comprising the S&P 500 had staggered boards. By the end of 2015, that number had decreased to only 55. Moreover, activists are locating more viable candidates to run against incumbents than they have in the past. While few expect fights for the majority or the entire board to become the norm, such fights are likely to grow in number in the ensuing years.[9]

---

9 See David Benoit, *Clash Over Board Will Be Measure of Activist Clout*, WALL ST. J., May 23, 2014, at C1.

According to FactSet Research Systems Inc.,[10] in 2016 the number of proxy fights for board seats reached 101, the highest number since 2009 (118). Of those contests, 34 went the distance. The company win rate in those 34 contests was 68 percent, a significant increase from 2015's 54 percent win rate. Importantly, proxy settlements have increased every year since 2013, as many companies are choosing to grant board seats to activists before a proxy contest develops. In 2016, 76 non-proxy fight activist campaigns led to at least one board seat for the activist in question. Thus, while companies appear more willing to provide a board seat without engaging in a fight, when they do choose to fight it is more likely than not that they will win. Indeed, they are choosing their battles wisely.

2. STOCK REPURCHASE PROGRAMS

A stock repurchase program is a program whereby a publicly traded company announces its plan to use the company's own money to repurchase shares of its own common stock in the open market. Typically, the company will commit to purchase "up to" a specified number of shares, which number is typically significant. Alternatively, it will commit to spend "up to" a specified number of dollars to repurchase shares. A stock repurchase program is fully disclosable to the public under Exchange Act Rule 10b–18 prior to its commencement given its manipulative effect on the company's stock price once launched.

A company's announcement of a stock repurchase program sends a positive or "bullish" signal to the market, and the company's stock price typically rises upon that announcement. It does so for several reasons. First, while the management of many companies lament that the market undervalues their companies, a management that engages in a stock repurchase program puts its money where its mouth is. That is, it signals that the best use of the company's cash is to invest in the company's own undervalued stock. Second, the additional (and artificial) demand for a company's stock stemming from a repurchase program naturally buoys the stock price (hence the need for advanced disclosure). Lastly, a company's earnings going forward will be spread over fewer shares once the repurchase program is completed, thus raising the company's earnings per share (EPS) assuming overall earnings stay at least constant.

In 2013, at the behest of Carl Icahn's Icahn Enterprises, technology giant Apple Inc. announced a stock repurchase program whereby the company would buy $60 billion of its own stock through 2015, a record stock repurchase program for any company. However, this proved insufficient from Mr. Icahn's perspective. Through a shareholder proposal, Mr. Icahn, who owned about 0.5 percent of Apple, pushed for at least an additional $50 billion in share repurchases during Apple's 2014 fiscal year. Apple's

[10] See Andrew Birstingl, *2016 Shareholder Activism Trends* (Dec. 12, 2016) (avail. at https://insight.factset.com/2016-shareholder-activism-trends).

management advised its shareholders to vote against Mr. Icahn's proposal, arguing that the company's cash was needed for other initiatives. In the end, Mr. Icahn ended his push for additional share repurchases. Nonetheless, as Anthony Filippo, a Toronto-based independent investment manager, pointed out, Apple would never have announced such a large repurchase program in 2013 "without an activist breathing down their neck."[11]

Despite Apple's rebuff of Mr. Icahn's request for additional share repurchases, Apple announced on April 23, 2014 that it was increasing its stock repurchase program from $60 billion to $90 billion. Inferring that Apple's stock was undervalued in the marketplace, CEO Tim Cook stated "That should show you how much confidence we have in the future of the company."[12]

3. SPIN-OFF STRATEGY

Activists also attempt to enhance shareholder value through a *spin-off* strategy. Here, a parent company will distribute the shares it holds in a subsidiary to the parent's shareholders, typically in the form of a special dividend. Once completed, the parent's shareholders still own stock in the parent (sans the subsidiary) but now also directly own stock in the former subsidiary itself. Activists often push for a spin-off because they believe the subsidiary will perform better once it is a stand-alone publicly traded company operating outside of its former parent's control.

In early 2014, Carl Icahn's Icahn Enterprises engaged in a campaign seeking two seats on the eBay Inc. board of directors and advocating for eBay to spin off its lucrative PayPal subsidiary. After eBay's board rebuffed the idea, Icahn began a vitriolic campaign (employing Twitter, blogs and cable television) against eBay's board. He accused the board of incompetence, particularly with respect to eBay's previous sale of its Skype subsidiary, which Icahn believed was sold for substantially less money than it was worth. He also claimed that two board members (tech venture capitalist Marc Andreessen and Intuit's Scott Cook) had a debilitating conflict of interest. With respect to PayPal, Mr. Icahn argued that an increasing majority of PayPal's business originated outside the eBay universe, and a separation therefore would improve PayPal's value and growth prospects. He later abandoned the idea of a complete spin-off of PayPal but pushed for a 20 percent stake in PayPal to be sold directly to eBay's shareholders.

---

[11] Jenifer Alban, *Icahn Gives Up Apple Buyback Plan After ISS Urges "No" Vote*, REUTERS.COM (Feb. 10, 2014) (avail. at http://www.reuters.com/article/2014/02/10/us-apple-icahn-idUSBREA1913T20140210).

[12] See Daisuke Wakabayashi, *Apple Boosts Buyback, Splits Stock To Reward Investors*, WSJ.COM (Apr. 23, 2014) (avail. at http://online.wsj.com/news/articles/SB1000142405270-2303834304579519880474287074).

By April 2014, eBay and Icahn had buried the hatchet in a manner viewed as a victory for eBay. In order to settle their differences, both agreed that a new independent director—David Dornman, the former CEO of AT&T—would be added to the eBay board.[13] Icahn, however, did not give up his push with respect to PayPal, as he continued to press his case through confidential discussions with the company. Nonetheless, he admitted at the time that "it's better to have peace than war."[14]

Despite making peace with Icahn, the eBay board, in an ironic twist of fate, unilaterally announced its decision to spin off the PayPal subsidiary. Apparently, eBay directors and executives shifted their stance on the spin-off strategy in June of 2014 after reviewing a six-month internal study of the future of the online payment industry.[15] The PayPal spin-off was completed on July 17, 2015.

4. PARTNERING WITH HOSTILE BIDDERS

A relatively new and highly unusual tactic for an activist investor is to partner with a strategic acquirer in pursuing a target company. The beauty of this alliance is that it combines an activist's rapid accumulation of target stock and call options on that stock with the financial wherewithal and gravitas of a strategic acquirer. Typically, the activist and the strategic acquirer form a new entity which purchases a significant toe-hold position in the target company. Purchasing call options is particularly useful as Hart-Scott-Rodino antitrust filings do not need to be made until the call options are exercised or the strategic acquirer launches its takeover. Due to the 10-day window for filing a Schedule 13D, the target company typically becomes aware of the activist's rapid accumulation at the same time it learns about (and has to defend against) the strategic acquirer's publicly announced bid.

The prime example of this strategy was the alliance between Bill Ackman's Pershing Square and Valeant Pharmaceuticals International Inc. ("Valeant") to pursue an acquisition of Allergan, Inc., the maker of Botox. Pursuant to a February 2014 letter agreement between Pershing Square and Valeant, hedge funds managed by Pershing Square as well as Valeant itself would contribute funds to a new entity (PS Fund I) managed by Pershing Square. Monies in PS Fund I would be invested solely in Allergan's common stock and stock options. Once PS Fund I acquired the

---

[13] See David Goldman, *Icahn Settles with eBay over Paypal*, CNN MONEY (Apr. 10, 2014) (avail. at http://money.cnn.com/2014/04/10/technology/ebay-icahn/).

[14] Michael J. De La Merced, *Ending Vitriol, Icahn and eBay Reach a Deal*, N.Y. TIMES (Apr. 10, 2014) (avail. at http://dealbook.nytimes.com/2014/04/10/ebay-settles-board-fight-with-icahn/?_php=true&_type=blogs&_r=0).

[15] See Deepa Seetharaman & Supantha Mukherjee, *EBay follows Icahn's advice, plans PayPal spinoff in 2015*, REUTERS.COM (Sept. 30, 2014) (avail. at http://www.reuters.com/article/2014-/09/30/us-ebay-divestiture-idUSKCN0HP13D20140930).

stock and options, Valeant would make a merger proposal to Allergan's board.

PS Fund I spent $3.2 billion in purchasing 28.8 million shares of Allergan common stock, although most of that was comprised of call options on Allergan stock. This represented approximately 9.7 percent of Allergan's outstanding shares of common stock. On April 21, 2014, Pershing Square and Valeant filed separate Schedule 13Ds as a "group." The following day Valeant publicly proposed a cash and stock merger deal worth $45.7 billion to Allergan's CEO and board.

After Allergan rebuffed Valeant's merger proposal, it began holding discussions with alternative business combination partners, including Salix Pharmaceuticals Ltd. Allergan believed that by making a major acquisition it could frustrate Valeant's takeover bid by making Allergan too large for Valeant to swallow.[16] Valeant, in turn, commenced a hostile exchange offer for Allergan in June 2014. PS Fund I was listed as a "co-bidder" in Valeant's Schedule TO under SEC rules. Allergan rejected the offer without ever discussing it with Valeant. Allergan's Schedule 14D–9 stated the offer price was inadequate from a financial point of view and highlighted that the offer itself was too risky given the long list of conditions that had to be satisfied before the offer could be consummated. Pershing Square immediately requested that Allergan hold a nonbinding vote among shareholders that would encourage the company to engage in good faith discussions with Valeant. Allergan called Pershing Square's efforts self-serving.

In July 2014, Pershing Square pushed for a special meeting of Allergan shareholders to consider the removal of six of the 10 incumbent directors and the appointment of Pershing Square's slate of six nominees. It later followed up by filing a lawsuit in Delaware Chancery Court seeking judicial intervention to ensure that a special meeting would occur before the end of 2014—and before Allergan could complete a defensive acquisition of its own. Success at the special meeting would give Pershing Square's nominees control of the Allergan board.

Allergan countered by suing Valeant and Pershing Square for alleged insider trading. Specifically, Allergan alleged that PS Fund I's purchase of Allergan shares and options violated Exchange Act Rule 14e–3. That Rule prohibits the purchase of shares in a target company based on material, nonpublic information about a tender offer if either substantial steps to commence a tender offer have occurred or the tender offer itself has commenced. Allergan alleged that Pershing Square and Valeant must have

---

16 David Benoit & Liz Hoffman, *Valeant Pushes Ahead in Fight for Allergan*, WALL ST. J., Aug. 25, 2014, at B3. Valeant had previously filed a lawsuit seeking judicial confirmation that seeking shareholder consents for calling a special meeting of shareholders would not trigger Allergan's poison pill. That suit was settled, and Valeant was allowed to move forward seeking consents. See *id.*

known Valeant's merger proposal would turn hostile at the time when PS Fund I first purchased Allergan shares and call options.

Pershing Square and Valeant denied the insider trading allegations. Pershing Square stated that "[a]t the time of the merger proposal to Allergan on April 22, 2014, neither Valeant nor Pershing Square had taken any steps whatsoever regarding a tender offer," adding that "[t]here is nothing illegal, unethical or improper in taking a toehold position before a merger is proposed, even if it is not wanted by the target's management."[17] Smelling smoke, the SEC joined the fray to search for fire. In August 2014 it launched a civil probe focusing on whether Valeant and Pershing Square potentially breached insider trading laws, including Exchange Act Rules 14e–3 and 10b–5. Pershing Square responded by stating "We welcome the SEC's review of the facts."[18]

In November 2014, Allergan accepted a "white knight" takeover bid from Actavis Plc. The offer valued Allergan at $66 billion, overshadowing Valeant's $53 billion bid. Valeant CEO Michael Pearson conceded that his takeover bid had come to an end when he stated, "Valeant cannot justify to its own shareholders paying a price of $219 or more per share for Allergan."[19]

In April 2015, both Ackman and Allergan agreed to drop their lawsuits against one another. Allergan voluntarily dismissed its claims against Ackman, Pershing Square and Valeant, and Ackman and Valeant did the same. Both parties paid for their own attorneys' fees.

Investors who sold Allergan shares from February 25 through April 21, 2014 brought a class action lawsuit over alleged insider trading against Pershing Square and Valeant. In November 2015, a California federal judge denied a motion to dismiss the lawsuit, leading to settlement talks. That litigation ultimately did settle for about $290 million in early 2018, with Pershing Square and Valeant agreeing to pay $193.25 million and $96.25 million, respectively. For Pershing Square investors, including Ackman himself, the settlement was a bitter and costly pill to swallow. Pershing Square, with over $9 billion in assets under management, is estimated to see its performance drop by a further 1.32 percent as monies are used to pay the settlement. Indeed, Pershing Square had previously reserved only $75 million to cover any settlement.

The status of the SEC's insider trading probe, much like the SEC itself, remains a mystery.

---

[17] Liz Hoffman & Jean Eaglesham, *SEC Is Examining Allergan Bid From Valeant, Ackman*, WALL ST. J., Aug. 15, 2014, at C3.

[18] *Id.*

[19] Paul Ackman, *Allergan Accepts Buyout Offer From Actavis, Valeant Bows Out*, 24/7 WALL ST. (Nov. 17, 2014) (avail. at http://247wallst.com/healthcare-business/2014/11/17/-allergan-accepts-219-per-share-offer-from-actavis-valeant-bows-out/).

5. WOLFPACKING

The tactic of *wolfpacking* involves several hedge funds or other activist investors circling a target company and pushing their agenda. One of the participants will act as the "lead" activist, while the others remain on the periphery. The purpose of wolfpacking is to provide the lead activist with more influence over a target company than its relatively small holdings would normally provide. The tactic was particularly prevalent during 2014.

Commentators have taken note of the potential viciousness with which wolf packs operate:

> The [wolf pack] members . . . quickly accumulate stock positions in the target that, although small individually, are significant in the aggregate. The market's knowledge of the formation of a wolf pack (either through word of mouth or public announcement of a destabilization campaign by the lead wolf pack member) often leads to additional activist funds entering the fray against the target corporation, resulting in a rapid (and often outcome determinative) *change in composition of the target's shareholder base* seemingly overnight.[20]

Importantly, the way in which a wolf pack is formed if fraught with securities law peril. The formation must appear to be *uncoordinated*. If the wolf pack establishes a *formal* coalition (which it may do so for purely tactical reasons[21]), then securities filings under the Williams Act (such as a group filing under Exchange Act Regulation 13D) must be made. By avoiding securities law filings, wolf packs do not trigger early warning systems upon which target corporations have relied historically. In fact, their failure to file frustrates the key purposes of the Williams Act, including advance notice to other investors, disclosure of their beneficial ownership of target shares, and disclosure of their intended plans for the target company. Moreover, because most shareholder rights plans (a.k.a. poison pills) incorporate a definition of "beneficial ownership" and "group" ownership found in the Williams Act, wolf packs collectively can own 20 percent or more of a target company's shares without triggering that company's poison pill.

6. SHAREHOLDER REFERENDA

Instead of waiting until the annual meeting of the target company's shareholders, or calling a special meeting of those shareholders (assuming

---

20 Mark D. Gernstein, Bradley D. Faris & Christsopher R. Drewry, *The Resurgent Rights Plan: Recent Poison Pill Developments and Trends*, at 11 (Latham & Watkins, Apr. 2009) (emphasis supplied) (avail. at https://corpgov.law.harvard.edu/wp-content/uploads/2009/05/the-resurgent-rights-plan.pdf).

21 E.g., a pack may choose to file required schedules with the SEC shortly before launching a proxy contest against a target company.

doing so is allowed under a target company's charter or bylaws[22]), an activist sometimes calls for a *shareholder referendum*. A referendum is an unofficial or unsanctioned shareholder "get together," as all target shareholders are invited to attend. The target company is not technically involved, which is why it is not an official meeting. Typically, the target shareholders will "vote" on a precatory resolution that furthers the activist's agenda, such as resolving that the target company should come to the table and negotiate with a hostile bidder. While nonbinding on the target company (i.e., precatory), any resolution approved by shareholders puts pressure on target management, especially in the context of a hostile takeover.

Of course, the charters or bylaws of many public companies do not allow shareholders to call special meetings. Thus, an activist is prevented from dictating when it can present its case to target shareholders. This is also the reason why some target companies opt out of control share acquisition statutes (which also may involve special meetings of shareholders) under state law. Referenda constitute end runs around the elimination of special meetings, which explains why target companies have great disdain for them.

Shareholder referenda put target companies in a bit of a pickle. Should target companies solicit shareholder votes in opposition to the activist's resolution(s)? Doing so lends a degree of legitimacy to the whole referendum process. However, a failure to do so allows the activist to address target shareholders on an empty stage without a dissenting opinion. Target companies must choose their poison.

7. PUTTING THE BRAKES ON A TARGET'S STRATEGY

While most activists push for change, others push to stop targets from *making changes* they view as ill-advised. For example, in 2018 activist Carl Icahn teamed up with fellow billionaire Darwin Deason in an attempt to kill Xerox Corp.'s proposed deal with FujiFilm Holdings Corp. Pursuant to that deal, Xerox would combine itself with a joint venture it has run with FujiFilm for 50 years, ceding control over the joint venture to FujiFilm. Icahn and Deason collectively owned 15.2 percent of Xerox's outstanding shares, thus creating a very significant roadblock to Xerox securing the necessary approval of its shareholders to consummate the deal. Messrs. Icahn and Deason wrote in a letter to Xerox shareholders: "To put it simply, the current board of directors [of Xerox] has overseen the systematic destruction of Xerox, and, unless we do something, this latest Fuji scheme

---

[22] See Del. Gen. Corp. L. § 211(d).

will be the company's final death knell. . . . We urge you—our fellow shareholders—do not let Fuji steal this company from us."[23]

However, nothing can top the bitter fued during 2013–14 between Jeffrey Smith's Starboard Value LP and Darden Restaurants, Inc. over the future of Darden. Starboard is a hedge fund which, at that time, had about $2 billion in assets under management. Darden Restaurants, Inc., a Florida corporation, was the parent company of Red Lobster, Longhorn Steakhouse, Olive Garden and several other restaurant chains at that time.

In December 2013, Darden's board announced its plan to sell the poorly performing Red Lobster chain. Starboard, owning 5.5 percent or about $350 million worth of Darden common stock, vehemently opposed what it believed was a deeply flawed and potentially destructive Red Lobster sale. Instead, it advocated for the company to undertake a comprehensive review that included an evaluation of all options relating to the company's real estate holdings, including a tax efficient sale or REIT spin-off of the company's owned properties. Jeffrey Smith of Starboard described Darden's decision to sell Red Lobster as "a hurried, reactive attempt, in the face of shareholder pressure, to do the bare minimum to appease shareholders."[24] Suffice it to say, Starboard was determined to protect its roughly $350 million investment from what it believed was a poor business decision that would devalue the company.

Consequently, in February 2014, Starboard solicited shareholder consents in an attempt to call a special meeting of shareholders. According to Darden's corporate charter and pursuant to Florida law, a special meeting of the company's shareholders may be called upon obtaining consents from the holders of at least a majority of all outstanding shares that are entitled to vote. The purpose of the special meeting, according to Starboard, was to approve a non-binding resolution urging the Board not to approve any agreement or proposed transaction involving a separation or spin-off of the company's Red Lobster business. Thus, even if Starboard successfully called the special shareholder meeting and subsequently obtained a majority vote at that meeting, the approved resolution would merely be precatory or non-binding on Darden's board. Nonetheless, even a non-binding shareholder-approved resolution would put significant pressure on the Darden board, as members who ignore the will of the shareholders risk the possibility of being voted out of office at the next election of directors.

---

23 The Icahn/Deason Letter is available at http://carlicahn.com/joint-statement-with-darwin-deason-regarding-xerox-2/.

24 *Starboard Wants to Put Red Lobster Spinoff Plan to a Vote—WSJ*, REUTERS.COM (Feb. 24, 2014) (avail. at http://www.reuters.com/article/2014/02/24/darden-starboard-idUSL3N0LT1A3201-40224).

Starboard was ultimately successful in obtaining the necessary shareholder consents to call the special meeting. However, with the date of the now legally permissible special meeting of shareholders fast approaching, Darden, in a bold move, signed a deal to sell Red Lobster to the private equity firm Golden Gate Capital for $2.1 billion. In response, Starboard sent a bitter letter condemning the board for rendering the special meeting moot by entering into a binding contract to sell Red Lobster. In addition, the letter stated in part: "The [Darden] Board has violated a clear shareholder directive and disenfranchised shareholders. [The Board has essentially] given away Red Lobster."[25]

Despite the sale of Red Lobster being a *fait accompli*, Starboard decided to pursue a Trojan Horse strategy. However, instead of seeking the election of a short slate of nominees, a frustrated and malcontent Starboard announced its intention to unseat Darden's *entire 12-person Board* and replace it with a full slate of Starboard-friendly nominees. While doing so is a much riskier (and more difficult) proposition than simply nominating a short slate of nominees for reasons discussed above, Starboard believed that replacing the entire existing board with new members was warranted given the actions of the incumbent directors.

After Darden's current chairman and chief executive, Clarence Otis, achieved his goal of selling Red Lobster, and with Darden's 2014 Annual Meeting of Shareholders fast approaching, Otis headed for the exit and resigned from the Darden board. This, however, did not placate Starboard, as it labeled Mr. Otis's departure "just one small step"[26] towards moving Darden in the right direction.

The Darden board received its comeuppance on October 10, 2014, as Darden shareholders voted to replace the entire Darden board with Starboard nominees. Starboard had convinced Darden shareholders that its plan for Darden was superior to that of the existing board members. Indeed, Starboard produced a slide presentation with *294 slides* covering what it would do to enhance shareholder value. That presentation was heavy on financial engineering, including calling for $200 million in expense cuts and the spinning off of chain restaurants such as The Capital Grille, Bahama Breeze and Yard House. Many of the suggestions related to improving the performance at Olive Garden and enhancing same store sales. *Starboard even suggested that Olive Garden should salt its pasta water!*[27]

---

[25] David Benoit, *Starboard Targets Darden Board After Red Lobster Sale*, WSJ.COM (May 22, 2014) (avail. at http://online.wsj.com/news/articles/SB10001424052702303749904579577834240760504).

[26] David Benoit & Julie Jargon, *Darden Restaurants CEO, Chairman To Step Down*, WSJ.COM (July 28, 2014) (avail. at http://online.wsj.com/articles/darden-chairman-ceo-to-step-down-1406581334).

[27] See Julie Jargon, Joann S. Lublin & David Benoit, *New Board Will Set Darden's Menu*, WALL ST. J., Oct. 11–12, 2014, at B3.

QUESTIONS

1. Assume that Darden Restaurants Inc. is a Delaware corporation rather than a Florida corporation. Darden's board of directors took unilateral action in entering into a deal to sell Red Lobster just a few days before the Darden special meeting of shareholders was to take place. If the board's actions are challenged in Delaware Chancery Court by Starboard or other Darden shareholders, which standard of review should the court apply? Please explain your choice.

2. What are the distinctions—legal, timing, procedural and strategic—between a shareholder referendum and a special meeting of shareholders? Be sure to examine the distinctions from both an activist's perspective and the target company's perspective.

3. Do the Federal Proxy Rules apply to shareholder referenda? If not, should they?

INDEX

References are to Pages